THIRD EDITION

ISSUES IN FEMINISM

An Introduction to Women's Studies

Sheila Ruth
Southern Illinois University of Edwardsville

Mayfield Publishing Company
Mountain View, California
London • Toronto

to Aunt Fay
with love and admiration

Library of Congress Cataloging-in-Publication Data

Issues in feminism : an introduction to women's studies / [compiled by] Sheila Ruth. — 3rd ed.
p. cm.
Includes bibliographical references and index.
ISBN 1-55934-224-2
1. Feminism—United States. 2. Women's studies—United States.
I. Ruth, Sheila.
HQ1426.I853 1995
305.42'0973—dc20 94-17305
CIP

Manufactured in the United States of America
10 9 8 7 6 5 4 3 2 1

Mayfield Publishing Company
1280 Villa Street
Mountain View, California 94041

Sponsoring editor, Franklin C. Graham; production editor, Sharon Montooth; manuscript editor, Carol Dondrea; cover designer, Jean Mailander; cover illustration, Tom Post. The text was set in 9/11 Palatino by Thompson Type and printed on 50# Text White Opaque by Maple Vail Book Manufacturing Group.

Contents

Preface

When I was preparing the first edition of *Issues in Feminism* in 1978, I wrote:

> *Women's studies was born out of the women's movement, which was born out of the concrete experience, realities, and possibilities of women's lives. No matter how much a part of the traditional, "respectable" university the research, faculty, or students of women's studies became, we never lose sight of our beginnings or continuing rootedness in women's liberation, because it is the rootedness in its issues that gives impetus and meaning to our work.*
>
> *Those of us engaged in what is currently called women's studies (research and learning in a feminist context) have come along different routes, yet almost without exception each of us is here because at some time in our personal history we have specifically experienced events or ideas that have propelled us into a reappraisal of our lives as women. Generally it was the power of those experiences and the shock of the appraisal that created in us the desire and the commitment to know more about women, womanhood, and the consequences of gender definition.*

In the years since this book's beginnings, a great deal has changed: society has changed; women's studies has changed; and I have changed.

The 1980s was not a good time for women or social activists: It was the decade of the reactionary. In national politics and in social attitudes, progressive liberalism was forced into retrenchment, and feminists found ourselves in an environment that seemed overtly more tolerant but was actually more hostile. In the United States, more women were working than ever before and were moving into the professions. More women were pursuing advanced education, and we saw some improvement in the income of certain groups of women, although there was scant improvement for women overall. (This was, after all, the era of the "feminization of poverty," and, according to the Coalition on Women and the Budget, during Ronald Reagan's first term in office nearly 2 million female-headed households were driven below the poverty line by government budget cuts.[1]) It became more respectable to be a single parent, or not to marry, and "liberated women" appeared as fixtures in television series.

Yet, the Equal Rights Amendment was defeated in 1982, twenty years into the second wave of the women's movement, and has been rarely spoken of since then in the halls of power; affirmative action for women was all but gutted by a national administration overtly opposed to women's rights; and we lost ground in reproductive autonomy. Worse, our young people were for the most part apolitical, and many young women—perhaps most—were accepting the proposition, advanced by the media and others, that feminism had become irrelevant, all important battles having been settled. Indeed, as the decade of conservatism wore on, it became unfashionable for women to use the "f" word at all. The term *feminazi* was born, a new version of the 1960s' epithet, "shrill libber," and it has become so common that even young, progressive women who are clearly feminist in orientation are averring, "Yes, I think women should be free to . . . but I'm no *feminazi*."

The late 1980s saw the birth of the "political correctness" debate, as *pc* became the ultimate accusation against anyone committed to cultural diversity and minority concerns. A situation that reflects the deepening determination of the old order to preserve the ancient hierarchy, in some ways this may be academia's (and women's studies') thorniest challenge yet to realistically combatting bigotry:

> *I am convinced we are poised at a dangerous political crossroads that could take us back much more than 40 years. . . . In academia this trend has gotten an insidious boost in the right-wing attack on "political correctness." . . . there has been a relentless assault on the views of those lumped together hyperbolically as "black activists, militant homosexuals and radical feminists," charging them . . . with "politicizing" curricula, pushing "intellectual conformity sometimes enforced by intimidation," and turning "whining" into the science of "victimology."*
>
> *I think that what is going on in the attack on us liberals and Little Rockers is nothing less than* intellectual blockbusting. *I remember when I was little, in the late fifties, two more black families moved into our neighborhood where for 50 years my family had been the only blacks. I remember the father of my best friend, Cathy, going from house to house, warning the neighbors, like Paul Revere with Chicken Little's brain, that the property values are falling, the values are falling. The area changed overnight. . . .*
>
> *The mass movement that turned my neighborhood into an "inner city" was part of the first great backlash to the civil rights movement. I think we are now seeing the second great backlash . . . .*
>
> *On campus, the enemies of diversity are trying to make universities more like fortresses against the siege of those who are perceived to be uncivilized heathen. . . . The cry has been sounded: the standards are falling, the standards are falling.*[2]

The new decade and the end of the Reagan–Bush era, long awaited and certainly welcome, has not yet given us the turnaround we all long for. Susan Faludi, author of *Backlash,* summed it up in a commentary on the "year of the woman":

> *1992 was and was not a "breakthrough" year for women. It was a year, to borrow from feminist poet Adrienne Rich, of woman born. It was a year* of *women's long overdue reaction to the string of setbacks and humiliations inflicted upon them in the past decade. It was a year* of *women naming names—in Washington, corporate America, the military. It was a year* of *women's words and* of *women's actions and, most of all,* of *women's anger. 1992 was the year women broke the sound barrier and threw away the etiquette books. Their fury unnerved even feminist-basher Rush Limbaugh, who complained that women were "standing up and shouting, demanding that what they are and what they believe be considered normal."*
>
> *. . . But just because women regained their voices and their ire doesn't mean they gained ground. And that's the pity: for all the* Sturm und Drang, *1992 was not a year* for *women. Women did not break through the glass ceiling. (More than 95 percent of executive suites are still inhabited by men.) Women did not break down the doors of political power. ("Tripling" our representation in the U.S. Senate is no triumph when the female faces go from two to six.) Women did not make a dent in Hollywood's rotten portrayal of women. Women did not win even the most basement-level basics—modest, very modest, federal bills for (unpaid) family leave, (minimal) child-care assistance, and freedom of choice went by the boards.*[3]

Nonetheless, there are signs now that in some quarters at least the political climate and the attitudes specifically of women may be changing. According to the 1992 special issue of *Extra! A Publication of Fair,* in 1989 a *New York Times* poll showed that "women overwhelmingly chose job discrimination as the most important problem facing women today"; 75 to 95 percent of women "credit the feminist campaign with improving their lives" (only 8 percent believed it made things worse); and 70 percent of the women polled "said the movement for women's rights had only just begun."

As the seeds of the activism of the 1960s had been sown in the reactionary 1950s, it would seem that our losses and the shocks of the 1980s may have propelled women back into action in the current decade. The spectacle of the rape trials of William Kennedy-Smith and Mike Tyson in rapid succession sparked a renewed awareness of the violence women are subject to and of society's apparent indifference toward it. Even more powerfully, the Clarence Thomas–Anita Hill hearings portrayed vividly not only women's vulnerability to sexual abuse, but our vulnerability in general to the insensitivity and the sexism of the men who are in charge of our social institutions. As former NOW president Eleanor Smeal remarked, "The Senate has done more in one week to underscore the critical need for more women in the Senate than feminists have been able to do in 25 years."[4] Dan Quayle's tirade against the fictional single mother Murphy Brown and the 1992 Republican National Convention's tirade against the very nonfictional feminist commitment to reproductive freedom (and to feminist values in general) brought all women's issues back into the forefront of public discussion. Finally, the woman-bashing heaped upon Hillary Clinton for her intelligence, assertiveness, and success, juxtaposed with her obvious competence, has created an awareness of the issue of fairness that is filtering into the public mind, especially of young women.

If, indeed, America is entering upon an era of renewed vitality for women's movement, then women's studies is faced with a vast responsibility in a complex situation. In the mid-1990s, women still constitute two-thirds of all the adult poor; more than 80 percent of full-time working women earn less than $20,000; and, according to the U.S. Bureau of the Census, "the average working women's salary lags as far behind the average man's as it did 20 years ago. American women face the worst gender-based pay gap in the developed world."[5] Violence of all kinds against women, including homophobic and other hate crimes, is increasing, the fanatical anti-woman forces of the religious right have vowed to redouble their opposition to reproductive autonomy, and women are ever more targeted for media and industry assaults on our appearance and health. We must prepare the present generation for its participation in women's struggle, but we must do so in an era of hardening antagonism and diminishing resources.

In these times of financial austerity, the fortunes of women's studies have been mixed and will continue to be precarious. On the one hand, we are everywhere. More than two-thirds of American colleges and universities has women's studies programs, a growing number with graduate offerings. The National Women's Studies Association, founded in 1977, has over 3,000 members, a journal of its own, and solid influence based on solid scholarship. In the late 1970s, careful women did not profess an interest in feminist scholarship until they had received tenure, and ambitious women avoided the field altogether. Today there are chairs in women's studies, joint appointments, and visiting lectureships. Women's studies today has luminaries, canons, "schools of thought," and a vast literature.

Let us not be mistaken, however, about our circumstances or our "place." We still live on the margin. Many programs continue to survive on the voluntary overwork of their faculty, and that is a situation likely to worsen—at least until the economy improves dramatically; many ambitious young academicians still think it prudent to avoid association with us, and we have had only the slightest impact on the traditional content or the traditional faculty of the traditional disciplines.

For those of us involved in women's studies, our evolution presents a two-edged sword. On the one hand, we have matured and grown in sophistication, having developed language, terminology, and concepts that help us to be more accurate in our analyses. We have opened up new areas of investigation. Very importantly, we are sensitizing ourselves to our own blind spots—racism, ethnocentrism, homophobia, agism, classism, and so on—sharpening our awareness regarding diversity among women and regarding the complexity of our subject. As women's studies has survived now over twenty-five years, we are seeing second-generation, even third-generation, feminist scholars, many of whom have been attracted to women's studies by the power of our scholarship and our classrooms rather than by direct experience on the streets.

On the other hand, although few would not delight in our growth, we must continue to be wary: Sophistication must not be allowed to degenerate into the vacuity we deplore in other fields. Women's studies must not be allowed to become irrelevant because it becomes another academic board game—full of cryptic lore and rules, but having little to do with life. Considerations of theory must be tempered with practical application. Today's young scholars must be encouraged to anchor their work firmly in the world outside the classroom. In the words of Barbara Smith:

> *The grass roots/community women's movement has given women's studies its life. How do we relate to it? How do we bring our gifts and our educational privilege back to it? Do we realize also how very much there is to learn in doing this essential work? Ask yourself what the women's movement is working on in your town or city. Are you a part of it? Ask yourself which women are living in the worst conditions in your town and how your work positively affects and directly touches their lives. If it doesn't, why not?*[6]

Today, as in the past, if we lose our rootedness in the women's movement, in concrete social action, we will lose not only our passion, but our heart and our meaning. In this I am reminded of the question Adrienne Rich put to the National Women's Studies Association regarding *disobedience:*

> *The question now facing Women's Studies, it seems to me, is the extent to which she has, in the past decade, matured into the dutiful daughter of the white, patriarchal university—a daughter who threw tantrums and played the tomboy when she was younger but who has now learned to wear a dress and speak and act almost as nicely as Daddy wants her to; the extent to which Women's Studies will remember that her mother was not Athena, but the Women's Liberation movement of the 1960s, a movement blazing with lesbian energy, whose earliest journals had names like* It Ain't Me, Babe, No More Fun and Games, off our backs, Up From Under, *and* The Furies. *In other words, how disobedient will Women's Studies be in the 1980s: how will this Association address the racism, misogyny, homophobia of the university and of the corporate and militarist society in which it is embedded; how will white feminist scholars and teachers and students practice disobedience to patriarchy?*[7]

It seems to me that this question is as relevant for us now as it was when it was formed in 1981.

As time and society and women's studies have moved along, so have I. Women's studies is past 20. I am past 50. Having been instructed by my work and my colleagues (dare I still use the word *sisters?*), I am losing some of my blind spots. I am becoming, for example, keenly aware of my own particularity—a white, middle-class, professional, Midwesterner, crusted around a working-class, Jewish, loner Bronx kid. I understand better what that enables me to say and what I should leave for others to say: I tend to be more careful in my speech—measuring, qualifying. I have given up what Mary Helen Osborne calls "certitude"; I know how much I don't know. I hope that this is reflected in this edition of *Issues in Feminism.*

What has not altered is my passionate belief in the women's movement, in the need for social change, in the possibilities of the future. I am still an unregenerate feminist, rooted, by choice, in the spirit of (dare I still use the phrase?) women's liberation. I hope that too is reflected in this edition.

This book is designed for beginners in feminism and women's studies, for those who have not yet had the experience of recognition and reappraisal, or who have had it only in the most inchoate way. The text and readings here are included not only to impart information; as their foremost goal they seek to precipitate the reader into an awareness of the self in contrast to gender. This is a primer in the most exact sense: it is directed at the prime, the spring, the level of consciousness out of which come the need and the decision to understand. It aims to engage students by revealing the gender issues embedded in the most familiar facets of life: family relationships, work, education, media, religion, popular culture. The ideas presented here comprise a *first* course in women's studies, first both logically and existentially.

The experiences we have, the awareness we develop, and the way we develop them are rarely ordered according to the patterns of academic disciplines. Reality, after all, is not disciplinary. Neither is this book, since it attempts, at least in part, to present ideas as life might. The readings are interdisciplinary, ranging across many fields of study and chosen to reveal issues in their interrelatedness. I have not necessarily selected the most recent pieces, the most erudite, or even the most reputable. I brought together statements from past and present that are representative of the prevailing notions that have had terrific impact on the lives of women (and hence of men). These readings, diverse as they are, go together. They have been selected for their collective power to provide a picture of the pattern of ideas about women. The readings are meant to educate in the broadest sense—not only to bring students face to face with their experience now, but also to provide them with a context, the sources of current beliefs in the ideas of the distant and not so distant past.

The theme of this book in both text and readings is twofold. First, in order to understand ourselves and our world we must be aware of all the notions regarding women, from the academic to the popular, from the scientific to the pseudoscientific, from the complex to the simplistic and from the thoughtful to the downright silly. Second, understanding can emerge only from critical analysis grounded in a sensitivity to even the homeliest events of our day-to-day lives.

After a short discussion of the nature of women's studies, we begin with an explication of the major themes of sex-role arrangements: the male and female ideals, the roles and expectations of gender as they have been expressed in various aspects of our culture and as they crisscross with class, race, ethnicity, sexual identity, and other social categories. We begin with these images—the Mars and Venus ideals—because they are at the root of social beliefs and attitudes toward the sexes. They have great explanatory value, both for the traditionalist, as justification for current behaviors, and for the feminist, as a schema to be explored. Then, following the presentation of some classic theories of why gender differences exist, the ideals of masculinity and femininity are traced through their appearances in such pertinent aspects of life as family, sexuality, education, work, and politics. Here, in the parts of our life we feel most deeply, the images are revealed in all their distortion and power. I hope that if students can recognize the destructive potential of the traditional images and stereotypes in their own lives, they will seek alternatives.

Although what follows covers a range of areas, from psychology to economics, from politics to anthropology, its place is primarily in the humanities. The driving questions in the issues presented are: What does this mean? How does this affect the quality of our lives? What would be better? Why does it matter?

If there is a discipline involved in the book, it is philosophy. Its process is to pose questions, articulate various responses, assess them, set the stage for further questions, and so on—the Socratic approach, all in the quest for knowledge. Its consequence is growth in wisdom and spirit. Nonetheless, what we will be doing here is women's studies, a nondisciplinary, multidisciplinary, counterdisciplinary feminist exploration of the conditions of our lives, where we ourselves set the boundaries of what may be asked and what we may ultimately do with the answers we devise.

To complete a project like *Issues in Feminism* requires many kinds of help and support. I am grateful to many colleagues who have reviewed the manuscript and offered guidance and suggestions, especially Joseph J. Arpad, California State University at Fresno; Susan Arpad, California State University at Fresno; Anne M. Butler, Utah State University; Carol Coburn, University of Kansas; Joan Hagman, Concordia College; Barbara S. Havira, Western Michigan University; Annis H. Hopkins, Arizona State University; Betty C. Safford, California State University at Fullerton; Tim Weinfeld, Western Maryland College; and Barbara A. White, University of New Hampshire. Special thanks go to Anne Bezdek for days spent in libraries searching bibliographies, chronologies, and statistical tomes and spent in my basement doing the same with publishers and authors, and permissions! It is most important that I thank Carol Keene, chairperson of philosophical studies at Southern Illinois University at Edwardsville, for so kindly granting me the precious time to write and teach in women's studies.

To Michael Allaband goes my deepest appreciation for respite on the river, dinners on the lake, and the certainty that partnership between the sexes is a possible and worthy ideal.

—Sheila Ruth

1. Quoted in *Extra! A Publication of FAIR,* Special Issue, 1992.
2. Patricia J. Williams, "Blockbusting the Canon," *Ms.* (September/October 1991), pp. 59–60.
3. "Looking Beyond the Slogans: The Author of 'Backlash' Evaluates the 'Year of the Woman.' " *Newsweek,* 28 December 1992, p. 31.

4. Quoted in Patricia Aburdene and John Naisbitt, *Megatrends for Women* (New York: Villard Books, 1992), p. 20.
5. Quoted in *Extra! A Publication of FAIR,* Special Issue, 1992.
6. Barbara Smith, "Racism and Women's Studies," in *All the Women Are White, All the Blacks Are Men, But Some of Us Are Brave,* ed. Gloria T. Hull, Patricia Bell Scott, and Barbara Smith (Old Westbury, NY: The Feminist Press, 1982); quoted in *Making Face, Making Soul, Haciendo Caras: Creative and Critical Perspectives by Women of Color,* ed. Gloria Anzaldúa (San Francisco: Aunt Lute Foundation Books, 1990), p. 27.
7. Adrienne Rich, "Disobedience and Women's Studies," in *Blood, Bread, and Poetry: Selected Prose 1979–1985* (New York: W. W. Norton, 1986), pp. 78–79.

1

An Introduction to Women's Studies

What Is "Women's Studies"?

In the middle to late 1960s, a scattering of courses focusing on feminist issues began to appear on college campuses. In 1970 the terms *women's studies* or *feminist studies* were first used to refer to them. Against strong resistance, two or three courses developed into thousands of courses, into programs, into a whole new educational and intellectual enterprise.

According to a study by Florence Howe, by 1980 university faculty were teaching more than twenty thousand such courses in institutions all over the country.[1] Today, there are programs at all levels of study—from the undergraduate minor to the doctorate—and the number is still increasing. According to the National Women's Studies Association, there was an increase of 23 percent in undergraduate programs listed between 1988 and 1990 (creating a total of more than 500 programs!), and by 1990 there were 102 programs offering work at the graduate level.[2] The extent of women's studies is even greater if we consider the thousands of noncredit courses offered through extension and continuing education programs and those offered in countries other than the United States.

In 1977 the number of people involved in feminist research had grown so large and their interests were so diverse that it became necessary to establish some formal means of communication and support. In January of that year, delegates from institutions all over the country participated in the founding of the National Women's Studies Association, which now has more than three thousand members.[3]

For contemporary university education and for some high schools, women's studies is a fact of life. But what is the nature of this new enterprise? What precisely does it do?

Because women's studies is still very young—only about twenty-five years old—it is difficult to give it an absolute definition. For one thing, scholars are still only beginning to articulate the challenging new insights and methods that are developing within the field. For another, women's studies is a field that has few models. It consciously rejects many traditional forms of inquiry, concepts, and explanatory systems; at the same time, it is developing new and sometimes unique traditions and authorities of its own.

In this chapter, you will learn how feminist researchers are discovering that most of the accepted theories in all the traditional fields—even their methods of pursuing knowledge—are rife with prejudice and misunderstandings about women in particular and humanity in general. Because the task is so complex, feminist thinkers are extremely hesitant to impose artificial limits on the work of those who seek to uncover this bias and restore balance in knowledge. We are committed to being tolerant toward new methodologies and analyses in order to avoid creating additional rigid principles that would discourage research. Therefore, we place a high value on freedom and self-determination. Ideologically, and often temperamentally, we are suspicious of hierarchies and of control, whether in social relations or in intellectual pursuits. Self-disciplined freedom and cooperative efforts, we believe, are more apt to produce constructive results in most endeavors. Thus, most of us try to encourage and be open to ideas even when they are very different from our own. You will see that openness and freedom from rigid preconception is not easy to attain, and the work is far from complete.

For many reasons, then—the rich diversity of perspectives and people engaged in women's studies; the newness of feminist research; the hesitancy to embrace constricting standards; and the unusually strong desire for tolerance, experimentation, and growth—the ideas, methods, curricula, and theories of women's studies exhibit great variety and resist easy definition. Those of us now working in women's studies have called it variously a process, a field of inquiry, a critical perspective, a center for social action, and/or the academic arm of the women's movement. It is all of these and more.

The "Study of Women"

For centuries, women have been "studied." Aristotle theorized that we were "misbegotten males," conceived instead of men when the winds were not propitious. Aquinas decided that because women were at least necessary for procreation, God had not, after all, made some terrible mistake in creating us. Freud "discovered" the vengeful, castrating, penis-envying character of us all, and the philosopher Karl Stern speculated about our "nonreflective," cosmically tied life of nature.[4]

Such concepts in past studies of women reflect the origin of these studies: They were carried on almost exclusively by men working together in institutions and disciplines absolutely closed to women. An examination of the many traditional works on women reveals certain characteristics:

- Women are generally looked *at;* we have rarely done our own looking and still more rarely have we been asked for our opinions concerning our own experience. Those ideas that women have offered have tended to be ignored or debunked unless they reinforced existing beliefs.
- Women are generally "studied" in a separate section or subsection of a work, as though we are some kind of extra appendage or anomaly, not readily understood within the general context of the inquiry. In Aristotle's *Politics,* for example, following a discussion of *human* excellence is a separate section asking whether women as well as men might have "excellence," and, if so, in what this excellence might consist.[5] (Aristotle decided that women's excellence is composed of obedience and silence.) An *Introduction to Islam*[6] contains fifteen chapters describing the fundamental beliefs and practices of the Muslim *people.* One chapter is entitled "The Muslim Woman." There is no chapter on "The Muslim Man."
- Professional and academic studies of women reflect the prejudices and attitudes that exist in the wider culture. Without women's own perspectives to balance the historical fund of ignorance and superstition surrounding our lives, conventional (misogynist) wisdom has been carried into research by so-called authorities on the subject, has hardened into accepted theories, and has ultimately become "science." As science, these myths about women have been used to justify all sorts of oppression from witch hunts to clitoridectomy.

Until recently, the accepted studies of women from primitive times to the present have examined women as if we were senseless, semihuman creatures unable to speak for ourselves; we have been prodded, dissected, categorized and filed, researched and resolved. No wonder the traditional products of the "study of women" are distorted and counterproductive.

Such an approach to understanding women's lives necessarily produces poor information. Try reversing the gender, and treat the male as the adjunct of humanity instead of the female. Can you imagine a history of westward expansion containing a chapter on the pioneer husband or the pioneer male? Or how would you evaluate an analysis of masculine attitudes on impotence that was researched and written entirely by women and was based on their observations alone, with no input from men?

Women's Studies and the Issue of Diversity Among Women

Gaining freedom from rigid preconception is not easy to attain. That is true for any thinker. As in the wider society, feminist scholars, too, have been subject to bias and misconception, to prejudice, and to narrowness of vision, which has been reflected in our work. Women's studies and the women's movement is now engaged in the arduous process of correcting serious errors. Among the *isms* with which we have been struggling are racism, ethnocentrism, heterosexism, classism, and ageism.

Early enthusiasm for "sisterhood," for cohesion among women *as* women, blinded many of us to the importance of understanding the *differences* among us as well as the similarities, and it led us into serious theoretical and practical mistakes. Elizabeth Spelman, in 1988, delineated the problem very sharply when she said that there is

> *a tendency in dominant Western feminist thought to posit an essential "womanness" that all women have and share in common despite the racial, class, religious, ethnic, and cultural differences among us. I try to show that the notion of a generic "woman" functions in feminist thought much the way the notion of generic "man" has functioned in Western philosophy: it obscures the heterogeneity of women and cuts off examination of the significance of such heterogeneity for feminist theory and political activity.*[7]

Spelman summed the issue up quite succinctly in citing Audre Lorde (whose selection you will see in Chapter 4): "There is a pretense to a homogeneity of experience covered by the word *sisterhood* that does not in fact exist."[8]

Earlier, sociologist Jessie Bernard, author of several books about women's experience, raised the matter this way:

> *Ruth Useem, a sociologist, once commented on the inadequacy of the single mark she had to make on all documents asking for "sex." All she could do was check the F box. But she knew that this "mark of Eve" told the reader very little about her. There were so many kinds of F: F_1, F_2, . . . F_n. . . . Whatever the difference may be between M and F, and whatever the origin of these differences may be, they are matched and in some cases exceeded by differences among women themselves. A woman may in many ways be more like the average man than she is like another woman. . . . In many situations F_1 may have more in common with M_1 than with any of the Fs. Rank, for example, is more important than sex in many situations. A princess has more in common with a prince than with a domestic; a professional woman often has more in common with a colleague than with a cleaning woman; an heiress with an heir than with a woman receiving welfare payments. Sometimes F_1 and F_2 have not only different but opposing points of view, each seeing the other as a threat either to a vested interest or to opportunity for achievement. The wife of a workingman may not agree with the woman worker on the principle of equal pay for equal work; she believes her husband should get more because he has to support his family. . . .*
>
> *It would, then, be more in line with the facts of life if, instead of compressing all women into the F category, the diversity among them could be recognized by allowing for F_1, F_2, . . . F_n.*[9]

For feminist research, understanding the diverse circumstances among women is critical. Obviously, we cannot allow ourselves to make the same mistakes we so abhor in other fields of study and in the wider society. Comprehending differences in perspective among women is not only required to maintain the kind of relationships we desire among ourselves, it is a prerequisite for making credible sense of reality. Masculine bias among men not only impairs women's lives, it deforms men's own lives as well because it distorts their discernment of reality. The pernicious *isms* among and in women have the same effect: They not only injure the women who are marginalized, they diminish the lives of all women, including those of the dominant group.

> *The reason racism is a feminist issue is easily explained by the inherent definition of feminism. Feminism is the political theory and practice that struggles to free all women: women of color, working-class women, poor women, disabled women, lesbians, old women—as well as white, economically privileged, heterosexual women. Anything less than this vision of total freedom is not feminism, but merely female self-aggrandizement.*
>
> *. . . White women don't work on racism to do a favor for someone else, solely to benefit Third World women.*

> *You have to comprehend how racism distorts and lessens your own lives as white women—that racism affects your chances for survival, too, and that it is very definitely your issue. Until you understand this, no fundamental change will come about.*
>
> –BARBARA SMITH, *Racism and Women's Studies*[10]

Our particular perspective affects the way we experience our lives in a patriarchal society, how we see ourselves, how we understand ourselves in relation to different groups of women and men, and how we seek solutions to our problems as women. When we explore women's studies, then, we all must come to terms with "particularity." In *Women's Realities, Women's Choices*, the Hunter College Women's Studies Collective explained the issue this way:

> *Individuals come to women's studies and feminism from a variety of cultural and social backgrounds. As members of different races, ethnic groups, economic classes, and age groups, we bring with us different interests and preoccupations which sometimes make it difficult to arrive at a consensus.*
>
> *Those of us who were brought up as members of oppressed racial and ethnic groups and social classes may find it particularly difficult to see what we have in common with those whom we have learned to classify as members of privileged, dominant groups. . . .*
>
> *Our identity as black, Jew, Chicana, Puerto Rican, Native American, Asian American, or member of a less privileged economic class depends on our consciousness of the history of our oppression by others. Freedom from racist, ethnic, or class oppression may rank highest among our priorities, and to focus attention on a division within our groups, between women and men, may seem to us a betrayal of our common cause. How can we concern ourselves with the problems of the women among our oppressors or even with our own experiences of sexism in our particular group when the men in our group daily suffer oppression from more privileged groups and classes?*[11]

Yet we are becoming more sophisticated in our analyses, and as we grow, we encompass and integrate more diverse perspectives, enlarge our understanding, and create the possibilities of connection. Said Robin Morgan, feminist activist and, until very recently, editor of *Ms.* magazine:

> *After all, on the one hand, as feminists we celebrate our diversity. On the other hand, we've all experienced how difficult attempts at dialogue among different women can be. So what do we mean when we say we "speak feminism"?*
>
> *It's nothing so sentimental (or arrogant) as presuming our differences don't exist. But it's nothing so cowardly (or lazy) as overemphasizing them to the point of justifying not engaging each other across them.*
>
> *It's a complex, delicate kind of "feminist diplomacy" that we're still in the process of developing. It involves respect, courtesy, risk, curiosity, and patience. It means doing one's homework in advance, being willing to be vulnerable, and attentively* listening *to one another. (A sense of humor never hurts, either.) Skill improves with practice, and practicing feminist diplomacy is challenging, exhilarating, rewarding—and at times exhausting.*
>
> *Feminism itself dares to assume that, beneath all our (chosen or forced) diversity, we are in fact much the same—yet the* ways *in which we are similar are not for any one woman or group of women to specify, but for all of us, collectively, to explore and define—a multiplicity of feminisms. In other words, our experience as female human beings in patriarchy may be the same, but our experiences of that experience differ.*[12]

Women's Studies and Feminism

What transforms the "study of women" into women's studies is reflected in the terms themselves. In the "*study of women,*" women are objects; in *women's studies,* we are subjects.

Women's studies has a feminist base. Feminists do not agree among themselves on one all-inclusive and universally acceptable definition of *feminism.* Depending on a number of factors, the term *feminism* can mean different things and have a variety of functions. We shall see later that several different theories of feminism exist, and considerable discussion centers on what it means to be a feminist, what goals feminism should have, and how feminists should behave. Feminism may be a perspective, a worldview, a political theory, a spiritual focus, or a kind of activism. Actually, one learns best what feminism means by listening to the assertions of women who consider themselves feminists and by understanding how they respond to events and conditions.

Just how much range in meaning there can be for the term is reflected in this partial list of the definitions of "Feminism" as reported in Cheris Kramarae and Paula A. Treichler's *Feminist Dictionary:*[13]

> *May be defined as a movement seeking the reorganization of the world upon a basis of sex-equality in all human relations; a movement which would reject every differentiation between individuals upon the ground of sex, would abolish all sex privileges and sex burdens, and would strive to set up the recognition of the common humanity of woman and man as the foundation of law and custom.*
>
> –THERESA BILLINGTON-GREIG, "Feminism and Politics," *The Contemporary Review,* November 1911

> *. . . has as yet no defined creed . . . [Is] the articulate consciousness of mind in women . . . in its different forms of expression.*
>
> "The Freewoman," 1911, *Votes for Women*

> *Feminism at heart is a massive complaint. Lesbianism is the solution. . . . Until all women are lesbians there will be no true political revolution. No feminist per se has advanced a solution outside of accommodation to the man.*
>
> –JILL JOHNSTON, *Lesbian Nation,* 1973

> *Begins but cannot end with the discovery by an individual of her self-consciousness as a woman. It is not, finally, even the recognition of her reasons for anger, or the decision to change her life, to go back to school, to leave a marriage. . . . Feminism means finally that we renounce our obedience to the fathers and recognize that the world they have described is not the whole world. . . . Feminism implies that we recognize fully the inadequacy for us, the distortion, of male-created ideologies, and that we proceed to think, and act, out of that recognition.*
>
> –ADRIENNE RICH, *Of Woman Born,* 1976

> *A method of analysis as well as a discovery of new material. It asks new questions as well as coming up with new answers. Its central concern is with the social distinction between men and women, with the fact of this distinction, with its meanings, and with its causes and consequences.*
>
> –JULIET MITCHELL AND ANNE OAKLEY, *The Rights and Wrongs of Women,* 1976

> *Is a mode of analysis, a method of approaching life and politics, a way of asking questions and searching for answers, rather than a set of political conclusions about the oppression of women.*
>
> –NANCY HARTSOCK, "Feminist Theory and the Development of Revolutionary Strategy," in Zillah Eisenstein, *Capitalist Patriarchy and the Case for Socialist Feminism,* 1979

> *Feminism is the political theory and practice to free all women; women of color, working-class women, poor women, physically challenged women, lesbians, old women, as well as white economically privileged heterosexual women. Anything less than this is not feminism, but merely female self-aggrandizement.*
>
> –BARBARA SMITH in Cherrie Moraga and Gloria Anzaldúa, *This Bridge Called My Back,* 1981

> *Is a commitment to eradicating the ideology of domination that permeates Western culture on various levels—sex, race, and class, to name a few—and a commitment to reorganizing U.S. society, so that the self-development of people can take precedence over imperialism, economic expansion, and material desires.*
>
> –BELL HOOKS, *Ain't I a Woman,* 1981

> *Is an entire world view or* gestalt, *not just a laundry list of "women's issues." Feminist theory provides a basis for understanding every area of our lives, and a feminist perspective can affect the world politically, culturally, economically, and spiritually.*
>
> –CHARLOTTE BUNCH, *Learning Our Way,* 1983

> *Third World feminism is about feeding people in all their hungers.*
>
> –CHERRIE MORAGA, *Loving in the War Years,* 1983

From Alice Walker we have the strong, jubilant definition of a *"womanist,"* a variation on the term *feminist.*

> *Womanist 1. From* womanish. *(Opp. of "girlish," i.e., frivolous, irresponsible, not serious.) A black feminist or feminist of color. From the black folk expression of mothers to female children, "You acting womanish,"*

> *i.e., like a woman. Usually referring to outrageous, audacious, courageous or* willful *behavior. Wanting to know more and in greater depth than is considered "good" for one. Interested in grown-up doings. Acting grown up. Being grown up. Interchangeable with another black folk expression: "You trying to be grown." Responsible. In charge.* Serious.
>
> 2. Also: *A woman who loves other women, sexually and/or nonsexually. Appreciates and prefers women's culture, women's emotional flexibility (values tears as natural counterbalance of laughter), and women's strength. Sometimes loves individual men, sexually and/or nonsexually. Committed to survival and wholeness of entire people, male and female. Not a separatist, except periodically, for health. Traditionally universalist, as in: "Mama, why are we brown, pink, and yellow, and our cousins are white, beige, and black?" Ans.: "Well, you know the colored race is just like a flower garden, with every color flower represented." Traditionally capable, as in: "Mama, I'm walking to Canada and I'm taking you and a bunch of other slaves with me." Reply: "It wouldn't be the first time."*
>
> 3. *Loves music. Loves dance. Loves the moon. Loves the Spirit. Loves love and food and roundness. Loves struggle. Loves the Folk. Loves herself.* Regardless.
>
> 4. *Womanist is to feminist as purple to lavender.*[14]

Notwithstanding our diversity, certain beliefs, values, and attitudes are common to all feminists. To set a context for comprehending the rich variety of feminist/womanist thought, these common points might be articulated as follows:

- *Feminism* means literally *"womanism."* As feminists we value women, not in the hypocritical fashion of centuries of male-dominated cultures in which women were valued for the work they could produce, the price they could bring, or the services they could render; nor do we value women provided they behave according to some externally imposed set of requirements. Rather we value women in and of themselves, as ends in themselves, and for themselves.
- As feminists we value the fact of being women as highly as we value the fact of being human. We do not accept the cultural images of women as incompetent, petty, irresponsible, or weak. In contrast, we affirm our capacities to be strong, capable, intelligent, successful, ethical human beings. Many of us believe that our history and special forms of experience have set the conditions of making us particularly "excellent" human beings.
- As feminists we value autonomy for ourselves as individuals and for women as a group. We mean to develop the conditions that will enable us to control our own political, social, economic, and personal destinies.
- As feminists we reject attitudes that regard the traditionally ascribed masculine characteristics of aggression, power, and competition as good and desirable and the ascribed feminine characteristics of compassion, tenderness, and compromise as weak and ridiculous. We tend to reject both the practice of separating human qualities into two categories—one of them for men and one for women—and the valuing of one of those categories above the other. Instead we recognize that all such characteristics may appear in either sex, and we evaluate each of them on its own merit.
- As feminists we understand that the majority of beliefs and attitudes regarding women both in our own culture and in most other cultures are false or wrongheaded, based on myth, ignorance, hate, and fear. It is necessary to replace myth with reality and ignorance with knowledge about women created by women, first for women and finally for all people.
- As feminists we point out that for centuries we have been denied our rights as citizens and as human beings. The right to vote, the right to earn a substantive living commensurate with effort, the freedom to determine whether to bear children—the denial of these and other freedoms constitutes concrete instances of oppression. We recognize that women possess persistent strength and spirit in the face of such oppression and are optimistic about the possibilities of change. Many of the qualities developed by women in the face of denial are precious and unique.

It is this feminist base—on the one hand, a realization that women's reality has been distorted, on the other, a positive and affirming stance toward women and womanhood—that transforms the "study of women" into women's studies. Women's studies might have been called feminist studies, and in some institutions it is; but some feminist educators have considered this term to be strategically imprudent since it evokes resistance from entrenched and powerful antifemale forces within institutions.

Resistance to Women's Studies

Women's programs, academic and nonacademic—even after twenty-five years of excellence—are still often met with derision or intolerance. The same forces that limit the freedom, status, and power of women in the wider society limit women within academe. For reasons we shall explore in this book, a pro-woman stance is threatening to traditional attitudes and institutional structures. The very word *feminism* carries fearful connotations for many people and evokes a defensive response.

Remarks that the student of women's studies may encounter express that defensive posture:

- "Are you taking that stuff?! What are you, a *man-hater*?"
- "Women's studies? What good is that going to do you?"
- "Since you've been reading that stuff you've been hard to get along with. I don't want to hear any more about it."

Faculty hear the same kind of comments, cast a little differently:

- "Feminism is biased. How do you expect to teach a course like that fairly? You can't be objective."
- "You were hired to teach political science, not waste your time getting sidetracked on trivia. *Women in Politics* is just too esoteric a course for this department to spend resources on."
- "Women's studies! Are you serious? When are we going to get a men's studies program?"
- "We've got to get back to basics. Women's studies is just a faddish trend."

It is interesting, and a little depressing, to note that after more than thirty years of a women's movement and twenty five years of women's studies, the issue of harassment of women, not just in universities but *in the women's studies classroom in particular,* is looming large enough to warrant increased attention. As recently as 1991, professors of women's studies Marcia Bedard and Beth Hartung raised the question of how to deal with the growing harassment of women faculty and students in women's studies classrooms.[15] Citing an expanding body of literature that examines various forms of harassment that is generally directed at female students and faculty by male students, they characterized the women's studies classroom as often a "specific site of harassment" on campus, sometimes a " 'Blackboard Jungle' revisited." Feminist teachers and scholars reported adversarial relationships, taunting of instructors and female students, passive resistance, and disruption of classes (among others) as examples of the hostile behavior they encounter. Pointing out that many of these behaviors need to be understood "in the larger context of campus violence against women," Bedard and Hartung describe some of the forms classroom harassment can take:

- claiming male victim status or challenging facts with particularistic anecdotes to undermine the credibility of feminist reading materials and instructors.
- dominating class discussions (talking too much and too long so that no one else has a chance to express their views or speaking so loudly and aggressively that other students are silenced and the instructor is irritated).
- aggressively pointing out minor flaws in statements of other students or the instructor, stating the exception to every generalization, and finding something wrong with everything from quizzes to books.
- changing the topic abruptly in the middle of a class discussion, often to claim male victim status or shift discussion to a less threatening topic.
- formulating a challenge after the first few sentences of an instructor's lecture, not listening to anything from that point on, and leaping in to argue at the first pause.
- taking intransigent and dogmatic stands on even minor positions and insisting that the instructor recognize the validity of the rigid positions.[16]

Although women constitute more than half the human population, serious examination of women's world and its implications for all humanity is simply not considered meaningful and important from a male-centered perspective. Feminist contentions that both women and the wider society are being deprived of female power are not seen as valid; the argument is dismissed, just as women are often dismissed. Rarely do the fruits of feminist research find their way from women's studies into the wider curriculum or the classrooms of other instructors—a situation that becomes a point of frustration for women's studies student and teacher alike.

Bias in Academe

Bias—which means prejudice, the absence of objectivity—derives from a term that means oblique, slanted, not standard or true, off-center. Bias implies some kind of distortion, usually unconscious. It is ironic that the enterprise of women's studies should be charged with bias.

When it is argued that feminist thinkers and women's studies are biased, at least two things are being said: (1) that feminists hold a set of beliefs that is somehow off-center, askew from "the truth"; and (2) that either we are unaware of having a distorted perspective, or we deliberately intend to impose slanted views on unsuspecting and vulnerable minds.

Feminism is perceived as a skewing of reality. Feminists would argue, however, that it is the traditional male-defined image of reality that is skewed.

Centuries ago, discerning thinkers in science, theology, and philosophy recognized the fallacy of mistaking the part for the whole. In philosophy and theology, it was recognized that to mistake human values and perspectives for universal ones was to be misled in analyses of God and reality. This mistake was called *anthropocentrism,* and cautious thinkers learned to avoid it. More recently, social scientists have become aware of the dangers of *ethnocentrism,* the practice of imposing the standards of one's own culture on another. *Egocentrism,* whether conceptual (as when an individual assumes that others see reality as he or she does) or ethical, also distorts understanding. The error here lies in assuming that one's own special view of the world is the true and only one, applicable everywhere to everyone and everything. Universally acknowledged to be fallacious, all such *isms* are guarded against—all, that is, except the most pervasive and distorting *ism* of all: *masculine-ism* or *masculism* (sometimes called *androcentrism*).

Masculism, as practiced in our culture, has many facets. We shall explore them in Chapter 2. Here we need only say that masculism is in part the mistaking of male perspectives, beliefs, attitudes, standards, values, and perceptions for all human perceptions. Masculism is pervasive in our culture except for the feminist challenge, and it is most frequently unconscious.

In almost every culture, the tools and conditions necessary for learning and analysis, the means of communication, and the forms of legitimization of knowledge have been jealously and effectively kept from women. In some societies, the artifacts of history, the symbols of religious significance, and the activities of power are all secreted in a special hut, the men's hut, taboo to women. In other cultures, men speak a private language that the women of the tribe are forbidden to utter; in that language, the policies of the tribe are decided. In our own culture, disfranchisement was effected in an analogous way. Reading and studying were deemed dangerous for women, contributing to discontent and rebellion against our "natural" roles as wives and helpmates. Too much learning, it was said, would drain away the energies we needed to produce children. Mathematics and science were particularly dangerous. They might rob women of a meek and gentle loveliness. Women were not supposed to have the stomach or the wit for politics. Such views have functioned as justifications for denying women the education, tools, and power to sustain ourselves and to direct society.

Women have been barred from the possibility of contributing all we can to the intellectual and scientific worldview. That has been reserved for men, who are in control of the academic disciplines, the universities, the learned societies, the presses, and the research foundations. With women virtually excluded from the intellectual power centers, the (male) minority opinion has been fallaciously equated with all that could be said. The male establishment has, in essence, appropriated reality for itself. Men have dominated the wider society. Their needs and goals have become official social goals. In learning, male thought has become official thought. The male stance has become the official human stance.

Consider, for example, the following analysis of the concept of respect by Joel Feinberg, a contemporary philosopher (italics added):[17]

> *In olden days, when power and authority went hand in hand . . . the scale of respect was one with the scales of power and status. This was the background against which the earliest moralists could begin demanding that respect be shown to various classes of the* deserving weak, *too. Hence our rude and unimpressed ancestors were urged to "show respect" for women, for the aged, for the clergy. . . . Christianity gave dignity even to the* meek and humble. *Respect could then be extended to the aged, to women, to the clergy. . . . To see a woman as having dignity now is to see her as in a moral position to make claims against* our *conduct, even though she may lack physical or political power over us. Certain minimal forms of consideration are her due, something she has coming, and can rightfully claim, even when she is in no position to make demands in the gunman sense. Insofar as* we *think of her that way* we *have respect for her . . . and insofar as she shares this image of herself she has self-respect.*[18]

Now, as I read this argument from my woman's perspective, I think: Indeed! And would any *man* in such a position—weak, meek, humble, and powerless—perceive himself with self-respect? Who is this author to speak for me? And who are the *we* (*us, our*) of whom Feinberg speaks? He is a philosopher addressing philosophers. But he could not mean that only philosophers grant respect in this fashion. (Besides, I am a philosopher). No, Feinberg is analyzing the concept of respect as it is used, given, and granted in society, among people. Which people? Society surely must include women. Do women grant respect that way? Am I part of that *we, us?* I certainly do not think of women and our worthiness that way. Generic *we?* Rather not. This is a mental involution impossible for me to make without self-alienation.

Feinberg's essay and his use of *we* (*us, our*) in juxtaposition to the term *women* is only one example among many of a worldview that constitutes humanity as male and relegates women to the status of out-group. Comfortable and confident that "we boys" are "we everyone," Feinberg exhibits the masculist usurpation of universality. The usurpation is conveniently masked by the linguistic device of generic *man* and is so generally accepted that it has become invisible to the naked (that is, nonfeminist) eye. For example, a film entitled *Why Man Creates* (1968), produced for the Kaiser Corporation and ostensibly an inquiry into the nature and motivation of *human* creativity, is composed of sequences in which scientists, artists, inventors, and symbols are all male; women appear only as wives, foils, or the subject of art. *The Uncommitted: Alienated Youth in Modern American Society* (1960), a sociopsychological study by Kenneth Keniston based on profiles of alienated young people, contained not one female profile, yet purported to be a study of alienated *youth.* The jacket of the book stated that "Mr. Keniston starts from an intensive study of alienated *youth,* asking why a group of talented and privileged young *men* should reject . . . " (italics added). An advertisement describes a work entitled *The States of Human Life: A Biography of Entire Man* (1974) as follows: "In this study of the career of the *individual,* the age-grades are considered as escarpments. . . . The perspective of the *individual* . . . shifts radically as *he* grows from infancy to young *manhood* and from maturity to old age" (italics added). In another example, a modern logic textbook asks the supposedly general reader, "She won't give you a date?" Finally, the Constitution of the United States declared, "We the people," although at the time women were totally disfranchised. The examples are endless.

The conceptual confusing of *human* and *male* historically and in the present in all disciplines and inquiries is so pervasive as to be the rule rather than the exception. Feminist criticism is revealing male bias, not creating a female one, as charged. Women's studies seeks to be the prophylactic of bias, not the cause.

Some researchers contend there are areas of investigation directly relevant to women's lives that may be pursued without a political perspective or a sex-theoretical stance: the female endocrine system, for example, or human reproduction. Such subjects, it is argued, are simply factual. It does not matter whether they are pursued by feminists or nonfeminists. Their content, being neutral in this respect, might be considered women's studies, but not feminist studies.

Feminist theoreticians in every field, however, are convinced that no purely factual studies exist. The way knowledge has been ordered, the methods of asking and answering questions, and the constructs used to understand data have all developed within a framework of male bias. Even an apparently true statement like the following becomes problematic from a feminist perspective: "The Renaissance took place during the fourteenth, fifteenth, and sixteenth centuries." A feminist historian illustrated the effect of a woman-oriented perspective on this traditionally accepted, so-called historical truth:

> *A young specialist in the Renaissance spoke to the obvious but unasked question, "Did women have a renaissance?" Her response was a jolt, for she suggested that the bourgeoisification of Italian society deprived women of power, created a patriarchal culture, and, in general, set women back in their quest for human liberty and autonomy. So what "renaissance" can be considered? What is progress, after all, if the transformation to a modern social order is achieved at the expense of half a population?*
>
> *Such questions would never have been asked within the context of traditional political and economic history, nor would they emerge in ordinary considerations of intellectual "revolutions." The Renaissance becomes problematic only as a question of social history, and it is precisely that field with which the women's movement has merged to create a wholly new way to regard the human past.*[19]

It is still a matter of argument whether truly neutral analyses with respect to sex orientation are possible. Perhaps a continuum of neutral to nonneutral is more relevant. Our developing conceptual tools will resolve this question. Whatever the resolution, though, the framework of the enterprise itself must be feminist.

An interesting development of the last few years has been the growth of two new fields, offshoots of women's studies: men's studies and gender studies. Prompted by the insights and new perspectives of feminist scholarship, some male scholars have begun to rethink the nature of masculinity, much as women have been analyzing the meanings of femininity and womanhood.

As Harry Brod explains, the new critique of the social constructions of manhood contains two main themes:

> *An acceptance of the obvious fact that most scholarship, in the conventional sense, has been about men, and the contention that such scholarship, in perhaps a more significant sense, has not really been about men at all. In my attempt to make "The Case for Men's Studies," I offer the following formulation:*
>
> > *While seemingly about men, traditional scholarship's treatment of generic man as the human norm in fact systematically excludes from consideration what is unique to men* qua *men. The over generalization from male to generic human experience not only distorts our understanding of what, if anything, is truly generic to humanity but also precludes the study of masculinity as a specific male experience, rather than a universal paradigm for human experience. The most general definition of men's studies is that it is the study of masculinities and male experiences as specific and varying social-historical-cultural formations. Such studies situate masculinities as objects of study on a par with femininities, instead of elevating them to universal norms.*
>
> *Men's studies questions assumptions that have passed beyond the horizons of usual scholarly inquiry to bring them back under critical purview. These assumptions about masculinity are so widely shared that they cease to appear as assumptions.*[20]

Gender studies is said to be an umbrella enterprise, encompassing both women's studies and men's studies. But some women's studies scholars are justifiably concerned about the development of gender studies programs. Certainly it is time that maleness and men's behavior be investigated in the same critical way as femaleness and by men as well as by women. Better understanding of men as men and the resultant changes in men's behavior and values can only accelerate the evolution of humane societies. Furthermore, it is natural that feminist insight should spur men to look into their own lives. Men's studies has real value and can complement feminist critique.

However, although women's studies is gender scholarship, not all gender scholarship can be or should be thought of as women's studies. Women's studies is and must be feminist. Gender studies may not be. If women's studies allows itself to be absorbed into gender studies, will it lose its feminist-activist foundations? Will its themes and goals be diluted or co-opted by men's interests under the guise of "universal" concerns, as they are in the wider curriculum and society? Might its women scholars and teachers, its methodologies, and its theories likewise be co-opted or displaced? Is gender studies one more example of women's interests being pushed to the peripheries of society, supplanted by the needs and desires of men?

> *. . . I am both interested in and wary of the emerging field of Gender Studies, which is in some places replacing efforts to develop Women's Studies. Just as many people early on encouraged us to stop focusing on women, to move quickly to the goal of studying humankind, others today are urging an immediate move to a study of gender. We need to notice that the pressure is to ensure that what we study includes men (as subject matter, as teachers, as students). Some give that advice in good faith, trying to get to what seems a deeper level of analysis, to look at what makes us women and men in a way that recognizes their profound mutual implication. For others, I fear, the motivation is akin to that of people who get nervous when we talk "too much" about women. There are threads here from the old tangle: study that does not involve men cannot really be significant, cannot become general enough, cannot raise "the basic and most important" questions or introduce works that are "good" enough to merit all that attention. Studying women feels like studying a* kind *of human, and a highly particular one at that . . . so let's hurry on to the "real stuff," which means that men* must *be more than present and in all roles.*
>
> *But if we do not study women, we will not become able to think about humans well, nor will our work on gender be equally informed by knowledge of and about women. It has taken millennia for the knowledge we have from and about men to develop; we can hardly critique it adequately in twenty or even a hundred years, nor can we discover or create knowledge of and about the equally diverse creatures who inhabit the category of women. I know very well how uncomfortable it makes men and some women to remain in the company of women for long, but that discomfort is precisely why we need to do so. Gender Studies requires Women's Studies, just as Women's Studies requires the study of gender. One does not substitute for the other; they are mutually enriching.*
>
> –Elizabeth Minnich, *Transforming Knowledge*[21]

The Goals of Women's Studies

Among the goals of women's studies is the uncovering of masculist bias in the history of knowledge as well as the creation of new knowledge and new values through positive research into women's experience. Women's studies seeks:

- to change women's sense of ourselves, our self-image, our sense of worth and rights, our presence in the world
- to change women's aspirations based on an increased sense of self-confidence and self-love, to allow women to create for ourselves new options in our own personal goals as well as in our commitments and/or contributions to society
- to alter the relations between women and men, to create true friendship and respect between the sexes in place of "the war between the sexes"
- to give all people, women and men, a renewed sense of human worth, to restore to the center of human endeavors a love for beauty, kindness, justice, and quality in living
- to erase from the world all the representations of unwholesome, illegitimate power of one group over another: sexism, racism, heterosexism, classism, and so on
- to end the race toward the destruction of the planet
- to reaffirm in society the quest for harmony, peace, and humane compassion

Such goals may appear presumptuous or at least not obviously related to the study of women's lives. But feminists have found that the movement that began in the concrete events of women's daily lives has implications that reach to the very foundations and quality of all life.

The Enfranchisement of Women in the University

Earlier, in the discussion of bias, I made reference to the exclusion of women from all the powerful policy-making institutions of our society and culture. That women all over the world should not have won suffrage until the turn of the century (New Zealand being first in 1893) is an indication of our exclusion from power in other areas of public life.

Until the end of the nineteenth century—except for the lowest paid, lowest status jobs—most women anywhere in the world had little access to economic independence. Within the family, they had small power over their possessions, their work, or their reproductive capacities. Legally they were at the mercy of male judges, lawyers, jurors, and laws. Women of any race or class found higher education barred to them. Oberlin was the first American college to admit women, in 1833, but its earliest programs for women were largely composed of home economics, religion, and other "female" subjects.

Today, in this country, because it is illegal to bar women from admission to any public educational institution on the basis of sex, we are entering universities and professional schools in increasing numbers (although the numbers are still disproportionate in terms of race and ethnicity). One would think, therefore, that, on campus, the priorities of women would become significantly more important and that the character of the institutions, too, would reflect the results of our particular input. But strong forces both within women and within institutions impel women to be absorbed into the male worldview rather than to create a new one. The masculine perspective in education; the preponderance of male faculty and administrators; male-oriented and authored textbooks and curricular materials; the pressures of husband care and child care; the conflicts between women's family roles and educational needs; the general contempt for women's views—all conspire to allow women on campus only a physical presence, not a sufficiently powerful intellectual/spiritual influence or full participation.

Certainly it is a major goal of women's studies to reverse discriminatory conditions in the educational system, and campus feminists engage in a number of activities to accomplish this end. Besides increasing the university community's awareness of the conceptual issues, we are often involved in activities directed toward changing policies in administration that have direct bearing on women's abilities to attend school: policies regarding admissions, affirmative action, financial assistance, health facilities, sexual harassment, child-care programs, part-time attendance, scheduling, and more. Feminist faculty, in or outside of women's studies, move for fairer decisions on salaries, promotion, and hiring, and we work toward increasing women's participation in decision making by seeking important administrative or committee appointments. The intent is to create balance and to eradicate the historical accumulation of masculist control.

Women have the right to full educational and professional opportunity, and this is the primary reason for ending university discrimination. But there is another reason as well, also profound and far-reaching: a desperately needed transformation of the university itself.

The Restoration of Humane Commitments

It has already been pointed out that education and learning have historically been the private preserve of men; that today, knowledge and the formation of knowledge are largely in the hands of men; and that masculism distorts conceptualization. But as we shall see in Chapter 2, masculism goes well beyond conceptual bias, beyond the universalization of male perspectives in thought, to a universalization of male perspectives and attitudes in values and behavior.

Masculism is not only the cause of misinterpretations of women's nature, it is also the reflection, the expression of an almost universal abhorrence for women themselves and for a whole set of characteristics historically ascribed to women in Western culture: sensitivity, compassion, compromise, aesthetic sensibility. These qualities, although officially regarded with respect, are actually only minimally valued except in women. In men, except in special circumstances and in measured amounts, they are generally regarded with contempt. The complementary qualities have been prescribed for and encouraged in men—the warrior virtues: strength, competitiveness, power, emotional reserve—and these are the qualities expected in the public sphere. In any environment dominated by men, the warrior virtues are likely to prevail. The university is no exception.

For more than a decade, educators have been decrying a growing dehumanization in universities, a waning of aesthetic and ethical commitment. Students and faculty alike question the university's mission; we fear our absorption into the wider technocracy, shudder at the absence of meaningfulness and the "cash mentality" among us. Some speak of a moral crisis or a failure of vision.

Of course something *is* wrong, and we can look to many factors involved. But as we shall see, the androcentric university is a microcosm of wider society, and its character defects reflect those of society.

Universities are products of the cultures that provide the individuals who people them and the ideas that govern them. In turn, by contributing the leaders of government, industry, art, and communication, and by bequeathing scientific and social theories or inventions and discoveries to society, the universities help to mold and direct cultural consciousness. An exchange of authority takes place between society and the halls of knowledge.

It can be easy to lose sight of the tremendous impact of much that is said and done in academe. What researchers and professors have learned and created in their institutions is passed on to their students, who in turn pass it to others through their work—in business, in government, in every phase of social life. The theories developed in lunchrooms and offices become tomorrow's "science," the "truths" that ultimately govern legal policy, psychotherapeutic techniques, media expression, and, finally, social behavior. If the truths of academe, developed in a masculist environment, seem to reflect and reinforce the warrior qualities, it is small wonder.

Consider the tone of university experience. It is not difficult to see that human compassion and caring, personal sensitivity, authenticity, love, and openness are not highly prized in formal education. Even talk of such things tends to embarrass people, to make them uneasy. Academic language is distant, cold, rife with jargon. Instructional faculty combat with administrators. Professors bore and bombard their students with disconnected facts not clearly relevant to life experience. Students distrust and deceive faculty. They are wary of participation in class or intimacy with one another. Courses and programs die and are born and die again, fitting students (however poorly) to meet the requirements of industry or government but rarely giving them the tools to live well. Academe is not typically a loving, caring environment.

It is, however, competitive, sometimes ruthless. Students learn to be "successful."

Faculty spar at intellectual gatherings, guard their positions, and compete for salary, status, and power. We are all reluctant to reveal our feelings and admit vulnerability. The warrior virtues prevail in contemporary education, blotting out the humane—a condition becoming increasingly obvious.

Human Redefinition and Social Values

Many feminists believe that women's reclamation of ourselves and our power may bring about a whole new way of being, a redefinition of human values. I agree but have to point out that such an idea must be based on a belief that is much debated—the idea that women are somehow in a special position with regard to value and better able to make ethical or humane judgments than most or many men.

For centuries, culminating in the Victorian period, a certain kind of woman—one who was removed from or had risen above her "carnal" nature—was thought to be especially sacred, especially like the Virgin Mary, a mother of the generations, a keeper of morality. In the nineteenth century, enshrined within the family, middle-class women were charged with the responsibility for maintaining human morality by keeping their own lives "pure," by investing the young with a love for virtue, and by creating a home where it could flourish. Women were to furnish society with a place and experience apart from the harsh realities of work and government.

The image of woman as keeper of morality was, however, double-edged. As we shall see in Chapter 3, it was based on all kinds of myths and misconceptions; and it placed impossible burdens on women, denying them their own freedom and requiring them to maintain public morality when they had no power to do so. Feminists quite rightly reject this image.

That women may be especially predisposed to human virtue carries yet another assumption that is problematic: that women and men really are different by nature, at least in this respect. The contention that women and men are constitutionally different has been used as the main justification for rigid role distinctions and female subordination for centuries, and feminists have taken great pains to gather evidence against it.

Yet the belief that women may be in a special position with regard to value and better able to make humane judgments is not necessarily based on the concepts described above. Rather it may be based on one or more of the following arguments: (1) In our culture women are trained and encouraged to develop caring or nurturing values and aesthetic sensibilities; (2) women's position outside the realms of power has also kept us from being fully absorbed into the psychodynamics of power and warrior values; (3) women's history of oppression makes us especially sensitive to the abuses of power and domination; (4) the concrete realities of women's lives—the creation of life, the intimate connection with rites of passage, the maintenance of the necessities of living—give us different perspectives on what is valuable and important in existence.

From infancy onward, women's lives are suffused with the affective (that is, feeling, experiential, noncognitive) aspects of living. Considerations of beauty, tenderness, warmth, compassion, and love have been prescribed as the special province of women. No doubt masculist society's motivation was not to make women especially humane, but to make us excellent servants. Nonetheless, our intimate relationship with the nonwarrior (or antiwarrior) virtues, our inculcated avoidance of domination together with our intact intellectual capacities may indeed render women especially insightful in matters of human value.

Women, particularly feminist women, hold a key to new perspectives on society. If new goals, values, and visions are to be infused into society, we must win for women access to all the centers of power and policy, from science and industry to art and communication. This is a major goal of women's studies.

Changes in Lifestyles and Self-Concepts

Nothing goes deeper in one's personal awareness or has more far-reaching implications for the whole of one's existence than her or his sexual identity. This accounts in part for the great resistance to feminism; it also accounts for the impact feminist learning and consciousness-raising have on students. Propelled into self-examination by the intensity of the search and the research, women and men alike report changes in attitudes and lifestyles that represent tremendous emotional, intellectual, spiritual, and professional growth.

Consciousness-raising means what it says: It raises the level of consciousness, of awareness one has about the feelings, behaviors, and experiences surrounding sex roles. The woman who learns how much of her personal being emanates from her social and political status as a woman must ask herself how much of that being she wants to keep, how much she wants to change, and how she plans to do it. Bewilderment, surprise, pain, joy, anger, and love accompany this growth.

Feminist instructors and students alike have been chided about consciousness-raising in women's studies courses. It has been argued that consciousness-raising (1) makes the courses "soft," (2) belongs in the women's movement, not in school; (3) is not a legitimate part of formal university education; (4) is brainwashing; and (5) sometimes causes great anguish with which some students are unable to cope.

You will discover as you read this book that women's studies is anything but soft. You will find that consciousness-raising occurs as a result of new insights and innovative ideas. Rather than brain-*washing,* raised consciousness comes as a result of brain-*opening*.

Consciousness-raising can be painful. Yet pain is not in itself something to avoid at all times for there are two kinds of pain: destructive and constructive. Destructive pain is suffered in a no-win situation. Embedded in the status quo, it leads to no benefits, no improvements. It just hurts. Such pain is best avoided. Constructive pain differs dramatically. It is like the physical distress we feel when we decide to get our bodies in shape after some disuse. Our muscles ache; we strain and groan, but we grow stronger. Much the same thing happens when we grow emotionally or spiritually. Our insight, memories, and feelings—not accustomed to such use—may cause us pain. Our new sense of autonomy and freedom, and the attendant responsibility, may make us anxious. We hurt, but we grow stronger. Emotional and spiritual strength are necessary to well-being.

Consider some of the comments taken from the journals of students in an introductory course in women's studies:

- "I feel like a ton of bricks has been lifted off my shoulders. I finally found me. For the first time in my life I really looked at myself and said, 'I like you!' I decided that there is only one companion that you can count on all through your life—yourself. If I don't like me, who will? I took a full survey of myself and decided what I liked and what I would like to change, not because I wanted to look good in someone else's eyes, but because I wanted to look good in *my* own eyes. I feel so free, happy; like I could lick the world. This is the way I want to stay—this is the way I always want to feel. And I will because I like me."

- "I have more pride; I am more confident in myself as a woman. I used to wonder if my womanhood would be a slight handicap. I now realize it is my strongest asset!"
- "While we were talking about fear and pain being all a part of growing, I found a great deal of consolation because I had felt both. . . . It took a while, but I now realize that all the things I learned and have become aware of will not allow me to keep silent. Also, those feelings of understanding and support will never really be left behind because I'll carry those feelings inside of me forever."

The Terms and Techniques of Women's Studies

Women's Studies must be pursued on its own terms if it is to maintain its integrity. Although the integration of feminist perspectives and insights into the regular curriculum is an ultimate goal of most feminist educators, the absorption of women's studies into the masculist domain is not something we seek. That might involve a loss of the unique configuration of methods and approaches we have developed. The feminist classroom typically differs from others, and feminist research bears the mark of its status outside the mainstream.

Feminist Pedagogy

Feminist faculty, like any other, gather information and ideas and impart them to students. Often they do this in traditional ways: They lecture, lead group discussions, show films, assign term papers, and give exams. Just as often, however, they opt for other, sometimes unorthodox, procedures.

Feminist faculty frequently diverge from their colleagues in attitudes, experiences, or methods. Many of us have come to academe from the learning laboratories of social action outside the university—from civil rights organizations, from feminist groups, from political parties and social change associations. From these experiences we have come to understand the strength of the entrenched power structures. Others of us, having lived within the established system and having tried its regular channels and found them resistant, have learned the same lesson in another way. Experiencing life, as philosopher Mary Daly puts it, "on the boundaries of patriarchal space,"[22] we have developed ways that are often contrary to traditional academic etiquette.

Although women's studies is beginning to generate some kinds of formal credentials, for the most part we enter this field as thinkers entered any field centuries ago—through experience and self-directed research. We have few models on which to style our activities. The criterion for our methods is productivity.

The result of these factors and others is a highly innovative, spontaneous, and authentic modus operandi. In a feminist classroom, one is apt to find group projects, small-group discussions, self-directed or student-directed study, credit for social change activities or for life experience, contracts or self-grading, diaries and journals, even meditation or ritual. Noticeable in a feminist classroom are two factors not typical in college classrooms: an acceptance of, and even emphasis on, the personal-affective element in learning; and a warm, human relationship among persons in the class, students and teacher. Feminist teachers are no longer at pains to maintain the manly aura of distance—from their work or from one another. Recognizing, too, that hierarchical structures can belie what is common to female experience, feminist faculty often seek alternatives to the traditional student–teacher dichotomy.

The Interdisciplinary Nature of Women's Studies

Almost all women's studies programs, curricula, and analyses are interdisciplinary. For the most part, the programs have avoided separating into discrete departments. Although this has raised some serious practical problems—of funding, staffing, and scheduling, for example—it serves important purposes. Some of these are pragmatic, having to do with survival in the institution, professional flexibility for instructors, and the like; but the most important reasons for the interdisciplinary structure of women's studies are philosophical.

Feminist theorists have found that insights into the elements of women's lives and their effects on the progress of humanity do not sensibly divide into the traditional academic disciplines. Understanding, for example, how the concept *human nature* is distorted by the omission of women from the subject requires sophisticated knowledge of history, sociology, psychology, linguistics, philosophy, and other fields. Feminist analysis requires global knowledge.

Sensitized by our own investigations, many feminists have gone on to challenge the entire departmental or disciplinary structure as it exists today. Some of us suggest that the division of knowledge into neat areas with boundaries that ought not to be crossed is analogous to (and possibly derived from) the warrior behavior of separating land into territories that then must be justified and guarded. Intellectual boundaries, we may argue, are not only artificial; they are destructive.

Feminist theoreticians, then, recognizing the importance of global knowledge and not typically given to territorial competition, are at least interdisciplinary. I tend to think of us as counterdisciplinary. Elizabeth Janeway, feminist educator, comments:

> *Women have both history and reality on their side. Our knowledge of the world as it is is really quite formidable, broadly based, aware of detail, and not afraid to make connections between areas which the traditionally minded see as separate. Our experience makes us interdisciplinary. Well, this is a most useful and needed ability in a fragmented society, and particularly in an educational system where the trend for years has been to know more and more about less and less. Research is valuable—if it is used; and to be used, it must be allowed to connect with other research and, even more, with everyday life.*[23]

The Scope of Women's Studies

Given what has been said about the global nature of feminist research, you can see how broad a scope women's studies must have. It ranges across history, psychology, art, economics, literature, philosophy, sociology, political science, biology, mathematics, law, and on through every area called an academic discipline. Of course, no one can be conversant with the details of all fields, but the study of women's experience requires some sophistication in each. Thus, women's studies scholars must be multifaceted in perspectives.

At the same time, however, there is specialization. A feminist psychologist is a psychologist with a woman orientation. She pursues her work with a feminist perspective and challenges the sexist bias and beliefs in her field, often—though not always—focusing on issues most pertinent to women. As a feminist philosopher, I have the traditional interests in metaphysics, ethics, and epistemology, but I add to their study my special feminist awareness. I might, for example, challenge the validity of Hobbes's argument that life is "a war of all against all," wondering whether this may be so for men (warriors?) but perhaps not so for women. I question the traditionally accepted basic assumptions of philosophy—its definition of *objectivity,* for example—and its relationship to prescribed male emotional reserve. But beyond a feminist analysis of traditional questions, I am involved in raising other questions crucial for women. What does the feminist idea of *matriarchy* imply for utopian visions? How does a notion of God as female change theology (thealogy?). What does my woman's understanding of the dehumanizing effect of rape tell me about the ethical implications of physical integrity?

Some Basic Concepts

This book is primarily about women—our experience, history, present situation, and future. It is about men, too, insofar as men's lives affect women. When we say that we are going to talk about women and men, when we use the words *woman, man, female, male, feminine, masculine,* what do we mean? What is a woman or a man? What possible different meanings do the terms *feminine* or *masculine* involve?

Perhaps the questions seem odd, their answers obvious. Yet it will become increasingly clear that such words as *woman, man, female,* or *male* are used in a variety of ways; they connote all sorts of meanings, and therefore have wide-ranging implications—psychological, political, social, and so on. Unless this is understood, one is apt to encounter a great deal of confusion in the analyses of sex roles.

To inquire into what it is to be a woman or a man, one must understand that various contexts exist in which to formulate definitions and make analyses, and though these may impinge on one another, their viewpoints are not the same. For example, the fact that females bear offspring (a biological aspect of womanhood) may be partly responsible for the kind of work a woman engages in (a cultural aspect), and that may have tremendous bearing on her status (political and social aspects). Furthermore, to understand that arrangements of these variables change from culture to culture (an anthropological aspect), it is necessary to know which economic and historical factors affect the others and how.

Before we continue, certain terms should be clearly understood because they are essential tools of our analysis. These are: *sex, gender, role, stereotype,* and *ideal.*

Sex is a term used by social scientists and biologists to refer to certain biological categories: female and male. Identification of sex is based on a variety of factors, including chromosomal patterns, hormonal makeup, and genital structure. The determination of sex is considerably more complex than is generally understood, but it is the least ambiguous of the five concepts we are considering.

Gender, on the other hand, is a social, not a physiological, concept. *Femininity* and *masculinity,* the terms that denote one's gender, refer to a complex set of characteristics and behaviors prescribed for a particular sex by society and learned through the socialization experience. For example, femininity (female gender) for certain groups of women in our culture requires passivity, fragility, and proclivities for nurturance. A little girl—given dolls to play with, prohibited from engaging in wild play, dressed in frilly or constricting clothing, and rebuked for so-called unladylike behavior—is reinforced in those behavior patterns here called feminine, and she learns to be passive, fragile, and nurturing.

The exact relation between sex and gender is controversial. Some argue that sexual characteristics are fixed in nature and account for gender and role arrangements; others disagree sharply. (This is part of what is called the "nature/nurture controversy.") Lionel Tiger, for example, argues that "leadership" or "dominance" is a characteristically male trait in animal as well as in human communities.[24] He contends that the trait is inheritable, therefore biological, and thus accounts for the dominance of men over women in human society. In other words, dominance or submission are biological (sexual) characteristics that account for the gender prescription of passivity in women and aggressiveness in men. Tiger is challenged by those who point to the tremendous variation of behavior both in the animal kingdom and in different societies. These commentators argue that the observed malleability and diversity of behavior imply a loose association between sex and gender.[25]

Gender is composed of a set of socially defined character traits. *Role* is composed of a pattern of behaviors prescribed for individuals playing a certain part in the drama of life. The sociologist Theodore R. Sarbin defined role as "The organized actions of a person in a given position."[26] For example, the role of teacher in our society requires such actions as imparting knowledge to students, attending classes, counseling, or grading papers; it might also include certain attitudes, values, and even appearance.

In almost every society, females and males—on the basis of their sex—are assigned separate and specific roles: the sex roles. Differing from culture to culture, and within a culture by a variety of factors (class, religion, race, age, and so on), the sex roles are made up of a set of expected behaviors, with accompanying gender traits. The role of a middle-class white female in our society includes playing with dolls, helping mother, getting married, having children, doing housekeeping, being sexy, typing, and so on. Many of these behaviors in their turn form other role configurations. Marrying, for example, requires that one be a wife, which entails another whole set of behaviors. The role of a woman, then, includes a series of subroles such as daughter, wife, mother, office worker, and so on. In this book, we shall be largely concerned with analyses of sex roles: their nature, composition, effects, and implications.

Stereotype is a concept related to role, yet distinct. Defined by one author as a "picture in our heads,"[27] a stereotype is a composite image of traits and expectations pertaining to some group (such as teachers, police officers, Jews, or women)—an image that is persistent in the social mind though it is somehow off-center or inaccurate. Typically, the stereotype is an overgeneralization of characteristics that may or may not have been observed in fact. Often containing a kernel of truth that is partial and thus misleading, the stereotype need not be self-consistent, and it has a remarkable resistance to change by new information; to wit, Lippmann's following remark:

> *If the experience contradicts the stereotype, one of two things happens. If the man is no longer plastic, or if some powerful interest makes it highly inconvenient to rearrange his stereotypes, he pooh-poohs the contradiction as an exception that proves the rule, discredits the*

witness, finds a flaw somewhere, and manages to forget it. But if he is still curious and open-minded, the novelty is taken into the picture, and allowed to modify it. Sometimes, if the incident is striking enough, and if he has felt a general discomfort with his established scheme, he may be shaken to such an extent as to distrust all accepted ways of looking at life, and to expect that normally a thing will not be what it is generally supposed to be.[28]

Not all stereotypes are pejorative, but many are. For example, one stereotypical image of a feminist is a woman incapable of fulfilling the traditional role requirements for femininity, unable to "catch a man," homely, dirty, aggressive, strident, shrill, sexually promiscuous (or frigid or a lesbian or all three), unkempt, ill-clothed, middle or upper middle class, childish, making speeches, carrying banners, and burning underwear. It is this image that is meant when clearly feminist women demur, "Now, I'm no feminist, but . . . ." Many feminists are not middle class or white or college educated. Feminists wear a variety of costumes and have differing sexual codes and identities.

Stereotypes can have wide-ranging effects on both the stereotyped group and those with whom the members of the group interact. Stereotypes can and do direct behavior.

An *ideal* is much like a stereotype. It, too, is a "picture in our heads"; it is resistant to change, frequently inconsistent, generally fits a very few, and is frequently based on false information. But the ideal contains only traits the society deems desirable. It functions as a standard and a goal, such as a "lady" or "the American girl."

All of these concepts are involved in the analyses of women's experience. Feminist investigators ask: What are the biological, physiological, and anatomical characteristics that distinguish women from men, and what are their implications? How are the sexes inherently different in makeup and behavior? What are the major psychological factors in women's lives; which, if any, are based on femaleness per se, and which come as a consequence of women's role in this and other societies? Since women's lives are apt to be markedly different across economic, educational, or racial lines, what traits or qualities, if any, can be said to characterize the category of women in general? How and why do they operate? How are the perceived female ideals different from the perceived stereotypes? What is their origin? How do they affect the daily lives of women in particular and people in general? In the following chapters, we shall be using the concepts of sex, gender, role, stereotype, and ideal to explore these and other questions.

Notes

1. Florence Howe, "The Power of Education," in *Women's Studies in the Curriculum* (Winston-Salem, NC: Salem College, 1983), p. 24, quoted in Catharine R. Stimpson with Nina Kressner Cobb, *Women's Studies in the United States* (New York: Ford Foundation, 1986), p. 4.

2. National Women's Studies Association, *Directory of Women's Studies Programs, Women's Centers, and Women's Research Centers,* cited in "Revolution and Reaction," *Women's Review of Books* 9, no. 5 (February 92): 13.

3. Mariam Chamberlain, "Enriching the Curriculum: Woman's Studies," *Thought and Action: The NEA Higher Education Journal* 4, no. 2 (Fall 1988) :24.

4. Karl Stern, *The Flight from Woman* (New York: Farrar, Straus & Giroux, 1965), pp. 21–22.

5. Aristotle, *Politics,* Book 1, Chap. 13, 1259b–1260a.

6. Muhammad Hamidullah, *Introduction to Islam,* 2d ed. (Paris: Centre Culturel Islamique, 1968). (c/o The Mosque, Place Puits de l'Ermite, Paris, France.)

7. Elizabeth V. Spelman, *Inessential Woman: Problems of Exclusion in Feminist Thought* (Boston: Beacon Press, 1988), p. ix.

8. Ibid., p. 1.

9. Jessie Bernard, *Women and the Public Interest* (New York: Aldine, 1971), pp. 7–13, *passim.*

10. Barbara Smith, "Racism and Women's Studies," in *All the Women Are White, All the Blacks Are Men, but Some of Us Are Brave,* ed. Gloria T. Hull, Patricia Bell Scott, and Barbara Smith (Old Westbury, New York: The Feminist Press, 1982), quoted in *Making Face, Making Soul, Haciendo Caras: Creative and Critical Perspectives by Women of Color,* ed. Gloria Anzaldúa (San Francisco: Aunt Lute Foundation Books, 1990), p. 27.

11. Hunter College Women's Studies Collective, *Women's Realities, Women's Choices* (New York: Oxford University Press, 1983), p. 11.

12. Robin Morgan, "Feminist Diplomacy," *Ms.* May/June 1991, p. 1.

13. Cheris Kramarae and Paula A. Treichler, with the assistance of Ann Russo, *A Feminist Dictionary* (New York: Pan-

dora Press, 1985), pp. 158–160, *passim*. Copyright © Cheris Kramarae and Paula A. Treichler, 1985. Reprinted with permission of Unwin Hyman Ltd. [A newer version of this book was published in 1992: *Amazons, Bluestockings, and Crones: A Feminist Dictionary* by Cheris Kramarae, Paula A. Treichler, with the assistance of Ann Russo (London: Pandora)].

14. Alice Walker, "Womanist" from *In Search of Our Mothers' Gardens* (New York: Harcourt Brace Jovanovich, 1983), pp. xi–xii. Copyright © 1983 by Alice Walker. Reprinted by permission of Harcourt Brace Jovanovich, Inc.

15. Marcia Bedard and Beth Hartung, "Blackboard Jungle Revisited," *Thought and Action: The NEA Higher Education Journal* 7, no. 1 (Spring 1991): 7–20.

16. Ibid., p. 11.

17. Some of the following discussion is included in my paper, "Methodocracy, Misogyny, and Bad Faith: Sexism in the Philosophic Establishment," *Metaphilosophy* 10, no. 1 (January 1979): 48–61.

18. Joel Feinberg, "Some Conjectures About the Concept of Respect," *Journal of Social Philosophy* 3, no. 2 (April 1973): 1–3.

19. Bari Watkins, "Women and History," in *Women on Campus: The Unfinished Liberation*, ed. Change Magazine Editors (New York: Change Magazine, 1975).

20. Harry Brod, "Introduction," *The Making of Masculinities: The New Men's Studies* (Boston: Allen & Unwin, 1987), p. 2.

21. Elizabeth Kamarck Minnich, *Transforming Knowledge* (Philadelphia: Temple University Press, 1990), p. 139.

22. Mary Daly, *Beyond God the Father* (Boston: Beacon Press, 1973).

23. Elizabeth Janeway, "Women on Campus: The Unfinished Liberation," in *Women on Campus*, ed. Change Magazine Editors (New York: Change Magazine, 1975), p. 27.

24. Lionel Tiger, *Men in Groups* (New York: Random House, 1969).

25. See, for example, Margaret Mead, *Sex and Temperament in Three Primitive Societies* (New York: Morrow, 1935).

26. Theodore R. Sarbin, "Role Theory," in *Handbook of Social Psychology*, ed. Gardner Lindzey (Reading, MA: Addison-Wesley, 1954), p. 225.

27. Walter Lippmann, *Public Opinion* (New York: Harcourt, Brace, 1922).

28. Ibid., p. 100.

A New Angle of Vision

Gerda Lerner

Noted historian Gerda Lerner is the author of eight books in women's history, among them Black Women in White America *(1972),* The Female Experience *(1979), and* The Majority Finds Its Past *(1979). She is past president of the Organization of American Historians and is Robinson-Edwards Professor of History, Emerita, at the University of Wisconsin-Madison. Her latest work is* Women and History, *2 volumes, from which the following selection is drawn.*

Here Lerner explains why examining the world from only one perspective, men's, is distorting. We require both perspectives—women's and men's—ultimately integrated, to view reality more accurately, to see with greater enrichment, and to transform consciousness.

Gerda Lerner, "A New Angle of Vision," from *The Creation of Patriarchy,* Vol. I of *Women and History.* New York: Oxford University Press, 1986, pp. 11–14. © 1986 Gerda Lerner. Used by permission of Oxford University Press, Inc., as approved by the author.

As we undertake this exploration, how are we, then, to think of women-as-a-group? Three metaphors may help us see from our new angle of vision:

In her brilliant 1979 article, Joan Kelly spoke of the new "doubled vision" of feminist scholarship:

> . . . woman's place is not a separate sphere or domain of existence but a position within social existence generally. . . . *[F]eminist thought is moving beyond the split vision of social reality it inherited from the recent past. Our actual vantage point has shifted, giving rise to a new consciousness of woman's "place" in family and society. . . . [W]hat we see are not two spheres of social reality (home and work, private and public), but two (or three) sets of social relations.*[1]

We are adding the female vision to the male and that process is transforming. But Joan Kelly's metaphor needs to be developed one step further: when we see with one eye, our vision is limited in range and devoid of depth. When we add to it the single vision of the other eye, our range of vision becomes wider, but we still lack depth. It is only when both eyes see together that we accomplish full range of vision and accurate depth perception.

The computer provides us with another metaphor. The computer shows us a picture of a triangle (two-dimensional). Still holding that image, the triangle moves in space and is transformed into a pyramid (three-dimensional). Now the pyramid moves in space creating a curve (the fourth dimension), while still holding the image of the pyramid and the triangle. We see all four dimensions at once, losing none of them, but seeing them also in their true relation to one another.

Seeing as we have seen, in patriarchal terms, is two-dimensional. "Adding women" to the patriarchal framework makes it three-dimensional. But only when the third dimension is fully integrated and moves with the whole, only when women's vision is equal with men's vision, do we perceive the true relations of the whole and the inner connectedness of the parts.

Finally, another image. Men and women live on a stage, on which they act out their assigned roles, equal in importance. The play cannot go on without both kinds of performers. Neither of them "contributes" more or less to the whole; neither is marginal or dispensable. But the stage set is conceived, painted, defined by men. Men have written the play, have directed the show, interpreted the meanings of the action. They have assigned themselves the most interesting, most heroic parts, giving women the supporting roles.

As the women become aware of the difference in the way they fit into the play, they ask for more equality in the role assignments. They upstage the men at times, at other times they pinch-hit for a missing male performer. The women finally, after considerable struggle, win the right of access to equal role assignment, but first they must "qualify." The terms of their "qualifications" are again set by the men; men are the judges of how women measure up; men grant or deny admission. They give preference to docile women and to those who fit their job-description accurately. Men punish, by ridicule, exclusion, or ostracism, any woman who assumes the right to interpret her own role or—worst of all sins—the right to rewrite the script.

It takes considerable time for the women to understand that getting "equal" parts will not make them equal as long as the script, the props, the stage setting, and the direction are firmly held by men. When the women begin to realize that and cluster together between the acts, or even during the performance, to discuss what to do about it, this play comes to an end.

Looking at the recorded history of society as though it were such a play, we realize that the story of the performances over thousands of years has been recorded only by men and told in their words. Their attention has been mostly on men. Not surprisingly, they have not noticed all the actions women have taken. Finally, in the past fifty years, some women have acquired the training necessary for writing the company's scripts. As they wrote, they began to pay more attention to what women were doing. Still, they had been well trained by their male mentors. So they too found what men were doing on the whole more significant and, in their desire to upgrade the part of women in the past, they looked hard for women who had done what men did. Thus, compensatory history was born.

What women must do, what feminists are now doing, is to point to that stage, its sets, its props, its director, and its scriptwriter, as did the child in the fairy tale who discovered that the emperor was naked, and say, the basic inequality between us lies within this framework. And then they must tear it down.

What will the writing of history be like when that umbrella of dominance is removed and definition is shared equally by men and women? Will we devalue the past, overthrow the categories, supplant order with chaos?

No—we will simply step out under the free sky. We will observe how it changes, how the stars rise and the moon circles, and we will describe the earth and its workings in male and female voices. We may, after all, see with greater enrichment. We now know that man is not the measure of that which is human, but men and women are. Men are not the center of the world, but men and women are. This insight will transform consciousness as decisively as did Copernicus's discovery that the earth is not the center of the universe. We may play our separate parts on the stage, sometimes exchanging them or deciding to keep them, as it works out. We may discover new talent among those who have always been living under the umbrella of another's making. We may find that those who had previously taken upon themselves the burden of both action and definition may now have more freedom for playing and experiencing the pure joy of existence. We are no more under an obligation to describe what we will find than were the explorers sailing to the distant edge of the world, only to find that the world was round.

We will never know unless we begin. The process itself is the way, is the goal.

Notes

1. Joan Kelly, "The Doubled Vision of Feminist Theory: A Postscript to the 'Women of Power' Conference," *Feminist Studies* 5: no. 1 (Spring 1979):221–22.

The Myth of the Male Orgasm

Bette-Jane Raphael

Bette-Jane Raphael, author of Can This Be Love? And Other Quandaries of Love in the Eighties *(1985), has been senior editor for* Viva *magazine and for* Working Woman.

Here Raphael presents with wonderful humor the absurdity of research and theories based on myth, false assumptions, and misplaced objectivity. Parodying Freud and other "experts" who presume to explain and describe the female sexual experience from their armchairs, so to speak, she shows what nonsense might have been produced if the tables had been turned and all that we knew about male sexuality (or, for that matter, male anything*) had been created by women looking at men.*

IS THERE SUCH A THING AS MALE ORGASM? FOR DECades, scientists have argued about it, written tracts about it, philosophized about it, and, in more recent years, conducted countless studies. But as Dr. Mary Jane Grunge, president of SMOS (the Society for Male Orgasmic Studies), said in her opening statement of the society's ninth annual cookout: "We still don't know."

But do we? Recent findings by Dr. Fern Herpes and her colleague, Dr. Lavinia Shoot, indicate that the mystery is at last on the brink of being unmasked. Working under a grant from NASA, which was disturbed by the cleaning bills for its last Apollo mission, Dr. Herpes and Dr. Shoot conducted a study of 300 middle-class men between the ages of 14 and 23. Their findings seem to indicate that not only is there a male orgasm, there may actually be two distinct kinds!

While 43 percent of the men in the Herpes/Shoot study were found to have trouble attaining orgasm consistently, or did not attain orgasm at all, and while another 4½ percent had no opinion, a whopping 50½ percent (four men fell asleep during their interviews, which accounts for the other two percent) admitted they had two distinctly different kinds of orgasms. After careful questioning, psychological testing, and physical examinations, Dr. Herpes came to the following conclusion (Dr. Shoot came to a different conclusion and left in a huff): there are two types of male orgasm. For purposes of clarification, Dr. Herpes called these penile orgasm and the spherical orgasm.

Of the two orgasms, Dr. Herpes hypothesizes that the spherical orgasm is the more mature. "Men who are enamored of their penises, who see their penises as the seat of all sexual pleasure, are just a bunch of babies. I hate them. Only the spherically oriented male can be thought of as mature because he can identify with the female to a much greater extent than the penile-oriented male. Thus the former's identification with his balls, which are the closest thing he has to female breasts."

Dr. Shoot, who consented to speak in rebuttal to Dr. Herpes, had this to say: "That woman is crazy. Men don't have two types of orgasm. They just think they do. My own findings reveal that they don't even have one kind of orgasm. Actually, there is no such thing as the male orgasm. What passes for orgasm in the male is really a mild form of St. Vitus dance. This afflicts more than 55 percent of the male population in this country, and if Herpes wasn't so hipped on orgasm she'd admit she's wrong. But as far as she's concerned, *everything* is orgasm!"

It should be noted that Dr. Amelia Leviathan is in close agreement with Dr. Shoot. She too believes that what passes for male orgasm is actually a disease. But contrary to Dr. Shoot, she believes the affliction is actually a form of epilepsy localized in the groin. She feels she proved this in her much publicized recent study of 100 male rats, 50 of whom had epilepsy. The epileptic rats, Dr. Leviathan found, could mate with the female rats, even if the female rats didn't want to. The nonepileptic rats just sat around exposing themselves.

Confusing the question of male orgasm even further is Dr. Jennifer Anis, who conducted a study of nearly 700 married males in their late 20s and 30s. According to the results of her study, the issue of male orgasmic or nonorgasmic capacity is clouded by the fact that many men simulate orgasm in order to please their partners. Nearly 25 percent of the men in the Anis group admitted they had at some time in their marriage faked orgasm either because they were tired, or because they knew their partners would be hurt if they didn't climax, or because they had headaches.

Nearly half the men in the Anis study had mild to severe orgasmic difficulties. (It was this group, incidentally, whose psychological profiles appeared in Dr. Anis's widely acclaimed paper, "The Prostate, the Penis, and You-oo," wherein it was revealed that all the orgasmically troubled men shared a common fear of their mothers' cuticles, a hatred of Speedwriting ads in subways, and a horror of certain kinds of peaked golf hats.) What has not been revealed until now, however, is that a great many of these men lead perfectly satisfactory sex lives *without* orgasm, a finding which would seem to put to rest the theory that men must achieve orgasm in order to enjoy sex.

Well, if men can enjoy sex without orgasm, can they also become fathers without achieving climax? Here again the answer is by no means clear. Dr. Herpes and Dr. Shoot, of course, disagree. Dr. Shoot says yes, they can, if they think they can. Dr. Herpes says no, not unless they have either a penile or a spherical orgasm. Dr. Anis believes they can fake it.

Lastly there is the question of the multiple orgasm. Do men have them? Unfortunately, here we are still very much in the dark. The only person ever to do research in this area was Dr. Helen Hager-Bamf, in 1971. From January through April of that year, Dr. Hager-Bamf personally tested more than 3,000 randomly selected men for duration and number of orgasms. Tragically dead at the age of 28, she never recorded her findings.

So where do we stand? Is there such a thing as male orgasm? Can men enjoy sex without it? Is a low orgasmic capacity psychologically or physiologically induced? To quote Dr. Grunge at her recent press conference, "Who knows?"

Perhaps the answers are not as important as the fact that the questions are finally being taken seriously. So that, someday, the boy who sells shoes, the young fellow in upholstery, and the man who sews alligators on shirts will no longer have to walk around in perplexity, confused and unnerved by the myth of the male orgasm.

When that day arrives, perhaps male sexuality will come out of the bathroom and into the bedroom where it belongs.

Gender & Race: The Ampersand Problem in Feminist Thought

Elizabeth V. Spelman

Elizabeth V. Spelman teaches in the Women's Studies program and is also professor of philosophy at Smith College in Northampton, Massachusetts. In addition to Inessential Woman: Problems of Exclusion in Feminist Thought *(1988), her works include* Unworthy Subjects: Suffering and the Economy of Attention, *which is in preparation for Beacon Press.*

In this selection Spelman analyzes a fundamental issue in feminist thought: the implications of differences among women, especially racial differences. She makes clear why it is an error to treat gender, race, class, or other differences among women in isolation from one another, and why it is equally mistaken to treat them "additively." She shows how "white solipsism," or solipsism of any kind, works against coming to see the world more accurately. Several terms are introduced that will serve us in following chapters, among them: identity, somatophobia, misogyny, gynephobia.

You don't really want Black folks, you are just looking for yourself with a little color to it.

–Bernice Johnson Reagon

In earlier chapters we have examined how attempts to focus on gender in isolation from other aspects of identity such as race and class can work to obscure the effect race, class, and gender have on each other.[1] In particular, we've looked at how gender can be treated in a way that obscures the race and class identity of privileged women—for example, of contemporary white middle-class women or the free women of ancient Greece—and simultaneously makes it hard to conceive of women who are not of that particular class and race as "women." Precisely insofar as a discussion of gender and gender relations is really, even if obscurely, about a particular group of women and their relation to a particular group of men, it is unlikely to be applicable to any other group of women. At the same time, the particular race and class identity of those referred to simply as "women" becomes explicit when we see the inapplicability of statements about "women" to women who are not of that race or class.

As mentioned in the Introduction, some of these points are illustrated tellingly in an article in the *New York Times* about how "women and Blacks" have fared in the U.S. military.[2] The author of the article does not discuss women who are Black or Blacks who are women. Indeed, it is clear that the "women" referred to are white, the "Blacks" referred to are male, even though, in a chart comparing the numbers and the placement of "women" and "Blacks," a small note appears telling the reader that Black women are included in the category "Blacks."[3] There are several things to note about the sexual and racial ontology of the article. The racial identity of those identified as "women" does not become explicit until reference is made to Black women, at which point it also becomes clear that the category "women" excludes Black women. In the contrast between "women" and "Blacks" the usual contrast between "men" and "women" is dropped, even though the distinction is in effect between a group of men and a group of women. But the men in question are not called men. They are called "Blacks."

It is not easy to think about gender, race, and class in ways that don't obscure or underplay their effects on one another. The crucial question is how the links between them are conceived. So, for example, we see that de Beauvoir tends to talk about comparisons between sex and race, or between sex and class, or between sex and culture; she describes what she takes to be comparisons between sexism and racism, between sexism and classism, between sexism and anti-Semitism. In the work of Chodorow and others influenced by her, we observe a readiness to look for links between sexism and other forms of oppression depicted as distinct from sexism. In both examples, we find an additive analysis of the various elements of identity and of various forms of oppression: there's sex *and* race *and* class; there's sexism *and* racism *and* classism. In both examples, attempts to bring in elements of identity other than gender, to bring in kinds of oppression other than sexism, still have the effect of obscuring the racial and class identity of those described as "women," still make it hard to see how women not of a particular race and class can be included in the description.

In this chapter we shall examine in more detail how additive analyses of identity and of oppression can work against an understanding of the relations between gender and other elements of identity, between sexism and other forms of oppression. In particular we will see how some very interesting and important attempts to link sexism and racism themselves reflect and perpetuate racism. Ironically, the categories and methods we may find most natural and straightforward to use as we explore the connections between sex and race, sexism and racism, confuse those connections rather than clarify them.

As has often been pointed out, what have been called the first and second waves of the women's movement in the United States followed closely on the heels of women's involvement in the nineteenth-century abolitionist movement and the twentieth-century civil rights movement. In both centuries, challenges to North American racism served as an impetus to, and model for, the feminist attack on sexist institutions, practices, and ideology. But this is not to say that all antiracists were antisexists, or that all antisexists were antiracists. Indeed, many abolitionists of the nineteenth century and civil rights workers of the twentieth did not take sexism seriously, and we continue to learn about the sad, bitter, and confusing history of women who in fighting hard for feminist ends did not take racism seriously.[4]

Recent feminist theory has not totally ignored white racism, though white feminists have paid much less attention to it than have Black feminists. Much of feminist theory has reflected and contributed to what Adrienne Rich has called "white solipsism": the tendency "to think, imagine, and speak as if whiteness described the world."[5] While solipsism is "not the consciously held belief that one race is inherently superior to all others, but a tunnel-vision which simply does not see nonwhite experience or existence as precious or significant, unless in spasmodic, impotent guilt-reflexes, which have little or no long-term, continuing momentum or political usefulness."[6]

In this chapter I shall focus on what I take to be instances and sustaining sources of this tendency in recent theoretical works by, or of interest to, feminists. In particular, I examine certain ways of comparing sexism and racism in the United States, as well as habits of thought about the source of women's oppression and the possibility of our liberation. I hope that exposing some of the symptoms of white solipsism—especially in places where we might least expect to find them—will help to eliminate tunnel vision and to widen the descriptive and explanatory scope of feminist theory. Perhaps we might hasten the day when it will no longer be necessary for anyone to have to say, as Audre Lorde has, "How difficult and time-consuming it is to have to reinvent the pencil every time you want to send a message."[7]

I shall not explicitly be examining class and classism, though at a number of points I suggest ways in which considerations of class and classism affect the topic at hand. Many of the questions I raise about comparisons between sexism and racism could also be raised about comparison between sexism and classism or racism and classism.

I

It is perhaps inevitable that comparisons of sexism and racism include, and often culminate in, questions about which form of oppression is more "fundamental."[8] Whether or not one believes that this way of thinking will bear any strategic or theoretic fruit, such comparisons have come to inform analyses of the nature of sexism and the nature of racism. To begin, I will examine some recent claims that sexism is more fundamental than racism, a highly ambiguous argument. In many instances the evidence offered in support turns out to refute the claim; and this way of comparing sexism and racism often presupposes the nonexistence of Black women, insofar as neither the description of sexism nor that of racism seems to apply to them. This is a bitter irony indeed, since Black women are the victims of both sexism and racism.

We need to ask first what "more fundamental" means in a comparison of racism and sexism. It has meant or might mean several different though related things:[9]

> It is harder to eradicate sexism than it is to eradicate racism.
>
> There might be sexism without racism but not racism without sexism: any social and political changes that eradicate sexism will eradicate racism, but social and political changes that eradicate racism will not eradicate sexism.
>
> Sexism is the first form of oppression learned by children.
>
> Sexism predates racism.
>
> Sexism is the cause of racism.
>
> Sexism is used to justify racism.
>
> Sexism is the model for racism.

We can trace these arguments in the work of two important feminist theorists: Kate Millett in *Sexual Politics* and Shulamith Firestone in *The Dialectic of Sex.* It is worth remembering that these authors did not ignore race and racism. But their treatments of the subjects enable us to see that as long as race is taken to be independent of sex, racism as independent of sexism, we are bound to give seriously misleading descriptions of gender and gender relations.

In *Sexual Politics,* Kate Millett seems to hold that sexism is more fundamental than racism in three senses: it is "sturdier" than racism and so presumably is harder to eradicate; it has a more "pervasive ideology" than racism, and so those who are not racists may nevertheless embrace sexist beliefs; and it provides our culture's "most fundamental concept of power."[10] But as Margaret Simons has pointed out, Millett ignores the fact that Black women and other women of color do not usually describe their own lives as ones in which they experience sexism as more fundamental than racism.[11] There is indeed something very peculiar about the evidence Millett offers in behalf of her view that sexism is the more endemic oppression.

On the one hand, she states that everywhere men have power over women. On the other hand, she notes with interest that some observers have described as an effect of racism that Black men do not have such power over Black women, and that only when racism is eradicated will Black men assume their proper position of superiority. She goes on to argue that "the military, industry, technology, universities, science, political office, and finance—in short, every avenue of power within the society, including the coercive force of the police, is entirely in male hands."[12] But surely that is white male supremacy. Since when did Black males have such institutionally based power, in what Millett calls "our culture"? She thus correctly describes as sexist the hope that Black men could assume their "proper authority" over Black women, but her claim about the pervasiveness of sexism is belied by her reference to the lack of authority of Black males.

There is no doubt that Millett is right to view as sexist the hope that racial equity will be established when Black males have authority over Black females, but it also is correct to describe as racist the hope—not uncommonly found in feminist arguments—that sexual equity will be established when women can be presidents or heads of business. That is no guarantee that they will not be running racist countries and corporations. As Elizabeth F. Hood said: "Many white women define liberation as the access to those thrones traditionally occupied by white men—positions in the kingdoms which support racism."[13] Of course, one might insist that any truly antisexist vision also is an antiracist vision, for it requires the elimination of all forms of oppression against all women, white or Black.[14] But, similarly, it can be said that any truly antiracist vision would have to be antisexist, for it requires the elimination of all forms of oppression against all Blacks and other people of color, women or men.

In arguing for the position in *The Dialectic of Sex* that racism is "extended sexism," Shulamith Firestone provides another variation on the view that sexism is more fundamental:

> *Racism is sexism extended. . . . Let us look at race relations in America, a macrocosm of the hierarchical relations within the nuclear family: the white man is father, the white woman wife-and-mother, her status dependent on his; the blacks, like children, are his property, their physical differentiation branding them the subservient class, in the same way that children form so easily distinguishable a servile class vis-à-vis adults. The power hierarchy creates the psychology of racism, just as, in the nuclear family, it creates the psychology of sexism.*[15]

It is clear that Firestone sees sexism as the model for racism; as the cause of racism, so that racism cannot disappear unless sexism does; and as the historical precursor of racism. Moreover, with this model she sees the goal of the Black man (male child) to be to usurp the power of the white man (father), which means that the restoration of the authority of the Black man will involve his domination of women.[16] Hence sexism according to Firestone is more fundamental than racism, in the sense that the eradication of racism is portrayed as compatible with the continuation of sexism.

Here, as in the case of Millett, the evidence Firestone offers actually undermines her claim. First of all, she points out, and her analogy to the family requires, that the Black man is not really "the *real* man."[17] However much the Black man tries to act like the white man, and however much his treatment of Black women resembles the white man's treatment of white women and Black women, he isn't really The Man. Now if this is so, it seems odd to claim that sexism is more fundamental than racism, since according to Firestone's own account the Black man's identity as a man is obscured or erased by his identity as a Black. Thus according to her own account, the racial identity of being an inferior assigned him by racists is more fundamental than the sexual identity of being a superior assigned him by sexists.

Firestone also claims that "the All-American Family is predicated on the existence of the black ghetto whorehouse. The rape of the black community in America makes possible the existence of the family structure of the larger white community."[18] But to say in these ways that racism makes sexism possible is to say that in the absence of racism, sexism could not exist—surely just the opposite of the claim that sexism is more fundamental than racism, the claim Firestone wishes to establish.

II

If Millett's and Firestone's accounts tend to ignore facts about the status of Black men, other similar accounts ignore the existence of Black women. In the process of comparing racism and sexism, Richard Wasserstrom describes the ways in which women and Blacks have been stereotypically conceived of as less fully developed than white men: In the United States, "men and women are taught to see men as independent, capable, and powerful; men and women are taught to see women as dependent, limited in abilities, and passive."[19] But who is taught to see Black men as "independent, capable, and powerful," and by whom are they taught? Are Black men taught that? Black women? White men? White women? Similarly, who is taught to see Black women as "dependent, limited in abilities, and passive"? If this stereotype is so prevalent, why then have Black women had to defend themselves against the images of matriarch and whore?

Wasserstrom continues:

> *As is true for race, it is also a significant social fact that to be a female is to be an entity or creature viewed as different from the standard, fully developed person who is male as well as white. But to be female, as opposed to being black, is not to be conceived of as simply a creature of less worth. That is one important thing that differentiates sexism from racism: the ideology of sex, as opposed to the ideology of race, is a good deal more complex and confusing. Women are both put on a pedestal and deemed not fully developed persons.*[20]

He leaves no room for the Black woman. For a Black woman cannot be "female, as opposed to being Black"; she is female *and* Black. Since Wasserstrom's argument proceeds from the assumption that one is either female or Black, it cannot be an argument that applies to Black women. Moreover, we cannot generate a composite image of the Black woman from Wasserstrom's argument, since the description of women as being put on a pedestal, or being dependent, never generally applied to Black women in the United States and was never meant to apply to them.

Wasserstrom's argument about the priority of sexism over racism has an odd result, which stems from the erasure of Black women in his analysis. He wishes to claim that in this society sex is a more fundamental fact about people than race. Yet his description of women does not apply to the Black woman, which implies that being Black is a more fundamental fact about her than being a woman and hence that her sex is not a more fundamental fact about her than her race. I am not saying that Wasserstrom actually believes this is true, but that paradoxically the terms of his theory force him into that position. If the terms of one's theory require that a person is either female or Black, clearly there is no room to describe someone who is both.

A similar erasure of the Black woman, through failure to note how sexist stereotypes are influenced by racist ones, is found in Laurence Thomas's comparison of sexism and racism.[21] Like Wasserstrom, Thomas believes that sexism is more deeply ingrained in our culture. Racist attitudes, he says, are easier to give up than sexist ones for two reasons: First, "sexism, unlike racism, readily lends itself to a morally unobjectionable description," and second, "the positive self-concept of men has been more centrally tied to their being sexists than has been the positive self-concept of whites to their being racists."[22]

Thomas argues that it is not morally objectionable that "a natural outcome of a sexist conception of women" is the role of men as benefactors of women—part of men's role vis-à-vis women is to "protect women and to provide them with the comforts of life."[23] But at best, Thomas's claim about the man's role as benefactor of woman only applies to men and women of the same race (and probably of the same class). It is of course difficult to explain how claims about roles are established, but the history of race relations in the United States surely makes ludicrous the idea that the role of white men is to be the benefactors of Black women—to "protect" them and to "provide them with the comforts of life." This neither describes what white men have done, nor what they have been told they ought to have done, with respect to Black women.

Thomas's description of sexism in relations between women and men leaves out the reality of racism in relations between Blacks and whites. If he wishes to insist that his analysis was only meant to apply to same-race sexual relations, then he cannot continue to speak unqualifiedly about relations between men and women. My point is not that Black men cannot in any way be sexist to white or to Black women, for indeed they can, just as white women can be racist to Black men or to Black women. My point, rather, is that a theory of sexism that describes men's and women's roles can itself reflect the racist society in which it develops, insofar as it is based on an erasure of the realities of white racism.

Thomas also holds that sexism is more central to the positive self-concept of men than racism has been to the positive self-concept of whites. He claims that, although being benefactors of women is essential to men's self-esteem as "real" men, for whites it is not necessary to own slaves or to hate Blacks in order to be "really" white.[24] Once again, we have to see what happens to Thomas's claim when we put "Black" or "white" in front of "men" or "women" in his formula: "For white men, being benefactors of Black women is essential to their self-esteem as 'real' men." That is false. Indeed, in a racist society, white men's self-esteem requires the opposite position and attitude toward Black women.

Reflection on this leads to doubts about the second part of Thomas's claim—that whites don't have to be racists in order to be "really" white. Does he mean to say that in our society a white man feels no threat to his self-esteem if a Black man gets the job for which they both are candidates? That a white man feels no threat to his self-esteem if a Black man marries the white woman the white man is hoping to marry? That a white man feels no threat to his self-esteem if he lives in a neighborhood with Blacks? Certainly not all white men's self-esteem is so threatened. But this is a racist society, and generally, the self-esteem of white people is deeply influenced by their difference from and supposed superiority to Black people.[25] Those of us who are white may not think of ourselves as racists, because we do not own slaves or hate Blacks, but that does not mean that much of what props up our sense of self is not based on the racism that unfairly distributes benefits and burdens to whites and Blacks.

For example, think for a moment about a case of self-esteem that seems on the surface most unlikely to be supported by racism: the self-esteem that might be thought to attend sincere and serious philosophical reflection on the problems of racism. How could this be said to be based on racism, especially if the philosopher is trying to eliminate racism? As the editors of the *Philosophical Forum* in an issue on philosophy and the Black experience pointed out, "Black people have to a disproportionate extent supplied the labor which has made possible the cultivation of philosophical inquiry."[26] A disproportionate amount of the labor that makes it possible for some people to have philosophy as a profession has been done by Blacks and others under conditions that can only be described as racist. If the connection between philosophy and racism is not very visible, that invisibility itself is a product of racism. Any feminist would recognize a similar point about sexism: it is only in footnotes and prefaces that we see a visible connection made between a man's satisfaction in having finished an article or book and a woman's having made that completion possible.[27]

At several points early in his essay, Thomas says that he is going to consider the "way in which sexism and racism each conceives of its object: woman and Blacks, respectively."[28] But there are many difficulties in talking about sexism and racism in this way, some of which we have noted, and others to which we now turn.

III

First of all, sexism and racism do not have different "objects" in the case of Black women. It is highly misleading to say, without further explanation, that Black women experience "sexism and racism." For to say merely that suggests that Black women experience one form of oppression, as Blacks (the same thing Black men experience) and that they experience another form of oppression, as women (the same thing white women experience). While it is true that images and institutions that are described as sexist affect both Black and white women, they are affected in different ways, depending upon the extent to which they are affected by other forms of oppression. Thus, as noted earlier, it will not do to say that women are oppressed by the image of the "feminine" woman as fair, delicate, and in need of support and protection by men. As Linda Brent succinctly puts it, "That which commands admiration in the white woman only hastens the degradation of the female slave."[29] More specifically, as Angela Davis reminds us, "the alleged benefits of the ideology of femininity did not accrue" to the Black female slave—she was expected to toil in the fields for just as long and hard as the Black male was.[30]

Reflection on the experience of Black women also shows that is is not as if one form of oppression is merely piled upon another. As Barbara Smith has remarked, the effect of multiple oppression "is not merely arithmetic."[31] This additive method informs Gerda Lerner's analysis of the oppression of Black women under slavery: "Their work and duties were the same as that of the men, while childbearing and rearing fell upon them as an added burden."[32] But as Angela Davis has pointed out, the mother/housewife role (even the words seem inappropriate) doesn't have the same meaning for women who experience racism as it does for those who are not so oppressed:

> *In the infinite anguish of ministering to the needs of the men and children around her (who were not necessarily members of her immediate family), she was performing the only labor of the slave community which could not be directly and immediately claimed by the oppressor.*[33]

The meaning and the oppressive nature of the "housewife" role has to be understood in relation to the roles against which it is contrasted. The work of mate/mother/nurturer has a different meaning depending on whether it is contrasted to work that has high social value and ensures economic independence or to labor that is forced, degrading, and unpaid. All of these factors are left out in a simple additive analysis. How one form of oppression is experienced is influenced by and influences how another form is experienced. An additive analysis treats the oppression of a Black woman in a society that is racist as well as sexist as if it were a further burden when, in fact, it is a different burden. As the work of Davis, among others, shows, to ignore the difference is to deny the particular reality of the Black woman's experience.

If sexism and racism must be seen as interlocking, and not as piled upon each other, serious problems arise for the claim that one of them is more fundamental than the other. As we saw, one meaning of the claim that sexism is more fundamental than racism is that sexism causes racism: racism would not exist if sexism did not, while sexism could and would continue to exist even in the absence of racism. In this connection, racism is sometimes seen as something that is both derivative from sexism and in the service of it: racism keeps women from uniting in alliance against sexism. This view has been articulated by Mary Daly in *Beyond God the Father.* According to Daly, sexism is the "root and paradigm" of other forms of oppression such as racism. Racism is a "deformity *within* patriarchy. . . . It is most unlikely that racism will be eradicated as long as sexism prevails."[34]

Daly's theory relies on an additive analysis, and we can see again why such an analysis fails to describe adequately Black women's experience. Daly's analysis makes it look simply as if both Black women and white women experience sexism, while Black women also experience racism. Black women, Daly says, must come to see what they have in common with white women—shared sexist oppression—and see that they are all "pawns in the racial struggle, which is basically not the struggle that will set them free as women."[35] But insofar as she is oppressed by racism in a sexist context and sexism in a racist context, the Black woman's struggle cannot be compartmentalized into two struggles—one as a Black and one as a woman. Indeed, it is difficult to imagine why a Black woman would think of her struggles this way except in the face of demands by white women or by Black men that she do so. This way of speaking about her struggle is required by a theory that insists not only that sexism and racism are distinct but that one might be eradicated before the other. Daly rightly points out that the Black woman's struggle can easily be, and has usually been, subordinated to the Black man's struggle in antiracist organizations. But she does not point out that the Black woman's struggle can easily be, and usually has been, subordinated to the white woman's struggle in antisexist organizations.

Daly's line of thought also promotes the idea that, were it not for racism, there would be no important differences between Black and white women. Since, according to her view, sexism is the fundamental form of oppression and racism works in its service, the only significant differences between Black and white women are differences that men (Daly doesn't say whether she means white men or Black men or both) have created and that are the source of antagonism between women. What is really crucial about us is our sex; racial distinctions are one of the many products of sexism, of patriarchy's attempt to keep women from uniting. According to Daly, then, it is through our shared sexual identity that we are oppressed together; it is through our shared sexual identity that we shall be liberated together.

This view not only ignores the role women play in racism and classism, but it seems to deny the positive aspects of racial identities. It ignores the fact that being Black is a source of pride, as well as an occasion for being oppressed. It suggests that once racism is eliminated, Black women no longer need be concerned about or interested in their Blackness—as if the only reason for paying attention to one's Blackness is that it is the source of pain and sorrow and agony. The assumption that there is nothing positive about having a Black history and identity is racism pure and simple. Recall the lines of Nikki Giovanni:

> and I really hope no white person ever has cause
> to write about me
> because they never understand Black love is
> Black wealth and they'll
> probably talk about my hard childhood
> and never understand that
> all the while I was quite happy.[36]

Or recall the chagrin of the central character in Paule Marshall's story "Reena," when she discovered that her white boyfriend could only see her Blackness in terms of her suffering and not as something compatible with taking joy and pleasure in life.[37] I think it is helpful too in this connection to remember the opening lines of Pat Parker's "For the white person who wants to know how to be my friend":

> The first thing you do is to forget that i'm Black.
> Second, you must never forget that i'm Black.[38]

Perhaps it does not occur to feminists who are white that celebrating being white has anything to do with our celebrating being women. But that may be so because celebrating being white is already taken care of by the predominantly white culture in which we live in North America. Certainly feminist theory and activity on the whole have recognized that it is possible, if difficult, to celebrate being a woman without at the same time conceiving of woman in terms of the sexist imagery and lore of the centuries. (That celebrating womanhood is a tricky business we know from the insidiousness of the "two-sphere" ideology of the nineteenth century and of the image of the "total woman"—in Daly's wonderful phrase, the "totaled woman"—of the twentieth century: as if by celebrating what men tell us we are, the burden magically disappears because we embrace it.) But just as it is possible and desirable to identify oneself as a woman and yet think of and describe oneself in ways that are not sexist, so it is possible and desirable to identify oneself as a Black woman and yet think of oneself in ways that are not racist.

In sum, according to an additive analysis of sexism and racism, all women are oppressed by sexism; some women are further oppressed by racism. Such an analysis distorts Black women's experiences of oppression by failing to note important differences between the contexts in which Black women and white women experience sexism. The additive analysis also suggests that a woman's racial identity can be "subtracted" from her combined sexual and racial identity: "We are all women." But this does not leave room for the fact that different women may look to different forms of liberation just because they are white or Black women, rich or poor women, Catholic or Jewish women.

IV

As we saw in the Introduction, feminist leaders such as Elizabeth Cady Stanton used racist arguments in pleas to better the condition of "women." Though such blatant racism is not as likely to appear in contemporary feminism, that doesn't mean that visions of a nonsexist world will also be visions of a nonracist world. In the rest of the chapter I will explore how some ways of conceiving women's oppression and liberation contribute to the white solipsism of feminist theory.

As I have argued in detail elsewhere, feminist theorists as politically diverse as Simone de Beauvoir, Betty Friedan, and Shulamith Firestone have described the conditions of women's liberation in terms that suggest that the identification of woman with her body has been the source of our oppression, and hence that the source of our liberation lies in sundering that connection.[39] For example, de Beauvoir introduces *The Second Sex* with the comment that woman has been regarded as "womb"; and she later observes that woman is thought of as planted firmly in the world of "immanence," that is, the physical world of nature, her life defined by the dictates of her "biologic fate."[40] In contrast, men live in the world of "transcendence," actively using their minds to create "values, mores, religions."[41] Theirs is the world of culture as opposed to the world of nature. Among Friedan's central messages is that women should be allowed and encouraged to be "culturally" as well as "biologically" creative, because the former activities, in contrast to childbearing and rearing, are "mental" and are of "highest value to society"—"mastering the secrets of atoms, or the stars, composing symphonies, pioneering a new concept in government or society."[42]

This view comes out especially clearly in Firestone's work. According to her, the biological difference between women and men is at the root of women's oppression. It is woman's body—in particular, our body's capacity to bear children—that makes, or makes possible, the oppression of women by men. Hence we must disassociate ourselves from our bodies—most radically—by making it possible, or even necessary, to conceive and bear children outside the womb, and by otherwise generally disassociating our lives from the thankless tasks associated with the body.[43]

In predicating women's liberation on a disassociation from our bodies, Firestone oddly enough joins the chorus of male voices that has told us over the centuries about the disappointments entailed in being embodied creatures. What might be called "somatophobia" (fear of and disdain for the body) is part of a centuries-long tradition in Western culture. As de Beauvoir so thoroughly described in *The Second Sex,* the responsibility for being embodied creatures has been assigned to women: we have been associated, indeed virtually identified, with the body; men (or some men) have been associated and virtually identified with the mind. Women have been portrayed as possessing bodies in a way man have not. It is as if women essentially, men only accidentally, have bodies. It seems to me that Firestone's (as well as Friedan's and de Beauvoir's) prescription for women's liberation does not challenge the negative attitude toward the body; it only hopes to end the association between the body, so negatively characterized, and women.

I think the somatophobia we see in the work of Firestone and others is a force that contributes to white solipsism in feminist thought, in at least three related ways. First, insofar as feminists ignore, or indeed accept, negative views of the body in prescriptions for women's liberation, we will also ignore an important element in racist thinking. For the superiority of men to women (or, as we have seen, of some men to some women) is not the only hierarchical relationship that has been linked to the superiority of the mind to the body. Certain kinds, or "races," of people have been held to be more body-like than others, and this has meant that they are perceived as more animal-like and less god-like. For example, in *The White Man's Burden,* Winthrop Jordan describes ways in which white Englishmen portrayed black Africans as beastly, dirty, highly sexual beings.[44] Lillian Smith tells us in *Killers of the Dream* how closely run together were her lessons about the evil of the body and the evil of Blacks.[45]

We need to examine and understand somatophobia and look for it in our own thinking, for the idea that the work of the body and for the body has no part in real human dignity has been part of racist as well as sexist ideology. That is, oppressive stereotypes of "inferior races" and of women (notice that even in order to make the point in this way, we leave up in the air the question of how we shall refer to those who belong to both categories) have typically involved images of their lives as determined by basic bodily functions (sex, reproduction, appetite, secretions, and excretions) and as given over to attending to the bodily functions of others (feeding, washing, cleaning, doing the "dirty work"). Superior groups, we have been told from Plato on down, have better things to do with their lives. It certainly does not follow from the presence of somatophobia in a person's writings that she or he is a racist or a sexist. But disdain for the body historically has been symptomatic of sexist and racist (as well as classist) attitudes.

Human groups know that the work of the body and for the body is necessary for human existence, and they make provisions for that necessity. Thus even when a group views its liberation in terms of being free of association with, or responsibility for, bodily tasks, its own liberation is likely to be predicated on the oppression of other groups—those assigned to do the body's work. For example, if feminists decide that women are not going to be relegated to doing such work, who do we think is going to do it? Have we attended to the role that racism and classism historically have played in settling that question? We may recall why Plato and Aristotle thought philosophers and citizens needed leisure from this kind of work and who they thought ought to do it.

Finally, if one thinks—as de Beauvoir, Friedan, and Firestone do—that the liberation of women requires abstracting the notion of woman from the notion of woman's body, then one might logically think that the liberation of Blacks requires abstracting the notion of a Black person from the notion of a black body. Since the body, or at least certain of its aspects, may be thought to be the culprit, the solution may seem to be: Keep the person and leave the occasion for oppression behind. Keep the woman, somehow, but leave behind her woman's body; keep the Black person but leave the Blackness behind. Once one attempts to stop thinking about oneself in terms of having a body, then one not only will stop thinking in terms of characteristics such as womb and breast, but also will stop thinking in terms of skin and hair. We would expect to find that any feminist theory based in part on a disembodied view of human identity would regard blackness (or any other physical characteristic that may serve as a centering post for one's identity) as of temporary and negative importance.

Once the concept of woman is divorced from the concept of woman's body, conceptual room is made for the idea of a woman who is no particular historical woman—she has no color, no accent, no particular characteristics that require having a body. She is somehow all and only woman; that is her only identifying feature. And so it will seem inappropriate or beside the point to think of women in terms of any physical characteristics, especially if their oppression has been rationalized by reference to those characteristics.

None of this is to say that the historical and cultural identity of being Black or white is the same thing as, or is reducible to, the physical feature of having black or white skin. Historical and cultural identity is not constituted by having a body with particular identifying features, but it cannot be comprehended without such features and the significance attached to them.

V

Adrienne Rich was perhaps the first well-known contemporary white feminist to have noted "white solipsism" in feminist theorizing and activity. I think it is no coincidence that she also noticed and attended to the strong strain of somatophobia in feminist theory. *Of Woman Born* updates the connection between somatophobia and misogyny/gynephobia that

Simone de Beauvoir described at length in *The Second Sex*.[46] But unlike de Beauvoir or Firestone, Rich refuses to throw out the baby with the bathwater: she sees that the historical negative connection between woman and body (in particular, between woman and womb) can be broken in more than one way. Both de Beauvoir and Firestone wanted to break it by insisting that women need be no more connected—in thought or deed—with the body than men have been. In their view of embodiment as a liability, de Beauvoir and Firestone are in virtual agreement with the patriarchal cultural history they otherwise question. Rich, however, insists that the negative connection between woman and body be broken along other lines. She asks us to think about whether what she calls "flesh-loathing" is the only attitude it is possible to have toward our bodies. Just as she explicitly distinguishes between motherhood as experience and motherhood as institution, so she implicitly asks us to distinguish between embodiment as experience and embodiment as institution. Flesh-loathing is part of the well-entrenched beliefs, habits, and practices epitomized in the treatment of pregnancy as a disease. But we need not experience our flesh, our body, as loathsome.

I think it is not a psychological or historical accident that having examined the way women view their bodies, Rich also focused on the failure of white women to see Black women's experiences as different from their own. For looking at embodiment is one way (though not the only one) of coming to recognize and understand the particularity of experience. Without bodies we could not have personal histories. Nor could we be identified as woman or man, Black or white. This is not to say that reference to publicly observable bodily characteristics settles the question of whether someone is woman or man, Black or white; nor is it to say that being woman or man, Black or white, just means having certain bodily characteristics (that is one reason some Blacks want to capitalize the term; "Black" refers to a cultural identity, not simply a skin color). But different meanings are attached to having certain characteristics, in different places and at different times and by different people, and those differences affect enormously the kinds of lives we lead or experiences we have. Women's oppression has been linked to the meanings assigned to having a woman's body by male oppressors. Blacks' oppression has been linked to the meanings assigned to having a black body by white oppressors. (Note how insidiously this way of speaking once again leaves unmentioned the situation for Black women.) We cannot hope to understand the meaning of a person's experiences, including her experiences of oppression, without first thinking of her as embodied, and second thinking about the particular meanings assigned to that embodiment. If, because of somatophobia, we think and write as if we are not embodied, or as if we would be better off if we were not embodied, we are likely to ignore the ways in which different forms of embodiment are correlated with different kinds of experience.

Rich—unlike de Beauvoir—asks us to reflect on the culturally assigned differences between having a Black or a white body, as well as on the differences between having the body of a woman or of a man. Other feminists have reflected on the meaning of embodiment and recognized the connection between flesh-loathing and woman-hatred, but they have only considered it far enough to try to divorce the concept of woman from the concept of the flesh. In effect, they have insisted that having different bodies does not or need not mean men and women are any different as humans; and having said that, they imply that having different colored bodies does not mean that Black women and white women are any different. Such statements are fine if interpreted to mean that the differences between woman and man, Black and white, should not be used against Black women and white women and Black men. But not paying attention to embodiment and to the cultural meanings assigned to different forms of it is to encourage sexblindness and colorblindness. These blindnesses are vicious when they are used to support the idea that all experience is male experience or that all experience is white experience. Rich does not run away from the fact that women have bodies, nor does she wish that women's bodies were not so different from men's. That healthy regard for the ground of our differences from men is logically connected to—though of course does not ensure—a healthy regard for the ground of the differences between Black women and white women.

> *"Colorblindness" . . . implies that I would look at a Black woman and see her as white, thus engaging in white solipsism to the utter erasure of her particular reality.*[47]

Colorblindness denies the particularity of the Black woman and rules out the possibility both that her history has been different and that her future might be different in any significant way from the white woman's.

VI

I have been discussing the ways in which some aspects of feminist theory exhibit what Adrienne Rich has called "white solipsism." In particular, I have been examining ways in which some prominent claims about the relation between sexism and racism ignore the realities of racism. I have also suggested that there are ways of thinking about women's oppression and about women's liberation that reflect and encourage white solipsism, but that thinking differently about women and about sexism might lead to thinking differently about Blackness and about racism.

First, we have to continue to reexamine the traditions which reinforce sexism and racism. Though feminist theory has recognized the connection between somatophobia and misogyny/gynephobia, it has tended to challenge the misogyny without challenging the somatophobia, and without fully appreciating the connection between somatophobia and racism.

Second, we have to keep a cautious eye on discussions of racism versus sexism. They keep us from seeing ways in which what sexism means and how it works is modulated by racism, and ways in which what racism means is modulated by sexism. Most important, discussions of sexism versus racism tend to proceed as if Black women—to take one example—do not exist. None of this is to say that sexism and racism are thoroughly and in every context indistinguishable. Certain political and social changes may point to the conclusion that some aspects of racism will disappear sooner than some aspects of sexism (see, for example, the statistics Diane Lewis cites in "A Response to Inequality: Black Women, Racism, and Sexism").[48] Other changes may point to the conclusion that some aspects of sexism will disappear sooner than some aspects of racism (e.g., scepticism about the possible effects of passage of the ERA on the lives of Black women in the ghetto). And there undoubtedly is disagreement about when certain changes should be seen as making any dent in sexism or racism at all. But as long as Black women and other women of color are at the bottom of the economic heap (which clearly we cannot fully understand in the absence of a class analysis), and as long as our descriptions of sexism and racism themselves reveal racist and sexist perspectives, it seems both empirically and conceptually premature to make grand claims about whether sexism or racism is "more fundamental." For many reasons, then, it seems wise to proceed very cautiously in this inquiry.

Third, it is crucial to sustain a lively regard for the variety of women's experiences. On the one hand, what unifies women and justifies us in talking about the oppression of women is the overwhelming evidence of the worldwide and historical subordination of women to men. On the other, while it may be possible for us to speak about women in a general way, it also is inevitable that any statement we make about women in some particular place at some particular time is bound to suffer from ethnocentrism if we try to claim for it more generality than it has. So, for example, to say that the image of woman as frail and dependent is oppressive is certainly true. But it is oppressive to white women in the United States in quite a different way than it is oppressive to Black women, for the sexism Black women experience is in the context of their experience of racism. In Toni Morrison's *The Bluest Eye*, the causes and consequences of Pecola's longing to have blue eyes are surely quite different from the causes and consequences of a white girl with brown eyes having a similar desire.[49] More to the point, the consequences of *not* having blue eyes are quite different for the two. Similarly, the family may be the locus of oppression for white middle-class women, but to claim that it is the locus of oppression for all women is to ignore the fact that for Blacks in America the family has been a source of resistance against white oppression.[50]

In short, the claim that all women are oppressed is fully compatible with, and needs to be explicated in terms of, the many varieties of oppression that different populations of women have been subject to. After all, why should oppressors settle for uniform kinds of oppression, when to oppress their victims in many different ways—consciously or unconsciously—makes it more likely that the oppressed groups will not perceive it to be in their interest to work together?

Finally, it is crucial not to see Blackness only as the occasion for oppression—any more than one sees being a woman only as the occasion for oppression. No one ought to expect the forms of our liberation to be any less various than the forms of our oppression. We need to be at least as generous in imagining what women's liberation will be like as our oppressors have been in devising what women's oppression has been.

Notes

1. This chapter is a slightly revised version of my "Theories of Race and Gender: The Erasure of Black Women," in *Quest: a feminist quarterly* 5, no. 4 (1982): 36–62.

2. Halloran, "Women, Blacks, Spouses Transforming the Military." See also Introduction, note 32.

3. See also Gloria T. Hull, Patricia Bell Scott, and Barbara Smith, eds., *All the Women Are White, All the Blacks Are Men, But Some of Us Are Brave: Black Women's Studies* (Old Westbury, N.Y.: Feminist Press, 1982).

4. See Eleanor Flexner, *Century of Struggle* (New York: Atheneum, 1972), especially chapter 13, on the inhospitality of white women's organizations to Black women, as well as Aileen S. Kraditor's *The Ideas of the Woman Suffrage Movement*, 1890–1920 (Garden City, N.Y.: Doubleday, 1971). See also DuBois, *Feminism and Suffrage;* Sara Evans, *Personal Politics* (New York: Vintage, 1979) on sexism in the civil rights movement; Dorothy Sterling, *Black Foremothers* (Old Westbury, N.Y.: Feminist Press, 1979), 147, on Alice Paul's refusal to grant Mary Church Terrell's request that Paul endorse enforcement of the Nineteenth Amendment for all women; Davis, *Women, Race, and Class;* Bettina Aptheker, *Women's Legacy: Essays on Race, Sex, and Class in American History* (Amherst: University of Massachusetts Press, 1982); Paula Giddings, *When and Where I Enter: The Impact of Black Women on Race and Sex in America* (New York: Morrow, 1984).

5. Adrienne Rich, "Disloyal to Civilization: Feminism, Racism, Gynephobia," in her *On Lies, Secrets, and Silence* (New York: Norton, 1979), 299 and passim. In the philosophical literature, solipsism is the view according to which it is only one's self that is knowable, or it is only one's self that constitutes the world. Strictly speaking, of course, Rich's use of the phrase "white solipsism" is at odds with the idea of there being only the self, insofar as it implies that there are other white people; but she is drawing from the idea of there being only one perspective on the world—not that of one person, but of one "race." (For further comment on the concept of race, see references in note 24 below.)

6. Ibid., 306.

7. Audre Lorde, "Man Child: A Black Lesbian Feminist's Response," *Conditions* 4 (1979): 35. My comments about racism apply to the racism directed against Black people in the United States. I do not claim that all my arguments apply to the racism experienced by other people of color.

8. See Margaret A. Simons, "Racism and Feminism: A Schism in the Sisterhood," *Feminist Studies* 5, no. 2 (1979): 384–401.

9. A somewhat similar list appears in Alison M. Jaggar and Paula Rothenberg's introduction to part 2 of *Feminist Frameworks*, 2d ed. (New York: McGraw-Hill, 1984), 86.

10. Kate Millett, *Sexual Politics* (New York: Ballantine, 1969), 33–34.

11. Simons, "Racism and Feminism."

12. Millett, *Sexual Politics*, 33–34.

13. Elizabeth F. Hood, "Black Women, White Women: Separate Paths to Liberation," *Black Scholar*, April 1978, 47.

14. This is precisely the position we found Richards attacking in chapter 2 above.

15. Shulamith Firestone, *The Dialectic of Sex* (New York: Bantam, 1970), 108.

16. Ibid., 117–18.

17. Ibid., 115. Emphasis in the original.

18. Ibid., 116.

19. Richard A. Wasserstrom, "Racism and Sexism," in *Philosophy and Women*, ed. Sharon Bishop and Marjorie Weinzweig (Belmont, Cal.: Wadsworth, 1979), 8. Reprinted from "Racism, Sexism, and Preferential Treatment: An Approach to the Topics," *UCLA Law Review* (February 1977): 581–615.

20. Ibid.

21. Laurence Thomas, "Sexism and Racism: Some Conceptual Differences," *Ethics* 90 (1980): 239–50.

22. I shall here leave aside the question of whether Thomas succeeds in offering a description of sexism that is not of something morally objectionable (see B.C. Postow's reply to Thomas, "Thomas on Sexism," *Ethics* 90 [1980]: 251–56). I shall also leave aside the question of to whom such a description is or is not morally objectionable, as well as the question of how its moral objectionableness is to be measured.

23. Thomas, "Sexism and Racism," 239 and passim.

24. Thomas says that "one very important reason" for this lack of analogy is that racial identity, unlike sexual identity, is "more or less settled by biological considerations" (ibid., 248). If Thomas means by this that there are such things as "races," and that the question of what race one belongs to is settled by biology, one must point out in reply that it is far from clear that this is so. See Ashley Montagu, "The Concept of Race: Part 1," *American Anthropologist* 64, no. 5 (1962) reprinted in *Anthropology: Contemporary Perspectives*, ed. David E. Hunter and Philip Whitten (Boston: Little, Brown, 1975), 83–95; and Frank B. Livingstone, "On the Nonexistence of Human Races," *The Concept of Race*, ed. Ashley Montagu (New York: Collier, 1964), reprinted in Hunter and Whitten. The existence of racism does not require that there are races; it requires the belief that there are races.

25. This is the kind of superiority that, as we saw in chapter 3, de Beauvoir described.

26. *Philosophical Forum,* 9, no. 2–3 (1977–78): 113.

27. See Carol Christ and Judith Plaskow Goldenberg, "For the Advancement of My Career: A Form Critical Study in the Art of Acknowledgement," *Bulletin of the Council for Religious Studies* (June 1972), for a marvelous study of the literary form of the "acknowledgement to the wife." See also the gruesomely delightful "Collecting Scholar's Wives," by Marilyn Hoder-Salmon, in *Feminist Studies* 4, no. 3 (n.d.): 107–14.

28. Thomas, "Sexism and Racism," 242–43.

29. Linda Brent, "The Trials of Girlhood," in *Root of Bitterness,* ed. Nancy F. Cott (New York: Dutton, 1972), 201.

30. Angela Y. Davis, "Reflections on the Black Woman's Role in the Community of Slaves," *Black Scholar* 3 (1971): 7.

31. Barbara Smith, "Notes For Yet Another Paper on Black Feminism, or Will the Real Enemy Please Stand Up," *Conditions* 5 (1979): 123–32. See also "The Combahee River Collective Statement," *Capitalist Patriarchy and the Case for Socialist Feminism,* ed. Zillah Eisenstein (New York: Monthly Review Press, 1979), 362–72.

32. Gerda Lerner, ed., *Black Woman in White America* (New York: Vintage, 1973), 15.

33. Davis, "Reflections on the Black Woman's Role," 7. Davis revises this slightly in *Women, Race, and Class.*

34. Mary Daly, *Beyond God the Father* (Boston: Beacon Press, 1975), 56–57.

35. Ibid.

36. Nikki Giovanni, "Nikki Rosa," in *The Black Woman,* ed. Toni Cade (New York: New American Library, 1980), 16.

37. Paule Marshall, "Reena," in *The Black Woman,* 28.

38. Pat Parker, *Womanslaughter* (Oakland: Diana Press, 1978), 13.

39. Spelman, "Woman as Body."

40. De Beauvoir, *The Second Sex,* xii, 57.

41. Ibid., 119.

42. Friedan, *The Feminine Mystique,* 247–77.

43. Firestone, *The Dialectic of Sex,* chap. 10.

44. Winthrop P. Jordan, *The White Man's Burden* (New York: Oxford University Press, 1974), chap. 1.

45. Smith, *Killers of the Dream,* 83–98.

46. Adrienne Rich, *Of Woman Born* (New York: Norton, 1976).

47. Rich, "Disloyal to Civilization," 300.

48. Diane Lewis, "A Response to Inequality: Black Women, Racism, and Sexism," *Signs* 3, no. 2 (1977): 339–61.

49. Toni Morrison, *The Bluest Eye* (New York: Pocketbooks, 1972).

50. See, for example, Carol Stack, *All Our Kin* (New York: Harper and Row, 1974).

Passion and Politics in Women's Studies in the Nineties

Renate D. Klein

Renate D. Klein is currently at Deakin University in Geelong, Victoria, Australia. She has been editor of the Athene Series in women's studies, and she has been active in the women's health movement. Her publications include Radical Voices: A Decade of Feminist Resistance from Women's Studies International Forum, *edited with Deborah Lynn Steinberg (1989) and* The Exploitation of a Desire: Women's Experience with In Vitro Fertilization *(1989).*

In this essay Klein celebrates the liberating power of early feminist scholarship and its origins in the activism of the 1960s and 1970s. She raises serious concerns, however, about more recent directions in women's studies: (1) the development of gender studies (which "reinforces the necessity of studying women and men in relation to one another: a much narrower aim than WS' claim to study the whole world from a feminist perspective!") and (2) the growth of theories that "deconstruct" realities so completely "that in the end what remains is total relativism." Finally, Klein suggests some strategies for women's studies to move "passionately forward" into the nineties and beyond.

Synopsis—This article first summarizes the origins and aims of Women's Studies—its "Idea Power"—which led to the impressive worldwide expansion of Women's Studies in the last twenty years as the educational arm of the Women's Liberation Movement. Then it discusses the "Woman Power" in Women's Studies and its promise of diversity followed by its subject matter, which is equally diverse and is conceptualized from revisionary to visionary and revisionary/visionary standpoints. Next are mentioned some obstacles to feminist vision and sisterhood, such as the libertarian ideology informing the theory and praxis of Gender Studies and post-structuralist discourse/deconstructionist epistemology. I contend that whilst there is much cause for celebrating the achievements of Women's Studies, there is also cause for concern with this latest resurgence of fragmented and disconnected theory, which mirrors similar developments in reproductive and genetic engineering. This article ends with some strategies of how Women's Studies might avoid colluding with compartmentalized frameworks and move "passionately forward" into the nineties and beyond.

Passion and politics, in interaction with a politics of curiosity *and* a politics of responsibility, are magic ingredients in the creation and distribution of the sort of feminist knowledge/vision that has the potential to move Women's Studies (WS)—and its participants with it—"out of the margins" in the 1990s and beyond. I first mention some of the dynamics of WS internationally,[1] and then list current developments in WS that I find troubling, and perceive as endangering the further growth of WS. I will suggest some strategies for how, hopefully, WS will move into the nineties with a vision of empowering feminist politics, towards ending all women's oppression internationally.

The Idea Power[2] of Women's Studies: Origins and Aims

It is important to remember that Women's Studies came into being as the educational arm of the Women's Liberation Movement in individual

"Passion and Politics in Women's Studies in the Nineties" by Renate D. Klein is reprinted from *Women's Studies International Forum,* Vol. 14, No. 3, 1991, pp. 125–134, with kind permission of Pergamon Press Ltd., Oxford, England.

This paper is the edited Plenary Address given at the Women's Studies Network (UK) Conference, Coventry Polytechnic, July 7–8, 1990.

It will also be published in *Out of the Margins: Women's Studies in the Nineties.* Edited by Jane Aaron and Sylvia Walby (Eds.), Falmer Press, Basingstoke, U.K.

western countries. In the late sixties and early seventies, feminists moved from the streets to the classrooms, in and outside higher education, and declared that enough was enough, women had been excluded, made invisible, and barred from creating and distributing knowledge for far too long. And what was needed was not just ANY knowledge, but knowledge that helped to *liberate* women, that gave us power to empower ourselves and that gave us strength, based on women's *diversity*. Contrary to what some history-makers are saying now, at that early time feminists wanted the liberation of ALL women of ALL classes, races, sexualities, ages, ethnicities, and professions—the collection *Sisterhood is Powerful,* edited by Robin Morgan in 1970 is a good example to demonstrate the inclusiveness of the early years. It is also important to remember how many lesbians and how many black women were actually involved in the origins of the Women's Liberation Movement in and outside the academy, and of course how lesbians and black women continue to be a most vital part of WS, which is not emphasized enough in public.

It was the particular position of women—the exclusion from the production and content of male culture—that WS set out to challenge. Canadian sociologist Dorothy Smith spoke of the "eclipsing of women" from what is supposed to be "our" culture (1978, pp. 281–295). Angry about the perpetuation of the seemingly unquestioned ideology of male dominance that "omitted, trivialized or distorted" women in what was presented as "knowledge" (Tobias, 1978, p. 88, attributed to Catharine Stimpson), promoters of WS said that WS must be an educational experience relevant to and positive for human beings living as women in today's society. Put differently, from its early days, the supporters of WS stated unequivocally that they were not simply seeking to change knowledge for knowledge's sake—to practice WS as an academic exercise—but that they were intent on *changing* the lives of *real live* women by improving the political, socio-economic, and psychological position of women worldwide. The slogan of the Women's Liberation Movement, "The personal is the political" thus was extended to "... is the intellectual" (Westkott, 1981/1983, p. 26).

Further, from the outset, WS made no secret that it aims to cross disciplinary boundaries. Since the drama of "life" does not take place in a glass-womb (although reproductive biologists would like us to *originate* there!), subject compartmentalization needs to be broken down in order to both study *and* survive in the *Politics of Reality* (Frye, 1987). What was emphasized in WS were inter-connections, continuity and inter-relationships: the *compartmentalization* of knowledge was—and by some of us still is—explicitly opposed.

What these goals make clear is that "the idea power" of WS from its origins amounted to a *"philosophy of life"* that embraces *all* human issues—and non-human issues as well. *Every* issue is a WS issue and WS is "not just a laundry list—it is a perspective on everything from budgets to biogenetics" (Bunch, 1980), and critically evaluates every facet of human existence from interpersonal relationships to established politics, from language to law, from the use and abuse of natural resources to the social construction of reality. Above all, WS is an *active* force: women are both (and often simultaneously) subject and object of the knowledge generated and transmitted, thus creating a *dynamic interaction* exemplary of the WS movement *per se.* Ideally, a common denominator of such work is the shift from a men centred perspective to a *women centred perspective* where women's varying needs and interests following from our diversity in the world are the point of departure; thus, in the words of Dorothy Smith (1978, p. 294), "... taking up the standpoint of women as an experience of being."

The "Woman Power" in Women's Studies: The Promise of Diversity

The "Idea Power" of WS is of course theorized and put into practice by the women who teach and study WS: the WS practitioners.[3] To find out who this group is—the "Woman Power" of WS as I have called them—was one of the main aims of my dissertation, which was an exploratory survey of 158 WS practitioners (88 teachers and 70 students) in the UK and the USA (including some women in (West) Germany and Australia) by means of a questionnaire, participant observation and in-depth interviews (Klein, 1986, pp. 104–282). Meeting with all the women was certainly the most enjoyable part of my dissertation: their originality, commitment, and hard labour to work for a better future, their originality of research and teaching, of inventing WS, and of "claiming an education" (Rich, 1977/79), their organizing skills and political "savvy" was inspiring. It is their *diversity*—or "different similarities", as I have called it—which is most impressive. In tandem with the equally diverse, all encompassing, holistic "idea power" (as described above), the breadth and depth is, in my view, an irrefutable argument why WS is much more than a new "subject" that can be integrated into the existing structure of knowledge. It is, in fact, a *new academic discipline,* which has already grown a multitude of its own "side" disciplines: like a healthy vigorous tree with lots of branches. However, a caveat is immediately needed here: then and now (I finished my research in 1986), the *ethnic* diversity among WS practitioners leaves much to be desired, that is "white dominance" in western WS continues to be cause for great concern, and racism, unfortunately, exists in WS too.

Briefly summarized, the *WS teachers* in my study range widely in disciplinary background,[4] age (a substantial number are reentry women), social class, sexuality, and with varying levels of participation in the Women's Liberation Movement, and their identification with non-heterorelational women-centredness.[5] Of particular importance in the discussion of WS as "discipline" is the fact that the WS teachers' particular "brands" of feminisms cover the whole gamut of feminism, which in turn greatly influences how they perceive WS. This means that women who define themselves as *reformist* or *liberal* feminists tend to see WS primarily as remedial: as the "study of women," as "adding women on" to the curriculum. A second group, women who identify as *socialist* feminists, tend to favour the integration of feminist courses into the traditional disciplines, and many of them are taken with the development of Gender Studies. Yet another group, *radical* feminists, are the main promoters of women-centred, "autonomous"[6] WS, preferably organized in independent programmes or departments. They perceive WS as an entity in its own right and see knowledge generated in WS as valid *qua* women.

The *WS students,* too, are a very mixed group. As with the WS teachers their "life profiles" vary greatly, and this extends to age (because a substantial number of WS students are also re-entry women).[7] A clear difference between WS teachers and students was the students' greater involvement with feminist activism.[8] They, too, adhere to many brands of feminism, and their political inclinations influence their view of WS in relation to its *usefulness* for their lives. The *reformist/liberal* feminists perceive sexism as left over "prejudice" and expect that WS will service them in acquiring skills to manoeuvre around remaining sexism and succeed in the world. More *socialist*-oriented students are deeply grateful for the existence of WS, which often changed their lives profoundly. They regard WS as a useful tool in contributing to social change, including the elimination of racism and classism. *Radical* feminists perceive WS as a women-centred power base, where they can acquire intellectual and political skills. They are very enthusiastic about its presence, and are committed to work for its continued existence.[9]

WS has clearly set itself an ambitious agenda: to try to accommodate, and cater to, the expectations, hopes and "dreams" of so many different women within the patriarchal reality of higher education, is no small goal. Needless to say, WS classrooms often bristle not only with the dynamics of intellectual excitement, but also with emotional energy. WS courses challenge participants to critically evaluate all knowledge and draw conclusions that often necessitate changes in our political/personal lives.[10]

The Subject Matter of WS: From Re-vision to Vision and Revision/Vision

Like the "Idea Power" and the "Woman Power" of WS, the nature of the subject matter in WS is by no means monolithic or uniform. I distinguish three main "types" of WS scholarship (although of course there are many overlaps):

1. *Re-action, re-vision*[11]*: assessing women within the androcentric worldview*
   Whether this approach is disciplinary or interdisciplinary, women are assessed in relation to the pervasive masculinism in existing scholarship: it is a critique of androcentricity and focuses on the absence and distortion of women from the non-feminist structure of knowledge. Examples include feminist critiques of literature, economics, biology, education, psychology, psychoanalysis, sociology, history. Courses taught include Women and the Law, Women and Work, Cross-Cultural Studies of Women, and so on. Such work might be

summarized as: "the study of women's oppression—gender roles, gender inequalities, discrimination, exclusion; their causes, nature and effects; women's perceptions of injustice and response to it" (Coyner, 1984, pp. 9–10).

2. *Action, vision: assessing women with a gynocentric world view*
   This type of WS scholarship and course content is rarely disciplinary, but creates its own women-centred definition of "cross-," "trans-," or multi-disciplinary (Bowles, 1983; Coyner, 1983). It is frequently, but not exclusively, produced by those who conceptualize WS as an "autonomous" entity (i.e., discipline) rather than by those whose main emphasis is to "transform" the other academic disciplines. Women are at the centre of research and teaching and are researched and assessed in their own right. The androcentric framework ceases to be the point of reference: what happens is a paradigmatic shift, creating new theories and methologies[12] for teaching and research. A visionary/action approach is used in courses that focus on similarities and diversities among and between women of various ethnicities, races, nationalities, sexualities, etc. Power differentials are discussed, both in material as well as ideological terms, and the nature of various theories of feminisms is assessed.

3. *Revision/vision, re-action/action combined: WS between criticism and vision*
   The most ambitious of the three "types," it conceptualizes WS research and curriculum as synthesising re-vision and vision i.e., as both critiquing androcentric scholarship as well as making an "imaginative leap" towards the creation of knowledge (vision, action). Janice Raymond's concepts of "Two Sights Seeing" (Raymond, 1986) can be adapted for the WS curriculum and scholarship which is between criticism and vision: "At one and the same time, vision is the exercise of the ordinary faculty of sight and something which is apparently seen otherwise than by ordinary sight (p. 85)." Examples include research/teaching about the "feminization of poverty." *Re-visionary* scholarship/teaching exposes its roots (e.g., male devaluation and appropriation of women's work, exploitation of cheap female labour, particularly that of poor women and women of color cross-culturally); the *visionary* part consists of devising theories for a non-sexist, non-racist international economic system that will benefit women and other oppressed groups (Mies, 1986; Waring, 1989), as well as implementing actions based on networks of "global feminism," Morgan, 1984) that will improve women's positions worldwide. Other examples of revisionary/visionary WS encompass work on violence against women including reproductive and genetic engineering (Klein, 1989b).

Summarizing the three "types" of WS scholarship, it is clear that the "re-vision/vision, re-action/action" approach is by far the most exciting, but also the most demanding framework for the production of WS knowledge. It needs both a combination of "idea power" and "woman power" and, importantly, access to resources, that is, grant monies to do research that incorporates both an avowedly feminist critique of androcentric research and ideas/theories for creating women-centred knowledge).[13] Such research also requires the administrative assurances of continuity that are most secure with departmental (or programme) status. As Bonnie Zimmerman, Chairperson of the WS Department at San Diego State University, U.S.A. put it: (personal communication March 20, 1990):

> *The best thing about being a Department is that we all work together and that we are in control. We control the curriculum, that is* we *take the decisions about* what *courses are offered when, and* who *teaches them, and we make all the faculty appointments. Equally important, we have the same access to resources and information as other departments.*

Women's Studies International at The Beginning of The 1990s

As we begin the 1990s, there is no doubt that WS is alive and well. In the U.S.A. there are more than 30,000 courses and over 600 programmes, including an increasing number of MA and PhD programmes and over 150 research centres. Moreover, in 1990, WS is a global movement. Without exception, all so-called "western" countries—including Australia and New Zealand—have some form or other of WS. Importantly, WS has also become a recognized phenomenon in Asia with courses in India, Bangladesh, the Philippines, Korea, Japan, China, to name but a few, and courses in Mexico and South American countries. In fact I think that Asia—and Central/South America—are the two continents where exciting developments are taking place, and western women can learn a lot about the interaction of theory and practice, and the activist role of WS practitioners.[14]

So, undoubtedly, there is much cause for celebrating the growth and proliferation of WS. But the undone work weighs heavily. While WS may be getting stronger and stronger globally, and more diversified, the feminization of poverty and women's illiteracy are increasing worldwide. Sheer survival is getting tougher: women's nutrition, and consequently women's and children's health is worsening, and male violence against women, be it incest, sexual harassment, date rape, rape in and outside marriage, criminal assault at home, pornography and prostitution—and with the latest toy of technopatriarchy, the crimes of gene and reproductive technology—are all increasing. Increasing, too, are the many forms of violence committed against our ecosystems, with particularly devastating effects in third world countries—committed by the west—from which women and children suffer most (see Shiva, 1989). And women's rights to integrity of body and soul are still not recognized as human rights; lesbian existence, for instance is by no means safe, and women's own decisions whether they wish to be—or can be—mothers or not, is being curtailed even further. It is therefore crucial to increase and solidify international feminist action. To this end, a strong feminist WS movement could contribute significantly: a movement which has as its core concept a fervent commitment to fostering a diversified sisterhood across cultural and national boundaries. Yet there are a number of shadows on the wall of such feminist unity, which I will examine next.[15]

Obstacles to Feminist Vision and International Sisterhood[16]

One thick cloud on the horizon of WS is the increasing tendency to rename Women's Studies and call it Gender Studies. In my view, this is the beginning of eclipsing WS, both by making women invisible (again)—gender is such a neutral term—and by allowing men into feminist space. (The first U.S. chair in Gender Studies went to Harry Brod.) Promoters of Gender Studies tell us that WS is really only about women, that we are marginalizing ourselves, and that what we need is a *broader* vision. The broader vision they propose is, however, precisely a masculine construction of knowledge that feminists have been fighting against for centuries (see for instance Spender, 1982); the very *limited* idea that the world centres around *hetero-relations* since ". . . it expresses woman in relation to man—as determined by the concept of gender which relies on *dichotomies*" (Hawthorne, 1989, p. 626; my emphasis).[17] Gender Studies thus reinforces the necessity of studying women and men in relation to one another: a much narrower aim than WS' claim to study the whole world from a feminist perspective! Given the continuing power differences in our patriarchal society—*and* the increasing number of men interested in (taking over) such "Hetero-Relations Studies"—my new term for Gender Studies—with its obsession with the concept of *difference* do not bode well for the future of a strong WS movement. This new form of hetero-reality might easily become compulsory through community support and financial resources available only to "balanced" Gender Studies and not to "marginal" WS.

Indeed, the obsession with "difference" seems to be a legacy from the 1980s for the early 1990s. Theories of sexualities, especially lesbian sexuality, are now celebrating eroticized power differences among women and ridiculing sexual relations based on equality. Diane Hamer, discussing difference among lesbians in butch and femme sexuality, praises it (1990, p. 147):

> *. . . as an antidote to the monolithic account of lesbianism within psychoanalysis (as well as to the rather* sexless *emphasis of* sameness *between lesbians supported by a certain current of lesbian feminism dominant in the late 70s and early 1980s; see Rich, 1980). (my emphases)*

This ideology creates, as Sheila Jeffreys puts it, ". . . otherness . . . through differences of age, race, class, the practice of sadomasochism or role playing" (1990, p. 301). There is much talk about "individual pleasure" promoted under the guise of "choice." Political thought and action is "out," "in" is a libertarian ideology that fosters individualism and is centred around "difference." And even in the lesbian context, the focus on differences between men and women appears; as Cindy Patton, interviewed by Sue O'Sullivan says ". . . it is possible at this point politically and culturally for lesbians to start looking at gay male porn. . . ." (O'Sullivan, 1990, p. 132), which is in line with Sara Dunn's comment in the same so-called feminist journal "to be firmly pro-pornography" (1990, p. 162). When sexual liberals teach such knowledge in WS classrooms, it defuses the inherent women-hating nature of patriarchal power and one of its cornerstones, pornography, in the making of which real live women are hurt, indeed sometimes killed. The students' sense of dignity and their/our embodied "right" to integrity of body and soul may be destabilized and numbed: the beginning of another generation of women perhaps, who justify the continuation of woman-hating ideologies with a tyranny of tolerance—anything goes as long as somebody "desires" it—at the expense of their own freedom?

The concept of difference rules supreme in post-structuralist discourse and deconstructionist epistemology. Through analytical tools, realities are taken apart, turned around, taken apart again, and turned around again . . . so that in the end what remains is total relativism: a multitude of subjectivities out of which, so the de-constructionist logic runs, it is excitingly impossible to name one as more real than the other. We are left with fragmented bits and pieces, vagueness and uncertainty. As Somer Brodribb puts it ". . . texts without contexts, genders without sexes, and sex without politics" (1991). Pluralism reigns supreme and "nothingness"—when all is deconstructed—precludes us from having clear concepts about, for instance, the power dynamics between the sexes, or feminism.

I began to seriously take notice of this "grand theory" (rather than just thinking it was a virus that could be avoided with lots of Vitamin C), when I realized that the theory of splitting realities and texts into fragments mirrors precisely what goes on in contemporary science, especially in reproductive and genetic engineering. Here, it is women with a fertility problem—or "bad" genes—who are split into bits and pieces. They are not conceptualized as whole human beings, but dismembered as "bad eggs," "diseased tubes," "hostile wombs." These bits are what is looked at—through the pornographic gaze of the "masters"—and what the "experts"—the techno-docs—will try to "fix up." That the other "bit" surrounding these body parts happens to be a whole person with the complications of a human life, human feelings, fears, and longings, does not matter, is not seen as "real."

Once I made this connection between reproductive and genetic engineering and deconstructionism, I began to see it as more than a fad, but, rather as the current *Zeitgeist:* a serious threat to everything that is connected, that is interactive and whole, that wants and insists on continuities and commonalities—which are, in fact some of the cherished values of feminism and WS. Instead, the cutters with words and knives prefer difference.[18] This not only splits women into non-entities, thereby seriously damaging a woman's sense of self and sense of identity, it also splits women from each other; one of patriarchy's best tools to keep women from forming a joint resistance movement. In fact these ideologies mimic patriarchy as described by Robin Morgan (1989, p. 51):

> *If I had to name one quality as the genius of patriarchy, it would be compartmentalization, the capacity for institutionalizing disconnection. . . . The personal isolated from the political. Sex divorced from love. The material ruptured from the spiritual. The past parted from the present disjointed from the future. Law detached from justice, vision dissociated from reality.*

Sisterhood Is Still Powerful: Strategies For The Future

Instead of colluding with such compartmentalized and life-endangering frameworks, what can we do to move "passionately forward" with our research/lives and keep the WS movement moving with us?

Going back to basics. Remembering that we *do* live in international (techno) patriarchy, which continues to oppress and kill women. U.S. philosopher, Janice Raymond suggested "putting the politics back into lesbianism" (1989). Paraphrasing her, I suggest putting politics back into WS: radical passionate politics. Politics that remember the goal of the Women's Liberation Movement to end patriarchal oppression in all its forms: sexism, racism, classism, to name but three—all thriving on "differences," on separation and division between people. Politics also, that remember our successes, our empowerment, our pleasures, the joys that often come from working with women, the knowledge that "sisterhood is *still* powerful" (Klein, 1989a), and that it is, in fact, our lifeline, which we cannot afford to sever. Politics, above all, that are emphatic and come from the heart as well as the brain.

Working hard towards making sisterhood more inclusive and validating *all* women, thus truly making the diversity in WS, as I have described it earlier in this article, into our strength. "Rethinking Sisterhood" and looking for "Unity in Diversity" (Klein, 1985). Changing and enlarging our limited frameworks by listening to women from other cultures and countries. Reading Vandana Shiva's *Staying Alive: Women, Ecology and Survival in India* (1989).

Recognizing how the increasingly cruel global technology machine is numbing us, swallowing us, killing some of us. Resisting such necrophilic politics with passion, with alliances among women around the globe. Working together if this is what all want, or respecting our different priorities by supporting one another's actions, if this is preferred. And western women being careful, also, not to be voyeuristic or to objectify women who are "foreign" and "exotic" (Hawthorne, 1989).

Remembering and using the enormous body of feminist knowledge we have generated in the last twenty years, including the wealth of empowering fiction, especially writings by women of colour from different continents and countries. Respecting women's "different similarities" in our own countries based on different abilities, ages, social status, cultures, and nationalities. Looking for commonalities instead of differences: it is bonds, not divisions, which will make us powerful. For women to disown one another, I think, is suicidal politics. As Kathleen Barry said (1989, p. 572):

> *Whenever differences are emphasized without first recognizing collectivity, commonality and unity among women, gender power is depoliticized.*

As we have a responsibility to pass on what has been created in the first twenty years of the WS movement to younger women, we need to work hard to maintain our continuity and continue our growth. We have the imagination, pragmatic shrewdness, and passion to turn "the margins" into *the centre* through using creative, wild, life-loving lateral thinking, and associating, connecting, and synthesizing the many threads of life into theories that we can put into action.[19] Acting with truly radical, passionate politics will contribute to *real* change for the better in the lives of *real* women globally, which is, after all, what WS set out to do.

Endnotes

1. The first part of this article draws on my PhD dissertation, *The Dynamics of Women's Studies* (Klein, 1986); see also Klein (1984a, 1984b).

2. I am indebted to Sarah Slavin Schramm for this expression, which she created to describe the conceptual origins of WS as an educational movement for change based on the collective intellectual power of women who are motivated by the ideology of the Women's Liberation Movement to end women's oppression (1978, pp. 3–12).

3. Florence Howe and Carol Ahlum introduced the term WS "practitioner" (1973). I believe it is useful as a common denominator to describe "those in WS" in spite of its usual meaning as "professional or practical worker, esp. in medicine" *The Concise Oxford Dictionary* (1979, p. 867).

4. It must be pointed out that no WS teacher in my study had a degree in WS. This is changing slowly, but there still is a great need for MA and PhD Programmes in WS.

5. The term "non-heterorelational" does not necessarily mean non-heterosexual. Rather, it is putting oneself and other women at the centre of analysis instead of perceiving women in relation to men (see note 17). A synonym might be "woman-identified."

6. "Autonomy" within an institution is of course relative and not comparable to autonomy in the sense of being totally *outside* an institution (as the term is used in Germany). Nevertheless, I believe it is a useful term, especially when comparing WS to other academic disciplines, that all have their autonomy when it comes to hiring and firing, resources, and university politics. For further discussion of the heated autonomy/integration debate of the early 1980s, see Gloria Bowles and Renate Duelli Klein (1983, p. 126).

7. I believe the proportion of older women students in WS is decreasing, and there are more very young women (i.e., in their early 20s). It remains to be seen how this change in balance influences WS.

8. The lesser involvement of WS teachers in feminist activism created a considerable amount of tension for many WS students in my study. They were disappointed that in some cases the teachers' feminism remained aloof and removed from women's "real lives", in particular with regard to the various forms of violence against women and feminist resistance against it in the form of anti-pornography campaigns or shelters for battered women.

9. The problem with this group is that they are usually overextended as student advocates, leaders in anti-racism workshops, environmental politics, anti-nuclear demonstrations, as well as work in feminist organizations (e.g., feminist health centres, rape-crisis centres, shelters for battered women, anti-pornography groups). There is a fourth student group too—separatist in their political orientation—who do not perceive WS as an alternative positive education for women. They think that by being part of the academy WS has "sold out." They show no commitment to the continued existence of WS, and the only satisfaction they draw from their involvement in WS is from getting to know other like-minded women.

10. This is indeed a very different mission from other courses taught at universities. At best WS "gynagogy" (a term I prefer to "pedagogy", see Klein, 1987) is passionate teaching in order to combine scholarship, reason, intellect, emotion, and intuition. For a detailed discussion of the "Dynamics of WS Gynagogy," see Chapter 2 C of my Dissertation (Klein, 1986) and my article on this topic (Klein, 1987). Of particular importance are the problems of cross-cultural similarity and diversity; white dominance; heterosexism; the relationship between WS and the Women's Liberation Movement; the hidden curriculum (e.g., hierarchies, power differences, grading); men in WS.

11. I use these terms in line with Adrienne Rich's (1975), Mary Daly's (1978), Helen Callaway's (1981) and Robyn Rowland's (1988) interpretations, that is as a positive way of "taking a second look" from a feminist perspective.

12. Feminist methodology is another crucial area of development, which I have no time to address in this paper. See Gloria Bowles and Renate Duelli Klein (1983) for references, as well as Liz Stanley (1990) and Shulamit Reinharz (in prep).

13. Feminist natural scientists could write research grants as WS scholars backed up by their department of WS, for which they have very little chance of receiving grant monies in their "traditional" disciplines (e.g., women-centred research that does not fall into the "high-tech" category that presently attracts most of the funding in the natural sciences).

14. Korea, for instance, has had WS courses on an undergraduate level since 1978, and at its oldest Women's University—the Ewha University—it has been possible to get an MA in WS since 1982 (Chang, 1989). India has an excellent network of WS courses including some research centres, such as at the S.N.D.T. Women's University at Bombay. WS in Japan is growing, too. In 1983 there were 94 courses; in 1988 there were 280 (and they have had a WS Association since 1979). A special feature of Asian WS—and this holds true also for WS in South America—is the fact that the colonization exploitation of the so-called "third world" by the west—or from within Asia by Japan—are very important topics. The other striking feature is how well organized and *activist* women in these countries are, and how most academics appear to be also involved in some of the many feminist campaigns against sex-determination, pornography, dowry, suttee, sex-tourism, to name just a few. Pilwha Chang pointed out that her WS graduates frequently became Korea's feminist activists!

15. I should mention that I will not focus on economic problems, which does not mean that I am not aware of the economic plight worldwide but especially in the UK and its serious implications for WS. But I also think it is important to examine obstacles to feminist vision and sisterhood that arise amongst ourselves.

16. The increasing presence of men in WS, in my view, is another problem. As I have elaborated on this topic at length elsewhere (Klein, 1983), for reasons of space suffice it to say here that whether men appear as "experts," "ignoramuses" or "poor dears" in WS classrooms, they usually manage to attract undue attention, divide the women on the course and, importantly, change the climate from one where female students take risks in speaking out, to a hetero-relationally controlled atmosphere. A further cause for concern is the proliferating number of "Men's Studies" courses in which men are the new experts on women, gender, and "masculinities studies" (Brod, 1987). They manage to thoroughly exploit feminist scholarship by selectively including—and reinterpreting—women's words, followed by the real "feminist" scholarship: by a male authority, of course. For a detailed exploration of this very masculinist phenomenon, which in true sexist fashion attempts to render women invisible again, see Jalna Hanmer (1990).

17. Janice Raymond describes *hetero-relations* as a world view (1986, p. 29): "I use the word hetero-relations to express the wide range of affective, social, political and economic relations that are ordained between men and women by men. The literature, history, philosophy and science of patriarchy have reinforced the supposedly mythic and primordial relationship of *woman for man.*"

18. One of the core concepts of patriarchal science is the value placed on differences at the expense of similarities. Research results that do not demonstrate differences are usually not publishable, as they are not seen as important. Feminists in the natural sciences have thoroughly critiqued this biased method over the last 20 years, particularly in relation to research on sex differences, and pointed to its sexist one-sidedness. It is therefore rather ironic that the feminists in literature and increasingly in philosophy, history, and education are so taken by the frenzied theorizing of differences, and regard it as a positive new conceptual framework (among the many critiques of science, see in particular Bleier, 1984, 1986).

19. Charlotte Bunch's collection *Passionate Politics* (1987) is an excellent example of putting feminist theory into action.

References

Barry, Kathleen
1989 Biography and the search for women's subjectivity. *Women's Studies International Forum, 12*(6), 561–577.

Bleir, Ruth
1984 *Science and Gender: A critique of biology and its theories of women.* New York: Pergamon Press. (The Athene Series)

Bleier, Ruth
1986 Sex differences research: Science or belief? In Ruth Bleier (Ed.), *Feminist approaches to science* (pp. 147–164). New York: Pergamon Press. (The Athene Series)

Bowles, Gloria, & Klein, Renate Duelli. (Eds.).
1983 *Theories of women's studies.* Boston: Routledge and Kegan Paul.

Bowles, Gloria
1983 Is women's studies an academic discipline? In Gloria Bowles & Renate Duelli Klein (Eds.), *Theories of women's studies* (pp. 32–45). Boston: Routledge and Kegan Paul.

Bowles, Gloria, & Klein, Renate Duelli
1983 Introduction: Theories of women's studies and the autonomy/integration debate. In Gloria Bowles & Renate Duelli Klein, (Eds.), *Theories of women's studies* (pp. 1–28). Boston: Routledge and Kegan Paul.

Brod, Harry
1987 *The making of masculinities. The new men's studies.* Boston: Allen and Unwin.

Brodribb, Somer
1991 Discarnate desires: Thoughts on sexuality and post-structuralist discourse. *Women's Studies International Forum, 14*(3), 135–142.

Bunch, Charlotte
1980, July *Global feminism.* Talk delivered at Women's Studies Forum, Copenhagen.

Bunch, Charlotte
1987 *Passionate politics, feminist theory in action.* New York: St. Martin's Press.

Callaway, Helen
1981 Women's perspectives. Research as re-vision. In Peter Reason & John Rowan (Eds.), *Human inquiry.* New York: John Wiley & Sons.

Chang, Pilwha
1989 The development of women's studies in Korea and its impact on Korean society. In *Proceedings of international seminar, global perspectives on changing sex roles* (pp. 432–441). Tokyo: National Women's Education Centre.

Concise Oxford Dictionary
1979 Oxford: Oxford University Press.

Coyner, Sandra
1983 Women's studies as an academic discipline: Why and how to do it. In Gloria Bowles & Renate Duelli Klein (Eds.), *Theories of women's studies* (pp. 46–71). Boston: Routledge and Kegan Paul.

Coyner, Sandra
1984 *The core concepts and central themes of women's studies viewed as an emerging academic discipline.* Unpublished manuscript.

Dunn, Sara
1990 Voyages of the valkyries: Recent lesbian pornographic writing. *Feminist Review,* [Perverse Politics: Lesbian Issues], pp. 161–170.

Daly, Mary
1978 *Gyn/ecology, The metaethics of feminism.* Boston: Beacon Press.

Frye, Marilyn
1987 *The politics of reality.* Trumansburg, NY: Crossing Press.

Hanmer, Jalna
1990 Men, power and the exploitation of women. *Women's Studies International Forum, 13*(5), 443–456.

Hamer, Diane
1990 Significant others: Lesbians and psychoanalytic theory. *Feminist Review,* [Perverse Politics: Lesbian Issues], pp. 134–151.

Hawthorne, Susan
1989 The politics of the exotic: The paradox of cultural voyeurism. *NWSA Journal, 1*(4), 617–629.

Howe, Florence, & Ahlum, Carol
1973 Women's studies and social change. In Alice Rossi & Ann Calderwood (Eds.), *Academic women on the move* (pp. 393–423). New York: Russell Sage.

Jeffreys, Sheila
1990 *Anticlimax, a feminist perspective on the sexual revolution.* London: Women's Press.

Klein, Renate Duelli
1983 The "men problem" in women's studies: Experts, ignoramuses and power dears. *Women's Studies International Forum, 6*(4), 413–421.

Klein, Renate Duelli
1984a Women studies: The challenge to man-made education. In Sandra Acker et al. (Eds.), *World year book of education* (pp. 292–306). New York: Kogan Page/Nichols Publication.

Klein, Renate Duelli
1984b The intellectual necessity for women's studies. In Sandra Acker & David Warren Piper (Eds.), *Is*

Higher Education Fair to Women? (pp. 220–241). University of Guilford, Surrey: SRHE and NFER Nelson.

Klein, Renate Duelli. (ed.).
1985 Rethinking sisterhood: Unity in diversity. [Special Issue]. *Women's Studies International Forum, 8*(1).

Klein, Renate Duelli
1986 *The dynamics of women's studies: An exploratory study of its international ideas and practices in higher education.* Unpublished doctoral dissertation, University of London, Institute of Education.

Klein, Renate D.
1987 The dynamics of the women's studies classroom: A review essay of the teaching practice of women's studies in higher education. *Women's Studies International Forum, 10*(2), 187–206.

Klein, Renate
1989a The Journey Forward: Sisterhood is *Still* Powerful. In Robyn Rowland (Ed.), *Girl's own annual.* Women's Studies Summer Institute. Geelong: Deakin University.

Klein, Renate D. (Ed.).
1989b *Infertility: Women speak out about their experiences of reproductive medicine.* Winchester, MA: Pandora Press/Unwin Hyman.

Mies, Maria
1986 *Patriarchy and accumulation on a world scale: Women and the international division of labour.* London: Zed Press.

Morgan, Robin. (Ed.).
1970 *Sisterhood is powerful: An anthology of writings from the women's liberation movement.* New York: Vintage Books.

Morgan, Robin. (Ed.).
1984 *Sisterhood is global: An anthology of writings from the women's liberation movement.* New York: Vintage Books.

Morgan, Robin.
1989 *The demon lover.* New York: W. W. Norton.

O'Sullivan, Sue
1990 Mapping: Lesbianism, AIDS and sexuality. *Feminist Review* [Perverse Politics: Lesbian Issues], 120–133.

Raymond, Janice G.
1986 *A passion for friends: Toward a philosophy of female affection.* Boston: Beacon Press.

Raymond, Janice G.
1989 Putting the politics back into lesbianism. *Women's Studies International Forum, 12*(2), 149–156.

Reinharz, Shulamit
in prep *Social research methods, feminist perspectives.* New York: Pergamon Press. (The Athene Series)

Rich, Adrienne
1975 Toward a women-centred university. In Florence Howe (Ed.), *Women and the power to change.* Berkeley: Carnegie Commission/MacGraw Hill.

Rich, Adrienne
1977/1979 Claiming an education. In *On lies, secrets and silences* (pp. 231–236). New York: W. W. Norton.

Rich, Adrienne
1980 Compulsory heterosexuality and lesbian existence. *Signs, 5*(4) 631–660.

Rowland, Robyn
1988 *Woman herself. A transdisciplinary perspective on women's studies.* Melbourne: Oxford University Press.

Shiva, Vandana
1989 *Staying alive: Women, ecology and survival in India.* London: Zed Press.

Slavin Schramm, Sarah
1978 Women's studies: Its focus, idea power and promise. In Kathleen O'Connor Blumhagen & Walter Johnson (Eds.), *Women's studies* (pp. 3–12). Westport: Greenwood Press.

Spender, Dale
1982/1983 *Women of ideas and what men have done to them: From Aphra Behn to Adrienne Rich.* London: Ark Paperbacks.

Smith, Dorothy
1978/1989 A peculiar eclipsing: Women's exclusion from man's culture. *Women's Studies International Quarterly, 1* (4), 281–295. [Reprinted in Renate D. Klein & Deborah Lynn Steinberg (Eds.), *Radical voices* (pp. 3–21). New York: Pergamon Press. (The Athene Series)]

Stanley, Liz
1990 *Feminist praxis.* London: Routledge and Kegan Paul.

Tobias, Sheila
1978 Women's studies: Its origins, its organisation, and its prospects. *Women's Studies International Quarterly, 1*(1) 85–97.

Waring, Marilyn
1989 *If women counted: A new feminist economics.* New York: Harper & Row.

Westkott, Marcia
1981/1983 Women's studies as a strategy for change: Between criticism and vision. In Gloria Bowles & Renate Duelli Klein (Eds.), *Theories of women's studies* (pp. 210–218). Boston: Routledge and Kegan Paul.

Constitution: Preamble and Statement of Purpose

National Women's Studies Association (NWSA)

The National Women's Studies Association was founded in 1977. The current formulation of its constitution, adopted in 1982, shows the close association between the women's movement and women's studies and between a social process, its values and goals, and an intellectual or academic enterprise. Clearly we can see why women's studies has been called "the academic arm of the women's movement."

Presented and passed at the February 1982 Meeting of the Coordinating Council (CC), passed at the Delegate Assembly (DA) in June 1982, and ratified by the membership in September 1982. Reprinted with permission of the National Women's Studies Association.

Preamble

The National Women's Studies Association was formed to further the social, political, and professional development of Women's Studies throughout the country and the world, at every educational level and in every educational setting. To this end, this organization is committed to being a forum conducive to dialogue and collective action among women dedicated to feminist education and change.

Women's Studies owes its existence to the movement for the liberation of women; the feminist movement exists because women are oppressed. Women's Studies, diverse as its components are, has at its best shared a vision of a world free from sexism and racism. Freedom from sexism by necessity must include a commitment to freedom from national chauvinism; class and ethnic bias; anti-Semitism, as directed against both Arabs and Jews; ageism; heterosexual bias—from all the ideologies and institutions that have consciously or unconsciously oppressed and exploited some for the advantage of others. The development of Women's Studies in the past decade, the remarkable proliferation of programs that necessitated this Association, is a history of creative struggle to evolve knowledge, theory, pedagogy, and organizational models appropriate to that vision.

Women's Studies is the educational strategy of a breakthrough in consciousness and knowledge. The uniqueness of Women's Studies has been and remains its refusal to accept sterile divisions between academy and community, between the growth of the mind and the health of the body, between intellect and passion, between the individual and society.

Women's Studies, then, is equipping women not only to enter society as whole and productive human beings, but to transform the world to one that will be free of all oppression. This Constitution reaffirms that commitment.

I. Purpose

Because

—Feminist education is a process deeply rooted in the women's movement and remains accountable to that community;

—Feminist aims include the elimination of oppression and discrimination on the basis of sex, race, age, class, religion, ethnicity, and sexual orientation, as well as other barriers to human liberation inherent in the structure of our society;

—Feminist education is not only the pursuit of knowledge about women, but also the development of knowledge for women, a force which furthers the realization of feminist aims;

Therefore

—The National Women's Studies Association actively supports and promotes feminist education, and supports the persons involved in that effort, at any educational level and in any educational setting.

Women's Studies

Sarah Stemler

Sarah Stemler was born in Smithton, Illinois, in 1971. She received her B.S. from Southern Illinois University at Edwardsville in 1993. She plans to become a teacher, and, in her own words, "raise the consciousness of her students as she educates them."

The following poem was written while she was still an undergraduate, during her introduction to women's studies. In it, one feels the many, often conflicting, emotions typically experienced by those newly introduced to feminist consciousness: surprise, anger, exhilaration, comprehension—but most of all, affirmation of self and of womanness.

Reprinted by permission of the author.

Women's studies
Women study
Women study women
Women study selves
Women study men
Women study men's studies of women
Men's studies
Men study selves
Men study MAN's effects on society
Men study men over MAN
Generic = MAN
Excluded = woman
History—the accomplishments of MAN
Politics—the power of MAN
Science—the creations of MAN
Religion—the ruling of MAN
MAN
Keeping WOMAN
Ignorant of her worth
Denying her knowledge
Restricting her rights
Laughing at her anger
Women's studies
Buried studies
Ignored studies
Mocked studies
Damned studies
Emerging as
Living studies
Powerful studies
Spirited studies
Dynamic studies
Women's studies
My studies
I study my mothers and sisters

I am subject
I study me
I find my fear
I find my fury
I find my joy
I find my strength
I find my value
I find myself
I accept myself
I love myself
I fight for the right to be
MYSELF
Women's studies

PART I

Consciousness: Concepts, Images, and Visions

Men know a lot about dying, but they don't know enough about living.

–MARGARET MEAD, speech before the Fourth Plenary Session, First National Women's Conference, International Women's Year, Houston, 20 November 1977

AS WE EXPLORE THE TOPICS IN THIS BOOK, WE WILL consider womanhood in all its perspectives—biological, social, political, and philosophical. We begin in this part with *sexual consciousness*—the abstract, symbolic, sometimes prelingual elements of our sexual reality. Meanings, associations, expectations, images, stereotypes, and ideals of both sexes form the underpinnings, the "mind set" of sexual reality, which in large part determines our social-sexual behavior. *We* begin here because much of *it* begins here.

We examine first in Chapter 2 the dynamics of patriarchy, the male-identified, male-governed, masculist society in which we live. It is both the setting in which traditional (male-identified) images of womanhood were created and the foil against which our new, woman-identified ideals are being forged. In Chapters 3 and 4 we explore images of women, patriarchal stereotypes and ideals, as well as women's responses to them and feminist affirmations. Chapter 5 closes this part with an analysis of some of the theories that attempt to explain the origins of the asymmetrical relations of the sexes.

2

The Dynamics of Patriarchy

Conceptions of Patriarchy

The terms *patriarchy* and *matriarchy* can have a multiplicity of meanings. Since the suffix *-archy* literally means "the rule of," patriarchy means literally "the rule of the fathers" and matriarchy, "the rule of the mothers." In social science, particularly anthropology, the terms have meanings very close to this literal sense: A patriarchy is a society in which formal power over public decision and policy-making is held by adult men; a matriarchy is a society in which policy is made by adult women.

Many contemporary anthropologists contend that although there have been, and still are, societies that are matrilineal (societies in which descent is traced through the females) and matrilocal (in which domicile after marriage is with the wife's family), there is little if any evidence to show that true matriarchies—societies ruled by women—have ever existed. Yet the concept of matriarchy flourishes in feminist theory.

This seeming contradiction could be confusing unless one realized that feminists use the terms *patriarchy* and *matriarchy* in various ways. Depending on the context, the terms may be scientific (as above), political, philosophic, or even poetic. In feminist thought, matriarchy can mean not only the actual rule of women (any women), but also the rule of what historically has been taken to be the female principle—in other words, the rule of feminist ideals. Patriarchy, then, would refer not simply to a society where men hold power, but rather to a society ruled by a certain kind of men wielding a certain kind of power—a society reflecting the values underlying the traditional male ideal. Thus, feminists frequently use the term *patriarchy* to denote a culture that embodies masculist ideals and practices.

Feminists argue that in contemporary Western culture we inhabit a patriarchy, both in the anthropological and in the political, feminist sense. Patriarchy, then, has determined almost entirely the character of our society: its values and priorities, the place and image of women within it, and the relation between the sexes. Thus, to comprehend our lives, we must understand the dynamics of patriarchy—what it is and how it works. To do this, we must ask the following questions:

- Since patriarchy is an embodiment of the masculist ideal, what is that ideal? How is it derived from the traditional picture of ideal masculinity?
- What are the underlying themes of the masculist ideal? How and why do they actually function in the real world?
- What is the effect of the ideal—on men, on women, and on society in general?

Let us begin with a discussion of the nature of the male ideal, its beliefs and its imperatives. We can then burrow more deeply, examining its underlying dynamic, to reveal the hidden implications of contemporary masculinity and its effects on the way we live.

The Male Ideal

We must begin with a caution: that in studying the male ideal we are examining *masculinity,* not human excellence. Because our masculist society has historically considered men to be the only fully human creatures, and because—as we saw in Chapter 1—the concepts *human* and *male* have frequently been confused, the concept of the human ideal has been similarly confused with that of the masculine. This blurring of concepts has led to a good deal of misunderstanding and mischief.

The "Human" and the "Male": A Preliminary Distinction

When I have asked students (women and men alike) to name people whom they believed represented human ideals, they have named Mahatma Gandhi, Abraham Lincoln, Martin Luther King, Jr., Jesus, and other great-hearted individuals. When I have asked them to name "ideal men," they have again listed Gandhi, Lincoln, King, and Jesus, but the same lists have also included such names as Tom Cruise, John Wayne, and Indiana Jones. Even the students were perplexed by the disparity of their choices. What, they asked, accounts for this confusion?

The students were confused by the ambiguity surrounding the term *man,* which can mean in our language either *human* or *male.* Such usage, feminists point out, derives from the ancient masculist presumption that humanity and masculinity are one and the same and that excellence in humanity is therefore the same as excellence in masculinity. By such reasoning, if a man enhances his masculine qualities, he must also be enhancing his "human" qualities; and as he develops excellence in human character, so must he as well become more "manly." Recognizing this ambiguity, we can understand why the terms *male ideal* and *ideal man* might not be distinguished and thus how the Bodyguard and Mahatma Gandhi might appear on the same list.

Until feminists crystallized the problem, researchers had given almost no consideration to the masculine element distinct from the human. But once the simple fact is realized that *human* and *masculine* are not the same, it is evident that ideal masculinity and ideal humanity are different too and that no sense can be made of either one until they are separated and compared.

The intellectual community has spent considerable energy identifying the qualities of human excellence. Philosophers of classical antiquity included intelligence, independence, temperance, honesty, courage, responsibility, altruism, justice, and rationality in their vision. Modern authors have added more characteristics, particularly the affective traits, such as humor, compassion, and sensibility. Now, to fully comprehend the male ideal, we must ask how these qualities of human excellence are related to the requirements of masculinity. Which of them are retained and which discarded? How are they adapted to the masculine image, and how are they changed? In a conflict between masculine and human ideals, which takes precedence for most men? Under what conditions? These are questions that must be explored if we are to understand more than superficially what contemporary images of masculinity mean to men and ultimately to women.

The Masculine Ideal

Consider the men, real or fanciful, who have come to be known as masculine heroes in our culture—figures like Babe Ruth, Tarzan, the Lone Ranger, Hulk Hogan, Sam Malone, Tom Cruise, Rambo, Elliot Ness, Axel Foley, or Batman.

An examination of these images begins to reveal the qualities of today's ideal male. Typically, our hero exhibits some version of the classical traits of human excellence, adapted though they may be to contemporary circumstances: He is intelligent (or canny), competent, courageous, essentially forthright (at least with the "right" people and under the "right" circumstances), healthy, and strong. Responsible and persevering, he pursues right as he sees it and lets no one deter him from his course. He has spirit or backbone. Thus, from the shores of Iwo Jima to the hills of Montana, soldier or cowboy or rugged ex-fighter-come-home, John Wayne gets the job done. Not an intellectual, though natively intelligent, he always knows just how to make things come out right. Fearless in the face of danger, he speaks truth to his adversaries—Indians, captors, crooks, townspeople—and always triumphs.

It becomes apparent that our image of the ideal male is not fully drawn using the classical qualities of intelligence, honesty, courage, and so on. Added dimensions transform the ideal man from the merely human to the masculine: The contemporary hero needs to be (1) "sexy" and (2) "tough"—that is, violent in a socially approved way. (As we shall see later, for masculists these two factors—sex and violence—coalesce.)

For the most part, the masculine heroes in our culture can be grouped into just a few categories: soldiers (warriors), cops and detectives (warriors against crime), cowboys (pioneer warriors against bad guys, Indians, and the untamed environment), tough doctors (warriors against disease, ignorance, or the hospital administration), rough but basically good crooks [warriors against . . . (fill in the blank)], and now a new high-tech version—the half-man, half-machine warrior like Robo-Cop and others. Our hero may be handsome or rugged, young or graying or bald, a good guy or a good bad guy, a learned professional or a street-educated bum, but one thing is certain—he is tough in a special and desirable way. He isn't afraid of pain; he doesn't shun a "necessary" fight; he can't be pushed; he perseveres in his will; he wins. Taciturn or talkative, he doesn't mince (words or movement), and whether in a lab coat or a three-piece suit, like the "Incredible Hulk," he communicates the untamed animal within, under control but nonetheless ready to surface should a challenge present itself.

The Warrior Imperative

Masculinity, manhood, is symbolized by the astrological symbol ♂, which represents Mars, the ancient god of war. That is no accident, for the essence of the masculine ideal is the warrior image. The true male, the "man's man," the virile, exciting hero is a warrior, regardless of what he battles. Without the aura of the fighter, a man may be important or powerful, or even humanly excellent, but he will not be masculine in the traditional sense. Indiana Jones is a scholar, a professor, successful in his profession, intelligent, capable. He is quiet—one might even say reserved and conservative. He is transformed into a symbol of potent masculinity, however, by the alter character within: the fearless, never defeated, unorthodox, knock-'em-down, shoot-'em-up, get-the-girl wise guy. Harrison Ford played the same character in *Witness* in a different venue: a competent, successful cop who succeeds because he is tough, relentless in a fight, breaks rules when he chooses, gives them what for, and gets the girl.

From *Lethal Weapon* to "L.A. Law," to *The Last of the Mohicans* to *Passenger 57*, the male heroes are fighters. Aggressive—often downright truculent and even violent—they epitomize the ideal of the primal warrior, the prototype of pure masculinity. In the words of Marc Feigen Fasteau, a lawyer and feminist, "men are brought up with the idea that there *ought* to be some part of them, under control until released by necessity, that thrives on [violence]. This capacity, even affinity, for violence, lurking beneath the surface of every real man, is supposed to represent the primal, untamed base of masculinity."[1]

But a proclivity for violence, though a necessary part, is not all there is to the warrior-hero. Within the ideal lies a further, nearly hidden prescription. It is the reverse side of the coin: The "real" man must never exhibit the complementary characteristics of the masculine ideal, those qualities that would render him unfit for battle—delicacy, sensitivity, fastidiousness, pity, emotionality, fearfulness, need, tenderness toward other men, and certain other humane traits. These are exactly the qualities reserved for women, expected and required of women, and symbolized by ♀, the sign of Venus, goddess of life. The masculine ideal is *all* "man," *all* Mars, *none* of Venus. Ultimately, it comes to this: The warrior virtues together with the negation of their complement (the affective qualities) compose the patriarchal ideal of masculinity.

Patriarchal Ideal of Masculinity

Warrior Virtues	*Not-Male (Complement)*
aggressiveness	passivity
courage	timidity
physical strength and health	fragility and delicacy
self-control and emotional reserve	expressiveness
perseverance and endurance	frailty
competence and rationality	emotionality
independence	needfulness
self-reliance, autonomy	dependence

individuality	humility
sexual potency	chastity, innocence or receptivity

The ideal patriarchal male must be not only brave, but never-timid; not only independent, but never-needful; not only strong, but never-weak. Committed to victory in battle, which is his first priority, he is a man of constraint and restraint, for violent emotions of any kind might deter him from his rationally designed course or strategy. For this man, control over himself and his needs or feelings is perceived to be the key to control over events.

The contemporary superhero is supersexed; yet with all the emphasis on potency (as a sign of strength and power), the version of sex presented by this masculist imperative is devoid of sensuality. According to the precepts of Mars, the warrior must not involve himself with commitments other than success; nor can he allow himself the luxury of compliance, of shared control or surrender—to himself or to his partner. If feeling must be denied—if sensitivity, delicacy, and needfulness are prohibited—then surely an experience as profoundly emotional and affective as full sensuality must also be denied. Instead of yielding to the affective self, as implied by sensuality, the warrior-hero must fight another battle, treating sex as war (between the sexes), making conquests and gaining victories. Even the contemporary vision of the sexual expert is more a matter of a "mission accomplished" than of shared delight. "Cheers" hero Sam Malone (Ted Danson) drives women mad with his rugged good looks and his adolescent charm, yet we can see that his own involvement is less than complete; even when "in love," he is distant, ambivalent, frequently exploitative.

Malone is an interesting character because he represents a bridge between the formal image of ideal masculinity (perfectly represented by John Wayne) and another of its aspects—culturally subliminal, slightly illicit, and only grudgingly acknowledged—the good guy who is so bad or the guy who is good because he's so bad, sharply characterized by such images as Sylvester Stallone in *Rambo,* Bruce Willis in *Die Hard,* or James Bond, 007.

The official portrait of the perfect man, à la Wayne, depicts a man accomplished and successful, a warrior, a fighter in socially approved arenas, strong, powerful, and dominating, fully controlled, emotionally detached, logical, orderly, duty-bound, and committed to the "right" side. He is law-abiding (for the most part) and motivated by the altruistic values of his society. He is, in the strictest sense, a hero.

Sam Malone, and a score of others quite like him—Crocodile Dundee, Rocky, the Beverly Hills Cop, or Mr. Baseball, for example—represents a uniquely contemporary variation on the theme, halfway between the classic strong man and the contemporary "new man." On the outside, this man is tough, cool, slick, proud; he is hot stuff. He charms women, takes what he wants, does what he likes, fights the system. As far as women are concerned, as one undergraduate woman put it, "he's a dick, but it's okay, because he's actually only half a dick (which is sexy) and half not a dick." That is, under the traditional masculist exterior roams a character more appealing (at least to this young woman), the boy inside the man—playful, sensitive, confused, needy, messing up by the numbers, ("a tear not quite on the cheek"). He is Star Man, an advanced being, yet a baby; Rocky, oh so tough but oh so dependent on his lady; Dundee, king of the outback, wielder of the big knife, who cannot fathom a bidet; Malone, jock and lady killer, brought down by his attraction to the wrong (bright, independent, educated, but safely goofy) woman.

Actually, although very up to date, this is not a new image. In the '30s and '40s, Jimmy Stewart, Cary Grant, and Clark Gable played this type very well. The '90s element is the degree of tension between the two poles and perhaps also the sheer immaturity of the personalities depicted.

On the far end resides the darker aspect of maleness, the character who is most defined by the martial ideals—the tough, hard, uncompromising, totally controlled warrior-man. On the "good" side of this role is James Bond, sex symbol of the '70s. He strayed a bit: He beat women (but only those on the other side), he killed (with a license), he was "b-a-a-a-d." In the '80s he was replaced by Charles Bronson's character in *Death Wish,* et al., or by Rambo; in the '90s by Chuck Norris or Caine, now an elderly but still undefeatable kung fu fighter—more savage, less controlled, less suave, reflecting perhaps the frustrations of their decade. These men are released from the rules of civilization by the unconscionable crimes of the enemy. That is, with "justification" they kill without quarter, pleasure themselves with the fruits of their fury, and bring order out of chaos with brute force, as a proper warrior should.

But what happens when the justification dissolves or the control goes awry? Then we have the monster-sergeant of *Platoon*, who is just a shade away from his acceptable counterpart.

The dark side of the masculine imperative is an alliance between violence, sexuality, a certain baseness, and mischief, pointedly manifest in events like the one during the Vietnam war described here:

> *Some of the GIs who conducted the My Lai massacre raped women before they shot them. The day after that "mission," an entire platoon raped a woman caught fleeing a burning hut. And a couple of days later a helicopter door gunner spotted the body of a woman in a field. She was spread-eagled, with an Eleventh Brigade patch between her legs. Like a "badge of honor," reported the gunner. "It was obviously there so people would know the Eleventh Brigade had been there."*[2]

Machismo: Bad Is Good

Under the gloss of the classic heroic ideal is a hidden agenda, a group of themes spawned by the warrior ideal and containing the underlying realities of patriarchal manliness. They take precedence over, or transform, the classical values, and they constitute the concrete fleshing out of the abstract formal ideal. The word for this aspect of masculinity is *machismo.*

Machismo is the Latin American word for the mystique of "manliness." It denotes a configuration of attitudes, values, and behaviors clearly articulated by a Michael Jackson hit on MTV: "I'm bad," he sings joyfully, skipping around and bumping hips and groin. All the associations are made: masculinity, genitalia, bad, . . . , desirable.

The machismo element of masculinity is that of the bad boy, of mischief that can and sometimes does slip into downright evil. This configuration is not an aberration, peripheral to masculinity. It is essential to it. Encouraged by parents ("Trouble, trouble, trouble, isn't he *all* boy?"), tolerated in school, and enhanced by sports, military traditions, and many rites of passage—for example, the bachelor dinner, Friday night with the boys, or "sowing wild oats"—machismo is real and present. Although its expression may vary with class, race, or location, it forms an important part of the male worldview, for its alternative is the sissy or goody-two-shoes, an object of ridicule and rejection.

Though the expression and the intensity of mischief may vary, the components are relatively stable.

General Naughtiness: Breaking the Rules El Macho does what he chooses, often the opposite of what is required. Christian society requires certain attitudes of temperance; el Macho drinks too much, spends too much, gambles, and engages in excessive and/or illicit sex. In the extreme, he may steal or kill; in polite society, he swears and fools around. The point of the behavior is in the fact of breaking the rules; too much concern for submission is clearly effeminate. Michael Douglas is depicted as evil but fascinating and sexy in the film *Wall Street.*

Sexual Potency Machismo is a cultural image, a human type, but it is a sexual identity as well. Potency—defined as the ability to have sex often and as rapidly as possible, to impregnate with ease—is tightly integrated into the other components described. Violence and sexuality are *not* juxtaposed in this context. Instead, they are different facets of the same thing. El Macho uses his sex like a weapon. In street language, you "deck'em and dick'em," you "tear off a piece," or "bang'em" or "hit'er"—all intensely violent metaphors. In the extreme, one rapes or gang-bangs; ordinarily, one simply exploits or insults.

Contempt for Women Since masculinity requires a commitment to Mars and an aversion to Venus, it is hardly surprising that el Macho should be contemptuous of Venus's earthly manifestations: women. The official macho attitude requires that women—in their delicacy, dependence, timidity, gullibility, and softness—be used and enjoyed, like a peach plucked from a tree and just as easily discarded. A young man told me that his father advised him to practice the four *f*'s: "Find'em, feel'em, fuck'em, and forget'em." Contempt blossoms into hatred: Women are stupid, dangerous, wheedling. The only exceptions are those who cannot be contemplated as sexual partners—mothers and sisters, for example, or nuns.

The women's movement reserves the word *macho* for behavior and attitudes expressive of these values wherever they appear. He who even jokingly brags of his macho orientation (and there are those who do) either misunderstands what he is saying or else he deserves the misapprobation he receives, for it is this aspect of the masculine imperative that transforms an inadequate lifestyle (the martial hero) into a destructive one.

The Male Role in the Twentieth Century

In a book that includes a variety of writings on the male role, Deborah S. David and Robert Brannon have translated the concepts given in the previous section into concrete dictates of masculinity for the contemporary Western man.[3] They contend that four major themes underlie prescribed behavior for men and boys. These themes appear early in life, function powerfully in the socialization process, and pervade the masculine conceptual environment.

1. "No sissy stuff"—the rejection of any of the characteristics reserved for femininity, either in the male's own behavior or in other men. This includes the fear of being labeled a sissy and discomfort in female environments, the rejection of vulnerability, and the flight from close male friendships.
2. "The Big Wheel"—the quest for wealth, fame, success, and signs of importance.
3. "The Sturdy Oak"—the aura of confidence, reliability, unshakable strength and toughness: "I can handle it."
4. "Give'em hell"—the enjoyment and expression of aggression, violence, and daring.[4]

The Effects of Patriarchy

Thus, a two-part image of masculinity characterizes our culture: on the one hand, the warrior-hero, a compilation of classical ideals and warrior qualities; on the other hand, the machismo syndrome, the undercurrent of mischief, composed of a predilection for violence, intemperate and exploitative sex, and recklessness.

The Commandments of Mars are:

Dominate and control—people, events, objects.

Succeed at any cost. Never admit defeat or error.

Control your emotions. Avoid strong feelings.

Strive for distance—from others and from self.

Banish needfulness (called "weakness").

Be contemptuous of needfulness in others.

Guard against the female within and without.

Protect your image (or ego).

Add the Machismo Orientation:

Exhibit a kind of reckless unconcern for rules.

Embrace violence.

Place sexuality in a power context.

Such are the imperatives of the masculine ideal in our patriarchy.

As we explore and observe the imperatives of the masculine mystique, it is essential to remember that we are dealing with an image, an ideal, or a stereotype. The image functions as a standard; it does not represent any individual or even a group of individuals. Although a man may strive to meet the requirements of the image, he cannot become the image in reality any more than a real woman can actually become all that is implied by the title "playmate of the year."

The sexual stereotypes—in this case, the masculine ideal—function as social mores in the culture. These are, as the sociologist William G. Sumner showed, values and attitudes that begin dimly somewhere in the past, become so habitualized that they take on an aura of cosmic validity, and ultimately become so embedded in the social fabric that they cannot allow for deviation or rejection.[5] They are usually perceived not as social rules but as enduring truths and realities. Learned through the process of socialization, mores—including sex-role prescriptions—are internalized by individuals and become extremely powerful determinants of behavior. As David and Brannon's discussion points out, the young boy learns truculence as a value for men the same way he learns that Americans eat beef but not horse meat. The picture of ideal manhood is presented to him as a required model, not as a choice.

Yet a variety of factors affect a male's response to the model: how strongly it is presented to him, the successes (or failures) he has within it, the values that are juxtaposed to it, the alternative lifestyles he may learn about and try, and many more. One way or another, by adoption, rejection, or adaptation, each male must reckon with these idealized images of masculinity. Insofar as he internalizes the masculist ideal, he will exhibit its characteristics, will try to control others with them, and will be controlled by them.

The sex-role prescriptions function in this way: Although they are male expressions, they are in large part independent of individual men; and although men may benefit or suffer from them and have a stake in maintaining or ending them, men as social beings are nevertheless subject to them, as are women.

Men Under Patriarchy

Men are not the greatest victims of patriarchy (as I have heard it said), but they are certainly victimized. If the sex roles, both female and male, are destructive, as feminists believe they are, then men as well as women are afflicted.

One might hypothesize that any externally imposed role model would create difficulties. After all, any prescriptive set of values will inevitably contain elements contrary to existing patterns and "natural" inclinations in individuals. What makes these sex roles particularly difficult to deal with, however, is their tremendous scope, the intensity of feelings surrounding them, their inflexibility, and the aspect of one's identity that they affect.

A role model for a pop musician, let us say, requires certain standards of competence with music and with instruments. It also prescribes other values related to the work, such as a tolerance of mobility and a willingness to hustle for engagements. Going a little deeper, one expects as well a particular personal style. To be really popular, a musician needs to look a certain way, talk a certain way, and so on, depending on the era. If the musician fails to meet these expectations, the penalty for deviation may adversely affect his or her musical career, but it is unlikely to be extreme beyond that point. That is, it is unlikely to ruin the player's very sense of being and human worth.

But deviation from the sex roles can have just that effect. In our culture, and possibly for all people, the sense of one's sexual identity and of one's sexual desirability are powerful components of the sense of self and worth. Accordingly, deviation from sexual norms incurs severe penalties, not only from others but often from oneself as well. In other words, the inability or even the refusal to meet sex-role prescriptions, for whatever reason, creates serious conflicts for the individual. Whether in terms of adapting to the culture or in terms of resolving inner confusion, the person who deviates from gender expectations experiences real difficulty.

In a genuine way, then—and in several respects—men in a patriarchy encounter a painful situation.[6] Certainly, should a man fail to adopt the masculine role expectations, either by default (because he cannot meet them) or by choice (because he rejects them on principle), he must confront and resolve both the social traumas and the conflicts within himself. Through rejection, ostracism, ridicule, or more formidable signs of hostility, people will punish him for his deviation. Because he is not a "man's man" or a "real" man, he is apt to find himself ill received both in traditional male environments and among many traditional women. Male students who do not submit to the masculine mold have described their surprise at being rejected not only by men (as they expected) but also by women, who consider them unmanly or unattractive as sexual partners.

If the pain of rejection from without is hard to bear, so is the pain of rejection from within. From childhood on, from our membership in the culture, we carry with us beliefs and attitudes that are extremely difficult to change. Even after we have deliberately altered our opinions in the light of a better considered set of ideals, the old, internalized value judgments continue in force, thwarting our resolve through doubt and self-contention and raising both anxieties and emotional turmoil. Breaking habits is hard; breaking these ancient and heavily prescribed habits of thought, feeling, and action is particularly hard. While part of the person opts for a new style, the other part rejects it. The result is inner war.

The problems entailed in rejecting traditional gender ideals are obvious; they are much the same problems involved in trying to reject any highly valued cultural norm. The problems that follow *accepting* the patriarchal image are far less obvious because they are so fully integrated into the culture, yet they are considerably more severe in their effects. The supermale image of masculinity is not a human image; machismo is not humane. The masculine mystique is directly at odds with a good portion of the classical and Christian ideals of human excellence; it is at odds with many of the known components of mental health; and it is certainly at odds with many elements that both philosophers and social scientists believe are essential to human happiness.

The classical ideal, although inadequate because it fails to treat the affective qualities of human life, still includes a certain tranquillity of spirit born of temperance, a strong commitment to the rights and needs of other individuals through social order, and thoughtful ethical awareness and responsibility. It is an ideal of intelligent, rational behavior, and although it contains a goodly element of physical strength, courage, and spirit, it is not given to violence per se or pugnacity as an end in itself.

The Christian ideal, too, is one of temperance and tranquillity. With greater emphasis on peace and gentleness than the classic ideal, it is yet disciplined and highly concerned with law.

The masculine mystique, however—particularly the machismo component—values violence, recklessness, intemperance, exploitativeness, and aggressive pursuit of success at all costs. Surely the man raised under the imperatives of both the classical and the martial visions suffers considerable conflict. Because our society officially teaches him the classical virtues and at the same time requires the martial, he is asked to exhibit incompatible qualities and behaviors: to love his neighbor or brother but to carry a bayonet; to be charitable and loving but also to succeed in business; to be a responsible father and husband but to prove his potency through untrammeled sex. To be pulled between contradictory values is not unusual in our changeable, diverse society. In fact, some social commentators suggest that the most important capacity for people in the coming era will be the capacity to adapt. But the martial imperative is such that it denies men the means to adapt in a substantive, meaningful, integrative way.

Adaptation and growth at the spiritual and emotional level requires a great deal of reflection, introspection, self-awareness, self-criticism, and emotional integrity. To flourish under conditions of stress and change, one must be capable of understanding one's feelings, of seeking assistance, and of nurturing an enduring internal sense of self. But these very capacities are denied by the masculist male ideal. The proper warrior has neither the time nor the patience for reflection and introspection. His imperative is direct action. He considers thinking as effete and equates it with indecisiveness.

And feelings? We all "know" that big boys don't cry. They also don't get scared and don't need anyone to help them. Although the martial virtue of emotional reserve refers primarily to feelings not convenient for a warrior—such as fear, anguish, grief, and hurt—the truly "manly" man is expected to be reserved in all his feelings. Anger and lust might be acceptable, but even these ought never to operate spontaneously, independent of plan, for they must not interfere with success. Even the so-called positive emotions of humor, love, joy must be controlled lest they interfere with duty. (Have we not been regaled with tales of foolish men who forsook their commitments for love and were dashed into dishonor? Think of *Anthony and Cleopatra* or *Of Human Bondage*.) Young boys are trained early not to feel—rather, to "take it like a man" and to "keep a stiff upper lip."

The key word in this image is *distance*—from the self, from one's feelings and needs, from other men, and from women. The perfect warrior trusts no one and has one loyalty: the battle and its success. He succeeds or he is worthless. In business, in science or debate, in relationships, or in sex, a man under patriarchy must win or set himself to winning. That is why weakness is contemptible: The "weak" (the needful, the feeling, or the tender) do not win (that is, dominate, control, overwhelm). A man must push, strive, never let up, and loathe himself if he fails.

Where Mars triumphs, men are shorn of their affective elements, impelled toward distance and truculence, and robbed of many precious experiences of life and self. They find themselves consigned to an arena of striving, pressure, anxiety, and threat. They must content themselves with the prescribed fruits of patriarchal success: status, power, and public praise. In such a context, even pleasure is transitory and shallow. Not a happy prospect. But happiness, in terms that Aristotle or Plato or Buddha might understand—an ongoing, profound experience—is not the issue for the warrior. He has no time for that kind of experience. He is too busy winning.

This is not a wholesome picture, to be sure. Men who pursue the macho ideal indeed lose a good deal in life, yet we must not be blind to a harsh reality: They hold a tremendous advantage in power, privilege, and position. And because masculist men have the presiding power in society, their perspectives and values, including the martial ideal, permeate our culture. These have become, in fact, the guiding ethos of much social behavior. That is why, feminists argue, we inhabit a patriarchy.

Social Priorities in Patriarchy

This discussion has shown that the essential element of the masculine ideal is warrior aggressiveness. The rationale is as follows: "Because this is a violent world, the man of the world must be violent." It is rarely considered that the world is violent because the ideal man of the world is violent. Feminists, however—both female and male—have suggested just that.

Shulamith Firestone, Andrea Dworkin, Gloria Steinem, Brian Easlea, and countless others have commented on the principle of violence in our patriarchal culture. Some argue that this element of masculism is the root of all the other destructive forces that plague us: war, racism, rape, and environmental abuse. Mary Daly, a feminist theologian, philosopher, and educator, argues that all of these problems are manifestations of the "phallocentric" commitment to domination (of people, events, and things). She calls the configuration of power-through-violence "phallic morality," and sees it expressed through "The Most Unholy Trinity: Rape, Genocide, and War."[7] If Daly's language seems extreme or exceptional, her thesis is not.

Sexism, Masculism, and Patriarchy

Before going on, let us pause to review some important concepts. Sexism, masculism, and patriarchy are related, as we have seen, but the terms may not always be used interchangeably.

Sexism is a way of seeing the world in which actual or alleged differences between males and females, are perceived as profoundly relevant to important political, economic, and social arrangements. One way to more easily understand the meaning of the term *sexism* is to think of some human trait that is not typically treated as relevant to such things and substitute it for sex differences—hair color, for example. To continue the analogy, *hairism* becomes a way of seeing the world in which differences in hair color are thought to be profoundly relevant to important political, economic, and social structures. In that case, ego identities, social roles, work assignments, rights and obligations, and human relationships would all be determined in large measure by the color of one's hair.

It seems absurd, doesn't it? After all, the color of one's hair has nothing to do with one's functioning in society. Hair color as a sociopolitically relevant trait is recognized as absurd because in our culture there are no claims that it is related in any way to other traits that *are* important to social function, such as intelligence, character, competence, maturity, and responsibility.

But this is exactly what happens in sexism. Sexists claim that important traits such as character, competence, and so on are related to, and in fact determined by, one's biological sexual identity: Males are intelligent, responsible, courageous; females are emotional, dependent, and flighty—hence, males rather than females are suited to authority.

Of course, the maintenance of such claims does not constitute the full meaning of sexism. If it did, sexism would simply be a strategy for ordering social functions that were essentially neutral in value. Men and women would be different and have different things to do, but they would still have equal worth. The argument would be much like this: Bananas and apples are different and, respectively, go better with certain foods, but neither fruit is superior to the other. In fact, many sexists claim that this is precisely what they do believe about sexual arrangements. However, their claim is false.

The essence of sexism (as of racism, nativism, heterosexism, and similar bigotries) is its inherent evaluative element. The term *sexism* may appear to be neutral, and some maintain that women, too, may be sexist (that is, female chauvinistic), but that is not the way sexism functions in our society. "Separate but equal" is a lie between the races; "complementary but equal" is a lie between the sexes. Sexists believe and require that men are superior to women in every way that matters. Both a dichotomy of sexual characteristics and a negative judgment about women (misogyny) are essential features of our culture's particular brand of sexism, *masculism*.

Masculism (or *androcentrism)* is the elevation of the masculine, conceptually and physically, to the level of the universal and the ideal. It is the valuing of men above women. It is, as well, an honoring of a male principle (conceived of as Mars, a warring configuration of qualities) above the female (conceived of as Venus, a serving and nurturing configuration). Some feminists have referred to this honoring of the male and the male principle as phallic worship, or *phallocentrism,* because male identity in a martial context is so intricately bound up with and expressed through their sexuality—more specifically, genital sexuality.

Women Under Patriarchy

Masculism in a political context is *patriarchy.* A consideration of the condition of women under patriarchy will fill the remainder of this book, but some general remarks are appropriate here because the misogynist, patriarchal treatment of women and womanhood is the quintessence of masculism, its culmination and fullest expression.

If masculism is at heart the worship of Mars and the embracing of phallic morality to the exclusion of its complement, then the rejection of Venus and the rejection of the traits symbolized by Her—love, beauty, tenderness—as well as the rejection of woman, her earthly manifestation, becomes predictable. No "real man" may tolerate (within himself, at least) the tender qualities. He must deny himself any tendency toward them, any personal experience of them. Instead, these traits must be projected outward. The complement of his masculine character is settled on his sexual complement, woman: "I am man; she is woman. I am strong; she is weak. I am tough; she is tender. I am self-sufficient; she is needful."

Woman serves this important function in patriarchy. As the negative image of man, his complement, she is the receptacle of all the traits he cannot accept in himself, yet cannot, as a *human* being, live without. The image Woman contains that element of humanity ripped from Man—an element she keeps for him, still in the world, available when and where needed, but sufficiently distant to avoid interfering with business. Yet even as negation, woman's place is not safe. As a man must flee from the Venus principle within himself, as he must hold that configuration in contempt, so he must hold woman in contempt as well, for *in patriarchy* she is the incarnation of Venus and nothing else. The outcome of this arrangement for man is ambivalence. He is both drawn to and repelled by patriarchal woman. Although she represents love, tenderness, compassion, nurture, passion, beauty, and pleasure, she is also, fashioned by him, the composite of all the reasons why these traits were banned for men: She is weak, emotional, dependent, imprudent, incompetent, timid, and undependable.

Woman's place, then, as we shall see in detail in Chapter 3, is precarious. She is the object of love and hate, fascination and horror. As Venus, she carries traits that are for men both beautiful and terrible, seductive and dangerous; hence, she may be desired and tolerated by men but only so long as she serves and is controlled, like feelings within. Adored and reviled, worshiped and enslaved, the image of woman as well as her "place" in patriarchy is the natural outcome of masculist values and needs. More than a convenience (which it is), the subordination of women is a necessity in patriarchy. Economically, politically, biologically, and psychologically, it is the foundation on which the entire structure rests.

Notes

1. Marc Feigen Fasteau, *The Male Machine* (New York: McGraw-Hill, 1974), p. 144.

2. Lucy Komisar, "Violence and the Masculine Mystique," *Washington Monthly* 2, no. 5 (July 1970): 45.

3. Deborah S. David and Robert Brannon, eds., *The Forty-Nine Percent Majority: The Male Sex Role* (Reading, MA: Addison-Wesley, 1976).

4. Ibid., pp. 13–35.

5. William G. Sumner, *Folkways* (Boston: Ginn and Co., 1907).

6. In Chapter 3 you will see that women face many of the same problems, although cast differently, that men face in dealing with their sex roles.

7. Mary Daly, *Beyond God the Father* (Boston: Beacon Press, 1973), ch. 4.

Men As "Gendered Beings"

Michael S. Kimmel and Michael A. Messner

Sociologist Michael S. Kimmel teaches courses on gender and social theory at State University of New York at Stony Brook. His books include Changing Men: New Directions in Research on Men and Masculinity *(1987) and* Men Confronting Pornography. *Michael A. Messner is associate professor in the department of sociology and the Program for the Study of Women and Men in Society at the University of Southern California. He is coeditor (with Michael S. Kimmel) of* Men's Lives *(Macmillan, 1992) and (with Donald F. Sabo)* Sport, Men and the Gender Order: Critical Feminist Perspectives *(Human Kinetics, 1990), and author of* Power at Play: Sports and the Problem of Masculinity *(Beacon Press, 1992).*

Kimmel and Messner explain that although men as well as women come to know themselves "through the prism of gender," for men that prism is generally invisible, and they often view themselves as society does: human, generic person. Since the women's movement, some men are beginning to examine themselves as males, *as gendered beings, and they are studying the effects of their masculinity on society.*

BUT WHAT DOES IT MEAN TO EXAMINE MEN "AS men"? Most courses in a college curriculum are about men, aren't they? But these courses routinely deal with men only in their public roles, so we come to know and understand men as scientists, politicians, military figures, writers and philosophers. Rarely, if ever, are men understood through the prism of gender.

But listen to some male voices from some of these "ungendered" courses. Take, for example composer Charles Ives, debunking "sissy" types of music; he said he used traditional tough guy themes and concerns in his drive to build new sounds and structures out of the popular musical idiom (cf. Wilkinson, 1986: 103). Or architect Louis Sullivan, describing his ambition to create "masculine forms": strong, solid, commanding respect. Or novelist Ernest Hemingway, retaliating against literary enemies by portraying them as impotent or homosexual.

Consider also political figures, such as Cardinal Richelieu, the seventeenth-century French First Minister to Louis XIII, who insisted that it was "necessary to have masculine virtue and do everything by reason" (cited in Elliott, 1984: 20). Closer to home, recall President Lyndon Baines Johnson's dismissal of a political adversary: "Oh him. He has to squat to piss!" Or his boast that during the Tet offensive in the Vietnam War, he "didn't just screw Ho Chi Minh. I cut his pecker off!"

Democrats have no monopoly on unexamined gender coloring their political rhetoric. Richard Nixon was "afraid of being acted upon, of being inactive, of being soft, or being thought impotent, of being dependent upon anyone else," according to his biographer, Bruce Mazlish. And don't forget Vice-President George Bush's revealing claim that in his television debate with Democratic challenger Geraldine Ferraro he had "kicked ass." (That few political pundits criticized such unapologetic glee concerning violence against women is again indicative of how invisible gender issues are in our culture.) Indeed, recent political campaigns have revolved, in part, around gender issues, as each candidate attempted to demonstrate that he was not a "wimp" but was a "real man." (Of course, the few successful female politicians face the double task of convincing the electorate that they are not the "weak-willed wimps" that their gender implies in the public mind while *at the same time* demonstrating that they are "real women.")

These are just a few examples of what we might call gendered speech, language that uses gender terms to make its case. And these are just a few of the thousands of examples one could find in every academic discipline of how men's lives are organized around gender issues, and how gender remains one of the organizing principles of social life. We come to know ourselves and our world through the prism of gender. Only we act as if we didn't know it.

Fortunately, in recent years, the pioneering work of feminist scholars, both in traditional disciplines and in women's studies, and of feminist women in the political arena has made us aware of the centrality of gender in our lives. Gender, these scholars have demonstrated, is a central feature of social life, one of the central organizing principles around which our lives revolve. In the social sciences, gender has now taken its place alongside class and race as the three central mechanisms by which power and resources are distributed in our society, and the three central themes out of which we fashion the meanings of our lives.

We certainly understand how this works for women. Through women's studies courses and also in courses about women in traditional disciplines, students have explored the complexity of women's lives, the hidden history of exemplary women, and the daily experiences of women in the routines of their lives. For women, we know how gender works as one of the formative elements out of which social life is organized.

The Invisibility of Gender: A Sociological Explanation

Too often, though, we treat men as if they had no gender, as if only their public personae were of interest to us as students and scholars, as if their interior experience of gender was of no significance. This became evident when one of us was in a graduate seminar on Feminist Theory several years ago. A discussion between a white woman and a black woman revolved around the question of whether their similarities as women were greater than their racial differences as black and white. The white woman asserted that the fact that they were both women bonded them, in spite of their racial differences. The black woman disagreed.

"When you wake up in the morning and look in the mirror, what do you see?" she asked.

"I see a woman," replied the white woman.

"That's precisely the issue," replied the black woman. "I see a black woman. For me, race is visible every day, because it is how I am not privileged in this culture. Race is invisible to you, which is why our alliance will always seem somewhat false to me."

Witnessing this exchange, Michael Kimmel was startled. When *he* looked in the mirror in the morning, he saw, as he put it, "a human being: universally generalizable. The generic person." What had been concealed—that he possessed both race and gender—had become strikingly visible. As a white man, he was able not to think about the ways in which gender and race had affected his experiences.

There is a sociological explanation for this blind spot in our thinking: the mechanisms that afford us privilege are very often invisible to us. What makes us marginal (unempowered, oppressed) are the mechanisms that we understand because those are the ones that are most painful in daily life. Thus, white people rarely think of themselves as "raced" people, rarely think of race as a central element in their experience. But people of color are marginalized by race, and so the centrality of race is both painfully obvious and urgently needs study. Similarly, middle-class people do not acknowledge the importance of social class as an organizing principle of social life, largely because for them class is an invisible force that makes everyone look pretty much the same. Working-class people, on the other hand, are often painfully aware of the centrality of class in their lives. [Interestingly, upper-class people are often more aware of class dynamics than are middle-class people. In part, this may be the result of the emphasis on status within the upper class, as lineage, breeding, and family honor take center stage. In part, it may also be the result of a peculiar marginalization of the upper class in our society, as in the overwhelming number of television shows and movies that are ostensibly about just plain (i.e., middle-class) folks.]

In this same way, men often think of themselves as genderless, as if gender did not matter in the daily experiences of our lives. Certainly, we can see the biological sex of individuals, but we rarely understand the ways in which *gender*—that complex of social meanings that is attached to biological sex—is enacted in our daily lives. For example, we treat male scientists as if their being men had nothing to do with the organization of their experiments, the logic of scientific inquiry, or the questions posed by science itself. We treat male political figures as if masculinity were not even remotely in their consciousness as they do battle in the political arena.

References

Brod, Harry, ed.
1987 *The Making of Masculinities.* Boston: Allen and Unwin.

Carrigan, Tim, Bob Connell, and John Lee
1985 "Toward a New Sociology of Masculinity" in *Theory and Society,* 5(14).

Chodorow, Nancy
1978 *The Reproduction of Mothering.* Berkeley: University of California Press.

Connell, R. W.
1978 *Gender and Power.* Stanford, CA: Stanford University Press.

David, Deborah, and Robert Brannon, eds.
1976 *The 49% Majority.* Reading, MA: Addison-Wesley.

Elliott, J. H.
1984 *Richelieu and Olivares.* New York: Cambridge University Press.

Epstein, Cynthia Fuchs
1986 "Inevitability of Prejudice" in *Society,* Sept./Oct.

Farrell, Warren
1975 *The Liberated Man.* New York: Random House.

Feigen-Fasteau, Marc
1974 *The Male Machine.* New York: McGraw-Hill.

Gilder, George
1986 *Men and Marriage.* Gretna, LA: Pelican Publishers.

Gilligan, Carol
1982 *In a Different Voice.* Cambridge, MA: Harvard University Press.

Goldberg, Steven
1975 *The Inevitability of Patriarchy.* New York.

———.
1986 "Reaffirming the Obvious" in *Society.* Sept./Oct.

Hearn, Jeff
1987 *The Gender of Oppression.* New York: St. Martin's Press.

Hrdy, Sandra Blaffer
1981 *The Woman That Never Evolved.* Cambridge, MA: Harvard University Press.

Kimmel, Michael S., ed.
1987 *Changing Men: New Directions in Research on Men and Masculinity.* Newbury Park, CA: Sage Publications.

Mead, Margaret
1935 *Sex and Temperament in Three Primitive Societies.* New York: McGraw-Hill.

Pleck, Joseph
1981 *The Myth of Masculinity.* Cambridge, MA: M.I.T. Press.

——— and Elizabeth Pleck, eds.
1980 *The American Man.* Englewood Cliffs, NJ: Prentice-Hall.

——— and Jack Sawyer, eds.
1974 *Men and Masculinity.* Englewood Cliffs, NJ: Prentice-Hall.

Tiger, Lionel, and Robin Fox
1984 *The Imperial Animal.* New York: Holt, Rinehart & Winston.

Trivers, Robert
1972 "Parental Investment and Sexual Selection" in *Sexual Selection and the Descent of Man* (B. Campbell, ed.). Chicago: Aldine Publishers.

Wilkinson, Rupert
1986 *American Tough: The Tough Guy Traditions and American Character.* New York: Harper and Row.

Wilson, E. O.
1976 *Sociobiology: The New Synthesis.* Cambridge, MA: Harvard University Press.

How Men Have (a) Sex

John Stoltenberg

Well known for his critiques of masculinity and gender, John Stoltenberg has long been an activist for social change. His published works include Refusing to Be a Man: Essays on Sex and Justice *(1989) and* The End of Manhood: A Book For Men of Conscience *(1993).*

"We are not born belonging to one or the other of two sexes," says Stoltenberg. Instead, the sense that we have of ourselves as masculine or feminine is created by an array of sociological and psychological factors. Sexedness is relative, and "we are a multisexed species." *This is a provocative idea. How does it change our interpretation of the terms* masculinity *and* femininity? *How does it affect our understanding of our own sexual identity? What are its implications for the idea that particular traits and behaviors are "natural" or necessary in one sex or the other?*

We are born into a physiological continuum on which there is no discrete and definite point that you can call "male" and no discrete and definite point that you can call "female." If you look at all the variables in nature that are said to determine human "sex," you can't possibly find one that will unequivocally split the species into two. Each of the so-called criteria of sexedness is itself a continuum—including chromosomal variables, genital and gonadal variations, reproductive capacities, endocrinological proportions, and any other criterion you could think of. Any or all of these different variables may line up in any number of ways, and all of the variables may vary independently of one another.[1]

What does all this mean? It means, first of all, a logical dilemma: Either human "male" and human "female" actually exist in nature as fixed and discrete entities and you can credibly base an entire social and political system on those absolute natural categories, or else the variety of human sexedness is infinite. As Andrea Dworkin wrote in 1974:

> *The discovery is, of course, that "man" and "woman" are fictions, caricatures, cultural constructs. As models they are reductive, totalitarian, inappropriate to human becoming. As roles they are static, demeaning to the female, dead-ended for male and female both.*[2]

The conclusion is inescapable:

> *We are, clearly, a multisexed species which has its sexuality spread along a vast continuum where the elements called male and female are not discrete.*[3]

"We are . . . a multisexed species." I first read those words a little over ten years ago—and that liberating recognition saved my life.

All the time I was growing up, I knew that there was something really problematical in my relationship to manhood. Inside, deep inside, I never believed I was fully male—I never believed

I was growing up enough of a man. I believed that someplace out there, in other men, there was something that was genuine authentic all-American manhood—the real stuff—but I didn't have it: not enough of it to convince *me* anyway, even if I managed to be fairly convincing to those around me. I felt like an impostor, like a fake. I agonized a lot about not feeling male enough, and I had no idea then how much I was not alone.

Then I read those words—those words that suggested to me for the first time that the notion of manhood is a cultural delusion, a baseless belief, a false front, a house of cards. It's not true. The category I was trying so desperately to belong to, to be a member of in good standing—it doesn't exist. Poof. Now you see it, now you don't. Now you're terrified you're not really part of it; now you're free, you don't have to worry anymore. However removed you feel inside from "authentic manhood," it doesn't matter. What matters is the center inside yourself—and how you live, and how you treat people, and what you can contribute as you pass through life on this earth, and how honestly you love, and how carefully you make choices. Those are the things that really matter. Not whether you're a real man. There's no such thing.

The idea of the male sex is like the idea of an Aryan race. The Nazis believed in the idea of an Aryan race—they believed that the Aryan race really exists, physically, in nature—and they put a great deal of effort into making it real. The Nazis believed that from the blond hair and blue eyes occurring naturally in the human species, they could construe the existence of a separate *race*—a distinct category of human beings that was unambiguously rooted in the natural order of things. But traits do not a race make; traits only make traits. For the idea to be real that these physical traits comprised a race, the race had to be socially constructed. The Nazis inferiorized and exterminated those they defined as "non-Aryan." With that, the notion of an Aryan race began to seem to come true. That's how there could be a political entity known as an Aryan race, and that's how there could be for some people a personal, subjective sense that they belonged to it. This happened through hate and force, through violence and victimization, through treating millions of people as things, then exterminating them. The belief system shared by people who believed they were all Aryan could not exist apart from that force and violence. The force and violence created a racial class system, *and* it created those people's membership in the race considered "superior." The force and violence served their class interests in large part because it created and maintained the class itself. But the idea of an Aryan race could never become metaphysically true, despite all the violence unleashed to create it, because there simply *is* no Aryan race. There is only the idea of it—and the consequences of trying to make it seem real. The male sex is very like that.

Penises and ejaculate and prostate glands occur in nature, but the notion that these anatomical traits comprise a sex—a discrete class, separate and distinct, metaphysically divisible from some other sex, *the* "other sex"—is simply that: a notion, an idea. The penises exist; the male sex does not. The male sex is socially constructed. It is a political entity that flourishes only through acts of force and sexual terrorism. Apart from the global inferiorization and subordination of those who are defined as "nonmale," the idea of personal membership in the male sex class would have no recognizable meaning. It would make no sense. No one could be a member of it and no one would think they *should* be a member of it. There would be no male sex to belong to. That doesn't mean there wouldn't still be penises and ejaculate and prostate glands and such. It simply means that the center of our selfhood would not be required to reside inside an utterly fictitious category—a category that only seems real to the extent that those outside it are put down.

We live in a world divided absolutely into two sexes, even though nothing about human nature warrants that division. We are sorted into one category or another at birth based solely on a visual inspection of our groins, and the only question that's asked is whether there's enough elongated tissue around your urethra so you can pee standing up. The presence or absence of a long-enough penis is the primary criterion for separating who's to grow up male from who's to grow up female. And among all the ironies in that utterly whimsical and arbitrary selection process is the fact that *anyone* can pee both sitting down and standing up.

Male sexual identity is the conviction or belief, held by most people born with penises, that they are male and not female, that they belong to the male sex. In a society predicated on the notion that there are two "opposite" and "complementary" sexes, this idea not only makes sense, it *becomes* sense; the very idea of a male sexual identity produces sensation, produces the meaning of sensation, becomes the meaning of how one's body feels. The sense and the sensing of a male sexual identity is at once mental and physical, at once public and personal. Most people born with a penis between their legs grow up aspiring to feel and act unambiguously male, longing to belong to the sex that is male and daring not to belong to the sex that is not, and feeling this urgency for a visceral and constant verification of their male sexual identity—for a fleshy connection to manhood—as the driving force of their life. The drive does not originate in the anatomy. The sensations derive from the idea. The idea gives the feelings social meaning; the idea determines which sensations shall be sought.

People born with penises must strive to make the idea of male sexual identity personally real by doing certain deeds, actions that are valued and chosen because they produce the desired feeling of belonging to a sex that is male and not female. Male sexual identity is experienced only in sensation and action, in feeling and doing, in eroticism and ethics. The feeling of belonging to a male sex encompasses both sensations that are explicitly "sexual" and those that are not ordinarily regarded as such. And there is a tacit social value system according to which certain acts are chosen because they make an individual's sexedness feel real and certain other acts are eschewed because they numb it. That value system is the ethics of male sexual identity—and it may well be the social origin of all injustice.

Each person experiences the idea of sexual identity as more or less real, more or less certain, more or less true, depending on two very personal phenomena: one's feelings and one's acts. For many people, for instance, the act of fucking makes their sexual identity feel more real than it does at other times, and they can predict from experience that this feeling of greater certainty will last for at least a while after each time they fuck. Fucking is not the only such act, and not only so-called sex acts can result in feelings of certainty about sexual identity; but the act of fucking happens to be a very good example of the correlation between *doing* a specific act in a specific way and *sensing* the specificity of the sexual identity to which one aspires. A person can decide to do certain acts and not others just because some acts will have the payoff of a feeling of greater certainty about sexual identity and others will give the feedback of a feeling of less. The transient reality of one's sexual identity, a person can know, is always a function of what one does and how one's acts make one feel. The feeling and the act must conjoin for the idea of the sexual identity to come true. We all keep longing for surety of our sexedness that we can feel; we all keep striving through our actions to make the idea real.

In human nature, eroticism is not differentiated between "male" and "female" in any clear-cut way. There is too much of a continuum, too great a resemblance. From all that we know, the penis and the clitoris are identically "wired" to receive and retransmit sensations from throughout the body, and the congestion of blood within the lower torso during sexual excitation makes all bodies sensate in a remarkably similar manner. Simply put, we all share all the nerve and blood-vessel layouts that are associated with sexual arousal. Who can say, for instance, that the penis would not experience sensations the way that a clitoris does if this were not a world in which the penis is supposed to be hell-bent on penetration? By the time most men make it through puberty, they believe that erotic sensation is supposed to *begin* in their penis; that if engorgement has not begun there, then nothing else in their body will heat up either. There is a massive interior dissociation from sensations that do not explicitly remind a man that his penis is still there. And not only there as sensate, but *functional and operational.*

So much of most men's sexuality is tied up with gender-actualizing—with feeling like a real man—that they can scarcely recall an erotic sensation that had no gender-specific cultural meaning. As most men age, they learn to cancel out and deny erotic sensations that are not specifically linked to what they think a real man is supposed to feel. An erotic sensation unintentionally experienced in a receptive, communing mode—instead of in an aggressive and controlling and violative mode, for instance—can shut down sensory systems in an instant. An erotic sensation unintentionally linked to the "wrong" sex of another person can similarly mean sudden numbness. Acculturated male sexuality has a built-in fail-safe: Either its political context reifies manhood or the experience cannot be felt as sensual. Either the act creates his sexedness or it does not compute as a sex act. So he tenses up, pumps up, steels himself against the dread that he be found not male enough. And his dread is not stupid; for he sees what happens to people when they are treated as nonmales.

My point is that sexuality does not *have* a gender; it *creates* a gender. It creates for those who adapt to it in narrow and specified ways the confirmation for the individual of belonging to the idea of one sex or the other. So-called male sexuality is a learned connection between specific physical sensations and the idea of a male sexual identity. To achieve this male sexual identity requires that an individual *identify with* the class of males—that is, accept as one's own the values and interests of the class. A fully realized male sexual identity also requires *nonidentification with* that which is perceived to be nonmale, or female. A male must not identify with females; he must not associate with females in feeling, interest, or action. His identity as a member of the sex class men absolutely depends on the extent to which he repudiates the values and interests of the sex class "women."

I think somewhere inside us all, we have always known something about the relativity of gender. Somewhere inside us all, we know that our bodies harbor deep resemblances, that we are wired inside to respond in a profound harmony to the resonance of eroticism inside the body of someone near us. Physiologically, we are far more alike than different. The tissue structures that have become labial and clitoral or scrotal and penile have not forgotten their common ancestry. Their sensations are of the same source. The nerve networks and interlock of capillaries throughout our pelvises electrify and engorge as if plugged in together and pumping as one. That's what we feel when we feel one another's feelings. That's what can happen during sex that is mutual, equal, reciprocal, profoundly communing.

Notes

1. My source for the foregoing information about so-called sex determinants in the human species is a series of interviews I conducted with the sexologist Dr. John Money in Baltimore, Maryland, in 1979 for an article I wrote called "The Multisex Theorem," which was published in a shortened version as "Future Genders" in *Omni* magazine, May 1980, pp. 67–73 ff.

2. Dworkin, Andrea. *Woman Hating* (New York: Dutton, 1974), p. 174.

3. Dworkin, *Woman Hating*, p. 183 (Italics in original).

Patriarchy, Scientists, and Nuclear Warriors

Brian Easlea

Brian Easlea received a doctorate in mathematical physics from London University in 1961 and, during the 1960s, taught nuclear physics in various countries. He later studied the history, philosophy, and social studies of science, which he taught at Sussex University until 1987. He has published on issues relating to both capitalism and science, and gender and science.

Lest anyone believe that masculism, martial values, or patriarchy is either not real or not important, this frightening piece should bring them up short. Easlea shows that the present "masculinity of science" may very well kill us. What is more, he offers an alternative perspective.

From Michael Kaufman, *Beyond Patriarchy.* Toronto: Oxford University Press, 1987. Reprinted by permission of the author.

IN A LECTURE AT THE UNIVERSITY OF CALIFORNIA IN 1980, the Oxford historian Michael Howard accused the world's scientific community, and particularly the Western scientific community, of an inventiveness in the creation and design of weapons that has made, he believes, the pursuit of a "stable nuclear balance" between the superpowers virtually impossible. At the very least, he found it curious that a scientific community that had expressed great anguish over its moral responsibility for the development of the first crude fission weapons "should have ceased to trouble itself over its continuous involvement with weapons-systems whose lethality and effectiveness make the weapons that destroyed Hiroshima and Nagasaki look like clumsy toys."[1] On the other hand, in the compelling pamphlet *It'll Make a Man of You: A Feminist View of the Arms Race,* Penny Strange expresses no surprise at the militarization of science that has occurred since the Second World War. While acknowledging that individual scientists have been people of integrity with a genuine desire for peace, she tersely states that "weapons research is consistent with the attitudes underlying the whole scientific worldview" and that she looks forward to "an escape from the patriarchal science in which the conquest of nature is a projection of sexual dominance."[2] My aim in this article is to explore the psychological attributes of patriarchal science, particularly physics, that contribute so greatly to the apparent readiness of scientists to maintain the inventive momentum of the nuclear arms race.

My own experiences as a physicist were symptomatic of the problems of modern science. So I begin with a brief account of these experiences followed by a look at various aspects of the masculinity of science, particularly physics, paying special attention to the ideology surrounding the concept of a scientific method and to the kinds of sexual rhetoric used by physicists to describe both their "pure" research and their contributions to weapons design. I conclude with some thoughts on the potential human integrity of a life in science—once patriarchy and its various subsystems have become relics of history.

A Personal Experience of Physics

Growing up in the heart of rural England, I wanted in my early teens to become a professional bird-watcher. However, at the local grammar school I was persuaded that boys who are good at mathematics become scientists: people just don't become bird-watchers. I did in fact have a deep, if romantic, interest in physics, believing that somehow those "great men" like Einstein and Bohr truly understood a world whose secrets I longed to share. So I went to University College London in 1954 to study physics and found it excruciatingly boring. But I studied hard and convinced myself that at the postgraduate level it would be different if only I could "do research"—whatever that mysterious activity really was. It didn't seem remarkable to me at the time that our class consisted of some forty men and only three or four women. At that time, I was both politically conservative and politically naive, a situation not helped by the complete absence of any lectures in the physics curriculum on "science and society" issues.

In my final year it was necessary to think of future employment. Not wanting to make nuclear weapons and preferring to leave such "dirty" work to other people, I considered a career in the "clean and beautiful" simplicity of the electronics industry. I came very close to entering the industry but in the end, to my great happiness, was accepted back at University College to "do research" in mathematical physics. It was while doing this research that I was to begin my drift away from a career in physics.

One event in my graduate years stands out. As an undergraduate I had only twice ever asked about the nature of reality as presented by modern physics, and both times the presiding lecturer had ridiculed my question. However, one day a notice appeared announcing that a famous physicist, David Bohm, together with a philosopher of science were inviting physics students to spend a weekend in a large country house to discuss fundamental questions of physics. That weekend was an enlightening experience that gave me the confidence to believe that physics was not solely a means for manipulating nature or a path to professional mundane achievement through the publication of numerous, uninteresting papers, but ideally was an essential part of human wisdom.

In the early 1960s, while I was on a two-year NATO Fellowship at the Institute of Theoretical Physics in Copenhagen, the first cracks and dents began to appear in my worldview. I met scientists from around the world, including the Soviet Union, who engaged me in animated political discussions. With a group of physicists I went on a ten-day tour of Leningrad and Moscow and, equipped with a smattering of Russian, I left the group to wander about on my own and kept meeting people who, at this high point of the Cold War, implored me to believe that Russia wanted peace. I couldn't square this image of Russia and the Russian people with what I had become accustomed to in Britain and would soon be exposed to while teaching at the University of Pittsburgh.

It seemed to be a world gone mad: my new university in Pittsburgh awarded honorary degrees to Werner von Braun, the former Nazi missile expert, and to Edward Teller, the father of the H-bomb. The Cuban blockade followed; Kennedy, Khrushchev, and physics were going to bring about the end of the world. I kept asking myself how the seemingly beautiful, breathtaking physics of Rutherford, Einstein, Heisenberg, and Niels Bohr had come to this.

New experiences followed which deepened my frustration with physics and increased my social and philosophic interests. University appointments in Brazil gave me a first-hand experience with the type of military regime that the United States so liked to support to save the world from communism. In the end I returned to the University of Sussex, where I taught "about science" courses to non-science students and "science and society" courses to science majors.

The more I learned, the more I became convinced that the reason physics was so misused and the reason the nuclear arms race existed was the existence of capitalist societies, principally the United States, that are based on profit making, permanent war economies, and the subjugation of the Third World. My pat conclusion was that if capitalism could be replaced by socialism, human behavior would change dramatically. But I felt uneasy with this belief since oppression and violence had not first appeared in the world in the sixteenth century. As the years went by and the feminist movement developed, I came to explore the profound psychological connections between the discipline of physics and the world of the warriors—connections that are ultimately rooted in the social institutions of patriarchy. That is the focus of this paper.

The Masculinity of Physics

Indisputably, British and American physics is male-dominated. In Britain in the early 1980s, women made up only 4 percent of the membership of the Institute of Physics, and in the United States women made up only 2 percent of the faculty of the 171 doctorate-awarding physics departments.[3] This male domination of physics has obviously not come about by chance; not until recently have physicists made serious attempts to encourage women to study the discipline and enter the profession. Indeed, in the first decades of the twentieth century strenuous attempts by physicists to keep women out of their male preserve were not unknown. Symbolic of such attempts in the 1930s was that of no less a man than the Nobel laureate Robert Millikan, who in 1936 wrote to the President of Duke University questioning the wisdom of the University's appointment of a woman to a full physics professorship.[4] As the statistics amply demonstrate, the male domination of physics continues despite publicized attempts by physicists to eliminate whatever prejudice still exists against the entry of women into the profession.

A second aspect of the masculinity of physics is that the men who inhabit this scientific world—particularly those who are successful in it—behave in culturally masculine ways. Indeed, as in other hierarchical male-dominated activities, getting to the top invariably entails aggressive, competitive behavior. Scientists themselves recognize that such masculine behavior, though it is considered unseemly to dwell upon it, is a prominent feature of science. The biologist Richard Lewontin even goes so far as to affirm that "science is a form of competitive and aggressive activity, a contest of man against man that provides knowledge as a side-product."[5] Although I wouldn't agree with Lewontin that knowledge is a mere "side-product" of such competition, I would, for example, agree with the anthropologist Sharon Traweek, who writes that those most prestigious of physicists—the members of the high-energy physics "community"—display the highly masculine behavioral traits of "aggressive individualism, haughty self-confidence, and a sharp competitive edge."[6] Moreover, Traweek's verdict is supported by the remarks of the high-energy physicist Heinz Pagels, who justifies such masculine behavior by explaining that a predominant feature in the conduct of scientific research has to be intellectual aggression, since, as he puts it, "no great science was discovered in the spirit of humility."[7] Scientists, then, physicists included, behave socially in a masculine manner.

A third aspect of the masculinity of physics is the pervasiveness of the ideology and practice of the conquest of nature rather than a human goal of respectful interaction and use. Although, of course, many attitudes (including the most gentle) have informed and continue to inform the practice of science, nevertheless a frequently stated masculine objective of science is the conquest of nature. This was expressed prominently by two of the principal promoters and would-be practitioners of the "new science" in the seventeenth century, Francis Bacon and René Descartes, the former even claiming that successful institutionalization of his method would inaugurate the "truly masculine birth of time." Although modern scientists usually attempt to draw a distinction between "pure" and "applied" science, claiming that pure science is the attempt to discover the fundamental (and beautiful) laws of nature without regard to possible application, it is nevertheless widely recognized that it is causal knowledge of nature that is sought, that is, knowledge that in principle gives its possessors power to intervene successfully in natural processes. In any case, most "pure" scientists know very well that their work, if successful, will generally find application in the "conquest of nature." We may recall how the first investigators of nuclear energy wrote enthusiastically in the early years of the twentieth century that their work, if successful, would provide mankind with an almost limitless source of energy. Both the "pure" and the technological challenges posed by the nucleus proved irresistible: the nucleus was there to be conquered and conquest was always incredibly exciting. Even in today's beleaguered domain of nuclear power for "peaceful" purposes, the ideology and practice of the conquest of nature has not disappeared. Thus, rallying the troops in 1979 at the twenty-fifth anniversary of the formation of the UK Atomic Energy Authority, the physicist chairman of the Authority, Sir John Hill, said that we will be judged "upon our achievements and not upon the plaintive cries of the faint-hearted who have lost the courage and ambitions of our forefathers, which made mankind the master of the earth."[8]

The masculine goal of conquest undoubtedly makes its presence felt in our images of nature and beliefs about the nature of reality; this constitutes a fourth aspect of the masculinity of physics and of science in general. That which is to be conquered does not usually emerge in the conqueror's view as possessing intrinsically admirable properties that need to be respected and preserved. Much, of course, could be written on specific images of nature, particularly with respect to "pure" and "applied" research objectives, and the subject does not lend itself to obvious generalizations. Nevertheless, it is clear that from the seventeenth century onwards, natural philosophers, men of science, and scientists tended to see the "matter" of nature as having no initiating, creative powers of its own (a point of view maintained only with some difficulty after the development of evolutionary theory in the nineteenth century). The historian of science, R. S. Westfall, is certainly not wrong when he writes that "whatever the crudities of the seventeenth century's conception of nature, the rigid exclusion of the psychic from physical nature has remained as its permanent legacy."[9] No matter what the cognitive arguments in favor of science's generally reductionist conception of "matter" and nature, it is clear that a nature that is seen as "the mere scurrying of matter to and fro" is a nature not only amenable to conquest but also one that requires no moral self-examination on the part of its would-be conqueror. "Man's place in the physical universe," declared the Nobel laureate physical chemist (and impeccable Cold-War warrior) Willard Libby, "is to be its master . . . to be its king through the power he alone possesses—the Principle of Intelligence."[10]

A fifth aspect of the masculinity of physics lies in the militarization the discipline has undergone in the twentieth century. Optimistically, Francis Bacon had expressed the hope in the seventeenth century that men would cease making war on each other in order to make collective warfare on nature. That hope has not been realized, nor is it likely to be. We may, after all, recall C. S. Lewis's opinion that "what we call Man's power over nature turns out to be a power exercised by some men over other men [and women] with nature as its instrument."[11] In the overall militarization of science that has occurred largely in this century and that was institutionalized during and after the Second World War, physics and its associated disciplines have indeed been in the forefront. For example, in a courageous paper to the *American Journal of Physics*, the physicist E. L. Woollett reported that at the end of the 1970s some 55 percent of physicists and astronomers carrying out research and development in the United States worked on projects of direct military value and he complained bitterly that physics had become a largely silent partner in the nuclear arms race.[12] It is estimated that throughout the world some half million physical scientists work on weapons design and improvement. As the physicist Freeman Dyson has reported, not only is the world of the scientific warriors overwhelmingly male-dominated but he sees the competition between physicists in weapons creation, allied to the (surely masculine) thrill of creating almost limitless destructive power, as being in large part responsible for the continuing qualitative escalation of the nuclear arms race.[13] Moreover, competition between weapons physicists is still a powerful motivating force in the nuclear arms race. Commenting on the rivalry at the Livermore Weapons Laboratory between two physical scientists, Peter Hagelstein and George Chapline, as to who would be the first to achieve a breakthrough in the design of a nuclear-bomb-powered X-ray laser, the head of the Livermore "Star Wars" Group, Lowell Wood, alleged: "It was raw, unabashed competitiveness. It was amazing—even though I had seen it happen before . . . two relatively young men . . . slugging it out for dominance in this particular technical arena."[14] And he then went on to agree with Richard Lewontin's unflattering description of motivation throughout the world of science:

> *I would be very surprised if very many major scientific endeavors, maybe even minor ones, happen because a disinterested scientist coolly and dispassionately grinds away in his lab, devoid of thoughts about what this means in terms of competition, peer esteem, his wife and finally, prizes and recognition. I'm afraid I'm sufficiently cynical to think that in excess of 90 percent of all science is done with these considerations in mind. Pushing back the frontiers of knowledge and advancing truth are distinctly secondary considerations.*[15]

One might, no doubt naively, like to believe that male scientists do not compete among themselves for the privilege of being the first to create a devastating new weapon. That belief would certainly be quite wrong.

Given such a sobering description of the masculine world of physics in Britain and North America, it isn't altogether surprising if girls, whose gender socialization is quite different from that of boys, are reluctant to study physics at school. What's more, it is in no way irrational, as British science teacher Hazel Grice points out, for girls to reject a subject that appears to offer "as the apex of its achievement a weapon of mass annihilation."[16]

Scientific Method for Scientists and Warriors

One common description of physics is that it is a "hard," intellectually difficult discipline, as opposed to "soft" ones, such as English or history. The hard-soft spectrum spanning the academic disciplines is, of course, well-known, and within the sciences themselves there is also a notorious hard-soft spectrum, with physics situated at the hard end, chemistry somewhere toward the middle, biology toward the soft end, and psychology beyond. Insofar as mind, reason, and intellect are (in a patriarchy) culturally seen as masculine attributes, the hard-soft spectrum serves to define a spectrum of diminishing masculinity from hard to soft.

But what is held to constitute intellectual difficulty? It seems that the more mathematical a scientific discipline, the more intellectually difficult it is believed to be and hence the "harder" it is. Mathematics not only makes a discipline difficult, it seems: it also makes it rigorous; and the discipline is thus seen to be "hard" in the two connecting senses of difficult and rigorous. The fact that physics, and especially theoretical physics, makes prodigious use of sophisticated mathematics no doubt contributes to their enviable position at the masculine end of the hard-soft spectrum. It is perhaps of more relevance, however, that mathematics and logical rigor are usually seen as essential components of the "scientific method" and it is the extent to which a discipline is able to practice the "scientific method" that determines its ultimate "hardness" in the sense of intellectual difficulty, the rigor of its reasoning, and the reliability and profundity of its findings. Physics, it is widely believed, is not only able to but does make excellent use of the "scientific method," which thus accounts for its spectacular successes both in the understanding of physical processes and in their mastery. While, of course, all the scientific disciplines aspire to practice the "scientific method," it is physics and related disciplines that are held to have succeeded best.

But does such a procedure as the "scientific method" really exist? If it does, it is deemed to enjoy masculine rather than feminine status insofar as it rigorously and inexorably arrives at truth about the natural world and not mere opinion or wishful thinking. Such a method must therefore, it seems, be ideally characterized by logically rigorous thinking aided by mathematics and determined by experimental, that is, "hard" evidence with no contamination by feminine emotion, intuition, and subjective desires. "The scientific attitude of mind," explained Bertrand Russell in 1913, "involves a sweeping away of all other desires in the interests of the desire to know—it involves the suppression of hopes and fears, loves and hates, and the whole subjective emotional life, until we become subdued to the material, able to see it frankly, without preconceptions, without biases, without any wish except to see it as it is."[17] Such a view of the scientific method remains incredibly influential. In 1974 the sociologist Robert Bierstedt could confirm that "the scientist, *as such,* has no ethical, religious, political, literary, philosophical, moral, or marital preferences. . . . As a scientist he is interested not in what is right or wrong, or good and evil, but only in what is true or false."[18] Numerous examples could be given. Emotion, wishful thinking, intuition, and other such apparent pollutants of cognition are held to betray and subvert the objectivity of the scientific method, which is the hard, ruthless application of logic and experimental evidence to the quest to understand and master the world. Thus while the philosopher of science Hans Reichenbach could tell the world in 1951 that "the scientific philosopher does not want to belittle the value of emotions, nor would he like to live without them" and that the philosopher's own life could be as passionate and sentimental as that of any literary man, nevertheless the truly scientific philosopher "refuses to muddle emotion and cognition, and likes to breathe the pure air of logical insight and penetration."[19] Perhaps that is why the Nobel laureate physicist, Isidor Rabi, then eighty-four years of age, could confide in the early 1980s to Vivian Gornick that women were temperamentally unsuited to science, that the female nervous system was "simply different." "It makes it impossible for them to stay with the thing," he explained. "I'm afraid there's no use quarrelling with it, that's the way it is."[20]

Now the view of successful "scientific method" as masculine logic, rigor, and experimentation necessarily untainted and uncontaminated with feminine emotion, intuition, and wishful thinking is completely and hopelessly wrong. Such a scientific method is as elusive as "pure" masculinity. If nothing else, the invention of theories demands considerable intuition and creative imagination, as every innovative scientist knows and often has proclaimed. Does this therefore mean that the masculine "objectivity" of scientific method is intrinsically compromised? The philosopher of science, Carl Hempel, explains that it doesn't, since "scientific objectivity is safeguarded by the principle that while hypotheses and theories may be freely invented and *proposed* in science [the so-called context of discovery], they can be *accepted* into the body of scientific knowledge only if they pass critical scrutiny [the context of justification], which includes in particular the checking of suitable test implications by careful observation and experiment."[21] Alas for this typical defense of scientific objectivity, for ever since the work of Thomas Kuhn in his 1962 essay *The Structure of Scientific Revolutions,* it is generally accepted that no hard and fast distinction can be readily drawn between such a feminine context of discovery and a masculine context of justification.[22]

For this is what seems to be at issue. Not only does the notion of scientific objectivity appear to entail a clear-cut distinction between the masculine investigator and the world of "feminine" or "female" matter, within the psyche of the masculine investigator there also appears to be a pressing need to establish an inviolable distinction between a masculine mode of "hard," rigorous reasoning determined by logic and experimental evidence and, should it operate at all, a feminine mode characterized by creative imagination, intuition, and emotion-linked preferences. However, such clear-cut distinctions neither exist nor are possible in scientific practice, no matter how much the masculine mode appears paramount in normal research. What certainly does exist (although not uniformly so) is a very impassioned commitment to deny an evaluative subjective component to scientific practice; we may see such a masculine commitment as stemming from an emotional rejection and repudiation of the feminine within masculine inquiry. In other words, the impassioned claim that there exists an unemotional, value-free scientific method (or context of justification) may be interpreted as an emotional rejection and repudiation of the feminine and, if this is so, it would mean that scientific practice carried out (supposedly) in an "objective," value-free, unemotional way is in fact deeply and emotionally repressive of the feminine. This is a hornets' nest with all kinds of implications, but it may help to explain why much of modern science has, I shall argue, been embraced so uncritically by a society that is misogynistic and, in the case of the war industries, misanthropic as well. It is partly because patriarchal science is fundamentally antifeminine that its practitioners are psychologically vulnerable to the attractions of the "defense" industry.

We learn from Freeman Dyson that the world of the warriors, which comprises military strategists, scientists, and Pentagon officials, is ostentatiously defined by a "deliberately cool," quantitative style that explicitly excludes "overt emotion and rhetoric"—it is a style modelled on "scientific method" and directly opposed to, for example, the "emotional, "anecdotal" style of the anti-nuclear campaigner Helen Caldicott, whose arguments, according to Dyson, the warriors find unacceptable even when they manage to take them seriously.[23] For her part, Helen Caldicott believes that great rage and hatred lie suppressed behind the seemingly imperturbable, "rational" mask of scientific military analysis.[24] The military historian Sue Mansfield has posed the problem at its starkest: the stress placed in the scientific world on "objectivity" and a quantitative approach as a guarantee of truth, together with the relegation of emotions to a peripheral and unconscious existence, has, she maintains, carried "from its beginnings in the seventeenth century the burden of an essential hostility to the body, the feminine, and the natural environment."[25]

Sexual Rhetoric by Scientists and Warriors

The stereotype of the sober male scientist dispassionately investigating the properties of matter with, obviously, not a single sexual thought in mind is singularly undermined by the extent to which scientists portray nature as female in their informal prose, lectures, and talks. Indeed, according to the historian of science, Carolyn Merchant, the most powerful image in Western science is "the identification of nature with the female, especially a female harbouring secrets."[26] Physicists often refer to their "pure" research as a kind of sexual exploration of the secrets of nature—a female nature that not only possesses great subtlety and beauty to be revealed only to her most skilful and determined admirers and lovers, but that is truly fearsome in her awesome powers.

"Nature," wrote the high-energy physicist Frank Close in the *Guardian,* "hides her secrets in subtle ways." By "probing" the deep, mysterious, unexpectedly beautiful submicroscopic world, "we have our eyes opened to her greater glory."[27] The impression is given of a non-violent, male exploration of the sexual secrets of a mysterious, profoundly wonderful female nature. From the end of the nineteenth century to the middle 1980s, such sentiments have frequently been expressed by famous physicists. Thus, addressing the annual meeting of the British Association in 1898, the physicist Sir William Crookes announced to his audience, "Steadily, unflinchingly, we strive to pierce the inmost heart of nature, from what she is to reconstruct what she has been, and to prophesy what she yet shall be. Veil after veil we have lifted, and her face grows more beautiful, august, and wonderful, with every barrier that is withdrawn."[28]

But no matter how many veils are lifted, ultimately the fearsome and untameable "femaleness" of the universe will remain.[29] Even if female nature is ultimately untameable, scientific research and application can reveal and make usable many of nature's comparatively lesser secrets. It is striking how successful scientific research is frequently described in the language of sexual intercourse, birth, and claims to paternity in which science or the mind of man is ascribed the phallic role of penetrating or probing into the secrets of nature—with the supposed hardness of successful scientific method now acquiring an obvious phallic connotation. Accounts of the origins of quantum mechanics and nuclear physics in the first decades of the twentieth century illustrate this well. In 1966 the physicist, historian, and philosopher of science, Max Jammer, admiringly announced that those early achievements of physicists in quantum mechanics clearly showed "how far man's intellect can penetrate into the secrets of nature on the basis of comparatively inconspicuous evidence"; indeed, Victor Weisskopf, Nobel laureate, remembers how the physicists at Niels Bohr's institute were held together "by a common urge to penetrate into the secrets of nature."[30] While Frederick Soddy was already proudly convinced by 1908 that "in the discovery of radioactivity . . . we had penetrated one of nature's innermost secrets,"[31] it was Soddy's collaborator in those early years, Sir Ernest Rutherford, who has been adjudged by later physicists and historians to have been the truly masculine man behind nuclear physics' spectacular advances in this period. Referring to Rutherford's triumphant hypothesis in 1911 that the atom consisted of an extremely concentrated nucleus of positively charged matter surrounded by a planetary system of orbiting electrons, one of Rutherford's assistants at the time, C. G. Darwin, later wrote that it was one of the "great occurrences" of his life that he was "actually present half-an-hour after the nucleus was born."[32] Successful and deep penetration, birth, and ensuing paternity: these are the hallmarks of great scientific advance.

At first sight it might seem that there is little untoward in such use of sexual, birth, and paternity metaphors, their use merely demonstrating that nuclear research, like scientific research in general, can be unproblematically described by its practitioners as a kind of surrogate sexual activity carried out by male physicists on female nature. However, not only did all the early nuclear pioneers (Rutherford included) realize that enormous quantities of energy lay waiting, as it were, to be exploited by physicists—"it would be rash to predict," wrote Rutherford's collaborator, W. C. D. Whetham, "that our impotence will last for ever"[33]—but, ominously, some of the sexual metaphors were extremely aggressive, reminding one forcibly of the ideology of (masculine) conquest of (female) nature. Indeed, since Rutherford's favorite word appears to have been "attack" it does not seem startling when one of the most distinguished physicists in the United States, George Ellery Hale, who was convinced that "nature has hidden her secrets in an almost impregnable stronghold," wrote admiringly to Rutherford in astonishingly military-sexual language. "The rush of your advance is overpowering," he congratulated him, "and I do not wonder that nature has retreated from trench to trench, and from height to height, until she is now capitulating in her inmost citadel."[34]

The implications of all this were not lost on everyone. Well before the discovery of uranium fission in 1939, the poet and Cambridge historian Thomas Thornely expressed his great apprehension at the consequences of a successful scientific assault on nature's remaining nuclear secrets:

Well may she start and desperate strain,
To thrust the bold besiegers back;
If they that citadel should gain,
What grisly shapes of death and pain
May rise and follow in their track![35]

Not surprisingly, just as military scientists and strategists have adopted the formal "scientific style" of unemotional, quantitative argument, so they also frequently make informal use of sexual, birth, and paternity metaphors in their research and testing. Now, however, these metaphors become frighteningly aggressive, indeed obscene: military sexual penetration into nature's nuclear secrets will, the metaphors suggest, not only shake nature to her very foundations but at the same time demonstrate indisputable masculine status and military paternity. We learn that the first fission bomb developed at the Los Alamos laboratory was often referred to as a "baby"—a baby boy if a successful explosion, a baby girl if a failure. Secretary of War Henry Stimson received a message at Potsdam after the successful Trinity test of an implosion fission weapon which (after decoding) read:

> *Doctor has just returned most enthusiastic and confident that the little boy [the uranium bomb] is as husky as his big brother [the tested plutonium bomb]. The light in his eyes discernible from here to Highhold and I could have heard his screams from here to my farm.*[36]

Examples are abundant: the two bombs (one uranium and one plutonium) exploded over Japanese cities were given the code names "Little Boy" and "Fat Man"; a third bomb being made ready was given the name "Big Boy." Oppenheimer became known as the Father of the A-Bomb and indeed the National Baby Institution of America made Oppenheimer its Father of the Year. Edward Teller, publicly seen as the principal physicist behind the successful design of the first fusion weapon or H-bomb, seemingly takes pains in his memoirs to draw readers' attention to the fact that it was a "phallic" triumph on his part.[37] After the enormous blast of the first H-bomb obliterated a Pacific island and all its life, Teller sent a triumphant telegram to his Los Alamos colleagues, "It's a boy."[38] Unfortunately for Teller, his paternity status of "Father of the H-Bomb" has been challenged by some physicists who claim that the mathematician Stanislaw Ulam produced the original idea and that all Teller did was to gestate the bomb after Ulam had inseminated him with his idea, thus, they say, making him the mere Mother.

Following the creation of this superbomb, a dispute over two competing plans for a nuclear attack against the Soviet Union occurred between strategists in the RAND think tank and the leading generals of the Strategic Air Command (SAC) of the U.S. Air Force. In a circulated memorandum the famous strategist Bernard Brodie likened his own RAND plan of a limited nuclear strike against military targets while keeping the major part of the nuclear arsenal in reserve to the act of sexual penetration but with withdrawal before ejaculation; he likened the alternative SAC plan to leave the Soviet Union a "smoking radiating ruin at the end of two hours" to sexual intercourse that "goes all the way."[39] His colleague Herman Kahn coined the term "wargasm" to describe the all-out "orgastic spasm of destruction" that the SAC generals supposedly favored.[40] Kahn's book *On Escalation* attempts, like an elaborate scientific sex manual, a precise identification of forty-four (!) stages of increasing tension culminating in the final stage of "spasm war."[41] Such sexual metaphors for nuclear explosions and warfare appear to be still in common use. In 1980 General William Odom, then a military adviser to Zbigniew Brzesinski on the National Security Council, told a Harvard seminar of a strategic plan to release 70 to 80 percent of America's nuclear megatonnage "in one orgasmic whump,"[42] while at a London meeting in 1984, General Daniel Graham, a former head of the Defense Intelligence Agency and a prominent person behind President Reagan's Strategic Defense Initiative, brought some appreciative chuckles from his nearly all-male audience in referring to all-out nuclear "exchange" as the "wargasm."[43]

What is one to make of such metaphors and in particular of an analogy that likens ejaculation of semen during sexual intercourse (an act, one hopes, of mutual pleasure and possibly the first stage in the creation of new life) with a nuclear bombardment intended to render a huge country virtually lifeless, perhaps for millennia to come? And what conception of pleasure was foremost in Kahn's mind when he coined the term "wargasm"—surely the most obscene word in the English language—to describe what he sees as the union between Eros and Thanatos that is nuclear holocaust? I find such comparisons and terminology almost beyond rational comment. Simone de Beauvoir's accurate observation that "the erotic vocabulary of males" has always been drawn from military terminology becomes totally inadequate.[44] Brodie's and Kahn's inventiveness has surely eclipsed Suzanne Lowry's observation in the *Guardian* that " 'fuck' is the prime hate word" in the English language.[45] Indeed, given the sexual metaphors used by some of the nuclear warriors, one can understand Susan Griffin's anguished agreement with Norman

Mailer's (surprising) description of Western culture as "drawing a rifle sight on an open vagina"—a culture, Griffin continues, "that even within its worship of the female sex goddess hates female sexuality."[46] We may indeed wonder why a picture of Rita Hayworth, "the ubiquitous pinup girl of World War II," was stenciled on the first atomic bomb exploded in the Bikini tests of 1946.[47]

Unconscious Objectives of Patriarchy and Patriarchal Physics

There has been much analysis of the Catholic Church's dichotomization of women into two stereotypes: the unattainable, asexual, morally pure virgin to which the Christian woman could aspire but never reach and the carnal whore-witch representing uncontrollable sexuality, depravity, wickedness, and the threat of universal chaos and disorder. During the sixteenth and seventeenth centuries such a fear and loathing of women's apparent wickedness came to a head in the European witch craze that was responsible for the inquisition and execution of scores of thousands of victims, over 80 percent of them female. A major historian of the witch craze, H. C. E. Midelfort, has noted that "one cannot begin to understand the European witch craze without recognizing that it displayed a burst of misogyny without parallel in Western history."[48]

Whatever the causes of the European witch craze, what may be particularly significant is that it coincided with the first phase of the scientific revolution, the peak of the witch craze occurring during the decades in which Francis Bacon, René Descartes, Johannes Kepler, and Galileo Galilei made their revolutionary contributions. In *one* of its aspects, I believe that the scientific revolution may be seen as a secularized version of the witch craze in which sophisticated men either, like Francis Bacon, projected powerful and dangerous "femaleness" onto nature or, like René Descartes, declared nature to be feminine and thus totally amenable to manipulation and control by (the mind of) man. We recall how Simone de Beauvoir declared that woman is seemingly "represented, at one time, as pure passivity, available, open, a utensil"—which is surely Descartes's view of "feminine" matter—while "at another time she is regarded as if possessed by alien forces: there is a devil raging in her womb, a serpent lurks in her vagina, eager to devour the male's sperm"—which has more affinity to Francis Bacon's view of "female" matter.[49] Indeed, Bacon likened the experimental investigation of the secrets of "female" nature to the inquisition of witches on the rack and looked forward to the time when masculine science would shake "female" nature to her very foundations. It is, I believe, the purified natural magical tradition advocated by Bacon (with considerable use of very aggressive sexual imagery) that contributed in a major way to the rise of modern science. Believing firmly in the existence of the secrets of nature that could be penetrated by the mind of man, Bacon predicted that eventually the new science would be able to perform near miracles. And indeed the momentous significance of the scientific revolution surely lies in the fact that, unlike the rituals of preliterate societies which in general failed to give their practitioners power over nature (if this is what they sought), the male practitioners of modern science have been rewarded with truly breathtaking powers to intervene successfully in natural phenomena (we have become blasé about the spectacular triumphs of modern science, but what a near miracle is, for example, a television picture). Bacon's prediction that the new science he so passionately advocated would inaugurate the "truly masculine birth of time" and eventually shake nature to her very foundations has been triumphantly borne out by the achievements of modern physics and the sad possibility of devastating nature with environmental destruction, nuclear holocaust, and nuclear winter.

Clearly modern science possesses what might be called a rational component. In this article I am taking for granted the fact that modern science produces knowledge of nature that "works" relative to masculine (and other) expectations and objectives and that the intrinsic interest and fascination of scientific inquiry would render a non-patriarchal science a worthy and central feature of a truly human society. What I am here concerned with is the "truly masculine" nature of scientific inquiry involving the discipline's would-be rigid separation between masculine science and "female" nature and the possibility of an underlying, if for the most part unconscious, hostility to "dangerous femaleness" in the minds of some, or many, of its practitioners—a hostility presumably endemic to patriarchal society. A case can be made—and has been both by Carolyn Merchant and myself—that a powerful motivating force, but not the only one, behind the rise of modern science was a kind of displaced misogyny.[50] In addition a case can be made that a powerful motivating force behind some (or much) modern science and particularly weapons science is a continuation of the displaced misogyny that helped generate the scientific revolution.

Certainly a counterclaim is possible that modern science might have had some misogynistic origins, but that this has no relevance today. In disagreement with such a counterclaim, however, it can be plausibly argued that the industrialized countries have remained virulently misogynistic, as seen in the prevalence of violence practiced and depicted by men against women. If there is indeed a link between misogyny, insecure masculinity, and our conceptions of science, particularly weapons science, then we are given a way to understand why nuclear violence can be associated in warriors' minds with sexual intercourse and ejaculation. Moreover, not only does Sue Mansfield suggest that at a deep level the scientific mentality has carried from its inception in the seventeenth century "the burden of an essential hostility to the body, the feminine, and the natural environment," but she also points out that, if human life survives at all after a nuclear holocaust, then it will mean the total restoration of the power of arm-bearing men over women. This leads her to make a significant comment that "though the reenslavement of women and the destruction of nature are not conscious goals of our nuclear stance, the language of our bodies, our postures, and our acts is a critical clue to our unexamined motives and desires."[51]

Of course, at the conscious level the scientific warrior today can, and does, offer a "rational" explanation for his behavior: his creation of fission and fusion weapons, he maintains, has made the deliberate starting of world war unthinkable and certainly has preserved peace in Europe for the last forty years. Whatever financial gain comes his way is not unappreciated but is secondary to the necessity of maintaining his country's security; likewise whatever scientific interest he experiences in the technological challenge of his work is again secondary to the all-important objective of preserving the balance of terror until world statesmen achieve multilateral disarmament. While well-known arguments can be made against the coherence of such a typical rationalization, what I am suggesting is that at a partly conscious, partly unconscious, level the scientific warrior experiences not only an almost irresistible need to separate his (insecure) masculinity from what he conceives as femininity but also a compulsive desire to create the weapons that unmistakably affirm his masculinity and by means of which what is "female" can, if necessary and as a last resort, be annihilated. (And it must be noted that scientific warriors can be supported by women or even joined by female warriors in their largely unconscious quest to affirm masculine triumph over the feminine and female.)

Conclusion

Looking over the history of humanity—the "slaughter-bench of history" as Hegel called it—I feel compelled to identify a factor—beyond economic and territorial rationales—that could help explain this sorry escalation of weaponry oppression, and bloodshed. It seems to me of paramount importance to try to understand why men are generally the direct oppressors, oppressing other men and women, why in general men allow neither themselves nor women the opportunity to realize full humanity.

While the political scientist Jean Bethke Elshtain may well be correct when she writes skeptically that no great movement will ever be fought under the banner of "androgyny," I suggest that it could well be fought under the banner of "a truly human future for everyone."[52] And that would entail the abolition of the *institutionalized* sexual division of labor. Men and women must be allowed the right to become complete human beings and not mutilated into their separate masculine and feminine gender roles. At the same time, I agree with Cynthia Cockburn when she writes in her book *Machinery of Dominance* that "men need more urgently to learn women's skills than women need to learn men's" and that "the revolutionary step will be to bring men down to earth, to domesticate technology and reforge the link between making and nurturing."[53]

In such a world "education" could not remain as it is now in Britain and the United States (and elsewhere). Certainly there would be no "physics" degree as it exists today, although there would be studies that would eventually take "students" to the frontiers of research in "physics." Needless to say, such an educational system would not be male-dominated (or female-dominated), it would not institutionalize and reward socially competitive aggressive behavior, and there would be no objective in "physics" education of the "conquest of nature," although it would certainly recognize the need to find respectful, ecologically sound ways of making use of nature. Moreover, images of nature would, I suspect, undergo some profound changes (with probably major changes to some theories as well), and clearly in a truly human world there would be no militarization of physics. As for the "scientific method," this would be recognized to be a somewhat mysterious activity, perhaps never completely specifiable, certainly an activity making use of the full range of *human* capacities from creative intuition to the most rigorous logical reasoning.

As for sexual imagery, that would surely thrive in the new truly human activity of scientific research, given that sexual relations—deprived of the hatred that now so greatly distorts sexuality—would continue to provide not only much of the motivation but also the metaphors for describing scientific activity (and much else). Consider, for example, the language of a woman who was awarded just about every honor the discipline of astrophysics could bestow (but only after she spent years challenging blatant sexism and discrimination). The images invoked by Cecilia Payne-Gaposchkin are more directly erotic than the "equivalent" sexual imagery used by male scientists and physicists (not to mention their frequent aggressive imagery); her language was of her friendship, her love, her delight, her ecstasy with the world of "male" stars and galaxies. Writing of nature as female, Payne-Gaposchkin advises her fellow researchers: "Nature has always had a trick of surprising us, and she will continue to surprise us. But she has never let us down yet. We can go forward with confidence,

> *Knowing that nature never did betray*
> *The heart that loved her.*"[54]

But it was an embrace of relatedness that Payne-Gaposchkin had sought and which had given her great satisfaction throughout her life, the satisfaction arising, in the words of Peggy Kidwell, from a sustained impassioned, loving endeavor "to unravel the mysteries of the stars."[55] In a truly human world, the principal purpose and result of science, as Erwin Schrödinger once said, will surely be to enhance "the general joy of living."[56]

Notes

I am most grateful to Michael Kaufman for his extremely skillful pruning of a very long manuscript.

1. Michael Howard, "On Fighting a Nuclear War," in Michael Howard, *The Causes of War and Other Essays* (London: Temple Smith, 1983), 136.

2. Penny Strange, *It'll Make a Man of You* (Nottingham, England: Mushroom Books with Peace News, 1983), 24–5.

3. These statistics are taken from *Girls and Physics: A Report by the Joint Physics Education Committee of the Royal Society and the Institute of Physics* (London, 1982), 8, and Lilli S. Hornig, "Women in Science and Engineering: Why So Few?" *Technology Review* 87 (November/December, 1984), 41.

4. See Margaret W. Rossiter, *Women Scientists in America: Struggles and Strategies to 1940* (Baltimore: Johns Hopkins University Press, 1982), 190–1.

5. Richard Lewontin, "'Honest Jim' Watson's Big Thriller, about DNA," Chicago *Sun Times*, 25 Feb. 1968, 1–2, reprinted in James D. Watson, *The Double Helix . . . A New Critical Edition*, edited by Gunther S. Stent (London: Weidenfeld, 1981), 186.

6. Sharon Traweek, "High-Energy Physics: A Male Preserve," *Technology Review* (November/December, 1984), 42–3; see also her *Beamtimes and Lifetimes: The World of High-Energy Physicists* (Boston: Harvard University Press, 1988).

7. Heinz Pagels, *The Cosmic Code: Quantum Physics as the Language of Nature* (London: Michael Joseph, 1982), 338.

8. Sir John Hill, "The Quest for Public Acceptance of Nuclear Power," *Atom*, no. 273 (1979): 166–72.

9. Richard S. Westfall, *The Construction of Modern Science* (1971; Cambridge: Cambridge University Press, 1977), 41. It should be noted, however, that quantum mechanics is essentially an antireductionist theory; see, for example, the (controversial) book by Fritjof Capra, *The Tao of Physics* (London: Fontana, 1976).

10. Willard Libby, "Man's Place in the Physical Universe," in John R. Platt, ed., *New Views of the Nature of Man* (Chicago: University of Chicago Press, 1965), 14–15.

11. C. S. Lewis, *The Abolition of Man* (1943; London: Geoffrey Bles, 1946), 40.

12. E. L. Woollett, "Physics and Modern Warfare: The Awkward Silence," *American Journal of Physics* 48 (1980): 104–11.

13. Freeman Dyson, *Weapons and Hope* (New York: Harper and Row, 1984), 41–2.

14. William J. Broad, *Star Warriors: A Penetrating Look into the Lives of the Young Scientists Behind Our Space Age Weaponry* (New York: Simon and Schuster, 1985), 204.

15. *Ibid.*

16. Hazel Grice, letter to the *Guardian*, 9 Oct. 1984, 20.

17. Bertrand Russell, "Science in a Liberal Education," the *New Statesman* (1913) reprinted in *Mysticism and Logic and Other Essays* (Harmondsworth: Penguin, 1953), 47–8.

18. Robert Bierstedt, *The Social Order* (1957; New York: McGraw-Hill, 1974), 26.

19. Hans Reichenbach, *The Rise of Scientific Philosophy* (1951; Berkeley and Los Angles: California University Press, 1966), 312.

20. Vivian Gornick, *Women in Science: Portraits from a World in Transition* (New York: Simon and Schuster, 1984), 36.

21. Carl Hempel, *Philosophy of Natural Science* (Englewood Cliffs, N.J.: Prentice-Hall, 1966), 16.

22. See, for example, Imre Lakatos and Alan Musgrave, eds., *Criticism and the Growth of Knowledge* (Cambridge: Cambridge University Press, 1970): Sandra Harding, "Is Gender a Variable in Conceptions of Rationality? A Survey of Issues," *Dialectica: International Journal of Philosophy of Knowledge* 36 (1982): 225–42: and Harry M. Collins, ed., special issue of *Social Studies of Science* 11 (1981): 3–158, "Knowledge and Controversy: Studies of Modern Natural Science."

23. Freeman Dyson, *Weapons and Hope*, 4–6.

24. Helen Caldicott, "Etiology: Missile Envy and Other Psychopathology," in her *Missile Envy: The Arms Race and Nuclear War* (New York: William Morrow, 1984).

25. Sue Mansfield, *The Gestalts of War: An Inquiry into Its Origins and Meaning as a Social Institution* (New York: Dial Press, 1982), 224.

26. Carolyn Merchant, "Isis' Consciousness Raised," *Isis* 73 (1982): 398–409.

27. Frank Close, "And now at last, the quark to top them all," the *Guardian*, 19 July 1984, 13, and "A shining example of what ought to be impossible," the *Guardian*, 8 Aug. 1985, 13.

28. Sir William Crookes, quoted in E. E. Fournier d'Albe, *The Life of Sir William Crookes* (London: Fisher Unwin, 1923), 365.

29. See, for example, the physicist Paul Davies's account of "black holes," "naked singularities," and "cosmic anarchy" in his *The Edge of Infinity: Naked Singularities and the Destruction of Space-time* (London: Dent, 1981), especially 92–3, 114, 145.

30. Max Jammer, *The Conceptual Development of Quantum Mechanics* (New York: McGraw-Hill, 1966), 61, and Victor Weisskopf, "Niels Bohr and International Scientific Collaboration," in S. Rozenthal, ed., *Niels Bohr: His Life and Work as Seen by His Friends and Colleagues* (Amsterdam: North Holland, 1967), 262.

31. Frederick Soddy, *The Interpretation of Radium* (London, 1909), 234.

32. C. G. Darwin quoted in A. S. Eve, *Rutherford* (Cambridge: Cambridge University Press, 1939), 199, 434.

33. W. C. D. Whetham, *The Recent Development of Physical Science* (London: Murray, 1904) 242.

34. G. E. Hale quoted in Helen Wright, *Explorer of the Universe: A Biography of George Ellery Hale* (New York: Dutton, 1966), 283, and in A. S. Eve, *Rutherford*, 231.

35. "The Atom" from *The Collected Verse of Thomas Thornely* (Cambridge: W. Heffer, 1939), 70–1, reprinted in John Heath-Stubbes and Phillips Salmon, eds., *Poems of Science* (Harmondsworth: Penguin, 1984), 245.

36. Richard G. Hewlett and Oscar E. Anderson, *A History of the United States Atomic Energy Commission* (Pennsylvania State University Press, 1962), vol. 1, *The New World*, 1939–1946, 386.

37. Edward Teller with Allen Brown, *The Legacy of Hiroshima* (London: Macmillan, 1962), 51–3.

38. Edward Teller, *Energy from Heaven and Earth* (San Francisco: W. H. Freeman, 1979), 151. See also Norman Moss, *Men Who Play God* (Harmondsworth: Penguin, 1970), 78 For general detail see my *Fathering the Unthinkable: Masculinity, Scientists and the Nuclear Arms Race* (London: Pluto Press, 1983), ch. 3.

39. Bernard Brodie's memorandum is referred to by Fred Kaplan in *The Wizards of Armageddon* (New York: Simon and Schuster, 1983), 222. I have not seen the text of Brodie's memorandum. The chilling phrase "smoking, radiating ruin at the end of two hours" comes from a declassified Navy memorandum on a SAC briefing held in March 1954; see David Alan Rosenberg, "A Smoking Radiating Ruin at the End of Two Hours': Documents on American Plans for Nuclear War with the Soviet Union 1954–55," *International Security* 6 (1981/82), 3–38.

40. Herman Kahn, *On Escalation: Metaphors and Scenarios* (London: Pall Mall, 1965), 194.

41. Note that Gregg Herken in *Counsels of War* (New York: Knopf, 1985), 206, writes that Bernard Brodie objected to Herman Kahn's "levity" in coining the term "wargasm."

42. Quoted in Thomas Powers, "How Nuclear War Could Start," *New York Review of Books*, 17 Jan. 1985, 34.

43. Roger Hutton, (personal communication), who attended the meeting when researching the Star Wars project.

44. Simone de Beauvoir, *The Second Sex* (1949; Harmondsworth: Penguin, 1972), 396.

45. Suzanne Lowry, "O Tempora, O Mores," the *Guardian*, 24 May 1984, 17.

46. Susan Griffin, *Pornography and Silence: Culture's Revenge Against Nature* (London: Women's Press, 1981), 217.

47. Paul Boyer, *By the Bomb's Early Light: American Thought and Culture at the Dawn of the Atomic Age* (New York: Pantheon, 1985), 83.

48. H. C. E. Midelfort, "Heartland of the Witchcraze: Central and Northern Europe," *History Today* 31 (February 1981): 28.

49. Simone de Beauvoir, *The Second Sex*, 699.

50. See, for example, Carolyn Merchant, *The Death of Nature: Women, Ecology and the Scientific Revolution* (San Francisco: Harper and Row, 1980), and my *Science and Sexual Oppres-*

sion: Patriarchy's Confrontation with Women and Nature (London: Weidenfeld, 1981), ch. 3 and *Fathering the Unthinkable,* ch. 1.

51. Sue Mansfield, *The Gestalts of War,* 223.

52. Jean Bethke Elshtain, "Against Androgyny," Telos 47 (1981), 5–22.

53. Cynthia Cockburn, *Machinery of Dominance* (London: Pluto Press, 1985), 256–7.

54. Katherine Haramundanis, ed., *Cecilia Payne-Gaposchkin: An Autobiography and Other Recollections* (Cambridge: Cambridge University Press, 1984), 237.

55. *Ibid.,* 28.

56. "Science, Art and Play," reprinted in E. C. Schrödinger, *Science, Theory and Man* (New York: Dover, 1957), 29; see, for example, Euan Squires, *To Acknowledge the Wonder: The Story of Fundamental Physics* (Bristol: Adam Hilger, 1985).

3

Images of Women in Patriarchy: The Masculist-Defined Woman

The "Naming" of Women

> *It is necessary to grasp the fundamental fact that women have had the power of* naming *stolen from us. We have not been free to use our own power to name ourselves, the world, or God. The old naming was not the product of dialogue—a fact inadvertently admitted in the Genesis story of Adam's naming the animals and the women. Women are now realizing that the universal imposing of names by men has been false because partial. That is, inadequate words have been taken as adequate.*
>
> *To exist humanly is to name the self, the world, and God.*
>
> –MARY DALY, *Beyond God the Father*[1]

In a society where men have controlled the conceptual arena and have determined social values as well as the structure of institutions, it is not surprising that women should have lost the power of *naming,* of explaining and defining for ourselves the realities of our own experience. In a patriarchal culture, men define (explain, analyze, describe, direct) the female just as they define nearly everything else. The issue is not only that men perceive women from masculine perspectives, but also that given the nature of socialization, all members of society—including women—perceive the female from the prevailing masculine perspective.

The Male Identification of Women

It is argued by many feminists, and properly so, that women—sometimes, directly, often indirectly—have had considerable impact on society.[2] In primitive times, women were very likely the inventors of pottery, food preservation, and other "domestic" technology; hence, they probably also originated early forms of social organization. As teachers of the young, women have always done much to form the individual attitudes and values within the community, and our personal influence on one another and on men has long been recognized (although often maligned).

But informal networks and personal power are not political power, and the influence that women do wield is frequently deflected and counterbalanced—often distorted—by the subordinate and peripheral place we have been assigned in society. The attitudes and values we teach, the influences we mean to effect are often alien to us, originating not in our own perspectives but in sources we have inherited and internalized. We learn our roles and their attendant behaviors from mothers who themselves were bent to the yoke as we are meant to be. We attend male-dominated schools and universities. We read books, manuals, and bibles written by men for male ends. We learn about and care for our bodies through male physicians, institutions, and medical societies. We are exhorted and chastised by male priests. We model ourselves after images presented in media controlled almost entirely by men, who publish the newspapers and magazines, manage the advertising agencies, produce and direct films, and determine fashion trends in the great couture houses of Europe. Finally, through societally cultivated dependence, we place ourselves in the position of bartering our self-definition for "protection."

The naming of women has been effected by men primarily through control of the social institutions that determine behavior and attitudes. As social beings subject to those institutions, we have commonly (although not without exception) adopted the images wrought by that naming, often unaware that the ideals and visions we live by are not of our own creation. From our first breath—from our entry into a world of pink and white ruffles; of dolls and docility; of behaving like a lady; of loving strokes for submission, quiet, and gentility; of cutout dolls in wedding gowns and Barbie dolls that develop breasts; of cheering on the sidelines; of applause for being picked; of frowns for "tomboy" behavior, assertiveness, intelligence, and independence—from that earliest time before we can even question, we absorb an environment that teaches us a vision of femininity so pervasive and complete that it appears real; it appears to be our own.

> *Being good at what was expected of me was one of my earliest projects. . . .*
>
> *Girls were different from boys, and the expression of that difference seemed mine to make clear. Did my loving, anxious mother, who dressed me in white organdy pinafores and Mary Janes and who cried hot tears when I got them dirty, give me my first instruction? Of course. Did my doting aunts and uncles with their gifts of pretty dolls and miniature tea sets add to my education? Of course. But even without the appropriate toys and clothes, lessons in the art of being feminine lay all around me, and I absorbed them all: the fairy tales that were read to me at night, the brightly colored advertisements I pored over in magazines before I learned to decipher the words, the movies I saw, the comic books I hoarded, the radio soap operas I happily followed whenever I had to stay in bed with a cold. I loved being a little girl, or rather I loved being a fairy princess, for that was who I thought I was.*
>
> –SUSAN BROWNMILLER, *Femininity*[3]

By the time we are old enough, wise enough, and angry enough to discard this vision, the seed planted in our infancy and constantly tended has so taken root—become so integral a part of us—that to reject it has almost the force of rejecting ourselves. Such is the meaning of saying that it is easier to fight an external enemy than one who has "outposts in your head."[4]

The alien definition of women, even more extreme than it first appears, goes beyond merely the producing and imposing of foreign images, beyond women's accepting these images as our own; it proceeds all the way to our accepting the status of not only less-than-standard humanity but of less-than-standard *being*, of "otherness."[5] "Otherness," in existentialist terms, is a social-moral as well as a personal-psychological assignment of women to the role of a less than primary, less than completely worthy human being. Otherness defines women as the "other half" of humanity, the half that helps, that *assists* in the work of society, whether by staying out of the way, or by relieving the primary beings of chores that would impede their work, or by procreating. Otherness defines woman as satellite, adjunct, alter to man, but not as an end in herself. It accounts for woman being tuned to a servant consciousness, to *care for* before being *cared for*, to keep to the background in a place of her own, to yield to man's will, which is valued in itself directly *for* the world whereas she is only *in* the world. It accounts for women being told not to take jobs away from men, as if the jobs were somehow the cosmically ordained property of men. It accounts for wanting sons and deeming daughters less valuable.

Woman Identification Versus Male Identification: The Alternatives

The woman created in and by the male perspective is called by the women's movement the *male-identified woman*. The alternative, the *woman-identified woman*, is surely a feminist vision. She is a person who indeed understands herself to be subject (self), not object (other); she respects both her womanhood and her humanity; she takes her direction and definition from values that are her own, born of her own self-perceived qualities and goals as well as those of other women; she contributes to society that which she takes to be meaningful and does so in her own way.

Such a woman is only now evolving. In a patriarchal environment, hostile as it is to assertive, self-defined women, the processes of woman identification and of growth toward that new identity are perplexing, confusing, and arduous. The new images that feminists are laboring to draw are necessarily influenced by the struggle in which we are engaged.

What we shall see, then, in this chapter and the next, is a contest of visions: on the one hand, the male-identified ideals and masculist stereotypes; on the other, feminist responses and affirmations. The pictures created—primarily of women but affecting all humanity—are intricately interwoven by circumstance, race, class, nationality, religion, sexuality, age, and a host of factors, yet they are so different from masculist ideals as to entail two separate realities: patriarchal perspective and feminist consciousness.

Ideals and Images: The Masculist Definition

It is an extraordinary fact of women's lives that for centuries, across space and time and from culture to culture, women have been consistently treated with ambivalence, misogyny, and subordination.[6] These constant themes in the naming of women by patriarchal societies may find different expressions and may vary in intensity and effect, but they recur almost universally.

Although there are many hypotheses, ranging from the scientific to the religious and from the acceptable to the vehemently opposed, the origins and causes of women's subordination have never been definitely explained. Certain things are clear, however. The masculist images of women and the roles that these images support are socially constructed to create a situation very convenient for men in many ways. The patriarchal definitions of femininity provide the masculist with excellent rationales for using women as they have as well as for granting themselves potent sociopsychological advantages. The female role of helpmate, for example, follows "naturally" from the patriarchal definition of women's nature; it provides men with tremendous privilege, power, and pleasure. Women are expected to serve men physically, taking care of their homes, property, clothing, or persons; economically, doing countless jobs for which women are ill paid or not paid at all; sexually, as wives, mistresses, or prostitutes; and reproductively, assuring men of paternity through female chastity. Because women do the "shitwork" of society (as the movement refers to all the work men do not wish to do), men are freed to spend their time on socially valued activities for which they receive all kinds of material and psychological rewards. From this use of women, men accrue extra time, energy, and power.

The image of woman as man's complement offers an extremely effective support mechanism for the masculist self-image: The softer, weaker, and more dependent the woman is, the stronger and more powerful the man appears; the more a servant the woman, the more a master the man. And the more the woman withdraws into home and gentility, the more the arenas of government and industry are left to the iron grasp of warriors and warrior values.

The misogynist picture of women as inferior—not quite human, incompetent, petty, evil, and lacking in responsibility and moral aptitude—stands as clear justification to the masculist for our subordination and suffering. After all, because we cause all the trouble in the world and instigate misfortune and disaster (Eve taking the apple, Pandora opening the box), it is natural and fitting that we should be punished for our deeds and controlled, lest we do further harm.

> *. . . in sorrow thou shalt bring forth children; and thy desire shall be to thy husband, and he shall rule over thee.*
>
> –Genesis 3:16

Patriarchal society has indeed been well served by these masculist images; it behooves us to understand them. Although neither the origin or cause of these images can be traced definitively, feminists have proposed cogent speculations that help clarify the issue.

Ambivalence: An Undercurrent

The images of women in our culture are fraught with contradiction: Woman is the sublime, the perfect, the beautiful; she is the awful, the stupid, the contemptible. She is the mother of god as well as the traitor of the garden. She is the tender young creature man marries and protects as well as the treacherous, manipulative sneak who tricked him into a union he never sought. Keeper of virtue, she is yet a base and petty creature, incapable of rational moral judgment, cosmically wise, concretely stupid. Explicitly or implicitly, women are represented as having dual natures, of being all that is desirable, fascinating, and wonderful yet also being extremely destructive and dangerous. Ambivalence toward a whole range of real and alleged female powers (birth, menstruation, seduction, intuition) expresses itself in a subliminal patriarchal belief that women have a great deal of "big magic," very much worth having but destined to go awry if not controlled and subdued.

No doubt, there are many sources for such attitudes, but, feminists argue, we must understand them all within this important context: In patriarchy, images of women—like other conceptualizations—have been male-created. The stereotypes of women, contradictory and conflicting, are male projections. As such, we must understand them as outward expressions of male attitudes. The dichotomy in the representation of women, therefore, is a strong indication of extreme ambivalence on the part of men.

In literature, psychology, philosophy, or religion, one comes face to face, again and again, with the ambivalence men feel toward women. They seek her, the eternal feminine. They want and desire her, but oh so much the worse for them! Men are exhorted by the stronger and more stoic among them to beware the lures and entrapments of females. In the first century A.D., Paul proclaimed the dangers of sin, sex, and uncontrolled women (all related). Centuries later, in language altered for "science," yet reminiscent of primitive mythology—toothed vaginas and grasping spiders—Freud advised the same caution.

Students of many disciplines try to account for the origin of these attitudes. Certain sociologists, for example, have pointed out that ambivalence is typical of feelings experienced by any dominant group toward those it colonizes or exploits—a mixture of need and contempt, guilt, anger, and fear.

Many anthropologists, tracing a long history of male fear of women, place great emphasis on attitudes toward female regenerative powers and organs, so magical, so powerfully important and stirring, yet so utterly female, and both mysterious and alien to men. Anthropologists such as H. R. Hays, Wolfgang Lederer, and Joseph Campbell point to the frequency of myths crediting the *first* birth to a man (like Adam). They point to menstrual taboos and blood magic, and they postulate that men feel strong envy for a power they themselves can never have.

Psychologists, from classical times to the present, have pointed to male fears surrounding the sex act: fear of impotence, detumescence, vaginal containment, and other, more abstract matters, such as absorption by the partner, possession, or even castration. That the act of intercourse[7] is simultaneously perceived as a most desirable and also a fearsome or dangerous experience may account for male ambivalence, in the view of many psychologists.[8]

That all these factors contribute to ambivalence is likely the case, yet like many other feminists, I am more apt to seek the major source of masculist attitudes toward women or womanhood in the intricate, primal dimensions of men's own gender identity, in the dynamics of the martial ideal.

Masculinity as defined in patriarchy, you remember, requires men to repudiate in themselves most of the affective components of human experience: It is imprudent to feel. It is very difficult, however, not to acknowledge feeling, and as a result at least two major facets of life are thrown into severe conflict for men: sex and an entire configuration of experience we may call *the tender.* These conflicts have direct bearing on male attitudes toward women.

Although it is surely true that the sex act is surrounded with certain fears and danger, I contend that it is not intercourse itself that provides the greatest conflict, but rather what sex represents. It is not the mechanical act of sex that has usually been presented as the great source of "sin" but rather the *enjoyment* of the act, the surrender to sex; it is sensuality and its attendant implications—fun, caprice, relaxation, nonstriving. Whether the language be religious (Paul warning against sin and damnation) or psychological (Freud fretting about the id and sublimation), sensuality and pleasure have been consistently presented as the foe of duty, the primary value of the martial ideal. The message is always the same: A man has a choice between duty (manhood) and indulgence (sensuality, pleasure, and self). If he chooses the former, he gains pride, identity, praise, and worthiness; if he chooses the latter, all he may expect is dissipation and disgrace.

For the masculist, *woman* and *sex* are nearly synonymous terms. The rejection of sensuality necessitates, then, a rejection of the object and instigator of sensuality: woman. If sex evokes mixed feelings—of approach and avoidance—most certainly woman must evoke the same feelings.

But the problem does not end here. The ambivalence goes further. Besides sensuality and pleasure, the warrior must also expunge from his character the parts of himself that either express vulnerability or render him vulnerable: fear, sensitivity, need, desire, grief, hurt, trust, and all the other traits, qualities, and feelings that are part of the tender. Because the tender is not allowable in men but is impossible to live without, patriarchy splits this element off from men and instead invests it in women, where men may enjoy it in greater safety. Yet even in this externalized form, the tender remains a danger that each man must guard against because he knows—though he would probably deny it—how easily he might yield to it, how much he wishes to yield.

In this light, we can understand male contempt for women's "emotionalism" as a rejection of emotions within; ridicule of female timidity as flight from timidity within; hatred of the woman without as of the woman within. The ambivalence, then, that men feel toward women is something we can understand, at least in part, as a displaced expression of an inner conflict so frustrating and frightening that it cannot be contained but must instead be projected outward, onto women.

That we should be the recipients of all these "bad" feelings is not surprising; it is common for minorities or out-groups to serve as scapegoats for the masters. But that we should function as the object of this particular displaced ambivalence is even more to be expected: We are, after all, the male-identified symbol of the entire configuration the male is required to excise.

Man has ordained woman as the carrier of all he dare not entertain in himself—and he hates her for it. It is as if mankind has said to woman: "Woman—be tenderness, be nurture, be vulnerability, be laughter, play, and fun for me, because I cannot be these things myself"; but then "You are all the things the great Mars has deemed evil and dangerous; and therefore you are evil and dangerous."

Misogyny: The Expression

Attitude is easily converted into judgment: *Woman is desirable* is quickly transformed into *woman is good; woman is frightening* readily becomes *woman is bad.*

Misogyny—the hatred or distrust of women—is an integral part of masculism and patriarchy. Veiled by chivalry or a mythic masking of female roles (called *mystification* in the women's movement), it is nonetheless a potent force in the relations of men and women—and readily apparent should the veil or mask be rent even slightly. It is misogyny that underlies not only rape, invective, and abuse but also beauty contests, work segregation, menstrual taboos, mother-in-law jokes, "old bag" themes, "Hooters" restaurants, patronizing etiquette, and current sexual mores.

Misogyny includes the beliefs that women are stupid, petty, manipulative, dishonest, silly, gossipy, irrational, incompetent, undependable, narcissistic, castrating, dirty, overemotional, unable to make altruistic or moral judgments, oversexed, undersexed, and a host of other ugly things. Such beliefs culminate in attitudes that demean our bodies, our abilities, our characters, and our efforts, and so imply that we must be controlled, dominated, subdued, abused, and used, not only for male benefit but for our own. St. Jerome, Freud, the Rolling Stones, and numerous others have all agreed that when it comes to punishment, women need it and love it.

The image of woman as victim is nowhere more acutely portrayed than in *Story of O,*[9] originally published in France and described by reviewers variously as "pornographic," "political,"[10] or "mystical"[11]—undoubtedly, all three. The plot is simple: O is a young woman subjected by her lover and his comrades to continual sadosexual torture and humiliation unto death, all of which (vividly portrayed in "erotic" images) both O and her lover willingly, consciously, even joyfully, accept as proof of O's love as well as punishment for her "wantonness" (any little bits of self-assertion). During the course of the book, O is transformed from an individual to a totally degraded, totally pliant, totally selfless (in the worst sense) creature—a sexual garbage pail, for "love."

Many feminists have pointed out that what is important about the book is not the plot but the theme, as it is interpreted and responded to by its commentators. Jean Paulhan, in a prefacing essay significantly titled "Happiness in Slavery," describes the "mystical" theme in these familiar terms:

> *At last a woman who admits it!*[12] *Who admits what? Something that women have always refused till now to admit (and today more than ever before). Something that men have always reproached them with: That they never cease obeying their nature, the call of their blood, that everything in them, even their minds, is sex. That they have constantly to be nourished, constantly washed and made up, constantly beaten. That all they need is a good master, one who is not too lax or kind: for the moment we make any show of tenderness they draw upon it, turning all the zest, joy, and character at their command to make others love them. In short, that we must, when we go to see them, take a whip along.*[13]

Paulhan praises woman's uniqueness, her greater "understanding" born of childlikeness, her more primitive decency, requiring "nothing less than hands tied behind the back . . . the knees spread apart and bodies spread-eagled, than sweat and tears."[14] The other "official" commentator, Mandiargues, proposes that the theme is "the tragic flowering of a woman."[15]

It is important that we look at such talk. It is not simply an aberration but rather the expression of a vital and common principle of masculism: that woman is most adored, most exquisite, most revered when she is sufficiently selfless to be martyred. In O, self-effacement that would be repulsive in men, inimical to all the classical values of human excellence, is deemed mystically beautiful, fulfilling, and sacrificial. The Sacred Principle of Victimization[16] means that women are more conveniently exploitable and indeed more sexually exciting when they are stripped not only of clothing but also of power, strength, assertiveness, and sense of self. Should one doubt the relevance of such an attitude here and today, consider how titillating men find the newspaper stories of rape, the torture-murders of *True Detective Magazine,* the bent-over beauties in *Hustler* magazine, and the tough sex of current movies and rock videos. Because women are bad, they must be punished. Misogyny earns women torture of one kind or another.[17]

Stereotypes: Good Women and Bad

The ultimate ambivalence finally expresses itself in the ultimate bifurcation into good women and bad. The judgments of good and bad, like the images themselves, are male projections, resting not only on the extent to which any woman meets the specifications of her role requirements or adheres to the standards set for her but also on a particular male's needs and his attitudes toward that role configuration at some moment in time. That is, an image may be judged good at one time and bad at another, depending on its serviceability to those making the judgment. As the image is judged, so is the woman expressing that image. Meeting the complex imperatives of femininity is a tenuous affair at best.

All male-identified ideals of women rest on one basic presupposition: that women are and ought to be completely defined and understood within their biological capacities, sexual or reproductive. These capacities determine our "place" in the world, and we are only "good," one way or another, when we are (willingly or unwillingly) in that place. Should we instead stray—particularly through our own assertiveness but even by accident—then we are bad women and can only be redeemed if we are returned to our proper sphere.

In patriarchy, for women, "anatomy is destiny," and our physical capacities determine for us two separate and often conflicting roles: that of procreator-mother and that of sexual partner.[18] The "good" woman, then, each in a different sense, is she who serves, either in the capacity of excellent mother or of excellent mistress or both.

Mother: The Primary Ideal

The Marian image, Mother, nurture incarnate, is patriarchy's most positive image for women. This lady, charged ostensibly with the care of the young, is the complement of male power—she is tenderness, fragility, love, charity, loyalty, submission, and sacrifice. Carrier of man's seed, she is the essence of purity, totally absorbed in the activities and qualities of caring. Serene and satisfied within her role, placing the needs of her charges above her own, she busies herself with feeding them, watching over them, making them happy. Intuitive, cosmically linked with lunar cycles, she has special powers and therefore little need for rationality.

> *Just as in sexual physiology the female principle is one of receiving, keeping and nourishing—women's* specific *form of creativeness, that of motherhood, is tied up with the life of nature, with a* non-reflective bios.

... Indeed, the four-week cycle of ovulation, the rhythmically alternating tides of fertility ... the nine months of gestation ... ties women deeply to the life of nature, to the pulse beat of the cosmos.[19]

I think, perhaps, that insofar as insight—the seeing into, the throwing of light into darkness, the intellectual illumination—aims at greater self-awareness and a more conscious functioning, it belongs into the mode or sphere of male development. The eternal feminine, static, perfect in itself, does not and need not develop. What any given woman does not know about it, insight therapy cannot ever teach her. Insight therapy, even in women, can only address itself to the masculine aspect. A given woman, through insight, can become more aware and more conscious, but not more feminine—although the balance of male and female within her may at times be shifted through insight which enables her to place less stress on male modes of functioning; in that case a covered-up femininity may emerge: but only as much of it as was there in the first place. One is a woman, one learns *to be a man. Therapeutic theories stressing insight deal primarily with men because only men—and the masculine aspects of women—can be approached by and can utilize insight.*[20]

Womanhood, it would seem then, is closer to nature than manhood, more compelling as well as more disastrous if denied. One might wonder (and feminists do) how anything so "natural" and "instinctive" *could* be denied. Yet according to theory it sometimes is, and then not only do women themselves suffer, but the whole world goes topsy-turvy; it is askew, even in danger. Men lose their manhood, children become psychotic, society dissolves, and the natural order is disturbed!

In the language of the women's movement, the mothering role is *mystified,* covered over with a whole set of myths, fantasies, and images that hide many realities of the role and the person who lives it.

Playmate: The Illicit Ideal

Mother is the *official* good woman of the Western world. But another kind of "good" woman exists, good in a different sense, good in an elbow-in-the-ribs or slightly déclassé kind of way—a sexy, naughty, fun-loving lady: the playmate.

The Marian image, the classic model of femininity in the West, born out of the fear and loathing of sex and sensuality rampant in the early Christian church, is pointedly asexual; pure, chaste, and virginal, despite marriage, wifehood, and childbirth. The good woman in this image, the Mother, is an asexual or even antisexual ideal, too pure for carnality. Sex is beneath her. She is patient, enduring, dutiful, submissive, and nurturing, *and she doesn't play around.* She's not supposed to, and she doesn't want to, not even with her husband. Hence, her converse, the Playmate.

For the playmate, playing around is her raison d'être. She is built "to take it" and to give it. You can tell by the seductive, compliant look in her eyes, the parted lips, the knowing smile, the receptive, open posture of her opulent young body. But the playmate is no ordinary whore. She is interesting (bright enough to be companionable but not so bright as to be uncooperative or threatening). She is independent (able to take care of herself but needful enough to succumb to male power). She is choosy (nobody wants something that anyone can have). She is even a little aggressive, a little dangerous—enough to make her a worthy trophy.

"There are two kinds of girls," a saying goes, "the kind you bring home to Mother and the kind you bring home to Father." To each of these types is attached a distinct set of male expectations and responses. The playmate is for playing, for fun, not for seriousness and heavy obligation. She has waived her claims to adulation from afar. She isn't chaste so one need not hide "baser" motivations and appetites. Because she's not timid or naive, one needn't be solicitous or protective. She's worldly wise—no need for protocol, courtship, and protestations of love. Having opted out of "purity" and the category of the primary ideal, she has abandoned the status and prerogatives of the "official" good woman. Mother and playmate, lady and tramp, Mary and Eve, the dichotomy—familiar in novels, movies, and sermons—creates tension that puts women in a bind.

The Wife

It should be obvious by now that the two female ideals, perfect mother and perfect mistress, are incompatible. No one can be chaste, submissive, timid, needful, innocent, loyal, tender, and serene and *at the same time* sexually wise, perky, naughty, independent, and so on. Yet that is exactly the position into which middle-class American patriarchy places women, for to be both Mary/Mother and Playmate is the prescribed role and image of the ideal woman—girlfriend, roommate, date, or wife. Like the "hell of a woman" in a popular song lyric, she is supposed to be all things to her hell of a man: not just *act* all things, but *be* them: "woman, baby, witch, lady." It's a difficult game, for even if she wins, she loses—her identity, her self-concept, her sense of autonomy, cohesion, and direction. It is a schizophrenic setup.

The Dichotomy Dichotomizes: The Misogynist Flip

All that effort, and as often as not, it doesn't even work. Each of us may indeed choose between a life modeled on Mary or a life modeled on Playmate, settling for the rewards of either role. We may even manage to negotiate the tricks and turns of playing both, but that still cannot guarantee us undying love.

Circumstances arise over which none have control and in which Mary, the Playmate, or even Helluvawoman may become a pain in the neck, an object of contempt, a creature to be avoided. Reflected visions, after all, ultimately depend on the minds of those who reflect. And the extent to which any of these roles is prized (and consequently the woman playing it praised) depends on how well it serves the function for which it was created and how long that function endures. Mary is desirable to one seeking nurture, understanding, and mothering (for himself or his children). But she rapidly becomes a nuisance when that same man sets out to find exuberant or illicit sex. The playmate is fun when playing is what he wants, but she is an unsuitable companion at the company dinner.

Each ideal is subject to a "serviceability" factor: The status of the role itself, its value and meaning, and even the language used to refer to it can shift radically as its utility shifts or its context changes. She who is "the little woman" in church becomes "the old lady" at the bar; she who was seen as "a good old girl" in graduate school may be seen as "a slut" when he joins the club.

Within a single moment, depending on changing attitudes or interests, the image may shift—good becomes bad, bad becomes good. The nurturing Mary becomes the old ball and chain, and very easily her innocence becomes stupidity; her chastity, frigidity; her nurture, suffocation; her loyalty, imprisonment; her beauty, vanity; her earthiness, carnality; her children, obligation. The Playmate becomes Eve, the Traitor of the Garden, she who is trouble—and contempt mushrooms into hatred.

> *And I have found a woman more bitter than death, who is the hunter's snare, and her heart is a net, and her hands are bonds. . . .*
>
> *More bitter than death, again, because that is natural and destroys only the body; but the sin which arose from woman destroys the soul . . . bodily death is an open and terrible enemy, but woman is a wheedling and secret enemy.*[21]

This serviceability factor in women's role manifests more clearly than all the rest—including the images that allege to portray her—that under patriarchy women's lives are meant to be lived not for ourselves, but for men's needs, and our cultural images are defined by that fact. The major factor in the flip from good to bad (that is, serviceable to not serviceable) is the matter of intrusiveness into male affairs; it has to do with women's self-assertion, self-direction, and will. It is important to have Mary; it is fun to have playmates—just so long as neither gets in the way. When a woman moves toward her own needs, gets "pushy," or stands in the way of *his* wishes, Mary becomes the Ball and Chain (alias the Wif'nkids), and the Playmate becomes the Bitch.

As you look at the following chart, remember that any or all of these images may be expected from any one woman, sometimes at the same time.

Variations on the Theme: Ethnic Overlay

Because the men who make up and direct the patriarchy in which we live are mostly white, Christian, and middle class, it is not surprising that the primary models of womanhood in our society are markedly WASP. Across racial, ethnic, and class lines, one composite image prevails. The fragile, pale-skinned Madonna and the saucily tanned Playmate with flowing blond hair are clearly white, Christian images not even marginally attainable for the very large segment of the female population comprising members of racial or ethnic subgroups. Yet, viable or not, these images continue to function as models, held up to us either as ideals we must strain to copy in whatever meager way possible or as evidence of our inferiority.

BASIC FEMALE STEREOTYPES

	Nonsexual	Sexual
	The Virgin Mary/Mother-Wife:	*The Playmate/Lover:*
Serviceable	chaste, pure, innocent, good proper-looking, conservative, matronly nurturing, selfless, loving, gentle, "mother of his children" submissive, pliable, receptive compromising, tactful, loyal fragile, needful, dependent feeling, nonrational, aesthetic, spiritual understanding, supportive	sensuous, sexually wise, experienced sexy, "built," stylish satisfying, eager, earthy, mysterious, slightly dangerous sexually receptive, agreeable, "game" challenging, exciting independent, carefree, "laid back" bright, fun-loving, playful, carnal responsive, ego-building
	The Old Ball and Chain/Wif' nkids:	*Eve/The Witch-Bitch Temptress:*
Nonserviceable	frigid, sexually uninteresting frumpy or slatternly cloying, suffocating, obligating incapable of decision, changeable, scatterbrained dumb, passive nagging, shrewish, harping helpless, burdensome overemotional, irrational, unreasonable shrewd, manipulative, sneaky	promiscuous, bad coarse, vulgar, trampy tempting, leads one into sin and evil undiscriminating she's "anybody's" bitchy, demanding, selfish; she "asks for it" immoral, makes trouble thoughtless, sinful, evil immodest, unladylike

The WASP quality of the cultural ideal puts minority women—African American, Chicana, Jew, or other—in an even more constricted double bind. Not only are we subject to all the usual contradictions of the bifurcated female image—sexual/nonsexual, good/bad—but we must also deal with a second set of problems compounded and enlarged by our particular ethnic status and circumstances. Oppressed as women, oppressed again as minorities, we are expected to choose between loyalties, between liberations. Caught between minority men's anger at WASP behavior and their unconscious acceptance of WASP ideals, minority women "cannot win for losing": If we strain to meet prevailing standards, we are selling out; if we do not, we are unattractive.

Whichever way we choose to go, however we resolve the cultural loyalties, the issue of our own self-image also arises. The traditional minority woman, as any other, seeks desirability as a mate, seeks the whole range of rewards that comes with being thought "beautiful." Should those standards be even farther removed from her real self than they are from other women, she must either work harder to meet them, risking proportionately deeper self-alienation, or she must accept defeat and wrestle with an intense sense of inferiority.

I vividly remember, as an adolescent Jewish girl of the 1950s, hooked on Marilyn Monroe and Ava Gardner, Debbie Reynolds and Liz Taylor, how I fretted at my unfashionable curly hair, trying tirelessly to straighten its resilient black locks. I remember, too, staring enviously at my *shiksa* girlfriends' straight noses. Anything, I thought, even being old, would be better than having this awful bumpy nose. At nineteen, I had it "fixed."

For the Jewish women who fix their noses, for the African-American women who straighten their hair, for the millions of us who attempt or contemplate "corrections" to body and character that must ever remain inadequate, there must always be a severe sense of either deceit or defeat. The experience is more than self-diminishing; it is crushing.

Although ideals and models rarely vary from one group to another, the pejorative stereotypes, born of particular history and circumstance, admit of a good deal of variation and adjustment. For example, the

Jewish woman, as a woman, may still function as the old ball and chain or the bitch temptress; but she may, as well, be placed within some other disparaging categories, exotic variations on the traditional themes. The young Jewish woman who is ethnically identified and hence esteemed by the Jewish community (and therefore *less* desirable to her male compatriots for the reasons pointed out above) is known as "the nice Jewish girl"—the NJG. Her more chic, less ethnically identified counterpart, the Jewish-American Princess (the JAP) is disparaged precisely because she avoids the social pitfalls of ethnic identification and strives so diligently to meet the WASP model. In either case, the racist, masculist mythology will ultimately turn both women into the Jewish Mother: aggressive, brassy, domineering, suffocating, unwholesomely self-inclined. If she cares too little, she's a shrew; if she cares too much, she's sick. Finally, any Jewish woman may be typed the "pushy Jewish broad," projecting onto her female self all the worst traits of the Jewish stereotype—a classic example of how an image, created by an external dominant group and internalized within the minority group, is applied to women by any men, in and out of the group, and even by women themselves.

Just as entangled in the dilemma of ethnic identification is the African-American woman, bound on one hand by white images of black women and on the other by black images of white women. For men, black or white, who adopt the traditional WASP models, the black woman functions both as a symbol of racial difference and as the usual receptacle of misogyny. Pejorative images of her only intensify the traditional dichotomies.

In the African-American context, the Mother-Nurturer gone wrong is not only the frigid nuisance, the nag of white society, she is also the destroyer of the race—the matriarch of the Moynihan Report, who controls the family, castrates the African-American man by displacing him as head of the household, and thereby contributes to the destruction of his manhood, the family unit, and African-American pride.[22] Rather than being prized and lauded, the strength, resiliency, and independence developed in the African-American woman through centuries of hardship are in true masculist style deflected and turned against her.

These same traits—strength and assertiveness—are the very ones that mark the African-American version of Eve. In this context, Eve is still the Playmate gone awry, only worse. Here we have the Hot Black Bitch, an image obviously constructed by the white overlord, yet at least partially reflected in the African-American community as well. Whereas the white playmate is naughty, her stereotypic black counterpart is depicted as without morals, without limits, sexually voracious, undiscriminating, and hard as nails, her behavior and character placing her completely outside the bounds of chivalry and masculine protection.

Each woman can and should analyze the particular version of the stereotype applicable to her background. This is certain: Whatever the ethnic, racial, and class variations, however the images are adapted and reflected, they all are born of masculist experience to serve masculist needs. They have little to do with women's undistorted natures.

Effects of the Stereotype

The patriarchal images of women—whether sexual or nonsexual, working class or middle class, black or white—have a common denominator. They all say that women as human beings are substandard: less intelligent; less moral; less competent; less able physically, psychologically, and spiritually; small of body, mind, and character; often bad or destructive. The images argue that we have done little in society (besides reproduce) to earn our keep; that we have made only small contribution to culture, high or low, yet always push for more than we deserve. Sometimes cute or adorable, sometimes consoling, but only in a controlled context, we are pleasant baubles to have around. In any other guise, we are a nuisance at best, a disaster at worst.

These and other stereotypical images of women work to destroy us. In their positive aspects, they are impossible to meet; in the negative, they are deprecatory and ugly, flourishing in the minds of women who are forced to live them. Functioning in large part as social norms, they have great power to direct attitudes and behavior among the group stereotyped, as well as in the larger community. The tragedy of the female stereotype is that it impels women not only to appear substandard but also to become substandard; it moves to form us into the loathed monster. If the work of the stereotype be done, we are reduced to the weak, hapless creatures required by social lore, living in the mold, even experiencing ourselves according to the myth.

Limited experience, opportunity, and education, deemed appropriate for beings who must not become "too smart for our own good"; restrictive clothing and play, tailored for our more "alluring" and refined bodies; disapproval for behavior (sports, for example, competition, and assertiveness) that might strengthen body or character; suitors who require subservience and fragility; adolescent girlfriends straining to become "desirable" women; parents prompting us to marriage or marriageability—these and countless other influences combine to make us believe the myth and copy the model.

The model requires that we be pretty, gentle, and kind; we can become pretty, gentle, and kind. The model, however, also requires that we be silly, weak, and incompetent. Are we not required then to become silly, weak, and incompetent? Haven't we sometimes tried? Then, as we work to fit the mold and exhibit the expected traits, we reinforce the stereotype and so perpetuate the cycle and give "truth" to the lie. And if the lie be true, then everything follows. Because women are incompetent and weak, we must be protected, set apart, and given a safe "place," guarded by "our" men. Since we are pretty and evil, unable to get along even with each other, we must be controlled for the good of ourselves and society. We deserve the contempt in which we are held.

Clearly, to live in the shadow of such attitudes is intolerable, even when they are hidden by chivalry or mystification, even when they are temporarily suspended for our good behavior. Life and personhood defined within such constraints is necessarily distorted, out of phase with even the barest elements of emotional and physical health, spiritual transcendence, and joy. But the misery brought on by these ideals extends beyond the psychological and spiritual elements of life. Because we are speaking here only about images, we have not yet raised the issue of more concrete oppression: poverty and physical abuse.

In the next chapter we examine feminist responses to these images, feminist insights into the nature and effects of patriarchal stereotypes, the struggles women experience in freeing ourselves, and the alternative, woman-identified images we are forging in the struggle.

Notes

1. Mary Daly, *Beyond God the Father* (Boston: Beacon Press, 1973), p. 8.

2. See, for example, Mary R. Beard, *Woman as Force in History* (New York: Macmillan, 1946). Some contemporary feminists make this argument from a cross-cultural perspective, pointing out that "power" is a highly complex notion that varies within and across social groups.

3. Susan Brownmiller, *Femininity* (New York: Fawcett Columbine, 1984), pp. 13–14.

4. Sally Kempton's terminology in "Cutting Loose," *Esquire*, July 1970, p. 57.

5. The treatment of "otherness" relative to women is most typically associated with the French existentialist philosopher Simone de Beauvoir, who developed the concept in her landmark work, *The Second Sex*, ed. and trans. H. M. Parshley (New York: Knopf, 1953).

6. There is a school of feminists who question the thesis of the universal subordination of women within patriarchal culture. They contend that women's power in some societies is different but real; hence, *subordination* is a term not universally applicable. I am not of this opinion.

7. For an interesting analysis of the meaning of the relation of carnality and femaleness for men, see Beauvoir, *Second Sex*, chap. 9.

8. Whether there are oedipal components to male fear of sex I hesitate to conjecture, although others have. Certainly it ought to be considered but in another, wider study of this problem.

9. Pauline Réage, *Story of O*, trans. Sabine d'Estre (New York: Grove Press, 1965).

10. Andrea Dworkin, *Woman Hating* (New York: E. P. Dutton, 1974), pp. 55–63.

11. Andre Pieyre de Mandiargues, "A Note on *Story of O*," in Réage, *Story of O*, p. xvi.

12. It is a sport among the readers and commentators of *Story of O* to guess at the sex of its author (who uses a pen name). Actually, it matters little whether it was written by a man or a woman; the book is the expression of one fully steeped in the perspectives and values of masculism, and, as I have pointed out, these are not gender-specific.

13. Jean Paulhan, "Happiness in Slavery," in Réage, *Story of O*, p. xxv.

14. Ibid., p. xxviii.

15. Mandiargues, "A Note," ibid., p. vii.

16. The idea that victimization per se is an essential principle of female excellence in patriarchy appeared in Dworkin's *Woman Hating*.

17. Some of this discussion appeared in Sheila Ruth, "Sexism, Patriarchy, and Feminism: Toward an Understanding of Terms" (Paper delivered at Pioneers for Century III Conference, Cincinnati, Ohio, March 1976).

18. "Anatomy is destiny," argued Sigmund Freud. For the female, he contended, the body, its makeup and potential, determines personality and character in a far more definitive way than is true for men.

19. Karl Stern, *The Flight from Woman* (New York: Farrar, Straus & Giroux, 1964), pp. 21–22.

20. Wolfgang Lederer, *The Fear of Women* (New York: Grune & Stratton, 1968), pp. 269–70. Note that Beauvoir argued just the opposite in *The Second Sex,* that one is "not born, but becomes a woman."

21. K. Kramer and J. Sprenger, *Malleus Maleficarum,* trans. M. Summers (London: Arrow Books, 1971), p. 112.

22. Daniel Patrick Moynihan, *The Negro Family: The Case for National Action* (U.S. Department of Labor, Office of Policy Planning and Research, 1965). Moynihan wrote this analysis of African-American needs and problems for the president of the United States, thereby launching many of the economic programs of the sixties. Moynihan argued that "In essence, the Negro community has been forced into a matriarchal structure, which . . . imposes a crushing burden on the Negro male, and in consequence on a great many Negro women as well" (p. 29).

Antifeminism

Andrea Dworkin

Active in the women's movement for more than two decades, Andrea Dworkin has been a speaker, activist, and author of many powerful books including Mercy *(1991),* Letters from a War Zone *(1989),* Pornography: Men Possessing Women *(1987),* Ice and Fire: A Novel *(1987),* Intercourse *(1987),* Right-Wing Women *(1983),* Our Blood: Prophecies and Discourses on Sexual Politics *(1976), and* Woman-Hating *(1974).*

As a speaker or a writer, Dworkin never minces words. In the following piece she argues that because feminism is the philosophy of liberation for women, antifeminism, in any guise, is an expression of misogyny, the hatred of women. Antifeminism supports the present abusive gender system as natural and desirable: it opposes women's freedom and it denigrates our selfhood.

From *Right-Wing Women* (New York: Perigree, 1983). Reprinted by permission of Andrea Dworkin.

FEMINISM IS A MUCH-HATED POLITICAL PHILOSOPHY. This is true all along the male-defined, recognizable political spectrum from far Right to far Left. Feminism is hated because women are hated. Antifeminism is a direct expression of misogyny; it is the political defense of woman hating. This is because feminism is the liberation movement of women. Antifeminism, in any of its political colorations, holds that the social and sexual condition of women essentially (one way or another) embodies the nature of women, that the way women are treated in sex and in society is congruent with what women are, that the fundamental relationship between men and women—in sex, in reproduction, in social hierarchy—is both necessary and inevitable. Antifeminism defends the conviction that the male abuse of women, especially in sex, has an implicit logic, one that no program of social justice can or should eliminate; that because the male use of women originates in the distinct and opposite natures of each which converge in what is called "sex," women are not abused when used as women—but merely used for what they are by men as men. It is admitted that there are excesses of male sadism—committed by deranged individuals, for instance—but in general the massive degradation of women is not seen to violate the nature of women as such. For instance, a man's nature would be violated if anyone forcibly penetrated his body. A women's nature is not violated by the same event, even though she may have been hurt. A man's nature would not provoke anyone to forcibly penetrate his body. A woman's nature does provoke such penetration—and even injury is no proof that she did not want the penetration or even the injury itself, since it is her nature as a woman to desire being forcibly penetrated and forcibly hurt. Conservatively estimated, in the United States a woman is raped every three minutes, and in each and every rape the woman's nature is at issue first and foremost, not the man's act. Certainly there is no social or legal recognition that rape is an act of political terrorism.

Antifeminism can accommodate reform: a recognition that some forms of discrimination against women are unfair to women or that some kinds of injustice to women are not warranted (or entirely warranted) by the nature of women. But underneath the apparent civility, there are facile, arrogant assumptions: that the remedies are easy, the problems frivolous; that the harm done to women is not substantial nor is it significant in any real way; and that the subordination of women to men is not in and of itself an egregious wrong. This assessment is maintained in the face of proved atrocities and the obvious intractability of the oppression.

Antifeminism is always an expression of hating women: it is way past time to say so, to make the equation, to insist on its truth. Antifeminism throws women to the wolves; it says "later" or "never" to those suffering cruel and systematic deprivations of liberty; it tells women that when their lives are at stake, there is no urgency toward either justice or decency; it scolds women for wanting freedom. It is right to see woman hating, sex hatred, passionate contempt, in every effort to subvert or stop an improvement in the status of women on any front, whether radical or reform. It is right to see contempt for women in any effort to subvert or stop any move on the part of women toward economic or sexual independence, toward civil or legal equality, toward self-determination. Antifeminism is the politics of contempt for women as a class. This is true when the antifeminism is expressed in opposition to the Equal Rights Amendment or to the right to abortion on demand or to procedures against sexual harassment or to shelters for battered women or to reforms in rape laws. This is true whether the opposition is from the Heritage Foundation, the Moral Majority, the Eagle Forum, the American Civil Liberties Union, the Communist Party, the Democrats, or the Republicans. The same antifeminist contempt for women is expressed in resistance to affirmative action or in defenses of pornography or in the acceptance of prostitution as an institution of female sex labor. If one sees that women are being systematically exploited and abused, then the defense of anything, the acceptance of anything, that promotes or continues that exploitation or abuse expresses a hatred of women, a contempt for their freedom and dignity; and an effort to impede legislative, social, or economic initiatives that would improve the status of women, however radical or reformist those measures are, is an expression of that same contempt. One simply cannot be both for and against the exploitation of women: for it when it brings pleasure, against it in the abstract; for it when it brings profit, against it in principle; for it when no one is looking, against it when someone who might notice is around. If one sees how exploited women are—the systematic nature of the exploitation, the sexual base of the exploitation—then there is no political or ethical justification for doing one whit less than everything—using every resource—to stop that exploitation. Antifeminism has been the cover for outright bigotry and it has been the vehicle of outright bigotry. Antifeminism has been a credible cover and an effective vehicle because the hatred of women is not politically anathema on either the Right or the Left. Antifeminism is manifest wherever the subordination of women is actively perpetuated or enhanced or defended or passively accepted, because the devaluation of women is implicit in all these stances. Woman hating and antifeminism, however aggressive or restrained the expression, are empirical synonyms, inseparable, often indistinguishable, often interchangeable; and any acceptance of the exploitation of women in any area, for any reason, in any style, is both, means both, and promotes both.

. . .

To achieve a single standard of human freedom and one absolute standard of human dignity, the sex-class system has to be dismembered. The reason is pragmatic, not philosophical: nothing less will work. However much everyone wants to do less, less will not free women. Liberal men and women ask, Why can't we just be ourselves, all human beings, begin now and not dwell in past injustices, wouldn't that subvert the sex-class system, change it from the inside out? The answer is no. The sex-class system has a structure; it has deep roots in religion and culture; it is fundamental to the economy; sexuality is its creature; to be "just human beings" in it, women have to hide what happens to them as women because they are women—happenings like forced sex and forced reproduction, happenings that continue as long as the sex-class system operates. The liberation of women requires facing the real condition of women in order to change it. "We're all just people" is a stance that prohibits recognition of the systematic cruelties visited on women because of sex oppression.

Feminism as a liberation movement, then, demands a revolutionary single standard of what humans have a right to, and also demands that the current sexual bifurcation of rights never be let out of sight. Antifeminism does the opposite: it insists that there is a double standard of what humans have a right to—a male standard and a female standard; and it insists at the same time that we are all just human beings, right now, as things stand, within this sex-class system, so that no special attention should be paid to social phenomena on account of sex. With respect to rape, for instance, the feminist starts out with a single standard of freedom and dignity: everyone, women as well as men, should have a right to the integrity of their own body. Feminists then focus on and analyze the sex-class reality of rape: men rape, women are raped; even in those statistically rare cases where boys or men are raped, men are the rapists. Antifeminists start out with a double standard: men conquer, possess, dominate, men take women; women are conquered, possessed, dominated, and taken. Antifeminists then insist that rape is a crime like any other, like mugging or homicide or burglary: they deny its sex-specific, sex-class nature and the political meaning undeniably implicit in the sexual construction of the crime. Feminists are accused of denying the common humanity of men and women because feminists refuse to fudge on the sex issue of who does what to whom, how often, and why. Antifeminists refuse to acknowledge that the sex-class system repudiates the humanity of women by keeping women systematically subject to exploitation and violence as a condition of sex. In analyzing the sex-class system, feminists are accused of inventing or perpetuating it. Calling attention to it, we are told, insults women by suggesting that they are victims (stupid enough to allow themselves to be victimized). Feminists are accused of being the agents of degradation by postulating that such degradation exists. This is a little like considering abolitionists responsible for slavery, but all is fair when love is war. In ignoring the political significance of the sex-class system except to defend it when it is under attack, antifeminists suggest that "we're all in this together," all us human beings, different-but-together, a formulation that depends on lack of clarity for its persuasiveness. Indisputably, we're all in rape together, some of us to great disadvantage. Feminism especially requires a rigorous analysis of sex class, one that is ongoing, stubborn, persistent, unsentimental, disciplined, not placated by fatuous invocations of a common humanity that in fact the sex-class system itself suppresses. The sex-class system cannot be undone when those whom it exploits and humiliates are unable to face it for what it is, for what it takes from them, for what it does to them. Feminism requires precisely what misogyny destroys in women: unimpeachable bravery in confronting male power. Despite the impossibility of it, there is such bravery: there are such women, in some periods millions upon millions of them. If male supremacy survives every effort of women to overthrow it, it will not be because of biology or God; nor will it be because of the force and power of men per se. It will be because the will to liberation was contaminated, undermined, rendered ineffectual and meaningless, by antifeminism: by specious concepts of equality based on an evasion of what the sex-class system really is. The refusal to recognize the intrinsic despotism of the sex-class system means that that despotism is inevitably incorporated into reform models of that same system: in this, antifeminism triumphs over the will to liberation. The refusal to recognize the unique abuses inherent in sex labor (treating sex labor as if it were sex-neutral, as if it were not intrinsically part of sex oppression and inseparable from it) is a function of antifeminism; the acceptance of sex labor as appropriate labor for women marks the triumph of antifeminism over the will to liberation. The sentimental acceptance of a double standard of human rights, responsibilities, and freedom is also the triumph of antifeminism over the will to liberation; no sexual dichotomy is compatible with real liberation. And, most important, the refusal to demand (with no compromise being possible) one absolute standard of human dignity is the greatest triumph of antifeminism over the will to liberation. Without that one absolute standard, liberation is mush; feminism is frivolous and utterly self-indulgent. Without that one absolute standard as the keystone of revolutionary justice, feminism has no claim to being a liberation movement; it has no revolutionary stance, goal, or potential; it has no basis for a radical reconstruction of society; it has no criteria for action or organization; it has no moral necessity; it has no inescapable claim on the conscience of "mankind"; it has no philosophical seriousness; it has no authentic stature as a human-rights movement; it has nothing to teach. Also, without that one absolute standard, feminism has no chance whatsoever of actually liberating women or destroying the sex-class system. Refusing to base itself on a principle of universal human dignity, or compromising, retreating from that principle, feminism becomes that which exists to stop it: anti-feminism. No liberation movement can accept the degradation of those whom it seeks to liberate by accepting a different definition of dignity for them and stay a movement for their freedom at the same time. (Apologists for pornography: take note.) A universal standard of human dignity is the only principle that completely repudiates sex-class exploitation and also propels all of us into a future where the fundamental political question is the quality of life for all human beings. Are women being subordinated to men? There is insufficient dignity in that. Are men being prostituted too? What is human dignity?

Two elements constitute the discipline of feminism: political, ideological, and strategic confrontation with the sex-class system—with sex hierarchy and sex segregation—and a single standard of human dignity. Abandon either element and the sex-class system is unbreachable, indestructible; feminism loses its rigor, the toughness of its visionary heart; women get swallowed up not only by misogyny but also by antifeminism—facile excuses for exploiting women, metaphysical justifications for abusing women, and shoddy apologies for ignoring the political imperatives of women.

One other discipline is essential both to the practice of feminism and to its theoretical integrity: the firm, unsentimental, continuous recognition that women are a class having a common condition. This is not some psychological process of identification with women because women are wonderful; nor is it the insupportable assertion that there are no substantive, treacherous differences among women. This is not a liberal mandate to ignore what is cruel, despicable, or stupid in women, nor is it a mandate to ignore dangerous political ideas or allegiances of women. This does not mean women first, women best, women only. It does mean that the fate of every individual woman—no matter what her politics, character, values, qualities—is tied to the fate of all women whether she likes it or not. On one level, it means that every woman's fate is tied to the fate of women she dislikes personally. On another level, it means that every woman's fate is tied to the fate of women whom she politically and morally abhors. For instance, it means that rape jeopardizes communist and fascist women, liberal, conservative, Democratic, or Republican women, racist women and black women, Nazi women and Jewish women, homophobic women and homosexual women. The crimes committed against women because they are women articulate the condition of women. The eradication of these crimes, the transformation of the condition of women, is the purpose of feminism: which means that feminism requires a most rigorous definition of what those crimes are so as to determine what that condition is. This definition cannot be compromised by a selective representation of the sex class based on sentimentality or wishful thinking. This definition cannot exclude prudes or sluts or dykes or mothers or virgins because one does not want to be associated with them. To be a feminist means recognizing that one is associated with all women not as an act of choice but as a matter of fact. The sex-class system creates the fact. When that system is broken, there will be no such fact. Feminists do not create this common condition by making alliances: feminists recognize this common condition because it exists as an intrinsic part of sex oppression. The fundamental knowledge that women are a class having a common condition—that the fate of one woman is tied substantively to the fate of all women—toughens feminist theory and practice. That fundamental knowledge is an almost unbearable test of seriousness. There is no real feminism that does not have at its heart the tempering discipline of sex-class consciousness: knowing that women share a common condition as a class, like it or not.

What is that common condition? Subordinate to men, sexually colonized in a sexual system of dominance and submission, denied rights on the basis of sex, historically chattel, generally considered biologically inferior, confined to sex and reproduction: this is the general description of the social environment in which all women live.

Whether Woman Should Have Been Made in the First Production of Things

St. Thomas Aquinas

St. Thomas Aquinas (1227–1274), medieval philosopher and theologian, was named the official philosophic authority of the Catholic Church by Pope Leo XIII in 1879. His reasoning forms the basis of Catholic doctrine and pervades much of Protestant theology as well. As such, it has exerted tremendous influence on Western culture and hence on women's lives. Through the church, Aquinas's ideas continue in importance today, having their effect on arguments regarding contraception and abortion, women's place in the priesthood, women's role in the family, women's role in the economy, and so on.

In the following discussion, Aquinas asks whether one could say that because women are defective and sinful (more so than men) they ought not to have been created in the first innocent beginning of things by an all-perfect God. Certainly, women should have been created, he replies, for nature decrees that men must have "helpers," not in cultural works, but in reproduction. That is, women are necessary as biological assistants.

*Aquinas was known for his reconciliation of Christian doctrine with the philosophy of Aristotle, increasingly important in the thirteenth century. The philosopher he refers to in his opening remarks is Aristotle, who theorized that "females are weaker and colder in nature, and we must look upon the female character as being a sort of natural deficiency" (*De Generatione Animalium*, IV, 6, 775a 15). Aristotle's analysis of woman as "misbegotten male" is one of a whole genre of theories, popular through the centuries, treating womanhood as a partial or defective instance of manhood.*

St. Thomas Aquinas. *Summa Theologicae.*

Question XCII
The Production of Woman

First Article
Whether Woman Should Have Been Made in the First Production of Things?

We proceed thus to the First Article:—

Objection 1. It would seem that woman should not have been made in the first production of things. For the Philosopher says that the *female is a misbegotten male.*[1] But nothing misbegotten or defective should have been in the first production of things. Therefore woman should not have been made at that first production.

Obj. 2. Further, subjection and limitation were a result of sin, for to the woman was it said after sin (*Gen.* iii. 16): *Thou shalt be under the man's power;* and Gregory says that, *Where there is no sin, there is no inequality.*[2] But woman is naturally of less strength and dignity than man, *for the agent is always more honorable than the patient,* as Augustine says.[3] Therefore woman should not have been made in the first production of things before sin.

Obj. 3. Further, occasions of sin should be cut off. But God foresaw that woman would be an occasion of sin to man. Therefore He should not have made woman.

On the contrary, It is written (*Gen.* ii. 18): *It is not good for man to be alone; let us make him a helper like to himself.*

I answer that, It was necessary for woman to be made, as the Scripture says, as a *helper* to man; not, indeed, as a helpmate in other works, as some say,[4] since man can be more efficiently helped by another man in other works; but as a helper in the work of generation. This can be made clear if we observe the mode of generation carried out in various living things. Some living things do not possess in themselves the power of generation, but are generated by an agent of another species; and such are those plants and animals which are generated, without seed, from suitable matter through the active power of the heavenly bodies. Others possess the active and passive generative power together, as we see in plants which are generated from seed. For the noblest vital function in plants is generation, and so we observe that in these the active power of generation invariably accompanies the passive power. Among perfect animals, the active power of generation belongs to the male sex, and the passive power to the female. And as among animals there is a vital operation nobler than generation, to which their life is principally directed, so it happens that the male sex is not found in continual union with the female in perfect animals, but only at the time of coition; so that we may consider that by coition the male and female are one, as in plants they are always united, even though in some cases one of them preponderates, and in some the other. But man is further ordered to a still nobler work of life, and that is intellectual operation. Therefore there was greater reason for the distinction of these two powers in man; so that the female should be produced separately from the male, and yet that they should be carnally united for generation. Therefore directly after the formation of woman, it was said: *And they shall be two in one flesh* (*Gen.* ii. 24).

Reply Obj. 1. As regards the individual nature, woman is defective and misbegotten, for the active power in the male seed tends to the production of a perfect likeness according to the masculine sex; while the production of woman comes from defect in the active power, or from some material indisposition, or even from some external influence, such as that of a south wind, which is moist, as the Philosopher observes.[5] On the other hand, as regards universal human nature, woman is not misbegotten, but is included in nature's intention as directed to the work of generation. Now the universal intention of nature depends on God, Who is the universal Author of nature. Therefore, in producing nature, God formed not only the male but also the female.

Reply Obj. 2. Subjection is twofold. One is servile, by virtue of which a superior makes use of a subject for his own benefit; and this kind of subjection began after sin. There is another kind of subjection, which is called economic or civil, whereby the superior makes use of his subjects for their own benefit and good; and this kind of subjection existed even before sin. For the good of order would have been wanting in the human family if some were not governed by others wiser than themselves. So by such a kind of subjection woman is naturally subject to man, because in man the discernment of reason predominates. Nor is inequality among men excluded by the state of innocence, as we shall prove.[6]

Reply Obj. 3. If God had deprived the world of all those things which proved an occasion of sin, the universe would have been imperfect. Nor was it fitting for the common good to be destroyed in order that individual evil might be avoided; especially as God is so powerful that He can direct any evil to a good end.

Notes

1. *De Gener. Anim.*, II, 3 (737a 27).
2. *Moral.*, XXI, 15 (PL 76, 203).
3. *De Genesi ad Litt.*, XII, 16 (PL 34, 467).
4. Anonymously reported by St. Augustine, *De Genesi ad Litt.*, IX, 3 (PL 34, 395).
5. Aristotle, *De Gener. Anim.*, IV, 2 (766b 33).
6. Q.96, a.3.

Femininity

Sigmund Freud

The Austrian psychologist Sigmund Freud (1856–1939) was one of the earliest theorists and probably the most influential in the areas of clinical psychology and psychoanalysis. Although extraordinarily creative and insightful as ground-breaker in a new dimension, his work has been severely criticized for its ethnocentricity, its lack of objective verification (or perhaps even verifiability), and more recently, its thorough sexism. Freud's theories on the nature of women's psychology include the following themes: (1) that for women, anatomy is destiny—more so than for men, women's lives and personalities are prescribed by their biological and reproductive nature; (2) that women are not only fundamentally different from men in character but inferior to them physically (in sexual capacity and equipment), emotionally (in stability and control), and ethically (in the sense of honesty and justice).

The essay reprinted here (written about 1933) is Freud's most famous treatise on femininity. It was at one time (until quite recently—into the forties or fifties) the official word on female psychology. Although Freud and this analysis have been challenged roundly from all quarters, its themes are still highly influential and pervade much of both contemporary clinical and popular thought.

LADIES AND GENTLEMEN,[1]—ALL THE WHILE I AM preparing to talk to you I am struggling with an internal difficulty. I feel uncertain, so to speak, of the extent of my licence. It is true that in the course of fifteen years of work psycho-analysis has changed and grown richer; but, in spite of that, an introduction to psycho-analysis might have been left without alteration or supplement. It is constantly in my mind that these lectures are without a *raison d'être.* For analysts I am saying too little and nothing at all that is new; but for you I am saying too much and saying things which you are not equipped to understand and which are not in your province. I have looked around for excuses and I have tried to justify each separate lecture on different grounds. The first one, on the theory of dreams, was supposed to put you back again at one blow into the analytic atmosphere and to show you how durable our views have turned out to be. I was led on to the second one, which followed the paths from dreams to what is called occultism, by the opportunity of speaking my mind without constraint on a department of work in which prejudiced expectations are fighting to-day against passionate resistances, and I could hope that your judgement, educated to tolerance on the example of psycho-analysis, would not refuse to accompany me on the excursion. The third lecture, on the dissection of the personality, certainly made the hardest demands upon you with its unfamiliar subject-matter; but it was impossible for me to keep this first beginning of an ego-psychology back from you, and if we had possessed it fifteen years ago I should have had to mention it to you then. My last lecture, finally, which you were probably able to follow only by great exertions, brought forward necessary corrections—fresh attempts at solving the most important conundrums; and my introduction would have been leading you astray if I had been silent about them. As you see, when one starts making excuses it turns out in the end that it was all inevitable, all the work of destiny. I submit to it, and I beg you to do the same.

To-day's lecture, too, should have no place in an introduction; but it may serve to give you an example of a detailed piece of analytic work, and I can say two things to recommend it. It brings forward nothing but observed facts, almost without any speculative additions, and it deals with a subject which has a claim on your interest second almost to no other. Throughout history people have knocked their heads against the riddle of the nature of femininity—

> Häupter in Hieroglyphenmützen,
> Häupter in Turban und schwarzem Barett,
> Perückenhäupter und tausend andre
> Arme, schwitzende Menschenhäupter. . . .[2]

Nor will *you* have escaped worrying over this problem—those of you who are men; to those of you who are women this will not apply—you are yourselves the problem. When you meet a human being, the first distinction you make is 'male or female?' and you are accustomed to make the distinction with unhesitating certainty. Anatomical science shares your certainty at one point and not much further. The male sexual product, the spermatozoon, and its vehicle are male; the ovum and the organism that harbours it are female. In both sexes organs have been formed which serve exclusively for the sexual functions; they were probably developed from the same [innate] disposition into two different forms. Besides this, in both sexes the other organs, the bodily shapes and tissues, show the influence of the individual's sex, but this is inconstant and its amount variable; these are what are known as the secondary sexual characters. Science next tells you something that runs counter to your expectations and is probably calculated to confuse your feelings. It draws your attention to the fact that portions of the male sexual apparatus also appear in women's bodies, though in an atrophied state, and vice versa in the alternative case. It regards their occurrence as indications of *bisexuality*,[3] as though an individual is not a man or a woman but always both—merely a certain amount more the one than the other. You will then be asked to make yourselves familiar with the idea that the proportion in which masculine and feminine are mixed in an individual is subject to quite considerable fluctuations. Since, however, apart from the very rarest cases, only one kind of sexual product—ova or semen—is nevertheless present in one person, you are bound to have doubts as to the decisive significance of those elements and must conclude that what constitutes masculinity or femininity is an unknown characteristic which anatomy cannot lay hold of.

Can psychology do so perhaps? We are accustomed to employ 'masculine' and 'feminine' as mental qualities as well, and have in the same way transferred the notion of bisexuality to mental life. Thus we speak of a person, whether male or female, as behaving in a masculine way in one connection and in a feminine way in another. But you will soon perceive that this is only giving way to anatomy or to convention. You cannot give the concepts of 'masculine' and 'feminine' *any* new connotation. The distinction is not a psychological one; when you say 'masculine', you usually mean 'active', and when you say 'feminine', you usually mean 'passive'. Now it is true that a relation of the kind exists. The male sex-cell is actively mobile and searches out the female one, and the latter, the ovum, is immobile and waits passively. This behaviour of the elementary sexual organisms is indeed a model for the conduct of sexual individuals during intercourse. The male pursues the female for the purpose of sexual union, seizes hold of her and penetrates into her. But by this you have precisely reduced the characteristic of masculinity to the factor of aggressiveness so far as psychology is concerned. You may well doubt whether you have gained any real advantage from this when you reflect that in some classes of animals the females are the stronger and more aggressive and the male is active only in the single act of sexual union. This is so, for instance, with the spiders. Even the functions of rearing and caring for the young, which strike us as feminine *par excellence,* are not invariably attached to the female sex in animals. In quite high species we find that the sexes share the task of caring for the young between them or even that the male alone devotes himself to it. Even in the sphere of human sexual life you soon see how inadequate it is to make masculine behaviour coincide with activity and feminine with passivity. A mother is active in every sense towards her child; the act of lactation itself may equally be described as the mother suckling the baby or as her being sucked by it. The further you go from the narrow sexual sphere the more obvious will the 'error of superimposition'[4] become. Women can display great activity in various directions, men are not able to live in company with their own kind unless they develop a large amount of passive adaptability. If you now tell me that these facts go to prove precisely that both men and women are bisexual in the psychological sense, I shall conclude that you have decided in your own minds to make 'active' coincide with 'masculine' and 'passive' with 'feminine'. But I advise you against it. It seems to me to serve no useful purpose and adds nothing to our knowledge.[5]

One might consider characterizing femininity psychologically as giving preference to passive aims. This is not, of course, the same thing as passivity; to achieve a passive aim may call for a large amount of activity. It is perhaps the case that in a woman, on the basis of her share in the sexual function, a preference for passive behaviour and passive aims is carried over into her life to a greater or lesser extent, in proportion to the limits, restricted or far-reaching, within which her sexual life thus serves as a model. But we must beware in this of underestimating the influence of social customs, which similarly force women into passive situations. All this is still far from being cleared up. There is one particularly constant relation between femininity and instinctual life which we do not want to overlook. The suppression of women's aggressiveness which is prescribed for them constitutionally and imposed on them socially favours the development of powerful masochistic impulses, which succeed, as we know, in binding erotically the destructive trends which have been diverted inwards. Thus masochism, as people say, is truly feminine. But if, as happens so often, you meet with masochism in men, what is left to you but to say that these men exhibit very plain feminine traits?

And now you are already prepared to hear that psychology too is unable to solve the riddle of femininity. The explanation must no doubt come from elsewhere, and cannot come till we have learnt how in general the differentiation of living organisms into two sexes came about. We know nothing about it, yet the existence of two sexes is a most striking characteristic of organic life which distinguishes it sharply from inanimate nature. However, we find enough to study in those human individuals who, through the possession of female genitals, are characterized as manifestly or predominantly feminine. In conformity with its peculiar nature, psycho-analysis does not try to describe what a woman is—that would be a task it could scarcely perform—but sets about enquiring how she comes into being, how a woman develops out of a child with a bisexual disposition. In recent times we have begun to learn a little about this, thanks to the circumstance that several of our excellent women colleagues in analysis have begun to work at the question. The discussion of this has gained special attractiveness from the distinction between the sexes. For the ladies, whenever some comparison seemed to turn out unfavourable to their sex, were able to utter a suspicion that we, the male analysts, had been unable to overcome certain deeply-rooted prejudices against what was feminine, and that this was being paid for in the partiality of our researches. We, on the other hand, standing on the ground of bisexuality, had no difficulty in avoiding impoliteness. We had only to say: 'This doesn't apply to *you*. You're the exception; on this point you're more masculine than feminine.'

We approach the investigation of the sexual development of women with two expectations. The first is that here once more the constitution will not adapt itself to its function without a struggle. The second is that the decisive turning-points will already have been prepared for or completed before puberty. Both expectations are promptly confirmed. Furthermore, a comparison with what happens with boys tells us that the development of a little girl into a normal woman is more difficult and more complicated, since it includes two extra tasks, to which there is nothing corresponding in the development of a man. Let us follow the parallel lines from their beginning. Undoubtedly the material is different to start with in boys and girls: it did not need psycho-analysis to establish that. The difference in the structure of the genitals is accompanied by other bodily differences which are too well known to call for mention. Differences emerge too in the instinctual disposition which give a glimpse of the later nature of women. A little girl is as a rule less aggressive, defiant and self-sufficient; she seems to have a greater need for being shown affection and on that account to be more dependent and pliant. It is probably only as a result of this pliancy that she can be taught more easily and quicker to control her excretions: urine and faeces are the first gifts that children make to those who look after them, and controlling them is the first concession to which the instinctual life of children can be induced. One gets an impression, too, that little girls are more intelligent and livelier than boys of the same age; they go out more to meet the external world and at the same time form stronger object-cathexes. I cannot say whether this lead in development has been confirmed by exact observations, but in any case there is no question that girls cannot be described as intellectually backward. These sexual differences are not, however, of great consequence: they can be outweighed by individual variations. For our immediate purposes they can be disregarded.

Both sexes seem to pass through the early phases of libidinal development in the same manner. It might have been expected that in girls there would already have been some lag in aggressiveness in the sadistic-anal phase, but such is not the case. Analysis of children's play has shown our women analysts that the aggressive impulses of little girls leave nothing to be desired in the way of abundance and violence. With their entry into the phallic phase the differences between the sexes are completely eclipsed by their agreements. We are now obliged to recognize that the little girl is a little man. In boys, as we know, this phase is marked by the fact that they have learnt how to derive pleasurable sensations from their small penis and connect its excited state with their ideas of sexual intercourse. Little girls do the same thing with their still smaller clitoris. It seems that with them all their masturbatory acts are carried out on this penis-equivalent, and that the truly feminine vagina is still undiscovered by both sexes. It is true that there are a few isolated reports of early vaginal sensations as well, but it could not be easy to distinguish these from sensations in the anus or vestibulum; in any case they cannot play a great part. We are entitled to keep to our view that in the phallic phase of girls the clitoris is the leading erotogenic zone. But it is not, of course, going to remain so. With the change to femininity the clitoris should wholly or in part hand over its sensitivity, and at the same time its importance, to the vagina. This would be one of the two tasks which a woman has to perform in the course of her development, whereas the more fortunate man has only to continue at the time of his sexual maturity the activity that he has previously carried out at the period of the early efflorescence of his sexuality.

We shall return to the part played by the clitoris; let us now turn to the second task with which a girl's development is burdened. A boy's mother is the first object of his love, and she remains so too during the formation of his Oedipus complex and, in essence, all through his life. For a girl too her first object must be her mother (and the figures of wet-nurses and foster-mothers that merge into her). The first object-cathexes occur in attachment to the satisfaction of the major and simple vital needs,[6] and the circumstances of the care of children are the same for both sexes. But in the Oedipus situation the girl's father has become her love-object, and we expect that in the normal course of development she will find her way from this paternal object to her final choice of an object. In the course of time, therefore, a girl has to change her erotogenic zone and her object—both of which a boy retains. The question then arises of how this happens: in particular, how does a girl pass from her mother to an attachment to her father? or, in other words, how does she pass from her masculine phase to the feminine one to which she is biologically destined?

It would be a solution of ideal simplicity if we could suppose that from a particular age onwards the elementary influence of the mutual attraction between the sexes makes itself felt and impels the small woman towards men, while the same law allows the boy to continue with his mother. We might suppose in addition that in this the children are following the pointer given them by the sexual preference of their parents. But we are not going to find things so easy; we scarcely know whether we are to believe seriously in the power of which poets talk so much and with such enthusiasm but which cannot be further dissected analytically. We have found an answer of quite another sort by means of laborious investigations, the material for which at least was easy to arrive at. For you must know that the number of women who remain till a late age tenderly dependent on a paternal object, or indeed on their real father, is very great. We have established some surprising facts about these women with an intense attachment of long duration to their father. We knew, of course, that there had been a preliminary stage of attachment to the mother, but we did not know that it could be so rich in content and so long-lasting, and could leave behind so many opportunities for fixations and dispositions. During this time the girl's father is only a troublesome rival; in some cases the attachment to her mother lasts beyond the fourth year of life. Almost everything that we find later in her relation to her father was already present in this earlier attachment and has been transferred subsequently on to her father. In short, we get an impression that we cannot understand women unless we appreciate this phase of their pre-Oedipus attachment to their mother.

We shall be glad, then, to know the nature of the girl's libidinal relations to her mother. The answer is that they are of very many different kinds. Since they persist through all three phases of infantile sexuality, they also take on the characteristics of the different phases and express themselves by oral, sadistic-anal and phallic wishes. These wishes represent active as well as passive impulses; if we relate them to the differentiation of the sexes which is to appear later—though we should avoid doing so as far as possible—we may call them masculine and feminine. Besides this, they are completely ambivalent, both affectionate and of a hostile and aggressive nature. The latter often only come to light after being changed into anxiety ideas. It is not always easy to point to a formulation of these early sexual wishes; what is most clearly expressed is a wish to get the mother with child and the corresponding wish to bear her a child—both belonging to the phallic period and sufficiently surprising, but established beyond doubt by analytic observation. The attractiveness of these investigations lies in the surprising detailed findings which they bring us. Thus, for instance, we discover the fear of being murdered or poisoned, which may later form the core of a paranoic illness, already present in this pre-Oedipus period, in relation to the mother. Or another case: you will recall an interesting episode in the history of analytic research which caused me many distressing hours. In the period in which the main interest was directed to discovering infantile sexual traumas, almost all my women patients told me that they had been seduced by their father. I was driven to recognize in the end that these reports were untrue and so came to understand that hysterical symptoms are derived from phantasies and not from real occurrences. It was only later that I was able to recognize in this phantasy of being seduced by the father the expression of the typical Oedipus complex in women. And now we find the phantasy of seduction once more in the pre-Oedipus prehistory of girls; but the seducer is regularly the mother. Here, however, the phantasy touches the ground of reality, for it was really the mother who by her activities over the child's bodily hygiene inevitably stimulated, and perhaps even roused for the first time, pleasurable sensations in her genitals.[7]

I have no doubt you are ready to suspect that this portrayal of the abundance and strength of a little girl's sexual relations with her mother is very much overdrawn. After all, one has opportunities of seeing little girls and notices nothing of the sort. But the objection is not to the point. Enough can be seen in the children if one knows how to look. And besides, you should consider how little of its sexual wishes a child can bring to preconscious expression or communicate at all. Accordingly we are only within our rights if we study the residues and consequences of this emotional world in retrospect, in people in whom these processes of development had attained a specially clear and even excessive degree of expansion. Pathology has always done us the service of making discernible by isolation and exaggeration conditions which would remain concealed in a normal state. And since our investigations have been carried out on people who were by no means seriously abnormal, I think we should regard their outcome as deserving belief.

We will now turn our interest on to the single question of what it is that brings this powerful attachment of the girl to her mother to an end. This, as we know, is its usual fate: it is destined to make room for an attachment to her father. Here we come upon a fact which is a pointer to our further advance. This step in development does not involve only a simple change of object. The turning away from the mother is accompanied by hostility; the attachment to the mother ends in hate. A hate of that kind may become very striking and last all through life; it may be carefully overcompensated later on; as a rule one part of it is overcome while another part persists. Events of later years naturally influence this greatly. We will restrict ourselves, however, to studying it at the time at which the girl turns to her father and to enquiring into the motives for it. We are then given a long list of accusations and grievances against the mother which are supposed to justify the child's hostile feelings; they are of varying validity which we shall not fail to examine. A number of them are obvious rationalizations and the true sources of enmity remain to be found. I hope you will be interested if on this occasion I take you through all the details of a psycho-analytic investigation.

The reproach against the mother which goes back furthest is that she gave the child too little milk—which is construed against her as lack of love. Now there is some justification for this reproach in our families. Mothers often have insufficient nourishment to give their children and are content to suckle them for a few months, for half or three-quarters of a year. Among primitive peoples children are fed at their mother's breast for two or three years. The figure of the wet-nurse who suckles the child is as a rule merged into the mother; when this has not happened, the reproach is turned into another one—that the nurse, who fed the child so willingly, was sent away by the mother too early. But whatever the true state of affairs may have been, it is impossible that the child's reproach can be justified as often as it is met with. It seems, rather, that the child's avidity for its earliest nourishment is altogether insatiable, that it never gets over the pain of losing its mother's breast. I should not be surprised if the analysis of a primitive child, who could still suck at its mother's breast when it was already able to run about and talk, were to bring the same reproach to light. The fear of being poisoned is also probably connected with the withdrawal of the breast. Poison is nourishment that makes one ill. Perhaps children trace back their early illnesses too to this frustration. A fair amount of intellectual education is a prerequisite for believing in chance; primitive people and uneducated ones, and no doubt children as well, are able to assign a ground for everything that happens. Perhaps originally it was a reason on animistic lines. Even to-day in some strata of our population no one can die without having been killed by someone else—preferably by the doctor. And the regular reaction of a neurotic to the death of someone closely connected with him is to put the blame on himself for having caused the death.

The next accusation against the child's mother flares up when the next baby appears in the nursery. If possible the connection with oral frustration is preserved: the mother could not or would not give the child any more milk because she needed the nourishment for the new arrival. In cases in which the two children are so close in age that lactation is prejudiced by the second pregnancy, this reproach acquires a real basis, and it is a remarkable fact that a child, even with an age difference of only 11 months, is not too young to take notice of what is happening. But what the child grudges the unwanted intruder and rival is not only the suckling but all the other signs of maternal care. It feels that it has been dethroned, despoiled, prejudiced in its rights; it casts a jealous hatred upon the new baby and develops a grievance against the faithless mother which often finds expression in a disagreeable change in its behaviour. It becomes 'naughty', perhaps, irritable and disobedient and goes back on the advances it has made towards controlling its excretions. All of this has been very long familiar and is accepted as self-evident; but we rarely form a correct idea of the strength of these jealous impulses, of the tenacity with which they persist and of the magnitude of their influence on later development. Especially as this jealousy is constantly receiving fresh nourishment in the later years of childhood and the whole shock is repeated with the birth of each new brother or sister. Nor does it make much difference if the child happens to remain the mother's preferred favourite. A child's demands for love are immoderate, they make exclusive claims and tolerate no sharing.

An abundant source of a child's hostility to its mother is provided by its multifarious sexual wishes, which alter according to the phase of the libido and which cannot for the most part be satisfied. The strongest of these frustrations occur at the phallic period, if the mother forbids pleasurable activity with the genitals—often with severe threats and every sign of displeasure—activity to which, after all, she herself had introduced the child. One would think these were reasons enough to account for a girl's turning away from her mother. One would judge, if so, that the estrangement follows inevitably from the nature of children's sexuality, from the immoderate character of their demand for love and the impossibility of fulfilling their sexual wishes. It might be thought indeed that this first love-relation of the child's is doomed to dissolution for the very reason that it is the first, for these early object-cathexes are regularly ambivalent to a high degree. A powerful tendency to aggressiveness is always present beside a powerful love, and the more passionately a child loves its object the more sensitive does it become to disappointments and frustrations from that object; and in the end the love must succumb to the accumulated hostility. Or the idea that there is an original ambivalence such as this in erotic cathexes may be rejected, and it may be pointed out that it is the special nature of the mother-child relation that leads, with equal inevitability, to the destruction of the child's love; for even the mildest upbringing cannot avoid using compulsion and introducing restrictions, and any such intervention in the child's liberty must provoke as a reaction an inclination to rebelliousness and aggressiveness. A discussion of these possibilities might, I think, be most interesting; but an objection suddenly emerges which forces our interest in another direction. All these factors—the slights, the disappointments in love, the jealousy, the seduction followed by prohibition—are, after all, also in operation in the relation of a *boy* to his mother and are yet unable to alienate him from the maternal object. Unless we can find something that is specific for girls and is not present or not in the same way present in boys, we shall not have explained the termination of the attachment of girls to their mother.

I believe we have found this specific factor, and indeed where we expected to find it, even though in a surprising form. Where we expected to find it, I say, for it lies in the castration complex. After all, the anatomical distinction [between the sexes] must express itself in psychical consequences. It was, however, a surprise to learn from analyses that girls hold their mother responsible for their lack of a penis and do not forgive her for their being thus put at a disadvantage.

As you hear, then, we ascribe a castration complex to women as well. And for good reasons, though its content cannot be the same as with boys. In the latter the castration complex arises after they have learnt from the sight of the female genitals that the organ which they value so highly need not necessarily accompany the body. At this the boy recalls to mind the threats he brought on himself by his doings with that organ, he begins to give credence to them and falls under the influence of fear of castration, which will be the most powerful motive force in his subsequent development. The castration complex of girls is also started by the sight of the genitals of the other sex. They at once notice the difference and, it must be admitted, its significance too. They feel seriously wronged, often declare that they want to 'have something like it too', and fall victim to 'envy for the penis', which will leave ineradicable traces on their development and the formation of their character and which will not be surmounted in even the most favourable cases without a severe expenditure of psychical energy. The girl's recognition of the fact of her being without a penis does not by any means imply that she submits to the fact easily. On the contrary, she continues to hold on for a long time to the wish to get something like it herself and she believes in that possibility for improbably long years; and analysis can show that, at a period when knowledge of reality has long since rejected the fulfilment of the wish as unattainable, it persists in the unconscious and retains a considerable cathexis of energy. The wish to get the longed-for penis eventually in spite of everything may contribute to the motives that drive a mature woman to analysis, and what she may reasonably expect from analysis—a capacity, for instance, to carry on an intellectual profession—may often be recognized as a sublimated modification of this repressed wish.

One cannot very well doubt the importance of envy for the penis. You may take it as an instance of male injustice if I assert that envy and jealousy play an even greater part in the mental life of women than of men. It is not that I think these characteristics are absent in men or that I think they have no other roots in women than envy for the penis; but I am inclined to attribute their greater amount in women to this latter influence. Some analysts, however, have shown an inclination to depreciate the importance of this first instalment of penis-envy in the phallic phase. They are of opinion that what we find of this attitude in women is in the main a secondary structure which has come about on the occasion of later conflicts by regression to this early infantile impulse. This, however, is a general problem of depth psychology. In many pathological—or even unusual—instinctual attitudes (for instance, in all sexual perversions) the question arises of how much of their strength is to be attributed to early infantile fixations and how much to the influence of later experiences and developments. In such cases it is almost always a matter of complemental series such as we put forward in our discussion of the aetiology of the neuroses.[8] Both factors play a part in varying amounts in the causation; a less on the one side is balanced by a more on the other. The infantile factor sets the pattern in all cases but does not always determine the issue, though it often does. Precisely in the case of penis-envy I should argue decidedly in favour of the preponderance of the infantile factor.

The discovery that she is castrated is a turning-point in a girl's growth. Three possible lines of development start from it: one leads to sexual inhibition or to neurosis, the second to change of character in the sense of a masculinity complex, the third, finally, to normal femininity. We have learnt a fair amount, though not everything, about all three.

The essential content of the first is as follows: the little girl has hitherto lived in a masculine way, has been able to get pleasure by the excitation of her clitoris and has brought this activity into relation with her sexual wishes directed towards her mother, which are often active ones; now, owing to the influence of her penis-envy, she loses her enjoyment in her phallic sexuality. Her self-love is mortified by the comparison with the boy's far superior equipment and in consequence she renounces her masturbatory satisfaction from her clitoris, repudiates her love for her mother and at the same time not infrequently represses a good part of her sexual trends in general. No doubt her turning away from her mother does not occur all at once, for to begin with the girl regards her castration as an individual misfortune, and only gradually extends it to other females and finally to her mother as well. Her love was directed to her *phallic* mother; with the discovery that her mother is castrated it becomes possible to drop her as an object, so that the motives for hostility, which have long been accumulating, gain the upper hand. This means, therefore, that as a result of the discovery of women's lack of a penis they are debased in value for girls just as they are for boys and later perhaps for men.

You all know the immense aetiological importance attributed by our neurotic patients to their masturbation. They make it responsible for all their troubles and we have the greatest difficulty in persuading them that they are mistaken. In fact, however, we ought to admit to them that they are right, for masturbation is the executive agent of infantile sexuality, from the faulty development of which they are indeed suffering. But what neurotics mostly blame is the masturbation of the period of puberty; they have mostly forgotten that of early infancy, which is what is really in question. I wish I might have an opportunity some time of explaining to you at length how important all the factual details of early masturbation become for the individual's subsequent neurosis or character: whether or not it was discovered, how the parents struggled against it or permitted it, or whether he succeeded in suppressing it himself. All of this leaves permanent traces on his development. But I am on the whole glad that I need not do this. It would be a hard and tedious task and at the end of it you would put me in an embarrassing situation by quite certainly asking me to give you some practical advice as to how a parent or educator should deal with the masturbation of small children.[9] From the development of girls, which is what my present lecture is concerned with, I can give you the example of a child herself trying to get free from masturbating. She does not always succeed in this. If envy for the penis has provoked a powerful impulse against clitoridal masturbation but this nevertheless refuses to give way, a violent struggle for liberation ensues in which the girl, as it were, herself takes over the role of her deposed mother and gives expression to her entire dissatisfaction with her inferior clitoris in her efforts against obtaining satisfaction from it. Many years later, when her masturbatory activity has long since been suppressed, an interest still persists which we must interpret as a defence against a temptation that is still dreaded. It manifests itself in the emergence of sympathy for those to whom similar difficulties are attributed, it plays a part as a motive in contracting a marriage and, indeed, it may determine the choice of a husband or lover. Disposing of early infantile masturbation is truly no easy or indifferent business.

Along with the abandonment of clitoridal masturbation a certain amount of activity is renounced. Passivity now has the upper hand, and the girl's turning to her father is accomplished principally with the help of passive instinctual impulses. You can see that a wave of development like this, which clears the phallic activity out of the way, smooths the ground for femininity. If too much is not lost in the course of it through repression, this femininity may turn out to be normal. The wish with which the girl turns to her father is no doubt originally the wish for the penis which her mother has refused her and which she now expects from her father. The feminine situation is only established, however, if the wish for a penis is replaced by one for a baby, if, that is, a baby takes the place of a penis in accordance with an ancient symbolic equivalence. It has not escaped us that the girl has wished for a baby earlier, in the undisturbed phallic phase: that, of course, was the meaning of her playing with dolls. But that play was not in fact an expression of her femininity; it served as an identification with her mother with the intention of substituting activity for passivity. *She* was playing the part of her mother and the doll was herself: now she could do with the baby everything that her mother used to do with her. Not until the emergence of the wish for a penis does the doll-baby become a baby from the girl's father, and thereafter the aim of the most powerful feminine wish. Her happiness is great if later on this wish for a baby finds fulfilment in reality, and quite especially so if the baby is a little boy who brings the longed-for penis with him.[10] Often enough in her combined picture of 'a baby from her father' the emphasis is laid on the baby and her father left unstressed. In this way the ancient masculine wish for the possession of a penis is still faintly visible through the femininity now achieved. But perhaps we ought rather to recognize this wish for a penis as being *par excellence* a feminine one.

With the transference of the wish for a penis-baby on to her father, the girl has entered the situation of the Oedipus complex. Her hostility to her mother, which did not need to be freshly created, is now greatly intensified, for she becomes the girl's rival, who receives from her father everything that she desires from him. For a long time the girl's Oedipus complex concealed her pre-Oedipus attachment to her mother from our view, though it is nevertheless so important and leaves such lasting fixations behind it. For girls the Oedipus situation is the outcome of a long and difficult development; it is a kind of preliminary solution, a position of rest which is not soon abandoned, especially as the beginning of the latency period is not far distant. And we are now struck by a difference between the two sexes, which is probably momentous, in regard to the relation of the Oedipus complex to the castration complex. In a boy the Oedipus complex, in which he desires his mother and would like to get rid of his father as being a rival, develops naturally from the phase of his phallic sexuality. The threat of castration compels him, however, to give up that attitude. Under the impression of the danger of losing his penis, the Oedipus complex is abandoned, repressed and, in the most normal cases, entirely destroyed, and a severe super-ego is set up as its heir. What happens with a girl is almost the opposite. The castration complex prepares for the Oedipus complex instead of destroying it; the girl is driven out of her attachment to her mother through the influence of her envy for the penis and she enters the Oedipus situation as though into a haven of refuge. In the absence of fear of castration the chief motive is lacking which leads boys to surmount the Oedipus complex. Girls remain in it for an indeterminate length of time; they demolish it late and, even so, incompletely. In these circumstances the formation of the super-ego must suffer; it cannot attain the strength and independence which give it its cultural significance, and feminists are not pleased when we point out to them the effects of this factor upon the average feminine character.

To go back a little. We mentioned as the second possible reaction to the discovery of female castration the development of a powerful masculinity complex. By this we mean that the girl refuses, as it were, to recognize the unwelcome fact and, defiantly rebellious, even exaggerates her previous masculinity, clings to her clitoridal activity and takes refuge in an identification with her phallic mother or her father. What can it be that decides in favour of this outcome? We can only suppose that it is a constitutional factor, a greater amount of activity, such as is ordinarily characteristic of a male. However that may be, the essence of this process is that at this point in development the wave of passivity is avoided which opens the way to the turn towards femininity. The extreme achievement of such a masculinity complex would appear to be the influencing of the choice of an object in the sense of manifest homosexuality. Analytic experience teaches us, to be sure, that female homosexuality is seldom or never a direct continuation of infantile masculinity. Even for a girl of this kind it seems necessary that she should take her father as an object for some time and enter the Oedipus situation. But afterwards, as a result of her inevitable disappointments from her father, she is driven to regress into her early masculinity complex. The significance of these disappointments must not be exaggerated; a girl who is destined to become feminine is not spared them, though they do not have the same effect. The predominance of the constitutional factor seems indisputable; but the two phases in the development of female homosexuality are well mirrored in the practices of homosexuals, who play the parts of mother and baby with each other as often and as clearly as those of husband and wife.

What I have been telling you here may be described as the prehistory of women. It is a product of the very last few years and may have been of interest to you as an example of detailed analytic work. Since its subject is woman, I will venture on this occasion to mention by name a few of the women who have made valuable contributions to this investigation. Dr. Ruth Mack Brunswick [1928] was the first to describe a case of neurosis which went back to a fixation in the pre-Oedipus stage and had never reached the Oedipus situation at all. The case took the form of jealous paranoia and proved accessible to therapy. Dr. Jeanne Lampl-de Groot [1927] has established the incredible phallic activity of girls towards their mother by some assured observations, and Dr. Helene Deutsch [1932] has shown that the erotic actions of homosexual women reproduce the relations between mother and baby.

It is not my intention to pursue the further behaviour of femininity through puberty to the period of maturity. Our knowledge, moreover, would be insufficient for the purpose. But I will bring a few features together in what follows. Taking its prehistory as a starting-point, I will only emphasize here that the development of femininity remains exposed to disturbance by the residual phenomena of the early masculine period. Regressions to the fixations of the pre-Oedipus phases very frequently occur; in the course of some women's lives there is a repeated alternation between periods in which masculinity or femininity gains the upper hand. Some portion of what we men call 'the enigma of women' may perhaps be derived from this expression of bisexuality in women's lives. But another question seems to have become ripe for judgement in the course of these researches. We have called the motive force of sexual life 'the libido'. Sexual life is dominated by the polarity of masculine-feminine; thus the notion suggests itself of considering the relation of the libido to this antithesis. It would not be surprising if it were to turn out that each sexuality had its own special libido appropriated to it, so that one sort of libido would pursue the aims of a masculine sexual life and another sort those of a feminine one. But nothing of the kind is true. There is only one libido, which serves both the masculine and the feminine sexual functions. To it itself we cannot assign any sex; if, following the conventional equation of activity and masculinity, we are inclined to describe it as masculine, we must not forget that it also covers trends with a passive aim. Nevertheless the juxtaposition 'feminine libido' is without any justification. Furthermore, it is our impression that more constraint has been applied to the libido when it is pressed into the service of the feminine function, and that—to speak teleologically—Nature takes less careful account of its [that function's] demands than in the case of masculinity. And the reason for this may lie—thinking once again teleologically—in the fact that the accomplishment of the aim of biology has been entrusted to the aggressiveness of men and has been made to some extent independent of women's consent.

The sexual frigidity of women, the frequency of which appears to confirm this disregard, is a phenomenon that is still insufficiently understood. Sometimes it is psychogenic and in that case accessible to influence; but in other cases it suggests the hypothesis of its being constitutionally determined and even of there being a contributory anatomical factor.

I have promised to tell you of a few more psychical peculiarities of mature femininity, as we come across them in analytic observation. We do not lay claim to more than an average validity for these assertions; nor is it always easy to distinguish what should be ascribed to the influence of the sexual function and what to social breeding. Thus, we attribute a larger amount of narcissism to femininity, which also affects women's choice of object, so that to be loved is a stronger need for them than to love. The effect of penis-envy has a share, further, in the physical vanity of women, since they are bound to value their charms more highly as a late compensation for their original sexual inferiority.[11] Shame, which is considered to be a feminine characteristic *par excellence* but is far more a matter of convention than might be supposed, has as its purpose, we believe, concealment of genital deficiency. We are not forgetting that at a later time shame takes on other functions. It seems that women have made few contributions to the discoveries and inventions in the history of civilization; there is, however, one technique which they may have invented—that of plaiting and weaving. If that is so, we should be tempted to guess the unconscious motive for the achievement. Nature herself would seem to have given the model which this achievement imitates by causing the growth at maturity of the pubic hair that conceals the genitals. The step that remained to be taken lay in making the threads adhere to one another, while on the body they stick into the skin and are only matted together. If you reject this idea as fantastic and regard my belief in the influence of lack of a penis on the configuration of femininity as an *idée fixe,* I am of course defenceless.

The determinants of women's choice of an object are often made unrecognizable by social conditions. Where the choice is able to show itself freely, it is often made in accordance with the narcissistic ideal of the man whom the girl had wished to become. If the girl has remained in her attachment to her father—that is, in the Oedipus complex—her choice is made according to the paternal type. Since, when she turned from her mother to her father, the hostility of her ambivalent relation remained with her mother, a choice of this kind should guarantee a happy marriage. But very often the outcome is of a kind that presents a general threat to such a settlement of the conflict due to ambivalence. The hostility that has been left behind follows in the train of the positive attachment and spreads over on to the new object. The woman's husband, who to begin with inherited from her father, becomes after a time her mother's heir as well. So it may easily happen that the second half of a woman's life may be filled by the struggle against her husband, just as the shorter first half was filled by her rebellion against her mother. When this reaction has been lived through, a second marriage may easily turn out very much more satisfying.[12] Another alteration in a woman's nature, for which lovers are unprepared, may occur in a marriage after the first child is born. Under the influence of a woman's becoming a mother herself, an identification with her own mother may be revived, against which she had striven up till the time of her marriage, and this may attract all the available libido to itself, so that the compulsion to repeat reproduces an unhappy marriage between her parents. The difference in a mother's reaction to the birth of a son or a daughter shows that the old factor of lack of a penis has even now not lost its strength. A mother is only brought unlimited satisfaction by her relation to a son; this is altogether the most perfect, the most free from ambivalence of all human relationships.[13] A mother can transfer to her son the ambition which she has been obliged to suppress in herself, and she can expect from him the satisfaction of all that has been left over in her of her masculinity complex. Even a marriage is not made secure until the wife has succeeded in making her husband her child as well and in acting as a mother to him.

A woman's identification with her mother allows us to distinguish two strata: the pre-Oedipus one which rests on her affectionate attachment to her mother and takes her as a model, and the later one from the Oedipus complex which seeks to get rid of her mother and take her place with her father. We are no doubt justified in saying that much of both of them is left over for the future and that neither of them is adequately surmounted in the course of development. But the phase of the affectionate pre-Oedipus attachment is the decisive one for a woman's future: during it preparations are made for the acquisition of the characteristics with which she will later fulfil her role in the sexual function and perform her invaluable social tasks. It is in this identification too that she acquires her attractiveness to a man, whose Oedipus attachment to his mother it kindles into passion. How often it happens, however, that it is only his son who obtains what he himself aspired to! One gets an impression that a man's love and a woman's are a phase apart psychologically.

The fact that women must be regarded as having little sense of justice is no doubt related to the predominance of envy in their mental life; for the demand for justice is a modification of envy and lays down the condition subject to which one can put envy aside. We also regard women as weaker in their social interests and as having less capacity for sublimating their instincts than men. The former is no doubt derived from the dissocial quality which unquestionably characterizes all sexual relations. Lovers find sufficiency in each other, and families too resist inclusion in more comprehensive associations.[14] The aptitude for sublimation is subject to the greatest individual variations. On the other hand I cannot help mentioning an impression that we are constantly receiving during analytic practice. A man of about thirty strikes us as a youthful, somewhat unformed individual, whom we expect to make powerful use of the possibilities for development opened up to him by analysis. A woman of the same age, however, often frightens us by her psychical rigidity and unchangeability. Her libido has taken up final positions and seems incapable of exchanging them for others. There are no paths open to further development; it is as though the whole process had already run its course and remains thenceforward insusceptible to influence—as though, indeed, the difficult development to femininity had exhausted the possibilities of the person concerned. As therapists we lament this state of things, even if we succeed in putting an end to our patient's ailment by doing away with her neurotic conflict.

That is all I had to say to you about femininity. It is certainly incomplete and fragmentary and does not always sound friendly. But do not forget that I have only been describing women in so far as their nature is determined by their sexual function. It is true that that influence extends very far; but we do not overlook the fact that an individual woman may be a human being in other respects as well. If you want to know more about femininity, enquire from your own experiences of life, or turn to the poets, or wait until science can give you deeper and more coherent information.

Notes

1. [This lecture is mainly based on two earlier papers: 'Some Psychical Consequences of the Anatomical Distinction between the Sexes' (1925*j*) and 'Female Sexuality' (1931*b*). The last section, however, dealing with women in adult life, contains new material. Freud returned to the subject once again in Chapter VII of the posthumous *Outline of Psycho-Analysis* (1940*a* [1938]).]

2. Heads in hieroglyphic bonnets,
Heads in turbans and black birettas,
Heads in wigs and thousand other
Wretched, sweating heads of humans. . . .
(Heine, *Nordsee* [Second Cycle, VII, 'Fragen'].)

3. [Bisexuality was discussed by Freud in the first edition of his *Three Essays on the Theory of Sexuality* (1905*d*). The passage includes a long footnote to which he made additions in later issues of the work.]

4. [I.e., mistaking two different things for a single one. The term was explained in *Introductory Lectures,* XX.]

5. [The difficulty of finding a psychological meaning for 'masculine' and 'feminine' was discussed in a long footnote added in 1915 to Section 4 of the third of his *Three Essays* (1905*d*), and again at the beginning of a still longer footnote at the end of Chapter IV of *Civilization and its Discontents* (1930*a*).]

6. [Cf. *Introductory Lectures,* XXI.]

7. [In his early discussions of the aetiology of hysteria Freud often mentioned seduction by adults as among its commonest causes (see, for instance, Section I of the second paper on the neuro-psychoses of defence (1896*c*), and Section II *(b)* of 'The Aetiology of Hysteria' (1896*c*). But nowhere in these early publications did he specifically inculpate the girl's father. Indeed, in some additional footnotes written in 1924 for the *Gesammelte Schriften* reprint of *Studies on Hysteria,* he admitted to having on two occasions suppressed the fact of the father's responsibility. He made this quite clear, however, in the letter to Fliess of September 21, 1897 (Freud, 1950*a,* Letter 69), in which he first expressed his scepticism about these stories told by his patients. His first published admission of his mistake was given several years later in a hint in the second of the *Three Essays* (1905*d*), but a much fuller account of the position followed in his contribution on the aetiology of the neuroses to a volume of Löwenfeld (1906*a*). Later on he gave two accounts of the effects that this discovery of his mistake had on his own mind—in his 'History of the Psycho-Analytic Movement' (1914*d*), and in his *Autobiographical Study* (1925*d*), (Norton, 1963). The further discovery which is described in the present paragraph of the text had already been indicated in the paper on 'Female Sexuality' (1931*b*).]

8. [See *Introductory Lectures,* XXII and XXIII.]

9. [Freud's fullest discussion of masturbation was in his contributions to a symposium on the subject in the Vienna Psycho-Analytical Society (1912*f*).]

10. [See below.]

11. [Cf. Section II of 'On Narcissism' (1914*c*).]

12. [This had already been remarked upon earlier, in 'The Taboo of Virginity' (1918*a*).]

13. [This point seems to have been made by Freud first in a footnote to Chapter VI of *Group Psychology* (1921*c*). He repeated it in the *Introductory Lectures,* XIII, and in Chapter V of *Civilization and its Discontents* (1930*a*). That exceptions may occur is shown by the example above.]

14. [Cf. some remarks on this in Chapter XII (D) of *Group Psychology* (1921*c*).]

I Am Unclean . . .

H. R. Hays

The novelist and anthropologist H. R. Hays studied at Cornell and Columbia and has taught at the University of Minnesota, Fairleigh Dickinson, and Southampton. He is the author of several works in social anthropology: From Ape to Angel, In the Beginnings, Children of the Raven, *and* The Kingdom of Hawaii.

The Dangerous Sex, *from which this selection is taken, is described by Frederic Wertham as "a long overdue and well-documented study of man's inhumanity to woman." Through an examination of the beliefs, customs, and mores of cultures from the primitive to the present, Hays chronicles the hostility and cruelty with which men have treated women and seeks reasons in male fears and ignorance. The chapter reprinted here describes the highly prevalent treatment of woman as dirty, woman as cosmically dangerous. The biological processes of women have "big magic"; they are fraught with serious consequences and thus surrounded by "big scare." Interestingly, the theme of male fear of women, not a new or uncommon idea, is increasingly a factor in analyses of male–female relations.*

WHEN MENSTRUATING, A SURINAM NEGRO WOMAN lives in solitude. If anyone approaches her, she must cry out, "I am unclean."

The notion that women's sexual processes are impure is worldwide and persistent; the magical fear of menstrual blood is particularly intense. In the first place, the fact that blood flows from the female genitals at regular intervals sets women off from the other sex and gives them the exceptional properties of mana in a world in which men set the norm. The taboos which surround the first menstruation are particularly severe. The phenomenon itself is frequently explained as a supernatural wound, the result of an attack by a bird, a snake or a lizard. The origin of the female genital as a result of castration or sadistic attack is also illustrated in myths concerning the creation of women. Since male fantasy is dominant in human institutions, a very early time is often referred to in which there were only men and no women. The Negritos of the Malay Peninsula maintain there was once an ancestral creator entity, the monitor lizard. Since his contemporaries were all men, the lizard caught one of them, cut off his genitals and made him into a woman who became the lizard's wife and the ancestor of the Negritos. When Christopher Columbus discovered the Indians inhabiting Haiti, whom he named Caribs, he left a friar among them as a missionary. Friar Pane recorded a story concerning the Indian ancestors who had no women yet felt they should have some. One day they observed certain creatures who were falling out of the trees or hiding in the branches. These alien beings had no sex organs whatsoever. The Carib ancestors bound them and tied woodpeckers to them in the proper place. The birds pecked out the desired sexual orifices. Not only do we have here the theme of women being created by castration appearing on opposite sides of the world but, significantly enough, the image of the vulva as a wound also occurs in the fantasies of male psychoanalytical patients.

New Guinea carvings show images of women with a crocodile attacking the vulva, a hornbill

---

H. R. Hays. *The Dangerous Sex.* N.Y.: Putnam's Sons, 1964. Reprinted by permission of Ann Elmo Agency.

plunging its beak into the organ or a penislike snake emerging from it. On the one hand there is the idea of castration and on the other an image of the female genital being created by a sadistic attack by the penis, symbolized by lizard, bird beak, or snake. The mysterious and dangerous nature of the wound is uppermost in primitive tradition.

Blood in all of its manifestations is a source of mana. In the case of menstrual blood the ancient ambivalence is in evidence with the harmful aspect predominating. The dangers of contact and contagion are so great that women are nearly always secluded or forced to reside apart during their monthly periods. Special huts are built for them by the Bakairi of Brazil, the Shuswap of British Columbia, the Gauri of northern India, the Veddas of Ceylon, and the Algonkian of the North American forest. From this it can be seen that the custom covers the globe.

Then, too, a sort of fumigating sometimes takes place. Siberian Samoyed women step over fires of burning reindeer skin. They must also refrain from cooking food for their men. Among the Nootka of the Canadian northwest coast, at her first period a girl is given her private eating utensils and must eat alone for eight months. The Chippewa girl also eats alone, cannot cross a public road or talk to any man or boy. Eskimo girls at their first period are taboo for forty days. They must sit crouching in a corner, their faces to the wall, draw their hoods over their heads, let their hair hang over their faces and only leave the house when everyone else is asleep. Hermann Ploss describes a still more curious segregation practiced by the Australians of Queensland. The girl is taken to a shady place. Her mother draws a circle on the ground and digs a deep hole into which the girl must step. "The sandy soil is then filled in, leaving her buried up to the waist. A woven hedge of branches or twigs is set around her with an opening toward which she turns her face. Her mother kindles a fire at the opening, the girl remains in her nest of earth in a squatting posture with folded arms and hands resting downward on the sand heap that covers her lower limbs."

We are not told how long she must remain in the condition of the heroine of Beckett's play, *Happy Days,* but it is evident that the soil is supposed to purify or nullify her dangerous condition.

Among the Dogon of East Africa the menstrual taboo is so strong that a woman in this condition brings misfortune to everything she touches. Not only is she segregated in an isolated hut and provided with special eating utensils, but if she is seen passing through the village a general purification must take place. The Wogeo of South Australia believe that if a man has contact with a menstruating woman he will die from a wasting disease against which there is no remedy whatsoever.

The Hindus observe an endless number of prohibitions during the first three days of a woman's period. She must not weep, mount a horse, an ox or an elephant, be carried in a palanquin or drive in a vehicle.

In Hebrew tradition the menstruating woman is forbidden to work in a kitchen, sit at meals with other people, or drink from a glass used by others. Any contact with her husband is a sin and the penalty for intercourse during her period is death for both. Indeed the misfortunes which men suffer when they break the menstrual taboo vary but they are always severe. A Uganda Bantu woman by touching her husband's effects makes him sick; if she lays a hand on his weapons, he will be killed in the next fight. The natives of Malacca believe that coitus, or even contact, will cause the man to lose his virility.

The prohibitions which we have just been discussing occur in ancient or primitive cultures. Menstrual anxiety, however, is so deeply ingrained in the male psyche that it lingers in folk tradition. The peasants of eastern Europe believe that a woman must not bake bread, make pickles, churn butter or spin thread during her period or all will go wrong. Here, of course, is a survival of the idea that food is particularly susceptible to the deadly contagion. In Silesian folklore women during their periods are forbidden to plant seedlings or work in the garden. The Roman author Pliny tells us that contact of menstruous women with new wine or ripe fruit will sour both. The same author provides us with examples of ambivalence: "Hailstorms, whirlwinds and lightnings even will be scared away by a woman uncovering her body while her courses are upon her. . . . Also if a woman strips herself naked while she is menstruating and walks around a field of wheat, the caterpillars, worms, beetles and other vermin will fall off the ears of corn [wheat]. Algonkian women walk around a cornfield for the same reason. Menstrual blood is also thought to cure leprosy and is actually by European peasants sometimes put into a man's coffee as a love charm. In Russian folklore it is said to cure warts and birthmarks. These instances are enough to show that the basic principle of ambivalent mana is involved. The overwhelming amount of evidence proves, however, that men do not envy the female ability to menstruate but fear it.

An example cited by Havelock Ellis shows that even in the late nineteenth century educated men were not free of this superstition. In 1891 a British doctor, William Goodell, wrote that he had to shake off the tradition that women must not be operated upon during their periods. "Our forefathers from time immemorial have thought and taught that the presence of a menstruating woman would pollute solemn religious rites, would sour milk, spoil the fermentation in wine vats, and much other mischief in a general way." Ellis also cites several instances of violinists who were convinced that the strings of their instruments continually broke while their wives were indisposed.

Even Hermann Ploss and Max Bartels in their gynecological and anthropological work *Woman,* first published in Germany in 1905, wrote: "But it seems very doubtful whether these superstitions and traditions will ever be eradicated. They are far too deeply and far too widely ramified in the mind and emotions of humanity."

It will be seen that all the basic predispositions to anxiety are involved. Women by their recurring supernatural wound are set apart as aliens from the male norm. Sensitivity to contact and contagion is aroused and the symbol of the whole complex is blood, the powerful magic liquid on which life depends.

But menstruation is not the only female process which is surrounded with precautions. Pregnancy and childbirth, although the focus of various ideas, again arouse anxiety connected with blood, impurity and contagion. In addition, the production of a live being from a woman's body undoubtedly endows her with the supernatural properties of mana. In most cases the woman must be segregated or else she must give birth alone in the forest as among the Negritos, some east coast African Negroes, the Kiwai Papuans and the Guaná of Paraguay. The Hottentots of South Africa, the Tahitians, the Todas of India and the Gilyaks of the island of Sakhalin are among those who build a special hut or tent.

The misfortunes brought about by pregnancy and childbirth parallel those of menstruation. Among the Indians of Costa Rica, a woman pregnant for the first time infects the whole neighborhood; she is blamed for any deaths which may occur and her husband is obliged to pay damages. Cape Town Bantu males believe that looking upon a lying-in woman will result in their being killed in battle. Some Brazilian Indians are sure that if the woman is not out of the house during childbirth weapons will lose their power. The Sulka of New Britain feel that in addition men will become cowardly and taro shoots will not sprout. A purification ceremony consists of chewing ginger, spitting it on twigs which are held in the smoke of a fire, and repeating certain charms. The twigs are then placed on the taro shoots, on weapons, and over doors and on roofs.

Those who aid the parturient woman are also sure to be infected by the contagion. Garcilaso de la Vega, the chronicler of the ancient Incas, wrote that no one must help a woman in childbirth, and any who did would be regarded as witches. Among the Hebrews the midwife was regarded as unclean. The whole concept of "lying in"—only recently dispelled by new medical theories requiring the new mother to be up and about as soon as possible—which was rationalized as necessary for the woman to regain her strength, originated in magical precautions, as is clearly shown by the extreme length of time during which primitive women were sequestered and by the ceremonies carried out to purify them. To cite a few examples: The time varied from forty days, among the Swahili of Africa, to two months among the Eskimo or two to three months in Tahiti. Significantly enough, the period was longer after the birth of a girl in India, among the Hebrews, among many New Guinea tribes, the Masai of West Africa, and the Cree Indians of North America.

An example of purification ceremonies is the bathing of Hebrew women in special bathhouses in which both menstruating and parturient women were cleansed. After her time of sequestration was over, the Hebrew woman was required to send a lamb and a dove to the priest as sacrifices. The Pueblo Indians treat the purification more lyrically. Five days after the child is born, its mother is ceremonially washed. She then walks in the retinue of a priest to view the sunrise, throwing up cornflowers and blowing them about in the air.

In accordance with the feeling that the exceptional is imbued with mana, miscarriage, being more abnormal than ordinary birth, is regarded with particular apprehension. The African Bantu consider it a cause of drought. They also believe that if a woman succeeds in aborting herself and at once has sexual relations with a man his death will follow.

The samplings just given are selected from a wealth of evidence which demonstrates that the male attitude toward female sexual functions is basically apprehensive; women, in short, are dangerous. Taboos and fears of contagion, however, are not limited to the physical crises in their lives. When we investigate the ideas of contact still further, a host of activities requires avoidance of women in general.

Since nutrition is one of the basic needs of human beings, and food is brought into contact with the body, it is not surprising that food and eating are universally involved with magical precautions. Women being intrinsically dangerous, their relation to food is a psychological problem. We have already cited food and eating taboos in relation to menstruation. Among preliterates and in ancient civilizations it is the rule rather than the exception that women do not eat with their husbands. Although in later periods the idea that the dominant male must be served first also enters the picture, the germ of the custom is certainly the notion that female impurity will contaminate a man's food and do him harm. Throughout Africa men and women eat separately, and the same is true of many South American tribes. In Melanesia and Polynesia the same segregation is observed. The Todas, those hill people of India who have already been cited, also observe the taboo, as do the sophisticated Hindus. If the wife of one of the Hindus were to touch his food it would be rendered unfit for his use. The same precaution was widespread in North America. The early traveler and artist George Catlin said he never saw Indians and squaws eating together. Henry Rowe Schoolcraft, the first American anthropologist, when he was an Indian agent among the Chippewa, married a half-Indian girl. Although his wife had been educated in England and helped him collect Algonkian folklore and her dark-skinned mother prevented a border incident by mediating between her people and the whites, the mother's conservatism was so intense that she could never be persuaded to eat with her son-in-law.

The two exclusive male activities of hunting and fighting are also very often associated with avoidance of women. Nothing is closer to man's maleness than his weapons and his hunting gear. In Tahiti, women are prohibited from touching weapons and fishing apparatus. In Queensland the natives throw away their fishing lines if women step over them, and elsewhere a woman is forbidden to step over objects, because in so doing the woman's sex passes over them and they are thus exposed to the seat of contagion. (When a Maori warrior wishes to absorb the phallic magic of a powerful chief, he crawls between his legs.) A Dakota Indian's weapons must not be touched by a woman and women of the Siberian hunting tribes must abide by the same taboo. If a woman touches a Zulu's assegai, he cannot use it again.

Cattle among the southern Bantu are an important form of male ego expression and in this case they are taboo to women. If women touch them the beasts will fall ill. Fighting cocks among the Malay are treated in the same way. This taboo, however, among the Bantu does not apply to girls who have not yet reached puberty or to old women who have passed the menopause, proving conclusively that it is the female sexual mana which is thought to do the damage.

The necessity of abstaining from intercourse with women before undertaking the chase and warfare has sometimes been explained as a fear of the debilitating effect of what is considered the weaker sex. Indeed it is often so rationalized by the primitives themselves. That this is a late addition is indicated by the fact that fasting often accompanies the ritual surrounding hunting and war and fasting can scarcely be construed as a method of conserving strength.

Sexual abstinence before war and hunting is practiced all over Polynesia and in many parts of Melanesia. The headhunters of Assam, in India, are particularly strict in observing this taboo. In one case the wife of a headman spoke to her husband, unaware that he was returning with a group of warriors who had taken trophy heads. When she learned what she had done she was so disturbed that she grew sick and died. In British Columbia and other areas of North America which were inhabited by the hunting tribes, the taboo against contact with women before hunting or fighting was carefully observed. The Huichol of Mexico did so, and explained that a deer would never enter the snare of a man who was sleeping with his wife. It would simply look at the trap, snort "pooh, pooh" and go away. Throughout Africa continence and avoidance were observed before war and hunting. Women were forbidden to approach the Zulu army except (as in the case of cattle) for old women past the menopause, because such women "have become men."

The hunting taboo can be exaggerated to the extent that the Bangalas of equatorial Africa remain continent while they are making nets to capture wild pigs and the Melanesian of the Torres Straits refrain from intercourse during the mating season of turtles (an important food), in a curious defiance of the principles of mimetic magic.

Most extreme of all is the taboo which functions on the principle that since the name is a part of the individual, its use will affect his well-being. The Bantu women of Nyasaland do not speak their husband's names or any words that may be synonymous. A Warramunga woman of Australia may not mention the ordinary name of a man, which she knows, and in addition he has a secret name which she does not even know. Similarly the Hindus, whom we have continually cited as taboo ridden, do not allow a woman to mention her husband's name. She must speak of him as the "man of the house" or "father of the household" and if she dreams of his name this will result in his untimely death.

The tiny Bushmen, who are one of the oldest peoples and who support life by the simplest of hunting and gathering techniques, exemplify nearly all of the avoidances we have been discussing. Men and women sit on different sides of their crude shelters of woven twigs or grasses—if a man occupies a woman's place he will become impotent. When a man sets out to shoot an eland or a giraffe, he must avoid intercourse or the poison on his arrows will lose its power. A Bushman woman gives birth secretly in the bush. If a man inadvertently steps over the spot he will lose his ability to hunt.

A Bushman myth emphasizes the alienation of the two sexes almost in terms of their being different tribes. In the early times men and women lived apart, the former hunting animals exclusively, the latter pursuing a gathering existence. Five of the men, who were out hunting, being careless creatures, let their fire go out. The women, who were careful and orderly, always kept their fire going. The men, having killed a springbok, became desperate for means to cook it, so one of their number set out to get fire, crossed the river, and met one of the women gathering seeds. When he asked her for some fire, she invited him to the feminine camp. While he was there she said, "You are very hungry. Just wait until I pound up these seeds and I will boil them and give you some." She made him some porridge. After he had eaten it, he said, "Well, it's nice food so I shall just stay with you." The men who were left waited and wondered. They still had the springbok and they still had no fire. The second man set out, only to be tempted by female cooking, and to take up residence in the camp of the women. The same thing happened to the third man. The two men left were very frightened. They suspected something terrible had happened to their comrades. They cast the divining bones but the omens were favorable. The fourth man set out timidly, only to end by joining his comrades. The last man became very frightened indeed and besides by now the springbok had rotted. He took his bow and arrows and ran away.

On the other side of the world, among the Pueblo and Zuñi Indians, myths which tell of the emergence of their forefathers from the ground also divide the sexes into two camps, although in this case the women are portrayed as less efficient than the men in their attempts to reach the upper world. In these traditional stories such matters as sex and marriage are completely ignored, the sexes are viewed as groups living apart, a theme which may be a reflection of the periodic segregation of women.

The earliest types of religion at any rate codify male anxiety by proclaiming that women shall remain inactive for a considerable portion of their lives. The same religious sanctions prohibit them from participating in many human activities, partly excluding them from the human condition. And all the evidence points to the fact that this situation began with the simplest types of group association, in all probability as far back as the Paleolithic.

Despite these barriers of alienation and fear, the sex drive after all does insure reproduction. The act of procreation, however, arouses still another type of ambivalence which affects the status of women and substantiates the view that the conditions of man's development as a social being prevent him from ever taking eros for granted.

References

Cazeneuve, Jean

1958 *Les rites et la condition humaine.* Paris.

Crawley, Ernest
1960 *The Mystic Rose.* (Meridian) New York.

Ellis, Havelock
1901–1928 *Studies in the Psychology of Sex,* Vol. I. Philadelphia.

Hays, H. R.
1963 *In the Beginnings.* New York.

Ploss, Hermann, and Bartels, M. C. A. and P. R. A.
1935 *Woman: An Historical, Gynaecological and Anthropological Compendium,* 3 Vols. London.

Woman as "Other"

Simone de Beauvoir

French existentialist Simone de Beauvoir (1908–1986) is one of the most important figures of the women's movement in the twentieth century. The Second Sex *was one of the earliest inquiries into the social construction of "femininity" and sparked a great deal of debate. Beauvoir was a political activist all her life and participated in the women's movement in France during the second wave.*

Le Deuxième Sexe (The Second Sex) *was published in France in 1949 and in the United States in 1953, a time and climate hospitable neither to feminist scholarship nor to activism. Coming at a time of transition for the women's movement, between the social-psychological debates of the twenties and thirties and the liberation movement of the sixties, the book was a work of great creativity and courage. Broad in range and at times complex in argument, it covers issues in philosophy, biology, psychology, sociology, anthropology, education, politics, history, and more. The unifying theme is summarized by H. M. Parshley in the translator's preface:*

> *. . . Since patriarchal times women have in general been forced to occupy a secondary place in the world in relation to men, a position comparable in many respects with that of racial minorities in spite of the fact that women constitute numerically at least half of the human race, and further that this secondary standing is not imposed of necessity by natural "feminine" characteristics but rather by strong environmental forces of educational and social tradition under the purposeful control of men. This, the author maintains, has resulted in the general failure of women to take a place of human dignity as free and independent existents, associated with men on the plane of intellectual and professional equality, a condition that not only has limited their achievement in many fields but also has given rise to pervasive social evils and has had a particularly vitiating effect on the sexual relations between men and women.*

Beauvoir's thesis is not new and was not new in 1949, but it had been ignored, and her treatment of it was unique. Today, she has been faulted for being nonpolitical in her orientation, not sufficiently concerned with remedy, and at times even sexist in her perspective. Although that may be true of the work in its present context, it was a criticism far less applicable in its day, and the book was widely read.

As a philosophy, existentialism emphasizes direct experience, feeling, awareness, choice, commitment, and honestly. It strives for living "authentically," being true to one's own values and insights, living fully and freely, taking responsibility for one's actions, sharpening one's understanding, and ultimately moving beyond the confines of the brute here and now as determined by the concrete social environment. In this, one is said to strive for transcendence. *A major theme of* The Second Sex *is that women's peripheral existence denies them the chance for transcendence.*

In the following selection, Beauvoir analyzes the female condition of otherness *or* alterity. *It is natural, she argues, for people—either individually or collectively—to understand their existence in terms of a fundamental duality: I (Self) and things not myself (Other). The mature adult juxtaposes her or his own needs and perceptions against those of others, understanding at the same time that the other person is doing so as well. To me, I am Self, you are Other; but to you, you are Self, I am Other. I realize and accept this as so. Beauvoir terms the equality of claims to Self and Otherness from different perspectives* reciprocity. *She points out, however, that the typical reciprocity of claims to Selfness does not obtain between women and men. Men perceive themselves as Self and women as Other. That is as it should be. The problem Beauvoir emphasizes is that women too perceive men as Self (as subject) and themselves as Other. Commonly, neither men nor women recognize the reciprocity of Selfness for women.*

A MAN WOULD NEVER GET THE NOTION OF WRITING a book on the peculiar situation of the human

---

male.[1] But if I wish to define myself, I must first of all say: "I am a woman"; on this truth must be based all further discussion. A man never begins by presenting himself as an individual of a certain sex; it goes without saying that he is a man. The terms *masculine* and *feminine* are used symmetrically only as a matter of form, as on legal papers. In actuality the relation of the two sexes is not quite like that of two electrical poles, for man represents both the positive and the neutral, as is indicated by the common use of *man* to designate human beings in general; whereas woman represents only the negative, defined by limiting criteria, without reciprocity. In the midst of an abstract discussion it is vexing to hear a man say: "You think thus and so because you are a woman"; but I know that my only defense is to reply: "I think thus and so because it is true," thereby removing my subjective self from the argument. It would be out of the question to reply: "And you think the contrary because you are a man," for it is understood that the fact of being a man is no peculiarity. A man is in the right in being a man; it is the woman who is in the wrong. It amounts to this: just as for the ancients there was an absolute vertical with reference to which the oblique was defined, so there is an absolute human type, the masculine. Woman has ovaries, a uterus; these peculiarities imprison her in her subjectivity, circumscribe her within the limits of her own nature. It is often said that she thinks with her glands. Man superbly ignores the fact that his anatomy also includes glands, such as the testicles, and that they secrete hormones. He thinks of his body as a direct and normal connection with the world, which he believes he apprehends objectively, whereas he regards the body of woman as a hindrance, a prison, weighed down by everything peculiar to it. "The female is a female by virtue of a certain *lack* of qualities," said Aristotle; "we should regard the female nature as afflicted with a natural defectiveness." And St. Thomas for his part pronounced woman to be an "imperfect man," an "incidental" being. This is symbolized in Genesis where Eve is depicted as made from what Bossuet called "a supernumerary bone" of Adam.

Thus humanity is male and man defines woman not in herself but as relative to him; she is not regarded as an autonomous being. Michelet writes: "Woman, the relative being. . . ." And Benda is most positive in his *Rapport d' Uriel:* "The body of man makes sense in itself quite apart from that of woman, whereas the latter seems wanting in significance by itself. . . . Man can think of himself without woman. She cannot think of herself without man." And she is simply what man decrees; thus she is called "the sex," by which is meant that she appears essentially to the male as a sexual being. For him she is sex—absolute sex, no less. She is defined and differentiated with reference to man and not he with reference to her; she is the incidental, the inessential as opposed to the essential. He is the Subject, he is the Absolute—she is the Other.[2]

The category of the *Other* is as primordial as consciousness itself. In the most primitive societies, in the most ancient mythologies, one finds the expression of a duality—that of the Self and the Other. This duality was not originally attached to the division of the sexes; it was not dependent upon any empirical facts. It is revealed in such works as that of Granet on Chinese thought and those of Dumézil on the East Indies and Rome. The feminine element was at first no more involved in such pairs as Varuna-Mitra, Uranus-Zeus, Sun-Moon, and Day-Night than it was in the contrasts between Good and Evil, lucky and unlucky auspices, right and left, God and Lucifer. Otherness is a fundamental category of human thought.

Thus it is that no group ever sets itself up as the One without at once setting up the Other over against itself. If three travelers chance to occupy the same compartment, that is enough to make vaguely hostile "others" out of all the rest of the passengers on the train. In small-town eyes all persons not belonging to the village are "strangers" and suspect; to the native of a country all who inhabit other countries are "foreigners"; Jews are "different" for the anti-Semite, Negroes are "inferior" for American racists, aborigines are "natives" for colonists, proletarians are the "lower class" for the privileged.

Lévi-Strauss, at the end of a profound work on the various forms of primitive societies, reaches the following conclusion: "Passage from the state of Nature to the state of Culture is marked by man's ability to view biological relations as a series of contrasts; duality, alternation, opposition, and symmetry, whether under definite or vague forms, constitute not so much phenomena to be explained as fundamental and immediately given data of social reality."[3] These phenomena would be incomprehensible if in fact human society were simply a *Mitsein* or fellowship based on solidarity and friendliness. Things become clear, on the contrary, if, following Hegel, we find in consciousness itself a fundamental hostility toward every other consciousness; the subject can be posed only in being opposed—he sets himself up as the essential, as opposed to the other, the inessential, the object.

But the other consciousness, the other ego, sets up a reciprocal claim. The native traveling abroad is shocked to find himself in turn regarded as a "stranger" by the natives of neighboring countries. As a matter of fact, wars, festivals, trading, treaties, and contests among tribes, nations, and classes tend to deprive the concept *Other* of its absolute sense and to make manifest its relativity; willy-nilly, individuals and groups are forced to realize the reciprocity of their relations. How is it, then, that this reciprocity has not been recognized between the sexes, that one of the contrasting terms is set up as the sole essential, denying any relativity in regard to its correlative and defining the latter as pure otherness? Why is it that women do not dispute male sovereignty? No subject will readily volunteer to become the object, the inessential; it is not the Other who, in defining himself as the Other, establishes the One. The Other is posed as such by the One in defining himself as the One. But if the Other is not to regain the status of being the One, he must be submissive enough to accept this alien point of view. Whence comes this submission in the case of woman?

There are, to be sure, other cases in which a certain category has been able to dominate another completely for a time. Very often this privilege depends upon inequality of numbers—the majority imposes its rule upon the minority or persecutes it. But women are not a minority, like the American Negroes or the Jews; there are as many women as men on earth. Again, the two groups concerned have often been originally independent; they may have been formerly unaware of each other's existence, or perhaps they recognized each other's autonomy. But a historical event has resulted in the subjugation of the weaker by the stronger. The scattering of the Jews, the introduction of slavery into America, the conquests of imperialism are examples in point. In these cases the oppressed retained at least the memory of former days; they possessed in common a past, a tradition, sometimes a religion or a culture.

The parallel drawn by Bebel between women and the proletariat is valid in that neither ever formed a minority or a separate collective unit of mankind. And instead of a single historical event it is in both cases a historical development that explains their status as a class and accounts for the membership of *particular individuals* in that class. But proletarians have not always existed, whereas there have always been women. They are women in virtue of their anatomy and physiology. Throughout history they have always been subordinated to men,[4] and hence their dependency is not the result of a historical event or a social change—it was not something that *occurred*. The reason why otherness in this case seems to be an absolute is in part that it lacks the contingent or incidental nature of historical facts. A condition brought about at a certain time can be abolished at some other time, as the Negroes of Haiti and others have proved; but it might seem that a natural condition is beyond the possibility of change. In truth, however, the nature of things is no more immutably given, once for all, than is historical reality. If woman seems to be the inessential which never becomes the essential, it is because she herself fails to bring about this change. Proletarians say "We"; Negroes also. Regarding themselves as subjects, they transform the bourgeois, the whites, into "others." But women do not say "We," except at some congress of feminists or similar formal demonstration; men say "women," and women use the same word in referring to themselves. They do not authentically assume a subjective attitude. The proletarians have accomplished the revolution in Russia, the Negroes in Haiti, the Indo-Chinese are battling for it in Indo-China; but the women's effort has never been anything more than a symbolic agitation. They have gained only what men have been willing to grant; they have taken nothing, they have only received.[5]

The reason for this is that women lack concrete means for organizing themselves into a unit which can stand face to face with the correlative unit. They have no past, no history, no religion of their own; and they have no such solidarity of work and interest as that of the proletariat. They are not even promiscuously herded together in the way that creates community feeling among the American Negroes, the ghetto Jews, the workers of Saint-Denis, or the factory hands of Renault. They live dispersed among the males, attached through residence, housework, economic condition, and social standing to certain men—fathers or husbands—more firmly than they are to other women. If they belong to the bourgeoisie, they feel solidarity with men of that class, not with proletarian women; if they are white, their allegiance is to white men, not to Negro women. The proletariat can propose to massacre the ruling class, and a sufficiently fanatical Jew or Negro might dream of getting sole possession of the atomic bomb and making humanity wholly Jewish or black; but woman cannot even dream of exterminating the males. The bond that unites her to her oppressors is not comparable to any other. The division of the sexes is a biological fact, not an event in human history. Male and female stand opposed within a primordial *Mitsein,* and woman has not broken it. The couple is a fundamental unity with its two halves riveted together, and the cleavage of society along the line of sex is impossible. Here is to be found the basic trait of woman: she is the Other in a totality of which the two components are necessary to one another.

One could suppose that this reciprocity might have facilitated the liberation of woman. When Hercules sat at the feet of Omphale and helped with her spinning, his desire for her held him captive; but why did she fail to gain a lasting power? To revenge herself on Jason, Medea killed their children; and this grim legend would seem to suggest that she might have obtained a formidable influence over him through his love for his offspring. In *Lysistrata* Aristophanes gaily depicts a band of women who joined forces to gain social ends through the sexual needs of their men; but this is only a play. In the legend of the Sabine women, the latter soon abandoned their plan of remaining sterile to punish their ravishers. In truth woman has not been socially emancipated through man's need—sexual desire and the desire for offspring—which makes the male dependent for satisfaction upon the female.

Master and slave, also, are united by a reciprocal need, in this case economic, which does not liberate the slave. In the relation of master to slave the master does not make a point of the need that he has for the other; he has in his grasp the power of satisfying this need through his own action; whereas the slave, in his dependent condition, his hope and fear, is quite conscious of the need he has for his master. Even if the need is at bottom equally urgent for both, it always works in favor of the oppressor and against the oppressed. That is why the liberation of the working class, for example, has been slow.

Now, woman has always been man's dependent, if not his slave; the two sexes have never shared the world in equality. And even today woman is heavily handicapped, though her situation is beginning to change. Almost nowhere is her legal status the same as man's,[6] and frequently it is much to her disadvantage. Even when her rights are legally recognized in the abstract, long-standing custom prevents their full expression in the mores. In the economic sphere men and women can almost be said to make up two castes; other things being equal, the former hold the better jobs, get higher wages, and have more opportunity for success than their new competitors. In industry and politics men have a great many more positions and they monopolize the most important posts. In addition to all this, they enjoy a traditional prestige that the education of children tends in every way to support, for the present enshrines the past—and in the past all history has been made by men. At the present time, when women are beginning to take part in the affairs of the world, it is still a world that belongs to men—they have no doubt of it at all and women have scarcely any. To decline to be the Other, to refuse to be a party to the deal—this would be for women to renounce all the advantages conferred upon them by their alliance with the superior caste. Man-the-sovereign will provide women-the-liege with material protection and will undertake the moral justification of her existence; thus she can evade at once both economic risk and the metaphysical risk of a liberty in which ends and aims must be contrived without assistance. Indeed, along with the ethical urge of each individual to affirm his subjective existence, there is also the temptation to forgo liberty and become a thing. This is an inauspicious road, for he who takes it—passive, lost, ruined—becomes henceforth the creature of another's will, frustrated in his transcendence and deprived of every value. But it is an easy road; on it one avoids the strain involved in undertaking an authentic existence. When man makes of woman the *Other,* he may, then, expect her to manifest deep-seated tendencies toward complicity. Thus, woman may fail to lay claim to the status of subject because she lacks definite resources, because she feels the necessary bond that ties her to man regardless of reciprocity, and because she is often very well pleased with her role as the *Other.*

But it will be asked at once: how did all this begin? It is easy to see that the duality of the sexes, like any duality, gives rise to conflict. And doubtless the winner will assume the status of absolute. But why should man have won from the start? It seems possible that women could have won the victory; or that the outcome of the conflict might never have been decided. How is it that this world has always belonged to the men and that things have begun to change only recently? Is this change a good thing? Will it bring about an equal sharing of the world between men and women?

These questions are not new, and they have often been answered. But the very fact that woman *is the Other* tends to cast suspicion upon all the justifications that men have ever been able to provide for it. These have all too evidently been dictated by men's interest. A little-known feminist of the seventeenth century, Poulain de la Barre, put it this way: "All that has been written about women by men should be suspect, for the men are at once judge and party to the lawsuit." Everywhere, at all times, the males have displayed their satisfaction in feeling that they are the lords of creation. "Blessed be God . . . that He did not make me a woman," say the Jews in their morning prayers, while their wives pray on a note of resignation: "Blessed be the Lord, who created me according to His will." The first among the blessings for which Plato thanked the gods was that he had been created free, not enslaved; the second, a man, not a woman. But the males could not enjoy this privilege fully unless they believed it to be founded on the absolute and the eternal; they sought to make the fact of their supremacy into a right. "Being men, those who have made and compiled the laws have favored their own sex, and jurists have elevated these laws into principles," to quote Poulain de la Barre once more.

Legislators, priests, philosophers, writers, and scientists have striven to show that the subordinate position of woman is willed in heaven and advantageous on earth. The religions invented by men reflect this wish for domination. In the legends of Eve and Pandora men have taken up arms against women. They have made use of philosophy and theology, as the quotations from Aristotle and St. Thomas have shown. Since ancient times satirists and moralists have delighted in showing up the weaknesses of women. We are familiar with the savage indictments hurled against women throughout French literature. Montherlant, for example, follows the tradition of Jean de Meung, though with less gusto. This hostility may at times be well founded, often it is gratuitous; but in truth it more or less successfully conceals a desire for self-justification. As Montaigne says, "It is easier to accuse one sex than to excuse the other." Sometimes what is going on is clear enough. For instance, the Roman law limiting the rights of woman cited "the imbecility, the instability of the sex" just when the weakening of family ties seemed to threaten the interests of male heirs. And in the effort to keep the married woman under guardianship, appeal was made in the sixteenth century to the authority of St. Augustine, who declared that "woman is a creature neither decisive nor constant," at a time when the single woman was thought capable of managing her property. Montaigne understood clearly how arbitrary and unjust was woman's appointed lot: "Women are not in the wrong when they decline to accept the rules laid down for them, since the men make these rules without consulting them. No wonder intrigue and strife abound." But he did not go so far as to champion their cause.

It was only later, in the eighteenth century, that genuinely democratic men began to view the matter objectively. Diderot, among others, strove to show that woman is, like man, a human being. Later John Stuart Mill came fervently to her defense. But these philosophers displayed unusual impartiality. In the nineteenth century the feminist quarrel became again a quarrel of partisans. One of the consequences of the industrial revolution was the entrance of women into productive labor, and it was just here that the claims of the feminists emerged from the realm of theory and acquired an economic basis, while their opponents became the more aggressive. Although landed property lost power to some extent, the bourgeoisie clung to the old morality that found the guarantee of private property in the solidity of the family. Woman was ordered back into the home the more harshly as her emancipation became a real menace. Even within the working class the men endeavored to restrain women's liberation, because they began to see the women as dangerous competitors—the more so because they were accustomed to work for lower wages.[7]

In proving women's inferiority, the antifeminists then began to draw not only upon religion, philosophy, and theology, as before, but also upon science—biology, experimental psychology, etc. At most they were willing to grant "equality in difference" to the *other* sex. That profitable formula is most significant; it is precisely like the "equal but separate" formula of the Jim Crow laws aimed at the North American Negroes. As is well known, this so-called equalitarian segregation has resulted only in the most extreme discrimination. The similarity just noted is in no way due to chance, for whether it is a race, a caste, a class, or a sex that is reduced to a position of inferiority, the methods of justification are the same. "The eternal feminine" corresponds to "the black soul" and to "the Jewish character." True, the Jewish problem is on the whole very different from the other two—to the anti-Semite the Jew is not so much an inferior as he is an enemy for whom there is to be granted no place on earth, for whom annihilation is the fate desired. But there are deep similarities between the situation of woman and that of the Negro. Both are being emancipated today from a like paternalism, and the former master class wishes to "keep them in their place"—that is, the place chosen for them. In both cases the former masters lavish more or less sincere eulogies, either on the virtues of "the good Negro" with his dormant, childish, merry soul—the submissive Negro—or on the merits of the woman who is "truly feminine"—that is, frivolous, infantile, irresponsible—the submissive woman. In both cases the dominant class bases its argument on a state of affairs that it has itself created. As George Bernard Shaw puts it, in substance, "The American white relegates the black to the rank of shoeshine boy; and he concludes from this that the black is good for nothing but shining shoes." This vicious circle is met with in all analogous circumstances; when an individual (or a group of individuals) is kept in a situation of inferiority, the fact is that he *is* inferior. But the significance of the verb *to be* must be rightly understood here; it is in bad faith to give it a static value when it really has the dynamic Hegelian sense of "to have become." Yes, women on the whole *are* today inferior to men; that is, their situation affords them fewer possibilities. The question is: should that state of affairs continue?

Many men hope that it will continue; not all have given up the battle. The conservative bourgeoisie still see in the emancipation of women a menace to their morality and their interests. Some men dread feminine competition. Recently a male student wrote in the *Hebdo-Latin:* "Every woman student who goes into medicine or law robs us of a job." He never questioned his rights in this world. And economic interests are not the only ones concerned. One of the benefits that oppression confers upon the oppressors is that the most humble among them is made to *feel* superior; thus, a "poor white" in the South can console himself with the thought that he is not a "dirty nigger"—and the more prosperous whites cleverly exploit this pride.

Similarly, the most mediocre of males feels himself a demigod as compared with women. It was much easier for M. de Montherlant to think himself a hero when he faced women (and women chosen for his purpose) than when he was obliged to act the man among men—something many women have done better than he, for that matter. And in September 1948, in one of his articles in the *Figaro littéraire,* Claude Mauriac—whose great originality is admired by all—could[8] write regarding woman: "*We* listen on a tone [*sic!*] of polite indifference . . . to the most brilliant among them, well knowing that her wit reflects more or less luminously ideas that come from *us.*" Evidently the speaker referred to is not reflecting the ideas of Mauriac himself, for no one knows of his having any. It may be that she reflects ideas originating with men, but then, even among men there are those who have been known to appropriate ideas not their own; and one can well ask whether Claude Mauriac might not find more interesting a conversation reflecting Descartes, Marx, or Gide rather than himself. What is really remarkable is that by using the questionable *we* he identifies himself with St. Paul, Hegel, Lenin, and Nietzsche, and from the lofty eminence of their grandeur looks down disdainfully upon the bevy of women who make bold to converse with him on a footing of equality. In truth, I know of more than one woman who would refuse to suffer with patience Mauriac's "tone of polite indifference."

I have lingered on this example because the masculine attitude is here displayed with disarming ingenuousness. But men profit in many more subtle ways from the otherness, the alterity of woman. Here is miraculous balm for those afflicted with an inferiority complex, and indeed no one is more arrogant toward women, more aggressive or scornful, than the man who is anxious about his virility. Those who are not fear-ridden in the presence of their fellow men are much more disposed to recognize a fellow creature in woman; but even to these the myth of woman, the Other, is precious for many reasons.[9] They cannot be blamed for not cheerfully relinquishing all the benefits they derive from the myth, for they realize what they would lose in relinquishing woman as they fancy her to be, while they fail to realize what they have to gain from the woman of tomorrow. Refusal to pose oneself as the Subject, unique and absolute, requires great self-denial. Furthermore, the vast majority of men make no such claim explicitly. They do not *postulate* woman as inferior, for today they are too thoroughly imbued with the ideal of democracy not to recognize all human beings as equals.

In the bosom of the family, woman seems in the eyes of childhood and youth to be clothed in the same social dignity as the adult males. Later on, the young man, desiring and loving, experiences the resistance, the independence of the woman desired and loved; in marriage, he respects woman as wife and mother, and in the concrete events of conjugal life she stands there before him as a free being. He can therefore feel that social subordination as between the sexes no longer exists and that on the whole, in spite of differences, woman is an equal. As, however, he observes some point of inferiority—the most important being unfitness for the professions—he attributes these to natural causes. When he is in a co-operative and benevolent relation with woman, his theme is the principle of abstract equality, and he does not base his attitude upon such inequality as may exist. But when he is in conflict with her, the situation is reversed: his theme will be the existing inequality, and he will even take it as justification for denying abstract equality.[10]

So it is that many men will affirm as if in good faith that women *are* the equals of man and that they have nothing to clamor for, while *at the same time* they will say that women can never be the equals of man and that their demands are in vain. It is, in point of fact, a difficult matter for man to realize the extreme importance of social discriminations which seem outwardly insignificant but which produce in woman moral and intellectual effects so profound that they appear to spring from her original nature.[11] The most sympathetic of men never fully comprehend woman's concrete situation. And there is no reason to put much trust in the men when they rush to the defense of privileges whose full extent they can hardly measure. We shall not, then, permit ourselves to be intimidated by the number and violence of the attacks launched against women, nor to be entrapped by the self-seeking eulogies bestowed on the "true woman," nor to profit by the enthusiasm for woman's destiny manifested by men who would not for the world have any part of it.

We should consider the arguments of the feminists with no less suspicion, however, for very often their controversial aim deprives them of all real value. If the "woman question" seems trivial, it is because masculine arrogance has made of it a "quarrel"; and when quarreling, one no longer reasons well. People have tirelessly sought to prove that woman is superior, inferior, or equal to man. Some say that, having been created after Adam, she is evidently a secondary being; others say on the contrary that Adam was only a rough draft and that God succeeded in producing the human being in perfection when He created Eve. Woman's brain is smaller; yes, but it is relatively larger. Christ was made a man; yes, but perhaps for his greater humility. Each argument at once suggests its opposite, and both are often fallacious. If we are to gain understanding, we must get out of these ruts; we must discard the vague notions of superiority, inferiority, equality which have hitherto corrupted every discussion of the subject and start afresh.

Notes

1. The Kinsey Report [Alfred C. Kinsey and others: *Sexual Behavior in the Human Male* (W. B. Saunders Co., 1948)] is no exception, for it is limited to describing the sexual characteristics of American men, which is quite a different matter.

2. E. Lévinas expresses this idea most explicitly in his essay *Temps et l'Autre.* "Is there not a case in which otherness, alterity [*altérité*], unquestionably marks the nature of a being, as its essence, an instance of otherness not consisting purely and simply in the opposition of two species of the same genus? I think that the feminine represents the contrary in its absolute sense, this contrariness being in no wise affected by any relation between it and its correlative and thus remaining absolutely other. Sex is not a certain specific difference . . . no more is the sexual difference a mere contradiction. . . . Nor does this difference lie in the duality of two complementary terms, for two complementary terms imply a pre-existing whole. . . . Otherness reaches its full flowering in the feminine, a term of the same rank as consciousness but of opposite meaning."

I suppose that Lévinas does not forget that woman, too, is aware of her own consciousness, or ego. But it is striking that he deliberately takes a man's point of view, disregarding the reciprocity of subject and object. When he writes that woman is mystery, he implies that she is mystery for man. Thus his description, which is intended to be objective, is in fact an assertion of masculine privilege.

3. See C. Lévi-Strauss: *Les Structures élementaires de la parenté.* My thanks are due to C. Lévi-Strauss for his kindness in furnishing me with the proofs of his work, which, among others, I have used liberally in Part II.

4. With rare exceptions, perhaps, like certain matriarchal rulers, queens, and the like—TR.

5. See Part II, ch. viii.

6. At the moment an "equal rights" amendment to the Constitution of the United States is before Congress.—TR. [*Note:* Today, nearly fifty years after the writing of *Second Sex,* that amendment is still before Congress—still not yet law.—S. Ruth]

7. See Part II.

8. Or at least he thought he could.

9. A significant article on this theme by Michel Carrouges appeared in No. 292 of the *Cahiers du Sud.* He writes indignantly: "Would that there were no woman-myth at all but only a cohort of cooks, matrons, prostitutes, and bluestockings serving functions of pleasure or usefulness!" That is to say, in his view woman has no existence in and for herself; he thinks only of her *function* in the male world. Her reason for existence lies in man. But then, in fact, her poetic "function" as a myth might be more valued than any other. The real problem is precisely to find out why woman should be defined with relation to man.

10. For example, a man will say that he considers his wife in no wise degraded because she has no gainful occupation. The profession of housewife is just as lofty, and so on. But when the first quarrel comes he will exclaim: "Why, you couldn't make your living without me!"

11. The specific purpose of Book II of this study is to describe this process.

4

Talking Back: Feminist Responses to Sexist Stereotypes

The Challengers

Subtract the effort to meet the stereotypic model; undo much of the indoctrination; add a streak of independence, self-affirmation, and self-respect; toss in a growing knowledge of women's history and circumstance, pride in womanhood, and concern for other women; wrap all in a strong awareness of the entire process—and you have some picture of the feminist woman who today is challenging old images and building new ones. If patriarchy is hostile to women in general, even those who conform to masculist standards and regulations, one can imagine the attitudes toward the feminist woman, who rejects patriarchy's regulations and constraints, refuses to accept the "place" constructed for her, and aspires instead to a space of her own regardless of its acceptability to the patriarchs. To the masculist, a feminist woman is the incarnation of a nightmare, the "feminazi" of Rush Limbaugh fame. According to this mythology, a woman unfettered by "respectable" convention—by the watchful eyes of fathers, brothers, and husbands—is dangerous. Now here are women not only unredeemed by their servitude but also questioning convention, rebelling, refusing their appointed labors, lusting after male jobs, intruding on male territory, demanding preposterous freedoms, and worst of all, making headway!

To verify this hostility, one need only turn to the common indicators of social attitudes: TV stories, letters to the editor in newspapers and magazines, commentaries in books and magazines, political campaign rhetoric and election results, church sermons, in-group jokes, and the other usual sources. Notice how the feminist and her demands are presented. Either ridiculed or despised, she is first of all *unfeminine*. This term implies not only a lack of "charm" and expertise in certain "womanly" behaviors, it suggests as well a particular appearance: either hard, "glitzy," and slick or dirty, unkempt, badly dressed, and not pretty—she is clearly disadvantaged in whatever it takes to attract men. She is perceived as in some way having trouble with sex and as having problems relating to men because of bad experiences either in childhood (with her father) or later on (with husband, lover, or rapist). In short, she is maladjusted. From a representative cross section of such hostile comments, one gathers that feminists want:

- to become like men, to "sleep around," to reject their maternal prerogatives and special "power," to emasculate men, and to destroy civilization (George Gilder)[1]
- to indulge themselves, abrogate familial responsibility, and avoid sex (Midge Decter)[2]

- to reject their true "femininity," castrate men, have a penis of their own, and disrupt society (Sigmund Freud)[3]
- to surrender their womanliness, become "phallic women," and distort the innate balance of complementarity in life and nature (Karl Stern)[4]
- to destroy the universities, academic freedom, scholarship, etc. (those against affirmative action)
- to give up all "the wonderful privileges" women in this country now enjoy (Phyllis Schlafly)
- the "suppression of modesty" and the "naturally given" sexual differentiation which makes "men and women always men and women"[5] and the "dismantling" of men's souls.[6] (Allan Bloom)
- to take jobs away from those who are "really oppressed"
- to turn their children over to communist-inspired day-care centers
- to kill babies

Feminists, it is said, tend to get "shrill" or "strident," which means literally high-pitched, grating on the ear. These are terms one would expect masculists to use; they are—and are meant to be—deprecating. They not only refer to the higher pitch of the female voice, but they also conjure up images of whining old crones and nagging shrews. They are a means of ridiculing and discounting feminist arguments: "Not only do I not accept the things you are saying, but I don't even take them seriously; I reduce them simply to the ugly noises of thwarted, aggressive women."

Yet I believe that, in a sense different from the intended one, the terms *shrill* and *strident* are accurate, for they reveal a deeper, perhaps unconscious, truth. Feminists' arguments *are* extremely grating—to masculist mind-sets. Feminists are striking at values and feelings that run deep and have powerful impact. If even the smallest changes in sex orientation (such as altering hair length) provoke marked reactions—which they seem to—then greater shifts will certainly beget proportionately greater response. Feminists can and do expect to incur a great deal of anger and abuse, whether that is expressed as ridicule or as outright attack.

Although we have had some gains in the last thirty years, women—feminist or nonfeminist—still live in a hostile environment. We live within a struggle. Feminists work within this struggle: We philosophize, analyze, act, try, and grow there. Our development—the way we grow, the things we learn, and the visions we create—all bear that mark and so we must understand them in that context.

To one degree or another, most feminists perceive themselves as revolutionaries. In Shulamith Firestone's words, "If there were another word more all-embracing than revolution we would use it."[7] Yet we are revolutionaries on peculiar terrain, for we do not typically seek war—that is, to exchange one hierarchy for another. We rarely hate our "enemies." In fact, we often hesitate to call anyone "enemy," not quite certain who or what that enemy might be. It is said that most of us live intimately in the homes of our oppressors, loving and caring for them. We are not decided on a firm, far-reaching revolutionary program for we have not agreed upon one set of strategies or goals. Yet with all, we *are* revolutionaries, for in altering the arrangements of work and relationships between women and men, in challenging the primacy of martial-masculist values, we mean to change the very nature of life and society for all people.

The women's movement has a saying: The personal is the political. This means several things. First, no gulf truly exists between the personal and social elements of our lives. It also means that much of what we have taken to be private matters—problems of communication with our men, for example, or the failures in our sexual relationships—are actually not purely personal but are also social and political, a consequence of the power arrangements between women and men. "The personal is the political" means also that the insights we gain into our private circumstances can ultimately have widespread political and social consequences.

Kate Millett defined politics as "power-structured relationships, arrangements whereby one group of persons is controlled by another."[8] If that is the case, then such questions as, "Why do I get up earlier than he does and prepare breakfast for the family before we both go off to our jobs?" are political questions because they refer to men's control of women's time and effort. It is a political issue that most women are still expected to wash, cook, clean, and serve and yet not be paid for their labors or even recognized as working. It is a political issue that society places the class of women in such a position and not so the class of men. This is no small matter for it represents one symptom of the exploitation and domination of 51 percent of the world population by the remaining 49 percent. If the exploitation of women by men is both model and manifestation of other forms of exploitation and oppression, as many feminists believe, then understanding male–female roles is profoundly important, and challengers' analyses of sexism—rather than being petty and inconsequential as charged—are highly significant, not only for the 51 percent, but for all humanity.

The personal is the political, and feminists are fomenting a revolution out of consciousness-raising.

The Process: Coming to Understand

The process of learning and unlearning, of coming to recognize the consequences that the images of woman have and of reorienting oneself toward them is difficult, painstaking, and time-consuming. Considering how long each of us has lived with these images and the extent of their power in our culture, it is not surprising that this is so.

Consciousness-Raising

Each of us has come to the task of becoming aware from her own set of circumstances and in her own way. Most women report a first moment, an event, when they experienced "the explosion," the first rush of awareness or insight into sexism and its intimate connection with them. Perhaps triggered by a personal crisis—an unwanted pregnancy and the social cruelties that often follow, or a divorce that left her burdened and impoverished, or perhaps job discrimination or social humiliation or even a feminist speech that freed the woman from some damaging beliefs—the explosion or insight, once begun, is almost always followed by a growing and developing awareness. Often the growth is conscious, sought after, and cultivated. Sometimes it happens despite resistance, for the awareness, though freeing and exciting, is painful and frightening as well.

This process of coming to understand sexism fully, at the highest level of awareness, is called "consciousness-raising." It both intensifies awareness of the implications of sexism and stimulates the search for alternatives. Consciousness-raising takes a variety of forms; it follows from various techniques (for example, self-examination, role reversal, shared discussion); and it takes different paths.

The Insight: It's a Lie

How does the experience of consciousness-raising proceed? Suppose you spent your youth learning the trade of "femininity." Suppose Mom and Dad taught you to make yourself just right so you could attract just the right man so he would care for you and make you happy because that is what women and men do, and it is right and proper and wonderful that it should be that way. Suppose you do just what is expected: You become feminine and sweet and sexy, and you find that man (or, rather, he finds you), and you marry and have three lovely children, and he has a lovely job and you have a lovely house and . . . then suppose it suddenly ends. Now suppose you find yourself in your thirty-third year with three lovely children, no husband, meager or no support, no income, no skills, no joy. Suppose you see him with freedom, mobility, job skills, income, future. What do you say? Usually you first say, "What did I do wrong?" But perhaps in time you gain some insight and recognize that what went wrong wasn't you—it was the whole thing: beliefs, assumptions, and expectations. Seeing this, you say, "Oh, it was a lie."

Suppose it doesn't end. Suppose you have the lovely children, the lovely home, the lovely husband, but you aren't happy. You're depressed or restless or grouchy. You're always busy, but you're also bored. What do you say? You say, "What's wrong with me? Why am I unsatisfied?" Or perhaps you look around and say, "It was a lie."

Suppose you did all the things you were advised to do in *Cosmopolitan* or *Woman's Day:* You were kind, thoughtful, playful, sexy, and supportive—but instead of undying love, you got misunderstanding, neglect, and hostility. What do you say?

Suppose it all went a different way. Suppose your youth was poor and hard. You learned to scratch and scrape. Now jobs are hard to find, and when they do come along they pay even less than a man's, and your men come and go, and you have some babies to support, but when you go to court and ask for support, the (male) judge decides that, after all, Mr. X has a new family to support and cannot be left penniless! What do you say?

Or suppose the scenario is very different. You spent your youth learning and preparing and studying, and the future is bright because America is a land of opportunity. You know things are harder for a woman and you have to be twice as good, but you *are* twice as good. But suppose you can't find the kind of job you want. They just ask how many words per minute you can type. Or suppose they do give you that job (EEOC and Title IX, you know), but you find you're the only sales associate answering the phone or having a typewriter on your desk. What do you say?

When at last, for whatever reason and in whatever way, you recognize one lie, you get suspicious, and you begin to look at it all. Soon you see just how many lies there are. Then you think: If women are stupid, incompetent, and petty, as they say, but I am female and *not* those things, either I am not a woman, or it's a lie. And if it's a lie about me, it's a lie about other women; and if that's a lie, then perhaps the rest is a lie. Perhaps it's a lie that women can't be trusted with important tasks; that for women love is more important than income; that women are best satisfied in the home of a he-male; that women don't need jobs or a salary; that men should make the decisions; that women should *never* be "slutty" or "pushy" or "ambitious" or "shrill."

Once begun, the questioning has no limits. We discover lie upon lie, myth upon myth. The response? If it is not true that women are bad or incompetent, then all our subordination is just plain wrong. If the role won't work, we'll have to find another way.

Where is it written that it must be the way it is?

What We Learn: The Images Tell Us

The heading of this section is presumptuous. What we learn when we begin to ask these kinds of questions is so vast that it could not be told in a thousand volumes. What I would like to describe here, though, are some of the insights feminists have had into themselves as women, into the effects of the myths and stereotypes, and into the possibilities open to women without them.

The Splitting of the Androgyne: Complements

The term *androgyne* is composed of the two ancient Greek words *andros* and *gyne*, "man" and "woman." In certain feminist theories, it refers to a person of either sex characterized by a combination of qualities that traditionally have been taken to be only male or only female.[9] The androgyne, or the androgynous person, may be strong *and* tender, rational *and* feeling, independent *and* receptive, and so on. Or they may be none of these but exhibit other traits true to their individuality.

As we saw earlier, what currently obtains in the ideals of women and men is the exact opposite: Instead of androgyny, there is *complementarity*. Women and men are expected to exhibit opposite and exclusive traits and behavior.

Patriarchal Ideals

Ideal Man	*Ideal Woman*
powerful, creative,	nurturant, supportive,
intelligent, rational,	intuitive, emotional, cunning,
independent, self-reliant,	needful, dependent,
strong,	tender,
courageous, daring,	timid, fragile,
responsible, resolute,	capricious, childlike,
temperate, cautious, sober,	ebullient, exuberant,
honest, forthright,	tactful, evasive, artful,
active, forceful,	passive, receptive,
honorable, principled, just,	obedient, loyal, kind, merciful,
self-affirming,	self-abnegating,
authoritative, decisive,	compliant, submissive,
successful, task-oriented,	contented, serene, being-oriented,
he does,	she cares,
he lives in the mind,	she lives in the heart,
he confronts the world	she withdraws from the world

Some sexists say that men and women are complements to one another; that their complementarity is natural, desirable, and beautiful; that together these two, different but interlocking, provide for themselves, their families, and society all that is necessary and harmonious for human living. Actually, the theory of complementarity is based on a division of labor: Men and women, each having different natural capacities and abilities, have different (but equally important) tasks and spheres that are appropriate to their "natures."

Feminists argue that this is a "mystification," an intentional camouflaging of reality by euphemistic social myths. They counter with concrete criticisms of this complementary arrangement:

- It may be appealing to envision two interlocking creatures walking hand in hand down life's highway, but in reality half a person and half a person equal two half-persons, not one whole.
- As Plato pointed out in the third century B.C., human beings require balance and excellence in all of their qualities to function well. The ideal man of patriarchy may be eminently successful so far as society is concerned, but if he lacks the ability to feel and to experience fully the affective elements of living, he gains only half of what life has to offer, and he is apt to be a rather unbalanced and unpleasant person. The ideal patriarchal woman may be very fetching and capable of deep feeling, but she is also unable to take care of herself in the material aspects of life, and hence she is at the mercy of other people and events.
- It is unrealistic to believe that two people, entirely different in capacity and outlook, could successfully manage meaningful communication, mutual respect, and love. Rather than interlocking, these people are locked together in destructive, though symbiotic, partnership. The traditional complementary arrangement is logical and functional only in terms of social and economic efficiency, not in terms of human needs. Complementarity, a "division of labor," may be an effective way of accomplishing a variety of social tasks; and when marriage functioned as a social arrangement for satisfying certain community needs, complementarity might have been a productive perspective. But if marriage is to function as a satisfying *personal* arrangement, as a primary source of emotional support and profound human interchange, then complementarity is dysfunctional, and "interlocking" symbiosis is a psychological and spiritual disaster.
- Even if it were possible for two people to relate well in complementarity, women would still be at a marked disadvantage. In fact, we are.

In the first place, the thesis that in our society the two elements, male and female, are different but equal in value and importance is a lie. The system—patriarchal in origin and serving patriarchal ends—is built on the principle that men rule and women obey, that men take care of themselves and women take care of everyone but themselves. Even in the most benevolent of all worlds, that is not a highly promising arrangement for women.

In the second place, though it is true that in a system of complementarity men and women are both in the position of using half and only half of their human capacities (and so losing half as well), the half that men keep is the half valued by society (which stands to reason, given the control of the masculists), and the half that women keep is devalued. Though women are praised, a patronizing undertone always accompanies that praise. The praise is awarded for traits that society deems substandard.

> Sigh no more, ladies
> Time is male
> and in his cups drinks to the fair.
> Bemused by gallantry, we hear
> our mediocrities over-praised,
> indolence read as abnegation,
> slattern thought styled intuition,
> every lapse forgiven, our crime
> only to cast too bold a shadow
> or smash the mould straight off.
> For that, solitary confinement,
> tear gas, attrition shelling.
> Few applicants for that honor.
>
> –ADRIENNE RICH,
> "Snapshots of a Daughter-in-Law"[10]

Human Versus Female

In Chapter 2, we looked at the historical confusion of the concepts *man* and *human*. In fact, the patriarchal schema of complementary ideals is both cause and effect of that confusion. The configuration of traits and qualities reserved for men is the configuration expected of excellent human beings: intelligence, independence, courage, honor, strength. Not so the configuration for a woman. Womanly perfection and human excellence in this schema are incompatible.

In effect, women are being asked to choose between their human selves and their sexual identities. Unlike men, who develop and improve their masculinity and humanity concurrently, women in patriarchy only destroy their acceptability as females if they develop their human excellence or else destroy their human potential if they become more "feminine."

A famous early feminist study, still important today, translated this issue into the language of psychology.

A study by Inge Broverman and her colleagues suggests that many clinicians today view their female patients the way Freud viewed his. They gave 79 therapists (46 male and 33 female psychiatrists, psychologists and social workers) a sex-role-stereotype questionnaire. This test consists of 122 pairs of traits such as "very subjective . . . very objective" or "not at all aggressive . . . very aggressive."

The investigators asked the subjects to rate each set of traits on a scale from one to seven, in terms of where a healthy male should fall, a healthy female, or a healthy adult (sex unspecified). They found:

1. *There was a high agreement among these clinicians on the attributes that characterize men, women and adults.*
2. *There were no major differences between the male and the female clinicians.*
3. *Clinicians have different standards of mental health for men and women. Their standards for a "healthy adult man" looked like those for a "healthy adult"; but healthy women differed from both by being: submissive, emotional, easily influenced, sensitive to being hurt, excitable, conceited about their appearance, dependent, not very adventurous, less competitive, unaggressive, unobjective—and besides, they dislike math and science. This "healthy woman" is not very likeable, all in all! (In fact, other studies have shown that these traits, characteristic of normal women, are the least socially desirable.) For a woman to be "healthy," then, she must adjust to the behavioral norms for her sex even though these norms are not highly valued by her society, her men—or her therapist.*[11]

Thus, behavior considered healthy for men was not considered healthy for women, and vice versa. Men and women were expected to display opposite characteristics. But the traits deemed *generally* healthy, desirable for *people* without regard to sex, were those expected of or prescribed for men. Women displaying those traits would be deemed "unfeminine." At the same time, women who were "feminine," who would be deemed healthy or adjusted as women, would by this schema have to be judged sick as people!

What an impossible dilemma. Women may choose to be considered "feminine," or we may choose to be mature, healthy human beings, but we may not be both. Put a slightly different way: While men may be thought of as human beings who happen to be male, women are cast as females who happen to be (in a lesser sense) human.

Feminists argue that complementarity is a disaster for both sexes, that the healthy person (of either sex) is the human being who excels in both configurations—or perhaps rejects *any* configuration—who has the wherewithal to cope with the necessities and challenges of life, as well as the sensibilities to do it in a way that is *for* life.

What's Wrong with "Femininity"?

In the preceding chapter we noted that the dichotomy in the female ideal required women to exemplify at once two incompatible characterizations, Mary and the Playmate, and we could see how destructive such a contradiction is. However, more is wrong with patriarchal female images, or "femininity," than just the contradictions wrought by dichotomy. For one thing, feminists argue, the pejorative stereotype of "Woman the Inferior" is false. For another, neither of the supposedly nonpejorative images, Mary or Playmate, is a desirable model. In fact, both are demeaning and destructive.

The Myth of Female Inferiority

According to misogynist ideology, women are inferior in two ways: (1) women are morally inferior, evil, bad, sinful, dangerous, harmful, and dirty; (2) women are inferior in ability—physically, intellectually, and spiritually.

Women Are Evil. That women are morally inferior to the point of being positively evil is a well-worn theme that comes down to us today from antiquity:

Woman is a pitfall—a pitfall, a hole, a ditch. Woman is a sharp iron dagger that cuts a man's throat.

–MESOPOTAMIAN POEM[12]

Man who trusts womankind trusts deceivers.

–HESOID[13]

The beauty of woman is the greatest snare.

–ST. JOHN CHRYSOSTOM[14]

You are the devil's gateway . . . the first deserter of the divine law; you are she who persuaded him whom the devil was not valiant enough to attack. You destroyed so easily God's image, man. On account of your desert—that is, death—even the son of God had to die.

–TERTULLIAN[15]

I have not left any calamity more detrimental to mankind than woman.

–ISLAMIC SAYING[16]

Art thou not formed of foul slime? Art thou not full of uncleanness?

–RULE FOR ANCHORESSES[17]

God made Adam master over all creatures, to rule over all living things, but when Eve persuaded him that he was lord even over God she spoiled everything. . . . With tricks and cunning women deceive men.

–MARTIN LUTHER[18]

I cannot escape the notion . . . that for women the level of what is ethically normal is different from what it is in man.

–SIGMUND FREUD[19]

So much for woman on a pedestal. These historical statements have only scratched the surface. Further evidence of the belief in female malevolence abounds—no less virulent today than it has been for centuries. In the past were the stories of Delilah and Salome; Medusa, the Gorgon who turned men into stone; Meanads, who tore men apart and ate them during drunken orgies; Sirens, who lived in the sea and lured sailors to their death with covert promises. Which of us did not grow up on the wicked women of the fairy tales: vain and murderous queens, dark fairies, bad witches, malevolent stepsisters and their cruel, ambitious, self-centered mothers. What these women all had in common was that they were not "good" like Snow White and Sleeping Beauty and Cinderella. They were not young and fair and victimized; they were not "sweet" and pliant, vulnerable, dependent, and utterly passive. Indeed, they were women on their own: autonomous, self-directed, unowned, *and therefore uncontrolled.* And that is why, furthermore, they all came to no good.

How different are these characters and these tales from those of today? Are there not still good, sweet, wholesome, back-home kinds of girls who follow their hearts and their men and their prescribed roles and win (the prince) in the end? The poor, sweet, innocent, good-hearted creatures of *Pretty in Pink, An Officer and a Gentlemen,* and *Pretty Woman* endure, remain loyal and loving even in the face of rejection and shame—and they triumph. Another fate befalls the tougher women in *Diary of a Mad Housewife* or *Kramer vs. Kramer, Fatal Attraction,* and *Working Girl;* after all, they rebelled, said no. Consider the movies *Nothing in Common* or *Fatal Attraction.* In each, a powerful, willful, independent, beautiful woman seems *for a while* to be in control. But she is vanquished in the end, supplanted by the sweet and proper lady; in each case, both women are raised or lowered in esteem by the choice of the male, who moves easily between them and always acts for his own interests in his own way.

To all such allegations of evil, feminists retort: Nonsense! While patriarchal society prattles of women's destructiveness, feminists ask: Who creates weapons and marches off to war? Who hunts and kills living creatures for fun? Who fights for kicks? Who pillages the earth for profit? Who colonizes and exploits? What destruction could we have wrought that even nearly compares? If Eve you call us, then we will be Eve in our sense, in the best sense, reconstructed according to our feminist perspectives:

> *They say: she violated the taboo, surrendered to the snake, ate the apple, corrupted the man, brought about the expulsion from the Father's garden, was responsible for the Fall, called down the Father's curse. Upon earth, upon labor, upon childbirth, upon woman. So far as they were concerned they told a tale of sin and its punishment, of gluttony and its consequences, of disobedience and the revenge taken by the primal father against those who eat.*
>
> *I say: Eve dared to break the taboo against eating, embraced the temptation offered by the snake, ate the*

apple, and returned symbolically to the maternal breast to regain an identity with the Mother Goddess. If eating caused her to be expelled from her Father's house, that precisely is what allowed her to give birth to the Woman Who Is Not Yet.

Eve's dilemma: a choice between obedience and knowledge. Between renunciation and appetite. Between subordination and desire. Between security and risk. Between loyalty and self-development. Between submission and power. Between hunger as temptation and hunger as vision.

It is the dilemma of modern women.

–KIM CHERNIN, *Reinventing Eve*[20]

Women Are Incompetent. The charge that both requires and easily admits of refutation is that women are simply not as able as men, not as competent at any task except those traditionally designated "women's work." It is said that women are less capable than men of doing any kind of work requiring a high degree of rationality, abstraction, and intelligence because women are intellectually inferior and are characteristically not given to rationality and logic. It is said that, in even the best of circumstances, even unusually intelligent women are still not the equals of men in important and difficult work because they are temperamentally unsuited to seriousness of purpose, sustained effort, and strain. It is said that women are unable to withstand the pressure of competition, either with people or with ideas, and are therefore always destined to defeat. And finally, it is said that women who are not thus characteristically inferior are not "normal," are not attractive or natural or feminine, and are not even really women—another double bind.

As evidence of women's inferiority, it is asserted that the great scientists, inventors, legislators, entrepreneurs, artists, humorists, authors, athletes, and warriors have always been men. Where are the female geniuses—the Beethovens, Shakespeares, and Platos? We are told that in business and industry, in the professions and professional schools, it is men who outnumber women, who outrank women, who achieve. Even today, argue the sexists, when women have all the opportunities of men, they still do not make it. Why? Because women do not have the intelligence, the instincts, the grit, the motivation, the stamina, or the strength of men. In every way that counts, women are inferior.

This is how the schema goes:

Part I—It is unnatural and undesirable for women to do what men do; women must expend their energies serving, supporting, and pleasing; they must not be allowed to do what men do.

Part II—Because women do not do the things men do, it is evident that they cannot do what men do and are therefore obviously inferior.

The argument is circular, superficial, and fallacious. It does, however, hold tremendous power in society—at least as a rationale for the status quo—and a majority, both female and male, believe it.

Feminists refute these arguments. We contend that the socialization process and the structure of society, not "natural" capacities, account for the different levels of achievement and motivation in women and men. Although the literature is mixed and the research inconclusive, there is no evidence that men and women differ in intellectual capacity or IQ, and a good deal of evidence to the contrary. Apparently males excel earlier in spatial perception and females in verbal perception, but even this difference may possibly be accounted for by social conditions. It is certainly not sufficient to account for the wide divergence in interest, abilities, motivations, and achievements.

A great deal of evidence suggests that "feminine" ideals—the images and values described in Chapter 3, including the constraints and circumstances imposed on women from childhood—are far more responsible for women's alleged and actual lack of motivation, grit, and aggressiveness than any inherent childlikeness or timidity. Differences in training, expectations, and experience produce ineffectualness and defeatism in women as they do in men. Yet there are and always have been women of incredible courage, stamina, and commitment:

And even though they keep me blindfolded forever, I will always be able to find my way back to Chile, my country, set between the Cordillera of the Andes and the sea, between a dialectic of landscapes, between the malevolent Pacific and the untamable Andes. Between these opposing confines I grew up, among things proper for little girls, beside my grandmothers who predicted a tranquil future for me, and also beside marvelous wise old women dressed in black, rebozos *around their shoulders, who bewitched me with their native wisdom and their universe of signs and symbols. . . .*

Our liberty as women will come from our own efforts. And it will come with the help of others strong enough to help us, those who will want to know and understand us, who will want to learn from those of us who have not forgotten how to live and how to sing. Bullets cannot kill us, bonds cannot bind the strength of our hands, blindfolds cannot imprison our vision. We hold in our own palms our ultimate truths.

–Marjorie Agosin, "Chile: Women of Smoke"[21]

Not now nor ever has equality of opportunity existed for women—in business, the professions, education, the arts, or any other socially prized and male-controlled venture. Today, doors are still only grudgingly opening to women. Women are still ill paid for our work, segregated in function, last hired and first fired. Even if this were not so, the separate but not equal conditioning of females and the hostility and ignorance of the men already in positions of power make any claims to equality of opportunity a farce.

Women's dual roles and incompatible cultural requirements render success in the community or in a profession painfully expensive if not impossible, physically, emotionally, spiritually:

I was a child when I first heard someone say, "Men work from sun to sun, but women's work is never done." For years I thought it proof that women, rather than being the "weaker" sex, were if anything superior to, stronger than men. I was a woman, very much grown, before I realized how heavy those words can weigh—the reality, the burden.

Black women work! *Yet the gruesome truth is that "women's work" is often dismissed, taken for granted or devalued. It's almost as if never-ending hard work and bearing burdens is what we were born to. Our plates are piled high with things we have to do or are expected to do or want to do or are pushed to.*

The pressures we women are under are intense. We are bombarded from all sides with all manner of things we gotta do: Gotta make ways for lasting meaningful social, economic and political change. Gotta stop analyzing and amening and get to practical solutions, then make 'em happen. Gotta do well on our jobs, gotta keep 'em or get better ones or make the ones we have pay off. Gotta keep our relationships thriving or get some going. Gotta look good and stay healthy. Told that we gotta be in control of our lives and our destinies. Gotta be past, present and future women all at the same time. Gotta keep our spirits and our sanity. Most important, or so it often seems, is that we Black women gotta be good women, gotta be strong.

–Marcia Ann Gillespie, "The Myth of the Strong Black Woman"[22]

The married woman who works outside the home usually carries two jobs—one paid (however humbly), one not paid. She is lawyer (teacher, doctor, pilot, secretary . . .), and she is homemaker and mother. The price of such demands, both for her profession and her personal health, are obvious. The unmarried professional faces different costs: slurs on her womanhood, social disapprobation, at times loneliness. According to the image, ideal women are intuitive but not rational, lovely but not effectual. The successful professional, according to the myth, is the unsuccessful *femme.* To opt for a career, the story goes, is to relinquish one's happily-ever-after. Such visions, even unfounded, are disturbing. They do not do much for professional motivation.

To the questions, "Why haven't women produced any geniuses? Why are there no female Shakespeares or Beethovens?" Virginia Woolf answered that we have not been allowed a "room of our own." We have been accorded bread but not roses. We have not been allowed the spiritual atmosphere, the creative space men are heir to, the amenities (not to mention the financial circumstances) that raise life above the mundane and encourage one to creativity.

The issues treated here all point to an important feminist argument: A range of factors in the environment conspire to impede women's competence and accomplishments in many areas: the hostile or deprecating attitudes of incumbent men, lack of support and assistance from all quarters, dual and/or incompatible professional and nonprofessional functions, pervasiveness of the male (alien, inhospitable) ambience, and socialization that erodes confidence and self-assertion. Rather than being inferior, women are hampered in developing competence in the most profound ways. To overcome the obstacles put in our way, we must indeed be twice as good but in more ways than we expected. It is not surprising that so many of us don't "succeed." What is extraordinary is that any of us do.

And what we do accomplish often disappears! In the history books, women of achievement are rarely given more than a few lines, and the experiences of ordinary women, unlike those of the "the common man," are simply not considered. Our successes have often gone underground—to be attributed to men or thought to be anonymous because women were not permitted success. Female authors or artists often used male pen names or "protectors" or "co-authors" who frequently co-authored them right out of their due. Ancient accomplishments are simply usurped by the patriarchy. Male historians and anthropologists "forget" to research the contributions of women to early civilization: the introduction of pottery, weaving, food preservation and preparation, perhaps even agriculture itself. Current anthologies of the arts do not bother to include women's works because these are "inferior," "narrow," or "lacking in grandeur."

And we cannot forget that at times and still in some places it is dangerous for women to succeed, that women die for assertiveness. Midwives were burned as witches, rebellious wives and daughters were imprisoned in convents or beaten or burned alive. Feminists in Nazi Germany went to concentration camps. In Iran they may be shot.

> *In December of 1970, Ms. Farrokhrou Parsa, the first woman to serve in the Iranian cabinet, was executed after a trial by hooded judges—a trial at which no defense attorney was permitted, no appeal possible, and the defendant had been officially declared guilty before the proceedings began. She was charged with "expansion of prostitution, corruption on earth, and warring against God." Aware of the hopelessness of her case, she delivered a reasoned, courageous defense of her career decisions, among them a directive to free female schoolchildren from having to be veiled and the establishment of a commission for revising textbooks to present a nonsexist image of women. A few hours after sentence was pronounced she was wrapped in a dark sack and machine-gunned. . . .*
>
> *. . . The years ahead will be difficult. To unite a torn and battered nation and rebuild what had been destroyed is a monumental task. But as I contemplate the future of Iran, a reassuring image gives me hope. I recall a young women I met in the southern village of Zovieh. She had finished her military service in the literacy corps to return to her home and establish a school in which she taught all subjects to all four grades. On the day I saw her, she was walking out of a village meeting in her faded uniform, flushed, and proud, followed by the old men who had just selected her* Kadkhoda, *or "elderman," of the village.*
>
> *Those who have struggled and those who have died sacrificed so that women like her may exist.*
>
> *She is the future.*
>
> –MAHNAZ AFKHAMI, "Iran: A Future in the Past—The 'Prerevolutionary' Women's Movement"[23]

The Dark Side of the "Good" Woman

Refuting the claim that women as a class are inferior does not constitute the entire feminist offensive against patriarchal female images. The so-called positive images of women in patriarchy are as much a target, for even the ideals—Perfect Woman, Mary, or the Playmate—are destructive. Despite the apparent praise, approval, and veneration, these ideals actually disparage women and cause us to disparage ourselves and assist in diminishing our lives.

Consider once again the major requirements of traditional femininity: beauty, self-effacement, fragility, and domesticity. History, poetry, literature, philosophy, and even science have eulogized the woman who embodies these qualities, but feminists have taken a closer look. Demystifying the image, translating myth into reality—through introspection and analysis—we have seen the dark side of this image.

Beauty Attractiveness in people is by and large a cultural phenomenon; beauty is socially defined. In patriarchy, men construct the ideal in their own interests, and women—whose lives have no purpose outside of being chosen, whose identities and fortunes have been made subject to their appeal to men—have little choice but to struggle with the imperious requirements of "beauty" even though the ideal is impossible. For no human being can be "perfect" in hair, skin, teeth, shape, proportion, and scent, and furthermore be so both "naturally" and endlessly. Constant comparison with the made-up and reconstructed figures of screen and magazine that more nearly realize the ideal always leaves us defeated, always at a disadvantage, always self-deprecating.

Women are called narcissistic. We are chided for our obsession with clothing and fashion. We are ridiculed for slathering cream on our skin and dye in our hair. And yet that is precisely what is demanded *if we accept* the traditional role that bids us to use our appearance to attract and keep a mate. Can we reject that option if any life other than "being chosen" is deemed undesirable or even unacceptable, if "attractive" and "sexy" are society's primary terms of approbation for women?

Self-effacement The concept of submissiveness for women has changed since the Middle Ages. Few today expect a women to lower her head and whisper, "Yes, sir." Yet the concept survives: No one likes an aggressive woman. We may quarrel, we may fight, but in the end, if we don't give in and lose often enough, we will lose our man. Assertiveness, the kind that goes beyond a little pluckiness, is still not considered acceptable in women; it is always translated into aggression.

And self-effacement? The husband who taunts in public is teasing. The wife who does the same is attacking her man's ego. She is not expected to say, "Yes, dear," but she is expected to yield the decisions (or pretend to), follow his job, entertain his friends. He drives when he chooses; he works late when he needs to. He storms out of the house when angry; she screams or she cries, but she stays put.

Women, it is said, are prone to depression. We get "neurotic," clingy, and nagging. What man who could not make his own decisions, place his own needs high in priority, satisfy his desires and wishes, please himself, and follow his goals would not get depressed and "neurotic"? What man barred from creating his own pleasures and diversions wouldn't nag others for entertainment? The logical outcome of self-effacement is depression.

Fragility Very close to self-effacement is fragility. Women are to be submissive because we are weaker, needful of protection and guidance. In gratitude and in our understanding of our best interests, we are to take direction from the stronger. Fragility—physical smallness, timidity, delicacy, needfulness—means vulnerability. It is, to be sure, very appealing to the male. But vulnerability of the sort required of women means dependence. To be fearful of strange situations, to be hesitant when decisions are called for, to avoid risk, to learn *not* to defend oneself, to feign or even encourage physical weakness, to shrink from the world—all these are to place oneself at the mercy of circumstances, to afford oneself dependence on others. Even if those on whom one depends are completely trustworthy, marvelously competent, and around forever, anyone in such a situation must feel some lack of self-respect, a sense of inferiority and ineffectualness. For such people, life is truncated; the pleasures and rewards of independence, accomplishment, and power are unknown. Further, in a culture that clearly values competence and where human excellence is said to include independence and self-reliance, the endlessly vulnerable and dependent person is a figure of ridicule and contempt. We saw earlier that for women this was so.

Domesticity *Kinder, Kirche, Küche*—"children, church, and cooking"—was the slogan of ideal womanhood for Hitler's Germany, the Third Reich. Similarly, housekeeping and all of its attendant duties; care of children, including teaching, nursing, and other service occupations; and worship (*not* theology) are said to be the only legitimate occupations for women in patriarchy. What is more, the work is to be task-oriented, not policy-oriented; that is, we are to execute our jobs according to prescribed procedure, not to define those jobs or to create their meaning. Ours is to carry out that part of any job that is repetitive, routine, uninteresting. Work that transcends the mundane belongs to men. Women may be cooks, not chefs; dressmakers, not designers; secretaries, not executives. We may busy ourselves with the pretties of making curtains or vases, but we are not to presume to art.

The imminent (as the existentialists call it), the mundane, the here-and-now, the "what," is dull and petty unless it is lifted by the transcendent, the eternal, the why and the wherefore. Tasks and things do not have the scope or the breadth of ideas. Interest, scope, and depth belong to creativity. Interesting people are living, growing people; they are people themselves interested, excited, challenged and challenging, learning and experiencing. *Kinder, Kirche, Küche*—however taxing of time and energy—cannot be creative unless so treated. In closing women to freedom of experience and movement, in disallowing as "unfeminine" an interest in the transcendent, in constricting our limits and our power, patriarchy confines us to the narrow and then condemns us for our "narrowness."

Patriarchal feminine ideals are monstrous. When successful, they destroy; and when we become the most perfect realizations of them, we are most damaged.

Responses: Feminist Reactions and Ideals

When feminist women look over the history of the tyranny of these beliefs and visions, when we note the destruction they have wrought and the exploitation they have legitimized, we are appalled and filled with anger, pain, grief, shock, and, finally, determination.

Some call feminists petty, prattling noisily about inconsequentials. But is the loss of potential, of self-respect and autonomy inconsequential? Are economic deprivation and financial dependency inconsequential, or the use and abuse of our bodies for the interests of others? What about infanticide, physical mutilation, footbinding, and other physical torture? Is ten thousand years of domination and exploitation of over half of humanity inconsequential?

We are advised to be ladylike, to go slow, ask nicely, develop a sense of humor. Are we to swallow our pride once again and plead prettily for our liberation from those who have withheld it for ten millennia until this day? Are we to chuckle good naturedly at centuries of restrictive clothing, at chastity belts and whalebone corsets, at enforced fatigue of body and mind, at slave labor and sexual servitude, at prostitution and rape? Are we to take these images in our stride, once more play the peacemakers, maintain the hated postures just a little longer while the masculists slowly adjust to the idea of change?

No, say the feminists, we won't do it. If we are angry, it is because we have seen the attack. If we are noisy, it is because women are suffering. If we sound strident, it is because the affirmation of women grates on the ears of masculists. "It is not that we are so radical," said Gloria Steinem, "but that there is something radically wrong with our world."

We have seen the visions of *woman the oppressed, woman the exploited, woman the outsider, woman the lost, woman the debased*—and we reject them all, opting instead for positive visions.

Feminists are building new visions. Throwing away the demands of "femininity" so badly conceived, canceling "ladylikeness," we are redefining what is desirable for us, what is commendable, what is possible. Our new heroines include *woman rediscovering herself* in history and for today; *woman redeeming herself* in her own eyes; *woman rightfully angry,* rightfully fighting; and *woman the leader,* the pillar, who in the words of Wilma Scott Heide may "create the kind of world where the power of love exceeds the love of power."[24] Indeed, our heroines include our own selves, to whom we are saying, yes!

What we shall be, what we should and can be, remains an open question. Feminists are still very much involved in the matter of what we are not and should not be. We have been asked what we would wish to be, how life would be if we could have our way, and many have answered that it is hard to say. We have never known a time when we have not been subordinated and devalued; we have never known a time of freedom and self-determination. We are only beginning to learn our history and to conceive our future—with few known models and precious little experience. In very large part, the question of what we ought to be is the question philosophers have pursued for centuries: What is human excellence and virtue? Women are, after all, human beings, and our strivings and hopes are those of all humanity. How our ideals may differ from those of men or how our insights may alter the notion of human excellence is yet to be discovered.

Certain things we do know: We are being born, coming into life. We are struggling, and in this birth struggle is joy. That has been expressed eloquently by feminist writers Germaine Greer and Erica Jong.

> *The surest guide to the correctness of the path that women take is* joy in the struggle. *Revolution is the festival of the oppressed. For a long time there may be no perceptible reward for women other than their new sense of purpose and integrity. Joy does not mean riotous glee, but it does mean the purposive employment of energy in a self-chosen enterprise. It does mean pride and confidence. It does mean communication and cooperation with others based on delight in their company and your own. To be emancipated from helplessness and need and walk freely upon the earth that is your birthright. To refuse hobbles and deformity and take possession of your body and glory in its power, accepting its own laws of loveliness. To have something to desire, something to make, something to achieve, and at last something genuine to give. To*

be freed from guilt and shame and the tireless self-discipline of women. To stop pretending and dissembling, cajoling and manipulating, and begin to control and sympathize. To claim the masculine virtues of magnanimity and generosity and courage. It goes much further than equal pay for equal work, for it ought to revolutionize the conditions of work completely. It does not understand the phrase "equality of opportunity," for it seems that the opportunities will have to be utterly changed and women's souls changed so that they desire opportunity instead of shrinking from it. The first significant discovery we shall make as we racket along our female road to freedom is that men are not free, and they will seek to make this an argument why nobody should be free. We can only reply that slaves enslave their masters, and by securing our own manumission we may show men the way that they could follow when they jumped off their own treadmill. Privileged women will pluck at your sleeve and seek to enlist you in the "fight" for reforms, but reforms are retrogressive. The old process must be broken, not made new. Bitter women will call you to rebellion, but you have too much to do. What will you do?

–GERMAINE GREER, *The Female Eunuch*[25]

Narrowing life because of the fears
narrowing it between the dust motes,
narrowing the pink baby
between the tree-limbed monsters,
& the drooling idiots,
& the ghosts of Thalidomide infants,
narrowing hope,
always narrowing hope.
Mother sits on one shoulder hissing:
Life is dangerous.
Father sits on the other sighing:
Lucky you.
Grandmother, grandfather, big sister:
You'll die if you leave us,
You'll die if you ever leave us.

Sweetheart, baby sister,
you'll die anyway
& so will I.

Even if you walk the wide greensward,
even if you
& your beautiful big belly
embrace the world of men & trees,
even if you moan with pleasure,
& smoke the sweet grass
& feast on strawberries in bed,
you'll die anyway—
wide or narrow,
you're going to die.
As long as you're at it,
die wide.
Follow your belly to the green pasture.
Lie down in the sun's dapple.
Life is not as dangerous
as mother said.
It is more dangerous,
more wide.

–ERICA JONG, "For Claudia, Against Narrowness"[26]

What might I, as representative of many feminists, include in an ideal? I would like to see:

- women bearing all the marvelous traits of excellence chronicled by the great philosophers: strength, intelligence, temperance, independence, courage, principle, honor, and the rest
- women, beautiful and healthy in our bodies, comfortable with them, understanding them, proud of them
- women free of the fetters of possession and exploitation, free to define our own female beings, to direct the rites, events, and progress of our own lives and experience
- women caring for one another, proud of our womanhood, caring for any living thing in the way that is meaningful to us
- women contributing wholeheartedly and equally with men to civilization in whatever way we enjoy and believe to be right.

Notes

1. George Gilder, *Sexual Suicide* (New York: Quadrangle, 1973), ch. 1.

2. Midge Decter, *The New Chastity and Other Arguments Against Women's Liberation* (New York: Coward, McCann & Geoghegan, 1972).

3. Especially in Sigmund Freud, "Femininity," Lecture XXXIII, in *The Standard Edition of the Complete Psychological Works of Sigmund Freud*, trans. and ed. James Strachey et al. (London: Hogarth Press, 1964), vol. 22.

4. Karl Stern, *The Flight from Woman* (New York: Farrar, Straus & Giroux, 1965).

5. Allan Bloom, *The Closing of the American Mind* (New York: Simon & Schuster, 1987), pp. 101–102.

6. Ibid., p. 129.

7. Shulamith Firestone, *The Dialectic of Sex* (New York: Bantam, 1971), p. 1.

8. Kate Millett, *Sexual Politics* (New York: Doubleday, 1970), p. 23.

9. The meaning and utility of the concept of androgyny is much debated. See Joyce Trebilcot, "Two Forms of Androgynism," in *Feminism and Philosophy*, ed. Mary Vetterling-Braggin, Frederick A. Elliston, and Jane English (Totowa, N.J.: Littlefield, Adams, 1977), among others.

10. The lines from "Snapshots of a Daughter-in-Law" are reprinted from COLLECTED EARLY POEMS, 1950–1970, by Adrienne Rich, by permission of the author and W. W. Norton & Company, Inc. Copyright © 1993 by Adrienne Rich. Copyright © 1967, 1963, 1962, 1961, 1960, 1959, 1958, 1957, 1956, 1955, 1954, 1953, 1952, 1951 by Adrienne Rich. Copyright © 1984, 1975, 1969, 1966, by W. W. Norton & Company, Inc.

11. Reported by Phyllis Chesler, "Men Drive Women Crazy," in *The Female Experience*, ed. Carol Tavris (Del Mar, CA: Communications Research Machines, 1973), p. 83.

12. Quoted in Vern L. Bullough, Brenda Shelton, and Sarah Slavin, *The Subordinated Sex* (University of Georgia Press, 1988), p. 24.

13. Ibid., p. 49.

14. Ibid., p. 84.

15. Ibid., p. 96–97.

16. Ibid., p. 122.

17. Ibid., p. 150.

18. Ibid., p. 169.

19. Quoted in Chesler, "Men Drive Women Crazy," p. 82.

20. Kim Chernin, *Reinventing Eve: Modern Woman in Search of Herself* (New York: Harper & Row, 1987), p. 182.

21. Marjorie Agosin, "Chile: Women of Smoke," trans. Cola Franzen from *SISTERHOOD IS GLOBAL: THE INTERNATIONAL WOMEN'S MOVEMENT ANTHOLOGY,* edited by Robin Morgan (New York: Anchor Books, 1984) pp. 138, 141. Copyright © 1984 by Robin Morgan. By permission of Edite Kroll Literary Agency.

22. Marcia Ann Gillespie, "The Myth of the Strong Black Woman," *Essence Magazine*, August 1982, p. 58.

23. Mahnaz Afkhami, "Iran: A Future in the Past," from *SISTERHOOD IS GLOBAL: THE INTERNATIONAL WOMEN'S MOVEMENT ANTHOLOGY,* edited by Robin Morgan, supra, pp. 330, 337. Copyright © 1984 by Robin Morgan. By permission of Edite Kroll Literary Agency.

24. Wilma Scott Heide in the Introduction to *Hospitals, Paternalism, and the Role of the Nurse,* by JoAnn Ashley (New York: Teachers College Press, 1976), p. viii.

25. Germaine Greer, *The Female Eunuch* (New York: McGraw-Hill, 1971), pp. 328–329. Copyright © 1970, 1971 by Germaine Greer. Reprinted by permission of the publishers, McGraw-Hill Book company.

26. "For Claudia, Against Narrowness." From LOVEROOT by Erica Jong. Copyright © 1968, 1969, 1973, 1974, 1975 by Erica Mann Jong. Reprinted by permission of Henry Holt and Company, Inc.

Woman—Which Includes Man, Of Course

Theodora Wells

Theodora Wells, who took an MBA at the University of Southern California, taught management and communication at the University of California at Los Angeles and at the University of Southern California. President of Wells Associates, a management consulting firm, she is also coauthor of Breakthrough: Women into Management *(1972) and* Keeping Your Cool Under Fire: Communicating Non-Defensively *(1980).*

The following selection is an "experience in awareness." Read and feel it slowly and deeply.

THERE IS MUCH CONCERN TODAY ABOUT THE FUture of man, which means, of course, both men and women—generic Man. For a woman to take exception to this use of the term "man" is often seen as defensive hair-splitting by an "emotional female."

The following experience is an invitation to awareness in which you are asked to feel into, and stay with, your feelings through each step, letting them absorb you. If you start intellectualizing, try to turn it down and let your feelings again surface to your awareness.

Consider reversing the generic term Man. Think of the future of Woman which, of course, includes both women and men. Feel into that, sense its meaning to you—as a woman—as a man.

Think of it always being that way, every day of your life. Feel the everpresence of woman and feel the nonpresence of man. Absorb what it tells you about the importance and value of being woman—of being man.

Recall that everything you have ever read all your life uses only female pronouns—she, her—meaning both girls and boys, both women and men. Recall that most of the voices on radio and most of the faces on TV are women's—when important events are covered—on commercials—and on the late talk shows. Recall that you have no male senator representing you in Washington.

Feel into the fact that women are the leaders, the power-centers, the prime-movers. Man, whose natural role is husband and father, fulfills himself through nurturing children and making the home a refuge for woman. This is only natural to balance the biological role of woman who devotes her entire body to the race during pregnancy.

Then feel further into the obvious biological explanation for woman as the ideal—her genital construction. By design, female genitals are compact and internal, protected by her body. Male genitals are so exposed that he must be protected from outside attack to assure the perpetuation of the race. His vulnerability clearly requires sheltering.

Thus, by nature, males are more passive than females, and have a desire in sexual relations to be symbolically engulfed by the protective body of the woman. Males psychologically yearn for this protection, fully realizing their masculinity at this time—feeling exposed and vulnerable at other times. The male is not fully adult until he has overcome his infantile tendency to penis orgasm and has achieved the mature surrender of the testicle orgasm. He then feels himself a "whole man" when engulfed by the woman.

If the male denies these feelings, he is unconsciously rejecting his masculinity. Therapy is thus indicated to help him adjust to his own nature. Of course, therapy is administered by a woman, who has the education and wisdom to facilitate openness leading to the male's growth and self-actualization.

To help him feel into his defensive emotionality, he is invited to get in touch with the "child" in him. He remembers his sister's jeering at his primitive genitals that "flop around foolishly." She can run, climb and ride horseback unencumbered. Obviously, since she is free to move, she is encouraged to develop her body and mind in preparation for her active responsibilities of adult womanhood. The male vulnerability needs female protection, so he is taught the less active, caring, virtues of homemaking.

Because of his clitoris-envy, he learns to strap up his genitals, and learns to feel ashamed and unclean because of his nocturnal emissions. Instead, he is encouraged to keep his body lean and dream of getting married, waiting for the time of his fulfillment—when "his woman" gives him a girl-child to carry on the family name. He knows that if it is a boy-child he has failed somehow—but they can try again.

In getting to your feelings on being a woman—on being a man—stay with the sensing you are now experiencing. As the words begin to surface, say what you feel from inside you.

Consciousness-Raising

Catharine A. MacKinnon

Catharine A. MacKinnon is professor of law at the University of Michigan Law School. She has been extremely active in the feminist antipornography movement in the United States and around the world. Her publications include Toward a Feminist Theory of the State *(1989),* Feminism Unmodified: Discourses on Life and Law *(1987), and* Sexual Harassment of Working Women: A Case of Sexual Discrimination *(1987).*

Here, MacKinnon describes the process of developing a feminist consciousness, of beginning to "see" previously invisible realities of gender and of women's lives. "The key to feminist theory consists in its way *of knowing," she says. This aspect of feminism is crucial, and explains in part the unique character of feminist politics, activism, and pedagogy.*

Consciousness raising is the process through which the contemporary radical feminist analysis of the situation of women has been shaped and shared. As feminist method and practice, consciousness raising is not confined to groups explicitly organized or named for that purpose. In fact, consciousness raising as discussed here was often not practiced in consciousness-raising groups. Such groups were, however, one medium and forum central to its development as a method of analysis, mode of organizing, form of practice, and technique of political intervention. The characteristic structure, ethic, process, and approach to social change which mark such groups as a development in political theory and practice are integral to many of the substantive contributions of feminist theory. The key to feminist theory consists in its *way* of knowing. Consciousness raising is that way. "[An] oppressed group must at once shatter the self-reflecting world which encircles it and, at the same time, project its own image onto history. In order to discover its own identity as distinct from that of the oppressor, it has to become visible to itself. All revolutionary movements create their own way of seeing."[1] One way to analyze feminism as a theory is to describe the process of consciousness raising as it occurred in consciousness-raising groups.

As constituted in the 1960s and 1970s, consciousness-raising groups were many women's first explicit contact with acknowledged feminism. Springing up spontaneously in the context of friendship networks, colleges and universities, women's centers, neighborhoods, churches, and shared work or workplaces, they were truly grassroots. Many aimed for diversity in age, marital status, occupation, education, physical ability, sexuality, race and ethnicity, class, or political views. Others chose uniformity on the same bases. Some groups proceeded biographically, each woman presenting her life as she wished to tell it. Some moved topically, using subject focuses such as virginity crises, relations among women, mothers, body image, and early sexual experiences to orient discussion. Some read books and shared literature. Some addressed current urgencies as they arose, supporting women through difficult passages or encouraging them to confront situations they had avoided. Many developed a flexible combination of formats. Few could or wanted to stick to a topic if a member was falling apart, yet crises were seldom so clarifying or continuous as entirely to obviate the need for other focus.

Participants typically agreed on an ethic of openness, honesty, and self-awareness. If a member felt she could not discuss an intimate problem or felt coerced to do so, this was typically taken as a group failure. Other usual norms included a commitment to attend meetings and to keep information confidential. Although leadership patterns often emerged, and verbal and emotional skills recognizably varied, equality within the group was a goal that reflected a value of nonhierarchical organization and a commitment to confronting sources of inequality on the basis of which members felt subordinated or excluded.

What brought women to these groups is difficult to distinguish from what happened once they were there. As with any complex social interaction, from laboratory experiment to revolution, it is often difficult to separate the assumptions from the discoveries, the ripeness of conditions from the precipitating spark. Where does consciousness come from? The effectiveness of consciousness raising is difficult to apportion between the process itself and the women who choose to engage in it. The initial recruiting impulse seems to be a response to an unspecific, often unattached, but just barely submerged discontent that in some inchoate way women relate to being female. It has not escaped most women's attention that their femaleness defines much of who they can be. Restrictions, conflicting demands, intolerable but necessarily tolerated work, the accumulation of constant small irritations and indignities of everyday existence have often been justified on the basis of sex. Consciousness raising coheres and claims these impressions.

Feminists tend to believe that most if not all women resent women's status on some level of their being; even women's defense of their status can be a response to that status. Why some women take the step of identifying their situation with their status as women, transforming their discontents into grievances, is a crucial unanswered question of feminism (or, for that matter, of marxism). What brings people to be conscious of their oppression as common rather than remaining on the level of bad feelings, to see their group identity as a systematic necessity that benefits another group, is the first question of organizing. The fact that consciousness-raising groups were there presupposes the discovery that they were there to make. But what may have begun as a working assumption becomes a working discovery: women are a group, in the sense that a shared reality of treatment exists sufficient to provide a basis for identification—at least enough to begin talking about it in a group of women. This often pre-articulate consensus shapes a procedure, the purpose of which becomes to unpack the concrete moment-to-moment meaning of being a woman in a society that men dominate, by looking at how women see their everyday experience in it. Women's lives are discussed in all their momentous triviality, that is, as they are lived through. The technique explores the social world each woman inhabits through her speaking of it, through comparison with other women's experiences, and through women's experiences of each other in the group itself. Metaphors of hearing and speaking commonly evoke the transformation women experience from silence to voice. As Toni McNaron put it, "within every story I have ever heard from a woman, I have found some voice of me. The details are of course unique to the speaker—they are our differences. But the meaning which they make is common to us all. I will not understand what is common without hearing the details which reveal it to me."[2] The particularities become facets of the collective understanding within which differences constitute rather than undermine collectivity.

The fact that men were not physically present was usually considered necessary to the process. Although the ways of seeing that women have learned in relation to men were very much present or there would be little to discuss, men's temporary concrete absence helped women feel more free of the immediate imperative to compete for male attention and approval, to be passive or get intimidated, or to support men's version of reality. It made speech possible. With these constraints at some remove, women often found that the group confirmed awarenesses they had hidden, including from themselves. Subjects like sexuality, family, body, money, and power could be discussed more openly. The pain of women's roles and women's stake in them could be confronted critically, without the need every minute to reassure men that these changes were not threatening to them or to defend women's breaking of roles as desirable. The all-woman context valued women to each other as sources of insight, advice, information, stimulation, and problems. By providing room for women to be close, these groups demonstrated how far women were separated and how that separation deprived women of access to the way their treatment is systematized. "People who are without names, who do not know themselves, who have no culture, experience a kind of paralysis of consciousness. The first step is to connect and learn to trust one another."[3] This context for serious confrontation also revealed how women had been trivialized to each other. Pamela Allen called these groups "free space."[4] She meant a respectful context for interchange within which women could articulate the inarticulate, admit the inadmissible. The point of the process was not so much that hitherto-undisclosed facts were unearthed or that denied perceptions were corroborated or even that reality was tested, although all these happened. It was not only that silence was broken and that speech occurred. The point was, and is, that this process moved the reference point for truth and thereby the definition of reality as such. Consciousness raising alters the terms of validation by creating community through a process that redefines what counts as verification. This process gives both content and form to women's point of view.[5]

Concretely, consciousness-raising groups often focused on specific incidents and internal dialogue: what happened today, how did it make you feel, why did you feel that way, how do you feel now? Extensive attention was paid to small situations and denigrated pursuits that made up the common life of women in terms of energy, time, intensity, and definition—prominently, housework and sexuality. Women said things like this:

> *I am nothing when I am by myself. In myself, I am nothing. I only know I exist because I am needed by someone who is real, my husband, and by my children. My husband goes out into the real world. Other people recognize him as real, and take him into account. He affects other people and events. He does things and changes things and they are different afterwards. I stay in my imaginary world in this house, doing jobs that I largely invent, and that no-one cares about but myself. I do not change things. The work I do changes nothing; what I cook disappears, what I clean one day must be cleaned again the next. I seem to be involved in some sort of mysterious process.*[6]

Intercourse was interrogated: how and by whom it is initiated, its timing, woman's feelings during and after, its place in relationships, its meaning, its place in being a woman.[7] Other subjects included interactions in routine situations like walking down the street, talking with bus drivers, interacting with cocktail waitresses. Women's stories—work and how they came to do it; children; sexual history, including history of sexual abuse—were explored. Adrienne Rich reflects the process many women experienced and the conclusion to which many women came:

> *I was looking desperately for clues, because if there were no clues then I thought I might be insane. I wrote in a notebook about this time: "Paralyzed by the sense that there exists a mesh of relationships—e.g., between my anger at the children, my sensual life, pacifism, sex (I mean sex in its broadest significance, not merely sexual desire)—an interconnectedness which, if I could see it, make it valid, would give me back myself, make it possible to function lucidly and passionately. Yet I grope in and out among these dark webs." I think I began at this point to feel that politics was not something "out there" but something "in here" and of the essence of my condition.*[8]

Woman's self-concept emerged: who she thinks she is, how she was treated in her family, who they told her she was (the pretty one, the smart one), how she resisted, how that was responded to, her feelings now about her life and herself, her account of how she came to feel that way, whether other group members experience her the way she experiences herself, how she carries her body and delivers her mannerisms, the way she presents herself and interacts in the group. Contradictions between messages tacitly conveyed and messages explicitly expressed inspired insightful and shattering criticism, as with women who behave seductively while complaining that men accost them. Complicity in oppression acquires concrete meaning as women emerge as shapers of reality as well as shaped by it. A carefully detailed and critically reconstructed composite image is built of women's experienced meaning of "being a woman." From women's collective perspective, a woman embodies and expresses a moment-to-moment concept of herself in the way she walks down the street, structures a household, pursues her work and friendships, shares her sexuality—a certain concept of how she has survived and who she survives as. A minute-by-minute moving picture is created of women becoming, refusing, sustaining their condition.

Interactions usually overlooked as insignificant if vaguely upsetting proved good subjects for detailed scrutiny. A woman mentions the way a man on the subway looked at her. How did this make her feel? Why does she feel so degraded? so depressed? Why can the man make her hate her body? How much of this feeling comes from her learned distrust of how men use her sexually? Does this show up in other areas of her life? Do other women feel this way? What form of power does this give the man? Do all men have, or exercise, such power? Could she have done anything at the time? Can the group do anything now? Women learn that the entire structure of sexual domination, the tacit relations of deference and command, can be present in a passing glance.

Realities hidden under layers of valued myth were unmasked simply by talking about what happens every day, such as the hard physical labor performed by the average wife and mother, the few women who feel strictly vaginal orgasms and the many who pretend they do. Women confronted collectively the range of overt violence represented in the life experience of their group of women, women who might previously have appeared "protected." They found fathers who raped them; boyfriends who shot at them; doctors who aborted them when they weren't pregnant or sterilized them "accidentally"; psychoanalysts who so-called seduced them, committing them to mental hospitals when they exposed them; mothers who committed suicide or lived to loathe themselves more when they failed; employers who fired them for withholding sexual favors or unemployment offices that refused benefits when they quit, finding their reasons personal and uncompelling. Women learned that men see and treat women from their angle of vision, and they learned the content of that vision.

These details together revealed and documented the kind of world women inhabit socially and some of what it feels like for them to inhabit it, how women are systematically deprived of a self and how that process of deprivation constitutes socialization to femininity. In consciousness raising, women become aware of this reality as at once very specific—a woman's social condition and self-concept as it is lived through by her—and as a social reality in which all women more or less participate, however diversely, and in which all women can be identified. Put another way, although a woman's specific race or class or physiology may define her among women, simply being a woman has a meaning that decisively defines all women socially, from their most intimate moments to their most anonymous relations. This social meaning, which is unattached to any actual anatomical differences between the sexes, or to any realities of women's response to it, pervades everyday routine to the point that it becomes a reflex, a habit. Sexism is seen to be all of a piece and so much a part of the omnipresent background of life that a massive effort of collective concentration is required even to discern that it has edges. Consciousness raising is such an effort. Taken in this way, consciousness means a good deal more than a set of ideas. It constitutes a lived knowing of the social reality of being female.

What women become conscious of—the substance of radical feminist analysis—is integral to this process. Perhaps most obviously, it becomes difficult to take seriously accounts of women's roles or personal qualities based on nature or biology, except as authoritative appeals that have shaped women according to them. Combing through women's lives event by event, detail by detail, it is no mystery that women are who they are, given the way they have been treated. Patterns of treatment that would create feelings of incapacity in anybody are seen to connect seamlessly with acts of overt discrimination to deprive women of tools and skills, creating by force the status they are supposed to be destined for by anatomy. Heterosexuality, supposed natural, is found to be forced on women moment to moment. Qualities pointed to as naturally and eternally feminine—nurturance, intuition, frailty, quickness with their fingers, orientation to children—or characteristics of a particular subgroup of women—such as married women's supposed talent for exacting, repetitive, simple tasks, or Black women's supposed interest in sex—look simply like descriptions of the desired and required characteristics of particular occupants of women's roles. Meredith Tax summarized this insight: "We didn't get this way by heredity or by accident. We have been molded into these deformed postures, pushed into these service jobs, made to apologize for existing, taught to be unable to do anything requiring any strength at all, like opening doors or bottles. We have been told to be stupid, to be silly."[9]

If such qualities are biological imperatives, women conform to them remarkably imperfectly. When one gets to know women close up and without men present, it is remarkable the extent to which their so-called biology, not to mention their socialization, has failed. The discovery that these apparently unchangeable dictates of the natural order are powerful social conventions often makes women feel unburdened, since individual failures no longer appear so individualized. Women become angry as they see women's lives as one avenue after another foreclosed by gender.

More than their content, it is the relation to lived experience which is new about these insights. It is one thing to read a nineteenth-century tract describing a common problem of women. It is quite another for women to hear women speak the pain they feel, wonder what they have to fall back on, know they need a response, recognize the dilemmas, struggle with the same denial that the pain is pain, that it is also one's own, that women are real. Susan Griffin expressed it: "We do not rush to speech. We allow ourselves to be moved. We do not attempt objectivity. . . . We said we had experienced this ourselves. I felt so much for her then, she said, with her head cradled in my lap, she said, I knew what to do. We said we were moved to see her go through what we had gone through. We said this gave us some knowledge."[10]

It was common for women in consciousness-raising groups to share radical changes in members' lives, relationships, work, life goals, and sexuality. This process created bonds and a different kind of knowledge, collective knowledge built on moving and being moved, on changing and being changed. As an experience, it went beyond empirical information that women are victims of social inequality. It built an experienced sense of how it came to be this way and that it can be changed. Women experienced the walls that have contained them as walls—and sometimes walked through them. For instance, when they first seriously considered never marrying or getting a divorce, women often discovered their economic dependency, having been taught to do little they can sell or having been paid less than men who sell comparable work. Why? To understand the precise causation would be to identify the supportive dynamics of male supremacy and capitalism. But an equivalency, at least, was clear: women's work is defined as inferior work, and inferior work is defined as work for women. Inferior work is often considered appropriate for women by the same standards that define it as inferior, and by the same standards that define "women's work" as inferior work—its pay, status, interest or complexity, contacts with people, its relation to cleanliness or care of bodily needs. Inextricably, women may find themselves inwardly dependent as well: conditioned not to think for themselves, to think that without a man they are nothing, or to think that they are less "woman" when without one. The point is not how well women conform to this standard but that there is such a standard and women do not create it. The power dynamic behind these facts is brought into the open when women break out, from the panic they feel at the thought and from the barriers they encounter when they try. It becomes clear, from one horror story after another, that men's position of power over women is a major part of what defines men as men to themselves, and women as women to themselves. Challenge to that power is taken as a threat to male identity and self-definition. Men's reaction of threat is also a challenge to women's self-definition, which has included supporting men, making men feel masculine, and episodically being treated better as a reward. Men's response to women's redefinition as in control is often to show women just how little control they have by threatening women's material or physical survival or their physical or sexual or emotional integrity. Women learn they have learned to "act independently in a dependent fashion."[11] And sometimes they find ways to resist all of this.

This place of consciousness in social construction is often most forcefully illustrated in the least materially deprived women, because the contrast between their economic conditions and their feminist consciousness can be so vivid:

> *As suburban women, we recognize that many of us live in more economic and material comfort than our urban sisters, but we have come to realize through the women's movement, feminist ideas and consciousness raising, that this comfort only hides our essential powerlessness and oppression. We live in comfort only to the extent that our homes, clothing, and the services we receive feed and prop the status and egos of the men*

> *who support us. Like dogs on a leash, our own status and power will reach as far as our husbands and their income and prestige will allow. As human beings, as individuals, we in fact own very little and should our husbands leave us or us them, we will find ourselves with the care and responsibility of children without money, jobs, credit or power. For this questionable condition, we have paid the price of isolation and exploitation by the institutions of marriage, motherhood, psychiatry and consumerism. Although our life styles may appear materially better, we are, as all women, dominated by men at home, in bed, and on the job, emotionally, sexually, domestically and financially.*[12]

Women found they face these conditions sharply through nonmarriage or divorce or on becoming openly lesbian. Women who do not need men for sexual fulfillment can suddenly be found "incompetent" on their jobs when their bosses learn of their sexual preference. Similarly, when a women's health clinic is opened, and women handle their own bodies, male-controlled hospitals often deny admitting privileges, threatening every woman who attends the clinic. These conditions arise when women suggest that if housework is so fulfilling men should have the chance to do it themselves: it is everybody's job, women just blame themselves or do it when it is not done or done well. Always in the background, often not very far, is the sanction of physical intimidation, not because men are stronger but because they are willing and able to use their strength with relative social impunity; or not because they use it, but because they do not have to. In addition, identity invalidation is a form of power a man has for the price of invoking it: you are an evil woman, you are a whore (you have sex on demand), you are a failure as a woman (you do not have sex on demand). Women learn they have to become people who respond to these appeals on some level because they are backed up by material indulgences and deprivations. The understanding that a social group that is accorded, possesses, and uses such tools over others to its own advantage is powerful and that it exercises a form of social control or authority becomes not a presupposition or rhetorical hyperbole but a substantiated conclusion.

Perhaps the most pervasive realization of consciousness raising was that men as a group benefit from these same arrangements by which women are deprived. Women see that men derive many advantages from women's roles, including being served and kept in mind, supported and sustained, having their children cared for and their sexual needs catered to, and being kept from the necessity of doing jobs so menial they consider them beneath them unless there is no other job (or a woman) around. But the major advantage men derive, dubious though it may seem to some, is the process, the value, the mechanism by which their interest itself is enforced and perpetuated and sustained: power. Power in its socially male form. It is not only that men treat women badly, although often they do, but that it is their choice whether or not to do so. This understanding of power is one of the key comprehensions of feminism. The reality it points to, because it is everywhere and relatively invariant, appears to be nowhere separable from the whole, from the totality it defines.

Women, it is said, possess corresponding power. Through consciousness raising, women found that women's so-called power was the other side of female powerlessness. A woman's supposed power to deny sex is the underside of her actual lack of power to stop it. Women's supposed power to get men to do things for them by nagging or manipulating is the other side of the power they lack to have their every need anticipated, to carry out the task themselves, to be able to deliver upon sharing the responsibility equally, or to invoke physical fear to gain compliance with their desires without even having to mention it. Once the veil is lifted, once relations between the sexes are seen as power relations, it becomes impossible to see as simply unintended, well-intentioned, or innocent the actions through which women are told every day what is expected and when they have crossed some line. From the male point of view, no injury may be meant. But women develop an incisive eye for routines, strategems, denials, and traps that operate to keep women in place and to obscure the recognition that it is a place at all. Although these actions may in some real way be unintentional, they are taken, in some other real way, as meant.[13]

These discussions explored the functioning of sex roles in even one's closest "personal" relations, where it was thought women were most "ourselves," hence most free. Indeed, the reverse often seemed to be the case. The measure of closeness often seemed to be the measure of the oppression. When shared with other women, one's most private events often came to look the most stereotypical, the most for the public. Each woman, in her own particular, even chosen, way reproduces in her most private relations a structure of dominance and submission which characterizes the entire public order. The impact of this insight can be accounted for in part by the fact that it is practiced on the level of group process, so that what could be a sociopsychological or theoretical insight becomes a lived experience. That is, through making public, through discussing in the group, what had been private, for example sexual relations, it was found that the split between public and private, at least in the context of relations between the sexes, made very little sense, except as it functioned ideologically to keep each woman feeling alone, particularly in her experiences of sexual violation.

> *After sharing, we* know *that women suffer at the hands of a male supremacist society and that this male supremacy intrudes into every sphere of our existence, controlling the ways in which we are allowed to make our living and the ways in which we find fulfillment in personal relationships. We know that our most secret, our most private problems are grounded in the way that women are treated, in the way women are allowed to live.*[14]

The analysis that the personal is the political came out of consciousness raising. It has four interconnected facets. First, women as a group are dominated by men as a group, and therefore as individuals. Second, women are subordinated in society, not by personal nature or by biology. Third, the gender division, which includes the sex division of labor which keeps women in high-heeled low-status jobs, pervades and determines even women's personal feelings in relationships. Fourth, since a woman's problems are not hers individually but those of women as a whole, they cannot be addressed except as a whole. In this analysis of gender as a nonnatural characteristic of a division of power in society, the personal becomes the political.

. . .

Consciousness raising has revealed that male power is real. It is just not the only reality, as it claims to be. Male power is a myth that makes itself true. To raise consciousness is to confront male power in its duality: as at once total on one side and a delusion on the other. In consciousness raising, women learn they have learned that men are everything, women their negation, but the sexes are equal. The content of the message is revealed as true and false at the same time; in fact, each part reflects the other transvalued. If "Men are all, women their negation" is taken as social criticism rather than as simple description, it becomes clear for the first time that women are men's equals, everywhere in chains. The chains become visible, the civil inferiority—the inequality—the product of subjection and a mode of its enforcement. Reciprocally, the moment it is seen that this life as we know it is not equality, that the sexes are not socially equal, womanhood can no longer be defined in terms of lack of maleness, as negativity. For the first time, the question of what a woman is seeks its ground in and of a world understood as neither of its making nor in its own image, and finds, within a critical embrace of woman's fractured and alien image, the shadow world women have made and a vision of the possibility of equality. As critique, women's communality describes a fact of male supremacy, a fact of sex "in itself": no woman escapes the meaning of being a woman within a gendered social system, and sex inequality is not only pervasive but may be universal (in the sense of never having not been in some form), though "intelligible only in . . . locally specific forms."[24] For women to become a sex "for itself"[25] is to move community to the level of vision.

Notes

1. Sheila Rowbotham, *Woman's Consciousness, Man's World* (Harmondsworth: Penguin, 1973), p. 27.

2. Toni McNaron, *The Power of Person: Women Coming into Their Own* (Minneapolis: Women's Caucus of the National Association of Social Workers, 1982).

3. Rowbotham, *Woman's Consciousness*, p. 27.

4. Pamela Allen, *Free Space: A Perspective on the Small Group in Women's Liberation* (New York: Times Change Press, 1970).

5. In addition to the citations in Chapter 1, note 4, see Jo Freeman, *The Politics of Women's Liberation: A Case Study of an Emerging Social Movement and Its Relation to the Policy Process* (New York: David McKay, 1975), chap. 4; Carol Hanisch, *Notes from the Second Year* (New York: Radical Feminism, 1970), pp. 76–77. For possible parallels in Chinese "speak bitterness" sessions, see Richard H. Solomon, *Mao's Revolution and the Chinese Political Culture* (Berkeley: University of California Press, 1971), pp. 195–197, 209, 439, 441, 514, 523, 571.

6. Meredith Tax, "Woman and Her Mind: The Story of Everyday Life," in *Radical Feminism*, ed. Ann Koedt, Ellen

Levine, and Anita Rapone (New York: Quadrangle Books, 1973), pp. 26–27.

7. An excellent example in writing, of which there are few, is Ingrid Bengis, *Combat in the Erogenous Zone: Writings on Love, Hate, and Sex* (New York: Alfred A. Knopf, 1973). See also Kate Millett, *Flying* (New York: Ballantine Books, 1974).

8. Adrienne Rich, "When We Dead Awaken: Writing as Re-Vision," in *On Lies, Secrets, and Silence: Selected Prose,* 1966–1978 (New York: Norton, 1979), p. 44.

9. Tax, "Woman and Her Mind," pp. 26–27.

10. Susan Griffin, *Woman and Nature: The Roaring Inside Her* (New York: Harper & Row, 1978), p. 197.

11. This is Steven Hymer's description of the results of Robinson Crusoe's socialization of Friday. Steven Hymer, "Robinson Crusoe and the Secret of Primitive Accumulation," *Monthly Review* 23 (September 1971): 16.

12. Westchester Radical Feminists, "Statement of Purpose, May, 1972," in Koedt, Levine, and Rapone, *Radical Feminism,* pp. 385–386.

13. Pat Mainardi, "The Politics of Housework," in *Sisterhood Is Powerful: An Anthology of Writings from the Women's Liberation Movement,* ed. Robin Morgan (New York: Random House, 1970), pp. 447–454, written in 1965, is an early and brilliant example of this perception.

14. Allen, *Free Space,* p. 27. See also Irene Peslikis, "Resistances to Consciousness," in Morgan, *Sisterhood Is Powerful,* pp. 337–339.

. . .

24. Michelle Z. Rosaldo, "The Use and Abuse of Anthropology: Reflections on Feminism and Cross-Cultural Understanding," *Signs: Journal of Women in Culture and Society 5* (Spring 1980): 417.

25. Marx discusses the in itself/for itself distinction in *Poverty of Philosophy,* p. 195 and in *The Eighteenth Brumaire of Louis Bonaparte,* in *Selected Works.* See L. Kolakowski, *Main Currents of Marxism,* trans. P. S. Falla, vol. 1 (Oxford: Clarendon Press, 1978), 356.

The Transformation of Silence into Language and Action

Audre Lorde

Audre Lorde, poet, essayist, fiction writer, and activist, was born in New York City in 1934 of West Indian parents. A graduate of Hunter College and Columbia University in New York, she later was professor of English at Hunter. Lorde was a founding member of Kitchen Table: Women of Color Press and the author of many works, including ten books of poetry; a novel, Zami; *and several important essays on racism, sexism, and peace. In 1993 she died of the cancer she refers to in the opening of this essay, having continued to write and work throughout her illness.*

Lorde's work is powerful, searingly honest, and always directed toward positive social change and personal action. In her essay "Eye to Eye," she said:

> *To search for power within myself means I must be willing to move through being afraid to whatever lies beyond. If I look at my most vulnerable places and acknowledge the pain I have felt, I can remove the source of that pain from my enemies' arsenals. My history cannot be used to feather my enemies' arrows then, and that lessens their power over me. Nothing I accept about myself can be used against me to diminish me. I am who I am, doing what I came to do, acting upon you like a drug or a chisel or remind you of your me-ness, as I discover you in myself.*[1]

After the heavy load of misogyny and deceit we encountered in the previous chapter, these are healing words.

I HAVE COME TO BELIEVE OVER AND OVER AGAIN that what is most important to me must be spoken, made verbal and shared, even at the risk of having it bruised or misunderstood. That the speaking profits me, beyond any other effect. I am standing here as a Black lesbian poet, and the meaning of all that waits upon the fact that I am still alive, and might not have been. Less than two months ago I was told by two doctors, one female and one male, that I would have to have breast surgery, and that there was a 60 to 80 percent chance that the tumor was malignant. Between that telling and the actual surgery, there was a three-week period of the agony of an involuntary reorganization of my entire life. The surgery was completed, and the growth was benign.

But within those three weeks, I was forced to look upon myself and my living with a harsh and urgent clarity that has left me still shaken but much stronger. This is a situation faced by many women, by some of you here today. Some of what I experienced during that time has helped elucidate for me much of what I feel concerning the transformation of silence into language and action.

In becoming forcibly and essentially aware of my mortality, and of what I wished and wanted for my life, however short it might be, priorities and omissions became strongly etched in a merciless light, and what I most regretted were my silences. Of what had I *ever* been afraid? To question or to speak as I believed could have meant pain, or death. But we all hurt in so many different ways, all the time, and pain will either change or end. Death, on the other hand, is the final silence. And that might be coming quickly, now, without regard for whether I had ever spoken what needed to be said, or had only betrayed myself into small silences, while I planned someday to speak, or waited for someone else's words. And I began to recognize a source of power within myself that

---

From *Sister Outsider: Essays & Speeches by Audre Lorde.* New York: Crossing Press, 1984.

comes from the knowledge that while it is most desirable not to be afraid, learning to put fear into a perspective gave me strength.

I was going to die, if not sooner then later, whether or not I had ever spoken myself. My silences had not protected me. Your silence will not protect you. But for every real word spoken, for every attempt I had ever made to speak those truths for which I am still seeking, I had made contact with other women while we examined the words to fit a world in which we all believed, bridging our differences. And it was the concern and caring of all those women which gave me strength and enabled me to scrutinize the essentials of my living.

The women who sustained me through that period were Black and white, old and young, lesbian, bisexual, and heterosexual, and we all shared a war against the tyrannies of silence. They all gave me a strength and concern without which I could not have survived intact. Within those weeks of acute fear came the knowledge—within the war we are all waging with the forces of death, subtle and otherwise, conscious or not—I am not only a casualty, I am also a warrior.

What are the words you do not yet have? What do you need to say? What are the tyrannies you swallow day by day and attempt to make your own, until you will sicken and die of them, still in silence? Perhaps for some of you here today, I am the face of one of your fears. Because I am woman, because I am Black, because I am lesbian, because I am myself—a Black woman warrior poet doing my work—come to ask you, are you doing yours?

And of course I am afraid, because the transformation of silence into language and action is an act of self-revelation, and that always seems fraught with danger. But my daughter, when I told her of our topic and my difficulty with it, said, "Tell them about how you're never really a whole person if you remain silent, because there's always that one little piece inside you that wants to be spoken out, and if you keep ignoring it, it gets madder and madder and hotter and hotter, and if you don't speak it out one day it will just up and punch you in the mouth from the inside."

In the cause of silence, each of us draws the face of her own fear—fear of contempt, of censure, or some judgment, or recognition, of challenge, of annihilation. But most of all, I think, we fear the visibility without which we cannot truly live. Within this country where racial difference creates a constant, if unspoken, distortion of vision, Black women have on one hand always been highly visible, and so, on the other hand, have been rendered invisible through the depersonalization of racism. Even within the women's movement, we have had to fight, and still do, for that very visibility which also renders us most vulnerable, our Blackness. For to survive in the mouth of this dragon we call america, we have had to learn this first and most vital lesson—that we were never meant to survive. Not as human beings. And neither were most of you here today, Black or not. And that visibility which makes us most vulnerable is that which also is the source of our greatest strength. Because the machine will try to grind you into dust anyway, whether or not we speak. We can sit in our corners mute forever while our sisters and our selves are wasted, while our children are distorted and destroyed, while our earth is poisoned; we can sit in our safe corners mute as bottles, and we will still be no less afraid.

In my house this year we are celebrating the feast of Kwanza, the African-american festival of harvest which begins the day after Christmas and lasts for seven days. There are seven principles of Kwanza, one for each day. The first principle is Umoja, which means unity, the decision to strive for and maintain unity in self and community. The principle for yesterday, the second day, was Kujichagulia—self-determination—the decision to define ourselves, name ourselves, and speak for ourselves, instead of being defined and spoken for by others. Today is the third day of Kwanza, and the principle for today is Ujima—collective work and responsibility—the decision to build and maintain ourselves and our communities together and to recognize and solve our problems together.

Each of us is here now because in one way or another we share a commitment to language and to the power of language, and to the reclaiming of that language which has been made to work against us. In the transformation of silence into language and action, it is vitally necessary for each one of us to establish or examine her function in that transformation and to recognize her role as vital within that transformation.

For those of us who write, it is necessary to scrutinize not only the truth of what we speak, but the truth of that language by which we speak it. For others, it is to share and spread also those words that are meaningful to us. But primarily for us all, it is necessary to teach by living and speaking those truths which we believe and know beyond understanding. Because in this way alone we can survive, by taking part in a process of life that is creative and continuing, that is growth.

And it is never without fear—of visibility, of the harsh light of scrutiny and perhaps judgment, of pain, of death. But we have lived through all of those already, in silence, except death. And I remind myself all the time now that if I were to have been born mute, or had maintained an oath of silence my whole life long for safety, I would still have suffered, and I would still die. It is very good for establishing perspective.

And where the words of women are crying to be heard, we must each of us recognize our responsibility to seek those words out, to read them and share them and examine them in their pertinence to our lives. That we not hide behind the mockeries of separations that have been imposed upon us and which so often we accept as our own. For instance, "I can't possibly teach Black women's writing—their experience is so different from mine." Yet how many years have you spent teaching Plato and Shakespeare and Proust? Or another, "She's a white woman and what could she possibly have to say to me?" Or, "She's a lesbian, what would my husband say, or my chairman?" Or again, "This woman writes of her sons and I have no children." And all the other endless ways in which we rob ourselves of ourselves and each other.

We can learn to work and speak when we are afraid in the same way we have learned to work and speak when we are tired. For we have been socialized to respect fear more than our own needs for language and definition, and while we wait in silence for that final luxury of fearlessness, the weight of that silence will choke us.

The fact that we are here and that I speak these words is an attempt to break silence and bridge some of those differences between us, for it is not difference which immobilizes us, but silence. And there are so many silences to be broken.

Notes

1. "Eye to Eye: Black Women, Hatred and Anger" in *Sister Outsider: Essays and Speeches by Audre Lorde* (New York: Crossing Press, 1984), p. 147.

2. Paper delivered at the Modern Language Association's "Lesbian and Literature Panel," Chicago, Illinois, December 28, 1977. First published in *Sinister Wisdom* 6 (1978) and *The Cancer Journals* (Spinsters Ink, San Francisco, 1980).

Myths to Divert Black Women From Freedom

Barbara Smith

Author, speaker, activist, Barbara Smith coedited Conditions: Five, The Black Women's Issue *(1979) and* All the Women Are White, All the Blacks Are Men, but Some of Us Are Brave: Black Women's Studies *(1982) and edited* Home Girls: A Black Feminist Anthology *(1983), from which this selection is taken. With Audre Lorde she cofounded Kitchen Table: Women of Color Press in 1980.*

"Black feminism is, on every level, organic to Black experience," argues Smith. The history, culture, and experience of African-American women is innately feminist, yet many Third World women have not been attracted to the contemporary women's movement. Smith addresses the reasons why this may be so: among others, a set of myths designed to divert women of color from organizing around political issues that are specifically women's.

Excerpted from "Introduction," *Home Girls* by Barbara Smith © 1983. Used by permission of the author and of Kitchen Table: Women of Color Press, P.O. Box 908, Latham, New York 12110.

Sources

THERE IS NOTHING MORE IMPORTANT TO ME THAN home.

The first house we lived in was in the rear. Hidden between other houses, it had a dirt yard that my twin sister Beverly and I loved to dig in, and a handful of flowers my grandmother had planted. We lived there with our mother and grandmother and with one of our great-aunts named Phoebe, whom we called Auntie. We seldom saw Auntie because she was a live-in cook for rich people. The house, however, was considered to be hers, not because she owned it, but because Auntie was the one who had originally rented it. She had been the first of the family to come North in the late 1920s, followed by the rest of her sisters and their children all during the 30s and 40s.

The house was old and small, but I didn't know it then. It had two bedrooms. The big one was Auntie's, though she only used it on her occasional visits home. The small one was where my grandmother, Bev, and I slept, our cribs and her bed crowding together. Our mother, who worked full time, slept downstairs on a daybed which she folded in half each morning, covered with a faded maroon throw, and pushed back against the wall. The kitchen, where we ate every meal except Sunday dinner, was the room Bev and I liked best. Our grandmother did most of the cooking. Unlike her sister Phoebe she was a "plain" cook, but she did make a few dishes—little pancakes with Alaga syrup and bacon, vanilla-ey boiled custards—which appealed even to Bev and my notoriously fussy appetites.

The house was on 83rd Street between Central and Cedar Avenues in what was called the Central Area, one of Cleveland's numerous ghettoes. The church the family had belonged to ever since they'd come North, Antioch Baptist, was a few blocks away at 89th and Cedar. Aunt LaRue, our mother's sister, also lived on 89th Street, on the second floor of a house half a block from the church.

When Bev and I were six we moved. Aunt LaRue and her husband had bought a two-family house (five rooms up, five rooms down) on 132nd Street off of Kinsman for us all to live in. They lived upstairs and the five of us lived downstairs, including Auntie, who became increasingly ill and was eventually bedridden. The "new" house was old too, but it was in a "better" neighborhood, had a front and a back yard, where my aunt and uncle planted grass, and there was more space.

One thing that was different about being at the new house was that for the first time we lived near white people. Before this we only saw them downtown, except for some of the teachers at school. The white people, mostly Italians and Jews, quickly exited from our immediate neighborhood but some remained in the schools. Most of our white classmates, however, were Polish, Czech, Yugoslavian, or Hungarian. Their families had emigrated from Eastern Europe following the World Wars. Despite the definite racial tensions between us, we had certain things in common. Cleveland was new to their people as it was to ours; the church figured heavily in their lives as both a spiritual and social force; they were involved in close-knit extended families; and they were working people many rungs below the rich white people who lived on the Heights.

Beverly and I lived in the house on 132nd Street until we were eighteen and went away to college. It is this house that I remember clearly when I think of home. It is this place that I miss and all the women there who raised me. It was undoubtedly at home that I learned the rudiments of Black feminism, although no such term even existed then. We were "Negroes" or "colored people." Except for our uncle, who lived upstairs briefly and soon departed because "LaRue was too wrapped up in her family," we were all women. When I was growing up I was surrounded by women who appeared able to do everything, at least everything necessary to maintain a home. They cleaned, cooked, washed, ironed, sewed, made soap, canned, held jobs, took care of business downtown, sang, read, and taught us to do the same. In her essay, "Women In Prison: How We Are," Assata Shakur perfectly describes the kind of women who filled my childhood. She writes:

> *I think about North Carolina and my home town and [I] remember the women of my grandmother's generation: strong, fierce women who could stop you with a look out the corners of their eyes. Women who walked with majesty. . . .*
>
> *Women who delivered babies, searched for healing roots and brewed medicines. Women who darned sox and chopped wood and layed bricks. Women who could swim rivers and shoot the head off a snake. Women who took passionate responsibility for their children and for their neighbors' children too.*
>
> *The women in my grandmother's generation made giving an art form. "Here, gal, take this pot of collards to Sister Sue"; "Take this bag of pecans to school for the teacher"; "Stay here while I go tend Mister Johnson's leg." Every child in the neighborhood ate in their kitchens. They called each other sister because of feeling rather than as the result of a movement. They supported each other through the lean times, sharing the little they had.*
>
> *The women of my grandmother's generation in my home town trained their daughters for womanhood.*[1]

The women in my family, and their friends, worked harder than any people I have known before or since, and despite their objective circumstances, they believed. My grandmother believed in Jesus and in sin, not necessarily in that order; my mother believed in education and in books; my Aunt LaRue believed in beauty and in books as well; and, their arguments aside, they believed in each other. They also seemed to believe that Beverly and I could have a future beyond theirs, although there was little enough indication in the 40s and 50s that Negro girls would ever have a place to stand.

Needless to say, they believed in home. It was a word spoken often, particularly by my grandmother. To her and her sisters, home meant Georgia. One of the last to leave, my grandmother never considered Cleveland anything but a stopping place. My older relatives' allegiance to a place we'd never seen was sometimes confusing, but their loyalty to their origins was also much to our benefit, since it provided us with an essentially Southern upbringing, rooting us solidly in the past and at the same time preparing us to face the unknowable future.

In the spring of 1982 I visited Georgia for the first time and finally saw the little town of Dublin where they had lived and farmed. Being in rural Georgia, I thoroughly understood their longing for it, a longing they had implanted sight unseen in me. It is one of the most beautiful, mysterious landscapes I have ever seen. I also understood why they had to leave. Though lynching and segregation are officially past, racial lines are unequivocally drawn. Dublin has become very modern and unmistakably prosperous, yet many streets in the Black section of town are, to this day, unpaved. I took a handful of red clay from the side of the road in Dublin and brought it home to remind me of where my family had walked and what they had suffered.

I learned about Black feminism from the women in my family—not just from their strengths, but from their failings, from witnessing daily how they were humiliated and crushed because they had made the "mistake" of being born Black and female in a white man's country. I inherited fear and shame from them as well as hope. These conflicting feelings about being a Black woman still do battle inside of me. It is this conflict, my constantly " . . . seeing and touching/Both sides of things" that makes my commitment real.[2]

In the fall of 1981, before most of this book was compiled, I was searching for a title. I'd come up with one that I knew was not quite right. At the time I was also working on the story which later became "Home" and thought that I'd like to get some of the feeling of that piece into the book. One day while doing something else entirely, and playing with words in my head, "home girls" came to me. Home Girls. The girls from the neighborhood and from the block, the girls we grew up with. I knew I was onto something, particularly when I considered that so many Black people who are threatened by feminism have argued that by being a Black feminist (particularly if you are also a Lesbian) you have left the race, are no longer a part of the Black community, in short no longer have a home.

I suspect that most of the contributors to *Home Girls* learned their varied politics and their shared commitment to Black women from the same source I did. Yet critics of feminism pretend that just because some of us speak out about sexual politics *at home,* within the Black community, we must have sprung miraculously from somewhere else. But we are not strangers and never have been. I am convinced that Black feminism is, on every level, organic to Black experience.

History verifies that Black women have rejected doormat status, whether racially or sexually imposed, for centuries. Not only is there the documented resistance of Black women during slavery followed by our organizing around specific Black women's issues and in support of women's rights during the nineteenth century, there is also the vast cultural record of our continuously critical stance toward our oppression. For example, in the late nineteenth and early twentieth centuries, poets Frances E. W. Harper (1825–1911), Angelina Weld Grimké (1880–1958), Alice Dunbar-Nelson (1875–1935), Anne Spencer (1882–1975), and Georgia Douglas Johnson (1886–1966) all addressed themes of sexual as well as racial identity in some of their work.

. . .

I have always felt that Black women's ability to function with dignity, independence, and imagination in the face of total adversity—that is, in the face of white America—points to an innate feminist potential. To me the phrase, "Act like you have some sense," probably spoken by at least one Black woman to every Black child who ever lived, is a cryptic warning that says volumes about keeping your feet on the ground and your ass covered. Alice Walker's definition of "womanist" certainly makes the connection between plain common sense and a readiness to fight for change. She writes:

> *WOMANIST: (According to Walker) From* womanish. *(Opp. of "girlish," i.e. frivolous, irresponsible, not serious.) A black feminist or feminist of color. From the colloquial expression of mothers to daughters, "You're acting womanish," i.e., like a woman. Usually referring to outrageous, audacious, courageous or* willful *behavior. Wanting to know more and in greater depth than is considered "good" for one. Interested in grown-up doings. Acting grown-up. Being grown-up. Interchangeable with other colloquial expression: "You're trying to be grown." Responsible. In charge.* Serious. . . .
>
> *2. Also: Herstorically capable, as in "Mama, I'm walking to Canada and I'm taking you and a bunch of other slaves with me." Reply: "It wouldn't be the first time."*[5]

Black women as a group have never been fools. We couldn't afford to be. Yet in the last two decades many of us have been deterred from identifying with a liberation struggle which might say significant things to women like ourselves, women who believe that we were put here for a purpose in our own right, women who are usually not afraid to struggle.

Although our involvement has increased considerably in recent years, there are countless reasons why Black and other Third World women have not identified with contemporary feminism in large numbers.[6] The racism of white women in the women's movement has certainly been a major factor. The powers-that-be are also aware that a movement of progressive Third World women in this country would alter life as we know it. As a result there has been a concerted effort to keep women of color from organizing autonomously and from organizing with other women around women's political issues. Third World men, desiring to maintain power over "their women" at all costs, have been among the most willing reinforcers of the fears and myths about the women's movement, attempting to scare us away from figuring things out for ourselves.

It is fascinating to look at various kinds of media from the late 1960s and early 1970s, when feminism was making its great initial impact, in order to see what Black men, Native American men, Asian American men, Latino men, and white men were saying about the irrelevance of "women's lib" to women of color. White men and Third World men, ranging from conservatives to radicals, pointed to the seeming lack of participation of women of color in the movement in order to discredit it and to undermine the efforts of the movement as a whole. All kinds of men were running scared because they knew that if the women in their midst were changing, they were going to have to change too. In 1976 I wrote:

> *Feminism is potentially the most threatening of movements to Black and other Third World people because it makes it absolutely essential that we examine the way we live, how we treat each other, and what we believe. It calls into question the most basic assumption about our existence and this is the idea that biological, i.e., sexual identity determines all, that it is the rationale for power relationships as well as for all other levels of human identity and action. An irony is that among Third World people biological determinism is rejected and fought against when it is applied to race, but generally unquestioned when it applies to sex.*[7]

In reaction to the "threat" of such change, Black men, with the collaboration of some Black women, developed a set of myths to divert Black women from our own freedom.

Myths

Myth No. 1: The Black woman is already liberated.

This myth confuses liberation with the fact that Black women have had to take on responsibilities that our oppression gives us no choice but to handle. This is an insidious, but widespread myth that many Black women have believed themselves. Heading families, working outside the home, not building lives or expectations dependent on males, seldom being sheltered or pampered as women, Black women have known that their lives in some ways incorporated goals that white middle-class women were striving for, but race and class privilege, of course, reshaped the meaning of those goals profoundly. As W.E.B. DuBois said so long ago about Black women: " . . . our women in black had freedom contemptuously thrust upon them."[8] Of all the people here, women of color generally have the fewest choices about the circumstances of their lives. An ability to cope under the worst conditions is not liberation, although our spiritual capacities have often made it look like a life. Black men didn't say anything about how poverty, unequal pay, no childcare, violence of every kind including battering, rape, and sterilization abuse, translated into "liberation."

Underlying this myth is the assumption that Black women are towers of strength who neither feel nor need what other human beings do, either emotionally or materially. White male social scientists, particularly Daniel P. Moynihan with his "matriarchy theory," further reinforce distortions concerning Black women's actual status.

. . .

Myth No. 2: Racism is the primary (or only) oppression Black women have to confront. (Once we get that taken care of, then Black women, men, and children will all flourish. Or as Ms. Luisah Teish writes, we can look forward to being "the property of powerful men.")[10]

This myth goes hand in hand with the one that the Black woman is already liberated. The notion that struggling against or eliminating racism will completely alleviate Black women's problems does not take into account the way that sexual oppression cuts across all racial, nationality, age, religious, ethnic, and class groupings. Afro-Americans are no exception.

It also does not take into account how oppression operates. Every generation of Black people, up until now, has had to face the reality that no matter how hard we work we will probably not see the end of racism in our lifetimes. Yet many of us keep faith and try to do all we can to make change now. If we have to wait for racism to be obliterated *before* we can begin to address sexism, we will be waiting for a long time. Denying that sexual oppression exists or requiring that we wait to bring it up until racism, or in some cases capitalism, is toppled, is a bankrupt position. A Black feminist perspective has no use for ranking oppressions, but instead demonstrates the simultaneity of oppressions as they affect Third World women's lives.

Myth No. 3: Feminism is nothing but man-hating. (And men have never done anything that would legitimately inspire hatred.)

It is important to make a distinction between attacking institutionalized, systematic oppression (the goal of any serious progressive movement) and attacking men as individuals. Unfortunately, some of the most widely distributed writing about Black women's issues has not made this distinction sufficiently clear. Our issues have not been concisely defined in these writings, causing much adverse reaction and confusion about what Black feminism really is.[11]

This myth is one of the silliest and at the same time one of the most dangerous. Anti-feminists are incapable of making a distinction between being critically opposed to sexual oppression and simply hating men. Women's desire for fairness and safety in our lives does not necessitate hating men. Trying to educate and inform men about how their feet are planted on our necks doesn't translate into hatred either. Centuries of anti-racist struggle by various people of color are not reduced, except by racists, to our merely hating white people. If anything it seems that the opposite is true. People of color know that white people have abused us unmercifully and it is only sane for us to try to change that treatment by every means possible.

Likewise the bodies of murdered women are strewn across the landscape of this country. Rape is a national pastime, a form of torture visited upon all girls and women, from babies to the aged. One out of three women in the U.S. will be raped during her lifetime. Battering and incest, those home-based crimes, are pandemic. Murder, of course, is men's ultimate violent "solution." And if you're thinking as you read this that I'm exaggerating, please go get today's newspaper and verify the facts. If anything is going down here it's woman-hatred, not man-hatred, a war against women. But wanting to end this war still doesn't equal man-hating. The feminist movement and the anti-racist movement have in common trying to insure decent human life. Opposition to either movement aligns one with the most reactionary elements in American society.

Myth No. 4: Women's issues are narrow, apolitical concerns. People of color need to deal with the "larger struggle."

This myth once again characterizes women's oppression as not particularly serious, and by no means a matter of life and death. I have often wished I could spread the word that a movement committed to fighting sexual, racial, economic, and heterosexist oppression, not to mention one which opposes imperialism, anti-Semitism, the oppressions visited upon the physically disabled, the old and the young, at the same time that it challenges militarism and imminent nuclear destruction is the very opposite of narrow. All segments of the women's movement have not dealt with all of these issues, but neither have all segments of Black people. This myth is plausible when the women's movement is equated only with its most bourgeois and reformist elements. The most progressive sectors of the feminist movement, which includes some radical white women, have taken the above issues, and many more, quite seriously. Third World women have been the most consistent in defining our politics broadly. Why is it that feminism is considered "white-minded" and "narrow" while socialism or Marxism, from verifiably white origins, is legitimately embraced by Third World male politicos, without their having their identity credentials questioned for a minute?

Myth No. 5: Those feminists are nothing but Lesbians.

This may be the most pernicious myth of all and it is essential to understand that the distortion lies in the phrase "nothing but" and not in the identification Lesbian. "Nothing but" reduces Lesbians to a category of beings deserving of only the most violent attack, a category totally alien from "decent" Black folks, i.e., not your sisters, mothers, daughters, aunts, and cousins, but bizarre outsiders like no one you know or *ever* knew.

Many of the most committed and outspoken feminists of color have been and are Lesbians. Since many of us are also radicals, our politics, as indicated by the issues merely outlined above, encompass all people. We're also as Black as we ever were. (I always find it fascinating, for example, that many of the Black Lesbian-feminists I know still wear their hair natural, indicating that for us it was more than a "style.") Black feminism and Black Lesbianism are not interchangeable. Feminism is a political movement and many Lesbians are not feminists. Although it is also true that many Black feminists are not Lesbians, this myth has acted as an accusation and a deterrent to keep non-Lesbian Black feminists from manifesting themselves, for fear it will be hurled against them.

Fortunately this is changing. Personally, I have seen increasing evidence that many Black women of whatever sexual preference are more concerned with exploring and ending our oppression than they are committed to being either homophobic or sexually separatist. Direct historical precedent exists for such commitments. In 1957, Black playwright and activist Lorraine Hansberry wrote the following in a letter to *The Ladder,* an early Lesbian periodical:

> *I think it is about time that equipped women began to take on some of the ethical questions which a male-dominated culture has produced and dissect and analyze them quite to pieces in a serious fashion. It is time that "half the human race" had something to say about the nature of its existence. Otherwise—without revised basic thinking—the woman intellectual is likely to find herself trying to draw conclusions—moral conclusions—based on acceptance of a social moral superstructure which has never admitted to the equality of women and is therefore immoral itself. As per marriage, as per sexual practices, as per the rearing of children, etc. In this kind of work there may be women to emerge who will be able to formulate a new and possible concept that homosexual persecution and condemnation has at its roots not only social ignorance, but a philosophically active anti-feminist dogma.*[12]

I would like a lot more people to be aware that Lorraine Hansberry, one of our most respected artists and thinkers, was asking in a Lesbian context some of the same questions we are asking today, and for which we have been so maligned.

Black heterosexuals' panic about the existence of both Black Lesbians and Black gay men is a problem that they have to deal with themselves. A first step would be for them to better understand their own heterosexuality, which need not be defined by attacking everybody who is not heterosexual.

Home Truths

Above are some of the myths that have plagued Black feminism. The truth is that there is a vital movement of women of color in this country. Despite continual resistance to women of color defining our specific issues and organizing around them, it is safe to say in 1982 that we have a movement of our own. I have been involved in building that movement since 1973. It has been a struggle every step of the way and I feel we are still in just the beginning stages of developing a workable politics and practice. Yet the feminism of women of color, particularly of Afro-American women, has wrought many changes during these years, has had both obvious and unrecognized impact upon the development of other political groupings and upon the lives and hopes of countless women.

The very nature of radical thought and action is that it has exponentially far-reaching results. But because all forms of media ignore Black women, in particular Black feminists, and because we have no widely distributed communication mechanisms of our own, few know the details of what we have accomplished. The story of our work and contributions remains untold. One of the purposes of *Home Girls* is to get the word out about Black feminism to the people who need it most: Black people in the U.S., the Caribbean, Latin America, Africa—everywhere. It is not possible for a single introduction or a single book to encompass all of what Black feminism is, but there is basic information I want every reader to have about the meaning of Black feminism as I have lived and understood it.

In 1977, a Black feminist organization in Boston of which I was a member from its founding in 1974, the Combahee River Collective, drafted a political statement for our own use and for inclusion in Zillah Eisenstein's anthology, *Capitalist Patriarchy and the Case for Socialist Feminism.* In our opening paragraph we wrote:

The most general statement of our politics at the present time would be that we are actively committed to struggling against racial, sexual, heterosexual, and class oppression and see as our particular task the development of integrated analysis and practice based upon the fact that the major systems of oppression are interlocking. The synthesis of these oppressions creates the conditions of our lives. As Black women we see Black feminism as the logical political movement to combat the manifold and simultaneous oppressions that all women of color face.

The concept of the simultaneity of oppression is still the crux of a Black feminist understanding of political reality and, I believe, one of the most significant ideological contributions of Black feminist thought.

We examined our own lives and found that everything out there was kicking our behinds—race, class, sex, and homophobia. We saw no reason to rank oppressions, or, as many forces in the Black community would have us do, to pretend that sexism, among all the "isms," was not happening to us. Black feminists' efforts to comprehend the complexity of our situation as it was actually occurring, almost immediately began to deflate some of the cherished myths about Black womanhood, for example, that we are "castrating matriarchs" or that we are more economically privileged than Black men. Although we made use of the insights of other political ideologies, such as socialism, we added an element that has often been missing from the theory of others: what oppression is comprised of on a day-to-day basis, or as Black feminist musician Linda Tillery sings, " . . . what it's really like/To live this life of triple jeopardy."[13]

This multi-issued approach to politics has probably been most often used by other women of color who face very similar dynamics, at least as far as institutionalized oppression is concerned. It has also altered the women's movement as a whole. As a result of Third World feminist organizing, the women's movement now takes much more seriously the necessity for a multi-issued strategy for challenging women's oppression. The more progressive elements of the left have also begun to recognize that the promotion of sexism and homophobia within their ranks, besides being ethically unconscionable, ultimately undermines their ability to organize. Even a few Third World organizations have begun to include the challenging of women's and gay oppression on their public agendas.

Approaching politics with a comprehension of the simultaneity of oppressions has helped to create a political atmosphere particularly conducive to coalition building. Among all feminists, Third World women have undoubtedly felt most viscerally the need for linking struggles and have also been most capable of forging such coalitions. A commitment to principled coalitions, based not upon expediency, but upon our actual need for each other is a second major contribution of Black feminist struggle. Many contributors to *Home Girls* write out of a sense of our ultimate interdependence. Bernice Johnson Reagon's essay, "Coalition Politics: Turning the Century," should be particularly noted. She writes:

You don't go into coalition because you just like *it. The only reason you would consider trying to team up with somebody who could possibly kill you, is because that's the only way you can figure you can stay alive. . . . Most of the time you feel threatened to the core and if you don't you're not really doing no coalescing.*

The necessity for coalitions has pushed many groups to rigorously examine the attitudes and ignorance within themselves which prevent coalitions from succeeding. Most notably, there has been the commitment of some white feminists to make racism a priority issue within the women's movement, to take responsibility for their racism as individuals, and to do anti-racist organizing in coalition with other groups. Because I have written and spoken about racism during my entire involvement as a feminist and have also presented workshops on racism for white women's organizations for several years during the 1970s, I have not only seen that there are white women who are fully committed to eradicating racism, but that new understandings of racial politics have evolved from feminism, which other progressive people would do well to comprehend.[14]

Having begun my political life in the Civil Rights movement and having seen the Black liberation movement virtually destroyed by the white power structure, I have been encouraged in recent years that women can be a significant force for bringing about racial change in a way that unites oppressions instead of isolating them. At the same time the percentage of white feminists who are concerned about racism is still a minority of the movement, and even within this minority those who are personally sensitive and completely serious about formulating an *activist* challenge to racism are fewer still. Because I have usually worked with politically radical feminists, I know that there are indeed white women worth building coalitions with, at the same time that there are apolitical, even reactionary, women who take the name of feminism in vain.

One of the greatest gifts of Black feminism to ourselves has been to make it a little easier simply to *be* Black and female. A Black feminist analysis has enabled us to understand that we are not hated and abused because there is something wrong with us, but because our status and treatment is absolutely prescribed by the racist, misogynistic system under which we live. There is not a Black woman in this country who has not, at some time, internalized and been deeply scarred by the hateful propaganda about us. There is not a Black woman in America who has not felt, at least once, like "the mule of the world," to use Zora Neale Hurston's still apt phrase.[15] Until Black feminism, very few people besides Black women actually cared about or took seriously the demoralization of being female *and* colored *and* poor *and* hated.

When I was growing up, despite my family's efforts to explain, or at least describe, attitudes prevalent in the outside world, I often thought that there was something fundamentally wrong with me because it was obvious that me and everybody like me was held in such contempt. The cold eyes of certain white teachers in school, the Black men who yelled from cars as Beverly and I stood waiting for the bus, convinced me that I must have done something horrible. How was I to know that racism and sexism had formed a blueprint for my mistreatment long before I had ever arrived here? As with most Black women, others' hatred of me became self-hatred, which has diminished over the years, but has by no means disappeared. Black feminism has, for me and for so many others, given us the tools to finally comprehend that it is not something we have done that has heaped this psychic violence and material abuse upon us, but the very fact that, because of who we are, we are multiply oppressed. Unlike any other movement, Black feminism provides the theory that clarifies the nature of Black women's experience, makes possible positive support from other Black women, and encourages political action that will change the very system that has put us down.

The accomplishments of Black feminism have been not only in developing theory, but in day-to-day organizing. Black feminists have worked on countless issues, some previously identified with the feminist movement and others that we, ourselves, have defined as priorities. Whatever issues we have committed ourselves to, we have approached them with a comprehensiveness and pragmatism which exemplify the concept "grassroots." If nothing else, Black feminism deals in home truths, both in analysis and in action. Far from being irrelevant or peripheral to Black people, the issues we have focused on touch the basic core of our community's survival.

Some of the issues we have worked on are reproductive rights, equal access to abortion, sterilization abuse, health care, child care, the rights of the disabled, violence against women, rape, battering, sexual harassment, welfare rights, Lesbian and gay rights, educational reform, housing, legal reform, women in prison, aging, police brutality, labor organizing, anti-imperialist struggles, anti-racist organizing, nuclear disarmament, and preserving the environment.

Notes

1. Shakur, Assata. "Women in Prison: How We Are," in *The Black Scholar,* Vol. 9, No. 7 (April, 1978), pp. 13 & 14.

2. Rushin, Donna Kate. "The Bridge Poem," in *This Bridge Called My Back: Writings by Radical Women of Color,* eds. Moraga and Anzaldúa. Watertown: Persephone Press, Inc., 1981, p. xxi.

. . .

5. Walker, Alice. *In Search of Our Mothers' Gardens,* (Forthcoming, 1983). Cited from manuscript, n.p. [*Note:* Alice Walker's book was published by Harcourt Brace Jovanovich (New York, 1983).—S. Ruth]

6. The terms Third World women and women of color are used here to designate Native American, Asian American, Latina, and Afro-American women in the U.S. and the indigenous peoples of Third World countries wherever they may live. Both the terms Third World women and women of color apply to Black American women. At times in the introduction Black women are specifically designated as Black or Afro-American and at other times the terms women of color and Third World women are used to refer to women of color as a whole.

7. Smith, Barbara. "Notes for Yet Another Paper on Black Feminism, Or Will the Real Enemy Please Stand Up?" in *Conditions: Five, The Black Women's Issue,* eds. Bethel & Smith. Vol. 2, No. 2 (Autumn, 1979), p. 124.

8. DuBois, W.E.B. *Darkwater, Voices from Within the Veil,* New York: AMS Press, 1969, p. 185.

. . .

10. Teish, Luisah. "Women's Spirituality: A Household Act," in *Home Girls,* ed. Smith. Watertown: Persephone Press, Inc., 1983. All subsequent references to work in *Home Girls* will not be cited.

11. See Linda C. Powell's review of Michele Wallace's *Black Macho and the Myth of the Super Woman* ("Black Macho and Black Feminism") in this volume and my review of Bell Hooks' (Gloria Watkins) *Ain't I A Woman: Black Women and Feminism* in *The New Women's Times Feminist Review,* Vol. 9, no. 24 (November, 1982), pp. 10, 11, 18, 19 & 20 and in *The Black Scholar,* Vol. 14, No. 1 (January/February 1983), pp. 38–45.

12. Quoted from *Gay American History: Lesbians and Gay Men in the U.S.A.,* ed. Jonathan Katz. New York: T.Y. Crowell, 1976, p. 425. Also see Adrienne Rich's "The Problem with Lorraine Hansberry," in "Lorraine Hansberry: Art of Thunder, Vision of Light," *Freedomways,* Vol. 19, No. 4, 1979, pp. 247–255 for more material about her woman-identification.

13. Tillery, Linda. "Freedom Time," *Linda Tillery,* Oakland: Olivia Records, 1977, Tuizer Music.

14. Some useful articles on racism by white feminists are Elly Bulkin's "Racism and Writing: Some Implications for White Lesbian Critics." *Sinister Wisdom 13* (Spring, 1980), pp. 3–22; Minnie Bruce Pratt's "Rebellion." *Feminary,* Vol. 11, Nos. 1 & 2 (1980), pp. 6–20; and Adrienne Rich's "Disloyal to Civilization: Feminism, Racism, Gynephobia." *On Lies, Secrets and Silence: Selected Prose* 1966–1978. New York: W.W. Norton, 1979, pp. 275–310.

15. Hurston, Zora Neale. *Their Eyes Were Watching God.* Urbana: University of Illinois, 1937, 1978, p. 29.

I Am What I Am

Rosario Morales

Rosario Morales is a writer, performer, and activist. Her publications include Getting Home Alive *(1986), which she coauthored with her daughter, Aurora Levins, and selections in several anthologies and journals. She has performed dramatic renderings of her work for organizations at various universities, including Haverford, Wellesley, Brandeis, and Brown. In 1987 she won the Boston Contemporary Writer's Award.*

Morales describes herself this way:

> *I'm a New York Puerto Rican born in 1930, raised in Manhattan and the Bronx. I married at 20 and moved to Puerto Rico where I farmed for five years and bore and raised three delightful people. I've also done ecological and other scientific work and I have an M.A. in Anthropology from the University of Chicago.*
>
> *I've written on and off all my life. I find bits stuck in envelopes or in dusty notebooks. I began writing in earnest and taking myself seriously as a writer in 1979. My writing reflects my upbringing in New York City. I grew up among children of Irish, European Jewish, Puerto Rican, Southern Black and Afro-Caribbean migrants.*
>
> *I look forward to old age. I feel freer than ever before to make choices for my own growth and pleasure. Despite what pain and obstacles I may have faced because of it, I'm glad I am Puerto Rican, a woman, born into the working class, and a radical. I am, at last, pleased to be myself.*

Such dynamic self-acceptance and pride is a goal and a tribute each of us may wish for ourselves—hard won, but worth the task. In the short piece that follows, they are all there: exuberance, defiance, self-assertion, humor, and more.

I am what I am and I am U.S. american I haven't wanted to say it because if I did you'd take away the Puerto Rican but now I say go to hell I am what I am and you can't take it away with all the words and sneers at your command I am what I am I am Puerto Rican I am U.S. American I am New York Manhattan and the Bronx I am what I am I'm not hiding under no stoop behind no curtain I am what I am I am Boricua as Boricuas come from the isle of Manhattan and I croon Carlos Gardel tangoes in my sleep and Afro-Cuban beats in my blood and Xavier Cugat's lukewarm latin is so familiar and dear sneer dear but he's familiar and dear but not Carmen Miranda who's a joke because I never was a joke I was a bit of a sensation See! here's a real true honest-to-god Puerto Rican girl and she's in college Hey! Mary come here and look she's from right here a South Bronx girl and she's honest-to-god in college now Ain't that something who wouda believed it Ain't science wonderful or some such thing a wonder a wonder And someone who did languages for a living stopped me in the subway because how I spoke was a linguist's treat I mean there it was yiddish and spanish and fine refined college educated english and irish which I keep mainly in my prayers It's dusty now I haven't said my prayers in decades but try my Hail Marrrry full of grrrace with the nun's burr with the nun's disdain It's all true and it's all me do you know I got an English accent from the BBC For years in the mountains of Puerto Rico when I was 22 and 24 and 26 all those young years I listened to the

BBC and Radio Moscow's English english announcers announce and denounce and then I read Dickens all the way through three of four times at least and then later I read Dickens aloud in voices and when I came back to the U.S. I spoke mockDickens mockBritish especially when I want to be crisp efficient I know what I'm doing and you can't scare me tough that kind I am what I am and I'm a bit of a snob too Shit! why am I calling myself names I really really dig the funny way the British speak and it's real it's true and I love too the singing of yiddish sentences that go with shrugs and hands and arms doing melancholy or lively dances I love the sound and look of yiddish in the air in the body in the streets in the English language noo so what's new so go by the grocer and buy some fruit oye vey gevalt gefilte fish those words hundreds of them dotting the English language like raisins in the bread shnook and schlemiel suftik tush schmata all those soft sweet sounds saying sharp sharp things I am what I am and I'm naturalized Jewish-American wasp is foreign and new but Jewish-American is old shoe familiar schmata familiar and it's me dears it's me bagels blintzes and all I am what I am Take it or leave me alone.

The Spiritual Significance of the Self-Identified Woman*

Elsa Gidlow

Elsa Gidlow (1898–1986), poet, essayist, activist, philosopher, was called the Poet Warrior. Her autobiography, ELSA: I Come With My Songs *(1986) was the first explicitly lesbian full-life autobiography published.*

Religion, traditional and institutionalized, has been one of the foremost enemies of liberation for women. Yet, Gidlow argues, without inner wholeness, without a spiritual center, life can become directionless and lack zest. Women must regain spiritual autonomy, must in fact become spiritually self-identified.

START WITH THE PREMISE THAT SPIRITUAL POWER grows from a ground of personal wholeness. Next, each human born comes into life as a whole being. Third, if the inner sense of wholeness is lost or discouraged from maturing, the individual becomes maimed and susceptible to indoctrination, manipulation and mastery.

I have made no mention of gender; persons are born as women or men. Are their prospects equal for realizing their spiritual personhood?

From earliest childhood a boy's sense of his wholeness is reinforced, encouraged. As he grows, the integrity of his personhood is emphasized. He probably learns he will have to fight for it, but it is his to fight for. Advancing in awareness, he absorbs the conviction that his maleness is the earthly manifestation of deity. He was *"created"* in God's image. Almost all of God's representatives are male. Even if he is atheistic, he is a beneficiary of the religious and philosophical climate of male supremacy. Most religious leaders are male, as are practically all the power figures in the secular world. However humble his social position or role, a man may take for granted that there is someone of lesser importance who can be called upon to serve him: a female someone. His mother was the first model for that and, with rare exceptions, was the instiller of that expectation.

A little girl, on the other hand, from her earliest years and throughout each phase of her education and development, receives both active and subliminal messages of her subsidiary role, of her incompleteness as a person, hence her need to realize and complete herself through others: children, a husband. Her identification with "god" is not one of being created in his image. Impossible. She is female. The alternative is to serve him, as she is expected to serve the needs, works and concerns of men at the secular level. It seems curious that the simple correlation between identifying

Reprinted from *Woman of Power,* Issue Twelve, Winter 1989, pp. 15–17. By permission of *Woman of Power* and Celeste West, Booklegger Publishing, San Francisco. Originally published in *Maenad,* Spring 1981, Vol. 1, No. 3, pp. 73–79.

deity with maleness and subservience with femaleness has not received more emphasis.

Ultimate spirituality, the Source, the creative energy that is incommunicable in words, obviously is beyond gender. Every human may be presumed to reflect equally that spiritual energy, by whatever name and in whatever image it is presented. The fact that nearly every figure embodying spiritual transcendence and human wisdom has been presented as male could hardly leave women unaffected. It is easy and natural for men to seek and find their spiritual selves reflected in these figures, and to draw on their power for worldly enterprise. But since the preemption or destruction of the Goddess religions, there has been no embodiment of woman's spirituality for like identification and power. Is it far-fetched to see in this exclusion from identification with and direct participation in the sacred at least one cause of women's sense of mental and physical limitations and dependence, the feeling of incompleteness pushing her to ally herself with a man in an attempt by indirection to benefit from the male repository of power?

That is how it has been and to a great extent continues to be. But change is well underway. Thoughtful women have come to realize that we must seek individually and collectively—for our survival and perhaps even the survival of the planet—our spiritual path guided by our own inner light. How and where do we begin?

Some start with a personal declaration of independence, as I did at an early age; this impulse culminated in celebration of my eightieth birthday on December 29, 1978, with what I called *"Creed for Free Women."* Here is a passage from that poem:

> As no free-growing tree serves another or requires
> to be served,
> As no lion or lamb or mouse is bound or binds,
> No plant or blade or grass nor ocean fish,
> So I am not here to serve or be served.
>
> I am Child of every Mother,
> Mother of each daughter,
> Sister of every woman,
> And lover of whom I choose or chooses me.[1]

Yes, once we get down to the roots of our power-in-wholeness, our roots can split rock. Clear-eyed on the path to full personhood, we do not ignore the presence of obstacles and seductive temptations. There are women, however, who acquiesce in subsidiary-sex roles in the hope of escaping the struggles of independence or because they fear they may fail to be equal to those struggles, just as some men, more than might admit it, join the Army with a sense of relief at being freed from daily decisions and even long-term responsibilities. The challenges are formidable; the inducements to give up are ever present. It is not and never has been easy to maintain our vision of freedom, but the rewards in selfhood are worth the pains and the risk.

Always, the first step for a woman to determine is whether she wants full personhood in freedom, to decide with her whole being whether she needs autonomy and is willing to pay the price. Not every woman does—yet. There is a useful exercise for determining if one is ready to start on the path of *self*-possession. For fifteen minutes or so before retiring, stand quietly, with inward attention, and ask: "What do I *really* want?" Resist any impulse to give answers. Such usually come from "out there," from the authorities, spiritual and secular, clamoring to enter and make us theirs. Remember, we are not asking, "What *should* I want?" but what do I *really* want? Need? Repeat the exercise night after night and go to sleep empty of answers. As I know from my own experience, sooner or later, almost magically, the answer will come of itself from our own depth.

Then the work begins—work that empowers one as the discoveries unfold. The woman in her revolt realizes that she is not an auxiliary, not a partial being needing to be completed by alliance with a male—not a womb, a pair of breasts, legs, a cunt—but that she emerged into life as a whole human person who was robbed of the recognition of her wholeness to one degree or another. The knowledge comes with a surge of energy. She sees that the source of spiritual autonomy is in herself and may be tapped for whatever course she may choose to pursue. Wide awake to that knowledge, she is flooded with wonder and delight at what she has known in her depths yet hidden from herself: spirituality is relationship—collaboration and interaction with the energies of the universe and with all other women coming into that knowledge.

She realizes what Sappho, the poet, the maker, the archetype of the independent, spiritually creative woman, knew twenty-five centuries ago (and women forgot): "I am forever virgin." One can hardly doubt that she meant being, thinking and acting autonomously, in her own right. As Esther Harding reminded us, virgin originally meant "one-in-herself," not necessarily abstaining from sex or marriage, but remaining independent.[2]

At this point of initial euphoria, many women choose to "become" Lesbian. That surely is one path, a rewarding one for those whom it fulfills. It was my choice because from childhood it appeared to be my original nature. But Lesbianism and liberation from stereotypes are not synonymous. There are millions of Lesbians, declared and undeclared, but multimillions more of women eager to achieve full personhood whose way of realizing their vision need not and will not require a choice between celibacy and erotically loving women. Nor will it require rejection of motherhood for women who genuinely desire to have and nurture children, as opposed to reproducing because of pressure from ecclesiastical or secular authorities who would convince her that childbearing is her sole destiny. A woman's control over her own body is a requisite of autonomy on all levels of her existence. She is not the property or means of production for the interests of church or state. We can see here an extended meaning of "I am virgin: one-in-myself."[3]

Having made the declaration signifying her resolve to reclaim spiritual identity and autonomy on all levels of her life, a woman must be willing to follow through on it. Obviously this involves purging herself of all the false, debilitating images of what a woman is supposed to be: weak, passive, incomplete without male insemination, both spiritual and physical, to give birth to anything of flesh or spirit.

Because she aims at reclaiming full and authentic womanhood, she will come into full realization and acceptance of her erotic capabilities. She discovers the regenerative and recreative powers of her sexuality. This too is an aspect of the knowledge that she has within herself all that is necessary for strength, creativity, autonomy and spiritual relatedness. In salvaging the role of pleasure from repressive puritanism, she discovers the satisfaction inherent in one more victory over stereotypes, in this case the myth of women's "frigidity" or weak libido. Yet, the contrary has been well documented.

Although we use the words "victory" and "battle," we are not speaking about war but leaps in evolution. No banners or fanfares are needed. The women's revolt is fundamentally a quiet one, as quiet and inevitable as a plant bursting into bloom when a long, inner growth has reached culmination. This evolution was necessary not only for women but for our whole society. Much of the clamor over "women's lib" has come from those deploring, contesting, or exploiting it. Those who prefer to think in terms of a "war" are mainly extremists who execute spasmodic and isolated guerrilla attacks. The majority of women aiming at spiritual/political wholeness disavow and avoid the causes of polarization, either between women and men and, even more important, between women, individually and collectively.

Surveying human existence with the needs of a whole person, I hope, I see no opposition between the spiritual and the political. They must permeate, even define, one another. If the political excludes the deep human awe induced by the mysteries of existence and our visions of human perfectibility, it is hollow. When the spiritual is intolerant of political necessity and activity, it is ungrounded, a "blue sky" indulgence. Actually, each is rooted in the other. Whole persons know the strength of integrating both into their lives and actions.[4]

Ignoring this, much harm has been done—fortunately short-range and reversible—by some of the bitter feuds between groups whose members would not or could not come into accord on tactics despite a common aim. Stridency, even cruelty, and acts of aggression that debilitate in the long run, have sometimes aped the least attractive qualities of the worst males. There is always the tendency of those involved in a "cause" to assume the masks and adopt the weapons of those who attack them and may be seen as stronger. But it would be fatal for a woman to lose her authentic womanhood in the process of retrieving it. There need be no repression or denial of a woman's gentler, receptive, compassionate qualities. Wholeness consists of integrating all of these within her strengthening Self. It is extremely important that this be recognized. Not only Western society but the entire world is suffering from a submergence of these female qualities, although they exist in all beings who have not been terminally twisted by patriarchal indoctrination.[5]

The future of humankind may depend on acceptance of the gentler, womanly qualities as a key to survival on this miraculously evolved and evolving Earth. Our gentler qualities in the service of the wholeness and strength we are reclaiming is the secret umbilical between all women who share our struggle toward wholeness. Our bond grows from the achievements and ecstasies that accompany acting out of fully realized personhood. And let us never forget that it is also the umbilical linking us to our long heritage of foremothers reaching back to a hardly imaginable past. We are the heirs to their sufferings, arduously won achievements and unrecorded triumphs. Many years ago, in a sort of ecstatic vision during a still dark early morning, lighting my fire, I felt the need to express gratitude to those women. I wrote a poem from which I quote now in the hope that our inner light and fire may lead—with work, hope and laughter—to women's fully human future:

> Each dawn, kneeling before my hearth,
> Placing stick, crossing stick
> On dry eucalyptus bark,
> Now the larger boughs, the log
> (With thanks to the tree for its life)
> Touching the match, waiting for creeping flame,
> I know myself linked by chains of fires
> To every woman who has kept a hearth.
>
> In the resinous smoke
> I smell hut and castle and cave,
> Mansion and hovel,
> See in the shifting flame my mother
> And grandmothers out over the world
> Time through, back to the paleolithic
> In rock shelters, where flint struck first sparks
> (Sparks aeons later alive on my hearth).
> I see mothers, grandmothers back to the
> beginnings,
> Huddled beside holes in the earth
> Of iglu, tipi, cabin,
> Guarding the magic no other
> being has learned.
> Awed reverent, before the sacred
> fire . . .[6]

Notes

*I have chosen the term "*self*-identified woman" for two reasons: "Woman-identified woman" has served well for years, but has come to connote Lesbianism only. "*Self*," as used here, is more inclusive, applicable to all women. *The American College Dictionary* says that in philosophical terminology it means "the individual consciousness in relationship to itself." Until we know our own selfhood, we are not ready to relate to the selfhood of other women. Ungrounded ideals and visions are not enough.

1. Elsa Gidlow, "A Creed for Free Women," *The Pacific Sun*, Mill Valley, Ca., December 29, 1978. This was published for my eightieth birthday.

2. Esther Harding, *Women's Mysteries, Ancient and Modern* (London: Rider and Co., 1971).

3. Unless the human race is faced with extinction, no female of our species should feel that she has an obligation to reproduce. The sole reason to decide affirmatively to lend herself to procreation must be her own will to motherhood and child nurturing and women's assessment of the ensuing benefit to society.

4. Speaking personally, in the fifties my own political activities were investigated by the California Un-American Activities Committee (known as The Tenney Committee, after the McCarthy-type senator of that name). In 1962, with Alan and Mary Jane Watts and one or two others, I helped found the Society for Comparative Philosophy; was its first vice-president, later treasurer, and in that capacity have continued to the present on its board of directors.

5. Males are also victims of stereotypes, although they derive benefits personally and on the world stage. While in the spiritual sense, they too have been robbed of wholeness by the over-emphasis on masculinity, they receive the constant reinforcement that they are the prototypes of humanness; hence, all but a few are spared recognition of their own maimed condition.

6. Elsa Gidlow, "Chains of Fires," in *Moods of Eros*, Druid Heights Books, Mill Valley, Ca., 1970, p. 20.

I Have a Motherland

Gena Corea

Gena Corea, born in 1946 in Hingham, Massachusetts, was educated at the University of Massachusetts and in 1971 became an investigative reporter. She edited a feminist feature for the Holyoke (Mass.) Transcript *until 1973 and then turned to freelance writing. Her articles have appeared in the* New York Times, Ms., *and* Glamour, *and she has written a weekly syndicated column, "Frankly Feminist," for the New Republic Syndicate. Active in women's health care, she is a coeditor of* Man-Made Women: How New Reproductive Technologies Affect Women *(1987) and author of* The Hidden Malpractice: How American Medicine Mistreats Women *(1977),* The Mother Machine *(1985), and* Invisible Epidemic: The Story of Women and AIDS *(1992).*

To all the distortions, the ultimate response is the search for truth and the affirmation of worth. Forceful and feeling, Corea's affirmation captures the emotions aroused in us when we recover the past and reconstitute our "place."

SIT DOWN, WRETCH, AND ANSWER ME: WHAT HAVE you done with my past?

Years ago you stood before me with a solemn face and told me I was an orphan. With the hand behind your back you pushed the heads of my parents—my proud, strong, angry ancestors—under time's river.

You hid the action of your right hand by pointing with your left to my entire history, one sentence in a book: "In 1920, in a battle largely led by Susan B. Anthony, women won the right to vote."

But you never told me how strong Anthony was. How, year after year, she suffered scorn, ridicule and defeat and kept on working, not merely for suffrage, but for woman's full liberation.

You never described to me, white man, the courage of hundreds of nameless women who, though raised to be timid, taught to be frightened, nonetheless defied decorum and walked down strange streets, knocked on doors, stood up before hostile faces, and suffered jeers to collect signatures for suffrage petitions—petitions later joked about in Congress and then ignored.

Why didn't you tell me I had such magnificent foremothers?

Why, white man, in your history books, did you never tell me about spunky Abigail Adams asking her husband John to assign women the legal status of human being, rather than property, in the Constitution of the young United States?

And of her warning that, if forgotten, women were "determined to foment a rebellion"? Women were forgotten and women have been fomenting a rebellion but you hid from me the uprisings of my foremothers.

Why did you reverently describe to me the political and military strategies with which earlier Kissingers entertained themselves but keep from me the stories of how ordinary women lived their lives?

I know all about the glorious deaths of soldiers on the battlefield but nothing about the deaths of women in childbed.

Where is the Tomb of the Unknown Mother? Why did she die?

You told me about Carrie Nation, whom you pictured as a ludicrous, axe-wielding teetotaller, but not about Margaret Sanger, who brought to women the most important discovery since fire: contraception.

Why did you hide Anne Hutchinson, Lucy Stone, Sojourner Truth and Mary Walker from me? I could have been stronger if I'd known of them.

You tried to disinherit me. When I trembled before you like an orphan dependent on your good will, you said, "Oh, I'll take care of you, little one."

You kept me meek and grateful for your very small favors. You told me how benevolent you were to an orphan like me. How chivalrous you were, you said.

(Oh, why did you never tell me that way back in 1848, Sarah Grimke had called chivalry "practical contempt"?)

And in gratitude for your chivalry, your patronizing protection, I cooked your food, washed your clothes, cleaned your house, bore and raised your children.

You fraud! I'm your equal and you hid that from me.

When I envied you your freedom, your adventures, and dreamed of being, say, a lawyer, you frowned and told me that if I began to use my brain, I'd be sure to have labor pains and it wouldn't do for me, while trying a case in a court of law, to give birth to a child.

You put on black robes, held a thick book to your heart, rolled your eyes to heaven and solemnly announced that God wanted me to be just as I was.

How cruel of God, I whispered.

Blasphemer! you shouted in my ear. Heretic!

Let me read the thick book, I said.

No, you snapped, your brain's too small. You'll hurt it and go mad.

And all that time, all that time when I thought I was a strange mutation of a woman with strange longings to be whole, all that time, damn it, my ancesters had felt the same, thought the same, said the same.

And you, white man, hid their words, their struggles, their very existences from me. You left my ancestors out of history.

But now I know. I have a tribe, a people, a history, a past, an identity, a motherland, a tradition. I'm not an orphan. I'm not alone.

And I'll tremble before you no more.

. . . To Form a More Perfect Union

Maya Angelou

Poet, novelist, playwright, screenwriter Maya Angelou has written a number of works including I Know Why the Caged Bird Sings *(1970),* And Still I Rise *(1978),* The Heart of a Woman *(1981),* Singin' and Swingin' and Gettin' Merry Like Christmas *(1985),* All God's Children Need Traveling Shoes *(1986), and* I Shall Not Be Moved *(1991).*

As commissioner for the observance of International Women's Year, appointed by President Jimmy Carter, she gave this speech at the First National Women's Conference in Houston, Texas, in 1977. That equality and freedom for women is squarely within the American tradition of progressive liberty for all citizens is reflected in Angelou's words.

Maya Angelou, "To Form a More Perfect Union . . . "reported in *THE SPIRIT OF HOUSTON: THE FIRST NATIONAL WOMEN'S CONFERENCE,* An official report to the President, the Congress, and the People of the U.S. National Commission on the Observance of International Women's Year. Washington, D.C., 1978.

WE AMERICAN WOMEN VIEW OUR HISTORY WITH equanimity. We allow the positive achievement to inspire us and the negative omissions to teach us.

We recognize the accomplishments of our sisters, those famous and hallowed women of history and those unknown and unsung women whose strength gave birth to our strength.

We recognize those women who were and are immobilized by oppression and crippled by prejudice.

We recognize that no nation can boast of balance until each member of that nation is equally employed and equally rewarded.

We recognize that women collectively have been unfairly treated and dishonorably portrayed.

We recognize our responsibility to work toward the eradication of negatives in our society and by so doing, bring honor to our gender, to our species, and to ourselves individually.

Because of the recognition set down above we American women unfold our future today.

We promise to accept nothing less than justice for every woman.

We pledge to work unsparingly to bring fair play to every public arena, to encourage honorable behavior in each private home.

We promise to develop courage that we may learn from our colleagues and patience that we may attack our opponent.

Because we are women, we make these promises.

5

The Origins of Female Subordination: Theories and Explanations

Asking the Question

As one becomes sensitized to women's situation, one is likely to ask, Why? How did this come to be, and why is it so resistant to change? Although great diversity exists among peoples of the world, we can see that, for the most part, in society after society and across time and space, men dominate the upper levels of political, economic, and social power, and women are rarely or only partially included.[1] The work of men is generally more highly valued than that of women and usually more highly compensated. Men are typically valued more in themselves as persons, a fact often expressed in social customs, rites, and laws. Men tend to outrank women in social status, and their privilege is frequently built on the service of women. The reverse is rarely the case.

What accounts for the fact that societies are so constructed that men dominate and disparage women? Has it always been so, or was there a time in the dim past when women were the equals of men or even, as some have suggested, the initiators and prime movers of civilization? If male dominance has indeed been universal in time, how is the superior position of men to be explained? Is it true, as the patriarchs contend, that men are superior to women in ability, or did they win their place by the choice of the gods? If, however, male dominance has not always been the case, how did it come to be? Was there a primordial revolution of magnificent proportions, as is sometimes figured in ancient myths, or did a gradual erosion of female power and autonomy occur, and what could have occasioned such an erosion?

Many have argued that men and women are "different" in a variety of ways and that these differences account for women's position. Are women different in ways that matter to the direction in which civilization has evolved? Or did the way civilization has evolved create the differences? Are behavioral differences biologically or culturally based? And what difference do the differences make, or *should* they make, for the way a culture is arranged—in apportioning political authority, economic benefits, and enjoyment of life's amenities?

Some answers to these questions are scientific or quasi-scientific; others appear in mythic context, in political or even poetic language. Some speak in purely pragmatic terms, arguing social efficiency or orderliness, whereas others center on women's personal choices or even on cosmic decrees.

The question of why this is as it is has been asked before, but now the women's movement has focused afresh on the issues it raises, and the analyses are becoming more urgent and often more sophisticated. In the religious communities, feminist theologians are challenging the traditional interpretations of language, dogma, and beliefs. In the sciences, feminists and nonfeminists alike are carrying on new and vigorous research into aspects of these issues barely touched or else treated prejudicially before. Controversy and debate are sharp. Many are gaining new, more reliable information and generating new techniques to deal with this ancient question.

New Data

Researchers in almost every field of intellectual endeavor are collecting new information regarding women's place, experience, and contributions to culture, past and present. Anthropologists have thrown new light on women's discoveries and inventions in early civilization—pottery, food preservation, tanning, and so on. Feminist historians have unearthed data on women never before recognized, events whose importance had been overlooked, activities never before understood. Psychologists and biologists are carefully reexamining studies of female–male differences, together with their relation to behavioral characteristics, in order to deal in a more objective way with traditional assumptions and theories. Linguists are discovering new connections between speech patterns and social effectiveness and power.

New Perspectives

The addition of feminist critique to intellectual dialogue is bringing a new degree of sophistication to the inquiry itself. Having challenged the reliability of traditional knowledge collected solely by men or within male structures, feminists are posing new questions that considerably alter the search for explanations. How viable and/or complete is much of the information we have on prehistory and primitive cultures, interpreted as it has been through masculist bias? Can we depend on unsensitized males to have asked the pertinent questions about women; would women have confided freely in male researchers? Would the male researcher have properly evaluated the female data he collected? If the masculist psychologist has imposed his expectations on his research findings, won't they have been distorted, and won't most of the theories of sex differences be unreliable? Might not there then have to be entirely new ways of piecing together the origins of patriarchy?[2]

The matter of terminology, for example, has been sharply challenged. The term *domestic* is an interesting case in point. Literally the word means "pertaining to the home," and social scientists use it to describe tasks, artifacts, or behavior directly related to the home site, to the group's family or living arrangements. Anthropologists generally agree that women have almost universally carried on the "domestic" activities of society. However, evidence also shows that almost any task assigned to women is likely to be deemed "domestic" by social scientists, whereas the same task assigned to men is likely to be categorized differently. For example, an ethnographer might categorize fashioning pottery for the tribe as a "domestic" activity if done by women but as an "artistic" one if done by men. In other words, because the assumption is that women do the domestic work of the group, their tasks are automatically categorized as domestic; then, in a real round robin, because women's work is termed "domestic," researchers feel safe in reporting that the domestic work of the tribe is always done by women!

Thus, one may realistically challenge such traditionally accepted theses as the claim that women are oppressed because they have never united in their own self-interest. New discussions have highlighted many events where women fought in our own behalf, events that were either unknown before the surge of feminist history or else neglected as irrelevant. If these factual events, such as the Roman women's opposition to the Oppian Laws; the movement of the Beguines in the Middle Ages; the later fights for temperance, birth control, and abortion rights are ignored and thus not integrated into the thesis, how reliable is the final thesis?

The current surge of interest in the quest for explanations gives us reason to be optimistic about discovery but not without careful attention to the many complicated problems before us. Our discussion must be preceded by certain cautions. First, no one as yet knows "the answer." Vast gaps in data and analysis exist. Second, there may not be one answer, but many. Third, the several theories presented here represent only examples of those that exist, and even the challenges put to them do not constitute the full array of those that should be made. This book has room only for a beginning.

The Matter of Definition

No one as yet knows "the answer" to what? That is, what exactly is our question? Are we asking why women and men are "unequal"? Unequal in what? In political or personal power? What constitutes power? What kind of power do women not have? Unequal in opportunity? Opportunity for what? We have opportunity to gain income—we can marry it. From a value-free standpoint, why is that mode of opportunity less acceptable than any other? Are we unequal in status? Or are we just "different," that is, separate but "equal"? How does one measure status and compare it? How does one compare the power and status of one group of women in a culture (say, middle-class American white women) with another (perhaps, wealthy black British women)?

If we ask why women are subordinate to men, what do we mean by "subordinate," and how do we indicate and include differences in subordination from culture to culture? How is subordination different from oppression, exploitation, discrimination, domination? What does the term *subordination* mean in the context of power? If it is true, as some have suggested, that though men hold formal power, women frequently hold great informal power over men, then who is subordinate to whom, and in what way?

As you can see, there are many relevant concepts and terms, and each has its nuances and their implications. One must be extraordinarily careful about how they are used.

Any good researcher will point out that effective problem-solving requires an accurate statement of the problem itself, as well as careful definitions of the terms employed. Consider the following two sentences, each of which has actually been used as a statement of the problem: How did it come about that men usurped the autonomy and labor of women? Why are men superior to women both in power and accomplishments? Neither of these formulations defines the problem adequately. They each contain assumptions and value judgments; they each express a particular perspective; and they each contain research expectations that have not been critically explored. In short, they are biased and circular: Each assumes an answer before it begins to search.

In tracking down reliable explanations, one must guard against hidden assumptions and values, charged language ("usurped," "equality," "superior"), and bias-prone terminology ("domestic," "aggressive," "technological"). This in itself is a monumental task. How does one ask a question that is free of prior assumptions and value-laden concepts, yet is still meaningful? For example: "Under what conditions did the present cultural sexual arrangements come to be?" What arrangements? What culture? What kind of origin—in time? in causative factors? Whereas the two formulations in the previous paragraph are too narrow and prejudicial, this one is too broad and omits the essence of the problem, which *is* valuational. Clearly, a balance of attention must exist between constructing formulations that are relatively objective and free of assumption yet sufficiently concrete in perspective to be substantive.[3]

Sexual Asymmetry

Searching for an expression that captures all of the issues that we have been raising, that is broad enough and relatively "objective," some feminists and social scientists have been using the term *sexual asymmetry*, which simply means a disproportion or dissimilarity based on sex. The term functions in a number of different contexts—scientific, political, religious, and so on—and also avoids many pitfalls. It is both meaningful and scientifically productive to ask, "What are the origins and causes of sexual asymmetry?" Yet, in its scientific purity, the term *sexual asymmetry* tends to be vague, and without the support of related concepts for fleshing it out (charged though they may be), discussion within its limits might tend to be thin.

For purposes of our discussion, let us say that sexual asymmetry refers to a whole range of situations where (1) policies regarding control over the wider community and the freedom to participate in activities affecting all members of the group are determined solely or primarily on the grounds of sex, and (2) judgments of worth are made solely or primarily on the basis of sex. For example, in a culture where the legal right to vote for a leader of the entire group is limited to men *because they are men* (not bright men or strong men or educated men) and prohibited to women *because they are women* (not stupid women or poor women or malicious women), political sexual asymmetry exists. In a culture where men are deemed intrinsically more valuable than women, more worthy, better humans, more desirable *solely on the ground of maleness,* valuational sexual asymmetry exists.

Asymmetry takes many forms. In most cultures, as we have said, the work of men is more highly prized than that of women; women are considered to be the inferiors of men (in a variety of ways); and people tend to disparage both the work and the personhood of women. Such societies are termed *misogynist,* women-hating. In our culture signs of misogyny range from the subtle to the blatant. Women are reputed to be stupid, petty, incompetent, or deceptive; they are underpaid and are excluded from many activities. Other cultures have featured infibulation,[4] the chastity belt, purdah, and suttee.

Although in some cultures women have considerable power within the family group or over other women, in every known society, for the most part, men make the policy that affects the group as a whole—men make policy for women (and for some other men), but women do not formally make policy for the majority of men. In such a case, women are *subordinate* to men; that is, women inhabit a lower order of rank, power, and privilege. For example, men in our culture control the institutions that determine the rules of our lives: the legislature, the judiciary, the police, the law, the economy. Women control the home, though *formally* only with the approval of the men they live with.

Oppression differs from subordination in that one person may be subordinate to another and yet not be oppressed, as when a child is subordinate to a benevolent parent or when a worker of lesser ability must yield to policy set by a more highly qualified person in a position of higher rank. To oppress means to bear down, to weigh upon, to burden. One is oppressed when one experiences life as a burden, when one is emotionally or spiritually crushed or tyrannized. A culture that demeans a woman's self-image, destroys her pride, misuses her person for ends not her own, or appropriates the fruits of her labor without proper compensation (that is, exploited her labor) is an oppressive culture. Many cultures oppress and exploit their women as our culture oppresses and exploits at least some of us, if not all (as many feminists argue). Through *discrimination* (different, disadvantageous treatment before the law), outright slavery, or social customs that serve to solidify male privilege, women are oppressed and exploited in most cultures.

When we ask here, "What are the origins and causes of sexual asymmetry?" we are seeking an answer to the entire range of asymmetry from discrimination to misogyny.

Problems of Method

How do we go about finding reliable answers to the questions we have asked? We are, after all, pursuing a situation that in myth is without beginning and in social science traces back at least ten thousand years into prehistory, that traverses diverse cultures around the globe, and that may even have parallels in other species.

Scientifically, how do we deal with origins when the beginnings are lost? And where shall we count the beginnings? With recorded history? With early primitive peoples? With primates and hominoids? How helpful is information gleaned from current "primitive" groups when they diverge so much even among themselves?

Under what circumstances and to what degree is the practice of drawing analogies between humans and other animals to count? And if they count, which animals? Shall we select those that meet one set of expectations, like the aggressive, asymmetrical gibbons or shall we focus on the ever-faithful, one-time-mating graylag goose or perhaps the lion with its tough female hunter? Shall we confine ourselves to primates? And to what degree are any animal studies helpful when investigating a creature as uniquely malleable as the human being?

A great deal of important information is coming from new research into certain primate groups such as the chimpanzees, which are believed to be closely related to the kind of African ape that some four million years ago may have given rise to the hominids (the earliest members of the human family, such as *Australopithecus* and *Homo erectus*). Because fossil records (bones and teeth, for example, or organic tools) of this period are scarce, and because it is difficult to speculate reliably on behavior patterns of groups that are not observable, anthropologists use several kinds of evidence to generate hypotheses about the nature of early human social activities. For example, changes in the relative size of canine and molar teeth, within and across sexual categories, may tell us about diet (and therefore food-getting patterns) or about modes of defense or even about degrees of sociability. Such speculations, supported or enlarged by the observation of existent populations of highly developed primates, offer possibilities for piecing together a picture of the evolution of early human organization.

Some social scientists, however, approach the problem differently. They contend that because *Homo sapiens* is a far more advanced and complex creature in terms of intelligence than the earliest hominids, and because reflective thinking is unique to humans, *Homo sapiens* is qualitatively different from its ancestors. Its behavior patterns and social organization, therefore, require a different kind and level of explanation, perhaps psychological or even mythic.

Studying the art and artifacts of lost civilizations further along the evolutionary scale, some claim that advanced cultures existed before our own that were matriarchal and matrilineal. Argued primarily from inferential information, such theories are very controversial.

What counts as evidence? It is commonly understood that personal testimony (called emic data) may be unreliable; issues of subjectivity, of perspective, of lack of insight, even of deceit arise. Yet even purely objective, researcher-based analysis (called etic data) may suffer from ethnocentrism or oversimplification, and even with physical evidence the problem of interpretation remains. How then are such speculations or hypotheses to be verified?

A Series of Hypotheses

So far, all we have for "answers" to our problem is conjecture. There are hypotheses, no firm theories. The hypotheses, except for certain themes that appear to be common to all, range across a variety of perspectives, levels of explanation, and conclusions, some of them quite contradictory.

Biological Approaches

When one argues that asymmetry occurs because women and men have different capacities and behaviors based on the *innate, inherited physical differences* (such as hormonal patterns, brain size, or bone structure), then one is arguing from the biological perspective or level. This approach has included arguments that females and males differ *constitutionally* in such varied factors as intelligence, temperament, IQ, capacity to lead, physical endurance, propensity to "bond" with members of the same sex, sexuality, aggressiveness, and even a sense of justice. Some have contended that these biologically based differences account for *and justify* sexual asymmetry.

Such a point of view has the advantage of focusing on factors that are more easily observable, hence more amenable to study and to verification than some others. And, as some of the discussion in the preceding chapter pointed out, research does indicate that real physical, behavior-related differences do exist between females and males. What remains, however, is to determine what these differences mean, and more important, what they should mean. If it should be found, for example, that males are constitutionally more aggressive and hence more likely to compete than females (there is some evidence to this effect) and thus more inclined to dominate or lead, one ought reasonably to ask whether this means that men *should* lead; or, since the world now suffers from an overabundance of aggressiveness, whether less aggressive persons (females?) should be socially encouraged to lead and males be discouraged from doing so.[5]

To say that women are "naturally" this and men are "naturally" that (leaving aside the question of the truth of such propositions) is an argument that is frequently used to maintain the status quo. Yet one must remember that the terms *natural* and *desirable* are different. It is natural for animals to kill or maim (usually for food or protection but sometimes for other reasons), but that does not make this behavior desirable. It is natural for humans to die painfully of disease, but that does not make this desirable. The human species has never rested content with what is "natural." That is our splendor as well as our infamy. We have survived because of adaptations that were not "natural." Cultures evolve because humans are malleable. We must not confuse the muddy scientific concept *natural* with the equally muddy ethical notion *desirable*.

Sociological or Cultural Theories

The factor of malleability raises the familiar issue of the "nature/nurture" controversy. Which is more responsible for human behavior, nature (physiological, inborn components) or nurture (the effects of society—socialization, enculturation, learning)? Although nature, our physical selves and our genes, constitutes the raw material of our beings and thus imposes its own limits on our development, social scientists generally agree that nurture contributes the lion's share to our development.

In a famous cross-cultural study of three existing societies, Margaret Mead described extremely divergent gender-based behavior.[6] The Arapesh society approved behavior for both men and women that our culture would term *feminine:* unaggressive, maternal, and cooperative rather than competitive. Mundugumor men and women were exactly opposite in behavior, all of them expected to be extremely aggressive, violent, and nonmaternal. The Tchambuli culture, a mirror image of our own, prized dominant, impersonal, and managing women and emotionally dependent, less effective men. Mead concluded that such data threw great doubt on the biological basis of gender difference and strongly supported the thesis that sex-linked behavioral characteristics are the result of social conditions.

The emphasis on enculturation as the main source of sex-role behavior continues today, yet both nonfeminists and feminists are moving toward reappraising biological and physiological factors. Sociological theories like Mead's generally argue that female–male behavioral differences are more a matter of social than of biological degree: The traits we take to be feminine or masculine are prescribed by the mores of our culture and are learned or internalized through formal education, religion, media, and all the other institutions that define experience. Unlike biological explanations, which account for the beginnings of asymmetry by saying simply, "It has always been that way, decreed by nature," sociological theories need additional elaboration to deal with origins. It is one thing to say that I as a woman have trait *x* because my society teaches it, and another to account for *why* my society teaches *x*. How and why did my society choose to teach *x*, and why does this society teach *x* while another teaches *y?*

There are those, feminist and otherwise, who say that it is not necessary to ask why or how gender norms originated. They argue that we need only evaluate them in the present context from the point of view of ethics (is it right, fair, or just to subordinate women?) or of social efficacy (does it benefit our society to maintain the present arrangement?). In common sense, this argument carries weight. One need not ask when or how the first war began in order to decide that war is undesirable and must be ended. A medical researcher need not ask who had the first cancer in order to search for its cause. But origins and causes are logically related. If we know how something comes to be, if we can determine *what factors precede and precipitate an event,* in effect we have found the cause, and only in understanding causes of events can we hope to control them.

The problem, however, becomes complicated. Just as some people confuse natural with desirable, others confuse origin with justification. For example, George Gilder, a well-known writer of antifeminist theories, argued that asymmetry originates in the males' exclusion from childbearing and in their drive to achieve parity through other modes of creativity.[7] This, he argued, explains why men feel the need to exclude women from their activities, why they become unpleasant if women refuse the place men have made for them, and *why women should not refuse that place.* Whatever one thinks of Gilder's first contention—that men dominate women to achieve reproductive parity—we can plainly see that the thesis cannot stand as a justification, an ethical argument, for asymmetry. To say that *people commit murder because they are hostile, antisocial, and pressured* may explain why they do it—how their murderous impulses originate—but it does not support the thesis that *they should do it;* that is, the explanation does not serve as a justification. Clearly, it is helpful to explore the origins of sexual asymmetry, but one must carefully distinguish what the exploration accomplishes and what it leaves undone. By and large, sociological-cultural theories of origin are either *evolutionary* or *psychomythic.* Evolutionary theories argue that individuals or entire cultures or both have developed certain traits or norms as adaptations, or survival mechanisms, in answer to the requirements of their environment.

Individual-Evolutionary Theories A famous example of the individual-evolutionary explanation is the "man-the-hunter" theory. Food, it begins, was the most important survival commodity in primitive society, and because scarce, meat was the most prized. As women in primitive circumstances were always with child or caring for them, it was not practical for them to go on the hunt, which often took one miles and days away from the safety of the home site and required activities hard to perform with an attached small child. For this reason, women stayed at home, raising children, foraging for vegetables and small game, and tending the hearth while men went hunting. Finally, each sex developed (evolved) physical and behavioral traits appropriate to their tasks. This, some evolutionists say, explains not only work segregation based on sex but also why men are prized above women (*they* brought the meat). It also reveals the origin of the different capabilities, traits, and personalities of females and males: Men are aggressive and bonding so they can hunt, whereas women are compliant and gentle because "the overall mood arising from such organic orientation, from so much waiting and letting grow and gentling and encouraging but never forcing, is a mood of compliance."[8]

For a time, this theory was in great vogue with many people, feminists and nonfeminists alike. But now the entire perspective has come into question. One may ask whether the male became aggressive because he had to hunt or hunted because he was aggressive. (After all, other sources of protein existed, usually provided by the woman, than what was sought after in the hunt—even meat.) Which came first, man the hunter or man the warrior, and are the two related? Did women really evolve "compliance" because that temperament is necessary to raising children, and who says that it is necessary? Mead's Mundugumors certainly do not believe so. Their women are aggressive, their children survive, and female aggressiveness does not lead to male unaggressiveness, as some theories suggest. How does one account for male aggressiveness and rites of courage in cultures (for example, in Polynesia) where food (including protein) is plentiful and hunting unnecessary?

Evolutionary theories that focus on the development of individual (male–female) differences are certainly more sophisticated than biological theories, but they leave much to be desired. Still paying scant attention to the power of socialization, they fail to take into account the changes in individual behavior that would be wrought by changing environments. Men no longer go off to hunt (however widely one chooses to define the term), and brute strength, size, and aggressiveness are no longer adaptive traits for social survival, yet the value persists. Some other, wider factor may be needed to explain the cultural definitions of woman and man.

Cultural-Evolutionary Theories Variations of the preceding kind of explanation, cultural-evolutionary theories, take the society rather than the individual as the basic unit to be explored.[9] In this case, it is the entire culture, as well as the individual, that evolves adaptive mechanisms; sexual mores, role definitions, and gender expectations are part of them. For example, if a society were located in an environment where conditions were particularly hard, with a high death rate, such a society would probably require a high birth rate to maintain an adequate population, and it might well develop values that encouraged women to conceive and bear many children, to view themselves primarily in their childbearing capacity, and so on. The cultural-evolutionary approach, then, seeks to understand sexual mores, attitudes, and behaviors in terms of the environmental conditions that give rise to them.

Psychomythic Theories None of the theories thus far developed fully accounts for the whole range of sexual asymmetry. Too many puzzling questions are left unanswered. The kinds of explanations we have considered do not adequately explain the reasons for sex segregation, political subordination, or the divisions of labor based on sex. They do not even begin to explain the other, more virulent aspect of asymmetry: misogyny.

It is one thing to categorize people on the basis of a certain trait—old people do this, young people do that; large people do this, small people do that—but what gives sexism its essential characteristic is the element of valuation. Not only are tasks separated by sex, but men's tasks are also judged more valuable, women's less valuable. Not only is the male's role to lead and the female's to follow, but leading is valued and following is disparaged. Not only are men and women to exhibit complementary character traits, but male traits are praised and female traits are held in contempt. Nor is it only that men tend to do or be better things and hence are more deserving of praise. Rather, it is the reverse: The things that are praised are simply the things that men do; they are praised *because men do them.* For the most part, a task socially assigned to women is debased. Cross-cultural studies bear this out.

We hear much of the fact, for example, that 75 percent of all physicians in the former USSR were women. However, it is rarely pointed out that in that society the practice of medicine, except for some highly specialized fields, was considered merely a technical job and was not highly paid; for the most part, the higher paid specialists and surgeons were men. In the United States, secretarial work had high status and was highly paid until it became a female occupation; so was teaching. Nursing, always female, has always suffered in power, prestige, and pay. The men who are now moving into the nursing field are being rewarded with preference in the highest paid, most select positions. Men are "encouraged" to enter nursing to "raise the level of the profession." Women are "permitted" to enter medicine or law because it is not just or legal to bar them; nothing is said about raising the level of the profession. More and more it becomes apparent that it is not simply that women do the "shitwork" of society, but it is equally the other way around: Tasks are deemed unworthy if women do them.

We can make the same analysis of human behaviors. For example, when men ask their wives more than once to do something, they are "reminding." Women who ask repeatedly are "nagging." When men are firm and resolute, they have backbone; women who act the same are stubborn or bitchy. When a man raises his voice in argument he is angry, but a woman is hysterical. Menstruation in most societies is surrounded with taboos, disgust, and even horror. In today's modern society where people can utter any obscenity, freely discuss publicly any body function from nose blowing to orgasm, open admission of having one's period is still an occasion for shock and embarrassment. Would that be the case if menstruation were a male function? Erections are a source of pride to their owners. Much fuss is made over the length and breadth of a penis. What is analogous for women? In patriarchy, it is as though the female carries with her an evil effusion and contaminates all that she touches.

Theories that explain only the *fact* of separation or categorization (men do this, women do that) and omit the *judgment* of devaluation (men and what they do are good; women and what they do are contemptible) or theories that disclaim the existence or importance of devaluation are missing the central point. The misogyny in sexual asymmetry is what renders it sexist and makes it oppressive. It is true that analyses of asymmetry are highly charged with value. One could argue that one's misogyny is another man's reality—it is not misogyny to say that women are inferior; it is true! Many of us, however, know better, and the fact of misogyny, almost universal though varying in degree, must be explained.

Psychomythic explanations function on a level where this issue can be treated. A myth is a story that serves to explain and/or to express some important reality of life or nature. The creation story in the Bible, for example, represented the ancient Hebrew explanation of the origin of the world, of life, and of human suffering. Sometimes the stories are avowedly fictitious; others are regarded as true.

Several theories try to explain myths: that they represent certain human verities, common to all people (such as the confrontation with one's own mortality); that they are modes of expressing experiences or feelings inexpressible in ordinary language; or that they symbolize beliefs and needs in a person that are too deep, to intense, or too socially bizarre to express directly. Their relation to psychological explanation, then, is clear.

A myth is generally taken to be an accurate representation of common, perhaps universal, human beliefs and attitudes. For this reason, myths are important for the analysis of sexual asymmetry. We study them to reveal their hidden message about attitudes toward women, and feminists often explain certain arrangements regarding women as the social acting out of basic psychomythic beliefs or psychological needs. The Adam and Eve story, for example, is a powerfully revealing myth that has parallels in many cultures. Many societies, primitive and otherwise, have stories that credit the first human life and the power of birth to a male and then relegate the life-giving function to women as a discredited and burdensome task. Does this story reveal a universal male envy of female procreative powers? Does it perhaps hark back to a primitive matriarchy, if not a historical one then a symbolic one (as in the paradigmatic Mother)? And does this tale not neatly justify the subordination and oppression of women? Have not numerous churchmen contended that women's suppression justly results from the primordial betrayal in the Garden of Eden? Does this story not express a statement of women's evil, untrustworthiness, guile, naivete, seduceability, and unworthiness before God? Does it not justify hatred and contempt?

Although the story expresses misogyny and presents a "justification" for the believer, we are still left with a question: Why is it necessary to create stories to justify the subordination and hatred of women? That is, why do men control and condemn women? The psychomythic theories attempt to approach this central issue through various themes, such as a yearning for maternal safety (Elizabeth Janeway), the model of family aggression—man upon woman (Shulamith Firestone), or even penis envy (Sigmund Freud). Each theory seeks some universal theme, some common human reality to explain this universal behavior: misogynous sexual asymmetry.

The major strength of psychomythic theories is that they seek wide-ranging explanations, sufficiently inclusive to cover all the variations of sexism. Also, they treat a psychological event—attitudes and beliefs—on a psychological level. The problem with psychomythic theories, however, is that they are almost impossible to verify—and if used exclusively, they omit references to the very essential sociocultural elements.

Conclusion

If we have no definitive theories of explanation, what can we do? Search the following explanations carefully. Ponder the points they have in common, such as the centrality of childbearing or of hunting, and consider whether these themes are viable and/or sufficient. Notice the gaps in all the theories; use these as further points of departure.

Ultimately, we can probably develop reliable explanations from a combination of levels and perspectives. Such explanations will undoubtedly require a great deal more in the way of research and data than is now available.

Notes

1. In the social sciences today, particularly anthropology, energetic dialogue surrounds the issue of the universality or near universality of female subordination. Well known in this debate is the work of Alice Schlegel [see Alice Schlegel, ed., *Sexual Stratification: A Cross-Cultural View* (New York: Columbia University Press, 1977)] and of Michelle Rosaldo and Nancy Chodorow in the anthology *Women, Culture, and Society*, ed. Michelle Rosaldo and Louis Lamphere (Stanford: Stanford University Press, 1974).

2. For an interesting discussion of the relation of politics to scientific inquiry, see Donna Haraway, "Animal Sociology and a Natural Economy of the Body Politic, Part I: A Political Physiology of Dominance," *Signs* 4, no. 1 (Autumn 1978): 21–36.

3. For two very different but very good approaches to the matter of definitions, see Cheris Kramarae and Paula A. Treichler, *A Feminist Dictionary* (Boston: Pandora Press, 1985); and Gerda Lerner, "Definitions" in *Creation of Patriarchy*, Appendix (New York: Oxford University Press: 1986), pp. 231–243.

4. *Infibulation:* the practice of excising the clitoris and labia of the vagina and sewing together the vulva to ensure chastity; *purdah:* the practice in Islam of totally sequestering women; *suttee:* the practice in India, surviving now only in rural areas, of widows immolating themselves on the burning funeral pyres of their husbands.

5. Steven Goldberg, in *The Inevitability of Patriarchy* (New York: Morrow, 1974), argued precisely that: Males *are* constitutionally more aggressive, more likely to compete energetically and hence win. Socialization patterns merely recognize and support this reality. Patriarchy, therefore, is the inevitable arrangement because it is the most orderly, stable, and reflective of nature.

6. Margaret Mead, *Sex and Temperament in Three Primitive Societies* (New York: Morrow, 1935).

7. George Gilder, *Sexual Suicide* (New York: Quadrangle, 1973).

8. Wolfgang Lederer, *The Fear of Women* (New York: Grune & Stratton, 1968), p. 87.

9. For an excellent review of these kinds of theories (and others) see Virginia Sapiro, *Women in American Society*, 3d ed. (Mountain View, CA: Mayfield, 1994), ch. 2 and 3.

Genesis

The myth that the origin of male authority rested in some great cataclysmic female sin is not peculiar to the Judeo-Christian tradition or to the Western world. Again and again, this idea appears in primitive and highly advanced societies: Woman is evil and dangerous and to make things right the gods decree that man should maintain order through control.

The Holy Scriptures, rev. by Alexander Harkavy. New York: Hebrew Publishing Company, 1951.

[26]AND GOD SAID, LET US MAKE MAN IN OUR IMAGE, after our likeness: and let them have dominion over the fish of the sea, and over the fowl of the air, and over the cattle, and over all the earth, and over every creeping thing that creepeth upon the earth. [27]So God created man in his *own* image, in the image of God created he him; male and female created he them.

[28]And God blessed them, and God said unto them, Be fruitful, and multiply, and replenish the earth, and subdue it: and have dominion over the fish of the sea, and over the fowl of the air, and over every living thing that moveth upon the earth.

[29]And God said, Behold, I have given you every herb bearing seed, which *is* upon the face of all the earth, and every tree, in which *is* the fruit of a tree yielding seed; to you it shall be for meat. [30]And to every beast of the earth, and to every fowl of the air, and to every thing that creepeth upon the earth, wherein *there is* life, *I have given* every green herb for meat: and it was so.

[31]And God saw every thing that he had made, and, behold, *it was* very good. And there was evening and there was morning, the sixth day.

2 Thus the heavens and the earth were finished, and all the host of them. [2]And on the seventh day God ended his work which he had made; and he rested on the seventh day from all his work which he had made. [3]And God blessed the seventh day, and sanctified it: because that in it he had rested from all his work which God created and made.

[4]These *are* the generations of the heavens and of the earth when they were created, in the day that the Lord God made the earth and the heavens.

[5]And no plant of the field was yet on the earth, and no herb of the field had yet grown: for the Lord God had not caused it to rain upon the earth, and *there was* not a man to till the ground. [6]But there went up a mist from the earth, and watered the whole face of the ground. [7]And the Lord God formed man *of* the dust of the ground, and breathed into his nostrils the breath of life; and man became a living soul.

[8]And the Lord God planted a garden eastward in Eden; and there he put the man whom he had formed. [9]And out of the ground made the Lord God to grow every tree that is pleasant to the sight, and good for food; the tree of life also in the midst of the garden, and the tree of knowledge of good and evil. [10]And a river went out of Eden to water the garden; and from thence it was parted, and became into four heads. [11]The name of the first *is* Pishon: that *is* it which compasseth the whole land of Havilah, where *there is* gold; [12]And the gold of that land *is* good: there *is* bdellium and the onyx stone. [13]And the name of the second river *is* Gihon: the same *is* it that compasseth the whole land of Ethiopia. [14]And the name of the third river *is* Hiddekel: that *is* it which goeth toward the east of Assyria. And the fourth river is Euphrates.

[15]And the Lord God took the man, and put him into the garden of Eden to till it and to keep it. [16]And the Lord God commanded the man saying, Of every tree of the garden thou mayest freely eat: [17]But of the tree of the knowledge of good and evil, thou shalt not eat of it; for in the day that thou eatest thereof thou shalt surely die.

[18]And the Lord God said, *it is* not good that the man should be alone; I will make a help meet for him. [19]And out of the ground the Lord formed every beast of the field, and every fowl of the air; and brought *them* unto Adam to see what he would call them: and whatsoever Adam called every living creature, that *was* the name thereof. [20]And Adam gave names to all cattle, and to the fowl of the air, and to every beast of the field; but for Adam there was not found a help meet for him. [21]And the Lord God caused a deep sleep to fall upon Adam, and he slept: and he took one of his ribs, and closed up the flesh instead thereof; [22]And the rib, which the Lord God had taken from man, made he a woman, and brought her unto the man. [23]And Adam said, This *is* now bone of my bones, and flesh of my flesh: she shall be called Woman, because she was taken out of Man. [24]Therefore shall a man leave his father and his mother, and shall cleave unto his wife: and they shall be one flesh.

[25]And they were both naked, the man and his wife, and were not ashamed.

3 Now the serpent was more subtle than any beast of the field which the Lord God had made. And he said unto the woman, Yea, hath God said, Ye shall not eat of every tree of the garden? [2]And the woman said unto the serpent, We may eat of the fruit of the trees of the garden: [3]But of the fruit of the tree which *is* in the midst of the garden, God hath said, Ye shall not eat of it, neither shall ye touch it, lest ye die. [4]And the serpent said unto the woman, Ye shall not surely die: [5]For God doth know that in the day ye eat thereof, then your eyes shall be opened, and ye shall be as gods, knowing good and evil. [6]And when the woman saw that the tree *was* good for food, and that it *was* pleasant to the eyes, and a tree to be desired to make *one* wise, she took of the fruit thereof, and did eat, and gave also unto her husband with her; and he did eat. [7]And the eyes of them both were opened, and they knew that they *were* naked; and they sewed fig leaves together, and made themselves aprons. [8]And they heard the voice of the Lord God walking in the garden in the cool of the day: and Adam and his wife hid themselves from the presence of the Lord God amongst the trees of the garden. [9]And the Lord God called unto Adam, and said unto him, Where *art* thou? [10]And he said, I heard thy voice in the garden, and I was afraid, because I *was* naked; and I hid myself. [11]And he said, Who told thee that thou *wast* naked? Hast thou eaten of the tree, whereof I commanded thee that thou shouldest not eat? [12]And the man said, The woman whom thou gavest *to be* with me, she gave me of the tree, and I did eat. [13]And the Lord God said unto the woman, What *is* this *that* thou hast done? And the woman said, The serpent beguiled me, and I did eat. [14]And the Lord God said unto the serpent, Because thou hast done this, thou *art* cursed above all cattle, and above every beast of the field; upon thy belly shalt thou go, and dust shalt thou eat all the days of thy life: [15]And I will put enmity between thee and the woman, and between thy seed and her seed; he shall bruise thy head, and thou shalt bruise his heel. [16]Unto the woman he said, I will greatly multiply thy sorrow and thy conception; in sorrow thou shalt bring forth children; and thy desire *shall be* to thy husband, and he shall rule over thee. [17]And unto Adam he said, Because thou hast hearkened unto the voice of thy wife, and hast eaten of the tree, of which I commanded thee, saying, Thou shalt not eat of it; cursed *is* the ground for thy sake; in sorrow shalt thou eat *of* it all the days of thy life; [18]Thorns also and thistles shall it bring forth to thee, and thou shalt eat the herb of the field; [19]In the sweat of thy face shalt thou eat bread, till thou return unto the ground; for out of it wast thou taken; for dust thou *art*, and unto dust shalt thou return.

[20]And Adam called his wife's name Eve; because she was the mother of all living.

[21]Unto Adam also and to his wife did the Lord God make coats of skins, and clothed them.

[22]And the Lord God said, Behold, the man is become as one of us, to know good and evil: and now, lest he put forth his hand, and take also of the tree of life, and eat, and live for ever: [23]Therefore the Lord God sent him forth from the garden of Eden, to till the ground from whence he was taken. [24]So he drove out the man; and he placed at the east of the garden of Eden the Cherubim, and a flaming sword which turned every way, to keep the way of the tree of life.

Rape

Susan Brownmiller

Susan Brownmiller was born in Brooklyn, New York, in 1935. She was educated at Cornell University, served as a reporter for NBC-TV and as a newswriter for ABC-TV, and has worked as a freelance writer. Brownmiller is the author of Shirley Chisholm *(1970) and the controversial and well-known* Against Our Will *(1975), which was revised in 1986. In 1984, she published* Femininity *and in 1989* Waverly Place, *a personal and fictionalized interpretation of a New York City child abuse and wife battering case.*

Her treatment of the concept of rape is historical, anthropological, and political. Her thesis here is psychological and mythical (in the positive sense) as well as sociological. Forcible rape, in its violence and cruelty, is a conscious act of intimidation. Women's fear and vulnerability force them to seek protection. Perhaps man's domination of women has its source in his exclusive ability to fend off other attackers.

MAN'S STRUCTURAL CAPACITY TO RAPE AND WOMAN'S corresponding structural vulnerability are as basic to the physiology of both our sexes as the primal act of sex itself. Had it not been for this accident of biology, an accommodation requiring the locking together of two separate parts, penis and vagina, there would be neither copulation nor rape as we know it. Anatomically one might want to improve on the design of nature, but such speculation appears to my mind as unrealistic. The human sex act accomplishes its historic purpose of generation of the species and it also affords some intimacy and pleasure. I have no basic quarrel with the procedure. But, nevertheless, we cannot work around the fact that in terms of human anatomy the possibility of forcible intercourse incontrovertibly exists. This single factor may have been sufficient to have caused the creation of a male ideology of rape. When men discovered that they could rape, they proceeded to do it. Later, much later, under certain circumstances they even came to consider rape a crime.

In the violent landscape inhabited by primitive woman and man, some woman somewhere had a prescient vision of her right to her own physical integrity, and in my mind's eye I can picture her fighting like hell to preserve it. After a thunderbolt of recognition that this particular incarnation of hairy, two-legged hominid was not the Homo sapiens with whom she would like to freely join parts, it might have been she, and not some man, who picked up the first stone and hurled it. How surprised he must have been, and what an unexpected battle must have taken place. Fleet of foot and spirited, she would have kicked, bitten, pushed and run, *but she could not retaliate in kind.*

The dim perception that had entered prehistoric woman's consciousness must have had an equal but opposite reaction in the mind of her male assailant. For if the first rape was an unexpected battle founded on the first woman's refusal, the second rape was indubitably planned. Indeed, one of the earliest forms of male bonding must have been the gang rape of one woman by a band of marauding men. This accomplished, rape became not only a male prerogative, but man's basic weapon of force against woman, the principal agent of his will and her fear. His forcible entry into her body, despite her physical protestations and struggle, became the vehicle of his victorious conquest over her being, the ultimate test of his superior strength, the triumph of his manhood.

Man's discovery that his genitalia could serve as a weapon to generate fear must rank as one of the most important discoveries of prehistoric times, along with the use of fire and the first crude stone axe. From prehistoric times to the present, I believe, rape has played a critical function. It is nothing more or less than a conscious process of intimidation by which *all men* keep *all women* in a state of fear.

In the Beginning Was the Law

From the humblest beginnings of the social order based on a primitive system of retaliatory force—the *lex talionis:* an eye for an eye—woman was unequal before the law. By anatomical fiat—the inescapable construction of their genital organs—the human male was a natural predator and the human female served as his natural prey. Not only might the female be subjected at will to a thoroughly detestable physical conquest from which there could be no retaliation in kind—a rape for a rape—but the consequences of such a brutal struggle might be death or injury, not to mention impregnation and the birth of a dependent child.

One possibility, and one possibility alone, was available to woman. Those of her own sex whom she might call to her aid were more often than not smaller and weaker than her male attackers. More critical, they lacked the basic physical wherewithal for punitive vengeance; at best they could maintain only a limited defensive action. But among those creatures who were her predators, some might serve as her chosen protectors. Perhaps it was thus that the risky bargain was struck. Female fear of an open season of rape, and not a natural inclination toward monogamy, motherhood or love, was probably the single causative factor in the original subjugation of woman by man, the most important key to her historic dependence, her domestication by protective mating.

Once the male took title to a specific female body, and surely for him this was a great sexual convenience as well as a testament to his warring stature, he had to assume the burden of fighting off all other potential attackers, or scare them off by the retaliatory threat of raping *their* women. But the price of woman's protection *by some men* against an abuse *by others* was steep. Disappointed and disillusioned by the inherent female incapacity to protect, she became estranged in a very real sense from other females, a problem that haunts the social organization of women to this very day. And those who did assume the historic burden of her protection—later formalized as husband, father, brother, clan—extracted more than a pound of flesh. They reduced her status to that of chattel. The historic price of woman's protection by man against man was the imposition of chastity and monogamy. A crime committed against her body became a crime against the male estate.

The earliest form of permanent, protective conjugal relationship, the accommodation called mating that we now know as marriage, appears to have been institutionalized by the male's forcible abduction and rape of the female. No quaint formality, bride capture, as it came to be known, was a very real struggle: a male took title to a female, staked a claim to her body, as it were, by an act of violence. Forcible seizure was a perfectly acceptable way—to men—of acquiring women, and it existed in England as late as the fifteenth century. Eleanor of Aquitaine, according to a biographer, lived her early life in terror of being "rapt" by a vassal who might through appropriation of her body gain title to her considerable property. Bride capture exists to this day in the rain forests of the Philippines, where the Tasadays were recently discovered to be plying their Stone Age civilization. Remnants of the philosophy of forcible abduction and marriage still influence the social mores of rural Sicily and parts of Africa. A proverb of the exogamous Bantu-speaking Gusiis of southwest Kenya goes "Those whom we marry are those whom we fight."

It seems eminently sensible to hypothesize that man's violent capture and rape of the female led first to the establishment of a rudimentary mate-protectorate and then sometime later to the full-blown male solidification of power, the patriarchy. As the first permanent acquisition of man, his first piece of real property, woman was, in fact, the original building block, the cornerstone, of the "house of the father." Man's forcible extension of his boundaries to his mate and later to their offspring was the beginning of his concept of ownership. Concepts of hierarchy, slavery and private property flowed from, and could only be predicated upon, the initial subjugation of woman.

When Women Throw Down Bundles: Strong Women Make Strong Nations

Paula Gunn Allen

Paula Gunn Allen was born in 1939. The daughter of a Laguna Pueblo, Sioux, and Scottish mother and a Lebanese-American father, she was raised in a small New Mexican village bounded by the Laguna Pueblo reservation on one side and an Acoma reservation on another. Paula spent eleven years at a convent school from the age of six to seventeen, yet she was strongly influenced by her mother's stories about Native American goddesses and traditions.

As one of the country's most visible spokespeople for Native American culture, she is also an award-winning writer and a professor of English at UCLA. A major Native American poet, writer, lecturer, and scholar, she has written numerous works, including: Grandmothers of the Light: A Medicine Woman's Sourcebook *(1991),* Spider Woman's Granddaughters: Native American Women's Traditional and Short Stories *(1989),* Skins and Bones, *a book of poetry (1988),* The Sacred Hoop: Recovering the Feminine in American Indian Traditions *(1986), the novel* The Woman Who Owned the Shadows *(1983), and an anthology,* Studies in American Indian Literature *(1982).*

In this essay, Allen shows us that the subordination and deprecation of women was not universal, but had its origins in particular cultures and particular philosophies. In detailing the enforced "patriarchalization" of one society, the overthrow of one gynocracy, she gives us a clue as to how the current subordination of women may have been accomplished, and she defeats the idea that patriarchy is natural or inevitable.

NOT UNTIL RECENTLY HAVE AMERICAN INDIAN women chosen to define themselves politically as Indian *women*—a category that retains American Indian women's basic racial and cultural identity but distinguishes women as a separate political force in a tribal, racial, and cultural context—but only recently has this political insistence been necessary. In other times, in other circumstances more congenial to womanhood and more cognizant of the proper place of Woman as creatrix and shaper of existence in the tribe and on the earth, everyone knew that women played a separate and significant role in tribal reality.

This self-redefinition among Indian women who intend that their former stature be restored has resulted from several political factors. The status of tribal women has seriously declined over the centuries of white dominance, as they have been all but voiceless in tribal decision-making bodies since reconstitution of the tribes through colonial fiat and U.S. law. But over the last thirty years women's sense of ourselves as a group with a stake in the distribution of power on the reservations, in jobs, and within the intertribal urban Indian communities has grown.

As writer Stan Steiner observes in *The New Indians*, the breakdown of women's status in tribal communities as a result of colonization led to their migration in large numbers into the cities, where they regained the self-sufficiency and positions of influence they had held in earlier centuries. He writes, "In the cities the power of women has been recognized by the extra-tribal communities. Election of tribal women to the leadership of these urban Indian centers has been a phenomenon in modern Indian life."[1]

Since the 1960s when Steiner wrote, the number of women in tribal leadership has grown immensely. Women function as council members and tribal chairs for at least one-fourth of the federally recognized tribes. In February 1981, the Albuquerque *Journal* reported that sixty-seven American Indian tribes had women heads of state. In large measure, the urbanization of large numbers of American Indians has resulted in their reclaiming their traditions (though it was meant to work the other way when in the 1950s the Eisenhower administration developed "Relocation" and "Termination" policies for Indians).

The coming of the white man created chaos in all the old systems, which were for the most part superbly healthy, simultaneously cooperative and autonomous, peace-centered, and ritual-oriented. The success of their systems depended on complementary institutions and organized relationships among all sectors of their world. The significance of each part was seen as necessary to the balanced and harmonious functioning of the whole, and both private and public aspects of life were viewed as valuable and necessary components of society. The private ("inside") was shared by all, though certain rites and knowledge were shared only by clan members or by initiates into ritual societies, some of which were gender-specific and some of which were open to members of both sexes. Most were male-dominated or female-dominated with helping roles assigned to members of the opposite gender. One category of inside societies was exclusive to "berdaches"—males only—and "berdaches"*—female only. All categories of ritual societies function in present-day American Indian communities, though the exclusively male societies are best recorded in ethnographic literature.

The "outside" was characterized by various social institutions, all of which had bearing on the external welfare of the group. Hunting, gathering, building, ditch cleaning, horticulture, seasonal and permanent moves, intertribal relationships, law and policy decisions affecting the whole, crafts, and childrearing are some of the areas governed by outside institutions. These were most directly affected by white government policies; the inside institutions were most directly affected by Christianization. Destruction of the institutions rested on the overthrow or subversion of the gynocratic nature of the tribal system, as documents and offhand comments by white interveners attest.

Consider, for example, John Adair's remark about the Cherokee, as reported by Carolyn Foreman: "The Cherokee had been for a considerable while under petticoat government and they were just emerging, like all of the Iroquoian Indians from the matriarchal period."[2] Adair's idea of "petticoat government" included the power of the Women's Council of the Cherokee. The head of the Council was the Beloved Woman of the Nation, "whose voice was considered that of the Great Spirit, speaking through her."[3] The Iroquoian peoples, including the Cherokee, had another custom that bespoke the existence of their "petticoat government," their gynocracy. They set the penalty for killing a woman of the tribe at double that for killing a man. This regulation was in force at least among the Susquehanna, the Hurons, and the Iroquois; but given the high regard in which the tribes held women and given that in killing a woman one killed the children she might have borne, I imagine the practice of doubling the penalty was widespread.[4]

The Iroquois story is currently one of the best chronicles of the overthrow of the gynocracy. Material about the status of women in North American groups such as the Montagnais-Naskapi, Keres, Navajo, Crow, Hopi, Pomo, Turok, Kiowa, and Natchez and in South American groups such as the Bari and Mapuche, to name just a few, is lacking. Any original documentation that exists is buried under the flood of readily available, published material written from the colonizer's patriarchal perspective, almost all of which is based on the white man's belief in universal male dominance. Male dominance may have characterized a number of tribes, but it was by no means as universal (or even as preponderant) as colonialist propaganda has led us to believe.

The Seneca prophet Handsome Lake did not appreciate "petticoat government" any more than did John Adair. When his code became the standard for Iroquoian practice in the early nineteenth century, power shifted from the hands of the "meddling old women," as he characterized them, to men. Under the old laws, the Iroquois were a mother-centered, mother-right people whose political organization was based on the central authority of the Matrons, the Mothers of the Longhouses (clans). Handsome Lake advocated that young women cleave to their husbands rather than to their mothers and abandon the clan-mother–controlled longhouse in favor of a

*The term *berdache* is applied (or rather misapplied) to both lesbians and gay males. It is originally an Arabic word meaning sex-slave boy, or a male child used sexually by adult males. As such it has no relevance to American Indian men or women.

patriarchal, nuclear family arrangement. Until Handsome Lake's time, the sachems were chosen from certain families by the Matrons of their clans and were subject to impeachment by the Matrons should they prove inadequate or derelict in carrying out their duties as envisioned by the Matrons and set forth in the Law of the Great Peace of the Iroquois Confederacy. By provision in the Law, the women were to be considered the progenitors of the nation, owning the land and the soil.[5]

At the end of the Revolutionary War, the Americans declared the Iroquois living on the American side of the United States–Canadian border defeated. Pressed from all sides, their fields burned and salted, their daily life disrupted, and the traditional power of the Matrons under assault from the missionaries who flocked to Iroquois country to "civilize" them, the recently powerful Iroquois became a subject, captive people. Into this chaos stepped Handsome Lake who, with the help of devoted followers and exigencies of social disruption in the aftermath of the war, encouraged the shift from woman-centered society to patriarchal society. While that shift was never complete, it was sufficient. Under the Code of Handsome Lake, which was the tribal version of the white man's way, the Longhouse declined in importance, and eventually Iroquois women were firmly under the thumb of Christian patriarchy.

The Iroquois were not the only Nation to fall under patriarchalization. No tribe escaped that fate, though some western groups retained their gynecentric egalitarianism[6] until well into the latter half of the twentieth century. Among the hundreds of tribes forced into patriarchal modes, the experiences of the Montagnais-Naskapi, the Mid-Atlantic Coastal Algonkians, and the Bari of Colombia,[7] among others, round out the hemisphere-wide picture.

Among the Narragansett of the area now identified as Rhode Island was a woman chief, one of the six sachems of that tribe. Her name was Magnus, and when the Narragansetts were invaded by Major Talcot and defeated in battle, the Sunksquaw Magnus was executed along with ninety others. Her fate was a result of her position; in contrast, the wife and child of the sachem known as King Philip among the English colonizers were simply sold into slavery in the West Indies.[8]

This sunksquaw, or queen (hereditary female head of state), was one of scores in the Mid-Atlantic region. One researcher, Robert Grumet, identifies a number of women chiefs who held office during the seventeenth and eighteenth centuries. Grumet begins his account by detailing the nonauthoritarian character of the Mid-Atlantic Coastal Algonkians and describes their political system, which included inheritance of rank by the eldest child through the maternal line. He concludes with the observation that important historians ignore documented information concerning the high-status position of women in the leadership structure of the Coastal Algonkians:

> *Both Heckewelder (1876) and Zeisberger (1910) failed to mention women in their lengthy descriptions of Delawaran leadership during the westward exile. Eight out of the eleven sources listed in Kinietz (1946) noted that women could not be chiefs. The remaining three citations made no mention of women leaders. These same sources stated that "women had no voice in council and were only admitted at certain times." Roger Williams translated the Narragansett term* saunks *as "the Queen, or Sachims Wife," with the plural "Queenes" translating out as* sauncksquuaog *(1866). He nowhere indicated that these* saunckssquuaog *were anything more than wives.*
>
> *The ethnographic record has indicated otherwise. Even a cursory scanning of the widely available primary documentation clearly shows the considerable role played by Coastal Algonkian women throughout the historic contact period. Many sources state that women were able to inherit chiefly office. Others note that women sachems were often the sisters of wives of male leaders who succeeded them upon their decease. This does not mean that every "sunksquaw's" husband or brother was a leader. Many women sachems were married to men who made no pretension to leadership.*[9]

The first sunksquaw Grumet mentions was noted in John Smith's journal as "Queene of Appamatuck." She was present during the council that decided on his death—a decision that Pocahontas, daughter of one of the sachems, overturned.[10] The Wampanoag Confederacy's loss of control over the Chesapeake Bay area did not cause an end to the rule of sunksquaws or of the empress: George Fox, founder of the Quaker religion, recorded that "the old Empress [of Accomack] . . . sat in council" when he was visiting in March 1673.[11] In 1705, Robert Beverley mentioned two towns governed by queens: Pungoteque and Nanduye. Pungoteque, he said, was a small Nation, even though governed by a Queen, and he listed Nanduye as "a seat of the Empress." He seemed impressed. For while Nanduye was a small settlement of "not above 20 families," the old Empress had "all the Nations of this shore under Tribute."[12]

From before 1620 until her death many years later, a squaw-sachem known as the "Massachusetts Queen" by the Virginia colonizers governed the Massachusetts Confederacy.[13] It was her fortune to preside over the Confederacy's destruction as the people were decimated by disease, war, and colonial manipulations. Magnus, the Narragansett sunksquaw whose name was recorded by whites, is mentioned above. Others include the Pocasset sunksquaw Weetamoo, who was King Philip's ally and "served as war chief commanding over 300 warriors" during his war with the British.[14] Queen Weetamoo was given the white woman Mary Rowlandson, who wrote descriptions of the sunksquaw in her captivity narrative.

Awashonks, another queen in the Mid-Atlantic region, was squaw-sachem of the Sakonnet, a tribe allied with the Wampanoag Confederacy. She reigned in the latter part of the seventeenth century. After fighting for a time against the British during King Philip's War, she was forced to surrender. Because she then convinced her warriors to fight with the British, she was able to save them from enslavement in the West Indies.[15]

The last sunksquaw Grumet mentions was named Mamanuchqua. An Esopus and one of the five sachems of the Esopus Confederacy, Mamanuchqua is said to be only one name that she used. The others include Mamareoktwe, Mamaroch, and Mamaprocht,[16] unless they were the names of other Esopus sunksquaws who used the same or a similar mark beside the written designation. Grumet wisely comments on the presence of women chiefs and the lack of notice of them in secondary documents—that is, in books about the region during those centuries.

> *Ethnohistorians have traditionally assigned male gender to native figures in the documentary record unless otherwise identified. They have also tended to not identify native individuals as leaders unless so identified in the specific source. This policy, while properly cautious, has fostered the notion that all native persons mentioned in the documentation were both male and commoners unless otherwise identified. This practice has successfully masked the identities of a substantial number of Coastal Algonkian leaders of both sexes.*[17]

And that's not all it successfully achieves. It falsifies the record of people who are not able to set it straight; it reinforces patriarchal socialization among all Americans, who are thus led to believe that there have never been any alternative structures; it gives Anglo-Europeans the idea that Indian societies were beneath the level of organization of western nations, justifying colonization by presumption of lower stature; it masks the genocide attendant on the falsification of evidence, as it masks the gynocidal motive behind the genocide. Political actions coupled with economic and physical disaster in the forms of land theft and infection of native populations caused the Mid-Atlantic Algonkians to be overwhelmed by white invaders.

Politics played an even greater role in the destruction of the Cherokee gynocracy, of a region that included parts of Georgia, Mississippi, and North Carolina. Cherokee women had the power to decide the fate of captives, decisions that were made by vote of the Women's Council and relayed to the district at large by the War Woman or Pretty Woman. The decisions had to be made by female clan heads because a captive who was to live would be adopted into one of the families whose affairs were directed by the clan-mothers. The clan-mothers also had the right to wage war, and as Henry Timberlake wrote, the stories about Amazon warriors were not so farfetched considering how many Indian women were famous warriors and powerful voices in the councils.[18]

The war women carried the title Beloved Women, and their power was so great "that they can, by the wave of a swan's wing, deliver a wretch condemned by the council, and already tied to the stake," Lieutenant Timberlake reports.[19] A mixed-blood Cherokee man who was born in the early nineteenth century reported knowing an old woman named Da'nawagasta, or Sharp War, which meant a fierce warrior.[20]

The Women's Council, as distinguished from the District, village, or Confederacy councils, was powerful in a number of political and socio-spiritual ways, and may have had the deciding voice on what males would serve on the Councils, as its northern sisters had. Certainly the Women's Council was influential in tribal decisions, and its spokeswomen served as War Women and as Peace Women, presumably holding those offices in the towns designated red towns and white towns, respectively. Their other powers included the right to speak in men's Council, the right to inclusion in public policy decisions, the right to choose whom and whether to marry, the right to bear arms, and the right to choose their extramarital occupations.

During the longtime colonization of the Cherokee along the Atlantic seaboard, the British worked hard to lessen the power of women in Cherokee affairs. They took Cherokee men to England and educated them in English ways. These men returned to Cherokee country and exerted great influence on behalf of the British in the region. By the time the Removal Act was under consideration by Congress in the early 1800s, many of these British-educated men and men with little Cherokee blood wielded considerable power over the Nation's policies.

In the ensuing struggle women endured rape and murder, but they had no voice in the future direction of the Cherokee Nation. The Cherokee were by this time highly stratified, though they had been much less so before this period, and many were Christianized. The male leadership bought and sold not only black men and women but also men and women of neighboring tribes, the women of the leadership class retreated to Bible classes, sewing circles, and petticoats that rivaled those worn by their white sisters. Many of these upper-strata Cherokee women married white ministers and other opportunists, as the men of their class married white women, often the daughters of white ministers. The traditional strata of Cherokee society became rigid and modeled on Christian white social organization of upper, middle, and impoverished classes usually composed of very traditional clans.

In an effort to stave off removal, the Cherokee in the early 1800s, under the leadership of men such as Elias Boudinot, Major Ridge, and John Ross (later Principal Chief of the Cherokee in Oklahoma Territory), and others, drafted a constitution that disenfranchised women and blacks. Modeled after the Constitution of the United States, whose favor they were attempting to curry, and in conjunction with Christian sympathizers to the Cherokee cause, the new Cherokee constitution relegated women to the position of chattel. No longer possessing a voice in the Nation's business, women became pawns in the struggle between white and Cherokee for possession of Cherokee lands.

The Cherokee, like their northern cousins, were entirely represented by men in the white courts, in the U.S. Congress, and in gatherings where lobbying of white officials was carried on. The great organ of Cherokee resistance, the *Cherokee Phoenix*, was staffed by men. The last Beloved Woman, Nancy Ward, resigned her office in 1817 sending her cane and her vote on important questions to the Cherokee Council, and "thus renounced her high office of Beloved Woman, in favor of written constitutional law."[21]

In spite of their frantic attempts to prevent their removal to Indian Territory by aping the white man in patriarchal particulars, the Cherokee were removed, as were the other tribes of the region and those living north and west of them, whom the Cherokee thought of as "uncivilized." Politics does make strange bedfellows, as the degynocratization of the Cherokee Nation shows. Boudinot and Ridge were condemned as traitors by the newly reconstituted Cherokee government in Indian Territory and were executed (assassinated, some say). The Cherokee got out from under the petticoats in time to be buried under the weight of class hierarchies, male dominance, war, and loss of their homeland.

While the cases cited above might be explained as a general conquest over male Indian systems that happened to have some powerful women functioning within them rather than as a deliberate attempt to wipe out female leadership, the case of the Montagnais women clarifies an otherwise obscure issue. The Montagnais-Naskapi of the St. Lawrence Valley was contacted early in the fifteenth century by fur traders and explorers and fell under the sway of Jesuit missionizing in the mid-sixteenth century. The Jesuits, under the leadership of Fr. Paul Le Jeune (whose name, appropriately, means The Little or The Young One), determined to convert the Montagnais to Christianity, resocialize them, and transform them into peasant-serfs as were the Indians' counterparts in France centuries earlier.

To accomplish this task, the good fathers had to loosen the hold of Montagnais women on tribal policies and to convince both men and women that a woman's proper place was under the authority of her husband and that a man's proper place was under the authority of the priests. The system of vassalage with which the Frenchmen were most familiar required this arrangement.

In pursuit of this end, the priests had to undermine the status of the women, who, according to one of Le Jeune's reports, had "great power . . . A man may promie you something and if he does not keep his promise, he thinks he is sufficiently excused when he tells you that his wife did not wish him to do it."[22]

Further, the Jesuit noted the equable relations between husbands and wives among the Montagnais. He commented that "men leave the arrangement of the household to the women, without interfering with them; they cut and decide to give away as they please without making the husband angry. I have never seen my host ask a giddy young woman that he had with him what became of the provisions, although they were disappearing very fast."[23]

Undaunted, Paul Le Jeune composed a plan whereby this state of affairs could be put aright. His plan had four parts, which, he was certain, would turn the Montagnais into proper, civilized people. He figured that the first requirement was the establishment of permanent settlements and the placement of officially constituted authority in the hands of one person. "Alas!" he mourned. "If someone could stop the wanderings of the Savages, and give authority to one of them to rule the others, we would see them converted and civilized in a short time."[24] More ominously, he believed that the institution of punishment was essential in Montagnais social relations. How could they understand tyranny and respect it unless they wielded it upon each other and experienced it at each other's hands? He was most distressed that the "Savages," as he termed them, thought physical abuse a terrible crime.

He commented on this "savage" aberration in a number of his reports, emphasizing his position that its cure rested only in the abduction or seduction of the children into attendance at Jesuit-run schools located a good distance from their homes. "The Savages prevent their [children's] instruction; they will not tolerate the chastisement of their children, whatever they may do, they permit only a simple reprimand," he complains.[25]

What he had in mind was more along the lines of torture, imprisonment, battering, neglect, and psychological torment—the educational methods to which Indian children in government and mission schools would be subjected for some time after Conquest was accomplished. Doubtless these methods were required, or few would have traded the Montagnais way for the European one. Thus his third goal was subsumed under the "education" of the young.

Last, Le Jeune wished to implement a new social system whereby the Montagnais would live within the European family structure with its twin patriarchal institutions of male authority and female fidelity. These would be enforced by the simple expediency of forbidding divorce. He informed the men that in France women do not rule their husbands, information that had been conveyed by various means, including Jesuit education, to other tribes such as the Iroquois and the Cherokee.

Le Jeune had his work cut out for him: working with people who did not punish children, encouraged women in independence and decision making, and had a horror of authority imposed from without—who, in Le Jeune's words could not "endure in the least those who seem desirous of assuming superiority over the others, and place all virtue in a certain gentleness or apathy,"[26] who

> *. . . imagine that they ought by right of birth, to enjoy the liberty of wild ass colts, rendering no homage to anyone whomsoever, except when they like. They have reproached me a hundred times because we fear our Captains, while they laugh at and make sport of theirs. All the authority of their chief is in his tongue's end, for he is powerful insofar as he is eloquent; and even if he kills himself talking and haranguing, he will not be obeyed unless he pleases the Savages.*[27]

The wily Le Jeune did not succeed entirely in transforming these gentle and humorous people into bastard Europeans, but he did succeed in some measure. While the ease of relationships between men and women remains and while the Montagnais retain their love of gentleness and nurturing, they are rather more male-centered than not.[28] Positions of formal power such as political leadership, shamanhood, and matrilocality, which placed the economic dependence of a woman with children in the hands of her mother's family, had shifted. Shamans were male, leaders were male, and matrilocality had become patrilocality. This is not so strange given the economics of the situation and the fact that over the years the Montagnais became entirely Catholicized.

With the rate of assimilation increasing and with the national political and economic situation of Indians in Canada, which is different in details but identical in intent and disastrous effect to that of Indians in the United States, the Montagnais will likely be fully patriarchal before the turn of the next century.

As this brief survey indicates, the shift from gynecentric-egalitarian and ritual-based systems to phallocentric, hierarchical systems is not accomplished in only one dimension. As Le Jeune understood, the assault on the system of woman power requires the replacing of a peaceful, nonpunitive, non-authoritarian social system wherein women wield power by making social life easy and gentle with one based on child terrorization, male dominance, and submission of women to male authority.

Montagnais men who would not subscribe to the Jesuit program (and there were many) were not given authority backed up by the patriarchy's churchly or political institutions. Under patriarchy men are given power only if they use it in ways that are congruent with the authoritarian, punitive model. The records attest, in contrast, that gynecentric systems distribute power evenly among men, women, and berdaches as well as among all age groups. Economic distribution follows a similar pattern; reciprocal exchange of goods and services among individuals and between groups is ensured because women are in charge at all points along the distribution network.

Effecting the social transformation from egalitarian, gynecentric systems to hierarchical, patriarchal systems requires meeting four objectives. The first is accomplished when the primacy of female as creator is displaced and replaced by male-gendered creators (generally generic, as the Great Spirit concept overtakes the multiplicitous tribal designation of deity). This objective has largely been met across North America. The Hopi goddess Spider Woman has become the masculine Maseo or Tawa, referred to in the masculine, and the Zuñi goddess is on her way to malehood. Changing Woman of the Navajo has contenders for her position, while the Keres Thought Woman trembles on the brink of displacement by her sister-goddess-cum-god Utset. Among the Cherokee, the goddess of the river foam is easily replaced by Thunder in many tales, and the Iroquois divinity Sky Woman now gets her ideas and powers from her dead father or her monstrous grandson.

The second objective is achieved when tribal governing institutions and the philosophies that are their foundation are destroyed, as they were among the Iroquois and the Cherokee, to mention just two. The conqueror has demanded that the tribes that wish federal recognition and protection institute "democracy," in which powerful officials are elected by majority vote. Until recently, these powerful officials were inevitably male and were elected mainly by nontraditionals, the traditionals being until recently unwilling to participate in a form of governance imposed on them by right of conquest. Democracy by coercion is hardly democracy, in any language, and to some Indians recognizing that fact, the threat of extinction is preferable to the ignominy of enslavement in their own land.

The third objective is accomplished when the people are pushed off their lands, deprived of their economic livelihood, and forced to curtail or end altogether pursuits on which their ritual system, philosophy, and subsistence depend. Now dependent on white institutions for survival, tribal systems can ill afford gynocracy when patriarchy—that is, survival—requires male dominance. Not that submission to white laws and customs results in economic prosperity; the unemployment rates on most reservations is about 50 to 60 percent, and the situation for urban Indians who are undereducated (as many are) is almost as bad.

The fourth objective requires that the clan structure be replaced, in fact if not in theory, by the nuclear family. By this ploy, the women clan heads are replaced by elected male officials and the psychic net that is formed and maintained by the nature of non-authoritarian gynecentricity grounded in respect for diversity of gods and people is thoroughly rent. Decimation of populations through starvation, disease, and disruption of all social, spiritual, and economic structures along with abduction and enforced brainwashing of the young serve well in meeting this goal.

Along the way, each of these parts of the overall program of degynocraticization is subject to image control and information control. Recasting archaic tribal versions of tribal history, customs, institutions, and the oral tradition increases the likelihood that the patriarchal revisionist versions of tribal life, skewed or simply made up by patriarchal non-Indians and patriarchalized Indians, will be incorporated into the spiritual and popular traditions of the tribes. This is reinforced by the loss of rituals, medicine societies, and entire clans through assimilation and a dying off of tribal members familiar with the elder rituals and practices. Consequently, Indian control of the image-making and information-disseminating process is crucial, and the contemporary prose and poetry of American Indian writers, particularly of woman-centered writers, is a major part of Indian resistance to cultural and spiritual genocide.

Notes

1. Stan Steiner, *The New Indians* (New York: Dell, Delta Books, 1968), p. 224. Steiner's chapter on Indian women,

"Changing Women," is an important contribution to our understanding of the shift in women's positions under colonization. It should be read by those interested in learning about contemporary processes of patriarchalization and tribal resistance or acquiescence to it.

2. Carolyn Foreman, *Indian Women Chiefs* (Washington, D.C.: Zenger Publishing Co., 1976), p. 7.

3. John P. Brown, *Old Frontiers* (Kingsport, Tenn.: State of Wisconsin, State Historical Society, Draper Manuscripts, 1938), p. 20. Cited in Foreman, *Indian Women Chiefs,* p. 7.

4. Foreman, *Indian Women Chiefs,* p. 9.

5. See William Brandon, *The Last Americans: The Indian in American Culture* (New York: McGraw-Hill, 1974), p. 214, for more detail. Also see "Red Roots of White Feminism" in Part 3 of this volume.

6. The terms *gynecentric* and *egalitarianism* are not mutually exclusive; in fact, I doubt that egalitarianism is possible without gynecentrism at its base.

7. See Elisa-Buenaventura-Posso and Susan E. Brown, "Forced Transition from Egalitarianism to Male Dominance: The Bari of Colombia," in *Women and Colonization: Anthropological Perspectives,* eds. Mona Etienne and Eleanor Leacock (New York: Praeger, 1980), pp. 109–134, for an informative discussion of contemporary attempts to force the last remaining traditional group of Bari to shift their social structure to authoritarian male dominance.

8. Foreman, *Indian Women Chiefs,* p. 32. *Squaw* is not a derogatory word in its own language. Like the Anglo-Saxon "forbidden" word *cunt,* which is mostly used as an insult to women, *squaw* means "queen" or "lady," as will be seen in the following discussion. The fact that it has been taken to mean something less is only another example of patriarchal dominance, under which the proudest names come to be seen as the most degrading epithets, which the conquered and the conquerer alike are forbidden to use without the risk of sounding racist.

9. Robert Steven Grumet, "Sunksquaws, Shamans, and Tradeswomen: Middle Atlantic Coastal Algonkian Women During the 17th and 18th Centuries," in Etienne and Leacock, *Women and Colonization,* p. 49. In his note to this passage, Grumet comments that Regina Flannery ("An Analysis of Coastal Algonquian Culture," *Catholic University Anthropological Series,* no. 7 [1939], p. 145) "listed women's inheritance of chiefly rank among the Massachusett, Natick, Caconnet, Martha's Vineyard (Wampanoag), Narragansett, Western Niantic, Scaticook, Piscataway, and Powhatan groups" (p. 60n).

10. Grumet, "Sunksquaws," p. 60.

11. Grumet, "Sunksquaws," p. 50.

12. Grumet, "Sunksquaws," p. 50.

13. Grumet, "Sunksquaws," p. 50.

14. Grumet, "Sunksquaws," p. 51.

15. Grumet, "Sunksquaws," pp. 51–52.

16. Grumet, "Sunksquaws," pp. 51–52.

17. Grumet, "Sunksquaws," pp. 52–53.

18. Lieutenant Henry Timberlake, *Lieut. Henry Timberlake's Memoirs* (Marietta, Ga., 1948), p. 94 and n. 56. Cited in Foreman, *Indian Women Chiefs,* p. 76.

19. Timberlake, *Memoirs,* p. 94 and 56. Cited in Foreman, *Indian Women Chiefs,* p. 77.

20. Colonel James D. Wofford, whose name is frequently spelled Wafford, cited in Foreman, *Indian Women Chiefs,* p. 85.

21. Foreman, *Indian Women Chiefs,* p. 79.

22. Eleanor Leacock, "Montagnais Women and the Jesuit Program for Colonization," in Etienne and Leacock, *Women and Colonization,* p. 27. She is citing R. G. Thwaites, ed., *The Jesuit Relations and Allied Documents,* 71 vols. (Cleveland: Burrows Brothers Co., 1906), 2:77.

23. Leacock, "Montaignais Women," p. 27. Le Jeune's remarks from Thwaites, *Jesuit Relations,* 6:233.

24. Leacock, "Montaignais Women," p. 27. Thwaites, *Jesuit Relations,* 12:169.

25. Leacock, "Montaignais Women," p. 28. Thwaites, *Jesuit Relations,* 5:197.

26. Leacock, "Montaignais Women," p. 30. Thwaites, *Jesuit Relations,* 16:165.

27. Leacock, "Montaignais Women," p. 30. Thwaites, *Jesuit Relations,* 6:243.

28. Leacock, "Montaignais Women," pp. 40–41.

Woman the Gatherer: Male Bias in Anthropology

Sally Slocum

Sally Slocum, born in Indiana in 1939 and educated at the University of California and the University of Colorado, is an anthropologist with a wide array of skills and experience. A stained-glass craftswoman, a professional dancer, and a participant in archeological surveys, she has taught courses in physical anthropology, paleontology, and ethnology, among other subjects. Slocum has also made major contributions to research and teaching in women's studies.

Crystallizing, then rejecting, the male bias in anthropology that allowed theories like man-the-hunter to develop uncritically, Slocum here proffers a different perspective: Central to human community and social organization is the sharing of food that for many reasons must precede organized hunting. Such sharing must have originated in the mother-infant relationship and then enlarged into wider bonding. This concept might prove a far more fruitful explanatory factor than the notions of hunting, weaponry, and male bonding.

From Sally Slocum, "Woman the Gatherer: Male Bias in Anthropology," in *Toward an Anthropology of Women*, ed. Rayna Reiter (New York: Monthly Review Press, 1975).

THE PERSPECTIVE OF WOMEN IS, IN MANY WAYS, equally foreign to an anthropology that has been developed and pursued primarily by males. There is a strong male bias in the questions asked, and the interpretations given. This bias has hindered the full development of our discipline as "the study of the human animal" (I don't want to call it "the study of man" for reasons that will become evident). I am going to demonstrate the Western male bias by reexamining the matter of evolution of Homo sapiens from our nonhuman primate ancestors. In particular, the concept of "Man the Hunter" as developed by Sherwood Washburn and C. Lancaster (1968) and others is my focus. This critique is offered in hopes of transcending the male bias that limits our knowledge by limiting the questions we ask.

Though male bias could be shown in other areas, hominid evolution is particularly convenient for my purpose because it involves speculations and inferences from a rather small amount of data. In such a case, hidden assumptions and premises that lie behind the speculations and inferences are more easily demonstrated. Male bias exists not only in the ways in which the scanty data are interpreted, but in the very language used. All too often the word "man" is used in such an ambiguous fashion that it is impossible to decide whether it refers to males or to the human species in general, including both males and females. In fact, one frequently is led to suspect that in the minds of many anthropologists, "man," supposedly meaning the human species, is actually synonymous with "males."

This ambiguous use of language is particularly evident in the writing that surrounds the concept of Man the Hunter. Washburn and Lancaster make it clear that it is specifically males who hunt, that hunting is much more than simply an economic activity, and that most of the characteristics which we think of as specifically human can be causally related to hunting. They tell us that hunting is a whole pattern of activity and way of life: "The biology, psychology, and customs that separate us from the apes—all these we owe to the hunters of time past" (1968:303). If this line of reasoning is followed to its logical conclusion, one must agree with Jane Kephart when she says:

> *Since only males hunt, and the psychology of the species was set by hunting, we are forced to conclude that females are scarcely human, that is, do not have built-in the basic psychology of the species: to kill and hunt and ultimately to kill others of the same species. The argument implies built-in aggression in human males, as well as the assumed passivity of human females and their exclusion from the mainstream of human development. (1970:5)*

To support their argument that hunting is important to human males, Washburn and Lancaster point to the fact that many modern males still hunt, though it is no longer economically necessary. I could point out that many modern males play golf, play the violin, or tend gardens: these, as well as hunting, are things their culture teaches them. Using a "survival" as evidence to demonstrate an important fact of cultural evolution can be accorded no more validity when proposed by a modern anthropologist than when proposed by Tylor.

Regardless of its status as a survival, hunting, by implication as well as direct statement, is pictured as a male activity to the exclusion of females. This activity, on which we are told depends the psychology, biology, and customs of our species, is strictly male. A theory that leaves out half the human species is unbalanced. The theory of Man the Hunter is not only unbalanced; it leads to the conclusion that the basic human adaptation was the desire of males to hunt and kill. This not only gives too much importance to aggression, which is after all only one factor of human life, but it derives culture from killing. I am going to suggest a less biased reading of the evidence, which gives a more valid and logical picture of human evolution, and at the same time a more hopeful one. First I will note the evidence, discuss the more traditional reading of it, and then offer an alternative reconstruction.

The data we have to work from are a combination of fossil and archeological materials, knowledge of living nonhuman primates, and knowledge of living humans. Since we assume that the protohominid ancestors of Homo sapiens developed in a continuous fashion from a base of characteristics similar to those of living nonhuman primates, the most important facts seem to be the ways in which humans differ from nonhuman primates, and the ways in which we are similar. The differences are as follows: longer gestation period; more difficult birth; neoteny, in that human infants are less well developed at birth; long period of infant dependency; absence of body hair; year-round sexual receptivity of females, resulting in the possibility of bearing a second infant while the first is still at the breast or still dependent; erect bipedalism; possession of a large and complex brain that makes possible the creation of elaborate symbolic systems, languages, and cultures, and also results in most behavior being under cortical control; food sharing; and finally, living in families. (For the purposes of this paper I define families as follows: a situation where each individual has defined responsibilities and obligations to a specific set of others of both sexes and various ages. I use this definition because, among humans, the family is a *social* unit, regardless of any biological or genetic relationship which may or may not exist among its members.)

In addition to the many well-known close physiological resemblances, we share with nonhuman primates the following characteristics: living in social groups; close mother-infant bonds; affectional relationships; a large capacity for learning and a related paucity of innate behaviors; ability to take part in dominance hierarchies; a rather complex nonsymbolic communication system which can handle with considerable subtlety such information as the mood and emotional state of the individual, and the attitude and status of each individual toward the other members of the social group.

The fossil and archeological evidence consists of various bones labeled Ramapithecus, Australopithecus, Homo habilis, Homo erectus, etc.; and artifacts such as stone tools representing various cultural traditions, evidence of use of fire, etc. From this evidence we can make reasonable inferences about diet, posture and locomotion, and changes in the brain as shown by increased cranial capacity, ability to make tools, and other evidences of cultural creation. Since we assume that complexity of material culture requires language, we infer the beginnings of language somewhere between Australopithecus and Homo erectus.

Given this data, the speculative reconstruction begins. As I was taught anthropology, the story goes something like this. Obscure selection pressures pushed the protohominid in the direction of erect bipedalism—perhaps the advantages of freeing the hands for food carrying or for tool use. Freeing the hands allowed more manipulation of the environment in the direction of tools for gathering and hunting food. Through a hand-eye-brain feedback process, coordination, efficiency, and skill were increased. The new behavior was adaptive, and selection pressure pushed the protohominid further along the same lines of development. Diet changed as the increase in skill allowed the addition of more animal protein. Larger brains were selected for, making possible transmission of information concerning tool making, and organizing cooperative hunting. It is assumed that as increased brain size was selected for, so also was neoteny—immaturity of infants at birth with a corresponding increase in their period of dependency, allowing more time for learning at the same time as this learning became necessary through the further reduction of instinctual behaviors and their replacement by symbolically invented ones.

Here is where one may discover a large logical gap. From the difficult-to-explain beginning trends toward neoteny and increased brain size, the story jumps to Man the Hunter. The statement is made that the females were more burdened with dependent infants and could not follow the rigorous hunt. Therefore they stayed at a "home base," gathering what food they could, while the males developed cooperative hunting techniques, increased their communicative and organizational skills through hunting, and brought the meat back to the dependent females and young. Incest prohibitions, marriage, and the family (so the story goes) grew out of the need to eliminate competition between males for females. A pattern developed of a male hunter becoming the main support of "his" dependent females and young (in other words, the development of the nuclear family for no apparent reason). Thus the peculiarly human social and emotional bonds can be traced to the hunter bringing back the food to share. Hunting, according to Washburn and Lancaster, involved "cooperation among males, planning, knowledge of many species and large areas, and technical skill" (1968:296). They even profess to discover the beginnings of art in the weapons of the hunter. They point out that the symmetrical Acheulian biface tools are the earliest beautiful man-made objects. Though we don't know what these tools were used for, they argue somewhat tautologically that the symmetry indicates they may have been swung, because symmetry only makes a difference when irregularities might lead to deviations in the line of flight. "It may well be that it was the attempt to produce beautiful, symmetrical objects" (1968:298).

So, while the males were out hunting, developing all their skills, learning to cooperate, inventing language, inventing art, creating tools and weapons, the poor dependent females were sitting back at the home base having one child after another (many of them dying in the process), and waiting for the males to bring home the bacon. While this reconstruction is certainly ingenious, it gives one the decided impression that only half the species—the male half—did any evolving. In addition to containing a number of logical gaps, the argument becomes somewhat doubtful in the light of modern knowledge of genetics and primate behavior.

The skills usually spoken of as being necessary to, or developed through, hunting are things like coordination, endurance, good vision, and the ability to plan, communicate, and cooperate. I have heard of no evidence to indicate that these skills are either carried on the Y chromosome, or are triggered into existence by the influence of the Y chromosome. In fact, on just about any test we can design (psychological, aptitude, intelligence, etc.) males and females score just about the same. The variation is on an individual, not a sex, basis.

Every human individual gets half its genes from a male and half from a female; genes sort randomly. It is possible for a female to end up with all her genes from male ancestors, and for a male to end up with all his genes from female ancestors. The logic of the hunting argument would have us believe that all the selection pressure was on the males, leaving the females simply as drags on the species. The rapid increase in brain size and complexity was thus due entirely to half the species; the main function of the female half was to suffer and die in the attempt to give birth to their large-brained male infants. An unbiased reading of the evidence indicates there was selection pressure on both sexes, and that hunting was not in fact the basic adaptation of the species from which flowed all the traits we think of as specifically human. Hunting does not deserve the primary place it has been given in the reconstruction of human evolution, as I will demonstrate by offering the following alternate version.

Picture the primate band: each individual gathers its own food, and the major enduring relationship is the mother-infant bond. It is in similar circumstances that we imagine the evolving protohominids. We don't know what started them in the direction of neoteny and increased brain size, but once begun the trends would prove adaptive. To explain the shift from the primate individual gathering to human food sharing, we cannot simply jump to hunting. Hunting cannot explain its own origin. It is much more logical to assume that as the period of infant dependency began to lengthen, *the mothers would begin to increase the scope of their gathering to provide food for their still-dependent infants.* The already strong primate mother-infant bond would begin to extend over a longer time period, increasing the depth and scope of social relationships, and giving rise to the first sharing of food.

It is an example of male bias to picture these females with young as totally or even mainly dependent on males for food. Among modern hunter-gatherers, even in the marginal environments where most live, the females can usually gather enough to support themselves and their families. In these groups gathering provides the major portion of the diet, and there is no reason to assume that this was not also the case in the Pliocene or early Pleistocene. In the modern groups women and children both gather and hunt small animals, though they usually do not go on the longer hunts. So, we can assume a group of evolving protohominids, gathering and perhaps beginning to hunt small animals, with the mothers gathering quite efficiently both for themselves and for their offspring.

It is equally biased, and quite unreasonable, to assume an early or rapid development of a pattern in which one male was responsible for "his" female(s) and young. In most primate groups when a female comes into estrus she initiates coitus or signals her readiness by presenting. The idea that a male would have much voice in "choosing" a female, or maintain any sort of individual, long-term control over her or her offspring, is surely a modern invention which could have had no place in early hominid life. (Sexual control over females through rape or the threat of rape seems to be a modern human invention. Primate females are not raped because they are willing throughout estrus, and primate males appear not to attempt coitus at other times, regardless of physiological ability.) In fact, there seems to me no reason for suggesting the development of male-female adult pair-bonding until much later. Long-term monogamy is a fairly rare pattern even among modern humans—I think it is a peculiarly Western male bias to suppose its existence in protohuman society. An argument has been made (by Morris, 1967, and others) that traces the development of male-female pair-bonding to the shift of sexual characteristics to the front of the body, the importance of the face in communication, and the development of face-to-face coitus. This argument is insufficient in the first place because of the assumption that face-to-face coitus is the "normal," "natural," or even the most common position among humans (historical evidence casts grave doubt on this assumption). It is much more probable that the coitus position was invented *after* pair-bonding had developed for other reasons.

Rather than adult male-female sexual pairs, a temporary consort-type relationship is much more logical in hominid evolution. It is even a more accurate description of the modern human pattern: the most dominant males (chief, headman, brave warrior, good hunter, etc.), mate with the most dominant females (in estrus, young and beautiful, fertile, rich, etc.), for varying periods of time. Changing sexual partners is frequent and common. We have no way of knowing when females began to be fertile year-round, but this change is not a necessary condition for the development of families. We need not bring in any notion of paternity, or the development of male-female pairs, or any sort of marriage in order to account for either families or food sharing.

The lengthening period of infant dependency would have strengthened and deepened the mother-infant bond; the earliest families would have consisted of *females and their children.* In such groups, over time, the sibling bond would have increased in importance also. The most universal, and presumably oldest, form of incest prohibition is between mother and son. There are indications of such avoidance even among modern monkeys. It could develop logically from the mother-children family: as the period of infant dependency lengthened, and the age of sexual maturity advanced, a mother might no longer be capable of childbearing when her son reached maturity. Another factor which may have operated is the situation found in many primates today where only the most dominant males have access to fertile females. Thus a young son, even after reaching sexual maturity, would still have to spend time working his way up the male hierarchy before gaining access to females. The length of time it would take him increases the possibility that his mother would no longer be fertile.

Food sharing and the family developed from the mother-infant bond. The techniques of hunting large animals were probably much later developments, after the mother-children family pattern was established. When hunting did begin, and the adult males brought back food to share, the most likely recipients would be first their mothers, and second their siblings. In other words, a hunter would share food *not* with a wife or sexual partner, but with those who had shared food with him: his mother and siblings.

It is frequently suggested or implied that the first tools were, in fact, the weapons of the hunters. Modern humans have become so accustomed to the thought of tools and weapons that it is easy for us to imagine the first manlike creature who picked up a stone or club. However, since we don't really know what the early stone tools such as hand-axes were used for, it is equally probable that they were not weapons at all, but rather *aids in gathering*. We know that gathering was important long before much animal protein was added to the diet, and continued to be important. Bones, sticks, and hand-axes could be used for digging up tubers or roots, or to pulverize tough vegetable matter for easier eating. If, however, instead of thinking in terms of tools and weapons, we think in terms of *cultural inventions,* a new aspect is presented. I suggest that two of the *earliest and most important* cultural inventions were containers to hold the products of gathering, and some sort of sling or net to carry babies. The latter in particular must have been extremely important with the loss of body hair and the increasing immaturity of neonates, who could not cling and had less and less to cling to. Plenty of material was available—vines, hides, human hair. If the infant could be securely fastened to the mother's body, she could go about her tasks much more efficiently. Once a technique for carrying babies was developed, it could be extended to the idea of carrying food, and eventually to other sorts of cultural inventions—choppers and grinders for food preparation, and even weapons. Among modern hunter-gatherers, regardless of the poverty of their material culture, food carriers and baby carriers are always important items in their equipment.

A major point in the Man the Hunter argument is that cooperative hunting among males demanded more skill in social organization and communication, and thus provided selection pressure for increased brain size. I suggest that longer periods of infant dependency, more difficult births, and longer gestation periods also demanded more skills in social organization and communication—creating selective pressure for increased brain size without looking to hunting as an explanation. The need to organize for feeding after weaning, learning to handle the more complex social-emotional bonds that were developing, the new skills and cultural inventions surrounding more extensive gathering—all would demand larger brains. Too much attention has been given to the skills required by hunting, and too little to the skills required for gathering and the raising of dependent young. The techniques required for efficient gathering include location and identification of plant varieties, seasonal and geographical knowledge, containers for carrying the food, and tools for its preparation. Among modern hunting-gathering groups this knowledge is an extremely complex, well-developed, and important part of their cultural equipment. Caring for a curious, energetic, but still dependent human infant is difficult and demanding. Not only must the infant be watched, it must be taught the customs, dangers, and knowledge of its group. For the early hominids, as their cultural equipment and symbolic communication increased, the job of training the young would demand more skill. Selection pressure for better brains came from many directions.

Much has been made of the argument that cooperation among males demanded by hunting acted as a force to reduce competition for females. I suggest that competition for females has been greatly exaggerated. It could easily have been handled in the usual way for primates—according to male status relationships already worked out—and need not be pictured as particularly violent or extreme. The seeds of male cooperation already exist in primates when they act to protect the band from predators. Such dangers may well have increased with a shift to savannah living, and the longer dependency of infants. If biological roots are sought to explain the greater aggressiveness of males, it would be more fruitful to look toward their function as protectors, rather than any supposedly basic hunting adaptation. The only division of labor that regularly exists in primate groups is the females caring for infants and the males protecting the group from predators. The possibilities for both cooperation and aggression in males lies in this protective function.

The emphasis on hunting as a prime moving factor in hominid evolution distorts the data. It is simply too big a jump to go from the primate individual gathering pattern to a hominid cooperative hunting-sharing pattern without some intervening changes. Cooperative hunting of big game animals could only have developed *after* the trends toward neoteny and increased brain size had begun. Big-game hunting becomes a more logical development when it is viewed as growing out of a complex of changes which included sharing the products of gathering among mothers and children, deepening social bonds over time, increase in brain size, and the beginnings of cultural invention for purposes such as baby carrying, food carrying, and food preparation. Such hunting not only needed the prior development of some skills in social organization and communication; it probably also had to await the development of the "home base." It is difficult to imagine that most or all of the adult primate males in a group would go off on a hunting expedition, leaving the females and young exposed to the danger of predators, without some way of communicating to arrange for their defense, or at least a way of saying, "Don't worry, we'll be back in two days." Until that degree of communicative skill developed, we must assume either that the whole band traveled *and hunted* together, or that the males simply did not go off on large cooperative hunts.

The development of cooperative hunting requires, as a prior condition, an increase in brain size. Once such a trend is established, hunting skills would take part in a feedback process of selection for better brains just as would other cultural inventions and developments such as gathering skills. By itself, hunting fails to explain any part of human evolution and fails to explain itself.

Anthropology has always rested on the assumption that the mark of our species is our ability to *symbol*, to bring into existence forms of behavior and interaction, and material tools with which to adjust and control the environment. To explain human nature as evolving from the desire of males to hunt and kill is to negate most of anthropology. Our species survived and adapted through the invention of *culture*, of which hunting is simply a part. It is often stated that hunting *must* be viewed as the "natural" species' adaptation because it lasted as long as it did, nine-tenths of all human history. However:

> *Man the Hunter lasted as long as "he" did from no natural propensity toward hunting any more than toward computer programming or violin playing or nuclear warfare, but because that was what the historical circumstances allowed. We ignore the first premise of our science if we fail to admit that "man" is no more natural a hunter than "he" is naturally a golfer, for after symboling became possible our species left forever the ecological niche of the necessity of any one adaptation, and made all adaptations possible for ourselves. (Kephart, 1970:23)*

That the concept of Man the Hunter influenced anthropology for as long as it did is a reflection of male bias in the discipline. This bias can be seen in the tendency to equate "man," "human," and "male"; to look at culture almost entirely from a male point of view; to search for examples of the behavior of males and assume that this is sufficient for explanation, ignoring almost totally the female half of the species; and to filter this male bias through the "ideal" modern Western pattern of one male supporting a dependent wife and minor children.

The basis of any discipline is not the answers it gets, but the questions it asks. As an exercise in the anthropology of knowledge, this paper stems from asking a simple question: what were the females doing while the males were out hunting? It was only possible for me to ask this question after I had become politically conscious of myself as a woman. Such is the prestige of males in our society that a woman, in anthropology or any other profession, can only gain respect or be attended to if she deals with questions deemed important by men. Though there have been women anthropologists for years, it is rare to be able to discern any difference between their work and that of male anthropologists. Learning to be an anthropologist has involved learning to think from a male perspective, so it should not be surprising that women have asked the same kinds of questions as men. But political consciousness, whether among women, blacks, American Indians, or any other group, leads to reexamination and reevaluation of taken-for-granted assumptions. It is a difficult process, challenging the conventional wisdom, and this paper is simply a beginning. The male bias in anthropology that I have illustrated here is just as real as the white bias, the middle-class bias, and the academic bias that exist in the discipline. It is our task, as anthropologists, to create a "study of the human species" in spite of, or perhaps because of, or maybe even by means of, our individual biases and unique perspectives.

References

Kephart, Jane
1970 "Primitive Woman as Nigger, or, The Origin of the Human Family as Viewed Through the Role of Women." M.A. dissertation, University of Maryland.

Washburn, Sherwood, and Lancaster, C.
1968 "The Evolution of Hunting." In *Man the Hunter,* edited by R. B. Lee and Irven DeVore. Chicago: Aldine.

Sociobiology Revisited

Mykol C. Hamilton
Shannon Stuart-Smith

Mykol C. Hamilton received a B.A. in psychology from Stanford University, an M.A. in women's studies from San Jose State University, and an M.A. and Ph.D. in social psychology at UCLA. She is currently an assistant professor of psychology at Centre College in Danville, Kentucky. She has published several studies on male-biased language, and has also done research on bias in perception of AIDS risk, and preference for sons versus daughters.

Shannon Stuart-Smith earned a B.A. in philosophy from UCLA with an emphasis on the philosophy of science, and received her JD degree from the University of Kentucky. She sometimes strays from her work in the thoroughbred racehorse industry to collaborate with Mykol Hamilton, as she has for this paper and for a study on the effects of masculine generic language in jury instructions.

Many sociobiologists have contended that the whole array of gender roles and behaviors we have seen described in earlier chapters have evolved in humans from our animal ancestors, and are, therefore, "natural" and inevitable. The consequence? Don't fight it; it won't work. To reveal the fallacies in this argument, Hamilton and Stuart-Smith turn the tables, as Theodora Wells did in the previous chapter, and create a universe where women dominate. The results are funny and enlightening.

A version of this paper was presented at the conference of the Association for Women in Psychology, Long Beach, CA, March 1992.

Introduction

"SOCIOBIOLOGY" IS A THEORY THAT ATTEMPTS TO explain complex behavioral patterns, rather than just physiology and instinctual behaviors, in terms of evaluation and natural selection. We're all familiar with the basics of natural selection. For example, if a moth has slightly darker coloration than usual and this helps it hide from predatory birds, it may live longer and have more offspring than other moths, passing its genes for darker coloration on to the next generation. Eventually, if darkness is highly adaptable and lightness is harmful, only dark moths may remain. Similarly, instinctual behaviors such as a human baby's suckling response are commonly accepted to have natural selection explanations. Sociobiology's version of natural selection goes beyond these simple examples, in that it argues that even very sophisticated and complex human behavioral patterns, such as gender roles and marriage arrangements, have evolutionary causes. Sociobiologists argue that it is natural and nearly universal for human and animal males to dominate females, to desire multiple sexual partners, and to compete with each other for female attention. Non-sociobiologists believe, in contrast, that we *learn* such behaviors from parents, peers, brothers and sisters, and, in modern-day culture, from school, movies, and MTV. In other words, these behaviors are seen as culturally rather than genetically transmitted.

Human sociobiologists have been criticized for unfairly generalizing animal evidence to humans, for ignoring all animal and human behavior that differs from the male-as-dominant-and-promiscuous model, for using circular reasoning, and for anthropomorphizing animal behavior (describing animal behaviors as motivated by human emotions and values). Despite these flaws in the theory, human sociobiology is compelling to many, and the criticisms mentioned above are sometimes ignored.

The paper you are about to read, therefore, uses

a novel approach to debunk human sociobiology. We portray a world in which gender roles and human sexual arrangements are inverted, then we use evolutionary mechanisms to explain why it was inevitable and adaptive for *females* to be dominant, promiscuous, and aggressive. We hope you'll be able to spot where we have "cheated" in the same ways regular human sociobiology does despite the fact that all of our animal evidence *is* real. We also hope that our journey to a parallel universe will convince you that human sociobiology is in a sense too good, since it can explain *everything and its opposite!* A decent theory predicts the future as well as explains the past, and clearly a theory that can be used to look back and explain both "reality" and its inverse must be a total failure in prediction.

Sociobiology Revisited

Through the centuries these questions have been asked: Why do women so thoroughly dominate culture, politics, and intellectual life? Why have there been no great male painters, composers, writers, mathematicians? How is it that men gravitate toward the "private sphere," women toward the "public sphere"? Countless theories have been advanced, with a fundamental debate forming between nature and nurture explanations of woman's essence (generic "woman," of course). That is, are gender characteristics and behaviors determined by our biology, or are they culturally created? It is important to stand outside the petty politics of the debate, and explore these questions with an open mind. Let us now consider woman in the free spirit of natural history, as though we were zoologists from another planet completing a catalog of social species on earth.[1]

Certainly the finer details of female–male differences and roles are culturally determined, as they do differ from group to group. But there is an undeniable thread of continuity running through all societies: for example, the greater power of women plays itself out in different manners but can be seen in all cultures, and men tend to do the larger share of childrearing and domestic work in every tribal or national group. Similar arrangements can even be seen in other animal species. The underlying consistency in overall pattern suggests that biology plays a significant role in determining gender characteristics. But what kind of biological mechanism could account for the variety of effects we see?

Parental Investment

The great Charlotte Darwin proposed a theory of natural selection, which provides just such a mechanism. This theory posits that any physical characteristic of an organism that enhances its chances of producing surviving offspring will be selected for; if a particular offspring, due to a precipitous combination of genes from its two parents, or due to genetic mutation, is favored in its current environment, it will survive longer than others of its kind, perhaps deriving superior reproductive success. Darwin called this advantage in survivability and procreation "reproductive fitness." Thus genes guide the creation of a phenotype, and the phenotype is designed to ensure propagation of these same genes into future generations. But how do we get from the genetic shaping of phenotype to the genetic shaping of behavior?

It is our assertion that a major driving force in forming both the phenotype and the behavior of the sexes is females' and males' differing parental investment in the task of reproduction. Parental investment begins with the premise that there are costs to the individual organism of producing offspring. The costs take the form of energy output, time, and wear and tear on the organism, all of which may lead to early death. The investment differs from species to species, with the period of investment for mammalian parents being quite long—it begins with gamete production, moves through gestation, birth, and lactation, and may not end until the next generation is ready to begin its own reproductive cycle. For human beings the time and energy invested between the end of lactation and the sexual maturity of offspring can easily span over a decade or two.

What is the relative parental investment of human females and males, and what are the consequences of this pattern? Starting with gamete production, the female produces one egg at a time, each of which could result in an offspring, whereas the male's gamete contribution is more energy-consuming. Not only must he produce seminal fluid and millions of sperm for every insemination attempt, but his ejaculate is wasted every time he engages in sex that does not succeed in reproducing. The egg, of course, may live to see another day if insemination occurs too early in the female's sexual cycle. If, on the other hand, the egg is shed in the monthly menstruation it will be replaced by another egg shortly, one which comes from a store of ova that the female has carried with her since birth. She does not have to invest repeated energy in the lifelong generation of gametes.[2]

It should also be noted that the nature of each sex is analogous to that of its gamete. The female produces the more aggressive egg, the male the bumbling, passive sperm. "First, a wastefully huge swarm of sperm weakly flops along, its members bumping into walls and flailing aimlessly through thick strands of mucus. Eventually, through sheer odds of pinball-like bouncing more than anything else, a few sperm end up close to an egg. As they mill around, the egg selects one and reels it in, pinning it down in spite of its efforts to escape. It's no contest, really. The gigantic, hardy egg yanks this tiny sperm inside, distills out the chromosomes, and sets out to become an embryo" (Freedman, 1992, p. 61).[3]

The male's exaggerated investment at the gamete level did not necessarily always tip the scales against him. At one time in our distant evolutionary history, the production of millions of sperm may have been coupled with rampant breeding on the male's part. This strategy might have worked quite well for our predecessors, as it does in a few other species living today, because of two reproductive issues. First, offspring which come forth capable of nearly immediate survival on their own (insects and horses, for instance) may require little to no parental investment subsequent to insemination. Second, if a species' reproductive strategy is to produce hundreds or thousands of progeny in the hopes that a few will survive, it may pay off for the male to spread his sperm far and wide for more survivors overall.

However, promiscuity is not visible for the human male for several reasons. The prolonged helplessness of human infants necessitates lengthy and intense care. Also, the human norm is a single birth every few years, so that even at a frantic pace the male cannot leave offspring in numbers approaching those of insects, fish, etc. And unless he can keep all other males from copulating with his sex partners, there's a great chance that he has not actually fathered at all.

Some species, such as the hamadryas baboon of Ethiopia, exclude other males in order to ensure their own parentage by setting up a "harem" arrangement (Goldsmith, 1991). This would not work for humans for several reasons. Human offspring's extremely long dependency period would put a strain on any male's resources. How could he provide for so many for so long, while simultaneously defending his harem against lone males trying to usurp his position? His reign would surely end after only a short period of reproduction. In contrast, if human males attach themselves to a single female, in other words, become monogynous, theirs becomes an energy investment of longer duration but less intensity, results in better assurance of paternity, more offspring, and an enhanced infant survival rate. Thus males fulfill their genetic mandate.

The Beggar Syndrome

Parental investment of women and men, up to this point, could be viewed as nearly equitable. How could parental investment possibly explain the extreme disparity in women's and men's social positions across cultures and times? The answer is that three aspects of the parental investment issue conspire to leave men with little control over their own genetic destiny. One: It is the female who carries the child and gives birth—thus the child "belongs" to her. Two: Only the female is equipped to give immediate sustenance and nurturance to the child through lactation, thus cementing further her connection with the infant. Three: The child belongs even more certainly to her mother because only the mother can know with assurance that a child is her own. The male is an outcast, an outsider, in the reproductive cycle.

He is indeed a beggar. In order to regain some reproductive control, to find some way of securing the survival of his own genetic material, he must overcome this inbuilt disparity. Fortunately the needs of both sexes are met in historical human social arrangements; a mutually advantageous bargain seems to have been struck, such that the woman gains a caretaker and helpmate for the rearing of the new generation, and the man gains the ability to contribute to the successful rearing of offspring, a degree of certainty as to his paternity, and inclusion in family and/or community life. Shortly after the female gives birth, she generally hands over the offspring to the househusband and nurturer, the man. Secure in the knowledge that the child is hers and that through birth and lactation early bonding has taken place between mother and child, she need only be involved now in the more pleasant aspects of child-rearing, so that she is free to accomplish in the wider world, whether it be through hunting, inventing, or creating great works of science or art.

This bargain has served both genders well in the evolutionary sense, but it is not without its social and personal costs to males. The male is still an outsider asking to be let in. In order to obtain what he desires, he must ingratiate himself to the more powerful female by taking on the rather retiring and passive male role. He must be subservient and sexually faithful. Needless to say, taking on these qualities and behaviors was not a conscious decision on his part; it was simply an evolutionary response to the conditions he faced. Male faithfulness, passivity, subservience, and love for children and the domestic pursuits were rewarded genetically, in that any male displaying such characteristics and behaviors had more reproductive success than other males.

Reciprocal Sexual Selection[4]

As we have seen, one result of the female human's superior reproductive strategy is in giving her a stronger connection to, and thus greater socializing influence over the child. This helps ensure that her genes are perpetuated in the next generation, even allowing her, through continued close contact with her children, to have some impact on whether her genetic material is passed on through the children of her children.

Considering these decisive female advantages, reproductive strategies could have evolved in such a way that the male remained merely a sperm donor—the bargain we mentioned before need not have been made. Why didn't females shut males out completely, copulating with many, but becoming closely allied with none? Under such an arrangement, present today in some animal species and a few human cultures, males would have remained disenfranchised forever. However, though females would have benefited in some ways under such a system, they might not have evolved to be the powerful beings they are today, not having been freed up by the fair sex's willingness to perform the more tedious aspects of child care and home-tending. In fact, a double evolutionary mechanism was at work here—the strategy we adopted was genetically beneficial to both sexes, and both sexes contributed to its development through natural selection. First, it was to the male's direct genetic advantage to be helpful and to serve females by contributing to the safety and upbringing of her, and presumably his, children. This strategy ensures that his genes live on. And as Goldsmith (1991) has said, "The female's genetic interest will be served by processes that decrease the chances of desertion and increase the parental investment of the male" (p. 51). It is in this way, then, that the class of "beggar males" was created to serve woman. (Let it be said here that many past civilizations and even some of today's societies have not been very kind to their men, and we find this reprehensible. Some forms of marriage equate to sexual slavery, for example, a harem with harem-mistress, dowried grooms, groom price, society-wide lesbian relationships with the keeping of males as drones, polyandrous arrangements of various sorts, etc. As a character in the Margaret Atwood (1985) novel *The Handmaid's Tale* cynically put it, "a man is just a woman's strategy for making other women" (p. 155). Of course we in America do not subscribe to this gynocentric view.)

From the above evolutionary picture follow logically many of our social arrangements, as well as the traits and characteristics we see in women and men today. Matriarchy, matrilineality, and matrilocality predominate. And the fact that men take over most responsibility in the domestic sphere means that women have been free to pursue higher intellectual and creative interests. As Darwin said, "if two lists were made of the most imminent men and women in poetry, painting, sculpture, music (inclusive both of composition and performance), history, science, and philosophy with half a dozen names under each subject, the two lists would not bear comparison" (cited in Hubbard, 1990, p. 96).

Another residual of evolution is women's proclivity for sexual promiscuity. Prior to evolution's creation of the beggar class of males, the female undoubtedly used a strategy of promiscuity to ensure conception. If she only had one egg, she needed to be sure it was fertilized—what if he was infertile? What if her timing was off? "Estrus" in the human female is hidden, unlike in other mammals. It was evolutionarily advantageous for women to be highly interested in sex, and women have been gifted with a nearly insatiable sexual appetite through their capacity for multiple orgasm, as described in Mary Jane Sherfey's ovarian work (1966). Males in comparison, because each sexual act involves a major biological investment, and because it was in their interest to settle down to keep an eye on their mate and offspring, were not blessed with a very strong sexual incentive—thus males' relative sexual incapacity, refractory period, and general boredom with sex. Related to this, of course, are women's propensity for manizing, men's inability to perform sexually under stress, and men's frequent frigidity.

Research Evidence

Why are we certain that the sexual arrangements derived by humans are due to evolutionary biology? One reason is that these same strategies exist in human societies around the world, and, as far as we know, have existed over time with some minor but few major variations. The disturbing result of tampering with natural roles has been demonstrated well in recent studies on children reared in some of today's counter-culture men's lib communities. As one famous sociobiologist states, there are great costs to fighting biology—children raised in nontraditional communities are "neglected, deprived, and emotionally disturbed," and men seeking liberation from total responsibility for child care are adopting the other sex's biological strategy and "denying their own" (Barash, 1979).[5]

The other reason is the animal evidence.[6] There is of course wide variation in reproductive strategies across species. However, there are numerous animals, some near us evolutionarily, that lend support to the idea that sex differences and sexual behaviors have undergone natural selection processes,[7] bringing us to our current pinnacle. What these more typical and highly advanced species have in common with us and each other is the female's greater power and her dominance over males, as well as the male's involvement in the rearing of the young.

Female Dominance and Aggressiveness

Cross-species evidence for the naturalness of female dominance and aggressiveness is found in the behavior of the Japanese macaque (Crawford, 1978), for example. While the males of this species do have a dominance hierarchy, status is not determined by a male's size and strength. Instead, it is the rank of a young male's mother that predicts where he will eventually settle in the male hierarchy. When youngsters' rough-and-tumble play gets out of hand, it is the mothers who come in to settle the conflict, with dominant females chasing the other youngsters and their mothers away. Rank is thus inherited matrilineally. Also, according to Crawford, "tamarin and howler monkey females are aggressive and competitive" (p. 537), and, among ring-tailed lemurs, "adult females are dominant over males" (Wilson, cited in Leibowitz, 1979, p. 40). Thelma Rowell (1972) observed forest-dwelling baboons for five years, finding that females and their young form a stable social core, with males moving periodically from troop to troop. Older, more powerful females decide when the troop should move, and where. Males have no hierarchy and are quite peaceable and cooperative with each other as they perform their lookout duties.

Promiscuity

There is also much evidence for the promiscuous nature of females across the animal world. Among primates, for example, the bonobo (pygmy chimp) female seems to enjoy casual and frequent sex with both females and males, even to the point of rejecting male advances in favor of sexuality with a preferred female partner (Small, 1992). Though the bonobo is rarer than, for example, the common chimpanzee, it is a superior species from which to generalize to human beings because it is so much more highly evolved, as evidenced by its similarity to humans.[8] (Female and male bonobos are nearly the same size, the bonobo has a more slender build and a larger clitoris than the common chimp, the bonobo exhibits a preference for frontal sex rather than mounting because of the forward orientation of the clitoris, and the species seems to take great pleasure in sex, separating sex from procreation.)

Non-primates also provide extensive evidence for the universality of female promiscuity. For instance, though a blackbird male has a harem of females, research shows that if he is vasectomized, the females continue to conceive, showing that they are mating with other males (Bray, Kennelly, & Guarino, cited in Hrdy, 1986). A non–egg-producing shiner perch will court and mate with numbers of males, collecting sperm to be stored in her ovaries until seasonal conditions are favorable for ovulation (Shaw & Darling, cited in Hrdy, 1986). Various female cats, including leopards, lions, and pumas, are extremely sexually active—the lion may mate up to 100 times a day for 6–7 days with many partners, when she is in estrus (Eaton, cited in Hrdy, 1986). And of course we are all aware of the rampant fachisma of many insects, such as the praying mantis and black widow spider.[9]

Care of the Young

What about the rearing of the young among primates? Again, there are many examples of highly evolved species in which the male does the bulk of the infant care. The tamarin monkey of South America is polyandrous, according to Goldizen and Terborgh (cited in Hrdy, 1986), with the female mating with several males, then enlisting the help of all her mates in the care of her twin young—the mother nurses the two infants and the males carry them for the remaining part of the day. It is believed that in fact most troop-dwelling primates' breeding systems are polyandrous, with multiple males contributing to the care of offspring. It has also been observed that a species' chances of survival are enhanced if males care for the young (Hrdy, 1986).

Bird species, according to Bleier (1984), show a variety of mating and offspring care patterns, some of which involve promiscuity on the part of the female, some also showing an extensive contribution of the male toward caring for the young. The male rhea bird incubates the 50 or so eggs laid in his nest by multiple females. An emperor penguin male carries the egg on his feet to keep it warm for two months until it hatches. Many shore birds exhibit shared parenting. The jacana of South America keeps a harem of males in her territory, fills each male's nest with eggs, and leaves them all to be tended by the males.

In many of the evolutionarily important fish species the male is the bearer or primary tender of the young. The male seahorse becomes pregnant. The river bullhead male guards the eggs after the female has laid them in a nest under a rock, then he remains in the area to protect the young until they leave the nest. And for 23 days, while abstaining from eating, the male West African black-chinned mouth brooder incubates the fertilized eggs in his mouth.

Conclusion

In short, there is reason to believe, considering the widespread use of human-like reproductive strategies among animals and the universality of these same strategies among humans around the world, that our current sexual division of labor and the relationship between women and men have adaptive significance. As thinking women, we may choose to exaggerate the natural order, allow it to run its own course, or go against it. Any strategy will have its costs. In the interest of fairness to the male sex, we may want to resist biology, but before we tamper with Father Nature, we must beware the costs to the men and children, and to society as a whole.

References

Atwood, Margaret
1985 *The handmaid's tale.* New York: Fawcett Crest.

Barash, David
1979 *The whisperings within.* New York: Harper & Row.

Bleier, Ruth
1984 *Science and gender: A critique of biology and its theories on women.* New York: Pergamon Press.

Crawford, Mary
1978 Evolution made me do it. Women, men, and animal behavior. *International Journal of Women's Studies* 1: 533–543.

Freedman, David H.
June 1992 The aggressive egg. *Discover,* 61.

Goldsmith, T. H.
1991 *The biological roots of human behavior.* New York: Oxford University Press.

Hrdy, Sarah B.
1986 Empathy, polyandry, and the myth of the coy female. In *Feminist approaches to science,* edited by Ruth Bleier. New York: Pergamon Press.

Hubbard, Ruth
1990 *The politics of women's biology.* New Brunswick, NJ: Rutgers University Press.

Leibowitz, Lila
1979 "Universals" and male dominance among primates: A critical examination. In *Genesis and gender II,* edited by Ethel Tobach and Betty Rosoff. New York: Gordian Press.

Rowell, Thelma
1972 *Social behavior of monkeys.* Baltimore: Penguin.

Sayers, Janet
1982 *Biological politics: Feminist and anti-feminist perspectives.* New York: Tavistock Publications.

Sherfey, Mary Jane
1966 The evolution and nature of female sexuality in relation to psychoanalytic theory. *Journal of the American Psychoanalytic Association* 14: 28–128.

Small, Meredith F.
June 1992 What's love got to do with it? *Discover,* 46–51.

Van Voorhies, Wayne A.
(3 December 1992). Production of sperm reduces nematode lifespan. *Nature,* 456–458.

Wilson, Edward O.
1975 *Sociobiology: The new synthesis.* Cambridge, MA: The Belknap Press of Harvard University Press.

Notes

1. This sentence is a misquote of the opening sentence in E. O. Wilson's chapter on human sociobiology in the famous tome, *Sociobiology: The New Synthesis* (1975). In place of the word "woman" he used "man."

2. After this paper was written, scientific support concerning the costliness of sperm production appeared in an article in *Nature* (Van Voorhies, 1992). At least for the roundworm, the energy-consuming production of sperm may actually shorten the male's life by about a third!

3. Recent discoveries about the nature of eggs and sperm make this discription more accurate than that found in traditional biology textbooks, which portrays the egg as passively awaiting the onslaught of valiant warrior sperm.

4. A play on Darwin's term "sexual selection," a part of evolutionary theory that says that in some species, natural selection forces are exerted more on males than females.

5. Sociobiologist Barash referred here to women seeking liberation, rather than men.

6. All of the animal evidence cited is from actual studies done in *this* universe—it is not made up!

7. There are dozens of documented examples in the literature, among primates and other mammals, birds, fish, and plants, but we will describe only a few of these.

8. Selective use of supposedly superior and more human-like species is common in "real" sociobiology. Of course, which species one decides are superior and more human-like depends on whether one is a sociobiologist from this universe or our parallel universe!

9. E. O. Wilson (1975) says that insects have evolved a "rampant machismo." Mary Crawford (1978) cites other such extremes of anthropomorphizing, in such article titles as "The Male Response to Female Adultery in the Bluebird," "Wife Sharing in the Tasmanian Native Hen," and "Prostitution Behavior in a Tropical Hummingbird," as well as in descriptions of rape among ducks and flowers, divorce among seagulls, and homosexual rape in parasitic worms.

PART II

Sexism Realized: Women's Lives in Patriarchy

We have been foreigners not only to the fortresses of political power but also to those citadels in which thought processes have been spun out. . . . Women are beginning to recognize that the value system that has been thrust upon us by the various cultural institutions of patriarchy has amounted to a kind of gang rape of minds as well as of bodies.

–MARY DALY, Beyond God the Father

SO FAR WE HAVE BEEN EXAMINING THE CONSCIOUSness, or worldview, of patriarchy, the abstract concepts, the myths, beliefs, and values that underlie the sexual caste system. We now turn to the material expression of that consciousness, the effects it has on the concrete lives of women. Sexism is built into almost everything that women do or that is done to us. It is lodged in the most personal facets of our lives as well as in the most public. In the following chapters, we explore the outward realizations of sexist consciousness, the patterns and structures, institutional and informal, that give our female lives their particular color and shape.

Chapter 6 focuses on the part of women's lives ordinarily called the private sphere—personal relationships, marriage and unmarriage, love, romance, and sex.

Chapter 7 directs attention to the institutional sphere, to work and economics, to women's legal status, and to the quality and character of women's participation in public policy-making, all of which are intricately interrelated.

Finally, Chapter 8 treats the psychological undergirding of the entire system, the strategies through which patriarchy creates a sexist consciousness not only in men but in women.

6

Women's Personal Lives: The Effects of Sexism on Self and Relationships

The Lady in the Space

Earlier we looked at the images and the "place" patriarchy constructs for women, but we have not yet explored the impact these ideas have for the woman within. How do these forces shape our private lives, the way we think and the way we live on the most intimate level with ourselves and others?

Although sexists have difficulty wrapping their minds around the idea, we, of course, know that women are simply people, human beings, with the needs, dreams, and desires all people are wont to experience. How we relate to others on a one-to-one basis; how we relate to ourselves, our bodies, and our feelings; and how we relate to the physical space around us are the concrete realities that make up our daily lives. But certain aspects of our lives as *women*, particularly women in a sexist world, profoundly influence those concrete human realities. It is in the tension between the two, our experience as people and our experience as women in a sexist world—and in the conflicts that arise between these divergent states—that we live out our days. Let us turn, then, to examine our private, personal lives.

A Story

Once upon a time there lived a very beautiful little girl named Cinderella (Snow White, Sleeping Beauty, Rapunzel, . . .). Her nature was as lovely as her face. Gentle, kind, accepting, modest, obedient, and sweet, she never complained or became peevish, though she suffered greatly at the hands of circumstance and of cruel people. Because she was good natured and uncomplaining, because she asked for little and gave a great deal, her beauty shone, and a handsome prince came along, fell in love with her, and took her away to his castle, where the pair lived happily ever after. Here the story always ends.

This is a story that in its many tellings is dear to the hearts of most little girls, who hear it practically in the crib, read and repeat it endlessly, playact and live it vicariously, and dream of its realization in their own lives. It tells us a great deal about the way women are expected to be and the way we learn to see our existence.

The story teaches us that we are born to be chosen, admired, and sought after, and that to succeed in this goal of being chosen certain attributes are required: physical beauty, "good nature" (willingness to take unwarranted abuse), modesty, self-effacement, piety, vulnerability, suffering, and good luck. We learn that even if we do not have these attributes or, for that matter, dislike them, we had better appear to have them—for the essence of the story is the fact of *being chosen* rather than choosing, of being noticed for our "feminine qualities," and of gaining success from endurance and patience rather than initiative, which belongs to the man. The story goes beyond the facade of his asking and her assenting straight to the unvarnished truth: It is the prince who picks what he wants; our chief responsibility is to make ourselves "pickable," as worthy of his interest as we can. Our only appropriate direct action lies in the orchestrating of an effect. The story teaches us, by extending the principles of passivity, that it is not by our own efforts that we are to be happy (or safe or comfortable) but rather through the intervention of a powerful protector who alone can bestow status and security on us. He alone has the power to make us happy, for clearly we are (or ought to be) unable to do that for ourselves.

It is the element in these tales of relinquishing initiative as well as the power to make ourselves happy or safe that is so potent a factor in molding the approved feminine character. We are to believe not only that we are too weak and small to take care of ourselves, that we are and must be dependent, but also that it is wrong to be any other way. Self-assertive women like Cinderella's stepmother and sisters are portrayed as wicked and ugly, and because of this they come to bad ends. These and other stories fix in our minds that women who take for themselves, by themselves, are selfish and wicked, whereas admirable females earn for themselves through renunciation what they do not take directly.

The attitude born of all this is a sense that only through intercession of another can we *be made* happy, that we are to receive the positive goods in life only from another in return for beauty of face, passivity of nature, and for services rendered. Most of us do not learn until much later that in giving up the right of, as well as the responsibility for, framing our own fortunes, we place ourselves at the mercy of circumstance and of anyone who may wish to exercise the power we have abrogated. We do not hear until later, after the pain it brings, that we have bartered our souls for the illusion of protection.

The Matter of Marriage

Enter Mr. Right (alias the "prince" or the "one"). He will "come along," we will "fall in love," we will know instinctively that we belong together—forever. We will marry, have children, and live happily ever after. The End.

That fantasy—the marriage myth, a mystical tale of love, romance, and marriage—for women who marry, for women who do not, and for those who unmarry, exercises incredible power over how we live our lives. Even though the very smallest minority of families fits the fairy tale version—Mama at home, Papa at work—and even though the very smallest minority of couples lives the happily-ever-after forever romance, the myth functions. It undergirds our expectations and colors our relationships. The marriage myth operates on our consciousness even when it is completely absent from reality, even though the story is utterly false.

The Myth

During the early 1960s, in a course I was teaching in introductory philosophy, I used to ask the students to begin the term's work with an essay entitled, "What I Want Out of Life." Those were the years before I had acquired what now is known as a feminist consciousness, and the results surprised me. With great regularity, the papers of the men in the class differed categorically from the women's. The men's papers generally followed a familiar theme: I want to finish school, get a good job, have a good income, a nice place to live, friends, fun things to do. Many said they wanted to be happy; a few remembered to hope for health. The women, too, said they wanted to be happy. They wanted to finish school, have an interesting career, fall in love, get married. Finis. Did the men, I asked, mean to get married? Oh sure, they said. That was understood: It came along the way. For the women, it *was* the way. Career, possessions, health, and all were only satisfying thoughts against the certainty of marriage. To play the successful "bachelorette" for a time was a kick—but then the Cinderella tale took over: The ultimate goal was "happily ever after."

It is most telling, I think, that the favorite female fairy tales end with the wedding, and all else is subsumed under the heading of "ever-after." It is as though these stories teach us that our whole existence is to be wrapped up in the quest for a mate; that once we acquire the mate, all else is decided; that the definition of what follows after the wedding is irrelevant because it is indistinguishable from any other ever-after; that what follows really has little importance because we have already done the all-important; that no matter what else we do, life with the prince in his castle is the only happily-ever-after that is important for us, there being no viable alternatives; that all the other aspects of our lives, public as well as private, are determined in large measure by the overwhelming pervasiveness of the wifely estate.

As children listening to stories and as young women creating our own, how closely do we really look at ever-after land? The dream tells us that we will be loved and appreciated, sharing a husband's life, supporting him as he encourages and helps us, fulfilling ourselves in the haven of our world. But is this so?

Even today, when the terms of marriage, families, and relationships are shifting so dramatically, this vision of "happily-ever-after" persists. The demographics of families have become more than familiar; trends include:

> *declining rates of marriage, later ages at first marriage, higher divorce rates, an increase in female-headed households, a higher proportion of births to unmarried mothers, larger percentages of children living in female-headed families, and a higher percentage of children living in poverty.*[1]

More than half of all first marriages end in divorce.[2] Young women are painfully aware of that statistic; it frightens them. Yet 90 percent of young people will marry,[3] and three out of four divorced women remarry,[4] half within four years.[5] What is more, divorced people are even more likely to remarry than those who have never married,[6] a fact cynically called the "triumph of hope over experience."[7] Notwithstanding all the frightening news, as recently as 1985–86, in surveys of high school students, 81 percent of females reported that they would choose to marry (compared to 74 percent of males).[8]

For even those few who do not or are not married, the dream often pervades their lives as a nightmare search: "Maybe tomorrow I'll find the right one." In the heterosexual community, and even to some extent in the gay community, the image of the perfect mate in the perfect eternal relationship provides the model against which most measure their personal lives.

Promise and Disillusionment

The traditional American mystique of marriage promises women a roster of assurances:

- You will have someone to make you happy.
- You will be loved and cherished.
- You will be cared for and protected from all the dangers of the world.
- You will have sexual intimacy and satisfaction.
- You will have someone to understand and support you.
- You will have companionship and safety from loneliness.
- You will have a father for your children.
- You will be socially secure as part of a couple.
- You will have a place in this world, a meaning, and you will love it.
- You will gain status and prestige as someone's chosen wife. You will not be an "old maid."
- You will be financially secure.
- You will be happy.

That's the promise.

Feminists cast a more objective glance at the promise. "Demystifying" marriage, we have drawn up a roster of our own: the data that tell the hard facts, the untruths and half-truths, the traps and games, the dissimulations and dangers of the traditional marriage mystique. It is not that feminism is in principle incompatible with marriage. (Although some feminists believe that it is, others do not, and many feminists marry.) Rather, it is that these presuppositions and traditional marriage arrangements can be destructive to women's lives in the most concrete ways, and feminists, discovering these realities, seek to both warn and redress.

The Case Against Traditional Marriage

Following Emile Durkheim, Jessie Bernard, a feminist sociologist, commented that "marriage is not the same for women as for men; it is not nearly as good."[9] Following extensive research, Bernard concluded that although men ridicule married life and pretend to have contempt for it, they benefit considerably from marriage, whereas women lose a great deal. Several studies, for example, found that married men have greater emotional health than single men, suffer depression and anxiety less frequently than their single counterparts, advance faster professionally and socially, and have greater incomes than single men. Furthermore, the remarriage rate for divorced men and widowers is very high; they remarry more often and sooner than either women or never-married men.[10] Apparently they know what is good for them.

Married women, on the other hand, experience greater depression, anxiety, and fear than single women, are more apt to experience severe neurotic symptoms, and have lower self-esteem than single women or married men. What is interesting as well, as Tavris and Offir reported, is that homemakers are even more apt to exhibit these problems than working wives, and single men in any category (never married, divorced, or widowed) are more likely to suffer from psychological difficulties than are single women.[11]

After all the ball-and-chain jokes, all the tavern mythology about carefree bachelors and manipulative women, and all the masculist assertions that marriage is a terrific deal for women and a disaster for men, are not these findings a revelation? Yet, they should really come as no surprise. In so many ways—in terms of emotional exchange, economics, work, independence, freedom and mobility, autonomy and authenticity—traditional marriage offers to women and men a double standard, and women's part of that standard is truly the less advantaged.

Conjugal Obligation

In the patriarchal myth, a man and a woman marry, each taking on certain responsibilities. He agrees to love, honor, cherish, and provide her with the physical necessities of life. She agrees to love and to obey (a term now mostly out of vogue in modern marriage ceremonies, although the power relationship in which it originated is not), and she takes on a whole composite of responsibilities that are diverse, unspecified, and generally lumped under the heading of being a wife or housewife. Though it might superficially appear to be an even exchange, actually, it is rather an extraordinary exchange, and an enigmatic one, for at base it differs radically from what it appears to be. Overladen with social mythology, marriage is rarely seen for what it is, and the parties concerned often perceive it very differently.

In the patriarchal barroom myth, marriage is a trap for men. A man in the excellent condition of bachelorhood, free and unencumbered, encounters a lady, wily and manipulative, who tricks him into "falling in love." He becomes so besotted with her that he loses his good sense and marries her. The door slams shut; he will find out only later that he has been entrapped and is now the captive of a "ball and chain" who, for the rest of his life, will nag him, keep tabs on him, spend his money, and bring him no end of difficulties. The lady, on the other hand, has a "good deal," having snared a meal ticket and a respectable place in life. Actually, of course, both women and men know the myth to be false, yet both are unclear as to just how false because at some level of awareness, in some form, and to some degree, the myth is believed (or else Jessie Bernard's findings would not surprise us). Because of this, it exerts considerable pressure on the attitudes and behaviors of husbands and wives.

Let us take a more objective look at traditional marriage—"demystified." In patriarchy, a man and a woman marry; they strike a bargain, make an exchange (not fully understood at the time of marriage), and each takes on certain responsibilities and privileges. The bare bones of the agreement require that the husband provide the physical necessities of life through his income—shelter, food, clothing, and so on—and that in return for these the wife provides care of the home and family. But what do these respective duties, obligations, and privileges actually entail for each?

The patriarchal husband's responsibilities are explicit: He must work or in some fashion secure financial maintenance of the home and family. Because he is "out in the world," and therefore worldly wise, he must act as "head of household," making policy decisions for the family and bearing responsibility for them. He is to protect his wife and children from danger, whatever that might be in their circumstances, and guide and mold their behavior and character. Although the law does not specify the quantity or quality of the provisions a man must secure for his family, the culture does, for according to the imperatives of Mars, a man proves his worthiness through success in the marketplace (the modern hunt). Society—and often his wife or children—may judge a man ill if he does not provide according to the standard of living decreed by the media. There is then an intense pressure on husbands to provide always bigger and better, and this pressure may be both burdensome and unremitting. What is more, such pressure may not be much reduced even when there are two incomes, since the marriage myth operates regardless of actual circumstances.

A different aspect to the prescription to "provide" is often overlooked, however, in discussions about masculine responsibility. "Provision" means work. It means one must have a job, of whatever nature, and must remain regularly at a job in order to obtain all one needs. Husbands frequently point out that they work very hard "to get you what you need" and therefore should be loved, respected, served, and accorded the right to make family decisions. What they do not say is that they would work in any event, married or unmarried, for one still needs to eat, dress, and have shelter. They do not say that they work for more than income, that even routine or laborious jobs provide a satisfaction in earning, and that life without work outside the house would drive them mad. They do not say that a tremendous satisfaction comes in looking about one's family home and noting that whatever is there, whatever its condition, has been provided by one's efforts and that because of those efforts, one is autonomous and worthy. We need not denigrate the value and importance of giving or the pressure of provision. We need only consider that such labor carries with it a highly positive and meaningful reward that we must not overlook in evaluating its claims to compensation. This satisfying experience of autonomy and self-worth that comes from providing is the reason many women give for returning to work outside the home, or even for leaving "comfortable" marriages.

The husband's duty to protect is enigmatic in the twentieth century. Certainly protection from physical danger is impossible in such a complex society. That work is now largely passed to public institutions, and the remainder of the responsibility is equally shared by husband and wife. In terms of children's safety, the mother usually accomplishes the lion's share of that work, typically taking almost total charge of her offspring. Even when she is not with them, it is she who worries and protects through vigilance with regard to a ride to school, an adequate babysitter, a competent physician, dental appointments, birthday parties, and countless other matters. It is she, too, who "guides"; fathers could hardly be expected to provide much guidance in the average twelve minutes a day they spend with their children![12]

Head of household, then, becomes an interesting concept. If it does not mean protection, guidance, or modeling; what it means in essence is power, control over household and family in return for breadwinning, which is neither all sacrifice nor peculiar to marriage. The head of household also has certain real privileges that he enjoys both as husband and as male: considerably more freedom, autonomy, and service—the service, by and large, provided by his wife.

One of the most extraordinary features of being a traditional wife in patriarchy is the unification of certain aspects of the role: The married woman *is* a housewife; she doesn't *do* housewifing. She is not simply a mate, a coworker, and a partner in the business of life; she is a certain identity, one that carries with it a particular (mixed) status, a "place," and some identifiable and rather unchanging tasks. Upon marriage, the patriarchal wife yields her own individual identity (a fact attested to by her change of name), subsumes it under her husband's, and commits her life—her time, interests, and energies—to the needs of the family group, husband and offspring. Regardless of whatever else a wife may do—work in the marketplace or community affairs or pursue a professional career—patriarchy defines as her first priorities her duties as wife/housewife. Should she choose not to keep house, she is no less the housewife; she is simply a housewife not doing her job.

A husband barters some of his income and freedom for the kind of services and satisfactions a wife provides. What does a wife barter? For the financial security (now not a clear return for the more than 58 percent of all married women who work outside the home[13]), for the status of being married, for love and companionship, women take on almost limitless labors of service to their home and family. Whereas a husband takes on a "job" involving specifiable hours, tasks, and rewards, a wife takes on a lifestyle. Her tasks are not wholly specified, but instead comprise the satisfaction of almost every kind of physical and emotional need her husband and children voice, as well as the many more services required for smooth maintenance of family life. Her labor is limited by neither time nor personal need. She is expected to perform at whatever hour needs arise—breakfast at whatever time the family must rise, dinner when they return home. Were this job to be advertised outside the home, it might carry the warning that the job makes tremendous demands on one's personal time, including split shifts and a great deal of overtime.

Unlike her husband, whose skills and education define the kind of work he will do, the wife is assigned work that is elemental and undifferentiated by skill. College educated or illiterate, the common denominator is housework—sweeping floors, washing clothes, scouring ovens, cleaning toilets, washing dishes, dumping garbage—and she who performs such menial tasks earns for herself the status incumbent upon them: low. She is "a housewife." Even if she works outside the home, as most women today do, she is no less the housewife in her household; she is simply a housewife who works both at home and in the marketplace, or a "working wife." (It is interesting that the husband is never referred to as a "working husband.")

The tasks of housekeeping are themselves no joy. However glorified in the media, housework in the real world is boring, ugly, tiresome, repetitive, unsatisfying, and lonely work. Factory or office work may be dull and tiresome, but there are people around; one can see and be seen, talk and interact, change scenes. One of the worst aspects of housewifing is the awful sense of being locked up with the sameness day after day or, if the woman has a job, evening after evening, weekend after weekend.

Labor to maintain the house itself is not the wife's only responsibility. Besides being responsible for the care of the home, she is also expected to manage the inhabitants of the home—and this really remarkable assignment makes the contemporary wife's role what it is. Most wives have nearly complete responsibility for the care of their children—not only to feed, clothe, and teach them, but also to monitor the quality of their school experience; organize their religious, social, and health needs; provide for child care when parents are not at home; and so on. More to the point, the mother is held responsible for the emotional needs of her children, and it is left very unclear at which point needs become demands. Given current child-centered sensitivities deriving from the warnings of gurus Freud and Spock, no matter how tired or time-pressed they are, many mothers are extremely hesitant to deny their children any demands on their time, privacy, or strength without suffering considerable worry and guilt. In essence, the endless demands of parenting are not shared, and most mothers—working out of the home or not—function for the most part as single parents. Thus, though both men and women have families, women are responsible for the family life.

Care of the inhabitants does not end with children, however, for a wife is also expected to care for her husband in much the same way as she cares for their offspring. She is to feed him, cook his favorite dishes, buy and maintain his clothes, arrange his home to suit him, pack his suitcase when he goes on a trip, arrange entertainment for him on Saturday night, entertain his business friends, arrange doctor's appointments for him (even against his will), listen to him, and support and "understand" him. In some circles a wife is even responsible for the spiritual health of her husband. Priests in some parishes advise that it is sinful for a wife to deny her husband sex lest he be led into temptation outside the home, and Jews believe it to be a wife's duty to provide a living environment for her husband in which he may successfully seek blessings from God.

Whereas a husband's contributions to family maintenance are "public" or communal, much of the wife's work is frequently personal or private, and it is this aspect of her labor, added to the rest, that renders it a form of service (in the sense of a servant). The husband may mow a lawn, repair a door, or dump garbage, tasks pertaining to the household collectively, but he would not be expected to mend his wife's slacks or gauge and replenish her toiletries. In the traditional household, wives render to their husbands a plethora of personal services; the reverse is rarely true.

Wives do not receive a salary for their work although their husbands share their incomes with them, and sometimes generously. But a great deal of difference exists between receiving an established and agreed-upon sum of money in return for one's labor and receiving money as a "gift"—that is, at the giver's choosing. Although wife labor is extensive, time-consuming, often taxing, and absolutely necessary for the household, and although most husbands could not advance professionally or be half so productive without it, wives who do not work outside the home are not perceived as earning; hence, they are considered dependents. Both institutions and individuals regard the money they receive from their husbands as a grant. Therefore, they must endure the disadvantages and indignities of pensioners. Dependent wives are cautioned as to how they are to spend their *husband's* money; they are to express gratitude for sums earmarked for their own personal use (such as clothing), and they must wait until their husbands decide it is time to replace the washer. To put aside savings of their own out of "granted" money is perceived as deceptive and is rarely done, and, as a result, wives can find themselves trapped in intolerable marriages by finances—or their lack thereof.

The cruelest jab in the wife's situation (and one not often recognized) is derogating this labor to the status of non-work. Because our society (unlike some others) affords no economic recognition of housework (such as social security or compensation), because the work is accomplished at home in the service of the family rather than in the public marketplace, and because "women's work" is *always* devalued and demeaned, housework is perceived and treated as non-work, as nonproductive—with all the stigmas and trials the term entails. "Does your wife work?" one might ask. "No, she stays home." "Do you work?" one woman asks another. "No, I'm just a housewife." Even women, housewives themselves, must be reminded that, paid or not, recognized or not, *homemaking is a job.*

The effects of classifying homemaking as non-work are far-reaching and powerful. The full-time housewife or the wife who works as a "supplement" is reduced to a state of financial dependence, which in turn diminishes her power in the family, her own self-image, and her standing in society. The problems, however, go much farther. By allowing herself to be dependent on her husband's income, by accruing little formally recognized history of labor (such as social security benefits or a pension) that could compensate her in later years, and by collecting no savings of her own, a wife makes her future financial security subject to the continuance of her marriage or her husband's goodwill. By reducing herself in the labor force and by not developing or enhancing marketable skills, she further erodes the possibility of financial independence in or out of marriage.

Consider a woman who, after twenty years as a traditional wife, finds herself in an intolerable marriage situation. With dependent children, no savings, a poor-paying job or none at all, and limited marketable skills, what can she do? She may remain trapped and unhappy, or she may leave. Divorced, she then suffers not only the loss of companionship and social status; she must also expect a terribly diminished standard of living, severe strains of economic survival with little experience to withstand them, and no career or professional interests to sustain her. Furthermore, alimony and child support are largely inadequate or nonexistent.[14]

The circumstances of a wife within such a traditional marriage are difficult enough, but in 1989, fewer than 16 percent of families with minor children conformed to this traditional "Leave It to Beaver" model; by 1995, 78 percent of all mothers are expected to be employed.[15] Just as the traditional homemaker often finds herself in a double bind, so the wife who opts for an alternative to dependence by working outside the home may also find herself severely hampered by the non-work status of homemaking. As of 1988, more than 56.5 percent of all married women were doing paid work outside the home. Over 72.5 percent had children between six and seventeen years of age, and 54.5 percent had children under three, with the number steadily rising.[16] Such women share the responsibilities of economic maintenance with their husbands. Do they commonly receive a proportional increase in status, power, privilege, and autonomy? Do they, in return, receive from their husbands equal participation in homemaking efforts? In this country, as in nearly every other in the world, the answer is usually no.

Regardless of circumstances, husbands rarely take equal responsibility for maintaining the household. Research shows that working women spend 2 ½ to 3 times as many hours at housework as their husbands do, and men married to women who work spend the same amount of time on housework as men married to full-time homemakers.[17] Furthermore, in the two-career family, fathers still spend less time with their children than their wives do and even *less* time intensely interacting with them at the end of the day than fathers in traditional families![18] Does time men spend in housework come out of the time they would be spending with their children? Do women have that option?

In the case of the wife working only at home, the logic goes this way: If homemaking is non-work, it is not a job with visible, recognized, and acknowledged demands. The homemaker has no right, therefore, to expect her husband to share in household tasks, for she is "not working," and he is! How can she legitimately expect him to add her responsibilities to his burden? The same logic holds even when the wife is publicly employed. Such a wife actually carries two jobs, a salaried and a nonsalaried one, but since homemaking is not recognized as "work," her two-job status is also not recognized. She merely has certain wifely "responsibilities" at home, and the husband's contributions are usually treated as a gift or favors rather than a rightful responsibility. (He "helps." He "babysits.")

We are familiar with the media images of the (double)-working wife: She must "organize her time" very carefully in order to meet all her responsibilities and not "neglect" her family. Smiling all the while, taking Geritol to maintain her health and her sex appeal, she hurries home from work to get supper on, and spends her evenings and weekends cleaning, washing, using Downy (to get noticed); somehow she also finds time to use sexy perfume and carry on all that follows.

Two jobs, however, are more than taxing. Parenting, cleaning, cooking, shopping, and then working for a salary as well take their toll: Physically, psychologically, and creatively, one runs down. It is a truism in the business and professional world that one cannot produce at peak performance if one is cut in too many ways. For this reason, most institutions have formal prohibitions against moonlighting. Yet moonlighting is a way of life for most married working women or single mothers. Worse, it is never even clear which job is *the* job and which is moonlighting because lots of women never stop to realize that they're handling two full-time jobs simultaneously.

But many women are becoming sensitive to their circumstances. They have begun to recognize that it is a cultural construction and not a cosmic imperative that burdens them with homemaking. They have begun to expect their mates to share the work at home. Many husbands have come to recognize the unfairness, too, and some of them are moving (however grudgingly) toward carrying *some* of the load. Full sharing is painfully rare.

The Emotional Economy

If the fairy tale image of marriage promises women anything, it promises abundant satisfaction of emotional needs. When the prince arrives, he is supposed to bring with him love everlasting, constant attention, affection, devotion, understanding, companionship, appreciation, and, most of all, the desire and wherewithal to make his princess happy. To be sure, a great deal of this fantasy is wrongheaded and ill-conceived. No one can make another person happy, however much he or she might want to, and no one can provide another with complete solace and total understanding. Nor can or should anyone shower another with constant attention. Yet, people still can and do care for one another. Sociologists tend to agree that marriage as an institution survives today primarily because it is seen as providing the major source of caring interactions.

Love, as we know, is an enigmatic idea. Love is different things to different people in varied circumstances, and it is often experienced and expressed in very individual ways. It is not as enduring, dependable, and consistent as it has been reputed to be, nor can it conquer all or justify every kind of action. Yet it would be wrong to lapse into cynicism. However difficult it is to understand or define, however changeable and distorted by myth, love as a concept persists in the human vocabulary. Ample evidence shows that human beings cannot thrive without the kind of succor provided by what is generally called love and that life can be arid and unwholesome without some measure of love's joy.

Certainly, we can glean the intense personal contact that either is or begets love from many different kinds of relationships. However, our society rarely affords us an environment in which such relationships can grow, and we are discouraged rather than encouraged to participate in the kind of encounter crucial to love. Marriage (and living arrangements like marriage), though, does include an expectation that the partners will have at least this: a sharing of communication, concern, and mutual support and an exchange of sensitivity, compassion, and nurture. We can term such sharing and mutuality the emotional economy of the relationship.

For various reasons, all lodged in patriarchy, it is in this exchange that women often experience their greatest disappointment in the traditional relationship. The emotional economy, like the work economy, is out of balance, and once more the woman typically occupies the disadvantaged position. Although women usually express a greater interest in love and emotional exchange and although women are thought to need and want more open expressions of affection, in the patriarchal marriage, women are apt to receive considerably less personal affection than their partners. Despite or because of the high priority women often place on the love relationship, women are more apt to love than be loved, support rather than be supported, nurture rather than be nurtured—even though they appear to seek the exchanges more than men do. The sexist role and character definitions of Venus and Mars decree that women should become more bound up with the behaviors and feelings of interpersonal contact. Ultimately, women become very good at loving, but for the patriarchal male it is a clumsy business at best. In 1971 Shulamith Firestone, one of the founders of the women's liberation movement, wrote in *The Dialectic of Sex:*

> *That women live for love and men for work is a truism. . . . There is also much truth in the cliches that "behind every man there is a woman," and that "women are the power behind [read: voltage in] the throne." (Male) culture was built on the love of women, and at their expense. Women provided the substance of those male masterpieces; and for millennia they have done the work, and suffered the costs, of one-way emotional relationships the benefit of which went to men and to the work of men. . . .*
>
> *Simone de Beauvoir said it: "The word love has by no means the same sense for both sexes, and this is one cause of the serious misunderstandings which divide them." . . . [In] parlor discussions of the "double standard," . . . it is generally agreed: That women are monogamous, better at loving, "clinging," more interested in (highly involved) "relationships" than in sex per se, and they confuse affection with sexual desire. That men are interested in nothing but a screw (Wham, bam, thank you M'am!), or else romanticize the woman ridiculously; that once sure of her, they become notorious philanderers, never satisfied; that they mistake sex for emotion. . . .*
>
> *I draw three conclusions based on these differences:*
>
> 1. *That men can't love. (Male hormones?? Women traditionally expect and accept an emotional invalidism in men that they would find intolerable in a woman.)*
> 2. *That women's "clinging" behavior is necessitated by their objective social situation.*
> 3. *That this situation has not changed significantly from what it ever was.*[19]

Men cannot love? Emotional invalidism? One-way emotional relationships built at women's expense? Are women "better at loving"?

There is a good deal of controversy in the women's movement over whether women do or do not have any special ability for love and feeling. Sexists have used that idea to exclude us from any activity *not* based on serving, *not* based on feeling. But such a division is more patriarchal than rational; the idea that one who is capable of emotion is incapable of discipline or reason is absurd. We need not be afraid to consider whether women's experiences in the world may have developed in us a particular ability to live more lovingly, more considerately. It bespeaks no *undesirable* softness (again, the martial belief that "softness" is contemptible), no lack of intellect or strength.

It appears that women are very much concerned with the human and the loving, and that most of us do exercise an immense ability to nurture and support, a fact of which we may be duly proud. A problem does arise, however, with our concern for caring, because in patriarchy our ability to love can get distorted. Because love and service are prescribed as women's only allowable activities, they are forced out of proportion. Loving can become disproportionate in at least two ways: first, when loving and serving others is not balanced with loving and caring for oneself; and second, when the interests of love are not balanced by other kinds of interests, and indeed crowd out other sources of pleasure, satisfaction, and meaning. Such a situation is destructive, creating an overdependence on the exchanges of love (or some distorted facsimile) and an inability to draw on other resources.

Romance and love are important to men but so are a lot of other things. Woman's prescribed role as subordinate and the prescription that she be passive, dependent, and emotional are at the heart of the saying that love is central for women but peripheral for men; that for women love is abstract, emotional, and spiritual, whereas for men it is concrete, physical, and sexual. In relation to love, women and men move in two different realities, and there is the rub.

Let us look at how the traditional relationship turns the differences in male and female loving into the asymmetry of its emotional economy. Women and men both need love and nurture, although their expression of that need and the way they relate to it may differ. But given traditional female–male role definitions, men are far more likely than women to have that need well satisfied. Women, trained as we are for caring and service, often treat fulfilling another's needs not only as a responsibility or task, but also as something we want to do. We are in a sense assertive about taking the initiative in caring: ferreting out, anticipating, or pursuing the emotional needs of those we love. We want to "help." Just as we might to a child, we often communicate to a lover (although not necessarily in these words), "Let me take care of you, let me 'mother' you."

But if that lover is a traditional man, who is mothering Mother? Trained to see tenderness as effeminate, uncomfortable with feeling in general and need in particular, the traditional male is not usually adept at that aspect of the emotional exchange termed *psychological nurturance.* For men in patriarchy, love is not to be expressed directly, emotionally, on a one-to-one basis, but rather indirectly through providing, modeling, and caring for the family's material well-being. Such indirect provision can be a form of expressing love, but in the traditional division of labor, it is a form of caring in which the woman makes equal, if not greater, contributions. Men work, but women work, too, only their work is not acknowledged. Furthermore, in terms of the emotional economy, a woman's work is considerably more direct, personal, and expressive. She not only prepares food but prepares his favorite food; not only cleans clothes but maintains his personal items in an intimate and personal way; not only listens but hears.

It is often said that men express their most intimate feelings through their sexual lovemaking, and this may be true. One cannot presume to know how often or in what degree this is true. Yet in journals, conferences, workshops, and consciousness-raising groups, women of all ages have revealed that they very often sense a lack of emotional connection with their mates even in sex. Although women and men are both capable of separating love and sex, women are apparently considerably less apt to do so, particularly with their mates.

Yet if there were no qualifications, if it were true that a man typically expresses his love equally, though differently, through providing and through sex, it would still not change the fact of his woman's not receiving adequate emotional support and nurturance. The need for intimate connection in the realm of feeling is profound and important; few can do well without it. The fact is that women report less of this kind of connection, less attention, less direct concern. Great imbalance characterizes the emotional economy of the patriarchal couple.

After-Marriage: Divorce and Widowhood

Few consider as they "walk down the aisle" that marriages often end, either in divorce or in death. Because, in our culture, one is never free of a once-married state but instead is always perceived as a "formerly married person," when a marriage ends, a period of after-marriage follows. This is a time with its own particular character, a time that ends in either remarriage or death. More women than men experience this time because women are more frequently widowed than men, more men than women remarry after widowhood or divorce, and men remarry sooner. Women also experience this time very differently than men do because social attitudes toward the unmarried person, customs (such as dating behavior), and economic circumstances are frequently determined by sex.

The character and quality of one's life and experience in after-marriage are largely determined by the life decisions the partners made earlier. Quite naturally, the seeds sown in marriage continue to be harvested after its end. As we might expect, the woman of a traditional marriage, who has built her life around the prescribed patriarchal model—truncated and distorted as it is—is apt to find her condition similarly truncated and distorted after marriage. Traditional expectations, even for the average working wife, fix a woman's whole identity within her marriage and make her dependent on it in a very profound way; the more traditional the arrangements of the relationship, the more profound the dependence. Passivity, economic or psychological dependence on one's mate, withdrawal from public life, and discouragement from developing resources outside of the couple do not bode well for life; discouragement from developing resources outside the couple is not a good prognosis for life outside of marriage—that is, after-marriage. To live life alone well and happily requires personal strength, preparation, and experience, none of which women in patriarchal marriage are encouraged to develop. Hence, the wife as ex-wife or widow is likely to suffer tremendously at her marriage's end and for some time thereafter, even if she grows considerably, for she has lost valuable time.

Although divorce and widowhood have some fundamental and important differences, in patriarchy these experiences have much in common. A widow and a divorcee are both "once-were wives," having had similar roles and identities in their former lives. They both may be treated as half-beings, anomalies in a universe of couples. They are generally unprepared both economically and psychologically for life alone; and they frequently have the same burdens: children to raise alone, hostility or tolerant contempt from outsiders, and increased responsibilities with decreased resources.

The Feminine Role in Traditional Marriage: A Setup

Generally in our culture a woman marries young, typically in her twenties. Often before or without settling career questions, before becoming independent or self-sufficient, she moves out of her parents' home, or away from her roommates, into the home she shares with her husband. Directly she settles into the wife's role and lifestyle, forming her adult character, norms, and expectations and determining her future through decisions made within the economic and social structures of her marriage.

The Economic Setup

Whether wives work only at home or work both at home and in the marketplace, as is most common, patriarchal marriage will likely cause her to be economically disadvantaged after marriage. If she works only at home, for a large portion of her life parenting and housekeeping are her primary occupations. In such work at home, she accrues neither savings of her own nor salary nor social security benefits nor workmen's compensation nor pension. She develops no special marketable skills, no experience, no work history, no seniority. In the job market, she's worth little or nothing, and the longer she has remained at home, the less she is worth outside.

A traditional wife may work outside the home, especially if her income is absolutely necessary for the family's subsistence, but her salary is generally treated as a supplement to her husband's. Because in the patriarchal context neither mate perceives the wife's job as primary, neither pays much attention to the quality of the job situation, its potential for growth or advancement, its benefits and status in the work world. Even professionally trained women often make decisions that subordinate their careers to the needs of their husbands and families. In one study of dual-career families, for example, where both husbands and wives were working as managers in large corporations, it was found that wives accommodated their careers to those of their husbands, even where both "professed an 'egalitarian' ideology":[20]

> *All of the couples in O'Reilly's sample professed an "egalitarian" ideology. Adherence to such an ideology was prerequisite to participating in the interview. Yet, despite the presence of a philosophy that affirmed the importance of both careers, their behavior as couples clearly furthered husbands' careers at the expense of the wives'. O'Reilly attributes this outcome to a web of factors operating both at home and at work.*
>
> *The web begins with Steihm's[21] observations about "invidious intimacy." Even among highly educated men and women, marriage choices are made such that the man is older, often taller, and perceived to be "smarter." The edge in age, even if the men and women are in the same occupation with the same opportunities (which is frequently not the case), gives the husband more work experience and hence higher earnings than his wife has. If, in addition, the couple believes that the husband's opportunities for promotion are greater than the wife's, which is frequently a correct perception, the couple will seek to maximize their joint income by furthering the career of the husband.*
>
> *O'Reilly found two behavior patterns that favored husbands' careers over wives'. First, in determining whether or not to accept promotions that required geographical moves, couples made decisions that favored husbands' careers, even at the expense of their wives' careers.[22] Second, the pattern of labor division in the home favored the husband's career, especially in families where there were children. Even when husbands participated in housework and child care, wives*

typically fulfilled the time- and energy-consuming role of home manager and also did more of those home tasks that tended to conflict with work.

Like the couples themselves, the corporation that employed at least one member of O'Reilly's couples professed an egalitarian ideology. Equal opportunity policies had long ago abolished formal barriers to women's career progress. But career structures and informal barriers remained. And of course, the more the wife's career progress was slowed, the more "sense" it made for the joining-maximizing couple to favor the husband's career.[23]

Because patriarchy prescribes that the husband's job is more important than the wife's, wives must quit work to follow transferred husbands; wives are the ones who stay home from work to care for sick babies or mate; they accommodate their work around the needs of their families. Such expectations and behaviors do not make for professionalism or the rewards that follow upon it. In essence, during marriage, a husband builds a career, a future, marketable skills, experience, and seniority. But a wife who invests her time, energy, and service in promoting her husband's financial future—mistakenly believing it to be her own—is impoverishing her own earning potential and independent economic security.

A majority of wives work as procurement officers for their households. They shop not only for groceries but also for furniture, household goods, and private and personal needs. For this reason, they often pay the bills, keep the checkbook and the records, and do the banking. Yet, despite claims to the contrary, wives do not "control" the money in the family or the nation, except as delegated. They execute policy; they do not form it. Patriarchal wives may make such decisions as which toilet paper to buy or where to purchase their vegetables (hence their manipulation by advertising media), but they must wait for their husbands to outline the larger budget: how *much* money to spend on food or clothes or mortgage and when to replace an appliance. The intricacies of insurance, long-range planning and budgeting, and investments are generally left to the male in the traditional household.

Furthermore, although the wife may sign the check or the credit card, she usually does so under her husband's name. Until recently (since the successes of the present women's movement), wives could not even have their own charge accounts, and the homemaker without salary still cannot. The result: The wife may accrue little credit of her own; it goes to Mr. and Mrs. X (or, more succinctly, to Mr. X). The bottom line in the economics of the traditional marriage is that when the marriage ends, the wife's "bottom line" is apt to be substantially lower than her husband's.

The Social Setup

One of the really delightful aspects of marriage, when it goes well, is the friendly companionship; the opportunity to talk and do things with one another, interact with others in a kind of community, share in work and play. And yet this very positive facet of the relationship is a two-edged sword; unbalanced by the functioning existence of two separate realms of being for each partner, "togetherness" can be a trap. In patriarchy, the wife usually lacks any separate realm of being.

A traditional wife's lifestyle, made up of the concrete details of her day, is built around her husband. She sleeps with him, rises with him, eats breakfast and dinner with him. She plans her day around him, work and play. Rarely does a traditional wife socialize in mixed company without her husband. Outside of occasional all-female events, socializing occurs in couples: One invites the Smiths and the Joneses for dinner or goes out for an evening with the Browns, two by two. It would be unusual for the typical wife to go to a party by herself, unescorted at least by another couple. She is not likely to travel any distance alone or to vacation or play or dine out or go to a theater by herself—or even with another woman except in rare instances. A traditional married friend of mine laughingly reported that she and her husband were "joined at the hip." In traditional marriage, coupledom reigns.

Such a "togetherness" marriage does not encourage women to develop companionship or buddy relationships with other women or even with men, and it inhibits the growth of a life outside of marriage. In her workplace or at home during the day, with the children and/or her husband in the evening, with couples on the weekend, the traditional wife develops a social existence that is based almost entirely within marriage and the world of couples.

A patriarchal wife's social status and identity, too, are solidly grounded within her marriage. She is

John's wife—John the mechanic, John whose last name (and therefore hers) is Smith, John whose social status (and therefore hers) is X. Her friends are friends of the marriage, attached to the couple collectively, rarely to either individually. These things are more true for a woman in marriage than for a man. It is she who takes on his name and the social standing of his work, she who must live where his work is, she who entertains his business friends or working buddies. It is she, moreover, with all her responsibilities at home, with reduced opportunity for people contact, with little interest in her own job or economic future, who builds her life around the world of her husband, whatever its character and potential.

Feminists often quip, "In marriage two become one, and he's the one!" In the traditional household, this is very nearly so. Imagine the extent of the trauma to a person completely absorbed in a marriage if that union should end.

Denouement: The Experience of After-Marriage

Typically, the patriarchal wife has put all her eggs into one basket. She has built her life around her marriage. How does she find herself at that marriage's end?

The Divorcee

The longer and more traditionally a woman has lived as a patriarchal wife, the more her whole being has adapted itself to one kind of existence, and the harder her transition into and the experience of a new life will be. A great proportion of divorces occur well into marriage, after ten, twenty, even thirty years.

The divorced patriarchal wife is apt to find herself financially strapped. She has probably been left with the house (after all, there are three children who must be sheltered), but maintenance of that home is likely to pose problems. Mortgage payments are usually too high for her salary if she has one (between 60 and 80 percent of former wives do not receive child support or alimony), and she is usually unable to deal with repairs herself. Because she is inexperienced, she must hire maintenance people, usually at exorbitant rates. Perhaps she has been awarded the family car. But how long will it be before it too begins to fail, and how able will she be to replace it and maintain payments?

A job is in order for the former full-time homemaker. But what is she trained for or ready for? Who wants her after ten or twenty years outside the job market? What salary is she likely to earn? If she worked during her marriage at an "auxiliary" job, how likely is her income to supply the entire needs of her family now, if it was only an auxiliary income earlier? If her children are young, she must bear the burden of full-time work and full-time single parenting in the intensely difficult emotional environment of after-marriage. If she is one of the minority of women who receive some financial contributions from their ex-husbands, she must bear the burden of continued dependence, fretful interactions with him, and all the problems that follow from that circumstance.

Responsibility lies heavily on her life. She must meet her children's psychological, financial, and material needs. She must work as sole earner—an alien experience—while maintaining the semblance of a stable home and at the same time dealing with her own sense of loss and anxiety. Altogether too little time, too little money, and too little peace is available to her.

Loneliness closes in. Inexperienced at cultivating friendships, at seeking out and encouraging camaraderie, and uncomfortable with the different modes of interaction in single life, she finds at the same time that her old friends are dropping away. They are couples; she, a single, is no longer part of their world, the world she had with her husband. To the community of couples, the single woman is a pariah—more so the divorcee, because the image she carries is of wantonness and threat. Seeking new relationships, she often finds something different from what she wants. When a women leaves her marriage, she takes on a new image and a new status in male–female encounters. It is assumed that she is "on the prowl," and she often finds herself treated as a sexual mark. A new "meaningful relationship"? The later the divorce, the more limited her range of options are.

Resentful, lonely, frightened, the divorced patriarchal wife has a good deal of building to do. She can do it, many have, but the prescriptions of patriarchy—"femininity," wifely subordination, and social discrimination—make this an intensely difficult challenge.

The Widow

Much that is true of the divorcee also fits the widow. Just as financially limited,[24] thrust into loneliness and new responsibilities, the widow discovers she has lost more than a husband. She has lost status and identity as well. No longer a part of a couple, she too becomes a pariah in her singleness, intensified as it is by the stigma of death that she is perceived to carry. Friends who were so kind "at the end" drift away, embarrassed by her grief, uncomfortable with her new condition as not quite whole.

Living With Oneself

Women have two alternatives: married or ________. What's the other term—unmarried, single? In our society each of these terms has the ring of "wrongness," *Unmarried* is clearly the negative of married, which is the norm, the "natural" and acceptable and positive state in our society. *Single* implies that there must be a double. The wrongness of the terms is the wrongness assigned to the state, and I cannot find a term in our language for the unmarried state in women (*bachelor* is male) that does not carry with it a stigma.

It would be better, feminists believe, to think of the matter in a wholly different way. The crucial question (although our culture would disagree) is not whether we are married or unmarried or aftermarried, but whether we are whole or not whole, whether we are living fully and well or not. If we can be successful at living *with* ourselves, then the matter of whether or not we live *by* ourselves becomes secondary (though not unimportant). The ability to function well and happily with oneself and for oneself, encouraged to some extent in men, is discouraged in women in patriarchy. Self-sufficient, viable women do not make good servants. They make happier people, however, and, should they choose, better companions.

Living well, achieving peace and what happiness may be afforded, requires many hard-earned qualities: personal strength, courage, discipline, balance, perspective, endurance, humor, compassion, and intelligence. It requires a sense of self-worth, a sense of the integrity and inviolability of one's own being, a sense of pride. It requires self-awareness and understanding. It requires preparation, training, and experience, the wherewithal to use one's power for one's advantage in whatever circumstances one finds oneself. It requires a commitment made to the self to live well, to choose life for its own sake. When a person comes to see that there is good in the experiencing of life, that there is joy in doing what is personally meaningful, then that person is prepared to live with herself, alone or in company. When one keeps in mind that ultimately we walk quite by ourselves in this life, that for many reasons other people and other circumstances come and go, that we must always depend first on ourselves to meet our needs, emotional or material, then one does not relinquish one's power or safety into another's keeping.

A woman, as well as a man, must foster and maintain her own personal integrity and viability whatever her circumstances or relationships and however much she may love another or commit herself. In that case, she does not, as a female, take upon herself any greater risks than are already presented to women quite naturally by life and society, but rather she diminishes them and greatly increases the likelihood of happiness. A woman so described—independent, capable, viable—may not be the darling of patriarchy. She may find herself out of step with many and even rejected by some. But she is far more a person, more fully able to relate to those who would accept her, more likely to contribute to her whole community. Besides, the alternative is self-destructive.

Our Bodies: Negotiable Chattel

With few exceptions, the history of ideas has rarely given much consideration to the way one relates to one's own body in the formation of self-image. Possibly because of masculist fear of sensuality and feelings or because men as a class have so long had control over their own bodies as well as ours, "intellectuals" (until very recently) have given the subject short shrift. Nonetheless, our bodies are the material representations of our selves, both to others and to ourselves. On many levels, from the superficial (such as the way we dress) to the deeply profound (such as the way we encounter and treat our own decay), the attitudes directed toward our bodies often determine how we see other aspects of ourselves. The relationship between our physical selves and our psychosocial selves is very close.

If we look, we can see many examples that show the importance to self-image of control over one's body and its needs. One of the first and most compelling forms of control the military exercises over new recruits, one that molds them into obedience and dependence, is the control over their physical selves, through appearance (in dress and hair), through management of body functions (eating, sleeping, elimination), and through providing for bodily needs (from medical treatment to cigarettes). It has been reported that one of the major factors in breaking the resistance of victims in Nazi concentration camps was the removal of their clothing and their subjection to other physical humiliations. To a lesser extent, the same thing is true in prisons. Studies in the psychology of nursing and hospital care point out that a patient's loss of control over the care of her or his own body, apart from the illness itself, often leads to a reduced sense of health and well-being; as a result, patients are encouraged as soon as possible to meet as many of their own physical needs as they can. Nowhere, of course, can we more clearly see the close relationship between body control and confident, independent maturity than in the development of children. With each new step toward meeting physical needs, with each step away from control through physical discipline, the child grows in independence.

But in patriarchy, in our world, it is the class of men as a whole, and not women, who wield power over the circumstances and exigencies of women's physical selves. Because of this, women can be reduced to the status of dependent children. Through the institutionalization of masculine authority—in medicine, education, politics, communication, and law enforcement—and through brute power, men have obtained for themselves the use, maintenance, even "protection" of women's bodies. Until conditions change, women are in the childlike position of seeking out the *pater* for the satisfaction of physical needs and for the disposition of our bodies.

Appearance

Let us begin with something that might seem superficial (but is not): our appearance. We saw in Chapter 4 that women are taught very early that the way we come into this world is not the way we ought to remain. Unlike men, who are expected to groom and reorder themselves in small ways, we are pressed to conform significantly to whatever the current ideal is of feminine physical attractiveness. Who sets the standards of female beauty? Certainly not women; properly conditioned and prodded, we avidly acquiesce to the entire business of "beauty" to gain the patriarchs' approval.

It is men who determine not only how we must behave but also how we must present ourselves. Through fashion, through law, through "science" or religion, we are told how we ought to appear. The bound foot, the pierced ear and nose, the covered head or face, the enormous breast, the excised clitoris, the never-too-thin torso—are these ours? The near nakedness of jeans and bathing suits, the oppressive discomfort of spiked heels or garter belts; the obsession with youth, size, "sexiness"—are any of these ours? Do we do this to please ourselves? It is men who design fashions and control the media, the advertising, the magazines, the films, the cosmetic firms, and the department stores, and who ultimately manipulate women into believing that it is we who set the trends.

It is difficult in a society so controlled by men for us to distinguish between what we think and feel genuinely, freely, and what we think and feel as accommodation to social expectation. We "love" the little bikini that leaves us practically undressed, but do we love it because it is a joyous expression of self or do we love it because it draws approval from men? What is that suit meant to accomplish? What do we have to do to our physical selves over the long term to look in that suit the way we are required to look—diet, starve, guard our movements?

We are told that today the average woman would like to lose 10 or 15 pounds, even when she is not objectively "overweight"; that fashion models weigh 23 percent less than the average woman (as opposed to 8 percent less a generation ago); that 20 to 25 percent of college women suffer from severe eating disorders; that according to the federal Centers for Disease Control "nearly half of all teen-age girls are on diets, even though the majority of them are not overweight"; that an astonishing number of young girls and women rely upon diet pills, vomiting, and other destructive strategies to control their weight.[25]

What would happen if we chose *not* to wear that little bikini but instead selected a swimsuit for comfort? Would we have to choose between approval and autonomy? What is the significance of that? What does it tell us? Why do we choose as we do?

To adorn one's body out of a *self-defined* love of play and color may be self-expressive and healthy. To reject one's natural self and instead subject it to the requirements of an *alien* mold created by a separate reigning group for their interests, to surrender one's physical appearance for another's approval and protection—this is destructive because it is too terribly close to surrendering one's entire sense of self. "I am, physically and nonphysically, who I am" is authentic. "I am and will become what the gaze of another wishes me to be, no matter what the cost" is fatally close to spiritual suicide. It may also be fatally close to physical suicide, captured nowhere more dramatically than in the growing willingness of women to submit to cosmetic surgery. Following the congressional hearings on the silicone implant industry and the consequences of breast reconstruction for women's health, Merle Hoffman, editor of *On the Issues,* wrote:

> *It appears that having a potentially fatal disease like breast cancer and being small breasted or flat chested have taken on the same life and death proportions to many women. While one can empathize with the ambivalence of the women on the panel who had to make choices about whether or not to allow one class of women to potentially risk their health and lives to have breast reconstruction, one also has to question the reality that women so eagerly make life-threatening decisions to fit someone else's definition of being sexually acceptable—an external definition that has been integrated into their own psychologies. . . . It was a purely democratic decision, one which said that all women should have the right to make the wrong choices for the wrong reasons. . . .*
>
> *It was a decision that in one sweeping move reinforced and imprinted once again that women were defined, judged and found wanting or acceptable according to the size of their breasts. The women on the panel who so agonized over disqualifying the implants for purely cosmetic reasons seemed not to give a thought to the system, culture or society that spawned these ideas in the first place, that created the need and the market for women to desire reconstructed breasts even at the risk of their own lives. The fact that these decisions on implants are made more for internal rather than external approval only reinforces the insidious nature of the conditioning.*[26]

Health

When children are troubled with physical ailments, they must seek out their guardians for help. So must women. Because relatively few women set or control health-care policy (a situation deftly arranged by patriarchy), when we are ill or face physical changes and "passages," *by law* and by custom we must turn to those formally charged with our care—for the most part, men. Consider how absurd and humiliating men would think it if they had to ask women for assistance whenever they had a urinary disorder, a dysfunction of the penis, or a sexual or reproductive problem! In any sane world, such exclusively female events as pregnancy and childbirth would be women's province. Yet in our world it is men, through such agencies as the American Medical Association (AMA) and the American Hospital Association (AHA), insurance companies, and legislatures, who determine almost entirely how these experiences are to proceed: where and how, for example, we may give birth, what procedures will be followed, who may accompany us, who may assist. Women, at home or in clinics, may not legally contribute even informally in these affairs unless they are licensed by male-controlled agencies of various kinds.

Research into female medical needs, into surgical techniques and drug therapy for a variety of female experiences from menopause to depression, is carried on almost exclusively by males with the aid and support of the giant (male-dominated) research and grant agencies. Under policy written by men, male physicians develop, prescribe, and test contraceptives for women and may withhold them if they choose. They research and develop policy and procedures for treating conditions of the breast, uterus, and ovaries (no wonder so many of them wind up in jars!); they write theories about women's attitudes during menopause and debate the use of estrogen therapy or tranquilizers. They inform their patients that severe menstrual cramping is a problem of the mind. They tell women how to mother children. Now they manipulate women's reproductive systems to make babies in test tubes and create parents or transfer parenthood from one to another or "modify" results for more control over the process.

Through entrance into medical schools, licensing, lobby, and legislation, patriarchy limits the participation and authority of women in health care—hence, over our own care. Historically the AMA and AHA have fought any growth of power and prestige in the nursing associations. Now men are being encouraged to join the nursing profession to "raise the level of the profession," and, in passing, to capture the more highly skilled and highly paid positions in hospital nursing programs and in the American Nursing Association.

Control over our reproductive and medical needs is exacerbated by masculist-masculine control over the law. Women have little power in the making of policy because, as you will see in the following chapter, we are systematically excluded from anything like full participation in government. Legal policy regarding reproduction, contraception, abortion, and illegitimacy is written, interpreted, and executed essentially by men upon the advice and perspectives of "scientists" (men) and in response to their (most powerful and wealthy) constituencies (insurance companies, for example, or drug companies, legal associations, and political action committees, or PACs), which have the inclination and wherewithal to make substantial contributions to campaigns and administrations.

In matters of health and reproduction, almost more than anywhere else, women as "other" are objectified, reduced to "things," denied our own interests, and robbed of our personhood. In the current intense interest in women's reproductive lives, we are increasingly being treated as "delivery systems" of the young. The treatment of Jennifer Clarise Johnson, single mother and cocaine addict, is a perfect case in point.

> *SANFORD, Fla.—A judge has opened a new avenue for the criminal prosecution of cocaine-using mothers by finding a woman guilty of delivering the drug to her newborn children through the umbilical cord.*
>
> *The decision Thursday marks the first time in the nation that a law normally used against drug dealers has been applied to a mother giving birth, a legal expert said. It applies only to the Florida judicial circuit where the woman lives, but could be applied by prosecutors in other jurisdictions, even outside Florida.*[27]

Johnson was sentenced to thirty years in prison under a law making it a felony to deliver drugs to a minor. The prosecutor, delighted with his "new tool" for solving this "great problem," centered the matter on the issue of whether newborns may be considered persons after birth and before the umbilical cord is cut. The judge decided that they may and that "delivery" could mean passing cocaine to a fetus through the umbilical! A nice argument. Never mind that the woman has a serious and viciously difficult health problem. Never mind that the woman did not intend to pass drugs to her offspring, nor does she profit from it. Never mind that the law was not meant to cover such a case or that this interpretation of the law involves a most extraordinary use of the term *deliver.*

Johnson—poor, powerless, female, a "delivery system" gone wrong—is now incarcerated in a drug treatment center apart from her children, who are being raised by someone else, and denied her place and her desire to "mother." In a television interview, the prosecutor said that he saw this as a case of child abuse, pure and simple, *no different* from the intentional beating or burning of a child. How are men treated when they *do* abuse children? Are they typically given thirty-year prison sentences, whether they be drunk or sober? How are male athletes treated when they become addicted to drugs?What does the difference in treatment say about the way (the male) judge and prosecutor view women, as childbearers, as mothers (quite a different concept), and as selves—as individual, independent human persons?

Abortion

The matter of reducing women to "delivery systems," of ignoring the fact that women are people, with needs, feelings, goals, values, even when we are reproducing, is a crucial concept, for it is the heart of the antiabortion issue. It is that, the erasing of our personhood, together with a similar but opposite logical maneuver—the elevation of a fetus to the status of a "person"—that makes the antichoice campaign work. It is what makes the rhetoric so effective, even though it is often false and generally misleading. It is what drives the slogans and makes them appear convincing to the unpracticed eye: "Abortion is murder!" screams a highway sign. But murder is defined as the "illegal killing of one human being by another, especially with premeditated malice" (*Webster's II New Riverside University*

Dictionary). If a fetus is *not* a human being—that is, a fully existent person (regardless of whether it is a potential person)—then murder is a misleading term. And if the intention of a woman choosing to abort a pregnancy is to care for her life, her happiness, her well-being (and in some cases the well-being of her present and future family and children), then it is not malevolence that is motivating her, and malice has nothing to do with her choice. In other words, there is very good reason to think that abortion is not at all murder, and the slogan is a lie. "It is a baby, not a choice!" reads a popular bumper sticker. Leaving aside the grammatical games being played here, this slogan too lies. Between the mass of tissue that is a fetus and a living, breathing, experiencing *baby,* there is a world of difference. There are very thoughtful and moral people who believe that *it* is not a baby. What is more, of course, there is a choice to be made—by the woman, by the person in the equation who has been erased. Put her back into the picture, and either choice is a legitimate consideration, or motherhood by coercion is the only logical end. There are more complex issues in the question of abortion than the great majority of the antichoice contingent want anyone to think about; but think we must, for the reality is critical to women's lives.

> *As a nation, we are being asked to deny women the fundamental right to control their own bodies. We are being asked to reformulate a major policy that has broad social consequences. We are being asked to return to a time when women got abortions from motorcycle mechanics and dishwashers. . . .*
>
> *Dr. Kinsey found that in 1955, when abortion was almost entirely illegal, almost one in four American women had had an abortion by the time she was forty-five. By 1992, nineteen years after* Roe, *more than twenty-four million American women had had legal abortions in their own country and often in their own hometown. An even greater number of women have come of age, in a biological sense, since 1973. For the most part, they have no knowledge of what abortion was like when it was against the law.*
>
> *Many of today's legislators and policymakers were not old enough to hold office or perhaps even to vote in the years before* Roe. *When these newcomers formulate abortion policy, they often have no idea what abortion was like in the United States before 1973. How many of them know the barbaric and dangerous techniques of the abortion underground? How many know about the untold millions of women who terminated their pregnancies by whatever means available for reasons known only to them? How many know about the sheer numbers of women who died from illegal abortions? How many know anything at all about the public health consequences of recriminalizing abortion? Indeed, how many understand that the real public policy question is not* whether *we will have abortions but* what kind *of abortions we will have?*
>
> –PATRICIA G. MILLER, The Worst of Times[28]

For the most part, the abortion debate is characterized by more smoke than light. The most vocal antiabortion activists have tended to deflect reasonable discussion by focusing on issues that are either already apparent but moot, for the most part irrelevant, but extremely inflammatory: Of course life exists at conception; cells are alive. Of course the fetus is *human* life; it certainly isn't canine or vegetable. But isn't it reasonable to ask whether it is *a* human life; that is, is it a person? Does it think, know, remember, make decisions, relate to others, and all the hundreds of things that persons do that constitute them as persons? A tumor is a lump of human life. Is it morally sinful to remove it from its host? A fetus is a *potential* individual, but there is a great deal of difference between a potential individual and an actual one. A human ovum is a potential human being. Am I guilty of murder every time I have my period and do not assist this egg to become an actual life by having it fertilized?

Does a potential human being become a person simply by fiat, by creating a fiction, labeling it a baby or a child (as opposed to determining if it is a baby or a child), and granting this fiction all the legal and moral rights of personhood, *all the rights denied the mother?* As women, we must ask, why is the mother less worthy of society's protection than an alleged or potential "baby"? Because she is a woman? Why is that same potential baby, carried to term, born and alive, less worthy of protection than it was in the womb? Why is all the clamor directed at a woman's completing a pregnancy but not then sustained in regard to the feeding, sheltering, and aiding of that child and its mother? The great majority of America's poor, homeless, and desperate are women and their dependent children. To be substantively "pro-life"—that is, *for life*—wouldn't one need to actively care for such people? Where are their "rescuers"?

Here in St. Louis, where the anti-abortion movement is one of the strongest in the nation, the infant mortality rate ranks among the highest in the industrialized world—and for each white infant who dies two black infants die. Although many doctors sign the anti-abortion ads each year, I could not find an obstetrician to care for a homeless refugee woman with a complicated pregnancy who wanted her baby. There has been no demand by the heavily funded Missouri "pro-life" movement for improved prenatal care, no outrage at the decline in health-clinic services for the poor. . . .

Here in Missouri, a mother with two children receives $282 maximum AFDC cash income, $228 maximum in food stamps. Even if she is lucky enough to have subsidized housing (and thus receive fewer benefits) she is poor, and she and her children are more likely to be ill, malnourished and badly educated than their middle-class peers.

Here in Missouri, one-fourth of the children who begin high school do not graduate, and one out of every five children lives at the poverty level. . . .

Where are the thousands of marchers, led by bishops, when Emerson Electric and McDonnell Douglas and General Dynamics hold their annual meetings here to proclaim the money they have made from the arms industry? . . .

My own fear, based on signs I have seen carried at demonstrations, is that many anti-abortion activists see birth as a punishment for sex, not as a gift.

–MARY ANN MCGIVERN[29]

In a series on "The Changing American Family" in Missouri, the home state of the Webster case, the *St. Louis Post Dispatch* told the story of Dawn Smith and her infant son, Benjamin. Abandoned by her boyfriend early in her pregnancy, with no place of her own to live, not yet out of business school, she was "at the point where if I couldn't talk to someone about my situation, I would explode." A Baptist crisis pregnancy center gave her a "sympathetic ear, a few baby care items," and a companion through delivery. When she went home after the delivery, however, "reality set in":

The phone had been disconnected because of a mix-up over her last payment. Instead of spending the next few weeks recuperating from childbirth and getting to know her son, Smith spent the time settling bills, finding a baby sitter, hauling laundry and checking out social programs that might provide them with help. . . .

"By the time he was 3 weeks old, I was out of money. Completely out," Smith said. Although she had hoped to take a six-week maternity leave from her job, she was forced to return to work Feb. 13 (the leave had paid her only $50 a week). Benji was 33 days old.

. . .

"I cried all the way to work, and I cried all day," Smith said. "When I left that day, I wanted to drive 90 miles per hour to get home."

. . .

Smith now spends all of her free time with her baby. "There are 10 hours a day that I'm not with him, and I worry that some day when I go to pick him up he'll want to stay with the baby sitter instead of come with me," she said. "I want to spend all my time holding and loving him, but there are also times when I'm so tired that I just want him to go to sleep."

. . .

The $672 Smith takes home each month barely covers her fixed bills—$295 for rent, $150 for a baby sitter, $90 for electricity, $25 for telephone service, and $13.20 for water. There's little left for food, gas and diapers, and nothing to make a dent in her outstanding bills—$200 for electricity, $250 for a 12-year-old car, $700 for past medical treatment and more than $7,000 for school loans.

. . .

On the day she was interviewed, Smith had $35 to her name, $32 of which was needed to pay a bill. For the second week in a row, she had been unable to buy groceries. Her refrigerator contained a jar of jelly, a frozen pizza and some stale doughnuts bought for 25 cents a box. Besides baby formula, her pantry held a box of tea bags, a jar of peanut butter, a jar of honey, a box of crackers and two cans of green beans. Payday was 13 days away.[30]

Somehow, after the delivery, when reality set in, the "helpers" were gone.

For several years and with growing intensity, the antifeminist, antichoice advocates have thrown up a smoke screen against their very real issues: control over women's lives, our self-determination, our right to make decisions for ourselves, and our personal, economic, and social destinies. The issue for me as a women is not simply whether I carry a pregnancy to term, but whether I wish to bear and raise a child. For whether I raise a child or give it up, whether it is healthy or damaged, whether it is loved or not, that child changes my personal life in dramatic and permanent ways. Who is to decide, besides myself, whether I shall lend my life to those changes? On what moral grounds do I make that decision? Who besides myself should have the right to do that?

Since 1973, when abortion was legalized through Roe v. Wade, *the anti-abortion movement has worked to limit the ability of women to "choose" abortion. These efforts became part of a larger backlash which opposed gains made in the late 1960s and early 1970s by the women's liberation movement. Legalized abortion was fought for and won by that movement as part of a new and comprehensive vision of women's potential. In the 1970s and 1980s, abortion came to symbolize that vision as the New Right, driven by anti-feminism, made opposition to abortion the centerpiece of its own social and political program. The attack on abortion was part of an overall attack on women's freedom. This included a successful campaign to defeat the Equal Rights Amendment; efforts to constrain the rights of teenage girls through "Squeal Laws" which would force providers to notify parents if a minor sought contraception or a pregnancy test; the "Chastity Bill," which provided 30 million federal dollars to promote chastity among teens; gutting of affirmative action programs; and, most recently, efforts to control women's behavior during pregnancy by incarceration and other punitive measures.*

In both the propaganda and policies of the Right, hostility to women's autonomy is the unifying link between opposition to abortion and opposition to other feminist goals. Abortion rights are central to and have come to symbolize women's control. The Right opposes that control in the broadest sense. That is why they oppose sex education, government-funded contraception and family planning clinics, gay rights, and government programs directed at the battering of women and children within their homes. But their fight against abortion is the most virulent, and they have made real gains.

–MARLENE GERBER FRIED, *From Abortion to Reproductive Freedom*[31]

Perhaps the most important gain that the anti-abortion, antiwoman forces have made is to push the discussion about abortion off-center. Women have begun to speak in whispers where once we shouted for the right to determine our destinies. Even feminists, even prochoice activists can be heard to say, "Well, of course, abortion is a terrible thing, but it's better than . . ." or "Sometimes it's necessary," or "It is the better of two terrible choices." Once we say yes, of course abortion is terrible, we have conceded the question, for expediency is not a sufficient moral counter to evil. In fact, there are good reasons to think that abortion is not terrible, not merely expedient. There are many reasonable, ethical people who believe that although abortion may be emotionally trying, it can be a most positive, moral, life-loving choice.

From time immemorial women have risked their lives, have placed themselves in the most dreadful of situations when they felt it was necessary, and moral, to secure an abortion. I don't think we should ever believe that these women will allow themselves to be denied abortions by people who do something as simple as get arrested in front of clinics. Prochoice opponents need to be told that in no uncertain terms. Indeed their actions are remarkably trivial when they are weighted against the courage and decency and dedication and tenacity of women who need this service and persevere to get it.

As you reflect on this phenomenon, try to envision Operation Rescue's antecedents. The exponents of Operation Rescue compare themselves to U.S. civil rights demonstrators of the 1960s, but they don't summon a positive picture for me. Instead, I see a group of school children trying to enter a school in the South, and I see two lines of people, adults, mothers and fathers, on either side of those children. There are people screaming, people hating, people with meanness and ruthlessness in their faces screaming at little children who want to enter a school and exercise the right to a quality, equal education. If we want to use the comparison of the civil rights movement, the comparison is very simple. Screaming people do not parallel the civil rights activists who were trying to exercise their rights; these screamers today parallel those zealots who were trying to prevent other citizens from exercising rights they legitimately held.

I think these are the images we need to keep before us: images of women willing to do whatever necessary to secure needed abortions; images of women acting unselfishly and with as much compassion as possible. They are courageous images that clearly contrast with pictures of individuals who are prepared to force or coerce others into following their ways and their visions of righteousness.

–FRANCES KISSLING, "Operation Rescue," in *Conscience: A Newsjournal of Prochoice Catholic Opinion*[32]

What is the proper response to those who would rob us of our right to choose? To those filled with hate and the need for power, the answer is obvious. For those whose arrogance is born of a belief in their own right to speak for God, the clearest rebuke would be to require them to look at their own hidden needs:

"Rescue" Activist Speaks

Twenty-five-year-old Mary Ann Baney is on the staff of Operation Rescue (OR) in Binghamton, New York. A Pittsburgh native, Baney has been active in the antiabortion movement since September, 1987. After hearing Randall Terry speak at a rally, she says, she was moved to activism. "I agreed with him that we have to act like abortion is murder. We have to do something."

Her first involvement took her to Cherry Hill, New Jersey, OR's first "rescue" site, a practice run for the week-long assault on New York City clinics that took place in May, 1988. "I saw men and women coming to kill their children," says Baney. "I cared about them and their children. Out of love for them, and obedience to God, I sat down. I know murder is against God's commandments."

Baney found her participation empowering. "It was the most valuable thing I ever did. It took courage to sit down. But I know one couple who changed their minds and had the baby; a boy was born a few months ago. He would not have been alive without that 'rescue'."

Raised Catholic, Baney is now part of the Roman Catholic Charismatic Renewal movement. "In a sense it's like being born again," says Baney. "I'm spirit filled."

After the Cherry Hill protest—at which 211 Operation Rescue members were arrested—Baney returned to Pittsburgh and helped form a local OR group there. Then in May she spent a week doing daily "rescues" in New York City. This was followed by participation in two "rescues" in Philadelphia. "The week before July 19, the start of the Democratic Convention in Atlanta, I was laid off by the lawn care company I worked for. Since I was free, I went to Atlanta and ended up spending 36 days in jail for protesting abortion. It was one of the highlights of my life. I grew so much spiritually because I was doing God's will. It was so valuable. I felt a great sense of doing something worthwhile."

Baney says she was particularly impressed by the sense of community forged during her month-long incarceration. "God moved in the jail. The pastors all worshipped together. As the group got smaller we were moved in with the other inmates and we shared the love of God with them. God's presence changed the jail to a place of peace and love." (OR members were released from prison when they gave the authorities their real names and addresses. Most identified themselves to police as Baby Jane or Baby John Doe when they were initially arrested. OR staffer Marti Hendrickson told me that this alias was used to allow participants to "take a stand on behalf of the unborn; to be their voice and show that we won't let any more babies be murdered.")

Baney started working with OR full-time upon her release from jail. There's nothing, she says, that she'd rather be doing. Single and childless, she sees herself as part of a generation that has come to its senses, the generation that came of age in the 1980s and "found out the hard way about love and values. Many of my friends wish they'd remained pure, waited till marriage to have intercourse," she says. "They now know that they are to obey God, rather than men. They read the Bible and know that they are to render to God things that are God's. These children we "rescue" are the children of God. It's God's will."[33]

Apparently such absolute belief justifies arson and chemical attacks, physical and verbal harassment, stalking of pregnant women, medical workers, and their families, and now even murder. A student in one of my ethics courses told the class that he'd like to "shake the hand of the guy that murdered that doctor in Florida." He was that prolife! And what's more he didn't want to talk about it any more. He was sick of the whole thing. (!)

The matter of abortion is extremely complex, both ethically and legally, and the reasonable arguments both for and against (and there are reasonable arguments both for and against) are numerous and complicated. The following three points are crucial: First, in determining the matter of abortion laws and statutes, Supreme Court decisions, and constitutional amendments, we must take great care to distinguish legal rights and responsibilities from what we perceive to be moral obligations. Many acts one might wish performed or not performed, on moral or ethical grounds, cannot and should not be compelled or prohibited by law. Second, we must pay attention to the matter of consistency. People not actively or even ideologically opposed to killing real adult human beings in war or by capital punishment are clamoring for laws against killing a fetus. People little concerned with the quality of the ensuing life of either mother or child are determined to maintain the biological life. Although it is fallacious to attack an argument on the basis of who proposes it, in ethics the question of motivation is always pertinent. Third, it is valuable to place the issue of reproductive freedom into historical context. Strong analogies exist between the reproductive freedom movement of today and the movement in the 1930s to legalize the prescription, use, and sale of contraceptives. Those in favor argued, as today, on the grounds of constitutionality, personal freedom, the quality of life for all, and the benefits of population control to society. Then, as now, their opponents accused them of immorality, murder (of future generations), opposition to God's will, and the destruction of the family and the social order.

Sexuality

The matter of women's sexuality is a many-faceted topic, rarely treated either sanely or seriously outside of women's studies. Yet in the analysis of our life space, our sexuality is an extremely important issue. It is ironic, as well as indicative of the role we play in a patriarchal society, that the aspect of our nature that is considered definitive of us by the male hegemony is also the aspect of ourselves from which we are commanded to be the most alienated.

In Chapter 3 we saw that, except for our role as Mother and Caretaker (procreator or nurturer), our only function in patriarchy is to serve as sexual Playmate. In the patriarchal environment, we are submerged in that guise. Our clothing is designed, our movements are trained, and our behavior is coached to be seductive. And yet, though sex and appearing "sexy" is a prescribed part of the curriculum, for women the enjoyment of sex or sensuality, the use of sex to women's own ends, has been prohibited.

The women's movement has argued that in patriarchy women are all reduced to the status of "sex objects." That does not mean simply that we are sometimes the object of sexual interest or desire (which we all, on some occasion, might wish to be) but that we are formally perceived and treated as objects for sex, sex-things. Unlike a human being, a thing is not thought to have feelings, needs, and rights because a thing is not thought of as a subjectivity, as a self.

In patriarchy, women in our sexual roles are to function ideally not as self-affirming, self-fulfilling human beings but rather as beautiful dolls to be looked at, touched, felt, experienced for arousal, used for titillation (for sexual release or the sale of merchandise), to be enjoyed, consumed, and ultimately used up and traded in for a different model thing. We may respond to sexual contact or even enjoy it, but not for our own pleasure (only bad women are selfish), only for the greater pleasure of the user. Our sexual role in patriarchy is to be acted upon, not to act ourselves, except insofar as this serves the users' interest or needs.

Full sexuality and sensuality are utterly conscious and healthily self-centered as well as other-centered. As long as we accept the patriarchal image of women as copulating machines, as long as we allow ourselves to be washed, perfumed, painted, and dressed, playing a part, totally selfless, we will experience alienation in sex and alienation from our bodies. In patriarchy, women are objectified, passive, and self-abnegating, but authentic functioning sexuality is subjective, forceful, and self-affirming.

We may have much to learn from lesbian love and sex. As women loving women because they are women, lesbians point out that they are in a special position with regard to liberating female sexuality. Free of the heterosexual politics of the usual gender-based roles and prescriptions, more positive and self-affirming as women, more acutely aware of the needs of their partners because, in a sense, they are their partners, lesbian women contend that they are more able to discover and express authentic female sexuality than their heterosexual counterparts. Although lesbian couples share the conflicts of any two people in an intimate relationship, the experiences of many lesbian couples have valuable implications for creating nonexploitive relationships.

Violence

Canadian novelist Margaret Atwood once asked a male friend why men feel threatened by women. He replied: "They are afraid women will laugh at them." She then asked a group of women why they felt threatened by men. They answered: "We're afraid of being killed."

–JANE CAPUTI AND DIANA E. H. RUSSELL[34]

The right of men to control the female body is a cornerstone of patriarchy. . . . There is a different kind of terrorism, one that so pervades our culture that we have learned to live with it as though it were the natural order of things. Its targets are females—of all ages, races and classes. It is the common characteristic of rape, wife battery, incest, pornography, harassment, and all forms of sexual violence. I call it sexual terrorism *because it is a system by which males frighten and, by frightening, control and dominate females.*

–CAROL J. SHEFFIELD[35]

Rape is the logical outcome if men act according to the "masculine mystique" and women act according to the "feminine mystique."

–DIANNE HERMAN[36]

Man's discovery that his genitalia could serve as a weapon to generate fear must rank as one of the most important discoveries of prehistoric times. . . . I believe rape has played a critical function. It is nothing more or less than a conscious process of intimidation by which all men *keep* all women *in a state of fear.*

–SUSAN BROWNMILLER[37]

Woman abuse is viewed here as an historical expression of male domination manifested within the family and currently reinforced by the institutions, economic "arrangements," and sexist division of labor within capitalist society.

–SUSAN SCHECHTER[38]

Violence against wives—indeed, violence against women in general—is as old as recorded history, and cuts across all societies and socioeconomic groups. There are few phenomena so pervasive and yet so ignored.

–LORI HEISE[39]

Male survivors charge that feminists see rape as a "man vs. woman" issue, emphasizing the central role male violence plays in stunting and destroying women's lives, and they're right. The distinction is that while many women, and some men, are victimized by rape, all women are oppressed by it, and any victimization of women occurs in a context of oppression most men simply do not understand. Rape for men is usually a bizarre, outrageous tear in the fabric of reality. For women, rape is often a confirmation of relative powerlessness, of men's contempt for women, and its trauma is reinforced every day in a thousand obvious and subtle ways.

–FRED PELKER[40]

There is no question within the women's movement that we live in a society permeated by male violence and that a great deal of that violence is directed against women.

Facts:

In 1987, 91,111 rapes were reported to law enforcement agencies in the United States.[41]

One rape is reported every six minutes.[42]

Only one out of every ten rapes is reported.[43]

According to *Uniform Crime Reports,* published by the F.B.I., one in four women are raped. One in ten rape victims brings charges. Of the cases that are reported, only 20 percent make it to court. Half of these lead to a conviction (D.C. Rape Crisis Center). In the end, an estimated 97 to 98 percent of all rapists go free. Most rape again. Men who are caught have committed, on average, 14 rapes. Nor is a conviction any guarantee that they'll stop. Convicted rapists have one of the highest recidivism rates of any class of criminals.[44]

One in three females will be sexually assaulted by age eighteen, about 70% by men they know.[45]

Reported in the higher education section of *What Counts: The Complete Harper's Index,* 35 percent of male college students say they might commit rape if there were no chance of being caught. 84 percent say that some women look as though they're just asking to be raped.[46]

Nearly 20 percent of all American women were sexually abused as children. In cases of incest, nine times out of ten, the victim is a girl. The first sexual abuse generally occurs at age ten—although 37 percent report abuse at an even earlier age. Approximately 70 percent of young prostitutes and 80 percent of female drug users were victims of incest.[47]

Within the next decade, 25 million girls will be sexually abused, half of them under the age of eleven.[48]

Bureau of Justice figures show approximately 456,000 cases of domestic violence per year more than half committed by a spouse or ex-spouse. It is estimated that only one case in ten is reported.[49]

In the United States, a woman is abused every eighteen seconds.[50]

One in every five women involved in an intimate relationship with a man is beaten repeatedly by that man.[51]

Twenty-two to 35 percent of women who seek help in emergency rooms show signs of battering. Among 18- to 20-year-old women who appear at the emergency room door for trauma injuries, 42 percent have been battered. And battered women don't try to keep it a secret; 75 percent will reveal the cause of their injuries if asked. But doctors, unless educated about what to look for and what to do about it, are able to recognize abuse only 3 to 6 percent of the time.[52]

3 to 4 million American women . . . become victims of domestic abuse every year, about 1320 of them fatally . . . Domestic violence is the leading cause of injury and violent death for American women, resulting in more injuries than rape, auto accidents and muggings combined, according to the National Woman Abuse Prevention Project.[53]

Forty percent of all women who are murdered in the U.S. are killed by their male partners.[54]

In the United States, at least 4 women are murdered by their partners every day (National Coalition Against Domestic Violence, 1988). . . . American homicide statistics compiled by the Centers for Disease Control in Atlanta, Georgia, were analyzed by psychologist Angela Browne and sociologist Kirk Williams. They found an increase in the number of women being killed by abusive partners in 35 states; in 25 states, most of these women were killed after they separated from or divorced their male partners.[55]

Some studies have found that at least 40 percent of women who kill do so in self defense. (*WIN News*)

A California state prison study found that 93 percent of the women who had killed their mates had been battered by them; 67 percent of these women indicated the homicide resulted from an attempt to protect themselves or their children. (National Woman Abuse Prevention Project, 1989)[56]

In the 1980s, almost half of all homeless women were refugees of domestic violence (*Time*, Special Issue, Fall 1990). As of 1988, one third of the 1 million battered women who sought emergency shelter each year could find none. (Women and Housing Task Force, National Low-Income Housing Coalition). In the U.S., there are three times as many animal shelters as there are shelters for victims of domestic abuse. (Senate Judiciary Committee).[57]

Feminists generally agree: Women are the victims of male violence. Such violence is an integral part of the gender system; it is largely sanctioned and reinforced by social institutions—the courts, the media, the economic system, religions, and others; it has an agenda, a goal—the control of women by men through fear. What is more, the social system has been manipulated so that women have been prohibited from defending ourselves. Not until the women's movement created women's self-help groups, coalitions against violence, rape crisis centers, and battered women's shelters did we have any recourse besides protection by men.

Protection

In the system of chivalry, men protect women against men. This is not unlike the protection relationship which the Mafia established with small businesses in the early part of this century. Indeed, chivalry is an age-old protection racket which depends for its existence on rape.

–SUSAN GRIFFIN, *Rape: The Power of Consciousness*[58]

Ordinarily, nations and cultures grant their citizens the right of self-protection. Self-defense is deemed a natural and appropriate right. In patriarchy, however, so far as women are concerned, that is not true. No written law prohibits us from defending ourselves against attack; that would be unthinkable! Instead, we are kept from defending ourselves by two main devices. First, the kinds of attack directed specifically against women (such as rape or many forms of prostitution) are simply defined away as not an attack or not a crime. The burden is shifted to the victim to prove not only that certain acts took place but that they are indeed criminal. Second, the entire set of rules and behaviors imposed on women through the requirements of "femininity" render us passive, weak, and unable to defend ourselves; nor are we allowed by law to compensate physically, with weapons or similar protective devices, for our lesser strength and size. In patriarchy, men as a class are charged with the protection of women. This is ironic because, for the most part, it is men as a class from whom we must be protected. It is men who rape, batter, exploit, and prostitute women for their own interests.

Nor is the issue easily explained away by the proposition that the part of the group that attacks is different from the part that defends. The same man who rapes may also be a husband or lover, though not necessarily of the raped woman. The same man who batters and beats a woman may be her own husband or lover. When one accepts friendship or companionship from a man—a date, a ride, a dinner—one cannot be sure what payment may be exacted, even forcibly, in return.

Those who—like slaves or prisoners—are not permitted or are not able to defend themselves against any kind of attack by any thing or person are deprived of a basic prerequisite to freedom, integrity, confidence, viability, and independence. It matters little whether the prohibition to self-defense is imposed by law or by lore. Total dependence on others for protection, particularly when those others are the very persons from whom one must be protected, is not workable.

It may be said that women are not protected simply by men, but by law, the courts, judges, and the police. Feminists point out that the percentage of women in legislatures, courts, and police forces is small; the number who have any power in those areas is still smaller, and they are hampered by a legacy of masculist decision making.

Women beaten and battered by their male partners are only now beginning to receive even meager attention by society, much of it reversed by the Reagan–Bush years. Women raped or abused—by strangers, lovers, or relatives—have had little recourse in the courts and received little restitution. A patriarchal economy an
to barter their bodies for
they are harassed and im
force by men against wo
which we may not defen
litical terror meant to ke
for us.

Conclusion

This chapter has barely begun to strip open the many layers of women's private experiences in patriarchy. Much more remains to examine, much more to tell. Up to now much of the story has been painful, but as feminists point out, recognition of some of the harsh realities is the first spur to change.

There are some important thoughts to keep firmly in mind. Having been excluded from the inner power circle of patriarchy, women have also not been absorbed by it. Women have a unique position in society in that we have a more rounded, more balanced perception of it. Having lived and grown and studied in patriarchy, we know it intimately. Having lived on its periphery, often in contest with it, we also understand it more critically. With our "consciousnesses" raised, we are therefore in a much stronger position to change it than those more nearly its captives in the center. We have extraordinary social contributions to make.

We have, too, special options in our personal lives. Many have contended that a more satisfying life flows from challenge. I believe that, and so do many other feminists.

It is extremely difficult to break from the familiar, which is comfortable even in its inadequacy. It is hard indeed to alter behaviors, relationships, and values that hold at least some attraction for us in order to move toward something that we can only dimly see at times, but something that we know must be better. May Sarton has said, "It is only when we can believe that we are creating the soul that life has any meaning, but when we can believe it—and I do and always have—then there is nothing we do that is without meaning and nothing that we suffer that does not hold the seed of creation in it."[59] Because the oppression of women has in large part been an oppression of our souls (our character, integrity, and spirit), feminist activism is as much as anything else an attempt to reclaim our souls, to rebuild them. This is the source of the buoyant

excitemen
side wi
our
Re

...t so many feminists carry, even side by ...th the pain of recognition. It is the source of ...pride in the achievements and successes we win. ...wards are only as great as the risks one has to take to gain them.

Notes

1. Quoted in Timothy H. Brubaker and Judy A. Kimberly, "Challenges to the American Family," in *Family Relations: Challenges for the Future,* ed. Timothy H. Brubaker (Newbury Park, CA: Sage, 1993), p. 4.

2. Sanford M. Dornbusch and Myra H. Strober, "Our Perspective," in *Feminism, Children and the New Families,* ed. Sanford M. Dornbusch and Myra H. Strober (New York: Guilford Press, 1988), pp. 3–24, *passim.*

3. Ibid.

4. Ibid.

5. Ibid.

6. Ibid.

7. Ibid., p. 17.

8. Kristine M. Baber and Katherine R. Allen, *Women and Families: Feminist Reconstructions* (New York: Guilford Press, 1992), p. 36.

9. "The Paradox of the Happy Marriage," in *Women in Sexist Society,* ed. Vivian Gornick and Barbara Moran (New York: Basic Books, 1971), p. 147.

10. Ibid. See also Jessie Bernard, *The Future of Marriage* (New York: Bantam, 1972).

11. Carol Tavris and Carole Offir, *The Longest War* (New York: Harcourt Brace Jovanovich, 1977), p. 222.

12. Ibid., p. 232.

13. U.S. Bureau of the Census, 1991.

14. For statistics on alimony and child support, see the reading "Women and the American Economy," by Elyce Rotella in Chapter 7.

15. U.S. Census Bureau and Bureau of Labor Statistics.

16. Elyce Rotella, "Women and the American Economy," in Chapter 7.

17. Dornbusch and Strober, "Our Perspective," p. 14.

18. Harriet Nerlove Mischel and Robert Fuhr, "Maternal Employment: Its Psychological Effects on Children and Their Families," in Dornbusch and Strober, *Feminism, Children and the New Families,* pp. 194–195.

19. Shulamith Firestone, *The Dialectic of Sex: The Case for Feminist Revolution* (New York: Bantam, 1971), pp. 127, 135.

20. W. B. O'Reilly, "Where Equal Opportunity Fails: Corporate Men and Women in Dual-Career Families" (Ph.D. dissertation, Stanford University, 1983); quoted in Myra H. Strober, "Two-Earner Families" in Dornbusch and Strober, *Feminism, Children, and the New Families,* p. 178.

21. [Footnote in Strober, "Two-Earner Families"] J. Steihm, "Invidious Intimacy," *Social Policy* 6(5): 12–16.

22. [Footnote in Strober, "Two-Earner Families"] "The empirical evidence is unclear on whether two-earner couples are less likely to move than one-earner couples, even when their occupations and incomes are relatively similar." See W. T. Markham, "Sex, Relocation, and Occupational Advancement" in *Women and Work; An Annual Review 2* ed. A. H. Stromberg, L. Larwood, and B. A. Gutek (Beverly Hills, CA: Sage, 1987).

23. Ibid.

24. Carol J. Barrett, "Women in Widowhood," *Signs* 2, no. 4 (Summer 1978): 856.

25. *St. Louis Post-Dispatch,* 4 November 1991, p. 2B.

26. Merle Hoffman, "Editorial," *On the Issues* 22 (Spring 1992): 38.

27. *St. Louis Post-Dispatch,* 17 July 1989, p. 5A. Copyright 1989 Pulitzer Publishing Company. Reprinted with permission.

28. Patricia G. Miller, *The Worst of Times* (New York: HarperCollins, 1993), pp. 1–2.

29. Mary Ann McGivern, *St. Louis Post-Dispatch,* 17 February 1989.

30. *St. Louis Post-Dispatch,* 26 March 1989, pp. 5D, 9D. Copyright 1989 Pulitzer Publishing Company. Reprinted with permission.

31. Marlene Gerber Fried, *From Abortion to Reproductive Freedom* (Boston: South End Press, 1990), p. 3.

32. Frances Kissling, "Operation Rescue," in *Conscience: A Newsjournal of Prochoice Catholic Opinion* 10, no. 1 (January/February 1989): 8.

33. Reported by Eleanor J. Bader in *New Directions for Women* 18, no. 2 (March/April 1989): 14. Reprinted with permission of *New Directions for Women.*

34. Jane Caputi and Diana E. H. Russell, "Femicide: Sexual Terrorism Against Women," in *Femicide: The Politics of Woman Killing,* eds. Jill Radford and Diana E. H. Russell (New York: Twayne, 1992), p. 13.

35. Carol J. Sheffield, "Sexual Terrorism" in *Women: A Feminist Perspective,* 4th ed., ed. Jo Freeman (Mountain View, CA: Mayfield, 1984), p. 3.

36. Dianne Herman, "Rape Culture," in *Women,* p. 34.

37. Susan Brownmiller, *Against Our Will* (New York: Bantam, 1976), p. 5.

38. Susan Schechter, *Women and Male Violence* (Boston: South End Press, 1982), p. 209.

39. Lori Heise, "Crimes of Gender," *World-Watch,* March/April 1989, p. 12.

40. Fred Pelker, "Raped: A Male Survivor Breaks His Silence," *On the Issues 22* (Spring 1992): 40.

41. U.S. Department of Justice Uniform Crime Reports, 1988.

42. Ibid.

43. Illinois Coalition Against Sexual Assault (ICASA).

44. Tiffany Devitt, "Media Circus at Palm Beach Rape Trial," *Extra! A Publication of FAIR,* Special Issue (1992): 9.

45. Ibid.

46. "The Hard Facts," statistics reprinted from the higher education section of *What Counts: The Complete Harper's Index,* published by Henry Holt & Company. Reported in *Lingua Franca* 2, no. 1 (October 1991): 5.

47. Susan Dworkin, "Can We Save the Girls?" *New Directions for Women* 20 no. 5 (September/October 1991): 3.

48. NOW Legal Defense and Education Fund.

49. Louise Bausch and Mary Kimbrough, *Voices Set Free: Battered Women Speak from Prison* (St. Louis: Women's Self-Help Center, 1986), p. ix.

50. Ibid., p. 3.

51. Illinois Coalition Against Sexual Assault and the Illinois Coalition Against Domestic Violence, "Male Violence Against Women," pamphlet.

52. *Ms.,* March/April 1992, p. 39.

53. Martha Shirk, "Domestic Violence Is a Leading Hazard for Women," *St. Louis Post-Dispatch,* 6 May 1992, p. 10A.

54. Ibid.

55. Constance A. Bean, *Women Murdered by the Men They Loved* (Binghamton, NY: Haworth Press, 1992), p. 6.

56. Merle Hoffman, "Editorial," *On the Issues: The Progressive Woman's Quarterly 21* (Winter 1991): 3.

57. *Extra! A Publication of FAIR,* Special Issue (1992).

58. Susan Griffin, *Rape: The Power of Consciousness* (San Francisco: Harper & Row, 1979), p. 10.

59. May Sarton, *Journal of a Solitude* (New York: Norton, 1973), p. 67.

The Beauty Myth

Naomi Wolf

Naomi Wolf was born in San Francisco in 1962. She was educated at Yale University and at New College, Oxford University, where she was a Rhodes Scholar. Her essays have appeared in various publications including: The New Republic, Wall Street Journal, Glamour, Ms., Esquire, The Washington Post, *and the* New York Times. *She speaks widely on college campuses.* The Beauty Myth *is her first book; a second, a manifesto for a new wave of feminism, is in preparation. She lives in Washington, D.C.*

Wolf describes the myth that refuses to die: the "beauty myth"—the quality called beauty objectively exists; women want to be *it, and men want to* have *it. She argues that even more than in the past, the myth pervades our lives. It endangers our health and limits our options.*

AT LAST, AFTER A LONG SILENCE, WOMEN TOOK TO the streets. In the two decades of radical action that followed the rebirth of feminism in the early 1970s, Western women gained legal and reproductive rights, pursued higher education, entered the trades and the professions, and overturned ancient and revered beliefs about their social role. A generation on, do women feel free?

The affluent, educated, liberated women of the First World, who can enjoy freedoms unavailable to any women ever before, do not feel as free as they want to. And they can no longer restrict to the subconscious their sense that this lack of freedom has something to do with—with apparently frivolous issues, things that really should not matter. Many are ashamed to admit that such trivial concerns—to do with physical appearance, bodies, faces, hair, clothes—matter so much. But in spite of shame, guilt, and denial, more and more women are wondering if it isn't that they are entirely neurotic and alone but rather that something important is indeed at stake that has to do with the relationship between female liberation and female beauty.

The more legal and material hindrances women have broken through, the more strictly and heavily and cruelly images of female beauty have come to weigh upon us. Many women sense that women's collective progress has stalled; compared with the heady momentum of earlier days, there is a dispiriting climate of confusion, division, cynicism, and above all, exhaustion. After years of much struggle and little recognition, many older women feel burned out; after years of taking its light for granted, many younger women show little interest in touching new fire to the torch.

During the past decade, women breached the power structure; meanwhile, eating disorders rose exponentially and cosmetic surgery became the fastest-growing medical specialty. During the past five years, consumer spending doubled, pornography became the main media category, ahead of legitimate films and records combined, and thirty-three thousand American women told researchers that they would rather lose ten to fifteen pounds than achieve any other goal. More women have more money and power and scope and legal recognition than we have ever had before; but in terms of how we feel about ourselves *physically*, we may actually be worse off than our unliberated grandmothers. Recent research consistently shows that inside the majority of the West's controlled, attractive, successful working women, there is a secret "underlife" poisoning our freedom; infused with notions of beauty, it is a dark vein of self-hatred, physical obsessions, terror of aging, and dread of lost control.

It is no accident that so many potentially powerful women feel this way. We are in the midst of a violent backlash against feminism that uses images of female beauty as a political weapon against women's advancement: the beauty myth. It is the modern version of a social reflex that has been in force since the Industrial Revolution. As women released themselves from the feminine mystique of domesticity, the beauty myth took over its lost ground, expanding as it waned to carry on its work of social control.

The contemporary backlash is so violent because the ideology of beauty is the last one remaining of the old feminine ideologies that still has the power to control those women whom second wave feminism would have otherwise made relatively uncontrollable: It has grown stronger to take over the work of social coercion that myths about motherhood, domesticity, chastity, and passivity, no longer can manage. It is seeking right now to undo psychologically and covertly all the good things that feminism did for women materially and overtly.

This counterforce is operating to checkmate the inheritance of feminism on every level in the lives of Western women. Feminism gave us laws against job discrimination based on gender; immediately case law evolved in Britain and the United States that institutionalized job discrimination based on women's appearances. Patriarchal religion declined; new religious dogma, using some of the mind-altering techniques of older cults and sects, arose around age and weight to functionally supplant traditional ritual. Feminists, inspired by Friedan, broke the stranglehold on the women's popular press of advertisers for household products, who were promoting the feminine mystique; at once, the diet and skin care industries became the new cultural censors of women's intellectual space, and because of their pressure, the gaunt, youthful model supplanted the happy housewife as the arbiter of successful womanhood. The sexual revolution promoted the discovery of female sexuality; "beauty pornography"—which for the first time in women's history artificially links a commodified "beauty" directly and explicitly to sexuality—invaded the mainstream to undermine women's new and vulnerable sense of sexual self-worth. Reproductive rights gave Western women control over our own bodies; the weight of fashion models plummeted to 23 percent below that of ordinary women, eating disorders rose exponentially, and a mass neurosis was promoted that used food and weight to strip women of that sense of control. Women insisted on politicizing health; new technologies of invasive, potentially deadly "cosmetic" surgeries developed apace to re-exert old forms of medical control of women.

Every generation since about 1830 has had to fight its version of the beauty myth. "It is very little to me," said the suffragist Lucy Stone in 1855, "to have the right to vote, to own property, etcetera, if I may not keep my body, and its uses, in my absolute right." Eighty years later, after women had won the vote, and the first wave of the organized women's movement had subsided, Virginia Woolf wrote that it would still be decades before women could tell the truth about their bodies. In 1962, Betty Friedan quoted a young woman trapped in the Feminine Mystique: "Lately, I look in the mirror, and I'm so afraid I'm going to look like my mother." Eight years after that, heralding the cataclysmic second wave of feminism, Germaine Greer described "the Stereotype": "To her belongs all that is beautiful, even the very word beauty itself . . . she is a doll . . . I'm sick of the masquerade." In spite of the great revolution of the second wave, we are not exempt. Now we can look out over ruined barricades: A revolution has come upon us and changed everything in its path, enough time has passed since then for babies to have grown into women, but there still remains a final right not fully claimed.

The beauty myth tells a story: The quality called "beauty" objectively and universally exists. Women must want to embody it and men must want to possess women who embody it. This embodiment is an imperative for women and not for men, which situation is necessary and natural because it is biological, sexual, and evolutionary: Strong men battle for beautiful women, and beautiful women are more reproductively successful. Women's beauty must correlate to their fertility, and since this system is based on sexual selection, it is inevitable and changeless.

None of this is true. "Beauty" is a currency system like the gold standard. Like any economy, it is determined by politics, and in the modern age in the West it is the last, best belief system that keeps male dominance intact. In assigning value to women in a vertical hierarchy according to a culturally imposed physical standard, it is an expression of power relations in which women must unnaturally compete for resources that men have appropriated for themselves.

"Beauty" is not universal or changeless, though the West pretends that all ideals of female beauty stem from one Platonic Ideal Woman; the Maori admire a fat vulva, and the Padung, droopy breasts. Nor is "beauty" a function of evolution: Its ideals change at a pace far more rapid than that of the evolution of species, and Charles Darwin was himself unconvinced by his own explanation that "beauty" resulted from a "sexual selection" that deviated from the rule of natural selection; for women to compete with women through "beauty" is a reversal of the way in which natural selection affects all other mammals. Anthropology has overturned the notion that females must be "beautiful" to be selected to mate: Evelyn Reed, Elaine Morgan, and others have dismissed sociobiological assertions of innate male polygamy and female monogamy. Female higher primates are the sexual initiators; not only do they seek out and enjoy sex with many partners, but "every nonpregnant female takes her turn at being the most desirable of all her troop. And that cycle keeps turning as long as she lives." The inflamed pink sexual organs of primates are often cited by male sociobiologists as analogous to human arrangements relating to female "beauty," when in fact that is a universal, nonhierarchical female primate characteristic.

Nor has the beauty myth always been this way. Though the pairing of the older rich men with young, "beautiful" women is taken to be somehow inevitable, in the matriarchal Goddess religions that dominated the Mediterranean from about 25,000 B.C.E. to about 700 B.C.E., the situation was reversed: "In every culture, the Goddess has many lovers. . . . The clear pattern is of an older woman with a beautiful but expendable youth—Ishtar and Tammuz, Venus and Adonis, Cybele and Attis, Isis and Osiris . . . their only function the service of the divine 'womb.'" Nor is it something only women do and only men watch: Among the Nigerian Wodaabes, the women hold economic power and the tribe is obsessed with male beauty; Wodaabe men spend hours together in elaborate makeup sessions, and compete—provocatively painted and dressed, with swaying hips and seductive expressions—in beauty contests judged by women. There is no legitimate historical or biological justification for the beauty myth; what it is doing to women today is a result of nothing more exalted than the need of today's power structure, economy, and culture to mount a counteroffensive against women.

If the beauty myth is not based on evolution, sex, gender, aesthetics, or God, on what is it based? It claims to be about intimacy and sex and life, a celebration of women. It is actually composed of emotional distance, politics, finance, and sexual repression. The beauty myth is not about women at all. It is about men's institutions and institutional power.

The qualities that a given period calls beautiful in women are merely symbols of the female behavior that that period considers desirable: *The beauty myth is always actually prescribing behavior and not appearance.* Competition between women has been made part of the myth so that women will be divided from one another. Youth and (until recently) virginity have been "beautiful" in women since they stand for experiential and sexual ignorance. Aging in women is "unbeautiful" since women grow more powerful with time, and since the links between generations of women must always be newly broken: Older women fear young ones, young women fear old, and the beauty myth truncates for all the female life span. Most urgently, women's identity must be premised upon our "beauty" so that we will remain vulnerable to outside approval, carrying the vital sensitive organ of self-esteem exposed to the air.

Though there has, of course, been a beauty myth in some form for as long as there has been patriarchy, the beauty myth in its modern form is a fairly recent invention. The myth flourishes when material constraints on women are dangerously loosened. Before the Industrial Revolution, the average woman could not have had the same feelings about "beauty" that modern women do who experience the myth as continual comparison to a mass-disseminated physical ideal. Before the development of technologies of mass production—daguerreotypes, photographs, etc.—an ordinary woman was exposed to few such images outside the Church. Since the family was a productive unit and women's work complemented men's, the value of women who were not aristocrats or prostitutes lay in their work skills, economic shrewdness, physical strength, and fertility. Physical attraction, obviously, played its part; but "beauty" as we understand it was not, for ordinary women, a serious issue in the marriage marketplace. The beauty myth in its modern form gained ground after the upheavals of industrialization, as the work unit of the family was destroyed, and urbanization and the emerging factory system demanded what social engineers of the time termed the "separate sphere" of domesticity, which supported the new labor category of the "breadwinner" who left home for the workplace during the day. The middle class expanded, the standards of living and of literacy rose, the size of families shrank; a new class of literate, idle women developed, on whose submission to enforced domesticity the evolving system of industrial capitalism depended. Most of our assumptions about the way women have always thought about "beauty" date from no earlier than the 1830s, when the cult of domesticity was first consolidated and the beauty index invented.

For the first time new technologies could reproduce—in fashion plates, daguerreotypes, tintypes, and rotogravures—images of how women should look. In the 1840s the first nude photographs of prostitutes were taken; advertisements using images of "beautiful" women first appeared in mid-century. Copies of classical artworks, postcards of society beauties and royal mistresses, Currier and Ives prints, and porcelain figurines flooded the separate sphere to which middle-class women were confined.

Since the Industrial Revolution, middle-class Western women have been controlled by ideals and stereotypes as much as by material constraints. This situation, unique to this group, means that analyses that trace "cultural conspiracies" are uniquely plausible in relation to them. The rise of the beauty myth was just one of several emerging social fictions that masqueraded as natural components of the feminine sphere, the better to enclose those women inside it. Other such fictions arose contemporaneously: a version of childhood that required continual maternal supervision; a concept of female biology that required middle-class women to act out the roles of hysterics and hypochondriacs; a conviction that respectable women were sexually anesthetic; and a definition of women's work that occupied them with repetitive, time-consuming, and painstaking tasks such as needlepoint and lacemaking. All such Victorian inventions as these served a double function—that is, though they were encouraged as a means to expend female energy and intelligence in harmless ways, women often used them to express genuine creativity and passion.

But in spite of middle-class women's creativity with fashion and embroidery and child rearing, and, a century later, with the role of the suburban housewife that devolved from these social fictions, the fictions' main purpose was served: During a century and a half of unprecedented feminist agitation, they effectively counteracted middle-class women's dangerous new leisure, literacy, and relative freedom from material constraints.

Though these time- and mind-consuming fictions about women's natural role adapted themselves to resurface in the post-war Feminine Mystique, when the second wave of the women's movement took apart what women's magazines had portrayed as the "romance," "science," and "adventure" of homemaking and suburban family life, they temporarily failed. The cloying domestic fiction of "togetherness" lost its meaning and middle-class women walked out of their front doors in masses.

So the fictions simply transformed themselves once more: Since the women's movement had successfully taken apart most other necessary fictions of femininity, all the work of social control once spread out over the whole network of these fictions had to be reassigned to the only strand left intact, which action consequently strengthened it a hundredfold. This reimposed onto liberated women's faces and bodies all the limitations, taboos, and punishments of the repressive laws, religious injunctions and reproductive enslavement that no longer carried sufficient force. Inexhaustible but ephemeral beauty work took over from inexhaustible but ephemeral housework. As the economy, law, religion, sexual mores, education, and culture were forcibly opened up to include women more fairly, a private reality colonized female consciousness. By using ideas about "beauty," it reconstructed an alternative female world with its own laws, economy, religion, sexuality, education, and culture, each element as repressive as any that had gone before.

Since middle-class Western women can best be weakened psychologically now that we are stronger materially, the beauty myth, as it has resurfaced in the last generation, has had to draw on more technological sophistication and reactionary fervor than ever before. The modern arsenal of the myth is a dissemination of millions of images of the current ideal; although this barrage is generally seen as a collective sexual fantasy, there is in fact little that is sexual about it. It is summoned out of political fear on the part of male-dominated institutions threatened by women's freedom, and it exploits female guilt and apprehension about our own liberation—latent fears that we might be going too far. This frantic aggregation of imagery is a collective reactionary hallucination willed into being by both men and women stunned and disoriented by the rapidity with which gender relations have been transformed: a bulwark of reassurance against the flood of change. The mass depiction of the modern woman as a "beauty" is a contradiction: Where modern women are growing, moving, and expressing their individuality, as the myth has it, "beauty" is by definition inert, timeless, and generic. That this hallucination is necessary and deliberate is evident in the way "beauty" so directly contradicts women's real situation.

And the unconscious hallucination grows ever more influential and pervasive because of what is now conscious market manipulation: powerful industries—the $33-billion-a-year diet industry, the $20-billion cosmetics industry, the $300-million cosmetic surgery industry, and the $7-billion pornography industry—have arisen from the capital made out of unconscious anxieties, and are in turn able, through their influence on mass culture, to use, stimulate, and reinforce the hallucination in a rising economic spiral.

This is not a conspiracy theory; it doesn't have to be. Societies tell themselves necessary fictions in the same way that individuals and families do. Henrik Ibsen called them "vital lies," and psychologist Daniel Goleman describes them working the same way on the social level that they do within families: "The collusion is maintained by directing attention away from the fearsome fact, or by repackaging its meaning in an acceptable format." The costs of these social blind spots, he writes, are destructive communal illusions. Possibilities for women have become so open-ended that they threaten to destabilize the institutions on which a male-dominated culture has depended, and a collective panic reaction on the part of both sexes has forced a demand for counterimages.

The resulting hallucination materializes, for women, as something all too real. No longer just an idea, it becomes three-dimensional, incorporating within itself how women live and how they do not live: It becomes the Iron Maiden. The original Iron Maiden was a medieval German instrument of torture, a body-shaped casket painted with the limbs and features of a lovely, smiling young woman. The unlucky victim was slowly enclosed inside her; the lid fell shut to immobilize the victim, who died either of starvation or, less cruelly, of the metal spikes embedded in her interior. The modern hallucination in which women are trapped or trap themselves is similarly rigid, cruel, and euphemistically painted. Contemporary culture directs attention to imagery of the Iron Maiden, while censoring real women's faces and bodies.

Why does the social order feel the need to defend itself by evading the fact of real women, our faces and voices and bodies, and reducing the meaning of women to these formulaic and endlessly reproduced "beautiful" images? Though unconscious personal anxieties can be a powerful force in the creation of a vital lie, economic necessity practically guarantees it. An economy that depends on slavery needs to promote images of slaves that "justify" the institution of slavery. Western economies are absolutely dependent now on the continued underpayment of women. An ideology that makes women feel "worth less" was urgently needed to counteract the way feminism had begun to make us feel worth more. This does not require a conspiracy; merely an atmosphere. The contemporary economy depends right now on the representation of women within the beauty myth. Economist John Kenneth Galbraith offers an economic explanation for "the persistence of the view of homemaking as a 'higher calling'": the concept of women as naturally trapped within the Feminine Mystique, he feels, "has been forced on us by popular sociology, by magazines, and by fiction to disguise the fact that woman in her role of consumer has been essential to the development of our industrial society. . . . Behavior that is essential for economic reasons is transformed into a social virtue." As soon as a woman's primary social value could no longer be defined as the attainment of virtuous domesticity, the beauty myth redefined it as the attainment of virtuous beauty. It did so to substitute both a new consumer imperative and a new justification for economic unfairness in the workplace where the old ones had lost their hold over newly liberated women.

Another hallucination arose to accompany that of the Iron Maiden: The caricature of the Ugly Feminist was resurrected to dog the steps of the women's movement. The caricature is unoriginal; it was coined to ridicule the feminists of the nineteenth century. Lucy Stone herself, whom supporters saw as "a prototype of womanly grace . . . fresh and fair as the morning," was derided by detractors with "the usual report" about Victorian feminists: "a big masculine woman, wearing boots, smoking a cigar, swearing like a trooper." As Betty Friedan put it presciently in 1960, even before the savage revamping of that old caricature: "The unpleasant image of feminists today resembles less the feminists themselves than the image fostered by the interests who so bitterly opposed the vote for women in state after state." Thirty years on, her conclusion is more true than ever: That resurrected caricature, which sought to punish women for their public acts by going after their private sense of self, became the paradigm for new limits placed on aspiring women everywhere. After the success of the women's movement's second wave, the beauty myth was perfected to checkmate power at every level in individual women's lives. The modern neuroses of life in the female body spread to woman after woman at epidemic rates. The myth is undermining—slowly, imperceptibly, without our being aware of the real forces of erosion—the ground women have gained through long, hard, honorable struggle.

The beauty myth of the present is more insidious than any mystique of femininity yet: A century ago, Nora slammed the door of the doll's house; a generation ago, women turned their backs on the consumer heaven of the isolated multiapplianced home; but where women are trapped today, there is no door to slam. The contemporary ravages of the beauty backlash are destroying women physically and depleting us psychologically. If we are to free ourselves from the dead weight that has once again been made out of femaleness, it is not ballots or lobbyists or placards that women will need first; it is a new way to see.

Notes

Page

238 Cosmetic surgery: *Standard and Poor's Industry Surveys* (New York: Standard and Poor's Corp., 1988).

238 Pornography main media category: See "Crackdown on Pornography: A No-Win Battle," *U.S. News and World Report*, June 4, 1984. The Association of Fashion and Image Consultants tripled its membership between 1984 and 1989 alone (Annetta Miller and Dody Tsiantar, *Newsweek*, May 22, 1989). During the five or six years prior to 1986, consumer spending rose from $300 billion to $600 billion.

239 Thirty-three thousand American women, University of Cincinnati College of Medicine, 1984: Wooley, S. C., and O. W. Wooley, "Obesity and Women: A Closer Look at the Facts," *Women's Studies International Quarterly*, vol. 2 (1979), pp. 69–79. Data reprinted in "33,000 Women Tell How They Really Feel About Their Bodies," *Glamour*, February 1984.

239 Recent research shows: See Dr. Thomas Cash, Diane Cash, and Jonathan Butters, "Mirror-Mirror on the Wall: Contrast Effects and Self-Evaluation of Physical Attractiveness," *Personality and Social Psychology Bulletin*, September 1983, vol. 9, no. 3. Dr. Cash's research shows very little connection between "how attractive women are" and "how attractive they feel themselves to be." All the women he treated were, in his terms, "extremely attractive," but his patients compare themselves only to models, not to other women.

239 Very little to me: Lucy Stone, 1855, quoted in Andrea Dworkin, *Pornography: Men Possessing Women* (New York: Putnam, 1981), p. 11.

239 A doll: Germaine Greer, *The Female Eunuch* (London: Paladin Grafton Books, 1970), pp. 55, 60.

239 Myth: See also Roland Barthes's definition: "It [myth] transforms history into nature. . . . Myth has the task of giving an historical intention a natural justification, and making contingency appear eternal." Roland Barthes, "Myth Today," *Mythologies* (New York: Hill and Wang, 1972), p. 129.

Anthropologist Bronislaw Malinowski's definition of "a myth of origin" is relevant to the beauty myth: A myth of origin, writes Ann Oakley, "tends to be worked hardest in times of social strain, when the state of affairs portrayed in the myth are called into question." Ann Oakley, *Housewife: High Value/Low Cost* (London: Penguin Books, 1987), p. 163.

240 Platonic: See Plato's discussion of Beauty in *Symposium*. For varying standards of beauty, see Ted Polhemus, *BodyStyles* (Luton, England: Lennard Publishing, 1988).

240 Sexual selection; Darwin . . . was unconvinced: See Cynthia Eagle Russett, "Hairy Men and Beautiful Women," *Sexual Science: The Victorian Construction of Womanhood* (Cambridge, Mass.: Harvard University Press, 1989), pp. 78–103.

On page 84 Russett quotes Darwin: "Man is more powerful in body and mind than woman, and in the savage state he keeps her in a much more abject state of bondage, than does the male of any other animal; therefore it is not surprising that he should have gained the power of selection. . . . As women have long been selected for beauty, it is not surprising that some of their successive variations should have been transmitted exclusively to the same sex; consequently that they should have transmitted beauty in a somewhat higher degree to their female than to their male offspring, and thus have become more beautiful, according to general opinion, than men." Darwin himself noticed the evolutionary inconsistency of this idea that, as Russett puts it, "a funny thing happened on the way up the ladder: among humans, the female no longer chose but was chosen." This theory "implied an awkward break in evolutionary continuity," she observes: "In Darwin's own terms it marked a rather startling reversal in the trend of evolution."

See also Natalie Angier, "Hard-to-Please Females May Be Neglected Evolutionary Force," *The New York Times,* May 8, 1990, and Natalie Angier, "Mating for Life? It's Not for the Birds or the Bees," *The New York Times,* August 21, 1990.

240 Evolution: See Evelyn Reed, *Woman's Evolution: From Matriarchal Clan to Patriarchal Family* (New York: Pathfinder Press, 1986); and Elaine Morgan, *The Descent of Woman* (New York: Bantam Books, 1979). See especially "the upper primate," p. 91.

240 Goddess: Rosalind Miles, *The Women's History of the World* (London: Paladin Grafton Books, 1988), p. 43. See also Merlin Stone, *When God Was a Woman* (San Diego: Harvest Books, 1976).

240 Wodaabe tribe: Leslie Woodhead, "Desert Dandies," *The Guardian,* July 1988.

In the West African Fulani tribe young women choose their husbands on the basis of their beauty: "The contestants . . . take part in the yaake, a line-up in which they sing and dance, stand on tip-toe and make faces, rolling and crossing their eyes and grimacing to show off their teeth to the judges. They keep this up for hours, aided by the consumption of stimulating drugs beforehand. Throughout all this, old ladies in the crowd hurl criticisms at those who do not live up to the Fulani idea of beauty." [Polhemus, op. cit., p. 21]

See also Carol Beckwith and Marion van Offelen, *Nomads of Niger* (London: William Collins Sons & Co. Ltd., 1984), cited in Carol Beckwith, "Niger's Wodaabe: People of the Taboo," *National Geographic,* vol. 164, no. 4, October 1983, pp. 483–509.

Paleolithic excavations suggest that it has been human males rather than females to whom adornment was assigned in prehistoric societies; in modern tribal communities men generally adorn at least as much as women, and often hold "a virtual monopoly" over adornment. The Sudanese Nuba, the Australian Waligigi, and the Mount Hagen men of New Guinea also spend hours painting themselves and perfecting their hairstyles to attract the women, whose toilette takes only minutes. See Polhemus, op. cit., pp. 54–55.

240 Technologies: See, for example, Beaumont Newhall, *The History of Photography from 1839 to the Present* (London: Secker & Warburg, 1986), p. 31. Photograph *Academie,* c. 1845, photographer unknown.

242 Powerful industries: Diet items are a $74-billion-a-year industry in the United States, totaling one-third the nation's annual food bill. See David Brand, "A Nation of Healthy Worrywarts?," *Time,* July 25, 1988.

242 $33-billion-a-year diet industry: Molly O'Neill, "Congress Looking into the Diet Business," *The New York Times,* March 28, 1990.

242 $300-million-a-year cosmetic surgery industry: *Standard and Poor's Industry Surveys,* op. cit. 1988.

242 $7 billion pornography industry, "Crackdown on Pornography," op. cit.

242 Vital lies: Daniel Goleman, *Vital Lies, Simple Truths: The Psychology of Self-Deception* (New York: Simon and Schuster, 1983), pp. 16–17, quoting Henrik Ibsen's phrase: "The vital lie continues unrevealed, sheltered by the family's silence, alibis, stark denial."

242 A higher calling: John Kenneth Galbraith, quoted in Michael H. Minton with Jean Libman Block, *What Is a Wife Worth?* (New York: McGraw-Hill, 1984), pp. 134–135.

242 Ugly Feminist: Marcia Cohen, *The Sisterhood: The Inside Story of the Women's Movement and the Leaders Who Made It Happen* (New York: Ballantine Books, 1988), pp. 205, 206, 287, 290, 322, 332.

243 Swearing like a trooper: Betty Friedan, *The Feminine Mystique* (London: Penguin Books, 1982), p. 79, quoting Elinor Rice Hays, *Morning Star: A Biography of Lucy Stone* (New York: Harcourt, 1961), p. 83.

243 Unpleasant image: Friedan, op. cit., p. 87.

Women and Love

Shere Hite

Shere Hite is a cultural historian who has done extensive research in the area of sexuality and love. She is active in the American Association for the Advancement of Science, The American Historical Association, and the Society for Women in Philosophy. She has lectured in many countries and has received numerous awards for her groundbreaking work. Her best known works are Sexual Honesty: By Women for Women *(1974),* The Hite Report: A Study of Male Sexuality *(1987), and* Women and Love: A Cultural Revolution in Progress *(1987).*

For Women and Love, *Hite analyzed the questionnaires of forty-five hundred women on their love relationships. Ninety-eight percent of the heterosexual women reported that they needed and wanted fundamental improvements in their relationships. They wondered why love started off so well and became painful so soon. They suffered, they said, because they felt that they worked so much harder at making their relationships work than their men did, because they gave so much more than they received, because it was so difficult to maintain their own identity and power in the context of a relationship.*

Hite asks, "What happens to love?" She explores the inner dynamic of love relationships for women, the imbalances in the female–male partnership, the feelings, the exchanges, and the "bargains" lovers make with each other, the highs and the letdowns, the consequences. She examines the differences and similarities between heterosexual and lesbian relationships.

If it is true, as the creed goes, that "love" occupies a major portion of women's attention, energy, and time, more so than for men, then "love" is not a trivial matter, but bears instead serious study.

What Happens to Love?

"INITIALLY, BEING IN LOVE IS FUN BUT SOMETHING happens and it becomes frustrating, painful, and disappointing. What is the thing that happens?"

"I try to open him up. I want to talk about our relationship, feelings and problems and develop solutions or compromises. He is quiet, so I have to initiate it and drag it out of him. I usually work the hardest to resolve the problem. Sometimes, when he finds it hard to express himself, he withdraws. Without communicating, how can you solve anything?"

"Although I find that I'm funny, sarcastic, and energetic when in mixed groups, 'the life of the party'—when my boyfriend's there . . . boom. I'm very quiet. Almost like I don't want to steal his 'spotlight.' Am I alone in this?"

"My father was somewhat affectionate, as much as he knew how to be—you know, that masculine way, by being insulting."

"When I was three or four, my mother was already teaching me to *see* dust and other people's feelings. ('Don't bother your father, he's tired.') Men don't learn the same sensitivity."

"Generally I like least about men their tendency to bottle up their thoughts and emotions so that you have to use all your energy trying to get them to speak out and share their inner selves."

"I don't know if my short relationships with men are at all typical. The main thing that struck me was that there was virtually no discussion of anyone's feelings. Most men seem to see women as women, never as people. Things that I kept finding myself doing/feeling around men: Feeling like they were the important ones. Feeling too big, in all ways. Too tall, too large, said too much, felt too much, occupied more space than I had a right to. Wanting to please them. Wanting to appear femininely pretty."

"I was so hurt by the emotional abuse that I can't even talk about it now. Funny how feminists always get excited about physical abuse. Me too. If he'd ever hit me I would have walked out forever. Emotionally is something different . . . but the sick cycle of lashing out and then being repentant, and of finally in the end giving the emotional 'gifts,' is the same. It is sick, sick, sick, but when you are in the middle of it, it is hard to see, hard to get the perspective. You keep giving, simply the fact that you have invested so much makes it harder to give up."

Most people live their "real" lives in an emotional world—a world of feelings and beliefs. These interior lives are more real to them, more present with them, than politics or the day's news. There is great beauty in sharing these worlds with another. As one woman puts it, "The times you feel really alive are times like when you are in love, or there is something very real and intense, when a contract between a deep part of yourself and another being is made real."

Why do things so often change or go less "right" after the first weeks of happiness? Why is "love the greatest blessing, and the scourge of the earth"? Is it the normal course of relationships that passion and even closeness just die after a while? Here women describe what it is that they believe is going wrong between people who truly do love each other—a chain of events so common that one often hears cynicism expressed over the possibility of two people ever living happily together.

Ninety-eight percent of the women in this study say they want to make basic changes in their relationships and marriages, improve the emotional relationships they have with men.* How do women analyze the issues—what do women say are the main problems in relationships?

. . .

The Ideology Behind the System—Women's Giving, Men's "Being"

The Emotional Contract

What most women are trying to describe here is an entrenched, largely unrecognized system of emotional discrimination—a system whose subterranean roots are entwined so deeply in the psyche of the culture that it underlies our entire social structure. As many women point out, the incidents that upset them can be small—and yet these incidents are troubling because they reflect an overall attitude, are part of a fabric of denial of women as complete human beings.

How does one begin to name and demonstrate a pattern that has had no name for so long—these subtle interactions and subliminal messages that are much more deadly to love than arguing over money or children?

The emotional contract in relationships hasn't really been looked at yet, as we are doing here: it is the core of a relationship—the implicit understanding between two people about how each should behave in a relationship, how each expects the other to express her or his emotions, how each interprets the emotional outcries and silences of the other. These tender and often brief moments are the lifeblood of the emotional closeness between two people, and small misunderstandings can lead to a chain reaction, ending empathy between the two—even though they may remain "married" or "together." But this emotional interaction is troubled by an unclear, demeaning, and gender-oriented set of subliminal attitudes, assumptions interwoven into our ideas of who men and women are. We believe that women are "loving and giving" and men are "doers," that one has more rights than the other.

Thus the emotional contract contains psychological stereotypes which put women at a disadvantage, and give men preferential treatment, superior psychological status that is built into the system, into the tiniest crevices of our minds. It is the fundamental cause of the problems between women and men in love relationships.

What is Emotional Equality?

One woman describes what it isn't:

"Men have all these power behaviors—you know, like turning their backs on you, and walking off, shutting the door, or 'going out for a walk' when you are trying to tell them something, or bring up something. They think they have the right not to listen, they don't have to be bothered with '*your* problem.' They do just as they please, no matter how much we (I or my girlfriends) talk or plead or shout or reason—they just show contempt for who we are, basically.

"Like today, R. just turned his back on me while I was talking to him, thinking that would be the end of

*A 1986 study by *Woman's Day* magazine found similar dissatisfaction; four out of five women asked said they would not marry the same men again, if they had it to do over. Also, large sales of "advice books" for women seem to indicate that this is an area women are intensely interested in.

it. Was he surprised when I grabbed him by the arm and jerked him around! I could tell he wanted to really hit me, but he didn't. Then he said something like 'You can't make me do anything you want. I don't take orders from you.' I suppose that refers to the chores I asked him to do. He could help me a *little*—like maybe screw in a light bulb without being asked. If I ask him, he says, 'Oh, I didn't notice it.' I can't believe it. Incredibly juvenile. Men can get away with it, because they run things. Or they think they can. But if women would stick together and not put up with this stuff, we could change it. If England could run the whole world for a time, and David could beat Goliath, we as women can get ourselves out of this hole and end the stupidity of the whole male thing."

The signs of this unequal emotional "contract"—the unspoken assumptions, the word choices—are thrown at women every day, as we have seen, in a thousand ways. Indeed, these patterns are so subtle and accepted, coloring everything, that they make discussion of the "problem" almost impossible, and arguments seem circular. As one woman puts it, "There are no words, to begin with, and when you *do* use words, they are viewed by men through a reversing telescope (when they are heard at all)—taking what I said for something totally NOT what I meant."

Another woman describes this dilemma in a typical "non-conversation" about an issue she is trying to discuss: "If we go out, we always end up going out with his friends and not mine. If I tell him this, he says, that's not true, my friends are just around more. I say, so why don't you make an effort to get to know my friends better—they're important to me. Him, totally missing my point: well, you know how it is when I hang out with the boys. How do I explain to him that it bothers me that I can't explain to him *why* it bothers me that his friends are more important than my friends—or that he seems to be saying that his friends are BETTER than my friends. That's it—he really thinks his friends are better! But I can't tell him that, because then he'll say, no they're not, I don't think that. And then we're at a dead end."

Lack of emotional equality is the fundamental stumbling block to love in relationships. Furthermore, the underlying inequalities are so taken for granted—often not even consciously noticed, built into the culture—that women can become angry without knowing exactly why. As one young woman says, "I wonder if our relationship could get better, because I resent him and don't know why. I feel on the defensive a lot."

It is our purpose here to unravel some of the traditional assumptions in relationships, to see more clearly what is going on.

Women: The Ones Who Try to "Make It Work"

Almost every woman says she feels she is trying harder to make relationships work than the man is:

"The biggest problem is that when there is a problem, I have to do most of the solving. It's part of his nature to be too laid back. I am always aware of our relationship, always defining it; when I want to change something, I work on it."

"I work more at keeping us together—being lively and exciting, planning things to do, trying to understand and hear how he feels. It takes a lot of energy."

"I always felt I tried harder to work at getting to the real issues that were causing problems, and that my partners weren't doing their part so we could get on with enjoying the good parts."

"Most men aren't willing to see through the changes in their women, and hang in there and grow from the experience and maybe learn something. When the going gets tough, they give up sooner, whereas the women (most) are more willing to stick through the tough times and weird changes their husbands go through, always trying to make things better."

96 percent of women say they are giving more emotional support than they are getting from men (although they get it from their women friends. . . .):

"Men are lucky. Their lovers cushion them emotionally and generally mother them, so they can be hard and competitive in the outside world."

"I sometimes think I give too much love. You might say I love right down to my bootstraps. Unfortunately, the men in my life were better at taking my love than giving any in return."

"Men are not taught the skills and attitudes that make a good spouse, lover, or (by my definition) friend. When I was three or four, my mother was already teaching me to see dust and other people's feelings. ('Don't bother your father, he's tired.') It is generally agreed that even big strong men need to be mothered a little, but who mothers the mothers?"

"Most men—while they take love seriously—expect more love from the woman. I don't think there's a difference in emotional needs, but men expect and demand more nurturance (and women give it)."

"I don't believe men are capable of loving me as much as I am them, because so many have been raised to believe they and what they want are more important than women, children, and nature."

"Men grow up with a different set of expectations for their emotional lives—that they will be served and loved, without much emotional expenditure on their part. They only must make money."

"He doesn't realize—perhaps even now—that he needs to spend time and thought and energy on the relationship. He realizes that to some degree now but not sufficiently, I think. It's always left up to the woman—still too much of the time. Therapy has helped, though."

"My husband and I could have had a great friendship if he had wanted 'all of it' and was willing to work for it. But he just wanted a good relationship when he desired it, similar to his television set—on and off at the touch of a finger."

Some women wonder, with frustration, if they can ever do enough emotionally to satisfy men:

"I finally broke up with my husband because I was beginning to grow, and he wanted me to stay quiet and let him 'rule the roost.' Devastating. It was so unnecessary, it's still sad to think about. But I was stifled! I have some regrets I didn't try harder with him, but everything I didn't try I tried the next go-around, and it still didn't work. I'm wondering if you can ever do enough in a relationship with a man."

"I give and give and give. Being always the peacemaker sometimes gets to me. I get angry that he doesn't care enough to try to work things out—he'd rather ride his anger than let his love help our reconciliation happen. I get tired of that, and angry, cold."

"I somehow feel a heavy responsibility for so much of his life, added onto an immense feeling of responsibility I already feel for my own. Sometimes, however, I manage to feel very happy."

"I have given heart and soul of everything I am and have. Somehow it is taken leaving me with nothing and lonely and hurt and he is still requesting more of me. *I* am tired, so tired."

Yet 84 percent of women say they believe that having loving relationships is one of the most important parts of life:

"I never have enough time to do all the things I want. I always have to choose between spending time with the children, making love with my husband, watching television (to relax me when I've been putting out a lot), writing letters to my family. Sometimes I get very frustrated, with all the demands on me, but really, much as I would like a little time to dawdle in the shower, etc., I want to spend time with those I love above all else. This is really the point of life—to see them happy, and feel us being together."

"Nothing else we do in this world can matter as much as loving people and being loved. I care deeply about the people in my life, I want to be there for them, notice when something goes wrong."

"My job is only secondary in importance to me; people and human relationships are the most important. If anything happened to my relationship with J. or my son, I would be a basket case. If I couldn't get my business going faster, I'd be frustrated but it wouldn't be the end of everything."

"I'm a romantic, being in love and growing together is the main thing for me. I believe that, most of all, I need someone to love me and to love them back."

. . .

Men's Emotional Demands on Women

Many women feel very confused by all of this—reality turns out not to be what it is said to be. Most women say that, after the first six months of a relationship, especially a marriage, men seem to be more emotionally dependent on them than vice versa—contrary to stereotypes which label women as "dependent" and "clinging."

This also represents a profound irony; that is, that men—no matter what negative behaviors they may display to women (we have seen that it is common for men to be emotionally withholding, condescending, and harassing)—still, at the same time, turn to women for love and emotional understanding, support. In other words, men harass women, but want and expect their love. Why? Because, despite "manliness," men need emotional support as much as women do. And yet, what effect does this have on women and their perception of men?

Women Are Questioning the Emotional Arrangements in Their Lives

79 percent of women are now questioning intensely whether they should put so much energy into love relationships, or give them the highest priority in their lives; 89 percent feel a conflict between men's demands on them to be loving—i.e., their "duty" to be loving and giving ("endlessly . . .")—and their own need to be themselves:*

"I am afraid I cannot love, that I don't love, and that since love is the most important feeling in the world to have, no matter how great my garden is or how slender and healthy I get, I will never be able to be a whole person. I feel happiest when I am working in my garden, or other alone times. And that is the problem because I am not living alone, I am a mother of two children and living with a man for fifteen years. I don't like my alone times to end until I am ready and when I can slip easily into family life. If someone comes to get me at the garden, if a creative time of writing, sewing, yoga is interrupted, I almost want to shout at them."

"I wish that I didn't spend so much mental energy thinking about relationships (friendships). I am a good student but too often my work gets put aside because I am focusing on the people in my life. I feel like I can't help it. People are so important to me. My work always comes second. I wish that I could find a balance. I still value love relationships highly but I am consciously trying to switch my priorities."

"During a relationship, so much time is spent on learning about the other person and just enjoying the feelings that it puts a stop on every other part of life. Too much time and effort is wasted (?) on just *being* with this other person—at least that's how it's always been for me. In school I never put enough thought into what it was that I wanted to *do* in life (except being a wife and mother)."

"He demands my total involvement. If I gaze out the window of the plane to study the cloud formations, he has to keep intruding on thoughts, to be the total center of my attention all the time. He phones from work several times a day, and pouts when I am in conference and cannot talk. The way to solve my dilemma would be to change the dead-bolt lock on the door. Oh, I'm oversimplifying . . . This man is mid-forties but his insecurities and needs will consume me if I don't try to find answers."

"In both my relationships I've become far too involved in making relationships work that should have worked on their energy or I should have let go down the drain. I had a lot of trouble doing anything good or useful for myself dating them, and this affected all my relationships with other people."

Many women feel a great conflict between having a relationship and still taking time for themselves, their own thoughts, or a job that they take seriously. Over half worry that they spend too much energy on relationships.

Women don't want love to be a conflict, don't want to be forced into a choice between being themselves and loving a man—but all too many women say that this is the very position they are in. They must choose between leaving, fighting for their rights, or losing some of the relationship—over and over again, every day.

. . .

Women Loving Women

Listening on Another Frequency

"The conversations with Anne-Marie would be so complete and involved—like 'Oh, this dinner we're going to, I have really mixed feelings about it. How do you feel about it?' And then we would speculate on our thoughts, talk about it. Or if we were having a fight, one of us would say, 'You're really taking advantage of me,' and then the other would say, 'Tell me why—explain to me how you feel about that—tell me what you mean, in depth,' and then she would listen to me for five or ten minutes—she might complain about what I said, but still she would listen. That's the relationship I had with her.

"With a woman in a relationship, nothing's taken for granted—whereas men sometimes have the attitude: we'll just cruise along here and everything will be O.K. With women, there's always a discussion, always, and the direction of the relationship is constantly up for revision. At least, it was like that with us. And I carried this on into my current relationship. I'm afraid that, really, my current partner can't deal

*For each year of data received, the number of replies questioning this idea grew.

with so much analyzing of feelings, there is too much intensity and focus on the relationship for her. . . .

"But I think that your identity develops through these discussions. Even though when you have two women together who are extremely introspective and always examining what's going on, always questioning, it can be really too much, the constant questioning—still, it's great."

Is love between women different? More equal? Do women get along better together than female/male lovers? Or is this the wrong way to put it: is what we are looking at here a different culture, of which we should ask different questions?

One woman remarks, "I think this is a window on a world that most women have no conception of whatsoever—an all-woman culture."

Are Love Relationships Between Women Different?

Another Way of Life

Is there a difference in the way women in gay relationships define love, compared with the types of love we have seen so far?

This *is* a separate culture, and yet it is also, inevitably, influenced by the culture at large. Speaking of this, one woman in her twenties asks, "*Are* women better? There are women I meet who are like 'soul sisters'—and then there are those who are just like most men—cold, distant, unable to communicate, using people, not taking other people's feelings into consideration. Have a lot of us been co-opted by male views of power—power as necessary to make a relationship attractive? We don't have many alternate models. Still, intense and maybe over-analyzed as they have been, I think my relationships with women have been closer and more rewarding than any relationship I have ever had with a man. Maybe we're not perfect, but we're definitely onto something."

Another woman, in her fifties: "People in the women's movement said the problem with relationships is that men are so macho—i.e., they never apologize and they don't ask about feelings. So gay relationships should be a lot better, because both women have the same basic equality. Is it easier to get along? I would say yes. The best types of relationships are same-sex relationships, especially between women. They have the best chance in the world: they are more equal, and time together is much better quality. But even with all this going for them, there is no way that disputes won't come up. What you learn is to negotiate those disputes, and try to remain a team anyway. Women understand this better, the team concept. I could never have a relationship with anyone except a woman. I think that's the best way in the world to go."

What is Love?

"How do I love her, now after ten years? I love her mind, her body, her abilities. She's very brave and strong, exceptionally brilliant, and a beautiful woman."

"Our love feels like a stream that flows on and on, growing ever stronger and deeper, giving me a sense of peace and center. Her sense of humor always makes me laugh; her constancy and the knowledge that she is eminently dependable give me strength; the wonderful sparkle of my passion for her—the sense of joy in her just being there—is a daily joy for me. We live near each other, we sleep together, bathe together, wash each other's hair, and rub suntan lotion on each other. I love the warmth and intimacy of that. We sort of roughly share money, whoever has some shares—we're both poor. We generally tell each other everything—intimate things, memories, dreams. We are monogamous."

"When we make love, she makes me feel as though I'm the most beautiful woman in the world. She plays with my long hair and tells me how sexy she things it is. She tells me she loves the shape of my breasts. I especially love it when she whispers, 'You are so soft.'"

"My lover is the one I live with twenty-four hours a day and go on holiday with. She is a spark strange to me. Close, but from far, far off, like no light I've ever seen. A sound that constantly catches my ear, and sets my mind reeling. I am in love with her comfortably, vigorously, and for a long term. I love her too. She is my lover, my soul mate; the one I think about when I see a certain smile, when my heart sings—a sister I have known from centuries ago. We were together once, and it was easier or more difficult than it is now—but someday, some life, it will not be hard; it will be as natural as it feels. I'm in love with her *depth,* her sparkle. It makes me secure to know I'm deeply loved."

"My lover is beautiful, courteous, intelligent, well read, and attentive. Her political and spiritual views are important to her and similar to mine. I feel happy when we are together, we have a lot of exciting adventures. For example, she had an idea of how we could start a business and get rich, and we are working on that now and have a good chance of succeeding. We live together and have a pleasant lifestyle. We don't fight but we do argue sometimes. As time passes things are working out. Our biggest difference is opposite tastes in silverware design—that and a few more serious issues! I have a greater fear of intimacy, which is slowly diminishing. I work too many hours. I neglect her sometimes and she suffers in silence. She is developing her assertiveness, and I am becoming more attentive. We share very well."

39 percent of gay women in relationships are currently "in love" with their lovers—as is the following woman:

"I am twenty-five years old, black—in love with a thirty-two-year-old woman. She's all I think about, I can't sleep, can't think straight, she's just constantly on my mind. I would like to settle down with her and be comfortable, also financially. My lover feels the same for me. When she first kissed me and told me she wanted me too, I was so happy. Being in love with her is a challenge—it's joy, pain, frustration, hurt, learning, happiness all rolled into one. My favorite love story is my own.

"I've been in this relationship for two years. I have one nineteen-month-old daughter from a previous relationship. She has one child from her ex-husband. The most important part of our relationship is communication, passion, love, and sexual intimacy, in that order. Worst is we lack time together. She lives with her relatives. If I could change things, I'd move into my own place and invite her to come with me. I love and adore her.

"I broke up with a man I used to date before I became gay. He's the father of my child. One day he just took off. I went through a lot of changes, but after a while I came to the conclusion it's his loss, not mine. I came out of it O.K. I was good to him and there was no appreciation for it. To me women are more sensitive, lovable, affectionate, better to get along with, and more faithful. I feel more emotional commitment when I have sex with a woman. This feels better to me.

"My lover is the woman I have loved the most and hated the most. She's sweet, loving, generous, kind, stubborn, selfish, good lover, confused. Not really sure what she wants out of life. We see each other often, we go shopping, to movies, out to lunch, events, etc. We talk on the phone about everything. We have a good time most of the time—except when she likes to make me jealous: I guess she likes to see how I react and if I care.

"I feel a lot of passion usually when we are out to dinner or a movie and we start teasing each other. My passions go wild. I like to explore all parts of her body, especially breasts and vagina and clitoris. The taste and smell really turn me on. Usually I orgasm the best with oral sex. Sex with someone I love is much more fulfilling.

"My woman feels it's not necessary to have a man or a lover or a baby to be a whole, complete woman. I agree. You can be a woman without any of these. A lot of women feel you must have a baby and a man in your life to be whole. I don't. You can just be yourself."

Gay women discuss as often as heterosexual women the differences between "passion" and "caring" musing over the choices:

"Being in love is a short-lived state. Loving someone is something which lasts."

"Being in love is basically selfish. While it seems to enfold the beloved, it's only one's joy at finding someone you think you won't have to work on. Loving over time means finding out what feels good to *them,* and learning to give it. Between and among those states are so many other ones. Maternal/paternal love, seeing another person as a child to be nurtured. Sometimes it seems more important to like someone than to love her. But being *in* love is a time of bonding that can't be replaced by logical manipulation."

"Love stories? I like Jane Austen, her vision of love as a mutually respectful state which grows out of friendship. But I think she missed the complications of sex—that is, she splits passion from respect. The problem is that people have to find both, at least if they're going to be monogamous."

"I think sexual passion suffers with life. Passion cannot be a constant because nothing else is. Illness changes passion. Death changes passion. Fear changes it, as do anger, poverty, drugs, pain, a phone call from the folks. That's life. Passion can return just like the return of wellness, hopefulness, money . . ."

"Often my passions have not meshed well with

the rest of my life—or rather, the object of my passion has not been the sort of person I want to live with."

"I know that when I felt the most passionate, that fit all my 'pictures' of being in love. But if I look at it in a detached way, I can see that it was mostly about sex. I am open emotionally—I must have some feeling for the person I'm having sex with, but I tend to confuse passion with love. I always thought being 'in love' would include that blinding passion, the need to tear at someone's clothes and make love constantly. And yet the person I had this feeling with is extremely screwed up, very immature emotionally, and not someone I could really have a healthy relationship with on a day-to-day basis. It's disconcerting to realize that my ideas about love have not been very realistic. I suppose that's not uncommon, but it makes for confusion."

"*In love* is explosive, obsessive, irrational, wonderful, heady, dreamy. *Loving* is long work, trust, communication, commitment, pain, pleasure."

"We have a lot of respect for each other's creative silence, for each other's interior life. We would feel totally lost without each other but it isn't a blind, confused desperation—because fundamentally we love and respect ourselves. But life would be less challenging, less inspiring without each other. Simpler, perhaps, but less rich."

"My current relationship is the first, for me, of its kind. It began in friendship, and it exists for me as a steady, sustaining sweetness of love, like happiness! I sometimes miss the heavy passion of a former relationship (a touch of masochism, perhaps) but I don't for a moment miss the panics, gnawings, or emotional scrapings of these earlier lovers. I love her less madly than earlier lovers, but far better, more deeply. The biggest problem between us is unsatisfying or perhaps unexciting sex. In some way, I suspect the failures here are related to the nature of the love, and that lust and mad passion aren't the core of our being together. That is brand-new for me. I haven't yet learned, perhaps I won't ever, how to translate the deep caring love and affection I feel for her into sexual excitement such as I'm accustomed to. I need to learn and I'm trying to. But I have more fun with my current lover than I've ever had. We talk, go to movies, play tennis, work out, travel, even work together sometimes. I love being with her."

"I think 'in love' feelings are a peak experience of contacting a higher point of ourselves and the universe, projected onto the other. But it's more important to *love* someone you are going to live with."

"I enjoy being in love, but wouldn't want it to be a lifelong feeling or state of being, it's basically frustrating for me. I think to live with someone, to love them, is vitally more important than to be in love with them. Love is the day-to-day strength needed to exist. To be 'in love' is like a drug, a euphoria, a hypnotic state where I take leave of my more responsible self and act like a kid again. Real love is trust, concern, caring, empathy. I usually can sense people I will love at the first or second meeting."

While 43 percent of gay women say they would "risk it all" for a relationship, more disagree: 57 percent of gay women say passionate love, being "in love," is too volatile to work. Still, the percentage of gay women who like *living* with a passionate relationship is significantly higher than among heterosexual women.

Here, as in "straight" replies, confusion and contradictions are frequent:

"I still desire that big passion though I know it doesn't last."

"Actually, I don't really know about working at love for a long period of time—it just hasn't worked for me."

But one woman says both passion and *stability are possible:*

"You do not have to choose between passion and stability. Sex grows much better. Daily details are a turn-on too. There is an ebb and flow to it—sparks at times."

Homophobia: A Weapon of Sexism

Suzanne Pharr

Suzanne Pharr has been an activist and organizer for more than twenty years. She has presented workshops on homophobia throughout the United States.

Pharr shows us that homophobia is every women's issue, every person's issue. As the "last acceptable bigotry" in this country, its damage to lesbians is incalculable. What is more, as Pharr makes clear, all women lose when homophobia wins, because it is a powerful weapon in the arsenal of the antifeminists.

HOMOPHOBIA—THE IRRATIONAL FEAR AND HATRED of those who love and sexually desire those of the same sex. Though I intimately knew its meaning, the word homophobia was unknown to me until the late 1970s, and when I first heard it, I was struck by how difficult it is to say, what an ugly word it is, equally as ugly as its meaning. Like racism and anti-Semitism, it is a word that calls up images of loss of freedom, verbal and physical violence, death.

In my life I have experienced the effects of homophobia through rejection by friends, threats of loss of employment, and threats upon my life; and I have witnessed far worse things happening to other lesbian and gay people: loss of children, beatings, rape, death. Its power is great enough to keep ten to twenty percent of the population living lives of fear (if their sexual identity is hidden) or lives of danger (if their sexual identity is visible) or both. And its power is great enough to keep the remaining eighty to ninety percent of the population trapped in their own fears.

Long before I had a word to describe the behavior, I was engaged in a search to discover the source of its power, the power to damage and destroy lives. The most common explanations were that to love the same sex was either abnormal (sick) or immoral (sinful).

My exploration of the sickness theory led me to understand that homosexuality is simply a matter of sexual identity, which, along with heterosexual identity, is formed in ways that no one conclusively understands. The American Psychological Association has said that it is no more abnormal to be homosexual than to be lefthanded. It is simply that a certain percentage of the population *is.* It is not healthier to be heterosexual or righthanded. What is unhealthy—and sometimes a source of stress and sickness so great it can lead to suicide—is homophobia, that societal disease that places such negative messages, condemnation, and violence on gay men and lesbians that we have to struggle throughout our lives for self-esteem.

Suzanne Pharr, *Homophobia: A Weapon of Sexism.* Chardon Press, 1988. Distributed by Women's Project, 2224 Main Street, Little Rock, Arkansas 72206.

The sin theory is a particularly curious one because it is expressed so often and with such hateful emotion both from the pulpit and from laypeople who rely heavily upon the Bible for evidence. However, there is significant evidence that the approximately eight references to homosexuality in the Bible are frequently read incorrectly, according to Dr. Virginia Ramey Mollenkott in an essay in *Christianity and Crisis:*

> *Much of the discrimination against homosexual persons is justified by a common misreading of the Bible. Many English translations of the Bible contain the word homosexual in extremely negative contexts. But the fact is that the word* homosexual *does not occur anywhere in the Bible. No extant text, no manuscript, neither Hebrew nor Greek, Syriac, nor Aramaic, contains the word. The terms* homosexual *and* heterosexual *were not developed in any language until the 1890's, when for the first time the awareness developed that there are people with a lifelong, constitutional orientation toward their own sex. Therefore the use of the word* homosexuality *by certain English Bible translators is an example of the extreme bias that endangers the human and civil rights of homosexual persons. (pp. 383–4, Nov. 9, 1987)*

Dr. Mollenkott goes on to add that two words in I Corinthians 6:9 and one word in Timothy 1:10 have been used as evidence to damn homosexuals but that well into the 20th century the first of these was understood by everyone to mean masturbation, and the second was known to refer to male prostitutes who were available for hire by either women or men. There are six other Biblical references that are thought by some to refer to homosexuals but each of these is disputed by contemporary scholars. For instance, the sin in the Sodom and Gommorah passage (Genesis 19:1-10) is less about homosexuality than it is about inhospitality and gang rape. The law of hospitality was universally accepted and Lot was struggling to uphold it against what we assume are heterosexual townsmen threatening gang rape to the two male angels in Lot's home. While people dwell on this passage as a condemnation of homosexuality, they bypass what I believe is the central issue or, if you will, *sin:* Lot's offering his two virgin daughters up to the men to be used as they desired for gang rape. Here is a perfectly clear example of devaluing and dehumanizing and violently brutalizing women.

The eight Biblical references (and not a single one by Jesus) to alleged homosexuality are very small indeed when compared to the several hundred references (and many by Jesus) to money and the necessity for justly distributing wealth. Yet few people go on a rampage about the issue of a just economic system, using the Bible as a base.

Finally, I came to understand that homosexuality, heterosexuality, bi-sexuality are *morally neutral.* A particular sexual identity is not an indication of either good or evil. What is important is not the gender of the two people in relationship with each other but the content of that relationship. Does that relationship contain violence, control of one person by the other? Is the relationship a growthful place for the people involved? It is clear that we must hold all relationships, whether opposite sex or same sex, to these standards.

The first workshops that I conducted were an effort to address these two issues, and I assumed that if consciousness could be raised about the invalidity of these two issues then people would stop feeling homophobic and would understand homophobia as a civil rights issue and work against it. The workshops took a high moral road, invoking participants' compassion, understanding, and outrage at injustice.

The eight-hour workshops raised consciousness and increased participants' commitment to work against homophobia as one more oppression in a growing list of recognized oppressions, but I still felt something was missing. I felt there was still too much unaccounted for power in homophobia even after we looked at the sick and sinful theories, at how it feels to be a lesbian in a homophobic world, at why lesbians choose invisibility, at how lesbian existence threatens male dominance. All of the pieces seemed available but we couldn't sew them together into a quilt.

As I conducted more workshops over the years I noticed several important themes that led to the final piecing together:

1. Women began to recognize that economics was a central issue connecting various oppressions;
2. Battered women began talking about how they had been called lesbians by their batterers;
3. Both heterosexual and lesbian women said they valued the workshops because in them they were given the rare opportunity to talk about their own sexuality and also about sexism in general.

Around the same time (1985–86), the National Coalition Against Domestic Violence (NCADV) entered into a traumatic relationship with the U.S. Department of Justice (DOJ), requesting a large two-year grant to provide domestic violence training and information nationally. At the time the grant was to be announced, NCADV was attacked by conservative groups such as the Heritage Foundation as a "pro-lesbian, pro-feminist, anti-family" organization. In response to these attacks, the DOJ decided not to award a grant; instead they formulated a "cooperative agreement" that allowed them to monitor and approve all work, and they assured conservative organizations that the work would not be pro-lesbian and anti-family. The major issue between NCADV and the DOJ became whether NCADV would let an outside agency define and control its work, and finally, during never-ending concern from the DOJ about "radical" and "lesbian" issues, the agreement was terminated by NCADV at the end of the first year. Throughout that year, there were endless statements and innuendoes from the DOJ and some members of NCADV's membership about NCADV's lesbian leadership and its alleged concern for only lesbian issues. Many women were damaged by the crossfire, NCADV's work was stopped for a year, and the organization was split from within. It was lesbian baiting at its worst.

As one of NCADV's lesbian leadership during that onslaught of homophobic attacks, I was still giving homophobia workshops around the country, now able to give even more personal witness to the virulence of the hatred and fear of lesbians and gay men within both institutions and individuals. It was a time of pain and often anger for those of us committed to creating a world free of violence, and it was a time of deep distress for those of us under personal attack. However, my mother, like many mothers, had always said, "All things work for the good," and sure enough, it was out of the accumulation of these experiences that the pieces began coming together to make a quilt of our understanding.

On the day that I stopped reacting to attacks and gave my time instead to visioning, this simple germinal question came forth for the workshops: "What will the world be like without homophobia in it—for everyone, female and male, whatever sexual identity?" Simple though the question is, it was at first shocking because those of us who work in the anti-violence movement spend most of our time working with the damaging, negative results of violence and have little time to vision. It is sometimes difficult to create a vision of a world we have never experienced, but without such a vision, we cannot know clearly what we are working toward in our social change work. From this question, answer led to answer until a whole appeared of our collective making, from one workshop to another.

Here are some of the answers women have given:

- Kids won't be called tomboys or sissies; they'll just be who they are, able to do what they wish.
- People will be able to love anyone, no matter what sex; the issue will simply be whether or not she/he is a good human being, compatible, and loving.
- Affection will be opened up between women and men, women and women, men and men, and it won't be centered on sex; people won't fear being called names if they show affection to someone who isn't a mate or potential mate.
- If affection is opened up, then isolation will be broken down for all of us, especially for those who generally experience little physical affection, such as unmarried old people.
- Women will be able to work whatever jobs we want without being labeled masculine.
- There will be less violence if men do not feel they have to prove and assert their manhood. Their desire to dominate and control will not spill over from the personal to the level of national and international politics and the use of bigger and better weapons to control other countries.
- People will wear whatever clothes they wish, with the priority being comfort rather than the display of femininity or masculinity.
- There will be no gender roles.

It is at this point in the workshops—having imagined a world without homophobia—that the participants see the analysis begin to fall into place. Someone notes that all the things we have been talking about relate to sexual gender roles. It's rather like the beginning of a course in Sexism 101. The next question is "Imagine the world with no sex roles—sexual identity, which may be in flux, but no sexual gender roles." Further: imagine a world in which opportunity is not determined by gender or race. Just the imagining makes women alive with excitement because it is a vision of freedom, often just glimpsed but always known deep down as truth. Pure joy.

We talk about what it would be like to be born in a world in which there were no expectations or treatment based on gender but instead only the expectation that each child, no matter what race or sex, would be given as many options and possibilities as society could muster. Then we discuss what girls and boys would be like at puberty and beyond if sex role expectations didn't come crashing down on them with girls' achievement levels beginning to decline thereafter; what it would be for women to have the training and options for economic equity with men; what would happen to issues of power and control, and therefore violence, if there were real equality. To have no prescribed sex roles would open the possibility of equality. It is a discussion women find difficult to leave. Freedom calls.

Patriarchy—an enforced belief in male dominance and control—is the ideology and sexism the system that holds it in place. The catechism goes like this: Who do gender roles serve? Men and the women who seek power from them. Who suffers from gender roles? Women most completely and men in part. How are gender roles maintained? By the weapons of sexism: economics, violence, homophobia.

Why then don't we ardently pursue ways to eliminate gender roles and therefore sexism? It is my profound belief that all people have a spark in them that yearns for freedom, and the history of the world's atrocities—from the Nazi concentration camps to white dominance in South Africa to the battering of women—is the story of attempts to snuff out that spark. When that spark doesn't move forward to full flame, it is because the weapons designed to control and destroy have wrought such intense damage over time that the spark has been all but extinguished.

Sexism, that system by which women are kept subordinate to men, is kept in place by three powerful weapons designed to cause or threaten women with pain and loss. As stated before, the three are economics, violence, and homophobia. The stories of women battered by men, victims of sexism at its worst, show these three forces converging again and again. When battered women tell why they stayed with a batterer or why they returned to a batterer, over and over they say it was because they could not support themselves and their children financially, they had no skills for jobs, they could not get housing, transportation, medical care for their children. And how were they kept controlled? Through violence and threats of violence, both physical and verbal, so that they feared for their lives and the lives of their children and doubted their own abilities and self-worth. And why were they beaten? Because they were not good enough, were not "real women," were dykes, or because they stood up to him as no "real woman" would. And the male batterer, with societal backing, felt justified, often righteous, in his behavior—for his part in keeping women in their place.

Economics must be looked at first because many feminists consider it to be the root cause of sexism. Certainly the United Nations study released at the final conference of the International Decade on Women, held in Nairobi, Kenya, in 1985, supports that belief: of the world's population, women do 75% of the work, receive 10% of the pay and own 1% of the property. In the United States it is also supported by the opposition of the government to the idea of comparable worth and pay equity, as expressed by Ronald Reagan who referred to pay equity as "a joke." Obviously, it is considered a dangerous idea. Men profit not only from women's unpaid work in the home but from our underpaid work within horizontal female segregation such as clerical workers or upwardly mobile tokenism in the workplace where a few affirmative action promotions are expected to take care of all women's economic equality needs. Moreover, they profit from women's bodies through pornography, prostitution, and international female sexual slavery. And white men profit from both the labor of women and of men of color. Forced economic dependency puts women under male control and severely limits women's options for self-determination and self-sufficiency.

This truth is borne out by the fact that according to the National Commission on Working Women, on average, women of all races working year round earn only 64 cents to every one dollar a man makes. Also, the U.S. Census Bureau reports that only 9 percent of working women make over $25,000 a year. There is fierce opposition to women gaining employment in the nontraditional job market, that is, those jobs that traditionally employ less than 25 percent women. After a woman has gained one of these higher paying jobs, she is often faced with sexual harassment, lesbian baiting, and violence. It is clear that in the workplace there is an all-out effort to keep women in traditional roles so that the only jobs we are "qualified" for are the low-paid ones.

Actually, we have to look at economics not only as the root cause of sexism but also as the underlying, driving force that keeps all the oppressions in place. In the United States, our economic system is shaped like a pyramid, with a few people at the top, primarily white males, being supported by large numbers of unpaid or low-paid workers at the bottom. When we look at this pyramid, we begin to understand the major connection between sexism and racism because those groups at the bottom of the pyramid are women and people of color. We then begin to understand why there is such a fervent effort to keep those oppressive systems (racism and sexism and all the ways they are manifested) in place to maintain the unpaid and low-paid labor.

Susan DeMarco and Jim Hightower, writing for *Mother Jones,* report that *Forbes* magazine indicated that "the 400 richest families in America last year had an average net worth of $550 million each. These and less than a million other families—roughly one percent of our population—are at the prosperous tip of our society. . . . In 1976, the wealthiest 1 percent of America's families owned 19.2 percent of the nation's total wealth. (This sum of wealth counts all of America's cash, real estate, stocks, bonds, factories, art, personal property, and anything else of financial value.) By 1983, those at this 1 percent tip of our economy owned 34.3 percent of our wealth. . . . *Today, the top 1 percent of Americans possesses more net wealth than the bottom 90 percent.*" (My italics.) (*May, 1988, pp. 32–33*)

In order for this top-heavy system of economic inequity to maintain itself, the 90 percent on the bottom must keep supplying cheap labor. A very complex, intricate system of institutionalized oppressions is necessary to maintain the status quo so that the vast majority will not demand its fair share of wealth and resources and bring the system down. Every institution—schools, banks, churches, government, courts, media, etc.—as well as individuals must be enlisted in the campaign to maintain such a system of gross inequity.

What would happen if women gained the earning opportunities and power that men have? What would happen if these opportunities were distributed equitably, no matter what sex one was, no matter what race one was born into, and no matter where one lived? What if educational and training opportunities were equal? Would women spend most of our youth preparing for marriage? Would marriage be based on economic survival for women? What would happen to issues of power and control? Would women stay with our batterers? If a woman had economic independence in a society where women had equal opportunities, would she still be thought of as owned by her father or husband?

Economics is the great controller in both sexism and racism. If a person can't acquire food, shelter, and clothing and provide them for children, then that person can be forced to do many things in order to survive. The major tactic, worldwide, is to provide unrecompensed or inadequately recompensed labor for the benefit of those who control wealth. Hence, we see women performing unpaid labor in the home or filling low-paid jobs, and we see people of color in the lowest-paid jobs available.

The method is complex: limit educational and training opportunities for women and for people of color and then withhold adequate paying jobs with the excuse that people of color and women are incapable of filling them. Blame the economic victim and keep the victim's self-esteem low through invisibility and distortion within the media and education. Allow a few people of color and women to succeed among the profitmakers so that blaming those who don't "make it" can be intensified. Encourage those few who succeed in gaining power now to turn against those who remain behind rather than to use their resources to make change for all. Maintain the myth of scarcity—that there are not enough jobs, resources, etc., to go around—among the middleclass so that they will not unite with laborers, immigrants, and the unemployed. The method keeps in place a system of control and profit by a few and a constant source of cheap labor to maintain it.

If anyone steps out of line, take her/his job away. Let homelessness and hunger do their work. The economic weapon works. And we end up saying, "I would do this or that—be openly who I am, speak out against injustice, work for civil rights, join a labor union, go to a political march, etc.—if I didn't have this job. I can't afford to lose it." We stay in an abusive situation because we see no other way to survive.

In the battered women's movement abusive relationships are said to be about power and control and the way out of them is through looking at the ways power and control work in our lives, developing support, improving self-esteem, and achieving control over our decisions and lives. We have yet to apply these methods successfully to our economic lives. Though requiring massive change, the way there also lies open for equality and wholeness. But the effort will require at least as much individual courage and risk and group support as it does for a battered woman to leave her batterer, and that requirement is very large indeed. Yet battered women find the courage to leave their batterers every day. They walk right into the unknown. To break away from economic domination and control will require a movement made up of individuals who possess this courage and ability to take risks.

Violence is the second means of keeping women in line, in a narrowly defined place and role. First, there is the physical violence of battering, rape, and incest. Often when battered women come to shelters and talk about their lives, they tell stories of being not only physically beaten but also raped and their children subjected to incest. Work in the women's antiviolence movement during almost two decades has provided significant evidence that each of these acts, including rape and incest, is an attempt to seek power over and control of another person. In each case, the victim is viewed as an object and is used to meet the abuser's needs. The violence is used to wreak punishment and to demand compliance or obedience.

Violence against women is directly related to the condition of women in a society that refuses us equal pay, equal access to resources, and equal status with males. From this condition comes men's confirmation of their sense of ownership of women, power over women, and assumed right to control women for their own means. Men physically and emotionally abuse women because they *can,* because they live in a world that gives them permission. Male violence is fed by their sense of their *right* to dominate and control, and their sense of superiority over a group of people who, because of gender, they consider inferior to them.

It is not just the violence but the threat of violence that controls our lives. Because the burden of responsibility has been placed so often on the potential victim, as women we have curtailed our freedom in order to protect ourselves from violence. Because of the threat of rapists, we stay on alert, being careful not to walk in isolated places, being careful where we park our cars, adding incredible security measures to our homes—massive locks, lights, alarms, if we can afford them—and we avoid places where we will appear vulnerable or unprotected while the abuser walks with freedom. Fear, often now so commonplace that it is unacknowledged, shapes our lives, reducing our freedom.

As Bernice Reagan of the musical group Sweet Honey in the Rock said at the 1982 National Coalition Against Domestic Violence conference, women seem to carry a genetic memory that women were once burned as witches when we stepped out of line. To this day, mothers pass on to their daughters word of the dangers they face and teach them the ways they must limit their lives in order to survive.

Part of the way sexism stays in place is the societal promise of survival, false and unfulfilled as it is, that women will not suffer violence if we attach ourselves to a man to protect us. A woman without a man is told she is vulnerable to external violence and, worse, that there is something wrong with her. When the male abuser calls a woman a lesbian, he is not so much labeling her a woman who loves women as he is warning her that by resisting him, she is choosing to be outside society's protection from male institutions and therefore from wide-ranging, unspecified, ever-present violence. When she seeks assistance from woman friends or a battered women's shelter, he recognizes the power in woman bonding and fears loss of her servitude and loyalty: the potential loss of his control. The concern is not affectional/sexual identity: the concern is disloyalty and the threat is violence.

The threat of violence against women who step out of line or who are disloyal is made all the more powerful by the fact that women do not have to do anything—they may be paragons of virtue and subservience—to receive violence against our lives: the violence still comes. It comes because of the woman-hating that exists throughout society. Chance plays a larger part than virtue in keeping women safe. Hence, with violence always a threat to us, women can never feel completely secure and confident. Our sense of safety is always fragile and tenuous.

Many women say that verbal violence causes more harm than physical violence because it damages self-esteem so deeply. Women have not wanted to hear battered women say that the verbal abuse was as hurtful as the physical abuse: to acknowledge that truth would be tantamount to acknowledging that *virtually every woman is a battered woman.* It is difficult to keep strong against accusations of being a bitch, stupid, inferior, etc., etc. It is especially difficult when these individual assaults are backed up by a society that shows women in textbooks, advertising, TV programs, movies, etc., as debased, silly, inferior, and sexually objectified, and society that gives tacit approval to pornography. When we internalize these messages, we call the result "low self-esteem," a therapeutic individualized term. It seems to me we should use the more political expression: when we internalize these messages, we experience *internalized sexism,* and we experience it in common with all women living in a sexist world. The violence against us is supported by a society in which woman-hating is deeply imbedded.

In "Eyes on the Prize," a 1987 Public Television documentary about the Civil Rights Movement, an older white woman says about her youth in the South that it was difficult to be anything different from what was around her when there was no vision for another way to be. Our society presents images of women that say it is appropriate to commit violence against us. Violence is committed against women because we are seen as inferior in status and in worth. It has been the work of the women's movement to present a vision of another way to be.

Every time a woman gains the strength to resist and leave her abuser, we are given a model of the importance of stepping out of line, of moving toward freedom. And we all gain strength when she says to violence, "Never again!" Thousands of women in the last fifteen years have resisted their abusers to come to this country's 1100 battered women's shelters. There they have sat down with other women to share their stories, to discover that their stories again and again are the same, to develop an analysis that shows that violence is a statement about power and control, and to understand how sexism creates the climate for male violence. Those brave women are now a part of a movement that gives hope for another way to live in equality and peace.

Homophobia works effectively as a weapon of sexism because it is joined with a powerful arm, heterosexism. Heterosexism creates the climate for homophobia with its assumption that the world is and must be heterosexual and its display of power and privilege as the norm. Heterosexism is the systemic display of homophobia in the institutions of society. Heterosexism and homophobia work together to enforce compulsory heterosexuality and that bastion of patriarchal power, the nuclear family. The central focus of the rightwing attack against women's liberation is that women's equality, women's self-determination, women's control of our own bodies and lives will damage what they see as the crucial societal institution, the nuclear family. The attack has been led by fundamentalist ministers across the country. The two areas they have focused on most consistently are abortion and homosexuality, and their passion has led them to bomb women's clinics and to recommend deprogramming for homosexuals and establishing camps to quarantine people with AIDS. To resist marriage and/or heterosexuality is to risk severe punishment and loss.

It is not by chance that when children approach puberty and increased sexual awareness they begin to taunt each other by calling these names: "queer," "faggot," "pervert." It is at puberty that the full force of society's pressure to conform to heterosexuality and prepare for marriage is brought to bear. Children know what we have taught them, and we have given clear messages that those who deviate from standard expectations are to be made to get back in line. The best controlling tactic at puberty is to be treated as an outsider, to be ostracized at a time when it feels most vital to be accepted. Those who are different must be made to suffer loss. It is also at puberty that misogyny begins to be more apparent, and girls are pressured to conform to societal norms that do not permit them to realize their full potential. It is at this time that their academic achievements begin to decrease as they are coerced into compulsory heterosexuality and trained for dependency upon a man, that is, for economic survival.

There was a time when the two most condemning accusations against a woman meant to ostracize and disempower her were "whore" and "lesbian." The sexual revolution and changing attitudes about heterosexual behavior may have led to some lessening of the power of the word *whore,* though it still has strength as a threat to sexual property and prostitutes are stigmatized and abused. However, the word *lesbian* is still fully charged and carries with it the full threat of loss of power and privilege, the threat of being cut asunder, abandoned, and left outside society's protection.

To be a lesbian is to be *perceived* as someone who has stepped out of line, who has moved out of sexual/economic dependence on a male, who is woman-identified. A lesbian is perceived as someone who can live without a man, and who is therefore (however illogically) against men. A lesbian is perceived as being outside the acceptable, routinized order of things.

She is seen as someone who has no societal institutions to protect her and who is not privileged to the protection of individual males. Many heterosexual women see her as someone who stands in contradiction to the sacrifices they have made to conform to compulsory heterosexuality. A lesbian is perceived as a threat to the nuclear family, to male dominance and control, to the very heart of sexism.

Gay men are perceived also as a threat to male dominance and control, and the homophobia expressed against them has the same roots in sexism as does homophobia against lesbians. Visible gay men are the objects of extreme hatred and fear by heterosexual men because their breaking ranks with male heterosexual solidarity is seen as a damaging rent in the very fabric of sexism. They are seen as betrayers, as traitors who must be punished and eliminated. In the beating and killing of gay men we see clear evidence of this hatred. When we see the fierce homophobia expressed toward gay men, we can begin to understand the ways sexism also affects males through imposing rigid, dehumanizing gender roles on them. The two circumstances in which it is legitimate for men to be openly physically affectionate with one another are in competitive sports and in the crisis of war. For many men, these two experiences are the highlights of their lives, and they think of them again and again with nostalgia. War and sports offer a cover of all-male safety and dominance to keep away the notion of affectionate openness being identified with homosexuality. When gay men break ranks with male roles through bonding and affection outside the arenas of war and sports, they are perceived as not being "real men," that is, as being identified with women, the weaker sex that must be dominated and that over the centuries has been the object of male hatred and abuse. Misogyny gets transferred to gay men with a vengeance and is increased by the fear that their sexual identity and behavior will bring down the entire system of male dominance and compulsory heterosexuality.

If lesbians are established as threats to the status quo, as outcasts who must be punished, homophobia can wield its power over all women through lesbian baiting. Lesbian baiting is an attempt to control women by labeling us as lesbians because our behavior is not acceptable, that is, when we are being independent, going our own way, living whole lives, fighting for our rights, demanding equal pay, saying no to violence, being self-assertive, bonding with and loving the company of women, assuming the right to our bodies, insisting upon our own authority, making changes that include us in society's decision-making; lesbian baiting occurs when women are called lesbians because we resist male dominance and control. And it has little or nothing to do with one's sexual identity.

To be named as lesbian threatens all women, not just lesbians, with great loss. And any woman who steps out of role risks being called a lesbian. To understand how this is a threat to all women, one must understand that any woman can be called a lesbian and there is no real way she can defend herself: there is no way to credential one's sexuality. ("The Children's Hour," a Lillian Hellman play, makes this point when a student asserts two teachers are lesbians and they have no way to disprove it.) She may be married or divorced, have children, dress in the most feminine manner, have sex with men, be celibate—but there are lesbians who do all those things. *Lesbians look like all women and all women look like lesbians.* There is no guaranteed method of identification, and as we all know, sexual identity can be kept hidden. (The same is true for men. There is no way to prove their sexual identity, though many go to extremes to prove heterosexuality.) Also, women are not necessarily born lesbian. Some seem to be, but others become lesbians later in life after having lived heterosexual lives. Lesbian baiting of heterosexual women would not work if there were a definitive way to identify lesbians (or heterosexuals.)

We have yet to understand clearly how sexual identity develops. And this is disturbing to some people, especially those who are determined to discover how lesbian and gay identity is formed so that they will know where to start in eliminating it. (Isn't it odd that there is so little concern about discovering the causes of heterosexuality?) There are many theories: genetic makeup, hormones, socialization, environment, etc. But there is no conclusive evidence that indicates that heterosexuality comes from one process and homosexuality from another.

We do know, however, that sexual identity can be in flux, and we know that sexual identity means more than just the gender of people one is attracted to and has sex with. To be a lesbian has as many ramifications as for a woman to be heterosexual. It is more than sex, more than just the bedroom issue many would like to make it: it is a woman-centered life with all the social interconnections that entails. Some lesbians are in long-term relationships, some in short-term ones, some date, some are celibate, some are married to men, some remain as separate as possible from men, some have children by men, some by alternative insemination, some seem "feminine" by societal standards, some "masculine," some are doctors, lawyers and ministers, some laborers, housewives and writers: what all share in common is a sexual/affectional identity that focuses on women in its attractions and social relationships.

If lesbians are simply women with a particular sexual identity who look and act like all women, then the major difference in living out a lesbian sexual identity as opposed to a heterosexual identity is that as lesbians we live in a homophobic world that threatens and imposes damaging loss on us for being *who we are,* for choosing to live whole lives. Homophobic people often assert that homosexuals have the choice of not being homosexual; that is, we don't have to act out our sexual identity. In that case, I want to hear heterosexuals talk about their willingness not to act out their sexual identity, including not just sexual activity but heterosexual social interconnections and heterosexual privilege. It is a question of wholeness. It is very difficult for one to be denied the life of a sexual being, whether expressed in sex or in physical affection, and to feel complete, whole. For our loving relationships with humans feed the life of the spirit and enable us to overcome our basic isolation and to be interconnected with humankind.

If, then, any woman can be named a lesbian and be threatened with terrible losses, what is it she fears? Are these fears real? Being vulnerable to a homophobic world can lead to these losses:

- *Employment.* The loss of job leads us right back to the economic connection to sexism. This fear of job loss exists for almost every lesbian except perhaps those who are self-employed or in a business that does not require societal approval. Consider how many businesses or organizations you know that will hire and protect people who are openly gay or lesbian.
- *Family.* Their approval, acceptance, love.
- *Children.* Many lesbians and gay men have children, but very, very few gain custody in court challenges, even if the other parent is a known abuser. Other children may be kept away from us as though gays and lesbians are abusers. There are written and unwritten laws prohibiting lesbians and gays from being foster parents or from adopting children. There is an irrational fear that children in contact with lesbians and gays will become homosexual through influence or that they will be sexually abused. Despite our knowing that 95 percent of those who sexually abuse children are heterosexual men, there are no policies keeping heterosexual men from teaching or working with children, yet in almost every school system in America, visible gay men and lesbians are not hired through either written or unwritten law.
- *Heterosexual privilege and protection.* No institutions, other than those created by lesbians and gays—such as the Metropolitan Community Church, some counseling centers, political organizations such as the National Gay and Lesbian Task Force, the National Coalition of Black Lesbians and Gays, the Lambda Legal Defense and Education Fund, etc.—affirm homosexuality and offer protection. Affirmation and protection cannot be gained from the criminal justice system, mainline churches, educational institutions, the government.
- *Safety.* There is nowhere to turn for safety from physical and verbal attacks because the norm presently in this country is that it is acceptable to be overtly homophobic. Gay men are beaten on the streets; lesbians are kidnapped and "deprogrammed." The National Gay and Lesbian Task Force, in an extended study, has documented violence against lesbians and gay men and noted the inadequate response of the criminal justice system. One of the major differences between homophobia/heterosexism and racism and sexism is that because of the Civil Rights Movement and the women's movement racism and sexism are expressed more covertly (though with great harm); because there has not been a major, visible lesbian and gay movement, it is permissible to be overtly homophobic in any institution or public forum. Churches spew forth homophobia in the same way they did racism prior to the Civil Rights Movement. Few laws are in place to protect lesbians and gay men, and the criminal justice system is wracked with homophobia.
- *Mental health.* An overtly homophobic world in which there is full permission to treat lesbians and gay men with cruelty makes it difficult for lesbians

and gay men to maintain a strong sense of well-being and self-esteem. Many lesbians and gay men are beaten, raped, killed, subjected to aversion therapy, or put in mental institutions. The impact of such hatred and negativity can lead one to depression and, in some cases, to suicide. The toll on the gay and lesbian community is devastating.

- *Community.* There is rejection by those who live in homophobic fear, those who are afraid of association with lesbians and gay men. For many in the gay and lesbian community, there is a loss of public acceptance, a loss of allies, a loss of place and belonging.
- *Credibility.* This fear is large for many people: the fear that they will no longer be respected, listened to, honored, believed. They fear they will be social outcasts.

The list goes on and on. But any one of these essential components of a full life is large enough to make one deeply fear its loss. A black woman once said to me in a workshop, "When I fought for Civil Rights, I always had my family and community to fall back on even when they didn't fully understand or accept what I was doing. I don't know if I could have borne losing them. And you people don't have either with you. It takes my breath away."

What does a woman have to do to get called a lesbian? Almost anything, sometimes nothing at all, but certainly anything that threatens the status quo, anything that steps out of role, anything that asserts the rights of women, anything that doesn't indicate submission and subordination. Assertiveness, standing up for oneself, asking for more pay, better working conditions, training for and accepting a non-traditional (you mean a man's?) job, enjoying the company of women, being financially independent, being in control of one's life, depending first and foremost upon oneself, thinking that one can do whatever needs to be done, but above all, working for the rights and equality of women.

In the backlash to the gains of the women's liberation movement, there has been an increased effort to keep definitions man-centered. Therefore, to work on behalf of women must mean to work against men. To love women must mean that one hates men. A very effective attack has been made against the word *feminist* to make it a derogatory word. In current backlash usage, *feminist* equals *man-hater* which equals *lesbian.* This formula is created in the hope that women will be frightened away from their work on behalf of women. Consequently, we now have women who believe in the rights of women and work for those rights while from fear deny that they are feminists, or refuse to use the word because it is so "abrasive."

So what does one do in an effort to keep from being called a lesbian? She steps back into line, into the role that is demanded of her, tries to behave in such a way that doesn't threaten the status of men, and if she works for women's rights, she begins modifying that work. When women's organizations begin doing significant social change work, they inevitably are lesbian-baited; that is, funders or institutions or community members tell us that they can't work with us because of our "man-hating attitudes" or the presence of lesbians. We are called too strident, told we are making enemies, not doing good.

The battered women's movement has seen this kind of attack: the pressure has been to provide services only, without analysis of the causes of violence against women and strategies for ending it. To provide only services without political analysis or direct action is to be in an approved "helping" role; to analyze the causes of violence against women is to begin the work toward changing an entire system of power and control. It is when we do the latter that we are threatened with the label of man-hater or lesbian. For my politics, if a women's social change organization has not been labeled lesbian or communist, it is probably not doing significant work; it is only "making nice."

Women in many of these organizations, out of fear of all the losses we are threatened with, begin to modify our work to make it more acceptable and less threatening to the male-dominated society which we originally set out to change. The work can no longer be radical (going to the root cause of the problem) but instead must be reforming, working only on the symptoms and not the cause. Real change for women becomes thwarted and stopped. The word *lesbian* is instilled with the power to halt our work and control our lives. And we give it its power with our fear.

In my view, homophobia has been one of the major causes of the failure of the women's liberation movement to make deep and lasting change. (The other major block has been racism.) We were fierce when we set out but when threatened with the loss of heterosexual privilege, we began putting on brakes. Our best-known nationally distributed women's magazine was reluctant to print articles about lesbians, began putting a man on the cover several times a year, and writing articles about women who succeeded in a man's world. We worried about our image, our being all right, our being "real women" despite our work. Instead of talking about the elimination of sexual gender roles, we stepped back and talked about "sex role stereotyping" as the issue. Change around the edges for middleclass white women began to be talked about as successes. We accepted tokenism and integration, forgetting that equality for all women, for all people—and not just equality of white middleclass women with white men—was the goal that we could never put behind us.

But despite backlash and retreats, change is growing from within. The women's liberation movement is beginning to gain strength again because there are women who are talking about liberation for all women. We are examining sexism, racism, homophobia, classism, anti-Semitism, ageism, ableism, and imperialism, and we see everything as connected. This change in point of view represents the third wave of the women's liberation movement, a new direction that does not get mass media coverage and recognition. It has been initiated by women of color and lesbians who were marginalized or rendered invisible by the white heterosexual leaders of earlier efforts. The first wave was the 19th and early 20th century campaign for the vote; the second, beginning in the 1960s, focused on the Equal Rights Amendment and abortion rights. Consisting of predominantly white middleclass women, both failed in recognizing issues of equality and empowerment for all women. The third wave of the movement, multi-racial and multi-issued, seeks the transformation of the world for us all. We know that we won't get there until everyone gets there; that we must move forward in a great strong line, hand in hand, not just a few at a time.

We know that the arguments about homophobia originating from mental health and Biblical/religious attitudes can be settled when we look at the sexism that permeates religious and psychiatric history. The women of the third wave of the women's liberation movement know that *without the existence of sexism, there would be no homophobia.*

Finally, we know that as long as the word lesbian can strike fear in any woman's heart, then work on behalf of women can be stopped; the only successful work against sexism must include work against homophobia.

The Problem That Has No Name

Betty Friedan

Betty Friedan, born in Peoria, Illinois, in 1921 and educated at Smith College and the University of California at Berkeley, has been active in the current wave of the women's movement almost from its beginning. Some have credited her book, The Feminine Mystique, *with precipitating the feminist dialogue among the general public. She took part in founding NOW, the National Organization for Women, in 1966; in organizing the Women's Strike for Equality (1970); and coconvened the National Women's Political Caucus (1971). Having taught at several universities, Friedan is now a member of many national boards and associations. She is the author of three other books on the women's movement:* It Changed My Life *(1976),* The Second Stage *(1981), and* The Fountain of Age (1993).

In this selection from the first chapter of The Feminine Mystique, *Friedan describes the inchoate sense of something wrong lodged in the minds and feelings of countless American housewives, a sense that puts the lie to the "feminine mystique," the cultural image of wifely and domestic bliss. Friedan's work is powerful not only because it so accurately delineates the nature of the mystique, but because it also captures the flaws in the image as well, the fall from grace of happily-ever-after-land and the dangers for those who believe in or seek it.*

THE PROBLEM LAY BURIED, UNSPOKEN, FOR MANY years in the minds of American women. It was a strange stirring, a sense of dissatisfaction, a yearning that women suffered in the middle of the twentieth century in the United States. Each suburban wife struggled with it alone. As she made the beds, shopped for groceries, matched slipcover material, ate peanut butter sandwiches with her children, chauffeured Cub Scouts and Brownies, lay beside her husband at night—she was afraid to ask even of herself the silent question—"Is this all?"

For over fifteen years there was no word of this yearning in the millions of words written about women, for women, in all the columns, books and articles by experts telling women their role was to seek fulfillment as wives and mothers. Over and over women heard in voices of tradition and of Freudian sophistication that they could desire no greater destiny than to glory in their own femininity. Experts told them how to catch a man and keep him, how to breastfeed children and handle their toilet training, how to cope with sibling rivalry and adolescent rebellion; how to buy a dishwasher, bake bread, cook gourmet snails, and build a swimming pool with their own hands; how to dress, look, and act more feminine and make marriage more exciting; how to keep their husbands from dying young and their sons from growing into delinquents. They were taught to pity the neurotic, unfeminine, unhappy women who wanted to be poets or physicists or presidents. They learned that truly feminine women do not want careers, higher education, political rights—the independence and the opportunities that the old-fashioned feminists fought for. Some women, in their forties and fifties, still remembered painfully giving up those dreams, but most of the younger women no longer even thought about them. A thousand expert voices applauded their femininity, their adjustment, their new maturity. All they had to do was devote their lives from earliest girlhood to finding a husband and bearing children. . . .

The suburban housewife—she was the dream image of the young American woman and the envy, it was said, of women all over the world. The American housewife—freed by science and labor-saving appliances from the drudgery, the dangers of childbirth and the illnesses of her grandmother. She was healthy, beautiful, educated, concerned only about her husband, her children, her home. She had found true feminine fulfillment. As a housewife and mother, she was respected as a full and equal partner to man in his world. She was free to choose automobiles, clothes, appliances, supermarkets; she had everything that women ever dreamed of.

In the fifteen years after World War II, this mystique of feminine fulfillment became the cherished and self-perpetuating core of contemporary American culture. Millions of women lived their lives in the image of those pretty pictures of the American suburban housewife, kissing their husbands goodbye in front of the picture window, depositing their stationwagonsful of children at school, and smiling as they ran the new electric waxer over the spotless kitchen floor. They baked their own bread, sewed their own and their children's clothes, kept their new washing machines and dryers running all day. They changed the sheets on the beds twice a week instead of once, took the rug-hooking class in adult education, and pitied their poor frustrated mothers, who had dreamed of having a career. Their only dream was to be perfect wives and mothers; their highest ambition to have five children and a beautiful house, their only fight to get and keep their husbands. They had no thought for the unfeminine problems of the world outside the home; they wanted the men to make the major decisions. The gloried in their role as women, and wrote proudly on the census blank: "Occupation: housewife." . . .

If a woman had a problem in the 1950's and 1960's, she knew that something must be wrong with her marriage, or with herself. Other women were satisfied with their lives, she thought. What kind of a woman was she if she did not feel this mysterious fulfillment waxing the kitchen floor? She was so ashamed to admit her dissatisfaction that she never knew how many other women shared it. If she tried to tell her husband, he didn't understand what she was talking about. She did not really understand it herself. For over fifteen years women in America found it harder to talk about this problem than about sex. Even the psychoanalysts had no name for it. When a woman went to a psychiatrist for help, as many women did, she would say, "I'm so ashamed," or "I must be hopelessly neurotic." "I don't know what's wrong with women today," a suburban psychiatrist said uneasily. "I only know something is wrong because most of my patients happen to be women. And their problem isn't sexual." Most women with this problem did not go to see a psychoanalyst, however. "There's nothing wrong really," they kept telling themselves. "There isn't any problem."

But on an April morning in 1959, I heard a mother of four, having coffee with four other mothers in a suburban development fifteen miles from New York, say in a tone of quiet desperation, "the problem." And the others knew, without words, that she was not talking about a problem with her husband, or her children, or her home. Suddenly they realized they all shared the same problem, the problem that has no name. They began, hesitantly, to talk about it. Later, after they had picked up their children at nursery school and taken them home to nap, two of the women cried, in sheer relief, just to know they were not alone.

Gradually I came to realize that the problem that has no name was shared by countless women in America. As a magazine writer I often interviewed women about problems with their children, or their marriages, or their houses, or their communities. But after a while I began to recognize the telltale signs of this other problem. I saw the same signs in suburban ranch houses and split-levels on Long Island and in New Jersey and Westchester County; in colonial houses in a small Massachusetts town; on patios in Memphis; in suburban and city apartments; in living rooms in the Midwest. Sometimes I sensed the problem, not as a reporter, but as a suburban housewife, for during this time I was also bringing up my own three children in Rockland County, New York. I heard echoes of the problem in college dormitories and semi-private maternity wards, at PTA meetings and luncheons of the League of Women Voters, at suburban cocktail parties, in station wagons waiting for trains, and in snatches of conversation overheard at Schrafft's. The groping words I heard from other women, on quiet afternoons when children were at school or on quiet evenings when husbands worked late, I think I understood first as a woman long before I understood their larger social and psychological implications.

Just what was this problem that has no name? What were the words women used when they tried to express it? Sometimes a woman would say "I feel empty somehow . . . incomplete." Or she would say, "I feel as if I don't exist." Sometimes she blotted out the feeling with a tranquilizer. Sometimes she thought the problem was with her husband, or her children, or that what she really needed was to redecorate her house, or move to a better neighborhood, or have an affair, or another baby. Sometimes, she went to a doctor with symptoms she could hardly describe: "A tired feeling . . . I get so angry with the children it scares me . . . I feel like crying without any reason." (A Cleveland doctor called it "the housewife's syndrome.") A number of women told me about great bleeding blisters that break out on their hands and arms. "I call it the housewife's blight," said a family doctor in Pennsylvania. "I see it so often lately in these young women with four, five and six children who bury themselves in their dishpans. But it isn't caused by detergent and it isn't cured by cortisone." . . .

In 1960, the problem that has no name burst like a boil through the image of the happy American housewife. In the television commercials the pretty housewives still beamed over their foaming dishpans and *Time's* cover story on "The Suburban Wife, and American Phenomenon" protested: "Having too good a time . . . to believe that they should be unhappy." But the actual unhappiness of the American housewife was suddenly being reported—from the *New York Times* and *Newsweek* to *Good Housekeeping* and CBS Television ("The Trapped Housewife"), although almost everybody who talked about it found some superficial reason to dismiss it. It was attributed to incompetent appliance repairmen (*New York Times*), or the distances children must be chauffeured in the suburbs (*Time*), or too much PTA (*Redbook*). Some said it was the old problem—education: more and more women had education, which naturally made them unhappy in their role as housewives. "The road from Freud to Frigidaire, from Sophocles to Spock, has turned out to be a bumpy one," reported the *New York Times* (June 28, 1960). "Many young women—certainly not all—whose education plunged them into a world of ideas feel stifled in their homes. They find their routine lives out of joint with their training. Like shut-ins, they feel left out. In the last year, the problem of the educated housewife has provided the meat of dozens of speeches made by troubled presidents of women's colleges who maintain, in the face of complaints, that sixteen years of academic training is realistic preparation for wifehood and motherhood."

There was much sympathy for the educated housewife. ("Like a two-headed schizophrenic . . . once she wrote a paper on the Graveyard poets; now she writes notes to the milkman. Once she determined the boiling point of sulphuric acid; now she determines her boiling point with the overdue repairman. . . . The housewife often is reduced to screams and tears. . . . No one, it seems, is appreciative, least of all herself, of the kind of person she becomes in the process of turning from poetess into shrew.")

Home economists suggested more realistic preparation for housewives, such as high-school workshops in home appliances. College educators suggested more discussion groups on home management and the family, to prepare women for the adjustment to domestic life. A spate of articles appeared in the mass magazines offering "Fifty-eight Ways to Make Your Marriage More Exciting." No month went by without a new book by a psychiatrist or sexologist offering technical advice on finding greater fulfillment through sex.

A male humorist joked in *Harper's Bazaar* (July, 1960) that the problem could be solved by taking away women's right to vote. ("In the pre-19th Amendment era, the American woman was placid, sheltered and sure of her role in American society. She left all the political decisions to her husband and he, in turn, left all the family decisions to her. Today a woman has to make both the family *and* the political decisions, and it's too much for her.")

A number of educators suggested seriously that women no longer be admitted to the four-year colleges and universities: in the growing college crisis, the education which girls could not use as housewives was more urgently needed than ever by boys to do the work of the atomic age.

The problem was also dismissed with drastic solutions no one could take seriously. (A woman writer proposed in *Harper's* that women be drafted for compulsory service as nurses' aides and baby-sitters.) And it was smoothed over with the age-old panaceas: "love is their answer," "the only answer is inner help," "the secret of completeness—children," "a private means of intellectual fulfillment," "to cure this toothache of the spirit—the simple formula of handing one's self and one's will over to God."[1]

The problem was dismissed by telling the housewife she doesn't realize how lucky she is—her own boss, no time clock, no junior executive gunning for her job. What if she isn't happy—does she think men are happy in this world? Does she really, secretly, still want to be a man? Doesn't she know yet how lucky she is to be a woman? . . .

Even so, most men, and some women, still did not know that this problem was real. But those who had faced it honestly knew that all the superficial remedies, the sympathetic advice, the scolding words and the cheering words were somehow drowning the problem in unreality. A bitter laugh was beginning to be heard from American women. They were admired, envied, pitied, theorized over until they were sick of it, offered drastic solutions or silly choices that no one could take seriously. They got all kinds of advice from the growing armies of marriage and child-guidance counselors, psychotherapists, and armchair psychologists, on how to adjust to their role as housewives. No other road to fulfillment was offered to American women in the middle of the twentieth century. Most adjusted to their role and suffered or ignored the problem that has no name. It can be less painful for a woman, not to hear the strange, dissatisfied voice stirring within her.

It is no longer possible to ignore that voice, to dismiss the desperation of so many American women. This is not what being a woman means, no matter what the experts say. For human suffering there is a reason; perhaps the reason has not been found because the right questions have not been asked, or pressed far enough. I do not accept the answer that there is no problem because American women have luxuries that women in other times and lands never dreamed of; part of the strange newness of the problem is that it cannot be understood in terms of the age-old material problems of man: poverty, sickness, hunger, cold. The women who suffer this problem have a hunger that food cannot fill. . . .

Can the problem that has no name be somehow related to the domestic routine of the housewife? When a woman tries to put the problem into words, she often merely describes the daily life she leads. What is there in this recital of comfortable domestic detail that could possibly cause such a feeling of desperation? Is she trapped simply by the enormous demands of her role as modern housewife: wife, mistress, mother, nurse, consumer, cook, chauffeur; expert on interior decoration, child care, appliance repair, furniture refinishing, nutrition, and education? Her day is fragmented as she rushes from dishwasher to washing machine to telephone to dryer to station wagon to supermarket, and delivers Johnny to the Little League field, takes Janey to dancing class, gets the lawnmower fixed and meets the 6:45. She can never spend more than 15 minutes on any one thing; she has no time to read books, only magazines; even if she had time, she has lost the power to concentrate. At the end of the day, she is so terribly tired that sometimes her husband has to take over and put the children to bed.

Thus terrible tiredness took so many women to doctors in the 1950's that one decided to investigate it. He found, surprisingly, that his patients suffering from "housewife's fatigue" slept more than an adult needed to sleep—as much as ten hours a day—and that the actual energy they expended on housework did not tax their capacity. The real problem must be something else, he decided—perhaps boredom. Some doctors told their women patients they must get out of the house for a day, treat themselves to a movie in town. Others prescribed tranquilizers. Many suburban housewives were taking tranquilizers like cough drops. "You wake up in the morning, and you feel as if there's no point in going on another day like this. So you take a tranquilizer because it makes you not care so much that it's pointless."

It is easy to see the concrete details that trap the suburban housewife, the continual demands on her time. But the chains that bind her in her trap are chains in her own mind and spirit. They are chains made up of mistaken ideas and misinterpreted facts, of incomplete truths and unreal choices. They are not easily seen and not easily shaken off.

How can any woman see the whole truth within the bounds of her own life? How can she believe that voice inside herself, when it denies the conventional, accepted truths by which she has been living? And yet the women I have talked to, who are finally listening to that inner voice, seem in some incredible way to be groping through to a truth that has defied the experts.

Note

1. See the Seventy-fifth Anniversary Issue of *Good Housekeeping,* May, 1960, "The Gift of Self," a symposium by Margaret Mead, Jessamyn West, *et al.*

The Strength of My Rebellion

Gloria E. Anzaldúa

Gloria E. Anzaldúa is coeditor of This Bridge Called My Back: Writings by Radical Women of Color *(1983), editor of* Making Face, Making Soul—Haciendo Caras: Creative and Critical Perspectives by Feminists of Color *(1990), and author of* Borderlands / La Frontera: The New Mestiza *(1987), from which this excerpt is taken. She has taught creative writing, Chicano studies, and women's studies at several universities.*

In her essay "Towards a New Consciousness," also in Borderlands, *Anzaldúa describes the consciousness of a new* mestiza *as a "struggle of borders," a constant shifting from the points of view, experiences, and values of one culture to those of another, from Mexican, to Indian, to Anglo. To integrate, to cope with such dizzying possibilities of perception requires flexibility, tolerance of ambiguity, strength, courage, and creativity. Therefore, the future belongs to the* mestiza *because survival depends on the ability to heal splits, to move among diverse cultures—not only for the* mestiza, *not only for women, but for humankind itself.*

In this essay, Anzaldúa reveals another aspect of feminism for women of color: the intersection of different—sometimes opposing—perspectives, interests, and loyalties.

"Movimientos de rebeldía y las culturas que traicionan," *Borderlands/La Frontera: The New Mestiza* (San Francisco: Spinsters / Aunt Lute Book Company, 1987).

ESOS MOVIMIENTOS DE REBELDÍA QUE TENEMOS EN LA sangre nosotros los mexicanos surgen como ríos desbocanados en mis venas. Y como mi raza que cada en cuando deja caer esa esclavitud de obedecer, de callarse y aceptar, en mi está la rebeldía encimita de mi carne. Debajo de mi humillada mirada está una cara insolente lista para explotar. Me costó muy caro mi rebeldía—acalambrada con desvelos y dudas, sintiendome inútil, estúpida, e impotente.

Me entra una rabia cuando alguien—sea mi mamá, la Iglesia, la cultura de los anglos—me dice haz esto, haz eso sin considerar mis deseos.

Repele. Hable pa' 'tras. Fuí muy hocicona. Era indiferente a muchos valores de mi cultura. No me deje de los hombres. No fuí buena ni obediente.

Pero he crecido. Ya no soló paso toda mi vida botando las costumbres y los valores de mi cultura que me traicionan. También recojo las costumbres que por el tiempo se han provado y las costumbres de respeto a las mujeres. But despite my growing tolerance, for this Chicana *la guerra de independencia* is a constant.

The Strength of My Rebellion

I have a vivid memory of an old photograph: I am six years old. I stand between my father and mother, head cocked to the right, the toes of my flat feet gripping the ground. I hold my mother's hand.

To this day I'm not sure where I found the strength to leave the source, the mother, disengage from my family, *mi tierra, mi gente,* and all that picture stood for. I had to leave home so I could find myself, find my own intrinsic nature buried under the personality that had been imposed on me.

I was the first in six generations to leave the Valley, the only one in my family to ever leave home. But I didn't leave all the parts of me: I kept the ground of my own being. On it I walked away, taking with me the land, the Valley, Texas. *Gané mi camino y me largué. Muy andariega mi hija.* Because

I left of my own accord *me dicen, "¿Cómo te gusta la mala vida?"*

At a very early age I had a strong sense of who I was and what I was about and what was fair. I had a stubborn will. It tried constantly to mobilize my soul under my own regime, to live life on my own terms no matter how unsuitable to others they were. *Terca.* Even as a child I would not obey. I was "lazy." Instead of ironing my younger brothers' shirts or cleaning the cupboards, I would pass many hours studying, reading, painting, writing. Every bit of self-faith I'd painstakingly gathered took a beating daily. Nothing in my culture approved of me. *Había agarrado malos pasos.* Something was "wrong" with me. *Estabá más allá de la tradición.*

There is a rebel in me—the Shadow-Beast. It is a part of me that refuses to take orders from outside authorities. It refuses to take orders from my conscious will, it threatens the sovereignty of my rulership. It is that part of me that hates constraints of any kind, even those self-imposed. At the least hint of limitations on my time or space by others, it kicks out with both feet. Bolts.

Cultural Tyranny

Culture forms our beliefs. We perceive the version of reality that it communicates. Dominant paradigms, predefined concepts that exist as unquestionable, unchallengeable, are transmitted to us through the culture. Culture is made by those in power—men. Males make the rules and laws; women transmit them. How many times have I heard mothers and mothers-in-law tell their sons to beat their wives for not obeying them, for being *hociconas* (big mouths), for being *callajeras* (going to visit and gossip with neighbors), for expecting their husbands to help with the rearing of children and the housework, for wanting to be something other than housewives?

The culture expects women to show greater acceptance of, and commitment to, the value system than men. The culture and the Church insist that women are subservient to males. If a woman rebels she is a *mujer mala.* If a woman doesn't renounce herself in favor of the male, she is selfish. If a woman remains a *virgen* until she marries, she is a good woman. For a woman of my culture there used to be only three directions she could turn: to the Church as a nun, to the streets as a prostitute, or to the home as a mother. Today some of us have a fourth choice: entering the world by way of education and career and becoming self-autonomous persons. A very few of us. As a working class people our chief activity is to put food in our mouths, a roof over our heads and clothes on our backs. Educating our children is out of reach for most of us. Educated or not, the onus is still on woman to be a wife/mother—only the nun can escape motherhood. Women are made to feel total failures if they don't marry and have children. *"¿Y cuándo te casas, Gloria? Se te va a pasar el tren." Y yo les digo, "Pos si me caso, no va ser con un hombre." Se quedan calladitas. Sí, soy hija de la Chingada.* I've always been her daughter. *No 'tés chingando.*

Humans fear the supernatural, both the undivine (the animal impulses such as sexuality, the unconscious, the unknown, the alien) and the divine (superhuman, the god in us). Culture and religion seek to protect us from these two forces. The female, by virtue of creating entities of flesh and blood in her stomach (she bleeds every month but does not die), by virtue of being in tune with nature's cycles, is feared. Because, according to Christianity and most other major religions, woman is carnal, animal, and closer to the undivine, she must be protected. Protected from herself. Woman is the stranger, the other. She is man's recognized nightmarish pieces, his Shadow-Beast. The sight of her sends him into a frenzy of anger and fear.

La gorra, el rebozo, la mantilla are symbols of my culture's "protection" of women. Culture (read males) professes to protect women. Actually it keeps women in rigidly defined roles. It keeps the girlchild from other men—don't poach on my preserves, only I can touch my child's body. Our mothers taught us well, *"Los hombres nomás quieren una cosa"*; men aren't to be trusted, they are selfish and are like children. Mothers made sure we didn't walk into a room of brothers or fathers or uncles in nightgowns or shorts. We were never alone with men, not even those of our own family.

Through our mothers, the culture gave us mixed messages: *No voy a dejar que ningún pelado desgraciado maltrate a mis hijos.* And in the next breath it would say, *La mujer tiene que hacer lo que le diga el hombre.* Which was it to be—strong, or submissive, rebellious or conforming?

Tribal rights over those of the individual insured the survival of the tribe and were necessary then, and, as in the case of all indigenous peoples in the world who are still fighting off intentional, premeditated murder (genocide), they are still necessary.

Much of what the culture condemns focuses on kinship relationships. The welfare of the family, the community, and the tribe is more important than the welfare of the individual. The individual exists first as kin—as sister, as father, as *padrino*—and last as self.

In my culture, selfishness is condemned, especially in women; humility and selflessness, the absence of selfishness, is considered a virtue. In the past, acting humble with members outside the family ensured that you would make no one *envidioso* (envious); therefore he or she would not use witchcraft against you. If you get above yourself, you're an *envidiosa.* If you don't behave like everyone else, *la gente* will say that you think you're better than others, *que te crees grande.* With ambition (condemned in the Mexican culture and valued in the Anglo) comes envy. *Respeto* carries with it a set of rules so that social categories and hierarchies will be kept in order: respect is reserved for *la abuela, papá, el patrón,* those with power in the community. Women are at the bottom of the ladder one rung above the deviants. The Chicano, *mexicano,* and some Indian cultures have no tolerance for deviance. Deviance is whatever is condemned by the community. Most societies try to get rid of their deviants. Most cultures have burned and beaten their homosexuals and others who deviate from the sexual common.[1] The queer are the mirror reflecting the heterosexual tribe's fear: being different, being other and therefore lesser, therefore subhuman, inhuman, non-human.

Half and Half

There was a *muchacha* who lived near my house. *La gente del pueblo* talked about her being *una de las otras,* "of the Others." They said that for six months she was a woman who had a vagina that bled once a month, and that for the other six months she was a man, had a penis and she peed standing up. They called her half and half, *mita' y mita',* neither one nor the other but a strange doubling, a deviation of nature that horrified, a work of nature inverted. But there is a magic aspect in abnormality and so-called deformity. Maimed, mad, and sexually different people were believed to possess supernatural powers by primal cultures' magico-religious thinking. For them, abnormality was the price a person had to pay for her or his inborn extraordinary gift.

There is something compelling about being both male and female, about having an entry into both worlds. Contrary to some psychiatric tenets, half and halfs are not suffering from a confusion of sexual identity, or even from a confusion of gender. What we are suffering from is an absolute despot duality that says we are able to be only one or the other. It claims that human nature is limited and cannot evolve into something better. But I, like other queer people, am two in one body, both male and female. I am the embodiment of the *hieros gamos:* the coming together of opposite qualities within.

Fear of Going Home: Homophobia

For the lesbian of color, the ultimate rebellion she can make against her native culture is through her sexual behavior. She goes against two moral prohibitions: sexuality and homosexuality. Being lesbian and raised Catholic, indoctrinated as straight, I *made the choice to be queer* (for some it is genetically inherent). It's an interesting path, one that continually slips in and out of the white, the Catholic, the Mexican, the indigenous, the instincts. In and out of my head. It makes for *loquería,* the crazies. It is a path of knowledge—one of knowing (and of learning) the history of oppression of our *raza.* It is a way of balancing, of mitigating duality.

In a New England college where I taught, the presence of a few lesbians threw the more conservative heterosexual students and faculty into a panic. The two lesbian students and we two lesbian instructors met with them to discuss their fears. One of the students said, "I thought homophobia meant fear of going home after a residency."

And I thought, how apt. Fear of going home. And of not being taken in. We're afraid of being abandoned by the mother, the culture, *la Raza,* for being unacceptable, faulty, damaged. Most of us unconsciously believe that if we reveal this unacceptable aspect of the self our mother/culture/race will totally reject us. To avoid rejection, some of us conform to the values of the culture, push the unacceptable parts into the shadows. Which leaves only one fear—that we will be found out and that the Shadow-Beast will break out of its cage. Some of us take another route. We try to make ourselves conscious of the Shadow-

Beast, stare at the sexual lust and lust for power and destruction we see on its face, discern among its features the undershadow that the reigning order of heterosexual males project on our Beast. Yet still others of us take it another step: we try to waken the Shadow-Beast inside us. Not many jump at the chance to confront the Shadow-Beast in the mirror without flinching at her lidless serpent eyes, her cold clammy moist hand dragging us underground, fangs barred and hissing. How does one put feathers on this particular serpent? But a few of us have been lucky—on the face of the Shadow-Beast we have seen not lust but tenderness; on its face we have uncovered the lie.

Intimate Terrorism: Life in the Borderlands

The world is not a safe place to live in. We shiver in separate cells in enclosed cities, shoulders hunched, barely keeping the panic below the surface of the skin, daily drinking shock along with our morning coffee, fearing the torches being set to our buildings, the attacks in the streets. Shutting down. Woman does not feel safe when her own culture, and white culture, are critical of her; when the males of all races hunt her as prey.

Alienated from her mother culture, "alien" in the dominant culture, the woman of color does not feel safe within the inner life of her Self. Petrified, she can't respond, her face caught between *los intersticios,* the spaces between the different worlds she inhabits.

The ability to respond is what is meant by responsibility, yet our cultures take away our ability to act—shackle us in the name of protection. Blocked, immobilized, we can't move forward, can't move backwards. That writhing serpent movement, the very movement of life, swifter than lightning, frozen.

We do not engage fully. We do not make full use of our faculties. We abnegate. And there in front of us is the crossroads and choice: to feel a victim where someone else is in control and therefore responsible and to blame (being a victim and transferring the blame on culture, mother, father, ex-lover, friend, absolves me of responsibility), or to feel strong, and, for the most part, in control.

My Chicana identity is grounded in the Indian woman's history of resistance. The Aztec female rites of mourning were rites of defiance protesting the cultural changes which disrupted the equality and balance between female and male, and protesting their demotion to a lesser status, their denigration. Like *la Llorona,* the Indian woman's only means of protest was wailing.

So *mamá, Raza,* how wonderful, *no tener que rendir cuentas a nadie.* I feel perfectly free to rebel and to rail against my culture. I fear no betrayal on my part because, unlike Chicanas and other women of color who grew up white or who have only recently returned to their native cultural roots, I was totally immersed in mine. It wasn't until I went to high school that I "saw" whites. Until I worked on my master's degree I had not gotten within an arm's distance of them. I was totally immersed *en lo mexicano,* a rural, peasant, isolated, *mexicanismo.* To separate from my culture (as from my family) I had to feel competent enough on the outside and secure enough inside to live life on my own. Yet in leaving home I did not lose touch with my origins because *lo mexicano* is in my system. I am a turtle, wherever I go I carry "home" on my back.

Not me sold out my people but they me. So yes, though "home" permeates every sinew and cartilage in my body, I too am afraid of going home. Though I'll defend my race and culture when they are attacked by non-*mexicanos, conosco el malestar de mi cultura.* I abhor some of my culture's ways, how it cripples its women, *como burras,* our strengths used against us, lowly *burras* bearing humility with dignity. The ability to serve, claim the males, is our highest virtue. I abhor how my culture makes *macho* caricatures of its men. No, I do not buy all the myths of the tribe into which I was born. I can understand why the more tinged with Anglo blood, the more adamantly my colored and colorless sisters glorify their colored culture's values—to offset the extreme devaluation of it by the white culture. It's a legitimate reaction. But I will not glorify those aspects of my culture which have injured me and which have injured me in the name of protecting me.

So, don't give me your tenets and your laws. Don't give me your lukewarm gods. What I want is an accounting with all three cultures—white, Mexican, Indian. I want the freedom to carve and chisel my own face, to staunch the bleeding with ashes, to fashion my own gods out of my entrails. And if going home is denied me then I will have to stand and claim my space, making a new culture—*una cultura mestiza*—with my own lumber, my own bricks and mortar and my own feminist architecture.

The Wounding of the *india*-Mestiza

Estas carnes indias que despreciamos nosotros los mexicanos asi como despreciamos y condenamos a nuestra madre, Malinali. Nos condenamos a nosotros mismos. Esta raza vencida, enemigo cuerpo.

Not me sold out my people but they me. *Malinali Tenepat,* or *Malintzin,* has become known as *la Chingada*—the fucked one. She has become the bad word that passes a dozen times a day from the lips of Chicanos. Whore, prostitute, the woman who sold out her people to the Spaniards are epithets Chicanos spit out with contempt.

The worst kind of betrayal lies in making us believe that the Indian woman in us is the betrayer. *We, indias y mestizas,* police the Indian in us, brutalize and condemn her. Male culture has done a good job on us. *Son los costumbres que traicionan. La india en mí es la sombra: La Chingada, Tlazolteotl, Coatlicue. Son ellas que oyemos lamentando a sus hijas perdidas.*

Not me sold out my people but they me. Because of the color of my skin they betrayed me. The dark-skinned woman has been silenced, gagged, caged, bound into servitude with marriage, bludgeoned for 300 years, sterilized and castrated in the twentieth century. For 300 years she has been a slave, a force of cheap labor, colonized by the Spaniard, the Anglo, by her own people (and in Mesoamerica her lot under the Indian patriarchs was not free of wounding). For 300 years she was invisible, she was not heard. Many times she wished to speak, to act, to protest, to challenge. The odds were heavily against her. She hid her feelings; she hid her truths; she concealed her fire; but she kept stoking the inner flame. She remained faceless and voiceless, but a light shone through her veil of silence. And though she was unable to spread her limbs and though for her right now the sun has sunk under the earth and there is no moon, she continues to tend the flame. The spirit of the fire spurs her to fight for her own skin and a piece of ground to stand on, a ground from which to view the world—a perspective, a homeground where she can plumb the rich ancestral roots into her own ample *mestiza* heart. She waits till the waters are not so turbulent and the mountains not so slippery with sleet. Battered and bruised she waits, her bruises throwing her back upon herself and the rhythmic pulse of the feminine. *Coatlalopeuh* waits with her.

Aquí en la soledad prospera su rebeldía.
En la soledad Ella prospera.

Note

1. Francisco Guerra, *The Pre-Columbian Mind: A Study into the Aberrant Nature of Sexual Drives, Drugs Affecting Behaviour, and the Attitude Towards Life and Death, with a Survey of Psychotherapy in Pre-Columbian America* (New York: Seminar Press, 1971).

Abortion: A Positive Decision

Patricia Lunneborg

Patricia Lunneborg retired from the University of Washington in 1987, having been professor of psychology, Fellow in the Division of Counseling Psychology of the American Psychological Association, and adjunct professor of women's studies. She authored over 100 professional papers. Since that time, she has authored four books: Women Police Officers: Current Career Profile *(1989);* Women Changing Work *(1990), which describes the unique aspects of women's socialization brought to the male-dominated workplace;* Abortion: A Positive Decision *(1992); and* O U Women: Undoing Educational Obstacles, *forthcoming.*

This discussion provides balance and sanity to the invective of the antichoice antifeminists: Abortion can be, and usually is, the most positive option for a woman when she does not wish to complete a pregnancy and have a child.

NO MATTER THAT LEGAL ABORTION IS AS SAFE A PROcedure as having your tonsils out or a penicillin injection or a wisdom tooth extracted. It is far more than a safe medical procedure because of the complicated decision making that is involved, and the fact that it has to do with sex and life and death. So there's really no comparison between the energy that goes into deciding whether to have an abortion and these other health and body decisions, which are essentially neutral. With the neutral procedures, you have them done. You stay healthy. But you don't think about the meaning of life in the process. With an abortion, you do.

And while you're trying to think it through, there is all this abortion-is-murder rhetoric, state legislatures making abortion criminal, presidents trying to get fetal rights into the Constitution, picketing and blockading of clinics. And who can you talk to when you never know who might turn on you in fury and accuse you of being a bad person?

But out of that thinking, when you decide to have an abortion, you can do more than simply terminate an unwanted pregnancy and more than simply get on with your life afterward. You can use your abortion as a stepping stone for thinking about and deciding other important issues in your life.

Returning to the personal aspect, I learned what it means to be publicly vilified midway in writing this book. I joined a writers support group, the idea being that we would all share our projects and get constructive criticism. At my second meeting I described *Abortion: A Positive Decision* and then had the group silently read several pages from the chapter on family planning. I knew I was in bad trouble when I saw the look on a certain woman's face: stony anger. I mumbled something about it being controversial, but still I hoped. . . . She spoke first when the silent reading was over.

She shrieked at me. Lies, you're lying to me. Some things in life are just bad, evil, negative, and

---

there's nothing that can be done about it. Some things must be suffered. That's the way it is. This is nothing but cliches and jargon. You are hiding behind these women. It's a lie to hide behind these women. Abortion is murder and there is nothing positive that can come from it. Lies, lies, lies.

Her words were numbing enough, but worse was that face rigid with rage. I just sat there frozen, thinking, Oh, I feel so awful, I hate being screamed at. This must be how it feels to walk past the gauntlet of protesters. Or how it feels when you're 14 and you tell your father you're pregnant and he whams you across the face. The accusation of lying hurt the most, because the highest value I hold for myself is truthfulness. Truth, honesty, telling it like it is—that great line from *Hamlet* about if you're true to yourself, you can't be false to anyone.

What I am trying to do here is expose this piece of the truth that continues to be covered up. I'm trying to lift the lid off a corner of reality that isn't a polite topic of conversation. And the reality is that for millions (billions?) of women the abortion decision is positive for their lives. And the truth as I see it is that an unwanted pregnancy, like any crisis, can be turned into an opportunity. An opportunity for growth, for maturation, for making wise, lifelong choices.

. . .

Who Has an Abortion?

Why write a chapter about *who* gets abortions? Because there are 1.6 million abortions in the United States every year (Henshaw & Van Vort, 1990). Because as of 1987, 21 percent of United States women between 15 and 44 had had an abortion, and if current rates persist, this percentage will grow to 46 percent of women by the time they reach menopause (Forrest, 1987). Also because there are two abortions for every five births in the United States, according to Colin Francome, a British sociologist whose specialty is abortion (1986, p. 100). His estimate was that more than four out of ten American women would have an abortion sometime in their lives. So why write this chapter? Because there's an enormous information gap that needs filling.

Anne Baker (1981), who has counseled thousands of women at the Hope Clinic in Granite City, Illinois, says it's a real eye-opener to discover all the "good" kinds of women who get abortions. She personally has helped many: religious women active in their churches—Catholics, Protestants, Jews, Muslims, Pentecostals; women in the Right to Life movement; women in all occupations—doctors, lawyers, day-care workers, Sunday school teachers; mothers who are the envy of other mothers because of how loving and patient they are with all the neighborhood kids; grandmothers in their fifties.

Anne Baker says that not only do good women have abortions, but they believe abortion is the morally right decision for themselves and others, the best alternative depending on one's situation.

. . .

The Very Good Reasons Women Give For Their Abortions

An unappreciated but primary reason women have abortions is that contraception so often fails. If you don't think so, consider this: under the caption "Sins of Emission," a 1990 *London Guardian* squib informs us that Canadian researchers found that condoms leak during intercourse nearly three times out of four. Three times out of four!

What are we supposed to do when our birth control method fails? When the cap fails, the pill fails, the condom fails? The fact is that contraceptive failure led to 1.6 to 2 million of the 3.3 million unwanted pregnancies in the United States in 1987. "Such pregnancies constitute about half of the 1.5 million abortions performed each year." This is not the conclusion of some fly-by-night quack institute or radical political group. This is the finding of the National Academy of Sciences in 1990 (Kaeser, 1990).

Now, against this very good reason for an abortion—leaky condoms and faulty IUDs—what reasons do women give researchers? Here are the latest findings. A 1987 survey of 1,900 women at 30 abortion facilities asked, "Why do women have abortions?" (Torres & Forrest, 1988). The women could give as many reasons as they wanted, and most women do not have just one reason, but a complex of motives. Here are the top six reasons all women gave, the percentages being those for women under 18:

1. Concerned about how having a baby could change her life, 92 percent
2. Not mature enough or too young to have a child, 81 percent
3. Can't afford baby now, 73 percent

4. Doesn't want others to know she has had sex or is pregnant, 42 percent
5. Has relationship problems and doesn't want to be a single parent, 37 percent
6. Unready for the responsibility, 33 percent

There have been many studies done with smaller groups that expressed exactly the same reasons. Older women are more likely to say their families are complete; younger women more likely to say a baby would interfere with their education, career, and personal freedom. At any age, women say they have too many responsibilities already and not enough money. Examples of such studies are Burnell, Dworsky, & Harrington, 1972; Faria, Barrett, & Goodman, 1986; Morin-Gonthier & Lortie, 1984; Moseley, Follingstad, Harley, & Heckel, 1981; and Shusterman, 1979.

The reasons for which the American public at large is most approving of abortion are not the foremost reasons why women have abortions. Women, in the main, do not have abortions because of rape, incest, deformed fetuses, or because their physical life is in danger. But these are the most appropriate reasons in the eyes of the American public. Being poor, too young, unmarried, and not wanting a baby are deemed less valid in public opinion polls. We have a huge disjunction here that needs to be resolved. And the pathetic thing, in terms of public opinion, is that "I don't want a baby at the moment" isn't considered the most valid reason at all.

Women have abortions because their contraception failed and because they did not want to have a baby at that time. But anyone who thinks women take those two realities lightly hasn't spent a day observing abortion providers.

> *It is a major life occasion. Especially seeing all these different women, it can be one of the most profound decisions that you make. Because, yes, it is a very safe medical procedure, but there are risks, just as there are to all medical procedures, and you could be one of those very few statistics. It is a life decision because if you carry to term, your entire life is going to change forever. And by choosing not to, you are also making a choice to lead your life in one particular direction. A lot of women say things like, I know this is right for me because I'm in school, I don't have any money, I want to be a lawyer and I haven't even finished high school yet. And I know I want to do these things, and to have a child right now would mean I could never do these things. A lot of people say that. It definitely makes people think and want to change, or reinforces their decision and their life choices.* (24-year-old abortion counselor)

Another fact related to reasons for abortion is that the majority of abortions are first abortions. Among Canadian women, 78 percent of women having abortions had no prior abortion, and among women in England and Wales, the figure is 82 percent. For 60 percent of American women who have abortions, it is their first (Henshaw, 1990).

If it is a second, third, or fourth abortion, the reason "I don't want a baby at the moment" is no less valid. If you are not comfortable with the idea of multiple abortions, the old adage of walking in someone else's shoes comes to mind.

> *Sometimes people who have three or four or five abortions are failing in every other area of their lives in terms of being victimized. And they're taking such responsibility in making those decisions—where they don't feel they have control in any other area—to have an abortion. When they clearly know they aren't capable of being a good parent, or being a parent again. I give these women a lot of credit. Sometimes people get down on women who have repeat abortions without looking at those women's lives. They aren't willing to look at each pregnancy as a separate event with its own set of circumstances. And it doesn't matter how many times a woman has had an abortion, it only matters in her own eyes and her own value system. The last thing women who are having more than one abortion need is to feel judged and put down and criticized. They're doing the best they can, and in some cases are doing a great job of making decisions when they don't feel much control in other parts of their lives.* (47-year-old social worker, abortion at 22)

. . .

Why Talk About Abortion

With this book I want to get people talking about abortion. Keeping it under wraps does immeasurable harm. I think we need to tell it like it is—abortion is a part of life. We need to normalize the abortion experience and that means striking it from the list of taboo topics.

Divorce, menopause, and interracial marriage used to be hush-hush subjects, too. But people talk more easily about them now. And that talk has made divorce, menopause, and interracial marriage more normal, less threatening, less emotionally charged. And talk has made the people talking and listening less ignorant, more tolerant, more understanding, and more comfortable with what it means to be human.

Abortion isn't a proper topic for discussion because of people who are antiabortion. They are responsible for our silence. They are why we bite our lips and hesitate to speak. Who wants to invite their verbal attacks, or be put on the defensive? So we, wanting to avoid social disapproval, are more likely to change the subject than face public condemnation. But I'm saying, So what if other people disapprove? Their disapproval is their problem.

One thing we need to talk about is how frequently people have abortions. How many of us have had abortions? I've said something about the numbers already, but what's the U.S. population? Around 260 million, about half of whom are women. And since *Roe v. Wade* in 1973 through 1988, 22.3 million legal abortions were done (Henshaw & Van Vort, 1990). We also know millions occurred before 1973, and over 1.5 million per year since 1988. So if we say, very conservatively, at least 26 million American women have had abortions, that's one in five. But how many people are conscious of how huge this number is?

How well-known is the fact that, around the world, 43 million abortions occurred in 1987 (Henshaw, 1990)? Legal abortions numbered 28 million and illegal abortions 15 million. How many people know that the trend worldwide is toward liberalization of abortion laws, so that 63 percent of the world's population now lives in countries where abortion is permitted on request of the woman (40 percent of world population) or allowed for social or social-medical reasons (23 percent of world population)? How widely known is it that national health insurance covers abortions needed to preserve the health of a pregnant woman in all developed countries except the United States?

Nonetheless, "although tens of millions of living veterans" are all around us, Beryl Benderly (1984) has said, most women are reluctant to talk about their abortion experiences. But talk points the way for others, especially young women, not to feel deviant and solitary. Talk, Benderly says, means other women will come to wise decisions with less pain. Lack of information about how millions of other women thought and felt leaves future millions with no role models, needlessly alone as they consider the alternatives.

For Benderly, the information consists of the facts that most women feel fine afterward, in a purely physical sense (p. 128), and that in a psychological sense, the lives of the great majority are a good deal better after than before. The great majority, she says, use the abortion experience creatively, to grow. They get social support and cope well and do not lose their self-esteem (p. 152). So talk about the truth of women's lives and abortion experiences is necessary to make the outcomes of the abortion decision positive for more women.

To people who say there are too many abortions in America and they want to reduce that number, we need to say, Fine, then support sex education in the schools starting in kindergarten. Support free family planning consultation and free birth control services and supplies nationwide. Lobby for a massive federally funded research program on contraception for men and women. Oh, by the way, just because a person says there are too many abortions in America is no reason to believe she never had one. At the Philadelphia clinic I was told one of the regular protesters had come in for an abortion the month before. A 31-year-old Seattle Planned Parenthood counselor had this anecdote:

> *When I worked in Albuquerque I went to a "right to choose" meeting. And the antichoice people were in the back. It was pretty common practice. We'd go to their meetings, they'd come to our meetings. I went with my boss and she pointed out someone in the back, See that woman in the green dress? Well, she was my client four weeks ago when she was in our clinic for her abortion. And I said, Oh, my. And she said, She's been antichoice for years and going to these meetings for years, but it was okay when she was confronted with the decision. She chose to have a safe and legal abortion, but for any other woman it needs to be illegal and dangerous. You see that over and over and over again. And how many mothers do we see out picketing but when their little 14-year-old comes up pregnant, they bring them in, because when it's* my *daughter, it's different. What bothers me is, it's a religious issue, and this is a country based on separation of church and state. And my God isn't their God. And it offends me*

that they want to change laws based on their God and their religious beliefs. If you're antichoice, don't have one. But they've all had them!

Talk to Change Public Attitudes

Another reason we need to talk about abortion is to change society's attitudes toward the prochoice position. Public opinion polls on abortion are very important to people both for and against abortion rights. Each group wants to win more voters in its side so that the laws of the land will support its position. To that end, each group publicizes whatever poll results, over the many years polls have been given, best support their stance.

I put my trust in Gallup, whose report in February 1989 said that American attitudes on abortion were favorable and had changed little since the Supreme Court's 1973 ruling. In September 1988, a 57 percent majority favored legal abortions under certain circumstances, 24 percent favored abortion under any circumstances, and only 17 percent felt abortions should not be allowed under any circumstances. This is somewhat better than 1975, when those percentages were 54 percent (sometimes legal), 21 percent (always legal), and 22 percent (always illegal). However, by April 1990, 31 percent said abortion should be legal under any circumstances, while the proportion stating that abortion should be illegal under all circumstances fell from 17 percent to 12 percent ("Public Opinion on Abortion Shifts," 1990).

Suppose the question is, Do you want to see *Roe v. Wade* overturned? No, said a resounding 61 percent to an October 1989 Gallup Poll, which again, is comparable to 1977 when 65 percent of people said yes to the question, "Do you feel a woman should be allowed to have an abortion in the early months of pregnancy if she wants it?" Gallup's conclusion: "The population as a whole favors the pro-choice position" (Colasanto & DeStefano, 1989).

One way to change public opinion toward even greater favorability, however, is to normalize abortion by speaking out and saying, I'm normal, I'm responsible, I'm proud, and I am one of millions. A smartly dressed, bright-eyed, ambitious, 28-year-old college student I met in an empty college classroom put it this way:

I see my need to step out more, my need to stand up and say, Well, I'm this nice, middle-class person who is a mother, a former Jewish housewife, who had an abortion and I'm not a bad person. They can't say that it's just real deviant parts of our society that have abortions. A year ago when I got my abortion we really started hearing through the media that we might lose this right. And I am finally understanding how this was a real exercise of my own rights that I did it. I don't understand not having this choice. I take for granted rights that are so new to American society.

The same feeling was expressed by a 23-year-old Ivy League graduate who had her abortion in her sophomore year. She now uses her ability to speak out to educate students in the public schools about *who* gets abortions.

It changed my behavior in being more outspoken about abortion issues because it wasn't just an issue that affected other people any more. At the time I felt it was this secret, shameful thing that I couldn't tell anybody else about. Now I feel much more comfortable talking about it and telling other people because I think part of the problem is if people can't talk about it, then it's going to stay this shameful, awful thing and it makes it so emotionally difficult for everybody.

We need to tell people that between 1967 and 1982, over 40 countries extended their grounds for abortion while only three—Hungary, Bulgaria, and Czechoslovakia (and now Poland?)—narrowed them. Two-thirds of women now live in countries where laws permit abortion on request or for a wide variety of grounds. Fewer than one in ten women lives in a country where abortion is totally prohibited. Abortion continues to be widely available in five of the six most populous countries in the world—India, China, the Soviet Union, Japan, and the United States (Francome, 1984, p. 1). We need to educate Americans to the acceptance of legal abortion around the world.

I don't believe we can be silent any longer. We need to be seen as real people, not as monsters. Women must take responsibility for their choices and they must voice it and say, I'm proud I did what I did, and I'm living today, and I'm happy, that's the important thing. If a woman's reproductive choices go, then her choices of where she will work and where she will live and who she can love will be at stake. Women's very existence is threatened, because we're all connected, and it doesn't matter if the woman is in Bangladesh or

New York City or Hawaii. The only way we're going to survive is if we go positive. (47-year-old social worker)

Politicians can become prochoice when we speak out. "Roemer Listened to Women in Veto Move," read a *Seattle Times* headline (Shogan, 1990). Louisiana Governor Buddy Roemer had before him the nation's strictest abortion bill when he decided to ask his estranged wife, his 23-year-old daughter, and the three women in his cabinet their opinions. After talking to them he concluded abortion was about the feelings, rights, and values of women. He said if he talked to 100 women, 80 of them would say they wanted a place in the decision process. They would say, "It's my body and my family and it ought to be my choice." So he vetoed that bill, which he said was not compassionate, not fair, not decent, and not prolife. It remains to be seen whether Roemer is truly converted, but even in a legislature operating in the nineteenth century, most politicians facing a prochoice majority will opt for political survival.

A home nurse, who had her abortion when she was 18, was just one year older than Roemer's daughter when I interviewed her in her airy apartment with an imposing view of the snowclad Cascades.

What we need is just talking about it and people coming out and telling the facts and making it not such an ominous, awful, scary thing. Just education. So many people don't talk about it, so when you get pregnant, you feel alone, you think you're the only one, and you feel judged. I told probably five people total because it's not something you talk about. But if anybody came to me and said, I'm pregnant, can you help me? I'd totally talk with them about it. And I'd tell them about my experience. But it's not ordinarily something people are ready to hear about. I talk about the statistics before and after, and I say, Most of my friends have had an abortion and they were on birth control and being very careful. But I guess the more people talk about it . . . just like with homosexuality, the more neighbors that you have that are gay and that you love, the more brothers and sisters, and mothers and fathers that you have that are homosexual, you get to realize it's not a big deal and we all need to talk about it. Of my friends that I have talked to about their abortions, I've never known anybody who had a negative consequence. They've felt good with their decision, but almost thankful to talk to somebody who has had the same experience. I had a good friend who had an abortion in high school and so when I was pregnant I talked to her about it a lot. I don't know how many people she told back then, I don't think very many. So I think she was glad to know it had happened to somebody else who was just like her.

We need to say that schooling goes along with favorability toward abortion, and ignorance with being antiabortion. The better educated people are, the more in favor of abortion rights they are. Opposition to overturning *Roe v. Wade* was voiced by 73 percent of college graduates versus 45 percent of high school graduates in the 1989 Gallup poll (Colasanto & DeStafano, 1989).

This education factor showed up in a National Opinion Research Center poll that found in 1987 that 63 percent of U.S. adults approved of legal abortions ("Average of 63% approve," 1987). The figure 63 percent represents the average over six reasons ranging from serious health endangerment to the desire to have no more children. However, there was only 47 percent approval among people with less than a high school education, while 72 percent approval among people who had some college.

. . .

Bibliography

Abortion refusals seen as traumatic
1991, May 4 *Seattle Times*, p. A5.

Abrams, Marilyn
1985 Birth control use by teenagers one and two years postabortion. *Journal of Adolescent Health Care, 6*, 196–200.

Abrams, Marilyn, DiBiase, Vilma, & Sturgis, Somers.
1979 Post-abortion attitudes and patterns of birth control. *Journal of Family Practice, 9*, 593–599.

Adler, Nancy E.
1975 Emotional responses of women following therapeutic abortion. *American Journal of Orthopsychiatry, 45*, 446–454.

Adler, Nancy E., David, Henry P., Major, Brenda N., Roth, Susan H., Russo, Nancy F., & Wyatt, Gail E.
1990, April 6 Psychological responses after abortion. *Science*, 41–44.

Ashton, J. R.
1980 The psychosocial outcome of induced abortion. *British Journal of Obstetrics and Gynaecology, 87,* 1115–1122.

Athanasiou, Robert, Oppel, Wallace, Michelson, Leslie, Unger, Thomas, & Yager, Mary
1973 Psychiatric sequelae to term birth and induced early and late abortion: A longitudinal study. *Family Planning Perspectives, 5,* 227–231.

Average of 63% approve of legal abortions
1987 *Family Planning Perspectives, 19,* 221.

Baker, Anne
1981 *After her abortion.* Granite City, IL: Hope Clinic for Women.

Baker, Anne
1989 *How to cope successfully after an abortion.* Granite City, IL: Hope Clinic for Women.

Benderly, Beryl L.
1984 *Thinking about abortion.* Garden City, NY: Dial Press.

Beresford, Terry
1990 *Unsure about your pregnancy?* Washington, DC: National Abortion Federation [booklet].

Blum, Robert W., & Resnick, Michael D.
1982 Adolescent sexual decision-making: Contraception, pregnancy, abortion, motherhood. *Pediatric Annals, 11,* 797, 800–802, 804–805.

Bonavoglia, Angela (Ed.)
1991 *The choices we made.* New York: Random House.

Bracken, Michael B., Grossman, Gerald, Hachamovitch, Moshe, Sussman, Diane, & Schrieir, Dorothy
1973 Abortion counseling: An experimental study of three techniques. *American Journal of Obstetrics and Gynecology, 117,* 10–20.

Bracken, Michael B., Hachamovitch, Moshe, & Grossman, Gerald
1974 The decision to abort and psychological sequelae. *Journal of Nervous and Mental Disease, 158,* 154–162.

Bracken, Michael B., Klerman, Lorraine, & Bracken, Maryann
1978 Coping with pregnancy resolution among never-married women. *American Journal of Orthopsychiatry, 48,* 320–334.

Branch, Benjamin N.
1973 Extramural abortions: Why bother? In Howard J. Osofsky & Joy D. Osofsky (Eds.), *The abortion experience* (pp. 122–134). New York: Harper & Row.

Brewer, Colin
1977 Incidence of post-abortion psychosis: A prospective study. *British Medical Journal, 1,* 476–477.

Burnell, George M., Dworsky, William A., & Harrington, Robert L.
1972 Post-abortion group therapy. *American Journal of Psychiatry, 129,* 134–137.

Burnell, George M., & Norfleet, Mary A.
1987 Women's self-reported responses to abortion. *Journal of Psychology, 121,* 71–76.

Buttenweiser, Sarah, & Levine, Reva
1990 Breaking silences: A post-abortion support model. In Marlene G. Fried (Ed.), *From abortion to reproductive freedom: Transforming a movement* (pp. 121–128). Boston: South End Press.

Butterfield, Leslie M.
1984 Working through abortion. In Arthur B. Shostak & Gary McLouth, *Men and abortion* (pp. 293–297). New York: Praeger.

Catholics For a Free Choice
undated *You are not alone.* Washington, DC: Author. [pamphlet]

Colasanto, Diane, & DeStefano, Linda
1989, October *"Pro-choice" position stirs increased activism in abortion battle* (Report No. 289, pp. 16–20). Princeton, NJ: Gallup.

Cvejic, Helen, Lipper, Irene, Kinch, Robert A., & Benjamin, Peter
1977 Follow-up of 50 adolescent girls 2 years after abortion. *Canadian Medical Association Journal, 116,* 44–46.

Dagg, Paul K. B.
1991 The psychological sequelae of therapeutic abortion—denied and completed. *American Journal of Psychiatry, 148,* 578–585.

Dauber, Bonnie, Zalar, Marianne, & Goldstein, Phillip J.
1972 Abortion counseling and behavioral change. *Family Planning Perspectives, 4,* 23–27.

David, Henry P.
1985 Post-abortion and post-partum psychiatric hospitalization. In Ruth Porter & Maeve O'Connor (Eds.), *Abortion: Medical progress and social implications* (pp. 150–164). London: Pitman Ciba Foundation Symposium, 115.

Dixon, Dazon
1990 Operation oppress you: Women's rights under siege. In Marlene G. Fried (Ed.), *From abortion to reproductive freedom: Transforming a movement* (pp. 185–186). Boston: South End Press.

Doane, Benjamin K., & Quigley, Beverly G.
1981 Psychiatric aspects of therapeutic abortion. *Canadian Medical Association Journal, 125,* 427–432.

Dreyfous, Leslie
1991, March 31 No children. *Seattle Times,* p. K4.

Eisen, Marvin, & Zellman, Gail L.
1984 Factors predicting pregnancy resolution decision satisfaction of unmarried adolescents. *Journal of Genetic Psychology, 145,* 231–239.

Evans, Jerome R., Selstad, Georgiana, & Welcher, Wayne H.
1976 Teenagers: Fertility control behavior and attitudes before and after abortion, childbearing or negative pregnancy test. *Family Planning Perspectives, 8,* 192–200.

Faria, Geraldine, Barrett, Elwin, & Goodman, Linnea M.
1986 Woman and abortion: Attitudes, social networks, decision-making. *Social Work in Health Care, 11,* 85–86.

Ferguson, Bruce
1990 Informed consent and abortion [Letter to the editor]. *Journal of the American Medical Association, 264,* (21), 2739.

Forrest, Jacqueline D.
1987 Unintended pregnancy among American women. *Family Planning Perspectives, 19,* 76–77.

Forrest, Jacqueline D., & Fordyce, Richard R.
1988 U.S. women's contraceptive attitudes and practice: How have they changed in the 1980s? *Family Planning Perspectives, 20,* 112–118.

Forrest, Jacqueline D., & Singh, Susheela
1990 The sexual and reproductive behavior of American women, 1982–1988. *Family Planning Perspectives, 22,* 206–214.

Francome, Colin
1984 *Abortion freedom: A worldwide movement.* London: Unwin & Allen.

Francome, Colin
1986 *Abortion practice in Britain and the United States.* London: Unwin & Allen.

Frater, Alison, & Wright, Catherine
1986 *Coping with abortion.* Edinburgh: Chambers.

Freeman, Ellen W.
1978 Abortion: Subjective attitudes and feelings. *Family Planning Perspectives, 10,* 150–155.

Gallup Report
1989, February *Attitudes on abortion little changed since Supreme Court's 1973 ruling* (Report No. 281). Princeton, NJ: Author.

Greer, H. S., Lal, Shirley, Lewis, S. C., Belsey, E. M., & Beard, R. W.
1976 Psychosocial consequences of therapeutic abortion: King's termination study III. *British Journal of Psychiatry, 128,* 74–79.

Griffiths, Malcolm
1990 Contraceptive practices and contraceptive failures among women requesting termination of pregnancy. *British Journal of Family Planning, 16,* 16–18.

Hatcher, Sherry L.
1976 Understanding adolescent pregnancy and abortion. *Primary Care, 3,* 407–425.

Henshaw, Stanley K.
1990 Induced abortion: A world review, 1990. *Family Planning Perspectives, 22,* 76–89.

Henshaw, Stanley K., & Martire, Greg
1982 Abortion and the public opinion polls: Women who have had abortions. *Family Planning Perspectives, 14,* 60–62.

Henshaw, Stanley K., & Silverman, Jane
1988 The characteristics and prior contraceptive use of U.S. abortion patients. *Family Planning Perspectives, 20,* 158–159, 162–168.

Henshaw, Stanley K., & Van Vort, Jennifer
1990 Abortion services in the United States, 1987 and 1988. *Family Planning Perspectives, 22,* 102–108, 142.

Institute of Medicine
1975 *Legalized abortion and the public health.* Washington, DC: National Academy of Sciences.

Kaeser, Lisa
1990 Contraceptive development: Why the snail's pace? *Family Planning Perspectives, 22,* 131–133.

Kirshenbaum, Gayle
September/October 1990 Abortion: Is there a doctor in the clinic? *Ms., 1,* pp. 86–87.

Koop, C. Everett
1989a, March 21 Health impact of abortion. *Congressional Record, Extensions of Remarks,* E906–909.

Koop, C. Everett
1989b A measured response: Koop on abortion. *Family Planning Perspectives, 21,* 31–32.

Lazarus, Arthur
1985 Psychiatric sequelae of legalized elective first trimester abortion. *Journal of Psychosomatic Obstetrics and Gynaecology, 4,* 141–150.

Lodl, Karen M., McGettigan, Ann, & Bucy, Janette
1984–1985 Women's responses to abortion: Implications for post-abortion support groups. *Journal of Social Work and Human Sexuality, 3,* 119–132.

Londono, Maria L.
1989 Abortion counseling: Attention to the whole woman. *International Journal of Gynecology & Obstetrics, Suppl. 3,* 169–174.

Marecek, Jeanne
1986 Consequences of adolescent childbearing and abortion. In Gary B. Melton (Ed.), *Adolescent abortion: Psychological and legal issues* (pp. 96–115). Lincoln: University of Nebraska Press.

Marecek, Jeanne
1987 Counseling adolescents with problem pregnancies. *American Psychologist, 42,* 89–93.

Margolis, Alan, Rindfuss, Ronald, Coghlan, Phyllis, & Rochat, Roger
1974 Contraception after abortion. *Family Planning Perspectives, 6,* 56–60.

McDonnell, Kathleen
1984 *Not an easy choice.* Boston: South End Press.

Monsour, Karem, & Stewart, Barbara
1973 Abortion and sexual behavior in college women. *American Journal of Orthopsychiatry, 43,* 804–814.

More on Koop's study of abortion
1990 *Family Planning Perspectives, 22,* 36–39.

Morin-Gonthier, Mariette, & Lortie, Gilles
1984 The significance of pregnancy among adolescents choosing abortion as compared to those continuing pregnancy. *Journal of Reproductive Medicine, 29,* 255–259.

Moseley, D. T., Follingstad, D. R., Harley, H., & Heckel, R. V.
1981 Psychological factors that predict reaction to abortion. *Journal of Clinical Psychology, 37,* 276–279.

National Abortion Rights Action League (NARAL)
1985 WA NARAL Speak Out letters. Seattle, WA: Author. [provided by Esther Herst]

Osofsky, Joy D., Osofsky, Howard J., Rajan, Renga, & Spitz, Deborah
1975 Psychosocial aspects of abortion in the United States. *Mt. Sinai Journal of Medicine, 42,* 456–467.

Payne, Edmund C., Kravitz, Arthur R., Notman, Malkah T., & Anderson, Jane V.
1976 Outcome following therapeutic abortion. *Archives of General Psychiatry, 33,* 725–733.

Perez-Reyes, Maria G., & Falk, Ruth
1973 Follow-up after therapeutic abortion in early adolescence. *Archives of General Psychiatry, 28,* 120–126.

Pfost, Karen S., Lum, Cheryl U., & Stevens, Michael J.
1989 Femininity and work plans protect women against postpartum dysphoria. *Sex Roles, 21,* 423–431.

Pipes, Mary
1986 *Understanding abortion.* London: Women's Press.

Public opinion on abortion shifts
1990 *Family Planning Perspectives, 22,* 197.

Researchers confirm induced abortion to be safer
1982 *Family Planning Perspectives, 14,* 271–272.

Robbins, James M., & DeLamater, John D.
1985 Support from significant others and loneliness following induced abortion. *Social Psychiatry, 20,* 92–99.

Romans-Clarkson, Sarah E.
1989 Psychological sequelae of induced abortion. *Australian and New Zealand Journal of Psychiatry, 23,* 555–565.

Rossi, Alice S., & Sitaraman, Bhavani
1988 Abortion in context: Historical trends and future changes. *Family Planning Perspectives, 20,* 273–301.

Routh Street Women's Clinic
undated *I know I made the right decision, but. . . .* Dallas, TX: Author. [pamphlet]

Routh Street Women's Clinic
undated *Is there love after abortion?* Dallas, TX: Author. [pamphlet]

Rowan, Carl
1991, May 30 Absurd ruling on abortion advice. *San Diego Union,* p. B-13.

Shepherd, Cybill
(1990, November/December) My brain's not blond. *Ms., 1* (3), pp. 84–85.

Shogan, Robert
1990, July 31 Roemer listened to women in veto move. *Seattle Times,* p. A7.

Shusterman, Lisa R.
1979 Predicting the psychological consequences of abortion. *Social Science and Medicine, 13A,* 683–689.

Sins of emission
1990, November 6 *London Guardian,* p. 10.

Skowronski, Marjory
1977 *Abortion and alternatives.* Millbrae, CA: Les Femmes.

Smith, Elizabeth M.
1973 A follow-up study of women who request abortion. *American Journal of Orthopsychiatry, 43,* 574–585.

Steinberg, Terry N.
1989 Abortion counseling: To benefit maternal health. *American Journal of Law & Medicine, 15,* 483–517.

Steinhoff, Patricia G.
1985 The effects of induced abortion on future family goals of young women. In Sachdev, Paul (Ed.), *Perspectives on abortion* (pp. 117–129). Metuchen, NJ: Scarecrow Press.

Torres, Aida, & Forrest, Jacqueline D.
1988 Why do women have abortions? *Family Planning Perspectives, 20,* 169–176.

Trussell, James
1988 Teenage pregnancy in the United States. *Family Planning Perspectives, 20,* 262–272.

Turell, Susan C., Armsworth, Mary W., & Gaa, John P.
1990 Emotional response to abortion: A critical review of the literature. *Women & Therapy, 9,* 49–68.

Wallerstein, Judith S., Kurtz, Peter, & Bar-Din, Marion
1972 Psychosocial sequelae of therapeutic abortion in young unmarried women. *Archives of General Psychiatry, 27,* 828–832.

Watters, W. W.
1980 Mental health consequences of abortion and refused abortion. *Canadian Journal of Psychiatry, 25,* 68–73.

Zabin, Laurie S., Hirsch, Marilyn B., & Emerson, Mark R.
1989 When urban adolescents choose abortion: Effects on education, psychological status and subsequent pregnancy. *Family Planning Perspectives, 21,* 248–255.

Zimmerman, Mary K.
1977 *Passage through abortion: The personal and social reality of women's experiences.* New York: Praeger.

Morning News

Maggi Ann Grace

Maggi Ann Grace is a poet and fiction writer. She holds an M.F.A. in creative writing from the University of North Carolina at Greensboro and has taught writing in public schools and domestic violence shelters. She lives in Durham, North Carolina.

I hold the paper
sliced in early light,
read past the trial of a father
who powdered
his toddler's disposables with Drano
to inside pages
where an infant was found
locked inside a pickup truck
sucking a beer-filled bottle
while the teen mom window-shopped.
I flip to the back page
where the eight month old found
in an unheated Chicago apartment
won't need amputation after all,
only treatment for frost
and rodent bites.

My coffee is glue
sliding down my throat
and I must dress to pass
parades of mothers,
robeless judges
who tow chapped kids,
balance signs that talk of rights,
not of adolescents
not of men and women
who make mistakes
but rights of the results:
unborns who may be dropped
like bread crumbs on church steps,
in toilet bowls or scalding baths.

"Morning News" by Maggi Ann Grace, from *IF I HAD MY LIFE TO LIVE OVER I WOULD PICK MORE DAISIES*, edited by Sandra Haldeman Martz (Watsonville, California: Papier-Mache Press, 1992). Reprinted by permission of the author.

Rape: The Power of Consciousness

Susan Griffin

Susan Griffin has taught women's studies at the University of California at Berkeley and at San Francisco State University. Her play Voices, *produced widely here and in Europe, won an Emmy for a television performance. One of the founders of the Feminist Writer's Guild, she considers her writing a political activity. She is the author of* Chorus of Stones: The Private Life of War *(1992),* Unremembered Country *(1987),* Pornography and Silence: Culture's Revenge Against Nature *(1981), and* Woman and Nature: The Roaring Inside Her *(1978). This article first appeared in* Ramparts *magazine in 1971. It is one of the classic pieces of writing of the second wave.*

Griffin analyzes the effect of rape not only upon the primary victim, but upon all women: We are all victims of rape, which is a political act of terror against the entire female sex.

Part 1

Politics 1971

I HAVE NEVER BEEN FREE OF THE FEAR OF RAPE. From a very early age I, like most women, have thought of rape as part of my natural environment—something to be feared and prayed against like fire or lightning. I never asked why men raped; I simply thought it one of the many mysteries of human nature.

I was, however, curious enough about the violent side of humanity to read every crime magazine I was able to ferret away from my grandfather. Each issue featured at least one "sex crime," with pictures of a victim, usually in a pearl necklace, and of the ditch or the orchard where her body was found. I was never certain why the victims were always women, nor what the motives of the murderer were, but I did guess that the world was not a safe place for women. I observed that my grandmother was meticulous about locks, and quick to draw the shades before anyone removed so much as a shoe. I sensed that danger lurked outside.

At the age of eight, my suspicions were confirmed. My grandmother took me to the back of the house where the men wouldn't hear, and told me that strange men wanted to do harm to little girls. I learned not to walk on dark streets, not to talk to strangers, or get into strange cars, to lock doors, and to be modest. She never explained why a man would want to harm a little girl, and I never asked.

If I thought for a while that my grandmother's fears were imaginary, the illusion was brief. That year, on the way home from school, a schoolmate a few years older than I tried to rape me. Later, in an obscure aisle of the local library (while I was reading *Freddy the Pig*) I turned to discover a man exposing himself. Then, the friendly man around the corner was arrested for child molesting.

My initiation to sexuality was typical. Every woman has similar stories to tell—the first man who attacked her may have been a neighbor, a family friend, an uncle, her doctor, or perhaps her own father. And women who grow up in New York City always have tales about the subway.

But though rape and the fear of rape are a daily part of every woman's consciousness, the subject is so rarely discussed by that unofficial staff of male intellectuals (who write the books which study seemingly every other form of male activity) that one begins to suspect a conspiracy of silence. And indeed, the obscurity of rape in print exists in marked contrast to the frequency of rape in reality, for *forcible rape is the most frequently committed violent crime in America today.* The Federal Bureau of Investigation classes three crimes as violent: murder, aggravated assault and forcible rape. In 1968, 31,060 rapes were *reported.* According to the FBI and independent criminologists, however, to approach accuracy this figure must be multiplied by at least a factor of ten to compensate for the fact that most rapes are not reported; when these compensatory mathematics are used, there are more rapes committed than aggravated assaults and homicides.

When I asked Berkeley California's Police Inspector in charge of rape investigation if he knew why men rape women, he replied that he had not spoken with "these people and delved into what really makes them tick, because that really isn't my job. . . ." However, when I asked him how a woman might prevent being raped, he was not so reticent, "I wouldn't advise any female to go walking around alone at night . . . and she should lock her car at all times." The Inspector illustrated his warning with a grisly story about a man who lay in wait for women in the back seats of their cars, while they were shopping in a local supermarket. This man eventually murdered one of his rape victims. "Always lock your car," the Inspector repeated, and then added, without a hint of irony, "Of course, you don't have to be paranoid about this type of thing."

The Inspector wondered why I wanted to write about rape. Like most men he did not understand the urgency of the topic, for, after all, men are not raped. But like most women I had spent considerable time speculating on the true nature of the rapist. When I was very young, my image of the "sexual offender" was a nightmarish amalgamation of the bogey man and Captain Hook: he wore a black cape, and he cackled. As I matured, so did my image of the rapist. Born into the psychoanalytic age, I tried to "understand" the rapist. Rape, I came to believe, was only one of many unfortunate evils produced by sexual repression. Reasoning by tautology, I concluded that any man who would rape a woman must be out of his mind.

Yet, though the theory that rapists are insane is a popular one, this belief has no basis in fact. According to Professor Menachem Amir's study of 646 rape cases in Philadelphia, *Patterns in Forcible Rape,* men who rape are not abnormal. Amir writes, "Studies indicate that sex offenders do not constitute a unique or psychopathological type; nor are they as a group invariably more disturbed than the control groups to which they are compared." Alan Taylor, a parole officer who has worked with rapists in the prison facilities at San Luis Obispo, California, stated the question in plainer language, "Those men were the most normal men there. They had a lot of hang-ups, but they were the same hang-ups as men walking out on the street."

Another canon in the apologetics of rape is that, if it were not for learned social controls, all men would rape. Rape is held to be natural behavior, and not to rape must be learned. But in truth rape is not universal to the human species. Moreover, studies of rape in our culture reveal that, far from being impulsive behavior, most rape is planned. Professor Amir's study reveals that in cases of group rape—(the "gangbang" of masculine slang) 90 percent of the rapes were planned; in pair rapes, 83 percent of the rapes were planned; and in single rapes, 58 percent were planned. These figures should significantly discredit the image of the rapist as a man who is suddenly overcome by sexual needs society does not allow him to fulfill.

Far from the social control of rape being learned, comparisons with other cultures lead one to suspect that, in our society, it is rape itself that is learned. (The fact that rape is against the law should not be considered proof that rape is not in fact encouraged as part of our culture.)

This culture's concept of rape as an illegal, but still understandable, form of behavior is not a universal one. In her study *Sex and Temperament,* Margaret Mead describes a society that does not share our views. The Arapesh do not " . . . have any conception of the male nature that might make rape understandable to them." Indeed our interpretation of rape is a product of our conception of the nature of male sexuality. A common retort to the question, why don't women rape men, is the myth that men have greater sexual needs, that their sexuality is more urgent than women's. And it is the nature of human beings to want to live up to what is expected of them.

And this same culture which expects aggression from the male expects passivity from the female. Conveniently, the companion myth about the nature of female sexuality is that all women secretly want to be raped. Lurking beneath her modest female exterior is a subconscious desire to be ravished. The following description of a stag movie, written by Brenda Starr in Los Angeles' underground paper, *Everywoman,* typifies this male fantasy. The movie "showed a woman in her underclothes reading on her bed. She is interrupted by a rapist with a knife. He immediately wins her over with his charm and they get busy sucking and fucking." An advertisement in the *Berkeley Barb* reads, "Now as all women know from their daydreams, rape has a lot of advantages. Best of all it's so simple. No preparation necessary, no planning ahead of time, no wondering if you should or shouldn't; just whang! bang!" Thanks to Masters and Johnson even the scientific canon recognizes that for the female, "whang! bang!" can scarcely be described as pleasurable.

Still, the male psyche persists in believing that, protestations and struggles to the contrary, deep inside her mysterious feminine soul, the female victim has wished for her own fate. A young woman who was raped by the husband of a friend said that days after the incident the man returned to her home, pounded on the door and screamed to her, "Jane, Jane. You loved it. You know you loved it."

The theory that women like being raped extends itself by deduction into the proposition that most or much of rape is provoked by the victim. But this too is only myth. Though provocation, considered a mitigating factor in a court of law, may consist of only "a gesture," according to the Federal Commission on Crimes of Violence, only 4 percent of reported rapes involved any precipitative behavior by the woman.

The notion that rape is enjoyed by the victim is also convenient for the man who, though he would not commit forcible rape, enjoys the idea of its existence, as if rape confirms that enormous sexual potency which he secretly knows to be his own. It is for the pleasure of the armchair rapist that detailed accounts of violent rapes exist in the media. Indeed, many men appear to take sexual pleasure from nearly all forms of violence. Whatever the motivation, male sexuality and violence in our culture seem to be inseparable. James Bond alternately whips out his revolver and his cock, and though there is no known connection between the skills of gunfighting and lovemaking, pacifism seems suspiciously effeminate.

In a recent treatment of the Manson case, Frank Conroy writes of his vicarious titillation when describing the murders to his wife:

> *"Every single person there was killed." She didn't move.*
>
> *"It sounds like there was torture," I said. As the words left my mouth I knew there was no need to say them to frighten her into believing that she needed me for protection.*

The pleasure he feels as his wife's protector is inextricably mixed with pleasure in the violence itself. Conroy writes, "I was excited by the killings, as one excited by catastrophe on a grand scale, as one is alert to pre-echoes of unknown changes, hints of unrevealed secrets, rumblings of chaos. . . ."

The attraction of the male in our culture to violence and death is a tradition Manson and his admirers are carrying on with tireless avidity (even presuming Manson's innocence, he dreams of the purification of fire and destruction). It was Malraux in his *Anti-Memoirs* who said that, for the male, facing death was the illuminating experience analogous to childbirth for the female. Certainly our culture does glorify war and shroud the agonies of the gunfighter in veils of mystery.

And in the spectrum of male behavior, rape, the perfect combination of sex and violence, is the penultimate act. Erotic pleasure cannot be separated from culture, and in our culture male eroticism is wedded to power. Not only should a man be taller and stronger than a female in the perfect love-match, but he must also demonstrate his superior strength in gestures of dominance which are perceived as amorous. Though the law attempts to make a clear division between rape and sexual intercourse, in fact the courts find it difficult to distinguish between a case where the decision to copulate was mutual and one where a man forced himself upon his partner.

The scenario is even further complicated by the expectation that, not only does a woman mean "yes" when she says "no," but that a really decent woman ought to begin by saying "no," and then be led down the primrose path to acquiescence. Ovid, the author of Western Civilization's most celebrated sex manual, makes this expectation perfectly clear:

> *. . . and when I beg you to say "yes," say "no." Then let me lie outside your bolted door. . . . So Love grows strong. . . .*

That the basic elements of rape are involved in all heterosexual relationships may explain why men often identify with the offender in this crime. But to regard the rapist as the victim, a man driven by his inherent sexual needs to take what will not be given him, reveals a basic ignorance of sexual politics. For in our culture heterosexual love finds an erotic expression through male dominance and female submission. A man who derives pleasure from raping a woman clearly must enjoy force and dominance as much or more than the simply pleasures of the flesh. Coitus cannot be experienced in isolation. The weather, the state of the nation, the level of sugar in the blood—all will affect a man's ability to achieve orgasm. If a man can achieve sexual pleasure after terrorizing and humiliating the object of his passion, and in fact while inflicting pain upon her, one must assume he derives pleasure directly from terrorizing, humiliating and harming a woman. According to Amir's study of forcible rape, on a statistical average the man who has been convicted of rape was found to have a normal sexual personality, tending to be different from the normal, well-adjusted male only in having a greater tendency to express violence and rage.

And if the professional rapist is to be separated from the average dominant heterosexual, it may be mainly a quantitative difference. For the existence of rape as an index to masculinity is not entirely metaphorical. Though this measure of masculinity seems to be more publicly exhibited among "bad boys" or aging bikers who practice sexual initiation through group rape, in fact, "good boys" engage in the same rites to prove their manhood. In Stockton, a small town in California which epitomizes silent-majority America, a bachelor party was given last summer for a young man about to be married. A woman was hired to dance "topless" for the amusement of the guests. At the high point of the evening the bridegroom-to-be dragged the woman into a bedroom. No move was made by any of his companions to stop what was clearly going to be an attempted rape. Far from it. As the woman described, "I tried to keep him away—told him of my Herpes Genitalis, et cetera, but he couldn't face the guys if he didn't screw me." After the bridegroom had finished raping the woman and returned with her to the party, far from chastising him, his friends heckled the woman and covered her with wine.

It was fortunate for the dancer that the bridegroom's friends did not follow him into the bedroom for, though one might suppose that in group rape, since the victim is outnumbered, less force would be inflicted on her, in fact, Amir's studies indicate, "the most excessive degrees of violence occurred in group rape." Far from discouraging violence, the presence of other men may in fact encourage sadism, and even cause the behavior. In an unpublished study of group rape by Gilbert Geis and Duncan Chappell, the authors refer to a study by W. H. Blanchard which relates,

> *The leader of the male group . . . apparently precipitated and maintained the activity, despite misgivings, because of a need to fulfill the role that the other two men had assigned to him. "I was scared when it began to happen," he says. "I wanted to leave but I didn't want to say it to the other guys—you know—that I was scared."*

Thus it becomes clear that not only does our culture teach men the rudiments of rape, but society, or more specifically other men, encourage the practice of it.

II

> *Every man I meet wants to protect me. Can't figure out what from.*
>
> –Mae West

If a male society rewards aggressive, domineering sexual behavior, it contains within itself a sexual schizophrenia. For the masculine man is also expected to prove his mettle as a protector of women. To the naive eye, this dichotomy implies that men fall into one of two categories: those who rape and those who protect. In fact, life does not prove so simple. In a study euphemistically entitled "Sex Aggression by

College Men," it was discovered that men who believe in a double standard of morality for men and women, who in fact believe most fervently in the ultimate value of virginity, are more liable to commit "this aggressive variety of sexual exploitation."

(At this point in our narrative it should come as no surprise that Sir Thomas Malory, creator of that classic tale of chivalry, *The Knights of the Round Table,* was himself arrested and found guilty for repeated incidents of rape.)

In the system of chivalry, men protect women against men. This is not unlike the protection relationship which the mafia established with small businesses in the early part of this century. Indeed, chivalry is an age-old protection racket which depends for its existence on rape.

According to the male mythology which defines and perpetuates rape, it is an animal instinct inherent in the male. The story goes that sometime in our prehistorical past, the male, more hirsute and burly than today's counterparts, roamed about an uncivilized landscape until he found a desirable female. (Oddly enough, this female is *not* pictured as more muscular than the modern woman.) Her mate does not bother with courtship. He simply grabs her by the hair and drags her to the closest cave. Presumably, one of the major advantages of modern civilization for the female has been the civilizing of the male. We call it chivalry.

But women do not get chivalry for free. According to the logic of sexual politics, we too have to civilize our behavior. (Enter chastity. Enter virginity. Enter monogamy.) For the female, civilized behavior means chastity before marriage and faithfulness within it. Chivalrous behavior in the male is supposed to protect that chastity from involuntary defilement. The fly in the ointment of this otherwise peaceful system is the fallen woman. She does not behave. And therefore she does not deserve protection. Or, to use another argument, a major tenet of the same value system: what has once been defiled cannot again be violated. One begins to suspect that it is the behavior of the fallen woman, and not that of the male, that civilization aims to control.

The assumption that a woman who does not respect the double standard deserves whatever she gets (or at the very least "asks for it") operates in the courts today. While in some states a man's previous rape convictions are not considered admissible evidence, the sexual reputation of the rape victim is considered a crucial element of the facts upon which the court must decide innocence or guilt.

The court's respect for the double standard manifested itself particularly clearly in the case of the People v. Jerry Plotkin. Mr. Plotkin, a 36-year-old jeweler, was tried for rape last spring in a San Francisco Superior Court. According to the woman who brought the charges, Plotkin, along with three other men, forced her at gunpoint to enter a car one night in October 1970. She was taken to Mr. Plotkin's fashionable apartment where he and the three other men first raped her and then, in the delicate language of the *S. F. Chronicle,* "subjected her to perverted sex acts." She was, she said, set free in the morning with the warning that she would be killed if she spoke to anyone about the event. She did report the incident to the police who then searched Plotkin's apartment and discovered a long list of names of women. Her name was on the list and had been crossed out.

In addition to the woman's account of her abduction and rape, the prosecution submitted four of Plotkin's address books containing the names of hundreds of women. Plotkin claimed he did not know all of the women since some of the names had been given to him by friends and he had not yet called on them. Several women, however, did testify in court that Plotkin had, to cite the *Chronicle,* "lured them up to his apartment under one pretext or another, and forced his sexual attentions on them."

Plotkin's defense rested on two premises. First, through his own testimony Plotkin established a reputation for himself as a sexual libertine who frequently picked up girls in bars and took them to his house where sexual relations often took place. He was the Playboy. He claimed that the accusation of rape, therefore, was false—this incident had simply been one of many casual sexual relationships, the victim one of many playmates. The second premise of the defense was that his accuser was also a sexual libertine. However, the picture created of the young woman (fully 13 years younger than Plotkin) was not akin to the light-hearted, gay-bachelor image projected by the defendant. On the contrary, the day after the defense cross-examined the woman, the *Chronicle* printed a story headlined, "Grueling Day For Rape Case Victim." (A leaflet passed out by women in front of the courtroom was more succinct, "rape was committed by four men in a private apartment in October; on Thursday, it was done by a judge and a lawyer in a public courtroom.")

Through skillful questioning fraught with innuendo, Plotkin's defense attorney James Martin MacInnis portrayed the young woman as a licentious opportunist and unfit mother. MacInnis began by asking the young woman (then employed as a secretary) whether or not it was true that she was "familiar with liquor" and had worked as a "cocktail waitress." The young woman replied (the *Chronicle* wrote "admitted") that she had worked once or twice as a cocktail waitress. The attorney then asked if she had worked as a secretary in the financial district but had "left that employment after it was discovered that you had sexual intercourse on a couch in the office." The woman replied, "That is a lie. I left because I didn't like working in a one-girl office. It was too lonely." Then the defense asked if, while working as an attendant at a health club, "you were accused of having a sexual affair with a man?" Again the woman denied the story, "I was never accused of that."

Plotkin's attorney then sought to establish that his client's accuser was living with a married man. She responded that the man was separated from his wife. Finally he told the court that she had "spent the night" with another man who lived in the same building.

At this point in the testimony the woman asked Plotkin's defense attorney, "Am I on trial? . . . It is embarrassing and personal to admit these things to all these people. . . . I did not commit a crime. I am a human being." The lawyer, true to the chivalry of his class, apologized and immediately resumed questioning her, turning his attention to her children. (She is divorced, and the children at the time of the trial were in a foster home.) "Isn't it true that your two children have a sex game in which one gets on top of another and they—" "That is a lie!" the young woman interrupted him. She ended her testimony by explaining "They are wonderful children. They are not perverted."

The jury, divided in favor of acquittal ten to two, asked the court stenographer to read the woman's testimony back to them. After this reading, the Superior Court acquitted the defendant of both charges of rape and kidnapping.

According to the double standard a woman who has had sexual intercourse out of wedlock cannot be raped. Rape is not only a crime of aggression against the body; it is a transgression against chastity as defined by men. When a woman is forced into a sexual relationship, she has, according to the male ethos, been violated. But she is also defiled if she does not behave according to the double standard, by maintaining her chastity, or confining her sexual activities to a monogamous relationship.

One should not assume, however, that a woman can avoid the possibility of rape simply by behaving. Though myth would have it that mainly "bad girls" are raped, this theory has no basis in fact. Available statistics would lead one to believe that a safer course is promiscuity. In a study of rape done in the District of Columbia, it was found that 82 percent of the rape victims had a "good reputation." Even the Police Inspector's advice to stay off the streets is rather useless, for almost half of reported rapes occur in the home of the victim and are committed by a man she has never before seen. Like indiscriminate terrorism, rape can happen to any woman, and few women are ever without this knowledge.

But the courts and the police, both dominated by white males, continue to suspect the rape victim, *sui generis,* of provoking or asking for her own assault. According to Amir's study, the police tend to believe that a woman without a good reputation cannot be raped. The rape victim is usually submitted to countless questions about her own sexual mores and behavior by the police. This preoccupation is partially justified by the legal requirements for prosecution in a rape case. The rape victim must have been penetrated, and she must have made it clear to her assailant that she did not want penetration (unless of course she is unconscious). A refusal to accompany a man to some isolated place to allow him to touch her does not in the eyes of the court, constitute rape. She must have said "no" at the crucial genital moment. And the rape victim, to qualify as such, must also have put up a physical struggle—unless she can prove that to do so would have been to endanger her life.

But the zealous interest the police frequently exhibit in the physical details of a rape case is only partially explained by the requirements of the court. A woman who was raped in Berkeley was asked to tell the story of her rape four different times "right out in the street," while her assailant was escaping. She was then required to submit to a pelvic examination to prove that penetration had taken place. Later, she was taken to the police station where she was asked the same questions again: "Were you forced?" "Did he penetrate?" "Are you sure your life was in danger and you had no other choice?" This woman had been pulled off the street by a man who held a 10-inch knife at her throat and forcibly raped her. She was raped at midnight and was not able to return to her home until five in the morning. Police contacted her twice again in the next week, once by telephone at two in the morning and once at four in the morning. In her words, "The rape was probably the least traumatic incident of the whole evening. If I'm ever raped again, . . . I wouldn't report it to the police because of all the degradation. . . ."

If white women are subjected to unnecessary and often hostile questioning after having been raped, third world women are often not believed at all. According to the white male ethos (which is not only sexist but racist), third world women are defined from birth as "impure." Thus the white male is provided with a pool of women who are fair game for sexual imperialism. Third world women frequently do not report rape and for good reason. When blues singer Billie Holliday was 10 years old, she was taken off to a local house by a neighbor and raped. Her mother brought the police to rescue her, and she was taken to the local police station crying and bleeding:

> *When we got there, instead of treating me and Mom like somebody who called the cops for help, they treated me like I'd killed somebody. . . . I guess they had me figured for having enticed this old goat into the whorehouse. . . . All I know for sure is they threw me into a cell . . . a fat white matron . . . saw I was still bleeding, she felt sorry for me and gave me a couple glasses of milk. But nobody else did anything for me except give me filthy looks and snicker to themselves.*
>
> *After a couple of days in a cell they dragged me into a court. Mr. Dick got sentenced to five years. They sentenced me to a Catholic institution.*

Clearly the white man's chivalry is aimed only to protect the chastity of "his" women.

As a final irony, that same system of sexual values from which chivalry is derived has also provided womankind with an unwritten code of behavior, called femininity, which makes a feminine woman the perfect victim of sexual aggression. If being chaste does not ward off the possibility of assault, being feminine certainly increases the chances that it will succeed. To be submissive is to defer to masculine strength; is to lack muscular development or any interest in defending oneself; is to let doors be opened, to have one's arm held when crossing the street. To be feminine is to wear shoes which make it difficult to run; skirts which inhibit one's stride; underclothes which inhibit the circulation. Is it not an intriguing observation that those very clothes which are thought to be flattering to the female and attractive to the male are those which make it impossible for a woman to defend herself against aggression?

Each girl as she grows into womanhood is taught fear. Fear is the form in which the female internalizes both chivalry and the double standard. Since, biologically speaking, women in fact have the same if not greater potential for sexual expression as do men, the woman who is taught that she must behave differently from a man must also learn to distrust her own carnality. She must deny her own feelings and learn not to act from them. She fears herself. This is the essence of passivity and, of course, a woman's passivity is not simply sexual but functions to cripple her from self-expression in every area of her life.

Passivity itself prevents a woman from ever considering her own potential for self-defense and forces her to look to men for protection. The woman is taught fear, but this time fear of the other; and yet her only relief from this fear is to seek out the other. Moreover, the passive woman is taught to regard herself as impotent, unable to act, unable even to perceive, in no way self-sufficient, and finally, as the object and not the subject of human behavior. It is in this sense that a woman is deprived of the status of a human being. She is not free to be.

III

Since Ibsen's Nora slammed the door on her patriarchical husband, woman's attempt to be free has been more or less fashionable. In this nineteenth-century portrait of a woman leaving her marriage, Nora tells her husband, "Our home has been nothing but a playroom. I have been your doll-wife just as at home I was papa's doll-child." And, at least on the stage, "The Doll's House" crumbled, leaving audiences with hope for the fate of the modern woman. And today, as in the past, womankind has not lacked examples of liberated women to emulate: Emma Goldman, Greta Garbo and Isadora Duncan all denounced marriage and the double standard, and believed their right to freedom included sexual independence; but still their example has not affected the lives of millions of women who continue to marry, divorce and remarry, living out their lives dependent on the status and economic power of men. Patriarchy still holds the average woman prisoner not because she lacks the courage of an Isadora Duncan, but because the material conditions of her life prevent her from being anything but an object.

In the *Elementary Structures of Kinship,* Claude Levi-Strauss gives to marriage this universal description, "It is always a system of exchange that we find at the origin of the rules of marriage." In this system of exchange, a woman is the "most precious possession." Levi-Strauss continues that the custom of including women as booty in the marketplace is still so general that "a whole volume would not be sufficient to enumerate instances of it." Levi-Strauss makes it clear that he does not exclude Western Civilization from his definition of "universal" and cites examples from modern wedding ceremonies. (The marriage ceremony is still one in which the husband and wife become one, and "that one is the husband.")

The legal proscription against rape reflects this possessory view of women. An article in the 1952–53 *Yale Law Journal* describes the legal rationale behind laws against rape:

> *In our society sexual taboos, often enacted into law, buttress a system of monogamy based upon the law of "free bargaining" of the potential spouses. Within this process the woman's power to withhold or grant sexual access is an important bargaining weapon.*

Presumably then, laws against rape are intended to protect the right of a woman, not for physical self-determination, but for physical "bargaining." The article goes on to explain explicitly why the preservation of the bodies of women is important to men:

> *The consent standard in our society does more than protect a significant item of social currency for women; it fosters, and is in turn bolstered by, a masculine pride in the exclusive possession of a sexual object. The consent of a woman to sexual intercourse awards the man a privilege of bodily access, a personal "prize," whose value is enhanced by sole ownership. An additional reason for the man's condemnation of rape may by found in the threat to his status from a decrease in the "value" of his sexual possession which would result from forcible violation.*

The passage concludes by making clear whose interest the law is designed to protect. "The man responds to this undercutting of his status as *possessor* of the girl with hostility toward the rapist; no other restitution device is available. The law of rape provides an orderly outlet for his vengeance." Presumably the female victim in any case will have been sufficiently socialized so as not to consciously feel any strong need for vengeance. If she does feel this need, society does not speak to it.

The laws against rape exist to protect rights of the male as possessor of the female body, and not the right of the female over her own body. Even without this enlightening passage from the *Yale Law Review,* the laws themselves are clear: In no state can a man be accused of raping his wife. How can any man steal what already belongs to him? It is in the sense of rape as theft of another man's property that Kate Millett writes, "Traditionally rape has been viewed as an offense one male commits against another—a matter of abusing his woman." In raping another man's woman, a man may aggrandize his own manhood and concurrently reduce that of another man. Thus a man's honor is not subject directly to rape, but only indirectly, through "his" woman.

If the basic social unit is the family, in which the woman is a possession of her husband, the superstructure of society is a male hierarchy, in which men dominate other men (or patriarchal families dominate other patriarchal families). And it is no small irony that, while the very social fabric of our male-dominated culture denies women equal access to political, economic and legal power, the literature, myth and humor of our culture depict women not only as the power behind the throne, but the real source of the oppression of men. The religious version of this fairy tale blames Eve for both carnality and eating of the tree of knowledge, at the same time making her gullible to the obvious devices of a serpent. Adam, of course, is merely the trusting victim of love. Certainly this is a biased story. But no more biased than the one television audiences receive today from the latest slick comedians. Through a media which is owned by men, censored by a state dominated by men, all the evils of this social system which make a man's life unpleasant are blamed upon "the wife." The theory is: were it not for the female who waits and plots to "trap" the male into marriage, modern man would be able to achieve Olympian freedom. She is made the scapegoat for a system which is in fact run by men.

Nowhere is this more clear than in the white racist use of the concept of white womanhood. The white male's open rape of black women, coupled with his overweening concern for the chastity and protection of his wife and daughters, represents an extreme of sexist and racist hypocrisy. While on the one hand she was held up as the standard for purity and virtue, on the other the Southern white woman was never asked if she wanted to be on a pedestal, and in fact any deviance from the male-defined standards for white womanhood was treated severely. (It is a powerful commentary on American racism that the historical role of Blacks as slaves, and thus possessions without power, has robbed black women of legal and economic protection through marriage. Thus black women in Southern society and in the ghettoes of the North have long been easy game for white rapists.) The fear that black men would rape white women was classic paranoia. Quoting from Ann Breen's unpublished study of racism and sexism in the South, *The New South: White Man's Country,* Frederick Douglass legitimately points out that, had the black man wished to rape white women, he had ample opportunity to do so during the Civil War when white women, the wives, sisters, daughters and mothers of the rebels, were left in the care of Blacks. But yet not a single act of rape was committed during this time. The Ku Klux Klan, who tarred and feathered black men and lynched them in the honor of the purity of white womanhood, also applied tar and feathers to a Southern white woman accused of bigamy, which leads one to suspect that Southern white men were not so much outraged at the violation of the woman as a person, in the few instances where rape was actually committed by black men, but at the violation of his property rights. In the situation where a black man was found to be having sexual relations with a white woman, the white woman could exercise skin-privilege, and claim that she had been raped in which case the black man was lynched. But if she did not claim rape, she herself was subject to lynching.

In constructing the myth of white womanhood so as to justify the lynching and oppression of black men and women, the white male has created a convenient symbol of his own power which has resulted in black hostility toward the white "bitch," accompanied by a fear on the part of many white women of the black rapist. Moreover, it is not surprising that after being told for two centuries that he wants to rape white women, black men have begun to actually commit that act. But it is crucial to note that the frequency of this practice is outrageously exaggerated in the white mythos. Ninety percent of reported rape is intra- not inter-racial.

In *Soul on Ice,* Eldridge Cleaver has described the mixing of a rage against white power with the internalized sexism of a black man raping a white woman.

> *Somehow I arrived at the conclusion that, as a matter of principle, it was of paramount importance for me to have an antagonistic, ruthless attitude toward white women. . . . Rape was an insurrectionary act. It delighted me that I was defying and trampling upon the white man's law, upon his system of values and that I was defiling his women—and this point, I believe, was the most satisfying to me because I was very resentful over the historical fact of how the white man has used the black woman.*

Thus a black man uses white women to take out his rage against white men. But, in fact, whenever a rape of a white woman by a black man does take place, it is again the white man who benefits. First, the act itself terrorizes the white woman and makes her more dependent on the white male for protection. Then, if the woman prosecutes her attacker, the white man is afforded legal opportunity to exercise overt racism. Of course, the knowledge of the rape helps to perpetuate two myths which are beneficial to white male rule—the bestiality of the black man and the desirability of white women. Finally, the white man surely benefits because he himself is not the object of attack—he has been allowed to stay in power.

Indeed, the existence of rape in any form is beneficial to the ruling class of white males. For rape is a kind of terrorism which severely limits the freedom of women and makes women dependent on men. Moreover, in the act of rape, the rage that one man may harbor toward another higher in the male hierarchy can be deflected toward a female scapegoat. For every man there is always someone lower on the social scale on whom he can take out his aggressions. And that is any woman alive.

This oppressive attitude towards women finds its institutionalization in the traditional family. For it is assumed that a man "wears the pants" in his family—he exercises the option of rule whenever he so chooses. Not that he makes all the decisions—clearly women make most of the important day-to-day decisions in a family. But when a conflict of interest arises, it is the man's interest which will prevail. His word, in itself, is more powerful. He lords it over his wife in the same way his boss lords it over him, so that the very process of exercising his power becomes as important an act as obtaining whatever it is his power can get for him. This notion of power is key to the male ego in this culture, for the two acceptable measures of masculinity are a man's power over women and his power over other men. A man may boast to his friends that "I have 20 men working for me." It is also aggrandizement of his ego if he has the financial power to clothe his wife in furs and jewels. And, if a man lacks the wherewithal to acquire such power, he can always express his rage through equally masculine activities—rape and theft. Since male society defines the female as a possession, it is not surprising that the felony most often committed together with rape is theft. As the following classic tale of rape points out, the elements of theft, violence and forced sexual relations merge into an indistinguishable whole.

The woman who told the following story was acquainted with the man who tried to rape her. When the man learned that she was going to be staying alone for the weekend, he began early in the day a polite campaign to get her to go out with him. When she continued to refuse his request, his chivalrous mask dropped away:

> *I had locked all the doors because I was afraid, and I don't know how he got in; it was probably through the screen door. When I woke up, he was shaking my leg. His eyes were red, and I knew he had been drinking or smoking. I thought I would try to talk my way out of it. He started by saying that he wanted to sleep with me, and then he got angrier and angrier, until he started to say, "I want pussy," "I want pussy." Then, I got scared and tried to push him away. That's when he started to force himself on me. It was awful. It was the most humiliating, terrible feeling. He was forcing my legs apart and ripping my clothes off. And it was painful. I did fight him—he was slightly drunk and I was able to keep him away. I had taken judo a few years back, but I was afraid to throw a chop for fear that he'd kill me. I could see he was getting more and more violent. I was thinking wildly of some way to get out of this alive, and then I said to him, "Do you want money? I'll give you money." We had money but I was also thinking that if I got to the back room I could telephone the police—as if the police would have even helped. It was a stupid think to think of because obviously he would follow me. And he did. When he saw me pick up the phone, he tried to tie the cord around my neck. I screamed at him that I did have the money in another room, that I was going to call the police because I was scared, but that I would never tell anybody what happened. It would be an absolute secret. He said, "okay,' and I went to get the money. But when he got it, all of a sudden he got this crazy look in his eye and he said to me, "Now I'm going to kill you." Then I started saying my prayers. I knew there was nothing I could do. He started to hit me—I still wasn't sure if he wanted to rape me at this point—or just to kill me. He was hurting me, but hadn't yet gotten me into a stranglehold because he was still drunk and off balance. Somehow we pushed into the kitchen where I kept looking at this big knife. But I didn't pick it up. Somehow, no matter how much I hated him at that moment, I still couldn't imagine putting the knife in his flesh, and then I was afraid he would grab it and stick it into me. Then he was hitting me again and somehow we pushed through the back door of the kitchen and onto the porch steps. We fell down the steps and that's when he started to strangle me. He was on top of me. He just went on and on until finally I lost consciousness. I did scream, though my screams sounded like whispers to me. But what happened was that a cab driver happened by and frightened him away. The cab driver revived me—I was out only a minute at the most. And then I ran across the street and I grabbed the woman who was our neighbor and screamed at her, "Am I alive? Am I still alive?"*

Rape is an act of aggression in which the victim is denied her self-determination. It is an act of violence which, if not actually followed by beatings or murder, nevertheless always carries with it the threat of death. And finally, rape is a form of mass terrorism, for the victims of rape are chosen indiscriminately, but the propagandists for male supremacy broadcast that it is women who cause rape by being unchaste or in the wrong place at the wrong time—in essence, by behaving as though they were free.

The threat of rape is used to deny women employment. (In California, the Berkeley Public Library, until pushed by the Federal Employment Practices Commission, refused to hire female shelvers because of perverted men in the stacks.) The fear of rape keeps women off the streets at night. Keeps women at home. Keeps women passive and modest for fear that they be thought provocative.

It is part of human dignity to be able to defend oneself, and women are learning. Some women have learned karate; some to shoot guns. And yet we will not be free until the threat of rape and the atmosphere of violence is ended, and to end that the nature of male behavior must change.

But rape is not an isolated act that can be rooted out from patriarchy without ending patriarchy itself. The same men and power structure who victimize women are engaged in the act of raping Vietnam, raping Black people and the very earth we live upon. Rape is a classic act of domination where, in the words of Kate Millett, "the emotions of hatred, contempt, and the desire to break or violate personality," take place. This breaking of the personality characterizes modern life itself. No simple reforms can eliminate rape. As the symbolic expression of the white male hierarchy, rape is the quintessential act of our civilization, one which, Valerie Solanis warns, is in danger of "humping itself to death."

"The Rape" of Mr. Smith

Unknown

This small piece is so clear on the injustices—legal, cultural, and attitudinal—that are visited upon women who are victims of rape that it is used everywhere—in women's studies courses, in rape crisis centers, in training seminars for police and social workers—yet no one seems to know its origin.

It must be remembered that we are all *subject to rape: those who have been raped, those who may be raped and therefore have their lives altered, and those who are related to the victims of rape.*

THE LAW DISCRIMINATES AGAINST RAPE VICTIMS IN a manner which would not be tolerated by victims of any other crime. In the following example, a holdup victim is asked questions similar in form to those usually asked a victim of rape.

"Mr. Smith, you were held up at gunpoint on the corner of 16th & Locust?"
"Yes."
"Did you struggle with the robber?"
"No."
"Why not?"
"He was armed."
"Then you made a conscious decision to comply with his demands rather than to resist?"
"Yes."
"Did you scream? Cry out?"
"No. I was afraid."
"I see. Have you ever been held up before?"
"No."
"Have you ever given money away?"
"Yes, of course—"
"And did you do so willingly?"
"What are you getting at?"
"Well, let's put it like this, Mr. Smith. You've given away money in the past—in fact, you have quite a reputation for philanthropy. How can we be sure that you weren't *contriving* to have your money taken from you by force?"
"Listen, if I wanted—"
"Never mind. What time did this holdup take place, Mr. Smith?"
'About 11 p.m."
"You were out on the streets at 11 p.m.? Doing what?"
"Just walking."
"Just walking? You know that it's dangerous being out on the street that late at night. Weren't you aware that you could have been held up?"
"I hadn't thought about it."
"What were you wearing at the time, Mr. Smith?"
"Let's see. A suit. Yes, a suit."
"An *expensive* suit?"
"Well—yes."

---

*Reprinted with permission from *Women Helping Women: Volunteer Resource Manual,* by Rape Crisis Services, Urbana, Illinois.

"In other words, Mr. Smith, you were walking around the streets late at night in a suit that practically *advertised* the fact that you might be a good target for some easy money, isn't that so? I mean, if we didn't know better, Mr. Smith, we might even think you were *asking* for this to happen, mightn't we?"

"Look, can't we talk about the past history of the guy who *did* this to me?"

"I'm afraid not, Mr. Smith. I don't think you would want to violate his rights, now, would you?"

Naturally, the line of questioning, the innuendo, is ludicrous—as well as inadmissible as any sort of cross-examination—unless we are talking about parallel questions in a rape case. The time of night, the victim's previous history of "giving away" that which was taken by force, the clothing—all of these are held against the victim. Society's posture on rape, and the manifestation of that posture in the courts, help account for the fact that so few rapes are reported.

'Til Death Do Us Part

Nancy Gibbs

There are estimates that in one out of two marriages in the United States, women will experience violence against them. Battering is one of the highest causes of death and injury in women, not only in the United States but in the world. In the United States, a woman is beaten every fifteen seconds and at least four women are killed by their batterers every day, according to the U.S. Department of Justice. In Peru 70 percent of all crimes reported to the police are of battering. In Bangkok, Thailand, it was reported that 50 percent of married women are beaten regularly. Austria reported that in 1985, 54 percent of all murders were committed in the family, 90 percent involving women and children.[1] *Violence against women is epidemic. It occurs among all classes, all races, all ages. It has been mainly through the efforts of women's organizations and movements that the issue of domestic violence is beginning to attract some public attention. But as you will see, it is hardly enough.*

THE LAW HAS ALWAYS MADE ROOM FOR KILLERS. Soldiers kill the nation's enemies, executioners kill its killers, police officers under fire may fire back. Even a murder is measured in degrees, depending on the mind of the criminal and the character of the crime. And sometime this spring, in a triumph of pity over punishment, the law may just find room for Rita Collins.

"They all cried, didn't they? But not me," she starts out, to distinguish herself from her fellow inmates in a Florida prison, who also have stories to tell. "No one will help me. No one will write about me. I don't have a dirty story. I wasn't abused as a child. I was a respectable government employee, employed by the Navy in a high position in Washington."

Her husband John was a military recruiter, a solid man who had a way with words. "He said I was old, fat, crazy and had no friends that were real friends. He said I needed him and he would take care of me." She says his care included threats with a knife, punches, a kick to the stomach that caused a hemorrhage. Navy doctors treated her for injuries to her neck and arm. "He'd slam me up against doors. He gave me black eyes, bruises. Winter and summer, I'd go to work like a Puritan, with long sleeves. Afterward he'd soothe me, and I'd think, He's a good man. What did I do wrong?"

The bravado dissolves, and she starts to cry.

"I was envied by other wives. I felt ashamed because I didn't appreciate him." After each beating came apologies and offerings, gifts, a trip. "It's like blackmail. You think it's going to stop, but it doesn't." Collins never told anyone—not her friends in the church choir, not even a son by her first marriage. "I should have , but it was the humiliation of it all. I'm a professional woman. I didn't want people to think I was crazy." But some of them knew anyway; they had seen the bruises, the black eye behind the dark glasses.

She tried to get out. She filed for divorce, got a restraining order, filed an assault-and-battery charge against him, forced him from the house they had bought with a large chunk of her money

---

[1]Lori Heise, "Crimes of Gender," *World-Watch,* March/April 1989, pp. 12–21.

when they retired to Florida. But still, she says, he came, night after night, banging on windows and doors, trying to break the locks.

It wasn't her idea to buy a weapon. "The police did all they could, but they had no control. They felt sorry for me. They told me to get a gun." She still doesn't remember firing it. She says she remembers her husband's face, the glassy eyes, a knife in his hands. "To this day, I don't remember pulling the trigger."

The jury couldn't figure it out either. At Collins' first trial, for first-degree murder, her friends, a minister, her doctors and several experts testified about her character and the violence she had suffered. The prosecution played tapes of her threatening her husband over the phone and portrayed her as a bitter, unstable woman who had bought a gun, lured him to the house and murdered him out of jealousy and anger over the divorce. That trial ended with a hung jury. At her second, nine men and three women debated just two hours before finding her guilty of the lesser charge, second-degree murder. Collins' appeals were denied, and the parole board last year recommended against clemency. Orlando prosecutor Dorothy Sedgwick is certain that justice was done. "Rita Collins is a classic example of how a woman can decide to kill her husband and use the battered woman's syndrome as a fake defense," she says. "She lured him to his death. He was trying to escape her." Collins says her lawyers got everything: the $125,000 three-bedroom house with a pool, $98,000 in cash. "I've worked since I was 15, and I have nothing," she says. "The Bible says, 'Thou shalt not kill,' and everybody figures if you're in here, you're guilty. But I'm not a criminal. Nobody cares if I die in here, but if I live, I tell you one thing: I'm not going to keep quiet."

If in the next round of clemency hearings on March 10, Governor Lawton Chiles grants Collins or any other battered woman clemency, Florida will join 26 other states in a national movement to take another look at the cases of abuse victims who kill their abusers. Just before Christmas, Missouri's conservative Republican Governor John Ashcroft commuted the life sentences of two women who claimed they had killed their husbands in self-defense. After 20 years of trying, these women have made a Darwinian claim for mercy: Victims of perpetual violence should be forgiven if they turn violent themselves.

More American women—rich and poor alike—are injured by the men in their life than by car accidents, muggings and rape combined. Advocates and experts liken the effect over time to a slow-acting poison. "Most battered women aren't killing to protect themselves from being killed that very moment," observes Charles Ewing, a law professor at SUNY Buffalo. "What they're protecting themselves from is slow but certain destruction, psychologically and physically. There's no place in the law for that."

As the clemency movement grows, it challenges a legal system that does not always distinguish between a crime and a tragedy. What special claims should victims of fate, poverty, violence, addiction be able to make upon the sympathies of juries and the boundaries of the law? In cases of domestic assaults, some women who suffered terrible abuse resorted to terrible means to escape it. Now the juries, and ultimately the society they speak for, have to find some way to express outrage at the brutality that women and children face every day, without accepting murder as a reasonable response to it.

But until America finds a better way to keep people safe in their own homes or offers them some means of surviving if they flee, it will be hard to answer the defendants who ask their judges, "What choice did I really have?"

Home Is Where The Hurt Is

Last year the A.M.A., backed by the Surgeon General, declared that violent men constitute a major threat to women's health. The National League of Cities estimates that as many as half of all women will experience violence at some time in their marriage. Between 22% and 35% of all visits by females to emergency rooms are for injuries from domestic assaults. Though some studies have found that women are just as likely to start a fight as men, others indicate they are six times as likely to be seriously injured in one. Especially grotesque is the brutality reserved for pregnant women: the March of Dimes has concluded that the battering of women during pregnancy causes more birth defects than all the diseases put together for which children are usually immunized. Anywhere from one-third to as many as half of all female murder victims are killed by their spouses or lovers, compared with 4% of male victims.

"Male violence against women is at least as old an institution as marriage," says clinical psychologist

Gus Kaufman Jr., co-founder of Men Stopping Violence, an Atlanta clinic established to help men face their battering problems. So long as a woman was considered her husband's legal property, police and the courts were unable to prevent—and unwilling to punish—domestic assaults. Notes N.Y.U. law professor Holly Maguigan: "We talk about the notion of the rule of thumb, forgetting that it had to do with the restriction on a man's right to use a weapon against his wife: he couldn't use a rod that was larger than his thumb." In 1874 North Carolina became one of the first states to limit a man's right to beat his wife, but lawmakers noted that unless he beat her nearly to death "it is better to draw the curtain, shut out the public gaze and leave the parties to forget and forgive."

Out of that old reluctance grew the modern double standard. Until the first wave of legal reform in the 1970s, an aggravated assault against a stranger was a felony, but assaulting a spouse was considered a misdemeanor, which rarely landed the attacker in court, much less in jail. That distinction, which still exists in most states, does not reflect the danger involved: a study by the Boston Bar Association found that the domestic attacks were at least as dangerous as 90% of felony assaults. "Police seldom arrest, even when there are injuries serious enough to require hospitalization of the victim," declared the Florida Supreme Court in a 1990 gender-bias study, which also noted the tendency of prosecutors to drop domestic-violence cases.

Police have always hated answering complaints about domestic disputes. Experts acknowledge that such situations are often particularly dangerous, but suspect that there are other reasons for holding back. "This issue pushes buttons, summons up personal emotions, that almost no other issue does for police and judges," says Linda Osmundson, who co-chairs a battered wives' task force for the National Coalition Against Domestic Violence. "Domestic violence is not seen as a crime. A man's home is still his castle. There is a system that really believes that women should be passive in every circumstance." And it persists despite a 20-year effort by advocates to transform attitudes toward domestic violence.

While most of the effort has been directed at helping women survive, and escape, abusive homes, much of the publicity has fallen on those rare cases when women resort to violence themselves. Researcher and author Angela Browne points out that a woman is much more likely to be killed by her partner than to kill him. In 1991, when some 4 million women were beaten and 1,320 murdered in domestic attacks, 622 women killed their husbands or boyfriends. Yet the women have become the lightning rods for debate, since their circumstances, and their response, were more extreme.

What Choice Did She Have?

"There is an appropriate means to deal with one's marital problems—legal recourse. Not a .357 Magnum," argues former Florida prosecutor Bill Catto. "If you choose to use a gun to end a problem, then you must suffer the consequences of your act." Defense lawyers call it legitimate self-protection when a victim of abuse fights back—even if she shoots her husband in his sleep. Prosecutors call it an act of vengeance, and in the past, juries have usually agreed and sent the killer to jail. Michael Dowd, director of the Pace University Battered Women's Justice Center, has found that the average sentence for a woman who kills her mate is 15 to 20 years; for a man, 2 to 6.

The punishment is not surprising, since many judges insist that evidence of past abuse, even if it went on for years, is not relevant in court unless it occurred around the time of the killing. It is not the dead husband who is on trial, they note, but the wife who pulled the trigger. "Frankly, I feel changing the law would be authorizing preventive murder," argued Los Angeles Superior Court Judge Lillian Stevens in the Los Angeles *Times*. "The only thing that really matters is, Was there an immediate danger? There can't be an old grievance." And even if a woman is allowed to testify about past violence, the jury may still condemn her response to it. If he was really so savage, the prosecutor typically asks, why didn't she leave, seek shelter, call the police, file a complaint?

"The question presumes she has good options," says Julie Blackman, a New Jersey-based social psychologist who has testified as an expert witness in abuse and murder cases. "Sometimes, they don't leave because they have young children and no other way to support them, or because they grow up in cultures that are so immersed in violence that they don't figure there's any place better to go, or because they can't get apartments." The shelter facilities around the country are uniformly inadequate: New York has about 1,300 beds for a state with 18 million people. In 1990 the Baltimore zoo spent twice as much money to care for animals as the state of Maryland spent on shelters for victims of domestic violence.

Last July, even as reports of violence continued to multiply, the National Domestic Violence Hotline was disconnected. The 800 number had received as many as 10,000 calls a month from across the country. Now, says Mary Ann Bohrer, founder of the New York City-based Council for Safe Families, "there is no number, no national resource, for people seeking information about domestic violence."

The other reason women don't flee is because, ironically, they are afraid for their life. Law-enforcement experts agree that running away greatly increases the danger a woman faces. Angered at the loss of power and control, violent men often try to track down their wives and threaten them, or their children, if they don't come home. James Cox III, an unemployed dishwasher in Jacksonville, Florida, was determined to find his ex-girlfriend, despite a court order to stay away from her. Two weeks ago, he forced her mother at gunpoint to tell him the location of the battered women's shelter where her daughter had fled, and stormed the building, firing a shotgun. Police shot him dead. "This case illustrates the extent to which men go to pursue their victims," said executive director Rita DeYoung. "It creates a catch-22 for all battered women. Some will choose to return to their abusers, thinking they can control their behavior."

"After the law turns you away, society closes its doors on you, and you find yourself trapped in a life with someone capable of homicide. What choice in the end was I given?" asks Shalanda Burt, 21, who is serving 17 years for shooting her boyfriend James Fairley two years ago in Bradenton, Florida. She was three months pregnant at the time. A week after she delivered their first baby, James raped her and ripped her stitches. Several times she tried to leave or get help. "I would have a bloody mouth and a swollen face. All the police would do is give me a card with a deputy's name on it and tell me it was a 'lovers' quarrel.' The battered women's shelter was full. All they could offer was a counselor on the phone."

Two weeks before the shooting, the police arrested them both: him for aggravated assault because she was pregnant, her for assault with a deadly missile and violently resisting arrest. She had thrown a bottle at his truck. Her bail was $10,000; his was $3,000. He was back home before she was, so she sent the baby to stay with relatives while she tried to raise bail. The end came on a Christmas weekend. After a particularly vicious beating, he followed her to her aunt's house. When he came at her again, she shot him. "They say I'm a violent person, but I'm not. I didn't want revenge. I just wanted out." Facing 25 years, she was told by a female public defender to take a plea bargain and 17 years. "I wanted to fight. But she said I'd get life or the electric chair. I was in a no-win situation."

It is hard for juries to understand why women like Burt do not turn to the courts for orders of protection. But these are a makeshift shield at best, often violated and hard to enforce. Olympic skier Patricia Kastle had a restraining order when her former husband shot her. Lisa Bianco in Indiana remained terrified of her husband even after he was sent to jail for eight years. When prison officials granted Alan Matheney an eight-hour pass in March 1989, he drove directly to Bianco's home, broke in and beat her to death with the butt of a shotgun. Last March, Shirley Lowery, a grandmother of 11, was stabbed 19 times with a butcher knife by her former boyfriend in the hallway of the courthouse where she had gone to get an order of protection.

The Mind of The Victim

Defense lawyers have a hard time explaining to juries the shame, isolation and emotional dependency that bind victims to their abusers. Many women are too proud to admit to their family or friends that their marriage is not working and blame themselves for its failure even as they cling to the faith that their violent lover will change. "People confuse the woman's love for the man with love of abuse," says Pace's Dowd. "It's not the same thing. Which of us hasn't been involved in a romantic relationship where people say this is no good for you?"

It was Denver psychologist Lenore Walker, writing in 1984, who coined the term battered-woman syndrome to explain the behavior of abuse victims. Her study discussed the cycle of violence in battering households: first a period of growing tension; then a violent explosion, often unleashed by drugs or alcohol; and finally a stage of remorse and kindness. A violent man, she argues, typically acts out of a powerful need for control—physical, emotional, even financial. He may keep his wife under close surveillance, isolating her from family and friends, forbidding her to work or calling constantly to check on her whereabouts. Woven into the scrutiny are insults and threats that in the end can destroy a woman's confidence and leave her feeling trapped between her fear of staying in a violent home—and her fear of fleeing it.

Many lawyers say it is virtually impossible to defend a battered woman without some expert testimony about the effect of that syndrome over time. Such testimony allows attorneys to stretch the rules governing self-defense, which were designed to deal with two men caught in a bar fight, not a woman caught in a violent relationship with a stronger man.

In a traditional case of self-defense, a jury is presented a "snapshot" of a crime: the mugger threatens a subway rider with a knife; the rider pulls a gun and shoots his attacker. It is up to the jurors to decide whether the danger was real and immediate and whether the response was reasonable. A woman who shoots her husband while he lunges at her with a knife should have little trouble claiming that she acted in self-defense. Yet lawyers still find jurors to be very uncomfortable with female violence under any circumstances, especially violence directed at a man she may have lived with for years.

Given that bias, it is even harder for a lawyer to call it self-defense when a woman shoots a sleeping husband. The danger was hardly immediate, prosecutors argue, nor was the lethal response reasonable. Evidence about battered-woman syndrome may be the only way to persuade a jury to identify with a killer. "Battered women are extraordinarily sensitive to cues of danger, and that's how they survive," says Walker. "That is why many battered women kill, not during what looks like the middle of a fight, but when the man is more vulnerable or the violence is just beginning."

A classic self-defense plea also demands a fair fight. A person who is punched can punch back, but if he shoots, he runs the risk of being charged with murder or manslaughter. This leaves women and children, who are almost always smaller and weaker than their attackers, in a bind. They often see no way to escape an assault without using a weapon and the element of surprise—arguing, in essence, that their best hope of self-defense was a pre-emptive strike. "Morally and legally a woman should not be expected to wait until his hands are around her neck," argues Los Angeles defense attorney Leslie Abramson. "Say a husband says, 'When I get up tomorrow morning, I'm going to beat the living daylights out of you,'" says Joshua Dressler, a law professor at Wayne State University who specialized in criminal procedures. "If you use the word imminent, the woman would have to wait until the next morning and, just as he's about to kill her, then use self-defense."

That argument, prosecutors retort, is an invitation to anarchy. If a woman has survived past beatings, what persuaded her that this time was different, that she had no choice but to kill or be killed? The real catalyst, they suggest, was not her fear but her fury. Prosecutors often turn a woman's history of abuse into a motive for murder. "What some clemency advocates are really saying is that that s.o.b. deserved to die and why should she be punished for what she did," argues Dressler. Unless the killing came in the midst of a violent attack, it amounts to a personal death-penalty sentence. "I find it very hard to say that killing the most rotten human being in the world when he's not currently threatening the individual is the right thing to do."

Those who oppose changes in the laws point out that many domestic disputes are much more complicated than the clemency movement would suggest. "We've got to stop perpetuating the myth that men are all vicious and that women are all Snow White," says Sonny Burmeister, a divorced father of three children who, as president of the Georgia Council for Children's Rights in Marietta, lobbies for equal treatment of men involved in custody battles. He recently sheltered a husband whose wife had pulled a gun on him. When police were called, their response was "So?" Says Burmeister: "We perpetuate this macho, chauvinistic, paternalistic attitude for men. We are taught to be protective of the weaker sex. We encourage women to report domestic violence. We believe men are guilty. But women are just as guilty."

He charges that feminists are trying to write a customized set of laws. "If Mom gets mad and shoots Dad, we call it PMS and point out that he hit her six months ago," he complains. "If Dad gets mad and shoots Mom, we call it domestic violence and charge him with murder. We paint men as violent and we paint women as victims, removing them from the social and legal consequences of their actions. I don't care how oppressed a woman is; should we condone premeditated murder?"

Only nine states have passed laws permitting expert testimony on battered-woman syndrome and spousal violence. In most cases it remains a matter of judicial discretion. One Pennsylvania judge ruled that testimony presented by a prosecutor showed that the defendant had not been beaten badly enough to qualify as a battered woman and therefore could not have that standard applied to her case. President Bush signed legislation in October urging states to accept expert testimony in criminal cases involving battered women. The law calls for development of training materials to assist defendants and their attorneys in using such testimony in appropriate cases.

Judge Lillian Stevens instructed the jury on the rules governing self-defense at the 1983 trial of Brenda Clubine, who claimed that she killed her police-informant husband because he was going to kill her. Clubine says that during an 11-year relationship, she was kicked, punched, stabbed, had the skin on one side of her face torn off, a lung pierced, ribs broken. She had a judge's order protecting her and had pressed charges to have her husband arrested for felony battery. But six weeks later, she agreed to meet him in a motel, where Clubine alleges that she felt her life was in danger and hit him over the head with a wine bottle, causing a fatal brain hemorrhage. "I didn't mean to kill him," she says. "He had hit me several times. Something inside me snapped; I grabbed the bottle and swung." The jury found Clubine guilty of second-degree manslaughter, and Judge Stevens sentenced her to 15 years to life. She says Clubine drugged her husband into lethargy before fatally hitting him. "It seemed to me [the beatings] were some time ago," Stevens told the Los Angeles *Times*. Furthermore, she added, "there was evidence that a lot of it was mutual."

It is interesting that within the legal community there are eloquent opponents of battered-woman syndrome—on feminist grounds—who dislike the label's implication that all battered women are helpless victims of some shared mental disability that prevents them from acting rationally. Social liberals, says N.Y.U.'s Maguigan, typically explain male violence in terms of social or economic pressures. Female violence, on the other hand, is examined in psychological terms. "They look to what's wrong with her and reinforce a notion that women who use violence are, per se, unreasonable, that something must be wrong with her because she's not acting like a good woman, in the way that women are socialized to behave."

Researcher Charles Ewing compared a group of 100 battered women who had killed their partners with 100 battered women who hadn't taken that fatal step. Women who resorted to violence were usually those who were most isolated, socially and economically; they had been the most badly beaten, their children had been abused, and their husbands were drug or alcohol abusers. That is, the common bond was circumstantial, not psychological. "They're not pathological," says social psychologist Blackman. "They don't have personality disorders. They're just beat up worse."

Women who have endured years of beatings without fighting back may reach the breaking point once the abuse spreads to others they love. Arlene Caris is serving a 25-year sentence in New York for killing her husband. He had tormented her for years, both physically and psychologically. Then she reportedly learned that he was sexually abusing her granddaughter. On the night she finally decided to leave him, he came at her in a rage. She took a rifle, shot him, wrapped him in bedsheets and then hid the body in the attic for five months.

Offering such women clemency, the advocates note, is not precisely the same as amnesty; the punishment is reduced, though the act is not excused. Clemency may be most appropriate in cases where all the circumstances of the crime were not heard in court. The higher courts have certainly sent the message that justice is not uniform in domestic-violence cases. One study found that 40% of women who appeal their murder convictions get the sentence thrown out, compared with an 8.5% reversal rate for homicides as a whole. "I've worked on cases involving battered women and who have talked only briefly to their lawyers in the courtroom for 15 to 20 minutes and then they take a plea and do 15 to life," recalls Blackman. "I see women who are Hispanic and don't speak English well, or women who are very quickly moved through the system, who take pleas and do substantial chunks of time, often without getting any real attention paid to the circumstances of their case."

The first mass release in the U.S. came at Christmas in 1990, when Ohio Governor Richard Celeste commuted the sentences of 27 battered women serving time for killing or assaulting male companions. His initiative was born of long-held convictions. As a legislator in the early '70s, he and his wife helped open a women's center in Cleveland and held hearings on domestic violence. When he became lieutenant governor in 1974 and moved to Columbus, he and his wife rented out their home in Cleveland as emergency shelter for battered women. He and the parole board reviewed 107 cases, looking at evidence of past abuse, criminal record, adjustment to prison life and participation in postrelease programs before granting the clemencies. "The system of justice had not really worked in their cases," he says. "They had not had the opportunity for a fair trial because vitally important evidence affecting their circumstances and the terrible things done to them was not presented to the jury."

The impending reviews in other states have caused some prosecutors and judges to sound an alarm. They are worried that Governors' second-guessing the courts undermines the judicial system and invites manipulation by prisoners. "Anybody in the penitentiary, if they see a possible out, will be claiming, 'Oh, I was a battered woman,'" says Dallas assistant district attorney Norman Kinne. "They can't take every female who says she's a battered woman and say, 'Oh, we're sorry, we'll let you out.' If they're going to do it right, it's an exhaustive study."

Clemency critics point to one woman released in Maryland who soon afterward boasted about having committed the crime. Especially controversial are women who have been granted clemency for crimes that were undeniably premeditated. Delia Alaniz hired a contract killer to pretend to rob her home and murder her husband in the process. He had beaten her and their children for years, sexually abusing their 14-year-old daughter. The prosecutor from Skagit County, Washington, was sufficiently impressed by the evidence of abuse that he reduced the charge from first-degree murder and life imprisonment to second-degree manslaughter with a sentence of 10 to 14 years. In October 1989, Governor Booth Gardner granted her clemency. "Delia was driven to extremes. The situation was desperate, and she viewed it that way," says Skagit County public defender Robert Jones. "The harm to those kids having a mom in prison was too much considering the suffering they went through. As a state, we don't condone what she did, but we understand and have compassion."

The Alternatives to Murder

There is always a risk that the debate over clemency will continue to obscure the missing debate over violence. "I grew up in a society that really tolerated a lot of injustice when it came to women," says Pace University's Dowd. "It was ingrained as a part of society. This isn't a woman's issue. It's a human-rights issue. Men should have as much to offer fighting sexism as they do racism because the reality is that it's our hands that strike the blows." The best way to keep battered women out of jail is to keep them from being battered in the first place.

In a sense, a society's priorities can be measured by whom it punishes. A survey of the population of a typical prison suggests that violent husbands and fathers are still not viewed as criminals. In New York State about half the inmates are drug offenders, the result of a decade-long War on Drugs that demanded mandatory sentences. A War on Violence would send the same message, that society genuinely abhors parents who beat children and spouses who batter each other, and is willing to punish the behavior rather than dismiss it.

Minnesota serves as a model for other states. In 1981 Duluth was the first U.S. city to institute mandatory arrests in domestic disputes. Since then about half the states have done the same, which means that even if a victim does not wish to press charges, the police are obliged to make an arrest if they see evidence of abuse. Advocates in some Minnesota jurisdictions track cases from the first call to police through prosecution and sentencing to try to spot where the system is failing. Prosecutors are increasingly reluctant to plea-bargain assault down to disorderly conduct. They have also found it helpful to use the arresting officer as complainant, so that their case does not depend on a frightened victim's testifying.

Better training of police officers, judges, emergency-room personnel and other professionals is having an impact in many cities. "We used to train police to be counselors in domestic-abuse cases," says Osmundson. "No longer. We teach them to go make arrests." In Jacksonville, Florida, new procedures helped raise the arrest rate from 25% to 40%. "Arrests send a message to the woman that help is available and to men that abuse is not accepted," says shelter executive director DeYoung, who also serves as president of the Florida Coalition Against Domestic Violence. "Children too see that it's not accepted and are more likely to grow up not accepting abuse in the home."

Since 1990 at least 28 states have passed "stalking laws" that make it a crime to threaten, follow or harass someone. Congress this month may take up the Violence Against Women bill, which would increase penalties for federal sex crimes; provide $300 million to police, prosecutors and courts to combat violent crimes against women; and reinforce state domestic-violence laws. Most women, of course, are not looking to put their partners in jail; they just want the violence to stop.

A Minneapolis project was founded in 1979 at the prompting of women in shelters who said they wanted to go back to their partners if they would stop battering. Counselors have found that men resort to violence because they want to control their partners, and they know they can get away with it—unlike in other relationships. "A lot of people experience low impulse control, fear of abandonment, alcohol and drug addiction, all the characteristics of a batterer," says Ellen Pence, training coordinator for the Domestic Abuse Intervention Project in Duluth. "However, the same guy is not beating up his boss."

Most men come to the program either by order of the courts or as a condition set by their partners. The counselors start with the assumption that battering is learned behavior. Eighty percent of the participants grew up in a home where they saw or were victims of physical, sexual or other abuse. Once imprinted with that model, they must be taught to recognize warning signs and redirect their anger. "We don't say, 'Never get angry,'" says Carol Arthur, the Minneapolis project's executive director. "Anger is a normal, healthy emotion. What we work with is a way to express it." Men describe to the group their most violent incident. One man told about throwing food in his wife's face at dinner and then beating her to the floor—only to turn and see his two small children huddled terrified under the table. Arthur remembers his self-assessment at that moment: "My God, what must they be thinking about me? I didn't want to be like that."

If the police and the courts crack down on abusers, and programs exist to help change violent behavior, victims will be less likely to take—and less justified in taking—the law into their own hands. And once the cycle of violence winds down in this generation, it is less likely to poison the next. That would be a family value worth fighting for.

Reported by Cathy Booth/Miami, Jeanne McDowell/Los Angeles and Janice C. Simpson/New York

With No Immediate Cause

Ntozake Shange

Ntozake Shange is Zulu for "she who comes with her own things"/"she who walks like a lion." It is the name taken by poet, playwrite, novelist Paulette Williams, born in 1948 in New Jersey. Educated at Barnard College in New York and the University of Southern California, her works include Ridin' the Moon in Texas: Word Paintings *(1988),* Betsey Brown *(1985),* Sassafrass, Cypress, and Indigo *(1983), and her very famous* For Colored Girls Who Have Considered Suicide/When the Rainbow Is Enuf, *which opened on Broadway in 1976.*

every 3 minutes a woman is beaten
every five minutes a
woman is raped/every ten minutes
a lil girl is molested
yet i rode the subway today
i sat next to an old man who
may have beaten his old wife
3 minutes ago or 3 days/30 years ago
he might have sodomized his
daughter but i sat there
cuz the young men on the train
might beat some young women
later in the day or tomorrow
i might not shut my door fast
enuf/push hard enuf
every 3 minutes it happens
some woman's innocence
rushes to her cheeks/pours from her mouth
like the betsy wetsy dolls have been torn
apart/their mouths
mensis red & split/every
three minutes a shoulder
is jammed through plaster & the oven door/
chairs push thru the rib cage/hot water or
boiling sperm decorate her body
i rode the subway today
& bought a paper from a
man who might
have held his old lady onto
a hot pressing iron/i dont know
maybe he catches lil girls in the
park & rips open their behinds
with steel rods/i cdnt decide
what he might have done i only
know every 3 minutes
every 5 minutes every 10 minutes/so
i bought the paper
looking for the announcement
there has to be an announcement
of the women's bodies found
yesterday/the missing little girl
i sat in a restaurant with my
paper looking for the announcement

"With no immediate cause" from *NAPPY EDGES* by Ntozake Shange (New York: St. Martin's Press, 1972).

a yng man served me coffee
i wondered did he pour the boiling
coffee/on the woman cuz she waz stupid/
did he put the infant girl/in
the coffee pot/with the boiling coffee/cuz she cried
too much
what exactly did he do with hot coffee
i looked for the announcement
the discovery/of the dismembered
woman's body/the
victims have not all been
identified/today they are
naked & dead/refuse to
testify/one girl out of 10's not
coherent/i took the coffee
& spit it up/i found an
announcement/not the woman's
bloated body in the river/floating
not the child bleeding in the
59th street corridor/not the baby
broken on the floor/
"there is some concern
that alleged battered women
might start to murder their
husbands & lovers with no
immediate cause"

i spit up   i vomit   i am screaming
we all have immediate cause
every 3 minutes
every 5 minutes
every 10 minutes
every day
women's bodies are found
in alleys & bedrooms/at the top of the stairs
before i ride the subway/buy a paper/drink
coffee/i must know/
have you hurt a woman today
did you beat a woman today
throw a child cross a room
are the lil girl's panties
in yr pocket
did you hurt a woman today

i have to ask these obscene questions
the authorities require me to
establish
immediate cause

every three minutes
every five minutes
every ten minutes
every day

7

Discrimination: The Effects of Asymmetry on Social Institutions and Their Effects on Us

Sexism affects not only women's personal lives; it is also reflected in all public institutions, and it is formalized in law and custom. In the economy, most women are poor; in politics and government, nearly powerless; before the law, discriminated against and deprived of many rights. But in each instance, the situation is denied, distorted, or justified by the same body of myth and mystification that governs women's personal lives. Let us look at the position that women actually occupy in the social system, in the economy, in politics, and before the law. Keep in mind that these social structures are interrelated and reinforcing. An intricate web determines women's standing in each area, and that in turn determines the experiences of our personal lives.

Women in the Economy

Much has been written in the last twenty-five years about the "great strides" women as a group have allegedly made in earning power, professional and social advancement, and opportunity. The truth is that although some women's economic lives have dramatically improved, the great majority of women have experienced little or no improvement, and for many women, the situation has grown much worse as the term *the feminization of poverty* becomes increasingly descriptive.

The Myth: Lucky Ladies

Everyone has heard the tales of pampered wives playing bridge and drinking coffee while their harried husbands labor to win the dollar so carelessly tossed away at the supermarket or dress shop. As the story goes, the wives earn no money of their own, but *because they spend it, they control it;* everyone in America "knows" that. There are tales of "palimony" winners or gay divorcees reveling in windfalls snatched from vanquished ex-husbands, merry widows collecting fat sums from hard-earned insurance policies and social security, lazy but comfortable welfare mothers stealing from the state to live on televisions, expensive make-up, and steak. Such types compose a partial list of the privileged, well-off women reputed to represent the majority of the female population.

The Reality: Women Are Poor

Compared with men, for the most part, women are disadvantaged. Within and across job classifications, women have lower salaries, generally have less disposable income, are more likely to fall below nationally set poverty standards, and in several ways have far less recourse to remedy.

Facts on Women's Earnings and Income At present, on the average and across all occupations, year round full-time women workers earn about two-thirds the salaries of men. In 1991 women's median income was $21,245; men's median income was $30,331.[1]

Women (who comprise 46 percent of the civilian labor force) are generally employed in the lowest paid occupations and jobs. About 80 percent of the female labor force in 1990 worked in clerical, sales, and service jobs. Women constituted 79.1 percent of all cashiers, 98.7 percent of all secretaries, 80.9 percent of all food-counter workers, 94.8 percent of all household workers (housekeepers, servants, child-care workers, etc.), but only 19.9 percent of all physicians, 9.1 percent of all engineers, and 24.5 percent of all lawyers. Women make up 65.5 percent of all salespeople, but women constitute only 10.6 percent of auto and boat salespeople, among the highest paid of the sales categories ($479 median weekly earnings in 1992, compared, for example, with $255 for apparel salespeople, of whom 81.3 percent are female).[2]

Even within each of the preceding occupations, women earn less than men. For example, in retail sales—the job category with the largest female–male disparity—women earned considerably less than men. In 1992 the median weekly earnings for women in retail sales was $233 compared to $332 for men. (As Gloria Steinem pointed out, in department stores men sell stoves and refrigerators; women sell men's underwear. Why? Surely not because of appropriate experience.) Even in clerical work, women's earnings fall seriously behind men's. In 1992 women's median weekly earnings for full-time clerical work (secretaries, stenographers, and typists) was $370 compared with men's $404! Could we hope that some women workers, perhaps female professionals, might escape this disparity? Unfortunately not. Women physicians' median weekly earnings was $859 compared with men's $1190, and women lawyers' and judges' was $884 compared to men's $1157.[3]

Only approximately 16 percent of divorced women are awarded alimony by the courts. Of the divorced women with children who were awarded child support in 1989, only half received that support. Over 25 percent received no payment at all.[4] The average amount awarded for child support is far less than half of what is required for support of that child, and fewer than half the fathers pay that support. It has been estimated that, after divorce, women's standard of living drops 73 percent in the first year, while their ex-husbands' standard rises 42 percent.[5] Of the 10 million women who are eligible for child support, a third live in poverty.[6]

Because women earn less over a lifetime, their social security and retirement benefits are smaller. Employed women whose husbands paid into the social security system receive only their husband's benefits, not both theirs and his if he dies. This situation is worsened because women often retire with benefits at 62 rather than 65, receiving, therefore, even lower rates and having even smaller monthly benefits.

Some Facts on Poverty By the mid-1980s, the term *feminization of poverty* had become commonplace because by 1986 women constituted 63 percent of all adults in poverty. Thirty-four percent of all households headed by women were poor (compared to 6 percent of married-couple families), and 54 percent of all children in households headed by women were poor.[7] Half of the African-American and Hispanic households headed by women were poor.[8] One-fifth of all women over 60 were poor, and elderly women were twice as likely to be poor as elderly men.[9] By 1990 there had been no improvement, and the situation was actually worsening. Today, half of the poor are children and the elderly, and half of the homeless are women and their children.

Some Facts on Women's Contribution to the Economy Women work because we need to. Of the female labor force in 1987, 25 percent was single; 20 percent was widowed, divorced, or separated; and 15 percent had husbands earning less than $15,000.

In 1992 more than half of married-couple families had wives in the paid labor force. Such families had median weekly incomes of $955 compared to $556 for families in which the wife did not work for pay.[10]

The income of working wives reduces the potential poverty level substantially, and incomes in households in which wives work is on the average 60 percent higher than in households where only husbands work.[11] (See Table 7.1.[12])

Discrimination Everywhere Women workers are channeled into occupations that are seen as "appropriate" for women. These are continuations of the roles females are expected to fulfill in the wider society: for example, serving and facilitating (secretaries, waitresses, nurses, "gal Fridays"), child care (teachers on the elementary level, pediatricians), sex and decoration (receptionists, airline hostesses, entertainers). Occupations historically reserved for women are notoriously underpaid regardless of the level of expertise needed to perform them, and they are generally controlled by male administrators who make it impossible, one way or the other, for women to set their own market and hence their own demands.

When women try to break out of these occupational ghettos, they face other problems. Various practices, official or otherwise, challenge entry into male-dominated work areas—apprenticeship programs in trade unions, employment traps (for example, odd hours, machines too heavy for females), discriminatory hiring, and so on. (In 1990, for example, only 1.7 percent of carpenters were women, a very tiny gain from the 1 percent of 1979.[13]) Women who do manage entry are generally channeled to the low-earning end of the spectrum. Sales, for example, was shown earlier to favor men financially; high-line items may be reserved for men by seniority rules, for example, which disadvantage women, who more frequently are temporary, part-time, new, or returning workers.

Unemployment rates are higher for women than for men, probably even higher than they appear to be, for the number of women who have not yet worked but want to cannot be properly evaluated.

Aid to Families with Dependent Children (AFDC), too, encourages and even ensures female poverty. AFDC benefits are barely sufficient for subsistence, yet the mother with children to care for, no husband, and few skills is in a bind. Although job "retraining" may be supported, "education" is not. Often the kinds of jobs an AFDC mother may train for will not yield sufficient income to secure both adequate child care and subsistence living, yet the education that would make work outside the home truly profitable remains generally out of her reach. If she works to earn income additional to AFDC to make her life more tolerable, she stands to lose her public aid, leaving her few alternatives. With aid for abortion and contraception denied her, the plight of the welfare mother worsens.

Why?

What are the ideological factors that underlie the economic position of women? It is not too difficult to guess. Shirley Bernard expresses them in terms of "dominance."

> *In a society where money means power, most of the money must come to the dominant group if it is to maintain the status quo. In our society white males are dominant. . . . they earn substantially more than non-whites and females.*[14]

The notion of dominance is a shorthand we can unpack to reveal the entire range of beliefs and attitudes inherent in the patriarchal mind-set. Once again, the nature of women's role and the gender ideal are the factors underlying women's disadvantaged position.

The Role: Woman's Work

In earlier chapters we saw that in patriarchy it is believed that women were created to be helpmeets to men, whereas men are seen as the central actors in society. In addition to performing the functions of procreation and nursing, it is women's central responsibility to serve as underlaborers to men, to manage for them the necessary minutiae that muddy the waters of real creativity. Women are ideally suited for this function, it is said, being less intelligent and less rational than men—hence, both less capable of true accomplishment and more tolerant of detail and routine.

On the Job

Until very recently—and then only because of advances pressed by the women's movement—the "branch offices" of the public economic sector have been very much a study in patriarchal dominance. In offices, factories, hospitals, schools, and elsewhere, men "did the job," and women "helped." He man-

Table 7.1 MEDIAN WEEKLY EARNINGS OF FAMILIES BY TYPE OF FAMILY, NUMBER OF EARNERS, RACE, AND HISPANIC ORIGIN

(Numbers in thousands)

Type of family, number of earners, race, and Hispanic origin	Number of families		Median weekly earnings	
	I 1992	I 1993	I 1992	I 1993
Total				
Total families with earners[1]	43,668	43,758	$680	$694
Married-couple families	34,011	34,220	769	790
One earner	12,099	12,239	464	470
Husband	8,416	8,412	556	546
Wife	2,955	3,013	291	317
Other family member	728	814	287	291
Two or more earners	21,913	21,981	930	961
Husband and wife	19,473	19,652	955	985
Husband and other family member(s)	1,610	1,517	809	855
Wife and other family member(s)	632	609	592	609
Other family members only	198	204	643	579
Families maintained by women	7,455	7,428	389	394
One earner	5,348	5,246	309	308
Householder	4,273	4,225	320	310
Other family member	1,075	1,021	266	294
Two or more earners	2,107	2,182	639	643
Families maintained by men	2,202	2,110	508	499
One earner	1,413	1,443	405	422
Two or more earners	789	667	731	673
White				
Total families with earners[1]	37,076	36,907	710	724
Married-couple families	30,137	30,145	783	804
One earner	10,774	10,738	480	483
Husband	7,605	7,496	571	568
Wife	2,551	2,554	296	317
Two or more earners	19,363	19,407	943	971
Husband and wife	17,239	17,439	967	992
Families maintained by women	5,182	5,164	410	414
Families maintained by men	1,757	1,598	522	517

(Continues)

Table 7.1 MEDIAN WEEKLY EARNINGS OF FAMILIES BY TYPE OF FAMILY, NUMBER OF EARNERS, RACE, AND HISPANIC ORIGIN

(Numbers in thousands)

Type of family, number of earners, race, and Hispanic origin	Number of families		Median weekly earnings	
	I 1992	I 1993	I 1992	I 1993
Black				
Total families with earners[1]	5,081	5,137	481	484
Married-couple families	2,700	2,723	641	650
One earner	877	988	303	340
Husband	472	568	356	377
Wife	327	325	265	302
Two or more earners	1,823	1,735	782	836
Husband and wife	1,595	1,513	801	873
Families maintained by women	2,010	1,994	324	321
Families maintained by men	372	419	446	408
Hispanic origin				
Total families with earners[1]	3,676	3,765		
Married-couple families	2,652	2,711	564	572
One earner	1,046	1,139	347	333
Husband	800	888	388	359
Wife	154	162	241	276
Two or more earners	1,606	1,572	743	761
Husband and wife	1,215	1,224	790	786
Families maintained by women	730	7386	332	367
Families maintained by men	295	316	419	422

[1]Data exclude families in which there is no wage or salary earner or in which the husband, wife, or other person maintaining the family is either self-employed or in the Armed Forces.
NOTE: Detail for the above race and Hispanic-origin groups will not sum to totals because data for the "other races" group are not presented and Hispanics are included in both the white and black population groups.

aged while she answered his phone, sharpened his pencils, typed his letters, and perked his coffee. He cured the sick while she followed his orders, applied his prescriptions, and perked his coffee. He flew the airplane while she checked the tickets, served the customers, and perked his coffee. The rare woman who got to run the show was considered a peculiarity, causing problems for her own self-image as well as for her male colleagues and subordinates.

Salaries reflected these relative positions, for line workers earn more than their assistants. Moreover, women *by virtue of being women*—regardless of position occupied, regardless of how much education and ability they needed to do their job—earned less, whether in women's occupations or in others. Thus, nurses, schoolteachers, professional secretaries, and others in traditionally female jobs have been notoriously underpaid relative to their education, skill, and experience. But even women in managerial or executive positions could not look forward to the same rank, salary, or privileges of men of the same status. A survey by *Fortune* magazine

> *exposed one of the most closely guarded secrets of today's CEOs—the pervasiveness of discrimination against women prevents all but a minuscule number of them from reaching the highest ranks of corporate America.*
>
> *The magazine examined the 1990 proxy statements of the 799 public companies on its combined list of the 1000 largest U.S. industrial and service companies. It found that of the 4012 people listed as the highest-paid officers and directors, only 19 are women—less than one-half of 1 percent.*
>
> *Discrimination against women in management also is reflected dramatically in a wide pay gap, according to Labor Department figures. This is shown in the following data on median weekly wages paid in four categories of managers:*
>
> - *Female financial managers, $558; male $837.*
> - *Female lawyers and judges, $834; male $1,184.*
> - *Female marketing, advertising and public relations managers, $616; male $902.*
> - *Female personnel and labor relations managers, $604; male $881.*[15]

This, despite the fact that more women are attaining better educations than ever before. More than 53 percent of all students in higher education are female. Increasing numbers of women are earning professional degrees in medicine, law, and engineering, and graduate degrees, including doctorates, in all fields. Yet, in 1991, the *median income of women with four years of college education and a Bachelors degree* ($20,967) *was below that of men who had earned only a high school diploma, including equivalency* ($21,546)![16]

Actually, the reality is even worse than the statistics would suggest. According to Susan Faludi, even with the dramatic increase in women lawyers, physicians, and other professionals in the last two decades, "only 2 percent more of all working women were in professional specialties in 1988 than 15 years earlier."[17] According to *The World's Women,* a "recent study of the 1000 most valuable publicly held companies in the United States in 1989 showed only two women among the chief executive officers.[18]"

It is a current myth that these conditions no longer exist. In reality, little has changed. In fact, women have lost ground in some ways. The average salary of full-time women workers relative to men has been slowly increasing and is projected to be near 70 percent by the year 2000, when women are expected to climb to 47 percent of the labor force.[19] But considering that the average age of the female labor force in 2000 will be older (35–54),[20] considering as well the incredible effort women have made to gain parity in opportunity and compensation, even 70 percent is totally unacceptable.

Even where things seem to have changed, the underlying reality often remains untouched. An executive secretary with ten years' experience may be "promoted" to district sales manager (entry-level position for managerial class) with men several years her junior, but she may be the only one of her group with a typewriter on her desk. A female high school teacher may now receive a salary equal to that of her male counterpart for teaching, but if her extra duties at home or her sex role preclude her from requesting playground duties or coaching, she may thereby be denied the extra income that raises the job above the average. "Maid" and "janitor" may both be redefined as "maintenance worker—2" and receive equal pay, but if only men make it to "maintenance worker—3" (supervisor), the apparent equal opportunity is only a sham.

It is important to recognize the power of the forces straining to maintain the status quo. The female sex role and gender ideal is a major, if not *the* major, determinant of women's position in the workplace. Michael Korda, a publishing executive in 1972, contended that in the workplace men perceive women workers, whether colleagues or subordinates, as extensions of their wives or other women in their personal lives. That is, they see women as females first and workers second, and this perception conditions men's attitudes and behavior toward women on the job.[21]

The anthropologist George Gilder offered a further, even more psychologically profound, insight into men's resistance to women's economic equality.[22] In primitive times, Gilder theorized, men proved their masculine identity through the hunt by facing hardship and death. Today, although industrialization has made the hunt per se unnecessary, men still need to reinforce their sense of masculinity. They have, therefore, substituted their work—whatever it is—making it a kind of symbolic hunt. It is thus crucial for men to maintain their job's aura of manliness, its rituals and traditions, and most of all its separation from women and all things female. As women encroach upon a field of endeavor, we throw doubt on its manliness, destroying its ability to function as a symbolic hunt, sending men scurrying to more distant bastions of masculinity. In essence, in Gilder's view, the plain fact of the workplace is that for psychosexual reasons men simply do not want women there: Other arguments are mere rationales. Whatever one thinks of the man-the-hunter theory, the truth probably lies somewhere in this deeper region: Men do not want equality with women at work. Gilder concluded that women should stay out, leave men their bastions and their sources of identity. Feminists, of course, go another way. Martyrdom on the altar of masculinity is a price too high either for women or for all of humankind. Women not only *need* to work, but as citizens, women have a right to work, just as men do. Men will have to find other ways to prove their masculinity. Women, however, must change as well.

Gender: Subliminal Effects

It is true that a woman's relationship to a job or career is often different from a man's. Part of that difference comes as a result of external conditions: the double burden of home and child care, barriers to opportunity, as well as misogynist attitudes and behaviors. But added factors in those different relations to work reside within ourselves as women, in our own attitudes and behavior. These are the often hidden or subliminal effects of our gender conditioning.

As detailed earlier, we are raised to see ourselves as being second to men, husbands, and employer-workers; we learn to see our interests as subordinate to their needs and wishes. As wives, our husbands' jobs, desires, and values are to supersede our own. According to traditional rules, we work or fulfill ourselves only after we have accomplished our "primary duties." Even the modern, liberated woman is subject to the tremendous force of that other commitment. Not wanting to choose between work and family—and highly subject to a social structure that decrees her responsible for her home and children—a woman in the workplace is truly doubly burdened. Like it or not, even aware of it or not, and married or not, the weight of that burden is real and does interfere with our work. Even under the best of conditions, no wife clears the bothersome details of living for us, manages child care or housekeeping, or guarantees us unhampered mobility.

Very few of us were raised to see ourselves primarily as workers of one kind or another in the public marketplace. Even for women who work full-time their entire lives, an inbred image remains of women as temporary or marginal workers, as supplementary rather than central earners. Many of us have often been more apt, then, to accept inadequate incomes, reduced benefits, or poor conditions. To meet home demands, we may settle for part-time shifts, poor hours, or local jobs, all of which can be terribly exploitive.

The problem goes deeper, though, for added to these reduced expectations of work, most of us are conditioned to carry reduced expectations of ourselves. Following our mothers' model as young girls, serving our brothers and fathers, we learned to serve in general. Comfortable with the familiar behavior of subordination, some of us tend not to feel uncomfortable when we experience the same things at work. Passively we may give in to inappropriate use of our energy and time in a way that men would not tolerate. Accustomed to placing our attachments to men above many things, we might be more loyal to an exploitive employer than to a union of sister employees.

But even when we learn these things and consciously try to transcend the inherited values of "femininity," we are still subject to the "outposts in our own head." We must not only unlearn the destructive patterns we have been taught, but we must also somehow make up for the experiences we did not have, those reserved for males only, experiences such as the competition of team sports or the support system of the male in-group.

Women Before the Law: Some Relevant Principles

We should keep some essential features of law in mind to help us understand women's relationship to the legal system: Laws are the rules of the game. When we speak of the law in our society, we mean a collection of rules and procedures codified, formalized, made explicit; we mean the conceptual framework within which such "rules" are written, a set of values, attitudes, and general principles toward people, community, and government; we also mean a kind of overriding loyalty to the concept of law as such, to living by the rules we set for ourselves; and finally we mean the whole system of legislation, courts, procedures, and people that actualizes the abstract concepts.

Because laws that contradict or clash with social mores are most likely to be disregarded or disobeyed, to carry weight and command obedience in its own right (without undue force) a law must express or coincide with the beliefs and attitudes of a majority of the people governed. Therefore, we can understand law as representing the formal expression of nonformal ideals—norms, mores, values—the unwritten rules of the game for any people.

Laws are written by people who hold power. In our society, law is enacted by legislatures made up of individuals said to represent a majority of voters. It is from this representativeness that legislators in a democracy are supposed to derive their power, and it is from their ability to express the will of the public that they maintain it. To a degree, legislators do express the public will—but to a degree, they do not. What is true, however, is that many of the laws we live by are written and enacted by those people who, one way or the other, maintain their place in the legislatures by being able to satisfy their constituents that they are expressing the common will. That is why laws so clearly reflect the character of current values and specifically the values of those who have and exercise power.

Our legal system relies heavily on precedent, continuity, and conservatism to give it stability and to ensure orderliness, credibility, and respect. Judicial decisions made today are largely based on decisions made earlier and on an interpretation of what is believed to be the original intent of the framers of any law. Change in the body of law is meant to come slowly and cautiously. To a large degree, the past directs the present and the future, and the system strongly tends to maintain the status quo.

Law, Women, and Men

When we relate these principles of law to women's position in society, we can see the source of certain aspects of our situation. The law, in conceptualization, policy, practice, execution, and application, is almost entirely masculine.

In overwhelming proportions, the people in power who have written the laws as well as interpreted, argued, used, and enforced them have been men. Legislators, judges, teachers and philosophers of law, court officials, lawyers, and police have been and still are predominantly male. Women, having been barred one way or another from power and decision making, are represented in absurdly small numbers in every aspect of politics and law. The representation of feminists—that is, women consciously committed to women's rights and needs—is even smaller. Until as recently as 1920, the entire constituency that legislators and public officials had to satisfy was male. Before suffrage in 1920, women had no formal power at all. Today, without unity of common goals, without significant spheres of public influence, women's clout is little better.

It is a small wonder, therefore, that the law should reflect a male perspective. Given that the creators of our legal system and the constituency for whom it was created were and are the sons of patriarchy—and thus conscious and unconscious heirs to all the beliefs, attitudes, and values it entails—our legal system is highly sexist. It clearly accepts and supports the traditional images of male and female, awards to men privilege and advantage in every sphere of life both public and private, and sanctions the subordination of women to men. Judicial decisions on every level and in every area of concern—domestic relations, civil rights, labor and employment, crime, and others—all reflect the common social themes regarding "femininity" and the sexes: That men and women, being "naturally" different in capacities, needs, and function, should occupy different spheres of activity;[23] that because women are weak and dependent, we should be "protected," both from the ugliness of life and the dangers of our own inferiority; that because women are both morally and intellectually less competent than men, less rational and trustworthy, we should be under greater constraint.

What this means to us as women is that the legal system, allegedly designed to protect all citizens, instead often thwarts us. It means that when we go to the courts for redress of crimes or injustice, we go as little girls to a father, as supplicants, and we go to a system that sees us and the world in a way that is very much to our detriment. Most frequently, male lawyers must argue for us (often missing issues central to our experience). Male judges apply masculist laws to our female circumstances (interpreting them from their privileged male position). Male police must accept the credibility of individuals (women) said to have no credibility. These circumstances make the legal system a very different place for women than for men. The statistics bearing on rape, wife battering, child support, or prison sentences for women—to name just a few conspicuous areas of uneven-handed justice—bear this out. We know, furthermore, that since the law tends to conserve the status quo, we cannot expect change easily or soon, especially without some very powerful catalysts.

Points and Instances: A Short History

Law is based on precedent, and so the past directs the future. Regarding the law, what kind of past do women have?

From earliest time in Western culture, as one might expect in patriarchy, the position of women has been both marginal and shaky. Jo Freeman, like Kate Millett, argues that we can understand our relationship to men in terms of caste.[24] Unlike a class, from which one may emerge, a caste is a rigid category of stratification based on characteristics one has no hand in determining—birth, color, or sex, for example. Women's caste, from which we cannot emerge, entails certain functions and behaviors. It imposes on us a whole separate set of expectations with attendant rewards and punishments. Maintaining this caste (this "place") has been a major occupation of the legal system.

According to Jo Freeman, the current legal status of women has its roots in the most ancient traditions and prejudices of the Western world. Says Freeman:

> *The sexual caste system is the longest, most firmly entrenched caste system known to Western civilization. . . . There is a long standing legal tradition reaching back to early Roman law which defines women as perpetual children. This tradition, known as the "Perpetual Tutelage of Women," has not been systematically recognized, but the definition of women as minors who never grow up, who must always be under the guidance of a male, has been carried down in modified form to the present day.*[25]

The early Roman tradition of treating women not as citizens, not even as adults, but rather as "daughters" first of their natural fathers, then of their husbands, found its way into canon law and from there through English common law into our own legal system.

It was Blackstone's *Commentaries on the Laws of England*, written in 1765—a veritable bible on the law in the early United States, according to Freeman—that codified the ancient rules for future generations. Women's status is most clearly reflected in Blackstone's treatment of marriage:

> *Single women were presumed to have the same rights in private law as single men. But when a woman married, these rights were lost, suspended under the feudal doctrine of "coverture." As Blackstone described: "By marriage, the husband and wife are one person in law; that is, the very being or legal existence of the woman is suspended during the marriage, or at least is incorporated and consolidated into that of the husband, under whose wing, protection, and cover, she performs everything."*[26]

Where Do We Go from Here? ERA?

Historically, ours was a system that, for good or ill, maintained separate justice for women and men. The effect has been a legacy of discrimination and inequality that heavily influences juridical behavior today and supports sexism in the society at large.

> *Our legal structure will continue to support and command an inferior status for women so long as it permits any differentiation in legal treatment on the basis of sex. This is so for three distinct but related reasons. First, discrimination is a necessary concomitant of any sex-based law because a large number of women do not fit the female stereotype upon which such laws are predicated. Second, all aspects of separate treatment for women are inevitably inter-related; discrimination in one area creates discriminatory patterns in another. Thus a woman who has been denied equal access to education will be disadvantaged in employment even though she received equal treatment there. Third, whatever the motivation for different treatment, the result is to create a dual system of rights and responsibilities in which the rights of each group are governed by a different set of values. History and experience have taught us that in such a dual system one group is always dominant and the other subordinate. As long as woman's place is defined as separate, a male-dominated society will define her place as inferior.*[27]

Attempts at change have been spotty and largely ineffectual. The protections of the Fifth and Fourteenth Amendments to the Constitution have not been consistently applied to women's cases; piecemeal legislative changes have been sparse and slow; judicial review has been "casual," peremptory, or sexist itself.[28]

Most feminists and many legislators and judicial experts maintain that what is necessary is a single consistent, coherent principle of equal rights for women and men, a principle of law that would serve as mandate and policy for the public sector and for the courts. The embodiment of that principle is, of course, the Equal Rights Amendment (ERA):

Section 1: Equality of rights under the law shall not be denied or abridged by the United States or by any state on account of sex.

Section 2: The Congress shall have the power to enforce, by appropriate legislation, the provisions of this article.

Section 3: This amendment shall take effect two years after the date of ratification.

Simply put, the question is whether women are finally to be counted as full human beings before the law and in society.

Opponents to the amendment argued on grounds both hysterical and spurious: (1) ERA would legitimate abortion (false), homosexual marriage (false), and extraordinary federal control over personal matters (false); (2) ERA would deny the sanctity of the family (false), a woman's right not to have outside employment (false), and "privacy" (false); (3) ERA will require equal numbers of women and men in the army and in combat (false), coed bathrooms (false), women to share barracks with men in the service (false), children to be placed in state-run child-care facilities (false).

Most of these issues were created precisely to frighten both women and men into rejecting ERA. It was argued, furthermore, that ERA is simply not necessary, the Fourteenth Amendment being sufficient to remedy instances of discrimination. Proponents of ERA pointed out, however, that review under the Fourteenth Amendment has been inconsistent and inefficient, and that ERA, in making sex an absolutely prohibited classification for law, would go much further toward guaranteeing women equality of economic, educational, and political opportunity.

With all the public controversy, it is sometimes surprising to discover that during the campaign to pass the ERA the great majority of voters were for passage. By 1978 the amendment had been passed by thirty-five states, and even in many states that did not ratify, polls consistently showed a majority of popular approval. The minority opposed to ERA were apparently entrenched in the power structure, better supported financially, and better organized (as are the minority opposed to women's reproductive freedom). In 1985 the Equal Rights Amendment was reintroduced in both houses of Congress.

The Equal Rights Amendment would be a valuable tool, to be sure, but we must keep in mind that ERA, like suffrage, cannot guarantee equality. It can function only as a tool, provided it is used properly. To gain equality, women must move to full participation in every sector of American life. Most particularly, women must develop influence in government, for there lies the heart of public power, the formal source of law, policy, and enforcement.

Women, Government, and Politics

To govern is to exercise authority, to wield power, to manage and guide the affairs of state for the citizenry. In this area, people make rules that affect every aspect of our lives, public and private, from how and where we work to whether or not we may terminate a pregnancy. Yet here again—in the creation of law and public policy, in its interpretation, and in its execution—female citizens are absurdly underrepresented.

On the federal level, in 1992 the House of Representatives broke a record with forty-seven women (only 11 percent of the votes) and the Senate with six. No woman has ever been president. Few women have ever occupied a top-level cabinet position, and few have had major power in national or international affairs.

So far as formal public power is concerned, at present women have very little. Yet perhaps it would be more accurate to say that we *exercise* very little, for our potential is strong. After all, we represent more than half the total population, and we are legally entitled to vote, hold office, and participate in the political process. Until very recently, we have simply failed to do so to any extent.

A variety of reasons explain women's minimal participation in the political process. Of course, a long history of enforced formal suppression, including disfranchisement and legal discrimination, has left a legacy of prejudicial attitudes and policies. Informal suppression, the effects of female roles and gender stereotypes, also functions effectively. The negative image of the authoritative woman, the burdens of child-rearing and homemaking, and the absence of social support for functioning outside of the assigned "place" have all coalesced to keep women from organizing and unifying to challenge discrimination, exploitation, and sexism in the political arena and the wider society.

Most important, until recently women did not identify themselves in the political process as women. That is, we failed to recognize ourselves as a distinct, meaningful category or class, as a legitimate pressure group formed around and appropriately pressing for our own self-defined needs and goals. We have seen ourselves as Republicans or Democrats, as working class or middle class, as black or white, as conservative or liberal, and so on—but we have failed to make a most important identification, of ourselves simply as women who, regardless of other loyalties, have common needs and problems and have the right to make civil demands.

The result of this inferior participation has been a lack of voice in the decisions that direct our lives. Without proportional representation in government, one is not a free citizen, and so one can only endure the whims of those in power; there is no recourse. Such a principle is clearly expressed in the early formulative documents of the American system, and it is obviously reflected in women's position today in society. Men hold power and generally make decisions that they believe to be suitable. Women's perspective can be reflected in law only to the degree that women have public power and a political vote. To achieve this, we must not see ourselves as dependents or supplicants. The U.S. government is based on the principle that all citizens have a right to make their wishes known and to press for them in orderly fashion so that social balance arises through the interplay of these pressures, and citizens ultimately gain social justice. We as women must affirm ourselves as full citizens, with the full complement of social responsibility and hence the full measure of social rights.

We are entering a new phase of feminism—call it Grass Roots Feminism, call it Feminism 2000, call it Global Feminism, call it Life-Preserving Feminism, call it simply New Phase Feminism—whatever it may be, it will make history, as did the first phase of modern feminism. Its horizons are unlimited. Never before have women become possibly the only salvation for the survival of humanity.

Not so long ago on a flight from Dallas to Chicago, I sat next to a young woman, not very politically aware, but very appealing, and as so often happens with passing acquaintances, people you never expect to see again, we told each other our life histories. At some point she turned to me and said, "You know, I would like to be an activist; I would like to fight for a cause, but I'm not that type."

"What type would you say you are?" I inquired.

"A dreamer," was her response.

"My dear young friend," I said. "The very first condition for being an activist is that you be a dreamer. Without dreams, without a vision, there can be no hope, and hope is the essence of motivating force in the struggle for social change."

–MARGARITA PAPANDREOU, president of the Women's Union of Greece, "Feminism and Political Power"[29]

Notes

1. U.S. Bureau of the Census, *Current Population Reports, Consumer Income,* series P-60, no. 180, "Money Income of Households, Families, and Persons in the United States: 1991," Table 24 (August 1992), provided by Urban Information Center, University of Missouri–St. Louis, July 1993.

2. U.S. Bureau of the Census, *Employment by Occupation, Race, Sex and Hispanic Origin,* 1990 U.S. Census, EEO Special Tabulation File; report produced by the Urban Information Center, University of Missouri–St. Louis.

3. U.S. Department of Labor, Bureau of Labor Statistics, *Employment and Earnings,* Table 56, "Median weekly earnings of full-time wage and salary workers by detailed occupation and sex" (January 1993).

4. U.S. Bureau of the Census, *Current Population Reports* series P-23, no. 173 (August 1992): No. 596, "Child Support—Award and Recipiency Status of Women: 1981 to 1989," and No. 597, "Child Support and Alimony—Selected Characteristics of Women: 1989."

5. Lenore Weitzman, "Women and Children Last: The Social and Economic Consequences of Divorce Law Reforms," in *Feminism, Children, and the New Families,* ed. Sanford M. Dornbusch and Myra H. Strober (New York: Guilford Press, 1988).

6. Jeanne L. Reid, "Making Delinquent Dad Pay His Child Support," *Ms.*, July/August 1992, p. 86.

7. U.S. Department of Labor, Women's Bureau, "20 Facts on Women Workers."

8. Francine D. Blau and Anna E. Winkler, "Women in the Labor Force: An Overview," in *Women: A Feminist Perspective*, 4th ed., ed. Jo Freeman (Mountain View, CA: Mayfield, 1984), p. 280.

9. Diane Schaffer, "The Feminization of Poverty," in *Women, Power and Policy: Toward the Year 2000*, 2d ed., ed. Ellen Boneparth and Emily Stoper (New York: Pergamon Press, 1988), p. 224.

10. U.S. Department of Labor, Bureau of Labor Statistics, *Employment and Earnings* 40, no. 4 (April 1993), p. 71.

11. Elyce Rotella, "Fact Sheet: Women in the U.S. Economy," unpublished paper, 1989.

12. Department of Labor, *Employment and Earnings.*

13. Bureau of the Census, *Employment by Occupation*, EEO Special Tabulation File.

14. Shirley Bernard, "Women's Economic Status: Some Cliches and Some Facts" in *Women: A Feminist Perspective*, p. 239.

15. Oliver Starr, Jr., "Shatter the Glass Ceiling: Male-Dominated Work Force Erects Barriers to Women's Advancement," *St. Louis Post Dispatch*, 5 November 1991, p. 3B.

16. Bureau of the Census, *Consumer Income.*

17. Susan Faludi, *Backlash: The Undeclared War Against Women* (New York: Crown, 1991); quoted in Laura Shapiro, "Why Women Are Angry," *Newsweek*, 21 October 1991, p. 43.

18. United Nations, *The World's Women 1970–1990: Trends and Statistics*, 1991, p. 26.

19. U. S. Department of Labor, Women's Bureau, Fact Sheet No. 88-1, "Women and Workforce 2000" (January 1988).

20. Ibid.

21. Michael Korda, *Male Chauvinism! How It Works* (New York: Random House, 1972).

22. George Gilder, *Sexual Suicide* (New York: Quadrangle, 1973).

23. Barbara A. Brown, Thomas I. Emerson, Gail Falk, and Ann E. Freedman, "The Equal Rights Amendment: A Constitutional Basis for Equal Rights for Women," *Yale Law Journal* 80 (1971): 876.

24. Jo Freeman, "The Legal Basis of the Sexual Caste System," *Valparaiso University Law Review* 5, no. 2 (1971): 203ff.

25. Ibid., p. 208.

26. Ibid., p. 210.

27. Brown et al., "The Equal Rights Amendment," pp. 873–874.

28. Ibid., p. 876.

29. Margaret Papandreou, "Feminism and Political Power: Some Thoughts on a Strategy for the Future," in *Women, Power, and Policy*, pp. xvii, xix.

Women and The American Economy

Elyce J. Rotella

Elyce J. Rotella is professor of economics and a member of the Women's Studies Program at Indiana University. She was educated at the University of Pittsburgh and the University of Pennsylvania, where she received her Ph.D. in economic history. Her research includes work on the growth of women's participation in the U.S. labor force, on clerical workers and school teachers, on the economics of marriage and divorce, on the determinants of urban mortality decline, and on the history of borrowing and saving. Among her published work is the book, From Home to Office: U.S. Women at Work, 1870–1930. *She has taught courses that focus on the role of women in the U.S. economy at the University of Pennsylvania, San Diego State University, Tufts University, and Indiana University.*

In this article Rotella explains concepts necessary to analyze women's position in the American economy and details some information on women's present condition and status.

Elyce J. Rotella wrote this article for this edition of *Issues in Feminism.*

ANY ECONOMY, NO MATTER HOW IT IS ORGANIZED, must decide how the resources of the society will be used to produce the goods and services that the members of the society consume. A large portion of the productive resources of any society consists of the labor power of people. Therefore, the amounts and kinds of work that people do is of fundamental interest to anyone trying to understand an economy, and for that reason economists and other social scientists have long been interested in the ways that tasks are divided among the members of society. There are many reasons for the division of labor among individuals: The most obvious are differences in interest, ability and acquired skills. If all people were equally able to obtain all kinds of training, we expect that persons would choose tasks simply according to their interests, abilities, and the remuneration offered. However, we know that in reality people's choices are limited in a number of ways. For example, some people are expected to follow in their parents' footsteps; some very able people do not go to college or receive other kinds of training because their families are poor; and some people's choices are limited by the expectations society has of the proper roles for them to play.

Both women's and men's choices are limited by sex roles. In all societies sex is an important determinant of the division of tasks. Most people believe that the sexual division of labor that prevails in their own society is natural and is determined by the biological differences between the sexes. However, there is actually considerable variation among societies in the tasks that are assigned to females and males. For example, farming is thought to be men's work in Western European societies, but in much of Africa farming was done by women until very recently. The one set of tasks that virtually all societies have assigned to women is child rearing, although there are cultures in which it is customary for men to be quite involved in the care of children.

In this paper we focus on the economic roles that women play in late twentieth-century American society. Although much of what will be said can also be applied to women in the rest of the world, it should be kept in mind that there are important differences between cultures in the sexual division of labor. In addition the sexual division of labor has changed considerably over time, so that there are some tasks women routinely perform today that it would have been unthinkable for them to perform in the past.

The Economic System

Everyone in the economic system plays two basic roles—producer and consumer. People fulfill their producer role by using the resources they control to make goods and provide services. For most people their most important productive resource is labor power, and they sell their labor to businesses or agencies that organize the production of goods and services sold in the market. In exchange for their labor people receive income in the form of wage earnings, which then makes it possible for them to fulfill their other basic economic role, that of consumer. In an advanced market economy, such as the modern U.S. economy, a very large proportion of goods and services produced are sold in markets. This differs from the situation in subsistence economies where most people consume the things they produce themselves and few goods are traded in markets.

Consumers use their earnings to purchase the goods and services they need and want. Clearly, those people who receive the highest earnings in exchange for their labor are able to enjoy the consumption of the largest amounts of goods and services. In addition to spending the earnings that they receive in exchange for their own resources, some people are able to consume more market goods and services because they can use the earned income of others. For example, children are able to consume market goods because of their parents' earnings, and full-time housewives consume on the basis of their husbands' earnings.

In this paper we will mostly be examining women's roles as producers in the American economy, but we must keep in mind the close connection that exists among production, earnings, and consumption.

The Changing Participation of Women in the U.S. Labor Force

Women may use all of their labor power to work in their homes producing goods and services for themselves and their families. In this case they do not receive a money wage directly in exchange for their labor. In order to consume market goods and services they must be able to use the income earned by someone else, usually other family members. Such women are full-time homemakers, and they are fulfilling the economic role that many in our culture have considered to be the preferred and "natural" role for married women.

Many other women work for pay, that is, they exchange their labor services for a money wage in the market. Women who work for pay or who are looking for a paying job are said to be members of the labor force. The proportion of all women who are members of the labor force is called the female labor force participation rate.

Column one (1) in Table 1 shows how the female labor force participation rate has changed over this century. We can see that in 1900 only 20 percent of all women were at work for pay and that by 1993 nearly 58 percent of all women were in the labor force. This rise in the proportion of all women who work for pay is one of the most dramatic changes that have taken place in the U.S. economy in this century. The pattern of increase in female labor force participation has not been the same in all time periods. The increase was fairly slow up until 1940. The very rapid increase from 1940 to 1945 was due to the movement of women into the labor force during the Second World War, when many men were fighting and there was a severe labor shortage. The growth in participation associated with the war was temporary, and it was not until the 1960s that female labor force participation was again as high as it had been in April 1945, when it reached 38.1 percent. Since 1960 the growth of women's labor force participation has been extremely rapid. We should note, however, that there has been a slowdown in the rate of increase in women's labor force participation in the 1990s. This slowdown has caused a great deal of comment and debate with some arguing that it is a temporary response to the recent recession and others arguing that women's labor force participation rate is nearing its maximum and will grow little in the future. It is still too soon to tell which side is correct.

Column two (2) in Table 1 shows how women's share of the total labor force has changed. In 1900 only 18 of every 100 paid workers were women. In 1993 women made up over 45 percent of the American labor force, and this number is still rising. Clearly then, paid employment is more important in the lives of American women today than it was in the past, and women are more important in the labor force.

This dramatic increase in women's participation in the labor force has caused economists to investigate the factors that affect women's decisions about how to structure their work lives. Marital status and family responsibilities have been found to have an important effect. Table 2 shows participation rates by marital status for selected years since 1950; and for married women, it shows the effect of the presence of children in the home. Participation by single (never married) and divorced women was higher than that of married women at all dates. Although work force participation by women in all marital status groups has increased, the most notable increases were those of married women (husband present). Since the great majority of American women marry (only 8 percent of women aged 40 to 45 in 1992 had never been married), it is these women whose actions dominate the female work force and who have been responsible for the bulk of the female labor force growth since the Second World War. Some of this increase in participation has also been due to the rise in the proportion of women who are not currently married because of the increase in the divorce rate and because of the recent trend toward later marriage for women.

Table 1 WOMEN'S LABOR FORCE PARTICIPATION RATE AND WOMEN'S SHARE OF THE LABOR FORCE

Year	(1) Women's labor force participation rate[a]	(2) Women's share of the labor force[b]
1900	20.0	18.1
1920	22.7	20.4
1930	23.6	21.9
1940	27.9	25.2
1945	35.8	29.1
1950	33.9	28.8
1955	35.7	30.2
1960	37.7	33.4
1965	39.3	35.2
1970	43.3	38.1
1975	46.3	40.0
1980	51.5	42.6
1985	54.5	44.2
1990	57.5	44.9
1993 (June)	57.9	45.3

[a]Women's labor force participation rate = $\frac{\text{women in the labor force}}{\text{women in the population}}$

[b]Women's share of the labor force = $\frac{\text{women in the labor force}}{\text{total labor force}}$

Sources: U.S. Department of Commerce, Bureau of the Census, *Historical Statistics of the United States, Colonial Times to 1970* (1975), pp. 131–132; U.S. Department of Commerce, Bureau of the Census, *Statistical Abstract of the United States, 1992*, p. 381; U.S. Department of Labor, Bureau of Labor Statistics, *Employment and Earnings* (July 1993), p. 10.

Because married women are usually expected to bear the primary responsibility for housework and child care, it is not surprising that marriage and children reduce the likelihood that women will work for pay. When such women do work in the market, they generally assume the "double burden" of working at a paid job while maintaining nearly complete responsibility for home work. Recent surveys show that husbands' help with housework does not increase substantially when their wives are employed. It is interesting (and perhaps surprising) to see that, even in the face of this "double burden," labor force participation by married women with children is rising very rapidly. Indeed, the greatest increases are occurring among women with young children. In 1960 only 18.6 percent of married women with children under 6 were in the labor force; in 1991 this figure was 59.9 percent, an increase of over threefold. In 1970, 24 percent of all married mothers with children one year old or younger were in the labor force. Just 21 years later, nearly 56 percent of these mothers of very young children were labor force participants.

Certainly then, the last forty years have seen dramatic changes in the ways that women organize their work lives. Huge changes in labor force participation by age are pictured in Figure 1. The solid lines in Figure 1 show the variation in women's labor force participation by age for various cross sections. Before

Table 2 WOMEN'S LABOR FORCE PARTICIPATION RATE BY MARITAL STATUS AND PRESENCE OF CHILDREN

	1960	1970	1980	1988	1991
Single (never married)	58.6	56.8	64.4	67.7	66.5
Widowed, divorced or separated	41.6	40.3	43.6	46.2	46.8
Divorced	NA	71.5	74.5	75.7	NA
Married (husband present)	31.9	40.5	49.9	56.7	58.5
Married (husband present)					
With children 6 to 17 only	39.0	49.2	61.7	73.6	73.6
With children under 6	18.6	30.3	45.1	58.9	59.9
With children under 3	15.3	25.8	41.5	55.5	56.8
With children 1 or under	NA	24.0	39.0	53.9	55.8

Sources: U.S. Department of Commerce, Bureau of the Census, *Statistical Abstract of the United States, 1991*, p. 391; *Statistical Abstract of the United States, 1982*, pp. 387–388; Howard Hayghe, "Rise in Mothers' Labor Force Activity Includes Those with Infants," *Monthly Labor Review* (February 1986): 45.

1950, the bulk of women in the labor force were young. In the 1950 cross section, we see the phenomenon that has come to be called "reentry," a return to the labor force by women over 35 when their children are in school or grown. This pattern is even more pronounced in the curve for 1960, where the highest participation rates belong to women aged 45 to 54. The curve for 1970 shows higher participation at all ages than was the case in 1960 though the pattern by age (with highest participation by the youngest women and by women ages 45–54) is basically unchanged. Between 1970 and 1980 there were large increases in participation by women in all except the oldest group. The growth in participation over the decade of the seventies was particularly rapid for younger women. For women ages 25–34, many of them mothers of young children, labor force participation was 45 percent in 1970, 65.5 percent in 1980, and 73.6 percent in 1990. Looking at the line for 1990, we see that female labor force participation growth continued in the 1980s, with particularly notable growth in participation by women in their mid-20s to mid-50s.

As interesting as is the information presented by the solid lines in Figure 1, we can get more insight into the lives of women by looking at the dashed lines. These lines show the experience of specific groups of women as they age over their lifetimes. The dashed lines show the experience of birth-cohorts, i.e., women who were born at the same time. For example, if we look at the line labeled Cohort I, we see the experience of women born 1906–1915. They were ages 35–44 in 1950 and ages 45–54 in 1960. These women increased their participation as they aged (from 35 percent when they were 35–44 to 49.3 percent when they were 45–54). Notice how different their behavior was from women who were ages 45–54 in 1950, only 33 percent of whom were in the labor force. If we had been around in 1950 and wanted to predict the future participation of women who were currently 35–44, we probably would have looked at the current behavior of 45–54-year-old women and predicted a slight decline in participation as the 35–44-year-old women aged. How wrong we would have been! In fact, we would have been very wrong if we had followed this strategy for almost any age group at any date. To take one other notable example, look at women who were ages 25–34 in 1980 (Cohort IV, the baby boom cohort born 1946–55). The other half of this group were ages 20–24 in 1970. They had higher rates of labor force participation when they were 25–34 than they had when they were younger. And they continued to increase their participation as they aged to 35–44. Suppose that these women had been building their expectations of their own futures on the lives of their older contemporaries. They would have formed very erroneous expectations.

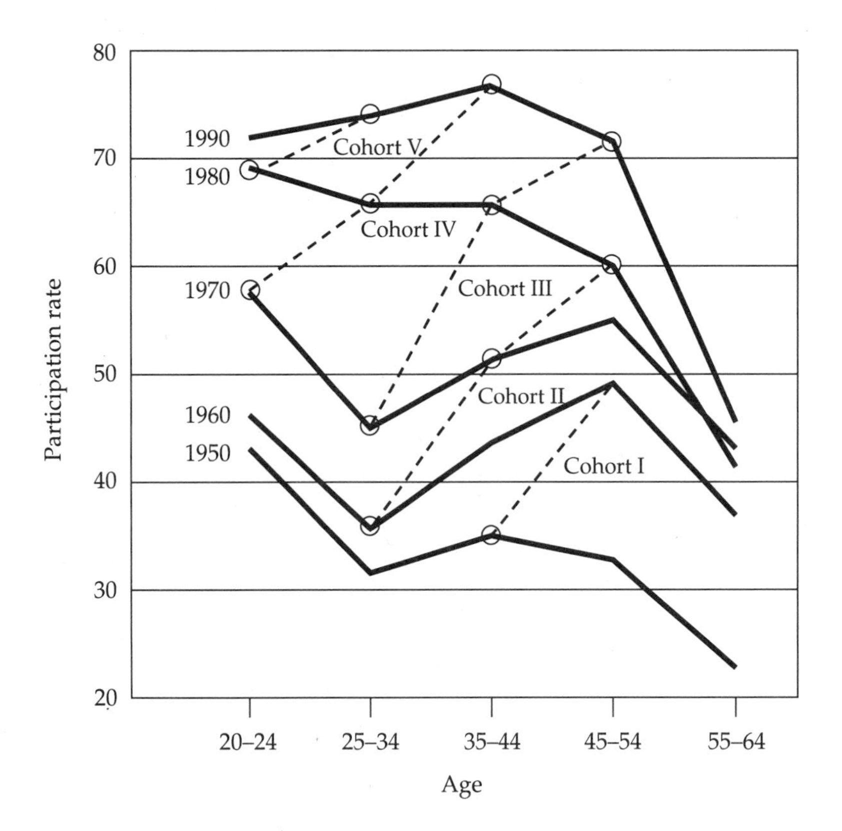

FIGURE 1
Female Participation in the Labor Force by Age, 1950–1990. Sources: U.S. Department of Labor, Bureau of the Census, *Statistical Abstract of the United States, 1953*, p. 185; *Statistical Abstract of the United States, 1964*, p. 217; *Statistical Abstract of the United States, 1988*, p. 366; *Statistical Abstract of the United States, 1992*, p. 381.

The Division of Women's Labor Between the Home and the Market: Explanations and Implications

We can gain understanding of the rise in women's labor force participation by focusing on the process through which people make decisions about how to use their time. For everyone time is a scarce resource, and we must all decide how to allocate our time among the various things that we would like to do. Everyone must spend time every day in sleep and in essential body maintenance functions. Beyond this we can decide to use our time for work or for leisure. All people (except workaholics) enjoy leisure and hope to have some leisure time each day. The time that we choose to work can be spent either working for pay or working in situations in which we are not paid for our labor. If we work for pay, we receive earnings, which allow us to enjoy consumption of goods and services that are bought in the market. If we engage in unpaid work, we produce goods and services that we ourselves or someone else consumes. Most unpaid work takes place in the home (dish washing, gardening, child care, and so on), but a substantial amount of unpaid work (e.g., volunteer work) is also performed in other settings. Everyone, of course, performs some unpaid work in the home so everyone must decide how to allocate their work time between paid work and unpaid work. However, because women are expected to be the major producers of goods and services in the home, the decision of dividing time between work at home and work in the market is particularly important for them.

Throughout this century, the wages that women can earn in the labor force have increased, and this increase is one factor that has been shown to be very important for explaining women's decisions about allocating time to paid work versus unpaid work. When the wage that a women can earn by being in the labor force increases, the cost to her and her family of having her stay out of the labor force and work at home to produce goods and services for the family to consume will also increase. For example, if a woman could earn $1000 per week by working as an engineer, she and her family would have to give up $1000 per week if she stays at home to be a full-time homemaker. And, if her potential earnings increase by $100 per week, the cost of staying home rises accordingly. Clearly then, the incentive for a woman to go into the labor force will increase when her market wage increases, and women with high potential wages will be less likely to be full-time homemakers. This is part of the reason that woman who have high levels of education are much more likely to be in the labor force. Educated women have higher potential earnings, and they are probably more able to find pleasant and fulfilling jobs.

As women increase their time in market work and reduce their time in home work, they substitute products they buy in the market for some of the goods and services they might have produced at home. This means that earning women and their families are more likely to eat in restaurants, to send out clothes to laundries, and to use institutional child care and baby sitters. It is not, however, possible to substitute purchased products for all home production. Therefore, studies have found that women who have the "double burden" of being homemakers and wage earners work more (and sleep fewer) hours per week than any other group in society.

The rise over time in women's wages and in women's labor force participation has a number of implications for the institutions of marriage and the family. In the traditional marriage common in Western cultures, the division of labor has been between the bread-winner husband and the homemaker wife. The husband specialized in paid market work, and the wife specialized in unpaid home work. In this arrangement the wife was dependent on her husband's earnings in order to be able to consume market goods and services, and a woman who was concerned with her economic well-being had to be careful to choose a husband with good earning potential. As more women work in the market, this dependency lessens, with the result that women may choose to marry later, and some may choose not to marry at all. Women with unhappy marriages may be more likely to divorce if they can earn their own income. In the last three decades, we have seen many changes in the marriage behavior of Americans—the kinds of changes that we would expect to result from greater female labor force participation. Overall women are marrying later; the median age at first marriage for women has risen from 20.3 in 1960 to 24.4 in 1992. It is quite possible that a substantial number of women may not marry at all; the proportion of women aged 25–29 who had never married rose from 10.5 percent in 1970 to 33.2 percent in 1992. The divorce rate has doubled since 1960. In addition to its implications for the incidence of marriage, we might expect that greater economic independence for women will have implications for courtship and the nature of the marriage relation as well. As they are more able to provide for themselves, women who wish to marry may be freer to choose husbands on the basis of affection and attraction rather than on the basis of men's potential as income providers. Perhaps these marriages will be more satisfying to both partners.

The analysis that stresses the increasing value of women's market time also has implications for the decisions that people make about how many children to have. As women's potential market wage rises, the cost of their time spent in household duties rises. Therefore, the cost to families of having children to care for goes up if the mother is to stay at home to provide child care instead of working for pay. This leads to the incentive to have smaller families and is undoubtedly part of the reason for the low fertility of American women.

The explanation offered above for increased labor force participation by American women emphasizes the central role played by the rising market value of women's time. As women's market wages have risen women have responded by reallocating time from non-market uses to market work. As powerful as this explanation is, we must not lose sight of the fact that women take jobs for the same reasons that men take jobs—they need money to support themselves and their families. Many employed women are married to men who earn low wages, and these women's earnings often make the difference between the family living below or above the poverty level. Earnings of families in which both husband and wife are employed are 60 percent higher on average than in families where only the husband is employed. As more and more families choose to send the wife into the labor force in pursuit of this higher income, the "Leave It to Beaver" family with a stay-at-home mother has become comparatively rare. In mid-1993, among all husband–wife families, only 20 percent had the husband as the only earner in the family.

As important as are women's earnings for husband–wife families, they are much more crucial for non-married women, especially for the rapidly growing number of non-married women who are supporting children. In 1991, 45 percent of all employed women did not have husbands (i.e., they were single, widowed, divorced, or married with an absent husband). Most of these women were dependent on themselves alone for financial support. In addition, many of these women were heads of families and used their earnings to support children. In the last quarter century there has been a dramatic increase in the incidence of divorce; more than half of all marriages are predicted to end in divorce. The greater prevalence of divorce has led to increased participation by women in the labor force through two avenues. First, as was seen in Table 2, divorced women have very high rates of labor force participation. This is because most divorced women bear almost complete responsibility for supporting themselves and their dependent children. Divorce commonly leads to substantially lower economic status for women and their children. In these days of no-fault divorce, alimony is very rare. In 1989, only 4 percent of divorced women were legally entitled to alimony payments. Child support awards are more common but are far from universal, often hard to collect, and generally cover only a portion of a child's needs. In 1989, only 58 percent of women with children of absent fathers had been awarded child support. Of the women who were supposed to receive child support payments in that year, 51 percent received the full payment and 25 percent received no child support payments at all. The average child support payment was $2995 per woman. Clearly divorced women need to be in the labor force to support themselves and their children. The prevalence of divorce also raises female labor force participation through a second avenue. It gives married women a strong incentive to maintain their attachment to the labor force and therefore their future earning potential. Because so many women will find themselves completely dependent on their own earnings in the future, they find it wise to insure themselves against a low post-marital living standard by remaining in the labor force while married.

In the past there has been a strong inverse relationship between husband's earnings and wife's labor force participation. Women with high-earning husbands were much less likely to work for pay than were women who were married to men with lower earnings. Since 1960 this association has been weakening as more highly educated women (who are usually married to high-earning men) enter the labor force. At present, there is no consistent relationship between husband's earnings and wife's likelihood of employment. From this we can conclude that married women are more responsive to the positive effects of their own wages, which tend to pull them into the work force, than they are to the negative effects of their husbands' earnings, which in the past have tended to keep them at home.

Women's Earnings

We have seen that women's earnings are an important factor affecting the decision of how women allocate their time between work at home and work for pay in the market. Women's earnings have increased over time which has tended to pull them into the labor force. In this section we turn our attention to the determinants of women's earnings and to the gap in earnings between women and men. The earnings of all American workers, males and females, have increased greatly in this century, reflecting the greater productivity of workers. These productivity increases reflect advances in production technology and the higher skill and education levels of workers.

Table 3 presents information on median earnings of workers employed full-year and full-time. We see that from 1960 to 1991, women's earnings rose by 49.2 percent after controlling for inflation. Over the same period, men's earnings rose by 29.6 percent. As a result of the faster growth of women's earnings, the earnings ratio (women's earnings as a percentage of men's earnings) rose from 60.7 percent in 1960 to 70 percent in 1991. Examination of the numbers in Table 3 reveals much about the performance of the U.S. economy in the recent past. For men, earnings rose to 1975, then declined. In contrast, women's earnings have grown except for a small decline in the recent recession. All the narrowing of the earnings gap is due to the faster growth of women's earnings in the 1980s. In fact, the earnings gap widened slightly from 1960 to 1975, a period when many women were joining the labor force. The recent narrowing of the earnings gap is all the more dramatic because it follows a long period during which the gap either remained constant or widened.

Why do women workers earn less than men, and how can we explain changes in the earnings gap over time? Some of the difference between the annual earnings of women and men is due to the fact that

Table 3 MEDIAN EARNINGS OF YEAR-ROUND, FULL-TIME WORKERS (IN 1991 DOLLARS)

Year	Female	Male	Earnings Ratio Female/Male
1960	13,777	22,706	60.7
1965	15,245	25,440	59.9
1970	17,554	29,568	59.4
1975	18,186	30,919	58.8
1980	18,530	30,801	60.2
1985	19,777	30,626	64.6
1990	20,656	28,843	71.6
1991	20,553	29,421	70.0
% increase 1960 to 1991	49.2	29.6	

Source: U.S. Department of Commerce, Bureau of the Census, Current Population Reports, series P-60, no. 180. *Money Income of Households, Families, and Persons in the U.S.: 1990,* pp. B-32–B-33.

more women work part-time and part-year. In 1991, 74 percent of employed women worked at full-time jobs compared with 90 percent of men. However, because Table 3 compared only the earnings of full-year, full-time workers, we have already controlled for this factor.

In general, economists think that the wages workers receive are related to their productivity. It is not surprising that highly productive workers in skilled jobs receive higher earnings than do less productive workers. We do not usually have accurate direct data on individual workers' productivity, but we do have expectations about the qualities that cause workers to be more productive. Education, job training, and experience on the job should lead to higher productivity and therefore to higher earnings. The gap between women's and men's earnings could reflect a gap between women's and men's productivities. The attempt to explain the earning gap by looking at differences between men and women in education, training, and experience and is called the *human capital approach.*

The human capital approach offers some powerful explanations of the pattern of the earnings gap over time. A part of the earnings gap reflects the fact that many women have lower levels of education and work experience than do men. Until recently, men were more likely to receive education and training beyond the college level and there were substantial sex differences in the kinds of post-secondary training received. As important as sex differences in education and training are differences in work experience. Women's lower levels of labor force participation meant that they had lower levels of market experience. Because employers reward education, training, and experience by higher earnings, some of the earnings gap reflects these differences.

Although there is more to explaining the earnings gap than just sex differences in education, training, and experience, we can get insight into the changing size of the earnings gap by focusing on these factors. The widening of the gap in the 1950s, 1960s, and 1970s seems to be due in part to the rapidly increasing participation by women who were new entrants (or reentrants) into the labor force. A large percentage of these women had low levels of prior experience. Many were older women who were either joining the labor force for the first time or reentering the labor force after a long absence. Such women commonly had low levels of experience and commanded low wages. Since there were so many of them in the labor force, they pulled down women's average earnings.

We can also understand the narrowing of the earnings gap in the 1980s as being due partly to the changing human capital characteristics of women workers. Women's educational levels have been rising steadily, and in the 1970s there was considerable change in the kinds of education that women got, with many more women attending graduate and professional schools and educating themselves for employment in nontraditional fields. For example, women received 47 percent of the bachelor's degrees in business and management awarded in 1988 compared with under 9 percent in 1970, and they received 33 percent of M.D. degrees compared with 8 percent in 1970. This rise in women's education was accompanied by a rise in women's experience levels. As we saw in Figure 1, the 1970s and 1980s were characterized by rapidly increasing labor force participation by women in their 20s and 30s. What happened was that a growing number of women joined the labor force when young and maintained their attachment while they married and had children. This is the pattern common to men, and produced a large number of young and middle-aged women with experience levels as high as men of the same age. It is likely that the rapid rise in women's earnings in the 1980s reflects this rise in education and experience.

Researchers have tried to see how much of the earnings gap can be explained by the human capital approach by comparing the earnings of women and men who have the same education and experience. What they have found is that some of the difference in earnings can be explained by differences in education and experience, but a substantial portion remains unexplained. Even when we compare the earnings of women and men in the same occupational categories we find that a gap persists.

The part of the earnings gap that cannot be attributed to human capital differences reflects discrimination against women in the labor market. Discrimination can take a number of different forms. When women are paid less than equally productive men, they are being discriminated against. When women are excluded from some jobs or training so that they are forced to work in jobs in which their productivity is not as high as it might be, their earnings are lowered due to discrimination. Sometimes employers assume that all women have the same characteristics and make employment decisions about individual women based on the expected average attributes of women as a group. For example, employers may believe that all women will have high labor market turnover because some women drop out of the labor force in order to fulfill household responsibilities. In such cases, the women, who are judged by the expected group characteristics rather than by their own individual characteristics, are said to be victims of statistical discrimination.

In most studies, discrimination has been found to be responsible for half or more of the earnings gap. However, the major form that discrimination takes is not "unequal pay for equal work," though there are many cases of women receiving lower pay for doing substantially the same work as men. The biggest cause of the earnings gap and the major form of discrimination against women is that women and men are, by and large, employed in different occupations; and the pay in women's occupations is lower than the pay in men's occupations.

The Sex Distribution of Occupations

In Table 4 we see how women and men workers are distributed among the major occupational categories of the U.S. labor force. Even at the high level of aggregation of these data, there are striking differences in the distributions. Over one-quarter of all female workers were in administrative support jobs (mostly clerical) compared to 5.9 percent of men. Nineteen percent of men, but only 2.1 percent of women, were precision production, craft, and repair (skilled blue collar) workers. Much higher proportions of women than men were employed as private household workers and as other service workers. In the professional and technical fields, where the figures for females and males are more similar, the degree of aggregation in the data hides the substantial differences that actually exist because a large proportion of female professionals are teachers, nurses, librarians, and social workers whereas male professionals are in a much broader mix of fields.

When we look at occupational breakdowns of the U.S. labor force that are more detailed than the breakdown in Table 4, we see even greater disparity between women's and men's jobs. Women's employment is concentrated in a much smaller number of occupations than is men's employment. Not only are women workers concentrated in a fairly small number of jobs, but many of the jobs that women hold are held almost exclusively by women. That is, the occupational structure is highly segregated by sex, with many women being employed in jobs in which the overwhelming majority of workers are women. We can get some sense of this by looking at the few detailed occupations listed in Table 4 and by concentrating on the last column which shows the percent of all workers in the occupation who are female. For example, we see that women are 98.3 percent of secretaries, stenographers, and typists but only 2.1 percent of construction workers. They are 74.8 percent of grade school and high school teachers but only 9.4 percent of engineers.

Despite the continuing high degree of concentration and sex segregation that persists in the U.S. occupational structure, there have been notable changes in the last two decades as women have made substantial inroads into some professional and managerial fields. For example, we can see in Table 4 that over 24 percent of all lawyers and judges are women; in 1970, only 5 percent were women. Women's employment has also grown very rapidly among physicians, dentists, accountants, and business executives. These occupational changes are concentrated among highly educated young women. The higher earnings

Table 4 OCCUPATIONAL DISTRIBUTION OF FEMALES AND MALES, JUNE 1993

	Percent of labor force in group		
Occupational Group	Females	Males	% Female
Executive, administrative, managerial	12.0	13.4	42.7
Professional specialty	15.9	11.8	52.8
Engineers			9.4
Teachers, college and university			40.1
Teachers, except college and university			74.8
Lawyers and judges			24.3
Technicians and related support	3.8	3.2	49.7
Sales occupations	12.5	11.7	47.3
Administrative support, including clerical	26.6	5.9	79.0
Secretaries, stenographers, and typists			98.3
Private household workers	1.6	0.1	94.0
Protective service workers	0.8	2.6	20.0
Other service workers	16.2	7.4	64.7
Precision production, craft, repair	2.1	19.1	8.3
Construction trades			1.8
Machine operators, assemblers, inspectors	5.1	6.8	38.5
Transportation and material moving	0.8	7.0	8.9
Handlers, equipment cleaners, helpers, laborers	1.5	5.9	17.5
Farming, forestry, and fishing	1.1	5.0	15.7
TOTAL	100.0	100.0	45.5

Source: U.S. Department of Labor, Bureau of Labor Statistics, *Employment and Earnings* (July 1993), pp. 31–32.

of these women is responsible for much of the narrowing of the earnings gap since 1980. For less educated women, there has been little change in occupational or earnings prospects. Few women are employed in the skilled blue-collar trades which provide the best earnings prospects for workers with less than college educations. The employment of women without higher education is still concentrated in clerical jobs, in a few traditionally female factory occupations, and in the service jobs of the "pink collar ghetto."

The concentration and segregation we observe in the occupational structure has implications for women's earnings and for the male–female earnings gap. If women's ability to enter occupations is limited so that they are able to take fewer kinds of jobs than men, then women's wages will be lowered because so many women are available to work for a limited number of opportunities. If more women enter the labor force and most of them try to get jobs in traditional women's occupations, then there will be extreme competition for these jobs and therefore downward pressure on women's wages. If discrimination limits women's access to some occupations, it increases competition for "women's jobs" and reduces competition for "men's jobs." The result is that women's wages are artifically low and men's wages are artificially high. Economists call this mechanism *occupational crowding*. The existence of occupational crowding implies that the gap between women's and men's earnings will persist until there is a widespread lessening of sex stereotyping of occupations.

Comparable Worth

The recognition of the crucial role played by occupational segregation in the earnings gap has fueled the drive for a movement to demand equal pay for jobs of comparable worth. The argument for comparable worth recognizes that "equal pay for equal work" will not narrow the earnings gap so long as most men and women are employed in different occupations. It therefore attempts to raise the earnings of women employed in female-dominated jobs by arguing that many of these jobs are of equal value to male-dominated jobs. In order to pursue this argument, a mechanism is needed whereby comparisons can be made among persons employed in different occupations. The basic principle behind comparable worth is that it is possible to compare jobs in terms of knowledge, skill, effort, responsibility, and working conditions, and that jobs equivalent in value in these terms should be paid equally.

Comparable worth has been the focus of a great deal of controversy in the political and legal arena. Business groups have generally been hostile to comparable worth, and during the 1980s and early 1990s the executive branch of the federal government was vocally hostile. Probably the most often quoted negative evaluation of comparable worth is that of Clarence Pendleton, chair of the U.S. Civil Rights Commission in the Reagan Administration who said that comparable worth is the "looniest idea since Looney Toons." Many of those who oppose comparable worth argue that it is impossible to evaluate the worth of dissimilar jobs and that the attempt to make such comparisons would produce unwarranted bureaucratic interference in the labor market. Such criticism, however, neglects to note that although it may seem very difficult to compare jobs in terms of knowledge, skill, effort, responsibility, and working conditions, such comparisons are routinely made, especially by large employers such as governments and major corporations.

Employers often use job evaluation schemes to develop salary structures for their organizations. Many people are familiar with the GS system of salary categories used by the federal Civil Service. Job evaluation schemes are so common that there are firms which specialize in evaluating jobs and are hired by organizations to perform evaluations and assign evaluation scores that can be compared across occupations. The most commonly used evaluation system assigns points (called Hay points) to each job classification. Since job evaluation schemes are common in large organizations and have existed for a long time, advocates of comparable worth are not asking for a major change in the way that employers operate. They ask only that whenever an evaluation scheme assigns the same number of points to male-dominated and female-dominated jobs that the jobs receive the same pay.

All instances where there have been specific struggles to reform salary scales according to comparable worth principles have involved government employees. For example, between 1983 and 1987 there was major reformation of the salary system of the State of Minnesota, which had previously assigned Hay points to all its job classifications. When the Minnesota Council on the Economic Status of Women examined salaries paid to state workers in 1982, they found many instances of dramatic differences in the pay of men and women in jobs that had been evaluated as being equal. For example, the maximum monthly salary of workers employed as clerk-stenographers grade 2 (Hay points = 135), 99.7 percent of whom were female, was $1171. By contrast, the maximum monthly salary of general repair workers (Hay points = 134), 99.3 percent of whom were male, was $1564. Licensed practical nurses (Hay points = 183; 94.7 percent female) received $1382, while highway maintenance workers (Hay points = 154, 99.9 percent male) received $139 per month more despite their much lower evaluation score. The discrepancies found in Minnesota between the salaries of workers in male-dominated and female-dominated jobs are common in the salary scales of many other state and local governments. In some areas, notably Washington State and the City of San Jose, California, readjustments of salary scales to move toward comparable worth have been made in response to pressure from women's advocacy groups and unions. While all the legal battles for comparable worth have involved public sector employment, a number of private firms have voluntarily adopted some aspects of comparable worth in their salary schedules. Among these are AT&T, IBM, Bank of America, and Tektronix. Despite these successes, comparable worth principles have not been widely adopted, and they remain very controversial.

The Feminization of Poverty

Over the same period that some American women have been improving their economic position, a very large number of women have suffered severe economic hardship. Women now make up a larger share of the population living in poverty—a phenomenon that has come to be called the "feminization of poverty." The most notable economic advances have been concentrated among young well-educated women who succeeded in entering nontraditional jobs, solidified their attachment to the labor force, and experienced above average increases in earnings. For women at the other end of the economic scale, the picture is bleak. Over 70 percent of persons with incomes under $5000 are women. Women's greater likelihood of living in poverty is due in large part to women's lower earnings; a great many women who work full-time, year round do not earn enough to support a family above the poverty line. The effect of low earnings combines with the fact that a large and rapidly growing number of families are maintained by women (i.e., families in which no adult male is present) to produce very high poverty rates for women and the children who are dependent on them.

Table 5

Proportion of U.S.families maintained by women (no husband present)

Year	Total	White	Black	Hispanic
1970	10.7	8.9	28.0	15.3
1980	14.6	11.6	40.3	20.1
1991	17.0	13.2	45.9	23.8

Proportion of U.S. families with children under 18 maintained by mothers (no husband present)

Year	Total	White	Black	Hispanic
1970	11.5	8.9	33.0	NA
1980	19.4	15.1	48.7	24.0
1991	25.0	19.3	58.0	28.7

Proportion of all families living below the poverty line, 1991

	Families maintained by women	Husband–wife families
Total	35.6	6.0
White	28.4	5.5
Black	51.2	11.0
Hispanic	49.7	19.1

Proportion of all families with children under 18 living below the poverty line, 1991

	Families maintained by women	Husband–wife families
Total	47.1	8.3
White	39.6	7.7
Black	60.5	12.4
Hispanic	60.1	23.5

Sources: U.S. Department of Commerce, Bureau of the Census, Current Population Reports, series P-20, no. 458, *Households and Family Characteristics: March 1991*, pp. 7, 10; Current Population Reports, series P-60, no. 181, *Poverty in the United States, 1991*, pp. 6–9.

Table 5 presents figures on poverty among American families. We can see that families maintained by women are much more likely to be poor than are husband–wife families; over 47 percent of families with children maintained by women are poor compared with 8.3 percent of husband–wife families with children. The increase in the share of the poverty population represented by families maintained by women is due to the marked rise in the prevalence of these families (see the top half of Table 5). Whereas in 1970, 10.7 percent of all American families were maintained by women, by 1991, this number had grown to 17 percent (25 percent of families with children under 18).

The growth in the number of families maintained by women and the attendant feminization of poverty is related to the increased incidence of divorce, the rise in the age at marriage, the apparent higher proportion of women not marrying at all, and the increase in childbearing by single women. As a result, in 1991, only 59.3 percent of women over age 17 were married and living with a spouse—a smaller proportion than at any other time in the last 50 years. This means that a large and growing proportion of women and their children are dependent on women's earnings, and we have already seen that women's earnings are much lower than men's.

Looking at Table 5, we see striking differences among black, white, and Hispanic women. Since the 1950s, racial differences in labor force participation, average earnings, and occupational distribution have declined substantially. The same cannot be said of racial differences in poverty. About half of all families maintained by black and Hispanic women are poor compared with 28.3 percent of families maintained by white women; the figures are considerably higher for families with children under 18. The top of the table shows that there are also substantial differences among the three groups in the proportion of families maintained by women. Black families are particularly likely to be economically dependent on women, with 45.9 percent of all black families and 58 percent of all black families with children being maintained by women. These figures reflect the recent rapid decline in the proportion of black women who are married. In 1991, only 41 percent of black women were married and living with a spouse, and over 66 percent of black babies were born to non-married women. These women and their children are very likely to live in poverty. Although the feminization of poverty is a phenomenon that cuts across racial and ethnic lines, the striking differences we see in proportions of families maintained by women has led to widening differences in incidence of poverty among the races.

Summary

This century has witnessed very dramatic increases in participation by women in the American labor force. The bulk of this increase has taken place since the Second World War and has been largely due to increased participation by married women. Before 1970, the greatest increases in participation were attributable to middle aged women returning to the labor force after their families were grown, but since then the most notable increases have come from young mothers and from young unmarried women. Studies of women's labor force participation have found that increases in women's wages are very important for explaining the greater propensity of women to work for pay. As women's education and experience levels have risen, thereby raising their potential market wage, the implied price of home-produced goods and services has also risen, thus increasing the incentive to work for pay instead of working full-time in the home.

After many years during which the gap between women's and men's average earnings either stayed constant or widened, the gap has narrowed somewhat since 1980. This narrowing seems to be related closely to the growth in experience levels of women who have maintained continuous attachment to the labor force and to changes in the amounts and kinds of education that women receive. For well-educated young women, there have been notable successes in gaining access to professional and managerial jobs that have traditionally not been held by women.

Although the earnings gap has narrowed somewhat, very large differences remain between the earnings of men and women. Studies have found that individual differences between women and men in education, training, and job experience can account for only a part of the earnings gap. The remainder reflects discrimination, particularly the kinds of discrimination that lead to widely differing occupational distributions of women and men workers. Women's employment tends to be concentrated in a relatively small number of low-paid jobs. Since the growth in women's labor force participation has not been accompanied by any very substantial decrease in the overall level of sex segregation in the occupational structure, most of new women workers have sought jobs in traditional women's fields. This development has increased competition for those jobs and exerted downward pressure on women's earnings. Any further substantial decrease in the size of the female–male earnings gap will require less sex segregation in the occupational structure and/or the widespread adoption of comparable worth principles in salary setting.

Despite economic gains by well-educated women workers, the picture for women who are close to the bottom of the economic ladder is disturbing. The number of families maintained by women is increasing rapidly as the incidence of marriage falls, the divorce rate rises, and the non-marital birth rate increases. Such families have a very high chance of falling into poverty and are unlikely to improve their position without major changes in social policy.

It is difficult to predict how women's economic roles will change in the future. We are seeing improvements for some women but increased difficulties for others. Most employed women bear the "double burden" of working in the labor force while they maintain primary responsibility for work in the home. Perhaps equality in the labor market will only come about when women achieve equality in other areas of life.

Suggestions for Further Reading:

Bergmann, Barbara R.
1986 *The Economic Emergence of Women.* New York: Basic Books.

Blau, Francine D., and Ferber, Marianne A.
1992 *The Economics of Women and Work.* 2d ed. Englewood Cliffs, NJ: Prentice-Hall.

Goldin, Caudia
1989 *Understanding the Gender Gap: An Economic History of American Women.* New York: Oxford University Press.

Women's Research and Education Institute.
1992 *The American Woman, 1992–93: A Status Report.* New York: W. W. Norton.

Two Observations on Sexual Harassment

The Nature of the Beast

Anita Hill

Anita Hill is professor of law at the University of Oklahoma College of Law. Her allegations of sexual harassment against Clarence Thomas at his confirmation hearings for appointment to the Supreme Court placed the issue of harassment against working women before the public as never before, and generated an awareness that was long overdue. It is interesting to note that although Hill was not believed, and vilified during and shortly after her revelations, one year later polls showed that the public had reversed its opinion.

THE RESPONSE TO MY SENATE JUDICIARY COMMITTEE testimony has been at once heartwarming and heart-wrenching. In learning that I am not alone in experiencing harassment, I am also learning that there are far too many women who have experienced a range of inexcusable and illegal activities—from sexist jokes to sexual assault—on the job.

My reaction has been to try to learn more. As an educator, I always begin to study an issue by examining the scientific data—the articles, the books, the studies. Perhaps the most compelling lesson is in the stories told by the women who have written to me. I have learned much; I am continuing to learn; I have yet ten times as much to explore. I want to share some of this with you.

"The Nature of the Beast" describes the existence of sexual harassment, which is alive and well. A harmful, dangerous thing that can confront a woman at any time.

What we know about harassment, sizing up the beast:

Sexual harassment is pervasive . . .

1. It occurs today at an alarming rate. Statistics show that anywhere from 42 to 90 percent of women will experience some form of harassment during their employed lives. At lease one percent experience sexual assault. But the statistics do not fully tell the story of the anguish of women who have been told in various ways on the first day of a job that sexual favors are expected. Or the story of women who were sexually assaulted by men with whom they continued to work.
2. It has been occurring for years. In letters to me, women tell of incidents that occurred 50 years

"The Nature of the Beast," by Anita Hill. *Ms.* 2, no. 4 (January/February, 1992).

ago when they were first entering the workplace, incidents they have been unable to speak of for that entire period.

3. Harassment crosses lines of race and class. In some ways, it is a creature that practices "equal opportunity" where women are concerned. In other ways it exhibits predictable prejudices and reflects stereotypical myths held by our society.

We know that harassment all too often goes unreported for a variety of reasons . . .

1. Unwillingness (for good reason) to deal with the expected consequences;
2. Self-blame;
3. Threats or blackmail by coworkers or employers;
4. What it boils down to in many cases is a sense of powerlessness that we experience in the workplace, and our acceptance of a certain level of inability to control our careers and professional destinies. This sense of powerlessness is particularly troubling when one observes the research that says individuals with graduate education experience more harassment than do persons with less than a high school diploma. The message: when you try to obtain power through education, the beast harassment responds by striking more often and more vehemently.

That harassment is treated like a woman's "dirty secret" is well known. We also know what happens when we "tell." We know that when harassment is reported the common reaction is disbelief or worse . . .

1. Women who "tell" lose their jobs. A typical response told of in the letters to me was: I not only lost my job for reporting harassment, but I was accused of stealing and charges were brought against me.
2. Women who "tell" become emotionally wasted. One writer noted that "it was fully eight months after the suit was conducted that I began to see myself as alive again."
3. Women who "tell" are not always supported by other women. Perhaps the most disheartening stories I have received are of mothers not believing daughters. In my kindest moments I believe that this reaction only represents attempts to distance ourselves from the pain of the harassment experience. The internal response is: "It didn't happen to me. This couldn't happen to me. In order to believe that I am protected, I must believe that it didn't happen to her." The external response is: "What did you do to provoke that kind of behavior?" Yet at the same time that I have been advised of hurtful and unproductive reactions, I have also heard stories of mothers and daughters sharing their experiences. In some cases the sharing allows for a closer bonding. In others a slight but cognizable mending of a previously damaged relationship occurs.

What we are learning about harassment requires recognizing this beast when we encounter it, and more. It requires looking the beast in the eye.

We are learning painfully that simply having laws against harassment on the books is not enough. The law, as it was conceived, was to provide a shield of protection for us. Yet that shield is failing us: many fear reporting, others feel it would do no good. The result is that less than 5 percent of women victims file claims of harassment. Moreover, the law focuses on quid pro quo, but a recent New York *Times* article quoting psychologist Dr. Louise Fitzgerald says that this makes up considerably less than 5 percent of the cases. The law needs to be more responsive to the reality of our experiences.

As we are learning, enforcing the law alone won't terminate the problem. What we are seeking is equality of treatment in the workplace. Equality requires an expansion of our attitudes toward workers. Sexual harassment denies our treatment as equals and replaces it with treatment of women as objects of ego or power gratification. Dr. John Gottman, a psychologist at the University of Washington, notes that sexual harassment is more about fear than about sex.

Yet research suggests two troublesome responses exhibited by workers and by courts. Both respond by . . .

1. Downplaying the seriousness of the behavior (seeing it as normal sexual attraction between people) or commenting on the sensitivity of the victim.
2. Exaggerating the ease with which victims are expected to handle the behavior. But my letters tell me that unwanted advances do not cease—and that the message was power, not genuine interest.

We are learning that many women are angry. The reasons for the anger are various and perhaps all too obvious . . .

1. We are angry because this awful thing called harassment exists in terribly harsh, ugly, demeaning, and even debilitating ways. Many believe it is criminal and should be punished as such. It is a form of violence against women as well as a form of economic coercion, and our experiences suggest that it won't just go away.
2. We are angry because for a brief moment we believed that if the law allowed for women to be hired in the workplace, and if we worked hard for our educations and on the job, equality would be achieved. We believed we would be respected as equals. Now we are realizing this is not true. We have been betrayed. The reality is that this powerful beast is used to perpetuate a sense of inequality, to keep women in their place notwithstanding our increasing presence in the workplace.

What we have yet to explore about harassment is vast. It is what will enable us to slay the beast.

Research is helpful, appreciated, and I hope will be required reading for all legislators. Yet research has what I see as one shortcoming: it focuses on our reaction to harassment, not on the harasser. How we enlighten men who are currently in the workplace about behavior that is beneath our (and their) dignity is the challenge of the future. Research shows that men tend to have a narrower definition of what constitutes harassment than do women. How do we expand their body of knowledge? How do we raise a generation of men who won't need to be reeducated as adults? We must explore these issues, and research efforts can assist us.

What are the broader effects of harassment on women and the world? Has sexual harassment left us unempowered? Has our potential in the workplace been greatly damaged by this beast? Has this form of economic coercion worked? If so, how do we begin to reverse its effects? We must begin to use what we know to move to the next step: what we will do about it.

How do we capture our rage and turn it into positive energy? Through the power of women working together, whether it be in the political arena, or in the context of a lawsuit, or in community service. This issue goes well beyond partisan politics. Making the workplace a safer, more productive place for ourselves and our daughters should be on the agenda for each of us. It is something we can do for ourselves. It is a tribute, as well, to our mothers—and indeed a contribution we can make to the entire population.

I wish that I could take each of you on the journey that I've been on during all these weeks since the hearing. I wish that every one of you could experience the heartache and the triumphs of each of those who have shared with me their experiences. I leave you with but a brief glimpse of what I've seen. I hope it is enough to encourage you to begin—or continue and persist with—your own exploration. And thank you.

This article is based on remarks delivered by Anita Hill (professor of law, University of Oklahoma) as part of a panel on sexual harassment and policymaking at the National Forum for Women State Legislators convened by the Center for the American Woman and Politics (CAWP) late last year. Other panel members were Deborah L. Rhode, professor of law at Stanford; Susan Deller Ross, professor of law and director of the Sex Discrimination Clinic at Georgetown University Law School; and Kimberle Williams Crenshaw, professor of law at UCLA. A transcript of the entire proceedings (the largest meeting of elected women ever held) is available from CAWP, Eagleton Institute of Politics, Rutgers University, New Brunswick, New Jersey 08901.

. . . And the Language Is Race

Eleanor Holmes Norton

Congresswoman Eleanor Holmes Norton is currently serving in her second term of office as Representative from Washington, D.C. She received her B.A. from Antioch College in Ohio and an M.A. and law degree from Yale. A tenured professor of law at Georgetown University, she chaired the Equal Employment Opportunity Commission under President Jimmy Carter (1977–1981). Even before seeking elective office, she had been named one of the 100 most important women in America and one of the most powerful women in Washington. She is a charter member of the Urban Caucus and is also a member of the Congressional Black Caucus and the Congressional Caucus on Women's Issues, among others. She is the author of the federal guidelines on sexual harassment in the workplace.

Following Clarence Thomas's confirmation, Ms. *magazine asked five African-American feminists to analyze what had happened—to women and to the black community. The preceding selection by Anita Hill focused on harassment itself. Congresswoman Norton's comments provide an additional perspective.*

I SELDOM VISIT MY COLLEAGUES ON THE SENATE side, although the Senate is a short walk from the House, and you can use the Capitol's long hallways or its Byzantine underground tunnels to get there. But on October 8, 1991, seven of us who are congresswomen took a walk to the Senate. Most of the 20 Democratic congresswomen also would have walked, but some remained on the House floor where the Republican men were raising parliamentary points against the one-minute speeches we were trying to make in support of Professor Anita Hill. The Republican men argued that House precedent barred discussion of proceedings in "the other body." They could raise their points of order if they liked, but nothing could keep us from reaching "the other body" in the most direct way. So we walked.

We were in step with U.S. women and men, who jammed the Senate and the House phones like nothing in memory, to stop the clock. It was incredible, but it was happening. The Senate was going to a vote in the face of a serious charge that could have two colossal consequences. If checked, it could disqualify Clarence Thomas for a seat on the Supreme Court. If not checked, it could strain the Court itself. An unresolved charge of sexual harassment would have followed Thomas to the Court, spreading the stain on an institution that must be spotless.

The best evidence of Hill's personal credibility was the desperation of Thomas' supporters to push for a vote without looking into her charges. Her press conference revealed a woman of awesome credibility, not to mention brains, dignity, attractiveness of person, and a personality so compelling that the official Thomas advocates never dared to attack her personally.

If Anita Hill was so credible, why did the public disbelieve her? Why did her revelations seem to drive Thomas' support up, capping her charges with irony? Or was it so ironic, after all?

If these allegations, made by a remarkably believable person with nothing to gain, had come out in the ordinary course of the hearings, they almost surely would have ended the nomination. Instead, the outcome was controlled by the law of unintended consequences—the leak caused an effect that was the reverse of what apparently was desired. The last-minute leak of lewd sex-based allegations during a hard-fought nomination gave the taint of unfairness to everything that followed. All of this was a major factor in saving Thomas. He should be grateful for small favors.

The leak that almost buried the nomination was universally seen as offensive, on that point uniting Thomas proponents and opponents alike. Disastrously, the leak also put the Judiciary Committee Democrats on the defensive, because their prior opposition to Thomas appeared to confer a motive. Moreover, Hill burst like a meteor with testimony much worse in the sexual crudeness it attributed to Thomas than anticipated. The testimony, said to betray the inner sex life of a man on his way to the Court, deeply embarrassed the public.

After all, the American people are not fools. During any normal hearing process, those who saw Hill (most did not; Thomas got to testify during evening hours) could figure out who had a motive to lie. Instead, the public was asked to respond with instant reflection to sexual crudeness so marginal most had never heard of the expressions used. Worse, a response against Thomas might seem to *condone* the leak through which the boorish pornographic conversation was revealed. In the minds of many Americans, Hill's charges and the sexual images they portrayed were not so much overcome as they were suppressed.

The leak sealed the matter for many African Americans, who were always the key to the success or failure of the nomination. Race had been responsible for the nomination and only race could undo it. Thus it is a mistake to read the outcome of the hearings as a comment on feminism; it is a comment on the continuing potency of race to push all else aside. Not surprisingly, with a nomination of a black man to the Supreme Court at stake, race trumped sex.

Thomas understood very well that his nomination was anchored to race, and that to save himself he must cling to that anchor. Faced with a black woman who was too honest to use race and too believable to be denied, Thomas reached below the belt. That Anita Hill was also black did not count for much; she declined to use her race (or her gender, for that matter) to enhance her charges, while Thomas made race his central, indeed his only, defense.

Though he had spent his entire career criticizing blacks for ascribing their condition to race, Thomas reached for a racial rock and angrily hurled it at the monolith that comprised the Senate Judiciary Committee. To many blacks the committee looked like nothing so much as an all-white jury. Thomas took no chance that this symbolism would be missed. Declining subtle racial allusions, he brought race front and center with brazenly undiluted charges of racism—"high-tech lynching" and the rest—sending the message, especially to blacks, that the leak and the public hearing had come *because* he was black. Thomas' charges lit a racial flame, the functional equivalent of screaming "Fire!" in a crowded theater.

Until Anita Hill's revelations, Thomas had been protected by his race, and by skillful administration handling of the Pin Point, Georgia, roots story to cover up his record. That chilling record began to come alive in documentation from witness after witness during the hearings: Thomas' career-long hostility to civil rights laws and to much of the current interpretation of the Bill of Rights. Slowly the man's own animus had begun to seep through the gauze that had seemed to seal off his government record and writings. In a New York *Times* poll three days after the first of Hill's revelations were published, only 36 percent of blacks said Thomas should be confirmed, down from 61 percent in September—when all that most blacks had known about Thomas was that he too was black.

By the end, most African Americans did not support Thomas, and the nomination barely survived—by a vote of 52 to 48, the closest since 1888. But southern senators, who were the decisive swing votes, did not get a clear enough message to oppose Thomas from southern blacks. Why not?

In addition to the racial confusion deliberately sown by Thomas, two motivations account for the black response.

First, the leak had a particularly deep effect. Victimized historically by racism and unfair tactics, some blacks found the leak especially suspect. More important, it reinforced the notion of racial dirty tricks. "They" (whoever was "behind" Anita Hill) came after the black guy just as he was about to cross the finish line. Historically conditioned to identify with black victims, some blacks felt the leak reinforced Thomas' charge that "they" were out to get him because he was an "uppity black."

Second, given a history impossible to ignore, many saw Thomas entirely through black-tinted glasses. Many blacks believed he was all they could expect or get from a conservative president who had vetoed one civil rights bill and was loudly promising to block yet another. For African Americans, the Supreme Court has been both the first and the last line of defense. In the lifetime of most, the Court had recognized rights the other branches of government had denied and had saved rights that Americans historically could not be trusted to ensure. Given this history, not having a black on the Supreme Court was unthinkable. Never mind that the Court seemed bent on marching backward. All the more reason for the appearance—and the hope—of racial fairness.

What was seldom stated, and what many blacks did not consider, is that an all-white Supreme Court probably could not long be left that way. Racism is still a salient part of this country's life and the Court's central role in its unraveling is too recent to be put aside. (Today, of course, the Court poses the opposite danger, as it retracts civil rights laws, most recently requiring the Congress to reenact the basic job discrimination statute, Title VII of the 1964 Civil Rights Act.) An all-white Court would lack the appearance of elementary fairness. If not this president, then surely the next one would have chosen an African American.

But race, and the race of the only nominee blacks could imagine from *this* president, blocked notions that there would be a better day. What if another black was not appointed for 40 years? Even some blacks who distrusted Thomas and others who opposed him on his record saw a bird in the hand. The far more ominous and obvious possibility receded: that Thomas could *block* for a very long time the appointment of a black in the tradition of the black legal experience. That of course is what has happened. Blacks who supported Thomas focused on the black nominee, hoping that he would allow, if not his racial identity, at least his racial memories, to overcome his expressed ideology.

Nothing can disturb the shining character of Anita Hill. In this period when high moral values are preached more than practiced, Anita Hill prevailed. She emerged with enhanced stature while Thomas was diminished. Most of us know from personal experience whereof she speaks, but few of us have the courage to attempt what she did. We are in her debt.

The African American community has been left with an old dilemma. We saw it first when the Fifteenth Amendment enfranchised black men but not black women and led Sojourner Truth to oppose it. It is race that has defined the black experience in this country. Everything else has been considered secondary.

Hill unintentionally brought forward the race-sex tension that is unavoidable when ethnicity is the mark of oppression. Color, country, culture, and language define an entire group; sex only half of it. This is a country where racism has been the longest standing national neurosis. Is it any wonder that it sometimes has been difficult for the black community to come to grips with its internal complexity? Some believe that even a concession to gender could threaten the solidarity necessary to resist and defeat racism. Nevertheless, after some initial confusion in the 1970s, many black women embraced feminism and women's rights. This proved far less difficult than had been imagined, in part because the two identities seldom competed on the same stage at the same time. This time the two emerged together when the prospect was all-white justice. It was not a fair fight.

Nevertheless, the majority of African Americans got past the race-sex confusion inherent in this conflict. Just before the confirmation vote, Thomas' support in the black community had risen, but only by four points, to 40 percent, and then only because it seemed to be a take-it-or-leave-it proposition. Blacks did not squarely veto Thomas, but whites carried Thomas over.

Anita Hill was everybody's daughter, every community's model student, every sister. At the same time, she was an enigma in the African American community, still struggling with racism, still searching for its rightful place in its own country, still sorting out race and sex and class. Anita was ahead of a time she has helped define—a time to be black and a woman.

Homeless in America

Jonathan Kozol

Jonathan Kozol was born in Boston, educated at Harvard, and awarded a Rhodes Scholarship to Magdalen College, Oxford. In 1964 he moved from Harvard Square into a poor black neighborhood of Boston and became a fourth grade teacher in the Boston public schools. Since then he has devoted himself to issues of education and social justice.

Combining teaching with activism, he taught at South Boston High during the city's desegregation crisis. Working with black and Hispanic parents, he helped set up a storefront learning center that became a model for many others.

Kozol's biographical note recalls: A few days before Christmas 1985, Kozol spent an evening at a homeless shelter in New York. Nightlong conversations with the mothers and children who befriended him led him to remain there for much of the winter, and finally to the writing of Rachel and Her Children: Homeless Families in America, *a portrayal of the day-to-day life struggles of the poorest people in America—living only one block from Fifth Avenue within our nation's richest city.*

Kozol's book Death at an Early Age, *a description of his first year as a teacher, was published in 1967 and received the 1968 National Book Award in Science, Philosophy and Religion. Other works include* Savage Inequalities: Children in America's Schools, Free Schools, The Night Is Dark and I Am Far from Home, *and* On Being a Teacher.

This reading gives flesh to the concept of "the feminization of poverty." We must not forget that the majority of America's poor are women and their children. The women's movement fails if it does not address itself to women's poverty.

IN TIME OF WAR, CIVILIANS SOMETIMES ARE OBLIGED to join a forced march with invading or retreating armies. Many people die along the way. Children and women are often the first victims.

The forced march undertaken by unsheltered children and their parents in New York is not often made on foot, more often by the public-transit system. Most survive: few without incurring an incalculable damage. At journey's end lies little comfort but a modernized internment.

At every step along the road they face the eyes of an impatient populace. Their transit papers will be subway tokens. Their rations will be food stamps, restaurant allowances, meal tickets to soup kitchens. Instead of visas they will be provided with referral slips that indicate to an anonymous and overburdened welfare system whether or not they meet requirements for sanctuary. Not orchestrated human love but punishment for having failed to navigate the economic mine field of America will be awarded to them as they pass the gates of every relocation center. Like displaced persons, each will be assigned a number.

References to prisons and to camps for displaced persons appear repeatedly in language used by homeless people. The theme is one of being under siege. "There is a sense of terror," says a man whose family has lived at the Martinique for several years. "But the physical fears are not the worst. There is this sense of darkness and foreboding. Doors are always banging late at night. They're made of metal and it echoes through the halls. It's hard to sleep. You feel like you're in jail."

The feeling of internment may be reinforced by rituals of lining up, of having one's room number written down, of receiving one serving—and one serving only—of a desperately needed meal. People who, one month before, may have been strong and full of pride are humbled rapidly. You see it in the corridor outside the ballroom of the Martinique at noon, when adults with their children wait to file past a table to receive a plate of food. "You can always tell the family . . . that's new," observes a priest who works with homeless families in Wisconsin. "Their heads are always down. . . . They're very grateful for everything. They eat very quickly, and then they quickly disappear."

A mother of three children in the Hotel Carter tells me this: She was a teacher's aide, had worked for three years with retarded children, and was living doubled up with relatives when the death of one and marriage of another forced her to the streets. She's been living in the Carter for two years.

"My rent allowance is $270. Places that I see start at $350. Even if you could pay it, landlords do not want you if you're homeless. 'Where do you live?' I say the Carter. That's the end of it. It's hard to do it. You psyche yourself. They want to check you out. You feel ashamed.

"It's the same with public school. The teacher asks: 'Where do you live?' You say the Carter. Right away they put you in a slot. Jennifer is in the fourth grade. She has had four teachers in one year. Teachers keep quitting. Too many kids for them to handle. They can't teach. So I have to see my kids losing their years. Do they put the homeless children into categories? 'Course they do! They know which ones they are."

Food is short: "By the eighteenth of the month I'm running out. I have to borrow. They have got to eat. When we're low we live on macaroni and french fries. I can make a lot from two potatoes. When you're running low you learn to stretch. I don't have the money to buy meat. Even if I did, there's no refrigerator. It won't keep.

"Christmas last year, we stayed in our room. Christmas this year, we'll be here again. It's a lonely time for everybody. I do what I can to keep the other women up. There are adults here who come to me. They think I'm stronger than I am. They're under stress. I'll talk them down. Do you know what scares them most? It's when the rent is due. You go to your welfare office. You're afraid there's a mistake. It happens for no reason. I can write but I cannot write all the things that come out of my heart."

The city pays the Hotel Carter $63 a night to keep her family in this room. Tourists who stay in newly renovated rooms on higher floors of the hotel pay $35 for a room of comparable size. The renovated rooms are clean and neat, with color television sets and air conditioners and new quilts and linens. The rooms for homeless families have roaches, water seeping through the ceilings, missing window panes, holes in the floor. The homeless families are restricted to three floors where they will not be seen by tourists.

"In the morning I'm up at six. The children go to school at eight. Some mornings there's no food. I give them a quarter if I have a quarter. They can buy a bag of chips. After school I give them soup—or bread with peanut butter. Cooking does pose certain dangers in a place like this. You're careful with a fry pan in this room. If you're using oil and it catches fire, it will go right up the wall."

These are the routine concerns of homeless families. Children in this building face an added injury. The management does not want them to be seen in front of the hotel. But they have to be outside to meet their school bus in the morning. They also have to be dropped off when they return. This is the solution: There is a rear exit, used primarily for trash collection. The exit can be reached through a back corridor. It opens on Forty-second Street next to a shop that sells drug paraphernalia in a block of pornographic movie theaters. This is the place the children wait to meet their bus.

"They told my kids: 'You have to use the back. You're not allowed to use the front.' They herd them down that corridor to the rear door. It doesn't hurt so much that they would want *me* to be hidden. It does hurt that they would want my children to be hid."

Do children know that they are viewed as undesirables? Using the same exit that is used by the hotel to throw away the trash is pretty vivid. They leave with the trash. Perhaps they carry some of its stench with them into school. "We aren't going to get away with this," said Daniel Moynihan. "We are *not* going to get away with this." The twenty-first century, he said, "is going to punish us. . . ." Perhaps he's right. The time of punishment may not be deferred so long.

A woman living on the tenth floor of the Martinique is told that she has cancer. She calls me late at night in Boston. It is, of course, the kind of news that terrifies all people, even in the best of economic situations. Most of us at least have systems of support. We live near neighbors. Some of us have family members near at hand; sometimes they are close enough to drive to our homes, sit up and talk with us, pack our clothes, our children's clothes, and take us back with them into their safer world. They can bring us to the hospital. If the information is unclear, they can bring us to another doctor to confirm the diagnosis, to be sure.

When you are homeless there are no supports.

Mrs. Andrews is forty-two. The first time that we met, before Thanksgiving, she told me she had worked for seventeen years as a secretary and bookkeeper—nine of those years for one firm. She'd lived in the same house for seven years.

How did she end up in the Martinique?

Like many people in this situation, she had been hit with two catastrophes in sequence. First, she had learned that she had cancer in her large intestine. Hospitalized for removal of a part of her intestine, she had to have a hysterectomy as well. Three successive operations coincided with a time in which the man to whom she had been married thirteen years fell into depression, caused by difficulties of his own. He had had a prior drinking problem and it now became much worse. Debilitated by her medical concerns, she had no strength to offer him support. He, in turn, became destructive and disorganized. She had to leave their home.

She had three children: two daughters and one son. With the breakup of her household and her inability to work for several months, she found her economic status dropping very fast. She turned to welfare. One night, six months after her third and final operation, she was sitting with her children in the office of the Church Street EAU.

For several nights the city is unable to assign her to a shelter. When a place is found, it is the Hotel Carter. Bad as it is, she never gets beyond the door. When she arrives at 1:00 A.M., the manager says he can't accommodate a family of four. Why was she sent here? She is too dazed to ask. At 2:00 A.M., she gets back on the subway and returns to the same EAU she has just left. On her return, a social worker seems annoyed. He asks: "Then you refuse this placement?" Although she explains what has transpired, she is forced to sign a paper formally refusing placement at the hotel which has just refused her.

I have asked her about this several times. "I had to *sign* the paper."

Mrs. Andrews is articulate, well organized, and neatly dressed. If this woman could be savaged with so little hesitation, how much more savage is the treatment meted out to women who don't have her middle-class appearance and do not display the style and articulation with which social workers might identify?

"We spent another seven days sitting in the welfare center, 9:00 to 5:00, and every evening 6:00 to 8:00 A.M., trying to sleep there at the EAU. All we had to eat that week was peanut butter, jelly, and cheese sandwiches." Not wanting to exaggerate, she adds: "They gave my children juice and little packages of milk."

After seven days she's given a week's placement at the Holland Hotel on West Forty-second Street, a few blocks from the Carter. This hotel, which has been likened by the *New York Times* to "a kiddie park designed by Hogarth and the Marquis de Sade," was cited in 1985 for nearly 1,000 health and building violations. The owner was later found to have been taking in $6 million yearly, half of which was profit.

At the time that Mrs. Andrews was sent by the city to the Holland, part of the building housed nonhomeless tenants. Only certain deteriorated floors were used to house the homeless. The fourteenth floor, to which the Andrews were assigned for their first night of sleep in thirteen days, had no running water. "Even the toilet had no water," Mrs. Andrews says. "We had to carry buckets to a bar across the street. There was a line of homeless families waiting to bring water back to the hotel. Only one elevator worked. You had to wait an hour."

Two days later, unable to face this any longer, she goes with her children to the EAU. There she is asked to sign another form refusing placement. " 'We gave you a room. You turned it down,' they said." She's given a referral slip and told that she must bring this to her welfare center. At the welfare center she presents the paper to her welfare worker, sits in a chair and waits until the office closes, then is sent back to the EAU to sit up in another chair until the morning. In this way, she and her children pass the next twenty-seven days.

During this time, Mrs. Andrews' fourteen-year-old daughter, Carol, becomes ill. She develops pain and swelling in her abdomen. Examination leads to the discovery of a tumor on her kidney. The kidney has to be removed. Also removed in the same operation are the ovary and fallopian tube on her right side. Carol's doctor tells her mother that she must not be allowed to sit up in a welfare office. Armed with a letter to this effect signed by the physician, the family goes back to the welfare center, then—after another day of waiting—to the EAU, only to repeat this ritual for three more days.

After forty-five days of homelessness, the Andrews are sent at 6:00 A.M., on a day in late September

1984, to a small room without a closet but with four beds in the Martinique Hotel. Seven months later they are moved into a slightly larger room two floors below. It is in this room that we first meet in 1986.

The room has the smell of fresh paint on the day I visit. Also, a new door has been installed. These changes, she believes, were made throughout the building and were prompted by some pressure from the Office of the Mayor. Unfortunately, the keys distributed to residents to match the locks on the new doors were incorrectly made. They are interchangeable in many cases. Mrs. Andrews has been robbed four times.

When we meet, she talks for hours of her fears. Fear is plainly written in her eyes. Forty-five days of destitution, sickness, subway travel, waiting lines, followed by two years of residence in the Martinique, have worn away much of her confidence.

"My mother and father are deceased. Except for the children I have only my grandparents. My grandmother is in a wheelchair. My grandfather is ninety-four years old. I pray for them. When they are gone I have nobody but the kids. I was not religious when I came here. People become religious here," she says, "because each day that you survive seems like a miracle."

Mrs. Andrews' husband has been in and out of psychiatric wards throughout the past two years. Her former boss has told her that he wants her back. She's reluctant to accept the job until she saves some money. If she returns to work she loses welfare and can't stay in the hotel. But welfare rules forbid her to save money. Any significant savings pose the risk of being cut from all support. So she cannot start a bank account in order to prepare for the unlikely chance of moving into an apartment. Even if she had her old job back, she couldn't pay a month's rent and deposit and security, buy furniture, or pay for health insurance. The city is said to have a program that sometimes assists with some of these expenses; few families have been given this assistance. Mrs. Andrews has not heard of such a program.

"I don't eat. I'd stopped smoking back in 1983. Now I smoke three packs a day."

Only in state prisons have I seen so many people craving cigarettes. She lights one cigarette after another, presses it out, looks for a match, hunts for another pack.

"Food is very scarce right now, worse than any time since I've been here." She had received $185 a month in food stamps on June 1. That was cut to $63 in August. It will be cut again to $44 in January. "I have trouble sleeping when we're short of food. I cannot sleep if I don't know that I can feed them breakfast."

Food-stamp cuts have forced her for the first time to accept free bags of food from local charities. "On Saturdays I go to St. Francis Church on Thirty-first Street. Tuesdays, I go to St. John's." In compensation for her loss of food stamps—a net loss of $122 each month—she receives an increase of $8.75 in restaurant allowance every two weeks from the city. Her room rent at the Martinique is about $2,000. Her rent allowance for a permanent apartment, if she were to find one, is $270.

She forces herself to eat one meal a day. Her children, knowing of her cancer history, have tried to get her to stop smoking. She wants to know: "How will I get them out of this?" I want to know: Why do we do this to her?

Her phone call brings me back to talk with her when cancer is again suspected, this time on her skin, just under her left eye. At the hospital, the spot in question has been tested. The results are positive. The doctor, she says, is also concerned about a lump that has developed on her throat. She has to go into the hospital but puts it off two weeks.

On New Year's Eve she phones again. She's going to go into the hospital. She'll have to leave her kids alone. She needs some cash so they can buy necessities until she's home. I send a postal money order for $250. The post office tells me: "It's as good as cash. Any postal clerk will honor it."

The money order is not honored. Even with identification, she is told that she needs someone else to "vouch" for her.

A friend in Manhattan helps me. He calls someone he knows at the post office and she finally gets the cash. She is embarrassed by the trouble she believes she's caused me. On the telephone she tells me that conditions in the building have grown worse. "There's been no light in the elevator for a month. People use cigarette lighters. Or you ride up in the dark. I can't face it. I walk up ten floors."

When she gets out of the hospital, she has good news. The spot on her face and lump on her throat turned out to be benign. By now, however, sleeplessness and fear have left her drained. She's also feeling the results of the last round of food-stamp cuts. Everyone in the hotel, she says, is short of food. The president this month requests a billion-dollar cut in food stamps and in child-nutrition funds for 1987.

The city, meanwhile, has run into shortages of shelter space. The shortage has been so acute that twenty-nine families have been sent to a hotel in Newark. The *Times* reports, however, that an HRA spokesperson "said the situation is by no means critical. . . ."

Government is not to blame for Mrs. Andrews' illnesses, her cancer surgery, her panic, her compulsive smoking. Government is certainly to blame for leaving a sick woman homeless more than forty days. It is to blame for sending her at 1:00 A.M. to a hotel from which she will be turned away. It is to blame for making any human being in New York City carry buckets from the fourteenth floor of an unsafe hotel in order to fetch water at a tavern.

The president, too, is certainly to blame for terrorizing women with the fear of hunger. He is no less to blame for the complacent ignorance that he displays when asked to comment on these matters. "If even one American child is forced to go to bed hungry at night . . . ," he says, "that is a national tragedy. We are too generous a people to allow this. . . ."

We are not too generous. The president is wrong. We have been willing to see hundreds of thousands of children go to bed, if they have any beds at all, too hungry to sleep and sometimes too weak to rise on the next morning to await the bus for school.

"Now you're hearing all kinds of horror stories," the president said on an earlier occasion, this time in Minnesota, "about the people that are going to be thrown out in the snow to hunger and [to] die of cold and so forth. . . . We haven't cut a single budget. . . ."

Hunger, cold and snow apart, what of this presidential reference to the budget? Dorothy Wickenden, in a *New Republic* article published in 1985, summarizes administration cuts affecting children of poor families in the previous four years: housing assistance ($1.8 billion); AFDC ($4.8 billion); child nutrition ($5.2 billion); food stamps ($6.8 billion); low-income energy assistance ($700 million). In housing, she writes, the Reagan administration "appears to have decided to renounce once and for all any meaningful federal support." HUD's budget authority to help additional low-income families "was cut from $30 billion to $11 billion" in the first Reagan term. "In his fiscal 1986 budget, he proposes to chop that by an additional 95 percent, to $499 million."

The president's first budget director, David Stockman, was noted for his straightforward speech: "I don't think people are entitled to services. I don't believe that there is any entitlement, any basic right to legal services or any other kind of services. . . . I don't accept that equality is a moral principle."

Will future generations read these words with pride?

"When men confront each other as men, as abstract universals," writes Ignatieff, "one with power, the other with none, then man is certain to behave as a wolf to his own kind." The claim of the less powerful—that because they are human they deserve to live—"is the weakest claim that people can make to each other: It is the claim addressed to anyone, and therefore to no one. When there is no family, no tribe, no state, no city to hear . . . , only the storm hears it."

For thousands of homeless people in New York, as in most cities of America during this era of acceptable abstraction, it is probably not true that only the storm can hear their pleas, but it is frequently the case that only the storm answers.

Stockman's theme—no rights, no services—finds application on the grand scale in withholding of essential funds for life support by government; but the idea, once established, finds expression in a multitude of small indignities that homeless people undergo day after day in places where one person exercises power over hundreds who have none.

The guards assigned to offer shelter residents some safety, for example, are frequently only a trifle better off than they; but, as in a prison where a favored inmate often brutalizes those from whom he can dissociate himself only by an overzealous application of the regulations set by his superiors, these are often the most vicious faces of authority that homeless people must confront.

November 27, 1986: On holidays like Thanksgiving, people in a homeless shelter face unusual depression. Those who are most fortunate may be invited elsewhere—some to have dinner with their family, if they have a family with the means to share a meal. Others may eat in one of those huge armories in which a charitable group, under the eyes of TV cameras, offers them a dinner with something the press invariably describes in a November formula as "all the fixings."

Many, however, never get the "fixings"—neither from their families nor from charitable groups.

They spend the day alone within their rooms. Sometimes a mother or grandmother who could not provide a meal at home brings something she has cooked and packaged carefully. Sometimes a friend appears.

Waiting here with about a dozen other people, most of them family members, I watch the guards hunched over at their guard post with their squawking intercoms hooked to their belts. I wonder why they seem so much more threatening today than usual. Generally their distaste for the job, or for the residents, is conveyed with lassitude; today it's energized. Is it because there are so few officials, volunteers or crisis workers to observe them? Do they, who have to work on holidays, regret the fact that others might enjoy an hour's respite from the colorless routine?

A woman sitting next to me has come from Brooklyn with a dinner wrapped in foil for her daughter and grandchildren. She arrived at 2:00 P.M. At three, she is still waiting.

"We're short of men," a guard remarks to no one in particular. "Holidays, we send up messages once every hour."

As the minutes tick away and people wait for recognition from the guards, she presses the corners of the foil together in a futile effort to preserve the warmth.

A well-dressed woman—middle-aged, soft-spoken—enters the lobby from the street and asks one of the guards to tell her sister that she's here.

"Fifteen-seven gets no visitors," the guard replies.

The woman begins a complicated explanation. She's here to take her sister to their mother's bed. Their mother is in the hospital. Her sister doesn't know. Their mother was taken ill last night.

"Fifteen-seven's on restriction," says the guard. Fixed in his meager station of authority, he seems reluctant to give up an opportunity to heighten panic, to create a needless little patch of pain.

She tells the guard she doesn't need to visit, only to send up a message. But the guard appears unmoved. "You cause us trouble," he says, "you got no rights."

"Would you tell her that her mother's ill?"

The guard replies: "She don't get no messages. Not until she gets her check."

I'm not sure those are the rules; but how is she to know and, even if she does, what can be done? She is about to speak again but he anticipates her words: "Don't block the desk. The waiting area is over there."

She looks confused. Does this mean he's relented? Will he send up the message? Why does he direct her to the waiting area? She's a black woman wearing an old-fashioned net around her hair. The guards are here presumably to keep out prostitutes and people who sell drugs. She doesn't look like either.

Another woman, white and elderly, comes in, makes her request, and is instructed to sit down. A Puerto Rican man gets up and offers her his chair. It has a jagged plastic edge; the back has been torn off. There are, in all, six chairs, one broken stool.

Across the lobby on the wall beside the elevator alcove is a poster about crack. Next to it, a crudely penciled sign I saw a year ago: "ABSOLUTELY NO GRAFFITI WILL BE TOLERATED." A young woman, heavily made up, walks past the desk on red stiletto heels. When she doesn't answer an obscene joke from a guard who seems to know her, he runs after her, pulls out his nightstick, and jams it between her legs. She pushes him away and heads off to the stairway in the rear.

All around me: tired, tired faces. The silence drips like water from a rainspout on the back porch of a house that someone left ten years before. Time stops. A damp and dreary afternoon.

"You cause us trouble, you go no rights." But even if you cause no trouble, you do not have many rights. The right to talk to a reporter is effectively denied. The publication of essential legal information, even in a casual newsletter, is prevented. I write in my notebook: "If we want to be sadistic, if we want to do it right, why not also take away their citizenship—withhold their right to vote?" Then I recall that this too was attempted but did not succeed. Court action finally restored the franchise for the homeless families of New York. But the idea remains attractive and is still proposed by policy advisors as another means of rendering dependent status undesirable.

"For adults, the stigma would be institutionalized," in Charles Murray's words, "by taking away the right to vote from anyone who had no source of income except welfare. . . ." Denial of the franchise, Murray has proposed, "would be an official stamp" of second-class status. While recognizing that "the balance" of this and other suggestions he has made to stigmatize poor single mothers "would probably be negative," Murray argues nonetheless that denial of the right to vote makes sense in that recipients of public funds should have no role in their disbursement. Notions like these, no matter how whimsically or speculatively offered, don't remain inert. Uncivilized contemplation is contagious.

"Fifteen-seven's got no rights."

The guard transmits the values of a decade that has brutalized him too. He doesn't even say the woman's name. For him, as for New York, she's been reduced to something that can be abstracted and computerized—a disobedient but expensive number.

I have not been in the Martinique for several months. The circumstances that brought me here today are rather special. Mrs. Allesandro knows I live alone and am unmarried and do not have children. She invited me to join her family for Thanksgiving dinner. I have been anticipating this for several days. As I learn later, she has gone to a great deal of trouble. It isn't easy to prepare a good Thanksgiving dinner on a hot plate. But a woman who's survived for over seventy years has had a lot of time to figure out some ways to make the best of hopeless situations. The guards have simply managed to destroy her happiness a little.

By the time they send the message up it's after four. The food is cold. The kids are hungry. While she warms the dinner, I go with her son to tell the woman in room 1507 that her mother's in the hospital and that her sister's waiting for her in the lobby.

Persistent Welfare Stereotypes

Renu Nahata

Renu Nahata is the administrative director of FAIR, which stands for Fairness & Accuracy in Reporting, a national media watch group which offers well-documented criticism of the media in an effort to correct bias and imbalance.

Consider these brief comments in the light of the previous selection and direct your feminist consciousness to the question: "Why do these stereotypes persist?"

"THERE IS NOW A FAIRLY WIDESPREAD FEELING, JUSTIFIED or not, that some welfare recipients are not doing enough to get off the dole." Thus began **ABC World News Tonight**'s "American Agenda" segment on welfare reform (4/14/92). While Peter Jennings' opening statement acknowledges that there may be disparities between public perception and reality, this segment and many others continue to rely heavily on widely held misconceptions about welfare.

With few exceptions, the mainstream media have portrayed the issue of welfare in terms and images not too far removed from Ronald Reagan's "welfare queens." Following news coverage, one might believe that most welfare recipients are black, unwed, unemployed, teenage mothers of several children, living in the inner city. She might be, as one article suggested, "a walking statistic: a single mother of five who dropped out of high school at 17, pregnant with her first child." (**Newsday,** 9/23/90). But the statistic she represents is quite small, since only two percent of all poor children live in such households (**Washington Post,** 6/3/91).

In fact, as Jack Smith acknowledged on **This Week With David Brinkley** (4/12/92), "most recipients of welfare are white, not black; most live in the suburbs, not the inner city; most want to work and stay on welfare less than two years." According to a Health and Human Services report, the average number of children in AFDC (Aid to Families with Dependent Children) families is only 1.9—well under the national average.

Whether "justified or not," several states have based their reform measures on the perception that the welfare system's failures derive from women abusing its benefits. In response, state legislatures have taken aim at those receiving assistance, while media have further fueled these concerns by offering up a parade of mothers, unwed, unrepentant and most often black.

The Wisconsin program, considered a model for other states, reduces benefits for a second child

Renu Nahata, "Persistent Welfare Stereotypes," *EXTRA!* Special Issue, 1992, is reprinted with permission of *FAIR/EXTRA,* 130 West 25th Street, N.Y., N.Y. 10001.

and eliminates them for a third, on the assumption that increased benefits will encourage women to have more children. However, according to the House Ways and Means Committee's 1991 Green Book, the average size of AFDC families has been decreasing steadily for 20 years. More to the point, the Center on Budget and Policy Priorities argues that there is no significant relationship between AFDC benefit levels and birth rates. Although these statistics are readily available, most news reports about such welfare "reforms" fail to use them.

ABC World News' April 14 segment on welfare relied on the "decline in values" critique made by many of welfare's detractors. Correspondent Rebecca Chase tried to demonstrate the corrosive social impact of welfare by interviewing several black mothers, most of them unwed and in their teens, one a mother of six who has been on welfare for the past 20 years. The two questions put to these women were, "How many of you are married?" and "Do you feel like you owe the taxpayers anything for them helping you support your children?"

Chase seemed to find the moral dilemma of unmarried motherhood, and the issue of gratitude for public support, far more compelling than soaring black unemployment (particularly for males), absence of affordable childcare and discriminatory hiring practices. Instead of addressing these kinds of issues, poverty and welfare are studied through the narrow lens of individual responsibility and moral double standards.

The same lens is used by **U.S. News and World Report**'s David Whitman (4/20/92), who approvingly describes the latest attitude toward those on welfare as the "new paternalism," i.e., "rewarding them for doing right and fining them for doing wrong." Given these absolute terms, Whitman's conclusion is not surprising: "No federal intervention . . . is likely to prompt legions of unwed, chronic welfare mothers to marry the fathers of their children."

This Week With David Brinkley (4/12/92), in a lengthy segment on Wisconsin's reform experiment, made an effort to dispel long-standing myths. But the show managed to undermine those facts by loading both the taped segment and the discussion that followed with repeated images of and references to urban blacks. Despite one guest's effort to raise the question of incentive in the absence of employment opportunities, larger societal factors lost ground to George Will's concern over "illegitimacy in our cities."

Even while attempting to dispel "social myths" about welfare, an Ellen Goodman column (**Boston Globe,** 4/16/92) focused on poor women with a sense of "entitlement" as the main problem with welfare. "Americans instinctively believe that the welfare poor should play by the same rules as the rest of us. A family that works does not get a raise for having a child. Why then should a family that doesn't work?"

The headline chosen by the **Globe** for Goodman's column, "Welfare Mothers With an Attitude," played up the worst aspects of the piece. And the graphic that accompanied the article, while apparently intended satirically, could just as easily be read as endorsing the stereotype of the African-American welfare mother with too many kids and too much money. At some point, repetition of stereotypical imagery merely hardens perceptions, rendering corrective caveats effectively useless.

Although most polls show that Americans still support public spending on the poor, James Patterson, a historian of social policy at Brown University, points out that "people support programs when they imagine the beneficiaries look a lot like themselves" (**New York Times,** 5/17/92). As if to substantiate this premise, just one month earlier the **Times** (4/13/92) ran "From Middle Class to Jobless: A Sense of Pride Is Shattered."

The primary concern of this article was the suffering, fear and loss of pride felt by recently unemployed white-color workers (illustrated by a photograph of a white accountant). Mounting welfare rolls in predominantly middle-class areas like Westchester, New York inspired the writer to feel compassion. In this case, the rise in chronic unemployment, family breakdowns, vanishing spouses, substance abuse and domestic violence are seen to stem from economic circumstances rather than vaguely defined social pathologies.

However, most welfare recipients we see in the media are black. And most efforts to reform welfare are directed at inner cities. There is little room for compassion here. The panacea generally offered for inner-city poverty and family breakdowns comes most often in the form of imposing "values."

Lawrence Mead, the author of an influential new book, *The New Politics of Poverty: The Nonworking Poor in America* demonstrates this tendency. One of the main sources in the **U.S. News** article about the "new paternalism," Mead argued in a **New York Times** op-ed (5/19/92) that "if poor adults behaved rationally, they would seldom be poor for long in the first place. Opportunity is more available than the will to seize it." Child care, he believes, can usually be found if one only looks for it, and "the ghetto mentality," more than racism or any other factor, is the main cause of unemployment. His solution to these personal failings is "a more authoritative social policy in which the needy are told how to live instead of merely being subsidized."

When President Bush can blame the L.A. uprising on Lyndon Johnson's Great Society programs, the official view is not far from Mead's. Stories like "White House Links Riots to Welfare" (**New York Times,** 5/5/92) display a certain skepticism, yet media assumptions about welfare and poverty—focusing on inner-city black women, their supposed unchecked fertility and lack of "individual responsibility"—differ little from the administration's. Despite the fact that most media outlets recognize the prevalence of stereotypes, few seem willing to give up those stereotypes as the basis for their coverage.

The Politics of Women and Medical Care

Hilary Salk, Wendy Sanford, Norma Swenson and Judith Dickson Luce
With special thanks to David Banta, Gene Bishop, Mary Fillmore, Mary Howell, Judy Norsigian, Sheryl Ruzek and Karen Wolf. 1992 Update by Amy Alpern, Robin Blatt, David Clarke, Judy Norsigian, Kathy Simmonds, Norma Swenson, and Nancy Worcester.

We usually do not think of the medical care system either as an institution or as an industry, but it is both. It affects the quality of our lives as profoundly as any other, and yet women have little influence over the practice of health care in America—delivery of services, costs, research, laws, or medical training. The argument in this selection is plain: Because women constitute the majority of workers and consumers of the health-care industry, we must play a major role in overseeing policy.

The American Medical Care System

I've repeatedly described my symptoms to physicians—disconcerting symptoms to say the least: sudden menses cessation, elevated temperature, weight loss, anxiety, extreme fatigue, nausea, joint pain, vertigo—but the doctors have made only the catch-all diagnosis of "menopause," unsupported by any testing. They advised me to go into counseling, expecting me to "live with it," despite the fact that I have told them that the symptoms seem extreme, are increasing and have impaired and even curtailed my work, my studies, my personal relationships.

From a letter to the Women's Health Collective in Providence, Rhode Island:

I think you would have been proud of the way I handled the situation with the surgeon. Despite a fair amount of crying on my part (to top it all off, my husband was away when all this happened), I was able to demand a second opinion for my diverticulosis treatment and the most conservative treatment possible. My surgeon was appalled *when I balked at surgery Monday without what I felt was adequate time to discuss the situation or get another opinion. By Friday I was able to deal with him, but it took about all I had. I really think that if it wasn't for my experience with the Women's Health Collective and the support of my friends and family, I would have a temporary colostomy right now.*

I, extremely well informed, well connected, verbally aggressive, have had to summon all my resources to get what I wanted in my treatment for breast cancer: medical care that was consistent with the findings of the latest literature and that took into account my needs as a woman.

As a young woman interested in one day having a family, I was never told that cimetidine "should not be used in pregnant patients or women of childbearing potential unless, in the judgment of the physician, the anticipated benefits outweigh the potential risks." I should have been informed of this and given the opportunity to make the decision myself in consultation with the doctor. This is one more indication of my rights and indeed my body being violated. My family raised me to trust doctors, but I no longer can do that.

In the words of a visiting nurse:

I learned to listen to patients, to speak their language, to let them set their own priorities for care, to teach them when they were ready. I also learned to evaluate the health care system through their eyes. Each day I confronted an irrelevant, noncaring, inadequate health care system that refused to consider the personal, social, cultural and economic needs of the patient.

It is a sobering time for women using the medical system in this country. Although some women are satisfied with the medical care they get, many are not.* The women quoted above are only a few of the thousands speaking out about the physicians and other medical personnel in medical settings who have:

- Not listened to them or believed what they said.
- Withheld knowledge.
- Lied to them.
- Treated them without their consent.
- Not warned of risks and negative effects of treatments.
- Overcharged them.
- Experimented on them or used them as "teaching material."
- Treated them poorly because of their race, sexual preference, age or disability.
- Offered them tranquilizers or moral advice instead of medical care or useful help from community resources (self-help groups, battered women's services, etc.).
- Administered treatments which were unnecessarily mutilating and too extreme for their problem, or treatments which resulted in permanent disability or even death (*iatrogenesis*).*
- Prescribed drugs which hooked them, sickened them, changed their entire lives.
- Performed operations they later found were unnecessary and removed organs that were in no way diseased.
- Abused them sexually.

Why Focus on Women and the Medical System?

Women are part of the medical care system, either for ourselves or our children, spouses or aging parents, more than twice as often as men are. We are 85 percent of all health care workers in hospitals and

*We are basing the analysis in this chapter both on thousands of personal accounts and on the work of a wide range of people and groups: feminist writers and other investigative journalists; feminist, radical and progressive physicians; public health researchers; health workers and practitioners of all kinds; medical historians and medical sociologists; public interest groups and government specialists; as well as social and feminist critics of many different persuasions.

**Iatrogenesis* is the process by which illness, impairment or death results from medical treatment. Some examples are cancers caused by DES, pelvic inflammatory disease (PID) or hysterectomy caused by an IUD, death or disability due to anesthesia accident (particularly when the surgery may not have been necessary), electrocution or burns from hospital equipment, infection from respirators, crippling or fatal strokes due to the birth control pill, addiction to tranquilizers and illness or death resulting from infant formula feeding in hospitals.

75 percent in the system as a whole.* We carry out most doctors' orders—treatment regimens like special diets, medications and bed rest, and so on—either as unpaid workers at home or as paid workers. We teach about health both in the home and in the system—what is good and not good for you. At home we are usually the first to be told when someone doesn't feel well, and we help decide what to do next. Some health care analysts even call us "primary health care workers" or the "layperson on the team." Most "patient" communication for and about family members flows through women: We report signs and changes, symptoms, responses to treatments and medications. The system also depends on women: Our direct reporting forms the basis of much of what medicine calls "scientific results," and our bodies provide the raw material for experimentation and research (e.g., the birth control pill), often without our knowledge and consent.[2]

Yet despite our overwhelming numbers and the tremendous responsibility we carry for people's health, we still have limited power to influence the medical system. Policymakers, usually male, have designed the system primarily for the convenience and financial gain of physicians, hospitals, administrators and the medical industries. *We believe that women, as the majority of consumers and workers, paid and unpaid, should have the major voice in health and medical care policy-making in this country.*

A previous edition of *Our Bodies, Ourselves* expressed considerable optimism that women would be able to work together to change medical care. In fact, women of all ages have joined together in local communities and nationwide: The resulting women's health movement has significantly changed the way many women look at medical care and is successfully fighting in legislatures, hospital administrations and law courts for improvements. Yet change comes slowly. The medical care system is too often unresponsive to women, deeply entrenched as it is in American economic, political and social structures, and the influence of medicine* in people's lives continues to grow. For example, the insurance and drug industries continue to make unrestrained profits, and physicians are still among the highest paid and among the least accountable of all U.S. professionals.† Despite a few governmental programs—Health Systems Agencies (HSAs) and neighborhood health centers—the medical establishment‡ has the money and status to contain most citizen attempts to achieve community control.

Our critique of medicine has taken on a new dimension. We see basic errors in its fundamental assumptions about health and healing. Although conventional medical care may at times be just what we need, in many situations it may be bad for our health because it emphasizes drugs, surgery, psychotherapy (especially for women) and crisis action rather than prevention.§ It is not enough to provide or improve medical care, to have more women physicians, to stop the abuses or to increase access to existing health and medical care for the poor and elderly—even though we support absolutely equal access to care for all classes and groups. We want to reclaim the knowledge and skills that the medical establishment has inappropriately taken over. We also want preventive

*While ailing men do report many of the same problems with the medical care system as women, men use the system less. They do not, like women, have to consult physicians for normal events in the reproductive cycle, such as pregnancy. Men tend to come into the system only during crises. Many different studies have shown that medical care providers treat male patients with more respect than women and offer fewer tranquilizers and less moral advice.[1] Also, since only 17 percent of doctors are women, most women see male physicians, a situation which severely exaggerates male-female power imbalances.

* We use "medicine" to mean both the *tangible* personnel and institutions of the medical system like physicians and hospitals, and the discipline, field or profession of medicine. We also mean the *intangible* institution of beliefs, ideology and assumptions that influence or control our daily habits in ways most of us are not aware of (as do "the family" and "religion").

† Accountability in the case of the medical profession would mean that they be more responsive to our perceived needs and wishes in recognition of the fact that, as taxpayers, we support medical education, research, hospital construction and much of the medical care given in hospitals, nursing homes and clinics.[3] See also the footnote on p. 660 which discusses accountability.

‡ By *medical establishment* we mean the cluster of organized physician, hospital, drug and insurance groups like the AMA (American Medical Association), the ACOG (American College of Obstetricians and Gynecologists), the AHA (American Hospital Association) and the PMA (Pharmaceutical Manufacturers Association), which pay large sums to influence public opinion, legislation and policy on health and medical matters.

§ Women consume far more prescription drugs, undergo much more unnecessary surgery and are referred for psychotherapy much more often than men, though crisis care is medicine's model for both sexes. (See relevant chapters for details.)

and nonmedical healing methods to be available to all who need them. We are committed to exposing how the medical establishment works to suppress these alternatives (home birth and nurse-midwifery, for example), contrary to the spirit of the antitrust laws of this country.

Pessimistic as we are about the present system, we believe in the healing powers within all of us—our ability to help one another by listening, talking, caring, touching—and in the power of small groups as sources of information sharing, support and healing. We still believe that we, as women, are the best experts on ourselves. The more we understand how vulnerable we become—both to disease and to dependency on experts—when isolated from one another, the more we see group experience and action as essential resources for health, from small consciousness-raising or self-help groups to large numbers of women organized for political action.

In this chapter we warn you of some of the dangers of this system and offer strategies to make it work for you as well as possible. We hope that you will feel entitled to demand more information about your health and medical needs, more able to distinguish when to turn to professionals, more empowered to take care of yourself and others when that is appropriate and more deeply convinced that good health is a fundamental right worth fighting for.

The Power of Medicine in Society

Why do most people have an almost religious belief in American medicine? Despite numerous bad or disappointing experiences, so many women say, "It must be my fault" or "I must just have had the wrong doctor," and fail to see that the system itself has serious faults. The institution and ideology of American medicine has penetrated so totally into the fabric of our lives over the past fifty years that most of us aren't even aware of its influence. Its power rests mainly on several widely held myths, which have in good part been created by an aggressive and highly successful public relations campaign of the wealthy AMA and other such groups.* Brought up as most of us were to "believe" in medicine, it is hard at first to realize how influenced (even at times manipulated) we have been by medical propaganda.

*Misleading tactics have been applied by organized medicine and the drug industry in a variety of situations through their skilled manipulation of the media. Gullible reporters have announced breakthroughs and false reassurances for anything from reselling menopausal estrogens to claiming that the Pill is now totally safe.

Myths and Facts

Myth: *American medical care is the best in the world.*

Fact: The United States spends more money on medical care, uses more medical technology per capita than any country on earth and has one of the highest ratios of doctors and hospitals to people. Yet it lags behind other industrialized countries in life expectancy and ranks twenty-fifth in infant mortality rates, two crucial basic indicators of health in the general population.[4] Clearly, we are not getting our money's worth.*

Myth: *Medical care has been responsible for the major improvements in world health.*

Fact: Many dread infectious diseases† were "conquered" in the past century, but this was most likely because of improved nutrition and sanitation, not medical care. *Their incidence rates were already falling* when medical treatments and vaccines were introduced. With the exception of smallpox, vaccines helped speed the decline of these diseases only minimally. *The disappearance of these diseases is the major source of our greater life expectancy in this century, leaving the chronic diseases, for which medicine has provided no cures.* Difficult as it is to believe, mortality from most of the chronic diseases, which are our leading causes of death today, has remained virtually unchanged throughout the century.[6]

Careful studies reveal that medical care has *not* been the most important factor in improving infant mortality rates. Factors such as education, income and race continue to be the most accurate predictors

*Some physician apologists have claimed that black and minority groups "drag down" our international standing in infant mortality (a clear case of racism and blaming the victim); however, even some of the most racially homogeneous U.S. communities lag considerably below Europe's best.[5] Furthermore, the resources we do spend have not improved certain disparities in health status. For example, in 1990 the National Commission to Prevent Infant Mortality reported that the death rate for black babies in the United States was twice that for white babies (17.9 deaths per 1,000 live births vs. 8.6). Also, from 1980 to 1987 the number of pregnant women not receiving prenatal care increased 50 percent.

†The diseases were typhoid, smallpox, scarlet fever, measles, whooping cough, diphtheria, influenza, tuberculosis, pneumonia, diseases of the digestive system and poliomyelitis.

of whether infants live or die. *General improvements, especially in nutrition and fertility control, have contributed most to improvements in neonatal mortality rates.*

Myth: *Medicine is a rigorous science.*

Fact: Medicine has prestige largely because it is associated with science in the public mind and claims objectivity and neutrality. Much of the theory on which modern medical practice is based actually derives from the untested assumptions and prejudices of earlier generations of medical leaders. Even though medical schools vaunt their "scientific method," they never actually teach it.[7] Furthermore, the scientific method is difficult to apply to human beings, since it is rarely possible or ethical to experiment on them as one would on inanimate objects or substances.* (However, animal researchers sometimes produce useful results.)

Myth: *Medical treatments in current use have been proven safe and effective.*

Fact: Most accepted treatments, therapies and medical technologies today have never been *scientifically* evaluated in terms of benefit.† Fetal monitors and radical mastectomies are only two examples of technology coming into widespread use before being fully evaluated. Scientific evaluation (in the form of randomized or controlled clinic trials [RCTs, CCTs])‡ is difficult, time- and labor-consuming and expensive and gets little funding from public sources. Most doctors have had no training in how to evaluate medical treatments and technology and often base their recommendations simply on what they think may work.

*There are always physicians willing to try if allowed to, which is one reason why ethical review boards have been set up in many institutions to set standards which all investigators must abide by (see Our Rights as Patients, p. 682).

†"No class of [medical] technologies is adequately evaluated for either cost effectiveness or social and ethical implications."[8]

‡Although there are other methods of evaluation, RCTs or CCTs are preferable. For these, very large numbers are required. Such trials also require that one group receiving treatment be compared with another (control) group receiving a different treatment or no treatment. This is the most difficult concept for the practicing physician, for whom the withholding of treatment is abhorrent. Without such evaluation, however, there is no way of *proving* that a certain type of medical treatment is effective, even if some people do seem to get better. "Only 10–20 percent of all procedures used in medical practice have been shown by Controlled Clinical Trials to be of benefit."[9]

As we were told by an assistant professor of medicine at Harvard Medical School:

> *Too frequently practicing physicians indulge in "cookbook medicine": They open the latest medical journal and inflict the latest recipe on patients, assuring their patients that on the one hand they are receiving "the latest thing" and on the other hand that they are "not guinea pigs." . . . In fact, the practicing physician is often extending some scientist's last experiment into the community setting—and without obtaining the patient's informed consent! At the same time, the scientist who performed the original experiment five years ago and who wrote the paper two or three years ago has long abandoned that approach in favor of something with more promise for a real cure.*

Fact: Most nonreproductive medical research has been done only on men and the results have been applied to women. Such a process is also far from scientific. In 1990, the National Institutes of Health (NIH) issued new guidelines to ensure that women would be adequately represented in all NIH-funded research of potential relevance to women. Thus, this situation should improve.

Myth: *Medical care keeps us healthy.*

Fact: Although deep down many of us believe that medicine has created and sustained our health through the technological advances of the past fifty years, public health* studies show that our health is primarily the result of the food we eat, the water we drink, the air we breathe, the environment we live in, the work we do and the habits we form. These factors in turn result primarily from the education we have, the money we are able to earn and the other resources we are able to command. Still other factors contribute to good health and long life: control over one's personal life, influence over the larger forces that affect all our lives, loving friendships and a supportive community.

Drugs, surgery and medical technology (kidney dialysis machines or blood transfusions, for example) are invaluable tools, and many people would not be alive today without them. While few of us would

**Public health,* which is the study of diseases or conditions in groups of people, is to be distinguished from *medicine,* the study and treatment of disease in the individual. *Epidemiology* is the basic science of public health.

want to live without these skills and emergency resources available to us and our families, it is fundamentally what *we* do or don't do, not what medicine does, that keeps us healthy.

By focusing on more profitable crisis care after people get sick rather than using its tremendous resources to help us prevent illness before it happens, the medical establishment shows itself unwilling to consider what really can and must be done to keep people healthy. This is a political issue, not simply a medical one, although many medical spokespeople argue that medicine is apolitical, scientific or politically neutral. Because Americans spend increasing health dollars on treating symptoms, we have less to spend on preventing chronic diseases in the first place.* *To consider reallocating the money available would force all of us to confront our economic, political and social system as major contributors to our ill health.*

When we go to a physician, clinic or hospital, every one of these myths encourages us to *trust* professionals, to lean on their reassurances and to follow their orders. Especially when we are sick, it is difficult to be anything but trusting and compliant; being sick is frightening and we *need* to feel comforted. Because medical professionals offer false reassurances more often than we'd like to think, we *must* be as critical as we can, get all the information possible and ask friends and family to help us in doing this.

Poverty, Racism and Health

Poverty is the most basic cause of ill health and early death in our society. The poor, who are mostly women and children and disproportionately people of color, have more illnesses and die in greater numbers and earlier than people with more income and education.[10] Many of their health problems are diseases that result from malnutrition, workplace dangers, inadequate housing, environmental pollution or excessive stress.

The medical system blames poor people for suffering the effects of poverty; for instance, accusing poor women of not taking proper care of themselves or their children and seeing alcoholism and depression in working-class families as individual, preventable failures. Medicaid and Medicare programs, which offered the poor and elderly at least minimal access to medical care, have been cut drastically and will take decades to reinstate.* The very programs that reduce people's need for costly medical care—job training, food-assistance programs, health education to the community—have been cut as well. The almost inevitable result will be increasing illness and death among the poor.† The United States and South Africa are the only modern industrialized nations without a universal health service or a national health program. Poor women are increasingly turned away from health facilities.

Racism is a serious threat to health and in some instances creates more barriers to obtaining needed care and to survival than does social class.[11] For example, even allowing for social class, black babies still die at higher rates than white babies living in the same geographic area, due mainly to low birth weight among black babies, which is almost entirely preventable.[12] In many communities, medicine's response to the widening infant death gap between those who are getting adequate nutrition and prenatal services and those who are not is to propose even more costly neonatal centers.‡ What's needed is not more expensive machines but a serious attempt to counter the effects of racism or class discrimination on the health of expectant mothers. Leadership for such an effort will not come from the medical establishment, which is heavily invested in technological and pharmacological solutions to problems, not social change.

Although people of color need medical care more often than white people do, they frequently get less.

*Prevention could reduce our illnesses by about half. (See Derek Bok, *Harvard Magazine*, May–June 1984, p. 430.)

*As it is, Medicaid covers only about 40 percent of the poor. Some states have expanded coverage for pregnant women beyond Medicaid through state-funded programs.

†In Michigan, which has one of the highest unemployment rates in the country, the infant mortality rate in Detroit increased 5.4 percent from 12.8 per 1,000 in 1980 to 19.7 in 1990.

‡For example, during the economically depressed period of the early 1980s, Rhode Island's Women and Infants Hospital proposed building a $50 million hospital to include a high-technology neonatal intensive care unit to save low-birth-weight infants in distress. Despite massive opposing testimony from citizens who argued that such deaths were preventable through community-based nutrition and midwifery-care programs, the building was approved. Such costly endeavors have become the national trend, displacing funds that could be used not only for nutrition and midwifery programs, but for drug treatment and AIDS prevention efforts as well, which pose increasing threats to women and their children.

For example, black people are less likely to get the most modern specialty treatment and follow-up care for cancer and do not survive as long after diagnosis. Similarly, even though hypertension is 82 percent higher among women of color, they do not receive any more treatment than white women.[13] Poor women and women of color often receive more abusive and damaging care than other women and are more likely to be used as "teaching material" in hospitals, so that physicians in training can practice the craft they will use later on wealthy private patients.[14] Sterilization abuse is far more frequent. When clients do not speak English fluently, they are often treated as though they are stupid. Stereotypes so govern practitioners' responses that a minority or poor patient who has the same symptoms as a white middle-class person will receive a different diagnosis and different treatment. In the words of a woman depicted in the film *Taking Our Bodies Back:*

> *It almost doesn't matter what I came in for, the place they send me is the "L" clinic ["L" is a code for sexually transmitted diseases]. They say, "She's black, she's got bladder trouble or a vaginal infection, she must be a prostitute—send her to the 'L' clinic."*[15]

When poor women are badly treated, they don't have the money to sue. They may hesitate to complain assertively, fearing that then they will get no care at all, since "free" care may be cut off at any time. Paradoxically, when women decide not to return for care, their absence gives rise to the health administrators' accusation that "they just won't come," although services are available. Again, women are blamed. Poor women also have little access to the more costly nonmedical alternative practices.

Though we are more critical than ever of the present medical system, at the same time we are working for the right of every woman, regardless of race or income, to have access to that system. Above all, we want to promote those social programs that would reduce people's need for expensive medical interventions and work for the deeper societal changes that will help eliminate poverty and racism.

Medicalization and Social Control of Women's Lives

Everywhere you turn, medical professionals are claiming expertise in matters never before considered medical: in criminality, adolescence, overactivity in children, sex, diet, child abuse, exercise and aging. In this takeover, called *medicalization,* medical people become the "experts" on *normal* experiences or social problems.[16] Surely the most striking example of this process is the medicalization of women's lives.

Consider how often we are expected to go to physicians for normal life events. For our early sexual encounters we may expect to go to gynecologists for most birth control devices and perhaps even for advice about sex.* During pregnancy we are urged to see obstetricians to be sure all is proceeding normally, and few of us have any alternative but the hospital for giving birth. The medicalizing of childbirth has become so complete that it resembles treatment for a severe, life-threatening illness. When birth goes well, we are often grateful to the physician and give her or him the credit for our success; when it goes badly, we are even more grateful for the interventions we believe saved us and our babies. And once the baby is born, we shift our gratitude and dependence to the pediatrician, so that even the first moments of mothering are conducted with an immediate sense of what our pediatrician thinks is right and proper.

When we are depressed or having difficulties in our personal relationships, we are encouraged to seek the advice and help of a psychiatrist instead of talking with friends. Women see psychiatrists in far greater numbers than men.

Medicine has stepped up its treatment of menopause and of aging as diseases. In a sense, the medical world defines women as inherently defective throughout life, in that we "require" a physician's care for all our normal female functions.

Medical "care" offered often extends to value judgments about our behavior, as we hear how a good girl, a good wife, a good mother should behave.

> *After advising me on when to put in my diaphragm ("Dinner, dishes, diaphragm," he said), my ob/gyn went on to speak about the fairly serious postpartum*

*Men do not go to urologists for their basic medical care; children are not segregated by sex when visiting pediatricians. Yet for decades many of us are expected to go to an obstetrician-gynecologist to obtain our basic care. We learn to do this without realizing that by doing so we begin to define ourselves and all our bodily needs in terms of our sex organs and reproductive capacities.

depression I was experiencing. "I like to tell my new mothers to get out to the library once in a while to keep their minds alive, but basically to find their happiness in the fact that they are taking care of their husbands and raising a new generation."

When I told my doctor (foolishly) that I'm a lesbian, the whole visit turned into a moral lecture and he never really paid attention to my problem. I walked out when he recommended a psychiatrist.

These moral judgments carry a weighty power, though they are no more "scientific" than the judgments of a priest or rabbi.[17]

We don't question the role that the physician has taken in our lives because, for one thing, our exposure and acceptance began early. When we were little, our mothers took us regularly to "the doctor," an extremely busy and important person, who may have ignored what our mothers said, and certainly what we said, and had their own answers. It may have seemed that our mothers allowed doctors to do all kinds of embarrassing or uncomfortable things to us and even that they did some of the same things themselves later on on the doctor's orders. Our mothers were very passive and compliant, in part because by the twentieth century male physicians had become the "authorities" on health. They had led a successful campaign during the late nineteenth and early twentieth centuries to eliminate midwives and sharply reduced the number of female physicians. For the first time in the history of the world, women were forbidden by law to be responsible for other women's childbirths and were replaced almost exclusively by male physicians. When this happened, women lost both female role models and caregivers and also the support of a whole system of woman-to-woman guidance.

During the mid-twentieth century, the gradual further moving of childbirth out of the home and into the hospital continued the process of isolating women from one another. Perhaps we have yet to measure how deeply our self-confidence as women may have been damaged by the loss of midwives as role models and respected sources of information and female authority.

All these factors together have brought us into an extreme and enforced dependency on professional experts—usually male physicians or those trained by them.[18]

Through these many medical encounters in the course of our normal life experiences, physicians gradually initiate women into the medical belief system, warning us against listening to other women, belittling the advice of our mothers, aunts, grandmothers and midwives—female lore—by calling it "old wives' tales." In this way, physicians prepare us to be their disciples. As we carry their message into our families and communities, we further contribute to the medicalization of society and a narrow, biological/technological perspective on the solution of human problems.*

It is difficult for most of us to recognize how "allopathic" medicine's proponents historically used women and women's central life experiences to initiate our entire society into a belief in and dependency on medicine. Despite much evidence to the contrary, most physicians believe sincerely that modern medicine has always helped women and that it deserves credit for society's overall health improvements since the turn of the century. Thus they tend to feel it is women's moral duty to teach children to place their faith in medicine.

Medicine as an Institution of Social Control

All societies establish institutions of social control, vested with the authority to define what is right or wrong, good or bad, sick or well. The schools, courts, and churches all play a role in defining our morality, but perhaps none more thoroughly than medicine does today. When we "deviate"—fail to conform to norms of womanhood—we discover how powerful medicine is.† Consider the ugly pronouncements medical authorities have made over the years, in the name of "science," about so-called inferior groups of people like women and blacks, and the way these

*For a thorough analysis of medicalization and iatrogenesis, see Ivan Illich, *Medical Nemesis: The Expropriation of Health*, New York: Pantheon Books, 1976; Bantam Books, 1977.

†For example, many poor women are sterilized without their knowledge or consent because they are unmarried or a physician thinks they have "too many babies" (see Sterilization, p. 300). Physicians have forced some women to accept cesarean sections, declaring them "unfit mothers" in court when they refuse a recommended section (despite the risk to the mother's own life); some women have had their children taken from them by the courts because a physician judged them "potential child abusers" for refusing medical treatments during pregnancy.[19]

pseudoscientific statements have been used to deprive these groups of social control and political power. For example, in the nineteenth century physicians claimed that to become a midwife or a doctor would "unsex" a woman: She would see things that would taint her moral character, cause her to "lose her standing as a 'lady' " and, because of the unusual physical and nervous excitement, "would damage her female organs irreparably and prevent her from fulfilling her social role as a wife and mother."[20] About blacks, a nineteenth-century physician wrote:

> *The grown-up Negro partakes, as regards his intellectual faculties, of the nature of the child, the female, and the senile White . . .*[21]

This misuse of power and these pronouncements continue today: Physicians dismiss females as too much "at the mercy of their hormones" to be trusted with serious responsibility, and cite blacks' "low-degree expectations" as a hurdle to parity in medical schools.*

Partly through the sanctity of the private physician-patient relationship, medicine (primarily obstetrics/gynecology and psychiatry) also achieves social control by encouraging us to see personal problems as individual isolated experiences rather than as problems we have in common with other women.

The Doctor–Patient Relationship

The relationship between a woman and her doctor is usually one of profound inequality on every level, an exaggeration of the power imbalance inherent in almost all male–female relationships in our society. The scales are even more unbalanced if the doctor is an ob/gyn with special knowledge about and power over our most intimate bodily selves or a psychiatrist with the authority to label us crazy or sane, to decide whether we can keep our children or not. *Doctors also frequently doubt our word simply because we are women.*

As in any relationship in which we are less powerful, we tend to evaluate what happens in a medical encounter in terms of *our* behavior rather than the doctor's. For example, if we don't understand something, we feel inadequate. Often we believe that a doctor's superior education, training, experience, sex and (sometimes) age automatically produce infallible judgment. "Well, he must know," many women say.

Many of us want to believe that we are in the hands of superior physicians—even though this may well not be true.

> *I knew that my doctor had a reputation for being one of the best in the city, and it made me feel good when I said his name and other people would say, "Oh, right, I've heard of him." I expected that he was going to do the best job he could possibly do. When he criticized me, I shrank inside. Sometimes I'd be annoyed that I had to travel so far for him to look at my stomach. But the mysteries still held. He was going to give me the baby. Once he confused me with someone else, and I was very depressed.*

There may always be something about the "laying on of hands" that calls up the child in us and makes us feel dependent, especially when pain and fear are present. Many physicians deliberately work to increase this natural phenomenon into a special kind of dependency (psychiatrists call it *transference*) in which the patient turns to the physician for guidance in all kinds of personal problems. Many medical schools and residency training programs teach techniques for eliciting this dependency as a useful way of "managing" patients, using the parent–child relationship as a model.* When a woman raises real, matter-of-fact questions, a doctor is apt to say, "What's the matter, don't you trust me?" For most doctors, the fact that the transference develops is justification for it—that is, a woman becomes overly dependent because she "needs" or wants to be.

> *Dr. G. sighed when he saw me. After examining me he sat down and said, "Let me be direct with you, hon." (I flinched at the "hon.") "You have called me or been here no less than four times this fall. You are com-*

*The kinds of biological (rather than societal) explanations for behavior and social position popular in the nineteenth century are becoming influential once again. Reinforced by such notions as "sociobiology," these myths have dangerous consequences for women, people of color and the poor.[22]

*As Diana Scully describes in her 1980 landmark study of obstetrician/gynecologists,[23] the training process prepares the surgeon to gain the patient's trust and confidence primarily for the purpose of controlling or "managing" her and then to *manipulate* her into doing something *the physician wants her to do*—undergoing surgery, for example, or some other procedure. Often, this is done either to gain experience or to generate income and is frequently not in her interests.

plaining about a pain that has no apparent organic basis. Quite frankly, my guess is that there are areas of your life you are having trouble facing, and the result is a funny pain in your chest and shoulder that flits around and is sometimes here and sometimes there and sometimes not anywhere at all."

"But I can feel exactly where it is," I broke in.

"Why don't you just leave the worrying to me?" he admonished. "I am the doctor. I have everything under control."[24]

The work of feminist sociologists such as Sue Fischer and Alexandra Todd shows the importance of changing this imbalance and improving communication. Our stories are crucial for correct diagnoses as well as for control over treatment options.

We can start needed change by pressing for real answers to our questions, using other sources of information besides our doctors (books, magazines, friends, nurses), seeking second opinions (not from a doctor who is our doctor's close colleague, on the same hospital staff or in the same specialty) and by bringing a friend to medical visits. Immersed in the propaganda about women's "need" for dependency, and comfortable with the fatherly, authoritarian role, many physicians react with surprise and even hostility at our "aggressiveness" when we insist on being partners in our health and medical care decisions. We must not let their reactions prevent us from persisting.

Occasionally, over time, you can build a satisfactory relationship with a doctor.

Friends now marvel at my close relationship with my current doctor and my ability to talk back, question and disagree with him and his colleagues. He respects me and trusts me to tell him what is going on, and I in turn trust him to listen, make suggestions and consult with me before any action is taken. When I don't want a procedure done or feel the psychological burden of making yet another trip to the lab or to his office is just too much for me on an occasion, I will tell him and he understands me most of the time. I have finally after many many years found someone willing to take into account my whole medical history and apply it to my current situation.

Sexual Abuse

Not only have women reported increasing numbers of cases of rape by their doctors, but between 5 and 10 percent of doctors have admitted in surveys and interviews to having sexual relations with their patients, sometimes saying that they believed such relations were either harmless or actually beneficial or "therapeutic" to the women involved. Because of the unequal power relationships involved, this sexual abuse may produce severe damage, akin to father–daughter incest.[25] When the woman turns to or is referred to a psychiatrist, she may be blamed for having "caused" the abuse.* Worse still, a few psychiatrists seduce the woman once again.[26]

It takes enormous courage for women to come forward and speak out about sexual abuse by doctors. Frequently no one believes them, and in one case, even nurses reporting their eyewitness experiences of patient abuse for three years were ignored by hospital administrators until another physician caught his anesthesiologist colleague in the act.[27]

The few cases that do reach state boards of registration in medicine frequently drag on for months and are then resolved with inadequate controls on future abuse. In spite of the fact that the Hippocratic oath and the ethics codes of all medical societies specifically forbid sexual relations with patients, doctors have made no serious effort to discipline those who breach the code. In fact, the medical profession often appears more concerned with covering up for a colleague who commits what are tactfully called "indiscretions." In the words of a woman psychiatrist:

I reported a psychiatrist who had had sex with two of his patients to the medical society. I called back two months later to find out what had been done. They told me the doctor denied everything, and it was his word against the patients'; so they were dropping the matter. When I persisted, the chairman of the ethics committee told me, "You know, my dear, we are not a consumer organization."

Physicians themselves may arrange for a problem physician to go to another community, without telling the unsuspecting new community about his assaultive behavior. In one famous case, medical school faculty members wrote glowing letters of recommendation for a convicted rapist who had moved to a new community.[28]

*Another 20 percent believe this. In California alone, one survey reported 36 percent of psychiatrists and 46 percent of psychologists had admitted affairs with clients during therapy.

It is common for women who are sexually abused by a doctor to be persuaded that he has fallen in love with them. This is not a sign of naiveté or psychopathology on our part. The physicians involved have abused a trust that every woman has learned to place in them.

We want to encourage women to notice any peculiar or irresponsible behavior and discuss these experiences with one another, to feel entitled to take action if necessary, protect ourselves and others and get our genuine needs for trust met appropriately. Keep a record of what happens; call a local women's group or rape crisis center; give serious consideration to mentioning your experience to a reliable lawyer.

WHERE DOES THE MONEY GO?

- About 12 percent of the U.S. gross national product, or $666 billion, now goes for health and medical care.
- This 12 percent is at least 25 percent more than Sweden or Canada, two-thirds more than Japan and twice that spent in Great Britain. Yet our infant mortality rate is higher and life expectancy lower than in all these countries.
- Per capita spending on hospital and physician services for the insured are 25 to 50 percent greater than for the uninsured.
- Nursing home costs increase more than 10 percent annually, inching toward $50 billion.
- Unnecessary services, administrative and advertising costs amount to at least $200 billion annually. Administrative costs, due largely to the many health insurers (over 1500), different billing systems and variations in coverage plans, account for more than 20 percent of total health and medical care expenditures—more than in any other nation.
- Physician earnings and hospital costs continue to rise well ahead of inflation; for many, profits are increasing.
- Technological innovations, largely of unproven value, account for 70 percent of health and medical care costs.
- Our tax dollars now support more than half the medical enterprise in all its forms, including medical education.

The Profit Motive in Medical Care

Why doesn't the present U.S. medical system provide affordable services and emphasize prevention and primary care? The profit motive has to be the main reason. From the many individuals who still want to be paid "fee for service" and build up a lucrative practice to the profit-making drug and insurance companies, medical care is now an industry in itself—the second-largest in the country—and a virtual monopoly.

The Medical Monopoly Our present type of medicine created a monopoly at the turn of the century through its control over state licensing laws which defined what the practice of medicine should be and who could be called a doctor. The laws provided state-sanctioned penalties for those who were not "properly" trained and licensed. At the same time the medical profession also gained absolute control over its education process, thus becoming a "legally enforced monopoly of practice."[29] Today medicine continues to set its own priorities and terms, with physicians controlling the majority of the medical decision-making and resource allocation processes. The profession decides what will be taught in medical schools, what medical services will be offered and how and where.* Surgeons generate most of their own income by self-referral ("I recommend this procedure and I will also perform it"), a practice judged unethical in other countries. Patients or third-party payors pay for services rendered. In many situations there is still no one but another doctor to decide whether or not these services are necessary, and no way of knowing whether or not they are effective. When review of costs occurs (as in the case of insur-

* Because medical care should always involve so much more than the application of technical skills and because it always occurs in a social context, society should be able to influence both the quality and quantity of medical care available. For example, we have too many specialists crowded into affluent communities and entirely more doctors than we need, although many inner city and rural areas in greater need have severe shortages of physicians. Yet 95 percent of physicians now specialize, despite a continuing shortage of primary-care physicians. Medical schools take no leadership in rectifying the problem, which leaves millions with inadequate access to quality care.

ance), it is often only physicians who undertake that review.

Medicine's monopoly was further consolidated when the government made federal funds available for hospital construction (Hill-Burton law), and the "Blues" (Blue Cross/Blue Shield) were created to reimburse in-hospital care. (Many of the Blue Crosses were created originally by local medical societies and are still physician dominated.) Backed up by the private insurance industry, hospitals became the base of medical care in this country. Substantial federal funding for Medicare, Medicaid and medical research increased the volume of federal money flowing into medicine. At the same time, profit-making hospital and nursing-home chains also began to proliferate. Today, expenditures for medical care grow faster than anything else. The whole system is completely out of control, despite growing cuts. Medicine has been allowed to expand continuously, and virtually without limits or accountability.*

In addition, there has been a phenomenal rise in the "corporatization" of medical care; that is, profit-making medical care chains that operate laboratories, "emergency rooms," mobile CAT scanners and so on, in addition to hospitals and nursing homes—a proliferation of separate services purely for profit.† Academic centers, medical schools and teaching hospitals have themselves created new and unprecedented arrangements amounting to millions of dollars with profit-making drug firms, all in the name of "scientific research"[30]—the medical-academic-industrial complex.

Those who profit from our illnesses are well organized politically and use their ample resources to keep the medical system free from government intrusion. Although they do not always agree among themselves, an informal coalition—physicians' lobbying groups like the AMA and ACOG, the pharmaceutical industry, hospital associations, the big voluntary "health" associations (Heart Association, Cancer Society, etc.), among others—tend to support the profit motive, the fee-for-service reimbursement system and the present crisis-care medical model.*

Health care has become a commodity or economic good, with profit as a blatant and legitimate goal. However inadequate government involvement in medical care was, it did make it possible for us to partially evaluate the system. It increased access to the system in some regions for a percentage of those who most needed it, and helped us to monitor or check a few of the system's most flagrant abuses. Government agencies were forced to respond *somewhat* to citizen pressure in the name of public interest. But federal regulations have been evaporating, with the result that profit-making enterprises have increased in number and monitoring their practices will be more difficult.

Our best hope is to form groups of workers and friends in the community and to work at the state level, making sure that reasonable options for care remain open to as many as possible at reasonable prices.

Insurance The insurance principle has become increasingly influential in shaping U.S. medical care. All third-party reimbursement systems, whether through private, profit-making insurance systems, non-profit Blue Cross/Blue Shield (the "Blues") or public programs (Medicare, Medicaid), reward doctors and hospitals by reimbursing them for doing the most expensive and complicated procedures on a fee-for-service basis. Yet they pay nothing or even require us to pay out of pocket for basic well-woman or pre-

*Because so much of our tax money is involved, we expect public utilities and our public education system, for example, to be somewhat accountable to the users. Through a public process we participate in decisions about cost, services and salaries, and sometimes even the budget itself. Though medical education, research and hospital operations are heavily subsidized by our taxes at all levels, we have virtually no say in how this money is spent. A few federally funded attempts were made in the past to make medicine more accountable, such as the formation of HSAs, but further attempts will now have to depend on local funding and initiative.

In addition, when there are errors or abuses in medical practice, physicians insist on "policing" themselves, leaving our range of options for redress short and unsatisfactory (see Medical Education and Training, p. 663, and Our Rights as Patients, p. 682).

†For example, recent surveys show that half of U.S. physicians are now on salary, many in profit-making corporations that are often physician owned. The fee-for-service system is changing, but not necessarily for the benefit of consumers, because only a few salaried doctors work in nonprofit settings such as health centers.

*The Center for Science in the Public Interest has played an important role in recently challenging how these extremely wealthy national organizations spend the money donated to them and in urging them to play a more effective role in health policy directed toward prevention. We can work locally by getting onto boards of chapters to help influence local projects (see Resources in Chapter 26, "Organizing for Change: U.S.A.").

ventive care. The insurance system thus acts as a kind of "blank check": We pay the premiums, directly or through our taxes (both continually rising); the doctors and hospitals bill the third parties (sometimes doctors also bill us for the "difference" between what insurance covers and what their real charges are), and there is no one looking to see if something cheaper or better (or sooner) might have been done. Medical costs skyrocket as a result. The chief beneficiaries of the insurance system are actually the doctors and stockholders, whose incomes and profits are all guaranteed.[31]

The insurance industry discriminates blatantly against women both as health and medical care workers and as consumers. Programs often do not reimburse directly for the services of nonphysician workers like nurse-midwives, nurse-practitioners, physical therapists and nutritionists, the majority of whom are women (this is changing now). Instead they reimburse the physicians, health departments or hospitals who hire or supervise them and indeed profit from their labor.

The Drug Industry Almost nowhere is the inherent conflict between profit-making and public safety more obvious than with the manufacture and sale of prescription drugs. Yet it is difficult to control the drug industry, which lies at the heart of both the medical system and the capitalist system. According to Dr. James L. Goddard, former commissioner of the Food and Drug Administration (FDA):

> *An American buying prescription drugs buys on faith what his doctor has prescribed. He is like a child who goes to the store with his mother's shopping list, which he cannot even read. He is totally unsophisticated as to the workings of the $5,000,000,000 [1972 figures] industry to which he is contributing and which his tax money is already helping to support. The consumer of drugs pays up and takes his medicine, and the Drug Establishment, about which he knows nothing, scores again.*[32]

Prescription drug sales in 1987 were estimated at about $23 billion, averaging twenty prescriptions per family in the United States. Pharmaceutical companies regularly show a return on investment of over 26 percent, outperforming any other part of the industrial sector. The drug industry is more than three times as price inflationary as all other U.S. industries. Americans have to pay more than twice or three times what Canadians and Europeans spend for drugs.

Although some drugs do save lives and enhance the quality of life for many sick people, research reveals increasing numbers of both new and older drugs to be dangerous or useless.* The GAO (the government's General Accounting Office) reports that Medicare/Medicaid pays $40 million a year for drugs shown to have no effectiveness. Each year, at least 1.5 million people to into the hospital because they have adverse reactions to drugs. Women receive about two-thirds of all prescription drugs, and the most profitable drugs made by the industry are oral contraceptives, injectable contraceptives (like Depo-Provera) and tranquilizers, all risky in some ways and all targeted mainly for women.

The drug industry spends 25 percent of its resources ($10 billion) on marketing—*more than on research*—and most of it for prescription drug promotion targeted to physicians.[34] Despite recent legislative efforts to curb gifts to medical students, the industry continues to woo successfully both practicing physicians, medical residents and medical schools by offering "research" opportunities and luxurious travel symposia, as well as sponsoring educational programs in hospitals and schools. Because medical school training in pharmacology is largely inadequate, doctors become permanently dependent on drug companies for information (or misinformation). As a result, physicians often cannot or do not protect us from ineffective or dangerous drugs. Often they don't know the possibly serious negative effects, or they continue to prescribe the drugs anyway,† based on personal observation or the belief that any negative findings (always challenged by the drug companies) have been inaccurate. Doctors also tend to prescribe the advertised brand-name drugs, which are more profitable to the drug companies, rather

*An industry-sponsored study of all drugs approved between 1938 and 1962 showed only 12 percent to be effective for their prescribed use and at least 15 percent to have no effectiveness whatsoever. *Yet most of these drugs are still on the market.*[33]

†For instance, physicians continued to prescribe progestin for pregnancy tests despite the discovery of a link to birth defects. The FDA warned against the use of the drug in the early stages of pregnancy, yet 75,000 prescriptions for progestin tests were given in 1978, years after the first FDA warning (testimony of Sidney Wolfe before Senator Edward Kennedy's Senate Health subcommittee August 1, 1979).

than using generic drugs, cheaper for the consumer, and often encourage patients' notions that a visit to the doctor is not complete without a prescription to "solve" the problem.

Regulation The FDA was ostensibly designed to protect the public from the dangers of adulterated food and harmful or useless drugs. (See Chapter 2, "Food," for more on the FDA.) Over many years, the efforts of some conscientious FDA staff, prompted and encouraged by the pressure of consumer groups, activists, investigative reporters and members of Congress, have sometimes led to effective, though limited, protection, as well as increased consumer participation in the regulatory process.

- Barbara Seaman, a founder of the National Women's Health Network and an early researcher on the Pill and menopausal estrogens, helped alert the public to the risk of these drugs in her testimony before Congress.
- Doris Haire, founder of the American Foundation for Maternal and Child Health, has repeatedly challenged the FDA, Congress and physician experts to demonstrate the safety to the infant and mother of drugs administered routinely during pregnancy, labor and delivery.
- Ralph Nader's Health Research Group has publicized the dangers and ineffectiveness of many drugs, successfully pressured the FDA to get them off the market, testified in Congress and worked extensively with the FDA staff on behalf of consumers.

However, these achievements are being increasingly threatened by the antiregulatory climate of a conservative government and also by the fact that the FDA's small budget has never been able to compete against the huge financial resources the drug industry musters for lobbying, court cases and the production of new products. The FDA is no match for many of the "best" drug companies, which often have substantial criminal records involving bribing of officials in foreign governments, falsifying of test data and failing to comply with FDA requirements to report adverse reactions to drugs.[35] Because drug companies are themselves required to test new drugs for safety and effectiveness, they also hire most of the researchers; if the research lab or doctor can make data look favorable to the company, it is more likely to continue to obtain funding.

At the very least, the drug industry should be required to submit to certain basic reforms, such as the severing of financial connections to those researching the safety and efficacy of the drugs they want to market, and the payment of much more severe penalties for misconduct. Consumer and public-interest groups have to be better watchdogs than ever before and also must serve as pressure groups to establish better regulatory systems at the state and local levels.

Medical Education and Training

Physicians have unusually broad powers. They decide which patients will be treated and where, who goes to the hospital, what treatment is given and for how long and which drugs are administered and in what quantities. They also have enormous influence in our most personal decisions. Why do many physicians misuse their power, consciously or unconsciously? Many of the behaviors we complain about in physicians—their authoritarian manner, their insensitivity and condescension—can be traced back to their education and training as doctors.

Who Gets into Medical School? Traditionally, upper- and upper-middle class white men have been the ones to survive the fierce competition for medical school entrance. In the words of one prestigious medical educator, "The years of premedical education, once considered so rewarding, have become a battleground of ruthless competition."[36] Some students tear out textbook pages so others cannot read them, and distort their fellow-students' experiments. Some also cheat, and it is known that those who do so will continue their deceptive behavior as doctors. Experienced educators have believed for some time that medicine is no longer attracting the best and brightest students, one reason being that they are repelled by the typical premed who would become their colleague. Although 1960s and 1970s activism resulted in a surge of women, poor and minority students, this number peaked around 1977 for poor and minority students, in part due to cutbacks in federal funding and in part to the fact that most medical schools were accepting these other candidates only under pressure.* Therefore, most physicians train alongside

*Enrollments for women are still increasing, however.

people more or less exactly like themselves, with teachers formed from the same mold. The result is a kind of cloning: The medical profession reproduces itself.

The Training Medical schools ask students to absorb an enormous quantity of highly technical information in compressed form, largely through one-way lectures. They place little emphasis on thinking and reasoning and none at all on questioning, criticizing or arguing. Few could learn to think critically in this environment if they did not know how before medical school. Students "are being driven to absorb an enormous amount of science at the sacrifice of just about everything else." Recall is poor after even a short period, however, and many in academic medicine admit that much of this material, irrelevant to competent medical practice, has crowded out crucial skills and subject matter. In the words of a woman physician:

> *The training program is disease-oriented, with life-threatening or rare conditions receiving the most attention, and the acquisition of skill in doing procedures (biopsies, punctures) and using diagnostic machines (EKG, X-ray, lab tests) being prized. The day-to-day ills of the public are ignored as "minor problems." The promotion of health and the prevention of disease are neglected almost entirely.*[37]

The training usually does not challenge students to become more aware of the social and political realities affecting people's health or to work through their own sexism, homophobia, class bias, ageism and racism. A woman doctor who does have a political awareness, wrote:

> *When I show a student her own cervix with a mirror, she is fascinated. When she is with me as a student and I offer my white middle-class patient the opportunity, the student thinks it is great. But when I offer a sixty-year-old woman the chance or a twenty-five-year-old working-class black woman, the student is amazed that "that kind" of patient would want to see her cervix. When I say, "This could be done in the clinic and would make women feel more in control," students say to me, "Oh, no, there's no time" (one extra minute?) or, worse, "*'Those people'* wouldn't be interested."*

Glaringly absent from medical training are most of the values, concerns and skills often thought of as "feminine": nurturance, empathy, caring, sensitive listening, encouraging others to take care of themselves, collaboration rather than competition. The medical hierarchy relegates these values and skills to the domain of nurses, other aides and (female) family members of the patients—physicians have "more important" things to attend to. Patients deprived of these elements of caring may not be as quick to recover, may miss absorbing important information about aftercare or preventive care and may end up feeling depressed about their experience because no one has paid attention to the emotional impact of their health problems. Women often complain bitterly of cold, abstract, impersonal or authoritarian doctors. A major study by the Institute of Medicine found that a majority of families were dissatisfied with their doctors and up to half had changed them as a result.[38] These qualities may have less to do with the physician's original personality than with the one-sidedness of her or his training. Similarly vital knowledge needed for optimum patient care—how to evaluate studies and risks accurately, what tests and treatments really cost, how to recognize a patient's rights and identify the ethical issues involved in medical decisions, what patients could do for themselves to prevent illness—is either absent altogether or relegated to the status of an elective. Students get the message: This material is not important.[39]

Many medical educators are now alarmed over the erosion of clinical skills caused by the overemphasis on technology in today's training, that is, by the increasing inability of younger physicians to make judgments based on experience, examination and careful listening to the patient rather than on readings from tests and machines.

The focus narrows further at the residency stage, where students aim to specialize because specialization promises more money, prestige and control over one's work.

> *Specialization and the rapid rate of advancement of knowledge and technology may tend to pre-empt the attention of both teachers and students from the central purpose of medicine, which is to heal the sick and relieve suffering.*[40]

Residency programs are grueling, low-paid, often demanding as much as thirty-six hours at a stretch

TOP PRIORITY FOR THE 1990S—A NATIONAL HEALTH PLAN

Except for South Africa, the United States is the only industrialized country in the world without a national health plan. During the 1990s this country will debate different legislative proposals designed to secure universal access to health and medical care. The National Women's Health Network and the Boston Women's Health Book Collective, along with other progressive organizations, believe that any successful system of universal access must include the following features:

- Comprehensive services, including preventive, routine, long-term care and independent living services;* noninstitutional alternatives, and access to caregivers such as midwives, chiropractors and homeopaths. For women, this means inclusion of such services such as Pap smears, birth control, mammography, and access to homebirth and freestanding birth centers (for low-risk childbearing women) and home-care services.
- Funding from a single source, publicly controlled, with most funds raised through progressive taxation.
- More systematic technology assessment, so that new (and increasingly more expensive) technologies will come under closer scrutiny before becoming accepted medical practice. (The internal fetal heart monitor is an excellent example of inappropriate and wasteful routine use of technology as a result of inadequate assessment.)
- No barriers to obtaining care, such as co-payments, deductibles and exemptions for previously existing conditions.
- Some significant degree of community input and control over the nature and type of services offered. This will require better education of the public about the most important determinants of health, so that increased community involvement will translate into improved decision making;
- Complete elimination of the fee-for-service model (which has encouraged unnecessary and often harmful treatment, especially for women). Already, close to half of U.S. physicians are on salary, so this may be a far less radical proposal today than twenty years ago.
- More equitable distribution of services and facilities to underserved populations and regions.
- A greater decision-making role for women and minorities, at least proportional to their presence in the community.
- High-quality, free and inexpensive resources for health- and medical-care information geared to laypersons.

The tremendous influence of the insurance industry, the current antitax climate and organized medicine may limit the political viability of some of these measures. The over 1500 insurance companies in the United States are especially opposed to the single-payor model, because it would essentially eliminate their current role in the provision of health and medical care. They, of course, prefer minor reform of the current insurance system. Interestingly, many members of Congress have expressed support for a "pay or play" approach (whereby employers either provide coverage to their employees or pay into a general fund that will cover their employees), usually because they state it is the most politically viable. Pay-or-play plans, as currently proposed, discriminate against part-time employees and thus hurt women more than men.

Surveys of the public show an overwhelming preference for the single-payor model (similar to that in Canada), suggesting that political viability is determined more by large lobbying interests than what the citizenry want. We hope that expanded public debate and activism on the question of a national health program will bring needed change before the turn of the decade—despite the opposition of powerful lobbies such as the insurance industry.

*Long-term care and independent living services for people with chronic illness and physical and mental disabilities are especially important for women given our longer life span. These services must include durable equipment, personal assistance services under the control of the individual, and backup hospice care.

and a hundred hours a week in consistently understaffed conditions, undesirable for both residents and patients alike. Teaching becomes haphazard, and not surprisingly, all types of residents have shown declining scores and performances in recent years, particularly in basic skills.

In short, specialty training is a dehumanizing process. Few working conditions in the industrial age have survived with so little change. Composed of one part sleep deprivation, one part shutting off of all feelings and one part automatic response to orders in what is probably the most militaristic of all civilian disciplines, this training resembles a kind of brainwashing.* The stress contributes to physicians' high rates of mental breakdown, drug addiction, alcoholism, suicide and family disruption.[41] Rates of incompetence among physicians in practice have also grown alarmingly. In addition to errors, they both perform many useless procedures and fail to perform needed ones.[42]

Studies have shown that while medical students may begin medical training with idealism and a sincere desire to help people, after years of training in the closed worlds of medical school and residency they become almost invariably more cynical, detached and mechanistic than at entry.[43] Their ability to communicate has actually deteriorated during the process.[44] Because of the enormous personal sacrifice medical training requires, and because most of the teachers and the doctors they admire are highly paid specialists, young physicians feel entitled to earn very large sums of money and to command interpersonal authoritarian power once the training is completed. Here is how another distinguished medical educator puts it: "What emerges are physicians without inquiring minds, physicians who bring to the bedside *not* curiosity and a desire to understand but a set of reflexes that allows them to earn a handsome living."[45]

These criticisms are not new; indeed, many were voiced as soon as the medical monopoly was created nearly a century ago. When *Our Bodies, Ourselves* came out in 1973, the then president of the American Association of Medical Colleges said every medical student should read it.

*The term *brainwashing* has been used repeatedly by medical educators, students and physicians in conversations with the authors. See also Allan Chamberlain, "Night Life: Sleep Deprivation in Medical Education," *The New Physician* (May 1981), p. 30, for use of this term.

A number of proposals to reform medical training have emphasized the importance of good communication skills and medical care that is culturally, linguistically and racially appropriate. For example, in response to pressure from the women's health movement, which had protested teaching medical students how to do pelvic exams on anesthetized women (often without their consent) and prostitutes, some medical schools now involve specially trained gynecological teaching associates (GTAs) in the teaching of the pelvic exam. These women can offer important, immediate feedback about how well a student is doing an exam, when s/he is doing something that may be hurting and so on.*

Even if educational reforms were to be realized, without substantial input from consumers and their communities, the experience of health and medical care will continue to be frustrating for women. Meanwhile, we can look to the many alternative and neighborhood facilities created by women and men over the past twenty years or so for examples of successful efforts to integrate competence, caring and community partnership.

Notes

1. Barbara Bernstein and Robert Kane. "Physicians' Attitudes Toward Female Patients," *Medical Care,* Vol. 19, No. 6 (June 1981), pp. 600–08. See Chapter 3 and Images of Women in Medical Textbooks and Women Physicians, on pp. 666 and 667.

2. Gena Corea. *The Hidden Malpractice: How American Medicine Mistreats Women.* New York: Harper & Row, 1985.

3. Arthur Owens. "Who Says Doctors Make Too Much Money?" *Medical Economics* (March 7, 1983), pp. 66–67. See also Peter Conrad and Rochelle Kern. *The Sociology of Health and Illness: Critical Perspectives,* 3rd ed. New York: St. Martin's Press, 1990. See figures quoted elsewhere in this chapter for taxpayer expenditures for medical care and training.

4. See United Nations Population and Vital Statistics Report in *U.N. Demographic Yearbook 1988.* In 1988 the U.S. infant mortality rate of 10 per 1000 live births was double that of Japan (5 per 1000 live births). The cities of Detroit, Washington and Baltimore all had rates above 19 deaths per 1000 live births. See also U.S. Department of Health and Human Services, *Report of the Secretary's Task Force on Black and Minority*

*For more information on GTAs, contact the Program in Introduction to Clinical Medicine, Tulane University Medical Center, 1430 Tulane Avenue, New Orleans, LA 70112.

Health, Vol. 6, *Infant Mortality and Low Birth Weight*, January 1986. Low-birth-weight babies are the major cause of high infant mortality rates. In poorer communities, there is what Professor Edward Sparer has called an "infant death gap" between haves and have-nots, which is getting wider.

5. Kathleen Newland. *Infant Mortality and the Health of Societies* (Worldwatch Paper #47). 1981, pp. 6–11. Available from Worldwatch Institute, 1776 Massachusetts Avenue NW, Washington, DC 20036. See also U.S. Department of Health, Education and Welfare, *Factors Associated with Low Birth Weight*, Hyattsville, MD: HEW, April 1980, p. 2.

6. John B. McKinlay and Sonja M. McKinlay. "Medical Measures and the Decline of Mortality," in Peter Conrad and Rochelle Kern, eds., *The Sociology of Health and Illness: Critical Perspectives*, New York: St. Martin's Press, 1981, pp. 12–30. Thomas McKeown. *The Role of Medicine: Dream, Mirage, or Nemesis.* London: Nuffield Provincial Hospitals Trust, 1976. René Dubos, *Mirage of Health: Utopias, Progress, and Biological Change.* New York: Harper Colophon, 1979, p. 23 ff.

7. Lack of teaching of scientific method in medical school is documented in David H. Banta, Clyde J. Behney and Jane Sisk Willems, *Toward Radical Technology in Medicine*, New York: Springer Publishing Co., 1981, p. 30. Additional discussion of the unscientific nature of modern medicine may be found in Rick Carlson, *The End of Medicine*, New York: Wiley-Interscience, 1976. A discussion of how medical decision making might be brought more into line with modern scientific thinking is presented in Harold Bursztajn, Richard I. Feinbloom, Robert M. Hamm and Archie Brodsky, *Medical Choices, Medical Chances*, New York: Routledge, 1990.

8. The Congressional Office of Technology Assessment. "Strategies for Medical Assessment," Publication 052-003-00887-4. Quoted in *The Nation's Health* (November 1982). Available from the U.S. Government Printing Office, Washington, DC 20052.

9. David H. Banta et al. *Toward Rational Technology in Medicine*, p. 122.

10. Leonard S. Syme and Lisa F. Berkman. "Social Class, Susceptibility, and Sickness," in *The Sociology of Health and Illness.*

11. National Academy of Sciences, Institute of Medicine, Division of Health Care Services. "Health Care in a Context of Civil Rights: A Report of a Study," No. 1804. Washington, DC: U.S. Government Printing Office, 1981.

12. Wornie L. Reed. "Racism and Health: The Case of Black Infant Mortality," *The Sociology of Health and Illness*, pp. 34–44.

13. S. Woolhandler et al. "Medical Care and Mortality: Racial Differences in Preventable Deaths," in Phil Brown, ed., *Perspectives in Medical Sociology.* Belmont, CA: Wadsworth, 1989, pp. 71–81.

14. Diana Scully. *Men Who Control Women's Health: The Miseducation of Obstetrician-Gynecologists.* Boston: Houghton-Mifflin, 1980. (See the footnote on p. 658, col. 2.)

15. *Taking Our Bodies Back: The Women's Health Movement*, a 33-minute 1973 color film. Available from Cambridge Documentary Films, Box 385, Cambridge, MA 02139.

16. Irving Zola. "Medicine as an Institution of Social Control," in *Socio-Medical Inquiries—Recollections, Reflections, and Reconsiderations.* Philadelphia: Temple University Press, 1983, p. 262 ff.

17. See Janice Raymond, "Medicine as Patriarchal Religion," *The Journal of Medicine and Philosophy*, Vol. 7 (1982), pp. 197–216.

18. See Barbara Ehrenreich and Deirdre English, *For Her Own Good: 150 Years of the Experts' Advice to Women.* New York: Doubleday/Anchor Books, 1978.

19. George J. Annas. "Forced Cesareans: The Most Unkindest Cut of All," *The Hastings Center Report* (June 1982), pp. 16–17. Also personal interviews with the authors of *Our Bodies, Ourselves.*

20. Dorothy Wertz and Richard W. Wertz. "The Decline of Midwives and the Rise of Medical Obstetricians," in *The Sociology of Health and Illness*, pp. 173–74.

21. Barbara Ehrenreich and Deirdre English. *For Her Own Good*, p. 117.

22. Estelle P. Ramey. "Men's Cycles (They Have Them Too, You Know)," in A. Kaplan and J. Bean, eds., *Beyond Sex-Role Stereotypes.* Boston: Little, Brown, 1976. See also Ruth Hubbard, Mary Sue Henifin and Barbara Fried, *Biological Woman—The Convenient Myth: A Collection of Feminist Essays and a Comprehensive Bibliography*, Cambridge, MA: Schenkman Publishing Co., 1982 (entire volume).

23. Diana Scully. *Men Who Control Women's Health.* See also Michelle Harrison, *A Woman in Residence.* New York: Random House, 1982.

24. From a woman who was later operated on for a rare form of cancer that had spread to her lungs. Stephani Cook, *Second Life*, New York: Simon & Schuster, 1981.

25. Anita Diamant. "Bedside Manners: Of Doctors, Patient Abuse, and Regulation. Again," *The Boston Phoenix* (November 10, 1981), Section 2, p. 14.

26. Personal communication, women's medical association members investigating physician sexual misconduct. See also "Therapist-Patient Sex Has Negative Effect for Most," *Ob/Gyn News*, Vol. 16, No. 24; D. Sobel, "Sex with Therapist Said to Harm Client"; John Kelly, "Sexually Abusive Doctors"; Ronald Kotulak, "Doctor-Patient Sex."

27. "New Case Alleges Sex Abuse by an M.D. at Rock's Sacramento," *Medical World News* (September 3, 1979), pp. 38–39. See also Anita Diamant. "Bedside Manners," p. 13.

28. "Harvard Medical School Dean's Statement on Letters of Recommendation," *Harvard Medical Area FOCUS* (October 8, 1981), p. 5. See also Fox Butterfield. "Doctors' Praise Assailed for Peer in Rape Case," *The New York Times* (September 24, 1981).

29. E. Freidson, quoted in Peter Conrad and Rochelle Kern, *The Sociology of Health and Illness,* p. 161.

30. Harvard University News Office for the Medical Area. "$6 Million Du Pont Gift for Genetics Research" (September 12, 1981), p. 8; "Johnson & Johnson Gives $500,000 for Basic Research" (September 12, 1981), p. 8; "Gift for Unrestricted Cancer Research from Bristol-Meyers" (April 8, 1982), p. 5. *Harvard Medical Area FOCUS,* 25 Shattuck Street, Boston, MA 02115. See also Barbara J. Culliton, "The Hoechst Department at Mass General (Hospital)" (News and Comment, second in a series on the Academic-Industrial Complex), *Science,* Vol. 216 (June 11, 1982), pp. 1200–03. For a critique, read Arnold S. Relman, "The New Medical-Industrial Complex" (Special Article), *New England Journal of Medicine,* Vol. 303, No. 17 (October 23, 1980), pp. 963–70.

31. William K. Stevens. "High Medical Costs Under Attack as Drain on the Nation's Economy," *The New York Times* (March 28, 1982), pp. 1, 50. Sandra Salmans. "Critics Say Lack of Incentives Hurt Insurers' Efforts to Curb Medical Costs," *The New York Times* (March 31, 1982).

32. *Science for the People,* Science and Society Series, No. 1 (November 1973).

33. Maryann Napoli. *Health Facts,* p. 15. See also "Ineffective Drugs," *The Public Citizen, 1981 Annual Report* (winter 1982), p. 22; Sidney M. Wolfe, Christopher M. Coley and the Health Research Group, *Pills That Don't Work: A Consumer's and Doctor's Guide to Six Hundred Prescription Drugs that Lack Evidence of Effectiveness.* New York: Warner Books, 1982.

34. Staff Report of the Special Select Committee on Aging, U.S. Senate, 102nd Congress, 1st Session, Committee Reprint. Washington, DC: U.S. Government Printing Office, 1991.

35. "Informed Consent," *Health Facts,* Vol. 4, No. 22 (July/August 1980), p. 3. See also Chapter 5, "Bribery and Other Strategies," in Milton Silverman, Philip R. Lee and Mia Lydecker, *Prescription for Death: The Drugging of the Third World,* Berkeley: University of California Press, 1982, pp. 119–30; Barbara Seaman and Gideon Seaman. *Women and the Crisis in Sex Hormones,* New York: Rawson Associates, 1977, pp. 73–74; Mark Dowie et al., "The Illusion of Safety," *Mother Jones* (June 1982), pp. 39, 43, 46–48; Ivan Illich, "The Pharmaceutical Invasion," in *Medical Nemesis,* New York: Pantheon Books, 1976, pp. 63–76; "Eli Lilly is Accused in FDA Documents of Not Reporting Adverse Drug Reactions," *The Wall Street Journal* (August 4, 1982), p. 6.

36. Dr. John Z. Bowers, as quoted in *Medical Area FOCUS* (Harvard Medical School), February 11, 1982.

37. Cynthia Carver. "The Deliverers," in Shelly Romalis, ed., *Childbirth: Alternatives to Medical Control.* Austin: University of Texas Press, 1981, p. 135.

38. Derek Bok, "Needed: A New Way to Train Doctors," president of Harvard University, in his annual report to the Board of Overseers, April 1984, *Harvard Magazine* (May–June 1984), p. 43.

39. Derek Bok, "Needed: A New Way to Train Doctors."

40. "Curriculum Review Panel for Medical School Education Initiated by the Association of American Medical Colleges," *The New York Times* (October 21, 1982).

41. Jack D. McCue. "The Effects of Stress on Physicians and Their Medical Practice," *New England Journal of Medicine,* Vol. 306, No. 8 (February 25, 1982), pp. 458–63.

42. President's Commission for the Study of Ethical Problems in Medicine and Biomedical Research. Washington, DC: U.S. Government Printing Office. *Securing Access to Health Care.* 1983. Also see Marcia Millman, *The Unkindest Cut: Life in the Backrooms of Medicine,* New York: William Morrow, 1977.

43. Howard S. Becker, E.C. Geer, Everett C. Hughes and Anselm L. Straus. *Boys in White.* Chicago: University of Chicago Press, 1961. Though over thirty years old, this classic study appears to apply to most of today's male students as well. No comparable work has yet been done on women. The work of psychiatrist Harold Lief, MD, at the University of Pennsylvania over a twenty-year period has provided similar corroboration, with special reference to sexuality. (The SKAT [Sex Knowledge and Attitude Tests] for physicians was developed by Dr. Lief.) See also Bryce Nelson. "Can Doctors Learn Warmth?" *The New York Times* (September 13, 1983).

44. Derek Bok. *Harvard Magazine,* p. 70.

45. Dr. J. Michael Bishop, in a speech to the American Association of Medical Colleges, November 8, 1983.

Women's Equality Through Law

Susan Gluck Mezey

Susan Gluck Mezey is professor of political science at Loyola University Chicago. She earned her M.A. and Ph.D. at Syracuse University and her J.D. at DePaul. Her articles on women and politics, women and law, abortion policy, social security policy, gender equality in education, and interspousal immunity in civil litigation have appeared in political science journals and law reviews, including the Journal of Politics, International and Comparative Law Quarterly, Rutgers Law Review, Women and Politics, *and the* Policy Studies Journal. *She is the author of two books,* No Longer Disabled: The Federal Courts and the Politics of Social Security Disability *(1988) and* In Pursuit of Equality: Women, Public Policy, and the Federal Courts *(1992). Her current research involves policymaking for children and the federal courts.*

Mezey outlines for us the current major legal issues for women and explains the relevant concepts and terms. She recounts the history of women's fight for legal equality in the nineteenth century and concludes that legal reform has only a limited ability to erase gender injustice.

Susan Gluck Mezey authored this article for this edition of *Issues in Feminism*.

Introduction

An early reminder of women's inequality appears in a letter Abigail Adams sent to her husband John, attending the Second Continental Congress in Philadelphia in 1777. Abigail implored him to "remember the ladies" when creating "a new code of laws" for the emerging nation. Despite her plea, the Founders did not accord women equal rights under the law in the new nation. Since then, women have struggled, individually and collectively, to alter their subordinate status.

The first women's movement grew out of the abolition struggle in the mid-1800s and ended with the ratification of the Nineteenth Amendment in 1920.[1] The next era, spearheaded by feminists, began in the 1960s when the second women's movement was born.[2] Arising out of women's participation in the civil rights and anti-war movements, the feminist movement was characterized in large part by legal battles over inequality between the sexes.[3]

As this chapter demonstrates, although the law is a useful weapon in fighting for social, political, and economic equality between men and women, legal solutions alone, that is, laws prohibiting discrimination or proclaiming women's equality with men, cannot entirely abolish inequality between the sexes.[4]

Constitutional Review

Early Decisions

The United States Supreme Court plays an important part in determining the legal status of women in America and its decisions are influenced by prevailing beliefs about the role of women in society. For most of its history, the Court turned a deaf ear to challenges to sexually discriminatory laws and interpreted the Constitution to allow states to bar women from a variety of occupations, to make it more difficult for them to serve on juries, and to prohibit them from voting.

The Court's belief in the legitimacy of restricting women's opportunities is illustrated in Supreme Court Justice Joseph Bradley's concurring opinion in an 1873 case challenging an Illinois statute limiting the practice of law to men only. Bradley stated that:

> *the constitution of the family organization . . . indicates the domestic sphere as that which properly belongs to the domain and functions of womanhood. The harmony . . . of interests and views which belong or should belong to the family institution, is repugnant to the idea of a woman adopting a distinct and independent career from that of her husband.*

This view of women, easily dismissed today as a relic of the nineteenth century, was manifest almost one hundred years later in a 1961 Florida case in which the Court upheld the constitutionality of a jury selection system that produced virtually all-male juries. The Court ruled that the state could allow women—but not men—to decide for themselves whether to register for jury duty because women were "the center of home and family life."

Equal Protection

The equal protection clause of the Fourteenth Amendment of the U.S. Constitution prohibits a state from "deny[ing] to any person within its jurisdiction equal protection of the laws." This clause tells states that they must justify legislative decisions to treat individuals differently; differential treatment is permissible when it is based on *relevant* distinctions. The courts have interpreted this to mean that "similarly situated" persons must be treated alike.

The modern phase of equal protection for women was ushered in with two signals from Congress: enactment of federal antidiscrimination legislation and congressional approval of the Equal Rights Amendment.[5] Another factor that led to the establishment of the new judicial doctrine was the rise of litigation activity sponsored by feminist law firms, the NAACP Legal Defense and Education Fund, the American Civil Liberties Union, as well as organized women's groups such as the National Organization of Women and the Women's Equity Action League.[6]

In 1971, for the first time in its history, the Supreme Court struck a law that distinguished between men and women. Since then the Court has invalidated most of the gender-classifications that have come before it, striking down laws that it believes are based on "archaic or overbroad generalizations" about men and women.[7]

In 1976 the Supreme Court insisted that gender classifications must be "substantially related" to the achievement of an "important" governmental interest. And in 1982 the Court added that the state must establish an "exceedingly persuasive justification" for such classifications.

Based on these criteria, the Supreme Court struck an Idaho law preferring male administrators to female administrators, a U.S. military regulation requiring women officers to prove their husband's dependency on them in order to receive benefits, a social security regulation limiting survivor's benefits to widows taking care of children, an Alabama law allowing alimony payments to women only, and a Mississippi law denying men admission to a state nursing college.

Nevertheless, despite its apparent commitment to gender equality, the Court has upheld a significant number of laws establishing legal differences between the sexes. It has allowed sex-based laws designed to rectify the effects of societal discrimination against women; for the most part, these laws were justified by the economic disparity between males and females. To this end the Court accepted two social security regulations allowing women a more favorable method of computing benefits, a Navy regulation permitting women more time in rank than men before being discharged, and a Florida law granting widows only a property tax exemption.

The majority of the laws upheld by the Court are directly or indirectly related to physical differences between the sexes because the Court is persuaded that states may classify in areas where men and women are not "similarly situated." On these grounds the Court approved a congressional statute limiting military registration to men only, a California law punishing men only for the crime of statutory rape, and several state laws with distinctions between mothers and fathers of illegitimate children.

In a much-criticized 1974 decision, the Supreme Court also upheld a California law denying working women pregnancy disability benefits on the grounds that differentiating on the basis of pregnancy was *not* an impermissible sex classification; in a now-famous footnote the Court explained that "the [California] program divides potential recipients into two groups—pregnant women and nonpregnant persons. While the first group is exclusively female, the second includes members of both sexes." This rather novel characterization of the relationship of women to pregnancy was ultimately reversed by Congress when it enacted the 1978 Pregnancy Discrimination Act.

The Role of Women on the Supreme Court

In 1981 Sandra Day O'Connor became the first woman justice to be appointed to the Supreme Court. Feminists, who lobbied the Senate on her behalf, were very pleased with her nomination. However, for a number of reasons, primarily because of her position in the abortion cases, O'Connor's performance on the Court has been disappointing to feminists.[8]

Ruth Bader Ginsburg, the second woman justice in U.S. history, was appointed to the Court in 1993. For the first time, the Supreme Court will have two women justices. Unlike O'Connor, Ginsburg proclaimed herself solidly in favor of abortion rights during her confirmation hearings. Moreover, before becoming a judge, Ginsburg was an advocate for women's rights issues and argued—and won—many important sex discrimination cases before the Supreme Court. Whether she will prove to be more pleasing to feminists remains to be seen.

Employment Discrimination

Equal Pay

In response to continuing pressure from women's advocates, in the 1960s and 70s, Congress enacted legislation that prohibited pay disparity between men and women, and barred sex discrimination in employment, credit, housing, and education. Because these laws did not provide immediate remediation, women increasingly turned to the courts to seek judicial enforcement of these rights.

The 1963 Equal Pay Act, requiring equal pay for men and women working at essentially the same jobs, was the federal government's first attempt to ameliorate job discrimination against women. This Act, passed during the administration of John F. Kennedy, commanded employers to provide "equal pay for equal work." Early federal court cases interpreting the Equal Pay Act held that the jobs need not be "identical," but only "substantially equal."

Early Pay Act challenges frequently succeeded in court because judges found that companies were paying women less than men for performing "substantially" the same work. Thus, wage differences between male and female "selector-packers" who inspected glass bottles were not justified even though the men also performed the additional job of "snap-up boy." The court ruled that the extra work occasionally performed by the men—essentially unskilled labor—did not merit the 21½ cents per hour pay differential. Another court held that male night shift factory workers could not be paid more than female day shift workers since the company did not treat the shifts differently in its own job classification scheme.

Equal Pay Act challenges can only succeed if women and men are working at the same kind of jobs. Therefore, despite victories in these and other cases, the Equal Pay Act has not eliminated the earnings gap between men and women in the U.S. because it has been unable to overcome the problem of sex segregation in employment. Sex segregation means that women work in jobs predominantly held by women and that these jobs generally command lower wages than jobs primarily held by men. The fight to overcome this situation has become known as the comparable worth, or pay equity, issue.

In the 1980s, comparable worth cases were brought by women working in female-dominated occupations, such as nursing or clerical work. And in these cases, the courts were asked to compare the jobs held by the women to jobs of "similar skill, effort, responsibility, and working conditions" held by men, often truck drivers or physical plant workers, and to decide whether the jobs were comparable and therefore should command comparable pay. Unlike Equal Pay Act cases, these comparable worth cases, brought as Title VII (of the 1964 Civil Rights Act) wage discrimination suits, frequently lost because the courts ruled that market conditions, such as the supply of available workers, the wages workers can command from other employers, and the rate of worker unionization, constituted sufficient nondiscriminatory reasons for pay disparity between men and women. Although some states have taken steps to remedy pay inequities, for the most part, occupational segregation persists and consequently so does pay discrimination.

Equal Employment Opportunity

The next major breakthrough in the battle against sex discrimination in employment came in Title VII of the 1964 Civil Rights Act which makes it unlawful for employers, labor unions, and employment agencies "to discriminate against any individual with respect to his compensation, terms, conditions or privileges of employment, because of such individual's race, color, religion, sex, or national origin."

As originally proposed, the bill was not intended to reach discrimination based on sex, but in the final vote on the floor of the House of Representatives, Democratic Congresswoman Martha Griffiths of Michigan proposed an amendment to include sex discrimination within its purview. Accepted in part by opponents hoping to defeat the entire bill, the prohibition on sex discrimination was included in the final version. Despite the initial lackluster support, Title VII of the 1964 Civil Rights Act became the single most important piece of legislation in the battle against sex discrimination in employment.[9]

In 1967 President Lyndon Johnson signed Executive Order 11375, which added sex as a protected category to earlier executive orders banning discrimination on the basis of race, color, creed, and national origin. Like its predecessors, Executive Order 11375 prohibited discrimination in federal contracts as well as required federal contractors to adopt affirmative action programs to promote equal employment goals.

In the years since its passage, the courts have fleshed out the parameters of Title VII in suits challenging discriminatory employment practices. But courts must follow congressional intent in interpreting statutes and the 1964 Congress did not believe that sex differences in employment were *wholly* unreasonable. Because of this belief, Title VII allows employers to draw distinctions among employees on the basis of sex where it is a "bona fide occupational qualification" (BFOQ) for the job, that is, when the business depends upon having either a male or female worker.

One of the first rulings on the BFOQ defense came in 1971 in a case in which an airline was sued by a man seeking a job as a flight attendant. The airline refused to hire him, arguing that sex was a BFOQ because customers preferred women flight attendants. In *Diaz* v. *Pan American,* the circuit court ruled that customer preference was not a "bona fide" reason to hire only women; in other words, the court held that sex is not a BFOQ for flight attendants.

The Supreme Court reinvigorated the BFOQ defense in 1977 in *Dothard* v. *Rawlinson* when it upheld Alabama's policy of not hiring women prison guards. Because women guards were less equipped to do the job and were at greater risk than men, the Court said, the state could restrict the jobs to men only.

Despite its support of the male-only prison guard policy in *Dothard,* the Court has interpreted the BFOQ defense narrowly. In its latest ruling on the BFOQ, the Court dealt with the difficult issue of employer fetal protection plans, policies that exclude women from jobs that expose them to chemicals or other toxins that might have detrimental effects on their unborn children. Under such policies, women seeking to work in restricted areas were forced to undergo sterilization or prove that they were infertile.

In 1991, in *United Automobile Workers* v. *Johnson Controls,* the Supreme Court held that an employer's fetal protection policy violated Title VII.[10] Sex was not a "bona fide occupational qualification," said the Court, because the employer was unable to prove that the pregnancy (or fertility) actually interfered with the woman's ability to perform the job. The Court believed that by passing Title VII (as amended by the Pregnancy Discrimination Act of 1978), Congress intended to allow the woman, not her employer, to decide whether, and where, to work while pregnant.

The courts also extended the reach of Title VII by prohibiting employers from making employment decisions on the basis of so-called neutral rules, such as height and weight requirements. Although such rules may not be discriminatory on their face, they frequently have the *effect* of keeping women out of jobs. In a 1971 case dealing with Title VII and racial discrimination, the Supreme Court ruled that these practices are illegal unless the employer can show that the requirements are related to the employee's ability to do the job.

Height and weight requirements were predominantly used as job qualifications by police and fire departments and, as a result, women were denied access to these jobs. In 1977, in the same Alabama prison case, the Supreme Court found that the state's minimum weight and height requirements (120 pounds and 5 feet 2 inches) had the effect of excluding women from prison guard work. Because the state could not prove that the requirements were necessary for the job, the Court held that the height and weight rules violated Title VII.

Although proof was often difficult and recovery uncertain in Title VII cases, until the late 1980s, the courts' interpretation of Title VII was generally expansive. Then in the Supreme Court's 1988–1989 term (beginning in October 1988 and ending in July 1989), the Court issued rulings in several civil rights cases that made it more difficult for employees to win employment discrimination suits. In *Wards Cove* v. *Atonio,* the most important of these cases, the Court altered the procedure for proving Title VII lawsuits, making it easier for employers to defeat actions against them.

After an earlier veto by President George Bush in 1990, Congress enacted the Civil Rights Act of 1991, reversing most of the Court's 1988–89 civil rights rulings. And although it included limits on the amount of money damages women could collect from employers found guilty of discrimination, the 1991 Civil Rights Act was a victory for all future victims of job discrimination.

Pregnancy in the Workplace

One of the most important debates about women and employment is over the rules governing the benefits for pregnant women. Some feminists argue that because pregnant women have special needs, employers *must* treat them differently to allow them to achieve equality with men. Others believe that making exceptions for the special condition of pregnancy denies equality between the sexes.

In the past, pregnancy-related policies restricted options for working women by forcing them to take unpaid maternity leaves and revoking their seniority if they were allowed to return to the job at all. Opposition to such laws led a number of feminists to argue for eliminating all laws relating to pregnancy and for treating pregnancy like any other disability—that is, like any other physical condition affecting the ability to work.

Other feminists claim that this hands-off approach fails to acknowledge that pregnancy imposes special constraints on women in the work force. Of course they agree that mandatory pregnancy leaves are detrimental to women, but they maintain that entirely ignoring the effects of pregnancy minimizes the physical and financial burden of childbearing on working women. According to this view, an equality approach that equates pregnancy with disability sends the wrong message; it portrays pregnancy as a workplace oddity rather than as a brief interlude in a woman's employment history.

In 1987 the Supreme Court upheld a California law that required employers to give pregnant employees special disability benefits, but it has refrained from taking an explicit position on the preferential treatment of pregnancy in the workplace.[11] To some extent this debate has been obviated by the passage of the Family and Medical Leave Act, signed into law on February 5, 1993 by President Bill Clinton. This law, applicable to employers with at least fifty workers, allows women or men employees to take up to twelve weeks of unpaid leave for the birth or adoption of a child, illness of a close family member, or the employee's own illness. Although the Family and Medical Leave Act will not solve all the problems of pregnant women workers, it will alleviate at least some of the concerns of women in the work force.

Sexual Harassment

The issue of sexual harassment was brought to national attention when, in October 1990, Professor Anita Hill of the University of Oklahoma Law School testified before a Senate committee that she had been sexually harassed by Supreme Court nominee (now Justice) Clarence Thomas almost ten years ago.

Sexual harassment reflects an imbalance of power in the workplace and is debilitating to the woman worker because it sends a message that she is viewed as an object of sexual gratification rather than as a serious employee. Although the law applies to male victims of harassment as well, the overwhelming number of complaints are brought by women. The problem of sexual harassment has existed for a long time, but it is only recently that women have been able to bring sexual harassment suits to the courts even though the federal law against sex discrimination in employment has been available to them since 1964 (in Title VII of the 1964 Civil Rights Act).

According to feminist scholar Catharine MacKinnon, there are two kinds of sexual harassment in employment. The first, called *quid pro quo,* is when women are forced to exchange sexual favors for employment benefits. The second, called "workplace (or environmental) harassment" occurs when the atmosphere in which women work is permeated with sexuality but no explicit demands are made on them as a condition of their employment.[12]

In the 1970s, women began suing their employers for sexual harassment on the job but the courts often dismissed their complaints. Some judges ruled that sexual harassment did not constitute sex discrimination because either sex *could* be harassed. Others held that sexual harassment was not sex discrimination because it simply involved an interpersonal relationship gone bad with no consequences for the woman's employment status—even when she was fired or demoted. The courts were also reluctant to hold companies liable for the acts of their employees, especially when there was a company policy against harassment.

After a number of cases, the courts eventually agreed that sexual harassment, if proven, was a form of sex discrimination in employment forbidden by Title VII. Judges were more willing to believe *quid pro quo* harassment claims because the victim was able to point to adverse employment consequences resulting from her refusal to comply with her employer's demands; that is, she could show that her employment status was negatively affected.

Eventually the courts also accepted the legitimacy of environmental harassment claims in which women complained that they were subject to physical or verbal abuse on the job. In the 1981 case of *Bundy* v. *Jackson*, the District of Columbia Circuit Court found that Sandra Bundy had been subject to a hostile work environment when her boss said to her, among other things, "any man in his right mind would want to rape you."

The Supreme Court agreed that workplace harassment, if "sufficiently severe or pervasive," constituted a violation of Title VII in the 1986 decision of *Meritor Savings Bank* v. *Vinson*, the Supreme Court's first ruling on sexual harassment in employment. In *Vinson*, in which a bank teller sued the Meritor Savings Bank for workplace harassment, the Court defined sexual harassment as "unwelcome" sexual advances. The Court did not settle the question of the employer's liability for harassing behavior by a supervisor; it ruled that while the company is not automatically liable for the supervisor's acts, it cannot simply escape liability by claiming ignorance of the harassment nor by pointing to a company policy against harassment.

Recently a federal court ruled that pornographic pictures of women in various stages of undress and suggestive and lewd remarks by male employees created a hostile work environment for a woman working in a Florida shipyard.[13]

Following the example set by the Ninth Circuit in a 1991 decision, many federal courts now view the man's behavior from the perspective of the "reasonable woman" in deciding whether there was sexual harassment.[14] In *Ellison* v. *Brady*, the court explained that it had adopted this approach because conduct that might appear perfectly normal to men could reasonably be seen by women as offensive, or abusive, or "hostile."

Education

In 1954 in *Brown* v. *Board of Education*, the Supreme Court announced that "separate but equal" has no place in public education and that schools segregated on the basis of race are unconstitutional. Apparently believing that this principle does not apply to sex-segregated education, the Court has refused to rule that "separate but equal" on the basis of sex is unconstitutional.

The Court's first ruling on "separate but equal" in sex-segregated education came in the 1982 case of *Mississippi University for Women* v. *Hogan*, in which nurse Joe Hogan sued to be allowed to attend the all-women nursing program at Mississippi University for Women (MUW). With Justice O'Connor announcing the decision, the Court ordered his admission to the nursing classes but refrained from declaring that a separate sex admission policy was always unconstitutional.

The most recent debate over "separate but equal" education arose over admitting women into the Virginia Military Institute (VMI) and the Citadel, state-funded, male only military schools. These continue to bar women from admission, arguing that the presence of women would undermine their institutional mission of training young men for the military. When the U.S. Justice Department brought suit against VMI on constitutional grounds of sex discrimination, the federal circuit court found that its policy of excluding women was unconstitutional. The court did not, however, order women to be admitted; rather, it commanded the state to devise a new educational policy. One of the court's suggested policy options included the establishment of a parallel military institution for women—in other words, "separate but equal."

In 1972 Congress addressed the question of sex inequality in education by passing Title IX of the Educational Amendments, an act providing that "no person in the United States shall, on the basis of sex, be excluded from participation in, be denied the benefits of, or be subjected to discrimination under any education program or activity receiving Federal financial assistance."

Title IX bans discrimination in vocational, professional, and graduate schools; it encompasses physical education classes, extracurricular activities, scholarships, and counseling. While the law represented an important step toward equality in education, it allows exceptions to sex equality in two major areas: admissions and athletics. Single-sex admissions remain legal in most elementary and secondary schools, private undergraduate schools, and traditionally single-sex public undergraduate institutions, as well as military and religious schools.

The Supreme Court's initial approach to Title IX was an expansive one, allowing individual discrimination suits and including employees as well as students within the ban on sex discrimination.[15] Then in 1984, in *Grove City College* v. *Bell,* the Court narrowed the statutory definition of "program or activity."

Grove City College argued that Title IX's prohibition against sex discrimination did not apply to it because it received no direct aid from the federal government and, even if it applied, it was only relevant to the program receiving the aid—in this case, Grove City's financial aid office.

Although it held that educational institutions receiving indirect aid through student grants and loans were subject to Title IX, the Court agreed with Grove City that Title IX only covered the specific program receiving the federal aid; other units within the college were not under the auspices of Title IX and hence not subject to the nondiscrimination rule.

In 1988, over President Ronald Reagan's veto, Congress enacted the Civil Rights Restoration Act to reverse the Court's *Grove City* decision. This Act defined "program or activity" to include the whole institution if any part of it received federal funds.

Reproductive Rights

In 1969, when Norma McCorvey, an unmarried carnival worker, learned she was pregnant, she discovered that Texas, like most states, allowed legal abortions only in cases where the woman's life was in danger. McCorvey's decision to challenge the Texas abortion law led to the famous *Roe* v. *Wade* case in 1973.[16]

In a 7–2 vote, the Supreme Court proclaimed that the constitutional right to privacy, formalized in *Griswold* v. *Connecticut* in 1965, was "broad enough to encompass a woman's decision whether or not to terminate her pregnancy." But, said Justice Harry Blackmun, the right was not "unqualified." Although the state could not ban abortions during the first three months (first trimester) of pregnancy, during the next three months (second trimester), it could make rules and regulations that reasonably relate to maternal health. During the last three months of pregnancy (third trimester), because of the medical likelihood that the fetus can exist outside the mother's womb, the state can prohibit abortion entirely except when the mother's life or health is at risk.

Although *Roe* v. *Wade* established a woman's right to terminate a pregnancy, it soon became clear that the right was largely limited to adult women with the financial resources to pay for it.[17] States were not compelled to make abortions available nor provide public funds for them.

With encouragement from the federal government, states denied public funding for poor women seeking abortions while continuing to pay the costs of childbirth out of the public fisc. In three 1977 cases, the Supreme Court upheld these practices, maintaining that while *Roe* established a woman's fundamental right to choose an abortion, the government was not obligated to fund the exercise of that right. And since the government's decision placed no obstacle "in the pregnant woman's path," her right of privacy was not diminished.

Following *Roe* states also enacted legislation limiting young women's access to abortion. In a series of decisions beginning in 1976, the Court upheld a variety of laws requiring minors seeking abortions to obtain their parent's consent, or at least notify them, before the abortion could be performed. The Court has not permitted parents to exercise full veto power over their daughter's decision to have an abortion though; state laws must contain judicial bypass provisions allowing the minor woman to petition the court for approval if the parents refuse to consent.

Beginning in 1973, in states such as Ohio, Pennsylvania, and Missouri, abortion opponents succeeded in enacting laws restricting the reproductive freedom women had secured in *Roe.* Until 1989, however, with the exception of restrictions on minors and public funding, the Court continued to adhere to the principles established in *Roe.* In two major abortion cases, in 1983 and 1986, the Court struck regulations requiring second trimester abortions to be performed in hospitals, specifying that the physician must provide the pregnant woman with information regarding fetal development and the risks of the abortion, establishing waiting periods, and requiring the presence of a second physician at abortions performed late in the pregnancy.

With the appointment of increasingly conservative justices by the Reagan–Bush administrations, support for *Roe* on the Court diminished. *Roe* had been decided by a 7 to 2 vote; the 1983 decision was carried by a 6 to 3 vote and the 1986 decision by a 5 to 4 vote. In 1989, the antiabortion forces won a victory when the Court upheld a Missouri law imposing significant restrictions on women's reproductive rights. Although the Supreme Court did not take the ultimate step of overturning *Roe* v. *Wade,* the 5–4 decision in *Webster* v. *Reproductive Health Services* moved it closer to an antiabortion position than it had been since 1973.

The case revolved around a 1986 Missouri abortion law, which included a preamble declaring life begins at conception; a provision requiring a test to determine fetal viability; a ban on using public funds to encourage or counsel women to have abortions not necessary to save their lives; and a prohibition on using public facilities for abortions—even for women willing and financially able to pay for the abortion themselves.

Speaking for the Court, Chief Justice William Rehnquist held that the Court need not decide on the constitutionality of the preamble because it simply reflected the state's view on the beginning of life. Rehnquist also found no constitutional problem in prohibiting the use of public funds or public facilities for abortion. Then, most importantly, the Court upheld the fetal testing provision even though it clashed with *Roe* by allowing viability tests during the second trimester.

Although the Court did not overrule *Roe,* it attacked the trimester approach that was the essence of the decision in 1973. Justice Blackmun, author of *Roe,* defended the opinion he announced almost twenty years ago. *Roe's* trimester approach, he argued, still represented the best way of balancing the state's interest in regulation with the woman's interest in privacy. He concluded his dissent by warning of dire consequences for the future: "for today, at least . . . the women of this Nation still retain the liberty to control their destinies. But the signs are evident and very ominous, and a chill wind blows."

Webster served as an invitation to states to enact new laws restricting access to abortion. Within months after the decision, state legislatures in Utah, Louisiana, Idaho, and Pennsylvania passed restrictive abortion laws, often with provisions that had been declared unconstitutional by the Supreme Court in earlier cases. The sponsors of the legislation hoped to force the Court to reexamine and overrule *Roe* v. *Wade.* One such statute, the Pennsylvania Abortion Control Act of 1989, among other provisions, required a woman to notify her husband of a planned abortion, or, if a minor, obtain her parent's consent; imposed a 24-hour waiting period; and ordered the doctor to deliver a lecture on the risks of abortion.

With two strongly pro-choice justices, Thurgood Marshall and William Brennan, retired from the bench, it seemed likely that the Court would overrule *Roe* v. *Wade* in the 1992 decision of *Planned Parenthood of Southeastern Pennsylvania* v. *Casey.* In a sharply divided ruling that satisfied neither side, the Court "reaffirmed the essential holding" of *Roe,* but at the same time upheld all the regulations except for the husband-notification provision. However, while the Court reaffirmed that the constitutional guarantee of liberty extended to the right to choose to terminate a pregnancy, it now permitted states to impose restrictions *throughout* a woman's pregnancy (thereby abolishing the trimester framework) as long as they were not "unduly burdensome." Because it felt the notification requirement was the only part of the law that constituted an "undue burden," the Court struck it while upholding the other provisions.

Even before *Casey* was decided, the Court had refused to overturn a "gag order" imposed on doctors working in family planning clinics receiving federal funds. The "gag order" prohibited these doctors from even discussing the possibility of abortion with their patients. Following *Casey,* in a 1993 decision, the Supreme Court barred federal courts from intervening to protect abortion clinics from increasingly violent antiabortion demonstrations led by a group calling itself Operation Rescue. Propelled by the *Casey* decision, the Freedom of Choice Act, a bill to codify the holding of *Roe* v. *Wade,* was introduced in Congress.

During his first few days in office, President Clinton signed executive orders that reversed some of the antiabortion policies of the Reagan–Bush administrations. The states remain political battlegrounds over abortion, though, and Congress continues to deliberate on passage of the Freedom of Choice Act and other abortion issues.

Ironically, the debate over abortion rights may become moot through the use of RU 486, a French drug that interrupts pregnancy at its earliest stage. So far, even though President Clinton has lifted the ban on the importation of the drug, antiabortion groups have been able to prevent the sale and manufacture of the drug in the United States.

Family Law

Marriage

Women's lives have always been bound by the legal, economic, and physical constraints of the family. The subordination of married women was reflected in the English common law doctrine of coverture which denied a married woman the right to own property and make contracts in her own name, and designated the husband as the head of the household with title to the marital property.

The Married Women's Property Acts, passed individually by states beginning in the 1830s, were the first halting steps to establish a separate legal identity for married women. Although these Acts did not create legal equality for women, they removed the worst of the restrictions on them. Women, however, remained burdened with the primary responsibility for the family and received little encouragement to move outside that arena. Indeed, on the contrary, they were constantly reminded that their place was at home.[18]

Because the family is sheltered from the reach of law, married women were—and still are to a great extent—subject to their husband's dominion. Under the common law women were obligated to perform domestic and sexual services, take care of the children and, in return, men were forced to provide basic necessities of food, clothing, and shelter; the level of support given to the wife was irrelevant to the "contract." This principle was demonstrated in a 1953 Nebraska case, *McGuire* v. *McGuire*, in which the Nebraska Supreme Court stated that

> *the living standards of a family are a matter of concern to the household, and not for the courts to determine, even though the husband's attitude toward his wife, according to wealth and circumstances, leaves little to be said in his behalf. As long as the home is maintained and the parties are living as husband and wife, it may be said that the husband is legally supporting his wife and the purpose of the marriage relation is being carried out.*

Although more than forty years have elapsed, the *McGuire* case is still considered the legal standard for cases challenging inadequate support by husbands.

Divorce

Conditions for divorce, such as residency requirements, grounds, and distribution of property, vary by state.[19] By the 1970s, a rising tide of no-fault divorce laws swept through the states and, by 1985, all states except South Dakota established a variation of a no-fault system; some states simply added no-fault provisions to their pre-existing fault grounds.

No-fault divorces are granted on the basis of "irreconcilable differences" or "irretrievable marital breakdown," meaning that neither spouse has to prove the other's guilt. Most states also demand that a period of time, often six months, lapse before granting a divorce decree. While the spread of no-fault divorce was largely applauded by feminists because it freed women from remaining trapped in unwanted marriages, there is a debate about whether it is beneficial for the divorced woman.[20]

Following divorce, wives are usually more economically disadvantaged than their husbands, often being forced for the first time to support themselves. Moreover, the "divorce may push them into the labor market under unfavorable circumstances."[21] Ironically, one of the consequences of the no-fault approach is that ex-husbands are often relieved of much of their financial responsibility for their former wives: Alimony (now called maintenance) has virtually disappeared and women who have never worked outside the home must now support themselves. Additionally, with the adoption of no-fault divorce, women lost much of their bargaining power in settlement negotiations.

The concept of spousal maintenance exemplifies the new approach to divorce; it is only awarded to a small fraction of divorced women and is primarily regarded as an interim measure to allow women to gain skills necessary to support themselves with appropriate employment.[22] Because fault no longer plays a role, courts base their decisions on such factors as the length of the marriage, the age, health, and earning capacity of the parties, as well as the possibility of each party returning to the standard of living enjoyed during the marriage.

Although divorce reform is consistent with the feminist philosophy of women taking responsibility for their lives, the reality is that women are often unprepared to assume financial responsibility for themselves and their children because their work experience has often been limited to unpaid labor in the home or underpaid labor outside the home.

Along with changes in no-fault divorce and spousal support, states also adopted new procedures for property division. Although the Married Women's Property Acts had ended the husband's explicit legal dominion over property by allowing women to manage and control their own property, they did little to change the fact that men are the primary wage earners who hold title to the bulk of the property obtained during marriage.

As with other rules of divorce, property distribution is determined by the state of residence. The fifty states of the United States fall into two categories: community property states and separate property states, the latter also known as common law states.

In the separate property states (forty-two states and the District of Columbia), separately owned property is not divided at divorce; only marital property, held jointly by both marriage partners, is divided between them. In community property states (seven western states plus Louisiana), husband and wife jointly own property acquired during the marriage and this property is distributed at divorce. Most separate property states now follow a community property model for dividing assets at divorce. Under this system, a spouse who made an economic contribution to the property, regardless of ownership, may claim a share of that property upon divorce.

A number of states allow a spouse, typically the woman, who has made a noneconomic contribution to the marriage, to claim assets at divorce. The major difficulty with this approach lies in the calculation of noneconomic contributions, that is, how to put a market value on the homemaking and parenting services of a stay-at-home spouse. Judges rely on factors such as the length of the marriage, the age, health, occupation and employability of the parties, as well as the amount and sources of income available to each party to determine the amount to be awarded.

Increasingly, one of the battlegrounds over what constitutes a fair divorce settlement involves the issue known as the "medical school syndrome."[23] This situation arises when one spouse, again usually the wife, has supported her husband through medical school and is asked for a divorce when he receives his diploma. She wants part of the increased earning power he *will* have; he wants property divisions and maintenance determined by their resources at the time of the divorce. Wrestling with this dilemma, courts have issued conflicting opinions, some favoring the wife, some favoring the husband. This area of law is clearly in a state of flux.[24]

Conclusion

More than two hundred years have elapsed since Abigail Adams appealed to John for laws establishing equality between the sexes. For most of U.S. history, Abigail's words were unheeded. As the chapter has illustrated, in the recent past, feminists have been more successful in attaining educational equity, equal employment opportunity, and reproductive freedom. Although these advances have been significant, there are still many legal and political battles to be fought. Many feminists have recognized that the law has been useful in furthering sexual equality, but that it will not solve all the problems women face in today's society.

Notes

1. The Nineteenth Amendment enfranchised women. See Aileen Kraditor, *The Ideas of the Woman Suffrage Movement 1890–1920* (New York: Anchor Books, 1971).

2. Rosemarie Tong, *Feminist Thought: A Comprehensive Analysis* (Boulder: Westview Press, 1989) for discussion of types of feminist theories.

3. See Sara Evans, *Personal Politics* (New York: Vintage Books, 1980) for discussion of the roots of the second women's movement.

4. Ava Baron, "Feminist Legal Strategies: The Powers of Difference," in *Analyzing Gender,* ed. Beth Hess and Myra Marx Ferree (Beverly Hills: Sage, 1987), p. 475. See also Nadine Taub and Elizabeth Schneider, "Perspectives on Women's Subordination and the Role of Law," in *The Politics of*

Law, ed. David Kairys (New York: Pantheon Books, 1982), pp. 117–139.

5. Ruth Bader Ginsburg, "The Burger Court's Grapplings with Sex Discrimination," in *The Burger Court,* ed. Vincent Blasi (New Haven: Yale University Press, 1983), pp. 132–133.

6. Karen O'Connor, *Women's Organizations' Use of the Courts* (Lexington: Lexington Books, 1980); Ruth Cowan, "Women's Rights Through Litigation: An Examination of the American Civil Liberties Union Women's Rights Project, 1971–1976," *Columbia Human Rights Law Review* 8 (Spring–Summer 1976):373–412; Jo Freeman, *The Politics of Women's Liberation* (New York: David McKay, 1975).

7. Susan Gluck Mezey, *In Pursuit of Equality: Women, Public Policy and the Federal Courts* (New York: St. Martin's Press, 1992).

8. Although Justice O'Connor has never voted to overrule *Roe,* she has been very critical of the decision and has upheld almost every state abortion regulation.

9. See Charles Whalen and Barbara Whalen, *The Longest Debate* (New York: New American Library, 1985) for history of the passage of the 1964 Civil Rights Act.

10. For a discussion of fetal protection policies, see Brian Hembacher, "Fetal Protection Policies: Reasonable Protection or Unreasonable Limitation on Female Employees," *Industrial Relations Law Journal* 11 (1989):32–44; Note, "Rethinking (M)otherhood: Feminist Theory and State Regulation of Pregnancy," *Harvard Law Review* 103:1325–1343; Wendy Williams, "Firing the Woman to Protect the Fetus: The Reconciliation of Fetal Protection with Employment Opportunity under Title VII," *Georgetown Law Journal* 69 (1981):641–704.

11. See Wendy Williams, "The Equality Crisis: Some Reflections on Culture, Courts and Feminism," *Women's Rights Law Reporter* 7 (Spring 1982):175–200 and Sylvia Law, "Rethinking Sex and the Constitution," *University of Pennsylvania Law Review* 132 (1984):955–1040 for opposing sides of the pregnancy and work debate.

12. Catharine MacKinnon, *Sexual Harassment of Working Women* (New Haven: Yale University Press, 1979).

13. *Robinson* v. *Jacksonville Shipyards,* 760 F.Supp. 1486 (M.D. Fla. 1991).

14. Naomi R. Cahn, "The Looseness of Legal Language: The Reasonable Woman Standard in Theory and Practice," *Cornell Law Review* 77 (1992):1398–1446.

15. Joyce Gelb and Martin Lief Palley, *Women and Public Policies* (Princeton: Princeton University Press, 1987); Rosemary Salomone, *Equal Education Under Law* (New York: St. Martin's Press, 1986).

16. Marian Faux, *Roe v. Wade* (New York: Macmillan, 1988).

17. See Barbara Hinkson Craig and David M. O'Brien, *Abortion and American Politics* (Chatham, NJ: Chatham House, 1993); Laurence H. Tribe, *Abortion: The Clash of Absolutes* (New York: Norton, 1992) for political and legal analysis of the years following *Roe.*

18. Liane Kosaki and Susan Gluck Mezey, "Judicial Intervention in the Family: Interspousal Immunity and Civil Litigation," *Women and Politics* 8 (1988):69–87.

19. Doris Jones Freed and Timothy Walker, "Family Law in the Fifty States: An Overview," *Family Law Quarterly* 18 (Winter 1985):369–471.

20. Lenore Weitzman, *The Divorce Revolution: The Unexpected Social and Economic Consequences for Women and Children in America* (New York: The Free Press, 1985); Martha Albertson Fineman, *The Illusion of Equality* (Chicago: University of Chicago Press, 1991); Susan Faludi, *Backlash* (New York: Anchor Books, 1991); Susan Moller Okin, *Justice, Gender, and the Family* (San Francisco: Basic Books, 1989).

21. Herbert Jacob, "No-Fault Divorce and Finances of Women," *Law and Society Review* 23 (1989): 98.

22. Herbert Jacob, *Law and Politics in the United States* (Boston: Little, Brown, 1986), p. 71.

23. Freed and Walker, "Family Law in the Fifty States," p. 411.

24. See *Drapek* v. *Drapek,* 399 Mass. 240, 503 N.E.2d 946 (Mass. 1987).

References

Baron, Ava
1987 "Feminist Legal Strategies: The Powers of Difference." In *Analyzing Gender,* edited by Beth Hess and Myra Marx Ferree, pp. 474–503. Beverly Hills: Sage.

Cahn, Naomi R.
1992 "The Looseness of Legal Language: The Reasonable Woman Standard in Theory and Practice," *Cornell Law Review* 77:1398–1446.

Cowan, Ruth
1976 "Women's Rights Through Litigation: An Examination of the American Civil Liberties Union Women's Rights Project, 1971–1976." *Columbia Human Rights Law Review* 8 (Spring-Summer):373–412.

Craig, Barbara Hinkson and O'Brien, David M.
1993 *Abortion and American Politics.* Chatham, NJ: Chatham House.

Evans, Sara
1980 *Personal Politics.* New York: Vintage Books.

Faludi, Susan
1991 *Backlash.* New York: Anchor Books.

Faux, Marian
1988 *Roe v. Wade.* New York: Macmillan.

Fineman, Martha Albertson
1991 *The Illusion of Equality.* Chicago: University of Chicago Press.

Freed, Doris Jonas, and Walker, Timothy
1985 "Family Law in the Fifty States: An Overview." *Family Law Quarterly* 18 (Winter):369–471.

Freeman, Jo
1975 *The Politics of Women's Liberation.* New York: David McKay.

Gelb, Joyce, and Palley, Marian Lief
1987 *Women and Public Policies.* Princeton: Princeton University Press.

Ginsburg, Ruth Bader
1983 "The Burger Court's Grapplings with Sex Discrimination." in *The Burger Court,* edited by Vincent Blasi, pp. 132–56. New Haven: Yale University Press.

Hembacher, Brian
1989 "Fetal Protection Policies: Reasonable Protection or Unreasonable Limitation on Female Employees," *Industrial Relations Law Journal* 11:32–44.

Jacob, Herbert
1986 *Law and Politics in the United States.* Boston: Little Brown and Company.

———.
1989 "No-Fault Divorce and Finances of Women." *Law and Society Review* 23:95–115.

Kosaki, Liane, and Mezey, Susan Gluck
1988 "Judicial Intervention in the Family: Interspousal Immunity and Civil Litigation." *Women and Politics* 8:69–87.

Kraditor, Aileen
1971 *The Ideas of the Woman Suffrage Movement 1890–1920.* New York: Anchor Books.

Law, Sylvia
1984 "Rethinking Sex and the Constitution." *University of Pennsylvania Law Review* 132:955–1040.

MacKinnon, Catharine
1979 *Sexual Harassment of Working Women.* New Haven: Yale University Press.

Mezey, Susan Gluck
1992 *In Pursuit of Equality: Women, Public Policy and the Federal Courts.* New York: St. Martin's Press.

Note, "Rethinking (M)otherhood: Feminist Theory and State Regulation of Pregnancy," *Harvard Law Review* 103: 1325–1343.

O'Connor, Karen
1980 *Women's Organizations' Use of the Courts.* Lexington: Lexington Books.

Okin, Susan Moller
1989 *Justice, Gender, and the Family.* New York: Basic Books.

Salomone, Rosemary
1986 *Equal Education Under Law.* New York: St. Martin's Press.

Taub, Nadine, and Schneider, Elizabeth
1982 "Perspectives on Women's Subordination and the Role of Law." In *The Politics of Law,* edited by David Kairys, pp. 117–139. New York: Pantheon Books.

Tong, Rosemarie
1989 *Feminist Thought: A Comprehensive Analysis.* Boulder: Westview Press.

Tribe, Laurence H.
1992 *Abortion: The Clash of Absolutes.* New York: Norton.

Weitzman, Lenore
1985 *The Divorce Revolution: The Unexpected Social and Economic Consequences for Women and Children in America.* New York: The Free Press.

Whalen, Charles, and Whalen, Barbara
1985 *The Longest Debate.* New York: New American Library.

Williams, Wendy
1982 "The Equality Crisis: Some Reflections on Culture, Courts and Feminism." *Women's Rights Law Reporter* 7(Spring):175–200.

———.
1981 "Firing the Woman to Protect the Fetus: The Reconciliation of Fetal Protection with Employment Opportunity under Title VII." *Georgetown Law Journal* 69:641–704.

The Equal Rights Amendment: What Is It, Why Do We Need It, And Why Don't We Have It Yet?

Riane Eisler
Allie C. Hixson

Riane Eisler was born in Vienna and studied anthropology, sociology, and law at the University of California at Los Angeles, where she also taught. She is the author of numerous articles and books, among them The E.R.A. Handbook *(1978),* The Chalice and the Blade: Our History, Our Future *(1987), and coauthor with David Loye of* The Partnership Way: New Tools for Living and Learning *(1990), a study and action guide. She is also an international activist for women, peace, and human rights issues. She is cofounder of the Center for Partnership Studies in Pacific Grove, California.*

Dr. Allie Corbin Hixson holds a master's degree in humanities and was the recipient of an American Association of University Women College Faculty Program Award leading to her doctorate in English from the University of Louisville (1969). She is the author of A Critical Study of Edwin Muir, Orcadian Poet. *After a fifteen-year teaching career, Hixson retired from academia to become a full-time volunteer activist for women's rights. She led the Kentucky International Women's Year (IWY) delegation to the 1977 First National Women's Conference in Houston, served as one of the vice chairs for that conference, and is past co-chair of the IWY continuing committee, the National Women's Conference Committee. Currently she is moderator of the National ERA Summit.*

The Equal Rights Amendment was first introduced in Congress in 1923 under the leadership of Alice Paul, not three full years after the passage of the Nineteenth Amendment, which guaranteed women the right to vote. After a well-organized and well-financed campaign by conservative and radical right forces such as the John Birch Society, the Eagle Forum, and fundamentalist religious groups, the ERA was defeated in 1982.

Down but not out, ERA was reintroduced in Congress on January 3, 1985. It is currently out of the news but not off the feminist agenda. It is astonishing and frightening how many young women are unfamiliar with ERA. Where do you stand on the issue?

The Equal Rights Amendment

> Section 1. Equality of rights under the law shall not be denied or abridged by the United States or by any State on account of sex.
>
> Section 2. The Congress shall have the power to enforce, by appropriate legislation, the provisions of this Article.
>
> Section 3. This Amendment shall take effect two years after the date of ratification.

The Statue of Liberty is the symbol of American opportunity, of the promise of equality and justice for all. For American women, in this year of 1986 when we celebrate her hundredth anniversary, our Statue of Liberty has a very special meaning. As she too is female, she has always stood for compassion, caring, and other qualities associated with women's great contribution to our nation, with our love for our country and our service to it. But at this time, when the promise of constitutional protection for the half of our nation born female has not yet been fulfilled—when the United States is the only major industrialized nation other than South Africa that does not yet have a constitutional clause guaranteeing women equal rights with men—she is also our inspiration: the emblem of our *inalienable* rights.

Throughout the world, the Statue of Liberty is the symbol of democracy. In our nation, the modern cradle of democracy, this noble female figure is also a reminder to all American women and men of good will that we cannot countenance any failure of the democratic process: that in a nation where poll after poll shows that the majority of the people favor the proposed Equal Rights Amendment to our Constitution, it is our responsibility as American citizens to see that the people's will is done.

The Moral Imperative: Justice and Equality for All Citizens

We hold this truth to be self evident: that all Americans are entitled to the equal protection of our laws. This is the American creed, the best and finest of the American spirit, the promise of the American dream. For over half a century, this promise has been expressed in twenty-four simple words: "Equality of rights under the law shall not be denied or abridged by the United States or by any state on account of sex."

That is the text of the proposed Equal Rights Amendment to the U.S. Constitution. When Americans are asked whether they approve or disapprove of these words, in poll after poll over 60% express approval. Until 1980, both the Democratic and the Republican Party platforms endorsed the ERA. Every major American women's organization from the National Organization for Women to the YWCA, the American Association of University Women, the National Federation of Business and Professional Women's Clubs, the National Council of Negro Women, the League of Women Voters, the National Women's Political Caucus, Federally Employed Women, the Older Women's League, the National Woman's Party and hundreds more support the ERA. So do the American Bar Association, the United Auto Workers, the AFL-CIO, the National Council of Churches, the National Assembly of Women Religious, the National Association of Social Workers, the American Federation of Governmental Employees, the American Jewish Congress, the National Council of Senior Citizens, and most other mainstream American organizations. Four American first ladies—Lady Bird Johnson, Patricia Nixon, Betty Ford, and Rosalyn Carter—backed the ERA. Why? Because, as Lady Bird Johnson said, "everyone in our democracy deserves to be treated with fairness and justice, and to have that right assured in our Constitution."

How, then, is it that we do not yet have an Equal Rights Amendment? As Betty Ford put it in 1981, when the ERA was only three states short of the thirty-eight states needed for ratification, "as a woman and as a Republican, I do not understand how we, as a people, can continue to hold our heads high and be proud of what this nation stands for if we have not guaranteed the rights of half our nation." When, as Ford summed it up, "all we are asking is that our rights be protected under the law," how could a handful of men in a handful of states deprive all American women of the constitutional protection that is our rightful due?

The answer is that these men voted their prejudices, aided and abetted by a well-financed campaign of slanderous lies against women and the ERA.

. . .

Public Information

Facts, Strategies, and Tactics

Proponents of the ERA sometimes have difficulty getting across the fact that women are legally "second class" citizens, particularly when those who feel threatened by the ERA are declaring vociferously that they do not "feel" second-class! A major reason is that until very recently there has been a dearth of FACTS about women, with most of what is taught us presenting primarily data about men.

Until the advent of "Women's Studies" departments on college campuses in the 1970s, the writing of history has been, by and large, the work of men. For nearly two centuries, female school children have suffered the drawing of a veil over their mind's eye as they have been fed a carefully controlled diet of the exploits of "great men" of history, interspersed only briefly with an anecdote about Betsy Ross sewing the flag or Molly Pitcher carrying water to the battlefield.

Not a word was there ever to enlighten a young

girl when she was taught to recite the Declaration of Independence that the glowing words of "all men are created equal" did not include her. Nor did she hear about the long and bitter struggle of our foremothers to gain their property rights and the right to vote.

Too many of these young girls have first had to grow up from being "cheerleaders" to "displaced homemakers" before the veil of illusion was pierced and they understood all too painfully the real status of females in the United States.

It is a sad fact that still today too many females, of all ages, cannot name the year or the number of the amendment to the Constitution that won for women the vote. Nor do they know about the long struggle women had even to obtain this most elementary of all political rights.

In June 1982, during the close contest over the ERA in the Illinois Legislature, the campaign for ratification was brought to a point of intensity with the arrival of the little band of "hunger fasters." Under the leadership of Sonia Johnson, the ex-communicated Mormon who wrote the story of her life and battle with the Mormon hierarchy in the book "From Housewife to Heretic" (Doubleday, 1981), these women gained attention for ERA by announcing they would fast until the critical vote. But, as she recounts in the film documentary about the Illinois campaign ("Fighting for the Obvious"), former Illinois Representative Susan Catania had to explain to her "shocked" colleagues in the Illinois Assembly—both pro-ERA women and men—that these tactics were hardly new. Quite the contrary, the "fast" and the incident of women chaining themselves to the chamber galleries were strictly in the tradition of the tactics used by the suffragists who had gone to jail, had fasted and were force-fed, beaten, with at least one woman dying in a dungeon for the right of women to go to the polls. Still, not one of these Illinois legislators was familiar with this story of the bitter struggles of the suffragists.

The general ignorance about our real history was undoubtedly a major factor behind the failure of the proposed twenty-seventh amendment to the Constitution. The next campaign in Illinois and elsewhere will be successful only if the American public has the indisputable historical facts about the necessity for the Equal Rights Amendment to perfect a flawed democratic blueprint. More women and men will be spokespersons for the Equal Rights Amendment when they have it clear in their own minds how women got into the current dilemma. And when this information is more widely spread, ERA opponents will no longer be able to delude our countrywomen and men with the myth that American women are—and have traditionally been—truly honored both in law and life.

. . .

Short History of the Equal Rights Amendment

1848 First Women's Rights Convention in Seneca Falls, New York, marks official birth of movement for equal rights in the United States. Elizabeth Cady Stanton proclaims all men *and women* are created equal.

1868 Fourteenth Amendment, including clause guaranteeing all persons equal protection under the law, becomes part of U.S. Constitution. Clause 2 provides for lowered representation for states that restrict right to vote of any qualified *male* citizen.

1870 Fifteenth Amendment guaranteeing black males right to vote becomes part of U.S. Constitution. Despite efforts by feminists, provision guaranteeing white and black women right to vote is not included.

1920 After more than three quarters of a century of struggle, Nineteenth Amendment guaranteeing women right to vote becomes part of U.S. Constitution.

1923 Because U.S. courts consistently fail to include women under the definition of persons protected under Equal Protection clause of the Fourteenth Amendment, under leadership of Alice Paul, Equal Rights Amendment is first introduced in U.S. Congress. Called the "Lucretia Mott Amendment," original version authored by Alice Paul reads: "Men and women shall have equal rights throughout the United States and in every place subject to its jurisdiction."

1943 Convinced that amendment would not pass with original wording, Alice Paul consents to rewording: "Equality of rights under the law shall not be denied or abridged by the United States or any state on account of sex."

1972 After introduction in Congress for forty-nine years, with numerous Congressional hearings, ERA is passed by U.S. Congress.

1973 ERA has been ratified by thirty-one states; only seven more states are needed.

1974 Two more states ratify ERA. The total is now thirty-three, so that only five more states are needed. But a well-financed, slanderous anti-ERA campaign is launched. John Birch Society, Phyllis Schlafly, and Christian Anti-Communist Crusade call ERA a subversive communist plot—even though Communist Party USA went on record in 1970 opposing ERA!

1975 North Dakota ratifies the ERA. Four more states are needed.

1977 January 18—Indiana becomes 35th state to ratify ERA. November 18–21—First National Women's Conference held in Houston, Texas, attended by 20,000 women, including Rosalyn Carter, Betty Ford, and Lady Bird Johnson. Conference is part of formal U.S. participation in First United Nations Decade for Women. It adopts a National Plan of Action which has passage of ERA as its first priority. National Women's Conference Committee is charged with implementation of National Plan of Action.

1978 Anti-ERA campaign has successfully blocked further state ratifications. As March 22, 1979, deadline approaches, ERA is still three states short of ratification. ERA Extension March for Equality of 100,000 in Washington, D.C. is spearheaded by NOW. U.S. Congress approves bill introduced by Representative Elizabeth Holtzman (D.N.Y.) extending ratification deadline to June 30, 1982.

1979 ERA opponents file suit in Federal Court challenging the constitutionality of the ERA deadline extension. Case is assigned to Judge Marion Callister, a high official in the Mormon Church, which that same year excommunicates Sonia Johnson for her activities in support of ERA.

1980 Republican Party platform and presidential candidate Ronald Reagan reverse Republican Party's traditional pro-ERA position.
Democratic National Convention reaffirms support for ERA and adds Platform pledge to withhold campaign funds and assistance from candidates who do not support ERA.

1981 Judge Callister rules ERA extension void, but Supreme Court stays ruling pending ERA ratification.

1982 Despite close votes in Florida, Illinois, and North Carolina, no more states ratify and ratification deadline expires.
Although ERA has been ratified by states representing the numerical majority of American population and polls show majority of Americans favor proposed amendment, it fails to be ratified by three additional states needed for it to become part of the United States Constitution. July 14, ERA is reintroduced in Ninety-seventh Congress.

1983 Equal Rights Amendment is again reintroduced in Congress (Ninety-eighth) on January 3rd with 230 co-sponsors in the House, but passage falls six votes short in November 1983 House vote.

1984 First woman in American history to be nominated for vice president, Geraldine Ferraro, runs on Democratic ticket, strongly endorsing ERA.

1985 Equal Rights Amendment is reintroduced in both houses of Ninety-ninth Congress on January 3, first day of new legislative session.

8

Distortions in Knowledge and Understanding: How Patriarchy Affects Our Minds

Mind Control as an Instrument of Patriarchy

Despite the incredible injustice done to women, few people of either sex take the matter seriously enough. In fact, many consider the women's movement deluded if not meaningless. Such people point out that women as well as men are in the nonfeminist or antifeminist camp: Don't many women, too, laugh at the jokes? Don't they back legislators and legislation against so-called women's rights? And even if all this nonsense has anything to it, women are their own worst enemies, now, aren't they?

It is true that some women have acted side by side with men in the control of women by patriarchy. If one thinks for a minute of what a tremendous feat it is for one-half of the world's population to have subjugated the other half, one sees that it has to be so. Women comprise and always have comprised more than half the human population, and had that numerical superiority been tapped, it could have given women great power. Women can be creative, resourceful, and courageous, and we could have stood on our own behalf. Yet for centuries women have very often supported the patriarchal status quo, have "backed our men," and have demanded that our daughters and granddaughters do so as well, binding their feet and their minds and instructing them in the duties of being "good girls" and women. How are we to account for that? Is there something to the charge that we women are our own worst enemies or that there is simply nothing to bother about? Or does the answer lie elsewhere?

People who study history and government often talk of the impossibility of world domination by a monolithic power on the grounds of size and space. It would be unlikely, they argue, that any power could maintain a policing network so encompassing or an executive agency so vast that it could preserve worldwide control. And yet, although patriarchal societies are not themselves monolithic, patriarchy per se is, and for centuries it has maintained control over women and over the institutions that guide the political, economic, and cultural arrangements governing our lives. How does it do this?

It is neither a new nor a surprising idea that

the most potent form of control is one that reigns not over the body but over the mind. Science fiction and cold war drama are full of stories about brainwashing and mind control. To place into the belief system of an individual the idea that the restraints governing her or him are inevitable, right, proper, and desirable is to place a perpetual sentry at the door to a free existence. Given this, there is no need for external guards. So long as the belief remains, the job is done and the control is intact.

Some time ago, at a conference of the Society for Women in Philosophy, as the members were discussing the nature of domination and control, one woman suggested that the most stable and effective form of slavery was one in which members of the oppressed group were socialized to love their slavery. A second woman countered that an even more perfect form of slavery was one in which the slaves were *unaware* of their condition, unaware that they were controlled, believing instead that they had freely chosen their life and situation. The control of women by patriarchy is effected in just such a way, by mastery of beliefs and attitudes through the management of all the agencies of belief formation.

For the most part, without ideas that challenge the patriarchal system, most women (and men) are unaware that their behavior, opportunities, and life possibilities are controlled by the gender system and that women do not freely come to choose "femininity" and its trappings. Women and men really live and move in two different conceptual universes. We see the world, value systems, and ourselves differently because in the most pointed ways patriarchy has arranged for education, media, art, science, philosophy, and many other such agencies to foster two separate conceptual environments in which to learn, grow, and act; our world has two separate images of reality to absorb. Not only are women and men trained to divergent perspectives on the world, but we also come to have divergent postures to life and to the inner reality. We come to answer differently the questions, Who am I? What am I? What shall I be?

If patriarchy is to prevail, it must instill its consciousness into the minds of its subjects, particularly women, because the rebellion of women would mean its demise. Let us sharpen our awareness of the many ways that patriarchal culture exerts control over our understanding. Let us look at some of the more powerful agencies of idea formation: how they work and what they produce.

Education

One learns patriarchal consciousness in many ways, from formal teaching to informal or subliminal messages. Schools, from the primary grades through college, teach not only the three Rs and the officially recognized "knowledge" we find in books and curricula. Self-consciously or not, they also foster values, attitudes, expectations, and worldviews. In functioning both as a trainer for participation in the wider society and as a reflection of that society, the schools generally transmit the traditional views on sexual identity, and very early they convey and reinforce in girls and boys the segregated conceptual systems of the sexes.

The Environment

Consider the hierarchy of the typical primary school and high school. Parallel to the arrangement of women and men in most institutions (male doctor to female assistants, male manager to clerks or secretaries, male pilot to his hostesses, male always in charge), the school presents to the students the traditional picture of masculine power. On the front lines, in the classrooms and in the outer offices behind typewriters, one finds women—accessible, concrete, "live" personnel. In the inner office, apart from the common folk, distant and powerful, resides the principal, who, in more than 95 percent of the cases in the United States, is a male. Further removed and even more powerful are the school boards and the superintendents, of whom approximately 97 percent are male.

Female teachers often function in relation to the principal in the same way that female parents often function in relation to male parents. The former maintain policy set by the latter (authority figure), but when children are very difficult, they are sent to that ultimate power for more "meaningful" discipline. When, on occasion, the principal visits the classroom, students can feel that something special is happening. The effect on both female and male children is powerful and enduring. The arrangement says something very different to boys and girls about what they may become, what they can expect of people in life, and what they can do and accomplish. Given such environmental cues, the consciousness of the two sexes forms rather differently.

The cues gain credence and deepen in meaning as they are played out in the same environment among the children themselves. Children are separated and reminded that they are different: *Boys on this side of the room, girls over there.* Their sense of competition is deepened: *Let's have a contest, boys against the girls.* Their place on the power–strength continuum is fixed: *I want three boys to carry the projector for me.* Little girls are taught to "behave like ladies": *Keep your legs down. Don't be rowdy.* Boys are told to be nice young *men* or to help little Suzy. In my daughter's kindergarten room, toys were arranged against two walls: dolls, cradle, ironing board, brooms, and cupboards on one side; trucks, blocks, and a horse on the other. Circumstances do not change in high school. Boys gravitate to science and technology, girls to literature. Boys begin to excel, and girls to channel their interest away from study and toward pleasing the boys. In my high school, girls were required to take shop, but we spent that semester making jewelry while the boys made wooden cabinets.

Physical education—with its different expectations for girls and boys—trains differently not only the body but also the mind. Boys' team sports—competitive, aggressive, and demanding—teach teamwork, the value of practice and readiness, the effectiveness of perseverance and determination, the willingness to face risk for gain. Girls interested in sports are poorly supported, financially or emotionally. The first-line women in high school sports lead cheers. They win their kudos standing on the sideline in tiny little frocks, tossing their hair and their bodies and shouting, "Come on, men!"

Consider for a moment the effects of those two different vantage points and the lessons gleaned from them. Think about those two, so different sets of perceptions—*I, player* and *I, cheerleader; I, center* and *I, periphery*—and how they will function twenty years later.

The Curriculum

The school system, through its administrative structures and through its curriculum, says different things to female and male students because it evolves out of a sexist society. So do the people within the system. Teachers, principals, authors, and scientists who grow and work in a sexist environment quite naturally develop sexist beliefs and perspectives. What they say and teach is therefore also sexist. Books, films, magazines, pamphlets, and papers are usually sexist; they are used by teachers who rarely notice or question that perspective, and so they are presented as truth. Sexist theories presented as truth in books have the weight of all history behind them. Even more than propositions about women and men that are pointedly spoken, the unspoken or subliminal statement has power because it is not even available for critique.

From nursery school through college, then, the learning experience—both formal and informal—is different for females and males. Different images of what women and men are and should be are communicated by the people in institutions and validated by the history of "truth" as maintained in the books.

Females are presented with the same vision of themselves that we meet in the culture at large. From books, teachers, counselors, extracurricular activities, and aptitude tests, we learn that we are expected to be passive, quiet, nurturing, surreptitiously bossy, incompetent ladies, wives, and mothers and all the rest of the baggage that makes up the content of sexism. Given the power of the school experience—and given its early, continuous, and pervasive entry into our lives—it is hardly surprising that we should absorb its formulations, believe them, and finally internalize them.

Education is, therefore, one of the major contributors to the fixing of a "feminine" (that is, masculist) consciousness in women, the consciousness that allows patriarchy to prevail in our own private worlds because it appears "right." If the schools, the teachers, and the textbooks say it is right, who then are we to say it is wrong?

Change

Since the impetus of the women's movement and Title IX, sensitivity to sexual asymmetry is increasing at the college level, in high schools, even in Parent-Teachers Associations and school boards. For teachers now in training, courses on sexism in education are frequently available. Book publishers, newly sensitized to the issue by groups such as the National Organization for Women (NOW) and the Women's Equity Action League (WEAL), are setting new, nonsexist guidelines. Schools are integrating physical education classes and even sports teams. Universities and professional schools are under pressure to add women to their faculty and staff not only for their own benefit but also as role models for the next generation of contributors. Antifeminists, of course, especially in religion and politics, are equally active in resisting such change.

In any society, the educational process, both formal or otherwise, is a primary effector of enculturation and a major arm of social control. We must, on the one hand, expect it to reflect the beliefs of the wider society and thus to be basically conservative. On the other hand, in our times education is supposed to be a purveyor of knowledge and truth, a foil to hardening of the intellectual arteries, a proponent of personal and social growth. That is an impressive image, believed by many, that carries with it an impressive responsibility: the duty to ensure that, however difficult the task, new understanding will be absorbed and integrated into the existing body of knowledge and passed on to the next generation. In that duty lies the hopeful optimism of women's studies and contemporary feminists. It is the reason for treating the educational system as a primary target for vigilance and activity.

The Media

A medium, in the sense referred to here, is a mode or agency for communicating ideas. In our society, the important media include newspapers, radio and television, magazines, art, advertising, books, and films. They are the primary means of carrying ideas among the various segments of the population. Media not only carry information, they are also very powerful in framing attitudes and forming opinions. In a word, media teach, and they teach not only with what they say but also with how they say it.

Television, Magazines, News Reporting

One of the most powerful media in our lives is television. More than any other modern invention, it has affected the content of our thinking because, beginning early in life for most of us, it so thoroughly pervades our waking time—for some people as much as five or six hours a day. During those hours, we see programs and advertising replete with the traditional stereotypes, the age-old misogynistic attitudes. On the sitcoms and weekly dramas are the long-suffering wives, the manipulative young beauties, the wronged lovers, the mindless child-women pursuing husbands, lovers, or other fantasies. In the Westerns, women are dance hall queens (prostitutes) or damsels in distress. In crime drama, they are the victims of bizarre crimes of murder and rape or perhaps the neglected wives of policemen or bad guys. Sometimes women manage to get on the police force, but they can usually be counted on to mess things up or become victimized in some way and to require saving by the male heroes. Exceptions now exist, thanks to the women's movement, but they are rare. The occasional single women, even the self-sufficient ones, tend to appear in light comedy. Seldom seen, except in "specials," are staunch women, older women, ordinary working women, realistically presented, wrestling with the simple human problems that we are all heir to.

Advertising, more insidious even than programming because it communicates beliefs more covertly, offers the same fare. Here we see women still groaning over which laundry soap will work best on their teenager's dirt, twittering to one another over the advantages of some toilet paper, and decaffeinating their husbands. Now and again we are presented with a professional woman, but she is generally a wife or mother madly juggling her time with the aid of product X so as not to neglect her family. We also see the straight sexual ads: This perfume, hair color, soap, or toothpaste will give you the sex appeal you now lack; if you buy it, you will finally capture your elusive prince. Worse yet are the ads that use female bodies as a shill to the male buyer: half naked sexpots smiling seductively, draped across speedboats or cooing over shaving cream.

Where are the real women, the millions of working women, the divorced and widowed women, the professional women, the intelligent competent women? Where are the ideas truly important to us, truly meaningful: dramas about women trying to break into decent jobs and decent salaries; working to stay emotionally intact; struggling to hold down jobs, care for children, and maintain peace of mind all at the same time? Where are the products truly useful to us, those that really might save work rather than create it?

Magazines and newspapers are no better. Most women's magazines are typically owned and published by men. It is they who select the articles and the advertising. It is they who decide and *tell us* what women want to see or think about. Women's magazines are most commonly found at the check-out counter of supermarkets and discount stores. They are easily identifiable. On their covers generally are pictures of food, artistically presented, side by side with the scoop on the latest quick weight loss diet, or pictures of movie and television stars. Inside, one finds details on how to fix the wonderful recipes and make the family sit up and take notice (finally); details on how to do that diet, lose pounds and inches, look young again, and make one's husband sit up and take notice (finally); and, failing that, how to lose oneself in the lives of those who *were* able to get people to sit up and take notice.

The problem of what is "real" and what is not is rather complex in terms of social presentation. The media not only reflect cultural images, but they also create, teach, and reify them as well. Girls and young women, constantly bombarded with certain images of beauty, are being taught that those images *are* beauty, that they should and must have it. Women who see themselves portrayed only as homemakers (happy or otherwise) or as sexy bombshells like the women of the soaps are being taught that women really are such things and are anomalous in any other guise. The woman who sees those images and does not fit them rarely says to herself, "Those images aren't real." Because she comes to those images with the unconscious working assumption that the media offer true representations of reality, she believes the images. For her, the images are real; thus, it is she who is not. She must either accept herself as the anomaly (with all the personal conflict that goes with it) or change to conform. Until alternative visions are given realistic treatment by the mass media, until they are given social approval by that treatment, they remain subversive, alien, or abnormal. Media treatment of alternative visions, however, has been sparse at best and generally well within the bounds of traditionally acceptable images. Women work, but they are models, highly paid executives in three-piece suits, or chic detectives. Unskinny women do occasionally show up, but, with very few exceptions, they are the clowns, not the lovers.

Language, of course, is central. The repeated use of certain language, particularly words in juxtaposition, can either hide the real meaning of a concept or distort it radically. Consider the term *beauty pageant*. The name alone proclaims that the contestants are beautiful, that they represent beauty per se. But standards of beauty are not absolute. In 1956, my nineteenth-century European grandmother, for example, worried about me endlessly, concerned that my size 9 frame was far too skinny ever to lure a husband; would she find the undernourished contestants of today's pageants beautiful? And I wonder if, after coming to terms with the artifice of contemporary feminine makeup and mannerisms, after spending time with and learning to admire very different kinds of women, most women would indeed find the pageant contestants beautiful. I find them silly and plastic. Can the term itself be wrong? The power of language is such that it can distort reality to its own image. That is why the language and images the media employ have been such a focal point of the movement.

Art and Films

In a university where I taught, a young art instructor was made to remove his painting from a student–faculty art exhibit because his subject was a nude male with full portrayal of genitals. Several nudes (female nudes are always referred to simply as "nudes") remained aloft without comment, their breasts and pubes in plain view.

An avant-garde festival of erotic film at another university was advertised by a poster picturing the face of the devil superimposed on the nude lower torso of a woman. Complaints to the administration by female faculty and students did not, however, bring it down.

Pop music, rock particularly, has become intensely misogynistic and savagely aggressive. Many all-male rock groups wear their sexuality as costume and chant diatribes against "silicone sisters" and delectable poison, even depicting how they would kill, rape, and cut them up. Album covers have appeared depicting chained women, naked or half-naked, their chests to the floor, their heads beneath the shoe of some arrogant male, the leader of the group. The girls in the audience, "liberated" and "modern," scream for more, pay for the concerts, and buy the albums. The number of female rock groups or females in the groups is minuscule.

The sexism of current rock music is particularly destructive today. Modern technology, with its plug-yourself-in, take-anywhere radios and its high-gloss videos, has made the popular music culture an even more prominent and more attitude-forming phenomenon than it has been for generations past. It is ever present, totally penetrating, and inside the head. Thus, its images come to pervade our awareness.

A popular video of the late 1980s, for example, *Addicted to Love,* presented a conservatively suited, well-dressed young man surrounded by several women, all identical. The women—each alike in costume, size, and thin, angular shape—were bizarrely made up so that only their lips, darkened eyes, and hairlines were prominent. Undulating in unison to the rhythm of the music, they were completely without expression or any sign of emotion. They were "sexy." The effect, in its way mesmerizing, was to depict the women not as persons but as caricatures, as clonelike robots, without individuality, identity, thought, or will. They had no humanity. They were props—interesting, decorative, seductive, but not fully alive. What lesson does such an image teach men about women? What lesson does it teach women about ourselves? What behaviors does it justify, does it create?

The point of these representative instances is that the perspective is male. Nude women are respectable because men find them "beautiful," men like to look at them and are accustomed to employing them. Nude males are not respectable because the blatant presentation of the unadorned male body removes the aura of godliness, distance, and power from their persons and reduces them to the common, as women have been reduced. It is fashionable today for women to dress so as to reveal their bodies, and modern chic decrees that those who object are just not "with it." Women who deplore videos, places (Hooters, for example), or fashions because of the contemptuous treatment of women are simply dismissed as prudes and poor sports.

The male hegemony of consciousness sets the rules and standards. This is art; this is not. This is presentable; this is not. The depiction of naked women, invitingly arranged, is presentable art; the same depiction of men is irresponsible (and probably perceived as antimale). Literature portraying war, the conflicts of manhood, or cataclysm is grandeur and art; that involving childbirth, families, or women's experiences is petty craft of marginal interest.

The same is true of the movies, that great shaper of American attitudes. In her study of the treatment of women in the movies, Molly Haskell explained that as the film industry has grown more and more to resemble an "art," with production of a film in the hands of one great "artist" (such as Bergman or Antonioni), the films increasingly reflect that (male) artist's point of view, and women's images have plunged.[1] Increasingly, the camera's eye is male; the film presents a man's view of reality, but, as Beauvoir pointed out, in patriarchy maleness equals universality. Both men and women fail to realize that the film reflects a masculine consciousness. What effect does this have on society? What is the effect on men and women respectively?

Social Science

Scientific theory is extremely important in the lives of twentieth-century people. Side by side with its data, procedures, and theories stands the scientific worldview, an entire way of looking at reality and of relating to life. Some social analysts have suggested that in contemporary times science functions much as a god or as a substitute for God, providing a basis for truth and knowledge, an agent to be trusted and depended on for salvation, even a ground of value.

Placing very high trust in the judgments of science and scientists is part of our cultural ethos. A large segment of the public maintains the belief that Science *is* Truth, the only dependable, sane truth for up-to-date, rational, right-minded people. The corollary to the Science-is-Truth theme is the notion that we should all live our lives in accordance with the truths of Science. Although the idea is rarely articulated in quite this way, a close appraisal of the new intellectual scene reveals the "modern" dictum: Live your life in such a way that Science would be proud of you. As medievals yearned to please God and stand in a state of grace, moderns yearn for a state of "health."

Because today's people want so badly to be judged "healthy," social science—that part of science that focuses specifically on human behavior—has become very much like a faith. On at least two levels—as a technical-academic enterprise and as a "philosophy" of life for popular culture—social science, and especially psychology, serves as a kind of religion. It forms eternal verities about human nature and goals, decrees standards of perfection (health) toward which one is advised to strive, separates the "good" people (healthy, normal, "okay") from the bad (unhealthy, abnormal, "not okay"), determines social priorities both for individuals and for the state, and carries sufficient esteem in the community to socialize the population according to a certain vision of behavior.

Clearly, the impact that theories of social science have on the conduct of our lives is tremendous. For women that spells disaster because both the technical enterprise of the social sciences and the contemporary ethic that has evolved from it are rabidly sexist.

The Formal Enterprise

For a variety of reasons—the newness of the study, the complexity of its subject matter, and the absence of clearly articulated concepts and procedures—social science, at least for now and possibly forever, requires a far greater degree of interpretive latitude than its natural science counterparts. That is a polite way of saying that social science is still quite subjective and thus resistant to the traditional forms of verification. Because of this, theories of the social sciences generally bear the mark of the people who develop them, and they tend to be "culture bound," reflective of both their time and place.

The majority of the people doing social science has always been male. For the most part, it was men who developed the methods of research and the procedures for verification; they also originated the earliest ideas from which current developments have evolved; and they ultimately fixed the application of those ideas, carrying theory out of the laboratory into the streets. With few exceptions, the women who gained some recognition for their work were adherents and popularizers of the existent male-identified systems rather than creators of their own models. In fact, their female support lent those anti-female systems greater weight, not only in academia but also in the minds of the people who received them. Theories from the pens of men immersed in the Victorian worldview brought all the familiar misogynistic stereotypes into greater respectability and enshrined them as science, or truth. At last it was not only taught by experience but was also explained by science that women are petty, self-centered, and unprincipled. Sigmund Freud, for example, showed how such traits were caused by penis envy and the castration complex.

Although some of the most blatant expressions of misogyny have changed (the expression, not the beliefs), the situation is little better today. Sexism in the social sciences is absolutely crucial in the formation of women's consciousness in contemporary society. The precepts of science and social science have become the theoretical underpinnings of education, social service, psychology, medicine, even law, and through them misogynistic doctrines masquerading as scientific truth are being formally infused into our entire conceptual environment. Every teacher, social worker, nurse, and doctor has received the rudiments of elementary psychology and has been properly oriented to the importance of social "adjustment," strong male models, and clear sexual identity distinction. It is a rare child who escapes Erikson or Piaget, a rare ob-gyn patient who eludes Freud. Women are getting extra doses of distortion, officially sanctioned and therefore extremely powerful and convincing.

The other branch of the formal enterprise, the so-called helping professions, is similarly suffused with sexist ideology and perspective. As Phyllis Chesler has pointed out in her book *Women and Madness*,[2] the helping professions may turn out to be more hindrance than help for the woman staggering under the collective weight of patriarchy's consciousness-shapers.

In the nineteenth century, science taught women that "self-abuse" (masturbation) was so damaging that it warranted removal of the clitoris if no other way could be found to stop the sinner-victim from practicing this "foul habit." It taught that "ladies" (if not women) never had orgasms and would not want to. Using the label "ladies nostrums," it dosed women up with morphine and barbiturates so that they would not mind their boredom or their overwork or their frustration or their resentment at being controlled. For those few who would not be so easily cured and who could afford it, science recommended lobotomies or incarceration in "rest homes" or mental asylums.

The twentieth century brought us Freud, Spock, and others who held us responsible for our family's mental health—as if responsibility for their physical health was not enough! Any slip in toilet training, any lack of vigilance in answering questions immediately as they arise, and *wham,* mother makes a crazy child. The scientific and pop literature of the 1950s was full of warnings about the hazards for children whose mother worked outside the home.

"Latch-key kids" were likely to be maladjusted at best, prone to crime and drugs at worst. Today, as the economy *requires* mothers and wives to work, studies are emerging that document the unreliability of any evidence that children reared in homes where mothers work are at all different from children of the Beaver Cleaver model home. In fact, evidence shows a slightly higher inclination to autonomy and adaptability in children whose moms work, not bad traits altogether. But how much guilt have women suffered and are still suffering because "science" scared them to death?

Today science tells us that comparable worth programs are unfeasible, that fetuses are babies, that healthy people are heterosexual (and preferably married), and that physical fitness requires us to be skinny. All of us must turn a critical eye to anything we are taught—and certainly to received opinion. That is the heart of learning and wisdom. But women must be especially wary because so often we are barred from participating in the creation of "received opinion." So often that opinion is an amalgam of flimsy data and a political agenda created by men.

Religion

Religion, as it is practiced through the social institutions of a people, is as much a reflection of that culture's ideals, attitudes, and needs as it is their creator. The Judeo-Christian tradition of the West is no exception. As Western culture is patriarchal, so is its religion, and so is its god.

Although most major religions say that God is without sex, neither female nor male, that contention is contradicted by a host of beliefs indicating the maleness of their anthropomorphic gods. Currently some fathers of the various Christian churches have opposed the ordination of women on the grounds that it would be sacrilegious because the maleness of Christ proves that only men were meant for the priestly office. In medieval times the Church explained that women rather than men were likely to be witches because, among other things, men had been saved from that most awful danger by the fact that Christ was male. Today, the use of feminine pronouns, *she* or *her*, to refer to the deity brings a very hostile response. Certainly, the Catholic imagery of the Church standing analogously to Christ as a wife stands to a husband once more supports the identification of the deity as male.

So in our culture we traditionally conceive of the god as male. What can we make of that? A great deal. The relationships among the concrete, material conditions of a culture, including its social organization and its myths, mores, and ideals, are intricate and close. The maleness of the Western god, his character and behavior, is as much a source of the content of our culture's masculist perspectives as it is an indicator. If men are to be gods, their god must be male. Likewise, if God in His heaven is male, then on earth men can be the only true gods. The entire conceptual system of Martial thought is elevated and deified by its incarnation in the person of the "One True God," ultimate male, just as the sociopolitical structures of patriarchy are reinforced by their justification through theology. The relationship between masculist theology and patriarchal society is the reason why it is both possible and necessary to insist on the masculinity of the priesthood or the authority of the hierarchy. It is the source of the masculine tone in biblical imagery and of male privilege in church doctrine.

Consider the Genesis story of Adam and Eve, a story whose theme appears in numerous mythologies in other cultures. Through feminist analysis, we can see how the story serves both as a resolution for a thorny male psychological conflict as well as a justification of male domination of women. Early in the creation, Adam appears, formed *in the likeness and image of God* (a concept, though unclear, frequently employed to support the ascendancy of maleness). Pure and happy, Adam spends his hours exercising his divinely given dominion over the earth until God decides that he needs a helpmeet. As Adam sleeps, Eve is taken by God from Adam's rib, from his body, formed into a "woman" (so called because she was "taken out of man") and presented to him. Shortly thereafter, Eve is beguiled into disobedience by a serpent, and taking Adam along with her into disfavor with God, she causes the expulsion from the Garden of Eden, the downfall of all humankind, and the spectre of death. The serpent is henceforth sentenced to the dust, Eve to her husband's yoke, and Adam, because he "hearkened to the voice of [his] wife," condemned to labor, sweat, and sorrow.

People have pulled many meanings from this story. Freud made much of the phallic symbolism of the serpent, building around the tale a sexual interpretation. Others have focused on the matter of human growth through separation from parental protection and subsequent trial by life. As feminists, however, we can see other, more pragmatic application.

We can see the masculist myth of Adam, the man, created "in the image of God" (in appearance? in power?), the first progenitor, the first earthly parent. So what if women and not men are able to conceive and bear young? Man did it *first* and produced woman, who produces young only secondarily. And man did it best—cleanly and neatly while he slept, without the fuss and mess of human conception, labor, and childbirth. We can see Eve, the woman—second in creation, an afterthought, a helpmeet—the first to be approached by the snake, easily seduced, equally seducing, placed for sinfulness and stupidity under the yoke of her husband, condemned to painful childbirth and suffering. In a single stroke, the awesome female power of procreation is discounted (as punishment for sin); supreme parenting is comfortably settled upon the male (God and Adam, a theme reiterated and developed in the doctrine of the Virgin Birth); the man is firmly fixed in a position of dominance over women (his wife and, one assumes, other females); and the exploitation and subjection of woman is justified: She sinned, she was stupid and led humanity into disgrace and misery, she was condemned to the yoke by God. Men go out and work (albeit in sweat), and women bring forth children. Men rule and leave off hearkening to their wives, whereas woman's desire is to her husband. All is conveniently explained, justified, and resolved.

As one might expect, the impact of the masculist character of theology and religion is vast, not only on women's lives and perspectives but on the entire culture as well.

Patriarchal Religion and Women

If the religion into which we are given and by which we are expected to live is masculist and misogynist, what does it mean to be a "religious" woman in that context? Although we may rarely focus on them, we are all aware of certain realities of Western religious tradition.

- The god of this tradition (Judaism, Christianity, and Islam) is referred to as "He." It is male. So are its priests, its potentates and hierarchies, its power centers; so are its philosophers, apologists, and policymakers; so are its favorite sons. Encyclicals of the Pope to this day are addressed: Honored Brothers and Dear Sons . . . .
- The savior and messiah of the tradition, Jesus, was himself male; so were the apostles and his disciples. Never did the question arise of his faithful female followers becoming disciples; it was outside the realm of consideration.
- In the tradition, women are conspicuously absent from power, from participation in theory or policy, from full human status. (Aquinas, remember, said that women's souls were not fully developed, and a Jewish male begins his morning prayers with thanksgiving for not having been born a woman.)
- In Judaism, Christianity, and Islam, the ideal woman is a fecund animal who tends to her young, to her husband's home and service, and who "humbly" accepts the dominion of her husband and the male hegemony. Docile, quiet, passive, obedient, and meek, she neither questions nor challenges.
- The Christian ideal, Mary, perfect in submission ("Thy will be done") and sexual purity, took no active part in the drama of Christ. Receptacle only of God's seed, she nurtured her young male god; she herself neither directed nor taught nor hazarded an intrusion into the march of events. She is the female model.
- According to the tradition, woman's progenitor was Eve, mother of evil, precipitator of the Fall. She resides in each of us.
- According to the early fathers, women's bodies are evil, seductive, damning, dirty. Women are carnal; men are spiritual. Women are body; men are mind. Women are sex, and sex is evil. Women are pleasure and passion, and that too is condemned.

Consider the impact on your self-image of being "in the likeness of God," like Jesus, the Pope, and the "Brothers of the Church" and contrast it with never finding yourself reflected in the sacred pronoun. Utter: God, He . . . ; God, Him. Now say: God,

She . . . . Imagine the experience of seeing oneself reflected in the sacred images of power: Christ walking on clouds, God forming Adam with His powerful arm. Imagine, instead, modeling after the suffering Mary or shamefully hiding one's inner Eve, one's sexuality. Think of looking high into the pulpit, seeing the Man proclaiming the Word of Him, knowing that this is ever out of the grasp of oneself or any of one's kind because of one's lesser excellence and status. Ask again: If one's religion is sexist, masculist, and misogynist, what does it mean to be a religious woman?

No wonder victimization is a sacred principle of womanhood, sacrifice a magic contribution, self-effacement a high.

> *Patriarchal religion adds to the problem by intensifying the process through which women internalize the consciousness of the oppressor. The males' judgment having been metamorphosed into God's judgment, it becomes the religious duty of women to accept the burden of guilt, seeing the self with male chauvinist eyes. What is more, the process does not stop with religion's demanding that women internalize such images. It happens that those conditioned to see themselves as "bad" or "sick" in a real sense become such. Women who are conditioned to live out the abject role assigned to the female sex actually appear to "deserve" the contempt heaped upon "the second sex."*
>
> –MARY DALY, *Beyond God the Father*[3]

God, Mars, and Culture

Consider the impact that the deification of maleness has on society. Remember that in any society the forms of religious worship are a reflection of cultural ideals, expressed in a different language. What makes the religious expression of those ideals so powerful is its claim to absolute validity and its subsequent persuasive force over people who believe it.

What we find when we analyze the patriarchal Western tradition is precisely what we would expect to find: a Martial god, an authoritarian ethic, and a warrior consciousness. The worship of Mars, the religion of masculism, means for society an obeisance to all the warrior values.

In patriarchy, God is a ruler, a king. Superior to all, He commands. He does not tolerate disobedience, rewards and punishes according to how well one meets his expectations, and trains his followers through a series of trials and challenges.

The masculinity of God is underscored smartly by comparison with Mary as the image of mercy and kindness. The Queen of Heaven, to whom most of the finest churches in the West are dedicated, is the Mother, free from the angry, frightening qualities of Mars/God: forgiving where he is stern, understanding where he is legalistic, accessible where he is distant.

God is good, we are told, although there are no standards outside of his own will against which we may judge him. He is good (right) because he is God; that is, King, the top of the hierarchy. Everybody else is expected to be good, too; that is, obedient to the will of the King. If one is not good (obedient), then God punishes. If one suffers sufficiently, one might be redeemed (forgiven), but that, too, is solely up to God. The pattern of the God–person relationship is clearly disciplinarian and authoritarian.

Other relationships in which God resides are equally authoritarian although in a different context. The relationships are generally expressed as dualistic oppositions in which God has ascendancy: God against nature, spirit against body, life against death, God vis-à-vis humanity. The relations are ones of strain, conflict.

The tone is certainly not humanistic: You are bad, it tells us. Your body is bad; sex is bad; pleasure is bad. You may be saved from yourself, but only if you deny your earthly self.

And of course the ethos of strain and contention permeates the lives of the people who are both its subject and its instigators. One strives constantly to "be good," to conform, to measure up to an image that is not in harmony with what it is to be human because, among other things, it is derived from only one aspect of humanity: maleness.

The character of this Mars-Father-God permeates our culture conceptually and spiritually. It is difficult to be self-affirming, constructively self-confident, healthily self-loving in the face of an image of humanity that is subordinated and debased.

Feminist Alternatives

There are other ways to treat religion than as the submission of one's will and understanding to the prescriptions of a powerful, antagonistic authority.

There are those who view worship as a total experience of life's elements, so beautiful, meaningful, and profound that they transcend temporary matters and deserve our most concentrated attention and respect. Perhaps such an experience may be possible through a very sensitive portrayal of the Western tradition, through Judaism or Christianity, but certainly not through the secularized, garden variety, patriarchal projections to which we are accustomed.

Many feminists question whether a reformed, nonsexist portrayal of the Judeo-Christian religions is possible, whether the historical identification of God as male can be reversed, whether its hierarchical, authoritarian character can be purged without obliterating its nature altogether.[4] Feminists ask whether women can or should participate in a religion that worships male gods and ideals in male language, demeans women's full humanity, and prohibits the full exercise of women's potentials. Can or should we participate in religious institutions that have historically been misogynistic and that even now form policy for our lives while blocking our power to contribute to those formulations? Is reform possible or even worthwhile?

Feminists both within and outside of the traditional religious institutions raise some rather intriguing questions about "God-talk"[5] and by doing so perhaps point the way to a revitalization of religious experience. We might wonder whether a feminist theology would be less authoritarian, less demanding and constraining than the ones we know? In such a perspective, would the deity Herself, free of masculist ideals, have been visualized as a more tolerant accepting being, and would such a religion have been more affirming? Is there need for a deity at all, or could we, as Mary Daly proposes, think of God not as a person at all, not as a noun, but rather as a verb, the Holy Verb *to be.* Thus, life itself and each moment in it are both deity and divine.

Some feminists reject entirely any forms of worship, arguing that religion channels one's energy in the wrong directions, that women's situation requires strong political action, not "wasteful dreaming." One can certainly sympathize with such a view, given the history of religion for women. On the other hand, I perceive feminism to be at base a spiritual movement. Feminists seek increased opportunity for participation and gain not as ends in themselves, not simply for the power they entail, but rather for the growth in the quality of life they represent, and that is a spiritual matter. In such a context, "religion," worship, or reverence may prove fruitful, and it should not be dismissed without careful scrutiny simply because of its past association and its usurpation by patriarchy.[6]

Conclusion

As we examine the agencies that form beliefs in our culture, we see a network of interlocking institutions and ideas that direct the consciousness of society.

Ideas that appear repeatedly in varying forms throughout the network become highly powerful forces of socialization and indoctrination because they are continually reinforced by their pervasiveness and their constant repetition in many languages and contexts. Their repetitiveness alone gives them a cumulative effect upon awareness that renders them nearly unquestionable, if not undeniable. We have seen, in case after case, that our society's institutions promote the traditional misogynistic themes of women's inferiority. The wonder is not that women absorb them; the wonder is not that we participate in our own oppression, but that any of us at all ever break through to a new vision!

And yet we do break through, we do come to recognize the falsehoods and the injustices, and we do strive to live by a more constructive point of view. That, in a nutshell, is what feminism is. However heterogeneous some of the theories, methods, or goals, feminism is constant in recognizing the falseness and perversity of masculist images of womanhood; it is constant in its affirmation of the worth of women. The following chapter is a small glimpse of the career of that affirmation.

Notes

1. Molly Haskell, *From Reverence to Rape: The Treatment of Women in the Movies* (New York: Holt, Rinehart & Winston, 1973).

2. Phyllis Chesler, *Women and Madness* (New York: Doubleday, 1972). Reissued with a new introduction by Harcourt Brace Jovanovich, 1989.

3. Mary Daly, *Beyond God the Father* (Boston: Beacon Press, 1973), p. 49.

4. See particularly the works of Mary Daly: *Beyond God the Father* (1973) and *Gyn/Ecology* (1978).

5. See the works of Rosemary Radford Ruether, Carol Christ, Starhawk, Merlin Stone, Margot Adler, Anne Kent Rush, Charlene Spretnak, Naomi Goldenberg, Judith Plaskow, Penelope Washbourn, Nelle Morton, Barbara G. Walker, Carol Ochs, Elaine Pagels, Elisabeth Fiorenza, and many other women now participating in the feminist "Womanspirit" movement.

6. For further discussion of feminist spirituality, see Sheila Ruth, *Take Back the Light: A Feminist Reclamation of Spirituality and Religion* (Lanham, MD: Rowman & Littlefield, 1994).

Myth America Grows Up

Rita Freedman

Rita Freedman, author of Beauty Bound *(1986) and* Bodylove: Learning to Like Our Looks—and Ourselves *(1988) has long been concerned with the place of appearance in the formation of women's self-concept. In this selection she details how little girls learn to please with their looks and mannerisms—indeed, how we all learn the trappings of femininity.*

I COMBED THE BEACHES LAST SUMMER COUNTING topless toddlers. Few could be found. On the Riviera, women freely bare their breasts to the Mediterranean sun. Here at home, the uncomplicated chests of little girls are discreetly covered. In this way young bodies are draped in gender, poured into the female mold, to be shaped, reshaped, and misshapen by it. Three-year-olds veiled behind bikini tops learn a small lesson in body awareness, one that often leads to heightened self-consciousness and sometimes to tormenting obsessions.

In every society, certain behaviors are considered more appropriate for one sex than for the other. Gender divergence includes occupational, recreational, and legal distinctions, as well as decorative and ornamental ones. How do children acquire this complex set of gender rules? A five-year-old confidently tells me that "girls play at being pretty, but boys play cars. . . ." How did she learn these components of masculinity and femininity so soon?

The socialization of gender begins in infancy, continues through adolescence, and involves almost every aspect of experience, including toys, clothes, media images, and, of course, parental expectations and behavior. Although studies of infants reveal few sex-based differences in emotional and cognitive functions, parents believe that their sons and daughters are quite different right from birth. Girls and boys do grow up in different "climates of expectation."

During pregnancy, parents prepare not just for a new baby but for a strong masculine son or a beautiful feminine daughter. Consequently, these are the qualities that they project onto their newborns. As noted . . . earlier . . . when parents rated firstborn infants, they saw their daughters as beautiful, soft, pretty, cute, and delicate, whereas they viewed their sons as strong, better coordinated, and hardier, even though the male and female infants had been carefully matched for equivalent physical characteristics.[1] People who played with a three-month-old dressed in yellow more often judged it a boy because of "the strength of his grasp and his lack of hair." Those who thought the baby was a girl remarked on her "roundness, softness, and fragility."[2] The cuter the baby, the more likely it is to be judged a girl.

Long before birth, babies are imagined through fantasies that devalue girls even while idealizing their appearance. In a song from the show *Carousel,* Bill ponders his unborn child. First a son "with head held high, feet planted firm"; a boy who, in his father's daydream, "grows tall and tough as a tree." Then, in the softer tones of an afterthought, Bill considers a daughter, "pink, and white as peaches and cream"; a girl with "ribbons in her hair, brighter than girls are meant to be," yet still needing to be "sheltered and dressed in the best that money can buy."

Old autograph books sometimes "wish you hope, wish you joy, wish you first a baby boy." A widespread preference for male offspring persists. In a recent American sample, over 90 percent of the couples wanted a firstborn son. Nearly all the men and three-fourths of the women said they would want a boy if they were to have only one child.[3] A frequent reason given by those few women who did prefer a girl was that "it would be fun to dress her and fuss with her hair."[4] When asked what kind of a person they want their child to become, parents mentioned "being attractive" far more often for daughters than for sons.

Imagine a growing girl who represents the collective experiences of many youngsters whose lives were studied for this chapter. The composite experiences of Linda typify the socialization process which teaches girls their role as members of the fair sex. Linda is initiated into the beautified female world through the subtle lessons of daily life. Her few strands of baby hair are swept into a curl in the hospital nursery. Her ears are pierced before her first birthday, her nails polished for her second. She is securely wrapped in a strawberry-shortcake universe: roses on her walls, ribbons in her hair, ruffles on her shirts. "Early in life, the pink world starts to process the girls to value it."[5]

Intuitively, children sense when and how they are touched or avoided, admired or ignored, complimented or criticized. Girls are initially sturdier than boys and developmentally ahead of them, but are perceived as more fragile. Handled more delicately, they receive less physical stimulation and less encouragement for energetic or exploratory behavior. Parents show greater anxiety about a girl's safety even while she is still in diapers. Fathers begin by engaging in more rough-and-tumble play with sons and by spending nearly twice as much time with sons as with daughters.[6] As Bill concludes in his song, "You can have fun with a son, but you gotta be a father to a girl."

Interestingly, fathers seem to sex-type youngsters even more consciously than mothers do, for example by giving children toys that are more gender-stereotyped. Men show greater anxiety over effeminate behavior in sons, while actively encouraging it in daughters. Fathers seem to want their little girls to fit their own personal image of an attractive female, within the bounds of what is appropriate for a child. Wives report that husbands urge them to keep their daughters' hair long and to "doll them up" even when the mothers themselves don't feel that these things are very important. Linda's father echoes the voices of many dads who describe their preschool daughters as "a bit of a flirt": "she cuddles and flatters in subtle ways"; "she's coy and sexy."[7]

Whether such descriptions of "daddy's little girl" are accurate, fathers enjoy and encourage seductive appearance in their daughters, which in turn enhances these Oedipal flirtations. In this way, Linda is more or less explicitly directed toward a kind of "predatory coquetry." Her enactment of the beauty role is therefore shaped by the way her father reinforces Linda's appearance, independently of how her mother may model feminine beauty.

According to Piaget's theory of intellectual growth, children strive to adapt to life by trying to understand their experiences. We are biologically programmed, says Piaget, to mentally reconstruct the world by forming concepts about ourselves and our surroundings. Mental file cards are written and rewritten to conform ever more closely to social "reality." Concepts of masculinity and femininity are learned as part of this general process of intellectual growth.

In acquiring her sense of gender, Linda first develops a rudimentary idea that people come in two separate forms. Her mental file cards are scribbled with vague notions of mommy/daddy, boy/girl, man/woman, along with perceptions about clothing, hair styles, and other gender markers. By her third birthday, she is well aware that girls and boys look and act differently, apart from any underlying genital structure. An anecdote describes two toddlers looking at a statue of Adam and Eve. "Which is which?" asks one. "I could tell if only they had their clothes on," replies the other.

Though she does not yet understand gender constancy (once a girl, always a girl), Linda knows her own gender membership. Confidently she asserts, "I'm a girl," because she has written "me" on the file card that is filled with "feminine" concepts. Once gender has been established internally, Linda begins to strive for consistency between what she knows about herself and what she knows about girls in general. The dialogue in her head runs something like this: "Since I'm a girl, and since girls look and act in certain ways, then I, too, should look and act the way they do." And so she begins to enact her feminine role. The need to establish consistency between oneself and one's gender role is the same for the toddler as for the adult. The problem for Linda (as for all women) is how to bring together her self-perception as a female with an understanding of gender role.

Femininity soon becomes associated with beauty, and to the internal dialogue a subtheme is added. "Since I'm a girl," Linda thinks intuitively, "and since girls are pretty, then I, too, should be (will be, must be) pretty, just like Mommy." In this way, beauty becomes part of her self-perception as a female. When she confirms the belief that she is a girl by enacting some part of the beauty role (such as putting ribbons in her hair), she achieves a sense of cognitive consistency that in turn feels satisfying. Hence, the inner dialogue concludes with the sentiment "I enjoy being a girl!" By maintaining harmony between two concepts (self-image and feminine image), Linda keeps her mental file cards in order, and in this way makes the world more comfortable and predictable.

Piaget explains that knowledge of one's gender role is partly imposed from within, that is, self-motivated through the basic drive to create intellectual order out of chaotic experiences. But gender role is also externally imposed. It is culturally conditioned through the direct experience of hearing Cinderella tales, dressing Barbie dolls, watching Miss America, Miss Teen, Miss Hemisphere. It is also overtly reinforced. Throughout the elementary school years, girls receive more compliments than boys on their appearance. They are given a bigger wardrobe to choose from and are admired especially when they wear dresses.[8] Linda repeatedly hears others say "You look so pretty," and eventually greets her own reflection with "I'm so pretty" or "Am I pretty? . . . as pretty as other girls? . . . as pretty as others expect me to be?" Finally she begins to wonder, "How can I be prettier?" *Pretty* becomes a framework within which she paints her feminine self-image.

Although parents are beginning to treat sons and daughters more similarly, they still give their children sex-typed clothing, toys, and books. These act as powerful conditioning agents that socialize the importance of female beauty. Emphasis on feminine attractiveness is obvious in fairy tales and in picture books for preschoolers, in which female animals are depicted with long curly eyelashes and ribbons on their tails. A study of school texts found that these books traditionally portrayed women as mothers who wear aprons and who "seem to want and do nothing personally for themselves." The notable exception was cited of a mother who "treated herself to some earrings on a shopping trip."[9]

Before 1970, textbooks rarely showed females engaged in independent activities. When the occupational world of women was presented, it consisted of either service jobs (nurse, teacher) or "glamour" jobs (model, dancer, actress), in which body display is an important component. A popular children's book of the 1970s shows a small boy and girl fantasizing about their future: when the boy becomes a jungle explorer and captures a lion, the girl "curls the lion's mane in her beauty shop for animals"; when he dreams of being a deep-sea diver, she becomes "a mermaid who serves him tea and ice cream."[10]

Books are somewhat less stereotyped today, although children's toys remain highly gender-typed. While boys are given action dolls equipped to capture the enemies of outer space, girls are given fashion dolls equipped with exotic outfits for capturing attention. Over 250 million Barbies have been sold in the past twenty-five years, a doll population that equals the number of living Americans. Over 20 million outfits a year are bought for Barbie and her friends, as the seeds of clothing addiction are sown. One collector concludes that Barbie remains the most popular fashion doll simply because she is the prettiest. (Barbie is both thinner and "sexier looking" than when first created in 1959.) Fashions for Barbie in 1984 featured her in elegant gowns because "glamour is back." Toy stores also sell makeup for dolls. With "Fashion Face," Linda can "put on Barbie's face, wash it off, change her look again and again." A single tube costs several dollars, and remember, this is makeup for a doll!

On Christmas morning, Linda eagerly unwraps her very own superdeluxe makeup set, "just like Mommy's." Here, packaged innocently with fun titles like "Fresh and Fancy" and "Pretty Party" are the sugar and spice that feed the beauty myth. These high-priced glamour rehearsal kits contain the essential tools of the trade. For Linda's hair there are rollers, styling combs, curling irons, "falls," wash-in color, and sparkles. For her face there are paints, gloss, frosting, liners, blush, shadow, and mascara. For her hands there are lotions, polish, nail crayons, and decals. Also included is gold foil for "beauty accents" and glitter for "today's metallic look." The tubes smell like candy and taste like soda pop. They come complete with magnifying mirror in a convenient carrying case so that she can take it anywhere and check her looks perpetually. Here is the making of a mirror junkie. The box covers of cosmetic kits carry reassuring messages to parents. "These toys are suitable for children as young as three"; they will help your child "personalize her own pretty face"; help her "create dozens of fashion looks and become a beauty consultant for her friends"; teach her the "fun way to learn beauty secrets."

What else do they teach Linda about herself and her role in society? That feminine beauty requires many faces and she can cultivate them all; that the easy way to impersonate a real grown-up lady is to put on the same disguise that Mommy wears; that playtime means narcissistic preening; that fantasy fun means enacting Cinderella; that spending time and money on beautifying oneself is approved by parents; that others like her to look fresh, fancy, and seductive; that her own face, though pretty, is somehow inadequate and needs to be made even lovelier—a double message that fosters negative body image and self-doubt.

For some girls, "glamouring up" is not just child's play. There has been a phenomenal growth in children's beauty contests since those protestors picketed the Miss America Pageant in 1968. Paradoxically, during the very years when the women's movement became a pervasive social force, beauty pageants for children . . . also gained in popularity. The Miss Hemisphere Pageant, with numerous divisions for girls ages three to twenty-seven, has mushroomed in size from a few hundred contestants in 1963 to hundreds of thousands of participants today. It is billed as the largest single beauty pageant in the world. Toddlers barely out of diapers (sometimes wearing false eyelashes and tasseled bikinis) are paraded before judges who scrutinize their "beauty, charm, poise and personality." The separate "masters" division for boys up to age nine attracts far fewer contestants.

Why do parents pay sizable entrance fees, invest in elaborate outfits, and drive hundreds of miles to these contests? Besides seeking prizes and modeling opportunities, many sincerely believe that they are helping girls to develop into "ambitious but feminine women, like Bess Myerson." Some experience a strong element of vicarious achievement. They describe the thrill of seeing their daughters on display. One father remarked, "Taking my girls around to pageants is my activity, like a hobby. The contests are flashier than Little League and the children don't get hurt."[11]

But perhaps they do get hurt, in ways less obvious yet more odious than a sprained ankle in a ballgame. Pediatrician Lee Salk warns that children's beauty contests do more harm than good. He describes them as perfect setups for failure, as girls experience tremendous pressure to accept and identify with exaggerated physical stereotypes. Realizing that they lack the winning look, many suffer deep feelings of inadequacy.

"Girls Like Rainbows, Boys Don't"

Although children start with only rudimentary concepts of masculinity and femininity, they soon fill in the details. Awareness of gender dualism expands and crystallizes with age, as cognitive file cards are refined. Each day, children learn from their books and toys, from parental reaction to their behavior, and from models that constantly surround them, that beauty is a critical part of femininity. When asked how boys and girls are different from each other, children's compositions show a clear understanding that beauty belongs to females. Although genital and reproductive differences are rarely mentioned, youngsters universally say that girls wear makeup, have pretty hair, "don't get as dirty and aren't as tough" as boys. It is tempting to think that times have changed, that the next generation is already liberated from gender stereotypes and is no longer bound by beauty myths. But consider this response written in 1982 by a fifth-grader:

> *Because I am a girl I am different in many ways. Girls put on eye shoudo and boys ware nothing like eye shoudo. And girls ware gowns and shoes and take a pocket book around. Boys don't do that. Alls they have to do is put on a tie and shine shoes. Girls put lipstick on their lips and girls put on earings, then they put on stockings and put thier hair in a bun or fix up the hair. Girls do housework and take care of a baby if they have*

one. Boys just sit around and watch football games and other sports.

The following comments from seven- and eight-year-olds are cited because they particularly reflect an awareness that beauty is central to the female role.[12]

"How Are Boys and Girls Different?"

- Girls play at being pretty but boys play cars. Boys' voices are louder. Girls wear more jewelry.
- Girls like pink, boys like blue. Boys take their shirts off when it's hot but girls don't.
- Girls are prettier and boys are bossy. Boys stay outside as long as they want, but girls can't.
- Boys don't clean house and girls don't get dirty. Most girls do not get hit by their mothers because girls are more beautiful.
- Girls are cute and harmless, don't get as muddy as boys. Girls like rainbows, but boys don't.
- Boys don't dance, or play hopscotch. Girls don't play rough or get sweaty (but they have the same rights as us).

More articulate ten- and eleven-year-olds made the following observations:

- Girls are very sensitive and delicate. They like perfume and like looking good and sweet. Boys are rough, tough, and insensitive.
- Girls can wear anything they like, but boys can only wear pants. Girls have more clothes. They are more into pink rooms and looking pretty.
- Girls put on makeup and boys don't because they don't want to look pretty. Girls like to stay clean and neat. Some boys say they don't want to take a bath and they want to stay smelly and dirty.
- Girls don't have a mustache, boys don't have a baby. Boys have short hair and drive better than girls. Girls can cook better but boys are stronger.
- Girls are soft like cotton but boys are rough like a truck. But we are nice to each other—that's what counts.

Clearly, these children believe that the male body is to be strengthened and developed, while the female body is to be protected and beautified. In fact, young children evaluate physical attractiveness in much the same way as adults do.[13] In nursery school, they can reliably judge the attractiveness of classmates and prefer to play with those who are better-looking.[14] Preschoolers also connect sex-related personality traits to appearance. They rate unattractive boys as more "scary and aggressive" but rate unattractive girls as more "fearful of things." (Good looks may inhibit assertive behavior in pretty girls who feel out of character when behaving more actively or aggressively than others expect.)

Children sex-typed a pretty face as feminine and a strong muscular physique as masculine. These stereotypes in turn influence the self-concepts of boys and girls in different directions. In a survey of eight- to fifteen-year-olds, girls at each age level worried more about their appearance than boys. Over half the fifth-grade girls in another sample ranked themselves as the least attractive person in their class. Follow-up interviews showed they were not simply motivated by modesty but were truly troubled by their "poor appearance."[15] The older the girl, the greater the influence of attractiveness on her popularity, as if children's understanding of the disproportionate social value of beauty to females gradually increases.

Linda grows up dressing and undressing Barbie, playing with her "Pretty Party" glamour kit, watching the selection of Miss Universe each year. She believes that beauty is something that happens at adolescence. Patiently she awaits it. While marking time, Linda may try on the role of the tomboy. Why do so many tomboys appear only to disappear? What can they teach us about the growing of little Myth America?

Tomboyism is a temporary detour on the road to female development, a last adventure before the final commitment to womanhood. Tomboys are familiar figures. Bred in every neighborhood, they roam like tomcats over the noisy, competitive, outdoor masculine turf. High on energy, they use their bodies freely to explore the world of people and things. The term *tomboy* traces back to the 1600s, when it was first directed at boys to censure them for "rude, boisterous or forward behavior." Soon the label was transferred to "girls who behave like unruly boys," and girls have worn it ever since.[16]

Tomboys not only act the part, they look it as well. We recognize them by their smudged faces and ragged clothes. The frills of Miss Muffet are not for them.

Patched, scruffy, and unkempt, they need shoes they can run in, pants they can climb in. A tomboy's appearance enables the very behavior it proclaims. For packaging can create both the image *and* the limits of a person. A female is what she looks like as much as what she does.

One of the most striking aspects of tomboyism is its current popularity. A majority of female college students describe themselves as former tomboys. With bright eyes and a tinge of nostalgia, they recount their tomboy adventures without shame or embarrassment. Tomboyism is the rule rather than the exception. More than half the adult women surveyed recall having been tomboys. Among growing girls, nearly three out of four currently place themselves in the tomboy category.[17]

Although tomboyism is almost universal in Western cultures, it has no counterpart among males Parents, especially fathers, react strongly against effeminate appearance in sons. A young boy in mommy's high heels, pearls, and nail polish, makes parents fidgety, to say the least. Such adornments remain a gender distinction reserved for the other sex. The term *sissy* is sometimes suggested as a parallel to *tomboy,* although the two are not really equivalent. Any child, whether boy or girl, who is noncombative, fearful, prim, and proper can be dubbed a sissy and ridiculed for possessing such "effeminate" qualities. Whereas *sissy* is clearly perjorative for both sexes, the term *tomboy* confers little stigma before puberty; it is never directed at boys and is often considered a tacit compliment for girls. Differences between the two terms clearly reflect the bias that male attributes are normative.

Why does our culture produce so many tomboys? Why do we first dichotomize gender roles and then permit and even encourage girls to "cross over" temporarily? Why do we set them apart with a distinct label?

Answers to these questions lead back to the belief in female deviance. Recall that one strategy women use to normalize their social position is to become one of the boys. Tomboyism has survived for centuries because it serves a purpose: to defer the full impact of being just another girl. As a tomboy, Linda straddles two gender roles and thereby expands the territory of the self into the valued male domain.

Both boys and girls internalize the cultural devaluation of females. Even preschoolers are aware that masculine traits are accorded higher value and yield greater rewards. In tests where children can express a preference for being one sex or the other, only one boy in ten chooses to be female, whereas one girl in three chooses to be male.[18] Similar results are found in age groups ranging from toddlers to adults. Fewer boys than girls believe it would be better to have been born the opposite sex. As one boy remarked, "If I'd been born a girl, I would have to be pretty and no one would be interested in my brains." Nearly a quarter of adult women surveyed recall a conscious desire to be a boy during childhood, but fewer than 5 percent of adult men remember ever wanting to be female.[19] At twelve Linda writes:

> *I am a female. I play football and baseball with a lot of boys. They sometimes beg me to play with them. I don't think it is fair that boys can do everything and girls can't. Boys have a baseball league but girls can't. . . . Nobody knows if girls could do more than boys or if boys could do more than girls. . . . Girls have to wash the dishes and suffer by doing everything while the boys have all the fun. One day, I want it to be fair.*

Tomboys gain temporary access to the valued masculine world. As "one of the boys," they shake off the girlish stigma and enjoy membership in a privileged club. In fact, rejection of personal adornment and adoption of a boyish look accomplishes for the prepubertal girl very much what beauty rituals accomplish for the adult woman. Both facilitate access to male company; both influence body image and self-esteem; and both defend against an underlying feeling of inferiority. Adopting tomboyism, like cultivating beauty, brings similar tangible rewards: visibility, attention, adventure.

Some young girls (like their mothers) maintain a dual repertoire of tomboy togs along with more coquettish drag, using one or the other as events require. In fact, such role diversity and flexibility may epitomize the best of an androgynous gender model. However, a time comes during adolescence when tomboyism evokes more anxiety than satisfaction, and its rewards no longer balance its costs. Though tolerated before puberty, tomboyism becomes increasingly threatening and is usually abandoned as gender file cards are updated. By the late teens, few girls continue to wear the title. When asked why they gave it up, college students replied:

I just outgrew it. It was more or less a natural process that happened over a long period of time. . . . I started wearing more dresses because I like them and because Mom decided I should look nice. . . . When dating, it was difficult to be myself, so I had to change my image in dressing and mannerisms.

Their responses convey an underlying feeling of loss. Some young women are searching for new labels that can link them to their former selves. At age nineteen Linda says, "If a tomboy is a woman who is very assertive or aggressive, I guess I'm still a tomboy. . . . I don't use the term *tomboy* because that connotes being very young, but I'm still very active, though less athletic, and still consider myself androgynous." The effects of tomboyism reach into adulthood. A survey showed that women who had been overtly tomboyish as children preferred a more tailored style of dress, wore more muted colors, and decorated their homes with a nonfrilly, functional design. Women who had never been tomboys preferred more ruffly clothes, were more marriage-oriented and less career-minded.

Attracting an Identity

"A boy expands into a man; a girl contracts into a woman." So goes an old saying. With each contraction Linda sheds a piece of her comfortable old skin to emerge naked and pink into the pastel shades of womanhood. Transforming into the fair sex, she delivers a new self. Yet labor is painful. Adolescence marks a major crisis in gender acquisition. Puberty rings out, sounding the death knell for a tomboy. Gentle curves on breast and hip expose her. In poetry, Anne Sexton assures her daughter: "There is nothing in your body that lies / All that is new is telling the truth."[20] Revealed as woman, Linda can no longer masquerade as an impostor in a tomboy's costume. Contracting, she abandons the ballfield for the prince's ball, trades in her old uniform, learns to play new games and to compete in new arenas. Contracting, she must outfit herself with the eleven traits that professionals in the Broverman study judged as feminine and must gradually abandon the long list of thirty-eight attributes they rated as masculine.

Puberty arrives uninvited—sometimes prematurely, other times long overdue. Many girls experience it as a turning point in their self-image. At age eleven, Linda was asked to describe herself by making a series of statements starting with "I am a . . ." She began: "I am a human being, I am a girl, I am a truthful person, I am not pretty. . . ." One of the striking sex differences to emerge at adolescence is a greater self-consciousness in females. Girls find it harder than boys do to measure up against the idealized norms for their own sex. In a study of fourth-through tenth-graders, the oldest girls had the poorest self-image of any group in the sample.[21] Nearly half the girls in a survey of twenty thousand teenagers reported they frequently felt ugly.[22] To the extent that adolescent girls dislike their bodies, they also dislike themselves.

Twice as many high school girls as boys want to change their looks. Girls are dissatisfied with a greater number of body parts than boys. They generally see themselves as less attractive than other girls, whereas boys tend to rate themselves as better-looking than their peers.[23] A correlation exists between intelligence and body satisfaction in boys, that is, the brighter the boy, the more satisfied he is with his appearance. No such relationship is found in girls, possibly because bright girls are all too aware that they can never attain the beauty ideal.[24]

By college age, 75 percent of males report they feel good about their overall looks and facial features, as compared with only 45 percent of females.[25] Adolescent girls are tormented by poor body image, partly because they have learned during childhood to overvalue, display, and mistrust their appearance. They enter puberty with a strong need to feel attractive, and therefore suffer greater insecurity than boys do when their developing bodies feel awkward and out of control. Moreover, girls are socialized to search for self-identity through male attention. To transform from tomboy to Tom's girl, Linda must depend in large part on being pretty.

Since good looks are stereotypically associated with desirable personality traits, an "unattractive" changing body threatens self-esteem. The connection between appearance and worthiness for females can become so deeply ingrained during puberty that it remains throughout a woman's life, making her continuously insecure about her appearance and, consequently, about herself. Looking back, women describe their teens as a time filled with awkwardness, embarrassment, feelings of inadequacy, fear of sexuality and of separation. Some become frozen into the negative body images that develop during this transitional stage and are never able to accept themselves as attractive women.

Even those girls who are naturally well endowed with beauty (or who manage to achieve it) report that good looks can be a mixed blessing. Pretty is nice but not always better. Nubile beauties become vulnerable to sexual exploitation, sometimes at a very young age. They may be shown off by parents or "used" by peers who seek social prestige through contacts with them. Many begin to resent attention that is based solely on looks and that disregards who they are as people. Good-looking boys rarely suffer from these special hazards. . . .

In their quest for a separate identity, adolescent girls become especially vulnerable to beauty problems that threaten their health and well-being. For example, sophisticated medical techniques now lure girls into cosmetic surgery even before they are fully grown. Nose jobs, chin implants, and breast reductions are being performed on minors as modern medicine perpetuates the myth of female beauty. The vast majority of teenage aesthetic surgery patients are girls, not boys. Before they can adjust to their own changing profiles, growing girls are considered suitable candidates for cosmetic overhaul. Parents are paying for it; professionals are providing it.

Girls as young as age fourteen are now undergoing breast alterations. This is a good example of how beauty stereotypes interact with the maturational process, producing adjustment problems that in turn prompt cosmetic surgery. Because breasts are so symbolic of feminine beauty (in Western cultures), many physically normal girls experience an almost paralyzing self-consciousness during breast development. Advertisements for bust "improvement" products abound in teen magazines. Breast development begins early in puberty, often by age ten. Girls start to mature before boys, and can be several years ahead of boys in the same grade. Full-breasted girls must carry the burden of their early maturation "up front." They suffer embarrassment, ostracism, and overt ridicule. (In fact, large-breasted females of any age are stereotyped as unintelligent, incompetent, immoral, and immodest.)[26] To these young girls, surgical correction of their breast problem seems to be a wonderful solution. In rare cases such a solution may be justifiable; usually it is pre-mature. . . .

The use of cosmetics is another beauty transformation that poses a special health hazard for adolescents. Makeup serves as a critical initiation rite into womanhood. It is an essential fashion prop that helps to exaggerate gender differences. An estimated one-third of the girls who regularly use cosmetics will develop a condition dermatologists are now calling acne cosmetica. Genetic in origin, acne is triggered by increasing hormone production during puberty. The potent ingredients used in cosmetics can induce serious skin problems even in girls who are not genetically prone. Since it takes several months for cosmetic acne to develop, the cause may go unsuspected. Once the acne has developed, a vicious cycle ensues: as it becomes worse, more makeup is used to cover it, which only further escalates the condition.[27] . . .

Pursuit of mythical beauty turns the adolescent girl into an active consumer. Giant industries create, define, and cater to her special beauty "needs" and siphon her babysitting money into the purchase of bust developers and Ultralash. A *New York Times* editorial asked, "Why does a fourteen-year-old Brooklyn girl need to spend $40 on a manicure and $700 on pants, sweaters, headbands and makeup to complete her back-to-school wardrobe?"[28] The very next day this newspaper carried a full back-page ad directed at potential advertisers for *Seventeen* magazine: "*Seventeen* readers don't love you and leave you. As adults 34% still rinse with the same mouthwash and 33% use the same nail polish. Talk to them in their teens and they'll be customers for life."

After analyzing magazine ads aimed at female adolescents, a researcher concludes that girls are bombarded with one essential message about their purpose in life: "learning the art of body adornment through clothing, cosmetics, jewelry, hair products, perfumes."[29] In these ads cosmetic transformations are made to seem a natural accentuation of what already exists. "I look myself, only better," says the young model, confiding the secret formula that brought out the highlights of her hair. Narcissism is fostered by ads that focus again and again on appearance as the primary source of female identity. Cosmetic advertisements have been shown to affect the "conception of social reality" of teenage girls. A single fifteen-minute exposure to a series of beauty commercials increased the degree to which they perceived beauty as being "important to their own personality and important to being popular with boys."[30]

Ads attempt to convince Linda that she must make up and make over in order to make it in life.

She is directed to her mirror to discover herself. In effect, the question "Who am I?" is translated into "What should I look like?" Her natural adolescent drive to attain a personal identity is distorted into a need to package herself as a product. In the end, costly and painful beauty rituals do not produce a sense of individuality. Just the opposite occurs: girls wind up all looking the same and are thus more easily stereotyped. "They look alike, think alike, and even worse . . . believe they are not alike."[31]

Notes

1. Rubin, J. et al., 1974.
2. Seavy, C. et al., 1975.
3. Hoffman, L., 1977.
4. Coombs, C. et al., 1975.
5. Bernard, J., 1981, 479.
6. Lamb, M., 1976.
7. Maccoby, E., & Jacklin, C., 1974, 329.
8. Joffe, C., 1971.
9. Weitzman, L. et al., 1972.
10. Williams, J., 1977, 176.
11. Vespa, M., 1975 and 1976.
12. Author's unpublished data.
13. Unger, R., & Madar, T., as cited in Unger, R., 1985.
14. Dion, K., 1973.
15. Simmons, R., & Rosenberg, F., 1975.
16. Fried, B., 1979, 37.
17. Hyde, J. et al., 1977.
18. Williams, J., 1983, 161.
19. Ibid., 161.
20. Sexton, A., "Little Girl, My String Bean, My Lovely Woman," 1966.
21. Bohan, J., 1973.
22. Offer, D. et al., 1981.
23. Musa, K., & Roach, M., 1973.
24. Offer, D. et al., 1981.
25. Dacey, J., 1979.
26. Kleinke, C., & Staneski, R., 1980.
27. Fulton, J., & Black, E., 1983.
28. *New York Times,* Sept. 13, 1983, editorial page.
29. Umiker-Sebeok, J., 1981, 226.
30. Tan, A., 1977.
31. Firestone, S., 1970, 151.

Bibliography

Bernard, J.
1981 *The Female World.* New York: Free Press.

Bohan, J.
1973 Age and sex difference in self-concept. *Adolescence, 8,* 379–384.

Coombs, C., Coombs, L., & McClelland, G.
1975 Preference scales for number and sex of children. *Population Studies, 29,* 273–298.

Dacey, J.
1979 *Adolescents Today.* Santa Monica, Calif.: Goodyear.

Dion, K.
1973 Young children's stereotyping of facial attractiveness. *Developmental Psychology, 10,* 772–778.

Firestone, S.
1970 *The Dialectic of Sex.* New York: William Morrow.

Hoffman, L.
1977 Changes in family roles, socialization and sex differences. *American Psychologist, 32,* 644–657.

Hyde, J., Rosenberg, B., & Behrman, J.
1977 "Tomboyism." *Psychology of Women Quarterly, 2,* 73–75.

Joffe, C.
1971 Sex role socialization and the nursery school: As the twig is bent. *Journal of Marriage and the Family, 33,* 467–475.

Kleinke, C., & Staneski, R.
1980 First impressions of female bust size. *Journal of Social Psychology, 10,* 123–124.

Lamb, M.
1976 (Ed.), *The Role of the Father in Child Development.* New York: Wiley.

Maccoby, E., & Jacklin, C.
1974 *The Psychology of Sex Differences.* Stanford, Calif.: Stanford University Press.

Musa, K., & Roach, M.
1973 Adolescent appearance and self-concept. *Adolescence, 8,* 385–394.

Offer, D., Ostrov, E., & Howard, K.
1981 *The Adolescent: A Psychological Self-Portrait.* New York: Basic Books.

Rubin, J., Provenzano, F., & Luria, Z.
1974 The eye of the beholder: Parents' views on sex of newborns. *American Journal of Orthopsychiatry, 44,* 512–519.

Seavey, C., Katz, P., & Zalk, S.
1975 Baby X: The effect of gender labels on adult responses to infants. *Sex Roles, 1,* 103–110.

Sexton, A.
1966 *Live or Die.* Boston: Houghton Mifflin.

Simmons, R., & Rosenberg, F.
1975 Sex, sex-roles, and self-image. *Journal of Youth and Adolescence, 4,* 229–258.

Tan, A.
1977 TV beauty ads and role expectations of adolescent female viewers. *Journalism Quarterly, 56,* 283–288.

Umiker-Sebeok, J.
1981 The seven ages of women. In C. Mayo & N. Henley (Eds.), *Gender and Non-Verbal Behavior* (pp. 220–239). New York: Springer-Verlag.

Unger, R., Hilderbrand, M., & Madar, T.
1982 Physical attractiveness and assumptions about social deviance: Some sex-by-sex comparisons. *Personality and Social Psychology Bulletin, 8,* 293–301.

Vespa, M.
1975, Feb. 9 The littlest vamps. *New York Sunday News.*

Vespa, M.
1976, Sept. A two year old in false eyelashes. *Ms.,* pp. 61–63.

Weitzman, L., Eifler, D., Hokada, E., & Ross, C.
1972 Sex role socialization in picture books for preschool children. *American Journal of Sociology, 77,* 1125–1150.

Williams, J.
1977 *Psychology of Women* (First Edition). New York: W. W. Norton.

———.
1983 *Psychology of Women* (Second Edition). New York: W. W. Norton.

Men's Power to Define and The Formation of Women's Consciousness

Gerda Lerner

You will remember historian Gerda Lerner from her selection in the first chapter, "A New Angle of Vision." Here she shows us how women have been systematically excluded from the power to name and define the "system of ideas that explain and order the world." We have been excluded by education, by philosophical and scientific systems, and by social organization.

Excerpted from *The Creation of Feminist Consciousness: From the Middle Ages to Eighteen-seventy* by Gerda Lerner, Vol II of *Women and History*. New York: Oxford University Press, 1993, pp. 3–12.

TRACING THE HISTORICAL DEVELOPMENT BY WHICH patriarchy emerged as the dominant form of societal order, I have shown how it gradually institutionalized the rights of men to control and appropriate the sexual and reproductive services of women. Out of this form of dominance developed other forms of dominance, such as slavery. Once established as a functioning system of complex hierarchical relationships, patriarchy transformed sexual, social, economic relations and dominated all systems of ideas. In the course of the establishment of patriarchy and constantly reinforced as the result of it, the major idea systems which explain and order Western civilization incorporated a set of unstated assumptions about gender, which powerfully affected the development of history and of human thought.

I have shown how the metaphors of gender constructed the male as the norm and the female as deviant; the male as whole and powerful; the female as unfinished, physically mutilated and emotionally dependent.

Briefly summarized the major assumptions about gender in patriarchal society are these:

> Men and women are essentially different creatures, not only in their biological equipment, but in their needs, capacities and functions. Men and women also differ in the way they were created and in the social function assigned to them by God.
>
> Men are "naturally" superior, stronger and more rational, therefore designed to be dominant. From this follows that men are political citizens and responsible for and representing the polity. Women are "naturally" weaker, inferior in intellect and rational capacities, unstable emotionally and therefore incapable of political participation. They stand outside of the polity.

> Men, by their rational minds, explain and order the world. Women by their nurturant function sustain daily life and the continuity of the species. While both functions are essential, that of men is superior to that of women. Another way of saying this is that men are engaged in "transcendent" activities, women—like lower-class people of both sexes—are engaged in "immanent" activities.
>
> Men have an inherent right to control the sexuality and the reproductive functions of women, while women have no such right over men.
>
> Men mediate between humans and God. Women reach God through the mediation of men.

These unproven, unprovable assumptions are not, of course, laws of either nature or society, although they have often been so regarded and have even been incorporated into human law. They are operative at different levels, in different forms and with different intensity during various periods of history. Changes in the way in which these patriarchal assumptions are acted upon describe in fact changes in the status and position of women in a given period in a given society. The development of concepts of gender should therefore be studied by any historian wishing to elicit information about women in any society.

. . .

The archaic states of the Ancient Near East which developed priesthood, kingship and militaristic elites did so in a context of developing male dominance over women and a structured system of slavery. It is not accidental that the time, leisure and education necessary for developing philosophy, religion and science was made available to an elite of priests, rulers and bureaucrats, whose domestic needs were met by the unpaid labor of women and slaves. In the second millennium B.C. this elite occasionally included female priestesses, queens and rulers, but by the time patriarchy was firmly established, approximately in the 6th century B.C., it was always male. (The appearance of an occasional queen to substitute for a missing male heir only confirms this rule.) In other words, it is patriarchal slave society which gives rise to the systems of ideas that explain and order the world for millennia thereafter. The twin mental constructs—the philosophical and the scientific systems of thought—explain and order the world in such a way as to confer and confirm power upon their adherents and deny power to those disputing them. Just as the distribution and allocation of resources give power to the rulers, so do the withholding of information and the denial of access to explanatory constructs give power to the system builders.

From the time of the establishment of patriarchy to the present, males of non-elite groups have struggled with increasing success for a share in this power of defining and naming. The history of the Western world can be viewed as the unfolding of that class-based struggle and the story of the process by which more and more nonelite males have gained access to economic and mental resources. But during this entire period, well into the middle of the 20th century, women have been excluded from all or part of that process and have been unable to gain access to it.

Not only have women been excluded through educational deprivation from the process of making mental constructs, it has also been the case that the mental constructs explaining the world have been androcentric, partial and distorted. Women have been defined out and marginalized in every philosophical system and have therefore had to struggle not only against exclusion but against a content which defines them as subhuman and deviant.[1] I argue that this dual deprivation has formed the female psyche over the centuries in such a way as to make women collude in creating and generationally recreating the system which oppressed them.

I have shown in Volume One how gender became the dominant metaphor by which Aristotle defended and justified the system of slavery. At the time of Aristotle's writing of *Politics* the question of the moral rightness of slavery was still problematical. It was certainly questionable in light of the very system of ethics and morals Aristotle was constructing. Why should one man rule over another? Why should one man be master and another be slave? Aristotle reasoned that some men are born to rule, others to be ruled. He illustrated this principle by drawing an analogy between soul and body—the soul is superior to the body and therefore must rule it. Similarly, rational mind is superior to passion and so must rule it. And "the male is by nature superior, and the female inferior; and the one rules and the other is ruled; this principle, of necessity extends to all mankind."[2] The analogy extends also to men's rule over animals.

> *And indeed the use made of slaves and of tame animals is equally not very different; for both with their bodies*

minister to the needs of life. . . . It is clear, then, that some men are by nature free, and others slaves, and that for these latter slavery is both expedient and right.[3]

The remarkable thing about this explanation is what is deemed in need of justification and what is assumed as a given. Aristotle admitted that there is some justification for a difference of opinion regarding the rightness of enslaving captive peoples in the event of an unjust war. But there is no difference of opinion regarding the inferiority of women. The subordination of women is assumed as a given, likened to a natural condition, and so the philosopher uses the marital relationship as an explanatory metaphor to justify slavery. By his efforts at justifying the moral rightness of slavery, Aristotle had indeed recognized the basic truth of the humanity of the slave. By denying and ignoring the need to explain the subordination of women, as well as by the kind of biological explanation Aristotle offered elsewhere, he had fixed women in a status of being less-than-human. The female is, in his words, "as it were, a mutilated male."[4]

More remarkable than Aristotle's misogynist construction is the fact that his assumptions remained virtually unchallenged and endlessly repeated for nearly two thousand years. They were reinforced by Old Testament restrictions on women and their exclusion from the covenant community, by the misogynist teachings of the Church fathers and by the continuing emphasis in the Christian era on charging Eve, and with her all women, with moral guilt for the Fall of humankind.

MORE THAN TWO THOUSAND years after Aristotle, the founding fathers of the American republic debated their Constitution. Once again, a group of revolutionary leaders, defining themselves as republicans and devoted to the creation of a democratic policy, was faced with the contradiction of the existence of slavery in their republic. The issue of how to deal with slavery was hotly contested and highly controversial. It ended in a pragmatic compromise which perpetuated a major social problem in the new republic.

The Declaration of Independence which states, "We hold these truths to be self-evident that all men are created equal and are endowed by their Creator with certain unalienable Rights, that among these are Life, Liberty and the pursuit of Happiness," implied that by natural right all human beings were endowed with the same rights. How were such principles to be upheld in the face of the existence of slavery in the Southern states? The issue surfaced in the constitutional debates on laws regulating the slave trade, assigning responsibility for the return of fugitive slaves and apportioning voting rights. The last issue proved to be the most difficult, the Northern states holding that slaves should be counted as property and not counted at all in voting apportionment. The Southern states wanted slaves to be counted as though they were citizens, with their votes being wielded by the men who owned them. What was at issue, more than the abstract principle of how to regard the Negro, was the relative regional strength in Congress. Since the Southern population including slaves was more numerous than the population of the free states, this would have given the Southerners predominance in the House of Representatives. The irony in the debate was that the proslavery forces argued the humanity of the slaves, while antislavery forces argued for their status as property. Definitions, in this case, were determined not by reason, logic or moral considerations, but by political/economic interest.

The compromise which was finally incorporated into the Constitution was couched in a language as devoid of concreteness and as abstract as possible. "Representatives and direct taxes" were to be apportioned by adding to the number of citizens in each of the states "including those bound to Service for a Term of Years, and excluding Indians not taxed, three fifths of all other Persons." In plain words, a slave was to be counted three-fifths of a man for purposes of voting apportionment. Implicit in both language and debate was the recognition that the Negro, although a chattel, was indeed human. The founders' uneasiness with the slavery issue was expressed in the outlawing of the external slave trade in 1808, which most men believed would doom slavery to wither of its own accord. It also found expression in the terms of the Northwest Ordinance of 1787, which explicitly stated that the territories then defined as the Northwest would remain free. This laid the basis for the constitutional argument of the antislavery campaigns of the antebellum period, that the power to keep slavery out of the territories lay with the Congress. Thus the Constitution in its unresolved contradiction over the slavery issue not only presaged the Civil War but set in motion the ideas and expectations that would fuel the struggle for the slaves' eventual emancipation and their admission to full citizenship.

It was different for women. There was no controversy or debate on the definition of a voter as a male. The American Constitution embodied the patriarchal assumption, shared by the entire society, that women were not members of the polity. It was felt necessary by the founders to define the status of indentured servants, persons "bound to Service for a Term of Years," and of Indians in regard to voting rights, but there was no need felt even to mention, much less to explain or justify, that while women were to be counted among "the whole number of free persons" in each state for purposes of representation, they had no right to vote and to be elected to public office (U.S. Constitution, Article I, 3). The issue of the civil and political status of women never entered the debate, just as it had not entered the debate in Aristotle's philosophy.

Yet women in large numbers had been involved in political actions in the American Revolution and had begun to define themselves differently than had their mothers and grandmothers in regard to the polity. At the very least, they had found ways of exerting influence on political events by fund-raising, tea boycotts and actions against profiteering merchants. Loyalist women made political claims when they argued for their property rights independent of those of their husbands or when they protested against various wartime atrocities. Several influential female members of elite families privately raised the issue of women's rights as citizens. Petitioners of various kinds thrust it into the public debate. Unbidden and without a recognized public forum and emboldened by the revolutionary rhetoric and the language of democracy, women began to reinterpret their own status. As did slaves, women took the preamble of the Declaration of Independence literally. But unlike slaves, they were not defined as being even problematic in the debate.[5]

The well-known exchange of private letters between John Adams and his wife Abigail sharply exemplifies the limits of consciousness on this issue. Here was a well-matched and loving couple, unusual in the wife's political interest and involvement, which would find active expression during her husband's later term as President when she handled some of his correspondence.[6] In 1776 Abigail Adams urged her husband in a letter to "remember the ladies" in his work on the legal code for the new republic, reminding him that wives needed protection against the "naturally tyrannical" tendencies of their husbands. Abigail's language was appropriate to women's subordinate status in marriage and society—she asked for men's chivalrous protection from the excesses of other men. John's reply was "As to your extraordinary code of laws, I cannot but laugh. . . ." He expressed astonishment that like children and disobedient servants, restless Indians and insolent Negroes "another tribe more numerous and powerful than all the rest [had] grown discontented." Chiding his wife for being "saucy," he trivialized her argument by claiming that men were, in practice "the subjects. We have only the name of masters."[7] A problem outside of definition and discourse could not be taken seriously. And yet, for an instant, John Adams allowed himself to think seriously on the subject—her code of laws, if enacted, would lead to social disorder: "Depend upon it, we know better than to repeal our Masculine systems."[8]

Here we see, in its extreme manifestation, the impact on History of men's power to define. Having established patriarchy as the foundation of the family and the state, it appeared immutable and became the very definition of social order. To challenge it was both ludicrous and profoundly threatening.

At the time Aristotle defined the rightness of slavery, the issue of the humanity of the slave was debatable but not yet political. By 1787 the founders of the new republic had to recognize the humanity of the slave and deal with its denial as a controversial political issue. The statement that the slave may be fully human yet for purposes of political power distribution (among the masters) may be counted as only three-fifths human and not at all as a citizen, was so profound a contradiction in a Christian nation founded on democratic principles that it made the end of slavery inevitable in less than a century. But for women nothing at all had changed in terms of the debate since the time of Aristotle. As far as the definition of humanity was concerned, they were still defined as incomplete and marginal, a sort of subspecies. As far as the polity was concerned, they were not even recognized sufficiently to be coddled with the sop of "virtual representation." The issue defined as a social problem can enter political debate and struggle. The issue defined out, remains silenced, outside the polity.

This ultimate consequence of men's power to define—the power to define what is a political issue and what is not—has had a profound effect on women's struggle for their own emancipation. Essentially, it has forced thinking women to waste much time and energy on defensive arguments; it has channeled their thinking into narrow fields; it has retarded their coming into consciousness as a collective entity and has literally aborted and distorted the intellectual talents of women for thousands of years.

In the literature dealing with the subject of women in history the emphasis has been on the various discriminations and disabilities under which women have lived. Structural, legal and economic inequalities between men and women have held the focus of attention, with educational deprivation seen mostly as yet another form of economic discrimination in that it restricted women's access to resources and self-support. I focus in this study on the educational disadvantaging of women as a major force in determining women's individual and collective consciousness and thus a major force in determining women's political behavior.

The systematic educational disadvantaging of women has affected women's self-perceptions, their ability to conceptualize their own situation and their ability to conceive of societal solutions to improve it. Not only has it affected women individually, but far more important, it has altered women's relationship to thought and to history. Women, for far longer than any other structured group in society, have lived in a condition of trained ignorance, alienated from their own collective experience through the denial of the existence of Women's History. Even more important, women have for millennia been forced to prove to themselves and to others their capacity for full humanity and their capacity for abstract thought. This has skewed the intellectual development of women as a group, since their major intellectual endeavor had to be to counteract the pervasive patriarchal assumptions of their inferiority and incompleteness as human beings. It is this basic fact about their condition which explains why women's major intellectual enterprise for more than a thousand years was to reconceptualize religion in such a way as to allow for women's equal and central role in the Christian drama of the Fall and Redemption. Women's striving for emancipation was acted out in the arena of religion long before women could conceive of political solutions for their situation.

The next issue through which women's quest for equality found expression was the struggle for access to education. Here, again, women were forced for hundreds of years not only to argue for their right to equal education, but first to prove their capacity to be educated at all. This exhausted the energies of the most talented women and retarded their intellectual development. Further, up until the end of the 19th century in Europe and the United States, women in order to be educated had to forgo their sexual and reproductive lives—they had to choose between wifehood and motherhood on the one hand and education on the other. No group of men in history ever had to make such a choice or pay such a price for intellectual growth.

For many centuries the talents of women were directed not toward self-development but toward realizing themselves through the development of a man. Women, conditioned for millennia to accept the patriarchal definition of their role, have sexually and emotionally serviced men and nurtured them in a way that allowed men of talent a fuller development and a more intensive degree of specialization than women have ever had. The sexual division of labor which has allotted to women the major responsibility for domestic services and the nurturance of children has freed men from the cumbersome details of daily survival activities, while it disproportionately has burdened women with them. Women have had less spare time and above all less uninterrupted time in which to reflect, to think and to write. The psychological support from intimacy and love has been far more readily available to talented men than to talented women. Had there been a man behind each brilliant woman, there would have been women of achievement in history equal to the numbers of men of achievement.

On the other hand it can be argued that throughout the millennia of their subordination the kind of knowledge women acquired was more nearly correct and adequate than was the knowledge of men. It was knowledge not based on theoretical propositions and on works collected in books, but practical knowledge derived from essential social interaction with their families, their children, their neighbors. Such knowledge was its own reward in making women aware of their essential role in maintaining life, family and community. Like men of subordinate castes, classes and races, women have all along had thorough knowledge of how the world works and how people work within it and with each other. This is survival knowledge for the oppressed, who must maneuver in a world in which they are excluded from structured power and who must know how to manipulate those in power to gain maximum protection for themselves and their children. The conditions under which they lived forced women to develop interpersonal skills and sensitivities, as have other oppressed groups. Their skill and knowledge were not made available to society as a whole because of patriarchal hegemony and instead found expression in what we now call women's culture. I will show in this book how women transformed the concepts and assumptions of male thought and subtly subverted male thought so as to incorporate women's cultural knowledge and viewpoint. This tension between patriarchal hegemony and women's re-definition is a feature of historical process we have hitherto neglected to describe and observe.

Women have also been deprived of "cultural prodding," the essential dialogue and encounter with persons of equal education and standing. Shut out of institutions of higher learning for centuries and treated with condescension or derision, educated women have had to develop their own social networks in order for their thoughts, ideas and work to find audiences and resonance. And finally, the fact that women were denied knowledge of the existence of Women's History decisively and negatively affected their intellectual development as a group. Women who did not know that others like them had made intellectual contributions to knowledge and to creative thought were overwhelmed by the sense of their own inferiority or, conversely, the sense of the dangers of their daring to be different. Without knowledge of women's past, no group of women could test their own ideas against those of their equals, those who had come out of similar conditions and similar life situations. Every thinking woman had to argue with the "great man" in her head, instead of being strengthened and encouraged by her foremothers. For thinking women, the absence of Women's History was perhaps the most serious obstacle of all to their intellectual growth.

Notes

1. An excellent discussion of the philosophical inadequacies of the patriarchal system of ideas, which corroborates my thinking, can be found in Elizabeth Kamarck Minnich, *Transforming Knowledge* (Philadelphia: Temple University Press, 1990).

2. Aristotle, *Politica* (tr. Benjamin Jowett), in W. D. Ross (ed.), *The Works of Aristotle* (Oxford: Clarendon Press, 1921), I, 2, 1254b, 4–6 12–16.

3. *Ibid.*, 1254b, 24–26; 1255a, 2–5.

4. J. A. Smith and W. D. Ross (tr.), *The Works of Aristotle* (Oxford: Clarendon Press, 1912), "De Generatione Animalium," II, 3, 729a, 26–31.

5. See Linda Kerber, *Women of the Republic: Intellect and Ideology in Revolutionary America* (Chapel Hill: University of North Carolina Press, 1980) and Mary Beth Norton, *Liberty's Daughters: The Revolutionary Experience of American Women, 1750–1800* (Boston: Little, Brown, 1980).

6. Kerber, *Women of the Republic*, p. 82.

7. L. H. Butterfield *et al.* (eds.) *The Book of Abigail and John: Selected Letters of the Adams Family, 1762–1784* (Cambridge: Harvard University Press, 1975). First quote, Abigail Adams to John Adams, Braintree, March 31, 1776, p. 121; second quote, John Adams to Abigail Adams, April 14, 1776, p. 123.

8. *Ibid.*

Transforming Knowledge

Elizabeth Kamarck Minnich

Elizabeth Kamarck Minnich is professor of philosophy and women's studies at the Graduate School of The Union Institute. She has also served as an administrator and faculty member at Barnard College, Sarah Lawrence College, Hollins College, The New School College, and (on a Fulbright) at Maharajah Sayajirao University in Gujerat, India. She has worked more than twenty-five years on curriculum transformation projects, and she writes and speaks extensively also on "Democracy, Diversity, and American Commitments." She coedited Reconstructing the Academy: Women's Education and Women's Studies *(1988). Her book* Transforming Knowledge *(1990), from which this selection was taken, received the Frederic W. Ness Award in 1991.*

Minnich begins her essay by telling us, "This is a book about transforming knowledge . . . so that we no longer perpetuate the old exclusions and devaluations of the majority of humankind that have pervaded our informal as well as formal schooling. . . . Such changes are necessary, I believe, not only to transform what is accepted as knowledge by the dominant culture and what is passed on to new generations, but for the sake of thinking itself. We cannot think well as long as we are locked into old errors that are so familiar as to be virtually invisible." She asserts: "All thinking is political."

As you read this selection, consider what it means that all thinking is political—that it is lodged in historical context, driven by social and individual interests, and influenced by status and authority. Consider the implications of those factors for groups that are not situated within the loop of power; and consider what effects they have probably had on you.

I BELIEVE THAT UNLESS FEMINIST SCHOLARSHIP IS accompanied by ongoing work on why and how the dominant liberal arts curriculum in all its varied expressions is not and, without fundamental reconception, *cannot be* receptive to the study of the majority of humankind, it remains at risk of disappearing as it has through the centuries before this wave of the Women's Movement. As we produce "the new knowledge of women," we must continue to work to understand why it is recurrently "new," rather than a further unfolding of all that has gone before. What is it, I ask through this book, that functions so effectively in the dominant meaning system to hold women and so knowledge of, by, and about women outside that which has been and is passed on, developed, taught?

This is a curricular matter. It is also more than that. The conceptual blocks to the comprehension and full inclusion of women that we find in familiar scholarly theories and arguments, as in their institutional expressions in organizations and systems, political and economic and legal, are at root the same blocks that are to be found within the curriculum. And if we do not remove them from the curriculum, much if not all that we achieve elsewhere may prove to be, once again, a passing moment. It is, after all, to a significant extent through what we teach to new generations that we bridge past, present, and future. That which is actively excluded from—or never makes it into—the curriculum is very likely to be forgotten and is almost certain to continue being devalued, seen as deviant and marginal at best.

Our educational institutions—those inspiring, impossible, frustrating, appealing, appalling systems within which we usually try simply to find the space and time to do our work of teaching and learning—are, not alone but preeminently, the shapers and guardians of cultural memory and hence of cultural meanings. Here too, then, we must do our work of critique, re-membering, creation.

As we do so, we also accept a number of risks. I am not referring only to the obvious risks of losing the privileges of participation in the Academy. As Linda Gordon puts it, "Existing in between a social movement and the academy, women's scholarship has a mistress and a master, and guess which one pays wages."[1] That these risks are complex and personally troubling does indeed need to be recognized. It is terribly difficult to work against the grain of what, after all, stands in our culture for "the life of the mind," particularly when one has had to struggle to achieve access to the institutions that have claimed to define it and have, indeed, succeeded all too well in professionalizing it, marking it as their own. I do not mean to trivialize even for a moment the struggle for access, the continuing difficulty of 'getting in.' But I want to point out here the risks that feminist scholars have warned one another about since the beginning of the curriculum change movement.

The dangers of such projects are indicated by the difference between the term "mainstreaming" and the phrase that, I am glad to say, has superseded it, "curriculum transformation projects." "Mainstreaming" implies that there is one main stream and what we want is to join it, that we are a tributary at best, and that our goal is to achieve the 'normalcy' of becoming invisible in the big river. "Transformation," on the other hand, puts the emphasis not on joining what is but on changing it.[2]

Teresa de Lauretis characterizes the problem, the risk, of "mainstreaming" as "the appropriation of feminist strategies and conceptual frameworks within 'legitimate' discourses or by other critical theories" in a way that "deflect[s] radical resistance and . . . recuperate[s] it as liberal opposition," which is "not just accommodated but in fact anticipated and so effectively neutralized."[3] That, indeed, would be the result of "mainstreaming." But it is something else again to work on transforming the curriculum with the full realization that women cannot be added to the present construction of knowledge because knowledge of, by, and for women is not simply more of the same; is not only knowledge of a subset of "mankind" that is conceptually compatible with that of which it is a subset; is not a category of exotica that can be tacked onto courses without implications for that which remains safely 'normal'; is not, indeed, neatly separable in any way from any knowledge that is adequate to human-kind.

The belief that knowledge about women *is* simply additive to, or a subset of, or a complement to, knowledge about men has been and is held both by nonfeminist scholars and educators and by some feminists involved with Women's Studies and curriculum-change projects. I understand those beliefs and know that some good work can indeed be done by those who hold them (just as valuable work is done in Women's Studies to find the women who did what women were not allowed to do so as to "prove that we can do it," that we "have been there"). But I do not believe such work is, by itself, adequate, because it remains within a system built on principles of exclusion and characterized by the conceptual errors those principles necessitate and perpetuate.

It is precisely to continue work on transforming the curriculum, not simply achieving access to it or joining its 'mainstream,' or providing it with an oppositional perspective that it can accommodate in the sense de Lauretis rightly fears, that this book is being written. Let me repeat here what I first wrote in 1979: what we are doing is as radical as undoing geocentrism, the notion that the earth is the center of the cosmos. If the earth—if Man—is not the center, then everything predicated on taking it/him to be so no longer stands as it has been formulated. This is not to say that there are no schools of thought with which we can join, or that there is nothing in the existing tradition we can draw on, use, and ourselves choose to perpetuate. It is not even to say that all feminist scholarship is or ought to be that radical, that it ought to work on that fundamental level. It *is* to say that as we do our work, we need to hold on to the radical critique, the effort to go to the root (*râdix*) of the tradition that is premised on our exclusion, or we will watch helplessly as the tree of knowledge continues to grow exactly as it did before.[4]

But making the case for that position is what this book is about, so I will leave the point now with the statement that refusal to engage in, or at least support, work on transforming the curriculum leaves us not pure but vulnerable to being, once again, excluded, rendered marginal, or brought into and utterly lost within the mainstream that has through the ages flooded and washed away the recurrent spring growth of feminist scholarship and thought.

Contextual Approaches: Thinking About

Access to The Curriculum: Some Background

It seems only right to recognize, however briefly and hence inadequately, that what we begin here, as we look at education and specifically at the curriculum, is itself another in a long history of beginnings. The struggles for women's education and for the study of women have their own histories. And it is also important to recognize at the same time, the parallels between and, still more important, the intimate intertwinings of, sex/gender, class, and race in the history of education as in all else. In a history of the curriculum in the United States, Frederick Rudolph reminds us that neither Black people nor white women have been included in the curricula even of institutions designed for us:

> *By 1900 . . . the curricular directions of colleges and universities for blacks had been established basically in imitation of the institutions that served the dominant caste. Acceptance of segregation as the defining practice in the relations between the races required of the southern colleges for blacks the education of trained, vocationally prepared graduates in many diverse fields. The curriculum of the black colleges was shaped by a policy of apartheid in a society sufficiently democratic in the abstract to encourage the development of a class of responsible professional leaders. . . . But the models for these institutions were those of the dominant caste: Fisk University's music department concentrated on classical European music to the exclusion of the music that expressed the black experience in America, and black history and sociology courses were rare and exceptional until after World War I.*

Similarly:

> *Colleges for women were . . . founded . . . as an experiment in applied psychology, philosophy, and physiology. Vassar, Smith, and Wellesley, in quick succession, using the classical liberal arts curriculum that was on the brink of collapse in the old men's colleges, proved that women were mentally and physically equal to a demanding collegiate course of study. . . . As was true of the colleges for blacks, colleges for women were often colleges in name only; those that deserved the name, having survived the opposition of critics who sought to discredit them with accusations of having failed to live up to the curricular standards of men's colleges, soon found themselves criticized for imitating the men's colleges too well and for not providing a course of study appropriate to women's work.*[1]

Women's work, in Rudolph's words, is "whatever men would not do."[2]

Thus, the majority of humankind was forced absurdly into proving that we were indeed fully human, that we could indeed think and learn, in curricula that either took no account whatsoever of us or were designed to keep us in our 'proper' place. The virtues (understood in a way that fluctuated oddly between the classical sense of *excellence of kind* and the Christian sense of *moral goodness*) of white middle- and upper-class women as of Black men and women, however different they were from each other, had in common being defined as different from the virtues of man-qua-citizen, or scholar. They were defined as virtues of service, not in the generalized Christian sense that calls all to act with *caritas,* but in a specific sense: those who were to serve the lives and interests of the small group of scholar–citizens were to develop the specific virtues of the 'naturally' servile.

This was the case even when some real pride and privilege went with fulfillment of the service role. For example, as Patricia Palmieri notes, "The American revolution made the entire society aware of the need to educate a populace capable of exercising democratic principles." Yet such civic arts and the virtue of their exercise were not to belong directly to all: "Women were to exert social influence through raising and educating sons. . . . Thus by 1800, while the vote was reserved for white men, white women could add to their domestic roles the role of 'Republican Mother.' "[3] Such provisions for influence—as distinct from power—were by no means extended to all those who served the dominant few. Even those who could proudly claim the mantle of "Republican Mother" did so through their relation to male citizens, their rearing of male children, the service they rendered the male order through those relations. Linda Kerber located for us the telling twist in such thinking, such provisions:

> *A revolution in women's education had been underway in England and America when the Revolution began; in postwar America the ideology of female education came to be tied to ideas about the sort of woman who would be of greatest service to the Republic. Discussions of female education were apt to be highly ambivalent. On one hand, republican political theory called for a sensibly educated female citizenry [from the privileged groups] to educate future generations of sensible republicans; on the other, domestic tradition condemned highly educated women as perverse threats to family stability. Consequently, when*

> *American educators discussed the uses of the female intellect, much of their discussion was explicitly anti-intellectual.*[4]

Black women, as always even more than privileged white women, have struggled continuously not only with the difficulty of achieving access to any education at all but with that of defining what Black people should be educated *for* even when slavery had been ended and some education could openly be sought and provided. They did so with great fortitude and ingenuity. Paula Giddings writes of the well-known debates about Black education around the turn of the century:

> *Though in many instances there was accommodation to [Booker T.] Washington's ideas—and power—Black women also operated independently of his influence. The educators, for example, believed in industrial education, but they also believed that Blacks should attain the highest academic level possible. One foot was in Booker T. Washington's camp on this issue, the other with W. E. B. DuBois, who supported the concept of the "talented tenth," a well-educated cadre of Black leaders. Anna Julia Cooper, for example, may have believed in industrial education with all her heart, but as an educator, and principal of Washington, D.C.'s The M Street School, she was best known for her success in channeling Black students into the most prestigious universities in the country. . . . Mary McLeod Bethune advocated "domestic science," but she also confronted (successfully) her White board members who wanted to maintain her school's curriculum below university status.*[5]

Mere access to schooling has clearly never been enough, and cannot become so, as long as any remnants of the old assumptions that we are by nature inferior and ought to be educated to serve white men remain within the curriculum, however deeply hidden. Such assumptions, such curricula, serve not equality but maintenance of an inegalitarian status quo: those who can pass as similar to higher-class white men are allowed to partake of the crumbs of privilege, while all others are to continue to be trained not only to serve but to admire those they serve. The present status hierarchy among institutions of higher education reflects the continuation of an exclusive history, however well-intentioned are those who bemoan the difficulty of finding 'qualified' women of all groups for their faculties and administrations, the supposed rarity of 'qualified' Black, Hispanic, and other students to be admitted to make a more diverse student body. Old assumptions, built into our modes of thought, our standards of judgment, our institutions and systems, keep inappropriate discrimination functioning long after many have consciously and seriously renounced, even denounced, it.[6]

Contemporary Movements for Equality

In the 1950s and early 1960s in America, dissatisfaction with the distortions of human lives and spirits effected by blithely inegalitarian social, political, educational, and economic systems began once again to bubble and rise to the surface. The old ambivalences so well described recently by Giddings, Kerber, Palmieri, and others (as, earlier, by Jane Addams, Anna Julia Cooper, Mary McLeod Bethune, Mary Beard, and others) had by no means been resolved. As a participant in that time of ferment (I was in college between 1961 and 1965, and started graduate work at the University of California/Berkeley in 1966), it would disturb me not to remember the political roots of Women's Studies in the movements that arose then. From them came a great deal of the passion and vision of feminist scholarship; from them, too, came some of the tensions that remain with us.

Remember: the Montgomery bus boycott took place in 1956, the struggle to desegregate Little Rock High School in 1957, and the sit-in movement that triggered mass Civil Rights protests against the exclusion of Black Americans began in early 1960, revealing the ferment that had been working with intensity and intelligence and great creativity in Black communities, in particular, for some time.[7] Betty Friedan published *The Feminine Mystique* in 1963, providing a rallying point for middle-class white women suffering from "the problem without a name." Educators (for example, Melissa Richter, Esther Rauschenbush, and Jean Walton) tried to do something about the inadequacies of women's education even at élite colleges such as Sarah Lawrence, Barnard, and Pomona, which did not recognize the reality that many women did and would work outside their own homes for pay (by necessity as well as by choice). The (largely white male) Beatniks and their male and female successors, the hippies of the late 1960s and 1970s (who had their own peculiar notions about what was 'proper' to men and to women) defied conventionality to find some meaning in a culture that seemed obsessed with 'success,' war, and materialism.[8] And Black nationalism gained new political and cultural impetus, often apart from, even in opposition to, efforts to desegregate white America.[9]

These were complex, multivoiced movements that were sometimes at odds with each other even as they shared a sometimes rather abstract passion for justice and equality, for full recognition of those excluded from the dominant culture. They were all felt within the Academy, too. The long quest for educational equality in the United States had by no means ended with the entrance of a few members of the excluded groups into the established halls of 'higher' learning in the United States, any more than the quest for political equality had ended with the winning of the franchise, first by Black men and then by all women. The intertwined, though often separately (even oppositionally) defined struggles that exploded again in the Civil Rights Movement of the 1960s and 1970s were extraordinarily complicated, conflictual, creative.

By the mid-to-late 1960s, some women involved in the Civil Rights Movement were discovering something wrong even within the struggle itself. The awareness re-emerged that prevailing generalizations about 'equality,' about 'justice,' somehow did not hold for women. That seed of understanding germinated quietly but released an intense and unstoppable energy. Slender blades of grass began to crack through pavement:

> *We've talked a lot, to each other and to some of you, about our own and other women's problems in trying to live in our personal lives and in our work as independent and creative people. In these conversations we've found what seem to be recurrent ideas or themes. Maybe we can look at these things many of us perceive, often as a result of insights learned from the movement.*[10]

The "recurrent ideas or themes" that white women began to see seemed at first not to speak to some of the Black women in the movement. The Civil Rights Movement was, after all, for Black women more 'their' movement, on the one hand, and, on the other, they knew themselves to have some real power in it. However, despite particular and by no means trivial differences in how it was experienced, discrimination based on sex/gender affected Black as well as white women. "Opposite ends of the spectrum" was Cynthia Washington's metaphor for the relation of Black and white women's experiences in the Movement: it described Black and white women's complex and differing realities, but the "spectrum" was indeed that of *women.* Many were beginning to realize that there was a problem in some, at least, of the ways men perceived and treated their female co-workers:

> *During the fall of 1964, I had a conversation with Casey Hayden about the role of women in SNCC. She complained that all the women got to do was type, that their role was limited to office work no matter where they were. What she said didn't make any particular sense to me because, at the time, I had my own project in Bolivar County, Miss. A number of other black women also directed their own projects. . . . Certain differences result from the way in which black women grow up. We have been raised to function independently. The notion of* retiring *to housewifery someday is not even a reasonable fantasy. Therefore whether you want to or not, it is necessary to learn to do all of the things required to do to survive. It seemed to many of us, on the other hand, that white women were demanding a chance to be independent while we needed help and assistance that was not always forthcoming. We definitely started from opposite ends of the spectrum. . . . [Yet even though] we did the same work as men . . . usually* with *men, . . . when we finally got back to some town where we could relax and go out, the men went out with other women. Our skills and abilities were recognized and respected, but that seemed to place us in some category other than female.*[11]

When some of the women in the Movement began to talk to each other, to explore their experiences *as women,* white and Black, sometimes together but also separately, and to take those experiences and one another seriously, tensions increased, splits developed even between long-time co-workers—and change was on the way. Expressions of personal and then of social discontent became increasingly politicized as a Movement carried by strong convictions and courage encountered the need to deal not only with those who crudely, and sometimes violently, opposed civil rights for Black Americans but also with the contradictions and tensions we all internalize in a segregated, class-divided, gender-hierarchical culture.

Long, often agonizing debates developed out of the earlier quiet, more personal conversations, and were sometimes broken up by confrontations that led to stunned silence, to deep hurt and anger, between and among individuals and groups. Black women, white women, Black men, white men, southerners and northerners, Civil Rights workers and local residents, students and non-students, political sectarians and those with beliefs but almost no ideology at all, painfully discovered their differences, struggled to continue to work together, broke apart to work separately. The deep divisions of the 'melting pot' of America, hidden behind 'the American dream,' cracked open in the crucible of the Civil Rights Movement. And even within the Movement, the dream cracked as tensions, as well as profound commitments, were exaggerated by the high tension of real danger surrounding the Civil Rights workers.

Those of us who lived through those times remember them vividly, and some of the dreams and nightmares, divisions and alliances, that developed then remain with us today. Much as some might like to think it, the sixties and early seventies were not just an aberration that is now, thank goodness, entirely over and done with. As I have traveled around the country working with faculty members and community groups, I have again and again encountered people who are still struggling to understand and learn from what happened then, when a people's movement succeeded in undoing most legally enforceable segregationist practices, converted many people to a lasting commitment to equality, spawned hundreds of grassroots organizations, many of which continue today,[12] and ended a war that the majority of Americans had come to believe was morally wrong. Some who are today faculty members became teachers because they came to believe then that education is indeed where and how a culture creates itself, and they wanted to be part of and have an effect on that critical process.

I have also met many faculty members who are still hurt, still angry, still frightened, by what happened in the late sixties and early seventies. Among these are some of the major opponents of curriculum transformation. They seem still to be fighting with the ideas, the actions, the people who so challenged them twenty years ago, and they are finding a startling number of allies across the nation. Some of us were enlivened by dreams as well as struggles for equality and justice; others were traumatized and remain terrified of anything that seems even vaguely "like the sixties." There was indeed frightening violence and hatred then, as well as peace and love. The era saw the undermining of some beliefs and traditions and values that may be necessary to our culture right along with some that locked it into terrible injustices.

But I cannot here re-enter that time of dream and anger. What matters now is that when Women's Studies and Black Studies began to appear on campuses, their creators were often motivated primarily by the renewed dream of an equitable world that had emerged, with pain as well as hope, from the Civil Rights Movement as well as the growing movement of women—most visibly white middle-class women, but also, and very importantly, Black, Hispanic, and other women whose activities tended to be 'overlooked' by the media. There was a shared, if by no means fully articulated or understood, realization that equity requires more than access to unchanged structures. But that does not mean that equity itself was fully understood. The meaning of "equity" remained a stubborn conceptual and political issue. It is arguable, for example, that with the turn to consciousness-raising, the Women's Movement that had emerged from the Civil Rights Movement began to develop in ways that deepened divisions between white and Black women, just as the early emphasis of white 'women's liberationists' on finding fulfilling work outside the home continued to do.[13]

Still, those who became involved in Women's Studies saw that in the Academy, as elsewhere, all women were denied full and equal entrance and, even once 'inside,' were not well treated as students, workers, teachers, and administrators. Sometimes naively assuming that the emerging new knowledge would be as inclusive as the old was exclusive, we set out to make ourselves not just present but significantly so—to be *recognized* in the fullest sense.

While we, all of us, remained strangers to the Academy, even if some of us were present in it, we could expect no more than token efforts toward such recognition. And tokenism reveals not so much bad faith as a profound lack of understanding of the nature and depth of the problems to which it is an inadequate response. Tokenism, after all, assumes that exclusion, which is an effect of complex hegemonic systems, is itself the problem. In this view, adding a few of those who have been excluded solves the problem, even though it actually leaves untouched the systems that produced (and, if left unfixed, will go on producing) exclusion and devaluation, both of which reflect also incomprehension. That is why tokens, even those included in (uncomprehending) good faith, even those who themselves fully intend otherwise, become available to play the role of "exceptions that prove the rule."

We added to our work toward political and professional equity efforts to bring full representation of our half of humankind into the body of what is taught. Many white women worked for Women's Studies without adequate efforts to learn from and with Black and other women, but not without awareness of the importance of doing so—a statement that is intended to be neither an excuse nor a judgment. Undoing racism in the Women's Movement—not just as exclusion perpetuated by bad feelings of whites toward Blacks but as an expression of the overarching oppressive system that benefits whites and exploits Blacks—is as complex as undoing it anywhere else. This is an acknowledgment that must be made and remade however painful it is, lest the pain block what must be done.[14]

It is in the direct feminist challenge to the knowledge the Academy preserves, enriches, and passes on that I locate one important context for the extraordinary explosion of thinking and new knowledge that no one should ignore any longer. Much has indeed changed, but the commitment to education that genuinely serves egalitarian democracy remains.[15]

Early—and Continuing—Questions

There is also another way to move into the subject of transforming knowledge, and the ways we think. We can change our perspective from the dramatic, stirring, inspiring, and troubling history of the times in which this commitment re-emerged, and focus on the unfolding thinking itself. To do so, it may be helpful to return to some of the early questions. We could start with the conclusions reached after much thought, making them as clear and accessible as possible, but some may find it more helpful to start where the thinking started, to move into the thinking as it actually developed rather than, or in addition to, focusing on its historical *or* its purely conceptual contexts. There are always lots of ways to begin, different contexts within which to locate that which we wish to understand, many perspectives on what we are trying to see.[16]

Scholarship vs. Politics? From the beginning, the commitments of feminist scholars have been complex and often in creative, demanding tension with each other. For example, an early conference in a continuing series run by the Barnard College Women's Center took on the question of the relation of scholarship to politics (the conferences, led by Jane Gould as director of the center, were in the late 1980s still called "The Scholar and the Feminist"). Were we, as many of those opposed to Women's Studies held, threatening to 'politicize' scholarship and the Academy in some new and dangerous way? Is it true that formal scholarship as traditionally conceived and practiced is disinterested, objective, removed from the interested, subjectively grounded advocacy efforts of the political realm? Are knowledge and action two separate human activities, and ought they to be so? Can one serve both equity and excellence, or does commitment to one threaten to undermine the other? To respond to such questions, we were faced with the need to rethink what scholarship has meant and should mean, and that effort led us to undertake an analysis and critique of the construction of knowledge.

The Disciplines Among the most evident characteristics of the prevailing construction of knowledge is its disciplinary nature, a characteristic that is given power by the discipline-based departments that are at the heart of academic institutions. Hence, we were faced with an obvious intellectual and institutional problem. Women's Studies put the study of women at the center of concern as no then-existing discipline did. In what discipline–department were we to work? Women as authors–scholars and as subject matter were largely or wholly invisible in all of them. Furthermore, the search for any *one* disciplinary–departmental 'home' quickly came to seem peculiar, since it is quite obvious that women cannot be studied adequately in only one discipline any more than men can. That is in part why Florence Howe issued her well-known call to "break the disciplines," and why we early claimed that Women's Studies must be "interdisciplinary."

But then we had also to ask whether even interdisciplinary work would suffice. Were *any* of the standing disciplines adequate to the study of women? Obviously not. How, then, could an amalgam of fields, none of which had proved open or adequate to the subject, transcend its component parts? It seemed clear that we would have to create a new field, not a pastiche of old ones, in order to be free to locate and when necessary create the theoretical frameworks, the methods and techniques of research and of teaching, that we might need to illuminate our complex subject.

A new debate arose. Should the goal of Women's Studies be the creation of a new discipline, and a new department, rather than the transformation of all the other standing disciplines? But the scholars who worked on Women's Studies were themselves trained in those disciplines, and the students who might take Women's Studies would also take other courses that would continue to exclude and/or devalue women. Our task seemed to require us not 'only' to create a whole new field, but also to rethink each discipline and all disciplines—separately, in relation to each other, and as they reflected and perpetuated this culture's understanding of knowledge. We realized that scholarship that refuses old exclusions and invidious hierarchies not only does not fit into any of the old fields, but, for that very reason, potentially transforms them all.

Therefore, we have worked to establish a new discipline, Women's Studies, and, simultaneously, to support that work with efforts to spread "the new scholarship on women" (as Catharine Stimpson early named it) to all fields through curriculum-transformation work. Despite the concern of some feminist activists and scholars that woman-focused work would be lessened by curriculum-transformation work, both undertakings have flourished side by side, one often leading to the other. The Academy has been changed by the burgeoning of feminist scholarship in general, its fostering in Women's Studies programs in particular, and its effects on all disciplines. The decision as to which kind of work to undertake has in fact usually been the result of realistic assessments of what is most possible and likely to succeed in a particular institutional setting at a particular time.[17]

"Lost Women" Both projects—the creation of Women's Studies programs and work toward the transformation of courses in and across all disciplines—depend, of course, on the availability of works by and about women. At first it seemed that, whatever anyone's intentions, it might be impossible to include knowledge of women in any courses at all until generations of dedicated scholars had produced enough sound new knowledge. Across the country some women and a very few men (notably, William Chafe and Joseph Pleck), while teaching what they had been hired to teach and struggling to continue the research on which jobs, promotions, and tenure depended, turned to finding the "lost women" whose lives, works, and perspectives could be brought into the curriculum. There was a sense that we had to prove that women and women's works really did exist, but—more important—there was an urgent desire to find our history. Stunning works of retrieval emerged with equally stunning speed: for example, Ann Sutherland Harris and Linda Nochlin's work locating, documenting, and studying women artists resulted in the ground-breaking show of women artists at the Brooklyn Museum of Art. The catalogue, later *Women Artists: 1550–1950,* was immediately picked up and used as a text. Also enriching our sense of continuity, culture, and complexity in women's lives were (and are) Gerda Lerner's anthology, *Black Women in White America,* and Rayna Rapp Reiter's anthology, *Toward an Anthropology of Women,* among many others, as well as Dorothy B. Porter's monumentally inspiring long-term work collecting, commenting on, and making available the story of Black women and men through the Moorland Spingarn Research Center at Howard University.[18]

As such work appeared, it allowed us to deepen the critique of the construction of knowledge, to question more concretely the notion that what had been taught was the product of disinterested, nonpolitical, objective scholars. Nochlin's early essay, "Why Are There No Great Women Artists?" that uncovered and analyzed the historical realities of discrimination faced by women began questioning of the very definitions of art that reflected and appeared to legitimize that discrimination.

The search for 'lost' women again pushed our quest for knowledge about women deeper than some had expected. We began to realize the full, complex implications of the obvious statement, "Women have always been here." We refined our understanding of the intellectual problems we faced when we realized that we have always been here *and* that we have been largely invisible in the body of knowledge passed on by the educational and research institutions whose purview is supposed to be the preservation, transmission, and enrichment of humankind's knowledge.

"Add Women and Stir" In a now-famous line, Charlotte Bunch characterized the problem: "You can't," she said, "just add women and stir."[19] It was an apt observation, crystallizing what many had learned in their own efforts to find 'lost' women and add them to their courses. The women could, in fact, be found. There have been women mathematicians, women physicists, women philosophers, women writers, women musicians. There have been women in history, in classical Greece and Rome, and women in politics. But, once found, they often didn't *fit*, couldn't just be dropped into standing courses. Why not? In looking for individual women who had done what men had done, we had not, after all, shifted anything very radically (as we would, and by now have). The problem was that although the now-found 'lost' women seemed to prove something that needed proving yet again—that women are by no means and in no ways inferior to men—we had not, in fact, learned much about *women.* In fact, we had not even proved anything about female abilities: exceptions, as we know, can easily be used simply to prove the rule. If some women were mathematicians, why were not more mathematicians women? There must be something about most if not absolutely all females that disqualifies us. That was not, of course, a reasonable conclusion. In finding the 'lost' women, we had also found more about why and how they were 'lost.' We began to know more about the practices of exclusion exercised against our sex.

But was the point of all our efforts to document that women had not performed as well as men in all the 'important' areas of life because we were discriminated against and actively excluded? Yes, of course that needed, and needs, to be acknowledged, studied, comprehended. But it leaves untouched some other critically important questions. What were women who led the lives prescribed for women doing in the past? What were *those* lives like? What do we all, women and men, need to learn from as well as about them? Those were the questions we could not ask within the constraints of the familiar courses and fields on our campuses. We realized that we did not need only to find the few women who did what men did, but to ask, Where were the women? What can we know about *women?* We needed to undo the established centrality of men.

What was required was a complete rethinking, first of the basic models of reality, truth, and meaning in the dominant tradition, and then of all the knowledge predicted on them. *If it is an intellectual, moral, and political error to think that Man has been, is, and should be the center of the human system, then we must rethink not only the basic models but all knowledge that reflects and perpetuates them.*

To be additive, knowledge must rest on the same basic premises, be of the same basic sort, as that to which it is to be added. But, in the language most often used in the earlier days of Women's Studies work, knowledge about women cannot be added to knowledge about men, because the center of the system has shifted radically when women are moved from "margin to center" (to use the phrase adopted by Bell Hooks for her second book).

That apprehension is sound, but it was not yet adequate to explain, or at least help us begin to explore fruitfully, the challenge of Women's Studies to the old male-centered curriculum. The basic errors that put some men (in their falsely universalized, singular representation as Man) at the center needed to be explored directly and in depth along with at least some of their conceptual consequences. Those errors began to appear as we realized that problems in each field were by no means unique, that there were striking commonalities on a deep level across all fields and outside the Academy as well.

There were many more issues debated and questions raised as we moved further into the effort to rethink a tradition that had excluded so many for so long, but perhaps those I have discussed will suffice to introduce that effort for now. What is important is to think through for oneself, as well as with others, how scholarship and politics are related, why the new scholarship on women did not become simply a subspecialty within the standing disciplines, why finding things that women had done that were as similar as possible to men's achievements did not tell us anything about the lives of *women,* and why, then, it would not suffice—was not even possible—just to add women on to scholarship that was premised on our devaluation and exclusion.

Clearly, we had to consider not just what was already known and how women could be added to it, but how knowledge was constructed, and what kind of thinking the dominant tradition has privileged. We need not give up all that has come to be known, or all the ways and forms and techniques of thinking that have been developed. Quite the contrary: we need to make use of whatever can help us think not only within but also about the dominant tradition. There is no articulable, communicable stance *utterly* outside the tradition for us to take. Should we try to find such a position, we risk falling back into silence just as surely as we do if we speak only within and in the established terms of the dominant culture.

Fortunately, humans are creatures of translation, transitive creatures able to understand more than one language and to move between languages without losing either what is unique to each or what is common enough to make translation possible. We are able to apprehend more than can be spoken in any one language, and can stretch that language in ways that change and enrich it. There are many ways to be both within and without our own cultures.

Critique and Reflexive Thinking

In addition to the personal, historical, political, and intellectual contexts within which efforts to change the curriculum developed, there is also what must, I suppose, be called a philosophical context. No one undertakes an effort to understand anything without bringing to that effort some more or less formulated, more or less conscious, philosophical assumptions, tools, frameworks, values. Certainly I do not; in fact, as I have said, some of the primary conversations that have informed my work have been with philosophers. *Furthermore, even more now than when I began, I believe that the effort to find out why and how our thinking carries the past within it is part of an on-going philosophical critique essential to freedom, and to democracy.* As we work on the curriculum, and so on understanding the dominant tradition, maintaining a critical stance will allow us to avoid tripping ourselves up precisely when we most need to think creatively and, often, in radically new ways.

Thinking With and Without the Tradition I found my thinking in this book on a commitment to critique in a generally Kantian sense, asking, What is *behind* this knowledge, this mode of thought? What were and are the conditions of its possibility? What makes, and keeps, it what, and as, it is? And I take the ground for the possibility of critique to be the human gift of reflexive thought, which is, I believe, not only a given possibility for us all but one of the primary bases of both the idea and the personal experience of freedom. Neither critique nor reflexive thinking is enough to give us freedom, but they help us comprehend and experience it in ways that help us know and value it as a necessity for full human be-ing.

Still, I must note that I am well aware that there is some irony in the project of thinking ourselves free, of transforming knowledge. The tradition to be critiqued is being used against itself. I count on some familiarity with the dominant tradition as part of the common ground we share as we communicate with each other about what needs to be changed, and I draw, to a large extent, on established forms and methods and rules of thought to try to speak with and persuade people. However, I believe in the liberatory quality of reflexive thinking. In thinking about thinking, we are not simply running around in circles like a squirrel in a cage, trapped despite all its frantic activity. We are working to see the thought displayed in particular ways of thinking from a standpoint that is relatively, not absolutely, outside them. I claim no 'higher' or more privileged—let alone absolute or definitive or 'pure'—perspective. I simply claim that it is possible for humans to think as and about ourselves, to think reflexively, self-consciously as we do when we observe ourselves becoming angry, or notice how we see something, or pay attention to how we learn and make discoveries. In what follows, I will discuss patterns of thought and of knowledge I have found in all disciplines as well as in the broader culture in the belief and hope that, having seen them, we may choose to use, vary, or discard them more freely.

That is, I do not believe that we are trapped by the fact that we learned to think in particular ways in this particular culture and in the Academy, nor do I believe that we can simply decide to be free of our formal and informal education. There is no either/or here, no "We are free *or* we are determined." Such dilemmas, created by abstracting two possible positions from all that grounds them in real experience and placing them artificially in opposition to each other, are part of a pattern of thought by which we may refuse to be coerced. In fact, we all know perfectly well that while we can and too often do think in ways that reflect a trap, we can also think about any specific trap and how it works to limit our thought in such a way that the problems it seemed to pose simply dissolve. We can think about our thinking as well as that of others and, in so doing, actualize a specific mode of human freedom that never suffices unto itself to effect genuine liberation but, as I have said, underlies and supports all other efforts—except, of course, those that are animated by a desire to replace one hegemonic system and ideology with another that is equally absolutized; and I, at least, do not consider those to be genuinely liberatory even if the new system seems in many ways better than the old.

Effects of Exclusion Analyzing the conceptual errors that lock the dominant meaning system shaping liberal arts curricula into exclusive, invidiously hierarchical sets of structures, values, principles, beliefs, and feelings is the basic task and challenge of this book. More, much more, will be said about the errors I introduced earlier. Here, I will simply summarize a major problem in including women and the excluded groups of men in the dominant meaning system by repeating that some conceptual errors are so fundamental to the dominant Western tradition that an additive approach to change simply cannot work. For example, work by and about women is not just missing from the academic curriculum; it is to a remarkable extent incompatible with it. That is, *knowledge that is claimed to be inclusive—claimed to be both about and significant for all humankind—but that is in fact exclusive must be transformed, not just corrected or supplemented.* Discoveries indicating that the world is round do not merely supplement knowledge shaped by and supportive of the theory that the world is flat. Similarly, feminist work by and about women is not just missing from the academic canon: it is incompatible with some of the canon's basic, founding assumptions. And that means *not* that feminist scholarship is 'out of order' but that whatever makes noninclusive knowledge unable to open to the subjects and perspectives so long devalued and/or excluded must itself be changed.[20]

I had the notion behind this idea for quite some time, but, as with many such flashes of understanding, it illuminated my thought only fitfully. I had not allowed it to stay, had not let myself think it through. But one day, after I had given my talk at a conference opening a curriculum-transformation project, it came to me. I was listening to other speakers on changes taking place in specific disciplines when suddenly I found myself whispering to the sociologist Margaret Anderson, who was sitting next to me, "We weren't *omitted*. We were *excluded*."

As I have said, that is obvious. But it remains hard to say. It sounds as if constant evil intent was involved, and so it threatens to move the attention of both speaker and audience from the *effects* of the intent to exclude that remain in the curriculum to the *motivation* of the excluders. And that shift is almost certain to make those who have not changed their courses, or their way of thinking about their work, suddenly feel attacked rather than included in an exciting effort to think about our thinking. But if I and others do not say, "We/women were excluded," we cannot get to the critical observation that *the reasons why it was considered right and proper to exclude the majority of humankind were and are built into the very foundations of what was established as knowledge.*

That is, women were not overlooked through a prolonged fit of the famous academic absentmindedness (much like that attributed to the British to 'explain' how they ended up with an empire), as the use of the word "omitted" tends to imply. Women were excluded from lives of scholarship, as from 'significant' subject matter, as from positions of authority and power, when the basic ideas, definitions, principles, and facts of the dominant tradition were being formulated. But does that mean that *all* the creators and guardians and transmitters of the dominant tradition were and are personally animated by a consistent, purposeful intent to think consciously about excluding women, and many men, every moment? No, it does not (although it does not preclude the observation that some, indeed, were and, I fear, still are so animated). It reminds us that *the principles that require and justify the exclusion of women, and the results of those principles appearing throughout the complex artifices of knowledge and culture, are so locked into the dominant meaning system that it has for a very long time been utterly irrelevant whether or not any particular person intended to exclude women.* The exclusion was and is effected by the forms and structures within which we *all* try to live, work, and find meaning.

Thus, although it at first sounds as if using the strong term "excluded" might divide us radically from each other, such that all who are not part of the solution are seen as actively, consciously, and willfully part of the problem, in fact it reminds us of something quite different. We are all, albeit to varying degrees that matter a great deal, a part of the problem. Insofar as we speak and think and act in ways that make sense to other people within the dominant meaning system, we cannot avoid participating (again to varying degrees) in precisely that which we wish to change. We have all at times thought, said, and done things that, as our consciousness grew through the use of our ability to think reflexively, we wish we could disavow or at least hope we have outgrown. And that "we" includes (again in critically different ways, and with critically different results) not only those who benefit but also those who suffer from the dominant system. One of the struggles of the oppressed, excluded, and colonized is always to break free of internalized oppression—which does *not* mean that "women are their own worst enemies," a ridiculous exaggeration of the reasonable insight that we tend to learn what the dominant culture teaches us, and reteaches us, sometimes harshly, when we begin to struggle free.

This is, of course, only another way of saying that prejudices such as sexism and the deeply related homophobia, racism, and classism are not just personal problems, sets of peculiar and troubling beliefs. Exclusions and devaluations of whole groups of people on the scale and of the range, tenacity, and depth of racism and sexism and classism are systemic and shape the world within which we all struggle to live and find meaning. I and other white women benefit to varying degrees from the system of racism, however strongly we oppose it, just as all men benefit to varying degrees from the sex/gender system. And those of us who work in various ways within and with the Academy benefit from it, too, however much our work is designed to change it. That all these systems also, and profoundly, damage in some ways those who benefit from them can be recognized without thereby excusing them/us from responsibility for their perpetuation.

Men and women sometimes say to me, "But men suffer, too. They aren't allowed to cry or be nurturant, and they die younger than women on the average because they carry an inordinate amount of responsibility." I recognize the problem and am very pleased to see men join in dismantling the systems that give them burdens related to their privileges. However, it must be noted that while some of the privileged of all groups understand and feel the harm done to them, most seem to want to get rid of the harm without giving up the privilege. The movements of many, many people we have come to associate with Mahatma Gandhi, Martin Luther King, and Susan B. Anthony provide striking examples of how the harm done to those in power as a result of their holding that power can indeed be brought to consciousness, and that consciousness can be enlisted in support of a collective (if by no means inclusively egalitarian) political movement. Each of these movements developed important methods of persuasion as well as coercion, of what we might call consciousness-raising, not only among movement activists but among those against whom they were protesting. They did not simply take up guns and try to force agreement; they used what Gandhi called *satyagraha*, soul-force, to convert others to the view that a *system* must be changed, a system that was unjust and so harmful for all.

But by itself consciousness of the costs of systems that also give privileges often does no more than make those in power a bit guilty and grumpy—harder, not easier, to live with.

The questions of 'harm' and 'benefit,' of 'consciousness' and 'false consciousness,' of 'oppression' and 'internalized oppression' are extraordinarily complex. Such complexities are important. They serve to hold us to the level of systemic analysis without allowing us to forget that it is individuals who participate in and rebel against systems. We can critique these systems from within, often using their own abstract principles against them. In the case of the Academy, it is clear that knowledge that is claimed to be objective and inclusive yet reflects and perpetuates societal discrimination and prejudices fails even on its own terms. Knowledge that was created and has been passed on within a culture that, until very recently indeed, excluded the majority of humankind from the activities, positions, and thinking that were considered most important can hardly be disinterested and politically neutral, as it is claimed to be. It replicates in what it covers, how it treats its subjects, how it explains and judges, the most basic assumptions of the dominant culture—not entirely, not absolutely, but consistently enough so that it remains related to the culture from which it arose. Such knowledge is almost certainly blind to some of its own basic assumptions and methods, but they are there to be found.

Consider the example of geocentrism. Copernicus's move to put the sun at the center of the cosmos was greeted as what it indeed was, a challenge to many of the most deeply held beliefs of his culture, and more—a challenge to a remarkable range of systems of explanation, of knowledge, even of mores and morals. Darwin's theory of evolution had, and for some still has, the same devastating effects. It dethrones Man, suggesting that he is *not* the center, is not a unique creation that is discontinuous with and superior in kind to all else. Shifting from an invidiously hierarchical view of humankind entailed then, and entails now, a concomitant shift in all areas of knowledge, of ethics, of politics. Consider, too, the deep differences between the knowledge of the English and Europeans who colonized this country and the knowledge of the Native Americans. One set of cultures saw the land as given to Man to tame, to use, to make his own so that thinking about the earth tended to be instrumental. The other saw the land as sacred; thinking about it tended to be descriptive, celebratory, mythic, with the instrumental entering in the mode of propitiation, not mastery.

Centering attention on women rather than on a particular group of men involves a shift in focus, a reconfiguration of the whole, that is just as profound and suggestive. To take only one example for now, we can return to one of the initial insights of the Women's Movement, the realization that the personal is political. The full implications of that simple statement are still unfolding, but from the start it reminds us that everything that appears in public needs to be seen in relation to the private, and vice versa, so the terms "public" and "private" themselves cease to be firmly distinct. Thus, among other effects, the whole panoply of 'women's virtues' is released from containment within the functions relegated to women to reveal its significance and value in and for everyone, rather than being shunned by the 'Real Man' who must, above all, display no 'effeminate' qualities, whether 'virtuous' or not. Heroism can then cease to be a singular individual quality expressed in highly visible deeds and become a quality of character developed in a whole life, a life led in relation to many others that expresses care, honesty, integrity, intimacy, constancy, as well as (even instead of) the ability to 'win' through dramatic confrontations and adventures. And leadership can then be understood not in terms of dominance but as an ability to empower others.

Consider the 'conquest' of the West in the United States. Was it really the work of single scouts, of brave men 'penetrating' the wilderness, of lone individuals developing a culture based primarily on an individualistic notion of self-reliance? What about women struggling to establish homes, to care for families, to find and build the community that was essential to efforts to survive? What about the sexual and physical abuse of women, which, while it remains an untold story, makes all other frontier stories not just incomplete but dangerously falsifying? What about the terrible dangers of childbirth in situations where little or no care was available?[21]

When we remember women, the story and its interpretation change, become much more complex; context and community reenter; the exigencies and heroism of everyday life, of reproducing and caring for life itself, take on the importance they really have.

Most basically, perhaps, we can say that when we focus on women the peculiarly abstract versions of the dominant Story of Mankind are undone so that the logics of connection, concreteness, context, and community can emerge. Such modes of relation cannot simply be added to a logic of externally related monads, of abstract individualism, of singular Great Deeds, of public life apparently ungrounded in and distinct from 'private' life. The coherence in many of the stories we have inherited was manufactured after the fact to make sense of characters, events, and motivations that had been removed from their real contexts. To uncover what women were doing and undergoing is to locate and ground a different and more truthful coherence, and that means, again, that we are not merely adding information but fundamentally reconceiving what we thought we knew.

Examples could be multiplied, but let us just note here the basic point: the shaping assumptions on which influential knowledge—which is always knowledge-accepted-as-such by a particular group in a particular culture—continues to be based are influential not *despite* but *because of* the fact that most people are unaware of them.

Thus knowledge and the whole culture and accepted process of knowledge-making need to be changed in their congruent basic claims and assumptions before that which has been defined as out of order, as rightly to be excluded, can be heard, seen, studied—comprehended. Old knots and tangles that are in all our minds and practices must be located and untied if there are to be threads available with which to weave the new into anything like a whole cloth, a coherent but by no means homogeneous pattern.[22]

Conceptual Approaches: Thinking Through

Conceptual Errors: The Root Problem

This is where all these beginnings, these different ways 'in' through our quick exploration of various contexts—personal, political, historical, philosophical—began, and arrive. We begin again, now circling toward the central root problem, discovering it, circling out again to see it differently, returning to reconsider it. Throughout what follows, I will continue to follow that kind of spiraling logic. I do so in part because, as I have said, my thinking has from the beginning been in conversation with many people, and I want to continue trying to keep open as many doors as possible. I do not want to argue anyone into agreement; that kind of agreement is entirely unstable, and rightly so. Argument by certain prevailing rules of logic is a kind of force; a good argument "compels agreement." I do not wish to compel agreement. I wish to invite it, and I would like the reasons for it to belong genuinely to each of those with whom I think. The whole point of this exploration is to try to think ourselves free, to free our own thinking.

The *root problem* reappears in different guises in all fields and throughout the dominant tradition. It is, simply, that while the majority of humankind was excluded from education and the making of what has been called knowledge, *the dominant few not only defined themselves as the inclusive kind of human but also as the norm and the ideal.* A few privileged men defined themselves as constituting mankind/humankind and simultaneously saw themselves as akin to what mankind/humankind ought to be in fundamental ways that distinguished them from all others. Thus, at the same time they removed women and nonprivileged men within their culture and other cultures from "mankind," they justified that exclusion on the grounds that the excluded were by nature and culture 'lesser' people (if they even thought of the others as having 'cultures'). Their notion of who was properly human was *both* exclusive *and* hierarchical with regard to those they took to be properly subject to them—women in all roles; men who worked with their hands; male servants and slaves; women and men of many other cultures.

Thus, they created root definitions of what it means to be human that, with the concepts and theories that flowed from and reinforced those definitions, made it difficult to think well about, or in the mode of, anyone other than themselves, just as they made it difficult to think honestly about the defining few.

"Know thyself," said the few ancient Greek men who had the leisure for and took the privilege of exploring "the life of the mind" and the "free life of the citizen"—and who are still mistakenly called "The Greeks" as if they were *all* the Greeks. Thus, they also created (indubitably *not* for the first time in human history) a haunting not-self that was essential to the admitted, recognized, claimed self. The not-self—the Barbarian (who was originally simply one who did not speak Greek), women, slaves, men who worked with their hands—surrounded the self they sought to know, setting its boundaries by constituting some activities, some feelings, some human functions, some deep desires, as forbidden because projected onto lesser others whom they must not be like.

This deep construction of a self inextricably tied to a not-self was, much later, brilliantly characterized in the concept of the Other that Simone de Beauvoir took up and transformed. *The Other* catches an existential reality as well as a conceptual trait that remains at the very heart of the Western tradition in a way that is particularly potent because it is far too often unrecognized. But it seems profoundly familiar once introduced:

> *In actuality the relation of the two sexes is not quite like that of two electrical poles, for man represents both the positive and the neutral, as is indicated by the common use of* man *to designate human beings in general; whereas woman represents only the negative, defined by limiting criteria, without reciprocity. . . . She is defined and differentiated with reference to man and not he with reference to her; she is the incidental, the inessential as opposed to the essential. He is the Subject, he is the Absolute—she is the Other.*[1]

The concept of the Other is a clue to the difficult conceptual tangles we must undo. It is very strange to maintain that one small group of people is simultaneously the essence, the inclusive term, the norm, *and* the ideal for all. Yet that is what we hear: "Man is a generic term," and, at the same time, "*Vive la différence,*" which positively celebrates the notion that "men and women are by no means the same." What, then, are we to do about the differences that mark women as not-men yet give no substantive, positive identity, no reality of their own? Those differences must be the marks of non-humans—if "man" is to be generic. Women then become beasts or gods (whores or virgins in the not-unfamiliar sexualized construction imposed on women), and/or non-entities, non-selves.

We hit absurdity fairly fast on this level. Consider the famous syllogism: "Man is mortal. Socrates is a man. Therefore, Socrates is mortal." Try it with a woman: "Man is mortal. Alice is ________" what? A man? No one says that, not even philosophers. "Man," the supposedly generic term, does not allow us to say, "Alice is a man." So we say, "Alice is a woman." Then what are we to deduce? "Therefore, Alice is ________" what? It is man, a supposedly universal category that is simultaneously neutral and masculine but *not* feminine ("masculine" is defined in contradistinction to "feminine"), who "is mortal." Is Alice, who is female and hence not in a category that is either neutral or masculine, then *immortal?* Is she mortal insofar as, for the purposes of such reasoning, she may be subsumed under the category *man,* but not insofar as she is, specifically, female? Are women, then, immortal insofar as we are female? Alice ends up in the peculiar position of being a somewhat mortal, somewhat immortal, creature. Or, we must admit, we cannot thus reason about Alice while thinking of her as female at all. We can think of Socrates as a man without derailing the syllogism; we cannot think of Alice as a woman. Reason flounders; the center holds, with Man in it, but it is an exclusive, not a universal or neutral, center. Alice disappears through the looking glass.

The fact is that "man" does not include (or "embrace," as witty grammarians used to like to say) women or all humans, any more than qualities derived from man as he has been understood represent either the norm or the ideal for all humankind.

That kind of tangle, and the errors it produces, is starkly evident in the curriculum.

Notes

1. Linda Gordon, "What's New in Women's History," in Teresa de Lauretis, ed., *Feminist Studies: Critical Studies* (Bloomington: Indiana University Press, 1986), p. 21.

2. For other reflections on the effects of terminology in this area, see Peggy McIntosh, "A Note on Terminology," *Women's Studies Quarterly* 11 (Summer 1983): 29–30.

3. Teresa de Lauretis, "Feminist Studies/Critical Studies: Issues, Terms and Contexts," in de Lauretis, ed., *Feminist Studies: Critical Studies,* p. 3.

4. Ibid., p. 7. See also Elizabeth Minnich, *Toward a Feminist Transformation of the Curriculum,* Proceedings of the 5th Annual GLCA Women's Studies Conference (Ann Arbor: GLCA, 1979).

Contextual Approaches: Thinking About

1. Frederick Rudolph, *Curriculum: A History of the American Undergraduate Course of Study since 1636* (San Francisco: Jossey-Bass, 1977), pp. 168, 169.

2. Ibid., p. 169.

3. Patricia Palmieri, "From Republican Motherhood to Race Suicide: Arguments on the Higher Education of Women in the United States, 1820–1920)," in Carol Lasser, ed., *Educating Men and Women Together* (Chicago: University of Illinois Press, 1987).

4. Linda Kerber, *Women of the Republic: Intellect and Ideology in Revolutionary America* (Chapel Hill: University of North Carolina Press, 1980), p. 10.

5. Paula Giddings, *When and Where I Enter . . . : The Impact of Black Women on Race and Sex in America* (New York: William Morrow, 1984), pp. 104–5.

6. For an excellent feminist analysis of the dominant tradition of thought about education, see Jane Roland Martin, *Reclaiming a Conversation: The Ideal of the Educated Woman* (New Haven: Yale University Press, 1985). For supportive analyses of the role of education and how it might be reconceived and practiced, see, for example, Paulo Freire, *Pedagogy of the Oppressed,* trans. Myra Bergman Ramos (New York: Seabury Press, 1970); Henry A. Giroux, *Ideology, Culture, and the Process of Schooling* (Philadelphia: Temple University Press, 1981); Ira Shor and Paulo Freire, *A Pedagogy for Liberation: Dialogues on Transforming Education* (South Hadley, Mass.: Bergin and Garvey, 1987).

7. See, for example, Barbara Christian, "The Race for Theory," in *Feminist Studies* 14 (Spring 1988): 67–79.

8. I have been drawn heavily, and with gratitude, on Sara Evans, *Personal Politics* (New York: Random House/Vintage Books, 1979).

9. For more work on the 1960s and 1970s movements, see also, for example, James Miller, *Democracy Is in the Streets: From Port Huron to the Siege of Chicago* (New York: Simon and Schuster, 1987); Clayborne Carson, *In Struggle: SNCC and the Black Awakening of the Nineteen Sixties* (Cambridge: Harvard University Press, 1981); Todd Gitlin, *The Sixties: Years of Hope, Days of Rage* (New York: Bantam Books, 1987); Wini Breines, *Community and Organization in the New Left: 1962–1968* (New York: Praeger Publishers, 1982); Sohnya Sayres

et al., eds., *The 60's Without Apology* (Minneapolis: University of Minnesota Press, in cooperation with Social Text, 1984).

10. "A Kind of Memo from Casey Hayden and Mary King to a Number of Other Women in the Peace and Freedom Movements, November 18, 1965," in Evans, *Personal Politics,* p. 235.

11. Cynthia Washington, "We Started from Different Ends of the Spectrum," ibid., pp. 238–40. See also Alice Walker, *Meridian,* a complex and fascinating novel about the Civil Rights Movement.

12. See, for example, the fine study by Harry C. Boyte, *The Backyard Revolution: Understanding the New Citizen Movement* (Philadelphia: Temple University Press, 1980).

13. See, for example, Evans, *Personal Politics;* Bell Hooks, *Ain't I a Woman: Black Women and Feminism* (Boston: South End Press, 1981), and *Feminist Theory: From Margin to Center* (Boston: South End Press, 1984); Giddings, *When and Where I Enter;* Elly Bulkin, Minnie Bruce Pratt, and Barbara Smith, *Yours in Struggle: Three Feminist Perspectives on Anti-Semitism and Racism* (New York: Long Haul Press, 1984); Johnella Butler, "Minority Studies and Women's Studies: Do We Want to Kill A Dream?" *Women's Studies International Forum 7,* no. 3 (1984): 135–38.

14. See also Audre Lorde, "An Open Letter to Mary Daly," and other essays in Cherrie Moraga and Gloria Anzaldua, eds., *This Bridge Called My Back: Writings by Radical Women of Color* (Watertown, Mass.: Persephone Press, 1981); Barbara Smith, ed., *Home Girls: A Black Feminist Anthology* (New York: Kitchen Table: Women of Color Press, 1983); Florence Howe, *Myths of Coeducation: Selected Essays, 1964–1983* (Bloomington: Indiana University Press, 1984); Robin Morgan, ed., *Sisterhood Is Powerful: An Anthology of Writings from the Women's Liberation Movement* (New York: Random House, 1970).

15. For some interesting thinking on a few of the early efforts to bring change to the Academy, see Charlotte Bunch and Sandra Rubaii, eds., *Learning Our Way: Essays in Feminist Education* (Trumansburg, N.Y.: Crossing Press, 1983), and Howe, *Myths of Coeducation;* see also the informal publications (by the Barnard College Women's Center) of proceedings of The Scholar and The Feminist Conferences. For an on-going record of efforts at institutional equity, see the publications of the Project on the Status and Education of Women headed by Bernice Sandler of the Association of American Colleges, 1818 R Street, N.W., Washington, DC 20009, and the American Council on Education's Offices of Women and of Minority Affairs, One Dupont Circle, Washington, DC 20036. For accounts of the development of Women's Studies courses and programs in the United States, see back issues of the *Women's Studies Quarterly* (Old Waterbury, N.Y.: Feminist Press); Elizabeth Minnich, Jean O'Barr, and Rachel Rosenfeld, eds., *Reconstructing the Academy: Women's Education and Women's Studies* (Chicago: University of Chicago Press, 1988), and Carol Pearson, Donna Shavlik, and Judith Touchton, eds., *Educating the Majority: Women Challenge Tradition in Higher Education* (New York: Macmillan, 1987), among other works.

16. See also Sandra Coyner, "The Ideas of Mainstreaming: Women's Studies and the Disciplines," in *Frontiers,* tenth anniversary issue: *A Decade of Women's Studies Inside the Academy* 8, no. 3 (1986): 87–96; and Marilyn R. Schuster and Susan R. Van Dyne, *Women's Place in the Academy: Transforming the Liberal Arts Curriculum* (Totowa, N.J.: Rowan and Allenheld, 1985), among others.

17. See also the report of the Association of American Colleges, *Liberal Education and the New Scholarship on Women: Issues and Constraints in Institutional Change,* from the Wingspread Conference, Racine, Wisc., 22–24 October 1981, and Elizabeth Kamarck Minnich, "Education for the Free Man?" in *Liberal Education* 68, no. 4 (1982): 311–21.

18. Linda Nochlin, "Why Are There No Great Women Artists?" in *Art News* 69 (1971): 22–39, 67–71; cf. also Ann Sutherland Harris and Linda Nochlin, *Women Artists: 1550–1950* (New York: Alfred A. Knopf, 1981).

19. This line has been quoted frequently among those involved with Women's Studies, spreading primarily through conversation rather than circulation of a text. However, we now have Charlotte Bunch's collected essays, *Passionate Politics: Essays 1968–1986—Feminist Theory in Action* (New York: St. Martin's Press, 1987); see p. 140. When asked, Bunch said that the idea cited here was developed in conversations with Mary E. Hunt.

20. Many people have found Thomas Kuhn's work on "paradigm shifts" helpful here: Thomas S. Kuhn, "The Structure of Scientific Revolutions," in *The International Encyclopedia of Unified Science,* vol. 2, no. 2, 2d ed. (Chicago: University of Chicago Press, 1962); see also Kuhn's *The Structure of Scientific Revolutions,* 2d ed. (Chicago: University of Chicago Press, 1970).

21. The idea that we need to rethink the story of the "conquest" of the West struck me first, I think, when I noticed a classic example of the root error in some popular magazine. The phrasing, all to familiar, went something like this: "The early pioneers followed their dreams West, taking with them all their worldly goods, their wives and children." "Pioneers," then, did/does *not* include women, who remain in the old stories on the level of worldly goods, a kind of baggage to be taken along by the 'real' pioneers. Once we have realized that, we can raise basic questions about what the women were doing and undergoing, and those questions immediately suggest that we consider the kinds of issues I have touched on here. Some of the scholars who have worked in this area include John Farragher, Elizabeth Hampsten, Glenda Riley, and Lillian Schlissel; for a compatible approach from the angle of communitarian and/or ec-

ological analyses, see, for example, work by Wendall Berry, Wes Jackson, Aldo Leopold, and John Tallmadge. Books dealing with different subjects that demonstrate how rethinking and re-envisioning women results in basic reconceptualizations and not merely additional information include Linda Gordon, *Woman's Body, Woman's Right: Birth Control in America* (New York: Penguin, 1977); John Berger, *Ways of Seeing* (London: Penguin, 1972); Jesse Bernard, *The Future of Marriage* (New York: World Publishing Co., 1972); and most of the other books and articles I cite throughout.

22. I was struck, and moved, by the Reverend Jesse Jackson's use of the image of a quilt (rather than the old "melting pot") to express the persistent and *not* undesirable patterned diversity of the peoples and cultures of the United States in his speech to the National Democratic Convention in Atlanta in the summer of 1988.

Conceptual Approaches: Thinking Through

1. Simone de Beauvoir, *The Second Sex*, trans. and ed., H. M. Parshley (New York: Random House/Vintage Books, 1974), p. xix.

Disappearing Tricks

Dale Spender

Dale Spender is a researcher, writer, editor, broadcaster, and teacher. She is a member of the Queensland Women's Consultative Council and the Australian Society of Authors. She is a consultant in the areas of information technology and management, in education and the construction of knowledge, as well as an international expert in the fields of language, communication, writing, editing, publishing, and equity. She has taught in universities in many countries, has given more than 300 keynote addresses, has appeared regularly on radio and television in Australia and overseas, and has written for many popular publications and newspapers. She contributes a regular column, "Data Crit" to the Australian Author. *Her more than 30 books include* Life Lines: Australian Women's Letters and Diaries 1788 to 1840 *(with Patricia Clarke, 1992);* The Knowledge Explosion: Generations of Feminist Scholarship *(with Cheris Kramarae, 1992);* The Writing or the Sex?: Or Why You Don't Have to Read Women's Writing to Know It's No Good *(1989);* Women of Ideas (and What Men Have Done to Them): From Aphra Behn to Adrienne Rich *(1988);* Reflecting Men at Twice Their Natural Size *(1987);* For the Record: The Making and Meaning of Feminist Knowledge *(1985);* Man Made Language *(1985);* There's Always Been a Women's Movement This Century *(1983);* Feminist Theorists: Three Centuries of Key Women Thinkers *(1983); and* Men's Studies Modified: The Impact of Feminism on the Academic Disciplines *(1981).*

Spender shows us how sexism inserts itself into our thinking process—in this case, through language.

MAN: 'Human being, especially *an adult male human being'*

–Webster's Collegiate Dictionary

Words are symbols. They stand for, or represent, an object. In the last decade there has been a debate about the symbol *man* (and its pronoun, *he*) for there is ambiguity about what these symbols represent. On the one hand, the prescriptive grammarians of the past not only ruled that *man* and *he* represented the male of the species; they also ruled that *man* and *he* represented the species as well, and therefore included women. Many people have taken the prescriptive grammarians at their word and accepted their ruling without always being familiar with their reasons. There are, however, individuals, many of them feminists, who have declared that this was a rather ridiculous rule partly because it has led to ambiguity and confusion, and partly because the reasons for the rule were blatantly sexist. While some may still be content to accept that the use of *man* and *he* which we have been taught is legitimate and inoffensive, and that its sexist overtones of rendering women invisible are nothing but a mere linguistic *accident,* there are others of us who regard this rule as most unacceptable and who wish to change it. There was nothing accidental about the way in which the rule was introduced and there is nothing accidental about the consequences which ensue. Because it was a rule which was intended to promote the primacy of *man* at the expense of *woman,* we are committed to its elimination and to the introduction of more equitable linguistic forms which favour neither sex.

The rationalisation that *man embraces woman* is a relatively recent one in the history of our language. Using *man* and *he* to encompass *woman* is a practice that was unknown in the fifteenth century. In 1553 we have the record of a certain Mr Wilson who argued that it was more 'natural' to place the man before the woman (as, for example, in male and female, husband and wife,

This extract from *Learning to Lose,* edited by Dale Spender and Elizabeth Sarah and published by the Women's Press Ltd (1980), 34 Great Sutton Street, London EC1V 0DX, is reprinted here by permission of the Women's Press Ltd.

brother and sister) and as he was writing for an almost exclusively male population of educated people who were interested in the art of rhetoric, there were few women in a position to protest against the so-called 'natural order'. By 1646, however, the argument had taken a different turn. Not only was it by then considered natural that the male should take precedence, it was also, according to one Mr Poole, that the male gender was the *worthier* gender and therefore deserved priority. Claims for the superiority of man over woman increased and were strengthened when, in 1746, Mr Kirkby invented his *Eighty-Eight Grammatical Rules;* Rule Twenty-One stated that the male gender was more *comprehensive* than the female. This marks an interesting shift in the argument. The Oxford English Dictionary defines *comprehensive* as *including much,* so Mr Kirkby was claiming that the male gender included much more than the female. This is of course a personal opinion which Mr Kirkby and his colleagues were entitled to hold, but it is not a linguistic opinion and these are not grounds for making linguistic judgements and for formulating rules to be imposed on all users of the language. Again, however, it seems that there were few protests about Rule Twenty-One; certainly Mr Kirkby had no women colleagues who could have objected to the rule and pointed to the flaws in his reasoning. And so the grammatical rule that *man embraces woman,* because *man* is more important, came into being and has been imposed upon the speakers of the language.

Mr Kirkby's rule however, was not always taken up with enthusiasm. Many people were unaware of it (and could therefore be labelled as ignorant) and some ignored it. People persisted in using *man* to mean male and *woman* to mean female, and *they* to refer to a person whose sex was unknown (as for example in 'Anyone can say what *they* like' or 'Everyone has *their* rights'). But the male grammarians were upset by this flagrant disregard of their rules and began to insist on *correctness*—meaning conformity to their rules—as a necessary characteristic of 'an educated man'. Their efforts were successful; being correct became important and so that there could be no doubt about what was correct or incorrect in the case of *man* and *he,* an Act of Parliament was passed in 1850 in which *man* was legally made to stand for *woman* (Bodine, 1975). There were of course no women members of parliament who could have cast opposing votes.

There can be no mistake about the reasons for the introduction of this rule and the consequent Act of Parliament. They were to give prominence and primacy to the male sex, and to give linguistic substance to the sexist bias of influential men. There is little likelihood that this usage would have evolved of its own accord; it required considerable intervention on the part of grammarians to introduce it and to insist on its use.

The current moves, then, by feminists to take out what the male grammarians put in, cannot be referred to as 'tampering' with the language. We are not trying to change something which is pure and unadulterated. On the contrary, we are trying to remove an artificial linguistic rule which should never have been given credence and which has never been justified on linguistic grounds. However, although the efforts of the male grammarians were not justified, they were, nonetheless, successful. We have in the past accepted their rule but if we continue to operate it we will help to support a practice of making man visible at the expense of woman. We will also be influenced by this practice for it has been found that one of the results of using the term *man* has been that the image of the male sex becomes foremost in our thoughts; while *man* is the favoured linguistic term, it is the male sex which is the favoured image in our consciousness.

There is evidence that people think of the male when they use the term *man.* Alleen Pace Nilsen (1973) found that young children thought that *man* meant male in sentences such as 'man needs food'; Linda Harrison (1975) found that science students thought of male people when talking of the evolution of *man;* J. Schneider and Sally Hacker (1972) found that college students thought of males when confronted with titles such as *Political Man* and *Urban Man.* And both Linda Harrison and Wendy Martyna (1978) found that men used the term *man* much more frequently than women. When Wendy Martyna asked the people in her sample what they thought of when they used the word *man,* the men said they thought of themselves. Women, however, said that they used the term *man* because they had been taught that it was grammatically correct. In Martyna's sample, at least, the women, who ranged from kindergarten to college students, recognised that they were not encompassed in the term *man;* they could not think of themselves when they used the word. If *man* was truly an encompassing word, a generic term, then women, as well as men, should be able to see their own image within it. That men think of themselves and not of women when they use the term *man* is an hypothesis which can readily be put to the test. Muriel Schulz (1978) examined the writings of many leading sociologists (past and present) and found that although they may have used terms like 'men of ideas' and 'the nature of man', supposedly to include *all* members of the species, they in fact meant only males. Alma Graham also found that many men revealed that although they may claim vehemently that man *includes* woman, their usage indicates otherwise:

> *In practice, the sexist assumption that man is a species of male becomes the fact. Erich Fromm certainly seemed to think so when he wrote that man's 'vital interests' were 'life, food, access to females etc.'. Loren Eisley implied it when he wrote of man that 'his back aches, he ruptures easily, his women have difficulties in childbirth. . .' . If these writers had been using* man *in the sense of the human species rather than male, they would have written that man's vital interests are life, food, and access to the opposite sex, and that man suffers backaches, ruptures easily, and has difficulties in giving birth (Graham, 1975; 62).*

With examples like this it is difficult to maintain the argument that *man* includes *woman* as the grammarians of old absurdly (but conveniently) claimed. For these are not just examples of occasional slips, they are the logical outcome of the grammarians' law that the world is to be considered male unless proven otherwise. There are yet more illustrations of the way in which the word *man* is used by us to mean just *men*. We can say that *man makes wars*, that *man plays football*, and that *he is an aggressive animal* without suggesting that we are mistaken or that we are being funny, even though we realise that these statements apply to only half the population. When women are left out of the activities that are being described, it seems that there is something wrong. But what happens when men are left out? The human species does a great deal more than make wars and play football but there is a problem when we use the word *man* to refer to other, equally human, but not necessarily male activities. Can we say *man devotes about forty hours a week to housework* without sounding as though we have made a mistake? Can we say *man lives an isolated life when engaged in childrearing*, or that *man is usually hospitalised for birth in our society* without saying something that sounds absurd? *Are menopause and menstruation significant events in the life of man?* When we think about it, it becomes increasingly clear that in our language, *man* means male. It is an example of the way in which the world is male unless proved otherwise; and housework, childcare and menstruation and menopause are otherwise. They are not classified with men and we therefore cannot use *man*, which means men, to refer to them!

> *One may be saddened but not surprised at the statement 'man is the only primate that commits rape'. Although, as commonly understood, it can apply to only half the human population, it is nevertheless semantically acceptable. But 'man, being a mammal breastfeeds his young' is taken as a joke. (Miller and Swift, 1976; 25-6).*

If we could say *man has been engaged in a constant search for the means to control his fertility*, we would have very different meanings embedded in our language; we would have a very different consciousness. We would be starting to make women with their problems and their pleasures visible and real.

While *woman* has been forced out of the language in many contexts, and the invisibility of women has been reinforced, our present society, which is predicated on the principle of male supremacy (and the accompanying male visibility) has not seen fit to protest because the issue has not been regarded as a problem. Women are socially devalued so it is not inconsistent to devalue them linguistically. Mainly as a response to feminist efforts, however, this issue is beginning to be seen as a problem and already there are changes underway. Many government agencies in America have tried to dismantle the mechanisms which maintain asymmetry between the sexes. When the evidence that *man* made *woman* invisible was put to certain government agencies, many were persuaded of its validity. The argument was enough to convince the United States Department of Labour to issue a revision of occupational titles in order to provide more equal employment opportunities. The old job titles were considered to be discriminatory towards women because they excluded women and suggested that their entry into such jobs was inappropriate.

Three thousand five hundred job titles were revised to eliminate reference to age and sex so that *policeman* became *police officer,* for example, and *salesman* became *sales agent.* Of course, the Manpower Administration had to begin with itself, changing its own title to that of The Employment and Training Administration and renaming its publication *Worklife,* recognising that the old name, *Manpower,* excluded the sizeable workforce of women:

> *Since children learn about society from language it is an easy lesson for girls to learn that many situations described by male identified words do not include them. Implicit in the omission is the understanding that a large part of the world is inappropriate to them. (Berger & Kachuk, 1977; 3).*

Of course, boys may learn the same things from language, but the words which exclude males are much less frequent, and of much lower status. Boys might not feel so offended by exclusion. Being left out of housework (*housewife*), or out of child care (*governess, au pair girl*), may not be as hard to take as being left out of politics (*congressman, chairman*), religion (*clergyman, priest*), work (*businessman, foreman, craftsman* and, of course, the verb *to man*) or society (*gentleman*).

The use of *man* to include *woman,* however, reveals not only sexist prejudice but also linguistic ignorance. It contradicts another grammatical rule, which is that English has *natural* gender. When a language has natural gender objects are supposed to be labelled on the basis of sex so that the world is divided into masculine, feminine and neuter according to its sexual attributes (or lack of them). English is *supposed* to have natural gender and this is *supposed* to make it superior to languages which have grammatical gender, such as French and German for example. Grammatical gender is not based on sex, but on arbitrary decisions (which are considered to be confusing) so that in German, for example, a tree is masculine, a tomcat is feminine and a wife neuter. English did once have grammatical gender (Anglo-Saxon was similar to modern German in this respect) and it is often claimed that the move to natural gender was a big improvement. The reason given for this is that natural gender is so much less confusing; people are classified according to their sex. In English, sex and gender are supposed to correspond and are therefore called *natural.*

But in describing the language in this way, one significant factor has been overlooked. English is only natural and unproblematic *if one is male.* There is nothing natural about women being referred to as *man* and *he;* they are not being classified on the basis of sex, and they do constitute half the population. The claim for natural gender in English is a claim based purely on the male experience of language and while *they* may not feel that there is any confusion, women may not share their assessment. It is confusing for women; it can be even more confusing than is the case with languages that have grammatical gender. At least if one is learning French or German one does not expect a correlation between sex and gender and one can become accustomed to being a woman and referred to as male or neutral. But in English we are specifically taught that sex and gender do correspond linguistically, and that it is wrong to refer to a tomcat as she, a tree as he, or a wife as it. But it is all right to refer to women as *men* or *he.*

So, there is inconsistency in the claims of the grammarians. If English does have natural gender then it is wrong to refer to women as *he/man.* And if *man* does include *woman* then it is wrong to claim that English has natural gender. One could ask why the male grammarians have not noticed this inconsistency?

In my work with secondary school students in a London mixed comprehensive I decided to investigate whether they felt excluded when they were excluded from the language. I wanted to find out how they felt about the use of *man* and *he* to encompass *woman,* so I tried to overcome any difficulties by presenting the concepts in a simple and concrete way. I began with a discussion of magic and that favourite conjuring trick of making things disappear. We talked about whether or not it was possible to make people invisible and I held out the carefully baited hook that it probably was possible and that, in fact, it wasn't even unusual as we were all magicians, making people invisible every day. The bait was taken and I began to focus upon language. I had some pictures of men and women which had captions using the so-called generic *he* and *man.* Illustrations of males and females reading were subtitled with 'Each student needs individual attention if *he* is to master reading'. Pictures of the Football Association Cup Final were accompanied with statements such as 'Everyone wants to grow up to be a football hero'. Newspaper photographs which prominently displayed

Ms Thatcher in her proverbial hat were followed by 'Politicians remove their hats in the presence of the Queen'. I do not think it would be biased on my part to state that the girls caught on to the idea more quickly than the boys. They took no more than three to four minutes to formulate the rule and the following is an extract from some of the comments made by one of the young women:

> *Can't you see you just pretend... You pretend you're talking about everybody, but you don't, you're not. It's only men... Look at this, no, look D, Come one. He says 'Everybody', but he doesn't mean that, you don't think he means* me *do you? That* I *want to be a football hero? He doesn't, course not!* Men's *everybody... and that's the trick.*

At this stage their involvement was in the 'game' and although they were able to use the rule (adequately summed up by this student as 'Men's everybody') there was no comment about the injustice of the rule in that it made only women disappear. The boys were very eager to play, we made a lot of magic and many women disappeared:

> *Australians are beer-drinking surfies.*
> *All Americans play baseball.*
> *Teenagers have to become members of gangs if they want to be accepted.*

These were some of the 'tricks' which were performed, but after having spent about twenty minutes making women disappear, I changed the focus. I reminded the students that only half the magic trick had been performed by making people invisible. There wouldn't be many magicians making a living if they could not complete the magic and bring people back again. I did not know what the students would do with this information. I envisaged that they would put women back into the picture in some way, but I neither predicted nor determined what that way should be. There was some discussion about bringing people back again and then C. began to alter some of the captions. She did so by simply applying the principle of reversal. Among some of her 'magic' was the following:

> *Adolescents think only of marriage and make-up.*
> *Australians look good in bikinis.*

She certainly made the female 'visible' by this process and was both pleased and amused by her efforts. Although I tried to indicate that she had made females visible at the expense of males, her only comment was 'About time' and with the other girls in the group she proceeded to give new captions to many of the pictures and to provide captions for those pictures which were without them and which included women and men.

It would be an understatement to say that the girls were thoroughly enjoying themselves. The boys, however, did not share their enthusiasm and passed from discomfort to hostility. They declared the whole thing 'stupid' and one of them withdrew from the group. I could only surmise that the feeling of exclusion which they experienced made them feel extremely uncomfortable and caused them to protest. Perhaps not being accustomed to 'not counting' and being made invisible, made it more difficult for them. My assumption about the reason for their behaviour was reinforced by an event described by Casey Miller and Kate Swift in which a group of males, who were being 'left out', also protested. Although the boys in my group had less sophisticated rationales for their behaviour, I suspect that their reaction might well have been the same.

> *Men who work in fields where women have traditionally predominated—as nurses, secretaries and primary school teachers for example—know exactly how... (the)... proposed generic pronoun... (she)... would affect them; they've tried it and they don't like it. Until a few years ago most publications, writers and speakers on the subject of primary and secondary education used* she *in referring to teachers. As the proportion of men in the profession increased, so did their annoyance with the generic use of feminine pronouns. By the mid 1960's, according to the journal of the National Education Association, some of the angry young men in teaching were complaining that references to the teacher as 'she' were responsible in part for their poor image and consequently, in part, for their low salaries. One man, speaking on the floor of the National Education Association Representative Assembly, said 'The incorrect and improper use of the English language is a vestige of the nineteenth-century image of the teacher and conflicts sharply with the vital image we attempt to set forth today. The interests of neither the women nor of the men in our profession are served by*

grammatical usage which conjures up an anachronistic image of the nineteenth-century school marm.'

Here is the male as norm argument in a nutshell. Although the custom of referring to elementary and secondary school teachers as 'she' arose because most of them were women, it becomes grammatically 'incorrect and improper' as soon as men enter the field in more than token numbers . . . Women teachers are still in the majority but the speaker feels that it is neither incorrect not improper to exclude them linguistically (Miller and Swift, 1976; 33–4).

References

Berger, G. and Kachuk, B.
1977 *Sexism, Language and Social Change,* US Dept. of Health, Education and Welfare, National Institute of Education

Bodine, A.
1975 'Androcentrism in Prescriptive Grammar: Singular "they", Sex Indefinite "he" and "he" and "she' ", *Language in Society,* Vol. 4, no. 2

Graham, A.
1975 'The Making of a Nonsexist Dictionary', in Thorne, B. and Henley, N. (eds), *Language and Sex: Difference and Dominance,* Newbury House, Rowley, Mass.

Harrison, L.
1975 'Cro-Magnon Woman–in Eclipse', *The Science Teacher,* April

Miller, C. and Swift, K.
1976 *Words and Women: New Language in New Times,* Penguin

Nilsen, A. P.
1973 'Grammatical Gender and its Relationship to the Equal Treatment of Males and Females in Children's Books', unpublished Ph.D thesis, University of Iowa

Schneider, J. and Hacker, S.
1972 'Sex role Imagery and the Use of the Generic "man" in Introductory Texts: A Case in the Sociology of Sociology', paper presented at Sociology of Sex Roles, American Sociological Association, New Orleans, August

Schulz, M.
1978 'Man (Embracing Woman): The Generic in Sociological Writing', paper presented at Sociolinguistics: Language and Sex, Ninth World Congress on Sociology, Uppsala, 14–20 August

How The Entertainment Industry Demeans, Degrades, and Dehumanizes Women

Martha Burk
Kirsten Shaw

Dr. Martha Burk is a political psychologist, cofounder and president of the Center for Advancement of Public Policy, a research and policy analysis organization in Washington, D.C. She has been a university research director, management professor, and advisor to political campaigns and organizations. She has served on the Commission for Responsive Democracy, the Advisory Committee of Americans for Workplace Fairness, the Sex Equity Caucus of the National Association for the Education of Young Children, and the board of directors of the National Organization for Women. Institutional consulting clients have included the U.S. Bureau of Indian Affairs, the U.S. Department of Education, the National Science Foundation, The Women's International News Gathering Service, and others. She is a frequent contributor to major newspapers on public policy and the progressive women's agenda.

Kirsten Shaw graduated in 1992 from Ohio Wesleyan University in Delaware, Ohio, where she studied international studies and history. She is currently administrator at the Institute for Policy Studies in Washington D.C. and is teaching English as a second language.

We support the entertainment industry—music, television, and film—with our dollars and our attendance. It returns the favor by exploiting us and fostering violence against women. The authors suggest: "If a few picketing police officers could force Time-Warner to stop selling violence against the police, imagine what a few million women could do if we decided to fight back with economic boycotts of companies that debase us for the bottom line."

Reprinted from *New Directions for Women* 21, no. 6 (November–December 1992): 4–5; 108 West Palisade Avenue, Englewood, New Jersey 07631. (201)568-0226/ Fax: (201)568-6532. $16/1 yr; $26/2 yrs.

WHEN 1992 DRAWS TO A CLOSE, HOW WILL MEDIA watchers remember it? As the year TV gave us a single mother who became the target of a phony "family values" crusade by the Republican party? Or the year when police and the "decent people" recruited by politicians shook their fists at the Time-Warner Corporation to get the anti-police song "Cop Killer" taken off the market?

Presumably few will notice that 1992 was the year in which neither politicians nor the public raised so much as an eyebrow about a song on the same album, entitled "KKK Bitch," that described the sodomizing of a Klansman's daughter. Nor did many protest the thousands of images of violence against women in movies, on TV, in advertising, and in music. 1992 will pass without remark as yet another year in which women were demeaned, degraded, and abused in the mass media.

The very survival of American women is being threatened by an epidemic of gender-specific violence that is legitimized and glamorized every day in the media while politicians and the public sit back and enjoy, even pay to see it. Battery is now the single largest cause of injury to women in America—more common than auto accidents, muggings, and rapes combined. You wouldn't know it from the media images pushed on society and the silent acceptance coming back in answer.

A woman is more likely to be killed by her husband or boyfriend than by anyone else. A woman is raped every five minutes. Yet popular movies such as **Basic Instinct,** opening with a gratuitous date-rape; **Batman Returns,** a "children's" movie depicting a woman thrown from a skyscraper by her boss; or **Unforgiven,** where a woman is knifed repeatedly in the face, trade on images of women as the passive victims of rape, murder and abuse.

This epidemic of violence against women has evoked only complacency that is shored up by the background noise of media images telling us it is acceptable.

"Gangster rap" has been roundly criticized for its promotion of violence against the police. Yet "bitches" and "ho's" are the only female characters it portrays. Women are objectified as sex objects and scorned as manipulators who must be controlled with a fist or a weapon: "If I have to go get a gun you girls will learn." N.W.A.'s recently released Niggaz4life album includes graphic lyrics boasting about the abuse, rape, and murder of women.

Opponents of Ice-T's "Cop Killer" worried that its malicious anti-police message demoralized officers working in an already hostile environment. Women live every day in a hostile world, though there has been no demonstration of concern about the malice continually expressed against them.

Gangster rap, of course, is only guilty of graphically depicting the messages that more mainstream media send out regularly—that women must be kept in their place through violence, and that they deserve and even enjoy being abused.

"Her body's beautiful so I'm thinkin' rape/ Shouldn't have had her curtains open so that's her fate." Such a rhyme is not really shocking in the context of an industry where one of every eight Hollywood movies depicts a rape theme. And it's not a modern phenomenon—in the classic **Gone with the Wind** Scarlett O'Hara is all smiles the morning after she is raped by her own husband.

Slasher movies, popular with teenagers, rely almost exclusively on the torture and murder of women for their plots. The same basic theme is churned out every year in sequels of **Halloween, Friday the 13th,** and **Nightmare on Elm Street:** young women are slaughtered one by one by an anonymous killer (typically cheered by the audience) who in the end escapes or is reborn. The murder and mutilation is broken only with a smattering of scenes of women undressing and engaging in sexual activity. The viewer is led to believe they got what they deserved.

Directors like Brian DePalma and David Lynch, hailed as artistic geniuses, derive an "aesthetic effect" from graphic images of torture, mutilation, and murder of females. Lynch's television series **"Twin Peaks"** featured abuse of most of its women characters, and a glamorous rape scene embellished his movie **Wild at Heart.**

Television embraces its share of violent themes as well, with women in "jep," (jeopardy) a common element. Sex and violence are the core of MTV fare, with 18 instances of aggression each hour and women's bodies the most common decorative element. Rivaling in frequency the image of woman as victim is that of woman as sex object. Popular series like "Married . . . with Children" get their laughs from the die-hard portrait of woman as empty-headed sex fiend. The devaluation of women through this kind of objectification lays the necessary groundwork for their exploitation and abuse.

Madison Avenue capitalizes on degrading images of women to sell everything from beer to blue jeans. Advertisements featuring sex, implied domination, and sometimes explicit bondage appear as often in women's magazines as those aimed at men. From roadside billboards to prime time television, gratuitous bikini-clad beauties ornamenting product slogans sustain society's perception of women as secondary, decorative and expendable. The September issue of **Vogue** featured a full color picture of a woman with a bare, bruised back dressed in a red formal gown against the backdrop of a dungeon complete with chains.

The connection between viewing an act of violence and committing one has been dismissed as ludicrous by supporters of unregulated corporate free speech. While there is more to violence than mere imitation, psychologists have demonstrated an association time and time again. When a person continually sees dehumanization and physical abuse glamorized and legitimized through television, movies, music and magazines, it is hard to imagine how that message could fail to be internalized and sometimes acted on.

Studies on children have shown that aggressive behavior increases after viewing aggression on television, even in cartoons. This violence, combined with the ever-present images of the victimization of women, is also sending powerful messages about inappropriate sex role behavior.

Adults are prone to the influence of media violence and victimization as well. Studies show that men watching movies depicting violence against women become progressively more callous toward the humanity of the victims and the reality of their suffering. Other research has shown that after viewing these films men are more inclined to believe that women want to be raped and actually enjoy the pain.

Trainers in the armed forces harden men for combat by desensitizing them to the sounds of screaming and the humanity of their enemies. In the same way, the profusion of images of violence and degradation of women make men (and even young boys) more callous toward women and more insensitive to their humanity.

And women are not immune to the messages. While men are learning to regard women with contempt and use force to deal with them, women are learning to expect and accept the abuse as their due.

Assumptions about women are formed at an early age. A now famous survey of Rhode Island youngsters found that at least half the boys and almost as many girls thought it was okay for a man to force a woman to kiss him if he had spent at least $15 on her. Rap fans in D.C. schools interviewed by the Washington Post this year expressed similar opinions. "Women get what they deserve," one eleven-year old commented.

Last summer politicians were stumbling all over each other to express their concern that children were being harmed by the images and language of "cop killer" music, since kids are unable to see it as metaphor and are likely to take it at face value. They should be equally concerned by the portrayals of women that the majority of children see daily in the mass media.

If politicians wish to concern themselves with whether "cop killer" music is offensive and soapbox on "family values," they need to look at what those values are. Are females valued equally?

Women must hold media corporations accountable. Women are 52% of the population, and despite our low pay compared to men, we have considerable economic clout. If a few picketing police officers could force Time-Warner to stop selling violence against the police, imagine what a few million women could do if we decided to fight back with economic boycotts of companies that debase us for the bottom line.

Women did not let the openly misogynist treatment of Anita Hill or the anti-feminist rhetoric of the Republican convention pass without comment. Neither should we ignore the daily barrage of anti-woman images that are pushed as entertainment. Images that influence both adults and children, male and female. These are the more subtle tools of indoctrination, and ultimately the more devastating.

Missing Voices: Women & The U.S. News Media

Susan J. Douglas

Susan Douglas is professor of media and American studies at Hampshire College in Amherst, Massachusetts. She is the author of Inventing American Broadcasting, 1899–1922, *and has written essays on media and cultural criticism for* In These Times, The Village Voice, *and other publications. Her column "Pundit Watch," appears each month in* The Progressive.

Douglas articulates disquieting trends in the news media: the exclusion of women as top executives in news organizations, the absence of women as spokespeople on vital issues, the trivialization of feminist issues and leaders, and others.

If indeed the news media are creating or adding to the negative stereotype of feminism, might not this be a major factor in the alleged "identity crisis" in the women's movement and young women's alienation from feminism?

A RANGE OF FACTORS HAVE COINCIDED, OVER TIME, to keep female voices, and particularly feminist voices, muted. Despite the increase in female journalists over the past 20 years, the top executives in news organizations (and in the conglomerates that own them) remain overwhelmingly male. Those few women who do become prominent journalists—Diane Sawyer, Leslie Stahl, Connie Chung—represent only a very small and privileged socioeconomic class of women.

The sources the mainstream media rely on time and again—from government "spokesmen" to political leaders and think tank analysts—are also male. A study published in **EXTRA!** (Jan/Feb '89) revealed that only 10.3 percent of the guests on **Nightline** were female, and of the 20 most frequent guests, none were women. Another study published in **Mother Jones** (2-3/90) found that the 10 individuals who appeared most frequently as experts or analysts on **CBS, ABC** and **NBC** nightly news (as often as 58 times in two years) were all men.

In addition to this institutional sexism, the ideological frameworks of the news media have served to marginalize much of the feminist agenda and to turn feminism into a dirty word. True, certain mainstream goals such as equal pay for equal work and equal access to educational opportunities have been legitimized over the years by the news media, especially because they resonate with our national conceits about this being the land of fairness and equal opportunity for all. But thoroughgoing critiques of how and why this society tolerates and promotes continued economic and physical predations on women are virtually absent from the airwaves and the printed page. In addition, the news media constantly tell feminists we're a discredited minority, when polls show feminism to be very much a majority movement.

News media seem to reason that to feature any news or commentary labeled as "feminist" would

Susan J. Douglas, "Missing Voices: Women & the U.S. News Media" *EXTRA!* Special Issue, 1992, is reprinted by permission of *FAIR/EXTRA!*, 130 West 25th Street, N.Y., N.Y. 10001.

alienate their audience, since most women, according to **Time's** cover story "Women Face the '90s" (12/4/89), reject the feminist label. "Ask a woman under the age of 30 if she is a feminist, and chances are she will shoot back a decisive, and perhaps even a derisive, no." This misrepresentation of feminism as an unpopular fringe movement has been a special source of concern for Ellie Smeal, head of the Fund for the Feminist Majority. According to the Fund's press secretary, Tamar Raphael, the Yankelovich poll **Time** relied on actually showed overwhelming support for feminist goals, especially among women under 30.

In response to the question "Are feminists in touch or out of touch with the average American woman," 77 percent of women between 16 and 21, and 71 percent of those between 22 and 29, said "in touch." Ratings for NOW and for feminist leaders were equally high, often twice as high as the ratings for Democrats or Republicans. To Ellie Smeal, the miracle is that feminist goals remain so popular given their constant marginalization in the news media.

"Hairy legs haunt the feminist movement," continued the **Time** article, "as do images of being strident and lesbian." The article goes on to blame feminists and the women's movement for "emphasizing the wrong issues" and for ignoring the "needs and values" of nonprofessional women, poor women and women of color.

What the article fails to acknowledge is that it is media coverage of women's issues that consistently emphasizes the wrong issues and ignores non-elite women. In its own reporting on the women's movement in the late 1960s and early 1970s, the news media played a major role in turning feminism into a dirty word. Feminists were repeatedly likened to witches who organized "covens" to proselytize the unsuspecting (**Time,** 11/21/69). The derisive and frequently used label "bra burners" was a media fabrication, based on a complete misrepresentation of the 1968 demonstration against the Miss America pageant, in which, it is worth noting, no bras were burned.

Under the headline "Very Volcanic," **Newsweek** (8/31/70) cast the women's movement as representing "only a small minority of American women" that couldn't possibly "unite women as a mass force." **Time** noted that "the movement has not produced much humor" and chose to point out that Kate Millet didn't wash her hair enough (8/31/70). Out of such dismissive and superficial coverage, the stereotype of the feminist as a strident, humorless, deliberately unattractive, man-hating harridan with an abiding contempt for the American family became entrenched in our popular culture and consciousness. And while white, liberal feminists made mistakes in dealing with working-class women, lesbians and women of color, the media routinely ignored the leaders and agendas of such women, and thus erased them from the national media landscape.

The consequences of the feminist stereotype have not been insignificant: The trivialization of feminism and the demonizing of feminist leaders have meant that the news media don't regard feminist analyses of politics, the economy or international relations as consequential or relevant. Also, it is risky for a public leader to describe herself as a feminist, for she will be pigeonholed as an extremist and thus shunned by a news media obsessed with what Herbert Gans has called "moderatism."

Another trend in the news media in the 1980s—the increased elitism of journalism and the rise of what **Washington Monthly** (7-8/85) called the "socialite journalist"—has exacerbated the upper-middle-class bias of the news media. Couple this with institutional sexism, and it follows that issues of desperate concern to working-class women and women of color are underrepresented. The media keep hidden the frustrating impact of seemingly unrelated legislative decisions—from changes in the tax code to corporate bailouts—on the poor and minority women who pay for such largesse through discontinued prenatal, nutritional and educational programs.

Women do get in the news when they serve the needs of sensationalism, so that Gennifer Flowers, Robin Givens and Marla Maples become household words, while less glamourous but critically important feminist leaders in all fields rarely get the spotlight. It remains one of the embarrassing truths of the news media that women's bodies are used as much to sell newsmagazines and papers as they are to sell soda and cars.

More than 20 years after the women's movement, the consciousness of the news media still needs to be raised. Yes, there is certainly more reporting than there was in 1970 about women's health issues, women in the workforce and the national childcare crisis. But such stories suffer from two consistent problems: their continued emphasis on upper-middle-class, professional white women; and their segregation, both spatially and conceptually, from other "hard news" stories. Thus, the interconnections between so-called "women's issues" and the nation's economic, political and international decisions are overlooked. Female perspectives on national priorities remain in ideological purdah.

PART III

Women Move

"So—against odds, the women inch forward."

–ELEANOR ROOSEVELT, 1946

AS WE LOOK AT SOME OF WOMEN'S PAST AND PRESENT activities on behalf of women, it is worthwhile to consider afresh a point made earlier—that the "history of history" has been prevailingly male. Given the masculist emphasis on political power and its contempt for things female, it is clear why women are, by and large, absent from history books and why the few appearances women do make are trivialized or distorted. If, as in this final chapter, we conceive of the women's movement as a centuries-old process of women coming to awareness of themselves as women, we can recognize that it is not enough to have learned about the past. To know and to understand the women's movement requires of us all that we search for the totality of women's experience throughout history, seek out previously hidden facts, look at old information in new ways, keep our minds open to reinterpretations of traditional recountings, and be ready for surprises from the lost past of women on the move.

9

Feminist Activism: Issues, Events, Documents

When Did the Women's Movement Begin?

It is often asked: When did the women's movement begin? Some *her*storians attempt to fix the origins of feminist ideas in relatively recent times, specifically in the Enlightenment and the French Revolution, in the drive for the abolition of slavery, or in the American civil rights and war resistance movements. These attempts have a certain logic, but they can be misleading. They tend to focus attention not on one movement but on many: on eighteenth-, nineteenth-, or twentieth-century movements, each with a discernible starting point, each built around distinct goals, and each with separate and characteristic political attitudes, personalities, and strategies. A traditional reading in this vein might be summed up as follows:

> *The first stirrings of the women's movement were felt with the publication of Mary Wollstonecraft's* A Vindication of the Rights of Woman *in 1792. The Women's Rights Movement in the United States was born during the drive for abolition, particularly in the activities and writings of the Grimke sisters in the 1830s. It culminated in the winning of the vote in 1920; and then, because women had exhausted themselves in the fight for suffrage, it died, until Betty Friedan's* The Feminine Mystique *brought it back to life in 1963.*

A way of looking at the women's movement that strikes me as more constructive is simply that of women moving toward greater strength and freedom, both in their awareness and in their sociopolitical position. This has been happening through the centuries, often for individuals, sometimes collectively. It has progressed, and it has receded; it has sometimes been subterranean, and sometimes it crests into waves of activism. It has expressed itself in many ways: in poetry, in marches on courthouses, or in the quiet but sturdy resistance of women in their households. It has been expressed in various contexts—political, economic, psychological, or even physical—and it is not easily confined to one model. From this perspective, no discernible "beginning" to the women's movement exists. We need not exclude the Roman women demonstrating in the forum in 195 B.C. for repeal of the antifemale Oppian laws or the poems of Sappho or the struggles for survival of a thirteenth-century group of women called the Beguines (who chose to abjure marriage, live and work together, help the poor in the name of Christianity but maintain independence from the control of the male church). We can include in our understanding of the women's movement the egalitarian ideals of the Quakers, of Anne Hutchinson, or of "Constantia."

Such an approach has manifold value. First, it reveals the universality of women's concerns. It also emphasizes the sisterhood of women. In addition, it reveals the startling continuity over time of feminist issues, values, goals, and challenges and in so doing allows us to see that each wave of activism is not separate and anomalous, destined for an end or for limited achievement at best but is rather an integral part of a progressive development. Finally, this approach affords us a context for evaluating challenges not only to feminist goals but also to the very legitimacy of feminism as a world movement.

Key Themes of Women's Movement

For centuries, in groups and as individuals, women have spoken out consistently on certain key issues. Although they may reflect the character of the times and the issues prominent in their age, the goals of feminist women's efforts have been remarkably consistent: They have to do with the *quality* of life for women and for the entire human community.

It is also interesting to note that opponents' reactions have been consistent as well. Adversaries generally attack feminists' "femaleness" (we aren't real women), good sense, and morality, and they charge activism on women's behalf with triviality or destructiveness or both (however inconsistent that may seem).

Major Issues for Women

It is a revelation to read, "The time has come to take this world muddle that men have created and strive to turn it into an ordered, peaceful, happy abiding place for humanity,"[1] and discover that those words, which sound so like the women's liberation movement since the 1960s, were spoken by Alva Belmont in 1922. Mary Wollstonecraft chides the affectations and destructive results of traditional "femininity," and were it not for the habits of language current in her time, she would sound quite like Gloria Steinem or Germaine Greer.

Again and again in poetry, political treatises, personal letters, speeches, and social analyses, we see these themes reiterated: the folly of grossly distorting women's physical, emotional and intellectual development; the injustice of denying to half the world's population their rights, opportunities, and contributions; the great need for humanitarian treatment of the young, the sick, and the powerless in the face of the insensitive and selfish values of traditional masculist institutions; the unlikeliness of peace and harmony in a world permeated with the aggressiveness and arrogance of martial power values.

The consistency of the themes in our history underscores the continuity of the movement, the character of feminist concerns, and, it would appear, the legitimacy of our claims. Feminist analysis is not transitory, but rather it is part of the mainstream of ongoing political thought, although it has not been perceived that way.

Charges and Countercharges

Feminist women all say to the masculists: You misunderstood and malign us; you thwart us; you deny to the world our abilities and contributions; you distort the quality of life; you cause war and unhappiness; you are arrogant and meanspirited. They answer: You, feminists, are misled and confused; your goals are contrary to reason, nature, and order; your behavior is unnatural and unseemly; you are either ill (unfeminine) or evil; your actions will cause your own downfall and that of your family, *the* family, the nation, and the world; you are unable to see this, or you don't care.

It crystallizes one's own sense of place and helps to resolve certain personal conflicts to realize that activist women in any age have met the same misogynist accusations. Cato exclaimed of the Roman women, "It is complete liberty, or rather complete license they desire. If they win in this, what will they not attempt? The moment they begin to be your equals, they will be your superiors."[2] Doesn't that sound like: Give them an inch and they'll take a mile; they want to dominate men? Mary Wollstonecraft commented in 1792: "From every quarter have I heard exclamations against masculine women."[3] The same charge of "masculinity" was made against nineteenth-century activists, and what contemporary feminist has not been called masculine or "unwomanly"? Lucy Stone reported in 1855: "The last speaker [at the National Convention, Cincinnati] alluded to this movement as being that of a few disappointed women."[4] How modern! Feminists today are called "disappointed" (that is, frigid, jilted, or crabby) and are always taken to be "in the minority," not in the mainstream of female life.

Just a Disappointed Few

The contention that feminists are not of the majority of women or are not like "normal" women bears looking at, first, because it is an attack so often made and, second, because it raises the question of how accurately feminists may claim to represent women's concern. The argument is phrased in various ways: "Feminists are just a bunch of losers who couldn't make it in the man–woman world." "Feminism is just a white middle-class movement." "Feminists are just a bunch of bored, selfish middle-class women trying to get more for themselves when there is *real* oppression in the world that affects millions of people." Let us consider those charges one by one.

A Bunch of Losers

To the charge that her movement was composed of a few disappointed women, Lucy Stone answered, "In education, in marriage, in religion, in everything, disappointment is the lot of woman! It shall be the business of my life to deepen this disappointment in every women's heart until she bows down to it no longer."[5] That, of course, is the proper answer. Women *are* losers in a patriarchal society—not losers in ourselves, as the epithet implies, not losers because of some personal inadequacy, but losers in a game where the rules and the rewards are so heavily stacked against us. It is the business of the movement to clarify to all women what we are losing and to help us understand that we are the victims and not the perpetrators of loss.

A White Middle-Class Movement

To a movement that proposes to speak to all women, a movement in which the term *sisterhood* is of first priority, the charge that we are composed of and concerned with only a small part of the female community, and that part the more privileged segment, is a serious matter.

For a period in feminism in the early part of the twentieth century, in seeking the vote, activist groups put aside their original convictions and exploited themes of ethnic, racial, and class bigotry. It was a period in feminist history that bears scrutiny for the lessons it reveals, yet I believe that it does not represent the greatest part of feminist history and thought but rather the smallest. Eighteenth-century analysis, growing as it did out of the Enlightenment, was strongly egalitarian. The next wave of activism, in the nineteenth century, developed out of abolition, out of the theory of human rights, and out of an absolute conviction in the worth and equality of all people. The first feminists of the second wave (1960s and following) came out of the civil rights and antiwar movements of the 1950s and 1960s. Their work, *in its intention,* is both internationalistic and egalitarian in its treatment of class, sex, and race.

Certainly, a great deal of writing and activism originated with middle-class women (some from working-class backgrounds). An examination of history reveals, however, that almost all movements for liberation and change have originated among those people who appear privileged beyond the means of those most sorely oppressed. It was they who had the education and training to see beyond their condition to reasons and alternatives, they who could articulate issues and instigate strategies for change, and it was they who had the time and the wherewithal to act. The themes *liberté, égalité,* and *fraternité* of the French Revolution originated among the well-educated, well-placed philosophers of the Enlightenment, not among the wretched poor who suffered most and most needed change, and to whom help eventually flowed. Marx and Lenin were intellectuals, and although they hoped for a rising of the masses, Lenin ultimately came to believe in the necessity of an educated vanguard of leadership.

Although the movement may appear to have been instigated by the white middle class (and even this appearance is misleading), it was not meant to be a movement *of* the white middle class. That is, it was not about only the white middle class, nor is it today. The drive for jobs and occupational equity certainly concerns working-class and poor women as much as it does middle-class women. Opening skilled and semiskilled unions to women, reforming clerical and secretarial occupations, and expanding women's place in government-funded poverty relief projects are all goals of the feminist movement. Securing the right of women to control our own bodies affects poor women even more than it does the affluent. Welfare reform has long been a feminist goal. The extinction of racism, homophobia, and other forms of bigotry is a major feminist target.

Where the women's movement originally erred was not in its intentions, but in individuals' failure to see; this was a result of lack of development, lack of sufficient perceptiveness. Like much of the society around us, feminists need greater sensitivity to *difference* and to the difference in our lives that difference makes. This has led many of us to lump all women into one category—woman—and to assume that female experience is always the same. Hester Eisenstein described the error as

> *a false universalism that generalized about the experience of women, ignoring the specificities of race, class, and culture. A feminist perspective assumed that all women in the world, whatever their race, religion, class, or sexual preference, had something fundamentally in common. Some versions of feminism took this assumption a step further: they insisted that what women had in common, by virtue of their membership in the group of women, outweighed all of their other differences, or (to put this another way) that the similarity of their situation as female was more fundamental than their economic and cultural differences. The second step in this argument is what I term "false" universalism. To some extent, this habit of thought grew inevitably from the need to establish gender as a legitimate intellectual category. But too often it gave rise to analysis that, in spite of its narrow base of white, middle-class experience, purported to speak about and on behalf of all women, black or white, poor or rich.*[6]

Feminists, like the wider society, suffered from ethnocentrism, or heterosexism, or classism, or agism, and so on, and it had the same effect as this always does: It was destructive.

Notable, however, is the seriousness of purpose with which the movement has responded to the problem. Efforts have been made to increase our sensitivity, to *listen*, to refrain from speaking for others, to make it possible for each to speak and act for herself, and for all to act for each other.

To the question, What are the central challenges for feminist scholars in the future? Catharine Stimpson replied:

> *To end stupid oversimplifications about "all women" and to speak of the differences among women created by race, class, religion, sexuality, nationality, region and age. I believe that the study of differences among women, which I have named "heterogeneity," is a laboratory in which we can learn how to think about and live with "human differences" themselves.*[7]

Tension arises over strategies and issues and between black and white, gay and straight, moderate and radical feminists—but diversity and interchange are creative. The ultimate values have stood.

A Diversion From "Real" Oppression

Feminists have been told that the movement, being about "peripheral" and "trivial" matters, dangerously diverts resources away from "real" problems that are far more serious than that of women. That charge is neither new nor unique to our times, as you will see in the selections ahead. When Abigail Adams—a young, intelligent, spunky woman of the emerging republic—wrote to her husband to "remember the ladies," she met with little success. Husband John, at that time a young firebrand in the cause of liberty but eventually the second president of the United States, cautioned her to be patient, for *more important matters* were at stake. In a letter to his compatriot James Sullivan, Adams revealed that although good reasons existed to consider the rights of "the ladies," it was consciously decided *not* to ensure the right of women citizens in the new society because it would be impractical and raise too many problems.[8] The egalitarian founders of the new republic were too busy to open such a messy can of worms as women's rights.

After the Civil War, when Congress forged the new constitutional amendments for human rights, feminists who had worked tirelessly for abolition asked that women be included among the newly protected persons. They were denied their request, told that it was the Negro's day. Paradoxically, only black men, not black women, were guaranteed their rights. You will see in the debate over ERA that the omission of women from those civil rights amendments (13–15) continues to haunt us into the present.

During the early 1920s, the new government of the USSR revoked gains made by women in the 1918 revolution on the grounds that Russia was under siege and other needs must take priority over women's rights. Last, women always come last.

In the 1970s feminists were chided for "muscling in" to affirmative action, federal programs, and educational opportunities; female activists in political parties are even now ridiculed for harping on "trivia" (women's issues) while men worry about "important" things like troop reductions and B-2 bombers.

Today there are those who would go cheerfully to prison for the protection of fetuses, but they would just as happily sacrifice the liberty, autonomy, and quality of life of the women who bear them. The right of a fetus to develop is important. The right of a woman to live well as she sees fit is trivial.

The charge of triviality is a constant in women's history and should not surprise us. Reducing women's suffering to trivia is not only an enduring masculist perspective but a misogynist strategy as well. To the sane and right-minded, it is self-evident that denial of autonomy and freedom, denial of political, economic, and educational equity, and daily exploitation are as destructive in women's lives as in men's. A revolution that only advanced the position of men could not justly be called a revolution for human rights. Similarly, "affirmative action" that guarantees jobs for men but not for women cannot claim to be a program for "equal" human rights. When political activists demand parity for the poor, the colonized, and the oppressed, they must remember that more than half of those poor, colonized, and oppressed are female, and that women are doubly tyrannized in being exploited even within their own subgroups, *as women*, by men. History shows that, when all is said and done, women's movement has been a drive to free all women from the tyranny of misogyny and all humanity from the tyrannies of masculism—hardly trivial.

Earlier Sisters, Ongoing Themes

To begin to get a clear picture of women's movement through the centuries, we need the widest treatment of history and anthropology. There are paintings on the walls of caves in France that are believed to have been put there by women who were recording their social organization; there are poems by ancient Sumerian and African mothers, letters written by a Renaissance woman to her daughter entering marriage, speeches attributed to condemned witches (practitioners of the "old religion"), psychological tracts and social treatises—and all carry powerful political messages and implications. By rights, a student of women's experience should see them all. Space, however, precludes so wide a sample. What this chapter presents is just a small segment of women's material, limited for the most part to the United States and to the last two centuries, selected primarily for its representativeness, in period or attitude, and for its fame.

As you sample the writings of foremothers at the end of this chapter, notice how the analyses and arguments of each woman reflect the currents and ideas of her time, yet maintain the continuity of the concerns just discussed. Many of the arguments remain powerful and timely today. Consider, too, how drives for progress in women's affairs have often come out of human liberation movements and how necessary it has been for women in every age to remind (male) society that its altruism must be extended to include women in its definition of "humanity."

Enlightenment Themes

The eighteenth century was a period of tremendous upheaval and change both in its social organization and in the philosophical themes that developed out of it. The major issues focused on what rights people should have in society and in government. Certain ideals, although hotly debated and often maintained more in principle than in fact, came to occupy a central position in political philosophy. New importance was given to the idea of *natural* human worth—that is, the value of the individual, which was held to be somehow cosmic in its source (Nature or God) and prior to any privilege or status that could be bestowed by "civilized" society. Men were said to be equal in that value, brothers to one another, rational, and essentially good. Education for all, freedom of opportunity, and the exercise of reason were seen as supplying the major ingredients of progress and harmonious community. Privilege, hereditary wealth and power, and unearned status were represented as villainous. Authority unchecked and exercised without consent was tyranny. Human excellence was composed of rationality, responsibility, emotional and physical health, independence, and tolerance. These were the major ideals of the political thought that we later called the Enlightenment. Although there was often great controversy over how these ideals might be instituted, the values themselves were taken as fundamental by a very large portion of the intelligentsia.

Note that *men* were said to be equal in worth. "All *men* are created equal"—not women. It was left to thinkers like Mary Wollstonecraft to remind the great liberal egalitarians that all they had said regarding worth, rights, opportunity, and freedom, as well as the condition and potential of the poor and oppressed, and uneducated, could and should be applied to women also. Although Abigail Adams's letter to her husband may have been, in her own words, "saucy," it revealed an important truth. The framers of the great experiment in political rights were themselves guilty of the same tyranny against which they had just rebelled in righteous indignation.

Human Rights and Abolition

Among radical activists of the 1960s, it was a common belief that the best way to attract people to reform movements was not to preach at them but rather to let them just once confront the establishment, and its barbarity would radicalize them. That indeed in large measure was what happened to women activists in the nineteenth century. Incensed by the injustice of slavery, they moved to correct that social sin; then, finding themselves equally sinned against, they became radicalized on their own behalf.

The women learned much from their work in the abolition movement. It was a combination of the Quaker conviction in the equality of people and the Enlightenment commitment to human liberty that they brought against slavery, and it was not a far distance from the rights of slaves to the rights of women. Many women learned for the first time about the effectiveness of political organization, and they experienced the potential and the joy of female unity and assertiveness. They learned to say openly, "me too." As women came to see clearly the hypocrisy and cruelty of black oppression, they gained the insight to recognize it in their own lives and the strength to reject the absurdity and meanness of masculist values, behavior, and rules.

Presenting so well the analogy between the oppression and liberation of blacks and that of women is the speech of Sojourner Truth at a rights convention in Ohio in 1851. An ex-slave who had become a lecturer and a preacher, Truth was described by the convention's president, Frances Gage, as an "almost Amazon form, which stood nearly six feet high, head erect, and eyes piercing the upper air like one in a dream." Truth's "Ain't I A Woman?" speech is a most powerful and stirring statement of masculist injustice and irrationality.

Themes of the First Half of the Twentieth Century

The first half of the twentieth century saw the people of the world drawing closer together, albeit painfully. The rise of industrialism, the need for increased trade, the Great War, the rise of Marxism, and other factors all brought internationalistic questions to the foreground and forced reexamination of many issues. People had to place themselves in a wider context and reconsider the limits of authority; the sources of government; the uses of knowledge; the concepts of community, social responsibility, and freedom; and even the nature of happiness. During this period the social sciences—sociology, psychology, and anthropology—were evolving, and they, too, were creating new questions for consideration: What have we learned about what is desirable and undesirable in our own society, and how should we change it for the better? What does the new study of human behavior tell us about possibilities for the future of life and society? What are the proper limits of science in changing our lives? That is, what should we not or could we not tamper with? What part of us comes from nature (and is therefore unchangeable), and what part originates somewhere else?

The debate over women's issues was affected by the emerging intellectual models. A belief, prevalent among many feminists and nonfeminists alike, is that the women's movement simply died in 1920 with the passage of the Nineteenth Amendment and the winning of suffrage. It is claimed that because the movement narrowed in the latter part of the nineteenth century from very wide-ranging concerns to a total involvement in suffrage, and because the winning of that goal required a Herculean effort, when it was won, activists simply folded in exhaustion. This argument has some basis. Certainly political activity on a scale of the preceding seven decades did diminish. One could look for reasons in the Depression of the 1930s, in the political turmoil of the entire world during that decade, and in the vast energy output in World War II during the 1940s. Such monumental events coupled with the belief that suffrage created the opportunity to cure all women's ills might indeed have led to a decrease in organized activism.

Yet we can bring the idea that the movement died (or even went to sleep) into different focus by placing it in the context of events from the wider intellectual scene. As general political activism in the thirties centered mainly in socialism and Marxism, so did feminism. Many of the questions raised by the original American feminists in the nineteenth century were debated by female socialists of this time—the isolation of housework, the opportunity for salaried work, the right to an independent identity, the oppressive elements of marriage and romance. (In fact, feminist groups of all kinds during these years were accused of Bolshevist tendencies.)

During this time, just as the impetus for social change often came out of the newly developing social sciences, so, too, did speculation about new possibilities for women's personal lives. In the 1920s, Freud's theories of female sexuality (among others, that females *had* sexuality) touched off a whole set of issues that were carried into the thirties and forties by psychologists like Karen Horney and her contemporaries. Reinforced by the research of various feministically inclined anthropologists, like Margaret Mead and Ruth Benedict, more positive attitudes toward women's sexuality occasioned lively activism on behalf of biological freedom. The birth control and planned parenthood movement was born and flourished between the 1920s and the 1950s, leading to advances in contraception in the 1960s.

In the 1920s, the suffragist Alice Paul and her coworkers of the radical Congressional Union introduced the Equal Rights Amendment and lobbied for its passage. The National Council of Women, the Women's International League for Peace and Freedom, the League of Women Voters, and other organizations like these, each with its own political agenda, came into existence during this period. Many still function today.

In the first half of the twentieth century, America's economic system underwent tremendous changes, as did women's participation in it. After World War I, women moved into the public workplace in growing numbers on every level. Frequently, as they grew in numbers, they organized. Women were particularly active in the trade union movement. In the professions, organizations such as Business and Professional Women (BPW) not only supported women in gaining better educational and business opportunities, but they also lobbied—and still do—for other women's goals in the legislatures and with presidential commissions.

Given all this activity, it is clearly not the case that exhausted women let their movement die. It is more accurate to say that many suffrage activists moved into different areas of activity, that new feminist women expressed their values through these different models. The movement—less centralized, less political, less visible in some ways, even less numerous—was nonetheless alive.

The Second Half and the Second Wave

Although women's issues as a major focus of public discussion receded in importance during the 1940s, conditions that would change this continued to ferment. The Depression had had a negative effect on women's position in the economy. What jobs existed had gone to men, and women lost ground in education, professional status, work rights, and salary. During World War II, however, conditions changed. Positions left empty by men gone to war and jobs in the burgeoning industrial sector had to be filled by women. In factories, offices, and industry, managing small businesses, running farms, teaching college, and building tanks, women did very well. Jobs which, until then, had been deemed "for men only" were effectively accommodated by women, and they learned an unforgettable lesson: There is no masculine or feminine occupation.

From 1945 on, even immediately after the war, when many women lost their jobs to returning veterans, the number and percentage of working women of all kinds—married and unmarried, young and mature, parent and nonparent—increased dramatically. Their numbers grew, and the realities of women's lives changed. What changed very little, and what eventually was to cause much of the conflict that crystallized in the fifties and exploded in the sixties, was the cultural mythology, the projected ideals of femininity and the "place" of women. Except for the brief wartime appearance of the patriotic Rosie the Riveter, America's dream-girl image never adjusted to women's new realities and changing needs. In fact, the gap between myth and reality widened. In the late forties and fifties, popular culture stressed the visions of the virginal, naive girl-next-door and the softly pliant housewife in cotton dress and three-inch spikes tending single-mindedly to family and home. On the surface, at least, it was a time of traditional values and "togetherness."

Betty Friedan, in *The Feminine Mystique,* credits the wars, especially the Korean War, for this period of retrenchment. Disillusioned and emotionally exhausted, people (particularly men) craved the security and nurturance of a stable family and home, and they retreated to the familiar comforting arrangement of marriage, or at least the image of it, and to the concept of the nurturing, tender wife-mother. This is at least partly true.

Again, however, one must be careful not to oversimplify, and one must seek explanations for women's situation with an eye to events in the wider culture. Although the fifties was a period of apparent quiescence, it harbored the seeds of turmoil. Although the decade was known for a kind of apathy toward political and national events, it also saw the cold war, the second "red scare," McCarthy and McCarthyism. It may have had "the corporation man" and the man in gray flannel, but it also had Jack Kerouac and anticonformist Beatniks. It was a day in 1955 when Rosa Parks refused to go to the back of the bus that touched off the civil rights movement. These and other events were as much a part of the personal history of the new feminist women of the sixties as were the television images of superwife.

Somewhere between the opposing realities, between prom gowns and Rosa Parks, between affluence and Vietnam, between maternal admonitions of purity and displaced homemakers, the feminists of the Second Wave emerged alive and kicking.

Contemporary Feminism: The Second Wave—Themes and Theories

Although there are issues upon which most feminists agree, there are others upon which there is great difference: in philosophic orientation, strategy, or treatment. These issues, which can generate conflict, are internal themes of contemporary feminism that have developed during and since the early sixties. Because they have a strong effect on the strategies that movement leaders choose, because they often determine how we articulate our concerns, and because opponents of feminism often seize upon them to split unity among women, these issues deserve our careful attention.

In the introduction to the first edition of their book *Feminist Frameworks,* Alison Jaggar and Paula Rothenberg (Struhl) outline four basic feminist frameworks or theoretical orientations: (1) *liberal* feminism (some call it *moderate* feminism), which essentially seeks opportunities for women's advancement in the existent society through institutional changes in education and the work place; (2) *Marxist* feminism, which locates the source of women's oppression in the general problems of a capitalist society and the remedy, therefore, in its dissolution; (3) *radical* feminism, which locates the source of women's oppression not in any particular economic system but in the nature and implications of gender (perhaps even sex) itself; and (4) *socialist* feminism, an amalgam of the last two, which holds both economic and gender/sex factors equally responsible.[9]

This approach represents one viable classification; others are possible. Some feminists believe that it is better not to classify, arguing that labels are misleading, restrictive, difficult to apply, and therefore counterproductive. This view has merit; categorization is always risky. And yet configurations of thought can be helpful in placing ideas into perspective and thereby rendering them more understandable.

Differences in Orientation: Moderate Versus Radical Feminism

The word *radical* is a relative term. Where anyone is placed on the spectrum of radical-to-conservative has at least as much to do with the person doing the placing as it does with the person described. Yet there have been strong differences of opinion among feminists regarding a number of issues: strategy (for example, militancy, demonstrations, and strikes versus painstaking political or legal action), procedural rules (for example, complete separatism versus male participation), and even language (for example, reform versus revolution).

Some theoreticians have associated moderation or conservatism with the women's rights organizations aimed basically at securing equality for women and men through institutional reform. They have reserved the term *radical* for those groups who wish to go beyond institutional reform, beyond equality, to bring about profound changes in the cultural as well as a complete redefinition of gender itself. It has been said that moderate feminists want to secure for women a piece of the pie; radical feminists want to change the pie. We must, however, use even this characterization with care, for clearly there is overlap. Radical feminists usually support institutional reform, and moderate or conservative activists realize that even small changes in society beget profound alterations in our lives.

The differences between radicals and moderates are based in their general philosophical orientation, ethical priorities, interpretation of causes, cultural vision, and even temperament. Compare, for example, the sharp differences in the tone, attitudes, explanatory constructs, strategies, and goals of the following documents:

> *Radical feminism recognizes the oppression of women as a fundamental political oppression wherein women are categorized as an inferior class based upon their sex. It is the aim of radical feminism to organize politically to destroy this sex class system. . . .*
>
> *A political power institution is set up for a purpose. We believe that the purpose of male chauvinism is primarily to obtain psychological ego satisfaction, and that only secondarily does this manifest itself in economic relationships. For this reason we do not believe that capitalism, or any other economic system, is the cause of female oppression, nor do we believe that female oppression will disappear as a result of a purely economic revolution. The political oppression of women has its own class dynamic; and that dynamic must be understood in terms previously called "non-political"—namely the politics of the ego.*[10]
>
> –ANN KOEDT, "Politics of the Ego"[11]

> *We, men and women who hereby constitute ourselves as the National Organization for Women, believe that the time has come for a new movement toward true equality for all women in America, and toward a fully equal partnership of the sexes, as part of the worldwide revolution of human rights now taking place within and beyond our national borders.*
>
> *The purpose of NOW is to take action to bring women into full participation in the mainstream of American society now, exercising all the privileges and responsibilities thereof in truly equal partnership with men. . . .*
>
> *We realize that women's problems are linked to many broader questions of social justice; their solution will require concerted action by many groups. Therefore, convinced that human rights for all are indivisible, we expect to give active support to the common cause of equal rights for all those who suffer discrimination and deprivation, and we call upon other organizations committed to such goals to support our efforts toward equality for women.*
>
> –from the National Organization for Women's "Statement of Purpose," 1966[12]

Into the Future: The Next Wave

Feminists must decide many issues for the future. We are feeling the full brunt of an antifeminist, antiwoman backlash, not only in the United States but all over the world. A strong wave of political and economic conservatism has reversed many of the hard-won victories of the past: affirmative action, comparable worth, professional upward mobility programs lie almost in tatters. The religious right has vowed absolute enmity to women's reproductive liberty, and they are making progress. Increasing numbers of women and their children are poor, homeless, and hungry. The earth we have vowed to protect is being devoured for its resources. All over the world, war, famine, and political repression hit women worst.

Fewer young women today are actively involved in politics or social activism. Indeed, they seem less aware, less concerned, than they were twenty years ago.

Yet, some observers of society, myself included, see the possibilities of the worm turning: Consider the renewed discussion of civil rights for all in the federal government; renewed awareness of social discrimination on American campuses, renewed vigor of prochoice activities in response to the relentless attacks upon our personal freedom. It is possible to see seeds of rebirth sown in the '80s flourish in the '90s, just as the worst repressions of the '50s gave birth to the energy of the '60s. This is already visible. Major factors in the last presidential election were the issues of reproductive freedom, educational and work opportunities for the next generation, and human rights.

We are the ones who can decide how the energy of the '90s will be employed. What shall we do? Where shall we put our greatest efforts? What should be our priorities? How can we revitalize the energy, optimism, and power of women's movement, and where shall we take it?

These questions are put to all of us. Ultimately, they are personal questions. What is *your* response?

For serious feminists, these tough questions should be asked and kept ever in mind as we go about our business. As we grow in sophistication and influence, we need greater unity, a better sense of our ultimate direction, effective strategies. We need ideas more carefully defined and strongly supported in order to communicate with one another, to persuade the outsider, and to counter our challengers.

Notes

1. *Ladies' Home Journal,* September 1922, p. 7; quoted in *Women Together* ed. Judith Papachristou (New York: Alfred A. Knopf, 1976), p. 203.

2. Quoted in Vern L. and Bonnie Bullough, *The Subordinate Sex* (Baltimore: Penguin, 1974), p. 88.

3. Author's Introduction to Mary Wollstonecraft, *A Vindication of the Rights of Woman* (New York: Dutton, Everyman Library, 1929), p. 3.

4. Quoted in Papachristou, *Women Together,* p. 32.

5. Ibid.

6. Hester Eisenstein, *Contemporary Feminist Thought* (Boston: G. K. Hall, 1983), p. 132.

7. Catharine R. Stimpson, "Setting Agendas, Defining Challenges," *The Women's Review of Books* 6, no. 5 (February 1989): 14.

8. See the Adams Letters in this chapter.

9. Alison M. Jaggar and Paula Rothenberg Struhl, eds., *Feminist Frameworks* (New York: McGraw-Hill, 1978), pp. xii–xiii. The second edition of *Feminist Frameworks* (McGraw-Hill, 1984) maintains the concept of "frameworks," or categories, but develops and deepens them.

10. *ego:* We are using the classical definition rather than the Freudian—that is, the sense of individual self as distinct from others. [Footnote in original source.]

11. Anne Koedt, "Politics of the Ego" was adopted as the manifesto of the New York Radical Feminists at its founding meeting in December 1969.

12. Reprinted in Aileen S. Kraditor, ed., *Up from the Pedestal* (Chicago: Quadrangle, 1968), pp. 363ff.

Rediscovering American Women: A Chronology Highlighting Women's History in the United States *and* Update—The Process Continues

The first part of this chronology was included in the The Spirit of Houston, *the report to President Carter following the conference in Texas of the National Commission on the Observance of International Women's Year, the First National Women's Conference, in 1977. No doubt it was meant to remind us that women* have *been a force in American history, sometimes against all odds.*

The update following the Houston Chronology was compiled by Kim Blankenship, a young feminist activist, a leader and an attorney in St. Louis, and Anne Bezdek, a returning graduate student studying philosophy and women's studies at Southern Illinois University at Edwardsville.

> *The reformation which we propose, in its utmost scope, is radical and universal. It is not the mere perfecting of a progress already in motion, a detail of some established plan, but it is an epochal movement—the emancipation of a class, the redemption of half the world, and a reorganization of all social, political, and industrial interests and institutions.*
> *—Paulina Wright Davis*
> *Woman's Rights Convention*
> *Worcester, Massachusetts, 1850*

Reprinted from *The Spirit of Houston,* The First National Women's Conference. An Official Report to the President, the Congress and the People of the United States, March 1978. Washington, D.C.: National Commission on the Observance of International Women's Year, U.S. Department of State, 1978.

1587
Virginia Dare, a girl, was the first baby born to English colonists in the New World. The daughter of Elenor White Dare and Ananias Dare, she was born on August 18 in Roanoke Island, Virginia.

circa 1600
The Constitution of the Iroquois Confederation of Nations guaranteed women the sole right and power to regulate war and peace. The women also selected tribal leaders.

1607
Princess Pocahantas saved the life of Captain John Smith, one of the founders of the Jamestown Colony, by interceding with her father, king of the Powhatan Confederacy.

1620
The Mayflower Compact was signed aboard ship by 39 men and male servants among the 102 passengers aboard the Pilgrim vessel. Women, who were not considered free agents, were not asked to sign. Only five of the 18 wives who arrived in Plymouth on the *Mayflower* survived the first harsh winter in the new land.

1638
Anne Hutchinson was excommunicated by the Puritan church in Boston for challenging its religious doctrines. One of her followers, Mary Dyer, later became a Quaker and was hanged in 1660 in Boston for refusing to accept a sentence of banishment. Another woman who fought for freedom of conscience was Lady Deborah Moody, who moved from Massachusetts to Gravesend, Long Island where she and her companions established a community based on religious tolerance and self-government.

1648
The first attempt by a white woman to obtain political power in America originated with Margaret Brent. In a petition to the Colony of Maryland House of Delegates she requested two votes in votes in the Assembly. She believed she merited one vote as a landowner, a vote a man would have obtained without question, and one vote as the executrix for the deceased brother of Lord Baltimore. Her request was denied.

1652
Elizabeth Poole formed a joint stock company in Taunton, Massachusetts to manufacture iron bars. This was one of the first successful iron production plants in the colonies.

1717
Twenty young women sent by King Louis XIV aboard a "brides' ship" to Louisiana to marry French settlers there refused to do so when they arrived in the primitive colony. Their revolt became known as the "petticoat rebellion."

1735
During the eight months that printer Peter Zenger was in jail in New York awaiting trial on charges of printing seditious materials, his wife, Catherine, kept his printshop running. She set type, read proof, wrote, and continued publication of his *New York Weekly Journal*. After her husband's death in 1746, Catherine Zenger continued to publish the newspaper.

The first woman publisher in the Colonies was believed to be Elizabeth Timothy, who took over her late husband's paper, the weekly *South Carolina Gazette*, in Charleston, South Carolina. An estimated 30 women were newspaper publishers in the 18th century Colonies.

1761
The first black poet whose work was to be preserved arrived in Boston harbor on a slave ship from western Africa. Then seven years old, Phyllis Wheatley was taught to read and write English and Latin, and her poetry became a focus for antislavery forces.

American Revolution
Women's groups, such as the Daughters of Liberty, organized to boycott tea and later to provide clothing and supplies for the Army. Deborah Sampson served as a soldier, for which she received a military pension, and Molly Pitcher assisted in the battlefield.

Groups of New Jersey women took vigorous action against husbands who abused their wives. Entering the home of a known wife-beater in the evening, they stripped the man and spanked him with sticks, shouting, "Woe to the men that beat their wives."

1777
Abigail Adams wrote to her husband, John Adams, and suggested, ". . . in the code of laws . . . I desire you to remember the ladies and be more generous and favorable to them than your ancestors. Do not put such unlimited power into the hands of the husbands. Remember all men would be tyrants if they could. If particular care and attention is not paid to the ladies, we are determined to foment a rebellion and will not hold ourselves bound by any laws in which we have no voice or representation." The future President replied: "Depend upon it, we know better than to repeal our Masculine systems."

In the years immediately following the American Revolution, women had the right to vote in some parts of Virginia and New Jersey. Later, the adoption of State constitutions limited the franchise to white males and excluded women.

1788
Mercy Otis Warren, the first American woman historian, a political satirist and playwright, wrote her *Observations on the New Constitution* in which she deplored the absence of a Bill of Rights. The first 10 Amendments (the Bill of Rights) were added to the Constitution in 1791.

1800–1820
Deborah Skinner operated the first power loom. In the first two decades of the 19th century, factories were established employing large numbers of women and children, particularly in the New England textile industry.

1804
Sacajawea, a young Indian woman, accompanied the Lewis and Clark expedition to the West. Her skill and courage were credited with helping to make the exploration a success.

1805
Mercy Otis Warren published a three-volume history of the American Revolution which is still used by historians.

1810
Mother Elizabeth Bayley Seton founded and became head of the first sisterhood in America, the Sisters of Charity of St. Joseph's. She was canonized as the Catholic Church's first U.S.-born Saint by Pope Paul VI in 1975.

1821
Emma Willard founded a female seminary at Troy, N.Y., the first effort to provide secondary education for women. In 1837 Mary Lyon founded Mt. Holyoke Seminary (later College), which provided education similar to that offered to men at the better men's colleges.

1828
The first known strike of women workers over wages took place in Dover, N.H. Similar strikes were waged in Lowell, Mass., in 1834 and 1836 by women textile workers protesting reduced real wages.

1833
Prudence Crandall opened a school for black girls in her Connecticut home. She was arrested, persecuted, and forced to give up the school to protect her pupils from violence.

1837
First national Anti-Slavery Convention of American Women met in New York City. This was the first national gathering of women organized for action without the assistance or supervision of men.

1839
After this time, most states began to recognize through legislation the right of married women to hold property. In New York State, Ernestine Rose and Susan B. Anthony led a petition campaign for women's rights. Mrs. Rose, Polish-born daughter of a rabbi, addressed the New York state legislature on at least five occasions until the body enacted a married women's property law in 1848.

1841
The first woman graduated from Oberlin College, having completed an easier "literary" course. At Oberlin, female students were required to wash male students' clothing, clean their rooms, serve them at meals, and were not permitted to recite in public or work in the fields with male students.

1845
Woman in the Nineteenth Century, written by Margaret Fuller, was an early and influential publication urging women's rights. Fuller wrote: "We would have every path laid open to Woman as freely as to Man."

1847
Trained by her father as an astronomer, Maria Mitchell at age 29 discovered a comet while standing on a rooftop scanning the sky with a telescope. In 1848 she became the first woman elected to the American Academy of Arts and Sciences in Boston.

1848
The first Women's Rights Convention was held in Seneca Falls, N.Y., led by Lucretia Mott and Elizabeth Cady Stanton. Its Declaration of Sentiments, paraphrased from the Declaration of Independence, stated that "all men and women are created equal." Eleven resolutions were approved, including equality in education, employment, and the law. A resolution advocating the right to suffrage passed by a narrow margin, with some delegates feeling that it was too daring a proposal.

The first issue of *The Lily,* a temperance paper, appeared with an editorial by Amelia Bloomer, later known for her experiment in clothing reform.

1849
Elizabeth Blackwell received her medical degree at Geneva, N.Y., becoming the first woman doctor in the United States.

1851
Sojourner Truth, ex-slave, electrified an audience in Akron, Ohio by drawing a parallel between the struggle for women's rights and the struggle to abolish slavery. In answer to arguments that women were delicate creatures who necessarily led sheltered lives, she described the hard physical labor she had done as a black woman slave and demanded, "And ain't I a Woman?"

1854
The first American day nursery opened in New York City for children of poor working mothers. In later years, licensing standards were established, but only minimal Federal funding was provided, except during the Depression and World War II.

1860
Elizabeth Peabody, a teacher, writer, and associate of the Transcendentalists, organized in Boston the first formal kindergarten in the United States. It was modeled on the Froebel kindergarten system in Germany.

Civil War
Women were responsible for the establishment of the U.S. Sanitary Commission. Dorothea Dix, Clara Barton, and Mother Bickerdyke served as nurses and trained others. Dr. Mary Walker was one of several women who served as doctors and surgeons at the front.

Susan B. Anthony organized the National Women's Loyal League to collect signatures for passage of the 13th amendment abolishing slavery. Women's rights leaders were prominent in the struggle to end slavery.

Women entered government offices to replace clerks who went to war. This established women not only in Government service but in clerical work. After the invention of the typewriter in 1867, women flocked to white collar office work, which began to be considered a women's specialty.

1864
Working Women's Protective Union was founded in New York to ensure fair treatment for women wage earners. Thousands of women were working in factories.

1865
Vassar College opened, offering the first college-level curriculum for women. Five years later, Wellesley and Smith Colleges were founded. Although women were admitted to some coeducational institutions, their opportunities to study with men were limited until the University of Michigan admitted women in 1870 and Cornell University became coeducational in 1872.

1866
Elizabeth Cady Stanton became the first woman candidate for Congress, although women could not vote. She received 24 votes.

1868
The first women's suffrage amendment to the Constitution was introduced by Senator S. C. Pomeroy of Kansas. In 1878 another proposal for woman suffrage, which came to be known as the Anthony Amendment, was introduced.

1869
After passage of the 14th and 15th amendments granting suffrage to all males, both black and white, leaders of the women's movement determined to press their own claims more vigorously. Because of differences over strategy, two organizations were formed. The National Woman Suffrage Association was led by Elizabeth Cady Stanton and Susan B. Anthony while the more conservative American Women Suffrage Association was directed by Lucy Stone and Julia Ward Howe. Unification of these two groups was not achieved until 1890.

1870
Women gained the right to vote and to serve on juries in the Territory of Wyoming.

1872
Susan B. Anthony attempted to vote in Rochester, N.Y. She was tried and convicted of voting illegally but refused to pay the $100 fine.

1873
Belva Lockwood was admitted to the bar of the District of Columbia and in 1879 won passage of a law granting women lawyers the right to practice law before the U.S. Supreme Court. She ran for President in 1884 as candidate of the National Equal Rights Party and got 4,149 votes.

1874
Under the leadership of Frances Willard, the Women's Christian Temperance Union became the largest women's organization in the Nation. During this same period, the Young Women's Christian Association evolved to meet the needs of working women away from home. Other women organized for cultural purposes and by 1890 the General Federation of Women's Clubs was formed. The Association of Collegiate Alumnae, organized in 1882 to investigate the health of college women, eventually became the American Association of University Women.

1878
The Knights of Labor advocated equal pay for equal work, the abolition of child labor under age 14, and in 1881 opened their membership to working women. By 1886, 50,000 women were members.

1880s
Lucy Gonzalez Parson, a labor organizer, traveled in 16 states to raise funds to help organize women gar-

ment workers and others. She founded *The Alarm* newspaper and edited *The Liberator.*

1890
Elizabeth Cady Stanton was elected first president of the unified suffrage organization, the National American Woman Suffrage Association. She also studied organized religion as a major source of women's inferior status and in 1895 published *The Woman's Bible.*

1893
Rebelling against an invitation to organize a Jewish women's committee to serve at receptions during Chicago's big Columbian Exposition, Hannah Greenbaum Solomon invited Jewish women from all over the country to attend a conference at the same time as the Exposition. The result was formation of the National Council of Jewish Women, dedicated to education, social reform, and issues of concern to women.

1896
The National Association for Colored Women, the first national organization of black women, was established, and Mary Church Terrell served as first president.

1898
Charlotte Perkins Gilman published *Women and Economics,* in which she decried the wasted efforts and the low economic status of the housewife. Gilman advocated the industrialization of housework and the socialization of child care.

1899
Florence Kelley became general secretary of the National Consumers League and worked for legislation in behalf of working women and children.

1900
The first decade of the 20th century showed the greatest increase in the female labor force of any period prior to 1940. New groups were formed to protect women and children from exploitation by industry. Several unions were organized at this time composed largely of women in the garment trades. Mother Jones, a labor organizer, led a march of children who worked in the Pennsylvania textile mills to the home of President Roosevelt in Oyster Bay, Long Island to call public attention to their plight.

1902
Carrie Chapman Catt organized the International Suffrage Alliance to help establish effective women's groups in other countries.

1904
Mary McLeod Bethune founded Bethune-Cookman College in Daytona Beach, Florida.

1907
The landmark case, *Muller* v. *Oregon,* established sex as a valid classification for protective legislation. The sociological type of evidence assembled by Florence Kelley and Josephine Goldmark to convince the court that overlong hours were harmful to the future of the race provided a model brief for later laws. While labor laws applying only to women were on the whole beneficial to women in the early part of the century, when jobs were largely sex segregated, the laws did result in loss of job opportunities for those seeking "male" jobs.

1908
A poem, "The New Colossus," written by Emma Lazarus, a poet who had died in 1887, was inscribed on a tablet in the pedestal of the Statue of Liberty in New York harbor. Its most famous lines: "Give me your tired, your poor, Your huddled masses yearning to be free . . ."

1909
The first significant strike of working women, "The Uprising of the 20,000," was conducted by shirtwaist makers in New York to protest low wages and long working hours. The National Women's Trade Union League (founded in 1903) mobilized public opinion and financial support for the strikers.

1911
The Triangle fire on March 25, in which 146 women shirtwaist operators were killed, dramatized the poor working conditions of immigrant women. A report of the Senate Investigation of the Condition of Women and Child Wage Earners led to establishment of the Children's Bureau (1912) and later the Women's Bureau of the Department of Labor (1920).

Liga Feminil Mexicanista was founded in Laredo, Texas to insure that the Mexican American culture and heritage would be preserved and transmitted.

1913
Harriet Tubman, ex-slave and most famous "conductor" on the Underground Railroad, died in poverty. Before the Civil War, she made 19 rescue trips to save hundreds of slaves. During the war, she served as a nurse, spy, and scout and led daring raids into the South.

1914
The Alaska Native Sisterhood was formed as an auxiliary of the Alaska Native Brotherhood, the most powerful union of native peoples in Alaska.

1915
Jane Addams, "the angel of Hull House," Carrie Chapman Catt and other women leaders held a meeting of 3,000 women in Washington, D.C. on January 10 which organized the Women's Peace Party. They called for the abolition of war.

Margaret Sanger, having studied birth control clinics abroad, returned home to campaign against the legal barriers to the dissemination of contraceptive information. She and other women, including Emma Goldman, were jailed for their efforts.

1916
Impatient with the slow pace of the woman suffrage campaign, Alice Paul organized the National Woman's Party to conduct a more militant strategy. Its followers organized suffrage parades, picketed the White House, and chained themselves to its fence. Repeatedly arrested and imprisoned, the women protested their illegal and harsh confinement by going on hunger strikes. They were force-fed by prison authorities. Their suffering aroused widespread public outrage and was credited with hastening ratification of the suffrage amendment.

1917
Jeannette Rankin, a Republican from Montana, was the first woman elected to serve in Congress. The first vote she cast opposed American entry into World War I. She was the only woman to serve in Congress before adoption of the Federal suffrage amendment.

1919
An outgrowth of women suffrage organizations, the League of Women Voters was set up to educate women for their new political and social responsibilities. The National Federation of Business and Professional Women's Clubs was also organized.

1919
Jane Addams led a delegation of American women to a Women's Conference in Zurich, which paralleled the official peace conference in Paris. They formed the Women's International League for Peace and Freedom, with Jane Addams as president and Emily Green Balch as secretary-treasurer.

1920
On August 26, the 19th amendment was ratified and 26 million women of voting age finally gained the right to vote.

1923
The Equal Rights Amendment, advocated by Alice Paul and the National Woman's Party, was introduced in Congress for the first time. Most women did not support this effort because they feared it would threaten protective legislation for women workers who labored in sweatshop conditions.

In the following years, the momentum of women's campaigns for access to equal education, employment, and professional achievement waned. Discrimination against women intensified. From 1925 to 1945 medical schools placed a quota of five percent on female admissions. Columbia and Harvard law schools refused to consider women applicants.

1928
Doris Stevens became the first president of the Inter-American Commission of Women, the Organization of American States.

1930
The Depression encouraged reaction against any change in women's traditional domestic role. Legislation restricted the employment of married women, and there was strong public disapproval of women working when men were unable to find employment. Nevertheless, many women performed low-paid labor to support their families. Opportunities for women to obtain college educations and graduate training were limited by lack of financial support.

1931
Suma Sugi, the first Nisei lobbyist (American born of Japanese ancestry), succeeded in amending the Cable Act of 1922 to permit American-born Asian women to regain their American citizenship upon termination of their marriage to an alien.

1933
Frances Perkins, the first woman to hold a Cabinet post, was appointed to head the Department of Labor by President Roosevelt and served in his cabinet for 12 years.

Eleanor Roosevelt turned her 12 years in the White House into a model of activism and humanitarian concern for future First Ladies.

1935
The National Council of Negro Women was founded in New York, with Mary McLeod Bethune as its first president.

1940
The percentage of working women was almost the same as it had been in 1900, when one of every five women worked for wages. After the U.S. entered World War II, wartime needs required the employment of large numbers of women. "Rosie the Riveter" became a national symbol. After the war, many women remained in the labor force, although many were displaced by returning veterans. Between 1940–60, the number of working women and the proportion of working wives doubled. More women over 35 were employed in rapidly expanding business and industry. Inequities in pay and advancement opportunities became more obvious limitations affecting large numbers of women. Economic conditions produced a favorable environment for the increasing demands for equity voiced by the women of the 1960's.

1950
A repressive decade for Chicana activists. Several were deported for their attempts to organize communities. Also deported was film actress Rosaura Revueltas, featured in the film, "Salt of the Earth," about striking miners in the Southwest.

1952
The Constitution of the Commonwealth of Puerto Rico was enacted, embodying the Equal Rights Amendment.

1953
Simone de Beauvoir's *The Second Sex,* a scholarly and historical analysis of the inferior status of women, was published in the United States.

1956
Rosa Parks, a black seamstress, refused to give up her bus seat to a white man and was arrested, touching off the Montgomery, Alabama, bus boycott.*

1957
Daisy Bates, coeditor with her husband of a black newspaper and president of the Arkansas National Association for the Advancement of Colored People, acted as spokesperson and counselor for the nine black youths who desegrated Little Rock Central High School.

*Rosa Parks' action took place in December of 1955, setting off the boycott, which came to fruition in 1956.

1960
Women Strike for Peace was formed as an outgrowth of protests against resumption of nuclear testing by the Soviet Union and United States.

1961
The President's Commission on the Status of Women, chaired by Eleanor Roosevelt, was established by Executive Order 10980, with a charge to study seven areas: education, private and Federal employment, social insurance and tax laws, protective labor laws, civil and political rights and family law, and home and community. Esther Peterson, Director of the Women's Bureau, was the moving force in its establishment, with the assistance of then Vice President Lyndon Johnson.

1962
In Michigan, the Governor's Commission on the Status of Women became the first State commission. Union women Mildred Jeffrey and Myra Wolfgang were the leaders in obtaining its establishment.

1962
Acting on a recommendation of his Commission on the Status of Women, President Kennedy issued an order requiring Federal employees to be hired and promoted without regard to sex. Prior to this order, Federal managers could restrict consideration to men or women.

1963
The National Federation of Business and Professional Women's Clubs adopted as its top priority the nationwide establishment of State commissions on the status of women. By June 1964 when the first national conference was held, there were 24 commissions, and by the end of the year there were 33.

The Equal Pay Act was passed in June, effective June 1964, after formation of a coalition of women's organizations and unions to support it in Congress.

The Feminine Mystique by Betty Friedan was published. Describing social pressures that sought to limit women to roles as wives and mothers, it became a national and influential best seller.

The Interdepartmental Committee on the Status of Women and Citizens Advisory Council on the Status of Women were established by Executive Order 11126, with Margaret Hickey as its first chairperson. The Committee and Council sponsored national meetings of the State commissions, issued annual reports on issues affecting women, and made legislative and administrative recommendations. Subsequent chairpersons were Maurine Neuberger and Jacqueline Gutwillig. (The Council was terminated on August 22, 1977 by Executive Order 12007.)

1964

The Spring issue of *Daedalus,* Journal of the American Academy of Arts and Sciences, devoted an entire issue to "The Woman in America," enhancing the academic respectability of the subject. Alice Rossi's "Equality Between the Sexes: An Immodest Proposal," probably the most widely reproduced article in the women's movement, first appeared here.

Title 7 of the Civil Rights Act, enacted in 1964, prohibited discrimination in employment because of sex, race, color, religion, and national origin.

The first meeting of the First National Institute on Girls' Sports was held "to increase the depth of experience and expand opportunities for women."

1965

The U.S. Supreme Court found that a Connecticut law banning contraceptives was unconstitutional because it violated the right to privacy. *Griswold* v. *State of Connecticut,* 381 U.S.C. 479.

1966

A Federal court declared that an Alabama law excluding women from State juries was in violation of the equal protection clause of the 14th amendment, the first time in modern times a Federal court had found a law making sex distinctions unconstitutional. *White* v. *Crook,* 251 F. Supp. 401.

The National Organization for Women (NOW) was organized at the Third National Conference of Governors' Commissions on the Status of Women as a culmination of dissatisfaction with the failure to enforce Title 7 of the Civil Rights Act. Among the 28 women who founded NOW were: Betty Friedan, Aileen Hernandez, Dr. Kathryn Clarenbach, Dr. Pauli Murray, Marguerite Rawalt, Catherine Conroy, Dorothy Haener, and Dr. Nancy Knaak.

1967

The first "women's liberation" group was formed in Chicago, partially in rebellion against the low status of young women in civil rights and "new left" campus movements. Similar groups were independently organized in New York, Toronto, Detroit, Seattle, San Francisco, and other cities. Initially concerned with analyzing the origins, nature, and extent of women's subservient status in society, some groups used the technique of "consciousness-raising" sessions to help women liberate themselves from restricting inferior roles. Most of the groups were small, egalitarian and opposed to elitism. They called for far-reaching and radical change in almost all aspects of American society.

Executive Order 11246, prohibiting discrimination by Federal contractors, was amended to include sex discrimination, with an effective date of October 1968.

A law repealing arbitrary restrictions on military rank held by women was signed by the President.

1968

The Church and the Second Sex by Dr. Mary Daly, a scholarly critique of Catholic Church doctrine, influenced Protestant as well as Catholic women. The first stirrings of Catholic feminist dissent occurred at the Second Vatican Council. The American branch of St. Joan's Alliance, an international Catholic feminist organization, had been formed in 1965 by Frances McGillicuddy.

Beginning in 1968, a number of distinguished Native American women, including Lucy Covington (Colville), Ramona Bennett (Puyallup), Joy Sundberg (Yurok), and Ada Deer (Menominee), were elected as tribal chairs.

Federally Employed Women was organized in September to press for equality in Federal employment, with Allie Weedon, a black attorney, as first president.

The Women's Equity Action League was organized in December by Dr. Elizabeth Boyer and other members of the National Organization for Women and concentrated on attacking sexism in higher education.

Women liberationists picketed the Miss America beauty pageant in Atlantic City. Contrary to myth, they did not burn bras. They carried signs that said: Women Are People, Not Livestock.

1969

Shirley Chisholm, Democrat of New York City, was the first black woman elected to Congress.

Weeks v. *Southern Bell Telephone Co.,* 408 F. 2d 228, was the first appeals court decision interpreting sex provisions of Title 7 of the Civil Rights Act of 1964. The lawsuit was brought by a blue collar union woman protesting discriminatory effects of State labor laws applying only to women. Marguerite Rawalt, NOW legal counsel, located a Louisiana lawyer, Sylvia Roberts, to represent Mrs. Weeks, and NOW paid court costs. The excellent decision, the great courage of the plaintiff, and the important victory of a volunteer woman lawyer and a women's organization over highly paid corporation lawyers were a great boost to the women's movement.

An equally important Title 7 case was decided by the Seventh Circuit Court of Appeals, *Bowe* v. *Colgate Palmolive,* 416 F. 2d 711. Union women and volunteer women attorneys were the pattern in this case, too. These and later Title 7 cases illustrated the real effects of State labor laws applying only to women and led to their early demise and broadened support for the Equal Rights Amendment.

The first Commission on the Status of Women appointed by a professional association began to function inside the Modern Language Association. In its early years, that Commission assumed responsibility for collecting and disseminating data on women's studies courses and programs. In December 1970 the Commission published a list of 110 women's studies courses taught at 47 colleges and universities. There were by then two Women's Studies Programs at Cornell University and San Diego State University.

In Fall 1972, the *Women's Studies Newsletter,* edited by Florence Howe, began to appear quarterly on the SUNY College at Old Westbury campus, published by The Feminist Press. *Annually,* the newsletter lists Women's Studies Programs; in 1977, there were 276. There are also groups of women's studies courses on more than 1,000 other campuses. The total number of courses now offered exceeds 15,000.

A women's caucus was organized at the Chicano Liberation Conference held in Denver.

The Boston Women's Health Collective was organized, one of a number of women's self-help groups that emerged in various parts of the country. The group researched and wrote *Our Bodies, Ourselves,* which later became a worldwide bestseller.

The four Republican Congresswomen—Florence Dwyer, Margaret Heckler, Catherine May, and Charlotte Reid—asked for an unprecedented audience with President Nixon to discuss women's issues. They presented a letter which outlined a proposed administration program and provided data on discrimination. Their program became the agenda of the President's Task Force on Women's Rights and Responsibilities, which the President later established with Virginia Allan as chair.

Women in the American Sociological Association formed the first caucus within a professional association, after presentation of a survey by Dr. Alice Rossi on the status of women in graduate departments of sociology. By the end of 1971 every professional association had an activist women's caucus or official commission to study the status of women.

1970

Women's Equity Action League officer, Dr. Bernice Sandler, filed the first formal charges of sex discrimination under Executive Order No. 11246 against the University of Maryland. The charges were well documented. By the end of 1971 women professors had filed formal charges of sex discrimination against more than 300 colleges, largely through the efforts of Dr. Sandler and WEAL.

The first statewide meeting of AFL-CIO women was held in Wisconsin in March. The women endorsed the ERA, opposing AFL-CIO national policy. The next month the United Auto Workers became the first major national union to endorse ERA. Later the AFL-CIO executive council changed its position and announced its support for the ERA.

The Subcommittee on Constitutional Amendments of the Senate Judiciary Committee, chaired by Senator Birch Bayh, held three days of hearings on the ERA in May. Leaders of women's organizations and unions, women lawyers, and Members of Congress testified.

The NAACP adopted a women's rights platform at its annual national convention in June.

The first national commercial newsletters to serve the women's movement—*Women Today,* published in Washington by Myra and Lester Barrer, and *Spokeswoman,* published in Chicago by Susan Davis—were issued.

The Interstate Association of Commissions on the Status of Women were organized to provide a national voice and greater autonomy for the State commissions. Elizabeth Duncan Koontz, newly appointed Director of the Women's Bureau, arranged the organized meetings, and Dr. Kathryn Clarenbach was elected first president.

The Women's Bureau held its 50th anniversary conference, attended by more than 1,000 women. The Conference endorsed the ERA and other recommendations of the President's Task Force on Women's Rights and Responsibilities.

On the first day of the Women's Bureau Conference, Congresswoman Martha Griffiths filed a petition to discharge the ERA from the House Judiciary Committee, where it had rested without hearings since 1948. The petition was successful, and the ERA was debated in the House on August 10, passing overwhelmingly. It was then defeated in the Senate by the addition of unacceptable amendments.

Hearings on discrimination in education were held in June and July by Congresswoman Edith Green, chairing a special House Subcommittee on Education. The two-volume report is a classic in documenting discrimination against women in education.

The Women's Affairs Division of the League of United Latin American Citizens was organized at the convention in Beaumont, Texas, with Julia Zozoya and Ada Pena in the forefront.

The National Conference of Commissioners on Uniform State Laws published the Uniform Marriage and Divorce Act, based on the assumption that marriage is an economic partnership and recognizing homemakers' contributions as having economic value.

A nationwide celebration of the 50th anniversary of the suffrage amendment, including a mammoth parade in New York City, was held in all major cities on August 26 by a wide spectrum of organizations and individual women. The parade became an annual event.

Sixty-three Native American women from 43 tribes and 23 States met at Colorado State University to discuss their common concerns. They organized the North American Indian Women's Association.

Patsy Mink, Democrat of Hawaii, was the first and only Asian woman elected to Congress. In New York City, Democrat Bella Abzug was the first woman elected to Congress on a women's rights platform. They were among only 11 women in the 435-member House of Representatives.

The Women's Action Organization of State, AID and ICA, the first women's caucus in the federal government, was formed to eliminate discrimination and promote equality of opportunity for women in the foreign affairs agencies.

1971

The National Women's Political Caucus was organized at a meeting in Washington in July, with Congresswoman Bella Abzug, Gloria Steinem, Aileen Hernandez, Fannie Lou Hamer, Edith Van Horn, Liz Carpenter, Koryne Horbal, Congresswoman Shirley Chisholm, Brownie Ledbetter, Betty Friedan, Bobby Kilberg, Jo Ann Gardner, LaDonna Harris, and Virginia Allan among the early leaders.

The U.S. Supreme Court held in *Reed* v. *Reed* that an Idaho law giving preference to males as executors of estates was invalid under the 14th amendment, the first in a series of Supreme Court cases expanding the application of the 5th and 14th amendments to sex discrimination, 404 U.S. 71, 1971.

A preview issue of *Ms.* magazine was published in December with Gloria Steinem as editor. Established to give voice to the ideas of the women's movement, it was an immediate success.

The Women's National Abortion Coalition was organized to work for repeal of anti-abortion laws.

1972

The Equal Rights Amendment was overwhelmingly approved by the Congress and submitted to the States for ratification. Hawaii was the first State to ratify.

The Equal Employment Opportunity Act of 1972, extending coverage and giving the EEOC enforcement authority, passed. The EEOC issued greatly improved sex discrimination guidelines.

Title 9 of the Education Amendments of 1972 was passed, prohibiting discrimination on account of sex in most Federally assisted educational programs. The Equal Pay Act was extended to cover administrative, professional, and executive employees, and the Civil Rights Commission was given jurisdiction over sex discrimination.

The Democratic and Republican Party platforms endorsed the ERA and vigorous enforcement of anti-discrimination laws. As a result of campaigns by the National Women's Political Caucus, the participation of women as convention delegates was higher than in previous conventions. At the Democratic convention, women were 40 percent of the delegates; at the Republican convention, 30 percent.

The National Conference of Puerto Rican Women was organized in Washington, with Carmen Maymi and Paquito Viva in leading roles.

The November elections brought more women into elective office. The number of women elected to State legislatures was 28.2 percent higher than those serving in the preceding year. In the House of Representatives, the number of Congresswomen increased to 16, but with the retirement of Margaret Chase Smith, the U.S. Senate once again became all-male.

Members of the National Council of Jewish Women conducted a study of day-care facilities in 176 areas. The NCJW report, written by Mary Keyserling, concluded that while the need for day-care centers was enormous, facilities were nonexistent in most places or were of poor quality, underfunded, and understaffed.

1973

AT&T signed an agreement with the EEOC and the Labor Department providing goals and timetables for increasing utilization of women and minorities. About $15 million in back pay was paid to some 15,000 employees.

In a historic decision on January 22, the U.S. Supreme Court held that during the first trimester of pregnancy, the decision to have an abortion must be left solely to a woman and her physician. The only restriction a State may impose is the requirement that the abortion be performed by a physician licensed by the State. In the second and third trimesters, the Court held, the States may impose increasingly stringent requirements. Lawyers for the plaintiffs were Sarah Weddington and Marjorie Hames. *Doe* v. *Bolton* and *Roe* v. *Wade,* 93 S. Ct. 739 and 755.

The National Black Feminists Organization was formed. Eleanor Holmes Norton, leading attorney and head of the New York City Human Rights Commission, was one of the leaders.

The Foreign Assistance Act (Public Law 93-189, 87 Stat. 714) included the Percy Amendment providing that in administering financial aid, particular attention be given to "programs, projects, and activities which tend to integrate women into the national status and assisting the total development effort." Dr. Irene Tinker and the Federation of Organizations for Professional Women were leading proponents.

Billie Jean King beat Bobby Riggs in straight sets in their "Battle of the Sexes" tennis match.

1974

The Coalition of Labor Union Women was organized in Chicago with over 3,000 women in attendance. Olga Madar, former UAW vice president, was elected president.

More than 1.5 million domestic service workers were brought under the coverage of the Fair Labor Standards Act by Public Law 93-259, approved April 8. A rate of $1.90 per hour was effective May 1, 1974, with increases slated for later periods.

The Wisconsin Commission on the Status of Women, chaired by Dr. Kathryn Clarenbach, inaugurated a series of six regional conferences to examine the status of the homemaker.

A national newsletter, *Marriage, Divorce and the Family,* edited by Betty Blaisdell Berry, began publication.

The Mexican American Women's Association (MAWA) was founded.

A study by Dr. Constance Uri, a Cherokee/Choctaw physician, revealed the widespread use and abuse of sterilization of Native American women in Indian health care facilities. The exposé led to the investigation of excessive sterilization of poor and minority women and to the 1977 revision of the Department of Health, Education, and Welfare's guidelines on sterilization.

Congresswoman Bella Abzug's bill to designate August 26 "Women's Equality Day" in honor of the adoption of the Suffrage Amendment became Public Law 93-392.

The Housing and Community Development Act of 1974, Public Law 93-383, prohibited sex discrimination in carrying out community development programs and in making federally related mortgage loans. The Civil Rights Act of 1968 was also amended to prohibit sex discrimination in financing, sale or rental of housing, or the provision of brokerage services.

The Equal Credit Opportunity Act became Public Law 93-495 after Congresswomen Bella Abzug, Margaret Heckler, and Leonor Sullivan led the fight for it in the House. It prohibited discrimination in credit on the basis of sex or marital status. Later, Congresswoman Abzug led a delegation of women members of Congress to meet with Chairman Arthur Burns of the Federal Reserve Board to protest unsatisfactory regulations designed to implement the new law. The regulations were revised.

The Screen Actors Guild reported a nationwide survey of 10,000 viewers on their opinions of women in the media. The majority wanted a more positive image of women, wanted to see women appearing on

TV in positions of authority and in leading roles, and felt the media did not encourage young girls to aspire to a useful and meaningful role in society.

Following a "Win With Women" campaign by the National Women's Political Caucus, 18 women were elected to the 94th Congress. A 19th member was elected in a special election in early 1975. In the State legislatures there was a 29.5 percent increase in the numbers of women (465 to 604). The first woman governor to be elected in her own right, Ella Grasso, was elected Governor of Connecticut. Mary Anne Krupsak was elected Lieutenant Governor of New York, and many more women were elected to statewide offices.

1975

The U.S. Supreme Court held in *Wiesenfeld* v. *Wineberger* that a widower with minor children whose deceased wife was covered by social security is entitled to a social security benefit under the same circumstances as a widow would be. The Court held unanimously that the fifth amendment prohibited the present difference in treatment. 43 USLW 4393.

The Supreme Court also held that, in the context of child support, a Utah statute providing that the period of minority extending for males to age 21 and for females to age 18 denies equal protection of the laws guaranteed by the 14th amendment. *Stanton* v. *Stanton*, 43 USLW 4167.

Ms. magazine published a petition for sexual freedom signed by 100 promiment women. They pledged to work for repeal of all laws and regulations that discriminate against homosexuals and lesbians.

The National Commission on the Observance of International Women's Year, 1975, was appointed by President Ford with Jill Ruckelshaus as presiding officer. Elizabeth Athanasakos became presiding officer in 1976. Members of the Commission represented the United States at the United Nations International Women's Year Conference in Mexico City in June.

The First American Indian Women's Leadership Conference met in New York City, sponsored by the International Treaty Council in conjunction with IWY.

A bill introduced by Congresswoman Bella Abzug directed the National Commission to organize and convene a National Women's Conference, preceded by State meetings. The bill was passed by both Houses, was signed by President Ford and became Public Law 94-167.

1976

The number of women delegates to the political party conventions rose to 31.4 percent at the Republican convention and declined to 34 percent at the Democratic convention. A large and effective women's caucus at the Democratic convention in New York met with Presidential nominee Jimmy Carter and obtained pledges from him to appoint significant numbers of women to his administration, to take other steps to improve the position of women, and to campaign for ratification of the ERA.

The major parties nominated 52 women for the House of Representatives, eight more than in 1974, but 31 ran against incumbents. Eighteen were elected, one less than in the previous Congress. Although women won seats in Maryland and Ohio and all incumbents won reelection, Congresswomen Bella Abzug and Patsy Mink gave up their seats to make unsuccessful campaigns for the Senate, and Congresswoman Leonor Sullivan retired. The number of women in State legislatures increased to 685, representing nine percent of legislative seats.

1977

President Carter named a new National Commission on the Observance of IWY and appointed Bella Abzug presiding officer. He named two women, Patricia Harris and Juanita Kreps, to his Cabinet and made other major appointments of women. An analysis of the Presidential personnel plum file appointments list in October, however, showed that of 526 top positions in the Carter administration, only 60 (11 percent) were held by women.

The drive for final ratification of ERA was stalled at 35 States, with three more States needed to meet the 1979 deadline for ratification.

The National Women's Conference met in Houston, Texas, November 18–21, attracted almost 20,000 people, including 2,005 delegates, adopted a National Plan of Action, and was acclaimed a success.

Editor's Note: In highlighting some of the notable women and events affecting women in American history, this chronology makes no pretense to being complete or even comprehensive. It is intended rather to remind readers that the role of women in America has too often been overlooked and that the struggle for equality for women is as old as our Nation.

Among the books which the editors found particularly useful in compiling this chronology were:

Chafe, William. The American Woman: Her Changing Social, Economic and Political Roles, 1920–1970. *Oxford University Press.*

DePauw, Linda Grant. Fortunes of War, New Jersey Women and the American Revolution. *New Jersey Historical Commission.*

Flexner, Eleanor. Century of Struggle. *Antheneum.*

Freeman, Jo. Women: A Feminist Perspective. *Mayfield.*

Hole, Judith, and Ellen Levine. Rebirth of Feminism. *Quadrangle.*

Lerner, Gerda. "The Lady and the Mill Girl: Changes in the Status of Women in the Age of Jackson." American Studies Journal, *Spring 1969.*

Lerner, Gerda. Black Women in White America. *Vintage.*

O'Neill, William. Everyone Was Brave. *Quadrangle.*

Papachristou, Judith. Women Together, A History in Documents of the Women's Movement in the United States. A *Ms.* Book.

Wertheimer, Barbara. We Were There: The Story of Working Women in America. *Pantheon.*

Special thanks to Catherine East for compiling the original chronology on which this is based, which appeared as an IWY publication in 1975.

Update—The Process Continues

Kim Blankenship and Anne Bezdek

1978

President Carter nominated Col. Margaret A. Brewer, forty-seven, as the first female general of the Marine Corps. She became the Director of Information.

Sea duty was opened to Navy women after a court battle. A U.S. district judge in Washington ruled a federal law unconstitutional which prohibited women from serving on anything other than transport and hospital ships. A few months later, in November, 8 women reported to serve on Navy ships. They were the first of 5,130 the Navy planned to assign over the following five years.

1979

The Jaycees ousted a chapter which retained women as members. Their national executive board revoked the charters of six units, five of which were in Alaska, for noncompliance with the bylaws that restricted the membership to men.

The first woman rabbi headed a congregation. Rabbi Linda Joy Holtzman became a recognized spiritual leader of Conservative Beth Israel Congregation in Coatesville, Pennsylvania. Rabbi Holtzman was a graduate of Reconstructionist Rabbinical College in Philadelphia.

Diana Nyad swam from the Bahamas to Florida. Nyad, a New Yorker, reached Juno Beach after a 60-mile swim in 27 hours and 38 minutes from North Bimini Island off the Bahamas. The thirty-year-old woman fought currents, sharks, and jellyfish.

1980

Firefighter Linda Eaton quit her job in Iowa City, alleging harassment after she had won a 16-month legal battle for the right to breastfeed her baby at the firehouse. The Iowa Civil Rights Commission found her the victim of sex discrimination. Eaton was the fire department's only female firefighter. Eaton received from the case back pay of $145, $2,000 in damages, and $26,000 in legal fees.

The first women graduated from service academies in May. The Coast Guard commissioned 14 women and 142 men at the New London academy's ninety-eighth graduation ceremony.

The U.S. Military Academy graduated 61 women in a class of 809.

At the Naval Academy, 55 women were a part of the graduating class of 938 midshipmen.

The Air Force Academy graduated 97 women and 970 men.

Women were placed on the AFL-CIO Executive Board for the first time. Joyce Miller, the president of the Coalition of Labor Union Women, was the first female to serve on the council since the federation's formation twenty-five years ago.

1981

The first woman Supreme Court justice was seated. On September 21 the Senate, with a 99–0 vote, confirmed Sandra Day O'Connor as a Supreme Court justice. O'Connor, a judge from Arizona, was the 102nd justice to sit on the Supreme Court. She was confirmed on September 25.

The first test-tube baby was born in a U.S. hospital. Elizabeth Jordan Carr—5 pounds, 12 ounces, and healthy—was delivered at Norfolk General Hospital in Virginia. She was conceived in a laboratory dish. She was the fifteenth child born in this manner; the others were born in Britain and Australia.

1982

The new editor of the *Roget's Thesaurus* eliminated

sexism from its publication. This edition of the 130-year-old book of synonyms and antonyms barred categories that the woman editor said were biased. "Mankind" became "humankind," and "countryman" was referred to as a "country dweller." The category heads were edited to be as neutral as possible.

The Equal Rights Amendment was defeated. It was three states short of the thirty-eight needed to ratify it as the twenty-seventh amendment to the Constitution. The supporters vowed to fight on.

1983

The first U.S. woman traveled in space. Sally Ride became the first U.S. woman to travel in space in June when the space shuttle *Challenger* was launched from Cape Canaveral, Florida. The *Challenger,* on its second flight, also carried four men in its crew. Ride, a physicist, held the position of mission specialist. The crew members deployed a Canadian communications satellite to hover over the Pacific Ocean at an altitude of 22,000 miles, and a similar satellite was deployed for Southeast Asian nations.

The House of Representatives defeated a plan to revive the proposed Equal Right Amendment by only six votes short of the two-thirds majority needed.

1984

The thirty-ninth Democratic National Convention nominated former Vice President Walter F. Mondale of Minnesota as candidate for president. He then chose Rep. Geraldine A. Ferraro of Queens, N.Y., by acclamation for vice-president. She was the first woman to be named for the office on a major party ticket.

The Jaycees finally admitted women members. The all-male civic organization bowed to the Supreme Court decision which opened up male-only organizations to female membership.

Marital rape was outlawed in New York. The State Court of Appeals, the highest tribunal, ruled that married men could be prosecuted for raping their wives.

1985

The Equal Rights Amendment was introduced in both houses of the Ninety-Ninth Congress in January.

The first woman conservative rabbi was ordained. Amy Eilberg entered the clergy with a ceremony in New York.

1987

A surrogate mother contract was tested in court for the first time in 1987, and the custody decision handed down favored the biological father and his wife over the surrogate. The case, known as the "Baby M" case, held that the contract was "constitutionally protected" and that the father was better able to care for the child than the biological mother.

In October, lesbian and gay rights supporters marched on Washington. Over 500,000 people attended the march, but major news sources opted not to report the event.

1988

The New Jersey Supreme Court overturned a lower court ruling on the "Baby M" case. The court in its ruling prohibited a natural parent from being deprived of parental rights absent any proof that the parent had neglected or abandoned the child. The court also ruled that surrogacy contracts were legal if there was no fee, and they had no binding agreement forcing the natural mother to give up the child.

1989

Rev. Barbara Harris was consecrated as the first female bishop in the Angelican Church.

In April a march on Washington supported a pro-choice stand on reproductive freedom. One of the largest such marches in U.S. history, it brought over 500,000 people to the Capitol steps.

The Bush administration attorneys requested the Supreme Court to overturn *Roe* v. *Wade.*

In *Webster* v. *Reproductive Health Services,* the Supreme Court upheld states' rights to regulate abortion, gutting much of *Roe* v. *Wade* and leaving abortion rights at risk. Feminists vowed never to give up the right to reproductive freedom.

A pro-choice "March for Women's Lives" sponsored by the National Organization for Women drew between 300,000 and 500,000 marchers to the Capitol.

1990

President George Bush vetoed the Civil Rights Act of 1990 on the grounds that it supported quotas in the workplace. He had also vetoed the family-leave bill that gave workers the right to take unpaid leave to care for sick family members or newborn or newly adopted babies.

Cardinal John J. O'Connor, Catholic archbishop of New York City, threatened politicians who supported abortion rights with excommunication.

Antonia C. Novello was the first woman to be appointed Surgeon General of the United States Health Service.

1991

Judge Clarence Thomas was confirmed by the Senate to serve on the Supreme Court after being accused of sexual harassment by Anita Hill, a law professor and Thomas's former aide.

The federal "gag rule" prohibiting federally funded family planning clinics from advising patients about abortion was upheld in the Supreme Court.

1992

The "Year of the Woman" saw a record number of women run for public office, placing record numbers in the House (47) and Senate (6). Carol Moseley Braun became the first black female to sit in the Senate. She defeated Senator Alan Dixon, long-time incumbent, who had supported Clarence Thomas's nomination to the Supreme Court after Anita Hill's accusation of sexual harassment.

The Church of England voted to allow women to become priests.

Colonel Margarethe Cammermeyer, a Vietnam veteran, was discharged from the Washington State Army National Guard because she was lesbian.

1993

Ruth Bader Ginsburg, an advocate for women's rights and avowedly pro-choice, was appointed the second female justice of the U.S. Supreme Court.

Opponents to reproductive rights became more violent. Two physicians known to perform abortions were shot, one of them killed. "Operation Rescue" and other abortion foes vowed to continue the fight with any means necessary, especially after the swearing in of President Bill Clinton, a supporter of abortion rights.

Sources

Facts on File, World News Digest, 1990–1993.

"Twenty Years of the U.S. Women's Movement," *Ms.* 3, no. 1, July/August 1992.

Phyllis J. Read and Bernard L. Witlieb
1992 *The Book of Women's Firsts* (New York: Random House).

The World Almanac,
1978–1992.

A Vindication of the Rights of Woman

Mary Wollstonecraft

It is not uncommon to begin the history of the nineteenth-century wave of feminism and women's rights movements with the work of the eighteenth-century British writer and radical thinker Mary Wollstonecraft. After all, her work had great influence in Europe and the United States, and The Rights of Woman *was read as inspiration by the founders of Seneca Falls, Lucretia Mott, Elizabeth Cady Stanton, and others.*

Born in Spitalfields, a poor district near London, in 1759, Wollstonecraft was destined to live a hard and extraordinary life for women of her time and to learn from experience both the value and the elusiveness of strength and independence in the lives of women. Her father became a drunkard after financial failure and periodically beat his wife and family and trifled away their remaining money. To escape conditions at home, her sister Eliza had married badly while still in her teens, and Wollstonecraft believed she had to spirit Eliza away to safety. On their own, the two sisters found it very hard to earn a living. All but two or three occupations were closed to them as women, and Eliza was not well. With a friend, Fanny Blood, they opened a school for girls; but, ill prepared and untrained, they failed financially, and the school closed.

Having educated herself, Wollstonecraft moved to London and began earning a living at writing—at first books about educating girls and stories for children. But through her publisher, she began to move in intellectual and radical circles and to grow in insight and awareness. In 1792 she published the Vindication of the Rights of Woman, *which was well read and earned her some fame. Later in that year, she moved to Paris to observe firsthand the revolution in France. There she began a history of the French Revolution, later published, and met the American Gilbert Imlay, with whom she lived and had a daughter, Fanny. After Imlay left her in 1795, she returned to London, depressed and heartbroken, to rebuild her life and move in once again with the friends she had known. Soon she met the radical philosopher William Godwin, whom she agreed to marry when she became pregnant. In 1797, shortly after the birth of her daughter Mary, she died at the age of thirty-eight.*

The following excerpts from The Rights of Woman *are from the introduction and the dedication, in which Wollstonecraft sets forth her main principles: Women are turned into weak, petty creatures—mere "alluring objects" (sex objects?)—by neglected education, by manners and morals (what we today would probably call sex-role socialization), and by flattery and dependence. She chides M. Talleyrand-Périgord, and with him the nation of men, to apply to women the same concern and commitment for "human" rights and freedom that they hold for men.*

Author's Introduction

After considering the historic page, and viewing the living world with anxious solicitude, the most melancholy emotions of sorrowful indignation have depressed my spirits, and I have sighed when obliged to confess that either Nature has made a great difference between man and man, or that the civilisation which has hitherto taken place in the world has been very partial. I have turned over various books written on the subject of education, and patiently observed the conduct of parents and the management of schools; but what has been the result?—a profound conviction that the neglected education of my fellow-creatures is the grand source of the misery I deplore, and that women, in particular, are rendered weak and wretched by a variety of concurring causes, originating from one hasty conclusion. The conduct and manners of women, in fact, evidently prove that their minds are not in a healthy state; for, like the flowers which are planted in too rich a soil, strength and usefulness are sacrificed to beauty;

---

and the flaunting leaves, after having pleased a fastidious eye, fade, disregarded on the stalk, long before the season when they ought to have arrived at maturity. One cause of this barren blooming I attribute to a false system of education, gathered from the books written on this subject by men who, considering females rather as women than human creatures, have been more anxious to make them alluring mistresses than affectionate wives and rational mothers; and the understanding of the sex has been so bubbled by this specious homage, that the civilised women of the present century, with a few exceptions, are only anxious to inspire love, when they ought to cherish a nobler ambition, and by their abilities and virtues exact respect.

In a treatise, therefore, on female rights and manners, the works which have been particularly written for their improvement must not be overlooked, especially when it is asserted, in direct terms, that the minds of women are enfeebled by false refinement; that the books of instruction, written by men of genius, have had the same tendency as more frivolous productions; and that, in the true style of Mahometanism, they are treated as a kind of subordinate beings, and not as a part of the human species, when improvable reason is allowed to be the dignified distinction which raises men above the brute creation, and puts a natural sceptre in a feeble hand.

Yet, because I am a woman, I would not lead my readers to suppose that I mean violently to agitate the contested question respecting the quality or inferiority of the sex; but as the subject lies in my way, and I cannot pass it over without subjecting the main tendency of my reasoning to misconstruction, I shall stop a moment to deliver, in a few words, my opinion. In the government of the physical world it is observable that the female in point of strength is, in general, inferior to the male. This is the law of Nature; and it does not appear to be suspended or abrogated in favour of woman. A degree of physical superiority cannot, therefore, be denied, and it is a noble prerogative! But not content with this natural preeminence, men endeavour to sink us still lower, merely to render us alluring objects for a moment; and women, intoxicated by the adoration which men, under the influence of their senses, pay them, do not seek to obtain a durable interest in their hearts, or to become the friends of the fellow-creatures who find amusement in their society.

I am aware of an obvious inference. From every quarter have I heard exclamations against masculine women, but where are they to be found? If by this appellation men mean to inveigh against their ardour in hunting, shooting, and gaming, I shall most cordially join in the cry; but if it be against the imitation of manly virtues, or, more properly speaking, the attainment of those talents and virtues, the exercise of which ennobles the human character, and which raises females in the scale of animal being, when they are comprehensively termed mankind, all those who view them with a philosophic eye must, I should think, wish with me, that they may every day grow more and more masculine.

This discussion naturally divides the subject. I shall first consider women in the grand light of human creatures, who, in common with men, are placed on this earth to unfold their faculties; and afterwards I shall more particularly point out their peculiar designation.

I wish also to steer clear of an error which many respectable writers have fallen into; for the instruction which has hitherto been addressed to women, has rather been applicable to *ladies,* if the little indirect advice that is scattered through "Sandford and Merton" be excepted; but, addressing my sex in a firmer tone, I pay particular attention to those in the middle class, because they appear to be in the most natural state. Perhaps the seeds of false refinement, immorality, and vanity, have ever been shed by the great. Weak, artificial beings, raised above the common wants and affections of their race, in a premature unnatural manner, undermine the very foundation of virtue, and spread corruption through the whole mass of society! As a class of mankind they have the strongest claim to pity; the education of the rich tends to render them vain and helpless, and the unfolding mind is not strengthened by the practice of those duties which dignify the human character. They only live to amuse themselves, and by the same law which in Nature invariably produces certain effects, they soon only afford barren amusement.

But as I purpose taking a separate view of the different ranks of society, and of the moral character of women in each, this hint is for the present sufficient; and I have only alluded to the subject because it appears to me to be the very essence of an introduction to give a cursory account of the contents of the work it introduces.

My own sex, I hope, will excuse me, if I treat them like rational creatures, instead of flattering their *fascinating* graces, and viewing them as if they were in a state of perpetual childhood, unable to stand alone. I earnestly wish to point out in what true dignity and human happiness consists. I wish to persuade women to endeavor to acquire strength, both of mind and body, and to convince them that the soft phrases, susceptibility of heart, delicacy of sentiment, and refinement of taste, are almost synonymous with epithets of weakness, and that those beings who are only the objects of pity, and that kind of love which has been termed its sister, will soon become objects of contempt.

Dismissing, then, those pretty feminine phrases, which the men condescendingly use to soften our slavish dependence, and despising that weak elegancy of mind, exquisite sensibility, and sweet docility of manners, supposed to be the sexual characteristics of the weaker vessel, I wish to show that elegance is inferior to virtue, that the first object of laudable ambition is to obtain a character as a human being, regardless of the distinction of sex, and that secondary views should be brought to this simple touchstone.

This is a rough sketch of my plan; and should I express my conviction with the energetic emotions that I feel whenever I think of the subject, the dictates of experience and reflection will be felt by some of my readers. Animated by this important object, I shall disdain to cull my phrases or polish my style. I aim at being useful, and sincerity will render me unaffected; for, wishing rather to persuade by the force of my arguments than dazzle by the elegance of my language, I shall not waste my time in rounding periods, or in fabricating the turgid bombast of artificial feelings, which, coming from the head, never reach the heart. I shall be employed about things, not words! and, anxious to render my sex more respectable members of society, I shall try to avoid that flowery diction which has slided from essays into novels, and from novels into familiar letters and conversation.

These pretty superlatives, dropping glibly from the tongue, vitiate the taste, and create a kind of sickly delicacy that turns away from simple unadorned truth; and a deluge of false sentiments and overstretched feelings, stifling the natural emotions of the heart, render the domestic pleasures insipid, that ought to sweeten the exercise of those severe duties, which educate a rational and immortal being for a nobler field of action.

The education of women has of late been more attended to than formerly; yet they are still reckoned a frivolous sex, and ridiculed or pitied by the writers who endeavour by satire or instruction to improve them. It is acknowledged that they spend many of the first years of their lives in acquiring a smattering of accomplishments; meanwhile strength of body and mind are sacrificed to libertine notions of beauty, to the desire of establishing themselves—the only way women can rise in the world—by marriage. And this desire making mere animals of them, when they marry they act as such children may be expected to act—they dress, they paint, and nickname God's creatures. Surely these weak beings are only fit for a seraglio! Can they be expected to govern a family with judgment, or take care of the poor babes whom they bring into the world?

If, then, it can be fairly deduced from the present conduct of the sex, from the prevalent fondness for pleasure which takes place of ambition and those nobler passions that open and enlarge the soul, that the instruction which women have hitherto received has only tended, with the constitution of civil society, to render them insignificant objects of desire—mere propagators of fools!—if it can be proved that in aiming to accomplish them, without cultivating their understandings, they are taken out of their sphere of duties, and made ridiculous and useless when the short-lived bloom of beauty is over,[1] I presume that *rational* men will excuse me for endeavouring to persuade them to become more masculine and respectable.

Indeed the word masculine is only a bugbear; there is little reason to fear that women will acquire too much courage or fortitude, for their apparent inferiority with respect to bodily strength must render them in some degree dependent on men in the various relations of life; but why should it be increased by prejudices that give a sex to virtue, and confound simple truths with sensual reveries?

Women are, in fact, so much degraded by mistaken notions of female excellence, that I do not mean to add a paradox when I assert that this artificial weakness produces a propensity to tyrannise, and gives birth to cunning, the natural opponent of strength, which leads them to play off those contemptible infantine airs that undermine esteem even whilst they excite desire. Let men become more chaste and modest, and if women do not grow wiser in the same ratio, it will be clear that they have weaker understandings. It seems scarcely necessary to say that I now speak of the sex in general. Many individuals have more sense than their male relatives; and, as nothing preponderates where there is a constant struggle for an equilibrium without it has naturally more gravity, some women govern their husbands without degrading themselves, because intellect will always govern.

To M. Talleyrand-Périgord Late Bishop of Autun

Sir,—Having read with great pleasure a pamphlet which you have lately published, I dedicate this volume to you—the first dedication that I have ever written, to induce you to read it with attention; and, because I think that you will understand me, which I do not suppose many pert witlings will, who may ridicule the arguments they are unable to answer. But, sir, I carry my respect for your understanding still farther; so far that I am confident you will not throw my work aside, and hastily conclude that I am in the wrong, because you did not view the subject in the same light yourself. And pardon my frankness, but I must observe, that you treated it in too cursory a manner, contented to consider it as it had been considered formerly, when the rights of man, not to advert to woman, were trampled on as chimerical—I call upon you, therefore, now to weigh what I have advanced respecting the rights of woman and national education; and I call with the firm tone of humanity, for my arguments, sir, are dictated by a disinterested spirit—I plead for my sex, not for myself. Independence I have long considered as the grand blessing of life, the basis of every virtue; and independence I will ever secure by contracting my wants, though I were to live on a barren heath.

It is then an affection for the whole human race that makes my pen dart rapidly along to support what I believe to be the cause of virtue; and the same motive leads me earnestly to wish to see woman placed in a station in which she would advance, instead of retarding, the progress of those glorious principles that give a substance to morality. My opinion, indeed, respecting the rights and duties of woman seems to flow so naturally from these simple principles, that I think it scarcely possible but that some of the enlarged minds who formed your admirable constitution will coincide with me.

In France there is undoubtedly a more general diffusion of knowledge than in any part of the European world, and I attribute it, in a great measure, to the social intercourse which has long subsisted between the sexes. It is true—I utter my sentiments with freedom—that in France the very essence of sensuality has been extracted to regale the voluptuary, and a kind of sentimental lust has prevailed, which, together with the system of duplicity that the whole tenor of their political and civil government taught, have given a sinister sort of sagacity to the French character, properly termed *finesse,* from which naturally flow a polish of manners that injures the substance by hunting sincerity out of society. And modesty, the fairest garb of virtue! has been more grossly insulted in France than even in England, till their women have treated as *prudish* that attention to decency which brutes instinctively observe.

Manners and morals are so nearly allied that they have often been confounded; but, though the former should only be the natural reflection of the latter, yet, when various causes have produced factitious and corrupt manners, which are very early caught, morality becomes an empty name. The personal reserve, and sacred respect for cleanliness and delicacy in domestic life, which French women almost despise, are the graceful pillars of modesty; but, far from despising them, if the pure flame of patriotism have reached their bosoms, they should labour to improve the morals of their fellow-citizens, by teaching men, not only to respect modesty in women, but to acquire it themselves, as the only way to merit their esteem.

Contending for the rights of woman, my main argument is built on this simple principle, that if she be not prepared by education to become the companion of man, she will stop the progress of knowledge and virtue; for truth must be common to all, or it will be inefficacious with respect to its influence on general practice. And how can woman be expected to cooperate unless she knows why she ought to be virtuous? unless freedom strengthens her reason till she comprehends her duty, and see in what manner it is connected with her real good. If children are to be educated to understand the true principle of patriotism, their mother must be a patriot; and the love of mankind, from which an orderly train of virtues spring, can only be produced by considering the moral and civil interest of mankind; but the education and situation of woman at present shuts her out from such investigations.

In this work I have produced many arguments, which to me were conclusive, to prove that the prevailing notion respecting a sexual character was subversive of morality, and I have contended, that to render the human body and mind more perfect, chastity must more universally prevail, and that chastity will never be respected in the male world till the person of a woman is not, as it were, idolised, when little virtue or sense embellish it with the grand traces of mental beauty, or the interesting simplicity of affection.

Consider, sir, dispassionately these observations, for a glimpse of this truth seemed to open before you when you observed, "that to see one-half of the human race excluded by the other from all participation of government was a political phenomenon that, according to abstract principles, it was impossible to explain." If so, on what does your constitution rest? If the abstract rights of man will bear discussion and explanation, those of woman, by a parity of reasoning, will not shrink from the same test; though a different opinion prevails in this country, built on the very arguments which you use to justify the oppression of woman—prescription.

Consider—I address you as a legislator—whether, when men contend for their freedom, and to be allowed to judge for themselves respecting their own happiness, it be not inconsistent and unjust to subjugate women, even though you firmly believe that you are acting in the manner best calculated to promote their happiness? Who made man the exclusive judge, if woman partake with him of the gift of reason?

In this style argue tyrants of every denomination, from the weak king to the weak father of a family; they are all eager to crush reason, yet always assert that they usurp its throne only to be useful. Do you not act a similar part when you *force* all women, by denying them civil and political rights, to remain immured in their families groping in the dark? for surely, sir, you will not assert that a duty can be binding which is not founded on reason? If, indeed, this be their destination, arguments may be drawn from reason; and thus augustly supported, the more understanding women acquire, the more they will be attached to their duty—comprehending it—for unless they comprehend it, unless their morals be fixed on the same immutable principle as those of man, no authority can make them discharge it in a virtuous manner. They may be convenient slaves, but slavery will have its constant effect, degrading the master and the abject dependent.

But if women are to be excluded, without having a voice, from a participation of the natural rights of mankind, prove first, to ward off the charge of injustice and inconsistency, that they want reason, else this flaw in your NEW CONSTITUTION will ever show that man must, in some shape, act like a tyrant, and tyranny, in whatever part of society it rears its brazen front, will ever undermine morality.

I have repeatedly asserted, and produced what appeared to me irrefragable arguments drawn from matters of fact to prove my assertion, that women cannot by force be confined to domestic concerns; for they will, however ignorant, intermeddle with more weighty affairs, neglecting private duties only to disturb, by cunning tricks, the orderly plans of reason which rise above their comprehension.

Besides, whilst they are only made to acquire personal accomplishments, men will seek for pleasure in variety, and faithless husbands will make faithless wives; such ignorant beings, indeed, will be very excusable when, not taught to respect public good, nor allowed any civil rights, they attempt to do themselves justice by retaliation.

The box of mischief thus opened in society, what is to preserve private virtue, the only security of public freedom and universal happiness?

Let there be then no coercion *established* in society, and the common law of gravity prevailing, the sexes will fall into their proper places. And now that more equitable laws are forming your citizens, marriage may become more sacred; your young men may choose wives from motives of affection, and your maidens allow love to root out vanity.

The father of a family will not then weaken his constitution and debase his sentiments by visiting the harlot, nor forget, in obeying the call of appetite, the purpose for which it was implanted. And the mother will not neglect her children to practise the arts of coquetry, when sense and modesty secure her the friendship of her husband.

But, till men become attentive to the duty of a father, it is vain to expect women to spend that time in their nursery which they, "wise in their generation," choose to spend at their glass; for this exertion of cunning is only an instinct of nature to enable them to obtain indirectly a little of that power of which they are unjustly denied a share; for, if women are not permitted to enjoy legitimate rights, they will render both men and themselves vicious to obtain illicit privileges.

I wish, sir, to set some investigations of this kind afloat in France; and should they lead to a confirmation of my principles when your constitution is revised, the Rights of Woman may be respected, if it be fully proved that reason calls for this respect, and loudly demands JUSTICE for one-half of the human race.

I am, Sir,

Yours respectfully,

M. W.

Notes

1. A lively writer (I cannot recollect his name) asks what business women turned of forty have to do in the world?

The Adams Letters

Abigail and John Adams

Abigail Adams (1744–1818) was born in Massachusetts the daughter of an upper-middle-class woman and her husband, who was a minister. Typical of her day, she received no formal education. Her husband, John, of course, fared differently. The son of a respected farmer, he graduated from Harvard in 1755, taught school for a while, studied law, and was admitted to the bar in 1758. Finally he carried on an active political life culminating in his becoming the second president of the United States in 1796.

How different, how predictably different, their lives were; how much opportunity to express his intelligence and energy John had and how little Abigail had. No wonder she had to request of him in 1776 that he "remember the ladies" as John Adams, together with Jefferson and Franklin, was composing the Declaration of Independence. No wonder he quite purposely (as his letter to Sullivan shows) turned her down, calling her a "saucy" girl.

It would be nearly three-quarters of a century later before another such declaration could be written—in Seneca Falls.

From Abigail to John

Braintree
March 31, 1776

—I long to hear that you have declared an independancy—and by the way in the new Code of Laws which I suppose it will be necessary for you to make I desire you would Remember the Ladies, and be more generous and favourable to them than your ancestors. Do not put such unlimited power into the hands of the Husbands. Remember all Men would be tyrants if they could. If perticuliar care and attention is not paid to the Laidies we are determined to foment a Rebelion, and will not hold ourselves bound by any Laws in which we have no voice, or Representation.

That your Sex are Naturally Tyrannical is a Truth so thoroughly established as to admit of no dispute, but such of you as wish to be happy willingly give up the harsh title of Master for the more tender and endearing one of Friend. Why then, not put it out of the power of the vicious and the Lawless to use us with cruelty and indignity with impunity. Men of Sense in all Ages abhor those customs which treat us only as the vassals of your Sex. Regard us then as Beings placed by providence under your protection and in immitation of the Supreem Being make use of that power only for our happiness.

From John to Abigail

April 14, 1776

As to your extraordinary Code of Laws, I cannot but laugh. We have been told that our Struggle has loosened the bands of Government every where. That Children and Apprentices were disobedient—that schools and Colledges were grown turbulent—that Indians slighted their Guardians and Negroes grew insolent to their Masters. But your Letter was the first Intimation that another Tribe more numerous and powerfull than all the rest were grown discontented.—This is rather too coarse a Compliment but you are so saucy, I wont blot it out.

Depend upon it, We know better than to repeal our Masculine systems. Altho they are in full Force, you know they are little more than Theory. We dare not exert our Power in its full Latitude. We are obliged to go fair, and softly, and in Practice you know We are the subjects. We have only the Name of Masters, and rather than give up this, which would compleatly subject us to the Despotism of the Peticoat, I hope General Washington, and all our brave Heroes would fight.

From John Adams to James Sullivan

Philadelphia, 26 May, 1776.

. . . It is certain, in theory, that the only moral foundation of government is, the consent of the people. But to what an extent shall we carry this principle? Shall we say that every individual of the community, old and young, male and female, as well as rich and poor, must consent, expressly, to every act of legislation? No, you will say, this is impossible. How, then does the right arise in the majority to govern the minority, against their will? Whence arises the right of the men to govern the women, without their consent? Whence the right of the old to bind the young, without theirs?

But let us first suppose that the whole community, of every age, rank, sex, and condition, has a right to vote. This community is assembled. A motion is made, and carried by a majority of one voice. The minority will not agree to this. Whence arises the right of the majority to govern, and the obligation of the minority to obey?

From necessity, you will say, because there can be no other rule.

But why exclude women?

You will say, because their delicacy renders them unfit for practice and experience in the great businesses of life, and the hardy enterprises of war, as well as the arduous cares of state. Besides, their attention is so much engaged with the necessary nurture of their children, that nature has made them fittest for domestic cares. And children have not judgment or will of their own. True. But will not these reasons apply to others? Is it not equally true, that men in general, in every society, who are wholly destitute of property, are also too little acquainted with public affairs to form a right judgment, and too dependent upon other men to have a will of their own? If this is a fact, if you give to every man who has no property, a vote, will you not make a fine encouraging provision for corruption, by your fundamental law? Such is the frailty of the human heart, that very few men who have no property, have any judgment of their own. They talk and vote as they are directed by some man of property, who has attached their minds to his interest. . . .

Your idea that those laws which affect the lives and personal liberty of all, or which inflict corporal punishment, affect those who are not qualified to vote, as well as those who are, is just. But so they do women, as well as men; children, as well as adults. What reason should there be for excluding a man of twenty years eleven months and twenty-seven days old, from a vote, when you admit one who is twenty-one? The reason is, you must fix upon some period in life, when the understanding and will of men in general, is fit to be trusted by the public. Will not the same reason justify the state in fixing upon some certain quantity of property, as a qualification?

The same reasoning which will induce you to admit all men who have no property, to vote, with those who have, for those laws which affect the person, will prove that you ought to admit women and children; for, generally speaking, women and children have as good judgments, and as independent minds, as those men who are wholly destitute of property; these last being to all intents and purposes as much dependent upon others, who will please to feed, clothe, and employ them, as women are upon their husbands, or children on their parents. . . .

Depend upon it, Sir, it is dangerous to open so fruitful a source of controversy and altercation as would be opened by attempting to alter the qualifications of voters; there will be no end of it. New claims will arise; women will demand a vote; lads from twelve to twenty-one will think their rights not enough attended to; and every man who has not a farthing, will demand an equal voice with any other, in all acts of state. It tends to confound and destroy all distinctions, and prostrate all ranks to one common level.

Historical Precedent: Nineteenth-Century Feminists

Judith Hole
Ellen Levine

At the time Rebirth of Feminism *was being written, Judith Hole was a producer for CBS television news. Her credits included shows on the value of homemaking, stepparents, mother-daughter profiles, and the politics of cancer. Ellen Levine, a writer, photographer, and lawyer, participated in the publication of* Notes from the Third Year *and the anthology* Radical Feminism. *She also published a book of her feminist cartoons,* All She Needs. *Here Hole and Levine introduce us briefly to the characters and events of nineteenth-century movement for suffrage and women's rights.*

Introduction: Historical Precedent

THE CONTEMPORARY WOMEN'S MOVEMENT IS NOT the first such movement in American history to offer a wide-ranging feminist critique of society. In fact, much of what seems "radical" in contemporary feminist analysis parallels the critique made by the feminists of the 19th century. Both the early and the contemporary feminists have engaged in a fundamental re-examination of the role of women in all spheres of life, and of the relationships of men and women in all social, political, economic and cultural institutions. Both have defined women as an oppressed group and have traced the origin of women's subjugation to male-defined and male-dominated social institutions and value-systems.

When the early feminist movement emerged in the 19th century, the "woman issue" was extensively debated in the national press, in political gatherings, and from Church pulpits. The women's groups, their platforms, and their leaders, although not always well received or understood, were extremely well known. Until recently, however, that early feminist movement has been only cursorily discussed in American history textbooks, and then only in terms of the drive for suffrage. Even a brief reading of early feminist writings and of the few histories that have dealt specifically with the woman's movement (as it was called then) reveals that the drive for suffrage became the single focus of the movement only after several decades of a more multi-issued campaign for women's equality.

The woman's movement emerged during the 1800's. It was a time of geographic expansion, industrial development, growth of social reform movements, and a general intellectual ferment with a philosophical emphasis on individual freedom, the "rights of man" and universal education.

In fact, some of the earliest efforts to extend opportunities to women were made in the field of education. In 1833, Oberlin became the first college to open its doors to both men and women. Although female education at Oberlin was regarded as necessary to ensure the development of good and proper wives and mothers, the open admission policy paved the way for the founding of other schools, some devoted entirely to women's education.[1] Much of the groundbreaking work in education was done by Emma Willard, who had campaigned vigorously for educational facilities for women beginning in the early 1820's. Frances Wright, one of the first women orators, was also a strong advocate of education for women. She viewed women as an oppressed group and argued that, "Until women assume the place in society which good sense and good feeling alike assign to them, human improvement must advance but feebly."[2] Central to her discussion of the inequalities between the sexes was a particular concern with the need for equal educational training for women.

It was in the abolition movement of the 1830's, however, that the woman's rights movement as such had its political origins. When women began working in earnest for the abolition of slavery, they quickly learned that they could not function as political equals with their male abolitionist friends. Not only were they barred from membership in some organizations, but they had to wage an uphill battle for the right simply to speak in public. Sarah and Angelina Grimké, daughters of a South Carolina slaveholding family, were among the first to fight this battle. Early in their lives the sisters left South Carolina, moved North, and began to speak out publicly on the abolition issue. Within a short time they drew the wrath of different sectors of society. A Pastoral letter from the Council of the Congregationalist Ministers of Massachusetts typified the attack:

> *The appropriate duties and influence of woman are clearly stated in the New Testament. . . . The power of woman is her dependence, flowing from the consciousness of that weakness which God has given her for her protection. . . . When she assumes the place and tone of man as a public reformer . . . she yields the power which God has given her . . . and her character becomes unnatural.*[3]

The brutal and unceasing attacks (sometimes physical) on the women convinced the Grimkés that the issues of freedom for slaves and freedom for women were inextricably linked. The women began to speak about both issues, but because of the objections from male abolitionists who were afraid that discussions of woman's rights would "muddy the waters," they often spoke about the "woman question" as a separate issue. (In fact, Lucy Stone, an early feminist and abolitionist, lectured on abolition on Saturdays and Sundays and on women's rights during the week.)

In an 1837 letter to the President of the Boston Female Anti-Slavery Society—by that time many female anti-slavery societies had been established in response to the exclusionary policy of the male abolitionist groups—Sarah Grimké addressed herself directly to the question of women's status:

> *All history attests that man has subjugated woman to his will, used her as a means to promote his selfish gratification, to minister to his sensual pleasures, to be instrumental in promoting his comfort; but never has he desired to elevate her to that rank she was created to fill. He has done all he could to debase and enslave her mind; and now he looks triumphantly on the ruin he has wrought, and says, the being he has thus deeply injured is his inferior. . . . But I ask no favors for my sex. . . . All I ask of our brethren is, that they will take their feet from off our necks and permit us to stand upright on that ground which God designed us to occupy.*[4]

The Grimkés challenged both the assumption of the "natural superiority of man" and the social institutions predicated on that assumption. For example, in her "Letters on the Equality of the Sexes," Sarah Grimké argued against both religious dogma and the institution of marriage. Two brief examples are indicative:

> *. . . Adam's ready acquiescence with his wife's proposal, does not savor much of that superiority* in strength of mind, *which is arrogated by man.*[5]

> *. . . man has exercised the most unlimited and brutal power over woman, in the peculiar character of husband—a word in most countries synonymous with tyrant. . . . Woman, instead of being elevated by her union with man, which might be expected from an alliance with a superior being, is in reality lowered. She generally loses her individuality, her independent character, her moral being. She becomes absorbed into*

him, and henceforth is looked at, and acts through the medium of her husband.[6]

They attacked as well the manifestations of "male superiority" in the employment market. In a letter "On the Condition of Women in the United States" Sarah Grimké wrote of:

... the disproportionate value set on the time and labor of men and of women. A man who is engaged in teaching, can always, I believe, command a higher price for tuition than a woman—even when he teaches the same branches, and is not in any respect superior to the woman. ... [Or] for example, in tailoring, a man has twice, or three times as much for making a waistcoat or pantaloons as a woman, although the work done by each may be equally good.[7]

The abolition movement continued to expand, and in 1840 a World Anti-Slavery Convention was held in London. The American delegation included a group of women, among them Lucretia Mott and Elizabeth Cady Stanton. In Volume I of the *History of Woman Suffrage,* written and edited by Stanton, Susan B. Anthony and Matilda Joslyn Gage, the authors note that the mere presence of women delegates produced an "... excitement and vehemence of protest and denunciation [that] could not have been greater, if the news had come that the French were about to invade England."[8] The women were relegated to the galleries and prohibited from participating in any of the proceedings. That society at large frowned upon women participating in political activities was one thing; that the leading male radicals, those most concerned with social inequalities, should also discriminate against women was quite another. The events at the world conference reinforced the women's growing awareness that the battle for the abolition of Negro slavery could never be won without a battle for the abolition of woman's slavery:

As Lucretia Mott and Elizabeth Cady Stanton wended their way arm in arm down Great Queen Street that night, reviewing the exciting scenes of the day, they agreed to hold a woman's rights convention on their return to America, as the men to whom they had just listened had manifested their great need of some education on that question.[9]

Mott and Stanton returned to America and continued their abolitionist work as well as pressing for state legislative reforms on woman's property and family rights. Although the women had discussed the idea of calling a public meeting on woman's rights, the possibility did not materialize until eight years after the London Convention. On July 14, 1848, they placed a small notice in the *Seneca* (New York) *County Courier* announcing a "Woman's Rights Convention." Five days later, on July 19 and 20, some three hundred interested women and men, coming from as far as fifty miles, crowded into the small Wesleyan Chapel (now a gas station) and approved a Declaration of Sentiments (modeled on the Declaration of Independence) and twelve Resolutions. The delineation of issues in the Declaration bears a startling resemblance to contemporary feminist writings. Some excerpts are illustrative:

We hold these truths to be self-evident: that all men and women are created equal; that they are endowed by their Creator with certain inalienable rights; that among these are life, liberty, and the pursuit of happiness;

.... The history of mankind is a history of repeated injuries and usurpations on the part of man toward woman, having in direct object the establishment of an absolute tyranny over her. To prove this, let facts be submitted to a candid world. ...

He has compelled her to submit to laws, in the formation of which she has no voice. ...

He has made her, if married, in the eye of the law, civilly dead. ...

He has monopolized nearly all the profitable employments, and from those she is permitted to follow, she receives but a scanty remuneration. He closes against her all the avenues to wealth and distinction which he considers most honorable to himself. As a teacher of theology, medicine, or law, she is not known.

He allows her in Church, as well as State, but a subordinate position, claiming Apostolic authority for her exclusion from the ministry, and, with some exceptions, from any public participation in the affairs of the Church.

He has created a false public sentiment by giving to the world a different code of morals for men and women, by which moral delinquencies which exclude women from society, are not only tolerated, but deemed of little account in man.

He has usurped the prerogative of Jehovah himself, claiming it as his right to assign for her a sphere of action, when that belongs to her conscience and to her God.

He has endeavored, in every way that he could, to destroy her confidence in her own powers, to lessen her self-respect, and to make her willing to lead a dependent and abject life.

Included in the list of twelve resolutions was one which read: "*Resolved,* That it is the duty of the women of this country to secure to themselves their sacred right to the elective franchise."

Although the Seneca Falls Convention is considered the official beginning of the woman's suffrage movement, it is important to reiterate that the goal of the early woman's rights movement was not limited to the demand for suffrage. In fact, the suffrage resolution was included only after lengthy debate, and was the only resolution not accepted unanimously. Those participants at the Convention who actively opposed the inclusion of the suffrage resolution:

. . . feared a demand for the right to vote would defeat others they deemed more rational, and make the whole movement ridiculous. But Mrs. Stanton and Frederick Douglass seeing that the power to choose rulers and make laws, was the right by which all others could be secured, persistently advocated the resolution. . . .[10]

Far more important to most of the women at the Convention was their desire to gain control of their property and earnings, guardianship of their children, rights to divorce, etc. Notwithstanding the disagreements at the Convention, the Seneca Falls meeting was of great historical significance. As Flexner has noted:

. . . [The women] themselves were fully aware of the nature of the step they were taking; today's debt to them has been inadequately acknowledged. . . . Beginning in 1848 it was possible for women who rebelled against the circumstances of their lives, to know that they were not alone—although often the news reached them only through a vitriolic sermon or an abusive newspaper editorial. But a movement had been launched which they could either join, or ignore, that would leave its imprint on the lives of their daughters and of women throughout the world.[11]

From 1848 until the beginning of the Civil War, Woman's Rights Conventions were held nearly every year in different cities in the East and Midwest. The 1850 Convention in Salem, Ohio:

. . . had one peculiar characteristic. It was officered entirely by women; not a man was allowed to sit on the platform, to speak, or vote. Never did men so suffer. *They implored just to say a word; but no; the President was inflexible—no man should be heard. If one meekly arose to make a suggestion he was at once ruled out of order. For the first time in the world's history, men learned how it felt to sit in silence when questions in which they were interested were under discussion.*[12]

As the woman's movement gained in strength, attacks upon it became more vitriolic. In newspaper editorials and church sermons anti-feminists argued vociferously that the public arena was not the proper place for women. In response to such criticism, Stanton wrote in an article in the Rochester, New York *National Reformer:*

If God has assigned a sphere to man and one to woman, we claim the right to judge ourselves of His design in reference to us, *and we accord to man the same privilege. . . . We have all seen a man making a jackass of himself in the pulpit, at the bar, or in our legislative halls. . . . Now, is it to be wondered at that woman has some doubts about the present position assigned her being the true one, when her every-day experience shows her that man makes such fatal mistakes in regard to himself?*[13]

It was abundantly clear to the women that they could not rely on the pulpit or the "establishment" press for either factual or sympathetic reportage; nor could they use the press as a means to disseminate their ideas. As a result they depended on the abolitionist papers of the day, and in addition founded a number of independent women's journals including *The Lily, The Una, Woman's Advocate, Pittsburgh Visiter* [sic], etc.

One of the many issues with which the women activists were concerned was dress reform. Some began to wear the "bloomer" costume (a misnomer since Amelia Bloomer, although an advocate of the loose-fitting dress, was neither its originator nor the first to wear it) in protest against the tight-fitting and singularly uncomfortable cinched-waisted stays and layers of petticoats. However, as Flexner has noted, "The attempt at dress reform, although badly needed, was not only unsuccessful, but boomeranged and had to be abandoned."[14] Women's rights advocates became known as "bloomers" and the movement for equal rights as well as the individual women were subjected to increasing ridicule. Elizabeth Cady Stanton, one of the earliest to wear the more comfortable outfit, was one of the first to suggest its rejection. In a letter to Susan B. Anthony she wrote:

> *We put the dress on for greater freedom, but what is physical freedom compared with mental bondage? . . . It is not wise, Susan, to use up so much energy and feeling that way. You can put them to better use. I speak from experience.*[15]

When the Civil War began in 1861, woman's rights advocates were urged to abandon their cause and support the war effort. Although Anthony and Stanton continued arguing that any battle for freedom must include woman's freedom, the woman's movement activities essentially stopped for the duration of the War. After the War and the ratification of the 13th Amendment abolishing slavery (for which the women activists had campaigned vigorously), the abolitionists began to press for passage of a 14th Amendment to secure the rights, privileges and immunities of citizens (the new freedmen) under the law. In the second section of the proposed Amendment, however, the word "male" appeared, introducing a sex distinction into the Constitution for the first time. Shocked and enraged by the introduction of the word "male," the women activists mounted an extensive campaign to eliminate it. They were dismayed to find no one, neither the Republican Administration nor their old abolitionist allies, had any intention of "complicating" the campaign for Negroes' rights by advocating women's rights as well. Over and over again the women were told, "This is the Negroes' hour." The authors of *History of Woman Suffrage* analyzed the women's situation:

> *During the six years they held their own claims in abeyance to the slaves of the South, and labored to inspire the people with enthusiasm for the great measures of the Republican party, they were highly honored as "wise, loyal, and clear-sighted." But again when the slaves were emancipated and they asked that women should be recognized in the reconstruction as citizens of the Republic, equal before the law, all these transcendent virtues vanished like dew before the morning sun. And thus it ever is so long as woman labors to second man's endeavors and exalt* his sex *above her own, her virtues pass unquestioned; but when she dares to demand rights and privileges for herself, her motives, manners, dress, personal appearance, character, are subjects for ridicule and detraction.*[16]

The women met with the same response when they campaigned to get the word "sex" added to the proposed 15th Amendment which would prohibit the denial of suffrage on account of race.[17]

As a result of these setbacks, the woman's movement assumed as its first priority the drive for woman's suffrage. It must be noted, however, that while nearly all the women activists agreed on the need for suffrage, in 1869 the movement split into two major factions over ideological and tactical questions. In May of that year, Susan B. Anthony and Elizabeth Cady Stanton organized the National Woman Suffrage Association. Six months later, Lucy Stone and others organized the American Woman Suffrage Association. The American, in an attempt to make the idea of woman's suffrage "respectable," limited its activities to that issue, and refused to address itself to any of the more "controversial" subjects such as marriage or the Church. The National, on the other hand, embraced the broad cause of woman's rights of which the vote was seen primarily as a *means* of achieving those rights. During this time Anthony and Stanton founded *The Revolution* which became one of the best known of the independent women's newspapers. The weekly journal began in January, 1868, and took as its motto, "Men, their rights and nothing more; women, their rights and nothing less." In addition to discussions of suffrage, *The Revolution* examined the institutions of marriage, the law, organized religion, etc. Moreover, the newspaper touched on ". . . such incendiary topics as the double standard and prostitution."[18] Flexner describes the paper:

> *. . . [It] made a contribution to the women's cause out of all proportion to either its size, brief lifespan, or modest circulation. . . . Here was news not to be found elsewhere—of the organization of women typesetters, tailoresses, and laundry workers, of the first women's clubs, of pioneers in the professions, of women abroad. But* The Revolution *did more than just carry news,*

or set a new standard of professionalism for papers edited by and for women. It gave their movement a forum, focus, and direction. It pointed, it led, and it fought, with vigor and vehemence.[19]

The two suffrage organizations coexisted for over twenty years and used some of the same tactics in their campaigns for suffrage: lecture tours, lobbying activities, petition campaigns, etc. The American, however, focused exclusively on state-by-state action, while the National in addition pushed for a woman suffrage Amendment to the federal Constitution. Susan B. Anthony and others also attempted to gain the vote through court decisions. The Supreme Court, however, held in 1875[20] that suffrage was not necessarily one of the privileges and immunities of citizens protected by the 14th Amendment. Thus, although women were *citizens* it was nonetheless permissible, according to the Court, to constitutionally limit the right to vote to males.

During this same period, a strong temperance movement had also emerged. Large numbers of women, including some suffragists, became actively involved in the temperance cause. It is important to note that one of the main reasons women became involved in pressing for laws restricting the sale and consumption of alcohol was that their legal status as married women offered them no protection under the law against either physical abuse or abandonment by a drunken husband. It might be added that the reason separate women's temperance organizations were formed was that women were not permitted to participate in the men's groups. In spite of the fact that temperance was in "women's interests," the growth of the women's temperance movement solidified the liquor and brewing industries' opposition to woman suffrage. As a result, suffrage leaders became convinced of the necessity of keeping the two issues separate.

As the campaign for woman suffrage grew, more and more sympathizers were attracted to the conservative and "respectable" American Association which, as noted above, deliberately limited its work to the single issue of suffrage. After two decades "respectability" won out, and the broad-ranging issues of the earlier movement had been largely subsumed by suffrage. (Even the Stanton-Anthony forces had somewhat redefined their goals and were focusing primarily on suffrage.) By 1890, when the American and the National merged to become the National American Woman Suffrage Association, the woman's movement had, in fact, been transformed into the single-issue suffrage movement. Moreover, although Elizabeth Cady Stanton, NAWSA's first president, was succeeded two years later by Susan B. Anthony, the first women activists with their catholic range of concerns were slowly being replaced by a second group far more limited in their political analysis. It should be noted that Stanton herself, after her two-year term as president of the new organization, withdrew from active work in the suffrage campaign. Although one of the earliest feminist leaders to understand the need for woman suffrage, by this time Stanton believed that the main obstacle to woman's equality was the church and organized religion.

During the entire development of the woman's movement perhaps the argument most often used by anti-feminists was that the subjugation of women was divinely ordained as written in the Bible. Stanton attacked the argument head-on. She and a group of twenty-three women, including three ordained ministers, produced *The Woman's Bible*,[21] which presented a systematic feminist critique of woman's role and image in the Bible. Some Biblical chapters were presented as proof that the Scripture itself was the source of woman's subjugation; others to show that, if reinterpreted, men and women were indeed equals in the Bible, not superior and inferior beings. "We have made a fetish [sic] of the Bible long enough. The time has come to read it as we do all other books, accepting the good and rejecting the evil it teaches."[22] Dismissing the "rib story" as a "petty surgical operation," Stanton argued further that the entire structure of the Bible was predicated on the notion of Eve's (woman's) corruption:

Take the snake, the fruit-tree and the woman from the tableau, and we have no fall, nor frowning Judge, no Inferno, no everlasting punishment,—hence no need of a Savior. Thus the bottom falls out of the whole Christian theology. Here is the reason why in all the Biblical researches and higher criticisms, the scholars never touch the position of women.[23]

Not surprisingly, *The Woman's Bible* was considered by most scandalous and sacrilegious. The Suffrage Association members themselves, with the exception of Anthony and a few others, publicly disavowed Stanton and her work. They feared that the image of the already controversial suffrage movement would be irreparably damaged if the public were to associate it with Stanton's radical tract.

Shortly after the turn of the century, the second generation of woman suffragists came of age and new leaders replaced the old. Carrie Chapman Catt is perhaps the best known; she succeeded Anthony as president of the National American Woman Suffrage Association, which by then had become a large and somewhat unwieldy organization. Although limited gains were achieved (a number of western states had enfranchised women) no major progress was made in the campaign for suffrage until Alice Paul, a young and extremely militant suffragist, became active in the movement. In April, 1913, she formed a small radical group known as the Congressional Union (later reorganized as the Woman's Party[24]) to work exclusively on a campaign for a *federal* woman's suffrage Amendment using any tactical means necessary no matter how unorthodox. Her group organized parades, mass demonstrations, hunger strikes, and its members were on several occasions arrested and jailed.[25] Although many suffragists rejected both the militant style and tactics of the Congressional Union, they nonetheless did consider Paul and her followers in large part responsible for "shocking" the languishing movement into actively pressuring for the federal Amendment. The woman suffrage Amendment (known as the "Anthony Amendment"), introduced into every session of Congress from 1878 on, was finally ratified on August 26, 1920.

Nearly three-quarters of a century had passed since the demand for woman suffrage had first been made at the Seneca Falls Convention. By 1920, so much energy had been expended in achieving the right to vote, that the woman's movement virtually collapsed from exhaustion. To achieve the vote alone, as Carrie Chapman Catt had computed, took:

> *... fifty-two years of pauseless campaign. ... fifty-six campaigns of referenda to male voters; 480 campaigns to get Legislatures to submit suffrage amendments to voters; 47 campaigns to get State constitutional conventions to write woman suffrage into state constitutions; 277 campaigns to get State party conventions to include woman suffrage planks; 30 campaigns to get presidential party conventions to adopt woman suffrage planks in party platforms, and 19 campaigns with 19 successive Congresses.*[26]

With the passage of the 19th Amendment the majority of women activists as well as the public at large assumed that having gained the vote woman's complete equality had been virtually obtained.

It must be remembered, however, that for most of the period that the woman's movement existed, suffrage had not been seen as an all-inclusive goal, but as a means of achieving equality—suffrage was only one element in the wide-ranging feminist critique questioning the fundamental organization of society. Historians, however, have for the most part ignored this radical critique and focused exclusively on the suffrage campaign. By virtue of this omission they have, to all intents and purposes, denied the political significance of the early feminist analysis. Moreover, the summary treatment by historians of the 19th and 20th century drive for woman's suffrage has made that campaign almost a footnote to the abolitionist movement and the campaign for Negro suffrage. In addition, the traditional textbook image of the early feminists—if not wild-eyed women waving placards for the vote, then wild-eyed women swinging axes at saloon doors—has further demeaned the importance of their philosophical analysis.

The woman's movement virtually died in 1920 and, with the exception of a few organizations, feminism was to lie dormant for forty years.

Notes

1. Mount Holyoke opened in 1837; Vassar, 1865; Smith and Wellesley, 1875; Radcliffe, 1879; Bryn Mawr, 1885.

2. Quoted in Eleanor Flexner, *Century of Struggle: The Woman's Rights Movement in the United States* (Cambridge, Mass.: The Belknap Press of Harvard University Press, 1959), p. 27.

3. *History of Woman Suffrage* (Republished by Arno Press and *The New York Times,* New York, 1969). Vol. I, p. 81. Hereafter cited as *HWS.* Volumes I to III were edited by Elizabeth Cady Stanton, Susan B. Anthony and Matilda Joslyn Gage. The first two volumes were published in 1881, the third in 1886. Volume IV was edited by Susan B. Anthony and Ida Husted Harper and was published in 1902. Volumes V and VI were edited by Ida Husted Harper and published in 1922.

4. Sarah M. Grimké, *Letters on the Equality of the Sexes and the Condition of Woman* (Boston: Isaac Kanapp, 1838, reprinted by Source Book Press, New York, 1970), p. 10 ff.

5. *Ibid.,* pp. 9–10.

6. *Ibid.,* pp. 85–86.

7. *Ibid.,* p. 51.

8. *HWS,* p. 54.

9. *HWS,* p. 61.

10. *HWS*, p. 73.

11. Flexner, p. 77.

12. *HWS*, p. 110.

13. *Ibid.*, p. 806.

14. Flexner, p. 83.

15. *Ibid.*, p. 84.

16. *HWS*, Vol. 2, p. 51.

17. The 13th Amendment was ratified in 1865; the 14th in 1868; the 15th in 1870.

18. Flexner, p. 151.

19. *Loc. cit.*

20. *Minor v. Happersett*, 21 Wall. 162, 22 L. Ed. 627 (1875).

21. New York, European Publishing Company, 1895 and 1898, Two Parts.

22. *Ibid.*, II, pp. 7–8.

23. Stanton, letter to the editor of *The Critic* (New York), March 28, 1896, quoted from Aileen S. Kraditor, *The Ideas of the Woman Suffrage Movement, 1890–1920* (New York: Columbia University Press, 1965), n. 11, p. 81.

24. See Chapter 2, National Women's Rights Organizations.

25. A total of 218 women from 26 states were arrested during the first session of the 65th Congress (1917). Ninety-seven went to prison.

26. Carrie Chapman Catt and Nettie Rogers Shuler, *Woman Suffrage and Politics* (New York, 1923), p. 107. Quoted from Flexner, p. 173.

Declaration of Sentiments and Resolutions

Seneca Falls Convention of 1848

The "woman question" had been bubbling heatedly among the intelligentsia and great reformers of the times and in the press at least since women had begun to emerge as strong and active movers in the antislavery societies. A major precipitating factor of early feminist activism occurred in 1840 in London at the World Anti-Slavery Convention attended by many Americans, among them Lucretia Mott, a strong, intelligent Quaker minister and delegate of the American Anti-Slavery Society, and Elizabeth Cady Stanton, then the bride of Henry Stanton, delegate of the American and Foreign Anti-Slavery Society. Although debate over the issue of women's participation in the abolition movement had been sharp in the United States, women had gained some degree of tolerance, if not wholehearted acceptance. Furthermore, the women involved here were educated, spirited women, accustomed to speaking out. They were not prepared for their reception in London: After a full day of debate on the question, on the grounds of morality and propriety (not to mention incompetence), women were finally allowed only to attend, not to participate actively in the discussion. Barred from the central gathering, they were required to sit in a separate curtained gallery, hidden from view, forbidden to speak. Humiliated and furious at the hypocrisy of liberals who could see one brand of oppression but not another, the American women determined to call their own convention on their own issue upon their return home.

Although diverted for nearly eight years, they made good their plan on July 19, 1848, at Seneca Falls, New York. The convention brought forth the following document, written primarily by Stanton and ultimately adopted by the gathering. The decision to use the language of the Declaration of Independence was done pointedly to remind all that women had been omitted from the concerns and safeguards of the original U.S. Constitution. The arguments are clearly in the tradition of eighteenth-century Enlightenment liberalism and nineteenth-century reformism. Notice the breadth of concerns voiced here, suffrage being only a part (and not a well-supported one!) of the commitment. Notice, too, the parallels between these ideas and those of today's women's liberation movement.

WHEN, IN THE COURSE OF HUMAN EVENTS, IT BEcomes necessary for one portion of the family of man to assume among the people of the earth a position different from that which they have hitherto occupied, but one to which the laws of nature and of nature's God entitle them, a decent respect to the opinions of mankind requires that they should declare the causes that impel them to such a course.

We hold these truths to be self-evident: that all men and women are created equal; that they are endowed by their Creator with certain inalienable rights; that among these are life, liberty, and the pursuit of happiness; that to secure these rights governments are instituted, deriving their just powers from the consent of the governed. Whenever any form of government becomes destructive of these ends, it is the right of those who suffer from it to refuse allegiance to it, and to insist upon the institution of a new government, laying its foundation on such principles, and organizing its powers in such form, as to them shall seem most likely to effect their safety and happiness. Prudence, indeed, will dictate that governments long established should not be changed for light and transient causes; and accordingly all experience hath shown that mankind are more disposed to suffer, while evils are sufferable, than to right themselves by abolishing the forms to which they

---

Stanton, Elizabeth Cady, Susan B. Anthony, and Matilda Joslyn Gage, eds. *History of Woman Suffrage,* 2nd ed., Vol. 1, Rochester, N.Y.: Charles Mann, 1889.

were accustomed. But when a long train of abuses and usurpations, pursuing invariably the same object evinces a design to reduce them under absolute despotism, it is their duty to throw off such government, and to provide new guards for their future security. Such has been the patient sufferance of the women under this government, and such is now the necessity which constrains them to demand the equal station to which they are entitled.

The history of mankind is a history of repeated injuries and usurpations on the part of man toward woman, having in direct object the establishment of an absolute tyranny over her. To prove this, let facts be submitted to a candid world.

He has never permitted her to exercise her inalienable right to the elective franchise.

He has compelled her to submit to laws, in the formation of which she had no voice.

He has withheld from her rights which are given to the most ignorant and degraded men—both natives and foreigners.

Having deprived her of this first right of a citizen, the elective franchise, thereby leaving her without representation in the halls of legislation, he has oppressed her on all sides.

He has made her, if married, in the eye of the law, civilly dead.

He has taken from her all right in property, even to the wages she earns.

He has made her, morally, an irresponsible being, as she can commit many crimes with impunity, provided they be done in the presence of her husband. In the covenant of marriage, she is compelled to promise obedience to her husband, he becoming, to all intents and purposes, her master—the law giving him power to deprive her of her liberty, and to administer chastisement.

He has so framed the laws of divorce, as to what shall be the proper causes, and in case of separation, to whom the guardianship of the children shall be given, as to be wholly regardless of the happiness of women—the law, in all cases, going upon a false supposition of the supremacy of man, and giving all power into his hands.

After depriving her of all rights as a married women, if single, and the owner of property, he has taxed her to support a government which recognizes her only when her property can be made profitable to it.

He has monopolized nearly all the profitable employments, and from those she is permitted to follow, she receives but a scanty remuneration. He closes against her all the avenues to wealth and distinction which he considers most honorable to himself. As a teacher of theology, medicine, or law, she is not known.

He has denied her the facilities for obtaining a thorough education, all colleges being closed against her.

He allows her in Church, as well as State, but a subordinate position, claiming Apostolic authority for her exclusion from the ministry, and, with some exceptions, from any public participation in the affairs of the Church.

He has created a false public sentiment by giving to the world a different code of morals for men and women, by which moral delinquencies which exclude women from society, are not only tolerated, but deemed of little account in man.

He has usurped the prerogative of Jehovah himself, claiming it as his right to assign for her a sphere of action, when that belongs to her conscience and to her God.

He has endeavored, in every way that he could, to destroy her confidence in her own powers, to lessen her self-respect, and to make her willing to lead a dependent and abject life.

Now, in view of this entire disfranchisement of one-half the people of this country, their social and religious degradation—in view of the unjust laws above mentioned, and because women do feel themselves aggrieved, oppressed, and fraudulently deprived of their most sacred rights, we insist that they have immediate admission to all the rights and privileges which belong to them as citizens of the United States.

In entering upon the great work before us, we anticipate no small amount of misconception, misrepresentation, and ridicule; but we shall use every instrumentality within our power to effect our object. We shall employ agents, circulate tracts, petition the State and National legislatures, and endeavor to enlist the pulpit and the press in our behalf. We hope this Convention will be followed by a series of Conventions embracing every part of the country.

WHEREAS, The great precept of nature is conceded to be, that "man shall pursue his own true and substantial happiness." Blackstone in his Commentaries remarks, that this law of Nature being coeval with mankind, and dictated by God himself, is of course superior in obligation to any other. It is binding over all the globe, in all countries and at all times; no human laws are of any validity if contrary to this, and such of them as are valid, derive all their force, and all their validity, and all their authority, mediately and immediately, from this original; therefore,

Resolved, That such laws as conflict, in any way, with the true and substantial happiness of woman, are contrary to the great precept of nature and of no validity, for this is "superior in obligation to any other."

Resolved, That all laws which prevent woman from occupying such a station in society as her conscience shall dictate, or which place her in a position inferior to that of man, are contrary to the great precept of nature, and therefore of no force or authority.

Resolved, That woman is man's equal—was intended to be so by the Creator, and the highest good of the race demands that she should be recognized as such.

Resolved, That the women of this country ought to be enlightened in regard to the laws under which they live, that they may no longer publish their degradation by declaring themselves satisfied with their present position, nor their ignorance, by asserting that they have all the rights they want.

Resolved, That inasmuch as man, while claiming for himself intellectual superiority, does accord to woman moral superiority, it is pre-eminently his duty to encourage her to speak and teach, as she has an opportunity, in all religious assemblies.

Resolved, That the same amount of virtue, delicacy, and refinement of behavior that is required of woman in the social state, should also be required of man, and the same transgressions should be visited with equal severity on both man and woman.

Resolved, That the objection of indelicacy and impropriety, which is so often brought against woman when she addresses a public audience, comes with a very ill-grace from those who encourage, by their attendance, her appearance on the stage, in the concert, or in feats of the circus.

Resolved, That woman has too long rested satisfied in the circumscribed limits which corrupt customs and a perverted application of the Scriptures have marked out for her, and that it is time she should move in the enlarged sphere which her great Creator has assigned her.

Resolved, That it is the duty of the women of this country to secure to themselves their sacred right to the elective franchise.

Resolved, That the equality of human rights results necessarily from the fact of the identity of the race in capabilities and responsibilities.

Resolved, therefore, That, being invested by the Creator with the same capabilities, and the same consciousness of responsibility for their exercise, it is demonstrably the right and duty of woman, equally with man, to promote every righteous cause by every righteous means; and especially in regard to the great subjects of morals and religion, it is self-evidently her right to participate with her brother in teaching them, both in private and in public, by writing and by speaking, by any instrumentalities proper to be used, and in any assemblies proper to be held; and this being a self-evident truth growing out of the divinely implanted principles of human nature, any custom or authority adverse to it, whether modern or wearing the hoary sanction of antiquity, is to be regarded as a self-evident falsehood, and at war with mankind.

Resolved, That the speedy success of our cause depends upon the zealous and untiring efforts of both men and women, for the overthrow of the monopoly of the pulpit, and for the securing to woman an equal participation with men in the various trades, professions, and commerce.

Ain't I A Woman?

Sojourner Truth

Sojourner Truth (1795–1883)—born Isabella, a slave, in New York State—became a well known antislavery speaker some time after gaining her freedom in 1827. This speech, given extemporaneously at a woman's rights convention in Akron, Ohio, 1851, was recorded by Frances Gage, feminist activist and one of the authors of the huge compendium of materials of the first wave, The History of Woman Suffrage. *Gage, who was presiding at the meeting, describes the event:*

> *The leaders of the movement trembled on seeing a tall, gaunt black woman in a gray dress and white turban, surmounted with an uncouth sunbonnet, march deliberately into the church, walk with the air of a queen up the aisle, and take her seat upon the pulpit steps. A buzz of disapprobation was heard all over the house, and there fell on the listening ear, "An abolition affair!" "Woman's rights and niggers!" "I told you so!" "Go it, darkey!" . . . Again and again, timorous and trembling ones came to me and said, with earnestness, "Don't let her speak, Mrs. Gage, it will ruin us. Every newspaper in the land will have our cause mixed up with abolition and niggers, and we shall be utterly denounced." My only answer was, "We shall see when the time comes."*
>
> *The second day the work waxed warm. Methodist, Baptist, Episcopal, Presbyterian, and Universalist ministers came in to hear and discuss the resolutions presented. One claimed superior rights and privileges for man, on the ground of "superior intellect"; another, because of the "manhood of Christ; if God had desired the equality of woman, He would have given some token of His will through the birth, life, and death of the Saviour." Another gave us a theological view of the "sin of our first mother."*
>
> *There were very few women in those days who dared to "speak in meeting"; and the august teachers of the people were seemingly getting the better of us, while the boys in the galleries, and the sneerers among the pews, were hugely enjoying the discomfiture as they supposed, of the "strong-minded." Some of the tender-skinned friends were on the point of losing dignity, and the atmosphere betokened a storm. When, slowly from her seat in the corner rose Sojourner Truth, who, till now, had scarcely lifted her head. "Don't let her speak!" gasped half a dozen in my ear. She moved slowly and solemnly to the front, laid her old bonnet at her feet, and turned her great speaking eyes to me. There was a hissing sound of disapprobation above and below. I rose and announced, "Sojourner Truth," and begged the audience to keep silence for a few moments.*
>
> *The tummult subsided at once, and every eye was fixed on this almost Amazon form, which stood nearly six feet high, head erect, and eyes piercing the upper air like one in a dream. At her first word there was a profound hush. She spoke in deep tones, which, though not loud, reached every ear in the house, and away through the throng at the doors and windows.*

One cannot miss that there were those who were staunch for women's rights but yet were racist. It was not until later, much later, that there was much sophisticated analysis linking sexism, racism, and expressions of other kinds.

Truth's speech is reproduced here exactly as Gage recorded it in History of Woman Suffrage.

"WALL, CHILERN, WHAR DAR IS SO MUCH racket dar must be somethin' out o' kilter. I tink dat 'twixt de niggers of de Souf and de womin at de Norf, all talkin' 'bout rights, de white men will be in a fix pretty soon. But what's all dis here talkin' 'bout?

"Dat man ober dar say dat womin needs to be helped into carriages, and lifted ober ditches, and to hab de best place everywhar. Nobody eber helps me into carriages, or ober mud-puddles, or gibs me any best place!" And raising herself to her full height, and her voice to a pitch like rolling

---

Elizabeth Cady Stanton, Susan B. Anthony, & Matilda Joslyn Gage eds. *History of Woman Suffrage,* 2nd ed. Vol. 1. Rochester, NY: Charles Mann, 1889.

thunder, she asked. "And a'n't I a woman? Look at me! Look at my arm! (and she bared her right arm to the shoulder, showing her tremendous muscular power). I have ploughed, and planted, and gathered into barns, and no man could head me! And a'n't I a woman? I could work as much and eat as much as a man—when I could get it—and bear de lash as well! And a'n't I a woman? I have borne thirteen chilern, and seen 'em mos' all sold off to slavery, and when I cried out with my mother's grief, none but Jesus heard me! And a'n't I a woman?

"Den dey talks 'bout dis ting in de head; what dis dey call it?" ("Intellect," whispered some one near.) "Dat's it, honey. What's dat got to do wid womin's rights or nigger's rights? If my cup won't hold but a pint, and yourn holds a quart, wouldn't ye be mean not to let me have my little half-measure full?" And she pointed her significant finger, and sent a keen glance at the minister who had made the argument. The cheering was long and loud.

"Den dat little man in black dar, he say women can't have as much rights as men, 'cause Christ wan't a woman! Whar did your Christ come from?" Rolling thunder couldn't have stilled that crowd, as did those deep, wonderful tones, as she stood there with outstretched arms and eyes of fire. Raising her voice still louder, she repeated, "Whar did your Christ come from? From God and a woman! Man had nothin' to do wid Him." Oh, what a rebuke that was to that little man.

Turning again to another objector, she took up the defense of Mother Eve. I can not follow her through it all. It was pointed, and witty, and solemn; eliciting at almost every sentence deafening applause; and she ended by asserting: "If de fust woman God ever made was strong enough to turn de world upside down all alone, dese women togedder (and she glanced her eye over the platform) ought to be able to turn it back, and get it right side up again! And now dey is asking to do it, de men better let 'em." Long-continued cheering greeted this. "'Bleeged to ye for hearin' on me, and now ole Sojourner han't got nothin' more to say."

Amid roars of applause, she returned to her corner, leaving more than one of us with streaming eyes, and hearts beating with gratitude. She had taken us up in her strong arms and carried us safely over the slough of difficulty turning the whole tide in our favor. I have never in my life seen anything like the magical influence that subdued the mobbish spirit of the day, and turned the sneers and jeers of an excited crowd into notes of respect and admiration. Hundreds rushed up to shake hands with her, and congratulate the glorious old mother, and bid her God-speed on her mission of "testifyin' agin concerning the wickedness of this 'ere people."

Speech Before the Legislature 1860

Elizabeth Cady Stanton

Elizabeth Cady was born in Johnstown, New York, in 1815. As the daughter of a judge of comfortable means, she encountered people and situations that afforded her more than the usual opportunities for education allowed girls of her time. Having displayed an earnest zest and ability for learning, she was granted special permission to attend the Boys Academy in Johnstown. Prevented by her sex from attending college, she was graduated from the rather conservative Emma Willard Seminary in Troy, New York. Afterward she studied law with her father but, again because of her sex, was prevented from gaining admission to the bar. She had learned, however, precisely how the law burdened women and wives.

Elizabeth's family and friends included many of the brightest thinkers of the Northeast, all of whom taught and influenced her. Her marriage to the activist Henry Stanton in 1840, their trip to the World Anti-Slavery Convention in London, and their move in 1842 to Boston further developed her social sensitivities, knowledge, and thirst for intellectual stimulation. After the family returned from Boston in 1846 to settle in Seneca Falls, New York, Elizabeth became isolated from friends and society. She became immersed in the duties and experiences of a housewife and mother of seven. It suffocated her. Only her visits to her friend Lucretia Mott in Waterloo, New York, revived her. There, with Lucretia and her sister Martha Wright, with Jane Hunt and Mary Ann McClintock, in what could only be called consciousness-raising sessions, seated around a table for tea, the women talked, vented their frustration, and finally planned the convention at Seneca Falls.

After that time, Elizabeth Cady Stanton worked determinedly for the whole range of women's freedoms—from discrimination in marriage and divorce to freedom from the misogyny of traditional religion (she published the Woman's Bible *in 1895), to suffrage, and more. In 1851, she met Susan B. Anthony, with whom she worked until the end. They founded a radical magazine,* The Revolution, *in 1868, and in 1869 Stanton was elected president of the National Woman's Suffrage Association, an organization she served for over twenty years. Stanton was always brave, outspoken, often ahead of her time, and sometimes considered too radical even for many of the feminists. She died still at work in New York City in 1902.*

Early in 1860, Stanton was invited to address the New York legislature on a pending bill (subsequently passed) for an enlargement of women's property rights. Her speech, presented here, expressed the themes of natural human rights, the necessary limits of authority, and the parallels between blacks and females. Here she introduced, furthermore, another extremely important concept, one that should be carried into the present, that of woman as citizen. We are, after all, citizens of the United States, and our inalienable right is full participation in all the opportunities of this country.

GENTLEMEN OF THE JUDICIARY:—THERE ARE CERtain natural rights as inalienable to civilization as are the rights of air and motion to the savage in the wilderness. The natural rights of the civilized man and woman are government, property, the harmonious development of all their powers, and the gratification of their desires. There are a few people we now and then meet who, like Jeremy Bentham, scout the idea of natural rights in civilization, and pronounce them mere metaphors, declaring that there are no rights aside from those the law confers. If the law made man too, that might do, for then he could be made to order to fit the particular niche he was designed to fill. But inasmuch as God made man in His own image, with capacities and powers as boundless as the universe, whose exigencies no mere human law can meet, it is evident that the man must ever

Elizabeth Cady Stanton, Susan B. Anthony, and Matilda Joslyn Gage, eds. *History of Woman Suffrage,* 2nd ed., vol. 1. Rochester, NY: Charles Mann, 1889. Currently available from Ayer Company Publishers, POB 958, Salem, NH 03079.

stand first; the law but the creature of his wants; the law-giver but the mouthpiece of humanity. If, then, the nature of a being decides its rights, every individual comes into this world with rights that are not transferable. He does not bring them like a pack on his back, that may be stolen from him, but they are a component part of himself, the laws which insure his growth and development. The individual may be put in the stocks, body and soul, he may be dwarfed, crippled, killed, but his rights no man can get; they live and die with him.

Though the atmosphere is forty miles deep all round the globe, no man can do more than fill his own lungs. No man can see, hear, or smell but just so far; and though hundreds are deprived of these senses, his are not the more acute. Though rights have been abundantly supplied by the good Father, no man can appropriate to himself those that belong to another. A citizen can have but one vote, fill but one office, though thousands are not permitted to do either. These axioms prove that woman's poverty does not add to man's wealth, and if, in the plenitude of his power, he should secure to her the exercise of all her God-given rights, her wealth could not bring poverty to him. There is a kind of nervous unrest always manifested by those in power, whenever new claims are started by those out of their own immediate class. The philosophy of this is very plain. They imagine that if the rights of this new class be granted, they must, of necessity, sacrifice something of what they already possess. They can not divest themselves of the idea that rights are very much like lands, stocks, bonds, and mortgages, and that if every new claimant be satisfied, the supply of human rights must in time run low. You might as well carp at the birth of every child, lest there should not be enough air left to inflate your lungs; at the success of every scholar, for fear that your draughts at the fountain of knowledge could not be so long and deep; at the glory of every hero, lest there be no glory left for you. . . .

If the object of government is to protect the weak against the strong, how unwise to place the power wholly in the hands of the strong. Yet that is the history of all governments, even the model republic of these United States. You who have read the history of nations, from Moses down to our last election, where have you ever seen one class looking after the interests of another? Any of you can readily see the defects in other governments, and pronounce sentence against those who have sacrificed the masses to themselves; but when we come to our own case, we are blinded by custom and self-interest. Some of you who have no capital can see the injustice which the laborer suffers; some of you who have no slaves, can see the cruelty of his oppression; but who of you appreciate the galling humiliation, the refinements of degradation, to which women (the mothers, wives, sisters, and daughters of freemen) are subject, in this the last half of the nineteenth century? How many of you have ever read even the laws concerning them that now disgrace your statute-books? In cruelty and tyranny, they are not surpassed by any slaveholding code in the Southern States; in fact they are worse, by just so far as woman, from her social position, refinement, and education, is on a more equal ground with the oppressor.

Allow me just here to call the attention of that party now so much interested in the slave of the Carolinas, to the similarity in his condition and that of the mothers, wives, and daughters of the Empire State. The negro has no name. He is Cuffy Douglas or Cuffy Brooks, just whose Cuffy he may chance to be. The woman has no name. She is Mrs. Richard Roe or Mrs. John Doe, just whose Mrs. she may chance to be. Cuffy has no right to his earnings; he can not buy or sell, or lay up anything that he can call his own. Mrs. Roe has no right to her earnings; she can neither buy nor sell, make contracts, nor lay up anything that she can call her own. Cuffy has no right to his children; they can be sold from him at any time. Mrs. Roe has no right to her children; they may be bound out to cancel a father's debts of honor. The unborn child, even by the last will of the father, may be placed under the guardianship of a stranger and a foreigner. Cuffy has no legal existence; he is subject to restraint and moderate chastisement. Mrs. Roe has no legal existence; she has not the best right to her own person. The husband has the power to restrain, and administer moderate chastisement.

Blackstone declares that the husband and wife are one, and learned commentators have decided that that one is the husband. In all civil codes, you will find them classified as one. Certain rights and immunities, such and such privileges are to be secured to white male citizens. What have women and negroes to do with rights? What know they of government, war, or glory?

The prejudice against color, of which we hear so much, is no stronger than that against sex. It is produced by the same cause, and manifested very much in the same way. The negro's skin and the woman's sex are both *prima facie* evidence that they were intended to be in subjection to the white Saxon man. The few social privileges which the man gives the woman, he makes up to the negro in civil rights. The woman may sit at the same table and eat with the white man; the free negro may hold property and vote. The woman may sit in the same pew with the white man in church; the free negro may enter the pulpit and preach. Now, with the black man's right to suffrage, the right unquestioned, even by Paul, to minister at the altar, it is evident that the prejudice against sex is more deeply rooted and more unreasonably maintained than that against color. As citizens of a republic, which should we most highly prize, social privileges or civil rights? The latter, most certainly.

To those who do not feel the injustice and degradation of the condition, there is something inexpressibly comical in man's "citizen woman." It reminds me of those monsters I used to see in the old world, head and shoulders woman, and the rest of the body sometimes fish and sometimes beast. I used to think, What a strange conceit! but now I see how perfectly it represents man's idea! Look over all his laws concerning us, and you will see just enough of woman to tell of her existence; all the rest is submerged, or made to crawl upon the earth. Just imagine an inhabitant of another planet entertaining himself some pleasant evening in searching over our great national compact, our Declaration of Independence, our Constitutions, or some of our statute-books; what would he think of those "women and negroes" that must be so fenced in, so guarded against? Why, he would certainly suppose we were monsters, like those fabulous giants or Brobdignagians of olden times, so dangerous to civilized man, from our size, ferocity, and power. Then let him take up our poets, from Pope down to Dana; let him listen to our Fourth of July toasts, and some of the sentimental adulations of social life, and no logic could convince him that this creature of the law, and this angel of the family altar, could be one and the same being. Man is in such a labyrinth of contradictions with his marital and property rights; he is so befogged on the whole question of maidens, wives, and mothers, that from pure benevolence we should relieve him from this troublesome branch of legislation. We should vote, and make laws for ourselves. Do not be alarmed, dear ladies! You need spend no time reading Grotius, Coke, Puffendorf, Blackstone, Bentham, Kent, and Story to find out what you need. We may safely trust the shrewd selfishness of the white man, and consent to live under the same broad code where he has so comfortably ensconced himself. Any legislation that will do for man, we may abide by most cheerfully. . . .

But, say you, we would not have woman exposed to the grossness and vulgarity of public life, or encounter what she must at the polls. When you talk, gentlemen, of sheltering woman from the rough winds and revolting scenes of real life, you must be either talking for effect, or wholly ignorant of what the facts of life are. The man, whatever he is, is known to the woman. She is the companion, not only of the accomplished statesman, the orator, and the scholar; but the vile, vulgar, brutal man has his mother, his wife, his sister, his daughter. Yes, delicate, refined, educated women are in daily life with the drunkard, the gambler, the licentious man, the rogue, and the villain; and if man shows out what he is anywhere, it is at his own hearthstone. There are over forty thousand drunkards in this State. All these are bound by the ties of family to some woman. Allow but a mother and a wife to each, and you have over eighty thousand women. All these have seen their fathers, brothers, husbands, sons, in the lowest and most debased stages of obscenity and degradation. In your own circle of friends, do you not know refined women, whose whole lives are darkened and saddened by gross and brutal associations? Now, gentlemen, do you talk to woman of a rude jest or jostle at the polls, where noble, virtuous men stand ready to protect her person and her rights, when, alone in the darkness and solitude and gloom of night, she has trembled on her own threshold awaiting the return of a husband from his midnight revels?—when, stepping from her chamber, she has beheld her royal monarch, her lord and master—her legal representative—the protector of her property, her home, her children, and her person, down on his hands and knees slowly crawling up the stairs? Behold him in her chamber—in her bed! The fairy tale of "Beauty and the Beast" is far too often realized in life. Gentlemen, such scenes as woman has witnessed at her own fireside, where no eye save Omnipotence could pity, no strong arm could help, can never be realized at the polls, never equaled elsewhere, this side the bottomless pit. No, woman has not hitherto lived in the clouds, surrounded by an atmosphere of purity and peace—but she has been the companion of man in health, in sickness, and in death, in his highest and in his lowest moments. She has worshiped him as a saint and an orator, and pitied him as madman or a fool. In Paradise, man and woman were placed together, and so they must ever be. They must sink or rise together. If man is low and wretched and vile, woman can not escape the contagion, and any atmosphere that is unfit for woman to breathe is not fit for man. Verily, the sins of the fathers shall be visited upon the children to the third and fourth generation. You, by your unwise legislation, have crippled and dwarfed womanhood, by closing to her all honorable and lucrative means of employment, have driven her into the garrets and dens of our cities, where she now revenges herself on your innocent sons, sapping the very foundations of national virtue and strength. Alas! for the young men just coming on the stage of action, who soon shall fill your vacant places—our future Senators, our Presidents, the expounders of our constitutional law! Terrible are the penalties we are now suffering for the ages of injustice done to woman.

Again, it is said that the majority of women do not ask for any change in the laws; that it is time enough to give them the elective franchise when they, as a class, demand it.

Wise statesmen legislate for the best interests of the nation; the State, for the highest good of its citizens; the Christian, for the conversion of the world. Where would have been our railroads, our telegraphs, our ocean steamers, our canals and harbors, our arts and sciences, if government had withheld the means from the far-seeing minority? This State established our present system of common schools, fully believing that educated men and women would make better citizens than ignorant ones. In making this provision for the education of its children, had they waited for a majority of the urchins of this State to petition for schools, how many, think you, would have asked to be transplanted from the street to the school-house? Does the State wait for the criminal to ask for his prison-house? the insane, the idiot, the deaf and dumb for his asylum? Does the Christian, in his love to all mankind, wait for the majority of the benighted heathen to ask him for the gospel? No; unasked and unwelcomed, he crosses the trackless ocean, rolls off the mountain of superstition that oppresses the human mind, proclaims the immortality of the soul, the dignity of manhood, the right of all to be free and happy.

No, gentlemen, if there is but one woman in this State who feels the injustice of her position, she should not be denied her inalienable rights, because the common household drudge and the silly butterfly of fashion are ignorant of all laws, both human and Divine. Because they know nothing of governments, or rights, and therefore ask nothing, shall my petitions be unheard? I stand before you the rightful representative of woman, claiming a share in the halo of glory that has gathered round her in the ages, and by the wisdom of her past words and works, her peerless heroism and self-sacrifice, I challenge your admiration; and, moreover, claiming, as I do, a share in all her outrages and sufferings, in the cruel injustice, contempt, and ridicule now heaped upon her, in her deep degradation, hopeless wretchedness, by all that is helpless in her present condition, that is false in law and public sentiment, I urge your generous consideration; for as my heart swells with pride to behold woman in the highest walks of literature and art, it grows big enough to take in those who are bleeding in the dust.

Now do not think, gentlemen, we wish you to do a great many troublesome things for us. We do not ask our legislators to spend a whole session fixing up a code of laws to satisfy a class of most unreasonable women. We ask no more than the poor devils in the Scripture asked, "Let us alone." In mercy, let us take care of ourselves, our property, our children, and our homes. True, we are not so strong, so wise, so crafty as you are, but if any kind friend leaves us a little money, or we can by great industry earn fifty cents a day, we would rather buy bread and clothes for our children than cigars and champagne for our legal protectors. There has been a great deal written and said about protection. We, as a class, are tired of one kind of protection, that which leaves us everything to do, to dare, and to suffer, and strips us of all means for its accomplishment. We would not tax man to take care of us. No, the Great Father has endowed all his creatures with the necessary powers for self-support, self-defense, and protection. We do not ask man to represent us; it is hard enough in times like these for man to carry backbone enough to represent himself. So long as the mass of men spend most of their time on the fence, not knowing which way to jump, they are surely in no condition to tell us where we had better stand. In pity for man, we would no longer hang like a millstone round his neck. Undo what man did for us in the dark ages, and strike out all special legislation for us; strike the words "white male" from all your constitutions, and then, with fair sailing, let us sink or swim, live or die, survive or perish together.

At Athens, an ancient apologue tells us, on the completion of the temple of Minerva, a statue of the goddess was wanted to occupy the crowning point of the edifice. Two of the greatest artists produced what each deemed his masterpiece. One of these figures was the size of life, admirably designed, exquisitely finished, softly rounded, and beautifully refined. The other was of Amazonian stature, and so boldly chiselled that it looked more like masonry than sculpture. The eyes of all were attracted by the first, and turned away in contempt from the second. That, therefore, was adopted, and the other rejected, almost with resentment, as though an insult had been offered to a discerning public. The favored statue was accordingly borne in triumph to the place for which it was designed, in the presence of applauding thousands, but as it receded from their upturned eyes, all, all at once agaze upon it, the thunders of applause unaccountably died away—a general misgiving ran through every bosom—the mob themselves stood like statues, as silent and as petrified, for as it slowly went up, and up the soft expression of those chiselled features, the delicate curves and outlines of the limbs and figure, became gradually fainter and fainter, and when at last it reached the place for which it was intended, it was a shapeless ball, enveloped in mist. Of course, the idol of the hour was now clamored down as rationally as it had been cried up, and its dishonored rival, with no good will and no good looks on the part of the chagrined populace, was reared in its stead. As it ascended, the sharp angles faded away, the rough points became smooth, the features full of expression, the whole figure radiant with majesty and beauty. The rude hewn mass, that before had scarcely appeared to bear even the human form, assumed at once the divinity which it represented, being so perfectly proportioned to the dimensions of the building, and to the elevation on which it stood, that it seemed as though Pallas herself had alighted upon the pinnacle of the temple in person, to receive the homage of her worshippers.

The woman of the nineteenth century is the shapeless ball in the lofty position which she was designed fully and nobly to fill. The place is not too high, too large, too sacred for woman, but the type that you have chosen is far too small for it. The woman we declare unto you is the rude, misshapen, unpolished object of the successful artist. From your stand-point, you are absorbed with the defects alone. The true artist sees the harmony between the object and its destination. Man, the sculptor, has carved out his ideal, and applauding thousands welcome his success. He has made a woman that from his low stand-point looks fair and beautiful, a being without rights, or hopes, or fears but in him—neither noble, virtuous, nor independent. Where do we see, in Church or State, in school-house or at the fireside, the much talked-of moral power of woman? Like those Athenians, we have bowed down and worshiped in woman, beauty, grace, the exquisite proportions, the soft and beautifully rounded outline, her delicacy, refinement, and silent helplessness—all well when she is viewed simply as an object of sight, never to rise one foot above the dust from which she sprung. But if she is to be raised up to adorn a temple, or represent a divinity—if she is to fill the niche of wife and counsellor to true and noble men, if she is to be the mother, the educator of a race of heroes or martyrs, of a Napoleon, or a Jesus—then must the type of womanhood be on a larger scale than that yet carved by man.

In vain would the rejected artist have reasoned with the Athenians as to the superiority of his production; nothing short of the experiment they made could have satisfied them. And what of your experiment, what of your wives, your homes? Alas! for the folly and vacancy that meet you there! But for your club-houses and newspapers, what would social life be to you? Where are your beautiful women? your frail ones, taught to lean lovingly and confidingly on man? Where are the crowds of educated dependents—where the long line of pensioners on man's bounty? Where all the young girls, taught to believe that marriage is the only legitimate object of a woman's pursuit—they who stand listlessly on life's shores, waiting, year after year, like the sick man at the pool of Bethesda, for some one to come and put them in? These are they who by their ignorance and folly curse almost every fireside with some human specimen of deformity or imbecility. These are they who fill the gloomy abodes of poverty and vice in our vast metropolis. These are they who patrol the streets of our cities, to give our sons their first lessons in infamy. These are they who fill our asylums, and make night hideous with their cries and groans.

The women who are called masculine, who are brave, courageous, self-reliant and independent, are they who in the face of adverse winds have kept one steady course upward and onward in the paths of virtue and peace—they who have taken their gauge of womanhood from their own native strength and dignity—they who have learned for themselves the will of God concerning them. This is our type of womanhood. Will you help us raise it up, that you too may see its beautiful proportions—that you may behold the outline of the goddess who is yet to adorn your temple of Freedom? We are building a model republic; our edifice will one day need a crowning glory. Let the artists be wisely chosen. Let them begin their work. Here is a temple to Liberty, to human rights, on whose portals behold the glorious declaration, "All men are created equal." The sun has never yet shone upon any of man's creations that can compare with this. The artist who can mold a statue worthy to crown magnificence like this, must be godlike in his conceptions, grand in his comprehensions, sublimely beautiful in his power of execution. The woman—the crowning glory of the model republic among the nations of the earth—what must she not be?

Constitutional Argument

Susan B. Anthony

Susan B. Anthony was born in Adams, Massachusetts, in 1820. Her father, a Quaker steeped in that religion's historic principle of sexual equality, held Susan in high regard. He educated her as he would a son, taught her responsibility and self-reliance, entrusted her with the management of his farm, and introduced her to the people and ideas of the liberal reform movements current in Rochester, New York, where they had come to live about 1839. In her teens, Susan taught at the Canajoharie Institute, but teaching was not a sufficient challenge for her. Later, having returned to Rochester, she became active in a reform movement to which several of her friends belonged—temperance. It was through the Rochester Daughters of Temperance that she met Amelia Bloomer of Seneca Falls who, in 1851, introduced her to Elizabeth Cady Stanton.

The women quickly became friends. Anthony was soon invited to Stanton's home to discuss ideas, and Anthony's views developed rapidly to coalesce with Stanton's. The two lectured, worked together, and founded The Revolution, *a radical magazine. In 1872, to bring to the test of the Supreme Court her conviction that as a citizen she was guaranteed by the Fourteenth Amendment the right to vote, Anthony "knowingly, wrongfully, and unlawfully" cast a vote in the election in Rochester. Arrested, convicted, and fined, she refused to pay, hoping for an appeal path, but the fine was not pursued. Nonetheless, she brought her principle into view and gained considerable sympathy. Later she was to lecture on coeducation (deemed radical at the time) and on all the various women's issues and to serve in the National American Woman's Suffrage Association and on the International Council of Women. In 1902, shortly after her retirement, she died.*

Like Stanton, Anthony was one of the strongest models in feminist history. The following selection is from a speech delivered during a tour of New York State prior to her trial in 1873. In it Anthony argued her thesis that both the original conception and the current law of the U.S. Constitution guaranteed her a citizen's right to vote.

DELIVERED IN TWENTY-NINE OF THE POST-OFFICE districts of Monroe, and twenty-one of Ontario, in Miss Anthony's canvass of those counties prior to her trial in June, 1873.

Friends and Fellow-Citizens:—I stand before you under indictment for the alleged crime of having voted at the last presidential election, without having a lawful right to vote. It shall be my work this evening to prove to you that in thus doing, I not only committed no crime, but instead simply exercised my citizen's right, guaranteed to me and all United States citizens by the National Constitution beyond the power of any State to deny.

Our democratic-republican government is based on the idea of the natural right of every individual member thereof to a voice and a vote in making and executing the laws. We assert the province of government to be to secure the people in the enjoyment of their inalienable rights. We throw to the winds the old dogma that government can give rights. No one denies that before governments were organized each individual possessed the right to protect his own life, liberty and property. When 100 or 1,000,000 people enter into a free government, they do not barter away their natural rights; they simply pledge themselves to protect each other in the enjoyment of them through prescribed judicial and legislative tribunals. They agree to abandon the methods of brute force in the adjustment of their differences and adopt those of civilization. Nor can you find a word in any of the grand documents left us by the fathers which assumes for government the power to create or to confer rights. The Declaration of Independence, the United States Constitution, the constitutions of the several States and the organic laws of the Territories, all alike propose to *protect* the people in the exercise of their God-given rights. Not one of them pretends to bestow rights.

Ida H. Harper, *Life and Work of Susan B. Anthony*, Indianapolis: Bowen-Merrill Co., 1898. Vol. II.

All men are created equal, and endowed by their Creator with certain inalienable rights. Among these are life, liberty and the pursuit of happiness. To secure these, governments are instituted among men, deriving their just powers from the consent of the governed.

Here is no shadow of government authority over rights, or exclusion of any class from their full and equal enjoyment. Here is pronounced the right of all men, and "consequently," as the Quaker preacher said, "of all women," to a voice in the government. And here, in this first paragraph of the Declaration, is the assertion of the natural right of all to the ballot; for how can "the consent of the governed" be given, if the right to vote be denied? Again:

Whenever any form of government becomes destructive of these ends, it is the right of the people to alter or abolish it, and to institute a new government, laying its foundations on such principles, and organizing its powers in such form, as to them shall seem most likely to effect their safety and happiness.

Surely the right of the whole people to vote is here clearly implied; for however destructive to their happiness this government might become, a disfranchised class could neither alter nor abolish it, nor institute a new one, except by the old brute force method of insurrection and rebellion. One-half of the people of this nation today are utterly powerless to blot from the statute books an unjust law, or to write there a new and a just one. The women, dissatisfied as they are with this form of government, that enforces taxation without representation—that compels them to obey laws to which they never have given their consent—that imprisons and hangs them without a trial by a jury of their peers—that robs them, in marriage, of the custody of their own persons, wages and children—are this half of the people who are left wholly at the mercy of the other half, in direct violation of the spirit and letter of the declarations of the framers of this government, every one of which was based on the immutable principle of equal rights to all. By these declarations, kings, popes, priests, aristocrats, all were alike dethroned and placed on a common level, politically, with the lowliest born subject or serf. By them, too, men, as such, were deprived of their divine right to rule and placed on a political level with women. By the practice of these declarations all class and caste distinctions would be abolished, and slave, serf, plebeian, wife, woman, all alike rise from their subject position to the broader platform of equality.

The preamble of the Federal Constitution says:

We, the people of the United States, in order to form a more perfect union, establish justice, insure domestic tranquillity, provide for the common defence, promote the general welfare and secure the blessings of liberty to ourselves and our posterity, do ordain and establish this Constitution for the United States of America.

It was we, the people, not we, the white male citizens, nor we, the male citizens; but we, the whole people, who formed this Union. We formed it not to give the blessings of liberty but to secure them; not to the half of ourselves and the half of our posterity, but to the whole people—women as well as men. It is downright mockery to talk to women of their enjoyment of the blessings of liberty while they are denied the only means of securing them provided by this democratic-republican government—the ballot. . . .

But I submit that in view of the explicit assertions of the equal right of the whole people, both in the preamble and previous article of the constitution, this omission of the adjective "female" should not be construed into a denial; but instead should be considered as of no effect. Mark the direct prohibition, "No member of this State shall be disfranchised, unless by the law of the land, or the judgment of his peers." "The law of the land" is the United States Constitution; and there is no provision in that document which can be fairly construed into a permission to the States to deprive any class of citizens of their right to vote. Hence New York can get no power from that source to disfranchise one entire half of her members. Nor has "the judgment of their peers" been pronounced against women exercising their right to vote; no disfranchised person is allowed to be judge or juror—and none but disfranchised persons can be women's peers. Nor has the legislature passed laws excluding women as a class on account of idiocy or lunacy; nor have the courts convicted them of bribery, larceny or any infamous crime. Clearly, then, there is no constitutional ground for the exclusion of women from the ballot-box in the State of New York. No barriers whatever stand today between women and the exercise of their right to vote save those of precedent and prejudice, which refuse to expunge the word "male" from the constitution. . . .

For any State to make sex a qualification, which must ever result in the disfranchisement of one entire half of the people, is to pass a bill of attainder, an ex post facto law, and is therefore a violation of the supreme law of the land. By it the blessings of liberty are forever withheld from women and their female posterity. For them, this government has no just powers derived from the consent of the governed. For them this government is not a democracy; it is not a republic. It is the most odious aristocracy ever established on the face of the globe. An oligarchy of wealth, where the rich govern the poor; an oligarchy of learning, where the educated govern the ignorant; or even an oligarchy of race, where the Saxon rules the African, might be endured; but this oligarchy of sex which makes father, brothers, husband, sons, the oligarchs over the mother and sisters, the wife and daughters of every household; which ordains all men sovereigns, all women subjects—carries discord and rebellion into every home of the nation. This most odious aristocracy exists, too, in the face of Section 4, Article IV, which says: "The United States shall guarantee to every State in the Union a republican form of government."

What, I ask you, is the distinctive difference between the inhabitants of a monarchical and those of a republican form of government, save that in the monarchical the people are subjects, helpless, powerless, bound to obey laws made by political superiors; while in the republican the people are citizens, individual sovereigns, all clothed with equal power to make and unmake both their laws and lawmakers? The moment you deprive a person of his right to a voice in the government, you degrade him from the status of a citizen of the republic to that of a subject. It matters very little to him whether his monarch be an individual tyrant, as is the Czar of Russia, or a 15,000,000 headed monster, as here in the United States; he is a powerless subject, serf or slave; not in any sense a free and independent citizen.

It is urged that the use of the masculine pronouns *he, his* and *him* in all the constitutions and laws, is proof that only men were meant to be included in their provisions. If you insist on this version of the letter of the law, we shall insist that you be consistent and accept the other horn of the dilemma, which would compel you to exempt women from taxation for the support of the government and from penalties for the violation of laws. There is no *she* or *her* or *hers* in the tax laws, and this is equally true of all the criminal laws.

Take for example the civil rights law which I am charged with having violated; not only are all the pronouns in it masculine, but everybody knows that it was intended expressly to hinder the rebel men from voting. It reads, "If any person shall knowingly vote without *his* having a lawful right." It was precisely so with all the papers served on me—the United States marshal's warrant, the bail-bond, the petition for habeas corpus, the bill of indictment—not one of them had a feminine pronoun; but to make them applicable to me, the clerk of the court prefixed an "s" to the "he" and made "her" out of "his" and "him;" and I insist if government officials may thus manipulate the pronouns to tax, fine, imprison and hang women, it is their duty to thus change them in order to protect us in our right to vote.

So long as any classes of men were denied this right, the government made a show of consistency by exempting them from taxation. When a property qualification of $250 was required of black men in New York, they were not compelled to pay taxes so long as they were content to report themselves worth less than that sum; but the moment the black man died and his property fell to his widow or daughter, the black woman's name was put on the assessor's list and she was compelled to pay taxes on this same property. This also is true of ministers in New York. So long as the minister lives, he is exempted from taxation on $1,500 of property, but the moment the breath leaves his body, his widow's name goes on the assessor's list and she has to pay taxes on the $1,500. So much for special legislation in favor of women! . . .

The only question left to be settled now is: Are women persons? I scarcely believe any of our opponents will have the hardihood to say they are not. Being persons, then, women are citizens, and no State has a right to make any new law, or to enforce any old law, which shall abridge their privileges or immunities. Hence, every discrimination against women in the constitutions and laws of the several States is today null and void, precisely as is every one against negroes. . . .

If once we establish the false principle that United States citizenship does not carry with it the right to vote in every State in this Union, there is no end to the petty tricks and cunning devices which will be attempted to exclude one and another class of citizens from the right of suffrage. It will not always be the men combining to disfranchise all women; native born men combining to abridge the rights of all naturalized citizens, as in Rhode Island. It will not always be the rich and educated who may combine to cut off the poor and ignorant; but we may live to see the hard-working, uncultivated day laborers, foreign and native born, learning the power of the ballot and their vast majority of numbers, combine and amend State constitutions so as to disfranchise the Vanderbilts, the Stewarts, the Conklings and the Fentons. It is a poor rule that won't work more ways than one. Establish this precedent, admit the State's right to deny suffrage, and there is no limit to the confusion, discord and disruption that may await us. There is and can be but one safe principle of government—equal rights to all. Discrimination against any class on account of color, race, nativity, sex, property, culture, can but embitter and disaffect that class, and thereby endanger the safety of the whole people. Clearly, then, the national government not only must define the rights of citizens, but must stretch out its powerful hand and protect them in every State in this Union.

If, however, you will insist that the Fifteenth Amendment's emphatic interdiction against robbing United States citizens of their suffrage "on account of race, color or previous condition of servitude," is a recognition of the right of either the United States or any State to deprive them of the ballot for any or all other reasons, I will prove to you that the class of citizens for whom I now plead are, by all the principles of our government and many of the laws of the States, included under the term "previous condition of servitude."

Consider first married women and their legal status. What is servitude? "The condition of a slave." What is a slave? "A person who is robbed of the proceeds of his labor; a person who is subject to the will of another." By the laws of Georgia, South Carolina and all the States of the South, the negro had no right to the custody and control of his person. He belonged to his master. If he were disobedient, the master had the right to use correction. If the negro did not like the correction and ran away, the master had the right to use coercion to bring him back. By the laws of almost every State in this Union today, North as well as South, the married woman has no right to the custody and control of her person. The wife belongs to the husband; and if she refuse obedience he may use moderate correction, and if she do not like his moderate correction and leave his "bed and board," the husband may use moderate coercion to bring her back. The little word "moderate," you see, is the saving clause for the wife, and would doubtless be overstepped should her offended husband administer his correction with the "cat-o'-nine-tails," or accomplish his coercion with blood-hounds.

Again the slave had no right to the earnings of his hands, they belonged to his master; no right to the custody of his children, they belonged to his master; no right to sue or be sued, or to testify in the courts. If he committed a crime, it was the master who must sue or be sued. In many of the States there has been special legislation, giving married women the right to property inherited or received by bequest, or earned by the pursuit of any avocation outside the home; also giving them the right to sue and be sued in matters pertaining to such separate property; but not a single State of this Union has ever secured the wife in the enjoyment of her right to equal ownership of the joint earnings of the marriage copartnership. And since, in the nature of things, the vast majority of married women never earn a dollar by work outside their families, or inherit a dollar from their fathers, it follows that from the day of their marriage to the day of the death of their husbands not one of them ever has a dollar, except it shall please her husband to let her have it.

In some of the States, also, laws have been passed giving to the mother a joint right with the father in the guardianship of the children. Twenty-five years ago, when our woman's rights movement commenced, by the laws of all the States the father had the sole custody and control of the children. No matter if he were a brutal, drunken libertine, he had the legal right, without the mother's consent, to apprentice her sons to rumsellers or her daughters to brothel-keepers. He even could will away an unborn child from the mother. In most of the States this law still prevails, and the mothers are utterly powerless.

I doubt if there is, today, a State in this Union where a married woman can sue or be sued for slander of character, and until recently there was not one where she could sue or be sued for injury of person. However damaging to the wife's reputation any slander may be, she is wholly powerless to institute legal proceedings against her accuser unless her husband shall join with her; and how often have we heard of the husband conspiring with some outside barbarian to blast the good name of his wife? A married woman can not testify in courts in cases of joint interest with her husband. . . .

I submit the question, if the deprivation by law of the ownership of one's own person, wages, property, children, the denial of the right as an individual to sue and be sued and testify in the courts, is not a condition of servitude most bitter and absolute, even though under the sacred name of marriage? Does any lawyer doubt my statement of the legal status of married women? I will remind him of the fact that the common law of England prevails in every State but two in this Union, except where the legislature has enacted special laws annulling it. I am ashamed that not one of the States yet has blotted from its statute books the old law of marriage, which, summed up in the fewest words possible, is in effect "husband and wife are one, and that one the husband."

Thus may all married women and widows, by the laws of the several States, be technically included in the Fifteenth Amendment's specification of "condition of servitude," present or previous. The facts also prove that, by all the great fundamental principles of our free government, not only married women but the entire womanhood of the nation are in a "condition of servitude" as surely as were our Revolutionary fathers when they rebelled against King George. Women are taxed without representation, governed without their consent, tried, convicted and punished without a jury of their peers. Is all this tyranny any less humiliating and degrading to women under our democratic-republican government today than it was to men under their aristocratic, monarchial government one hundred years ago? . . .

Is anything further needed to prove woman's condition of servitude sufficient to entitle her to the guarantees of the Fifteenth Amendment? Is there a man who will not agree with me that to talk of freedom without the ballot is mockery to the women of this republic, precisely as New England's orator, Wendell Phillips, at the close of the late war declared it to be to the newly emancipated black man? I admit that, prior to the rebellion, by common consent, the right to enslave, as well as to disfranchise both native and foreign born persons, was conceded to the States. But the one grand principle settled by the war and the reconstruction legislation, is the supremacy of the national government to protect the citizens of the United States in their right to freedom and the elective franchise, against any and every interference on the part of the several States; and again and again have the American people asserted the triumph of this principle by their overwhelming majorities for Lincoln and Grant. . . .

It is upon this just interpretation of the United States Constitution that our National Woman Suffrage Association, which celebrates the twenty-fifth anniversary of the woman's rights movement next May in New York City, has based all its arguments and action since the passage of these amendments. We no longer petition legislature or Congress to give us the right to vote, but appeal to women everywhere to exercise their too long neglected "citizen's right."

Marriage and Love

Emma Goldman

Anarchist, author, lecturer, and activist, Emma Goldman was born in Lithuania in 1869 and emigrated to the United States in 1886, settling in Rochester, New York. After working in a factory there for a short time, she moved to New York City and began her lifelong participation in radical political activity. Militantly involved in the labor movement, accused of complicity in the assassination of President McKinley, and active in the antidraft-antiwar movement of World War I, she was jailed twice, was deported to Russia in 1919, and spent the rest of her life traveling, writing, lecturing, and agitating on a variety of social issues. From 1906 to 1917, she copublished a radical American journal, Mother Earth, *and she wrote several books, among them* Anarchism and Other Essays *(1910), excerpted here, and* Living My Life *(1934), an autobiography. She died in Toronto, Canada, in 1940.*

As an anarchist, Goldman opposed any state interference in personal life. As a feminist, therefore, she opposed institutional marriage, the dependency it fostered, and laws relating to contraception and abortion. The following essay considers the relationship of love, sex, marriage, and parenthood and calls for the freeing of women from the "insurance pact" of state-sanctioned wedlock. Goldman's issues are classic in the women's movement, although she treats them in the context of her own particular political beliefs. She is an excellent example of the twentieth-century shift in feminist activism from a purely women's movement to more comprehensive organizations or models.

From ANARCHISM AND OTHER ESSAYS by Emma Goldman. Port Washington, NY: Kennikat Press, 1910, pp. 233–242. By permission of Gordon Press Publishers, New York, NY.

THE POPULAR NOTION ABOUT MARRIAGE AND LOVE is that they are synonymous, that they spring from the same motives, and cover the same human needs. Like most popular notions this also rests not on actual facts, but on superstition.

Marriage and love have nothing in common; they are as far apart as the poles; are, in fact, antagonistic to each other. No doubt some marriages have been the result of love. Not, however, because love could assert itself only in marriage; much rather is it because few people can completely outgrow a convention. There are today large numbers of men and women to whom marriage is naught but a farce, but who submit to it for the sake of public opinion. At any rate, while it is true that some marriages are based on love, and while it is equally true that in some cases love continues in married life, I maintain that it does so regardless of marriage, and not because of it.

On the other hand, it is utterly false that love results from marriage. On rare occasions one does hear of a miraculous case of a married couple falling in love after marriage, but on close examination it will be found that it is a mere adjustment to the inevitable. Certainly the growing-used to each other is far away from the spontaneity, the intensity, and beauty of love, without which the intimacy of marriage must prove degrading to both the woman and the man.

Marriage is primarily an economic arrangement, an insurance pact. It differs from the ordinary life insurance agreement only in that it is more binding, more exacting. Its returns are insignificantly small compared with the investments. In taking out an insurance policy one pays for it in dollars and cents, always at liberty to discontinue payments. If, however, woman's premium is a husband, she pays for it with her name, her privacy, her self-respect, her very life, "until death doth part." Moreover, the marriage insurance condemns her to life-long dependency, to parasitism, to complete uselessness, individual as well as social. Man, too, pays his toll, but as his sphere is wider, marriage does not limit him as much as woman. He feels his chains more in an economic sense.

Thus Dante's motto over Inferno applies with equal force to marriage. "Ye who enter here leave all hope behind."

That marriage is a failure none but the very stupid will deny. One has but to glance over the statistics of divorce to realize how bitter a failure marriage really is. Nor will the stereotyped Philistine argument that the laxity of divorce laws and the growing looseness of woman account for the fact that: first, every twelfth marriage ends in divorce; second, that since 1870 divorces have increased from 28 to 73 for every hundred thousand population; third, that adultery, since 1867, as ground for divorce, has increased 270.8 per cent.; fourth, that desertion increased 369.8 per cent.

Added to these startling figures is a vast amount of material, dramatic and literary, further elucidating this subject. Robert Herrick, in *Together;* Pinero, in *Mid-Channel;* Eugene Walter, in *Paid in Full,* and scores of other writers are discussing the barrenness, the monotony, the sordidness, the inadequacy of marriage as a factor for harmony and understanding.

The thoughtful social student will not content himself with the popular superficial excuse for this phenomenon. He will have to dig down deeper into the very life of the sexes to know why marriage proves so disastrous.

Edward Carpenter says that behind every marriage stands the life-long environment of the two sexes; an environment so different from each other that man and woman must remain strangers. Separated by an insurmountable wall of superstition, custom, and habit, marriage has not the potentiality of developing knowledge of, and respect for, each other, without which every union is doomed to failure.

Henrik Ibsen, the hater of all social shams, was probably the first to realize this great truth. Nora leaves her husband, not—as the stupid critic would have it—because she is tired of her responsibilities or feels the need of woman's rights, but because she has come to know that for eight years she had lived with a stranger and borne him children. Can there be anything more humiliating, more degrading than a life-long proximity between two strangers? No need for the woman to know anything of the man, save his income. As to the knowledge of the woman—what is there to know except that she has a pleasing appearance? We have not yet outgrown the theologic myth that woman has no soul, that she is a mere appendix to man, made out of his rib just for the convenience of the gentleman who was so strong that he was afraid of his own shadow.

Perchance the poor quality of the material whence woman comes is responsible for her inferiority. At any rate, woman has no soul—what is there to know about her? Besides, the less soul a woman has the greater her asset as a wife, the more readily will she absorb herself in her husband. It is this slavish acquiescence to man's superiority that has kept the marriage institution seemingly intact for so long a period. Now that woman is coming into her own, now that she is actually growing aware of herself as a being outside of the master's grace, the sacred institution of marriage is gradually being undermined, and no amount of sentimental lamentation can stay it.

From infancy, almost, the average girl is told that marriage is her ultimate goal; therefore her training and education must be directed towards that end. Like the mute beast fattened for slaughter, she is prepared for that. Yet, strange to say, she is allowed to know much less about her function as wife and mother than the ordinary artisan of his trade. It is indecent and filthy for a respectable girl to know anything of the marital relation. Oh, for the inconsistency of respectability, that needs the marriage vow to turn something which is filthy into the purest and most sacred arrangement that none dare question or criticize. Yet that is exactly the attitude of the average upholder of marriage. The prospective wife and mother is kept in complete ignorance of her only asset in the competitive field—sex. Thus she enters into life-long relations with a man only to find herself shocked, repelled, outraged beyond measure by the most natural and healthy instinct, sex. It is safe to say that a large percentage of the unhappiness, misery, distress, and physical suffering of matrimony is due to the criminal ignorance in sex matters that is being extolled as a great virtue. Nor is it at all an exaggeration when I say that more than one home has been broken up because of this deplorable fact.

If, however, woman is free and big enough to learn the mystery of sex without the sanction of State or Church, she will stand condemned as utterly unfit to become the wife of a "good" man, his goodness consisting of an empty brain and plenty of money. Can there be anything more outrageous than the idea that a healthy, grown woman, full of life and passion, must deny nature's demand, must subdue her most intense craving, undermine her health and break her spirit, must stunt her vision, abstain from the depth and glory of sex experience until a "good" man comes along to take her unto himself as a wife? That is precisely what marriage means. How can such an arrangement end except in failure? This is one, though not the least important, factor of marriage, which differentiates it from love.

Ours is a practical age. The time when Romeo and Juliet risked the wrath of their fathers for love, when Gretchen exposed herself to the gossip of her neighbors for love, is no more. If, on rare occasions, young people allow themselves the luxury of romance, they are taken in care by the elders, drilled and pounded until they become "sensible."

The moral lesson instilled in the girl is not whether the man has aroused her love, but rather is it, "How much?" The important and only God of practical American life: Can the man make a living? can he support a wife? That is the only thing that justifies marriage. Gradually this saturates every thought of the girl; her dreams are not of moonlight and kisses, of laughter and tears; she dreams of shopping tours and bargain counters. This soul poverty and sordidness are the elements inherent in the marriage institution. The State and the Church approve of no other ideal, simply because it is the one that necessitates the State and Church control of men and women.

Doubtless there are people who continue to consider love above dollars and cents. Particularly is this true of that class whom economic necessity has forced to become self-supporting. The tremendous change in woman's position, wrought by that mighty factor, is indeed phenomenal when we reflect that it is but a short time since she has entered the industrial arena. Six million women wage workers; six million women, who have the equal right with men to be exploited, to be robbed, to go on strike; aye, to starve even. Anything more, my lord? Yes, six million wage workers in every walk of life, from the highest brain work to the mines and railroad tracks; yes, even detectives and policemen. Surely the emancipation is complete.

Yet with all that, but a very small number of the vast army of women wage workers look upon work as a permanent issue, in the same light as does man. No matter how decrepit the latter, he has been taught to be independent, self-supporting. Oh, I know that no one is really independent in our economic treadmill; still, the poorest specimen of a man hates to be a parasite; to be known as such, at any rate.

The woman considers her position as worker transitory, to be thrown aside for the first bidder. That is why it is infinitely harder to organize women than men. "Why should I join a union? I am going to get married, to have a home." Has she not been taught from infancy to look upon that as her ultimate calling? She learns soon enough that the home, though not so large a prison as the factory, has more solid doors and bars. It has a keeper so faithful that naught can escape him. The most tragic part, however, is that the home no longer frees her from wage slavery; it only increases her task.

According to the latest statistics submitted before a Committee "on labor and wages, and congestion of population," ten per cent. of the wage workers in New York City alone are married, yet they must continue to work at the most poorly paid labor in the world. Add to this horrible aspect the drudgery of housework, and what remains of the protection and glory of the home? As a matter of fact, even the middle-class girl in marriage can not speak of her home, since it is the man who creates her sphere. It is not important whether the husband is a brute or a darling. What I wish to prove is that marriage guarantees woman a home only by the grace of her husband. There she moves about in *his* home, year after year, until her aspect of life and human affairs becomes as flat, narrow, and drab as her surroundings. Small wonder if she becomes a nag, petty, quarrelsome, gossipy, unbearable, thus driving the man from the house. She could not go, if she wanted to; there is no place to go. Besides, a short period of married life, of complete surrender of all faculties, absolutely incapacitates the average woman for the outside world. She becomes reckless in appearance, clumsy in her movements, dependent in her decisions, cowardly in her judgment, a weight and a bore, which most men grow to hate and despise. Wonderfully inspiring atmosphere for the bearing of life, is it not?

But the child, how is it to be protected, if not for marriage? After all, is not that the most important consideration? The sham, the hypocrisy of it! Marriage protecting the child, yet thousands of children destitute and homeless. Marriage protecting the child, yet orphan asylums and reformatories overcrowded, the Society for the Prevention of Cruelty to Children keeping busy in rescuing the little victims from "loving" parents, to place them under more loving care, the Gerry Society. Oh, the mockery of it!

Marriage may have the power to bring the horse to water, but has it ever made him drink? The law will place the father under arrest, and put him in convict's clothes; but has that ever stilled the hunger of the child? If the parent has no work, or if he hides his identity, what does marriage do then? It invokes the law to bring the man to "justice," to put him safely behind closed doors; his labor, however, goes not to the child, but to the State. The child receives but a blighted memory of its father's stripes.

As to the protection of the woman,—therein lies the curse of marriage. Not that it really protects her, but the very idea is so revolting, such an outrage and insult on life, so degrading to human dignity, as to forever condemn this parasitic institution.

It is like that other paternal arrangement—capitalism. It robs man of his birthright, stunts his growth, poisons his body, keeps him in ignorance, in poverty, and dependence, and then institutes charities that thrive on the last vestige of man's self-respect.

The institution of marriage makes a parasite of woman, an absolute dependent. It incapacitates her for life's struggle, annihilates her social consciousness, paralyzes her imagination, and then imposes its gracious protection, which is in reality a snare, a travesty on human character.

If motherhood is the highest fulfillment of woman's nature, what other protection does it need, save love and freedom? Marriage but defiles, outrages, and corrupts her fulfillment. Does it not say to woman, Only when you follow me shall you bring forth life? Does it not condemn her to the block, does it not degrade and shame her if she refuses to buy her right to motherhood by selling herself? Does not marriage only sanction motherhood, even though conceived in hatred, in compulsion? Yet, if motherhood be of free choice, of love, of ecstasy, of defiant passion, does it not place a crown of thorns upon an innocent head and carve in letters of blood the hideous epithet, Bastard? Were marriage to contain all the virtues claimed for it, its crimes against motherhood would exclude it forever from the realm of love.

Love, the strongest and deepest element in all life, the harbinger of hope, of joy, of ecstasy; love, the defier of all laws, of all conventions; love, the freest, the most powerful moulder of human destiny; how can such an all-compelling force be synonymous with that poor little State and Church-begotten weed, marriage?

Free love? As if love is anything but free! Man has bought brains, but all the millions in the world have failed to buy love. Man has subdued bodies, but all the power on earth has been unable to subdue love. Man has conquered whole nations, but all his armies could not conquer love. Man has chained and fettered the spirit, but he has been utterly helpless before love. High on a throne, with all the splendor and pomp his gold can command, man is yet poor and desolate, if love passes him by. And if it stays, the poorest hovel is radiant with warmth, with life and color. Thus love has the magic power to make of a beggar a king. Yes, love is free; it can dwell in no other atmosphere. In freedom it gives itself unreservedly, abundantly, completely. All the laws on the statutes, all the courts in the universe, cannot tear it from the soil, once love has taken root. If, however, the soil is sterile, how can marriage make it bear fruit? It is like the last desperate struggle of fleeting life against death.

Woman and the New Race

Margaret Sanger

Nothing has contributed so much to women's growing liberation as the increasing control women can exercise over their reproductive capacities. Although some forms of birth control had been practiced in antiquity, it did not become a major force in the lives of ordinary women, especially poor women, until the twentieth century. In this country, into the 1930s, the so-called Comstock Laws of 1873 forbade the distribution of birth control information through the mails, and many states had laws prohibiting the use and sale of contraceptives. The efforts of the Birth Control League and particularly Margaret Sanger eventually resulted in the social acceptance of "planned parenthood."

Sanger was born in Corning, New York, in 1883. She studied nursing in White Plains and New York City. Early in her first marriage, she worked as an obstetrical nurse on New York's impoverished Lower East Side, where she saw the destructive burdens unchecked reproduction imposed on the poor and underprivileged. After studying contraception in Europe in 1913, she returned to New York, where she founded the magazine Woman Rebel *and, in 1916, opened her first clinic with her sister, Ethel Byrne, and a friend, Fania Mindell. All were arrested, and Byrne was subsequently jailed and mistreated. The episode brought this until-then rarely discussed issue into public view, and 1917 saw the founding of the National Birth Control League, with a growing membership.*

Although the birth control campaign did not have the support of many of the established women's rights organizations, who feared the controversy, various reform groups (including some trade unions) and women activists, many from the suffrage movement, pressed vehemently for birth control. Circumstances were in many ways analogous to today's abortion debate. Then, as now, opposition was highly charged and well organized in both religious and political circles; the poor were in even greater need of the reform than were the more affluent; and issues centered on matters of morality and "nature." Sanger ultimately won her fight. By 1952 in Bombay, she was well respected and was named first president of the International Planned Parenthood Federation. She died in Arizona in 1966. She had founded various journals and leagues and had written six books, including Woman and the New Race *(1920). In the section reprinted here, Sanger argues the claims of women's right to personal freedom and autonomy in procreative decisions, points out the implications for the world community of unchecked reproduction, and focuses on the centrality of women alone in carrying the burdens and responsibilities of having and rearing children. These remain contemporary themes.*

Woman's Error and Her Debt

The most far-reaching social development of modern times is the revolt of woman against sex servitude. The most important force in the remaking of the world is a free motherhood. Beside this force, the elaborate international programmes of modern statesmen are weak and superficial. Diplomats may formulate leagues of nations and nations may pledge their utmost strength to maintain them, statesmen may dream of reconstructing the world out of alliances, hegemonies and spheres of influence, but woman, continuing to produce explosive populations, will convert these pledges into the proverbial scraps of paper; or she may, by controlling birth, lift motherhood to the plane of a voluntary, intelligent function, and remake the world. When the world is thus remade, it will exceed the dream of statesman, reformer and revolutionist.

Only in recent years has woman's position as the gentler and weaker half of the human family been emphatically and generally questioned. Men assumed that this was woman's place; woman

---

Margaret Sanger, *Woman and the New Race*. New York: Brentano's Publishers, 1920.

herself accepted it. It seldom occurred to anyone to ask whether she would go on occupying it forever.

Upon the mere surface of woman's organized protests there were no indications that she was desirous of achieving a fundamental change in her position. She claimed the right of suffrage and legislative regulation of her working hours, and asked that her property rights be equal to those of the man. None of these demands, however, affected directly the most vital factors of her existence. Whether she won her point or failed to win it, she remained a dominated weakling in a society controlled by men.

Woman's acceptance of her inferior status was the more real because it was unconscious. She had chained herself to her place in society and the family through the maternal functions of her nature, and only chains thus strong could have bound her to her lot as a brood animal for the masculine civilizations of the world. In accepting her rôle as the "weaker and gentler half," she accepted that function. In turn, the acceptance of that function fixed the more firmly her rank as an inferior.

Caught in this "vicious circle," woman has, through her reproductive ability, founded and perpetuated the tyrannies of the Earth. Whether it was the tyranny of a monarchy, an oligarchy or a republic, the one indispensable factor of its existence was, as it is now, hordes of human beings—human beings so plentiful as to be cheap, and so cheap that ignorance was their natural lot. Upon the rock of an unenlightened, submissive maternity have these been founded; upon the product of such a maternity have they flourished.

No despot ever flung forth his legions to die in foreign conquest, no privilege-ruled nation ever erupted across its borders, to lock in death embrace with another, but behind them loomed the driving power of a population too large for its boundaries and its natural resources.

No period of low wages or of idleness with their want among the workers, no peonage or sweatshop, no child-labor factory, ever came into being, save from the same source. Nor have famine and plague been as much "acts of God" as acts of too prolific mothers. They, also, as all students know, have their basic causes in over-population.

The creators of over-population are the women, who, while wringing their hands over each fresh horror, submit anew to their task of producing the multitudes who will bring about the *next* tragedy of civilization.

While unknowingly laying the foundations of tyrannies and providing the human tinder for racial conflagrations, woman was also unknowingly creating slums, filling asylums with insane, and institutions with other defectives. She was replenishing the ranks of the prostitutes, furnishing grist for the criminal courts and inmates for prisons. Had she planned deliberately to achieve this tragic total of human waste and misery, she could hardly have done it more effectively.

Woman's passivity under the burden of her disastrous task was almost altogether that of ignorant resignation. She knew virtually nothing about her reproductive nature and less about the consequences of her excessive childbearing. It is true that, obeying the inner urge of their natures, *some* women revolted. They went even to the extreme of infanticide and abortion. Usually their revolts were not general enough. They fought as individuals, not as a mass. In the mass they sank back into blind and hopeless subjection. They went on breeding with staggering rapidity those numberless, undesired children who become the clogs and the destroyers of civilizations.

To-day, however, woman is rising in fundamental revolt. Even her efforts at mere reform are, as we shall see later, steps in that direction. Underneath each of them is the feminine urge to complete freedom. Millions of women are asserting their right to voluntary motherhood. They are determined to decide for themselves whether they shall become mothers, under what conditions and when. This is the fundamental revolt referred to. It is for woman the key to the temple of liberty.

Even as birth control is the means by which woman attains basic freedom, so it is the means by which she must and will uproot the evil she has wrought through her submission. As she has unconsciously and ignorantly brought about social disaster, so must and will she consciously and intelligently *undo* that disaster and create a new and a better order.

The task is hers. It cannot be avoided by excuses, nor can it be delegated. It is not enough for woman to point to the self-evident domination of man. Nor does it avail to plead the guilt of rulers and the exploiters of labor. It makes no difference that she does not formulate industrial systems nor that she is an instinctive believer in social justice. In her submission lies her error and her guilt. By her failure to withhold the multitudes of children who have made inevitable the most flagrant of our social evils, she incurred a debt to society. Regardless of her own wrongs, regardless of her lack of opportunity and regardless of all other considerations, *she* must pay that debt.

She must not think to pay this debt in any superficial way. She cannot pay it with palliatives—with child-labor laws, prohibition, regulation of prostitution and agitation against war. Political nostrums and social panaceas are but incidentally and superficially useful. They do not touch the source of the social disease.

War, famine, poverty and oppression of the workers will continue while woman makes life cheap. They will cease only when she limits her reproductivity and human life is no longer a thing to be wasted.

Two chief obstacles hinder the discharge of this tremendous obligation. The first and the lesser is the legal barrier. Dark-Age laws would still deny to her the knowledge of her reproductive nature. Such knowledge is indispensable to intelligent motherhood and she must achieve it, despite absurd statutes and equally absurd moral canons.

The second and more serious barrier is her own ignorance of the extent and effect of her submission. Until she knows the evil her subjection has wrought to herself, to her progeny and to the world at large, she cannot wipe out that evil.

To get rid of these obstacles is to invite attack from the forces of reaction which are so strongly entrenched in our present-day society. It means warfare in every phase of her life. Nevertheless, at whatever cost, she must emerge from her ignorance and assume her responsibility.

She can do this only when she has awakened to a knowledge of herself and of the consequences of her ignorance. The first step is birth control. Through birth control she will attain to voluntary motherhood. Having attained this, the basic freedom of her sex, she will cease to enslave herself and the mass of humanity. Then, through the understanding of the intuitive forward urge within her, she will not stop at patching up the world; she will remake it.

Birth Control—A Parents' Problem or Woman's?

The problem of birth control has arisen directly from the effort of the feminine spirit to free itself from bondage. Woman herself has wrought that bondage through her reproductive powers and while enslaving herself has enslaved the world. The physical suffering to be relieved is chiefly woman's. Hers, too, is the love life that dies first under the blight of too prolific breeding. Within her is wrapped up the future of the race—it is hers to make or mar. All of these considerations point unmistakably to one fact—it is woman's duty as well as her privilege to lay hold of the means of freedom. Whatever men may do, she cannot escape the responsibility. For ages she has been deprived of the opportunity to meet this obligation. She is now emerging from her helplessness. Even as no one can share the suffering of the overburdened mother, so no one can do this work for her. Others may help, but she and she alone can free herself.

The basic freedom of the world is woman's freedom. A free race cannot be born of slave mothers. A woman enchained cannot choose but give a measure of that bondage to her sons and daughters. No woman can call herself free who does not own and control her body. No woman can call herself free until she can choose consciously whether she will or will not be a mother.

It does not greatly alter the case that some women call themselves free because they earn their own livings, while others profess freedom because they defy the conventions of sex relationship. She who earns her own living gains a sort of freedom that is not to be undervalued, but in quality and in quantity it is of little account beside the untrammeled choice of mating or not mating, of being a mother or not being a mother. She gains food and clothing and shelter, at least, without submitting to the charity of her companion, but the earning of her own living does not give her the development of her inner sex urge, far deeper and more powerful in its outworkings than any of these externals. In order to have that development, she must still meet and solve the problem of motherhood.

With the so-called "free" woman, who chooses a mate in defiance of convention, freedom is largely a question of character and audacity. If she does attain to an unrestricted choice of a mate, she is still in a position to be enslaved through her reproductive powers. Indeed, the pressure of law and custom upon the woman not legally married is likely to make her more of a slave than the woman fortunate enough to marry the man of her choice.

Look at it from any standpoint you will, suggest any solution you will, conventional or unconventional, sanctioned by law or in defiance of law, woman is in the same position, fundamentally, until she is able to determine for herself whether she will be a mother and to fix the number of her offspring. This unavoidable situation is alone enough to make birth control, first of all, a woman's problem. On the very face of the matter, voluntary motherhood is chiefly the concern of the woman.

It is persistently urged, however, that since sex expression is the act of two, the responsibility of controlling the results should not be placed upon woman alone. Is it fair, it is asked, to give her, instead of the man, the task of protecting herself when she is, perhaps, less rugged in physique than her mate, and has, at all events, the normal, periodic inconveniences of her sex?

We must examine this phase of her problem in two lights—that of the ideal, and of the conditions working toward the ideal. In an ideal society, no doubt, birth control would become the concern of the man as well as the woman. The hard, inescapable fact which we encounter to-day is that man has not only refused any such responsibility, but has individually and collectively sought to prevent woman from obtaining knowledge by which she could assume this responsibility for herself. She is still in the position of a dependent to-day because her mate has refused to consider her as an individual apart from his needs. She is still bound because she has in the past left the solution of the problem to him. Having left it to him, she finds that instead of rights, she has only such privileges as she has gained by petitioning, coaxing and cozening. Having left it to him, she is exploited, driven and enslaved to his desires.

While it is true that he suffers many evils as the consequence of this situation, she suffers vastly more. While it is true that he should be awakened to the cause of these evils, we know that they come home to her with crushing force every day. It is she who has the long burden of carrying, bearing and rearing the unwanted children. It is she who must watch beside the beds of pain where lie the babies who suffer because they have come into overcrowded homes. It is her heart that the sight of the deformed, the subnormal, the undernourished, the overworked child smites first and oftenest and hardest. It is *her* love life that dies first in the fear of undesired pregnancy. It is her opportunity for self expression that perishes first and most hopelessly because of it.

Conditions, rather than theories, facts, rather than dreams, govern the problem. They place it squarely upon the shoulders of woman. She has learned that whatever the moral responsibility of the man in this direction may be, he does not discharge it. She has learned that, lovable and considerate as the individual husband may be, she has nothing to expect from men in the mass, when they make laws and decree customs. She knows that regardless of what ought to be, the brutal unavoidable fact is that she will never receive her freedom until she takes it for herself.

Having learned this much, she has yet something more to learn. Women are too much inclined to follow in the footsteps of men, to try to think as men think, to try to solve the general problems of life as men solve them. If after attaining their freedom, women accept conditions in the spheres of government, industry, art, morals and religion as they find them, they will be but taking a leaf out of man's book. The woman is not needed to do man's work. She is not needed to think man's thoughts. She need not fear that the masculine mind, almost universally dominant, will fail to take care of its own. Her mission is not to enhance the masculine spirit, but to express the feminine; hers is not to preserve a man-made world, but to create a human world by the infusion of the feminine element into all of its activities.

Woman must not accept; she must challenge. She must not be awed by that which has been built up around her; she must reverence that within her which struggles for expression. Her eyes must be less upon what is and more clearly upon what should be. She must listen only with a frankly questioning attitude to the dogmatized opinions of man-made society. When she chooses her new, free course of action, it must be in the light of her own opinion—of her own intuition. Only so can she give play to the feminine spirit. Only thus can she free her mate from the bondage which he wrought for himself when he wrought hers. Only thus can she restore to him that of which he robbed himself in restricting her. Only thus can she remake the world.

The world is, indeed, hers to remake, it is hers to build and to recreate. Even as she has permitted the suppression of her own feminine element and the consequent impoverishment of industry, art, letters, science, morals, religions and social intercourse, so it is hers to enrich all these.

Woman must have her freedom—the fundamental freedom of choosing whether or not she shall be a mother and how many children she will have. Regardless of what man's attitude may be, that problem is hers—and before it can be his, it is hers alone.

She goes through the vale of death alone, each time a babe is born. As it is the right neither of man nor the state to coerce her into this ordeal, so it is her right to decide whether she will endure it. That right to decide imposes upon her the duty of clearing the way to knowledge by which she may make and carry out the decision.

Birth control is woman's problem. The quicker she accepts it as hers and hers alone, the quicker will society respect motherhood. The quicker, too, will the world be made a fit place for her children to live.

The Class Roots of Feminism

Karen Sacks

Karen Brodkin Sacks directs the Women's Studies Program at UCLA and is a member of the Anthropology Department. She is the author of Sisters and Wives, Caring by the Hour *(1988) and coeditor of* My Troubles Are Going To Have Trouble With Me *(1984).*

Generally speaking, we tend to hear most about the political and psychosocial issues raised during the nineteenth century and carried into the twentieth. But one ought to also recall that economic issues were at the heart of both the abolition and the women's rights movements. Karen Sacks traces those issues in the following article. She describes separate trends in the women's movement: black women's drive for legal and economic equality, middle-class women's push for educational opportunity and full legal membership in their class, and working-class women's drive for economic progress. Sacks's discussion reveals some of the sources of tension among those groups today in their differing needs and priorities, but she demonstrates the fallacy of identifying the entire impetus of women's desires for change as a "white middle-class movement."

DURING THE NINETEENTH CENTURY (SAY FROM 1820 to 1920) the women's movement in the United States was not a single movement, but rather three movements which were consciously movements for the rights of women. There was an industrial-working-class women's movement for economic improvement and equality which began with the earliest factories in the United States, the New England textile mills of the 1830s. Second, there was a black women's movement made up of working- and middle-class black women against racism and for both economic improvement and legal equality with whites. This also had its roots in the 1830s, in the black convention movements.* And finally, there was the white middle-class movement for legal equality which had its beginnings in women's attempts to become full legal members of their class, also in the 1830s.

While two well-known histories of the women's movement[1] show clearly that the white middle-class movement did not speak for all women, they do not examine the demands, priorities, and alliances of all three movements from the viewpoint of class roots and class interests. I would like to sketch such an analysis.

Class is the key, in the sense that the material conditions of black and working-class women, as well as the social ideology regarding them, have been very different from the material conditions of white middle-class women and their corresponding social ideologies. In both the colonial period and after independence, the only woman whose place was in the home was the woman of property. Neither slave women nor free propertyless women "belonged" there. Before the growth of industry, the United States had a domestic and agrarian economy in which men and women both could play a productive role "at home," so to speak—provided they owned or leased or otherwise had access to a home with farm (means of production), which most whites and some free blacks did. But those without their own household means of production, both men and women, had

This paper originally appeared in *Monthly Review,* 27, No. 9 (February 1976).

This article is a revised version of a paper read at the University of Connecticut Anthropology Department and at the 1973 meetings of the American Anthropological Association. The following people gave various kinds of assistance and very helpful criticism: Mary Clark, Soon Young Yoon, Bill Derman, Bobbye Ortiz, Rayna Reiter, Susan Reverby, the N.Y. Women's Anthropology Conference, and the librarians at the Archives of Labor History and Urban Affairs at Wayne State University. [K. Sacks's note] to work for someone else. Puritan religion and law in the North and slavery in the South were in agreement that those without property, free or slave, male or female, had an obligation to work for those with property. The terrible stigma attached to idleness by the Puritan religion largely served the interests of employers of labor. Efforts to stimulate a cloth-making industry, dating from the colonial period, emphasize the labor of "our own women and children who are now in a great measure idle."[2] Propertyless people who were not working for a master were a "public nuisance," the "public" in this phrase meaning, of course, people with property (especially manufacturing interests). Several New England states had laws compelling the binding out of children of the poor until the age of marriage. Adult poor, female as well as male, could be punished for "idleness." Thus for free as well as slave women, work outside the home was not looked down upon as unfeminine; rather, it was demanded as the only virtuous activity of propertyless women.

Propertied women, on the other hand, were virtuous and productive mistresses of households—until factories operated by propertyless women began to transform the domestic economy into an industrial one. Then they became ladies ("of leisure" being implicit in the word). The Southern transformation from domestic to industrial economy lay earlier, in the development of plantation slavery, with cotton grown partly by black women and a household run by the labor of black women. Thus, a double standard based on class came into being for women.

The self-consciously feminist movements and groups which developed—chiefly in the North during the nineteenth century—reflect the different circumstances of middle- and working-class women in the pre-Civil War years. Goals and tactics differed by class. Working-class women fought for more wages, equal wages with men, shorter hours, health, safety, and protective legislation. These were clearly class demands, and collective action was used to get them: strikes and unions mainly, but electoral pressure too (even without the vote). But working-class women also formed protective societies which got together for the purpose of self-"improvement" or of coping with various facets of a difficult life, rather than for the purpose of fighting to change social conditions.

The middle-class movement used analogous tactics, but in different proportions. Here, struggles of women to obtain and provide professional education and professional jobs for women, and to speak in public as full members of the anti-slavery movement, were, by and large, waged individually by women, rather than as part of a collective movement. It was the Abolition movement which gave birth to a self-conscious women's movement in the middle class, one which engaged in collective action, largely in the form of legislative petitions.

The pre-Civil War struggles were more social and thus collective among working-class women, and more self-help among middle-class women. This was due largely to the nature of the demands themselves and to the identity of the enemy, or obstacle. Education involved attacking no enemies. Likewise, both black and white women's improvement or protective societies were self-help ventures and did not identify enemies. The economic demands of women factory workers, on the other hand, were pursued solely by collective action directed against both mill owners and legislators.

Along with mill work, teaching school was a widespread women's occupation throughout this period. Not only were teachers and mill girls from the same background (farm families), but some women did both, alternating teaching and mill work. Though mill work paid badly, teaching paid worse. Schools were tiny affairs with few teachers, but factories often had several thousand workers. Despite the relatively better pay, it was the collective situation which allowed women to define "relatively better" as absolutely unsatisfactory by forming their own organization. Teachers, isolated and scattered, seem to have suffered in silence.

In the middle-class movement, collective action focused on those aspects of domestic law which prevented married women from having an independent economic status. Women's right to own inherited property was petitioned for and won without much opposition. But such a law had little relevance to working-class women. The situation in New York, the first state to pass such a law (1848), is illuminating. Its moving force was largely propertied males: "Fathers who had estates to bequeath to their daughters," and "husbands in extensive business operations [who could] see the advantage of allowing the wife the right to hold separate property."[3]

Middle-class women led two other important struggles in the legal realm of household affairs which did have relevance to working-class women: for the right of the woman to her own wages and to custody of children. By 1880 these were won in most states. New York was again the first state in which public sentiment for these changes was organized, beginning in 1854 via a petition campaign throughout the state. Middle-class feminists organized a delegation of working-class women to present this petition to the legislature and argue for it.[4] When it failed to move the legislature, Susan B. Anthony campaigned again throughout the state. Precisely what happened between 1855 and 1860 is not clear. But in 1860 the legislature passed a bill giving women property ownership, the right to collect their own wages, to sue in court, and to inherit the husband's property. It seems, though, that the majority of advances in civil law pertained to property law and thus to the middle and upper classes. While legislatures may have had to be persuaded, there were solid class interests for such reforms among propertied males and females.

As regards working-class women, the middle-class women who gathered at the Rochester women's convention in 1848 seem to have been both conscious of their own class and divided on class vs. sex interests. While all other resolutions passed clearly stated beliefs and principles, this one hedged: Resolved "*that those who* believe the laboring classes of women are oppressed, ought to do all in their power to raise their wages, beginning with their own household servants."[5]

Collective action by textile-mill women preceded that of middle-class women. Textile mills, centered in New England and staffed almost totally by women, were the nuclei of pre-Civil War U.S. industry. The first factory strike took place in 1824, just after the birth of the factories themselves, and involved both men and women. The 1830s saw a large number of strikes and the beginnings of many labor organizations, labor parties and papers, all short-lived. In this context, the record is full of male-female labor cooperation and independent women's actions and organizations. One of these labor parties, the Association of Working People of New Castle, Delaware, demanded the vote for women in 1831.[6]

Women were in the forefront and leadership of trade-union development in the 1840s and the focus was in the textile industry. The mills of the 1830s had been staffed by single women, largely daughters of farmers, who worked for a short time or a specific purpose. In the crisis of 1837 many farms were wiped out, and the workers in the mills during the forties and fifties were, by and large, landless native-born and Irish immigrants who could no longer quit if wages and hours were unsatisfactory. Out of this milieu came a whole host of factory-worker papers and organizations. The New England Female Labor Reform Association (FLRA) under its president, Sarah Bagley, a Lowell factory worker, became the main group for factory women. In addition to organizing in New England, this group stimulated and kept in contact with branches of women textile-worker groups in New York and western Pennsylvania. Though officially an affiliate of the New England Workingmen's Association (NEWA), in reality it was the center of it and provided much of its leadership, particularly in the fight for the ten-hour day. The FLRA argued for a ten-hour law in the Massachusetts legislature and, despite the fact that women could not vote, ran a successful campaign to defeat the re-election of Lowell's state representative, a mill owners' man who opposed the ten-hour bill.

Though women workers were centered in New England, the biggest women's struggle took place in the western Pennsylvania textile mills. Here the workers struck in 1845 for a ten-hour day. After a month, some workers began returning to the mills. But women strikers, aided by a "men's auxiliary," stormed the gates of one factory and threw out the strikebreakers. Despite this militancy, the strikers were told that they would get a ten-hour day only when New England workers did. They then appealed to the NEWA and the FLRA for help. Apparently only the women in New England were ready to call a general strike. In the face of the NEWA's hopelessness, they gave it up. Again in 1848 the Pennsylvania workers went out on strike, and again it looked like defeat. This time, the women, armed with axes, stormed the factory, took on a company of police, captured the strikebreakers, and then closed it down again. The leaders were arrested, but the strike continued. Though they finally won a ten-hour day only by accepting a wage cut, it is not clear whether they soon increased their wages to what they had been for twelve hours' work.[7] In any case, these early textile battles show the militance and leadership women gave to the early labor movement.

Though largely separate, the working-class and middle-class movements had a common ground in the anti-slavery movement. Abolition joined white well-to-do and professional people with free black men and women, and in the 1840s with a growing number of white workers, particularly from the New England textile mills. In Abolition one finds the seeds of class and race conflicts which pitted the women's movements against each other. In the 1830s the anti-slavery movement had split over women's participation, with particularly strong objections coming from the clergy. Middle-class women saw Abolition and women's rights as part of a single movement for extending democracy. In 1832 Lowell factory women formed a Female Anti-Slavery Society, and by 1845 they were fund-raising and circulating anti-slavery petitions, despite hostility on the part of the mill owners.[8] But their reasons for favoring Abolition differed from those of middle-class women. The mill women argued that a labor force in slavery degraded free labor as well as slave labor, and that all labor had a two-faced enemy: "the lord of the loom and the lord of the lash."

Abolition, whether spoken by middle- or working-class people, faced much more organized opposition than women's rights. Mobs in the North were "organized and led by prominent, respected members of the community." And, according to R. B. Nye, the major root of pro-slavery force was economic: fear of displeasing the Southern planter on whom much of New York commerce and rising New England textiles depended.[9] Indeed, H. Josephson has shown how assiduously the New England magnates of the 1840s and 1850s courted the planters and reviled the Abolitionists.[10]

Yet the anti-slavery movement contained much of the racism and class antagonisms which led to three separate and generally antagonistic women's movements after the Civil War. Many white middle-class Abolitionists were violently anti-labor, and most crafts excluded free black workers. While many Abolitionist groups spoke out against job discrimination against black workers in the North, some of their members were at the same time also practicing this same discrimination. In 1852 a number of black men applied for jobs at the businesses of members of the American and Foreign Anti-Slavery Society. Some were rejected outright; others got only menial jobs.[11] The widespread exclusion of black men and women from craft and factory jobs is well known. What has not received adequate treatment is the extent to which employers and workers were responsible for it.

These class and race antagonisms among the Abolitionists (important divisions to be inherited by the women's movement) were deepened by pro-slavery forces. Before the 1830s its defenders rationalized slavery as a necessary evil. To counter anti-slavery forces they developed a whole pseudo-science of white supremacy. Together with nativist corollaries, this became a cornerstone of post-Civil War bourgeois ideology. The war itself gave birth to accelerated industrialization and thus to the development of an industrial working class as well as a more powerful bourgeoisie. The latter took governmental power from the Southern agrarian bourgeoisie. Once in power, the Northern industrialists re-allied themselves with the Southern planters to defeat Reconstruction and entrench their common position against the black and white working class. Economic, political, and legal discrimination against black people was made a virtue through the newly developed national policy of white supremacy; at the same time an anti-foreignism was directed against white working-class immigrants in the North. Racism and nativism were important to the new capitalists because neither black nor white workers passively accepted the conditions of industrial wage slavery. Against this general background, we may better understand the divisions in the developing women's movement.

From the end of the Civil War until 1920, when it collapsed, the white middle-class women's movement defined itself as middle class by excluding black and working-class women. As such women moved from the liberalism of the Reconstruction period to the racist and anti-working-class mainstream of the "progressive era," they took for granted this status quo—a status quo with a sharp division between middle and working classes and with hierarchical divisions within the working class based on race, nationality, and sex. Black men and women were to be confined to agrarian and domestic work; native-born and immigrant white men and women would make up the industrial working class, with skilled crafts largely excluding all save native-born white men.

The Civil War itself led to middle-class women's widespread involvement in a variety of service and professional positions—from nursing and teaching to office work. By and large, the new war opportunities were important for middle-class kinds of jobs, mainly for whites, but some black women also entered, particularly in teaching, through the Freedmen's Bureau. Opportunities were there, but they were not equal. For example, the federal government was delighted to have women replace the male office workers, not least because they worked for half pay. Black women received even less for their work—if they received anything at all. Harriet Tubman had to fight almost until her death before the government would pay her for her very considerable services, both military and civilian, during and after the war. Even then she received a pittance, and that as a pension for her husband. Tubman was nationally famous. It is thus probable that the thousands of less famous black women were treated much worse.

Postwar years, then, saw the growth in numbers of middle-class women as independent earners in largely professional or so-called semi-professional occupations. Materially, they were members of a growing middle class. As such (and like the women factory workers of prewar years) they began developing a stronger class identity. They began to see themselves less as a socially excluded and oppressed segment of humanity and more as second-class members of the white middle class. Black middle-class women were largely prevented from claiming *class* rights by the practice of segregation and white supremacy. As black women they struggled against racial oppression, including the ideological stereotyping of black women as immoral.

The Civil War affected working-class women in some basically different ways than it affected middle-class women, even though there were some superficial similarities. While groups of middle-class women might get together to sew uniforms for the Union army as their patriotic duty, for working-class women taking in sewing of uniforms was wage work for survival in a period of inflation. However, they were often not paid for this work. Apparently the government felt that since middle-class women did not need to be paid, neither did working-class women. The war and postwar years saw working-class women developing their own unions and protective associations, at least in part to combat situations like the above. By and large, these were localized efforts. To some extent, though, they were integrated into the National Labor Union (NLU). Thus, in 1863, women collar workers in Troy, New York, formed a local union and struck successfully for higher wages. Kate Mullaney, their president, became assistant secretary of the NLU. But this women's local disbanded with the demise of the NLU.

To some extent, women's locals were joined with men's local or national organizations in the same industry. The men and women weavers in Fall River exemplify this pattern. In the face of a pay cut in 1875, the men's union voted to acquiesce; the women, knowing the results of the men's meeting, held their own and voted to strike three mills. The men then followed their lead and they won.[12]

Women workers did form one national organization. The Daughters of St. Crispin, begun by women shoe-stitchers in Lynn, Massachusetts, was an organization parallel to the men's Knights of St. Crispin. New England shoe workers, particularly women, had organized before the Civil War. In 1860 they had gone on strike throughout New England in the most extensive pre-Civil War strike.[13] The Daughters of St. Crispin, formed in 1869, had 24 chapters, most of which were in New England—the center of the shoe industry—and in six other states as well. They demanded equal pay for equal work. Though they affiliated with the NLU, they managed to outlast it, staying in existence through much of the 1873 depression, and continuing in New England until 1876. For those days it was a long-lived organization.

The Knights of Labor, the first enduring national labor organization in the United States, saw women and black people as important parts of the working class, and on this basis supported equality within the organization and demanded it of employers. At its first national convention in 1878, they voted for equal pay for equal work, and began from the outset to include women workers in separate locals as well as in male-female locals. The first all-women local, of Philadelphia shoe workers, joined in 1878. By 1886, at the peak of the Knights of Labor, there were about 194 women's locals and about 50,000 women members (8–9 percent of the total). In Massachusetts the proportion was higher: 1 in 7 members were women.[14] The Knights followed the same direction with regard to black workers, organizing them in the South and the North into both black-white and separate black locals. In 1886 there were about 60,000 black Knights out of about 700,000; in 1887 some 90,000 out of about half a million.[15] The Knights did seem to try in practice as well as rhetoric to fight for equal rights for all workers.

By contrast, the newly formed American Federation of Labor, an association of craft unions, supported few working-class women's issues, even though its membership included male-female as well as all-female locals, especially in the United Garment Workers (UGW). But if the UGW is any example of female participation, the AFL did not take the needs of its women members seriously.[16] The AFL did have some unofficial women organizers in the early years. Hannah Morgan organized some 23 women's locals in a variety of jobs; she also built the Illinois Women's Alliance, which led mass campaigns for protective legislation for women and children (and she organized secondarily for suffrage). Also under the AFL, the collar and shirt workers of Troy pulled together again, struck and won in 1891. The leader of the Working Women's Society of New York City unofficially organized women into the AFL, while the society organized support for strikes and for factory legislation.[17]

Meanwhile, the middle-class movement had become mainly a suffrage movement. But it too was divided. The National Women's Suffrage Association (NWSA) Stanton-Anthony wing, though biased in favor of the middle class by its suffrage focus, was willing to join with labor. Anthony and other suffrage leaders organized women's protective societies, supported and helped organize women's unions. For a time Susan Anthony was a member of the Knights of Labor (which favored suffrage). The rival group of suffragists, the American Women's Suffrage Association (AWSA), was anti-labor, narrowly suffragist, and drew its support from professional and leisured middle-class women, mainly through women's clubs.

Until 1890, then, there was a strong organization in the Knights of Labor fighting for equal rights for all labor, as well as a middle-class organization willing to join its main fight for suffrage with the economic demands of working women. Class determined the priorities, but on these issues there was no necessary conflict between them.

But the balance of forces favoring such inter-class cooperation changed in the 1890s. With the demise of the Knights, the AFL faced no competition and freely moved to organize skilled crafts only, largely the province of white, native-born men. Not only by focusing on skilled labor but also by deliberately excluding black and female skilled and semi-skilled workers, the AFL spread racism and sexism during its long-term domination of trade unionism. (It seems to me that modern-day notions about working-class racism and sexism are based heavily on the AFL's practice.) Women continued to form unions, some independent, which had a hard time, and some affiliated with the AFL, which seem to have faced almost equal difficulties.[18] At the same time that the unity of labor was weakened by this organizational practice, the ruling class stepped up its propaganda to cultivate and fix black-white, native-immigrant divisions and conflicts. The suffrage movement, represented by the National American Women's Suffrage Association (NAWSA, the merger of the two suffrage groups), fell solidly into line with them, abandoning even the divided support they had given working-class women in the 1860s.

In 1892, when the Homestead Steel workers struck and were embroiled in a nearly full-scale war to save job and union from Carnegie, the Pinkertons, and federal troops, Lucy Stone wanted to know why the workers didn't start their own businesses if they didn't like their jobs.[19] And Susan Anthony went to labor asking for suffrage support, but refused to do anything about working women's demands until the vote was won. Likewise, she raised her influential voice to argue that NAWSA should do nothing to fight Jim Crow laws barring black people (including black women) from decent railroad seats.

Their arguments for suffrage, as Kraditor has clearly shown,[20] came explicitly to be arguments for enfranchising white, American-born, and educated women as allies with their male counterparts against black and immigrant workers.

> *This government is menaced with great danger. . . . That danger lies in the votes possessed by the males in the slums of the cities, and the ignorant foreign vote which was sought to be brought up by each party, to make political success. . . . In the mining districts, the danger has already reached this point—miners are supplied with arms, watching with greedy eyes for the moment when they can get in their deadly work of despoiling the wealth of the country. . . . There is but one way to avert the danger—cut off the vote of the slums and give to woman, who is bound to suffer all, and more than man can, of the evils his legislation has brought upon the nation, the power of protecting herself that man has secured for himself—the ballot.*[21]

NAWSA closed ranks against working-class women, not so much by the demand for suffrage itself as by their arguments claiming it should be granted and by their hostility to more pressing needs of women workers and black women of both classes. Thus the 1893 convention of NAWSA passed the following resolution directed against black people in the same way that Catt's speech attacked immigrants and the working class:

> Resolved, *that without expressing any opinion on the proper qualifications for voting, we call attention to the significant facts that in every State there are more women who can read and write than all negro* [sic] *voters; more American women who can read and write than all foreign voters; so that the enfranchisement of such women would settle the vexed question of rule by illiteracy, whether of home-grown or foreign-born production.*[22]

They lashed out at "foreigners" not only for being "ignorant" in general, but for being a major force in opposing women's rights. Kraditor summed up suffrage explanations of why voting in wards with large immigrant populations went against suffrage: "Foreign-born men had been brought up in a culture in which women were inferior [here the suffragists forgot earlier arguments and proudly pointed to the respected position of women in their own society]; . . . the ignorance of the foreign born disqualified them from voting wisely; . . . the new voters generally used alcoholic beverages and feared that woman suffrage would bring prohibition; . . . foreign-born workers in cities voted as dictated by saloonkeepers, rich employers, or party machines."[23] Ironically, when New York finally passed its suffrage referendum in 1917, it was working-class and immigrant New York City which carried it over the opposition from non-worker, native-born upstate! By this time, though, some members of NAWSA had begun to overcome their aversion to the working class, and to campaign in working-class districts. As late as 1916, however, NAWSA had made little effort to communicate across class lines.

While the overt anti-working-class, racist, and nativist arguments remained until the end, there were growing numbers of NAWSA members after the turn of the century who believed it important to speak to the working class. Thus Florence Kelley worked hard to fight the exploitation of workers in the sweatshops and to obtain protective legislation for women workers. She even criticized the anti-foreign mouthings of NAWSA. Yet she too resented being forced to campaign among workers: "[It was] an ignominious way to treat us, to send us to the Chinamen *[sic]* in San Francisco, to the enfranchised Indians of other western states, to the negroes *[sic]*, Italians, Hungarians, Poles, Bohemians and innumerable Slavic immigrants in Pennsylvania and other mining States to obtain our rights of suffrage."[24]

Jessie Ashley, treasurer of NAWSA and a socialist, also criticized the association for its anti-worker attitudes, in particular for not addressing its campaigns to the real needs of working-class women—economic needs. But she did accept some very middle-class stereotypes of working-class women. Remarking on the contrast made in another article between the "handsome ladies" at a suffrage parade and the working girls getting onto the subway, Ashley wrote,

> *For it is those "handsome ladies," and they alone, who have begun to see that women must stand and think and work together, and they, alas, are not the ones whose need to do so is the greatest. . . . For the most part the handsome ladies are well satisfied with their personal lot, but they want the vote as a matter of justice, while the fluttering, jammed-in subway girls are terribly blind to the whole question of class oppression and of sex oppression. Only the women of the working class are really oppressed, but it is not only the working-class women to whom injustice is done. Women of the leisure class need freedom, too.*[25]

Considering that this was written less than two years after the massive women's garment strike in New York (where Ashley lived), her talk of working-class women being blind to class oppression flies in the face of reality, as does her notion that only the "handsome ladies" know they must work together. Essentially, Ashley is reflecting the stereotype of the ignorant and docile working girl.

Along with the general racist stereotyping of black people, which NAWSA accepted and propagated, there existed the stigmatizing of black women as "loose" and "immoral." Sometimes this stereotyping was done "sympathetically":

> *The negro* [sic] *women of the South are subject to temptations, of which their white sisters of the North have no appreciation, and which come to them from the days of their race enslavement. They are still the victims of the white man under a system tacitly recognized, which deprives them of the sympathy and help of the Southern white women, and to meet such temptations the negro* [sic] *women can only offer the resistance of a low moral standard, an inheritance from the*

> *system of slavery, made still lower from a life-long residence in a one-roomed cabin.*[26]

But it propagates the same false stereotype of the immoral black woman, adding another kind of fuel to racist propaganda.

Black women, led by black middle-class and professional women, had long before formed their own clubs and expressed a desire to work with the white clubs, which in general the latter refused to do. To combat this racism they formed the National Association of Colored Women. The conditions facing black women differed in many ways from those facing white middle-class women. Black women's clubs organized around providing a particular social service, since public facilities were even less available in black communities than in white working-class communities. They also exposed and organized against lynching and terror campaigns directed against black men and women. At least one club maintained a settlement house and served the poor and working-class neighborhoods through militant action as well as services. Moreover, the membership, if not the leadership, of black women's clubs differed from their white counterparts. While the white clubs were middle class and professional, black club members were often workers, tenant farmers, or poor women.[27]

Even though the suffrage movement somewhat weakened its anti-worker attitude and to some extent its anti-immigrant posture, it never publicly mitigated its racism. This was largely due to the strategy of allying with Southern white middle-class women, who wanted the vote at least as much to maintain white supremacy as to have the vote. As a result of this "Southern strategy," black women were all but kept out of the association.[28] While support for racial equality was ruled out of order as an extraneous issue, the numerous white-supremacy speeches never met any such objection, or any other kind of public objection, for that matter.

What little amelioration there was of NAWSA's anti-worker and anti-immigrant stance came about largely because of the growth of city-wide women's strikes, notably in the garment and textile industries, in 1909 in New York, 1910 in Chicago, and 1912 in Lawrence. Prior to that time a number of white middle-class women—radicals, reformers, and socialists like Jessie Ashley, Ella Reeve Bloor, etc.—had urged concentration on working women's needs. But they were mainly rebuffed by NAWSA.

It was largely through the National Women's Trade Union League (NWTUL), formed in 1903, that the suffrage movement saw possible allies in working-class women. Made up of women trade unionists, but run mainly by middle-class reformers, many of whom were active suffragists, the NWTUL tried to serve two functions. First, in the face of AFL indifference to women workers, it organized women to improve their working conditions through trade unionism. Specifically, it organized women into AFL locals and supported AFL strikes. Its second role was to make trade unionism "respectable" through publicity and by winning middle-class support for strikes. It did succeed in organizing women into the AFL and in making *certain kinds* of unions "respectable." But it did not reform the AFL, which sold out the Chicago clothing strike in 1911. And the following year, despite anger over Chicago, the NWTUL actually helped the AFL break a strike, in Lawrence, Massachusetts.

In this case, the AFL had organized only among skilled (white, male, native-born) workers. But the vast majority were unskilled female, as well as male and immigrant, workers. The IWW [International Workers of the World] represented these workers; and when they walked out, it was the IWW that led this Lawrence strike. Together with the AFL, the Boston TUL set up a relief council which aided only those who pledged to go back to work.[29]

So while they did unionize women and ameliorate some of the anti-worker attitudes in the middle class, their role within the working-class movement was to be in the midst of things, to see that events did not get out of control, and to make sure women workers stayed respectable in bourgeois eyes.

Many women in the Boston TUL were disgusted with the role of their own organization in Lawrence. "Are we, the NWTUL, to ally ourselves inflexibly with the 'stand-patters' of the Labor Movement or are we to hold ourselves ready to aid the 'insurgents,' those who are freely fighting the fight of the exploited, the oppressed, and the weak among the workers?"[30] While this may have been a widespread feeling among NWTUL members, publicly they stood pat with the stand-patters of the AFL. Their official stance appeared in *Life and Labor,* the NWTUL paper:[31] the AFL "refused to take any action during the first fortnight of the strike while it was being led by enemies of organized labor [the IWW], but now that it shows every symptom of collapse they do not propose to allow the misled workers to suffer or lose any opportunity to bring them into recognized trade organizations."[32]

Working-class women, the IWW, the radicals reacted to this suffragist and middle-class bias. One working woman wrote to Leonora O'Reilly of her experience at a New York suffrage conference:

> *I feel as if I have butted in where I was not wanted. Miss Hay gave me a badge and was very nice to me but you know they had a school teacher represent the Industrial workers if you ever herd her it was like trying to fill a barrell with water that had no bottom not a word of labor spoken at this convention so far . . . after the hole thing was over some people came to me and said I had a right to speak for labor but they kept away until it was over. . . . I am not goying to wait for sunday meeting I am goying home satturday.*[33]

In the New York shirtwaist strike, two upper-class women rented the Hippodrome for a strike-support rally, attended by approximately 8,000 people. Though much has been made of rich women's generosity, Theresa Malkiel, a striker, wrote another side to it in her diary:

> *The most of our girls had to walk both ways in order to save their car fare. Many came without dinner, but the collection baskets had more pennies than anything else in them—it was our girls themselves who helped make it up, and yet there were so many rich women present. And I'm sure the speakers made it plain to them how badly the money was needed, then how comes it that out of $300 collected there should be $70 in pennies?*[34]

The IWW saw the vote as irrelevant and the suffrage movement as making working women "the tail of a suffrage kite in the hands of women of the very class driving the girls to lives of misery and shame."[35] Yet Elizabeth Gurley Flynn, then an IWW organizer, speaks approvingly of socialists in 1904 organizing working-class women to demand the vote so they can vote on labor issues.[36] Emma Goldman saw suffrage as a "modern fetish" of women who swore loyalty to every institution which oppresses them. "Else how is one to account for the tremendous, truly gigantic effort set in motion by those valiant fighters for a wretched little bill which will benefit a handful of propertied ladies, with absolutely no provision for the vast mass of working women?"[37]

Through the efforts of middle-class NWTUL women, and to some degree those of the militant suffragists' Women's Party, Wage Earners' Suffrage Leagues did come into being and working-class women did march in suffrage demonstrations. But even where working-class women participated in suffrage demands, they did so separately from the middle-class organizations, in a labor-based organization. Suffrage in this context never had a high priority for working-class women as a whole.

The years 1909–1912 marked a huge upsurge in working-class women's activity. The 1909 New York dressmakers' strike, or the "Uprising of 20,000," was the largest women's strike in history. It was followed by many large and small garment and textile strikes and the formation of enduring unions, steps toward the elimination of sweatshops, cutting hours, and increasing pay for women workers. By and large, women won these victories without the ballot.

As a rule, next to nothing is said of black working-class women in these struggles. Though black women were largely excluded from industry before the First World War, and hence from unions, there were black women working in the packinghouses of Chicago, in tobacco warehouses in the South, and as pressers in the garment industry in New York. In 1902 two packinghouse women organized a women's local which included black women. But more significant is a white garment worker and organizer's account of the beginning of the 1909 New York strike. She writes of her anxiety as to whether the women of the shop would walk out at the appointed time. They did, fifteen minutes early, when the fifty-three black women of the pressing department dropped their work and led the whole shop out.[38] Even where black women were employed during and after the First World War, they were largely in the worst jobs, with little or no chance for advancement, and often paid one half or one third what white women received. For example, pressers in the garment industry had the most physically difficult job in that industry. This was the job given to black women.[39]

Whom the women's movements perceived as the enemy illuminates the primacy of class lines over sex. In the working-class movement it was clearly the employer. The suffragists saw their enemies mainly as the liquor interests and, to some extent, big-business interests. Only the Women's Party actually saw the President and much of Congress as real enemies of women. For this breach of class loyalty they got the same treatment as working-class women strikers: jail, police brutality, etc.

The working-class women's movement, rather than dying in 1920, continued in the drives of the 1920s and 1930s to organize in Southern textile and tobacco shops. Here, black and white working-class women not only struggled to overcome racism, but had to take on the AFL[40] directly. Neither before nor since 1920 have women won equal pay for equal work, one of the two long-standing working-class women's demands. However, to the extent that women have won union representation, male-female pay scales have made moves in that direction. The other demand, for unionization itself, also continues. As middle-class women's jobs have become collectivized (teaching, white-collar, health, social work, clerical), middle-class women have also moved into union situations, which at least provide a material basis for middle-class women to join working-class women rather than the ruling class.

Notes

*I could find very little information on the class composition of black women's organizations, or on the organizations and struggles of working-class black women. Thus there is a data bias of which the reader should be aware. Though there were national black conventions from 1830, the earliest specific mention of women's rights, support for the Seneca Falls Declaration, is in 1848 (R. E. Paulson, *Women's Suffrage and Prohibition* [Glenview: Scott Foresman, 1973], p. 34). The 1848 convention in Cleveland resolved for equality for women with men and for full citizenship, including the vote for black men and women (H. H. Bell, ed., *Minutes and Proceedings of the National Negro Conventions 1830–1864* [New York: Arno Press and the *New York Times*, 1969]).

1. A. Kraditor, *The Ideas of the Woman Suffrage Movement, 1890–1920* (New York: Columbia University Press, 1965); E. Flexner, *Century of Struggle* (New York: Atheneum, 1968).

2. E. Abbott, *Women in Industry* (New York: Appleton and Company, 1913), pp. 21–22.

3. E. C. Stanton, S. B. Anthony, and M. J. Gage, *History of Woman Suffrage*, vol. 1 (Rochester: Chas. Mann), p. 16.

4. A. Henry, *The Trade Union Woman* (New York: Appleton and Company, 1915), p. 254.

5. Stanton, Anthony, and Gage, p. 809. Italics added.

6. On early struggles by women the major source is J. B. Andrews and W. D. P. Bliss, *History of Women in Trade Unions* (vol. 10 of *Report on Conditions of Women and Child Wage Earners in the U.S.*, in 19 vols., U.S. Senate Doc. 645, 61st Cong., 2d Sess.); see also Flexner; Abbott; P. Foner, *History of the Labor Movement in the United States*, vol. 1 (New York: International, 1947); Henry, 1915; and A. Henry, *Women and the Labor Movement* (New York: Doran, 1923). Flexner claims men feared women's competition but gives no specifics. For this early period, only the printers and cigarmakers manifested the conservative stance, though it was later a strong position among conservative skilled trades unions. The instances of early cooperation between men's and women's unions are more impressive: in 1834 the Lady Shoe Binders of Lynn struck for higher wages and were supported by the men's cordwainers union in the form of money, a pledge not to work for any manufacturer who refused the women's demands, and an attempt to organize a boycott of such (Foner, pp. 108–111). In 1833 the Baltimore seamstresses and tailoresses were supported by the men journeymen tailors (Henry 1923, p. 41). In 1835 the Philadelphia Journeymen Cigarmakers opposed the low wages paid to women and recommended a joint strike. In this city, too, the men cordwainers and Ladies Shoe Binders Society waged a joint strike. In 1831 the New England Farmers, Mechanics and Other Workingmen tried, though without success, to spread unionism from skilled workers to factory women (Foner, pp. 105, 108–111).

7. For differing accounts see Andrews and Bliss, p. 65; Foner, p. 212; Flexner, p. 56.

8. Foner, p. 267.

9. R. B. Nye, *Fettered Freedom: Civil Liberties and the Slave Controversy, 1830–1860* (East Lansing: Michigan State University Press, 1963), p. 194.

10. H. Josephson, *Golden Threads: New England's Mill Girls and Magnates* (New York: Duell, Sloan and Pearce, 1949), pp. 300–303.

11. C. H. Wesley, *Negro Labor in the United States, 1850–1925* (New York: Russell and Russell, 1967), pp. 78–79.

12. In addition to Andrews and Bliss, pt. 2, see Abbott, p. 131; and Henry, 1923, p. 48.

13. Foner, p. 241; Henry, 1923, p. 47.

14. Foner, vol. 2, p. 61; Flexner, p. 194.

15. R. Logan, *The Betrayal of the Negro* (New York: Macmillan, 1970), pp. 150–151.

16. M. H. Willett, *The Employment of Women in the Clothing Trade* (New York: AMS Press, 1968).

17. Foner, vol. 2, pp. 189–193.

18. *Ibid.*, pp. 364–366; Foner, vol. 3, pp. 724–727.

19. Kraditor, p. 159.

20. *Ibid.*, chap. 6.

21. Carrie Chapman Catt, in *The Woman's Journal*, 1894; quoted in Flexner, p. 125.

22. *Ibid.*, p. 131.

23. *Ibid.*, p. 128.

24. *Ibid.*, p. 139.

25. *The Woman's Journal*, 1911; quoted in Flexner, p. 157.

26. *Ibid.*, p. 187.

27. G. Lerner, *Black Women in White America* (New York: Pantheon, 1972), pp. 198, 437.

28. Kraditor, pp. 170, 212–214; Logan, pp. 239–241.

29. Foner, vol. 4, pp. 338–339.

30. Letter from Mrs. Clark to Mrs. Robins; quoted in G. Boone, *The Women's Trade Union Leagues in Great Britain and the United States of America* (New York: AMS Press, 1968), p. 106.

31. *Life and Labor*, vol. 2, pp. 73, 77, 196.

32. *Ibid.*, p. 77.

33. Quoted in Kraditor, p. 160.

34. Quoted in R. Jacoby, "Feminism and Class Consciousness in the British and American Women's Trade Union Leagues, 1890–1925." Unpublished ms. (History Dept., University of Michigan, 1973), p. 21.

35. Quoted in Foner, vol. 4, p. 168.

36. E. G. Flynn, *I Speak My Own Piece* (New York: Masses and Mainstream, 1955), p. 46.

37. E. Goldman, *Anarchism and Other Essays* (New York: Mother Earth Publishing Association, 1917), p. 212.

38. A. Hourwich, *I Am a Woman Worker: A Scrapbook of Autobiographies* (New York: Affiliated Schools for Workers, Inc., 1936), p. 110.

39. On pressers' work: J. Laslett, *Labor and the Left* (New York: Basic Books, 1970), p. 103. On discrimination against black women: Henry 1923, pp. 203–206.

40. Supported again by a dying NWTUL. See *Life and Labor Bulletin* (July 1928 and January 1931).

The Civil Rights History of "Sex": A Sexist, Racist Congressional Joke

Elizabeth Roth

Elizabeth Roth is a partner in the Sunnyvale, California, law firm of General Counsel Associates, specializing in counseling companies on employment law matters. A member of the California bar since 1982, she was formerly a litigator with an employment law group in Palo Alto, California. She received her J. D. from Duke University School of Law and also holds a Ph.D. and M.A. in English from the University of Washington and a B.A. from Cornell. She is an editor of the American Bar Association's Litigation News *and publishes and speaks frequently on such employment law issues as the Americans with Disabilities Act, sexual harassment, privacy in the workplace, part-time policies, and women in the legal profession. Her articles have appeared in publications ranging from the* American Journal of Legal History *to* California Lawyer *and* Ms.

The sex discrimination component of the 1964 Civil Rights Act has been the basis of a large part of the litigation challenging sexist policies in our society. Dr. Roth tells the bizarre story of how and why it was introduced and how a bad joke backfired against the jokesters.

WHEN WE ARE TRYING TO INTERPRET LEGISLATION, we lawyers often talk about the intent of drafters. Once in a great while, it is clear what such intent was.

One February day 29 years ago, certain southern members of the U.S. House of Representatives had a jocular debate about sex. Hoping to defeat the Civil Rights Act of 1964, they decided, as a joke, to add sex discrimination to the proposed statute. It seems the joke was on them.

It was a Saturday afternoon, February 8, 1964. Although the U.S. had sent 109 athletes to Innsbruck during the Winter Olympics, the dour New York *Times* sportswriters had rated U.S. chances of even one gold medal as "dim." On January 31, the *Times* reported ruefully that the best U.S. showing so far had been a fourth place tie by "two New York girls"—Jeanne Ashworth and Janice Smith—in the 500-meter skating race. "So the United States was shut out of the first, second, and third place medal ceremonies in this event as it had been in every event at the games so far." The next day's headline said, U.S. FAILS AGAIN, and the grim story continued, "On a negative note, the United States still has no medal of any kind." Then, on February 1, Jean Saubert, an Oregon state junior from Ogden, Utah, won a bronze medal in the women's slalom and on February 3 she won the silver medal in the women's giant slalom. "With the IX Winter Games half over, the United States has won only two medals, one silver and one bronze, courtesy of Miss Saubert," reported the *Times*.

In the U.S. House of Representatives other games were afoot. Representative Howard W. Smith of Virginia introduced an amendment to add the word "sex" after the word "religion" as an additional type of unlawful employment discrimination.

The notion that sex discrimination in employment was a problem in the United States was an

"The Civil Rights History of 'Sex': A Sexist, Racist Congressional Joke," by Elizabeth Roth, *Ms.*, Vol. III, No. 5, March/April 1993. Reprinted by permission of Ms. Magazine, © 1993 and the author.

idea whose time had definitely not come. Referring to Saubert's medals, Representative Frances P. Bolton of Ohio pointed out to her colleagues: "[T]o read the sports news about the winter games in Innsbruck, I think it was a woman who rather saved the United States. . . ." But admiration for female athletes did not translate into serious concern about sex discrimination in employment.

Representative Smith introduced his amendment with mock protestations that he was "very serious about this amendment." (He used the word "serious" the way Mark Antony uses "honorable" for Brutus.) He read into the Congressional Record what he claimed was a relevant letter from a constituent. The author of this whimsical letter complained bitterly about the fact that there were more women than men in the U.S.A., making marriage more difficult to achieve, and asked the Congress to stop sending men to war so that spinsters could find nice husbands and families.

An Alice in Wonderland debate began in the august chamber. For the most part, supporters of the Civil Rights Act opposed the amendment. Representative Emanuel Celler of New York said that the amendment was "illogical, ill timed, ill placed, and improper." Representative Smith countered, "Your surprise at my offering the amendment does not nearly approach my surprise, amazement, and sorrow at your opposition to it."

It became clear as the debate progressed that those who were openly hostile to the Civil Rights Act supported the sex discrimination amendment, apparently hoping to derail the entire bill. Representative Mendel Rivers of South Carolina rose in support of the sex discrimination amendment, because it would make "it possible for the white Christian woman to receive the same consideration for employment as the colored woman." Making it clear what he thought of the Civil Rights Act itself, he went on: "It is incredible to me that the authors of this monstrosity—whomever they are—would deprive the white woman of mostly Anglo-Saxon or Christian heritage equal opportunity before the employer. I know this Congress will not be a party to such an evil."

The southern gentlemen in the House of Representatives rose in support of the sex amendment, wrapping themselves in the language of chivalry. "Some men in some areas of the country might support legislation which would discriminate against women, but never let it be said that a southern gentleman would vote for such legislation," said Representative J. Russell Tuten of Georgia. Representative George William Andrews of Alabama added his special concern: "Unless this amendment is adopted, the white women of this country would be drastically discriminated against in favor of a Negro woman."

The chivalric Representative Smith had said, upon introducing his legislation, that he wanted "to prevent discrimination against another minority group, the women." One matter-of-fact and sarcastic response to this concern came from a female, Representative Bolton, who commented: "[I]t is always perfectly delightful when some enchanting gentleman, from the South particularly, calls us the minority group. We used to be, but we are not anymore." She noted the 1960 U.S. census figures of 88,331,494 males and 90,991,681 females.

Representative Bolton and other female legislators spoke up that afternoon to such an extent that Representative Edith Green of Oregon remarked, "I suppose that this may go down in history as 'women's afternoon,' but the women of the House, I feel sure, recognize that you men will be the ones who finally make the decision." Representative Green herself, a strong women's rights advocate, opposed the amendment, stating that it would "clutter up the bill" and that the amendment would be used later to destroy the fair employment section of the bill. She stressed that the focus of the bill was to end racial discrimination in voting, public accommodations, education, and employment.

Noting the curious overnight conversion of the southern legislators to women's rights advocates, Representative Green dryly observed: "[T]hose gentlemen of the House who are most strong in their support of women's rights this afternoon, probably gave us the most opposition when we considered the bill which would grant equal pay for equal work just a very few months ago. I say I welcome the conversion and hope it is of long duration."

The women representatives in the House that afternoon were not all of one mind. To some of the female legislators, the amendment made perfect sense. Representatives Martha Wright Griffiths of Michigan and Katharine St. George of New York noted painful and real examples of employment discrimination on the basis of sex, and argued for the addition of "that little terrifying word 's-e-x,'" as St. George put it. Griffiths didn't find the levity amusing: "I presume that if there had been any necessity to have pointed out that women were a second-class sex, the laughter would have proved it."

The vote on the "sex" amendment was: ayes 168, noes 133. So the bizarre alliance of disingenuous southern gentlemen and women's rights pioneers produced a federal statute oddly ahead of its time. The House passed the bill on February 10, 1964; the Senate passed it on June 19; and President Johnson signed it on July 2. In the emotional aftermath of the assassination of President Kennedy, the focus of the Congress was racial discrimination. Johnson had called the passage of the Civil Rights Act of 1964 the best eulogy the Congress could provide. Quickly lost in the emotional shuffle were the implications of the "sex" amendment. Only now, in the complex context of hostile environment sexual harassment cases, are we beginning to sort it out.

When the Supreme Court ruled on its first hostile environment sexual harassment case in 1986, *Meritor Savings Bank* v. *Vinson*, then Associate Justice Rehnquist tried to discern the genesis of the word "sex" in Title VII of the Civil Rights Act of 1964. Noting that the word was added at the last minute, and that some had argued against it, the court observed: "This argument was defeated, the bill quickly passed as amended, and we are left with little legislative history to guide us in interpreting the act's prohibition against discrimination based on 'sex.'" Actually, we have more legislative history than the associate justice acknowledged. And it's pretty ironic.

Sexual Politics

Kate Millett

Kate Millett, feminist, author, and sculptor, was born in 1934 in St. Paul, Minnesota. She studied English at the University of Minnesota and at Oxford University and finished a doctorate at Columbia University with a dissertation that became the book Sexual Politics. *Millett has taught English and women's studies, worked as a sculptor, and codirected a film,* Three Lives. *An activist early in her career, she served in CORE (Congress of Racial Equality) in the 1950s, supported student strikes while teaching at Barnard, and served in NOW as chair of the Education Committee. During the early days of the Iranian revolution, she traveled to Iran to study the effects of the revolution on women there and to talk to feminist leaders. In addition to* Sexual Politics, *her works include* The Prostitution Papers *(1973),* Flying *(1974),* Sita *(1976), and* Going to Iran *(1982).*

The publication of Sexual Politics *in 1970 was an important development in the current movement. It received wide press attention, focused public attention on women's liberation, and was one of the first books to articulate a broad theoretical base for the ideas of the growing movement. Millett widens the term* politics *(which traditionally means simply "that which pertains to the* polis, *or city") to refer to "power-structured relationships . . . whereby one group of persons is controlled by another" then shows how this concept captures the essence of male-female arrangements. Using literary and historical models to support her thesis, she argues that social and sexual relations between women and men are not-so-nice power arrangements, grounded in misogyny, expressing themselves as a life view (patriarchy), and resulting in the worldwide oppression of women on both an institutional and a personal level.*

Theory of Sexual Politics

. . . In introducing the term "sexual politics," one must first answer the inevitable question "Can the relationship between the sexes be viewed in a political light at all?" The answer depends on how one defines politics.[1] This essay does not define the political as that relatively narrow and exclusive world of meetings, chairmen, and parties. The term "politics" shall refer to power-structured relationships, arrangements whereby one group of persons is controlled by another. By way of parenthesis one might add that although an ideal politics might simply be conceived of as the arrangement of human life on agreeable and rational principles from whence the entire notion of power *over* others should be banished, one must confess that this is not what constitutes the political as we know it, and it is to this that we must address ourselves.

The following sketch, which might be described as "notes toward a theory of patriarchy," will attempt to prove that sex is a status category with political implications. Something of a pioneering effort, it must perforce be both tentative and imperfect. Because the intention is to provide an overall description, statements must be generalized, exceptions neglected, and subheadings overlapping and, to some degree, arbitrary as well.

The word "politics" is enlisted here when speaking of the sexes primarily because such a word is eminently useful in outlining the real nature of their relative status, historically and at the present. It is opportune, perhaps today even mandatory, that we develop a more relevant psychology and philosophy of power relationships beyond the simple conceptual framework provided by our traditional formal politics. Indeed, it may be imperative that we give some attention to defining a theory of politics which treats of power relationships on grounds less conventional than those to which we are accustomed.[2] I have therefore found it pertinent to define them on grounds of personal contact and interaction between members of well-defined and coherent groups: races, castes, classes, and sexes. For it is precisely because certain groups have no representation in a number of recognized political structures that their position tends to be so stable, their oppression so continuous.

In America, recent events have forced us to acknowledge at last that the relationship between the races is indeed a political one which involves the general control of one collectivity, defined by birth, over another collectivity, also defined by birth. Groups who rule by birthright are fast disappearing, yet there remains one ancient and universal scheme for the domination of one birth group by another—the scheme that prevails in the area of sex. The study of racism has convinced us that a truly political state of affairs operates between the races to perpetuate a series of oppressive circumstances. The subordinated group has inadequate redress through existing political institutions, and is deterred thereby from organizing into conventional political struggle and opposition.

Quite in the same manner, a disinterested examination of our system of sexual relationship must point out that the situation between the sexes now, and throughout history, is a case of that phenomenon Max Weber defined as *herrschaft*, a relationship of dominance and subordinance.[3] What goes largely unexamined, often even unacknowledged (yet is institutionalized nonetheless) in our social order, is the birthright priority whereby males rule females. Through this system a most ingenious form of "interior colonization" has been achieved. It is one which tends moreover to be sturdier than any form of segregation, and more rigorous than class stratification, more uniform, certainly more enduring. However muted its present appearance may be, sexual dominion obtains nevertheless as perhaps the most pervasive ideology of our culture and provides its most fundamental concept of power.

This is so because our society, like all other historical civilizations, is a patriarchy.[4] The fact is evident at once if one recalls that the military, industry, technology, universities, science, political office, and finance—in short, every avenue of power within the society, including the coercive force of the police, is entirely in male hands. As the essence of politics is power, such realization cannot fail to carry impact. What lingers of supernatural authority, the Deity, "His" ministry, together with the ethics and values, the philosophy and art of our culture—its very civilization—as T. S. Eliot once observed, is of male manufacture.

If one takes patriarchal government to be the institution whereby that half of the populace which is female is controlled by that half which is male, the principles of patriarchy appear to be two fold: male shall dominate female, elder male shall dominate younger. However, just as with any human institution, there is frequently a distance between the real and the ideal; contradictions and exceptions do exist within the system. While patriarchy as an institution is a social constant so deeply entrenched as to run through all other political, social, or economic forms, whether of caste or class, feudality or bureaucracy, just as it pervades all major religions, it also exhibits great variety in history and locale. In democracies,[5] for example, females have often held no office or do so (as now) in such miniscule numbers as to be below even token representation. Aristocracy, on the other hand, with its emphasis upon the magic and dynastic properties of blood, may at times permit women to hold power. The principle of rule by elder males is violated even more frequently. Bearing in mind the variation and degree in patriarchy—as say between Saudi Arabia and Sweden, Indonesia and Red China—we also recognize our own form in the U.S. and Europe to be much altered and attenuated by the reforms described in the next chapter.

I Ideological

Hannah Arendt[6] has observed that government is upheld by power supported either through consent or imposed through violence. Conditioning to an ideology amounts to the former. Sexual politics obtains consent through the "socialization" of both sexes to basic patriarchal polities with regard to temperament, role, and status. As to status, a pervasive assent to the prejudice of male superiority guarantees superior status in the male, inferior in the female. The first item, temperament, involves the formation of human personality along stereotyped lines of sex category ("masculine" and "feminine"), based on the needs and values of the dominant group and dictated by what its members cherish in themselves and find convenient in subordinates: aggression, intelligence, force, and efficacy in the male; passivity, ignorance, docility, "virtue," and ineffectuality in the female. This is complemented by a second factor, sex role, which decrees a consonant and highly elaborate code of conduct, gesture and attitude for each sex. In terms of activity, sex role assigns domestic service and attendance upon infants to the female, the rest of human achievement, interest, and ambition to the male. The limited role allotted the female tends to arrest her at the level of biological experience. Therefore, nearly all that can be described as distinctly human rather than animal activity (in their own way animals also give birth and care for their young) is largely reserved for the male. Of course, status again follows from such an assignment. Were one to analyze the three categories one might designate status as the political component, role as the sociological, and temperament as the psychological—yet their interdependence is unquestionable and they form a chain. Those awarded higher status tend to adopt roles of mastery, largely because they are first encouraged to develop temperaments of dominance. That this is true of caste and class as well is self-evident.

IV Class

It is in the area of class that the castelike status of the female within patriarchy is most liable to confusion, for sexual status often operates in a superficially confusing way within the variable of class. In a society where status is dependent upon the economic, social, and educational circumstances of class, it is possible for certain females to appear to stand higher than some males. Yet not when one looks more closely at the subject. This is perhaps easier to see by means of analogy: a black doctor or lawyer has higher social status than a poor white sharecropper. But race, itself a caste system which subsumes class, persuades the latter citizen that he belongs to a higher order of life, just as it oppresses the black professional in spirit, whatever his material success may be. In much the same manner, a truck driver or butcher has always his "manhood" to fall back upon. Should this final vanity be offended, he may contemplate more violent methods. The literature of the past thirty years provides a staggering number of incidents in which the caste of virility triumphs over the social status of wealthy or even educated women. In literary contexts one has to deal here with wish-fulfillment. Incidents from life (bullying, obscene, or hostile remarks) are probably another sort of psychological gesture of ascendancy. Both convey more hope than reality, for class divisions are generally quite impervious to the hostility of individuals. And yet while the existence of class division is not seriously threatened by such expressions of enmity, the existence of sexual hierarchy has been re-affirmed and mobilized to "punish" the female quite effectively.

The function of class or ethnic mores in patriarchy is largely a matter of how overtly displayed or how loudly enunciated the general ethic of masculine supremacy allows itself to become. Here one is confronted by what appears to be a paradox: while in the lower social strata, the male is more likely to claim authority on the strength of his sex rank alone, he is actually obliged more often to share power with the women of his class who are economically productive; whereas in the middle and upper classes, there is less tendency to assert a blunt patriarchal dominance, as men who enjoy such status have more power in any case.[7] . . .

One of the chief effects of class within patriarchy is to set one woman against another, in the past creating a lively antagonism between whore and matron, and in the present between career woman and housewife. One envies the other her "security" and prestige, while the envied yearns beyond the confines of respectability for what she takes to be the other's freedom, adventure, and contact with the great world. Through the multiple advantages of the double standard, the male participates in both worlds, empowered by his superior social and economic resources to play the estranged women against each other as rivals. One might also recognize subsidiary status categories among women: not only is virtue class, but beauty and age as well.

Perhaps, in the final analysis, it is possible to argue that women tend to transcend the usual class stratifications in patriarchy, for whatever the class of her birth and education, the female has fewer permanent class association than does the male. Economic dependency renders her affiliations with any class a tangential, vicarious, and temporary matter. Aristotle observed that the only slave to whom a commoner might lay claim was his woman, and the service of an unpaid domestic still provides working-class males with a "cushion" against the buffets of the class system which incidentally provides them with some of the psychic luxuries of the leisure class. Thrown upon their own resources, few women rise above working class in personal prestige and economic power, and women as a group do not enjoy many of the interests and benefits any class may offer its male members. Women have therefore less of an investment in the class system. But it is important to understand that as with any group whose existence is parasitic to its rulers, women are a dependency class who live on surplus. And their marginal life frequently renders them conservative, for like all persons in their situation (slaves are a classic example here) they identify their own survival with the prosperity of those who feed them. The hope of seeking liberating radical solutions of their own seems too remote for the majority to dare contemplate and remains so until consciousness on the subject is raised.

As race is emerging as one of the final variables in sexual politics, it is pertinent, especially in a discussion of modern literature, to devote a few words to it as well. Traditionally, the white male has been accustomed to concede the female of his own race, in her capacity as "his woman" a higher status than that ascribed to the black male.[8] Yet as white racist ideology is exposed and begins to erode, racism's older protective attitudes toward (white) women also begin to give way. And the priorities of maintaining male supremacy might outweigh even those of white supremacy; sexism may be more endemic in our own society than racism. For example, one notes in authors whom we would now term overtly racist, such as D. H. Lawrence—whose contempt for what he so often designates as inferior breeds is unabashed—instances where the lower-caste male is brought on to master or humiliate the white man's own insubordinate mate. Needless to say, the female of the nonwhite races does not figure in such tales save as an exemplum of "true" womanhood's servility, worthy of imitation by other less carefully instructed females. Contemporary white sociology often operates under a similar patriarchal bias when its rhetoric inclines toward the assertion that the "matriarchal" (e.g. matrifocal) aspect of black society and the "castration" of the black male are the most deplorable symptoms of black oppression in white racist society, with the implication that racial inequity is capable of solution by a restoration of masculine authority. Whatever the facts of the matter may be, it can also be suggested that analysis of this kind presupposes patriarchal values without questioning them, and tends to obscure both the true character of and the responsibility for racist injustice toward black humanity of both sexes. . . .

VI Force

We are not accustomed to associate patriarchy with force. So perfect is its system of socialization, so complete the general assent to its values, so long and so universally has it prevailed in human society, that it scarcely seems to require violent implementation. Customarily, we view its brutalities in the past as exotic or "primitive" custom. Those of the present are regarded as the product of individual deviance, confined to pathological or exceptional behavior, and without general import. And yet, just as under other total ideologies (racism and colonialism are somewhat analogous in this respect) control in patriarchal society would be imperfect, even inoperable, unless it had the rule of force to rely upon, both in emergencies and as an ever-present instrument of intimidation.

Historically, most patriarchies have institutionalized force through their legal systems. For example, strict patriarchies such as that of Islam, have implemented the prohibition against illegitimacy or sexual autonomy with a death sentence. In Afghanistan and Saudi Arabia the adulteress is still stoned to death with a mullah presiding at the execution. Execution by stoning was once common practice through the Near East. It is still condoned in Sicily. Needless to say there was and is no penalty imposed upon the male corespondent. Save in recent times or exceptional cases, adultery was not generally recognized in males except as an offense one male might commit against another's property interest. In Tokugawa Japan, for example, an elaborate set of legal distinctions were made according to class. A samurai was entitled, and in the face of public knowledge, even obliged, to execute an adulterous wife, whereas a chōnin (common citizen) or peasant might respond as he pleased. In cases of cross-class adultery, the lower-class male convicted of sexual intimacy with his employer's wife would, because he had violated taboos of class and property, be beheaded together with her. Upper-strata males had, of course, the same license to seduce lower-class women as we are familiar with in Western societies.

Indirectly, one form of "death penalty" still obtains even in America today. Patriarchal legal systems in depriving women of control over their own bodies drive them to illegal abortions; it is estimated that between two and five thousand women die each year from this cause.[9]

Excepting a social license to physical abuse among certain class and ethnic groups, force is diffuse and generalized in most contemporary patriarchies. Significantly, force itself is restricted to the male who alone is psychologically and technically equipped to perpetrate physical violence.[10] Where differences in physical strength have become immaterial through the use of arms, the female is rendered innocuous by her socialization. Before assault she is almost universally defenseless both by her physical and emotional training. Needless to say, this has the most far-reaching effects on the social and psychological behavior of both sexes.

Patriarchal force also relies on a form of violence particularly sexual in character and realized most completely in the act of rape. The figures of rapes reported represent only a fraction of those which occur,[11] as the "shame" of the event is sufficient to deter women from the notion of civil prosecution under the public circumstances of a trial. Traditionally rape has been viewed as an offense one male commits upon another—a matter of abusing "his woman." Vendetta, such as occurs in the American South, is carried out for masculine satisfaction, the exhilarations of race hatred, and the interests of property and vanity (honor). In rape, the emotions of aggression, hatred, contempt, and the desire to break or violate personality, take a form consummately appropriate to sexual politics. In the passages analyzed at the outset of this study, such emotions were present at a barely sublimated level and were a key factor in explaining the attitude behind the author's use of language and tone.[12]

Patriarchal societies typically link feelings of cruelty with sexuality, the latter often equated both with evil and with power. This is apparent both in the sexual fantasy reported by psychoanalysis and that reported by pornography. The rule here associates sadism with the male ("the masculine role") and victimization with the female ("the feminine role").[13] Emotional response to violence against women in patriarchy is often curiously ambivalent; references to wife-beating, for example, invariably produce laughter and some embarrassment. Exemplary atrocity, such as the mass murders committed by Richard Speck, greeted at one level with a certain scandalized, possibly hypocritical indignation, is capable of eliciting a mass response of titillation at another level. At such times one even hears from men occasional expressions of envy or amusement. In view of the sadistic character of such public fantasy as caters to male audiences in pornography or semi-pornographic media, one might expect that a certain element of identification is by no means absent from the general response. Probably a similar collective *frisson* sweeps through racist society when its more "logical" members have perpetrated a lynching. Unconsciously, both crimes may serve the larger group as a ritual act, cathartic in effect.

Hostility is expressed in a number of ways. One is laughter. Misogynist literature, the primary vehicle of masculine hostility, is both an hortatory and comic genre. Of all artistic forms in patriarchy it is the most frankly propagandistic. Its aim is to reinforce both sexual factions in their status. Ancient, Medieval, and Renaissance literature in the West has each had a large element of misogyny.[14] Nor is the East without a strong tradition here, notably in the Confucian strain which held sway in Japan as well as China. The Western tradition was indeed moderated somewhat by the introduction of courtly love. But the old diatribes and attacks were coterminous with the new idealization of woman. In the case of Petrarch, Boccaccio, and some others, one can find both attitudes fully expressed, presumably as evidence of different moods, a courtly pose adopted for the ephemeral needs of the vernacular, a grave animosity for sober and eternal Latin.[15] As courtly love was transformed to romantic love, literary misogyny grew somewhat out of fashion. In some places in the eighteenth century it declined into ridicule and exhortative satire. In the nineteenth century its more acrimonious forms almost disappeared in English. Its resurrection in twentieth-century attitudes and literature is the result of a resentment over patriarchal reform, aided by the growing permissiveness in expression which has taken place at an increasing rate in the last fifty years.

Since the abatement of censorship, masculine hostility (psychological or physical) in specifically *sexual* contexts has become far more apparent. Yet as masculine hostility has been fairly continuous, one deals here probably less with a matter of increase than with a new frankness in expressing hostility in specifically sexual contexts. It is a matter of release and freedom to express what was once forbidden expression outside of pornography or other "underground" productions, such as those of De Sade. As one recalls both the euphemism and the idealism of descriptions of coitus in the Romantic poets (Keats's *Eve of St. Agnes*), or the Victorian novelists (Hardy, for example) and contrasts it with Miller or William Burroughs, one has an idea of how contemporary literature has absorbed not only the truthful explicitness of pornography, but its anti-social character as well. Since this tendency to hurt or insult has been given free expression, it has become far easier to assess sexual antagonism in the male.

The history of patriarchy presents a variety of cruelties and barbarities: the suttee execution in India, the crippling deformity of footbinding in China, the lifelong ignominy of the veil in Islam, or the widespread persecution of sequestration, the gynacium, and purdah. Phenomenon such as clitoroidectomy, clitoral incision, the sale and enslavement of women under one guise or another, involuntary and child marriages, concubinage and prostitution, still take place—the first in Africa, the latter in the Near and Far East, the last generally. The rationale which accompanies that imposition of male authority euphemistically referred to as "the battle of the sexes" bears a certain resemblance to the formulas of nations at war, where any heinousness is justified on the grounds that the enemy is either an inferior species or really not human at all. The patriarchal mentality has concocted a whole series of rationales about women which accomplish this purpose tolerably well. And these traditional beliefs still invade our consciousness and affect our thinking to an extent few of us would be willing to admit.

Notes

1. The American Heritage Dictionary's fourth definition is fairly approximate: "methods or tactics involved in managing a state or government." *American Heritage Dictionary* (New York: American Heritage and Houghton Mifflin, 1969). One might expand this to a set of strategems designed to maintain a system. If one understands patriarchy to be an institution perpetuated by such techniques of control, one has a working definition of how politics is conceived in this essay.

2. I am indebted here to Ronald V. Samson's *The Psychology of Power* (New York: Random House, 1968) for his intelligent investigation of the connection between formal power structures and the family and for his analysis of how power corrupts basic human relationships.

3. "Domination in the quite general sense of power, i.e. the possibility of imposing one's will upon the behavior of other persons, can emerge in the most diverse forms." In this central passage of *Wirtschaft und Gesellschaft* Weber is particularly interested in two such forms: control through social authority ("patriarchal, magisterial, or princely") and control through economic force. In patriarchy as in other forms of domination "that control over economic goods, i.e. economic power, is a frequent, often purposively willed, consequence of domination as well as one of its most important instruments." Quoted from Max Rheinstein's and Edward Shil's translation of portions of *Wirtschaft und Gesellschaft* entitled *Max Weber on Law in Economy and Society* (New York: Simon and Schuster, 1967), pp. 323–24.

4. No matriarchal societies are known to exist at present. Matrilineality, which may be, as some anthropologists have held, a residue or a transitional stage of matriarchy, does not constitute an exception to patriarchal rule, it simply channels the power held by males through female descent—, e.g. the Avunculate.

5. Radical democracy would, of course, preclude patriarchy. One might find evidence of a general satisfaction with a less than perfect democracy in the fact that women have so rarely held power within modern "democracies."

6. Hannah Arendt, "Speculations on Violence," *The New York Review of Books*, Vol. XII No. 4, February 27, 1969, p. 24.

7. Goode, *op. cit.*, p. 74.

8. It would appear that the "pure flower of white womanhood" has at least at times been something of a disappointment to her lord as a fellow-racist. The historic connection of the Abolitionist and the Woman's Movement is some evidence of this, as well as the incident of white female and black male marriages as compared with those of white male and black female. Figures on miscegenation are very difficult to obtain: Goode (*op. cit.*, p. 37) estimates the proportion of white women marrying black men to be between 3 to 10 times the proportion of white men marrying black women. Robert K. Merton "Intermarriage and the Social Structure" *Psychiatry*, Vol. 4, August 1941, p. 374, states that "most intercaste sex relations—not marriages—are between white men and Negro women." It is hardly necessary to emphasize that the more extensive sexual contacts between white males and black females have not only been extramarital, but (on the part of the white male) crassly exploitative. Under slavery it was simply a case of rape.

9. Since abortion is extralegal, figures are difficult to obtain. This figure is based on the estimates of abortionists and referral services. Suicides in pregnancy are not officially reported either.

10. Vivid exceptions come to mind in the wars of liberation conducted by Vietnam, China, etc. But through most of history, women have been unarmed and forbidden to exhibit any defense of their own.

11. They are still high. The number of rapes reported in the city of New York in 1967 was 2432. Figure supplied by Police Department.

12. It is interesting that male victims of rape at the hands of other males often feel twice imposed upon, as they have not only been subjected to forcible and painful intercourse, but further abused in being reduced to the status of a female. Much of this is evident in Genet and in the contempt homosexual society reserves for its "passive" or "female" partners.

13. Masculine masochism is regarded as exceptional and often explained as latently homosexual, or a matter of the subject playing "the female role"—e.g., victim.

14. The literature of misogyny is so vast that no summary of sensible proportions could do it justice. The best reference on the subject is Katherine M. Rogers, *The Troublesome Helpmate, A History of Misogyny in Literature* (Seattle, University of Washington Press, 1966).

15. As well as the exquisite sonnets of love, Petrarch composed satires on women as the "De Remediis utriusque Fortunae" and *Epistolae Seniles*. Boccaccio too could balance the chivalry of romances (Filostrato, Ameto, and Fiammetta) with the vituperance of Corbaccio, a splenetic attack on women more than medieval in violence.

NOW Bill of Rights

National Organization for Women

The National Organization for Women (NOW) was formed in 1966 by a group of feminist legislators, authors, professionals, labor workers, and academics. Set off by a series of events—the publication of Friedan's Feminine Mystique, *the addition of "sex" to the Civil Rights Act of 1964, the decade's climate of social criticism and change—the formation of the organization was one of the major events responsible for increasing feminist activism of the second wave. Notice that among its goals were passage of ERA and access to day care and to legal abortion, issues that at the time were controversial and yet galvanizing to many women, even those who might not have formerly been politically active.*

Adopted by NOW at their First National Conference, Washington, DC (© NOW), 1967.

Bill of Rights

National Organization for Women (NOW)

- **I** Equal Rights Constitutional Amendment
- **II** Enforce Law Banning Sex Discrimination in Employment
- **III** Maternity Leave Rights in Employment and in Social Security Benefits
- **IV** Tax Deduction for Home and Child Care Expenses for Working Parents
- **V** Child Care Centers
- **VI** Equal and Unsegregated Education
- **VII** Equal Job Training Opportunities and Allowances for Women in Poverty
- **VIII** The Right of Women to Control Their Reproductive Lives

WE DEMAND

Exception

I That the United States Congress immediately pass the Equal Rights Amendment to the Constitution to provide that "Equality of rights under the law shall not be denied or abridged by the United States or by any State on account of sex," and that such then be immediately ratified by the several States.

II That equal employment opportunity be guaranteed to all women, as well as men, by insisting that the Equal Employment Opportunity Commission enforces the prohibitions against sex discrimination in employment under Title VII of the Civil Rights Act of 1964 with the same vigor as it enforces the prohibitions against racial discrimination.

III That women be protected by law to ensure their rights to return to their jobs within a reasonable time after childbirth without loss of seniority or other accrued benefits, and be paid maternity leave as a form of social security and/or employee benefit.

IV Immediate revision of tax laws to permit the deduction of home and child care expenses for working parents.

V That child care facilities be established by law on the same basis as parks, libraries, and public schools, adequate to the needs of children from the pre-school years through adolescence, as a community resource to be used by all citizens from all income levels.

VI That the right of women to be educated to their full potential equally with men be secured by Federal and State Legislation, eliminating all discrimination and segregation by sex, written and unwritten, at all levels of education, including colleges, graduate and professional schools, loans and fellowships, and Federal and State training programs such as the Job Corps.

VII The right of women in poverty to secure job training, housing, and family allowances on equal terms with men, but without prejudice to a parent's right to remain at home to care for his or her children; revision of welfare legislation and poverty programs which deny women dignity, privacy and self-respect.

VIII The right of women to control their own reproductive lives by removing from penal codes laws limiting access to contraceptive information and devices and laws governing abortion.

Declaration of American Women, 1977

Mim Kelber

Writer, researcher, and peace activist Mim Kelber was policy adviser and speech writer for Congresswoman Bella Abzug when she became planning coordinator for the National Commission on the Observance of International Women's Year in 1977. She was the chief writer and editor of the report on the National Women's Conference, The Spirit of Houston, *which was delivered to President Jimmy Carter. Since then, she has published many articles on women and on peace and is currently editorial director for the Women's Foreign Policy Council in New York City.*

This declaration is the opening statement of The Spirit of Houston. *It has been more than a decade since the women in Houston, "expecting and entitled to serious attention" to their proposals demanded action. How much has changed? How much has not?*

Mim Kelber, The Spirit of Houston: The First National Women's Conference, ed. Helene Mandelbaum. Washington, DC: National Comm. on Observance of International Women's Year, 1978, DECLARATION OF AMERICAN WOMEN 1977.

WE ARE HERE TO MOVE HISTORY FORWARD.

We are women from every State and Territory in the Nation.

We are women of different ages, beliefs and lifestyles.

We are women of many economic, social, political, racial, ethnic, cultural, educational and religious backgrounds.

We are married, single, widowed and divorced.

We are mothers and daughters.

We are sisters.

We speak in varied accents and languages but we share the common language and experience of American women who throughout our Nation's life have been denied the opportunities, rights, privileges and responsibilities accorded to men.

For the first time in the more than 200 years of our democracy, we are gathered in a National Women's Conference, charged under Federal law to assess the status of women in our country, to measure the progress we have made, to identify the barriers that prevent us from participating fully and equally in all aspects of national life, and to make the recommendations to the President and to the Congress for means by which such barriers can be removed.

We recognize the positive changes that have occurred in the lives of women since the founding of our nation. In more than a century of struggle from Seneca Falls 1848 to Houston 1977, we have progressed from being non-persons and slaves whose work and achievements were recognized, whose needs were ignored, and whose rights were suppressed to being citizens with freedoms and aspirations of which our ancestors could only dream.

We can vote and own property. We work in the home, in our communities and in every occupation. We are 40 percent of the labor force. We are in the arts, sciences, professions and politics. We raise children, govern States, head businesses and institutions, climb mountains, explore the ocean depths and reach toward the moon.

Our lives no longer end with the childbearing years. Our lifespan has increased to more than 75 years. We have become a majority of the population, 51.3 percent and by the 21st century, we shall be an even larger majority.

But despite some gains made in the past 200 years, our dream of equality is still withheld from us and millions of women still face a daily reality of discrimination, limited opportunities and economic hardship.

Man-made barriers, laws, social customs and prejudices continue to keep a majority of women in an inferior position without full control of our lives and bodies.

From infancy throughout life, in personal and public relationships, in the family, in the schools, in every occupation and profession, too often we find our individuality, our capabilities, our earning powers diminished by discriminatory practices and outmoded ideas of what a woman is, what a woman can do, and what a woman must be.

Increasingly, we are victims of crimes of violence in a culture that degrades us as sex objects and promotes pornography for profit.

We are poorer than men. And those of us who are minority women—blacks, Hispanic Americans, Native Americans, and Asian Americans—must overcome the double burden of discrimination based on race and sex.

We lack effective political and economic power. We have only minor and insignificant roles in making, interpreting and enforcing our laws, in running our political parties, businesses, unions, schools and institutions, in directing the media, in governing our country, in deciding issues of war or peace.

We do not seek special privileges, but we demand as a human right a full voice and role for women in determining the destiny of our world, our nation, our families and our individual lives.

We seek these rights for all women, whether or not they choose as individuals to use them.

We are part of a worldwide movement of women who believe that only by bringing women into full partnership with men and respecting our rights as half the human race can we hope to achieve a world in which the whole human race—men, women and children—can live in peace and security.

Based on the views of women who have met in every State and Territory in the past year, the National Plan of Action is presented to the President and the Congress as our recommendations for implementing Public Law 94-167.

We are entitled to and expect serious attention to our proposals.

We demand immediate and continuing action on our National Plan by Federal, State, public, and private institutions so that by 1985, the end of the International Decade for Women proclaimed by the United Nations, everything possible under the law will have been done to provide American women with full equality.

The rest will be up to the hearts, minds and moral consciences of men and women and what they do to make our society truly democratic and open to all.

We pledge ourselves with all the strength of our dedication to this struggle "to form a more perfect Union."

What Will You Reap; What Will You Sow?

Barbara Jordan

Legislator and political leader Barbara Charline Jordan was born in Houston, the daughter of a Baptist minister. She was the first black student to graduate from Boston University Law School, and, after serving for a time in the Texas Senate, she was the first black woman elected to Congress from the deep South. She gained national attention in 1974 when, as a member of the House Judiciary Committee, she distinguished herself during the impeachment hearings of Richard Nixon. In 1976, she delivered an electrifying address as the keynote speaker at the Democratic Convention. That same year, she decided not to run again for Congress and took a position at the University of Texas at Austin. Her books include Local Government Election Systems *(with Terrell Blodgett) and her autobiography (with Shelby Hearon)* Barbara Jordan: A Self Portrait *(1979).*

Jordan told women in 1977, "Not making a difference is a cost we cannot afford." Is it any different now?

Keynote Speech by Congresswoman Barbara Jordan, First Plenary Session, The First National Women's Conference, November 19, 1977. Reported in *The Spirit of Houston* as the foregoing.

. . . IF YOU READ THE 31ST CHAPTER, IT BEGINS A litany of praise for the worthy woman. It begins this way: "Who can find a virtuous woman for her price is far above others." From virtue to power. What we are about here now will require no small amount of virtue and a great deal of power.

The value of women mostly in a narrowly construed fashion has been recognized throughout the ages, but the value of women has been periodically re-evaluated and is sometimes devaluated.

American history is peppered with efforts by women to be recognized as human beings and as citizens and to be included in the whole of our national life. . . .

If Americans were asked to differentiate or distinguish between what characterized other countries and what characterizes us, we would say our high regard for the individual. That's the thing which makes us different.

We endorse personal and political freedom as a national right of human pride. Human rights are more than abstractions, particularly when they are limited or non-existent. Human rights apply equally to Soviet dissidents, Chilean peasants and American women.

Women are human. We know our rights are limited. We know our rights are violated. We need a domestic human rights program. . . .

Not making a difference is a cost we cannot afford. . . .

What will you reap?

What will you sow?

Bibliography and Further Readings

Abbott, Franklin, ed.
1990 *Men & Intimacy: Personal Accounts Exploring the Dilemmas of Modern Male Sexuality.* Freedom, CA: Crossing Press.

———
1987 *New Men, New Minds: Breaking Male Tradition.* Freedom, CA: Crossing Press.

Abbott, Sidney, and Barbara Love
1972 *Sappho Was a Right-on Woman.* New York: Stein & Day.

Aburdene, Patricia, and John Naisbitt
1992 *Megatrends for Women.* New York: Villard Books.

Afshar, Haleh, ed.
1993 *Women in the Middle East: Perceptions, Realities and Struggles for Liberation.* New York: St. Martin's Press.

———
1987 *Women, State, and Ideology: Studies from Africa and Asia.* New York: SUNY Press.

Aiken, Susan Hardy, Karen Anderson, Myra Dinnerstein, Judy Nolte Lensink, and Patricia MacCorquodale
1988 *Changing Our Minds: Feminist Transformations of Knowledge.* Albany, NY: SUNY Press.

Albrecht, Lisa, and Rose M. Brewer, eds.
1990 *Bridges of Power: Women's Multicultural Alliances.* Santa Cruz, CA: New Society Publishers.

Allen, Jeffner
1990 *Lesbian Philosophies and Cultures.* NY: State University of New York Press.

———
1986 *Lesbian Philosophy: Explorations.* Palo Alto, CA: Institute of Lesbian Studies.

Allen, Paula Gunn
1991 *Grandmothers of the Light: A Medicine Woman's Sourcebook.* Boston: Beacon Press.

———
1986 *The Sacred Hoop: Recovering the Feminine in American Indian Traditions.* Boston: Beacon Press.

Amott, Teresa L., and Julie A. Matthaei
1991 *Race, Gender, and Work: A Multicultural Economic History of Women in the United States.* Boston: South End Press.

Amundsen, Kirsten
1971 *The Silenced Majority: Women and American Democracy.* Englewood Cliffs, NJ: Prentice-Hall.

Anderson, Lorraine, ed.
1991 *Sisters of the Earth: Women's Prose and Poetry About Nature.* New York: Vintage.

Anderson, Sherry Ruth, and Patricia Hopkins
1991 *The Feminine Face of God: The Unfolding of the Sacred in Women.* New York: Bantam Books.

Angelou, Maya
1981 *The Heart of a Woman.* New York: Random House.

———
1969 *I Know Why the Caged Bird Sings.* New York: Random House.

———
1991 *I Shall Not Be Moved.* New York: Bantam.

Angelou, Maya et al.
1993 *Double Stitch: Black Women Write About Mothers and Daughters.* New York: Harper & Row.

Anzaldúa, Gloria, ed.
1987 *Borderlands/La Frontera: The New Mestiza.* San Francisco: Spinsters/Aunt Lute.

———

1990 *Making Face, Making Soul/Haciendo Caras: Creative and Critical Perspectives by Women of Color.* San Francisco: Aunt Lute Foundation Books.

Apple, Rima D., ed.
1990 *Women, Health, and Medicine in America: A Historical Handbook.* New York: Garland.

Ardrey Robert
1966 *The Territorial Imperative.* New York: Atheneum.

Ashley, Jo Ann
1976 *Hospitals, Paternalism, and the Role of the Nurse.* New York: Teachers College Press.

Babcox, Deborah, and Madeline Belkin, comps.
1971 *Liberation Now!* New York: Dell.

Bacon, Margaret Hope
1986 *Mothers of Feminism: The Story of Quaker Women in America.* San Francisco: Harper & Row.

Baehr, Ninia
1990 *Abortion Without Apology: Radical History for the 1990s.* Boston: South End Press.

Bammer, Angelika
1991 *Partial Visions; Feminism and Utopianism in the 1970s.* New York: Routledge.

Banner, Lois W.
1983 *American Beauty.* New York: Alfred A. Knopf.

———

1980 *Elizabeth Cady Stanton: A Radical for Women's Rights.* Boston: Little, Brown.

———

1984 *Women in Modern America: A Brief History.* 2d ed. San Diego: Harcourt Brace Jovanovich.

Bardwick, Judith M.
1991 *Danger in the Comfort Zone: From Boardroom to Mailroom—How to Break the Entitlement Habit That's Killing American Business.* New York: AMACOM.

———

1981 *Feminine Personality and Conflict.* Westport, CT: Greenwood Press. (Originally published by Brooks/Cole, 1970.)

———

1979 *In Transition: How Feminism, Sexual Liberation, and the Search for Self-Fulfillment Have Altered America.* New York: Holt, Rinehart, and Winston.

———

1972 *Readings on the Psychology of Women.* New York: Harper & Row.

Barker-Benfield, G. J.
1976 *The Horrors of the Half-known Life.* New York: Harper Colophon.

Baron, Ava, ed.
1991 *Work Engendered: Toward a New History of American Labor.* Ithaca, NY: Cornell University Press.

Barrington, Judith, ed.
1991 *An Intimate Wilderness: Lesbian Writers on Sexuality.* Portland, OR: The Eighth Mountain Press.

Barry, Kathleen
1984 *Female Sexual Slavery.* New York: New York University Press.

———

1988 *Susan B. Anthony: A Biography of a Singular Feminist.* New York: New York University Press.

Bart, Pauline B., and Eileen Geil Moran
1993 *Violence Against Women: The Bloody Footprints.* Newbury Park, CA: Sage Publications.

Bart, Pauline B., and Patricia H. O'Brian
1985 *Stopping Rape: Successful Survival Strategies.* New York: Pergamon Press.

Bartky, Sandra Lee
1990 *Femininity and Domination: Studies in the Phonomenology of Oppression.* New York: Routledge.

Bean, Constance A.
1993 *Women Murdered by the Men They Loved.* New York: Haworth Press.

Beauvoir, Simone de
1953 *The Second Sex.* Translated and edited by H. M. Parshley. New York: Alfred A. Knopf.

Belenky, Mary Field, Blythe McVicker Clinchy, Nancy Rule Goldberger, and Jill Mattuck Tarnle
1986 *Women's Ways of Knowing: The Development of Self, Voice, and Mind.* New York: Basic Books.

Bem, Sandra Lipsitz
1993 *The Lenses of Gender: Transforming the Debate on Sexual Inequality.* New Haven, CT: Yale University Press.

Benhabib, Seyla, and Drucilla Cornell, eds.
1987 *Feminism as Critique: On the Politics of Gender.* Minneapolis: University of Minnesota Press.

Bernard, Jessie
1973 *American Family Behavior.* New York: Russell & Russell.

———

1981 *The Female World.* New York: Free Press.

———

1987 *The Female World from a Global Perspective.* Bloomington: Indiana University Press.

———

1973 *The Future of Marriage.* New York: Bantam.

———

1974 *The Future of Motherhood.* New York: Dell.

———

1971 *Remarriage.* New York: Russell & Russell.

———

1972 *The Sex Game.* New York: Atheneum.

———

1971 *Women and the Public Interest.* Chicago: Aldine.

———

1975 *Women, Wives, Mothers: Values and Options.* Chicago: Aldine.

Berry, Mary Frances
1986 *Why ERA Failed: Politics, Women's Rights and the Amending Process of the Constitution.* Bloomington: Indiana University Press.

Birke, Lynda, Susan Himmelweit, and Gail Vines
1990 *Tomorrow's Child: Reproductive Technologies in the 90s.* London: Virago Press.

Blea, Irene I.
1991 *La Chicana and the Intersection of Race, Class, and Gender.* New York: Praeger.

Bleier, Ruth H., ed.
1991 *Feminist Approaches to Science.* New York: Pergamon.

———

1984 *Science and Gender: A Critique of Biology and Its Theories on Women.* New York: Pergamon.

Bly, Robert
1990 *Iron John: A Book About Men.* Reading, MA: Addison-Wesley.

The Boston Women's Health Book Collective
1992 *The New Our Bodies, Ourselves: Updated and Expanded for the 90s.* New York: Simon & Schuster.

Boulding, Elise
1992 *The Underside of History: A View of Women Through Time.* Rev. ed. Vols. 1 and 2. Newbury Park, CA: Sage Publications.

Braun, Lily
1987 *Selected Writings on Feminism and Socialism.* Translated and edited by Alfred G. Meyer. Bloomington: Indiana University Press.

Bridenthal, Renate, Claudia Koonz, and Susan M. Stuard, eds.
1987 *Becoming Visible: Women in European History.* 2d ed. Boston: Houghton Mifflin.

Brod, Harry
1987 *The Making of Masculinities: The New Men's Studies.* Boston: Allen and Unwin.

———

1988 *A Mensch Among Men: Explorations in Jewish Masculinity.* Freedom, CA: Crossing Press.

Brown, Lyn M. and Carol Gilligan
1992 *Meeting at the Crossroads: Women's Psychology and Girls' Development.* Cambridge, MA: Harvard University Press.

Brown, Rita Mae
1988 *Bingo.* New York: Bantam.

———

1988 *In Her Day.* New York: Bantam.

———

1987 *The Poems of Rita Mae Brown.* Freedom, CA: Crossing Press.

———

1979 *Rubyfruit Jungle.* New York: Bantam Books.

———

1988 *Starting From Scratch: A Different Kind of Writer's Manual.* New York: Bantam Books.

———

1983 *Sudden Death.* New York: Bantam Books.

———

1993 *Venus Envy.* New York: Bantam.

Brown, Wendy L.
1988 *Manhood and Politics: A Feminist Reading in Political Theory.* Lanham, MD: Rowman & Littlefield.

Brownmiller, Susan
1975 *Against Our Will: Men, Women, and Rape.* New York: Simon & Schuster.

———

1984 *Femininity.* New York: Simon & Schuster.

———

1989 *Waverly Place.* New York: Grove Press.

Buechler, Steven M.
1990 *Women's Movements in the United States.* New Brunswick, NJ: Rutgers University Press.

Bullough, Vern L., Brenda Shelton, and Sarah Slavin
1988 *The Subordinated Sex.* Athens: University of Georgia Press.

Bunch, Charlotte
1987 *Passionate Politics: Feminist Theory in Action.* New York: St. Martin's Press.

Bunch, Charlotte, and Nancy Myron, eds.
1974 *Class and Feminism: A Collection of Essays from the Furies.* Baltimore: Diana Press.

———

1975 *Lesbianism and the Women's Movement.* Baltimore: Diana Press.

Bunch, Charlotte, and Sandra Pollack, eds.
1983 *Learning Our Way: Essays in Feminist Education.* Trumansburg, NY: Crossing Press.

Burgess, Ann Wolbert, ed.
1991 *Rape and Sexual Assault Research Handbook III* (I and II, 1988). New York: Garland.

Bynum, Caroline Walker, Steven Harrell, and Paula Richman
1986 *Gender and Religion: On the Complexity of Symbols.* Boston: Beacon Press.

Cade, Toni, ed.
1970 *The Black Woman: An Anthology.* New York: Signet.

Caine, Lynn
1974 *Widow.* New York: Morrow.

Caraway, Nancie
1991 *Segregated Sisterhood: Racism and the Politics of American Feminism.* Knoxville: University of Tennessee Press.

Case, Sue-Ellen
1988 *Feminism and Theatre.* New York: Methuen.

Chafetz, Janet Saltzman
1986 *Female Revolt: Women's Movements in World and Historical Perspective.* Totowa, NJ: Rowman and Allenheld.

———
1978 *Masculine/Feminine or Human?: An Overview of the Sociology of Gender Roles.* Itasca, IL: Peacock.

Chernin, Kim
1987 *The Flame Bearers.* New York: Perennial Library, Harper & Row.

———
1985 *The Hungry Self: Women, Eating, and Identity.* New York: Perennial Library, Harper & Row.

———
1983 *In My Mother's House.* New Haven, CT: Ticknor & Fields.

———
1982 *The Obsession: Reflections on the Tyranny of Slenderness.* New York: Harper & Row.

———
1987 *Reinventing Eve: Modern Woman in Search of Herself.* New York: Harper & Row.

———
1989 *Sex and Other Sacred Games: Love, Desire, Power, and Possession.* New York: Times Books.

Chesler, Ellen
1992 *Woman of Valor: Margaret Sanger and the Birth Control Movement in America.* New York: Simon & Schuster.

Chesler, Phyllis
1978 *About Men.* New York: Simon & Schuster. Reissued by Harcourt, Brace, Jovanovich, 1989.

———
1986 *Mothers on Trial: The Battle for Children and Custody.* New York: McGraw-Hill. Reprinted by Harcourt Brace Jovanovich, 1991.

———
1989 *Sacred Bond: The Legacy of Baby M.* New York: Times Books.

———
1979 *With Child: A Diary of Motherhood.* New York: Crowell.

———
1972 *Women and Madness.* New York: Doubleday. Reissued with a new introduction by Harcourt, Brace, Jovanovich, 1989.

Chesler, Phyllis, and Jane Goodman
1976 *Women, Money, and Power.* New York: Morrow.

Chisholm, Shirley
1971 *Unbought and Unbossed.* New York: Avon.

Chodorow, Nancy J.
1989 *Feminism and Psychoanalytic Theory.* New Haven, CT: Yale University Press.

———
1978 *The Reproduction of Mothering: Psychoanalysis and the Sociology of Gender.* Berkeley, CA: University of California Press.

Chopin, Kate
1972 *The Awakening* (1899). New York: Avon Books.

Christ, Carol P.
1986 *Diving Deep and Surfacing: Women Writers on Spiritual Quest.* 2d ed. Boston: Beacon Press.

———
1987 *Laughter of Aphrodite: Reflections on a Journey to the Goddess.* San Francisco: Harper & Row.

———
1989 *Weaving the Visions: New Patterns in Feminist Spirituality.* San Francisco: Harper & Row.

Christ, Carol P., and Judith Plaskow, eds.
1992 *Womanspirit Rising: A Feminist Reader in Religion.* 2d ed. San Francisco: Harper & Row.

Cline, Sally
1990 *Just Desserts: Women and Food.* London: Andre Deutsch.

Cline, Sally, and Dale Spender
1987 *Reflecting Men at Twice Their Natural Size.* New York: Seaver Books/Henry Holt.

Cohen, Sherrill, and Nadine Taub, eds.
1989 *Reproductive Laws for the 1990s.* Clifton, NJ: Humana Press.

Collard, Andree, and Joyce Contrucci
1989 *Rape of the Wild: Man's Violence Against Animals and the Earth.* Bloomington: Indiana University Press.

Collins, Patricia Hill
1990 *Black Feminist Thought: Knowledge, Consciousness, and the Politics of Empowerment.* Boston: Unwin Hyman.

Conover, Pamela Johnston, and Virginia Gray
1983 *Feminism and the New Right: Conflict over the American Family.* New York: Praeger.

Cook, Blanche Wiesen
1992 *Eleanor Roosevelt: A Life, 1884–1933.* New York: Viking.

Cooke, Joanne, Charlotte Bunch-Weeks, and Robin Morgan, eds.
1970 *The New Women.* Greenwich, CT: Fawcett.

Coole, Diana H.
1988 *Women in Political Theory: From Ancient Misogyny to Contemporary Feminism.* Boulder, CO: Lynne Rienner Publishers.

Corea, Gena
1985 *The Hidden Malpractice: How American Medicine Mistreats Women.* New York: Harper & Row.

———
1992 *Invisible Epidemic: The Story of Women and AIDS.* New York: HarperCollins.

———
1985 *The Mother Machine.* New York: Harper & Row.

Corea, Gena et al.
1987 *Man-Made Women: How New Reproductive Technologies Affect Women.* Bloomington: Indiana University Press.

Cotera, Martha P.
1976 *The Chicana Feminist.* Austin, TX: Information Systems Development.

———
1976 *Diosa y Hembra: The History and Heritage of Chicanas in the United States.* Austin, TX: Information Systems Development.

Cott, Nancy F.
1987 *The Grounding of Modern Feminism.* New Haven, CT: Yale University Press.

———
1991 *A Woman Making History: Mary Ritter Beard Through Her Letters.* New Haven, CT: Yale University Press.

Craig, Steve, ed.
1992 *Men, Masculinity, and the Media.* Research on Men and Masculinity Series, edited by Michael Kimmel, vol. 1. Newbury Park, CA: Sage Publications.

Crosby, Faye J.
1991 *Juggling: The Unexpected Advantages of Balancing Career and Home for Women and Their Families.* New York: Free Press.

Culliver, Concetta C., ed.
1992 *Female Criminality: The State of the Art.* New York: Garland.

Daly, Mary
1973 *Beyond God the Father.* Boston: Beacon Press.

———
1975 *The Church and the Second Sex.* New York: Harper Colophon.

———
1978 *Gyn/Ecology: The Metaethics of Radical Feminism.* Boston: Beacon Press.

———
1992 *Outercourse: The Be-Dazzling Voyage. Containing Recollections from* My Logbook of a Radical Feminist Philosopher *(Being an Account of My Time/Space Travels and Ideas—Then, Again, Now, and How).* San Francisco: HarperSanFrancisco.

———
1984 *Pure Lust.* Boston: Beacon Press.

Daly, Mary, in cahoots with Jane Caputi
1987 *Webster's First New Intergalactic Wickedary of the English Language.* Boston: Beacon Press.

Darty, Trudy, and Sandee Potter, eds.
1984 *Women-Identified Women.* Palo Alto, CA: Mayfield.

Davis, Angela
1974 *Angela Davis: An Autobiography.* New York: Random House.

———
1971 *If They Come in the Morning: Voices of Resistance.* New Rochelle, NY: Okapaku Communications Corporation.

———
1971 "Reflections on the Black Woman's Role in the Community of Slaves." *The Black Scholar* 3, no. 4 (December): 2–16.

———
1989 *Women, Culture, and Politics.* New York: Random House.

———
1981 *Women, Race, and Class.* New York: Random House.

Davis, Elizabeth Gould
1971 *The First Sex.* New York: Putnam.

Davis, Flora
1991 *Moving the Mountain: The Women's Movement in America Since 1960.* New York: Simon & Schuster.

DeCrow, Karen
1975 *Sexist Justice.* New York: Vintage.

Decter, Midge
1972 *The New Chastity and Other Arguments Against Women's Liberation.* New York: Coward, McCann & Geoghegan.

Delaney, Janice, Mary Jane Lupton, and Emily Toth
1988 *The Curse: A Cultural History of Menstruation.* Rev. ed. Champaign: University of Illinois Press.

Diamond, Irene, and Gloria F. Orenstein, eds.
1990 *Reweaving the World: The Emergence of Ecofeminism.* San Francisco: Sierra Club Books.

Dixon, Penelope A.
1990 *Mothers and Mothering: An Annotated Feminist Bibliography.* New York: Garland.

Doress, Paula Brown, Diana Laskin Siegal, and the Midlife and Older Women Book Project
1987 *Ourselves Growing Older: Women Again with Knowledge and Power.* New York: Simon & Schuster.

Dornbusch, Sanford M., and Myra H. Strober, eds.
1988 *Feminism, Children and the New Families.* New York: Guilford.

Dworkin, Andrea
1987 *Ice and Fire: A Novel.* New York: Weldenfeld & Nicolson.

———
1987 *Intercourse.* New York: Free Press.

———
1991 *Mercy.* New York: Four Walls Eight Windows.

———
1976 *Our Blood: Prophecies and Discourses on Sexual Politics.* New York: Harper & Row.

———
1987 *Pornography: Men Possessing Women.* New York: Free Press.

———
1983 *Right-Wing Women.* New York: Putnam.

———
1974 *Woman-Hating.* New York: E. P. Dutton.

Dynes, Wayne R., ed.
1990 *Encyclopedia of Homosexuality.* New York: Garland.

Easlea, Brian
1983 *Fathering the Unthinkable: Masculinity, Scientists and the Nuclear Arms Race.* London: Pluto Press.

Edson, Sakre Kennington
1988 *Pushing the Limits: The Female Administrative Aspirant.* Albany: State University of New York Press.

Ehrenreich, Barbara
1990 *The Worst Years of Our Lives.* New York: Pantheon.

Eisenstein, Hester
1983 *Contemporary Feminist Thought.* Boston: G. K. Hall.

———
1991 *Gender Shock: Practicing Feminism on Two Continents.* Boston: Beacon Press.

Eisler, Riane
1987 *The Chalice and the Blade.* New York: Harper & Row.

Eisler, Riane, and David Loye
1990 *The Partnership Way: New Tools for Living and Learning, Healing Our Families, Our Communities, and Our World.* San Francisco: Harper.

Ellman, Mary
1968 *Thinking About Women.* New York: Harcourt Brace Jovanovich.

Elshtain, Jean Bethke, and Sheila Tobias, eds.
1989 *Women, Militarism, and War: Essays in History, Politics, and Social Theory.* Lanham, MD: Rowman & Littlefield.

English, Jane, ed.
1977 *Sex Equality.* Englewood Cliffs, NJ: Prentice-Hall.

Epstein, Cynthia Fuchs
1988 *Deceptive Distinctions: Sex, Gender, and the Social Order.* New Haven, CT: Yale University Press.

———
1970 *Woman's Place.* Berkeley: University of California Press.

Erikson, Erik H.
1964 "Inner and Outer Space: Reflexions on Womanhood." *Daedalus* 93:582–606.

Espin, Oliva M., and Ellen Cole
1993 *Refugee Women and Their Mental Health.* New York: Haworth Press.

Estrich, Susan
1987 *Real Rape: How the Legal System Victimizes Women Who Say No.* Cambridge, MA: Harvard University Press.

Evans, Judith
1986 *Feminism and Political Theory.* Beverly Hills, CA: Sage Publications.

Evans, Sara
1990 *Born For Liberty: A History of Women in America.* New York: Free Press.

———
1978 *Personal Politics: The Roots of Women's Liberation in the Civil Rights Movement and the New Left.* New York: Alfred A. Knopf.

Evans, Sara M., and Barbara J. Nelson
1989 *Wage Justice: Comparable Worth and the Paradox of Technocratic Reform.* Chicago: University of Chicago Press.

Faludi, Susan
1991 *Backlash: The Undeclared War Against American Women.* New York: Crown.

Farrell, Warren
1986 *Why Men Are the Way They Are.* New York: McGraw-Hill.

Fasteau, Marc Feigen
1974 *The Male Machine.* New York: McGraw-Hill.

Feinman, Clarice, ed.
1992 *The Criminalization of Woman's Body.* New York: Haworth Press.

Ferguson, Mary Anne, ed.
1986 *Images of Women in Literature.* 4th ed. Boston: Houghton Mifflin.

Ferrato, Donna
1991 *Living With the Enemy.* Introduction by Ann Jones. New York: Aperture.

Figes, Eva
1971 *Patriarchal Attitudes.* Greenwich, CT: Fawcett.

Filene, Peter
1986 *Him/Her/Self: Sex Roles in Modern America.* 2d ed. Baltimore: John Hopkins.

Firestone, Shulamith
1971 *The Dialectic of Sex.* New York: Bantam.

Fisher, Dexter, ed.
1980 *The Third Woman: Minority Women Writers of the United States.* Boston: Houghton Mifflin.

Flexner, Eleanor
1973 *A Century of Struggle.* New York: Atheneum.

Forster, Margaret
1986 *Significant Sisters: The Grassroots of Active Feminism, 1839–1939.* New York: Oxford University Press.

Frankfort, Ellen
1972 *Vaginal Politics.* New York: Quadrangle.

Frazer, Elizabeth, Jennifer Hornsby, and Sabina Lovibond, eds.
1992 *Ethics: A Feminist Reader.* Cambridge, MA: Blackwell.

French, Marilyn
1986 *Beyond Power: On Women, Men, and Morals.* New York: Ballantine.

———
1985 *Bleeding Heart.* New York: Ballantine.

———
1988 *Her Mother's Daughter.* New York: Ballantine.

———
1992 *The War Against Women.* New York: Ballantine Books.

———
1977 *The Women's Room.* New York: Jove Publications.

Fried, Marlene Gerber, ed.
1990 *From Abortion to Reproductive Freedom: Transforming a Movement.* Boston: South End Press.

Friedan, Betty
1963 *The Feminine Mystique.* New York: Dell. (Twentieth Anniversary Edition, New York: W. W. Norton, 1983.)

———
1976 *It Changed My Life: Writings on the Women's Movement.* New York: Random House.

———
1986 *The Second Stage.* Rev. ed. New York: Summit.

Fuchs, Victor R.
1988 *Women's Quest for Economic Equality.* Cambridge MA: Harvard University Press.

Fudge, Judy, and Patricia McDermott, eds.
1991 *Just Wages: A Feminist Assessment of Pay Equity.* Toronto, Ontario: University of Toronto Press.

Gates, Henry Louis, ed.
1990 *Reading Black, Reading Feminist: A Critical Anthology.* New York: Meridian/Penguin Books.

Gearhart, Sally, and William R. Johnson
1974 *Loving Women—Loving Men: Gay Liberation and the Church.* San Francisco: Glide.

Gergen, Mary McCanney, ed.
1988 *Feminist Thought and the Structure of Knowledge.* New York: New York University Press.

Gifford, Carolyn De Swarte, and Donald Dayton, eds.
1988 *The American Ideal of the "True Woman" as Reflected in Advice Books to Young Women.* New York: Garland.

Gilligan, Carol
1982 *In a Different Voice.* Cambridge MA: Harvard University Press.

———
1988 *Mapping the Moral Domain: A Contribution of Women's Thinking to Psychological Theory and Education.* Cambridge, MA: Harvard University Press.

Gilman, Charlotte Perkins
1973 *The Yellow Wallpaper* (1892). New York: Feminist Press.

———
1979 *Herland: A Lost Feminist Utopian Novel.* New York: Random House.

Goldberg, Steven
1974 *The Inevitability of Patriarchy.* New York: Morrow.

Goldenberg, Naomi
1990 *Returning Words to Flesh: Feminism, Psychoanalysis, and the Resurrection of the Body.* Boston: Beacon Press.

Goldin, Claudia
1990 *Understanding the Gender Gap: An Economic History of American Women.* New York: Oxford University Press.

Gordon, Linda
1992 *Good Boys and Dead Girls (And Other Essays).* New York: Penguin.

———
1988 *Heroes of Their Own Lives: The Politics and History of Family Violence.* New York: Viking.

———
1976 *Woman's Body, Woman's Right: A Social History of Birth Control.* New York: Viking.

———, ed.
1991 *Women, the State, and Welfare.* Madison: University of Wisconsin Press.

Gordon, Margaret T., and Stephanie Riger
1988 *The Female Fear.* New York: Free Press.

Gordon, Vivian
1987 *Black Women, Feminism, and Black Liberation: Which Way?* Chicago: Third World Press.

Grauerholz, Elizabeth, and Mary Koralweski, eds.
1991 *Sexual Coercion: A Sourcebook on its Nature, Causes, and Prevention.* New York: Lexington Books.

Greer, Germaine
1992 *The Change: Women, Aging, and Menopause.* New York: Alfred A. Knopf.

———
1990 *Daddy We Hardly Knew You.* New York: Alfred A. Knopf.

———
1971 *The Female Eunuch.* New York: McGraw-Hill.

———
1986 *The Madwoman's Underclothes: Essays and Occasional Writings.* New York: Atlantic Monthly Press.

———
1979 *The Obstacle Race: The Fortunes of Women Painters and Their Work.* New York: Farrar, Straus & Giroux.

———
1984 *Sex and Destiny: The Politics of Human Fertility.* New York: Harper & Row.

Griffin, Susan
1992 *A Chorus of Stones: The Private Life of War.* New York: Doubleday.

———
1981 *Pornography and Silence: Culture's Revenge Against Nature.* New York: Harper & Row.

———
1979 *Rape: The Power of Consciousness.* San Francisco: Harper & Row.

———
1987 *Unremembered Country.* Port Townsend, WA: Copper Canyon.

———
1978 *Woman and Nature: The Roaring Inside Her.* New York: Harper & Row.

Grimké, Sarah
1988 *Letters on the Equality of the Sexes and Other Essays.* Edited by Elizabeth Ann Bartlett. New Haven, CT: Yale University Press.

Gubar, Susan, and Joan Hoff, eds.
1989 *For Adult Users Only: The Dilemma of Violent Pornography.* Bloomington: Indiana University Press.

Gurko, Miriam
1976 *The Ladies of Seneca Falls: The Birth of the Women's Movement.* New York: Schocken.

Hall, Kermit L., ed.
1987 *Women, the Law, and the Constitution.* New York: Garland.

Hammer, Jalna, and Mary Maynard, eds.
1987 *Women, Violence and Social Control.* Atlantic Highlands, NJ: Humanities Press International.

Harding, Sandra
1991 *Whose Science? Whose Knowledge? Thinking from Women's Lives.* Ithaca, NY: Cornell University Press.

Hays, H. R.
1964 *The Dangerous Sex.* New York: Putnam.

Hekman, Susan J.
1990 *Gender and Knowledge: Elements of a Postmodern Feminism.* Boston: Northeastern University Press.

Henley, Nancy, Mykol Hamilton, and Barrie Thorne
1984 *Womanspeak and Manspeak: Sex Differences and Sexism in Communication, Verbal and Nonverbal.* St. Paul, MN: West.

Herdt, Gilbert, ed.
1993 *Gay Culture in America: Essays from the Field.* Boston: Beacon Press.

Hill, George H., Lorraine Raglin, and Chas Floyd Johnson
1990 *Black Women in Television: An Illustrated History and Bibliography.* New York: Garland.

Hite, Shere
1987 *The Hite Report: A Study of Male Sexuality.* New York: Ballantine.

———
1974 *Sexual Honesty: By Women for Women.* New York: Warner.

———
1987 *Women and Love: A Cultural Revolution in Progress.* New York: Alfred A. Knopf.

Hoagland, Sarah Lucia
1988 *Lesbian Ethics: Toward New Values.* Palo Alto, CA: Institute of Lesbian Studies.

Hoff, Joan
1991 *Law, Gender, and Injustice: A Legal History of U.S. Women.* New York and London: New York University Press.

Hole, Judith, and Ellen Levine
1971 *Rebirth of Feminism.* New York: Quadrangle.

Holmes, Helen Bequaert, ed.
1992 *Issues in Reproductive Technology I: An Anthology.* New York: Garland.

hooks, bell
1981 *Ain't I a Woman: Black Women and Feminism.* Boston: South End Press.

———
1992 *Black Looks: Race and Representation.* Boston: South End Press.

———
1984 *Feminist Theory: From Margin to Center.* Boston: South End Press.

———
1989 *Talking Back: Thinking Feminist, Thinking Black.* Boston: South End Press.

———
1992 *A Woman's Mourning Song.* New York: Writers and Readers.

———
1990 *Yearnings: Race, Gender, and Cultural Politics.* Boston: South End Press.

Horner, Matina
1969 "A Bright Young Woman is Caught in a Double Bind," *Psychology Today* 3, no. 6 (November).

Howe, Florence, and Marsha Saxton
1987 *With Wings: An Anthology of Literature by and about Women With Disabilities.* New York: Feminist Press at CUNY.

Hubbard, Ruth
1989 *Authors of Pictures, Draughtsmen of Words.* Portsmouth, NH: Heinemann.

———
1990 *The Politics of Women's Biology.* New Brunswick, NJ: Rutgers University Press.

Hubbard, Ruth, and Mary S. Henefin, eds.
1979 *Women Look at Biology Looking at Women: A Collection of Feminist Critiques.* Boston: G. K. Hall.

Hubbard, Ruth, and Brenda Miller Power, eds.
1991 *Literacy in Process.* Portsmouth, NH: Heinemann.

Hubbard, Ruth, and Margaret Randall
1988 *The Shape of Red: Insider-Outsider Reflections.* San Francisco: Cleis Press.

Hughes, Jean O., and Bernice R. Sandler
1987 *"Friends" Raping Friends: It Could Happen to You.* Washington, DC: Association of American Colleges, Project on the Status and Education of Women.

Humm, Maggie
1990 *The Dictionary of Feminist Theory.* Columbus: Ohio State University Press.

Hurston, Zora Neale
1991 *Dust Tracks on the Road: An Autobiography.* New York: HarperCollins.

———
1986 *The Gilded Six-Bits.* Minneapolis, MN: Redpath Press.

———
1979 *I Love Myself When I am Laughing . . . and Again When I Am Looking Mean and Impressive: A Zora Neale Hurston Reader.* Edited by Alice Walker. Old Westbury, NY: Feminist Press.

———
1985 *Spunk: The Selected Stories of Zora Neale Hurston.* San Francisco: Turtle Island Foundation.

———
1978 *Their Eyes Were Watching God.* Champaign: University of Illinois Press.

Jack, Dana Crowley
1991 *Silencing the Self: Depression and Women.* Cambridge, MA: Harvard University Press.

Jacobus, Mary, Evelyn Fox Keller, and Sally Shuttleworth, eds.
1990 *Body/Politics: Women and the Discourses of Science.* New York: Routledge.

Jaggar, Alison M.
1988 *Feminist Politics and Human Nature.* Lanham, MD: Rowman & Littlefield.

———
1989 *Gender/Body/Knowledge: Feminist Reconstructions of Being and Knowing.* New Brunswick, NJ: Rutgers University Press.

Jaggar, Alison M., and Paula S. Rothenberg, eds.
1993 *Feminist Frameworks: Alternative Theoretical Accounts of the Relations Between Women and Men.* 3d. ed. New York: McGraw-Hill.

Janeway, Elizabeth
1982 *Cross Sections from a Decade of Change.* New York: Morrow.

———
1987 *Improper Behavior.* New York: Morrow.

———
1971 *Man's World, Woman's Place: A Study in Social Mythology.* New York: Delta Books.

———
1980 *Powers of the Weak.* New York: Alfred A. Knopf.

Jaquith, Cindy
1988 *Surrogate Motherhood, Women's Rights and the Working Class.* New York: Pathfinder Press.

Jardine, Alice, and Paul Smith, eds.
1987 *Men in Feminism.* New York: Methuen.

Jayawardena, Kumari
1986 *Feminism and Nationalism in the Third World.* New Delhi: Kali for Women. Distributed by Biblio Distribution Center, Totowa, NJ.

Johnson, Kim
1985 *If You Are Raped.* Holmes Beach, FL: Learning Publications.

Johnson, Sonia
1989 *From Housewife to Heretic.* Albuquerque, NM: Wildfire Books.

———
1987 *Going Out of Our Minds: The Metaphysics of Liberation.* Freedom, CA: Crossing Press.

———
1991 *The Ship That Sailed into the Livingroom: Sex and Intimacy Reconsidered.* Albuquerque, NM: Wildfire Books.

Johnston, Jill
1973 *Lesbian Nation.* New York: Simon & Schuster.

Jong, Erica
1989 *Any Woman's Blues.* New York: Harper & Row.

———
1979 *At the Edge of the Body.* New York: Holt, Rinehart, and Winston.

———
1992 *Becoming Light: Poems New and Selected.* New York: HarperCollins.

———
1980 *Fanny: Being the True History of the Adventures of Fanny Hackabout-Jones.* New York: New American Library.

———
1973 *Fear of Flying.* New York: Holt, Rinehart and Winston.

———
1977 *How to Save Your Own Life.* New York: Holt, Rinehart and Winston.

———
1976 *Loveroot.* New York: Holt, Rinehart and Winston.

———
1983 *Ordinary Miracles: New Poems.* New York: New American Library.

———
1984 *Parachutes and Kisses.* New York: New American Library.

———
1987 *Serenissima: A Novel of Venice.* Boston: Houghton Mifflin.

———
1981 *Witches.* New York: H. A. Abrams.

Kamen, Paula
1991 *Feminist Fatale: Voices from the "Twentysomething" Generation Explore the Future of the "Women's Movement."* New York: Donald I. Fine.

Kaminer, Wendy
1990 *A Fearful Freedom: Women's Flight from Equality.* New York: Addison-Wesley.

Kandal, Terry R.
1988 *The Woman Question in Classical Sociological Theory.* Gainesville: University Presses of Florida.

Kass-Simon, G., and Patricia Farnes, eds.
1990 *Women of Science: Righting the Record.* Bloomington: Indiana University Press.

Kessler-Harris, Alice
1982 *Out to Work: A History of Wage-Earning Women in the United States.* New York: Oxford University Press.

———
1990 *A Woman's Wage: Historical Meanings and Social Consequences.* Lexington: University Press of Kentucky.

Kimball, Gayle
1986 *Life After College: Combining a Career and Family.* Chico: Women's Studies, California State University.

Kimmel, Michael S., ed.
1987 *Changing Men: New Directions in Research on Men and Masculinity.* Sage Focus Editions, vol. 88. Newbury Park, CA: Sage.

Kimmel, Michael S., and Thomas E. Mosmiller
1993 *Against the Tide: Pro-Feminist Men in the United States 1776–1990.* Boston: Beacon Press.

Kirkland, Gelsey
1986 *Dancing on My Grave.* New York: Doubleday.

Klein, Renate D., and Deborah Lynn Steinberg, eds.
1989 *Radical Voices: A Decade of Feminist Resistance from Women's International Forum.* New York: Pergamon.

Korda, Michael
1972 *Male Chauvinism! How It Works.* New York: Random House.

Kraditor, Aileen S.
1965 *The Ideas of the Women Suffrage Movement, 1890–1920.* New York: Columbia University Press.

———, ed.
1968 *Up From the Pedestal.* Chicago: Quadrangle.

Kramarae, Cheris
1983 *Language, Gender, and Society.* Rowley, MA: Newbury House.

———
1984 *Language and Power.* Thousand Oaks, CA: Sage.

———, ed.
1988 *Technology and Women's Voices.* New York: Routledge & Kegan Paul.

Kramarae, Cheris, and Dale Spender, eds.
1992 *The Knowledge Explosion: Generations of Feminist Scholarship.* Athene Series. New York: Teachers College Press.

Kramarae, Cheris, and Paula Treichler, eds.
1985 *A Feminist Dictionary.* Boston: Pandora Press.

Kuhn, Annette
1988 *Cinema, Censorship and Sexuality, 1909–1925.* New York: Routledge, Chapman and Hall.

Lawless, Elaine J.
1988 *Handmaidens of the Lord: Pentecostal Women Preachers and Traditional Religion.* Philadelphia: University of Pennsylvania Press.

Lederer, Wolfgang
1968 *The Fear of Women.* New York: Grune & Stratton.

Lerner, Gerda
1993 *The Creation of Feminist Consciousness: From the Middle Ages to Eighteen-Seventy.* New York: Oxford University Press.

———
1986 *The Creation of Patriarchy.* New York: Oxford University Press.

———
1992 *The Female Experience: An American Documentary.* Updated edition with new preface. New York: Oxford University Press. (Original Bobbs, Merrill edition, 1977).

———
1979 *The Majority Finds Its Past: Placing Women in History.* New York: Oxford University Press.

———, ed.
1973 *Black Women in White America: A Documentary History.* New York: Vintage.

Lessing, Doris
1976 *The Golden Notebook.* New York: Simon & Schuster.

Lowe, Marian, and Ruth Hubbard, eds.
1983 *Woman's Nature: Rationalizations of Inequality.* New York: Pergamon.

Lunneborg, Patricia
1992 *Abortion: A Positive Decision.* Westport, CT: Greenwood.

Lystra, Karen
1989 *Searching the Heart: Women, Men and Romantic Love in Nineteenth Century America.* New York: Oxford University Press.

Maccoby, Eleanor E., ed.
1966 *The Development of Sex Differences.* Stanford, CA: Stanford University Press.

Maccoby, Eleanor E., and C. N. Jacklin
1974 *The Psychology of Sex Differences.* Stanford, CA: Stanford University Press.

Maccoby, Eleanor E., and Robert H. Mnookin
1992 *Dividing the Child: Social and Legal Dilemmas of Custody.* Cambridge, MA: Harvard University Press.

MacKinnon, Catherine A.
1987 *Feminism Unmodified: Discourses on Life and Law.* Cambridge, MA: Harvard University Press.

———
1987 *Sexual Harassment of Working Women: A Case of Sexual Discrimination.* New Haven, CT: Yale University Press.

———
1989 *Toward a Feminist Theory of the State.* Cambridge, MA: Harvard University Press.

Maio, Kathi
1988 *Feminist in the Dark: Reviewing the Movies.* Freedom, CA: Crossing Press.

Manning, Beverly
1988 *We Shall Be Heard: An Index to Speeches by American Women 1978–1985.* Metuchen, NJ: Scarecrow Press.

Marshall, Paule
1981 *Brown Girl, Brownstones.* New York: Feminist Press. (First published 1959).

———
1969 *The Chosen Place, The Timeless People.* New York: Harcourt, Brace and World.

———
1991 *Daughters.* New York: Atheneum.

———
1983 *Praisesong for the Widow.* New York: Putnam.

———
1984 *Reena & Other Stories.* New York: Feminist Press.

Martin, Wendy
1972 *The American Sisterhood.* New York: Harper & Row.

Martz, Sandra Haldeman, ed.
1992 *If I Had My Life to Live Over: I Would Pick More Daisies.* Watsonville, CA: Papier-Mache Press.

Mathews, Donald G., and Jane Sherron De Hart
1990 *Sex, Gender, and the Politics of ERA: A State and the Nation.* New York: Oxford University Press.

Matthews, Glenna
1987 *"Just a Housewife": The Rise and Fall of Domesticity in America.* New York: Oxford University Press.

A Matter of Simple Justice
1970 Report of the President's Task Force on Women's Rights and Responsibilities. Washington, DC: Government Printing Office.

Mead, Margaret
1928 *Coming of Age in Samoa.* New York: Morrow.

——
1949 *Male and Female.* New York: Dell.

——
1935 *Sex and Temperament in Three Primitive Societies.* New York: Morrow.

Medea, Andrea, and Kathleen Thompson
1974 *Against Rape: A Survival Manual for Women.* New York: Farrar, Straus, and Giroux.

Mernissi, Fatima
1975 *Beyond the Veil: Male-Female Dynamics in Modern Muslim Society.* Bloomington: Indiana University Press.

——
1991 *The Veil and the Male Elite: A Feminist Interpretation of Women's Rights in Islam.* Translated by Mary Jo Lakeland. Reading, MA: Addison-Wesley.

Messer, Ellen, and Kathryn E. May
1988 *Back Rooms: Voices from the Illegal Abortion Era.* New York: St. Martin's Press.

Mezey, Susan Gluck
1992 *In Pursuit of Equality: Women, Public Policy, and the Federal Courts.* New York: St. Martin's Press.

Miller, Patricia G.
1993 *The Worst of Times: Illegal Abortions—Survivors, Practitioners, Coroners, Cops, and Children of the Women Who Died Talk About Its Horrors.* New York: HarperCollins.

Millett, Kate
1979 *The Basement: Meditations on a Human Sacrifice.* New York: Simon & Schuster.

——
1990 *Flying.* New York: Simon & Schuster Trade.

——
1990 *The Loony Bin Trip.* New York: Simon & Schuster Trade.

——
1970 *Sexual Politics.* New York: Doubleday.

——
1992 *Sita.* New York: Simon & Schuster Trade.

Mills, Patricia J.
1987 *Woman, Nature, and Psyche.* New Haven, CT: Yale University Press.

Minh-ha, Trinh T.
1989 *Woman, Native, Other: Writing Postcoloniality and Feminism.* Bloomington: Indiana University Press.

Mitchell, Juliet
1975 *Psychoanalysis and Feminism.* New York: Vintage.

——
1973 *Woman's Estate.* New York: Vintage.

——
1984 *Women: The Longest Revolution.* New York: Pantheon Books.

Mitchell, Juliet, and Ann Oakley, eds.
1986 *What Is Feminism?* New York: Pantheon Books.

Mitter, Sara S.
1991 *Dharma's Daughters: Contemporary Indian Women and Hindu Culture.* New Brunswick, NJ: Rutgers University Press.

Mitter, Swasti
1986 *Common Fate, Common Bond: Women in the Global Economy.* London: Pluto Press.

Modleski, Tania
1991 *Feminism Without Women: Culture and Criticism in a "Postfeminist" Age.* New York: Routledge.

Moghadam, Valentine M.
1993 *Modernizing Women: Gender and Social Change in the Middle East.* Boulder, CO: Lynne Rienner Publishers.

Mohanty, Chandra Talpade, Ann Russo, and Lourdes Torres, eds.
1991 *Third World Women and the Politics of Feminism.* Bloomington: Indiana University Press.

Moi, Toril
1990 *Feminist Theory and Simone de Beauvoir.* Cambridge, MA: Basil Blackwell.

Momsen, Janet Henshall, and Janet Townsend, eds.
1987 *Geography of Gender in the Third World.* New York: SUNY Press.

Money, J., and A. A. Ehrhardt
1972 *Man and Woman, Boy and Girl.* Baltimore: Johns Hopkins Press.

Montague, Ashley
1974 *The Natural Superiority of Women.* New York: Collier Books.

Moraga, Cherrie
1986 *Giving up the Ghost: Teatro in Two Acts.* Los Angeles: West End Press.

———
1983 *Loving in the War Years: Lo Que Nunca Paso Por Sus Labios.* Boston: South End Press.

Moraga, Cherrie, and Gloria Anzaldúa, eds.
1983 *This Bridge Called My Back: Writings by Radical Women of Color.* 2d ed. New York: Kitchen Table: Women of Color Press.

Morgan, Elaine
1972 *The Descent of Woman.* New York: Stein & Day.

Morgan, Robin
1984 *The Anatomy of Freedom: Feminism, Physics and Global Politics.* Garden City, NY: Anchor Books/ Doubleday.

———
1989 *The Demon Lover: On the Sexuality of Terrorism.* New York: Norton.

———
1978 *Going Too Far: The Personal Chronicle of a Feminist.* New York: Vintage Books.

———
1992 *The Word of a Woman: Feminist Dispatches, 1968–1992.* New York: W. W. Norton.

Morgan, Robin, ed.
1984 *Sisterhood Is Global: The First Anthology of Writings from the International Women's Movement.* New York: Doubleday.

———
1970 *Sisterhood Is Powerful: An Anthology of Writings from the Women's Movement.* New York: Vintage.

Morris, Desmond
1968 *The Naked Ape.* New York: McGraw-Hill.

Morrison, Toni
1987 *Beloved.* New York: Alfred A. Knopf.

———
1972 *The Bluest Eye.* New York: Washington Square Press.

———
1992 *Jazz.* New York: McKay.

———
1978 *Song of Solomon.* New York: NAL-Duton.

———
1973 *Sula.* New York: Alfred A. Knopf.

———
1981 *The Tar Baby.* New York: Alfred A. Knopf.

Morrison, Toni, ed.
1992 *Race-ing Justice, En-genderinging Power: Essays on Anita Hill, Clarence Thomas, and the Construction of Social Reality.* New York: Pantheon Books.

Moynihan, Patrick
1965 *The Negro Family: The Case for National Action.* Washington, DC: U.S. Department of Labor.

Mueller, Carol M., ed.
1988 *The Politics of the Gender Gap: The Social Construction of Political Influence.* Beverly Hills, CA: Sage Publications.

Muldoon, Maureen
1991 *The Abortion Debate in the United States and Canada: A Source Book.* New York: Garland.

Murray, Pauli
1989 *Pauli Murray: The Autobiography of a Black Activist, Feminist, Lawyer, Priest, and Poet.* Knoxville: University of Tennessee Press.

National Commission of the Observance of International Women's Year
1976 *"To Form a More Perfect Union . . .": Justice for American Women.* Washington, DC: U.S. Department of State.

Nicholson, Linda, ed.
1989 *Feminism/Postmodernism.* New York: Routledge.

Nye, Andrea
1989 *Feminist Theory and the Philosophies of Man.* New York: Routledge.

———
1990 *Words of Power: A Feminist Reading of the History of Logic.* New York: Routledge.

Oakley, Ann
1974 *The Sociology of Housework.* New York: Pantheon.

———
1976 *Woman's Work: The Housewife Past and Present.* New York: Vintage.

Ochs, Carol
1989 *An Ascent to Joy: Transforming Deadness of Spirit.* New York: Meyer Stone Books.

———
1977 *Behind the Sex of God: Toward a New Consciousness Transcending Matriarchy and Patriarchy.* Boston: Beacon Press.

———
1992 *When I'm Alone.* Minneapolis, MN: Carolrhoda Books.

———
1983 *Women and Spirituality.* Lanham, MD: Rowman & Littlefield.

Okin, Susan Moller
1989 *Justice, Gender, and the Family.* New York: Basic Books.

———
1979 *Women in Western Political Thought.* Princeton, NJ: Princeton University Press.

Papachristou, Judith, ed.
1976 *Women Together: A History in Documents of the Women's Movement in the United States.* New York: Alfred A. Knopf.

Parrot, A.
1988 *Coping with Date Rape and Acquaintance Rape.* New York: Rosen Publishing Group.

Patton, Cindy, and Janis Kelly
1987 *Making It: A Woman's Guide to Sex in the Age of AIDS.* Spanish translation by Papusa Molina. Ithaca, NY: Firebrand Books.

Penelope, Julia
1992 *Call Me Lesbian: Lesbian Lives, Lesbian Theory.* Introduction by Sarah Hoagland. Freedom, CA: Crossing Press.

Penley, Constance, ed.
1988 *Feminism and Film Theory.* New York: Routledge, Chapman and Hall.

Peterson, V. Spike, ed.
1992 *Gendered States: Feminist (Re)Visions of International Relations Theory.* Boulder, CO: Lynne Rienner Publishers.

Pharr, Suzanne
1988 *Homophobia: A Weapon of Sexism.* Little Rock, AR: Chardon Press.

Plath, Sylvia
1971 *The Bell Jar.* New York: Harper & Row.

Pleck, J. H., and J. Sawyer
1974 *Men and Masculinity.* Englewood Cliffs, NJ: Prentice-Hall.

Pleck, Joseph
1981 *The Myth of Masculinity.* Cambridge, MA: MIT Press.

Pogrebin, Letty Cottin
1991 *Deborah, Golda, and Me: Being Female and Jewish in America.* New York: Crown Publishing Group.

Pozzetta, George E., ed.
1991 *Ethnicity and Gender: The Immigrant Woman.* New York: Garland.

Pribram, Deidre, ed.
1988 *Female Spectators: Looking at Film and Television.* New York: Verso.

Rabuzzi, Kathryn Allen
1988 *Motherself: A Mythic Analysis of Motherhood.* Bloomington: Indiana University Press.

Radford, Jill, and Daina E. H. Russell, eds.
1992 *Femicide: The Politics of Woman Killing.* New York: Twayne.

Rakow, Lana, and Cheris Kramarae, eds.
1990 *The Revolution in Words: Righting Women, 1868–1871.* New York: Routledge.

Randall, Margaret
1987 *This Is About Incest.* Ithaca, NY: Firebrand Books.

Ranke-Heinemann, Uta
1991 *Eunuchs for the Kingdom of Heaven: Women, Sexuality and the Catholic Church.* New York: Penguin.

Rapp, Sandy
1991 *God's Country: A Case Against Theocracy.* New York: Haworth Press.

Raymond, Janice
1986 *A Passion for Friends: Toward a Philosophy of Female Affection.* Boston: Beacon Press.

Raymond, Janice et al.
1991 *RU-486: Myths, Misconceptions, and Morals.* North Amherst, MA: Institute on Women and Technology.

Réage, Pauline
1965 *The Story of O.* Translated by Sabine d'Estree. New York: Grove Press.

Redfern, Bernice J.
1989 *Women of Color in the United States: A Guide to the Literature.* New York: Garland.

Reed, Evelyn
1971 *Problems of Women's Liberation.* New York: Pathfinder Press.

———
1970 *Woman's Evolution.* New York: Pathfinder Press.

Rhode, Deborah I., ed.
1992 *Theoretical Perspectives on Sexual Difference.* New Haven, CT: Yale University Press.

Rich, Adrienne
1975 *Adrienne Rich's Poetry.* New York: Norton.

———
1991 *An Atlas of the Difficult World: Poems, 1988–1991.* New York: Norton.

———
1986 *Blood, Bread, and Poetry: Selected Prose, 1979–1985.* New York: Norton.

———
1978 *The Dream of a Common Language: Poems, 1974–1977.* New York: Norton.

———
1986 *Of Woman Born: Motherhood as Experience and Institution.* New York: Norton.

———
1979 *On Lies, Secrets, and Silence: Selected Prose, 1966–1978.* New York: Norton.

———
1983 *Sources.* Woodside, CA: Heyeck Press.

———
1990 *Women and Honor: Some Notes on Lying.* Pittsburgh, PA: Cleis Press.

———
1986 *Your Native Land, Your Life: Poems.* New York: Norton.

Richards, Dell
1990 *Lesbian Lists: A Look at Lesbian Culture, History, and Personalities.* Boston: Alyson Publications.

Richardson, Laurel, and Verta Taylor, eds.
1992 *Feminist Frontiers.* 3d. ed. New York: McGraw-Hill.

Roman, Leslie, Linda K. Christian-Smith, and Elizabeth Ellsworth, eds.
1988 *Becoming Feminine: The Politics of Popular Culture.* New York: Falmer.

Rosser, Sue V.
1992 *Biology and Feminism: A Dynamic Interaction.* New York: Twayne.

———
1989 *Feminism and Science: In Memory of Ruth Bleier.* New York: Pergamon.

———
1988 *Feminism Within the Science and Health Care Professions: Overcoming Resistance.* New York: Pergamon.

———
1986 *Teaching Science and Health from a Feminist Perspective: A Practical Guide.* New York: Pergamon.

———, ed.
1990 *Female-Friendly Science: Applying Women's Studies Methods and Theories to Attract Students to Science.* New York: Pergamon.

Rossi, Alice S., ed.
1988 *The Feminist Papers: From Adams to de Beauvoir.* Boston: Northeastern University Press.

Rossiter, Amy
1988 *From Private to Public: A Feminist Exploration of Early Mothering.* Toronto, Ontario: Women's Press.

Rothenberg, Paula S.
1992 *Race, Class, and Gender in the United States: An Integrated Study.* New York: St. Martin's Press.

Rothman, Barbara Katz
1989 *Recreating Motherhood: Ideology and Technology in a Patriarchal Society.* New York: W. W. Norton.

Rothman, David J., and Sheila M. Rothman, eds.
1988 *Divorce: The First Debates.* New York: Garland.

Rountree, Cathleen
1991 *Coming into Our Fullness: On Women Turning Forty.* Freedom, CA: Crossing Press.

Rowbotham, Sheila
1976 *Hidden from History.* New York: Vintage.

———
1991 *The Past Is Before Us: Feminism in Action Since the 1960s.* Boston: Beacon Press.

———
1973 *Woman's Consciousness, Man's World.* Baltimore: Penguin.

———
1992 *Women in Movement: Feminism and Social Action.* New York: Routledge.

———
1974 *Women, Resistance and Revolution.* New York: Vintage.

Ruether, Rosemary Radford
1992 *Gaia & God: An Ecofeminist Theology of Earth Healing.* San Francisco: HarperSanFrancisco.

———
1974 *Religion and Sexism.* New York: Simon & Schuster.

———
1983 *Sexism and God-Talk: Toward a Feminist Theology.* Boston: Beacon Press.

———
1985 *Womanguides: Readings Towards a Feminist Theology.* Boston: Beacon Press.

Ruether, Rosemary, and Rosemary Skinner Keller, eds.
1986 *Women and Religion in America.* San Francisco: Harper & Row.

Ruether, Rosemary, and Eleanor McLaughlin, eds.
1979 *Women of Spirit: Female Leadership in the Jewish and Christian Traditions.* New York: Simon & Schuster.

Russell, Diana
1993 *Making Violence Sexy: Feminist Views of Pornography.* Athene Series. New York: Teachers College Press.

———
1984 *Sexual Exploitation: Rape, Child Sexual Assault and Workplace Harassment.* Beverly Hills, CA: Sage Publications.

Russo, Ann, and Cheris Kramarae, eds.
1991 *The Radical Women's Press of the 1850s.* New York: Routledge.

Ryan, Barbara
1992 *Feminism and the Women's Movement: Dynamics of Change in Social Movement, Ideology, and Activism.* New York: Routledge.

Salem, Dorothy
1990 *To Better Our World: Black Women in Organized Reform, 1890–1920.* Brooklyn, NY: Carlson.

Sapiro, Virginia
1984 *The Political Integration of Women: Roles, Socialization, and Politics.* Champaign: University of Illinois Press.

———
1992 *A Vindication of Political Virtue: The Political Theory of Mary Wollstonecraft.* Chicago: University of Chicago Press.

———
1986 *Women in American Society.* Palo Alto, CA: Mayfield.

———
1988 *Women, Political Action, and Political Participation.* Women and Politics Series. Washington, DC: American Political Science Association.

Sayers, Janet
1991 *Mothers of Psychoanalysis: Helen Deutsch, Karen Horney, Anna Freud, Melanie Klein.* New York: W. W. Norton.

Scarf, Mimi
1988 *Battered Jewish Wives: Case Studies in the Response to Rage.* Lewiston, NY: E. Mellen Press.

Scharf, Lois, and Joan M. Jensen
1983 *Decades of Discontent: The Women's Movement, 1920–1940.* Westport, CT: Greenwood Press.

Schecter, Susan
1982 *Women and Male Violence: The Visions and Struggles of the Battered Women's Movement.* Boston: South End Press.

Schmidt, Alvin John
1989 *Veiled and Silenced: How Culture Shaped Sexist Theology.* Macon, GA: Mercer University Press.

Schneir, Miriam, ed.
1971 *Feminism: The Essential Historical Writings.* New York: Random House.

Scott, Hilda
1985 *Working Your Way to the Bottom: The Feminization of Poverty.* Boston: Pandora.

Seidler, Victor
1991 *Recreating Sexual Politics: Men, Feminism and Politics.* New York: Routledge, Chapman & Hall.

Sharma, Arvind, ed.
1987 *Women in World Religions.* New York: SUNY Press.

Shulman, Alix Kates
1972 *Memoirs of an Ex-Prom Queen.* New York: Alfred A. Knopf.

Sidel, Ruth
1990 *On Her Own: Growing Up in the Shadow of the American Dream.* New York: Viking Penguin.

———
1986 *Women and Children Last: The Plight of Poor Women in Affluent America.* New York: Penguin. (Revised ed. 1992.)

Simon, Barbara Levy
1987 *Never Married Women.* Philadelphia: Temple University Press.

Simon, Rita J., and Jean Landis
1991 *The Crimes Women Commit, The Punishments They Receive.* New York: Lexington.

Sinclair, Marianne
1988 *Hollywood Lolitas: The Nymphet Syndrome in the Movies.* New York: Henry Holt.

Sloan, Irving J.
1988 *The Law Governing Abortion, Contraception and Sterilization.* New York: Oceana Publications.

Soble, Alan, ed.
1991 *The Philosophy of Sex: Contemporary Readings.* 2d ed. Lanham, MD: Rowman & Littlefield.

Sochen, June
1987 *Enduring Values: Women in Popular Culture.* Westport, CT: Greenwood Press.

———
1974 *Herstory.* Sherman, CA: Alfred Publishing.

———
1974 *Movers and Shakers: American Women Thinkers and Activists, 1900–1970.* New York: Quadrangle.

———
1991 *Women's Comic Visions.* Detroit, MI: Wayne State University Press.

Spallone, Patricia
1989 *Beyond Conception: The New Politics of Reproduction.* Granby, MA: Bergin & Garvey.

Spallone, Patricia, and Deborah Lynn Steinberg, eds.
1987 *Made to Order: The Myth of Reproductive and Genetic Progress.* Athene Series. New York: Pergamon Press.

Spelman, Elizabeth
1988 *Inessential Woman: Problems of Exclusion in Feminist Thought.* Boston: Beacon Press.

Spender, Dale
1987 *The Education Papers: Women's Quest for Equality in Britain.* Boston: Routledge.

———
1983 *Feminist Theorists: Three Centuries of Key Women Thinkers. New York: Pantheon.*

———
1985 *For the Record: The Making and Meaning of Feminist Knowledge.* London: Women's Press.

———

1985 *Man Made Language.* 2d ed. Boston: Routledge, Chapman and Hall.

———

1981 *Men's Studies Modified: The Impact of Feminism on the Academic Disciplines.* New York: Pergamon Press.

———

1986 *Mothers of the Novel: 100 Good Women Writers Before Jane Austen.* London: Pandora Press.

———

1983 *There's Always Been a Women's Movement This Century.* Boston: Pandora.

———

1984 *Time and Tide Wait For No Man.* London: Pandora Press.

———

1988 *Women of Ideas (and What Men Have Done to Them): From Aphra Behn to Adrienne Rich.* Boston: Pandora.

———

1988 *Writing a New World.* London: Pandora Press.

———

1989 *The Writing or the Sex?: Or Why You Don't Have to Read Women's Writing to Know It's No Good.* New York: Pergamon.

Spender, Dale, and Elizabeth Sarah
1988 *Learning to Lose: Sexism and Education.* London: Women's Press.

Spender, Dale, and L. Spender, eds.
1984 *Gatekeeping: The Denial, Dismissal, and Distortion of Women.* Tarrytown, NY: Pergamon.

Spiegel, Marcia Cohn, and Deborah Lipton Kremsdorf, eds.
1987 *Women Speak to God: The Prayers and Poems of Jewish Women.* San Diego, CA: Women's Institute for Continuing Jewish Education.

The Spirit of Houston: The First National Women's Conference
1978 Washington, DC: U.S. Department of State, National Commission on the Observance of Women's Year.

Stacey, Judith
1990 *Brave New Families: Stories of Domestic Upheaval in Late Twentieth Century America.* New York: Basic Books.

Stacey, Judith, Susan Bereaud, and Joan Daniels, eds.
1974 *And Jill Came Tumbling After: Sexism in American Education.* New York: Dell.

Stanton, Elizabeth Cady
1972 *The Woman's Bible.* New York: Arno Press.

Stanton, Elizabeth Cady, Susan B. Anthony, and Matilda Joslyn Gage, eds.
1881–1886 *History of Woman Suffrage.* Vols. 1–3. New York: Fowler and Wells. (1886–1904, vols. 4–6, edited by Ida Husted Harper, National Woman Suffrage Association.)

Starr, Tama
1991 *The "Natural Inferiority" of Women: Outrageous Pronouncements by Misguided Males.* New York: Poseidon.

Steinem, Gloria
1983 *Outrageous Acts and Everyday Rebellions.* New York: Holt, Rinehart and Winston.

———

1992 *Revolution from Within: A Book of Self-Esteem.* Boston: Little, Brown.

Stephenson, June
1991 *Men Are Not Cost-Effective.* Napa, CA: Smith Publishing.

———

1991 *The Two-Parent Family Is Not the Best.* Napa, CA: Diemer, Smith.

Stimpson, Catharine R.
1988 *Where the Meanings Are: Feminism and Cultural Spaces.* New York: Methuen.

———

1987 *Women, Households, and the Economy.* New Brunswick, NJ: Rutgers University Press.

Stone, Merlin
1979 *Ancient Mirrors of Womanhood: Our Goddess and Heroine Heritage.* Vols. 1 and 2. New York: New Sibylline Books.

———

1978 *When God Was a Woman.* New York: Harcourt Brace Jovanovich.

Stoner, K. Lynn, ed.
1989 *Latinas of the Americas: A Source Book.* New York: Garland.

Sumrall, Amber Coverdale, and Patrice Vecchione
1992 *Catholic Girls.* New York: New American Library.

Swirski, Barbara, and Marilyn P. Safir
1991 *Calling the Equality Bluff: Women in Israel.* New York: Athene Series, Pergamon Press.

Szekely, Eva
1988 *Never Too Thin.* Toronto, Ontario: Women's Press.

Tanner, Leslie B., ed.
1970 *Voices from Women's Liberation.* New York: Signet.

Taylor, Dena
1988 *Red Flower: Rethinking Menstruation.* Freedom, CA: Crossing Press.

Terborg-Penn, Rosalyn, Sharon Harley, and Andrea Benton Rushing, eds.
1988 *Women in Africa and the African Diaspora.* Washington, DC: Howard University Press.

Thiam, Awa
1986 *Black Sisters, Speak Out.* Translated by Dorothy Blair. London: Pluto Press.

Thompson, Mary Lou, ed.
1970 *Voices of the New Feminism.* Boston: Beacon Press.

Thorne, Barrie
1993 *Gender Play: Girls and Boys in School.* Newark, NJ: Rutgers University Press.

———
1992 *Rethinking the Family: Some Feminist Questions.* Revised ed. Boston: Northeastern University Press.

Thorne, Barrie, and Nancy Henley, eds.
1975 *Language and Sex: Difference and Dominance.* Rowley, MA: Newbury House.

Tiger, Lionel
1969 *Men in Groups.* New York: Random House.

Tiger, Lionel, and Robin Fox
1971 *The Imperial Animal.* New York: Holt, Rinehart and Winston.

Tilly, Louise A., and Patricia Gurin, eds.
1990 *Women, Politics and Change.* New York: Russell Sage Foundation.

Tinker, Irene
1990 *Persistent Inequalities: Women and World Development.* New York: Oxford University Press.

Todd, Janet, ed.
1988 *Women and Film.* New York: Holmes and Meier.

Tong, Rosemarie
1993 *Feminine and Feminist Ethics.* Belmont, CA: Wadsworth Publishing.

———
1989 *Feminist Thought: A Comprehensive Introduction.* Boulder, CO: Westview Press.

———
1984 *Women, Sex and the Law.* New Feminist Perspective Series. Savage, MD: Rowman and Littlefield.

Trebilcot, Joyce, ed.
1984 *Mothering: Essays in Feminist Theory.* Lanham, MD: Rowman & Littlefield.

Tucker, Susan
1988 *Telling Memories Among Southern Women: Domestic Workers and Their Employees in the Segregated South.* Baton Rouge: Louisiana State University Press.

Volgy, Sandra S., ed.
1991 *Women and Divorce/Men and Divorce: Gender Differences in Separation, Divorce and Remarriage.* Binghamton, NY: Haworth Press.

Walker, Alice
1982 *The Color Purple.* New York: Harcourt Brace Jovanovich.

———
1991 *Her Blue Body Everything We Know: Earthling Poems 1965–1990 Complete.* New York: Harcourt Brace Jovanovich.

———
1973 *In Love and Trouble: Stories of Black Women.* New York: Harcourt Brace Jovanovich.

———
1983 *In Search of Our Mother's Gardens: Womanist Prose.* San Diego, CA: Harcourt Brace Jovanovich.

———
1992 *Possessing the Secret of Joy.* New York: Harcourt Brace Jovanovich.

———
1989 *The Temple of My Familiar.* New York: Harcourt Brace Jovanovich.

———
1981 *You Can't Keep a Good Woman Down: Stories.* New York: Harcourt Brace Jovanovich.

Walker, Barbara G.
1992 *Amazon: A Novel.* San Francisco: HarperSanFrancisco.

———
1985 *The Crone: Woman of Age, Wisdom, and Power.* San Francisco: Harper & Row.

———
1986 *The I Ching of the Goddess.* San Francisco: Harper & Row.

———
1987 *The Skeptical Feminist: Discovering the Virgin, Mother, and Crone.* San Francisco: Harper & Row.

———
1988 *The Woman's Dictionary of Symbols and Sacred Objects.* San Francisco: Harper & Row.

———
1983 *The Woman's Encyclopedia of Myths and Secrets.* San Francisco: Harper & Row.

———
1990 *Women's Rituals: A Sourcebook.* San Francisco: Harper & Row.

Walker, Robbie Jean
1992 *The Rhetoric of Struggle: Public Address of African-American Women.* New York: Garland.

Wegner, Judith Romney
1988 *Chattel or Person? The Status of Women in the Mishnah.* New York: Oxford University Press.

Weis, Lois, ed.
1988 *Class, Race, and Gender in American Education.* New York: SUNY Press.

Weitzman, Lenore
1987 *The Divorce Revolution: The Unexpected Social and Economic Consequences for Women and Children In America.* New York: Free Press.

Welter, Barbara
1966 "The Cult of True Womanhood: 1820–1860." *American Quarterly* 18, no. 2, pt. 1: 151–174.

White, Evelyn C., ed.
1990 *The Black Women's Health Book: Speaking for Ourselves.* Seattle, WA: Seal Press.

Wilkinson, Sue, and Celia Kitzinger, eds.
1993 *Heterosexuality: A Feminism and Psychology Reader.* Newbury Park, CA: Sage Publications.

Williams, Patricia J.
1991 *The Alchemy of Race and Rights.* Cambridge, MA: Harvard University Press.

Wilson, Edward O.
1975 *Sociobiology: The New Synthesis.* Cambridge, MA: Harvard University Press.

Wittig, Monique
1973 *Les Guérillères.* Translated by David Le Vay. New York: Avon.

———
1992 *The Straight Mind and Other Essays.* Boston: Beacon Press.

Wolf, Naomi
1991 *The Beauty Myth.* New York: William Morrow.

Yayori, Matsui
1989 *Women's Asia.* Translated by Mizuko Matsuda. London: Zed Books.

Young, Elise G.
1991 *Keepers of the History: Women of the Israeli-Palestinian Conflict.* Athene Series. New York: Pergamon Press.

Young, Kate, ed.
1988 *Women and Economic Development: Local, Regional and National Planning Strategies.* New York: St. Martin's Press/Berg/UNESCO.

Zakaria, Rafiq
1990 *Women & Politics in Islam: The Trial of Benazir Bhutto.* New York: New Horizons Press.

Zanardi, Claudia
1990 *Essential Papers on the Psychology of Women.* New York: New York University Press.

Zappone, Katherine
1991 *The Hope for Wholeness: A Spirituality for Feminists.* Mystic, CT: Twenty-Third Publications.

Zopf, Paul E., Jr.
1989 *American Women in Poverty.* Westport, CT: Greenwood Press.

Zophy, Angela Howard, and Frances M. Kavenik, eds.
1990 *Handbook of American Women's History.* New York: Garland.

Index